A Flexible Organization for Instructors

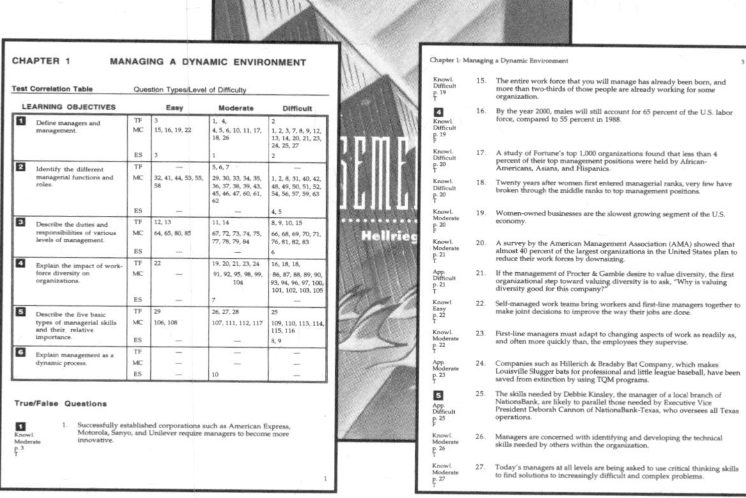

CHAPTER 1 MANAGING A DYNAMIC ENVIRONMENT

Test Correlation Table Question Types/Level of Difficulty

LEARNING OBJECTIVES		Easy	Moderate	Difficult
1 Define managers and management.	TF	3	1, 4,	2
	MC	15, 16, 19, 22	4, 5, 6, 10, 11, 17, 18, 26	1, 2, 3, 7, 8, 9, 12, 13, 14, 20, 21, 23, 24, 25, 27
	ES	3	1	2
2 Identify the different managerial functions and roles.	TF	—	5, 6, 7	—
	MC	32, 41, 44, 53, 55, 58	29, 30, 33, 34, 35, 36, 37, 38, 39, 43, 45, 46, 47, 60, 61, 62	1, 2, 8, 31, 40, 42, 48, 49, 50, 51, 52, 54, 56, 57, 59, 63
	ES	—	—	4, 5
3 Describe the duties and responsibilities of various levels of management.	TF	12, 13	11, 14	8, 9, 10, 15
	MC	64, 65, 80, 85	67, 72, 73, 74, 75, 77, 78, 79, 84	66, 68, 69, 70, 71, 76, 81, 82, 83
	ES	—	—	6
4 Explain the impact of work-force diversity on organizations.	TF	22	19, 20, 21, 23, 24	16, 18, 18,
	MC	—	91, 92, 95, 98, 99, 104	86, 87, 88, 89, 90, 93, 94, 96, 97, 100, 101, 102, 103, 105
	ES	—	7	—
5 Describe the five basic types of managerial skills and their relative importance.	TF	29	26, 27, 28	25
	MC	106, 108	107, 111, 112, 117	109, 110, 113, 114, 115, 116
	ES	—	—	8, 9
6 Explain management as a dynamic process.	TF	—	—	—
	MC	—	—	—
	ES	—	10	—

True/False Questions

1 Knowl. Moderate p. 3 T — 1. Successfully established corporations such as American Express, Motorola, Sanyo, and Unilever require managers to become more innovative.

1

Chapter 1: Managing a Dynamic Environment 3

Knowl. Difficult p. 19 T — 15. The entire work force that you will manage has already been born, and more than two-thirds of those people are already working for some organization.

4 Knowl. Difficult p. 19 F — 16. By the year 2000, males will still account for 65 percent of the U.S. labor force, compared to 55 percent in 1988.

Knowl. Difficult p. 20 T — 17. A study of Fortune's top 1,000 organizations found that less than 4 percent of their top management positions were held by African-Americans, Asians, and Hispanics.

Knowl. Difficult p. 20 T — 18. Twenty years after women first entered managerial ranks, very few have broken through the middle ranks to top management positions.

Knowl. Moderate p. 20 F — 19. Women-owned businesses are the slowest growing segment of the U.S. economy.

Knowl. Moderate p. 21 T — 20. A survey by the American Management Association (AMA) showed that almost 40 percent of the largest organizations in the United States plan to reduce their work forces by downsizing.

App. Difficult p. 21 T — 21. If the management of Procter & Gamble desire to value diversity, the first organizational step toward valuing diversity is to ask, "Why is valuing diversity good for this company?"

Knowl Easy p. 22 T — 22. Self-managed work teams bring workers and first-line managers together to make joint decisions to improve the way their jobs are done.

Knowl. Moderate p. 22 T — 23. First-line managers must adapt to changing aspects of work as readily as, and often more quickly than, the employees they supervise.

App. Moderate p. 23 T — 24. Companies such as Hillerich & Bradsby Bat Company, which makes Louisville Slugger bats for professional and little league baseball, have been saved from extinction by using TQM programs.

5 App. Difficult p. 25 F — 25. The skills needed by Debbie Kinsley, the manager of a local branch of NationsBank, are likely to parallel those needed by Executive Vice President Deborah Cannon of NationsBank-Texas, who oversees all Texas operations.

Knowl. Moderate p. 26 T — 26. Managers are concerned with identifying and developing the technical skills needed by others within the organization.

Knowl. Moderate p. 27 T — 27. Today's managers at all levels are being asked to use critical thinking skills to find solutions to increasingly difficult and complex problems.

Test Manual Questions are grouped by learning objective, so that you can thoroughly test all objectives – or emphasize the ones you feel are most important. Correlation tables at the beginning of each chapter make it easy to prepare tests that cover the objectives at the level of difficulty appropriate for your students.

MicroExam 4.0

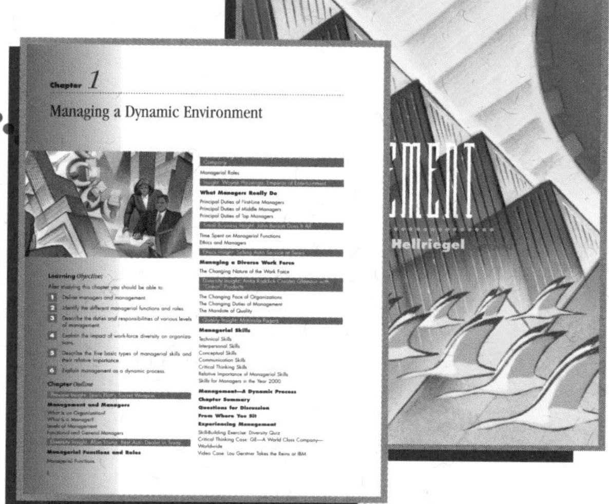

Text Learning Objectives form the framework for organizing your lectures, selecting support materials, and customizing tests for your students.

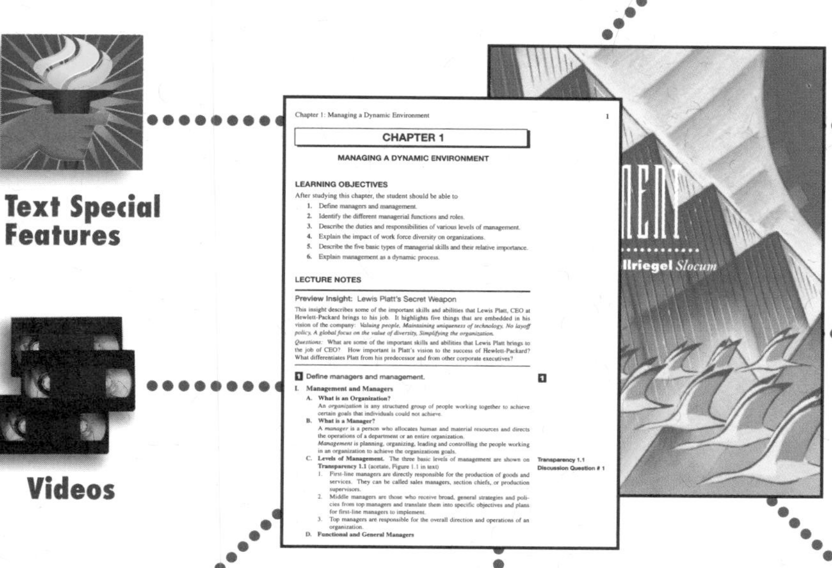

Chapter 1: Managing a Dynamic Environment 1

CHAPTER 1

MANAGING A DYNAMIC ENVIRONMENT

LEARNING OBJECTIVES

After studying this chapter, the student should be able to

1. Define managers and management.
2. Identify the different managerial functions and roles.
3. Describe the duties and responsibilities of various levels of management.
4. Explain the impact of work force diversity on organizations.
5. Describe the five basic types of managerial skills and their relative importance.
6. Explain management as a dynamic process.

LECTURE NOTES

Preview Insight: Lewis Platt's Secret Weapon

This insight describes some of the important skills and abilities that Lewis Platt, CEO at Hewlett-Packard brings to his job. It highlights five things that are embedded in his vision of the company: *Valuing people, Maintaining uniqueness of technology, No layoff policy, A global focus on the value of diversity, Simplifying the organization.*

Questions: What are some of the important skills and abilities that Lewis Platt brings to the job of CEO? How important is Platt's vision to the success of Hewlett-Packard? What differentiates Platt from his predecessor and from other corporate executives?

1 Define managers and management. 1

I. **Management and Managers**
   A. **What is an Organization?**
   An *organization* is any structured group of people working together to achieve certain goals that individuals could not achieve.
   B. **What is a Manager?**
   A *manager* is a person who allocates human and material resources and directs the operations of a department or an entire organization.
   Management is planning, organizing, leading and controlling the people working in an organization to achieve the organizations goals.
   C. **Levels of Management.** The three basic levels of management are shown on **Transparency 1.1** (acetate, Figure 1.1 in text) — Transparency 1.1 / Discussion Question # 1
      1. First-line managers are directly responsible for the production of goods and services. They can be called sales managers, section chiefs, or production supervisors.
      2. Middle managers are those who receive broad, general strategies and policies from top managers and translate them into specific objectives and plans for first-line managers to implement.
      3. Top managers are responsible for the overall direction and operations of an organization.
   D. **Functional and General Managers**

Text Special Features

Videos

Transparencies

Videodisc

PowerPoint

CRITICAL THINKING CASE

EXPERIENCING MANAGEMENT

End-Of-Chapter Cases

QUESTIONS FOR DISCUSSION

FROM WHERE YOU SIT

End-Of-Chapter Questions

…s come …tructor's …rage of …mes to integrate transparencies, videos, text special features, enrichment modules, and end-of-chapter pedagogy into your lectures – a smorgasbord of teaching aids from which to choose.

ANNOTATED INSTRUCTOR'S EDITION

SEVENTH EDITION

MANAGEMENT

Don **Hellriegel**

College of Business Administration and Graduate School of Business Texas A&M University

John W. **Slocum**, Jr.

Edwin L. Cox School of Business Southern Methodist University

Annotations by Cliff **Cheng**

University of California, Riverside

SOUTH-WESTERN College Publishing

An International Thomson Publishing Company

About the Cover

The graceful V pattern of geese in flight is a beautiful example of teamwork in nature. The lead goose breaks the wind so that the rest can fly with less resistance. When the lead goose tires, another takes the lead. In this way, the entire flock can reach its destination with less expenditure of its precious energy resource than could individuals flying alone. What better metaphor for today's organizations?

Acquisitions Editor: Randy G. Haubner
Developmental Editor: Cinci Stowell
Production Editor: Sharon L. Smith
Copyeditor: Jerrold A. Moore
Production House: WordCrafters Editorial Services, Incorporated
Photo Research: Ferret Research, Inc./Mary Goljenboom
Internal Design: Ellen Pettengell Design
Icon Illustrator: Steve Musgrave
Cover Design: Tin Box Studio/Sandy Weinstein
Cover Illustration: Arden von Haeger
Computer Illustration: Photonics/Alan Brown
Marketing Manager: Stephen E. Momper

The Library of Congress Cataloging-in-Publication Data
reads as follows in the student edition of the text:

Library of Congress Cataloging-in-Publication Data
Hellriegel, Don.
Management/Don Hellriegel, John W. Slocum, Jr.—7th ed.
p. cm.
Includes bibliographical references and index.
ISBN 0-538-84077-3
1. Management. I. Slocum, John W. II. Title.
HD31.H447 1995
658.4—dc20 95-16618
CIP

ISBN: 0-538-84082-X
1 2 3 4 5 6 7 VH 0 9 8 7 6 5

Printed in the United States of America

I(T)P
International Thomson Publishing

South-Western College Publishing is an ITP Company. The ITP trademark is used under license.

Brief Contents

Contents

Part *Two* The Environment and Managing Strategically 74

Part *Six* Controlling and Evaluating 582

Part *Seven* Change and Innovation 676

Special Features *Guided Tour* **for Students**

Before you begin your journey through this text, set aside a few minutes to take our guided tour through the special features that will make your journey a valuable—and memorable—learning experience. Whether your life plans include becoming a manager some day or not, management skills are essential to your future. Decision-making, thinking critically, working in teams, managing conflict, and working and living in an environment of diversity are just a few of the skills you will develop with the aid of this text—skills for everyday life, not just for managers. Your tour begins on the next page.

Bon voyage!

Build *Critical Thinking* Skills

◀ **Critical** *Thinking Cases*

Intriguing short cases at the end of every chapter challenge you to critically evaluate a situation, using the chapter concepts. To answer the case questions, you will have to sort through the data, isolate the true issues, and decide what you would do.

▼ **Video** *Cases*

Chapter-end Video Cases are similar to Critical Thinking Cases, except that they have an additional element—an accompanying video. The video gives a real-world feel to the case, as you learn about the company or issue by seeing and listening as well as reading.

CRITICAL THINKING CASE

Ford *Had* a Better Idea . . . Who Will Have It Next?

The future of Detroit as the center of automaking depends to some degree on the ability of U.S. companies to develop a generation of ultraclean, ultraefficient vehicles. The industry has been in turmoil for nearly two decades. The first sign of trouble came in the mid-1970s with the OPEC oil embargo and a sudden perception of the doubtful future of fossil fuels. Chrysler, Ford, and GM were forced to take notice of the smaller Japanese imports that were outselling their larger, gas-guzzling vehicles. As consumers continued to buy Japanese cars, they became aware of the much higher defect rates of U.S. vehicles.

At first, U.S. automobile manufacturers were puzzled by how the Japanese could produce high-quality, fuel-efficient, and (at the time) cheaper cars. They soon discovered that Japanese car companies were using a totally different type of technology to design and manufacture their vehicles. Known as Design for Flexible Manufacturing Systems (DFMS), or concurrent engineering, ... feedback from many sources in additi... plant engineers. No part of the vehicle... assemblies and components were red... process, Toyota reduced the number ... 14 to 5. New information technologie... This change from a sequential, mass-... mental and affected the entire industr...

Each U.S. auto manufacturer res... Ford was the first to try to reproduce ... by combining defect-free vehicles wit... price. The Team Taurus experiment c... the early 1990s. Chrysler attempted a ... before it finally introduced its "cab fo... Intrepid, Concord, and Vision models... combining customers' desires, Chrysl... ers' dreams—have received acclaim ... Canadian auto-workers at the newly r... Ontario. General Motors designed an... from all its other facilities. The Satur... lems, has nevertheless been a consum...

With auto quality problems bare...

into decline, causing a slowdown in sales and forcing U.S. car manufacturers to lay off workers. The recovery from this recession was different from that of previous recessions. A full recovery and return to high-wage work did not occur. Automakers were forced to rethink their product lines and the ways in which cars were purchased. This rethinking led to a trimming of product lines and promotion of leasing as an option to buying. The General Motors Acceptance Corporation is the most profitable of GM's businesses at present.

But the pressures for change have not let up. The problem of the 1990s is pressure from the regulatory environment. California has passed legislation mandating that 20 percent of the vehicles driven there be powered by electricity by 1998. Concurrently, the federal government initiated a $1 billion program to create an affordable family sedan with three times the fuel efficiency of today's average car. Undoubtedly, the fu-

VIDEO CASE

Glaxo Gets Ready for a New Health Care System

Ulcers, headaches, asthma, and upset stomachs are common complaints of the 1990s. However, Glaxo Pharmaceuticals, the U.S. division of Britain's Glaxo holdings, has products to treat these ailmen... its Zantac ulcer treatment product. In addition, ... with facilities in the Research Triangle Park, N... Imitrex for treating migraine headaches, Vento... for counteracting nausea.

Until recently, Glaxo has maintained a pr... prescription drugs with the support of reimbu... plans. Several recent developments threaten G...

The first is the change in the regulatory e... care. Large purchasing blocks responsible for ... services are balking at the high price of some ... such as Zantac. This drug currently provides a... revenues for the company. Although Zantac is ... 2002, health care providers are pressing for a ... Access to this global $8.4 billion market is sha... costliest scramble for market share in drug ind... Glaxo's largest competitor, SmithKline Beecham... On May 17, 1994, SmithKline's anti-ulcer block... patent protection in the United States, unleashi... generics onto the American market. Already, S... cuts of up to 80 percent to protect Tagamet's $... thirds of it in the United States, from ten gener... the fray. Novopharm, a generic drug company ... nearly identical product that sells for about hal... company has been attempting to get a U.S. cou... is no longer a proprietary drug. The new comp... corporate earnings, but it should prove to be a...

The second threat comes from changes i... are purchased. Until the mid-1990s, most of th... at physicians, who made the medication decisi... system changes, however, insurers are limiting... pharmaceuticals. These lists typically include s... for the more expensive patented, or "name-br... vey of 288 U.S. drug buyers, Goldman, Sachs, ... plan to reduce their use of Zantac or negotiate... generic Tagamet becomes available at less tha... Goldman, Sachs analyst says that Zantac's $2 b...

drop by 10 percent a year starting in 1996, when generic competition begins in earnest.

The third threat comes for pharmaceutical dispensers such as drug stores and mail-order pharmacies. Most of these outlets currently advise

104 PART 2 The Environment and Managing ...

PART THREE INTEGRATIVE CASE

Meyers & Morrison: A Question of Professional Ethics

Michael Morrison, partner in the accounting firm of Meyers & Morrison, didn't know what to think after the telephone conversation with one of his firm's oldest clients. The client had stated that he had received a letter from Stephen Adams, an associate with Meyers & Morrison, asking the client to switch to a new firm that he, Adams, was about to start. Morrison remarked to his partner, Phillip Meyers, "I can't believe that Adams would actually do this. He hasn't even left the firm yet. I thought he was going to wait to see what we could offer him to stay with the company." Meyers responded, "This isn't what I expected from someone in this office. We've always treated everyone like family here. This isn't a big impersonal, public accounting firm. I thought we all got along pretty well. This doesn't make a lot of sense."

Morrison paused, looked back at Meyers, and asked, "What do we do now?"

Background

Phillip Meyers had started his own small certified public accounting firm thirty years earlier in the seacoast town of Portsmouth, New Hampshire. For several years, he worked independently, establishing a small, but loyal, customer base. As his business continued to grow, he realized that he needed to hire additional employees to capitalize on his firm's excellent reputation.

Thus, after ten years on his own, Meyers hired Michael Morrison, the son of one of his largest clients. Morrison was a graduate of the MBA program at Boston University and had worked for five years for KPMG Peat Marwick in its Boston office. However, he had indicated that he wanted to move back to the Portsmouth area. He also had mentioned that he preferred the style and pace of a small firm to that of a branch of a Big Eight accounting firm. Together, Meyers and Morrison continued to expand the firm's client list by emphasizing customer service. They focused on small business and professional clients such as Morrison's father.

Through the years the firm continued to grow. Morrison was rewarded for his effort and dedication with a partnership in the firm, now called Meyers & Morrison. The partners gradually expanded the staff until it comprised ten employees, including a computer operator, payroll specialist, staff accountants, and clerical personnel. Only Meyers and Morrison were CPAs, however.

A few years after Morrison became a partner, however, the firm encountered some minor setbacks. One of its clients, which was responsible for over 40 percent of the firm's revenues, went bankrupt. The two partners were forced to lay off some of their employees to keep the firm profitable. After this incident, they vowed never again to become dependent on any one firm or client for a significant portion of their business.

Owing to the combined efforts of the partners and the remaining employees, Meyers & Morrison regained the profitability it had once enjoyed. Eventually the firm was able to expand the staff to its previous level. Then, as a result of continued expansion, the partners decided to hire an additional CPA. Morrison stated, "Our intent was to find someone who was like us and would be able to share some of this increased auditing and tax load. We also wanted someone who would help us to continue our expansion. Besides, my partner wanted to start withdrawing from active involvement with the firm." As a result the partners hired Stephen Adams, who was in his early thirties. He had an undergraduate degree in business from a local business school with a concentration in accounting. Hoping that Adams would prove his ability, the partners offered him a position that could lead to a partnership in the firm. Morrison stated that "the process of bringing Adams in was somewhat loose and informal, much the way we do everything around here." The partners believed that the offer, which included an extremely generous salary and benefits package, compared to those of associates in other small firms in the area. They admitted that they hadn't done a full salary analysis of the local market, however.

Stephen Adams came to Meyers & Morrison from another small public accounting firm in Massachusetts. He was married but had no children. His adjustment to the firm appeared to go well, according to Morrison. He stated that "Adams was looked upon favorably by the office staff. He worked long hours serving the needs of his clients and spent additional hours recruiting new business." Morrison added that "after the first twelve months, all in all, we were very happy with Stephen Adams's performance. Everyone in the office seemed to be getting along well."

Source: Case prepared by William Naumes, Michelle Wilson, and Sherry Walters, University of New Hampshire, Durham, N.H. Copyright 1995 by North American Case Research Association and William Naumes. Adapted and used with permission of the senior author and the *Case Research Journal*, 1995.

Integrative *Part Cases* ▶

These part cases require you to apply concepts from several chapters. The cases present more information and challenge your critical thinking skills more than do the chapter cases. Your instructor may choose to assign these integrative cases as individual or team projects.

Assess *and Apply Your Own* Skills

Skill Building *Exercises* ▶

"Skill-Building Exercises" at the end of each chapter challenge you to learn more about yourself and your skills. What are your strengths that you can offer an employer? What weaknesses should you improve to make yourself more marketable? These exercises are fun—and the results may sometimes surprise you!

EXPERIENCING MANAGEMENT

SKILL-BUILDING EXERCISE

Assessing Tolerance for Ambiguity

Intolerance for ambiguity is defined as the tendency to perceive ambiguous situations as threatening. Conversely, tolerance for ambiguity is the tendency to perceive ambiguous situations as acceptable or desirable. Ambiguity arises from novelty, complexity, or problems that have no obvious solutions. Complex/changing task environments usually possess these characteristics. The following statements will permit you to assess your own tolerance for ambiguity. Answer the following questions *yes* if you agree or *no* if you disagree with the statement.

1. An expert who doesn't come up with a definite answer probably doesn't know too much. ______
2. There is really no such thing as a problem that can't be solved. ______
3. A good job is one where what is to be done and how it is to be done are always clear. ______
4. In the long run, more can get done by tackling small, simple problems rather than large complicated problems. ______
5. What we are used to is always preferable to what is unfamiliar. ______
6. A person who leads an even, regular life in which few surprises or unexpected happenings arise really has a lot to be grateful for. ______
7. I like parties where I know most of the people more than parties where all or most of the people are strangers. ______
8. The sooner we all acquire similar values and ideals, the better. ______
9. I would like to live in a foreign country for a while. ______
10. People who fit their lives into a schedule probably miss most of the joy of living. ______
11. Tackling a complicated problem is more fun than solving a simple one. ______
12. Often the most interesting and stimulating people are those who don't mind being original or different. ______
13. People who insist on a yes or no answer just don't know how complicated things really are. ______

...l on insufficient information. ______

...signments give you a chance to show initiative and originality. ______

...bout your way of looking at things. ______

...1 point for every *Yes*.
...d 1 point for every *No*.
...omfortable you might be with ambiguity and ambiguous situations.
...ts for items 1, 2, and 14. This score indicates your tolerance for situations that cannot be
...2, 13, 15, and 16. This score indicates your tolerance for ambiguity caused by the complexity
...dicates your tolerance for ambiguity caused by the novelty of the situation.[50]

...ally

and goals are displayed visually in a table. The Pareto diagram is a graph that helps individuals or teams to determine which problems should be solved and in what order. The Pareto diagram is frequently used in total management quality programs to establish priorities for quality-related problems.

4 ***Describe Osborn's creativity model and the cause and effect diagram as aids to innovative decision making.***
Osborn's creativity model and the cause and effect diagram help decision makers solve unstructured and ambiguous problems, which often call for unique and innovative decisions. The creative process as a whole includes five interconnected elements: preparation, concentration, incubation, illumination, and verification. For innovation to flourish in organizations, a creative climate is needed. Such a climate generally includes attributes such as trust, open communication, and diversity. Osborn's creativity model is designed to stimulate and reduce blocks to creativity and innovation. The cause and effect diagram provides a process for getting at the root causes of a problem (an effect).

QUESTIONS FOR DISCUSSION

1. What are the key differences between rules and SOPs and artificial intelligence (AI)?
2. Review the Preview Insight. How might Andersen's *Window of Knowledge* be adapted to provide additional services to prospective or current customers? What are some potential problems that Andersen must avoid in using this system?
3. What are the similarities between break-even analysis and the payoff matrix?
4. By the time coffee arrived, Zita Thurman and Tom Namura were deeply involved in an after-dinner discussion about a problem at work. Thurman, manager of the small-parts division of a manufacturing company, had just taken a management science course. Namura, human resource director of the same company, had not. "I tell you," Thurman claimed, "chances are you *cannot* make a decision without having your emotions color it. Answer this for me. You have two options: A, a 100 percent chance to win \$3,000; and B, an 80 percent chance to win \$4,000. Which one would you take?" Namura thought for a few seconds and chose option A, the guaranteed \$3,000. Was Tom Namura correct? Why?[44]
5. Which of the following alternatives should Lois Garcia choose: (a) a 100 percent chance to lose \$3,000, or (b) an 80 percent chance to lose \$4,000 with a 20 percent chance to lose nothing?[45] Why?
6. What are two limitations to the use of the Pareto diagram?
7. How does Osborn's creativity model differ from the cause and effect diagram?

FROM WHERE YOU SIT

1. Describe one way in which you have been affected personally by an application of AI.
2. Apply a normative decision-making aid to your studying practices.
3. Develop a cause and effect diagram for one personal problem, such as getting a grade in a course or an overall grade point average lower than you desire.
4. You should do this activity in a discussion group with four to six other students. Each person should take five minutes and write down the five things that irritated them most while eating at local restaurants during the past three months. From this data, the group should develop a Pareto diagram. Does it offer any clues for needed changes to restaurant operators in the area?
5. Develop a preliminary cause and effect diagram related to one problem that you have experienced at your college or university. This task may require some speculation on your part. You may also undertake this assignment with four to six other students in this class.
6. Describe a personal situation that occurred within the past six months for which Osborn's creativity model would have been useful. Why would it have been?

CHAPTER 9 Decision-Making Aids 289

◀ **From Where** *You Sit*

"From Where You Sit" questions will prompt you to think about the concepts you just learned in terms of your own experiences or point of view. As you will see, management concepts don't just exist in a textbook—they are happening all around you.

Explore *Current Topics*

In the news you constantly hear about events that affect business operations. But what do these developments really mean? What are their implications for business? In this text, we will help you answer questions like these as they apply to the most current topics affecting business today. Here is a sampling.

Technological *Advances* ▲ ▶

Technological advances change the nature of business. Organizations can embrace new technologies and prosper from them, or risk falling behind competitors who do. In the text you will see how businesses are taking advantage of new technologies, such as virtual reality, the internet, and artificial intelligence.

Types of environmental variables used in a simulation might include inflation rate, short-term interest rate, tax rate, and unemployment level. Strategies used in a simulation could affect price, sales, dividends, cash flow, depreciation, or production capacity. The performance measure used to present the outcome of a simulation model might be an income statement, a financial ratio (e.g., debt-to-equity ratio, return on equity, or earnings per share), or a balance sheet (assets and liabilities).

Manufacturing processes have been studied using computer simulation. In the past, simulations of manufacturing systems were performed mainly by mathematical experts who believed in the results. However, managers often did not believe in them because the results were presented in the form of hard-to-interpret computer printouts. Simulation of manufacturing systems now utilizes a new technology—computer graphics—that is much clearer and easier to understand. Using graphic displays, the simulation evolves step by step on the screen for the user and others to see. As a result, many managers are gaining confidence in simulation results.[14]

virtual reality A surrogate environment created by communications and computer systems.

Virtual Reality. A new technology, **virtual reality,** is a surrogate environment created by communications and computer systems.[15] The term denotes a simulated environment into which a user "enters," moves around, and interacts with objects. Virtual reality fulfills the sensory requirements of human beings for sight, sound, and movement. One of the earliest practical uses of virtual reality was the training of pilots in flight simulators. Its entertainment uses are becoming increasingly common in video games. Some dentists are even using it to relax their patients while performing oral surgery.

The advantage of virtual reality as a planning aid is the freedom it allows for experimentation. The pace of action may be slowed down or speeded up. Processes that occur very rapidly can be slowed down for more careful study. Processes that extend over very long periods of time can be speeded up to reveal more clearly the consequences of particular actions. Actions that cannot be replayed in the real world can be

A Caterpillar engineer tests an electronic prototype of a wheel loader using virtual reality—a surrogate environment created by communications and computer systems.

Electronic mail has become popular with managers for several reasons. First, a manager doesn't have to wait "maybe a week" for a response because information usually can be sent, returned, and recalled in moments. Second, e-mail is relatively inexpensive because it can "piggyback" on computers and other equipment that companies already have in place. Third, it increases productivity by eliminating the need for the paper-handling steps required in traditional interoffice or intercompany communication systems. Mort Meyerson, CEO of Perot Systems, sends and receives more than 7,000 e-mail messages a month. In some months, IBM employees exchange more than 580,000 messages with outside suppliers and customers because staying in touch with these people with e-mail is easier and faster than by using the traditional written communication medium—letters.[20] One significant disadvantage has been observed in companies that use e-mail extensively. Employees who might never confront a co-worker face to face are less hesitant to explode at others via e-mail, a phenomenon called *flaming*. The following account describes the benefits of using e-mail at Intel—without flaming.

Global *Insight*

E-Mail at Intel Corporation

Intel Corporation began using electronic mail more than a decade ago. Today thousands of PCs connect Intel's more than 29,500 employees at locations throughout the world, along with its more than 2,000 customers. The system covers the United States and plants in more than twelve foreign countries.

To illustrate how e-mail works, consider the options available to President Andrew Grove for communicating with a manager in Tsukuba, Japan. Grove can use traditional mail but may not get a reply for weeks. He can send a message via a telex center. To do so, he must dictate a letter containing the message, which has to be retyped at the telex center. The telex message may not arrive in Japan for up to eight hours. (The same procedure, in the opposite direction, must be followed for Grove to receive a reply.) Of course, Grove can call Tsukuba. However, 5:00 P.M. in California is equivalent to 4:00 A.M. in Tsukuba, so timing (as well as cost) make the telephone a less-than-optimal method. E-mail enables Grove to send a message before leaving work in the evening and to have an answer waiting on his computer when he arrives for work the next morning. In terms of cost, e-mail is 90 percent less expensive than overseas calls and letters and 75 percent less costly than telex.

Grove estimates that e-mail and other automated office techniques, such as ProShare©—a system that provides users with video-conferencing capabilities—have had a positive effect on research and development at Intel. Producing state-of-the-art products and services at affordable prices requires that everyone in the organization have access to global information that could affect their efforts.[21]

Internet

Internet A loosely configured, rapidly growing web of 25,000 corporate, educational, and research computer networks around the world.

The **Internet** is a loosely configured, rapidly growing web of 25,000 corporate, educational, and research computer networks around the world.[22] It was created by the Defense Department in 1969 and designed to survive a nuclear war. Rather than route messages through central computers, the Internet makes use of thousands of computers linked by thousands of different paths. Each message sent bears an address code that lets any computer in the Internet forward it toward its destination. Messages usually arrive in seconds; only on rare occasions do they vanish into cyberspace. The Internet is like any other communications device in that a user can get a busy signal. With thousands of Internet groups and e-mail lists, sometimes the traffic is heavy and a user might have to wait. Also, there is no privacy. The information on the Internet is available to anyone.

Trade Agreements
and Economic Partnerships ▶

The news is full of reports about the latest agreements that affect trade among nations. You will learn about agreements like NAFTA, GATT, and the European Union and their implications for strategic management.

tions equipment. Formulas also were established to measure the rate of progress in opening Japan's markets.[60]

North American Free Trade Agreement[61]

The North American Free Trade Agreement (NAFTA) went into effect on January 1, 1994. It created a U.S., Canadian, and Mexican trade zone of 8.2 million square miles, 364 million consumers, and $7 trillion in economic activity. NAFTA represents an extension of the Canada-United States Free Trade Agreement, which went into effect on January 1, 1989.[62]

Actually, NAFTA didn't create free trade, but it certainly liberalizes trade. Over a fifteen-year period, NAFTA initially is intended to reduce and eliminate all tariffs and most nontariff barriers between Canada, Mexico, and the United States. Although full elimination of tariffs will take fifteen years, about 68 percent of the goods imported from Mexico may now enter the United States without tariffs. At the same time, 50 percent of U.S. exports to Mexico are now tariff-free. The agreement also realizes long-held goals of liberalizing trade in services and foreign investment rules abroad, and it tightens the protection of intellectual property (copyrights and patents, in particular).

Although NAFTA further opens Canadian and U.S. markets, the most significant liberalization applies to Mexico. NAFTA expands Canadian and U.S. companies' ability to establish or purchase a business in Mexico and facilitates their ability to sell if they want to leave. NAFTA also loosens previous restrictions on expanding operations for such companies, and it removes restrictions on transferring profits to other countries.

Despite much liberalization, NAFTA retains protectionist elements, some of which may persist indefinitely. NAFTA protects sensitive sectors (e.g., agriculture, minerals, banking, textiles, and apparel) by stretching out the phase-in time, but this protection is temporary. NAFTA also contains other types of protection that not only are permanent but appear to raise trade barriers above pre-NAFTA levels. In some sectors—notably automobiles, textiles, and apparel—NAFTA imposes higher North American content rules. Under the previous Canada-United States Free Trade Agreement, for example, automobiles could be imported duty-free if they contained at least 50 percent Canadian-U.S. inputs. For auto imports to receive NAFTA benefits, the North American rule is now 62.5 percent. For textiles or apparel to qualify for "free" trade under NAFTA, all components—beginning with the yarn or fiber—must be made in North America.

The services that received the most attention in the NAFTA negotiations were finance, insurance, transportation, and telecommunications. NAFTA doesn't change requirements for foreign banks' entry into the United States and Canada. But the opening of the Mexican financial system is among the agreement's most significant achievements. Requirements for entry into brokerage, bonding, insurance, leasing, and warehousing are even more liberal than for banking.

NAFTA and GATT do not eliminate all trade problems among the member countries. But they do provide frameworks through which these problems can be resolved. The less restricted trade resulting from these agreements increases the competitive forces on firms. The ultimate intent is to achieve greater efficiency and consumer satisfaction. GATT and NAFTA are political documents that attempt to cope with competing
omic and cultural interests among countries. As such, they contain loopholes and
tions that will be tested over the decades to come. The provisions of these agree-
no doubt will be welcomed or resisted, depending on their effect on a particular
ry and industry.[63]

pean Union

uropean Union (EU), called the European Community (EC) until 1994, has twelve
ers: Belgium, Denmark, France, Germany, Greece, Ireland, Italy, Luxemburg, the
rlands, Portugal, Spain, and the United Kingdom. These countries contain some
illion consumers. Austria, Finland, Norway, and Sweden are expected to join the

CHAPTER 4 Strategic Management: Global Forces 125

Review Results

The last phase in this process calls for a review of results to measure progress, identify and resolve problems, and revise (drop or add) goals or even the core mission. If these reviews are conducted properly, managers, teams, and individual employees can learn significant lessons from the immediate past and apply those lessons to future planning and actions.[33] Recall from the Preview Insight about Emerson Electric that James Berges, an executive vice-president, holds discussions on profit results with the key managers from Emerson's fifty divisions.

Goals and strategies are the basis of the review process. Managers and teams must review their own results and actively participate in evaluating them. Ideally, the review of results is a mutual problem-solving process involving managers and teams. Managers encourage the teams to identify obstacles or problems that affected the achievement of their goals and to suggest ways to improve performance. These reviews provide feedback to both managers and teams, letting them know how well they are achieving agreed-on goals. Knowledge of results is essential to maintaining and increasing effectiveness and the development of new plans.

Team-based management by goals calls on superiors to shift from being judgmental and critical to being helpful and willing to engage in mutual problem solving.[34] Some managers wrongly interpret this type of review process as "soft." People may be demoted, dismissed, and otherwise held fully accountable under this approach. However, the bases for such actions are less subjective. As a result, making well-founded demotion or dismissal decisions, when corrective actions have failed, should be easier. Moreover, this process should reduce the need for such decisions.[35]

4
Describe benchmarking and the Deming cycle, two planning aids specifically designed to improve quality.

PLANNING FOR QUALITY

Many issues and methods must be considered in planning for total quality. We have already addressed some of them in the Quality Insights and the text of Chapters 1–5. Here and in the remaining chapters we present additional concepts, techniques, and examples for achieving total quality in an organization.

quality Value (linking different grades of a product and price), conformance to established specifications or standards, excellence (providing the best), or meeting and/or exceeding customers' expectations.

Planning for quality starts with the recognition that there is no single indicator of quality. **Quality** has variously been defined as value (linking different grades of products and price), conformance to established specifications or standards, excellence (providing the best), and meeting and/or exceeding customers' expectations. The most common definition of quality is the extent to which a good or service meets and/or exceeds customers' expectations.[36] Consumers often apply the value definition of quality when making purchasing decisions. *Consumer Reports* magazine ranks products and services on both quality and price to arrive at recommendations of "best-buys." Thus alternative perspectives of quality are appropriate in different circumstances.[37]

Let's now turn to two planning aids that focus specifically on enhancing quality: benchmarking and the Deming cycle. Both may be used effectively in the team-based management by goals approach.

Benchmarking

benchmarking The continuous process of comparing an organization's functions, products, or processes with those of best-in-class organizations.

Benchmarking is the continuous process of comparing an organization's strategies, products, or processes with those of *best-in-class* organizations. It is intended to help employees learn how such organizations achieved excellence and then set out to match or exceed them.[38] Benchmarking may be used to assess virtually any aspect of an organization. It identifies and assesses the "best" that is occurring elsewhere to aid a firm in developing its own strategic or tactical plans and processes to reach that level.

Basic Steps. As noted in Figure 6.3, the benchmarking process includes seven basic steps.[39] Step 1 involves *defining the domain* to be benchmarked. This step includes a careful study of the organization's own products and processes that are to be compared

CHAPTER 6 Strategic Management: Planning Aids and Implementation 185

◀ **Total Quality** *Management*

Whether you call it "total quality managment," "continuous improvement," "creating customer value," or any of the other labels, the fact is that the tools of TQM are what managers are using now. To function in business after graduation, you will need to understand and have the skills to apply concepts like benchmarking, the Deming cycle, self-managed work teams, and others. This text will help you do that.

Gain Insights *Into Real Issues Facing* **Real Organizations**

Preview *Insight*

U.S. Sugar Cleans the Everglades

To many travelers, tourists, and Florida residents, the Everglades is a national park characterized by sawgrass, whooping cranes, and alligators. To the U.S. Sugar Company, however, it is a 700,000 acre Everglades agricultural area of which 400,000 acres is their home. In this fragile wetland, the company produces and refines over 20 percent of the sugar consumed in the United States. Recently, U.S. Sugar and other food growers in the Everglades have confronted environmentalists who have put the future of the companies at risk.

Sugar-cane and other vegetable growers historically have used phosphorous fertilizers to improve the quality and yield of their crops. But in the Everglades, the nutrient-poor wetland is below sea level.

1

Describe the m
the external bu
ment and how
organizations.

◀ Preview *Insights*

Each chapter begins with the story of a real organization's experience with current problems and issues. This opening example previews for you the upcoming chapter concepts. After reading the chapter, think back to the "Preview Insight"...Did the company act according to good management practice? Would you have acted differently?

Turbulent Times, author and management consultant Peter Drucker concluded: "Some time during the 1970s, the longest period of continuity in economic history came to an end. At some time during the last ten years, we moved into turbulence."[21]

Turbulent environments aren't limited to large corporations. Consider the competitive, regulatory, and technological changes faced by dentists who run their own practices. Their task environment has changed rapidly and become very complex over the past ten years, as the following Small Business Insight illustrates.

Small Business *Insight*

Dentist Wears Space Garb to Clean Teeth!

The practice of dentistry has changed dramatically in the past ten years: Dentists now wear space suits! Well, they aren't actually space suits; they simply are protection against infectious disease. Sally Marx is no exception. She has been practicing family dentistry in Louisville, Kentucky, since 1963. At that time, the typical dentist graduated from an accredited college of dentistry, established an office, and waited for patients to come. Those who did show up paid for their own dental work. The population was gr
fluoride, so findin
But practic
ment has been re
Let's look at these
loan money to bu
observing contin
Compliance with
to be successful.
In the 1990s
diseases threaten
the dentists provi
dental equipment
ance companies a
patient assigned
petition has incre
duce new proced
because of emplo
When Dr. M
sleeves. Her offic
modem to transm
dicate environme
use in restoring
changed? Not mu
Just ask Dr. Marx

Obviousl
One is the ch
placed perso
the past fifte
hepatitis, a li
Moreover
straints impo
new constrain
ance. In addit
to protect de

◀ Small Business *Insights*

Many of you will work in small businesses upon graduation. Today's business climate presents special problems and opportunities for small business. Every chapter presents at least one insight into the world of the entrepreneur and the small organizations that play such a large role in our economy.

Three primary reasons often are suggested for embracing the stakeholder social responsibility concept: (1) enlightened self-interest, (2) sound investment, and (3) interference avoidance.[58] Under the rationale of enlightened self-interest, management uses social responsibility to justify numerous decisions and actions. The general idea is that a better society creates a better environment for business. Under the rationale of sound investment, management believes that social responsibility has a positive effect on a company's net worth. Socially responsible firms claim that their stocks sell at higher prices than those of less socially responsible firms. Higher stock prices, in turn, reduce the cost (interest rate) of capital and increase earnings. As you might expect, this view is highly controversial.[59] Under the rationale of interference avoidance, management aims to minimize control of company decisions by powerful stakeholders, such as government agencies and pressure groups. Industry self-regulation often is justified on the basis of interference avoidance.

Although there is virtually no research on the subject, we suspect that the stakeholder concept is the concept most widely supported by the general public and many managers. More and more organizations are likely to apply the stakeholder concept proactively in the future when considering complex issues and alternative courses of action. The following Quality Insight reviews AT&T's application of the stakeholder concept in improving environmental quality. It illustrates that multiple stakeholders—environmental groups, governmental agencies, the general public, and shareholders—can be winners through lower costs.

Quality *Insight*

AT&T Goes Green

American Telephone & Telegraph (AT&T) established goals for reducing air emissions, CFCs, solid waste, and hazardous waste in 1990. Under the direction of David R. Chittick, AT&T's vice-president of environment and safety, the company has either surpassed its goals or been ahead of schedule in meeting them. To engineer ozone-depleting emissions out of its operations, AT&T invested $25 million to develop an array of alternative technologies. One, called low solids spray fluxer, eliminates the need for CFC solvents to clean excess flux from electronic circuit boards. AT&T is now selling this technology to some twenty-five other companies, among them IBM. AT&T even gives its ideas away at times. Engineers developed an alternative for 1,1,1-tricholroethane, another ozone-depleting solvent used to clean circuit boards. AT&T managed to eliminate virtually all its ozone-depleting substances a year and a half before the company's goal, and 2fi years ahead of the worldwide ban.

Now AT&T doesn't have to worry about the new U.S. law that requires companies to put warning labels on all goods that contain or are manufactured with ozone-depleting substances. The company figures that the cost of tracking and labeling all the tiny components and switching systems that it once manufactured with CFCs would add up to hundreds of thousands of dollars. The early phaseout also will save AT&T $25 million annually in supply costs because taxes on CFCs have helped boost its price from about $0.80 per pound in 1986 to more than $11 per pound in 1993. The substitutes developed for CFCs average $0.50 per pound.

In addition, AT&T embraced total quality management (TQM) principles to solve the universal office pollution problem of too much paper. First, the company established a corporate paper reduction goal of 15 percent by 1995; then it created a corporate TQM team to figure out how to meet it. Following classic TQM techniques, the team identified AT&T's heaviest paper users, called "fat rabbits." The fat rabbits in turn formed TQM teams to help meet the companywide goal. The internal information management unit, fat bunny No. 2 behind copying centers, accounted for about a quarter of AT&T's total paper use for such things as marketing and financial reports. The department's TQM teams suggested simple ways to decrease paper consumption, such as eliminating cover pages and using electronic rather than printed media. The department was consuming 22 percent less paper within a year.[60]

228 PART 3 Decision Making

Quality *Insights* **▶**

The 29 "Quality Insight" boxes located throughout the text will help you see how TQM tools are applied at real companies. Organizations today strive for quality in everything they do—from physical products to customer services to even internal processes for cost control.

Ethics *Insights* ▶

Business decisions often contain an ethics component. Pressures to increase profits can tempt an employee to cut corners. Sometimes honest attempts to motivate employees can result in unethical practices. "Ethics Insight" boxes contained in almost every chapter will give you an opportunity to test your own standards. These insights present examples of actions by real companies. You be the judge—were their actions ethical or unethical?

Ethics *Insight*

Computer Monitoring of Employees

Every morning for nearly two years, Meg Narducci came to work, logged onto her computer, logged on again to her terminal, plugged in her headphones, hit the ready button, and started to answer more than 200 calls in rapid succession, starting each one with "Hello, national customer service department. This is Meg."

Throughout the day, every second of her time was accounted for. Every conversation she had was subject to surveillance. Her manager knew everything she did. The computer she logged onto matched her name to every message she typed. The terminal next to her computer functioned like a high-tech stopwatch. It told her manager what time she punched in and out for the day, what time she took her scheduled lunch break, when she went to the bathroom, how long she stayed in the bathroom, how much time she was available to take calls, how many she took, and how long she spent on each one. For example, if she spent an extra minute in the bathroom that minute would be deducted from the six min-

...ck pain, ...at their man-

...d that all U.S. ...the increased ...yers to report ...and employer ...1988 requires ...will maintain ...datory imple-...ployee aware-

...ated $100 bil-...cts, workplace ...dent rates are ...1,000 organi-...21 percent just ...ost of the na-...ing of current

...b applicant to ...e is tested by ...-hand coordi-...a preference ...performance, ...screening test.

...al exam ques-

Global *Insights* ▶

The world is getting smaller. Relaxation of trade barriers by agreements such as NAFTA and GATT, as well as joint ventures, economic partnerships like the European Union, and technological advances that make communication easier are among the many developments bringing nations closer together. Throughout the text, "Global Insights" help you understand the nature of the global environment in which business operates.

technologies. And personal communicators made by an AT&T/IBM joint venture will permit phone, fax, and computing with a pen input screen.[37]

As a result, organizations will change the way they conduct business, and new companies that have developed and manufactured such devices will become household words like AT&T and IBM. The following Global Insight describes how some companies are gambling that access to the information highway will control the future of information technology.

Global *Insight*

Traveling the Information Superhighway

While the politicians try to decide what it is, the information superhighway is being put together by entrepreneurs, corporations, and universities around the world. This superhighway, unlike the Interstate Highway System begun in the 1950s, is an invisible web of machines, software, data, and graphics that interconnects users from throughout the world. This superhighway offers vast opportunities to those who design and develop its component parts and to those who use it to speed up organizational activities. Let's look at some of the organizations competing in this industry.

Oracle is a $1.6 billion Silicon Valley company that hasn't yet become a household word. The company is the number one producer of database software used by large corporations today. But CEO and part owner Larry Ellison isn't satisfied with his company's successes. He sees its database technology ex-...that global merchandising bazaars can bring together such ...in Iowa and a lender in Germany, or a bronze manufacturer

...of the whole. To access the database, both industrial and end ...digital signal processing (DSP) methods—a U.S. created and ...new generations of displays called high-definition television ...logy, and new generations of wired telephone connections. ...much larger amounts of data, particularly graphics, can be ...ly.

...such as Sprint, have been leaders in the global effort to create ...established players are not out of the race. Microsoft has in-...ntial research and development budget in developing operat-...rmation superhighway appealing to even the most unsophisti-...American telephone companies also are racing to update their ...ect to the communications companies of other countries. ...nts a change in technology for all companies. Like the com-...evitalized manufacturing, the information superhighway has ...people communicate at work and home. Consider the ...th this information system, Seal and other cargo carriers can ...ll let the shipper visually inspect the location, condition, and ...iner is on land, the signal is sent via cellular carrier. When ...ommunication satellite program (GPS) can track the cargo. ...s a major cost for shippers; more than $5 billion in losses ...one. ...is the wave of the future. It presents unparalleled opportuni-...demise for those firms who don't.[38]

...y will affect every organization in the years ahead. ...ogy, this element of the task environment undoubt-...olitical-legal environment as customers and managers

Philosophy and Management Style

Team-based management by goals reflects a positive philosophy about people and a participative management style. In Figure 6.2, it is phase 1 and provides the foundation for all subsequent planning and implementation actions. It has the following attributes.

- Mutual problem solving by individuals and teams across departmental lines and at different organizational levels.
- Trusting and open communication.
- Emphasis on win-win relationships in which all parties can benefit through cooperation.
- Rewards and promotions based directly on job- and team-related performance and achievement.
- Minimal use of political games, fear, and/or force.
- A positive, proactive, and challenging organizational culture.

This philosophy and management style fosters broad participation by teams and individuals in the development and review of goals and plans. However, some goals have to come from the top. For example, the U.S. Environmental Protection Agency (EPA) has required companies to achieve environmental goals within a specified period of time or pay stiff fines. Consequently, top management may require managers and teams to set departmental goals to reduce environmental hazards.

As suggested in the following Diversity Insight, strong leadership may be crucial in providing the spark to develop goals and plans on difficult and sensitive issues. It emphasizes the essential role that participation, teams, and incentives played in implementing Hoechst Celanese's diversity plan.

Diversity *Insight*

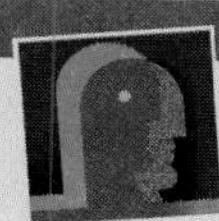

Hoechst Celanese Diversity Plan

Ernest H. Drew, the CEO of Hoechst Celanese, the chemical giant, remembers exactly when he became an advocate of a more diverse work force. He was attending a 1990 conference for Hoechst's top 125 officers. They were mostly white men, who were joined by 50 or so lower level women and members of minority groups. The group split into problem-solving teams; some were mixed by race and gender, but others were all white and male. The main issue was how the corporate culture affected the business and what changes might be made to improve results. When the teams presented their findings, a light clicked on for Drew. "It was so obvious that the diverse teams had the broader solutions," he recalls. "They had ideas I hadn't even thought of. For the first time, we realized that diversity is a strength as it relates to problem solving. Before, we just thought of diversity as the total number of minorities and women in the company, like affirmative action. Now we knew we needed diversity at every level of the company where decisions are made."

Under Drew's direction, work-force diversity is one of four performance criteria equally weighted in determining managers' salaries and bonuses. The other three are financial success, customer satisfaction, and environmental and safety improvements. Hoechst Celanese's diversity goal is specific: at least 34 percent representation of women and minorities at all levels of the company by the year 2001. This top-to-bottom target, which Drew refers to as reaching "vertical parity," mirrors the company's future work force—the percentage of women and minorities graduating with relevant majors from colleges where the company recruits.

The diversity plan includes a comprehensive set of strategies and proposed actions. One strategy is the requirement that the top twenty-six officers join two organizations in which they are a minority. Drew is a board member of the African-American Hampton University and of SER-Jobs for Progress, a Hispanic association. He explains why management put this policy in place: "The only way to break out of comfort zones is to be exposed to other people. When we are, it becomes clear that all people are similar."[29]

◀ **Diversity** *Insights*

A diverse work force is a strength to use to advantage, not a problem to be solved. In the 29 "Diversity Insights" throughout the text, you will explore cultural differences and see how the trend toward diversity affects business today.

Integrated *Learning* System

◄ ▼ The learning objectives listed at the beginning of every chapter briefly state the skills you will acquire from reading the chapter. Each objective, with its numbered icon, then appears in the chapter margin where the objective is fulfilled. The summary at the end of the chapter is organized around the learning objectives as well, reinforcing these key skills.

Chapter 9

Decision-Making Aids

Chapter *Outline*

Preview Insight: Andersen's Window of Knowledge

Normative Decision Making

Routine Decision Making

Learning *Objectives*

After studying this chapter, you

1. State the benefits and lim making.
2. Discuss rules and standar artificial intelligence as a ing.
3. Explain break-even analy Pareto analysis as aids to
4. Describe Osborn's creati effect diagram as aids to

Preview *Insight*

Andersen's Window of Knowledge

Andersen Windows, Inc., of Baypoint, Minnesota, makes windows in various shapes and sizes. They include made-to-order units designed for diverse home and office needs. Multimedia software called *Window of Knowledge* provides Andersen dealers with an interactive, on-line tool that they can use to demonstrate and design customized window systems. The same software provides specifications for Andersen products and information about competitors' products. It also supports a full range of administrative and sales tasks. These tasks include creating proposals, pricing installations, calculating the energy efficiency of designs, placing and tracking orders, and managing accounts.

Dave Coraccio of Harvey Industries, Inc., a supplier to building contractors in Woburn, Massachusetts, is a big fan of the *Window of Knowledge* system. "The system has enabled me to work with customers faster, more accurately and with more professional-looking results," Coraccio says. A customer ...

1 State the benefits and limitations of normative decision making.

normative decision making Any prescribed step-by-step process that individuals may use to help them make choices.

268 PART 3 Decision Making

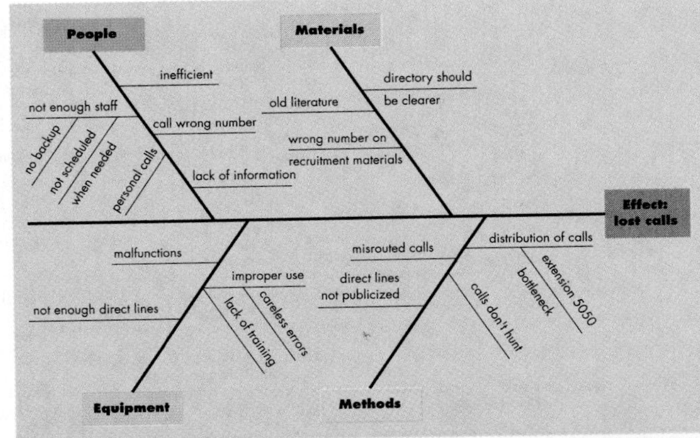

FIGURE 9.4

Cause and Effect Diagram for Phone Project

Source: DeCosmo, Richard D., Parker, Jerome S., and Haverly, Mary Ann. "Total Quality Management Goes to Community College," from p. 18. In L.A. Sherr and D.J. Teeter (eds.), *Total Quality Management in Higher Education*, no. 71. Copyright 1991 Jossey-Bass Inc., Publishers.

CHAPTER SUMMARY

1 ***State the benefits and limitations of normative decision making.*** Normative decision-making aids provide step-by-step procedures for helping individuals make effective decisions. Their purpose is to reveal hidden assumptions, clarify underlying reasoning processes, improve judgments, increase awareness of emotional responses, and reduce judgmental biases. They are limited by the impossibility of eliminating all emotional and attitudinal biases, of foreseeing all future events, and of acquiring complete data.

2 ***Discuss rules and standard operating procedures and artificial intelligence as aids to routine decision making.*** Rules and standard operating procedures (SOPs) prescribe specific ways of solving organizational problems and making decisions. Artificial intelligence (AI) refers to a wide range of computer systems programmed to manipulate data and make limited humanlike judgments based on information that users enter into the systems.

3 ***Explain break-even analysis, the payoff matrix, and Pareto analysis as aids to adaptive decision making.*** Break-even analysis shows graphically the relationships between sales (revenues) and costs and identifies the break-even point where revenues and costs are equal. The payoff matrix helps decision makers mathematically evaluate alternative solutions after goals have been set and alternative strategies specified. The alternatives

288 PART 3 Decision Making

▼ ▶ The Study Guide is also organized around the learning objectives. The chapter outline shows where each objective is covered. The true-false and multiple-choice questions are grouped by objective. Your instructor's materials are also tied to the text content through the learning objectives, so your objectives and the ones your instructor has for you are the same.

Chapter 9: Decision Making Aids 145

CHAPTER OUTLINE

1

I. **Normative Decision Making**—is any step-by-step process that individuals use to help them make choices.[1]

1. The rational model is an example of normative decision making.

   a. The steps in the rational model of decision making are: 1) define and diagnose the problem, 2) set goals, 3) search for alternative solutions, 4) compare and evaluate alternative solutions, 5) choose among alternative solutions, 6) implement the solution selected, and 7) follow-up and control.

2. The bounded rationality and political models are descriptive models (representations of how individuals actually make decisions).

...llowing assumptions:

...nd agreed upon.

...ailable.

...ranges from certainty to risk to uncer-

...s are likely to be brought into the open and

...be communicated to others effectively.

...ecting relevant information, and quantify-
...lihood of making a decision based on sound

...of powerful emotional forces, such as the
...g alternatives.

...m decision making can be reduced.[3]

...de in response to relatively well-defined

...e followed in dealing with a particular

Chapter 9: Decision-Making Aids 155

TRUE OR FALSE

Directions: Write True or False in the space provided.

1

_____ 1. The bounded rationality model of decision making is an example of normative decision making.

_____ 2. One assumption of normative decision making is that some information about the problem is available.

_____ 3. One benefit of normative decision making aids is that hidden assumptions and their implications are likely to be brought into the open and clarified.

2

...ide employ-

...e extensive

...ore they can

...disseminate

...ision situa-

...y cause the

...l occur.

...ased on an

...of identify-

Chapter 9: Decision-Making Aids 159

MULTIPLE CHOICE

Directions: Select the best answer in the space provided.

1

____ 1. The _______ model of decision making is an example of normative decision making.
a. bounded rationality
b. rational
c. Osborn
d. political

____ 2. Normative decision making is based on which of the following assumptions?
a. The goals can be stated and agreed upon.
b. The nature of the problem can be defined and agreed upon.
c. Some information about the problem is available.[9]
d. All of the above.

2

____ 3. _______ are standard choices made in response to relatively well-defined and well-known problems and solutions.
a. innovative
b. adaptive
c. routine
d. normative

____ 4. Plastic Co, a plastic manufacturing company, requires every employee to wear safety glasses. This is referred to as a(n):
a. policy
b. rule
c. SOP
d. standard

____ 5. The _______rule is a guide to which decisions and actions are ethical and which are not.
a. golden
b. pareto
c. moral
d. golden parachute

____ 6. _______ is the ability of a properly programmed computer system to perform functions normally associated with human intelligence.
a. artificial intelligence
b. computer matrix
c. artificial electronics
d. computer analysis

3

____ 7. The 7-Up Company uses _______ analysis to make year-by-year comparisons of product-line (such as diet versus regular) profits.
a. budget
b. matrix
c. break-even
d. data

The purpose of organizing the text and supplements around the objectives is to create a tightly integrated learning system. The initial list of objectives serve as a preview of the competencies that you will be expected to demonstrate after studying the chapter. The objectives in the margin show you where to find the applicable material, and the summaries review what you have learned about each objective.

After reading the chapter, review the chapter summary and work the Study Guide questions. If you find from these review activities that you need further study on a particular objective, you can easily locate all applicable material by simply looking for the numbered icon. Also, your instructor will be testing your knowledge of these key concepts as the final link in the learning system.

Preface

Our vision for the seventh edition of *Management* can be conveyed in one word—*insights.* Through *insights,* students develop understanding, skills, competencies, knowledge, judgment, and intuition. This vision required us to help develop the competencies, knowledge, and skills needed by both employees and managers today and in 21st-century organizations. Our vision of nourishing *insights* drove every aspect of this book—from text content, to special features, to design, to the supplemental learning packages. Throughout this preface, we convey the many ways this book implements our vision.

Our editorial team at South-Western Publishing also proposed a unique vision that complements our own. They proposed the creation of an *integrated learning system* to support the process by which students may acquire the skills, knowledge, and competencies they will need upon graduation as professionals and team members, and eventually as team leaders or managers. We soon discovered that these two visions were mutually supportive. However, it was a new challenge and learning experience in implementing our vision through the student-oriented *integrated learning system.* This required significant adjustments and closer coordination than ever with the ancillaries' authors. The results were well worth the added demands along the way. Students and instructors will be delighted by the merging of our *insights vision* and the *integrated learning system vision.* Read on to see how these two visions created a special synergy.

The text is packed with skill-building features, interesting cases, and new intriguing insights. They enable students to experience the excitement of contemporary organizational and managerial concepts, methods, and practices. Real-world examples are brought into the classroom throughout the text. We include fresh, relevant coverage of people and organizations that students know and might like to know. In keeping with this reality-based perspective, we focus on *telling it like it is* as well as *telling it like it should be.* Thus, students will learn from both good and bad applications of methods, practices, and concepts.

In addition, we go beyond text presentations by challenging students to develop deeper insights and a portfolio of skills. That way, students who study this text should come away equipped with new skills and the confidence they need to develop their own professional potential.

Focus on Skill-Building and Competencies

The development of skills and competencies are emphasized within each chapter. For example, we present *Skill-Building Exercises* and *From Where You Sit* questions at the end of each chapter. These features engage students in applying chapter concepts to their own experiences. In the process, students also learn about themselves as future professionals.

Developing Conceptual and Critical-Thinking Skills. To become successful professionals, students need to learn to process large quantities of information, deal with risks and uncertainties, sort out relevant facts, identify assumptions, creatively devise alternatives, and draw conclusions. These skills and competencies are nourished through the integration of *Critical Thinking Cases* and different types of *Insights* into every chapter of the text. These applications give students first-hand experience with the complexities and subtleties of organizational problems, issues, and opportunities. This exposure not only builds conceptual and critical thinking skills, but also highlights their importance and relevance.

Developing Total Quality Competencies. We greatly increased our discussion of total quality management—including the philosophy, methods, tools and processes that aid in the quest for high-quality goods and services. Total quality concepts are blended throughout the text. For example, we include: the quality viewpoint in the discussion of the evolution of management (Chapter 2), benchmarking (Chapter 6), Deming cycle (Chapter 6), Pareto analysis (Chapter 9), cause and effect diagram (Chapter 9), performance appraisal under total quality management (Chapter 12), teams and total quality (Chapter 16), activity-based costing for quality control (Chapter 18), Deming's prescriptions and the Baldrige framework and award (Chapter 20). *Quality Insight* boxes guide students to continuously think in terms of total quality—a philosophy and goal that more and more organizations recognize as critical for competitive survival. In addition, twenty-one chapters include a *Quality Insight* feature.

Developing Diversity Competencies. We develop the theme of diversity as a competitive and cultural strength throughout the text. We show students how effective team members, team leaders, and managers draw upon the strengths of people with differing backgrounds and life experiences to help their teams, departments, and organizations prosper. As organizations move increasingly toward global operations, diversity competencies become even more salient. The text guides students to gain insights regarding diversity concepts, issues, and controversies. Through this process, they strengthen the interpersonal and communication skills and competencies needed to succeed in a culturally diverse work environment. In addition, twenty chapters include a new *Diversity Insight* feature.

Developing Interpersonal and Communication Skills. The ability to perform effectively as a team member or leader to achieve goals, engage in creative decision making, and solve problems is another core theme we weave throughout *Management*. In every chapter, students may participate in skill-building exercises to enhance interpersonal and communication skills, as well as comptencies in team building, creative decision making, and conflict management. We also emphasize the need for self-diagnosis and self-insight in job-related roles.

Developing Global Competencies. We devote an entire chapter to the discussion of global forces and their linkages to organizations. In addition, we present global insights that are relevant to the content of each chapter. Even if students do not have careers in global operations, the text demonstrates the relevance of global issues and provides insight into global competitive, technological, political-legal, and cultural issues. In addition, twenty-one chapters include a *Global Insight* feature.

Developing Ethical Competencies. A wide range of issues is presented to guide students through the ethical challenges experienced by employees and organizations, which do not always have simple right or wrong answers. From promotion policies to offering "gifts" to foreign officials, the text leads students through the ethical complexities often faced by employees and managers. Chapter 7 presents the concepts, uses, and limitations of three foundation ethical approaches. These approaches serve as the basis for three types of social responsibility. We present admirable and questionable ethical practices and challenge students to think through some tough issues. In addition, nineteen chapters include an *Ethics Insight* feature.

Developing Small Business Competencies. The unique opportunities and problems of small business management and entrepreneurship are networked through the whole text. We help students to understand and sample the competencies necessary for success in this area. Many students may eventually have careers in small business management. Thus, we devote a whole chapter (Chapter 22) to the unique challenges of small business and entrepreneurship. In addition, twenty-two chapters include a *Small Business Insight* feature that applies the chapter's content to a small business situation.

Developing Technical Skills. Technical skills are the ability to apply specific methods, procedures, and techniques for achieving organizational goals. We added a variety of total quality methods, tools, and processes that aid in the quest for high-quality goods and services. We also improved our presentations for developing the skills needed to use such methods and aids as breakeven analysis, payoff matrix, Delphi technique, Devil's advocacy method, program evaluation and review technique (PERT), corrective control model, and reengineering, among others.

Coverage of Current Topics

The following is a sample of the many current topics discussed in this new edition:

- Managing a diverse work force, plus global and domestic work force trends.
- The quality viewpoint as a unique perspective in the evolution of management.
- The ecosystem and information technologies as environmental forces that affect managing strategically.
- The General Agreement on Tariffs and Trade (GATT) and the North American Free Trade Agreement (NAFTA), including their implications for strategic management.
- Benchmarking, virtual reality, and the Deming cycle as planning aids in strategic management.
- The linkages between total quality management, environmental policies and actions, and social responsibility.
- Pareto analysis and the cause and effect diagram as decision-making aids in total quality management initiatives.
- Customer departmentalization as a way of organizing to increase service quality.
- Network organization design.
- The movement toward small business as a result of downsizing.
- Self-managed work teams.
- Impacts of information technologies on changing patterns of interpersonal and organizational communications.
- Types of organizational cultures.
- Negotiation in conflict management.
- Activity-based accounting as a method of improving control and total quality.
- Advanced information management technologies.
- Agile manufacturing and reengineering for total quality.
- The learning organization as a process and system for facilitating change.

As previously noted, our intention was to simply provide a snapshot—which we did for only the first five chapters, and there are seventeen more—of the new value-added topics and approaches in this edition.

Competency and Skill-Building Cases

One primary path for implementing our vision is through the use of real-life examples to guide students in learning organizational and managerial concepts, methods, and practices. Current users tell us that our chapter-end cases are just the right length and level of difficulty for their students. We retain this feature with twenty-two *Critical Thinking Cases,* nineteen of which are new to this edition. In addition, we present seven *Integrative Part Cases* for a greater challenge and seventeen *Video Cases* that reflect elements of the experiential learning process.

Critical Thinking Cases. We designed our popular end-of-chapter cases—nineteen of them new to this edition—to stimulate students by applying and enriching their conceptual, critical thinking, and technical skills. These cases are purposely short, provocative, and relevant to the concepts in the chapter. Each case engages students with the opportunity to apply concepts, assess clues, identify assumptions, use various methods, and make decisions.

Integrative Part Cases. The *Integrative Part Cases* are new this edition. The seven cases enrich the challenge to students by networking issues, concepts, and methods across chapters. These longer, more complex cases provide an excellent opportunity for the further deepening of conceptual, critical thinking, technical and communication skills in the areas of ethics, quality, diversity, global, entrepreneurial and small business issues.

Video Cases. The *Video Cases* are new to this edition. They create added variety in your students' learning about organizations, teams, and management. The seventeen video cases present a variety of issues, organizations, and people. Each video is supported by a written video case in the text with questions to aid diagnosis and analysis. These provocative, newsworthy videos feature well-known organizations such as Saturn, IBM, and The Body Shop. Hundreds of videos were screened to select those that are the most consistent with the vision of this text. Students will enjoy the variety created by this new feature and will learn from it.

Insights Deliver Real-World Perspective

Throughout the book, seven special and general *Insights* bring real-world organizations, employees, and issues into the classroom. Through Microsoft to Taco Bell, students gain a portfolio of insights. In addition to the six types of special insights, there are twenty-seven general *Insights,* of which twenty-three are new to this edition.

Preview Insights. *Preview Insights* invite students into the chapter concepts through real-world issues, such as *Nike's Network Organization* in Chapter 11. Twenty-one of the twenty-two *Preview Insights* are new to this edition. They are crafted to stimulate students' interest in the chapter content and assist them in understanding the relevance of the chapter topics.

Diversity Insights. *Diversity Insights* are new to this edition. They reveal concepts, methods, and examples of how organizations deal with and resolve diversity issues. We show how diversity issues and practices impact the effectiveness of organizations. This demonstrates to students how they may benefit from the unique ideas and behaviors of a culturally diverse environment. There are twenty-one *Diversity Insights,* nineteen of which are totally new to this edition.

Ethics Insights. *Ethics Insights* are new to this edition. They demonstrate how ethical issues and problems will continue as organizations expand abroad and strive to serve diverse stakeholders, including customers, stockholders, and government regulators. Within this coverage, we emphasize the ethical concepts and practices needed to acquire insights into individual and team decisions and actions within all types of organizations. There are nineteen *Ethics Insights,* of which eighteen are totally new to this edition.

Global Insights. *Global Insights* offer perspectives on how issues, concepts, and practices may vary or be consistent across cultures and nations. They also present problems faced by employees and managers in global operations. This feature appears in twenty-one chapters, and twenty-four of the twenty-nine *Global Insights* are new to this edition. In addition, we devote Chapter 4 to a comprehensive discussion of the linkages among global forces and organizations.

Quality Insights. *Quality Insights* are new to this edition. They influence students in developing the competencies needed for total quality, which are increasingly valued by organizations. The quality philosophy, concepts, methods, and practices are threaded throughout the book. There are twenty-nine *Quality Insights,* of which twenty-seven are new to this edition.

Small Business Insights. *Small Business Insights* are new to this edition. They note how concepts, methods, and practices are applied by small business entrepreneurs, managers, and employees. Many students will eventually work for, do business with, or own small-scale firms. In addition, we devote Chapter 22 to the special questions and concerns of small businesses and entrepreneurs. There are twenty-four *Small Business Insights,* of which twenty-three are new to this edition.

Integrated Learning System

In order to ease the course organization, we use an *integrated learning system* to develop insights through the concepts, methods, and practices. This system provides a comprehensive, cohesive pedagogy. The text and all major ancillaries are organized according to the specific learning objectives listed at the beginning of each chapter. A numbered icon like this (1) precedes each learning objective in the text. These icons and their objectives then appear in the text margins and summaries to mark where each learning objective is fulfilled. Matching objective icons carry the system throughout the *Instructor's Resource Manual, Test Manual,* and *Student Study Guide.* The applicable content and support materials for a particular objective are found by simply looking for the icon.

Chapter Summaries. Concise chapter summaries are also organized around the learning objectives. We included this "boiled down" information to provide students with a helpful, convenient way to review each objective's main points.

Key Terms. To help students absorb new terminology, we present each new key term in bold, and then provide a concise definition of that term in the margin.

Glossary. A comprehensive glossary of all key terms appears at the end of the book for easy reference.

Indexes. We complied three indexes to assist students in quickly finding needed information. These indexes include an *Organizations Index,* a *Subject Index,* and an *Author Index.*

Superb Ancillaries

Working closely with us, the ancillary authors crafted a rich array of truly superb supplements to assist in the preparation of effective lectures and tests. All ancillaries—from the learning-based Test Manual to the comprehensive *Instructor's Resource Manual,* to the colored transparencies, to the timely videos, to the *Annotated Instructor's Edition*—are designed to facilitate teaching in the instructor's own style. They are organized around the chapter learning objectives and their corresponding icons to create a cohesive, integrated learning system.

Annotated Instructor's Edition. The margins in the *Annotated Instructor's Edition* of the text are rich in useful tips, additional examples, and information to enhance the learning process. Instructors can choose from over thirty-five annotations per chapter of the following types:

Real-World Examples. Numerous current examples are provided from the popular press to support the text concepts. These examples do not appear in the student text, so instructors can choose the ones they want to enhance class presentations.

Teaching Tips. These annotations are notes to instructors about activities, alternative approaches to the material, and discussion topics to help clarify difficult concepts.

Ethics. Ethics continues to be a core issue in organizations. These annotations describe ethical issues that relate to the topics being discussed at that point in the text. By incorporating them into presentations, instructors have another avenue for revealing how most decisions have an ethics component.

Ask Students. These annotations supply provocative questions to stimulate class discussion on the text topics.

Discussion Questions. To help instructors engage the end-of-chapter discussion questions, they are reproduced in the instructor's edition margin at the appropriate points in the discussion. These questions can be used to check student understanding or to prompt class discussion.

Instructor's Resource Manual. The *Instructor's Resource Manual* is another cornerstone to the integrated learning system. The comprehensive lecture notes, integrated with the text and major ancillaries through the learning objectives, refer instructors to the support materials at the appropriate points in the lecture:

- Insight box summaries
- Learning objectives
- Enrichment modules
- Transparency cues
- Discussion questions
- "From Where You Sit" questions
- Skill-building exercises

These features assist in organizing lectures, choosing support materials, bringing in outside enrichment materials, and taking full advantage of the integrated learning system. The lecture notes are something instructors can use—not just a list of headings.

The enrichment modules are a particularly valuable resource. They contain relevant information from outside the text for extending lectures and challenging students. Transparency masters accompany most enrichment modules.

In addition to the lecture notes and enrichment modules, the *Instructor's Resource Manual* supplies solutions to all end-of-chapter questions, critical thinking cases, video cases, and part cases. The end of each chapter provides a list of relevant videos and films, with a short description of each.

Videos and Video Cases. Excellent and professionally produced videos from CNBC Business News and other organizations are provided to bring action-based insights right into the classroom. The seventeen videos are supported through written video cases at the end of seventeen chapters. Helpful previews, comments, and suggested answers to the questions are provided in the *Instructor's Resource Manual.*

Transparencies. Approximately 120 colored acetates are provided free to adopters of the text. Transparency masters accompany most Enrichment Modules and are included in the *Instructor's Resource Manual.*

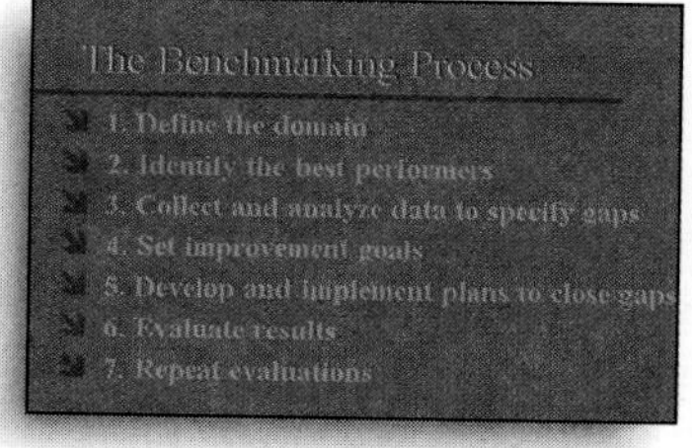

PowerPoint. The images of the approximately 120 acetate transparencies are also available on PowerPoint software. The user only needs Windows to run the PowerPoint viewer and an LCD panel for classroom display.

Test Manual. The printed *Test Manual* contains 3,324 test items, including the correct answers. Question types include multiple choice, true/false and essays for each chapter. Many questions require application or analysis, not just memorization. South-Western's new computerized test bank called *MicroExam 4.0* includes all of the objective questions from the printed test and operates on IBM compatible PCs for easy customization. Answer keys are included.

Student Study Guide. Students have told us that they use study guides to prepare for tests. Therefore, the guide presents additional questions for each chapter that parallel, but do not duplicate, test manual questions. The guide also includes outlines of key concepts, organized by learning objectives. The questions, too, are grouped by learning objective. If students find they need to review material to master a particular objective, they can easily find the relevant text material by looking for the icon.

Videodisc Technology. The latest videodisc technology can bring multimedia capabilities to classroom presentations. The *Management* videodisc contains over 90 minutes of text-related video, definitions, transparencies, and text illustrations for classroom projection. The content can be viewed in any order choosen. With optional computer and South-Western software, a complete video *script* of classroom presentations can be made ahead of time. An accompanying Videodisc Guide describes how to integrate this technology in the classroom. A compatible "CAV-type" videodisc player is required to use this feature.

How To Pack Your Career Parachute. We know that many students are concerned about finding the right job. This concise, easy-to-read ancillary gives them specific information on how to develop a résumé, prepare for an interview, and make career decisions.

Acknowledgments

We give special thanks to A. Benton Cocanougher, Dean of the College of Business Administration and Graduate School of Business, and Richard W. Woodman, head of the Department of Management at Texas A&M University, as well as Tom Barry and Mick McGill at Southern Methodist University for their personal support and encouragement. Our thanks to them for creating an environment that made possible the completion of this book project. For their outstanding help with many critical tasks and manuscript preparation, we express our deep gratitude to Kim Bravenec of Texas A&M University and Billie Boyd of Southern Methodist University. Their professionalism and dedication were central to this project from the very beginning to the submission of the last element.

Many individuals at South-Western College Publishing applied their ample professional skills in developing this text and the related supplements. Because of them and others, we feel this is an outstanding text with superb supplements—all of which are networked through an *integrated learning system*. Those most directly involved at South-Western include: Randy Haubner, the sponsoring editor for this book; Cinci Stowell, the senior development editor whose expertise is reflected in every chapter; Robert Runck, the development editor who provided many sage suggestions for enhancing each chapter; Sharon Smith, the production editor who handled the many interface issues in the production process; Mike Elinger, who is chiefly responsible for the attractive and supportive art program; Mary Goljenboom, who obtained the photos to enrich the written words; and Debbie Kokoruda, who lead the development of the professional design.

In addition, we are grateful to Ben Welch (Texas A&M University), who selected the videos and wrote the video cases that appear in seventeen chapters; Jerrold A. Moore, our copyeditor, whose superb professional skills enhanced the flow and readability of the manuscript; and Michael K. McCuddy (professor of human resource management at Valparaiso University), who served as the primary author in revising Chapters 12 and 13.

Thanks also to our excellent team of ancillary authors. They worked extremely hard to include all of the necessities, exercised their ample creativity in developing the *extras* to make their ancillaries special, and contributed to the team effort of implementing the *integrated learning system*.

Valerie Yates
California State University, Los Angeles
Instructor's Resource Manual and Transparencies

Cliff Cheng
University of California, Riverside
Annotated Instructor's Edition

G. Scott King
Sinclair Community College
How To Pack Your Career Parachute

Ben Welch
Texas A&M University
Test Manual

Elizabeth Cameron
Alma College
Student Study Guide

We worked with all of the ancillary contributors to assure compatability and coordination with the text material.

Our colleagues and friends at Texas A&M University and Southern Methodist University have created the environment that nurtures our continuous professional development. We thank them. We are grateful to our families for their empathy and understanding in *letting us go* for over a year to devote evenings and weekends on our *authors' island*. With the completion of this text, we look forward to having more time with our families.

A number of reviewers made insightful suggestions and comments on one or more chapters. Although there were some differences among them as to what to include, modify, or delete, their comments and suggestions resulted in substantial improvements. We are very grateful to the following reviewers for sharing their professional insights:

Peggy Brewer
Eastern Kentucky University

Elizabeth Cameron
Alma College

Janice Feldbauer
Austin Community College

George Foegen
Metropolitan State College

William McCusker
Southern Illinois University at Carbondale

Mel Schnake
Valdosta State University

Ram Subramanian
Grand Valley State University

Herman Theeke
Central Michigan University

Bernard Weinrich
St. Louis Community College

Valerie Yates
California State University, Los Angeles

Don Hellriegel
Texas A&M University

John W. Slocum, Jr.
Southern Methodist University

About the Authors

DON HELLRIEGEL

Don Hellriegel is Professor of Management and holds the Bennett Chair in Business Administration at Texas A&M University. He received his B.S. and M.B.A. from Kent State University and his Ph.D. from the University of Washington. Dr. Hellriegel has been a member of the faculty at Texas A&M since 1975 and has served on the faculties of Pennsylvania State University and the University of Colorado.

His research interests include interorganizational relationships, corporate venturing, effects of organizational environments, managerial cognitive styles, and organizational innovation and strategic management processes. His research has been published in a number of leading journals.

Professor Hellriegel served as Vice President and Program Chair of the Academy of Management (1986), President Elect (1987), President (1988), and Past President (1989). He served a term as Editor of the *Academy of Management Review* and served as a member of the Board of Governors of the Academy of Management (1979–1981); (1982–1989). Dr. Hellriegel has occupied many other leadership roles, among which include: President, Eastern Academy of Management; Division Chair, Organization and Management Theory Division; President, Brazos County United Way; Co-Consulting Editor, West Series in Management; Head (1976–1980 and 1989–1994), Department of Management (TAMU); Interim Dean, College of Business Administration (TAMU); and Interim Executive Vice Chancellor (TAMUS).

He has consulted with a variety of groups and organizations, including—among others—3DI, Sun Ship Building, Penn Mutual Life Insurance, Texas A&M University System, Ministry of Industry and Commerce (Nation of Kuwait), Ministry of Agriculture (Nation of Dominican Republic), American Assembly of Collegiate Schools of Business, and Texas Innovation Group.

JOHN W. SLOCUM, JR.

John Slocum holds the O. Paul Corley Professorship in Organizational Behavior at the Edwin L. Cox School of Business, Southern Methodist University. He was the dean ad-interim at the Cox School where he now teaches management and organizational behavior. He has also taught on the faculties of the University of Washington, Ohio State University, Pennsylvania State University, and the International University of Japan. He holds a B.B.A. from Westminster College, an M.B.A. from Kent State University, and a Ph.D. in organizational behavior from the University of Washington.

Professor Slocum has held a number of positions in professional societies. He was elected as a Fellow to the Academy of Management in 1976 and a Fellow to the Decision Sciences Institute in 1984. He was awarded the Alumni Citation for Professional Accomplishment by Westminster College, and both the Nicolas Salgo and Rotunda Outstanding Teaching Awards from SMU. He served as President of the Eastern Academy of Management in 1973. From 1975 to 1986, he served as a member of the Board of Governors, Academy of Management. In 1983–1984, he served as 39th President of the 10,000 member Academy and Chairman of the Board of Governors of that organization.

Dr. Slocum has co-authored 17 books and has authored or co-authored over 115 journal articles. He has presented his research at numerous professional meetings and has presented executive development programs to managers employed with Holiday Inns, Beatrice Foods, Westinghouse, Brooklyn Union Gas, Southland Corporation, Henry C. Beck, Price Waterhouse, Celanese, GTE, Tenneco, Midwest Energy Corporation, Xerox, IBM, LVS, Southwestern Bell Telephone, and Allstate, among others.

Professor Slocum has served as a consultant to such organizations as Mellon National Bank, Westinghouse, Corning Glass Works, Fort Worth Museum of Science & History, Pier 1 Imports, Henry C. Beck Company, Kodak, Price Waterhouse, Mutual Benefit Life, Hershey Foods, Xerox, U.S. Forest Service, Pennsylvania Bell Telephone, Mack Trucks, government of Indonesia, GTE, NASA, Southland Corporation, Transnational Trucks, and Brooklyn Union Gas. He has also been on the Industrial Relations Staff of B.F. Goodrich, and in 1969 was a National Science Foundation Fellow.

Part *One*

An Overview of Management

Chapter 1

Managing a Dynamic Environment

Learning *Objectives*

After studying this chapter you should be able to:

1. Define managers and management.
2. Identify the different managerial functions and roles.
3. Describe the duties and responsibilities of various levels of management.
4. Explain the impact of work-force diversity on organizations.
5. Describe the five basic types of managerial skills and their relative importance.
6. Explain management as a dynamic process.

Chapter *Outline*

Preview Insight: Lewis Platt's Secret Weapon

Management and Managers

What Is an Organization?
What Is a Manager?
Levels of Management
Functional and General Managers

Diversity Insight: Alan Young: Best Auto Dealer in Texas

Managerial Functions and Roles

Managerial Functions

Quality Insight: The Company That Isn't a Whole Company

Managerial Roles

Insight: Wayne Huizenga, Emperor of Entertainment

What Managers Really Do

Principal Duties of First-Line Managers
Principal Duties of Middle Managers
Principal Duties of Top Managers

Small Business Insight: John Burson Does It All

Time Spent on Managerial Functions
Ethics and Managers

Ethics Insight: Selling Auto Service at Sears

Managing a Diverse Work Force

The Changing Nature of the Work Force

Diversity Insight: Anita Roddick Creates Glamour with "Green" Products

The Changing Face of Organizations
The Changing Duties of Management
The Mandate of Quality

Quality Insight: Motorola Pagers

Managerial Skills

Technical Skills
Interpersonal Skills
Conceptual Skills
Communication Skills
Critical Thinking Skills
Relative Importance of Managerial Skills
Skills for Managers in the Year 2000

Management—A Dynamic Process

Chapter Summary

Questions for Discussion

From Where You Sit

Experiencing Management

Skill-Building Exercise: Diversity Quiz
Critical Thinking Case: GE—A World Class Company—Worldwide
Video Case: Lou Gerstner Takes the Reins at IBM

Preview *Insight*

Lewis Platt's Secret Weapon

When Lewis Platt took the reins from John Young, long-time CEO at Hewlett-Packard in 1992, many outsiders assumed that this successful high-technology company was going to maintain the status quo. Hewlett-Packard is a company best known for its laser printers and sophisticated calculators. However, it also is a global computing giant that sold $3.9 billion of computing equipment in the quarter ending April 1993, second only to IBM. In addition, its orders are rising at an annual rate of 19%. What does Hewlett-Packard do to achieve this ongoing success, and what role does Lewis Platt play in it?

Platt was charged with running a company in an industry where advancement meant forming partnerships of computing and telecommunication giants, such as Hitachi, IBM, and AT&T. Platt decided to exploit HP's own secret weapon: a unique mix of well-developed technologies that would be difficult to duplicate in their entirety by the competition. One key to his success was that, as a three-decade veteran of HP, he understood the implications of these innovations.

In addition to knowing how to exploit unique product technology, Platt brought other vital management skills to the job. He reemphasized the importance of people in the organization by implementing policies that minimize downsizing with a no-layoff goal. He also invested in teleconferencing equipment for all of HP's facilities so that employees can receive a daily company update.

Five convictions are embedded in Platt's vision for the company:

- *Valuing people.* HP should continue to stress that people are an important priority, as exemplified by the high visibility of its human resources management efforts.
- *Maintaining uniqueness of technology.* HP should continue to capitalize on the three-part mix of computing, measurement instrumentation, and wired and wireless networks.
- *No-layoff policy.* HP should continue to emphasize organizational balancing so that existing employees can be reallocated by internal draft, voluntary reclassifications, and voluntary retirements.
- *A global focus on the value of diversity.* HP should continue to stress its mentioning programs for women, a showcase on women in technology, and an action plan to hire and promote women, people with disabilities, and older workers, on a global basis.
- *Simplifying the organization.* HP should broaden its use of cross-functional teams and total quality techniques to simplify customer access to HP products because it, like other giant companies, became so complex that customers were being ignored.

Why is Platt different from his predecessor and from other corporate executives? His most important skill is understanding the strengths and hidden assets of Hewlett-Packard as a company, and the importance of people to its success.[1]

1

Define managers and management.

MANAGEMENT AND MANAGERS

Even if you aren't planning to be a manager for a large global company, these are challenging and exciting times for managers and for the people who report to them. Effective and innovative management like that demonstrated by Lewis Platt is essential to any organization's overall success. Even established corporations such as American Express, Motorola, Sanyo, and Unilever now demand that their managers become more innovative to meet the challenges that lie ahead. Lou Gerstner, CEO of IBM, was president of Travel Related Services at American Express in the late 1980s. At that time, *VISA* and MasterCard were cutting into that company's profits, a trend Gerstner felt he had to reverse. He began by challenging two longstanding corporate beliefs: that there should be only one card, the green card, and that it had limited potential for growth and innovation.

To broaden the customer base and encourage new ways of thinking about American Express, Gerstner quickly offered two new cards: Platinum and a revolving-credit card, Optima. He also used new ad campaigns to target two markets that American Express had neglected: college students and women. In addition, in 1988 American Express started a direct-mail merchandise program for all its cardholders. Cardholders can now use their cards to buy a variety of products, such as watches, luggage, clothing, jewelry, and furs, through the mail. What has been the result of such innovation? Since 1978, sales at Travel Related Services have increased more than 500 percent, and profits are up 28 percent.[2] In the case at the end of this chapter, we describe how Gerstner is applying his skills to resolve similar turnaround problems at IBM.

Real-World Example
The recently approved General Agreement on Trades and Tariffs (GATT) promises to increase the number of U.S. jobs by removing trade barriers between countries (*Business Week*, December 12, 1994).

In addition to becoming more innovative, managers in the twenty-first century must expand their focus. One reason is that U.S. firms are rapidly becoming part of a much broader—often global—economic community. The North American Free Trade Agreement has created a trading block of Canada, the United States, and Mexico. Other significant industrialized regions of the world, such as Europe and the Pacific Rim, are following suit. Managers of both U.S. and global corporations have yet to feel the full repercussions from these economic and political changes. One result of reform in Russia is that McDonald's opened its first restaurant in Moscow on January 31, 1990, with the capacity to serve 30,000 customers a day. Customers wait in long lines to buy a drink, fries, and a Big Mac for US$9.50.

Today's managers also face expanding public relations duties. They must be able to respond quickly to crises that may create image problems. President Bill Clinton recognized the importance of CEO visibility when he visited Los Angeles after the earthquake of January 1994. When the *Exxon Valdez* spilled 10.4 million gallons of crude oil in Alaska's Prince William Sound, killing thousands of birds and other wild creatures, it immediately affected management decisions at Exxon. Exxon's CEO, Lawrence Rawl, was besieged by reporters who portrayed the world's third-largest industrial company as uncaring, incompetent, and penny pinching.[3] Recently, Exxon was ordered to pay more than $248 million to 10,000 fishermen whose working lives were disrupted. In today's global economic community, managers can't assume that their organization's image will never be tarnished, that money will always be available for expansion, that other nations' governments will be stable, or that consumers will be satisfied with less than top quality.

In the twenty-first century, managers will need to expand their focus to include a global economic community. McDonald's opened its first restaurant in Moscow in 1990—a result of political and economic changes in Russia.

What Is an Organization?

But let's back up and talk about the immediate world in which you will operate as a manager. So far, we've cited examples of managers in large organizations. That's because organizations are the setting for all managers, and managers don't exist outside of them. An **organization** is any structured group of people working together to achieve certain goals that individuals could not reach alone. Although alike in their need to achieve specific goals, organizations differ with respect to what those goals are. A goal at American Airlines is to improve its market share relative to that of other major airlines, such as Delta, USAir, and JAL, by providing extraordinary customer service. At Southwest Airlines, a goal is to offer on-time service at the lowest prevailing price to increase its market share. The goal at Polaroid is to create innovative instant cameras, whereas at Minolta the goal is to produce high-quality lenses for cameras and other optical devices. Organizations differ in many other ways, too. Some are large and others small; some provide services and others products. Some organizations, such as the armed forces, spend millions of dollars on recruiting members and develop methods to make sure that they abide by formal rules. Others, such as the local MADD (Mothers Against Drunk Drivers) chapter, spend little money to attract members and impose few controls on their behavior.

Organizations have existed throughout history, so why are they, their goals, and their managers so important *today*? The reason is that during the past fifty years, all developed nations have become societies of organizations, and the United States is no exception. Each of you could write your autobiography as a series of experiences with organizations, both large and small: hospitals, schools, sports teams, governments, banks, stores, clubs, and community groups. Some have been well managed, but others have not.

In this book we look at organizations of all types and sizes and how their managers set and achieve goals. Our primary purposes are to help you understand how managers accomplish organizational goals and to teach you some of the skills you will need to be an effective manager in the 1990s and beyond. We haven't tried to cover every issue a manager might face—just those confronting *most* managers, regardless of their background or their organization's goals or size.

What Is a Manager?

Ask Students
Do you think that effective management is the key to an organization's success?

We've been talking about managers for several pages, so it's time to clarify exactly what the term means. A **manager** is a person who allocates human and material resources and directs the operations of a department or an entire organization.

Managers represent only a fraction of the employees in large firms. Most employees do nonmanagerial work. Receptionists, computer programmers, machine operators, secretaries, graphic designers, and maintenance workers—all are important, but they aren't managers. What sets managers apart? Simply put, the difference is that *managers are evaluated on how well others do their jobs*. Furthermore, it is the responsibility of managers to try to determine and plan for the most effective and efficient way to achieve the organization's goals.

Teaching Tip
Create enthusiasm in your students for the field of management. Students are motivated by relating personal experiences. Ask: "What are some of the characteristics of the best and worst managers you have had or have read about?" List the responses on the board or an overhead transparency.

For American Airlines to reach its overall profitability goal, for example, its managers have established five plans: (1) to reduce costs by buying fuel-efficient aircraft; (2) to reduce personnel by hiring only those who are most needed; (3) to restructure the route system to an efficient hub-and-spoke pattern of connecting airports, with about 80 percent of all traffic coming through Dallas–Fort Worth; (4) to maintain American's number one position in customer service; and (5) to expand marketing efforts by using customers for targeted promotions of vacations, car rentals, hotels, and the like.[4] These plans are specific to American Airlines, but all managers face similar challenges. That is, they must find ways to motivate employees and to increase their companies' overall productivity, efficiency, service, quality, and innovation.

Managers achieve an organization's or department's goals for the most part by arranging for others to do things—not by performing all the tasks themselves. **Management,** then, involves planning, organizing, leading, and controlling the people working in an organization to achieve the organization's goals. Those goals give direction to the tasks and activities undertaken.

The term *manager* covers many types of people. It includes operators of small businesses, chief executive officers (CEOs) of multinational corporations, plant managers, and supervisors—both generalists and specialists. Managers are also employed by not-for-profit organizations (e.g., government agencies and religious groups) and trade associations (e.g., the American Management Association and the Professional Golfers Association). We refer to all of these types of managers throughout this book.

Levels of Management

Discussion Question 1
What are the major differences in managerial responsibilities for first-line, middle, and top managers?

Teaching Tip
Students relate well to real-world applications. Invite a guest lecturer from a successful local business to discuss the differences in duties and responsibilities of the various levels of management in his or her organization. Have students prepare questions for the speaker in advance.

Managers are classified by their level within the organization. For example, entrepreneur Ray Kroc opened his first McDonald's restaurant in Des Plaines, Illinois, on April 15, 1955, and his cash register rang up sales of $366.12 for the day. After this initial success he was able to convince others to join him. He became president and chief executive officer of McDonald's, a management position he held for more than twenty-five years. Today, the franchise system he founded has sales of more than $7.4 billion, is the biggest owner of commercial real estate in the United States and employs more than 80,000 people in its more than 14,100 stores worldwide.[5] In contrast, the operator of a McDonald's restaurant in Moscow with twenty-five employees also is a manager. Although both men can be called *managers,* their jobs aren't the same. The goals, tasks, and responsibilities of the store manager are much different from those of the CEO.

Figure 1.1 shows the three basic management levels. We define these levels with a broad brush here, returning to add detail later in the chapter and throughout the book.

First-Line Managers. In general, **first-line managers** are directly responsible for the production of goods or services. They may be called sales managers, section chiefs, or production supervisors, depending on the organization. Employees who report to them do the organization's basic production work—whether of goods or of services. For example, a first-line manager at Freedom Forge supervises employees who make steel, operate and maintain machines, and write shipping orders. The sales manager at a U.S. Toyota dealership supervises the salespeople who sell cars to customers in the showroom. A Toyota sales manager in Japan works in an office that has computers and telephones similar to a telemarketing center and supervises sales people who go to people's homes to sell them their cars.

This level of management is the link between the production or operations of each department and the rest of the organization. However, first-line managers in most companies spend little time with higher management or with people from other organizations. Most of their time is spent side-by-side with the people they supervise.

First-line managers often lead hectic work lives full of interruptions. They commu-

FIGURE 1.1
Basic Levels of Management

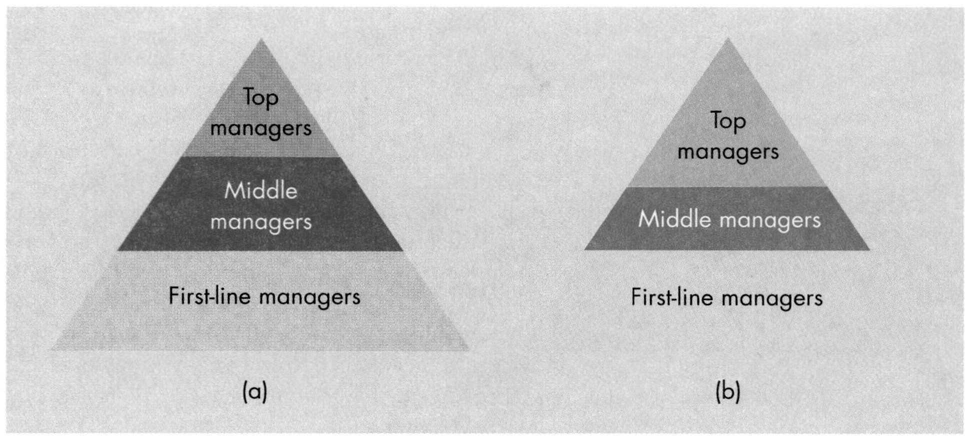

nicate and solve problems within their own work areas. Many first-line managers today are team leaders in self-managed work groups. Regardless of the type of departmentalization found in today's organizations, these people are on the "firing line."

Teaching Tip
Have students bring a Sunday newspaper section of help-wanted ads to class. Divide the students into groups of 3-5 each. Have them go through the ads and sort the jobs by organizational level.

Middle Managers. Small organizations can function successfully with only one level of management. As an organization grows, however, so do its problems. Some managers at larger organizations must focus on coordinating employee activities, determining which products or services to provide, and deciding how to market these products or services to customers. These are the problems of **middle managers,** who receive broad, general strategies and policies from top managers and translate them into specific goals and plans for first-line managers to implement. Middle managers typically have titles such as department head, plant manager, and director of finance. They are responsible for directing and coordinating the activities of first-line managers and, at times, such nonmanagerial personnel as clerks, receptionists, and staff assistants.

Top Managers. The overall direction and operations of an organization are the responsibility of **top managers.** Linda Wachner, CEO of Warnaco, and Doug Key, CEO of Medstar Ambulance, are such managers. They have built their companies into large, successful firms. Typical titles of top managers are chief executive officer, president, chairman, division president, and executive vice-president. Top managers develop goals, policies, and strategies for the entire organization. They set the goals that are handed down through the hierarchy, eventually reaching each worker.

Top managers often represent their organizations in community affairs, business deals, and government negotiations. They spend most of their time talking with other top managers in the company and with people outside the company. For example, Lou Gerstner of IBM spends more than half of his time traveling, dealing with the media, and creating an impression of IBM that will influence customers and shareholders.

Functional and General Managers

Teaching Tip
Invite one functional manager and one general manager to class. Have them describe their duties and discuss the differences in their jobs.

Our brief descriptions of the three management levels should help you understand the jobs different managers perform. However, in large organizations managers also are identified by the *scope* of the activities they manage.

Functional managers supervise employees having specialized skills in a single area of operation, such as accounting, human resources, sales, finance, marketing, or production. A typical functional manager, for example, is the head of a payroll department. That person doesn't determine companywide employee salaries, as a general manager might, but does make sure that payroll checks are issued on time and in the correct amounts.

General managers are responsible for the operations of a more complex unit, such as a company or a division, and usually oversee functional managers. Top and middle managers, by definition, are general managers. The following Diversity Insight indicates why Alan Young, owner–manager of an automobile dealership in Ft. Worth, Texas, has succeeded.

Diversity *Insight*

Alan Young: Best Auto Dealer in Texas

Alan Young, highlighted recently as the Black Enterprise Automobile Dealer of the year, has the spunk generally associated with entrepreneurs as well as the managerial savvy to run a Buick–GMC Truck dealership in Ft. Worth, Texas, whose sales increased 300% in four years, from $15.7 million in 1988 to nearly $50 million in 1991. A graduate of the University of Illinois at Urbana–Champaign, he started in 1968 as a service representative for Shell Oil. After a short time on the job, he cleaned out his bank account to open a Shell station on Chicago's South Side. After the OPEC oil crisis in the early 1970s, he decided that he didn't want to spend the rest of his life pumping gas.

Luck came to him in the form of his insurance agent, who told Young that he was quitting his job to join GM's Minority Dealer Development program. Young also applied, was accepted, and shut down the service station to prepare for a new career. During his two years in the GM program, he learned about retailing and dealerships. His mentor and teacher in the GM program, Michael Christopolous, reported that Young's people-handling skills were excellent and that he was willing to work hard. Young learned how to sell cars to anyone, even to people who couldn't speak English. From selling cars in ethnically diverse neighborhoods, he learned an important lesson for managers who deal across cultures: If you approach people in the right way, they will not reject you because of your race or ethnic origin.

After finishing his GM training, Young moved to Lincoln, Nebraska, where he opened his first Buick dealership. There he was able to turn customer curiosity about his race into sales that grew from $12 million in 1979 to $16 million in 1984. He also gained experience in the car dealership business that would prove invaluable when he moved to Texas in 1984. Two years after he opened his Ft. Worth dealership, the Texas economy was hit by declines in the oil and real estate industries—and Young sold fewer than 1,000 new Buicks. To compensate, he relied on his managerial skills to balance human resources with advertising needs. His strategy worked, and his position as the Black Enterprise Automobile Dealer of the Year is evidence of that.[6]

Although Young's domain is small compared to Platt's at Hewlett-Packard, his job has all the complexity of that of a general manager. He oversees all marketing functions, including advertising campaigns and sales; he manages the financial side of the business; he is active in the community as a member of the Ft. Worth Chamber of Commerce and other civic organizations; and he sponsors a high school basketball tournament.

2

Identify the different managerial functions and roles.

Discussion Question 3
Define the four managerial functions.

MANAGERIAL FUNCTIONS AND ROLES

Now that we've described various types of managers, let's consider what managers do—their managerial functions—and how they do it—the managerial roles they play. Managerial functions and roles are merely one way of describing a manager's job. Functions and roles may overlap somewhat, but you need to understand both to appreciate the nature and scope of management.

Managerial Functions

The successful manager capably performs four basic managerial functions: planning, organizing, leading, and controlling. Most managers perform these functions more or less simultaneously—rather than in a rigid, preset order—to achieve company goals. This point is illustrated graphically in Figure 1.2. In this section we briefly examine the four functions without looking at their interrelationships. Throughout this text frequent references to the relationships among them help explain exactly how managers do their jobs.

Planning. In general, **planning** involves defining organizational goals and proposing ways to reach them. Managers plan for three reasons: (1) to establish an overall direction for the organization's future, such as increased profit, expanded market share, and social responsibility; (2) to identify and commit the organization's resources to achieving its goals; and (3) to decide which activities are necessary to do so. We discuss the planning function in more detail in Chapter 6.

FIGURE 1.2

Basic Managerial Functions

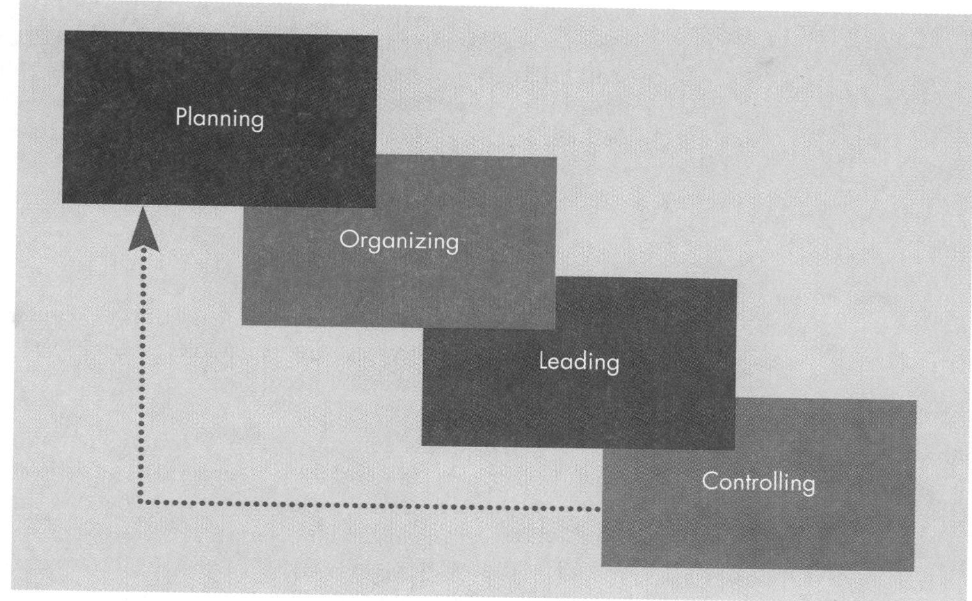

Organizing. After managers have prepared plans, they must translate those relatively abstract ideas into reality. Sound organization is essential to this effort. **Organizing** is the process of creating a structure of relationships that will enable employees to carry out management's plans and meet its goals. By organizing effectively, managers can better coordinate human and material resources. An organization's success depends largely on management's ability to utilize those resources efficiently and effectively.

Organizing involves setting up departments and job descriptions. In this sense, staffing proceeds directly from planning and organizing. For example, the U.S. Postal Service uses a different type of structure than does UPS. At the U.S. Postal Service, most employees think of themselves as production workers. Relatively little attention is paid to the marketing function. Most of the decisions are made by top managers, with mail carriers and postal clerks having little to do with decision making. Carriers and clerks are promoted to other jobs as they gain seniority, and the degree of job specialization is low.

In contrast, UPS is organized into two distinct divisions: an airline and a ground carrier. The ground carriers also are the people who have the most customer contact. But the truck drivers do not fly airplanes nor do the pilots drive the trucks. Parcel sorters are located in major hubs throughout the world and sort parcels for delivery by drivers. At UPS, the degree of job specialization is high.[7] We present the organizing function in more depth in Chapters 10–12.

Ethics
Think of situations involving ethical questions. For example: (1) Should managers and other employees stick to the plans that their boss made for them or risk upsetting the boss right before Christmas bonuses are to be given out? (2) Should a vendor play off one department of an organization against another when trying to get a higher price for her products because "one hand doesn't know what the other hand is doing?" (3) Should managers use their positions to demand personal favors (e.g., football or basketball tickets) from suppliers? (4) Should an employer use surveillance cameras to monitor employees?

Ask Students
What types of tasks must a sorority or fraternity president perform while planning, organizing, leading, and controlling?

Leading. After management has made plans, created a structure, and hired the right personnel, someone must lead the organization. Some managers call this process *directing* or *influencing*. Whatever it's called, **leading** involves communicating with and motivating others to perform the tasks necessary to achieve the organization's goals. And leading isn't done only after planning and organizing end; it is crucial to those functions, too. Chapters 13–17 focus on leading.

Controlling. The process by which a person, group, or organization consciously monitors performance and takes corrective action is **controlling.** Phil Knight is CEO of NIKE, the global athletic apparel and shoe company based in Oregon, with sales of over \$3.8 billion.[8] He likes to point out to his employees that of the 500 companies listed in *Fortune* in 1980, only 200 remain on that list today and NIKE ranks twenty-eighth. Why? Knight believes that it's NIKE's competitive spirit, ability to respond to customers' needs with diverse and genuine products, and its control procedures. NIKE establishes budgets for each shoe line, such as cross-training, aerobic, walking, basketball, and football, and holds employees responsible for meeting production and financial goals. If a shoe line can't meet its goals, the line is replaced. Knight also spends time traveling globally, visiting retailers. He reinforces the message that a retailer in Singapore or Shanghai is just as important as one in New York City and that every consumer can count on a consistent commitment to quality.

In the control process, managers

- set standards of performance.
- measure current performance against those standards,
- take action to correct any deviations, and
- adjust the standards if necessary.

Ethics
Workers who were laid off when their companies shifted manufacturing and/or assembly operations to lower cost labor sources abroad complained that management had behaved unethically. What do you think?

Just as a thermostat sends signals to a heating system that the room temperature is too high or too low, so a control system sends signals to managers that things aren't working as planned and that corrective action is needed. In Chapters 18–20 we present and discuss typical organizational control processes.

The following Quality Insight illustrates how new challenges in carrying out managerial functions are created for the managers of companies that outsource production, marketing or other functional areas. **Outsourcing** means letting other organizations perform a service and/or manufacture parts or a product. NIKE outsources the production of its shoes to low-cost plants in South Korea and China and imports the shoes for distribution in North America. These same plants also ship shoes to Europe and other parts of Asia for distribution.

Quality *Insight*

The Company That Isn't a Whole Company

Today's managers face a new challenge: to plan, organize, lead and control a company whose operating functions are performed by other companies. This type of company is known as a modular, virtual, or hollow corporation. The **modular corporation** is most common in three industries: apparel, auto manufacturing, and electronics. The most commonly outsourced function is production. By outsourcing production, a company can switch suppliers around and even change suppliers from time to time. Managers can select the supplier best suited to meet a customer's needs.

Most experts believe that the decision to contract production to another company is a sound business decision. It appears to hold down the unit cost of production by relieving the company of some overhead, and it frees the company to allocate its scarce resources to activities for which the company holds a competitive advantage. Some well-known examples of modular companies are Dell Computer, NIKE, Liz Claibourne fashions, and chip designer Cyrix. For example, the Liz Claibourne line of clothing is manufactured in Asia.

Chrysler's new compact car, the Neon, is being manufactured as a modular project. The entire car is shipped to Neon assembly plants in four easy-to-assemble modules from separate suppliers. Other U.S. car manufacturers are expected to follow its lead. In the future, a car may be designed on the super CAD/CAM system at IBM's Boca Raton facility, built by suppliers in various countries, and assembled for delivery at a site closest to its targeted customer. Currently, the Neon is being made both in the United States and in Mexico to accommodate customers in both countries.[9]

This new form of company seems to be a solution to various problems in the rapidly changing business environment. Today's managers are being challenged to carry out the functions of planning, organizing, leading, and controlling even when the "parts" don't belong to the whole!

Managerial Roles

Managers perform the four basic managerial functions while playing a variety of managerial roles. A **role** is an organized set of behaviors. Henry Mintzberg studied various managerial jobs to arrive at the ten most common managerial roles. They may be grouped into three categories: interpersonal, informational, and decisional, as shown in Figure 1.3.[10]

Ask Students
Discuss President Clinton's job with respect to Mintzberg's ten Managerial Roles. For example: He is a figurehead when he places a wreath of flowers on the Tomb of the Unknown Soldier. He is a liaison when he acts as a go-between in trying to broker peace in the Middle East. He is a negotiator when he tries to sell tax reforms.

Before discussing each of the ten managerial roles, we need to make four points: (1) every manager's job consists of some combination of these roles; (2) these roles often influence the characteristics of managerial work (discussed in the next section); (3) these roles are highly interrelated; and (4) the relative importance of each role varies considerably by managerial level and function.

Interpersonal Roles. As you might expect, interpersonal roles involve relationships among people. In their roles as figureheads, leaders, and liaisons, managers relate directly to other people.

In the **figurehead role,** the most basic and simplest of all managerial roles, the manager represents the organization at ceremonial and symbolic functions. The mayor who presents a local hero with a key to the city, the supervisor who attends the wedding of a machine operator, the sales manager who takes an important customer to lunch—all are performing duties of the figurehead role necessary to an organization's image and success. Although figurehead duties may not seem important, they are expected of managers because they symbolize management's concern for employees, customers, and the community.

The **leader role** involves responsibility for directing and coordinating the activities of subordinates in order to accomplish organizational goals. Some aspects of the leader role have to do with staffing: hiring, promoting, and firing. Other aspects involve motivating subordinates to meet the organization's needs. Still other aspects relate to projecting a vision with which employees can identify. Steve Jobs at neXt and Wayne Huizenga of Viacom created visions that employees could rally around. Jobs is leading his new company into the future by creating operating systems that tie multimedia hardware products together. Huizenga is building a new generation of family entertainment businesses. Both have created a vision of the future that can be seen now by employees and customers alike.

FIGURE 1.3
The Manager's Roles

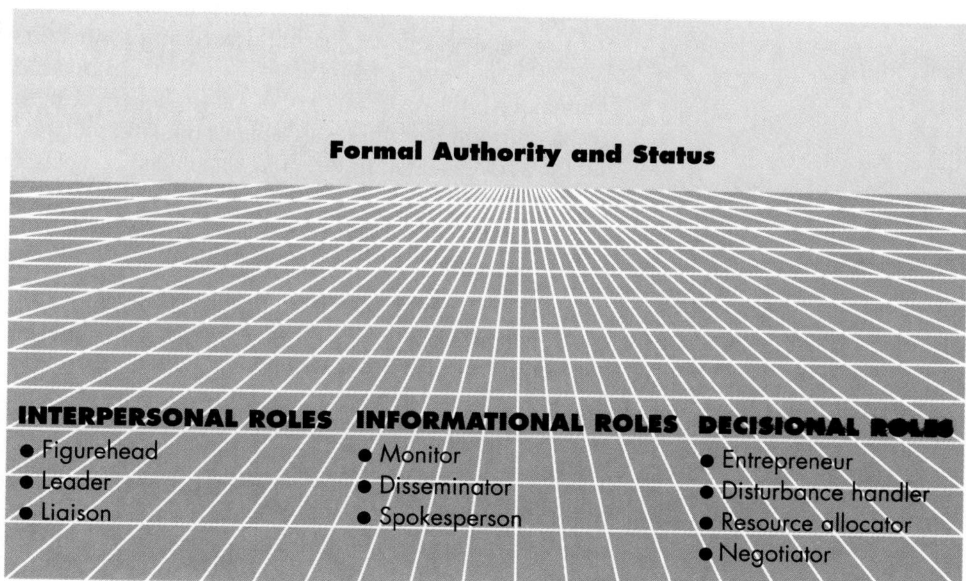

The **liaison role** refers to managers' dealings with people outside the organization. Such people include clients, government officials, customers, and suppliers. In the liaison role, the manager seeks support from people who can affect the organization's success.

Informational Roles. Effective managers build networks of contacts. The many contacts made while performing figurehead and liaison roles give managers access to important information. Because of these contacts, managers are the nerve centers of their organizations. Three roles—monitor, disseminator, and spokesperson—comprise the informational aspects of managerial work.

The **monitor role** involves seeking, receiving, and screening information. Like radar units, managers scan their environments for information that may affect their organizations. Because much of the information received is oral (from gossip and hearsay, as well as from formal meetings), managers must test it and decide whether to use it. Herb Kelleher, CEO of Southwest Airlines, receives daily information on number of seats filled, percentage of planes on time, and other aspects of the airline's operations. He also gathers data on United Airlines, a major employee-owned airline, that competes against Southwest in California. Information about intended governmental changes in California and FAA regulations is presented and discussed in meetings with his top managers.[11]

In the **disseminator role,** the manager shares information with subordinates and other members of the organization. Some managers pass along special, or "privileged," information to certain subordinates who would not ordinarily have access to it and who can be trusted not to let it go further. In practice, passing information along to subordinates can be time-consuming and nonproductive. Successful managers do a good job of deciding which and how much information will be useful to others.

Finally, in the **spokesperson role,** managers pass on information to others, especially those outside the organization, about the official position of the company. The spokesperson role is growing in importance—at least in part because the press and public are demanding more information. Many companies, in fact, have created a department of public information to handle such demands.

An example of a mishandled spokesperson role was the case of Lawrence Rawl and the *Exxon Valdez* oil spill. When the president and CEO of Exxon faced the press concerning that event, he found out how crucial the spokesperson role can be. When interviewed on programs such as CBS's "This Morning" and PBS's "MacNeil/Lehrer News Hour," Rawl claimed that it wasn't his job to know details of the cleanup plan. As CEO, Rawl might legitimately not know the details, but his going on the offensive and attacking the Coast Guard and others in government, accusing them of delaying the cleanup, made it appear that he was hiding something from the media.

The result was a financial and public relations nightmare for Exxon, as the media continually publicized images of oil-drenched dead birds, rocks coated with viscous crude, and other examples of environmental spoilage. Rawl learned from this incident that the spokesperson role requires managers to acknowledge the public's legitimate interest in their organization's actions.

Decisional Roles. Managers use the information they receive to decide when and how to commit their organization to new goals and actions. Decisional roles are perhaps the most important of the three classes of roles. As entrepreneurs, disturbance handlers, resource allocators, and negotiators, managers are at the core of the organization's decision-making system.

The **entrepreneur role** involves designing and starting a new project, enterprise, or business. When the late Sam Walton founded Wal-Mart in 1962 and Sam's Wholesale Clubs in 1983, his main objective was to offer quality goods at low prices. To achieve the low-price objective, Wal-Mart keeps inventory low, has few managerial levels, and locates its stores mostly in small towns. Wal-Mart is now the largest discounter in the United States. It has more than 1,400 stores in the United States, Canada, and Mexico, and over $45 billion in annual sales. As an entrepreneur, Walton was a designer and initiator of change in the discount retail industry.[12] The entrepreneur role can also be played within an existing organization when the organization encourages it. We call this approach *intrapreneurship*. For instance, Arthur Fry at 3M played this role when he invented Post-it self-stick notes.

Managers play the **disturbance handler role** when dealing with problems and changes beyond their immediate control. Typical problems include strikes by labor unions, bankruptcy of major suppliers, and breaking of contracts by customers. Sometimes disturbances arise because an ineffective manager ignores a situation until it turns into a crisis. However, even effective managers can't possibly anticipate all the results of their decisions or control the actions of others. In the summer of 1994, baseball players went on strike. The mediator selected by the secretary of labor and accepted by the owners and players is an example of a person's playing a disturbance handler role.

The **resource allocator role** involves choosing among competing demands for money, equipment, personnel, a manager's time, and other organizational resources. Managers have to ask themselves questions such as: What portion of the budget should be earmarked for advertising and what portion for improving an existing product line? Should a second shift of workers be added or overtime be paid to handle new orders? Lou Gerstner, for example, had to decide whether to keep employees on the IBM payroll or to hire temporaries to manage and work on short-term projects. His decision to hire workers on a project basis has provided employment for more than 2,000 people in the Boca Raton Research facility (IBM's "skunkworks") and has resulted in the development of a CAD/CAM system that designed the fastest bobsled built yet for use in the 1994 Olympics.

Closely linked to the resource allocator role is the **negotiator role.** In this role, managers meet with individuals or groups to discuss differences and reach an agreement. Negotiations are an integral part of a manager's job. They are especially tough, though, when a manager must deal with people or groups (such as unions or political action committees) who don't share all of the manager's goals.

Teaching Tip
Students need to relate the roles of management to their everyday lives. Ask students to analyze the role of student, spouse, or parent in terms of the ten managerial roles.

Role Interdependence. Although discussed separately, the ten managerial roles actually are interdependent and sometimes are played simultaneously. As a top manager at Viacom and former CEO of Blockbuster Entertainment, Wayne Huizenga certainly plays multiple roles. Some of them are identified in brackets in the following Insight.

Insight

Wayne Huizenga, Emperor of Entertainment

Wayne Huizenga is a lifelong entrepreneur. He is best known for his Blockbuster Video stores that blanket the United States and Europe. However, video and game rentals is not the first venture for Huizenga; he was the founder of Waste Management Corporation, one of the largest waste disposal companies in the world. In that venture, he introduced the dumpster as a replacement for individual trash cans in garbage collection at planned communities and strip shopping centers [entrepreneur].

Huizenga's world is characterized not only by the rental of commodity video movies, but is part of a massive entertainment kingdom [resource allocator]. Huizenga owns Sound Warehouse, a chain of stores that sells compact disks, tapes, and records; Discovery Zone, a chain of indoor playgrounds located in strip malls that are made up of inflatable slides and bouncers; and ownership of a baseball team (Florida Marlins), a hockey team (Florida Panthers), and a football team (Miami Dolphins). A sports theme park is underway that will match Disney World in size and include sports arenas for professional sports teams, as well as a world-class golf course.

All of the entertainments have a standard signature that has become Huizenga's hallmark: They are family entertainment at its cleanest and finest. All Wayne's world features are priced to appeal to a wide set of consumers. The announcement of his purchase of the Miami Dolphins early in 1994 promised "reasonably priced tickets and moderately priced concessions."

When asked about business leadership in South Florida, most people respond with Huizenga's name. What does he do to make himself so visible? The first thing that he does is maintain visibility ***inside*** his company. He does so by holding regular staff meetings with first-line managers and their employees, and by speaking regularly to the media rather than depending on a public relations officer [figurehead and liaison roles]. Thus he acts as a spokesperson both on internal and external issues.

He also is an entrepreneur and a visionary decision maker. When Viacom was trying to acquire Paramount Communications, Huizenga brought Blockbuster in as a merger partner for Viacom in the acquisition. He did so for two reasons:

1. It gave Blockbuster access to Paramount's large library of movies and data [entrepreneur and negotiator roles].
2. It permitted Huizenga to step aside as the Chief Executive Officer and Chairman of a company so that he could devote his energy to his new sports enterprises [entrepreneur role].[13]

The relative importance of each managerial role varies by management level and from one organization to another. The personality, achievements, and ambitions of a manager will also affect the relative importance of each role.

3

Describe the duties and responsibilities of various levels of management.

WHAT MANAGERS REALLY DO

Among the thousands of books and articles written about managers, relatively few examine what they actually do. These few give the impression that managers spend most of their time in air-conditioned offices reading reports and attending meetings, rushing to and from airports, entertaining important customers, and solving complicated problems.

Teaching Tip
Students can experience first-hand the life of a manager by spending some time with one. Have them do so and report on their experiences.

To some extent this impression may be accurate for top managers. But is it true for first-line and middle managers? A recent survey of more than 1,400 managers, summarized in Table 1.1, was designed to answer the question.[14] These managers identified seven major tasks performed by all managers. Let's look briefly at how the day-to-day work of managers differs at the three levels of management.

TABLE 1.1

What's Really Important in Different Management Jobs

	Management Level*		
Key Management Tasks	**First-line**	**Middle**	**Top**
Managing individual performance	63	56	45
Instructing subordinates	40	36	27
Planning and allocating resources	47	66	61
Coordinating groups	39	51	54
Managing group/department performance	22	48	43
Monitoring business environment	13	20	34
Representing own staff	51	55	53

Source: Kraut, A.I., Pegrego, P.R., McKenna, D.D., and Dunnette, M.D. The role of the manager: What's really important in different management jobs. *Academy of Management Executive,* 1989, 3, 286–293.

*Numbers are the percentages of managers who said that each task is important.

Principal Duties of First-Line Managers

Ask Students
Many students experience culture shock when they get their first job after graduating, for they didn't really know what managers actually do. How will you prevent this from happening to you?

Teaching Tip
Have students brainstorm a list of functions that first-line managers perform and a list of skills that they must possess in order to be successful. Ask students to identify problems that newly hired or promoted first-line managers might encounter.

Newly appointed first-line managers have much to learn—and also to unlearn. For example, a recently promoted production worker must learn to let others do the work that she has been used to doing and to put aside thoughts about how much better and faster she did it. Instead, a manager gains satisfaction from the accomplishments of others. New first-line managers must learn to plan and schedule the work formerly laid out for them and not wait for orders. In the process they must also learn how their group fits into the total organization and how to share staff services with other managers.

First-line managers usually need strong technical skills to teach subordinates and supervise their day-to-day tasks. Effective first-line managers learn to "lean on" their technical expertise. Sometimes, though, a first-line manager is a recent college graduate who is responsible for the work of both hourly workers and professionals. This type of first-line manager is likely to have little hands-on experience. This lack of experience isn't a problem if the manager has good interpersonal skills. They include the ability to communicate with diverse types of people, to coach and counsel subordinates, and to provide constructive feedback.

Table 1.1 shows that managing individual performance was rated the single most important managerial task performed by first-line managers. Motivating and disciplining subordinates, keeping track of performance and providing feedback, and improving communications and individual productivity are all vital parts of that task.

Principal Duties of Middle Managers

Teaching Tip
Divide the class into teams of 5 to 8 students. Give the teams a list of jobs commonly found at different organizational levels. Ask the students to see who can be the first to rank those jobs in descending order of responsibility. Give the teams some incentive (e.g. the side that wins gets to leave 15 minutes early).

Many middle managers began their careers as first-line managers. Typically, a middle manager has spent several years as a first-line manager, gaining knowledge about the business and honing technical skills. Even so, promotion from first-line to middle management is often difficult and sometimes traumatic. In fact, the percentages in Table 1.1 show a greater difference between first-line and middle management tasks than between those of middle and top management.

The heavier emphases on managing group performance and on allocating resources represent the most important differences between first-line and middle managers. The middle manager often is involved in reviewing the work plans of various groups, helping them set priorities, and negotiating and coordinating their activities. Middle managers are involved in establishing target dates for work or services to be performed; developing evaluation criteria for performance; deciding which projects should be given money, personnel, and materials; and translating top management's general goals into specific operational plans, schedules, and procedures.

Middle managers carry out top management's directives primarily by delegating authority and responsibility to their subordinates and by coordinating schedules and resources with other managers. The major roles these managers play are interpersonal and informational because they face problems that are people-centered, rather than technical. Middle managers often spend much of their day talking on the phone, attending committee meetings, and preparing reports.

Middle managers also are removed from the technical aspects of production work. Lacking hands-on experience, many middle managers must develop new skills to cope with top management's demands. One important skill is the ability to negotiate successfully with first-line managers to gain acceptance of top management's goals. Another is the ability to compromise and achieve consensus in order to win support. Attending meetings with other middle managers and with top managers demands greater interpersonal skills than those required of most first-line managers. And, finally, middle managers must be adept at developing their subordinates, opening lines of communication for them, and making them visible to other middle managers and to top managers.

Principal Duties of Top Managers

Pressures and demands on top managers can be intense. Tightly scheduled workdays, heavy travel requirements, and work weeks of sixty or more hours are common. During

Ask Students
Would you want to have a life as stressed and fast paced as the top managers the authors describe? Why or why not?

a typical day a top manager disposes of thirty-six pieces of mail, handles five telephone calls an hour, and goes to eight meetings. A true break is a luxury. Coffee is swallowed on the run, and lunch often is eaten during meetings with other managers, business associates, community representatives, or government officials. When there is some free time, eager subordinates vie for a piece of it.

A top manager spends days *and* nights working for the company. One night may be spent working late at the office and another entertaining business associates. On other nights the typical top manager goes home, not to relax but to use it as a branch office. Many recreational activities and social events are arranged for business purposes. Thus the top manager seldom stops thinking about the job or playing the roles it demands. Such an approach to time management may get the work done, but it also creates stress in most families. The following Small Business Insight shows how the top manager in a small business handles the demands of all three levels of management.

Small Business *Insight*

John Burson Does It All

John Burson is the sole owner of a one-year-old general contracting firm in South Florida. Although his family has been in the construction business for two generations, he recently started a separate company that specialized in light industrial construction. Burson's special skill is the metal framing and walls used in small strip shopping centers, small apartment complexes, and light industry buildings. However, he oversees the entire construction process on a job by subcontracting for the services that he cannot perform himself.

Burson, like many small business owners, carries out the jobs, roles and responsibilities of all three levels of management. As the CEO and President, he is responsible for creating the community relations that make his small company attractive to customers. He also must establish good rapport with other contractors who will do the portion of the construction that his company does not do. If he uses union labor, he must be familiar with union work requirements and pay scales. If he hires employees of his own, he must make policy provisions to comply with Affirmative Action and Equal Employment Opportunity (EEO) guidelines.

As a "middle manager," he must coordinate all aspects of every project so that it is completed according to the contract and time. As a "first-line" manager, he supervises the crews for the metal framing and wall-building activities and may actually operate machinery or participate in the building process.

Burson depends on new electronic devices such as cellular phones, pagers, voice mail, and FAX machines to communicate from an office that is alternately in his home, his car, and his work site. Although he may not spend as much time communicating as the CEO of a larger company, he does share the long work days associated with completing the responsibilities of top managers. In a typical day, he will examine his company's financial performance, bid on a job, meet electronically or face-to-face with customers and suppliers, and even attend a meeting of a voluntary association.[15]

As Burson's activities demonstrate, owners of small businesses do not differentiate among levels of management. As a company grows, however, the owner has to narrow the job's scope in order to concentrate on certain tasks at a specific managerial level. In Chapter 10 we show how increasing company size leads to the creation of departments and levels of management.

Teaching Tip
Most students are surprised at the fragmented, hectic pace of managerial life. Ask them whether they are surprised by the way managers spend their time. If so, why?

Time Spent on Managerial Functions

Figure 1.4 compares the distribution of time in a typical day among the four basic managerial functions by first-line, middle, and top managers. Note that first-line managers spend relatively little time planning and organizing. These functions are performed to a greater degree by middle and top managers. On the other hand, first-line managers spend 50 percent of their time leading (directing the actions of employees who actually do production work or deliver services) and 25 percent of their time controlling (making sure that parts arrive, settling disputes among employees, scheduling vacations and overtime, and inspecting products).

In contrast, middle managers spend much of their time planning, organizing, and leading to enable first-line managers and their subordinates to work as efficiently as possible. Ordering parts, dealing with customer complaints, and voicing first-line managers' concerns to top management are activities performed by middle managers.

Top managers spend most of their day (over 75 percent) planning and leading. Although middle managers spend almost half of their time leading, this time is focused on their subordinates. Top managers spend the bulk of their leading time with key people and organizations external to their own organization. Note that middle and top managers spend little time *directly* controlling the work of others.

Ethics and Managers

Ethics
Any employee can face ethical dilemmas, but they are especially troubling for those just out of school. How can you help them prepare to meet those dilemmas?

Managers, especially top managers, create the culture and climate that affect both the ethics and the social responsibility of an organization. **Ethics** represent a set of moral principles, values, and conduct that decision makers apply to issues that are not specifically addressed by law.[16] In other words, ethics help describe and determine right and wrong conduct. **Social responsibility** is the degree to which a company recognizes what being a good community and global citizen means and acts accordingly.

A discussion of ethics generally centers on one of three schools of thought. The first, the *utilitarian* school, stresses the resolution of ethical issues from the perspective of the greatest good for the greatest number of people involved. Utilitarian ethics are

FIGURE 1.4

A Distribution of Managerial Time by Function

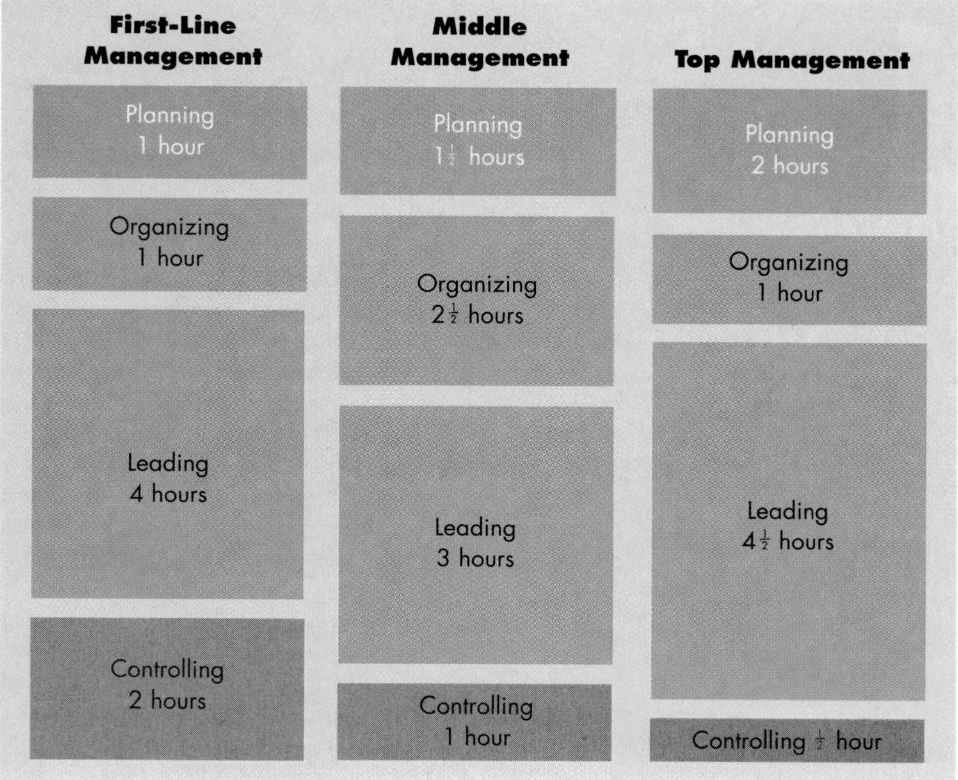

part of the foundation of democratic forms of government. An application of utilitarian ethics is a team's resolution of a flexible scheduling problem by accepting the will of the majority.

The second, the *moral rights* school, emphasizes the rights of the individual. An application of moral rights ethics is employee entitlement to a safe workplace or timely notification of a layoff.

The third, *social justice,* applies the fairness doctrine. The social justice test is the action that might be taken by an impartial observer such as an arbitrator. President Clinton acted in this capacity when he ordered airline flight attendants back to work in November 1993. That action prevented the disruption of air travel during the Thanksgiving holiday—the busiest travel time of the year.

Whereas ethics usually involves the individual's values, social responsibility puts the burden on the company as a whole. Thus, when we discuss whether a company is a "responsible citizen," we look at whether it is behaving appropriately toward customers, suppliers, employee groups, other competitors, and the community at large. Some insurance companies, such as Metropolitan Life and Humana, have acted irresponsibly by misleading their customers about the exact nature of their insurance benefits. Phelps Dodge's copper smelting operations in southern Arizona polluted the surrounding communities with hydrogen sulfide emissions. And there is some suspicion that companies, as a part of their downsizing efforts, have terminated older, more experienced, and more *expensive* employees. Such employees often have a difficult time finding another job and often lose their health insurance coverage and at least some of their future retirement benefits.

The following Ethics Insight focuses on Sears and its auto repair business. After reading it, you should be able to identify the ethical—utilitarian, moral rights, and/or social justice—and social responsibility concepts that Sears managers and employees failed to apply.

Ethics *Insight*

Selling Auto Service at Sears

In 1992, consumers filed hundreds of complaints against Sears for its automobile repair and service business. They accused the company of selling unnecessary parts and services in more than forty states. Sears management didn't set out to deliberately defraud customers—so what went wrong?

Faced with declining revenues and reduced market share, Sears attempted to improve the profitability of its auto repair centers. Management adopted new incentive goals and performance programs. Service representatives received higher sales quotas and mechanics received higher minimum work quotas. For example, goals called for larger numbers of parts and services such as springs, shocks, alignments, and brake jobs—to be sold each shift. Failure to meet quotas could result in transfers or a reduction in hours. Employees felt pressure to achieve the stated goals.

An analysis of what went wrong, conducted internally by Sears, concluded that management failed to clarify the line between legitimate preventive maintenance and unnecessary service. Pressures from top management on service managers and mechanics left some of them few legitimate options for meeting their goals. Under these pressures, some employees resorted to unethical behaviors and careless repairs to meet their goals.

Sears has discontinued the sales commissions and quotas for selling specific parts and services that led to the fraudulent practices. Mechanics who determine what repairs are needed no longer earn commissions from performing those repairs. Furthermore, Sears has instituted a plan to monitor auto repair and sales continuously. In addition, Sears has agreed to repay customers who had unneeded work done and all court costs. These costs could exceed $60 million.[17]

Cheating and not satisfying customers obviously tarnished Sears's reputation. Solving those problems was costly, time-consuming, and embarrassing to the company and its employees. We present an in-depth discussion of both ethical issues and social responsibility as they affect managerial decisions in Chapter 7. Throughout the book, we also present various business practices in ways that can help you further develop your own sense of ethical behavior.

4

Explain the impact of work-force diversity on organizations.

MANAGING A DIVERSE WORK FORCE

Work-force diversity is a term that refers to the racial, gender, age, and ethnic mix of today's labor force. During the past twenty years, the composition of the work force has changed dramatically: It is ethnically more mixed (more non-Caucasian) and older, and has more women. Because you may become a manager someday, let's consider what that job will be like if and when you do.

The entire work force that you will manage has already been born, and over two-thirds of those people are already working for some organization. As you think about managing such people, you need to consider three important issues: the changing nature of the work force, the changing nature of organizations, and the demand for better quality by customers. These factors will have an increasingly large effect on the duties of all employees and managers.

The Changing Nature of the Work Force

Teaching Tip

Students may have difficulty absorbing abstract demographic data. Ask them to name people they know in various age groups. What characteristics and values might people in each of the groups have in common? How could they affect management? For example, many young people in the 1960s protested the Vietnam War and rebelled against authority in other ways. How might such experiences have shaped their willingness to take and give direction? Are their large numbers in the work force likely to cause organizations to change to a more participatory management style?

Compared to the baby-boom generation (those born between 1946 and 1961), there are fewer of you to enter the job market. The size of that generation created a huge work-force influx. Thus, in the 1960s and 1970s, organizations could be highly selective in their hiring practices. In the late 1970s, for instance, about 3 million people entered the 18- to 24-year-old age group each year. But, in 1990, only 1.3 million new workers were in this age group, and this number continues to shrink. One implication is that you will have to get more work done with fewer people. For your organization to survive, you will have to foster an environment that increases productivity.[18]

The skills of entry-level employees will present you with another challenge. When the labor force was large, organizations could be highly selective, retaining the skilled and not hiring the undereducated and unskilled. In the future, organizations may have to hire workers who need remedial work in simple math and writing. In 1993 and 1994, organizations spent more than $220 billion on training. For example, Motorola requires every employee to attend thirty hours of education and training in its Motorola University program each year. To help ensure the success of this program, the company requires that all production employees demonstrate the ability to read and compute at a third-grade level and be free from chemical substances. The reason for this standard is the higher skill levels now required to perform many jobs, such as monitoring robots and maintaining computerized equipment.

Discussion Question 2

Of what significance to organizations are current work-force diversity trends?

Real-World Example

Only thirteen Fortune 500 companies have a woman as one of their top five officers, including Mattel, Merck, Pitney Bowes, and U.S. Surgical Corporation (*Wall Street Journal*, November 22, 1994:A1).

You also need to be aware of the influx of women and minority groups into the work force. By the year 2000, women will account for 65 percent of the U.S. labor force, and only 15 percent of the *entering* work force will be white men—compared to 45 percent women and over 43 percent white men in 1988. Moreover, these are global trends. Worldwide, over 34 percent of the work force is female. In developed nations, it is almost 60 percent. A major problem for both women and minorities has been the lack of managerial positions for members of these groups. At MCI, in the early 1990s, for example, where 42 percent of the 20,400 employees are female, women still hold only 12 percent of the top 350 management jobs—and that is double the number of three years earlier. Although affirmative action programs created hiring mandates, they didn't provide for advancement of women and minorities after they were hired.

Large organizations are having trouble finding, promoting, and retaining good female and minority managers. Many of the most capable women get fed up with orga-

Real-World Example
Alpine Banks of Colorado, located in the Aspen area, outmaneuvered its competitors by hiring bilingual employees to serve the thousands of Spanish speakers who moved there to work at ski resorts (*Nations Business*, December 1994).

nizational life when they fail to advance into top management. Twenty years after women first entered managerial ranks, very few have broken through the middle ranks to top management positions. A recent study by the editors of *Fortune* magazine found that less than 4 percent of the organizations surveyed had women in top management positions.

Similarly, a study of *Fortune*'s top 1,000 organizations found that less than 4 percent of their top management positions were held by African-Americans, Asians, and Hispanics. When it came to Boards of Directors, the group Working Women estimated that more than 90 percent of the positions of publicly held corporations were occupied by white males.[19] As the following Diversity Insight reveals, women CEOs, although still rare, have created and manage substantial and successful businesses. In fact, women-owned businesses are the fastest growing segment of the U.S. economy. Bureau of the Census statistics indicate that women own about 35 percent of all small businesses. That number is expected to increase to 40 percent by the year 2000.

Diversity *Insight*

Anita Roddick Creates Glamour with "Green" Products

The Body Shop, a company that originated in the United Kingdom, is hardly a household word today. Yet British-born owner and CEO Anita Roddick has franchises of her bath and body products company in forty-five countries. The products sold in these stores are made from natural ingredients supplied by vendors who guarantee that the components have not been tested on animals in the previous five years, and come from indigenous populations—rather than foreign investors who may exploit underdeveloped countries. Roddick sells a holistic, feminist concept that goes beyond the Avocado Body Butter and Honey Stick Lip Balm through the attention provided to the customer by the sales force.

Roddick is a woman on a mission. As she travels the world searching for new products, she helps meet local needs through education and participation in local social programs. Does she sacrifice her bottom line for these programs? Not a chance. In October 1993, she announced pretax profits of $15 million for the first half of the company's fiscal year—a 20 percent increase over the same period in the preceding year. And she has a global expansion plan for opening over 400 more stores.

Why is Roddick such a role model for others? One reason arises from the history of The Body Shop. She opened the first store in 1976 to support herself and two young children while her husband bicycled from Buenos Aires, Argentina, to New York City. She studied the project carefully, including product and store ambience, prior to opening. From the beginning, she held costs down by asking customers to refill their containers rather than use new ones. She engaged in sound business practices that were dictated by her personal values. Her gender makes her a role model and a mentor to other female entrepreneurs.[20]

Ask Students
In what types of situations could illiterate workers cause problems?

Solutions to some diversity problems are hampered by the educational system. More than half of minority group workers entering the work force come from school systems that haven't adequately prepared them with the skills they need to advance within organizations. In fact, Labor Secretary Robert Reich suggests that a major barrier to employment generally is the lack of proper training. This issue affects a larger percentage of minority workers than the population as a whole.[21]

Another issue that must be addressed by management in the mid-1990s and beyond is child care. Many of the women entering the work force have or will have children. A recent survey by the Society for Human Resource Management reported that only 10 percent of U.S. organizations provide child care assistance, a shortage made even more acute by the increasing number of **dual-career couples** (both husband and wife work).[22]

Diversity presents both challenges and opportunities for the organization and the manager. As Table 1.2 illustrates, the successful manager must recognize the benefits and changes in the skill base offered by different employees, as well as the opportunities to introduce new products and services. For example, a company introducing self-managed teams might benefit by using workers who come from countries more oriented toward the group than to the individual. And with the increasing diversity of the U.S. population, companies can successfully introduce niche products generated by the creativity of employees who reflect that diversity. Avon has capitalized on this competitive advantage by using its diverse employee pool to help develop cosmetics designed for non-Caucasian and African-American skin types and coloring.

The Changing Face of Organizations

Between 1990 and 2000, the number of people aged 35 to 47 will increase by 38 percent, and the number between 48 and 53 will increase by 67 percent. What this means for you is increased competition for high-level management jobs, traditionally held by people in those age groups. In 1987, one manager in twenty was promoted into a top management position; in 2001, the ratio is expected to be one in fifty. The traditional lure of promotion as an incentive to work long, hard hours appears to be weakening.[23] Other forces changing organizations include mergers and acquisitions, which have affected an estimated 15 million workers. One management tactic currently popular is downsizing an organization. **Downsizing** is the process of reducing the size of a firm by laying off or retiring workers early in an attempt to cut payroll costs. A recent survey by the American Management Association (AMA) showed that almost 40 percent of the largest organizations in the United States plan to reduce their work forces by downsizing. As a result of downsizing, an estimated 500,000 middle managers at more than 300 corporations lost their jobs or were eased out with special early retirement incentives. For example, IBM has restructured its organization and terminated more than

Real-World Example
5.6 million white-collar jobs were lost permanently from the U.S. economy between 1987 and 1991 (*The Academy of Management Executive*, January 1993, 95–104).

TABLE 1.2

Organizational Steps Toward Valuing Diversity

Why is valuing diversity good for this company?	**What modifications do we make?**
Compliance with the law	Change recruitment and promotion patterns
Community relations, social/ethical responsibility	Develop new systems (mentoring, sponsorship, promotion)
Leads to competitive edge	Change models of acceptable managerial behavior
What is my vision of a diverse work force?	**What kind of support will people need?**
Values women and minorities at all levels	Recognition that people are "pioneers"
Keeps people's identities intact	Dealing constructively with conflict
Is diverse and offers opportunities	Training and helping as people change
What is my definition of diversity?	**What can we do to help us value diversity?**
Race, gender, religion, country of origin, ethnicity, age	Keep affirmative action programs, but move beyond
Sexual orientation, background, education	Keep the doors of the organization open
"Differences" among people	Open doors at higher levels in the organization
What is the corporate culture in my organization?	
Values (Who is important here?)	
Myths (Who are the heroes?)	
Norms (How should I act in order to get ahead?)	
Can differences be accommodated?	

Source: Adapted from Thomas, R., Jr. From affirmative action to affirming diversity. *Harvard Business Review,* March–April 1990, 107–117.

Ask Students
Brainstorm problems caused by having to manage people you cannot see in person. How will managers who rely heavily on nonverbal cues get these cues to determine whether they are being told the truth and whether they are being understood? Will people who can't be seen be remembered at promotion and pay raise time?

100,000 employees—many at the middle management level. Many of the IBM managers have been replaced with temporary people to finish projects. As a result of such moves, many people are becoming concerned more with simply holding onto their jobs than with doing their work.[24]

The focus for many of tomorrow's organizations will be on service, not manufacturing. In 1990, the service sector accounted for more than 67 percent of the nation's gross domestic product (GDP) and 71 percent of its employment. Traditionally, service-oriented organizations have recruited people with low skill levels and have provided little in the way of training. The possibility of "electronic offices" means that eventually many people may be able to work at home instead of commuting to an office.[25] Your task will be to manage people who may not have the skills needed to perform their jobs and whom you may not even see on a daily basis. You will have to learn how to motivate people you can't talk with face-to-face.

The Changing Duties of Management

As you launch your career in management, your challenge will be to lead and manage during a time that will feature an older and more culturally diversified work force, changes within and to organizations, and redefined product–service mixes. The following paragraphs sketch the effects of these broad changes on the duties of first-line, middle, and top managers.

First-Line Managers in the 1990s and Beyond. The first-line manager's job will change in several ways. First, because of downsizing, first-line managers will have to assume greater responsibility for the work of their departments. At Muratec Business Systems, which makes fax machines, specialists in the areas of quality control, human resources, and industrial engineering provide guidance and support. First-line managers participate in the production processes and other line activities, and coordinate the efforts of the specialists to get the job done.

Second, the workers that first-line managers supervise will be less willing to put up with authoritarian management. They will expect more job satisfaction and will want to participate in decisions affecting their work. **Self-managed work teams** bring workers and first-line managers together to make joint decisions to improve the way their jobs are done. Such teams already are being used by organizations ranging from manufacturers of cars and airplanes to banks and fast-food restaurants.[26] Employees want their jobs to be more creative, challenging, and fun.

Third, the work itself will change. The design and manufacture of products are being changed to meet new market requirements, global competition, increased energy efficiency standards, and more stringent safety and health regulations. Finally, diversity of the work force will present challenges to first-line managers. The **multicultural organization,** with a work force representative of the population at large, will require mentoring for women, minorities, and newly hired older employees. Diversity will challenge managers to monitor and balance ethnic and cultural behavioral differences in groups. For example, employees who are raised in cultures that emphasize collective behavior—found in many parts of Asia—are more likely to cooperate with each other in group decision-making situations than those raised in cultures that emphasize the role of the individual, such as in Germany and the United States.[27]

Other changes arise from the use of robots to displace people who perform routine or dangerous jobs. Robots, in turn, create new technical or software-related jobs that require greater skill and knowledge. Employees in service organizations will deal more and more with words and symbols than with materials and products. First-line managers must adapt to all these changing aspects of work as readily as, if not more quickly than, the employees they supervise.

Middle Managers in the 1990s and Beyond. Middle managers will face a different set of challenges. They will have to improve efficiency, quality, productivity, and service—with fewer people. A wave of corporate mergers, acquisitions, divestitures, and leveraged buyouts (LBOs) has made entire levels of management redundant. (A **leveraged buyout** is the acquisition of a company, financed through borrowing by a group of investors.) Middle managers have been the hardest hit, and with survival a key issue, many middle managers feel powerless and anxious.[28]

Although their ranks have been depleted, middle managers still play an important role in bridging the gap between top and first-line managers. They implement the strategies devised by top managers and remain a significant source of innovation when given the freedom to make decisions. For example, Janet Young, an administrative manager at Palmetto General Hospital in Hialeah, Florida, has saved her hospital thousands of dollars by implementing a new quality control system for purchasing supplies.

Top Managers in the 1990s and Beyond. Top managers must strive to make their companies competitive in a global economy. Globalization increasingly requires **joint ventures** (partnerships between two or more firms to create another business to produce a product or service). For example, Thomson, S.A., of France recently formed a joint venture with JVC of Japan.[29] Thomson hopes to learn skills vital to competing in consumer electronics, such as manufacturing technologies in optical and compact discs, from its Japanese partner. In turn, JVC hopes to acquire from Thomson the marketing skills needed to compete in fragmented European markets. Another option in meeting global competition is cooperative management arrangements, such as that between the Russian government and Motorola to launch communication satellites.

To accommodate these new global arrangements, organizational structures that resemble a network of relationships, rather than the traditional organizational hierarchy, will become common. Top managers also will have to streamline their organizations. That means fewer layers of management and fewer middle managers. The first step in this process is for top managers to develop a clear vision for their organizations. In addition, they will have to work more closely with customers to learn customer preferences and how to cater to them. Finally, top managers are increasingly being held accountable to society for their organizations' actions on issues ranging from employee wellness to air and water pollution to hiring practices. Planning and implementing new programs related to these issues will consume much of top managers' time and energy.

The Mandate of Quality

Teaching Tip
Write the HRM practices of Baldrige TQM Award winners on the board (*The Academy of Management Executive,* June, 1993, 49–66): (1) communicate the importance of each employee's contribution to total quality, (2) stress quality-related synergies available through teamwork, (3) empower employees to "make a difference," (4) reinforce individual and team commitment to quality with a wide range of reward and reinforcement. Break the students into groups of 5 to 8. Ask one student in each group to volunteer to discuss his or her work in an organization. The others in the group should question the volunteer about whether the organization meets the Baldrige criteria. What TQM improvements can be made?

Companies have changed the focus of their activities from an internal, production orientation to an external, customer orientation. Much of this change is the result of a mini-industrial revolution in this country and worldwide called total quality management (TQM). In a **total quality management** system managers and other employees continually seek to improve processes and products. It emphasizes the reduction of defects in products while they are being manufactured and the needs of customers who purchase products or services. The most dramatic example of the need for improving quality was the decline of the U.S. automobile industry. It was brought on by declining quality of U.S. cars and the efforts of low-wage and quality conscious competitors in Asia, especially in Japan. As a result, many companies, including those in the auto industry, have embraced the redesign of jobs and departments and again are stressing quality and customer satisfaction. Companies such as Hillerich & Bradsby Bat Company, which makes Louisville Slugger bats for professional and little league baseball, have been saved from extinction by using TQM programs.

Quality has become such an important part of our country's national industrial policy that, in 1987, the federal government created an award called the **Malcolm Baldrige National Quality Award.** This award is an incentive for companies to work toward improved operations and performance by setting up standards for all aspects of company activity. Companies that have received the coveted award include FedEx (Federal Express), Xerox, Motorola, and AT&T.

Many U.S. companies adopted a total quality management system. Jobs and company departments are being redesigned and quality and customer satisfaction are being stressed.

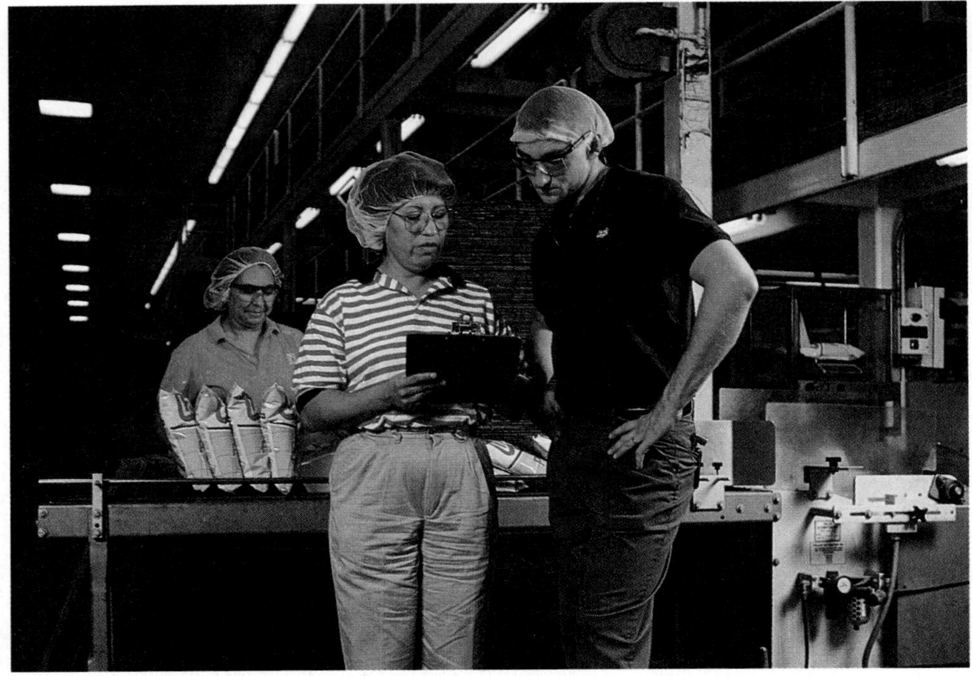

In addition to improving product quality, which helps companies compete globally, employee satisfaction also seems to be enhanced through the additional training and participation in decision making that is part of TQM. On FXTV, the in-house TV station at FedEx, key managers respond to employee questions on a call-in talk show. At Cadillac Division of General Motors, employees receive regular updates and answers to questions through a special feature on the company voice-mail system.[30]

Regardless of the specific type of program chosen, managers have attempted to introduce TQM into their companies for both external customers who purchase the service or product and internal customers in other departments. Because they extend to the entire company, and frequently involve suppliers as well as customers of the company, these organizationwide programs are quite different from the quality circle programs of the 1980s. As demonstrated in the following Quality Insight, the Motorola Paging Division effort is a good example of a TQM system that has resulted in happy consumers around the world and happy employees at work.

Quality *Insight*

Motorola Pagers

Pagers and paging devices are a part of the telecommunication revolution of the 1990s. No longer limited to medical doctors and emergency personnel, these small devices are used by dual-career families who need to maintain contact with each other and their children, as well as salespeople who must be on call to their customers. At Motorola in Boynton Beach, Florida, all pagers are custom built in unique job lots for the purchaser. They are built by robots and a team of workers trained to monitor the robots. The robots tune the crystals inside the pagers to the proper frequencies and inspect the finished products. Several minifactories exist within a larger "plant." Each factory is specialized by the type of pager it builds. One group builds a wristwatch pager that has little attraction for the Western consumer, but is extremely popular with the Japanese.

This plant was not always in this condition. In 1987, the Paging Division was experiencing large numbers of defective products. The company decided to use its Boynton Beach plant as an experiment. All employees were permitted to stay on the payroll as long as they met the basic human resources requirement of third-grade reading and writing skills. Factory workers were then trained to monitor robots, tune crystals, and take full responsibility for the product as it was assembled. They were given a target defect level of Six Sigma (about 1 defect in 14 million pagers). They were permitted to experiment with work-flow and product assembly procedures in their self-managed work teams. An automation manager with engineering training supervised the process. Successes were heralded throughout the facility by bulletin boards, in-house newspapers, and festivities to celebrate success.

As the number of defects fell toward targeted levels, the project was expanded to include interdepartmental teams who volunteered to solve problems involving nonproduction issues. One example was a team that set up the word processing system. Some internal "customers" in production and marketing who used "product" from the word processing system of the plant helped select the computer hardware and software. The system adopted permitted needed information to flow without paper to internal customers.

How long did the overall project take? It's not over. Good TQM programs involve continuous improvement not only in product but in customer–supplier relations. It is still evolving almost a decade later. Three years elapsed before any discernible economic benefit was achieved. But total quality is now well embedded in the work teams at the Motorola pager plant.[31]

Motorola isn't alone in discovering that producing quality products and services makes economic sense. Xerox Corporation has come up with a problem-solving process to improve customer billing accuracy at its Omaha district office. This project was undertaken as a result of a customer survey. It indicated that 18 percent of Xerox's customers were unhappy with billing accuracy and that 40 percent were dissatisfied with the way in which billing was corrected. The team, which called itself Billing Bloopers QIT, was formed from employees in customer relations, marketing support, service, business operations, and sales. Customers were happy with the outcome, and the amount of "rework" was cut significantly, thus reducing staff time and costs.

Ethics
Students often think that problems come in neat categories that correspond to textbook chapter topics. Make the observation that the Billing Bloopers QIT at Motorola not only improved quality and reduced rework cost, but also acted ethically on the customer's behalf by sending out fair bills.

Total quality programs require organizationwide attention. Thus we discuss the implications of total quality management in terms of the business environment and global competition in Chapters 3 and 4, in terms of group and team formation and performance in Chapter 16, in terms of organizational controls in Chapter 18, and in looking at specific techniques for total quality management in Chapter 20.

5

Describe the five basic types of managerial skills and their relative importance.

MANAGERIAL SKILLS

We've now talked about basic levels of management, what managers do, and what the future holds in store for them. But you may still be wondering exactly what it takes to be an effective manager. Should you develop certain basic managerial skills? **Skills** are abilities related to performance that are not necessarily inborn. For our purposes here, we group managerial skills into five categories: technical, interpersonal, conceptual, communication, and critical thinking.[32] In practice, however, telling where one skill begins and another ends may be difficult. Throughout this book, both within the text and in the exercises and critical thinking cases at the end of each chapter, we focus on the basic skills you should develop to be effective as both a manager and a subordinate.

Ask Students
How do the skills needed by managers in charge of jet aircraft fabrication differ from those needed by the manager of the campus bookstore?

The relative mix of skills required depends on the manager's level, responsibilities, and functions. For example, skills needed by Debbie Kinsley, the manager of a local branch of NationsBank, are likely to be quite different from those needed by Executive Vice-President Deborah Cannon of NationsBank-Texas, who oversees all Texas operations. The branch manager probably needs relatively high technical and interpersonal skills, whereas the executive vice-president needs relatively high conceptual, interpersonal, communication, and critical thinking skills.

Technical Skills

Technical skills involve the ability to apply specific methods, procedures, and techniques in a specialized field. Imagining the technical skills needed by design engineers, market researchers, accountants, and computer programmers is relatively easy. Their skills are concrete and can usually be taught in college courses or on-the-job training programs. Managers use technical skills to varying degrees. Generally, however, they are concerned with identifying and developing the technical skills needed by others in the organization.

Interpersonal Skills

Interpersonal skills include the abilities to lead, motivate, manage conflict, and work with others. Whereas technical skills involve working with things (techniques or physical objects), interpersonal skills focus on working with people. Because every organization's most valuable resource is people, interpersonal skills are a key part of every manager's job, regardless of level (from supervisor to president) or function (from production to marketing and finance).

A manager with excellent interpersonal skills encourages participation in decision making and lets subordinates express themselves without fear of embarrassment. A manager with good interpersonal skills respects other people and is liked by them. Managers who lack effective interpersonal skills often are rude, abrupt, and unsympathetic, making others feel inadequate and resentful.

Conceptual Skills

Conceptual skills involve the ability to view a problem, an issue, or the organization as a whole and how its parts are interrelated. Managers with good conceptual skills are able to see how the organization's various departments and functions relate to one another and how changes in one department or process can affect others. They use conceptual skills to diagnose and assess different types of management problems and issues that might arise.

Discussion Question 4
What changes in managerial skills occur as someone is promoted from a first-line to a middle management position?

Ask Students
Do you have sufficient skills in each of these five skill areas for the job you want when you graduate? What can you do to improve them?

Conceptual skills are among the most difficult to develop because they involve the way a person thinks. To use conceptual skills well requires thinking in terms of (1) relative priorities rather than ironclad goals and criteria, (2) relative chances and probabilities rather than certainties, and (3) rough correlations and overall patterns rather than clear-cut, cause-and-effect relationships. Conceptual skills are especially important to the manager's decisional roles of entrepreneur, disturbance handler, resource allocator, and negotiator—all of which require an ability to scan the environment for trends.

All managers, but especially top managers, need conceptual skills. Top managers must perceive changes in the organization's environment and respond to them promptly. For example, Citicorp is widely regarded as one of the most innovative banks in the world. It pioneered the negotiable certificate of deposit, was one of the first to use automated teller machines, has issued more credit cards than any other bank, and is the world's largest private foreign lender. It was able to do so because Walter B. Wriston, Citicorp's recently retired CEO, had the foresight to steer the bank toward innovative ways of thinking about the problems that would be facing the world's economy in the 1990s.[33]

Communication Skills

Communication skills are the ability to send and receive information, thoughts, feelings, and attitudes. The ten managerial roles are based on the assumption that managers have at least basic written, oral, and nonverbal (facial expression, body posture) communication skills. Because managers spend much of their time communicating, management recruiters look for people who can communicate effectively. In fact, the importance of good communication skills cannot be stressed enough. At a time when organizations increasingly expect employees to work with minimal supervision and to show more initiative, competent communication skills are a must.

The need to employ productive workers of both sexes and varied cultural and ethnic backgrounds is yet another reason to develop good communication skills. Managing diversity, after all, isn't just adapting to the new realities of the U.S. labor force; it also means getting all workers to contribute their best ideas and efforts in an intensely competitive global market. But being able to evaluate the qualifications and performance of workers whose cultural backgrounds and languages are unfamiliar to you isn't always easy.

Critical Thinking Skills

Critical thinking is the careful consideration of the implications of all known aspects of a problem. What does this mean? It means using the human mind to *evaluate* a problem rather than simply to respond in a prescriptive, predetermined way. Many years ago, educator B. S. Bloom proposed a hierarchy of learning that ranged from basic knowledge (e.g., knowing how to operate a lathe or assemble cars) to synthesis and evaluation of future strategies.[34] Today's managers at all levels are being asked to use critical thinking to find solutions to increasingly difficult and complex problems. Thus they are required to operate at a higher level of Bloom's hierarchy.

In the auditing department at Arthur Andersen, for example, Marc Charnas uses critical thinking skills to link the accounting practices of his clients with the needs of internal management and the requirements of the Federal Accounting Standards Board (FASB). At Armstrong World Industries in Pensacola, Florida, Susan Priller manages accounts payable. She is required not only to handle the bookkeeping function but also to determine whether suppliers are complying with Armstrong's ethical standards. In doing so, she uses both her basic knowledge and her ability to evaluate the quality of the product and the supplier's compliance with Armstrong's other requirements.

Managers and employees at all levels are being challenged to use these skills to perform their jobs better. You will have an opportunity to practice your critical thinking ability in the case at the end of each chapter and in responding to the end-of-chapter questions called "From Where You Sit."

Relative Importance of Managerial Skills

Teaching Tip
Have students bring a section of the Sunday newspaper help-wanted ads to class. Break the students into groups of 5 to 8. Ask them to go through the ads and sort the jobs by the five skills, weighing the relative importance of each skill to each job.

The relative importance of the five types of managerial skills at each level of management is shown in Figure 1.5. Note that communication and critical thinking skills are equally important at all management levels. In fact, basic communication skills are necessary to utilize competently the interpersonal, technical, and conceptual skills. A manager's best ideas and intentions will have little impact if they cannot be communicated effectively to others.

As Figure 1.5 indicates, the most striking difference among the levels of management is the shift from an emphasis on technical skills to an emphasis on conceptual skills. This transition is often very difficult for managers. First-line managers may be promoted into middle management positions because they have excellent technical skills. These new managers then often make the mistake of relying on their technical skills, rather than learning new conceptual skills and developing their interpersonal skills. As a result, many middle managers fail to get promoted to top positions.

The higher a manager's position in the organization, the more the manager is involved in making complex decisions. Top managers need conceptual abilities to recognize important factors in their businesses and how they interrelate. Many of the responsibilities of top managers, such as resource allocation and overall business strategy,

FIGURE 1.5

Relative Importance of Managerial Skills by Management Level

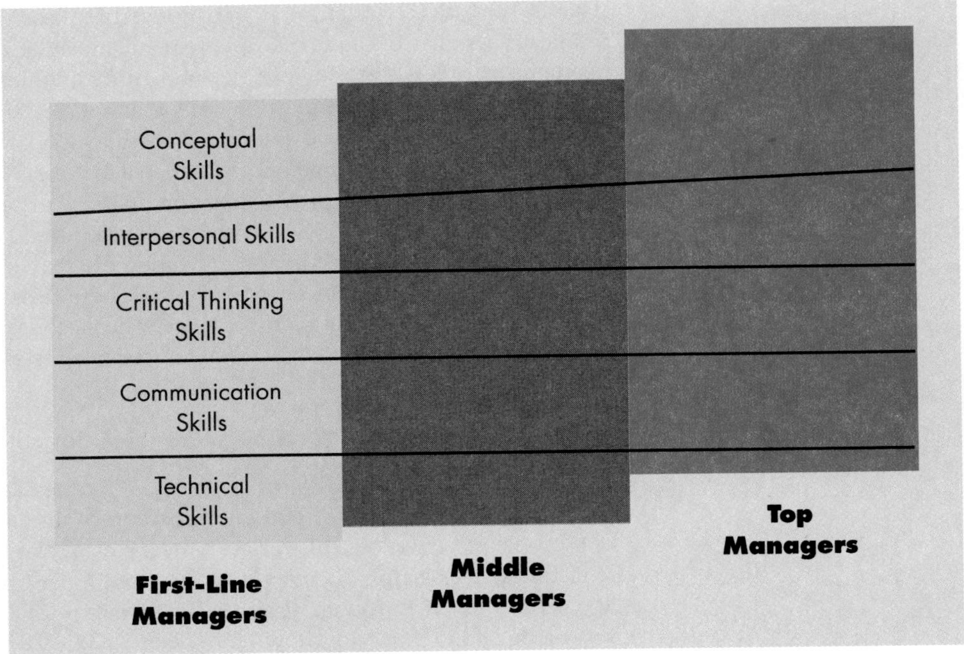

require a broad view. Without conceptual skills, managers cannot take actions that are in the best interests of the entire organization.

Skills for Managers in the Year 2000

Real-World Example
Today's managers need to develop a global perspective and learn to work with people from diverse cultures (*The Academy of Management Executive,* November 1992).

With the development of a single European market and the blossoming of the Pan-Pacific market, managers in the twenty-first century will need a different mix of skills than today's managers if they are to be successful. The 1990s are a decade in which markets are shrinking (like that for oil) and expanding overnight (like that for pharmaceuticals). However, new technologies will constantly change methods of manufacturing and distributing goods and services, and new competition will arise from unexpected places. For example, all U.S. car producers and computer companies have entered into some form of joint venture or other alliances with either Japanese or South Korean manufacturers to learn new manufacturing technologies.[35] Ford Motor Company and Mazda worked together for six years to design and manufacture the Ford Escort, a model that lasted five years. They repeated that success with the Ford Mustang. These cars are built both in the United States and Mexico.

Table 1.3 indicates the relative importance of managerial skills at the beginning and end of the 1990s. These data were taken from surveys conducted by *Fortune* magazine, General Electric Company, and others.

Real-World Example
John Bryant has a vision that doing business in South Central Los Angeles, which is still recovering from the 1992 riot, should be as easy as doing business anywhere else. Although other businesses have fled or won't consider locating there, Bryant started two successful tour bus companies and is active in community affairs (*California Business,* September 1993).

The ability to provide visionary leadership will be the most highly valued managerial skill in the year 2000. Such leadership means creating a vision with which people can identify and to which they can commit. The frequency of communication with both customers and employees will rise dramatically. With more operations spread throughout the world, managers will have to spend more time building consensus to meet the organization's goals. Because of leveraged buyouts, corporate downsizing, and international joint ventures, many employees may have to be reassigned to unfamiliar tasks. Unsatisfactory performers will be fired as companies cut costs to improve their operations and meet the financial goals of shareholders.

To cope with increasing globalization, managers will have to expand their communication skills by learning to speak other languages and becoming familiar with the culture, history, economics, and business practices of other countries. Organizations will

TABLE 1.3

Importance of Managerial Skills in 1990 and 2000

MANAGERIAL SKILL/BEHAVIOR	YEAR* 1990	YEAR* 2000
Technical		
Computer literacy	3	7
Marketing and sales	50	48
Production	21	9
Interpersonal		
Emphasize ethics	74	85
Manage human resources	41	53
Reassign or terminate unsatisfactory employees	34	71
Conceptual		
Formulate strategy	68	78
Convey strong sense of vision	75	98
Plan for management succession	56	85
Understand international economics and politics	10	19
Communication		
Communicate frequently with customers	41	78
Communicate frequently with employees	59	89
Handle media and public speaking	16	13
Be sensitive to cultural differences	10	40

Source: Kraut, A.I., Pegrego, P.R., McKenna, D.D., and Dunnette, M.D. The role of the manager: What's really important in different management jobs. *Academy of Management Executive,* 1989, 3, 286–293.

*Numbers are the percentages of managers who believe that each behavior is important.

need to establish training programs that expose middle managers to the company's long-range plans. This information will enable middle managers to deal more effectively with multinational joint ventures and to recognize the broad social and economic implications of their decisions. Training programs will also show employees how to conduct productive meetings with customers and address customers' concerns. Top managers Ron Golden at Radcure and Eileen Broyles at American Express Travel-Related Services frequently visit customers at their places of business to learn first hand their views on service and quality.

6

Explain management as a dynamic process.

MANAGEMENT—A DYNAMIC PROCESS

The *process* of obtaining and organizing resources and achieving goals through other people—that is, managing—is dynamic rather than static. You can begin to get a sense of its dynamic nature in Figure 1.6.

Managerial thought evolves whenever new theories are presented or new practices are tried. If the theories seem to have merit or the practices appear to succeed, their use spreads to more and more organizations until, over a period of time, they become accepted ways of managing. The adoption of Japanese quality control methods by many U.S. firms is an example of evolution in management thought. In 1950, W. Edward Deming's total quality control method was rejected by U.S. companies but were received warmly in Japan. We describe Deming's method more fully in Chapter 20, but its essence is that poor quality is unacceptable. To improve quality, data should be gathered to spot errors before and during the production process, not at its end. Moreover, employees should be rewarded for spotting quality problems, not punished. To honor and immortalize his contributions to their industries, the Japanese created the Deming Prize, awarded annually to the Japanese company that has attained the highest level of quality. An increasing number of U.S. firms, such as Ford Motor Company, Whirlpool, and Texas Instruments, are now using Deming's ideas to improve product quality.[36] The

Ethics
Not only should spotting quality problems be rewarded, but the reporting of ethical problems also should be rewarded.

Discussion Question 5
What is the relationship between TQM and a manager's ethical behaviors?

FIGURE 1.6

Managing in a Dynamic World

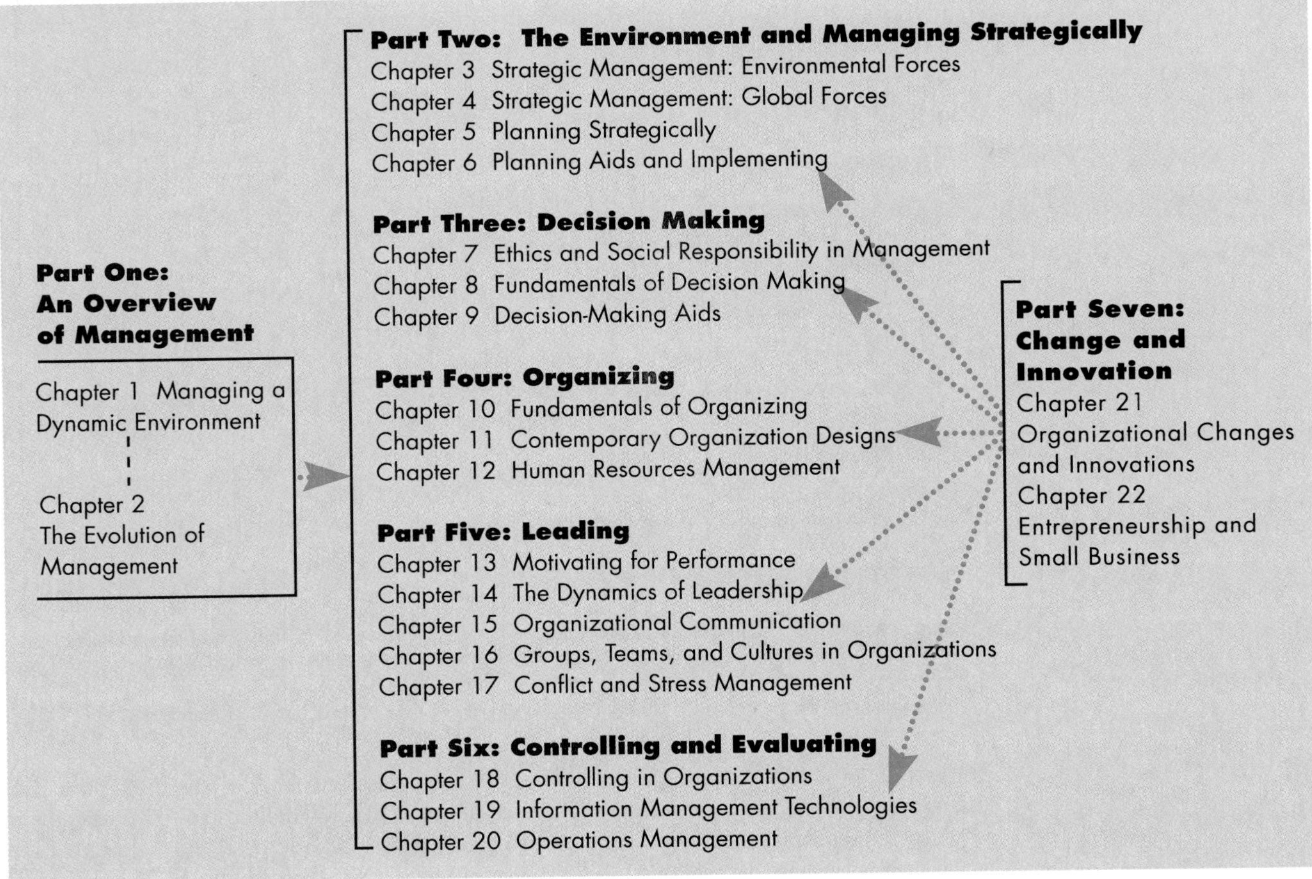

U.S. equivalent of the Deming Prize is the coveted Malcolm Baldrige Award described earlier.

Ethics
Ask students whether they think the trend of doing business faster increases or decreases the likelihood of ethical problems? If so, why?

Furthermore, many U.S. managers are eager to experiment with new solutions to urgent problems created by various internal and external forces. In recent years managerial decision making has felt the impact of a series of external forces: wireless communication technologies (environmental force); the explosion in computing, telecommunication, and multimedia technology, fueled by development and production of the silicon chip (environmental force); changing oil prices and limits on production (international force); serious competition from imports in terms of quality, price, and market share (international force); and public policy, expressed in laws and regulations aimed at improving the physical environment and the health and safety of consumers and workers (ethical and social forces).

Discussion Question 6
How has global competition affected organizations?

Ask Students
What is the stress level likely to be in companies that are undergoing constant change? What can you do to prepare for such an eventuality?

Managers of companies affected by such forces face immediate challenges to traditional ways of thinking, planning, and acting. If they can't adjust their decision making to these new realities, their companies will be unable to compete successfully and will decline. Perhaps the best example of an industry's response to external forces is that of U.S. automakers. Their recent joint ventures with Japanese and South Korean competitors have led managers to rethink company goals and ways of doing business. Nissan has collaborated with Ford and Mercury to create a better minivan. Ford and Mazda undertook broad restructuring of their decision-making processes. Zenith Data Systems is in a joint venture with the French conglomerate Groupe Bull to globalize its desktop computer systems. These organizations experienced change at all levels and, to some degree, in most internal functions; these changes, in turn, affected suppliers and the their decision-making processes. Thus constant change gives management a dynamic dimension. The success of managers and their companies depends largely on how well they can accommodate change.

CHAPTER SUMMARY

In this chapter, we introduced concepts that you should understand to be successful in the years ahead. Managers, management, and successful companies are changing. New skills are needed to lead and tackle a variety of organizational issues.

After reading the chapter, you should be able to:

1 ***Define managers and management.***
Managers establish organizational goals and then direct the work of subordinates, whom they depend on to achieve those goals. Managers acquire and allocate the human and material resources without which organizations could not exist. Effective management is essential to the success of an organization.

2 ***Identify the different managerial functions and roles.***
The managerial functions—planning, organizing, leading, and controlling—define what managers do. The managerial roles—interpersonal, informational, decisional—define how managers do their jobs. Managerial functions and roles go hand in hand: Managers perform the functions while playing one or more roles.

3 ***Describe the duties and responsibilities of various levels of management.***
The three basic levels of management are first-line, middle, and top. First-line managers are directly responsible for the production of goods and services. They supervise workers and solve specific problems. Middle managers coordinate the work of several first-line managers or direct the operations of a functional department. They translate top management's goals into specific goals and programs for implementation. Top managers establish overall organizational goals and direct the activities of an entire organization or a major business unit or segment.

Managers at different levels divide their time among the managerial functions quite differently. First-line managers spend about three-fourths of their time leading and controlling and the rest planning and organizing. Middle managers spend about two-thirds of their time organizing and leading and the rest planning and controlling. Top managers spend most of their time planning and leading and very little time directly organizing and controlling the work of others.

4 ***Explain the impact of work-force diversity on organizations.***
Today's managers and their employees are more diverse than they were in the past. The population is older, more racially and ethnically diverse, and more equally divided among men and women. Thus organizations must accommodate diversity in their hiring and human resources practices and focus attention on potentially exciting new products and services that may be desired by the changing population. Total quality management programs are being used to reengineer older, larger companies so that they can remain responsive and competitive and control costs.

5 ***Describe the five basic types of managerial skills and their relative importance.***
The five types of managerial skills are technical, interpersonal, conceptual, communication, and critical thinking. Technical skills are most important to first-line managers, who have to deal directly with specific methods of production. Interpersonal skills are important at all levels of management, because managing is the process of motivating other people in order to get something done. Conceptual skills are especially important to top managers, who have to think in more abstract terms and see parts in relation to the whole. Communication and critical thinking

skills are important to all managers. Such skills enable managers to lead, motivate, and change the organization's objectives. Critical thinking skills allow the manager to put together seemingly unrelated pieces of information, introducing creativity in the management process.

6 ***Explain management as a dynamic process.***
With the changes in today's work force and the globalization of many companies, management is not standing still. Managers must adapt to the changes created by diversity, quality, and international trade pacts. In addition, organizations are changing their shape and form from largely monolithic to networked and modular companies.

QUESTIONS FOR DISCUSSION

1. What are the major differences in managerial responsibilities for first-line, middle, and top managers?
2. Of what significance to organizations are current work-force diversity trends?
3. Define the four managerial functions.
4. What changes in managerial skills occur as someone is promoted from a first-line to a middle management position?
5. What is the relationship between TQM and a manager's ethical behaviors?
6. How has global competition affected organizations?

FROM WHERE YOU SIT

1. Write a letter to a local bank highlighting your skills and background for an entry-level management job. Why did you emphasize the skills that you did?
2. Is a large company (e.g., Hewlett-Packard) or a small company (e.g., Burson Construction) likely to provide you with the best learning experience for your first job?
3. Observe a manager at a local convenience store. What role(s) did that person play? Why?
4. Write an essay describing what managers can and should do to promote diversity in the workplace?
5. Imagine yourself in a job interview. The recruiter says that the organization is very concerned with developing a strong code of ethical conduct. Using insights from this chapter, respond to that statement.
6. How are organizations changing in today's workplace?

SKILL-BUILDING EXERCISE

Diversity Quiz

We have provided you with a chance to gain some insights into the practical realities of the diverse work force. Please answer the following twenty questions in the spaces provided. A sample of actual managers' responses is included for your information.

1. Throughout the 1990s, the U.S. pool of labor will shrink by ____________ million.
2. The management group most affected by the different mix of *new* workers in the U.S. work force is ____________.
3. White males make up ____________ percent of *new* workers in the United States.
4. Talent is blind to ____________, ____________, ____________, and ____________.
5. In addition to age, gender, nationality, and race, diversity includes these eight factors:

   ____________ ____________

   ____________ ____________

   ____________ ____________

   ____________ ____________

6. In 1970, the age of the average U.S. worker was ____________.
7. By the year 2000, the age of the average U.S. worker will be ____________.
8. Women make up about ____________ percent of *new* workers in the United States.
9. People of color made up about ____________ percent of the U.S. work force in 1985.
10. People of color make up about ____________ percent of *new* workers in the United States.
11. By the year 2000, immigrants will comprise almost ____________ percent of the new hires in the United States.
12. Before 1970, 79 percent of the immigrants to the United States were from these areas (be specific): ____________ and ____________.
13. Since 1970, 78 percent of the immigrants have come from these areas (be specific): ____________ and ____________.
14. An estimated ____________ percent of the people who graduate from high school cannot read or write at the ____________ grade level.
15. Adults who cannot read at this level (in item 14) would have trouble reading a ____________ menu and ____________ signs.
16. The most competitive country is ____________.
17. The country that values individuality most is ____________.
18. The group is more valued than the individual in ____________ percent of the world.
19. In cultures that respect ____________, it is considered impolite to ____________ or ____________ the boss.

20. People in the countries of ____________ and ____________ respect authority more than do people in the United States.

Diversity Quiz Answers

1. Throughout the 1990s, the U.S. labor pool will have shrunk by 4 to 5 million.
2. The management group most affected by the different mix of new workers is first-line supervisors.
3. White males make up 15 percent of the *new* workers.
4. Talent is blind to age, gender, nationality, and race.
5. In addition to the characteristics in item 4, diversity includes education, values, physical ability, mental capacity, personality, experiences, culture, and the way that work is approached.
6. In 1970, the age of the average U.S. worker was 28.
7. By the year 2000, the age of the average worker will be 40.
8. Women make up 66 percent of the new workers.
9. People of color made up 10 percent of the U.S. work force in 1985.
10. People of color make up 20 percent of the new workers.
11. By the year 2000, immigrants will make up almost 25 percent of the work force.
12. Before 1970, 79 percent of the immigrants to the United States were from Canada and Europe.
13. Since 1970, 78 percent of the immigrants to the United States have come from Asia and Latin America.
14. An estimated 25 percent of the people who graduate from high school cannot read or write at the eighth-grade level.
15. Adults who read below this level would have trouble reading a McDonald's menu and traffic signs.
16. The most competitive country is Japan.
17. The country that values individuality the most is the United States.
18. The group is valued more than the individual in 70 percent of the world.
19. In cultures that respect authority, it is considered impolite to disagree or argue with the boss.
20. People in Mexico and Japan respect authority more than do people in the United States.[37]

CRITICAL THINKING CASE

GE—A World-Class Company—Worldwide

Reinventing a company is not easy, even for General Electric's CEO Jack Welch. But that is exactly what he did. In just over a decade at the helm, he shed more than 200,000 employees while net income on sales of more than $57 billion nearly tripled. The most interesting part of the change at GE was that the company was not in trouble. However, Welch was astute enough to know that the stable manufacturer of jet engines and home appliances was facing global competition that would eventually erode company profits.

What has changed at GE? The first change is the level of productivity. One example is the GE Appliance Park in Louisville, Kentucky, which developed a Quick Response Program. This employee-designed program cut the production cycle time for GE Appliances by 75 percent, reducing the order-to-delivery time of a finished product from eighty to twenty days. That reduction cut inventory by $200 million, increasing return on investment from the plant by 8.5 percent. Employees who learned through training and education to work smarter instead of just harder made these improvements in productivity.

The lean, flexible systems used by GE and others are very different from the old, rigid systems previously used. The most significant features of these systems are that employees are cross-trained in several skills and work in teams, the customer order pulls the product through the factory, suppliers are involved and informed, and there is continuous improvement in the product or service and in its delivery.

But continuous improvement in quality isn't the only secret ingredient. Welch recognizes that the size of the U.S. market limits the company's potential for the future, and he has turned to global markets through a series of joint ventures. For example, the Appliance Division is making low-cost ovens in India through a joint venture with Godrej, a local company, and builds gas ranges in Mexico with its partner Mabe. The Medical Systems Division has a joint venture in China (GE Hangwei) to develop low-cost imaging equipment for both the local Chinese market and export. Jet engines are being sold in China and serviced in Indonesia. And the Power Systems Division is the leader of a consortium building a $600 million thermoelectric power plant in Mexico. To do all these things, Welch moved his most capable managers to the front line in these lesser developed countries. At the same time, he has flattened the organization and brought more employees into the management process.

To bring people into the process, Welch starts by presenting the realities of a situation to *all* employees. Despite Louisville's successful Quick Response Program, the Louisville appliance complex has not been profitable. So GE leadership announced to the union stewards and the workers its intention to leave the Louisville site. The employees responded quickly by assuring Welch that they could make the system work if GE would turn its management over to them. This experiment, which is not over yet, has made the employees completely responsible for the success or failure of a potentially profitable business.

Will it work? If the company's previous successes at continuous improvement are any signal, it should work. Will the change be over when that facility is profitable? Not likely. Welch's philosophy is "it's just begun!"[38]

Questions

1. What managerial roles is Jack Welch most likely to play in creating a culture that values continuous improvement?
2. When the Louisville facility was turned over to its employees, how might the responsibilities of the onsite managers have changed? Were the managers likely required to use a different "mix" of skills? What problems might that cause?
3. In a company that is involved in so many joint ventures in lesser developed countries, how might cultural diversity be an issue?

VIDEO CASE

Lou Gerstner Takes the Reins at IBM

The changes at IBM Corporation since CEO Louis V. Gerstner, Jr., took over in April 1993 have been far-reaching and revolutionary for Big Blue—a traditional company in every sense of the word. Gerstner was the first outsider ever to be appointed CEO of the company. Why was Gerstner chosen for the company at such a critical time in its history? One reason is that he had demonstrated a variety of important skills in his previous top management positions at RJR and American Express. At RJR, he used his technical and conceptual skills in engineering a leveraged buyout of the former tobacco company. Recall from the chapter text that he also had demonstrated strong conceptual skills in identifying new markets and products that turned American Express into a profitable company.

Let's explore some of the issues that IBM faced. The computing giant had alienated customers and insulated itself from the marketplace by focusing on internal maintenance of the organization. When Gerstner spoke with IBM's European managers, they expressed surprise that he wasn't comfortable with the traditional company concept of sovereignty. In the company's annual report Gerstner stated, "We have been too bureaucratic and too preoccupied with our own view of the world." He noted further that the company had earned a reputation for arrogance.

Gerstner has worked to dismantle the old IBM culture by permitting each facility to establish its own dress code, ordering his top managers to bear-hug five customers per month, and rightsizing the company so that it will be more responsive to the changing world of information technology. Gerstner was roundly criticized for a statement made during a press conference to announce IBM's financial results that "the last thing IBM needs right now is a vision." Instead, he stated that IBM was working on strategy statements. On March 24, 1994, Gerstner outlined six strategic themes that will guide the company. Broadly, they called for IBM to push its core technology across more product lines and to sell more components such as chips to outsiders; become a player in client-server computing; offer network services to large companies; reengineer the sales force to cut costs; jump into new geographic markets, particularly Asia; and leverage IBM's size and scale. Gerstner is committed two tasks: (1) eliminating unnecessary cost, duplication, and bureaucracy; and (2) implementing the newly developed business strategies.

Gerstner has banned some of IBM's internal jargon such as LOB (line of business), nonconcur (to disagree), PROFS me (PROFS is IBM's electronic mail system), and buck it up to CHQ (send an issue to Armon, New York, IBM's headquarters). He has commented that IBM needs some loosening and continually pounds away at interdivisional communications and cooperation issues. At the same time, he is continuing efforts to improve morale. Gerstner said that he doesn't want to foster a "stable" environment, stating, "I do not want the company to always feel insecure, hungry—somebody breathing down our neck. Stable to me means complacent, and I don't think you can be stable." He sees his job as providing a culture that manages change and being "the person that creates the change. And once everyone else catches up to you, start the change process all over again."

Let's look at how Gerstner spends his time. His work day is ten to twelve hours long, six and half-days per week. In the first four months of his tenure on the job, he visited every facility worldwide. He continues to travel among facilities and threatens to move the corporate headquarters from its "palace" in New York to more humble and accessible office space outside the city. Whenever he meets with a manager, he asks about customers, competitors, strengths, weaknesses, and challenges. He also talks regularly with outsiders. In the evening he reads his e-mail notes, which contain suggestions from managers and employees, as well as other information regularly disseminated throughout the company. He also spends some of his time becoming familiar with IBM's product lines and the technologies that support them. He wants the critical technologies to become a platform for products that are developed across divisional lines. For example, he believes that the company should use the PowerPC chip throughout its computer lines.

Gerstner continues to be disrespectful of IBM's culture, seeking to replace the notion of processes with the more tasteful concept of values. This view is exemplified by a sign in his office saying that a desk is a dangerous place from which to view the world. Thus Gerstner believes that his job is to create a new IBM out of the old company by capitalizing on its human and financial resources, improving internal and external communication through a more effective hierarchy, and rebuilding the norms of the organization through cultural change.[39]

Questions

1. Which managerial roles does Lou Gerstner use most extensively?
2. Which managerial skills are being used by Gerstner in his efforts to restore IBM to its former market-leading position?
3. Is Gerstner's lack of a technological background likely to hinder his ability to make a cultural change? Why or why not?

Chapter 2

The Evolution of Management

Learning *Objectives*

After studying this chapter, you should be able to:

1. Describe the three branches of the traditional viewpoint of management: bureaucratic, scientific, and administrative.
2. Explain the behavioral viewpoint's contribution to management.
3. Describe the systems viewpoint and the use of quantitative techniques to manage organizations.
4. Explain the place of the contingency viewpoint in modern management.
5. Describe the impact of the quality viewpoint on management practices.

Chapter *Outline*

Preview *Insight*

Hewlett-Packard's Information Highway

Organizations around the world will spend $3.25 billion in 1996 to buy intelligent hardware and software devices that sit at the center of computer networks. These networks connect people to people and people to data in ways that permit information to flow freely. Today, information is power, and it has changed the nature of managerial work as many people have known it. Consider Hewlett-Packard's customer-response system.

When a customer reports a problem, the call goes electronically to one of four hubs around the world, depending on the time of day. Operators get a description of the problem and its urgency, typing the information into a database and transferring the customer's file to one of 27 data centers, where a team specializing in the customer's problem can be quickly assembled. Anyone with access to the data can search for a solution to the problem.

If the first center can't solve the problem, the customer's problem follows the sun: When it's 5:00 P.M. in Dallas, for example, it's 7:00 A.M. the following day in Tokyo. The file is already there, so H-P employees can get to work on it quickly. Whenever the problem is solved, an employee instantly updates the file so that every center around the globe has access to the problem and solution.

Tools like e-mail and teleconferencing let people work together despite distance and time. Every month Hewlett-Packard's 97,000 employees exchange more than 20 million e-mail messages. A person might spend most of the day with a team of people from different departments led by someone from another part of the world doing work on a customer's project that their boss may know little about.[1]

1

Describe the three branches of the traditional viewpoint of management: bureaucratic, scientific, and administrative.

Discussion Question 1
Why should you know about the evolution management?

THE EVOLUTION OF MANAGEMENT THOUGHT

Working for a company on the information superhighway is a recent event. Only in the past ten years or so have companies such as Boeing, Hewlett-Packard, and Lotus with complex systems challenged their employees to manage these systems. Hewlett-Packard managers now lead employees who they do not see on a daily basis and who may know more about solving a problem than they do. New methods of managing employees are needed to keep pace with changes in today's organizations. But let's not discard what happened in management before the arrival of the information superhighway. Management today reflects the evolution of concepts and viewpoints and experience gained over many decades.

During the thirty years following the Civil War, the United States emerged as a leading industrial nation. The shift from an agrarian to an urban society was abrupt and, for many Americans, meant drastic adjustment. Never before in the nation's history had so many individuals made so much money so quickly. By the end of the century a new corporate capitalism ruled by a prosperous professional class had arisen. Captains of industry freely wielded mergers and acquisitions and engaged in cutthroat competition as they created huge monopolies in the oil, meat, steel, sugar, and tobacco industries. The federal government did nothing to interfere with these monopolies. On the one hand, new technology born of the war effort offered the promise of progress and growth. On the other hand, the rapid social change and a growing disparity between rich and poor caused increasing conflict and instability.

The year 1886 marked several important turning points in business and management history. Henry R. Towne (1844–1924), an engineer and cofounder of the Yale Lock Company, presented a paper titled "The Engineer as an Economist" to the American Society of Mechanical Engineers. In that paper Towne proposed that the American Society of Mechanical Engineers create an economic section to act as a clearinghouse and forum for "shop management" and "shop accounting." Shop management would deal with the subjects of organization, responsibility, reports, and the "executive management" of industrial works, mills, and factories. Shop accounting would treat the nuts and bolts of time and wage systems, cost determination and allocation, bookkeeping methods, and manufacturing accounting. The society would develop a body of literature, record members' experiences, and provide a forum for exchanging managers' ideas.

Other events in 1886 influenced the development of modern management thought and practice. During this boom period in U.S. business history, employers generally regarded labor as a commodity to be purchased as cheaply as possible and maintained at minimal expense. Thus it was also a peak period of labor unrest—during 1886 more than 600,000 employees were out of work because of strikes and lockouts. On May 4, 1886 a group of labor leaders led a demonstration in Chicago's Haymarket Square in support of an eight-hour work day. During the demonstration someone threw a bomb, killing seven bystanders. The Haymarket Affair was a setback for organized labor, because many people began to equate unionism with anarchy.

In his pioneering study of labor history in 1886, *The Labor Movement in America*, Richard T. Ely advocated a less radical approach to labor-management relations. Ely cautioned labor to work within the existing economic and political system. One union that followed Ely's advice was the American Federation of Labor (AFL), organized in 1886 by Samuel Gompers and Adolph Strasser. A conservative, "bread and butter" union, the AFL avoided politics and industrial unionism and organized skilled workers along craft lines (as carpenters, plumbers, bricklayers, and so on). Like other early unions, the AFL protected its members from unfair management practices. Gompers's goal was to increase labor's bargaining power within the existing capitalistic framework. Under his leadership the AFL dominated the American labor scene for almost half a century.

Chicago in 1886 also was the birthplace of an aspiring mail-order business called Sears, Roebuck and Company. From its beginning Sears—founded by railroad station agent Richard W. Sears, who sold watches to farmers in his area—characterized the mass distribution system that promoted the country's economic growth. For the first time affordable fine goods were available to both rural and urban consumers. Today Sears also operates thousands of retail stores and offers a wide range of insurance through Allstate. Also in 1886 the first Coca-Cola was served in Atlanta. This scarcely noticed event launched an enterprise that grew into a gigantic multinational corporation. Other companies that began in 1886 and remain in operation today include Avon Products, *Cosmopolitan* magazine, Johnson & Johnson, Munsingwear, Upjohn, and Westinghouse.

Thus 1886 marked the origins of several well-known, large-scale enterprises, modern management thought and practice, and major labor unions. Even as these events were unfolding, a new symbol of optimism and opportunity took final form on an island in New York harbor: The Statue of Liberty was dedicated in October 1886.

Why are we recounting century-old events in a book that claims to teach management for the twenty-first century? One reason is to learn from the past, yet understand that professional management hasn't been around all that long. In earlier, preindustrial societies, men and women paced their work according to the sun, the seasons, and the demand for what they produced. Small communities encouraged personal, often familial, relationships between employers and employees. The explosive growth of urban industry—the factory system, in particular—changed the face of the workplace forever. Workers in cities were forced to adapt to the factory's formal structure and rules and to labor long hours for employers they never saw. Many were poorly educated and needed considerable oral instruction and hands-on training in unfamiliar tasks.

The emergence of large-scale business enterprises in Canada, the United States, and Western Europe raised issues and created challenges that previously had applied only to governments. Businesses needed the equivalent of government leaders—managers—to hire and train employees and to then lead and motivate them. Managers also were needed to develop plans and design work units and, while doing so, make a profit—never a requirement for governments! In this chapter we briefly review how management viewpoints have evolved since 1886 to meet those needs.

During the past century theorists have developed numerous responses to the same basic management question: What is the best way to manage an organization? We continue to study those responses because they still apply to the manager's job. The following sections discuss the five most widely accepted viewpoints of management that have evolved since about 1886: traditional (or classical), behavioral, systems, contingency, and quality. These viewpoints are based on different assumptions about the behavior of people in organizations, the key goals of an organization, the types of problems faced, and the methods that should be used to solve those problems. Figure 2.1 shows when each viewpoint emerged and began to gain popularity. As you can see, all five of these viewpoints still influence managers' thinking. In fact, one important source of disagreement among today's managers is the degree of emphasis that should be placed on each of them. Thus a major purpose of this chapter is to show you not only how each viewpoint has contributed to the historical evolution of modern management thought, but also how each can be used effectively in different circumstances now and into the future.

The oldest and perhaps most widely accepted view of management is the **traditional** (or classical) **viewpoint.** It is split into three main branches: bureaucratic management, scientific management, and administrative management. All three emerged during roughly the same time period—the late 1890s through the early 1900s, when engineers were trying to make organizations run like well-oiled machines. The founders of these three branches came from Germany, the United States, and France, respectively.

Teaching Tip

Have students name three bureaucracies that they have had experience with as an employee or customer. Write one student's three names on the horizontal axis of a chart on the board as an example. Write each of the characteristics of bureaucracy on the vertical axis. Discuss each characteristic and ask the student whether each of the three bureaucracies meets the criteria and really is a bureaucracy. Then ask other students to come to the board and repeat the evaluation for their choices.

Bureaucratic Management

Bureaucratic management is a system that relies on rules, a set hierarchy, a clear division of labor, and detailed rules and procedures. Max Weber (1864–1920), a German social historian, is most closely associated with bureaucratic management (so named because Weber based his work on studies of Germany's governmental bureaucracy). Although Weber was one of the first theorists to deal with the problems of organizations, he was not widely recognized until his work was translated into English in 1947. He was concerned primarily with the broad social and economic issues facing society; his writings on bureaucracy represent only part of his total contribution.[2]

Bureaucratic management provides a blueprint of how an entire organization should operate. It prescribes seven characteristics: a formal system of rules, imperson-

FIGURE 2.1

History of Management Thought

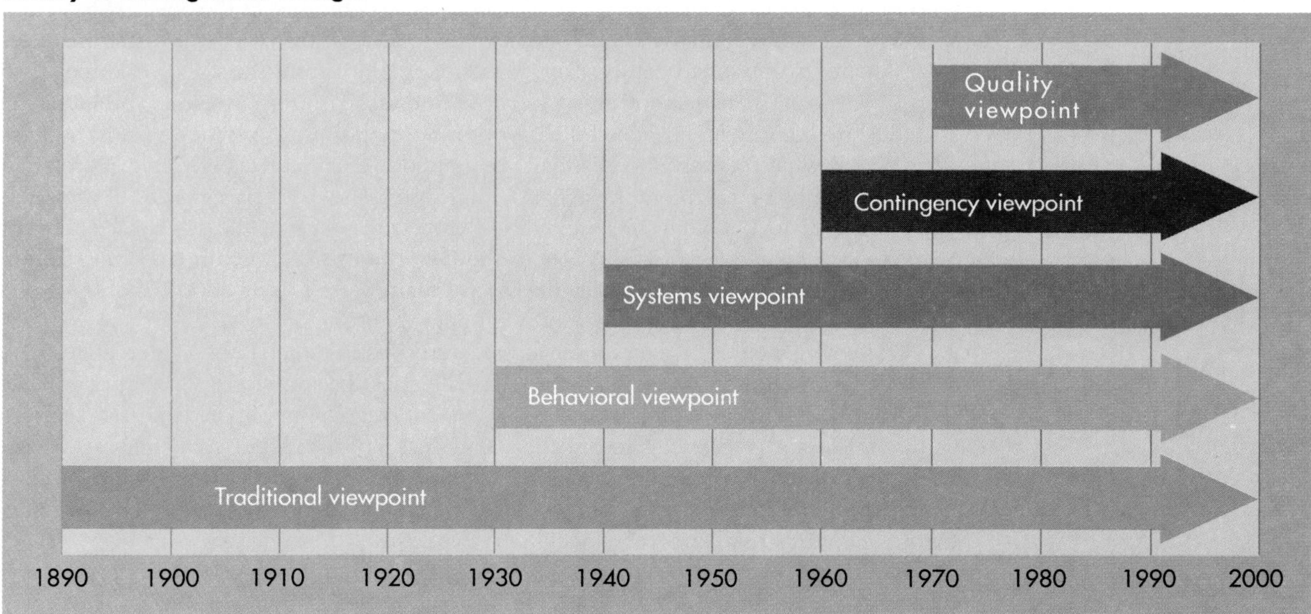

ality, division of labor, hierarchical structure, a detailed authority structure, lifelong career commitment, and rationality. Together these characteristics represent a formal, somewhat rigid method of managing. Let's take a look at this method, setting aside for the moment all the negative connotations the term *bureaucratic* has today and focusing on the system's strengths—consistency and predictability.

Ask Students
Have you run into organizational rules recently that you thought were dysfunctional? If so, what were they? What might the organization say in their defense?

Rules. Rules are formal guidelines for the behavior of employees while they are on the job. Viewed in a positive light, rules can help provide the discipline an organization needs if it is to reach its goals. Adherence to rules ensures uniformity of procedures and operations and helps maintain organizational stability, regardless of individual manager's or employee's personal desires.

Ask Students
Tell of an incident in which you experienced bureaucratic impersonality when you were the customer. Ask a volunteer to argue for bureaucratic impersonality as a top bureaucrat would. Ask a second volunteer to argue the total customer satisfaction viewpoint. Then ask the students to make up their own minds.

Impersonality. Reliance on rules leads to treating employees impersonally. That is, all employees are evaluated according to rules and objective data, such as sales or units produced. Although the term *impersonally* can also have negative connotations, Weber believed that this approach guaranteed fairness for all employees—an impersonal superior does not allow subjective personal or emotional considerations to color his or her evaluations of subordinates.

Ask Students
What are some examples of organizations that use high division of labor with high-skill jobs? (Examples: hospitals, universities, hi-tech firms.)

Division of Labor. The division of labor involves dividing duties into simpler, more specialized tasks. It enables the organization to use personnel and job-training resources efficiently. Managers and employees are assigned and perform duties based on specialization and personal expertise. Unskilled employees can be assigned tasks that are relatively easy to learn and do. For example, employee turnover at fast-food restaurants such as McDonald's, Burger King, Hardee's, and Wendy's is over 100 percent a year. Because of the narrow division of labor, most fast-food jobs can be learned quickly and require only unskilled labor. Thus high turnover may not create serious service problems.

Hierarchical Structure. Most organizations have a pyramid-shaped hierarchical structure, as illustrated in Figure 2.2. This type of structure ranks jobs according to the amount of authority (the right to decide) given to each. Typically, authority increases at each higher level to the top of the hierarchy. Those in lower level positions are under the control and direction of those in higher level positions. According to Weber, a well-defined hierarchy helps control employee behavior by making clear exactly where each stands in relation to everyone else in the organization.

Real-World Example
A monarchy, such as the United Kingdom's, is a real-world example of traditional authority. Often the monarch tends to be a figurehead leader who has little actual political power.

Real-World Example
Cult leaders often are charismatic leaders. Ask students to name recent charismatic leaders who used their power over people negatively. (Examples: Jim Jones of the Jonestown mass suicides and David Koresh of the Waco, Texas cult standoff.)

Ask Students
Rational-legal authority depends on its followers' recognizing it. What would happen if no one recognized it?

Authority Structure. A system based on rules, impersonal supervision, division of labor, and a hierarchical structure is tied together by an authority structure. It determines who has the right to make decisions of varying importance at different levels within the organization. Weber identified three types of authority structures: traditional, charismatic, and rational-legal.

- *Traditional authority* is based on custom, ancestry, gender, birth order, and the like. The divine right of kings and the magical influence of tribal witch doctors are examples of traditional authority.
- *Charismatic authority* is evident when subordinates suspend their own judgment and comply voluntarily with a leader because of special personal qualities or abilities they perceive in that individual. Social, political, and religious movements often are headed by charismatic leaders (Jesus, Joan of Arc, Gandhi, Martin Luther King). Leaders in business organizations seldom rely solely on charismatic authority, but some, such as Anita Roddick (CEO, The Body Shop), Herb Kelleher (CEO, Southwest Airlines), Mary Kay Ash (CEO, Mary Kay Cosmetics), and former president Ronald Reagan, have used their charisma to motivate and influence subordinates.
- *Rational-legal authority* is based on established laws and rules that are applied uniformly. A superior is obeyed because of the position he or she occupies within the organization's hierarchy. This authority depends on employees' acceptance of the organization's rules.

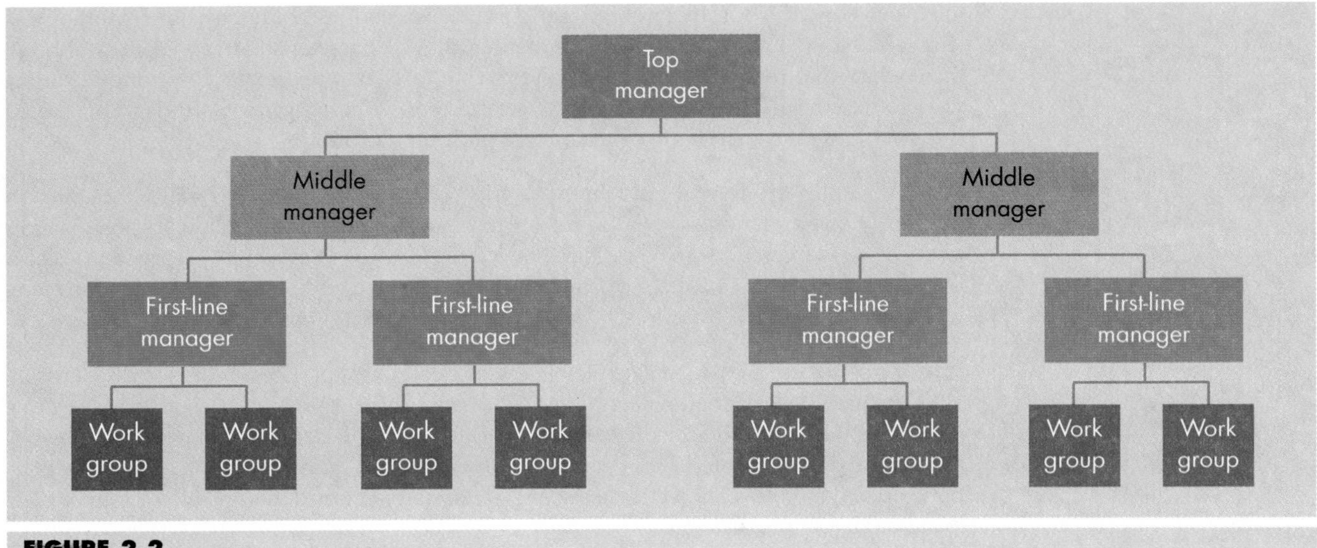

FIGURE 2.2

Hierarchical Organization Structure

Lifelong Career Commitment. In a bureaucratic management system, employment is viewed as a lifelong career commitment. That is, both the employee and the company view themselves as being committed to each other over the working life of the employee. Traditionally, Japanese and Korean organizations have hired key workers with the expectation—by both parties—that a permanent employment contract was being made. In general, lifelong career commitment means that job security is guaranteed as long as the employee is technically qualified and performs satisfactorily. Entrance requirements, such as level of education and experience, ensure that hiring is based on qualifications rather than friendship or family connections. The organization uses job security, tenure, step-by-step salary increases, and pensions to ensure that employees satisfactorily perform assigned duties. Promotion is granted when an employee demonstrates the technical competence required to handle the demands of the next higher position. Organizational level is assumed to correspond closely with expertise. Managers in bureaucratic organizations, such as the civil service, often rely on the results of written and physical tests, amount of formal education, and previous work experience in making hiring and promotion decisions.

Ask Students
What are some examples of organizations having these characteristics?

Rationality. The last characteristic of bureaucratic management is rationality. Rational managers are those who use the most efficient means possible to achieve the organization's goals. Managers in a bureaucratic management system run the organization logically and "scientifically," with all decisions leading directly to achieving the organization's goals. When activities are goal-directed, the organization uses its financial and human resources efficiently. In addition, rationality allows general organizational goals to be broken down into more specific goals for each part of the organization. At Xerox, for example, the overall corporate goals are to provide customers with copying machines and services of superior quality at a fair price and to earn enough profit to maintain the company's growth. A goal of its research and development (R&D) department is to pursue new xerographic technology and to transform technological breakthroughs into high-quality products and services. If all departments in the company reach their individual goals, the corporation reaches its overall goals.[3]

Ask Students
Do rational bureaucratic managers always know what will happen before it happens so that they can plan for it? Why or why not? Cite some examples.

Ranking Organizations by Bureaucratic Orientation. We can use the seven characteristics of bureaucratic management to rank organizations from low to high with respect to their bureaucratic orientation. As Figure 2.3 shows, government agencies (e.g., the U.S. Postal Service) and some private companies (e.g., United Parcel Service)

FIGURE 2.3

Continuum of Bureaucratic Orientation

rank high. Some creative and innovative companies (e.g., Disney Studios and Hewlett-Packard) rank low.

Such rankings have to be interpreted judiciously, however, because differences within organizations make precise measurement difficult. One organization may be highly bureaucratic in its division of labor but only slightly bureaucratic in its use of rules. In another organization these levels may be reversed. Are the organizations equally bureaucratic? No one can say for sure. Moreover, the degree of bureaucracy within an organization may vary considerably among departments and divisions. For example, Sony falls near the middle of the bureaucratic continuum, but its manufacturing plants, which produce standardized household goods (e.g., TVs, radios, clocks, and VCRs), tend to be more bureaucratic than its R&D departments, whose creativity would be stifled by too many rules.

Benefits of Bureaucracy. The expected benefits of bureaucratic management are efficiency and consistency. A bureaucracy functions best when many routine tasks need to be done. Then lower level employees can handle the bulk of the work by simply following rules and procedures. The fruits of their labor should be of standard (high) quality and produced at the rate necessary to meet organizational goals.

Teaching Tip
Have students watch TV newsmagazine shows, such as "60 Minutes" or "20/20," to obtain examples of bureaucratic excess and waste.

Costs of Bureaucracy. The same aspects of bureaucratic management that can increase one organization's efficiency can lead to great inefficiency in another. Managers at Xerox, Ernst & Young, Andersen Consulting, and others report that the orderliness of a bureaucracy often leads to inefficiencies that cannot be tolerated by companies operating in today's changing times. The following are five often unanticipated drawbacks of bureaucratic management.[4]

Ask Students
Have you ever encountered an understanding bureaucratic worker who sincerely wanted to help you but couldn't because "it was against the rules"?

1. ***Rigid rules and red tape.*** Rigid adherence to rules and routines for their own sake is a frequent complaint of employees in and customers of many organizations. Such a system leaves little room for individual freedom and creativity. This rigidity may foster low motivation, entrenched "career" employees, high turnover among the best employees, and shoddy work. A significant amount of time and money can be wasted, as is made clear by the Insight on the Beltway Bog.

Insight

Beltway Bog

Cindy Johnson, a county employment and training counselor, sits and waits for her 19 workshop participants to show up at 5:20 P.M. for class. Of the 5,000 county residents who receive food stamps, about 700 a year are supposed to take part in the training program, but only about 400 a year show up. Of those, only 41 obtained jobs through the program. Finally, three people trudge in.

Johnson passes around purple file folders containing job-hunting tips and forms to be completed. "I can't read," blurts out one person. Johnson carefully explains the program's sole requirement: Apply for two dozen jobs in the next sixty days or risk losing your food stamps. Ten job contacts must be made in person. The meeting this afternoon counts as one. Walking across the hall to the state employment bureau, she tells them, will count as another contact. She advises them that shops across the street are another quick stop. The trainees leave. This is the government's definition of "job training" and these practices are repeated in government agencies throughout the United States. Last year, some 1.5 million people were herded through this program. How can such programs last?

The federal bureaucracy is woven together by employees and congressional committees who zealously guard every corner of their turf. To please them all, training dollars must be spread thinly across all programs, diluting their effectiveness. The bureaucrats who run the programs have a keen interest in keeping them running. If the Agriculture Department, which runs only one program—the one for food stamps—eliminated its program, the agency would lose jobs and budget dollars. In addition, merging funding sources requires congressional approval, which usually isn't easy to get.[5]

Discussion Question 2
What are some of the problems of bureaucratic organizations identified in the Beltway Bog Insight?

2. ***Protection of authority.*** Managers in a bureaucratic organization may ignore issues of employee productivity while protecting and expanding their own authority. Caterpillar attacked the problem head on. Management believes that the company cannot afford to support a maze of corporate buck-passers. Caterpillar changed the system by focusing on customer satisfaction. Employees use their PCs to swap essential information and determine exactly what type of engine the customer wants. A computer-controlled monorail system and robots bring employees the engine, parts, and computer-generated information about what to do. This system requires 29 percent fewer people than the old system. Employees work at their own pace until they are satisfied that the job has been done right.
3. ***Slow decision making.*** Large, complex organizations depend heavily on timely decisions. In a highly bureaucratic organization, adherence to rules and procedures may take precedence over effective, timely decision making, as indicated in the Beltway Bog Insight. When that happens, rules take on a life of their own. Formality and ritual delay decisions at every level until all the red tape has been cleared, petty insistence on power and status privileges has been satisfied, and any chance of blame for errors in judgment has been minimized.
4. ***Incompatibility with changing technology.*** Advancing technology may make bureaucratic management inappropriate. Grahame Clark of Banctec believes that narrowly defined jobs based on rules and regulations generate little trust and sharing of information. At Banctec, the technology changes rapidly and employees must be able to go to whomever has the information they need to do their jobs.

Ask Students
What are some of the types of bureaucratic organizations that have gone out of business because their technology didn't keep up with technological change? (Examples: electronic tube manufacturers and phonograph manufacturers.)

5. ***Incompatibility with professional values.*** More and more professionals are being hired by bureaucratic organizations to fill important decision-making positions. Professional values include advancing knowledge, serving clients and customers, and finding innovative solutions to problems. These values often are incompatible with the bureaucratic need for efficiency, order, and consistency. Furthermore, bureaucratic authority is related to hierarchical position. However, the professional views authority as stemming from personal competence and technical knowledge. John Karlsten, a Hewlett-Packard manager, says that "I have to rely more on the professionalism and commitment of my people than on rules and regulations." Lotus is developing a performance appraisal system that allows team members, peers, and even external customers to evaluate employees' work. They are doing so because the boss might not know enough to evaluate a person's contributions.

Assessing Bureaucratic Management. Not all bureaucratic organizations are inefficient and unprofitable. In fact, bureaucratic management is still widely and successfully used. This approach is most effective when (1) large amounts of standard information have to be processed and an efficient processing method has been found (as in banks, insurance companies, the IRS, and traffic courts); (2) the needs of the customer are known and aren't likely to change (as in the registration of drivers in most states); (3) the technology is routine and stable, so employees can be easily and quickly taught how to operate machines (as at Taco Bell, McDonald's, Burger King, and in toll booths); and (4) the organization has to coordinate the activities of numerous employees in order to deliver a standardized service or product to the customer (as by the IRS, UPS, and the U.S. Postal Service).[6]

Teaching Tip
Some students mistakenly assume that, when we teach the evolution of management thought, no one uses scientific management anymore. Stress that all of the viewpoints covered in this chapter are currently in use.

Scientific Management

As manufacturing firms became larger and more complex in the late 1800s, not all managers could continue to be directly involved with production. Many began to spend more of their time administratively—in planning, scheduling, and staffing activities. Also, managers were hard-pressed to keep up with advances in the new, machine-oriented production technology. The distancing of management from the physical production of goods created a need for operations specialists who could solve the personnel and productivity problems that accompanied rapid industrialization and threatened operating efficiency.

Frederick W. Taylor. The stage was set for Frederick Winslow Taylor (1856–1915) to do his pioneering work in scientific management. Whereas bureaucratic management looks at broad organizational structures and work systems, **scientific management** focuses on individual worker-machine relationships in manufacturing plants. Its philosophy is that management practices should be based on proven fact and observation, not on hearsay or guesswork.[7]

Taylor, an American mechanical engineer influenced by Towne, started out as a foreman at Midvale Steel Company in Philadelphia. He believed that increased productivity ultimately depended on finding ways to make workers more efficient. One of Taylor's goals was to study and define precisely all aspects of the worker-machine relationship by using objective, scientific techniques.

When Taylor worked as a consultant to Bethlehem Steel, for example, he made a science of shoveling. Through observation and experimentation he looked for answers to questions such as:

1. Will a first-class worker do more work per day with a shovelful of five, ten, fifteen, twenty, thirty, or forty pounds?
2. What kinds of shovels work best with which materials?
3. How quickly can a shovel be pushed into a pile of coal and pulled out properly loaded?
4. How long does it take to swing a shovel backward and throw the load a specified horizontal distance at a specified height?

As Taylor accumulated answers to his questions, he developed views on how to increase the total amount shoveled per day. He started a program that matched workers, shovel sizes, materials, and the like for each job. By the end of the third year his program had reduced the number of shovelers needed from 600 to 140, while the average number of tons shoveled per worker per day rose from 16 to 50. Workers' earnings also increased from $1.15 to $1.88 a day.

Real-World Example
Have students observe real-world jobs (e.g., delivery drivers and fast-food workers), identify mechanical jobs that probably were subjected to time-and-motion studies, and present the reasons for their conclusions.

Taylor analyzed work flows, supervisory techniques, and worker fatigue using time-and-motion studies. A **time-and-motion study** involves identifying and measuring a worker's physical movements when performing a task and then analyzing the results. Movements that slow down production are dropped. One goal of a time-and-motion study is to make a job highly routine and efficient. Eliminating wasted physical effort and specifying an exact sequence of activities reduce the amount of time, money, and effort needed to produce a product.

Taylor thought that there was *one best* way to perform any task. Like Weber, he concluded that an organization operated best with definite, predictable methods, logically determined and set down as rules. Taylor was convinced that efficiency could be increased by having workers perform routine tasks that didn't require them to make decisions. Performance goals expressed quantitatively (such as number of units produced per shift) addressed a problem that had begun to trouble managers—how to judge whether an employee had put in a fair day's work.

Scientific management advocates specialization. It holds that expertise is the only source of authority and that a single foreman could not be expert at all the tasks supervised. Each foreman's particular area of specialization, therefore, should be made an area of authority. This solution is called **functional foremanship,** a division of labor that assigned eight foremen to each work area. Four of the foremen would handle planning, production scheduling, time-and-motion studies, and discipline. The other four would deal with machinery maintenance, machine speed, feeding material into the machine, production on the shop floor, and similar concerns.

Ethics
Unions argue that standard wage rate jobs, also called piece work jobs, are unethical because they give the edge to younger workers who tend to be faster than older workers. What do you think?

What motivates employees to work to their capacity? Taylor believed that money was the answer. He supported the individual piecework system as the basis for pay. If workers met a certain production standard, they were to be paid at a standard wage rate. Workers who produced more than the standard were to be paid at a higher rate for all the pieces they produced, not just for those exceeding the standard. Taylor assumed that workers would be economically rational; that is, they would follow management's orders to produce more in response to financial incentives that allowed them to earn more money. Taylor argued that managers should use financial incentives if they were convinced that increases in productivity would more than offset higher employee earnings.

The Gilbreths. Frank (1868–1924) and Lillian (1878–1972) Gilbreth formed an unusual husband-and-wife engineering team who made significant contributions to scientific management. Frank used a revolutionary new tool—motion pictures—to study the motion. For instance, he identified eighteen individual motions that a bricklayer uses to lay bricks. By changing the bricklaying process, he was able to reduce the eighteen motions to five. This resulted in a more than 200 percent increase in the worker's overall productivity. Many of today's industrial engineers have combined Frank Gilbreth's methods with Taylor's to redesign jobs for greater efficiency.[8]

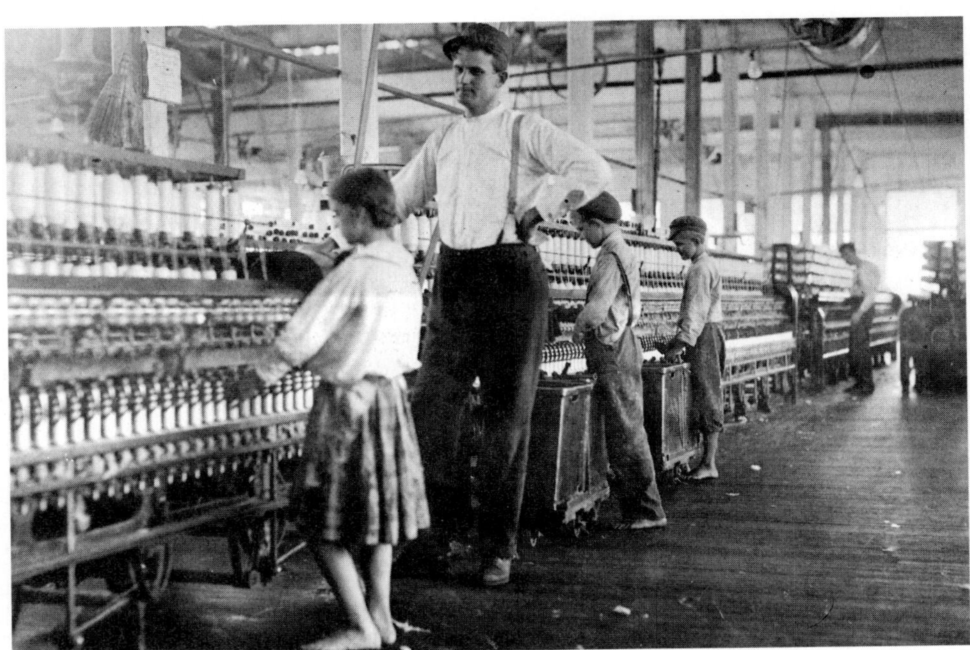

Lillian Gilbreth was concerned with the human side of industrial engineering. Her work influenced the U.S. Congress to establish child labor laws and develop rules to protect workers from unsafe conditions.

Real-World Example
In Cheaper by the Dozen, Gilbreth's children tell how Frank shaved with two razors so as to save two seconds' shaving time. He stopped doing so because he had to spend two minutes putting bandages over all the nicks.

Lillian Gilbreth carried on Frank's work *and* raised their twelve children after his death. She was concerned with the human side of industrial engineering. She championed the idea that workers should have standard days, scheduled rest breaks, and normal lunch periods. Her work influenced the U.S. Congress to establish child labor laws and develop rules for protecting workers from unsafe working conditions. Frank and Lillian Gilbreth also were the inspiration for two best-selling books, *Cheaper by the Dozen* and *Belles on Their Toes,* written by their son, Frank Bunker Gilbreth.

Henry Gantt. Taylor's associate, Henry Gantt (1861–1919), focused on "control" systems for production scheduling. His Gantt charts are still widely used to plan project timelines and have been adapted for computer scheduling applications. The **Gantt chart** is a visual plan and progress report. It identifies various stages of work that must be carried out to complete a project, sets a deadline for each stage, and documents accomplishments. Gantt also established quota systems and bonuses for workers who exceeded their quotas.[9]

Kentucky Fried Chicken (KFC) increased its quality through the application of scientific management ideas. Now owned by PepsiCo, KFC has more than 5,000 restaurants, annual sales in excess of $3.5 billion, and serves more than 600 million customers each year. The competitive pressures on all fast-food restaurants means that quick service and high quality are needed to attract and retain customers. The following Quality Insight highlights how KFC used the principles of scientific management to improve quality.

Quality *Insight*

Hang Time at KFC

Recognizing the importance of expectations, KFC conducts customer surveys and tracks its performance against its competitors (e.g., McDonald's, Wendy's, and Boston Chicken). From such data, senior management in KFC's South Central division realized that its restaurants were experiencing serious problems. Profits were down by more than 50 percent and its outlets were ranked in the bottom half of performance for speed of service and value for money spent by customers. As more than 50 percent of a McDonald's business is generated through the drive-through window operation, management decided to improve that operation.

Managers formed a team of employees and trained them to use time-and-motion studies and Gantt charts. The team also benchmarked competitors. Through the time-and-motion studies, KFC found that employees took almost two minutes to complete a customer's order, whereas its competitors took less than sixty seconds. The team then proceeded to measure (1) the time a customer spent at the menu board placing the order, (2) the time required for a customer to drive from the menu board to the drive-through window, including waiting time, and (3) the time a customer waits at the window to get the order, make payment, and drive away. The timing device used had to sense the customer's car in the driveway, alert store employees, and measure the time needed to serve a customer. To improve KFC's performance, the team made several recommendations: (1) all customers should be acknowledged within three seconds of arriving at the speaker; (2) customer orders should be filled within sixty seconds of arriving at the drive-through window; and (3) the total service time should average less than ninety seconds.

To implement those recommendations, the team developed procedures for eliminating wasted motion by employees, such as (1) do not take more than two steps to get what is needed to fill a customer's order, (2) do not lift anything that is needed to fill a customer's order, and (3) reach up and pull down napkins, straws, cups, and other items needed to fill a customer's order. Based on the team's recommendations, management totally reorganized the drive-through service area. This change included rearranging the placement of products, bags, boxes, cups, and salads and streamlining the movement of products from the kitchen to the packing area. High demand items were positioned closest to the employees. The ten-piece chicken meal was priced at $11.18 so that, including tax, it totaled $12.00, eliminating a lot of effort and time on the part of the customer and cashier in counting change. From experience, KFC learned that a customer whose bill was an even-dollar amount averaged 15 to 20 seconds less at the window than a customer whose bill was an odd-dollar amounts.

What were the results of all these changes? First, customer sales improved by 17.5 percent. Second, employee productivity improved by 12.3 percent. Third, the majority of all customers are now served in less than sixty seconds.[10]

Assessing Scientific Management. Taylor and other early proponents of scientific management would applaud the efforts of KFC, Honda, Canon, Owens-Corning, and other organizations that have successfully used their concepts. These firms make finished products faster and cheaper than Taylor could ever have dreamed. Organizations are increasingly taking for granted his idea that managers cannot expect employees to do their jobs properly without proper skills and training. Taylor's work has led today's managers to improve their employee selection and training processes and to seek the one best way to perform each task.

Unfortunately, most proponents of scientific management misread the human side of work. When Frederick Taylor and Frank Gilbreth formulated their principles and methods, they thought that workers were motivated primarily by a desire to earn money to satisfy their economic and physical needs. They failed to recognize that workers also have social needs and that working conditions and job satisfaction often are more important than money. For example, workers have struck in protest over working conditions, the speedup of an assembly line, or harassment by management—even when a fair financial incentive system was in place. Managers today cannot assume that workers are interested only in higher wages. Dividing jobs into their simplest tasks and setting clear rules for accomplishing those tasks won't always lead to a quality product, high morale, and an effective organization. Today's employees often want to participate in decisions that affect their performance. They may want to be independent and to hold jobs that give them self-fulfillment.

Ask Students
Have you ever worked for a boss who still thought that higher wages were the only thing workers were interested in? If so what was it like working there?

Administrative Management

Administrative management focuses on the manager and basic managerial functions. It evolved early in this century and is most closely identified with Henri Fayol (1841–1925), a French industrialist. However, his most important writings on management weren't translated into English until 1930. Fayol credited his success as a manager to the methods he used, rather than to his personal qualities. He felt strongly that, to be successful, managers had only to understand the basic managerial functions—planning, organizing, leading, and controlling—and to apply certain management principles to them. He was the first person to group managers' functions in this way.[11]

Like the other traditionalists, Fayol emphasized formal structure and processes, believing that they are necessary for the adequate performance of all important tasks. In other words, if people are to work well together, they need a clear definition of what they're trying to accomplish and how their tasks help meet organizational goals.

Fayol developed the following fourteen management principles and suggested that managers receive formal training in their application.

Ask Students
Ask a student volunteer to discuss how his or her employer follows Fayol's principles.

1. ***Division of labor.*** The more people specialize, the more efficiently they can perform their work.

2. ***Authority.*** Managers have the right, the authority, to give orders in order to get things done.
3. ***Discipline.*** Members of an organization need to respect the rules and agreements that govern it.
4. ***Unity of command.*** Each employee must receive instructions about a particular operation from only one person in order to avoid conflicting instructions and any confusion.
5. ***Unity of direction.*** The efforts of employees working on projects should be coordinated by managers, but only one should be responsible for the employee's behavior.
6. ***Subordination of individual interest to the common good.*** The interests of individual employees should not take precedence over the interests of the entire organization.
7. ***Remuneration.*** Pay for work done should be fair to both the employee and the employer.
8. ***Centralization.*** Managers should retain final responsibility but should also give their subordinates enough authority to do their jobs properly.
9. ***Scalar chain.*** A single uninterrupted line of authority (often represented by the neat boxes and lines of an organization chart) should run rank to rank from top management to the lowest level position in the company.
10. ***Order.*** Materials and people should be in the right place at the right time. In particular, people should be in the jobs or positions best suited to them.
11. ***Equity.*** Managers should be both friendly and fair to their subordinates.
12. ***Stability and tenure of staff.*** A high rate of employee turnover is not efficient.
13. ***Initiative.*** Subordinates should be given the freedom to formulate and carry out their own plans.
14. ***Esprit de corps.*** Promoting team spirit gives the organization a sense of unity.

Managers still use many of Fayol's principles of administrative management, but different managers seldom apply them in exactly the same way. Situations vary and so, too, does the application of these principles. At Freedom Forge, a steel company, the maintenance superintendent receives direction from the plant manager, the chief engineer, and the production manager—violating the unity of command principle. The maintenance superintendent has the authority to set priorities for plant maintenance—illustrating the initiative principle.

Assessing Traditional Management

Traditional management's three branches—bureaucratic, scientific, and administrative—still have their proponents, are often written about, and continue to be applied effectively. Let's summarize what the three branches of traditional management have in common and some of their drawbacks. Table 2.1 highlights the points discussed.

All three branches emphasize the formal aspects of organization. Traditionalists are concerned with the formal relations among an organization's departments, tasks, and processes. Weber, Taylor, the Gilbreths, Gantt, and Fayol replaced seat-of-the-pants management practices with sound theoretical and scientific principles. Managers began to stress the division of labor, hierarchical authority, rules, and decisions that would maximize economic rewards.

Teaching Tip
Point out to students that theorists such as Taylor or Weber were well intentioned, though naive, about human behavior. Their followers took their ideas to the extreme and misapplied them. We study management and organizational behavior so as not to repeat their mistakes.

Traditional management stresses the manager's role in a hierarchy. In bureaucratic management the relationship between expertise and organizational level is strong. Because of their higher position and presumed greater expertise, superiors are to be obeyed by subordinates. Administrative and scientific managements' emphases on logical processes and strict division of labor are based on similar reasoning.

Although traditionalists may recognize that people have feelings and are influenced by their friends at work, their overriding focus is on efficient and effective job performance. Taylor considered the human side of work in terms of eliminating bad feelings

TABLE 2.1

Characteristics of Traditional Management

BUREAUCRATIC	SCIENTIFIC	ADMINISTRATIVE
Characteristics		
Rules Impersonality Division of labor Hierarchy Authority structure Lifelong career commitment Rationality	Training in routines and rules "One best way" Financial motivation	Defining of management functions Division of labor Hierarchy Authority Equity
Focus		
Whole organization	Employee	Manager
Benefits		
Consistency Efficiency	Productivity Efficiency	Clear structure Professionalizing of managerial roles
Drawbacks		
Rigidity Slowness	Overlooks social needs	Internal focus Overemphasizes rational behavior of managers

between workers and management and providing employees with financial incentives to increase productivity. Job security, career progression, and protection of workers from employers' whims are considered important by traditionalists. However, they do not recognize informal or social relationships among employees at work. Taylor and Frank Gilbreth focused instead on well-defined rules intended to ensure efficient performance—the primary standard against which employees were to be judged.

In assessing the work of the early traditional theorists, you need to keep in mind that they were influenced by the economic conditions facing them at the time. The United States was moving toward becoming an industrial nation, unions were forming to protect workers' rights, and more laws were being passed to improve unsafe working conditions. Organizations operated in a relatively stable environment with few competitors. Much traditionalist thinking may still be found in some large organizations. For example, Fayol's principles are widely used as basic management building blocks at Nestlé, Gillette, Coca-Cola, and other global corporations.

Ask Students
Would you want to work in an organization having a traditional viewpoint of management? Why or why not?

2

Explain the behavioral viewpoint's contribution to management.

BEHAVIORAL VIEWPOINT

During the 1920s and 1930s the United States and other industrialized nations experienced radical social and cultural changes. Mass production triggered a second industrial revolution. Assembly lines released a flood of inexpensive goods—cars, appliances, and clothing—into an increasingly consumer-oriented society. The overall standard of living rose, and working conditions in many industries improved. As productivity shot up, the average work week plunged from seventy hours to less than fifty hours in the United States. Hard-pressed to satisfy consumer demand, manufacturers eagerly tried to attract workers from the farms by making industrial employment more appealing than it was during Taylor's tenure at Midvale Steel.

Ask Students
Do you think that those who are calling for shortening the forty-hour workweek are justified in doing so when their grandparents had to work a seventy-hour workweek? Why or why not?

During the Great Depression of the 1930s, the federal government began to play a more influential role in people's lives. By the time President Franklin D. Roosevelt took office in 1933, the national economy was hovering on the brink of collapse. To provide employment the government undertook temporary public works projects—constructing dams, roads, and public buildings and improving national parks. It also created agencies, such as the Social Security Administration, to assist the aged, the unemployed, and the disabled.

During the 1920s and 1930s, mass production triggered a second industrial revolution. Inexpensive goods such as automobiles were available to an increasingly consumer-oriented society.

In one of the era's most dramatic changes, unskilled workers increased their ability to influence management decisions by forming powerful labor unions. During the 1930s Congress aided unions by enacting legislation that deterred management from restricting union activities, legalized collective bargaining, and required management to bargain with unions. As a result the American Federation of Labor (AFL) grew rapidly, and the Congress of Industrial Organizations (CIO) was formed. In 1937 the autoworkers and steelworkers won their first big contracts. Eventually professionals and skilled workers, as well as unskilled laborers, formed unions to bargain for better pay, increased benefits, and improved working conditions. Following the depression and World War II, a new wave of optimism swept the U.S. economy.

Against this backdrop of change and reform, managers were forced to recognize that people have needs, cherish values, and want respect. They were now leading workers who did not appear to exhibit what the early traditional management theorists had thought was rational economic behavior. That is, workers weren't always performing up to their physiological capabilities, as Taylor had predicted rational people would do. Nor were effective managers consistently following Fayol's fourteen principles. By exploring these inconsistencies, those who favored a behavioral viewpoint of management gained recognition. The **behavioral** (human relations) **viewpoint** focuses on dealing more effectively with the human aspects of organizations. It looks at how managers do what they do, how managers lead subordinates and communicate with them, and why managers need to change their assumptions about people if they want to lead high-performance teams and organizations.

Follett's Contributions

Teaching Tip
Mary Follett Parker was the first major woman management theorist in a field virtually dominated by men.

In the early decades of this century, Mary Parker Follett (1868–1933) made important contributions to the behavioral viewpoint of management. She believed that management is a flowing, continuous process—not a static one—and that if a problem has been solved, the method used to solve it probably generated new problems. She stressed (1) involving workers in solving problems and (2) the dynamics of management, rather than static principles. Both of these ideas contrasted sharply with the views of Weber, Taylor, and Fayol.[12]

Follett studied how managers did their jobs by observing them at work. Based on these observations, she concluded that coordination is vital to effective management. She developed four principles of coordination for managers to apply.

1. Coordination is best achieved when the people responsible for making a decision are in direct contact.
2. Coordination during the early stages of planning and project implementation is essential.
3. Coordination should address all the factors in a situation.
4. Coordination must be worked at continuously.

Teaching Tip
These principles may seem obvious in a classroom, but they often are forgotten in the hectic pace and complexity of organizational life.

Follett believed that the people closest to the action could make the best decisions. For example, she was convinced that first-line managers are in the best position to coordinate production tasks. And by increasing communication among themselves and with workers, these managers can make better decisions than managers up the hierarchy regarding such tasks. She also believed that first-line managers should not only plan and coordinate workers' activities, but also involve them in the process. Simply because managers told employees to do something a certain way, Follett argued, they should not assume that the employees would do it. She argued further that it is the job of managers, at all levels, to maintain good working relationships with their subordinates. One way to do this is to involve subordinates in the decision-making process whenever they will be affected by the decision. Drawing on psychology and sociology, Follett urged managers to recognize that each person is a collection of beliefs, emotions, and feelings.

Follett also believed that managers should find ways to help resolve interdepartmental conflict. Properly handled, conflict can stimulate and integrate managerial and production efforts. The best way to resolve conflict is for managers to communicate directly with each other and with employees. As part of this process, managers and workers should try to understand the others' views and situations they face.

Discussion Question 3
How did John Mackey of Whole Foods put the advice of Mary Parker Follett to use in his grocery markets?

The following Small Business Insight describes how one small business has implemented many of Follett's recommendations to improve its grocery store operations. When Whole Foods opened on September 20, 1980, only a handful of natural food supermarkets existed in the United States. Whole Foods today operates nineteen markets in Texas, California, Louisiana, and Massachusetts.

Small Business *Insight*

Whole Foods Markets

John Mackey, president of Whole Foods, believes that people have powerful needs for affiliation and cooperation. Each Whole Foods market typically employs between 60 and 140 people, and each is organized into various teams to develop a sense of cooperation. Each team is responsible for doing its own work and selecting new team members. A candidate must be voted on by the team and receive a two-thirds majority to become a team member. Every four weeks, each team meets to discuss problems and make decisions.

Employees also practice self-responsibility. Mackey believes that, by placing responsibility and authority at the store and team level rather than at corporate headquarters, employees are encouraged to make decisions that affect their daily work. Mackey knows that employees will make mistakes because of their inexperience. However, the company is dedicated to learning and growing, and he believes that employees can learn from their mistakes. Recognizing that there are many different approaches to getting things done, Mackey encourages creativity and experimentation at each store and by each employee. He is convinced that only through experimentation can new information be gathered and communication increased among all employees.[13]

Barnard's Contributions

Chester Barnard (1886–1961) studied economics at Harvard but failed to graduate because he didn't finish a course in a laboratory science. He was hired by AT&T, and in 1927 he became president of New Jersey Bell. Barnard made two significant contributions to management that are detailed in his book *The Functions of the Executive.*[14]

Barnard viewed organizations as social systems that require employee cooperation if they are to be effective. In other words, people should continually communicate with one another. According to Barnard, managers' major roles are to communicate with employees and motivate them to work hard to help achieve the organization's goals. In his view, successful management also depends on maintaining good relations with people outside the organization with whom managers deal regularly. He stressed the dependence of the organization on investors, suppliers, customers, and other outside interests. Barnard introduced the idea that managers have to examine the organization's external environment and adjust its internal structure to balance the two.

Discussion Question 4
How do Bernard's management recommendations differ from those of Weber?

Another of Barnard's significant contributions is the **acceptance theory of authority.** This theory of *buy in* holds that employees have free wills and thus will choose whether or not to follow management's orders. They will follow orders if they (1) understand what is required, (2) believe that the orders are consistent with organizational goals, and (3) see positive benefits to themselves in carrying out the orders.

The Hawthorne Contributions

The strongest support for the behavioral viewpoint emerged from studies carried out between 1924 and 1933 at Western Electric Company's Hawthorne plant in Chicago.[15] The Hawthorne Illumination Tests, begun in November 1924 and conducted in three departments of the plant, initially were developed and directed by Hawthorne's engineers. They divided employees into two groups: a test group, whom they subjected to deliberate changes in lighting, and a control group, for whom lighting remained constant throughout the experiment. When lighting conditions for the test group were improved, the group's productivity increased, as expected. The engineers were mystified, though, by a similar jump in productivity upon reducing the test group's lighting to the point of twilight. To compound the mystery, the control group's output kept rising, even though its lighting condition didn't change. Western Electric called in Harvard professor Elton Mayo to investigate these peculiar and puzzling results.

Mayo and Harvard colleagues Fritz Roethlisberger and William Dickson devised a new experiment. They placed two groups of six women each in separate rooms. They changed various conditions for the test group and left conditions unchanged for the control group. The changes included shortening the test group's coffee breaks, allowing it to choose its own rest periods, and letting it have a say in other suggested changes. Once again, output of both the test group and the control group increased. The researchers decided that they could rule out financial incentives as a factor because they hadn't changed the payment schedule for either group.

The researchers concluded that the increases in productivity weren't caused by a physical event but by a complex emotional chain reaction. Because employees in both groups had been singled out for special attention, they had developed a group pride that motivated them to improve their performance. The sympathetic supervision they received further reinforced that motivation. These experimental results led to Mayo's first important discovery: When employees are given special attention, productivity is likely to change regardless of whether working conditions change. This phenomenon became known as the **Hawthorne effect.**

However, an important question remained unanswered: Why should a little special attention and the formation of group bonds produce such strong reactions? To find the answer Mayo interviewed employees. These interviews yielded a highly significant discovery: Informal work groups—the social environment of employees—greatly influence productivity. Many Western Electric employees found their lives inside and outside the factory dull and meaningless. Their workplace friends, chosen in part because of mutual antagonism toward "the bosses," gave meaning to their working lives. Thus peer pressure, rather than management demands, had a significant influence on employee productivity.[16]

The writings of Mayo, Roethlisberger, and Dickson influenced the basic conclusions that emerged from the Hawthorne studies and helped outline the behavioral viewpoint of management. These theorists believed that individual work behavior rarely is a result of simple cause-and-effect relationships based on scientific and economic principles, as the traditionalists believed. Instead it is determined by a complex set of factors. The informal work group develops its own set of norms to mediate between the needs of individuals and the work setting. The social system of such informal groups is maintained through symbols of prestige and power. They also concluded that managers need to consider the personal context (e.g., family situation and friendships) in order to understand each employee's unique needs and sources of satisfaction. They suggested that awareness of employee feelings and encouragement of employee participation in decision making can reduce resistance to change.

One organization that has dedicated itself to providing a better quality of life for its employees is Stride Rite. Stride Rite manufactures shoes such as Keds™ and Sperry Top-Sider™. With sales of more than $582 million, many of the practices recommended by the behavioral viewpoint are put into use in managing diversity at Stride Rite, as the following Diversity Insight illustrates.

Diversity *Insight*

Family Issues at Stride Rite

Fingerpainting. Walking canes. Toy trucks. Sandboxes. Trifocal glasses. This curious mixture of artwork and artifacts isn't found in most organizations, but it is at Stride Rite. Stride Rite sees these as critical to managing work-force diversity at its Boston locations. It provides employees with on-site child care and elder care serving fifty-five children and thirty elders. Stride Rite designed this intergenerational facility to help employees better understand the issues that both generations are facing and manage their personal problems. Many employees have the responsibility for both generations of dependents at the same time.

Stride Rite quickly learned that this intergenerational center lowers absenteeism. Because employees can now count on quality care for an elder or child dependent, they can focus on their work better. According to Connie Wentworth, "Being able to come to work and bring my child with me is really wonderful. Overall, it makes my performance a lot better." The company encourages workers to get involved with their communities—and pays them to do so. Stride Rite believes that it should create a workplace that's more than just a place to get a paycheck. It should be a place where employees can achieve their goals and appreciate the goals of others who might not look or think like they do. As Stride Rite opens new facilities, the needs of the employees will determine the programs offered.[17]

Discussion Question 5
What concepts from the behavioral viewpoint did Stride Rite effectively put to use in its diversity program?

Assessing the Behavioral Viewpoint

The behavioral viewpoint of management goes beyond the traditionalists' mechanical view of work by stressing the importance of group dynamics, complex human motivations, and the manager's leadership style. It emphasizes the employee's social needs and economic needs and the influence of the organization's social environment on the quality and quantity of work produced. The following are the basic assumptions of the behavioral viewpoint.

1. Employees are motivated by social needs and get a sense of identity through their associations with one another.

2. Employees are more responsive to the social forces exerted by their peers than to management's financial incentives and rules.
3. Employees are most likely to respond to managers who can help them satisfy their needs.
4. Managers need to coordinate the work of their subordinates participatively in order to improve efficiency.

Ask Students
Would you want to work in an organization having a behavioral viewpoint of management? Can an organization be a combination of the traditional and behavioral viewpoints? Why or why not?

These assumptions don't always hold in practice, of course. Improving working conditions and managers' human relations skills won't always increase productivity. Economic aspects of work are still important to the employee, as Taylor believed. The major union contracts negotiated in recent years, for instance, focus on job security and wage incentives. And, although employees enjoy working with co-workers who are friendly, low salaries tend to lead to absenteeism and turnover. The negative effects of clumsy organizational structure, poor communication, and routine or boring tasks won't be overcome by the presence of pleasant co-workers. The human aspect of the job in the 1990s is even more complex than was imagined by those advocating the behavioral viewpoint in the 1930s.[18]

3

Describe the systems viewpoint and the use of quantitative techniques to manage organizations.

SYSTEMS VIEWPOINT

During World War II the British assembled a team of mathematicians, physicists, and others to solve various wartime problems. These professionals formed the first operations research (OR) group. Initially, they were responsible for analyzing the makeup, routes, and speeds of convoys and probable submarine locations. The team developed ingenious ways to analyze complex problems that couldn't be handled solely by intuition, straightforward mathematics, or experience. The British and Americans further developed this approach (called *systems analysis*) throughout the war and applied it to many problems of war production and military logistics. Later, systems analysis became an accepted tool in the Department of Defense (DoD) and the space program, as well as throughout private industry.[19]

Systems Concepts

A **system** is an association of interrelated and interdependent parts. The human body is a system with organs, muscles, bones, nerves, and a consciousness that links all the parts. An organization also is a system with many employees, teams, departments, and levels that are linked to achieve the organization's goals. It also is linked to suppliers, customers, shareholders, and regulatory agencies. A competent systems-oriented manager makes decisions only after identifying and analyzing how other managers, departments, or customers might be affected by the decisions.

The **systems viewpoint** of management represents an approach to solving problems by diagnosing them within a framework of inputs, transformation processes, outputs, and feedback (see Figure 2.4). The system involved may be an individual, a work group, a department, or an entire organization.

Inputs are the physical, human, material, financial, and information resources that enter a transformation process. At a university, for example, inputs include students, faculty, money, and buildings. **Transformation processes** comprise the technologies used to convert inputs into outputs. Transformation processes at a university include lectures, reading assignments, lab experiments, term papers, and tests. **Outputs** are the original inputs (human, physical, material, information, and financial resources) as changed by a transformation process. Outputs at a university include the graduating students. For a system to operate effectively, it must also provide for feedback. **Feedback** is information about a system's status and performance. One form of feedback at a university is the ability of its graduates to get jobs. In an organization, feedback may take the form of marketing surveys, financial reports, production records, performance ap-

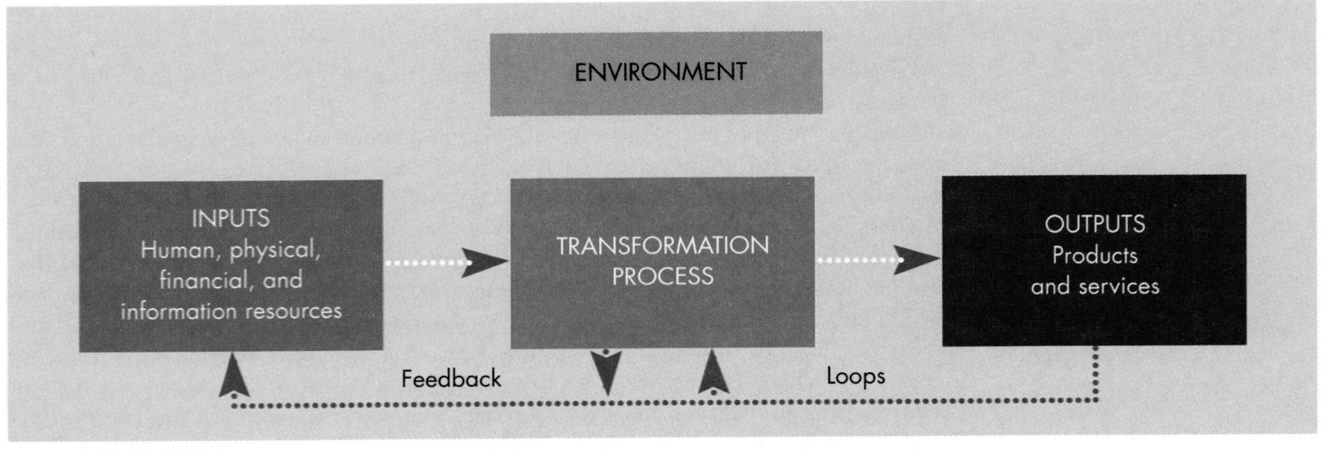

FIGURE 2.4

Basic Systems View of Organization

praisals, and the like. In the systems viewpoint, management's role is to facilitate transformation processes by planning, organizing, leading, and controlling.

System Types and Levels

There are two types of systems: closed and open. A **closed system** limits its interactions with its environment. Some production departments operate as closed systems: They produce standardized products in an uninterrupted stream. An **open system** interacts with the external environment. Managers in MCI's marketing department, for example, constantly try to develop new products or services to satisfy customers' telecommunications desires. They monitor what competitors are doing, then develop ways to deliver better quality and service at a lower price. Recall the opening Preview Insight on Hewlett-Packard. It clearly demonstrates an open system in action.

We can also think of a person, group, or organization as a **subsystem,** or a component consisting of one or more parts of a system. The subsystems at J.C. Penney Insurance Company include its marketing, human resources, claims, accounting, and finance departments. In turn, the insurance company is a subsystem of its parent corporation, J.C. Penney. With sales of over $20 billion, J.C. Penney is a subsystem of the United States' overall economic subsystem, which is part of the world's economic system. Figure 2.5 illustrates systems and subsystems in the world economy. We call each a level of the overall system. Note that each level represents a successively simpler part of the overall system. One system's output is another system's input.[20]

Teaching Tip
To promote critical thinking, ask students to generate questions they would ask a systems analyst if one were to be guest speaker in the class.

How can a manager use a systems viewpoint to integrate diverse aspects of one business? Gillette uses a systems approach to recruit and train its global managers. In the past, Gillette hadn't put much effort into developing managers. But, because of Gillette's aggressive expansion into many different countries, senior management decided to create such a system to train newly hired employees. Currently, Gillette has fifty-seven manufacturing plants in twenty-eight countries. Its human resource system now grooms recent college graduates for jobs in their home countries. The Global Insight on page 58 shows how Gillette's system operates. The systems concepts used are indicated in parentheses.

Discussion Question 6
What types of problems does systems analysis tackle?

Quantitative Techniques

While some advocates of systems analysis were suggesting that managers look at inputs, transformation processes, and outputs before making a decision, other systems advo-

FIGURE 2.5
System Levels

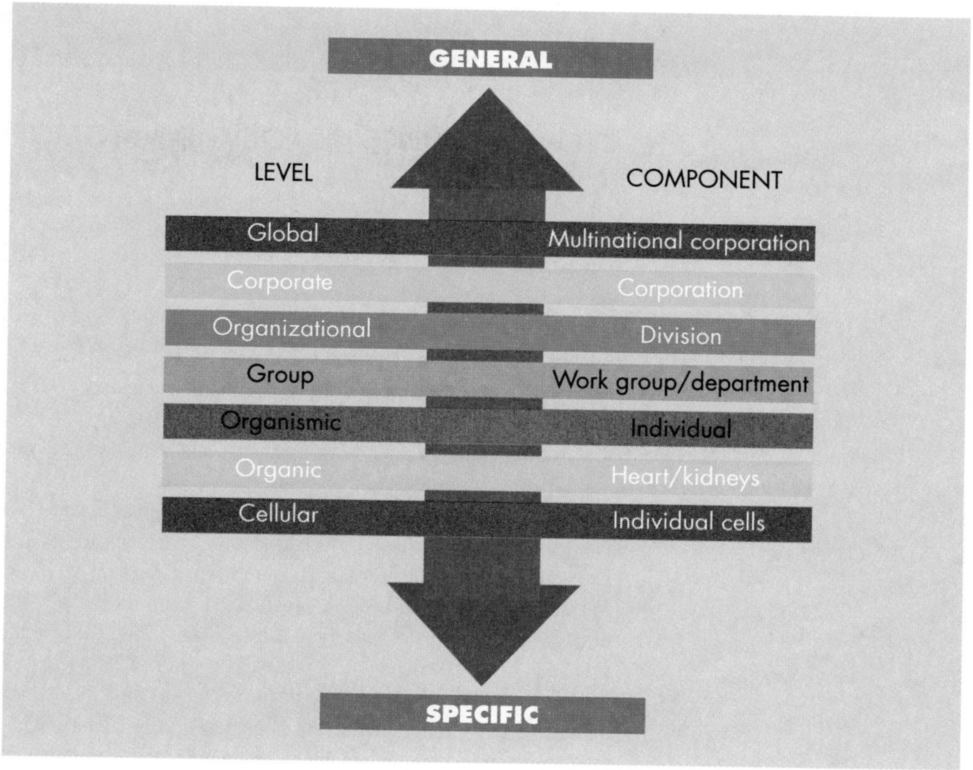

cates were developing quantitative techniques to aid in managerial decision making. Quantitative techniques have four basic characteristics.

1. ***The primary focus is on decision making.*** The solution identifies direct actions that managers can take.
2. ***Alternatives are based on economic criteria.*** Alternative actions are presented in terms of measurable criteria, such as costs, revenues, return on investment, and tax implications.
3. ***Mathematical models are used.*** Situations are simulated and problems are analyzed by means of mathematical models.
4. ***Computers are essential.*** Computers are used to solve complex mathematical models that would be too costly and time-consuming to process manually.

The range of quantitative decision-making tools available to management has expanded greatly during the past two decades. Today's managers have inventory decision models, statistical decision theory, linear programming, and many other types of aids for solving complex problems. Many of those tools are literally at their fingertips in the form of software that can be run on desktop computers. In the past, small businesses such as retail stores, medical offices, mom-and-pop restaurants, and farmers couldn't use systems analysis techniques. Today, many small businesses own their own computers. Ready-to-use software packages, such as Microsoft Windows and Lotus 1–2–3, enable small-business owners and managers to utilize programs for accounts payable, accounts receivable, and inventory control. A medical office system will do patient scheduling and create and maintain a database for patients' medical records. In the largest companies groups of management scientists tackle a broad range of business problems by devising their own sophisticated mathematical models for use on mainframe and personal computers.

Gambling casinos such as Caesar's Palace, Bally's, and Harrah's in Atlantic City spend millions of dollars on complimentary services (including food, rooms, and trans-

Global *Insight*

How Gillette Grooms Global Talent

What kinds of people is Gillette looking to hire as future managers (input)? They are looking for

- university graduates with a business background,
- adaptable people with good social skills,
- people who are mobile and globally career-oriented,
- people who are fluent in English, and
- young people—under thirty—who are enthusiastic and aggressive.

What happens after they are hired? The management trainee is paired with a Gillette senior manager in one of its major businesses, such as shaving, personal care, or stationery. The trainee will spend as long as eighteen months learning about marketing, accounting, finance, or manufacturing and how to work effectively within the Gillette organization (transformation process). Trainees typically work in two of the three areas during their training assignments. In addition to their daily assignments, trainees participate in monthly seminars on topics such as dressing for success, finance for nonfinancial managers, and presentation skills. Trainees make presentations while on assignment (output) and receive suggestions (feedback) from managers for honing their presentation skills.

Upon completion of the training program (output), graduates return to their home country to take entry-level positions (input). If the graduates continue to be successful, they move on to assignments in other countries. Eventually, they end up back in their home countries as general managers.[21]

portation) for high rollers. To reduce the cost of these services and improve the odds that these people will play—and, therefore, lose—in their establishments, casino managers utilize sophisticated information systems that analyze customers' favorite games, betting patterns, accommodation preferences, food and drink choices, and other habits. Similarly, Hertz uses information systems to attract customers. Available in several languages (including English, French, German, Italian, and Spanish), the Hertz destination printout specifies expressways, exits, turns, and time duration of the trip. In some cities the computer prints a grid on a map to depict geographic information.

Assessing the Systems Viewpoint

Systems analysis and quantitative techniques have been used primarily to manage transformation processes and in the technical planning and decision-making aspects of management. These techniques have not yet reached the stage where they can be used effectively to deal with the human aspects of management. Variables representing behavioral considerations and human values are difficult—if not impossible—to build into a mathematical model. Because these subjective variables must still be taken into account, judgments about people will continue to be a vital part of managerial decision making.

Research and development continues to expand the application of information systems in business. (Chapter 19 fully explores how.) As we discuss in Chapter 20, systems analysis is already having a great impact on manufacturing through the use of computer-aided design (CAD) and computer-aided manufacturing (CAM). Moreover, systems analysis is helping computer experts develop hardware, as well as software, with humanlike intelligence. These experts are trying to design computers capable of reasoning and pro-

Ask Students

Would you want to work in an organization having a systems viewpoint of management? Can an organization be a combination of the traditional, behavioral, and systems viewpoints? Why or why not?

cessing spoken language. When machines can reason, they, like us, will be able to learn from past experience and apply what they have learned to solve new problems.

Organizations no doubt will continue to develop more sophisticated systems in order to increase productivity. Such systems will require them to change many aspects of their day-to-day operations. These changes will not come without struggle and pain. Yet for organizations to survive they must install and utilize sophisticated systems to help managers make decisions.

4

Explain the place of the contingency viewpoint in modern management.

CONTINGENCY VIEWPOINT

The **contingency viewpoint** (sometimes called the *contingency* or *situational approach*) is summarized in Figure 2.6. It was developed in the mid-1960s by managers and others who tried unsuccessfully to apply traditional and systems concepts to actual managerial problems. For example, why did providing workers with a bonus for being on time decrease lateness at one Marriott hotel but have little impact at another? Proponents of the contingency viewpoint contend that different situations require different practices. As one manager put it, the contingency viewpoint really means "it all depends."

The contingency viewpoint advocates using the other three management viewpoints independently or in combination, as necessary, to deal with various situations. However, this viewpoint doesn't give managers free rein to indulge their personal biases and whims. Rather, managers are expected to determine which methods are likely to be more effective than others in a given situation. Applying the contingency view-

FIGURE 2.6

Contingency Viewpoint

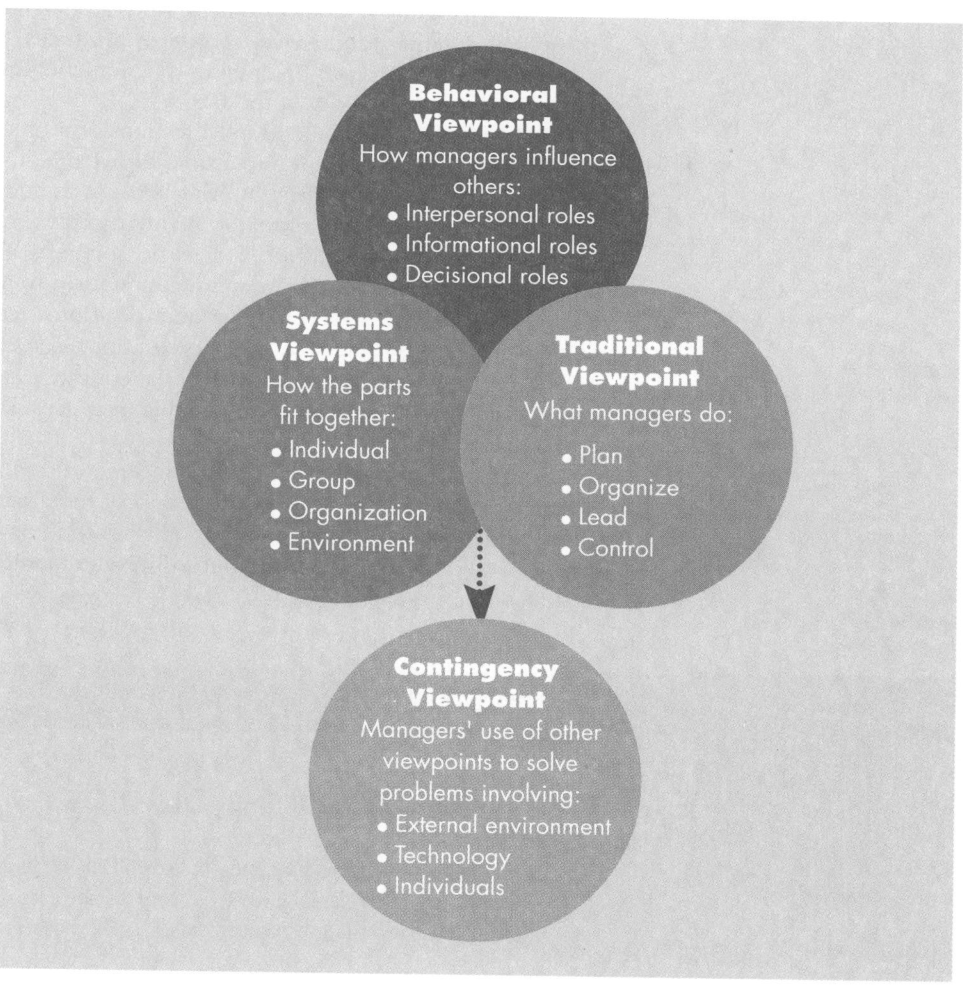

point requires the development and use of conceptual skills. Managers must be able to diagnose and understand a situation thoroughly—to determine which approach is most likely to succeed—before making a decision. The manager's interpersonal and communications skills are essential for actually implementing the decision.

Teaching Tip
Divide the class into three groups. Assign each group the traditional, behavioral, or systems viewpoint of management. Choose a management problem from a current news story. Have each group report on how it would handle the problem from its management viewpoint.

The contingency viewpoint holds that the effectiveness of different managerial styles, guidelines, or techniques will vary according to the situation. Managers who subscribe to this viewpoint use the concepts developed by traditionalists, behavioralists, and systems analysts—but go beyond them to identify the best approach for each particular situation. This blending process is illustrated in Figure 2.6. The contingency viewpoint, by its very nature, has yet to reach the point of offering detailed prescriptions for the best way to manage in *all* situations.

Contingency Variables

The essence of the contingency viewpoint is that management practices should be consistent with the requirements of the external environment, the technology used to make a product or deliver a service, and the people who work for the organization.[22] The relative importance of each contingency variable depends on the type of managerial problem being considered. For example, in designing an organization's structure, a manager should consider the nature of the company's external environment and the corresponding information processing requirements. Hence the IRS's structure is different from that of Southwest Airlines. The IRS has a fairly stable set of customers, most of whom must file their tax returns by April 15 each year. It hires many part-time people during the peak tax season to process returns and answer questions, then lays them off after the peak has passed. Southwest Airlines, however, has many competitors and a constantly changing set of customers whose demands for information (about ticket costs, flight numbers, and arrival and departure times) must be processed immediately. Its continuous information processing requirements call for more reliance on full-time personnel than is necessary at the IRS.

Teaching Tip
Students may have trouble understanding the different viewpoints of management. To promote discussion and understanding, ask: "What impact do the continuing increase of women in the work force and management, the Equal Employment Opportunity Act, and affirmative action currently have on the evolution of management?

Technology is the method used to transform organizational inputs into outputs.[23] It is more than machinery; it also is the knowledge, tools, techniques, and actions applied to change raw materials into finished goods and services. The technologies that employees use range from simple to highly complex. A simple technology involves decision-making rules to help employees do routine jobs. For example, IRS clerks who keyboard tax information into computers perform routine tasks and work under such rules, requiring few (if any) independent decisions. A complex technology is one that requires employees to make numerous decisions, sometimes with limited information to guide them. A doctor treating an AIDS patient must answer many questions and make many decisions without having much guidance because the technology for treating the disease hasn't been perfected.

Joan Woodward was one of the pioneers in developing the contingency viewpoint of management. The findings of her group of researchers in England helped managers understand how one contingency variable—technology—could determine how organizations should be structured in order to become more effective as the following Insight illustrates.

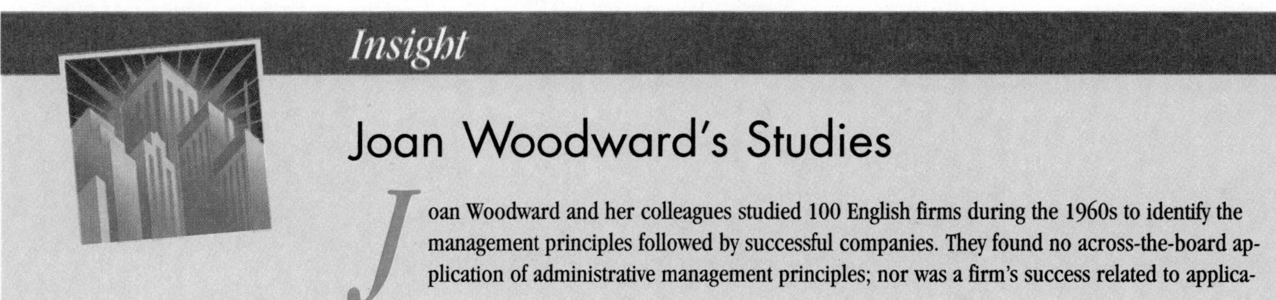
Insight

Joan Woodward's Studies

Joan Woodward and her colleagues studied 100 English firms during the 1960s to identify the management principles followed by successful companies. They found no across-the-board application of administrative management principles; nor was a firm's success related to applica-

tion of any one set of management principles. These results directly refuted the traditional viewpoint of management. There was apparently no "one best way"! Not satisfied with these negative results, Woodward looked for alternative explanations. She discovered that a firm's organizational characteristics and how they relate to its technology seemed to affect the likelihood of its success. Her group identified three types of technology.

1. ***Small-batch technology.*** Firms using small-batch technology are job-shop operations where highly skilled workers apply their knowledge and skills to produce custom-made products. Custom home builders use this technology to build finely crafted new homes.
2. ***Mass-production technology.*** Firms using mass-production technology manufacture standardized goods on an assembly line. They use standardized parts and standard ways of producing the product. Companies utilizing this type of technology include automobile manufacturers (GM, Ford, Hyundai, Nissan), soft drink bottlers (PepsiCo, Dr Pepper/7-UP), and fast-food outlets (Wendy's, McDonald's, Long John Silver's).
3. ***Continuous-process technology.*** Continuous-process technology is highly automated and programmed. Machines handle the production process almost entirely, and output is highly predictable. Firms using this type of technology include petroleum refineries (Texaco, Shell, and Exxon), chemical plants (Dow Chemical and Du Pont), nuclear power plants, and large breweries (Coors and Miller). Because of the expense involved in stopping production in such firms, excess output is stored for later distribution. Companies lower their prices to stimulate demand for their products if necessary.

Studying the technology utilized by effective firms, Woodward found a fairly consistent relationship between certain organizational characteristics and type of technology. These relationships are shown in the table below. Firms using mass-production methods are more effective operating under bureaucratic management. Numerous rules and highly formalized communication systems are needed to coordinate and control the production of standard outputs. However, firms using small-batch and continuous-process technologies have little or no need for bureaucratic methods. The study's conclusion was that a firm choosing an organizational design that complements its technology is more likely to be successful than a firm choosing a design that doesn't fit its technology.[24]

WOODWARD'S FINDINGS

	Technology		
Organizational Characteristic	*Small Batch*	*Mass Production*	*Continuous Process*
Number of hierarchical levels	3	4	6
Number of rules and regulations	Few	Many	Few
Amount of verbal communication between workers and managers	High	Low	High
Amount of written communication between workers and managers	Low	High	Low
Bureaucratic orientation	Low	High	Low

Source: Adapted from Woodward, J. *Industrial Organization: Theory and Practice,* 2nd ed. London: Oxford University Press, 1980.

Assessing the Contingency Viewpoint

The contingency viewpoint of management is useful because of its diagnostic approach, which clearly departs from the one-best-way approach of the traditionalists. The contingency viewpoint encourages managers to analyze and understand situational differences and to choose the solution best suited to the firm, the process, and the individual in each situation.[25]

Ask Students
Would you want to work in an organization having a contingency viewpoint of management? Can an organization be a combination of the traditional, behavioral, systems, and contingency viewpoints? Why or why not?

Critics argue that the contingency viewpoint really is nothing new. They say that it is merely a meshing of techniques from the other viewpoints of management. The contingency viewpoint does draw heavily from the other approaches. However, it is flexible, applying principles and tools from those approaches selectively and where most appropriate. It holds that a manager should rely on absolute principles from the traditional, behavioral, and systems viewpoints only after properly diagnosing the realities of the situation. Such a diagnosis looks at the nature of a situation and the means by which the manager can influence it.

Attitudes toward business ethics often vary more widely around the world than production practices and procedures, which have tended to become standardized in many countries and industries. The complex issues that arise in global business often create ethical problems for employees. The following Ethics Insight presents you with four situations and asks you to decide what you would do. We indicate how most employees working for global organizations responded to these issues at the end of this feature.

Ethics *Insight*

Bribery in Global Business

1. One of your top managers in an Asian country has been kidnapped by a terrorist group that has demanded a ransom of US$2 million plus food assistance for refugees in a camp. If the ransom is not paid, they threaten to kill the manager. *What do you do?*
2. On a business trip, you see a nice leather briefcase for a reasonable price in local currency (the equivalent of US$200). In this country, however, getting U.S. dollars is difficult for locals. The shop clerk offers you the briefcase for $100 if you pay in U.S. dollars. *What do you do?*
3. Your company has been trying to get foreign contracts in a certain country for months. Yesterday, the brother-in-law of the Finance Minister offered to work as a consultant to help you secure contracts. He charges two times more than anyone else. *What do you do?*
4. You are driving to a nearby country. In your car are a several expensive gifts for family and friends in the country you are visiting. When you cross the border, the customs official tells you the duty will be equivalent to US$200. Then he smiles, hands back your passport and whispers for you to put a smaller sum, US$35, in the passport and hand it back to him. *What do you do?*

What would you do in each situation? Our sample of managers responded as follows: Situation 1: Caving into the terrorist demands may save a life, but will surely help escalate the problem in the long run. It should not be done. Situation 2: Buying or selling goods on the black market is questionable. Situation 3: Bribery is clearly forbidden under U.S. law. Bribery is a payment for doing something a person should do without special or extra payment. Don't hire the brother-in-law. Situation 4: A "tip" is a reward for providing a service, but this is a bribe. Don't pay it.[26]

5

Describe the impact of the quality viewpoint on management practices.

QUALITY VIEWPOINT

In the twenty-first century are new management viewpoints—beyond the contingency viewpoint—likely to emerge? The answer is yes. Today's organizations are dynamic and—whether large or small, local or global—face formidable new management challenges. Organizations feel pressure from customers and competitors to deliver high-quality products and/or services on time, reward ethical behavior of employees, and develop plans to effectively manage highly diverse work forces. Customer demand for high-quality products and services may be the dominant theme for the foreseeable future. We recognize its importance throughout this book in Quality Insights. Managers in successful organizations are quality conscious and understand the link between high-quality goods and/or services, and competitive advantage.

Recall from Chapter 1 that, for an organization to be successful, it must satisfy customer wants and needs. The **quality viewpoint** emphasizes achieving customer satisfaction through the provision of high-quality goods and services. The focus of the quality viewpoint is the customer, who ultimately defines quality in the marketplace. Quality must be stressed throughout an organization so that it becomes second nature to everyone in that organization and its suppliers. Training, strategic planning, product design, management information systems, marketing, and other key activities all play a role in meeting quality goals. For example, at Marlow Industries, a Dallas-based firm and a winner of the Malcolm Baldrige National Quality Award, requires all employees to undergo fifty hours of training to learn how to use statistical and other measurement tools to ensure quality in its products.

The godfather of the quality movement was W. Edwards Deming (1900–1993).[27] Initially, U.S. managers rejected his ideas, and not until his ideas had helped rebuild Japan's industrial might after World War II were his ideas accepted in the United States. He taught eager Japanese managers how to use statistics to assess and improve quality. In 1951, Japan established the Deming Prize for corporate quality in his honor. Highly esteemed in Japan, this annual prize recognizes the company that has attained the highest level of quality that year.

In 1979, William Conway, president of Nashua Corporation, an office and computer products manufacturer, faced intense competitive pressure from the Japanese. On trips to Japan, he heard competitors praise Deming as a quality guru. Upon his return, Conway hired Deming. Deming stressed the need for all employees to use statistics to improve quality and productivity, build trust, and work closely with customers. Deming believed that poor quality is 85 percent a management problem and 15 percent a worker problem. After implementing Deming's methods, Nashua's quality and profits rose markedly.

In Chapter 20, we explore Deming's contributions more fully and emphasize differences between traditional quality control methods and his quality methods. Being aware of some of his methods is essential to an understanding of the Quality Insights presented throughout this book. His ideas and methods include the following.

- Poor quality is unacceptable. Defective workmanship, products, and service are not to be tolerated.
- Gather statistical evidence of quality during the process, not at the end of the process. The earlier an error is caught, the less the cost to correct it.
- Rely on a few suppliers that have historically provided quality, not on sampling inspections to determine the quality of each delivery.
- Depend on training and retraining employees to use statistical methods on their jobs, not on slogans, to improve quality.
- Employees should feel free to report any conditions that detract from quality.

Ask Students
Would you want to work in an organization having a quality viewpoint of management? Can an organization be a combination of the traditional, behavioral, systems, contingency, and quality viewpoints?

CHAPTER SUMMARY

1 ***Describe the three branches of the traditional viewpoint of management: bureaucratic, scientific and administrative.***

Max Weber developed a theory of bureaucratic management that stresses the need for a strict hierarchy governed by clearly defined regulations and lines of authority. His theory contains seven principles: a formal system of rules, impersonal management, division of labor, a hierarchical structure, a detailed authority structure, lifelong career commitment, and rationality. Scientific management theorists tried to find ways to make workers more productive. Frederick Taylor thought that management's job was to make individual workers more efficient. It was to be accomplished by improving worker-machine relationships, based on time-and-motion studies. Frank and Lillian Gilbreth also studied how to make workers more efficient. Frank Gilbreth focused on the various physical motions workers used, and Lillian Gilbreth emphasized the welfare of workers. Henry Gantt thought that workers' performance could be charted and thus improved through setting deadlines. Administrative management theorists focused on principles that managers, rather than workers, could use to become more effective. Henry Fayol outlined four functions—planning, organizing, leading, and controlling—that he believed all successful managers use in their work.

2 ***Explain the behavioral viewpoint's contribution to management.***
The behavioral viewpoint emphasizes employees' human and social needs. One of its first proponents, Mary Parker Follett, believed that management should coordinate the efforts of all employees to achieve organizational goals. Chester Barnard's contribution was similar to Follett's. He held, in part, that a manager doesn't have the authority to tell a worker what to do unless the worker accepts that authority. Studies conducted at the Hawthorne plant of the Western Electric Company led to the conclusion that social and human factors can be more important than physical and financial factors in influencing productivity.

3 ***Describe the systems viewpoint and the use of quantitative techniques to manage organizations.***
The systems viewpoint looks at organizations as a series of inputs, transformation processes, and outputs. A system may either be open or closed. Systems analysis advocates that managers use quantitative techniques to solve problems.

4 ***Explain the place of the contingency viewpoint in modern management.***
The contingency viewpoint, or the situational approach, encourages managers to use the concepts and methods of the traditional, behavioral, and systems viewpoints, depending on the circumstances that they face at the time. The three key contingency variables that managers should consider before making a decision are the environment, technology, and people.

5 ***Describe the impact of the quality viewpoint on management practices.***
The quality viewpoint stresses the provision of high-quality products and services at all times. One of the founders of the quality movement was W. Edwards Deming. After he had helped Japanese organizations make statistical quality control improvements, his contributions were recognized by U.S. managers. His recommendations include planning for quality, striving for zero defects, using only a few suppliers who have demonstrated that they can deliver quality, and inspecting for quality during the process and not after.

QUESTIONS FOR DISCUSSION

1. Why should you know about the evolution of management?
2. What are some of the problems of bureaucratic organizations identified in the Beltway Bog Insight?
3. How did John Mackey of Whole Foods put the advice of Mary Parker Follett to use in his grocery markets?
4. How do Barnard's management recommendations differ from those of Weber?
5. What concepts from the behavioral viewpoint did Stride Rite effectively put to use in its diversity program?
6. What types of problems does systems analysis tackle?

FROM WHERE YOU SIT

1. How likely is it that you will work for a manager who uses the principles of scientific management to improve quality?
2. What factors are influencing the quality movement?
3. Visit your local bank. Identify the inputs, transformation processes, and outputs it uses to serve customers.
4. You have been asked to address a local business group on the subject of the human relations viewpoint of management. Prepare an outline of your talk.
5. Which management practices from the traditional viewpoint are used in many fast-food restaurants today?
6. Why will the systems viewpoint be important for managers in the twenty-first century? How does this viewpoint help organizations achieve their quality goals?

SKILL-BUILDING EXERCISE

Diagnosing Bureaucratic Tendencies

In this Skill Building Exercise you are to focus on either your university or an organization for which you currently work in a full- or part-time capacity or for which you have worked in the past. Please circle the letter on the scale indicating the degree to which you agree or disagree with each statement. There is no "right" answer; simply respond according to how you see the organization being managed.

		Strongly Agree	Agree	Neutral	Disagree	Strongly Disagree
1.	People in this organization are urged to be innovative.	____	____	____	____	____
2.	There are a lot of rules to follow in this organization.	____	____	____	____	____
3.	People who pay attention to details are likely to get ahead in this organization.	____	____	____	____	____
4.	A person has a secure job in this organization.	____	____	____	____	____
5.	Precision in one's work is valued by the organization.	____	____	____	____	____
6.	This company operates with a stable set of competitors.	____	____	____	____	____
7.	People in this organization are urged to take risks and experiment with new ways of doing things.	____	____	____	____	____
8.	Jobs in this organization are very predictable.	____	____	____	____	____
9.	There are few rules in this organization.					
10.	Employees are very careful in performing their work.	____	____	____	____	____
11.	Employees are treated impersonally by managers in this organization.	____	____	____	____	____
12.	Lines of authority are closely followed in this organization.	____	____	____	____	____
13.	Job opportunities in this organization are limited to employees who play by the rules.	____	____	____	____	____
14.	Being highly organized is expected and rewarded in this organization.	____	____	____	____	____
15.	Being people-oriented is a characteristic of this organization.	____	____	____	____	____
16.	People are not constrained by many rules in this organization.	____	____	____	____	____

Scoring. On the scoring grid, circle the number that corresponds to your response to each of the 16 questions. Add the numbers in each column. Enter the total for each column on the line below. Add the column totals and enter as a total score. This is your organization's score.

Question	Strongly Agree	Agree	Neutral	Disagree	Strongly Disagree
1	1	2	3	4	5
2	5	4	3	2	1
3	5	4	3	2	1
4	5	4	3	1	1
5	5	4	3	2	1
6	5	4	3	2	1

Question	Strongly Agree	Agree	Neutral	Disagree	Strongly Disagree
7	1	2	3	4	5
8	5	4	3	2	1
9	1	2	3	4	5
10	5	4	3	2	1
11	5	4	3	2	1
12	5	4	3	2	1
13	5	4	3	2	1
14	5	4	3	2	1
15	1	2	3	4	5
16	1	2	3	4	5
Scores:	______	______	______	______	______

Total Score: (Add the scores for each column) __________

Interpretation. A high score (90–64 points) indicates that your organization has many of the features characteristic of the bureaucratic viewpoint. A low score (32–16 points) indicates that your organization has more features usually associated with the behavioral, or human relations, viewpoint. A score in the middle range (63–33 points) indicates that your organization incorporates features of both the bureaucratic and the behavioral viewpoints.[28]

CRITICAL THINKING CASE

Northern Industries

Northern Industries has asked you to help it resolve some racial issues that, according to President Jim Fisher, are "festering" in their manufacturing plant in Springfield, Massachusetts. Northern Industries is a family-owned enterprise that manufactures greeting cards and paper and plastic holiday decorations. It employs 125 people full time, including some African-Americans and Asians. About 80 percent of the full-time work force is female. During the peak production months of September and January (to produce orders primarily for Christmas/Hanukkah and Mother's Day), the company runs a second shift and adds about 50 part-time workers, most of whom are also women and minorities.

All orders are filled with batch runs made to customer specifications. In a period of a week, filling seventy different orders requiring different paper stocks, inks, plastics, and set-ups isn't unusual. Since these orders vary greatly in size, the company has a long-term policy of giving priority to high-volume customers and processing other orders on a first-come first-served basis. Half a dozen of the company's largest customers have been doing business with Northern for more than twenty years, having been signed up by Jim Fisher's father (now retired).

To begin your orientation to the company, Fisher asks his production manager, Walter Beacon, to take you around the plant. Beacon points out the production areas responsible for each step in the manufacture of a greeting card, from purchasing to printing to quality control to shipping. The plant is clean, but the two large printing rooms—each of which is the workplace for about twenty-five workers—are quite noisy. You catch snatches of employees' conversations, but you can't figure out what language they're speaking. In the shipping and receiving department you notice that most workers are African-American. Beacon confirms that eight out of ten of the workers in that department are African-American men, as is their boss, Adam Wright.

Jim Fisher had agreed that you could attend a meeting of top management to get a feel for the problems facing the company. The president introduces you and notes that several of his managers have expressed concerns about certain problems. He says that one of these problems is that "Each of the minority groups sticks together. The African-Americans and Orientals rarely mix." Another recent problem has been "the theft of finished product, especially on the second shift, and we had to fire a Thai worker."

Then Fisher described what he recently had read about self-directed teams and the success of these teams at the San Diego Zoo and Kodak. He stated that implementing such a concept at Northern would require a lot of employee training in different functions, such as printing, shipping, and quality control to give all employees an understanding of how their jobs affect those of others in the organization. He also said that flow charts would be needed to track the activities of employees from the time an order is received until the order is shipped. With flow charts, a team of employees could pinpoint inefficiencies in the manufacturing process better than managers could. Employees could then suggest ways to manufacture cards and other products more profitably.

Fisher then turns to his executive team to discuss its daily business. The others present are the general manager, human resources manager (the only woman), sales manager, quality control manager, production manager (Beacon), and the shipping and receiving manager (the only nonwhite manager). Soon an angry debate erupts between the sales and shipping/receiving managers. Apparently orders are not being shipped quickly enough, according to the sales manager, and several complaints have been received from smaller customers about the quality of the product. The shipping/receiving manager argues that he needs more hands to do the job and that the quality of incoming supplies is lousy anyhow. While this debate continues, the other managers are silent and seemingly uncomfortable. Finally one of them attempts to break up the argument with a joke. Fisher and the other men laugh loudly, and the discussion shifts to other topics.[29]

Questions

1. What are Northern's obvious and not so obvious problems?
2. Which of the management viewpoints helps you most in understanding Northern's problems? Explain.
3. What changes would you recommend to Jim Fisher?

What problems might you face in trying to implement your recommendations?

CRITICAL THINKING CASE

What Is Scientific Management?

The following is excerpted and adapted from the testimony by Frederick W. Taylor at hearings before the Special Committee of the House of Representatives to Investigate the Taylor and Other Systems of Shop Management, January 25, 1912, pp. 1387–1389.

In its essence scientific management involves a complete mental revolution on the part of the working man engaged in any particular establishment or industry—a complete mental revolution on the part of these men as to their duties toward their work, toward their fellow men, and toward their employees. And it involves the equally complete mental revolution on the part of those on management's side—the foreman, the superintendent, the owner of the business, the board of directors—a complete mental revolution on their part as to their duties toward their fellow workers in management, toward their workmen, and toward all their daily problems. And without this complete mental revolution on both sides scientific management does not exist.

The great revolution that takes place in the mental attitude of the two parties under scientific management is that both sides take their eyes off the division of the surplus as the all-important matter, and together turn their attention toward increasing the size of the surplus until this surplus becomes so large that it is unnecessary to quarrel over how it shall be divided. They come to see that when they stop pulling against one another, and instead both turn and push shoulder to shoulder in the same direction, the size of the surplus created by their joint efforts is truly astounding. They both realize that when they substitute friendly cooperation and mutual helpfulness for antagonism and strife they are together able to make this surplus so enormously greater than it was in the past that there is ample room for a large increase in wages for workmen and an equally great increase in profits for the manufacturer.

This change in the mental attitude of both sides toward the "surplus" is only a part of the great mental revolution which occurs under scientific management. There is one more change in viewpoint which is absolutely essential to the existence of scientific management. Both sides must recognize as essential the substitution of exact scientific investigation and knowledge for the old individual judgment or opinion, either of the workman or the boss, in all matters relating to the work done in the establishment. And this applies both as to the methods to be employed in doing the work and the time in which each job should be done.

Questions

1. What key assumptions underlie Taylor's testimony before the U.S. Congress? Explain.
2. Are the practices of scientific management consistent with the mental revolution suggested by Taylor?
3. Are there any similarities between Taylor's mental revolution and the behavioral viewpoint? Explain.

Jonathan Ward

On his way home on Friday afternoon, Jonathan Ward turned onto the entrance ramp leading to the Tappan Zee Bridge to cross the Hudson River. The bridge was badly congested, as it was every Friday. He'd just passed Peter Roberts's home in Tarrytown, New York. Roberts had been temporarily assigned to the company's new plant in Milwaukee for five or six months. Several other people on the same assignment were being brought home every two or three weeks, but Roberts wasn't.

Ward had talked with the chief industrial engineer, George Kosciusko, earlier that afternoon and had learned that Roberts wasn't being brought home at all for the entire assignment period. The engineer said that Roberts was being treated properly, but Ward found this assurance hard to accept. He muttered to himself that Kosciusko sure had a weird analysis of the situation. In the slow traffic, Ward started wondering whether he should take any action. If so, what should it be? How would his choice square with his ethical standards? He also worried about how his choice might affect his new position.

Jonathan Ward's Background

Ward had worked for Harrison Motors for more than four years, at its main factory near Yonkers, New York. Previously, he had worked for a large manufacturer of machine tools in Detroit for six years after graduating from Stevens Institute of Technology with a B.S. in industrial engineering. That job ended when the firm lost over half its sales volume, which was typical of that industry at the time. Fortunately, Ward had anticipated his layoff. Already in negotiation with Harrison Motors, he had started work at Harrison three weeks after his job in Detroit ended. He had moved his family to northern New Jersey only after selling their home in Detroit, which meant a five-month separation from his family (a nonworking wife and three young children). Although Ward got to Detroit three times during that period, both he and his wife had found the transition to be very difficult, and had looked forward to regaining stability in their lives. Ward's managerial ambitions had led him to start an evening MBA program in Detroit. After the move, he looked for two years before finding a suitable evening program, at Fordham University. He was allowed to transfer only six credit hours to the new program, and at the time of the events described here, he still had almost half the Fordham program to complete.

Harrison was a major producer of large diesel and gasoline engines used in ships and auxiliary power plants, and for stationary power generation. Eight weeks earlier Ward had been promoted to supervise thirteen industrial engineers who were responsible for planning engine block machining and with whom he had previously worked. Peter Roberts was part of another group of industrial engineers who were responsible for machining major precision parts, including crankshafts, camshafts, and valve stems. Roberts's boss and Ward both reported to George Kosciusko.

Co-Workers or Friends?

Jonathan Ward and Peter Roberts frequently had lunch together, usually with two or three others in positions similar to theirs. For some time, Ward had intended to plan a get-together with Roberts and their wives. It hadn't happened, partly because they lived 20 miles apart across the Hudson River. Twice Ward had dropped Roberts off at his home, where he had met Barbara, Peter's wife. Ward considered Roberts more than an acquaintance, but not yet a close personal friend. Ward now had managerial responsibilities, while Roberts remained a nonsupervisory worker.

The New Plant

Harrison was building a new plant near Milwaukee, to improve service to customers in the Midwest. Great Lakes shipbuilders, who had bought few Harrison engines to date, were one target market. Midwest power companies and paper mills were others. Product lines to be produced had been selected, and the plant was under construction.

Five months earlier, a project team of about twenty engineers had been assembled to select machinery and materials handling equipment for the new plant and to prepare detailed layouts for its installation. An unused portion of an old building was provided for the team, the first such project organization in anyone's memory at Harrison. Ward was assigned temporarily to this team. He headed a group of four who selected and laid out equipment for use in the new plant's engine block machining and assembly operation.

Ward's team completed its task in ten weeks, four weeks earlier than had been estimated by the project manager. They had caught several mistakes in the initial planning in time to avoid costly corrections,

Source: This case was prepared by Timothy W. Edlund, Morgan State University. It was published in the *Business Case Journal*, 1994, 2(1), 105-109. Adapted and used with permission of the author and the Society for Case Research, 1995.

and Ward had already been told by the manager of the new plant that the engine block part of facility was being installed more easily than any other part despite its greater complexity—thanks to his team's good work. The team also had completed successfully an additional, smaller assignment for the new plant. A promotion for Ward had been talked about, and George Kosciusko said that these results clinched it.

On-Site Installation

As the new plant neared completion, many complex machines had to be installed, tested, and "proven in" (demonstrated to actually produce the planned results). Many of these machines had been shipped from Harrison's existing plants and required substantial reconditioning. George Kosciusko had selected eight engineers to oversee installation at the Milwaukee plant. Their assignment was expected to last five months, perhaps six. Peter Roberts had left about five weeks before, with three other engineers; the other four had followed shortly after.

Where was Peter Roberts?

Earlier that Friday, Ward had run into three of the engineers assigned to the Milwaukee project, two of them for the second time since they had left. He'd had lunch with one of them, Bill Black. Black said that they were visiting home at company expense every two or three weekends, generally with Monday or Friday off to compensate for the time away from home. While waiting for their food, Ward asked, "What weekends does Peter Roberts get home? I haven't seen or heard from him. We often had lunch together before you all started work in Wisconsin."

Black replied, "You know, that's funny. Now that I think of it, I don't think he has been back here. He's there all the time I am, and it's clear his installation work has been continuing while I've been back here. I don't know what his schedule is." Their food arrived, and they talked about other matters.

A Conference with George Kosciusko

That afternoon, Ward was scheduled to meet Kosciusko at 2:00 o'clock. When they'd completed the planned agenda, Kosciusko asked Ward whether they needed to talk about anything else. Ward then asked what weekends Peter Roberts would be home. Kosciusko said that he wasn't coming home until the job was done, at least at company expense. Ward replied: "How come? Bill Black and Jenny Crawford have been back twice already, Earl Johnson once, and I understand all the others have been brought back too. Why not Peter—surely five or six months is too long away from home." Kosciusko replied, "He didn't ask for it." Ward sputtered, "But surely he's entitled to it anyway."

Kosciusko answered, "Well, the policy manual says that employees may be brought home twice every five weeks, if their assignments are from 500 to 1,500 miles away from their regular workplace. All the others asked how often they were entitled to get home, and I told them; that's why they're getting these weekends at home. But Roberts didn't ask; therefore he's not getting those weekends. He agreed to take this assignment, knowing that it would last five or six months. I'm not going to bring up the policy; this way I'm saving the company the cost of bringing him back nine or ten times. He hasn't complained."

Ward said, "What policy? I haven't seen that. Did Peter?" "Oh no, that policy is confidential. It's held in the personnel department. Only managers sending people out of town get to see it," Kosciusko declared. "So Peter doesn't even know about that policy," Ward replied. "That doesn't seem fair! Aren't you going to let Peter know, so that he too can get back here and visit his family once in a while?" Kosciusko's response was negative, and he assured Ward that he viewed the arrangement as completely proper. Ward left shaking his head. His boss sure was unpredictable! Meanwhile, he had to get on with his own work and put his concern for Roberts temporarily on hold.

Jonathan Ward's Dilemma

On the way home, Ward thought about Roberts's situation. Passing the Roberts's home, he remembered the last time he'd dropped Peter off, about seven weeks ago. He'd stopped in for a cup of coffee. He learned that Peter and Barbara Roberts, in addition to their regular jobs and raising their two children, were doing most of the construction of their home themselves. There were no stairs in the front hall to get upstairs (just a ladder), a gaping hole down to the basement, and much other work to be done to complete the house. They had hoped that the prefabricated stairs would arrive before Peter had to leave for Milwaukee, but it hadn't. Jon wondered how Barbara Roberts would manage and what any delay in completing the house might mean.

Ward thought about his boss's strengths and weaknesses. He had fought for and won justified pay increases for his staff and had gotten Ward a promotion. His previous boss had made similar recommendations but hadn't been willing to fight for them, and so none were approved. Together, Ward and Kosciusko had developed an effective way to prepare and submit negative recommendations on proposed projects when appropriate, which was something no one in the company had done before.

However, George Kosciusko was unpredictable. A week earlier he had prepared a memo requiring other departments to follow some changes in procedure, only to file it. He said that the memo would take care of getting people to change procedures. When Ward asked how others could comply when they hadn't seen the memo, his boss said not to worry; they would have to comply. Another time, six months earlier, when Ward was recovering from an injured hip, Kosciusko had insisted that the two of them take a walk through the many buildings in their factory. Ward believed that his recovery had been delayed by at least a week and that the information gained during the tour could have been obtained from drawings in the department.

Ward wondered whether such behavior could result from Kosciusko's background. His parents were Polish, but he had been raised in Italy. He had obtained his engineering degree from a French-speaking university in Quebec, where he met his French-Canadian wife. He claimed that English was his best language, but understanding him could be very difficult because at times he left out essential words when speaking.

His handling of Peter Roberts didn't seem to be in character. George Kosciusko asked people to do strange things sometimes, but he had always tried to get them proper job classifications and to win pay increases for them. It didn't make sense.

Ward wasn't sure how his boss might react if he meddled further. He'd recently read that whistleblowers—those who report their companies for unethical or illegal acts—often were subjected to harsh retribution. Sometimes they lost their jobs. The courts seemed to offer little protection, even when a company's violation was obvious. And the issues in this case were far from obvious!

At Harrison, Ward had noticed that new ideas weren't always welcome. Before contacting someone in another part of the organization, an employee customarily notified his or her own superior. Soon after going to work for Harrison he'd gotten burned for not doing so! And he'd heard vivid tales of abrupt firings of anyone found to be seeking employment elsewhere.

As he drove across the bridge without his usual car pool companions, Ward was conscious of two conflicting emotions. He was glad to be going home and hoped that he could forget company problems over the weekend. A neighbor was having a TGIF (thank God it's Friday) party. He thought, "That party will sure be welcome *this* week."

He also thought that Peter Roberts was being treated shabbily. He wondered what he might do to help. Among the people he could talk to were his boss, Peter (if he could reach him) and Barbara Roberts, Peter Roberts's boss, the manager of the new plant, and the project manager. He might also casually mention the situation to his car pool companions Monday and see what Ed Wilson, the assistant personnel manager and a neighbor, would say.

Questions

1. What managerial roles are illustrated? Be specific.
2. How would Jonathan Ward diagnose his situation in terms of the behavioral approach?
3. How should Ward resolve his ethical dilemma?

Part *Two*

The Environment and Managing Strategically

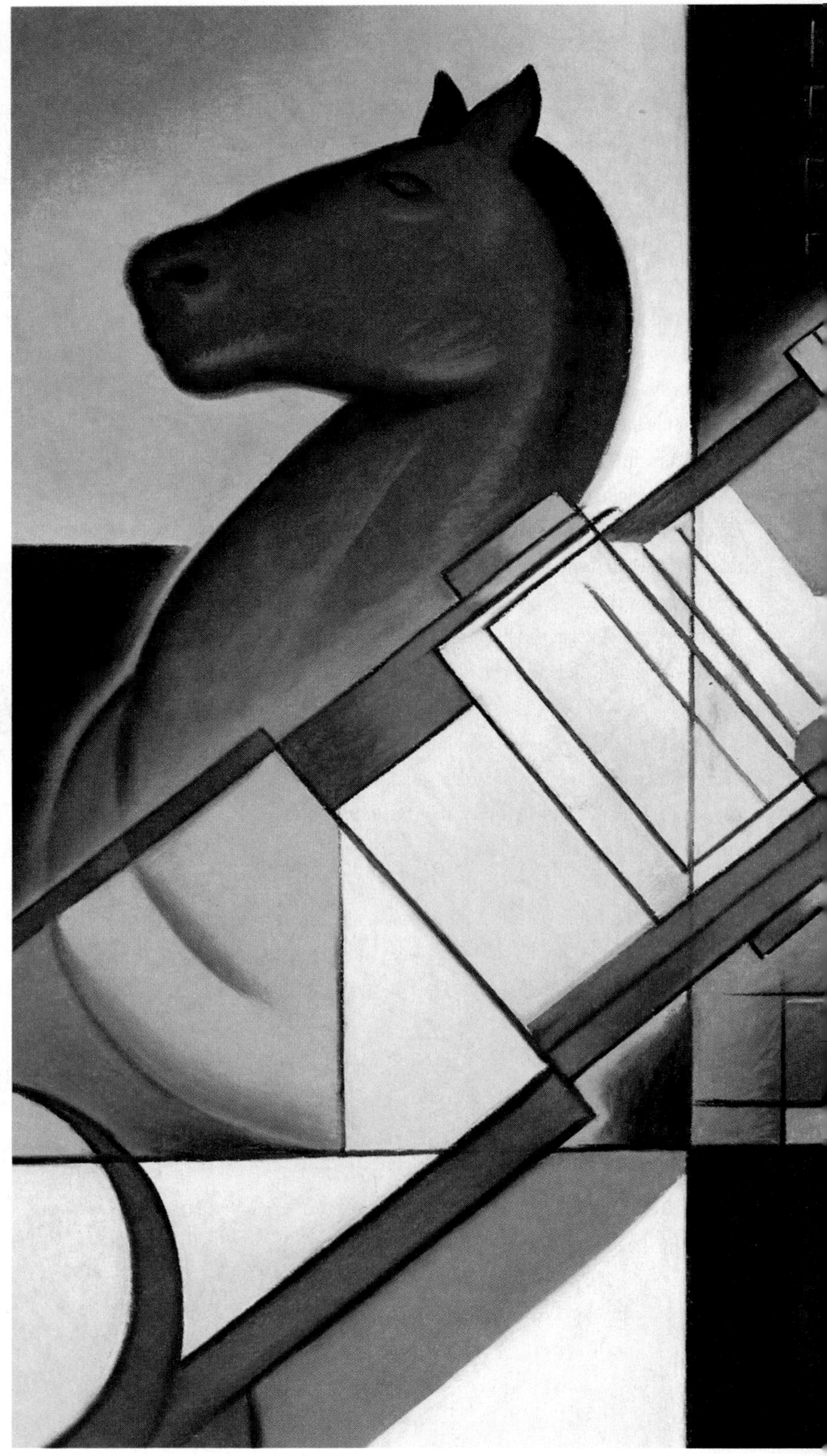

Chapter *3*

Strategic Management: Environmental Forces

Learning *Objectives*

After studying this chapter you should be able to:

1. Describe the main forces in the external business environment and how they influence organizations.
2. Define the role of the task environment and how it changes.
3. Identify the five competitive forces that directly affect organizations in an industry.
4. Explain why technological forces have become increasingly important in strategic planning.
5. Describe the principal political strategies used by managers to cope with external political-legal forces.

Chapter *Outline*

Preview *Insight*

U.S. Sugar Cleans the Everglades

To many travelers, tourists, and Florida residents, the Everglades is a national park characterized by sawgrass, whooping cranes, and alligators. To the U.S. Sugar Company, however, it is a 700,000 acre Everglades agricultural area of which 400,000 acres is their home. In this fragile wetland, the company produces and refines over 20 percent of the sugar consumed in the United States. Recently, U.S. Sugar and other food growers in the Everglades have confronted environmentalists who have put the future of the companies at risk.

Sugar-cane and other vegetable growers historically have used phosphorous fertilizers to improve the quality and yield of their crops. But in the Everglades, the nutrient-poor wetland is below sea level. Runoff from the fields has put fertilizer into a shallow aquifer. This "nutritious" water has been blamed for several significant ecological disturbances.

One is that water no longer flows freely to the Bay of Florida, southwest of Miami, because the nutrient-rich water has stimulated the growth of plants that block the water flow. Coupled with droughts in 1986 and 1987, the entire ecology of the Everglades has changed, creating a hostile environment for the animals and plants in the area. The second and more important issue is that less freshwater is flowing through the Everglades. This reduced flow has allowed seawater to creep into the aquifer, which provides drinking water for nearly 2.5 million people in the greater Miami area.

For years, environmentalists pressed U.S. Sugar, Flo-Sun, and other Everglades sugar and vegetable growers to engage in a voluntary cleanup and reduction in phosphorous discharge. When these efforts failed, they brought a class-action lawsuit, first heard in 1988 in a U.S. District Court. After five years of negotiation and costly legal battles, the farm combines and the U.S. Department of the Interior finally reached an accord. In 1993, U.S. Sugar and other companies agreed to pay at least $223 million and as much as $332 million to remove phosphorous pollutants from their water discharges.

For U.S. Sugar, this settlement has affected its decision-making process in three ways. First, the company has had to invest money in research to develop systems that permit the proper fertilization of its sugar cane and leafy vegetable crops while protecting the water that naturally runs off the fields. Second, it has built a series of filtering canals that eventually channel cleaner water to the aquifer. Finally, it has begun to cooperate in the development of marsh buffers on land that historically has been used for cash crops.[1]

1

Describe the main forces in the external business environment and how they influence organizations.

THE BUSINESS ENVIRONMENT

The events that led to the lawsuit and subsequent cleanup efforts in the Everglades are, to some degree, external to U.S. Sugar. Although U.S. Sugar contributed to the degradation of the Everglades, the situation has been complicated by events over which the company had no control, called **environmental forces.** One force is the U.S. Army Corps of Engineers, which built canals to drain land and to divert floodwater from Lake Okeechobee during hurricanes. These canals were erroneously channeled into the ocean and Intracoastal Waterway instead of into Florida Bay. This artificial water control increases the impact of drought, as occurred in the mid-1980s.

The second problem facing U.S. Sugar is the removal of some of the barriers to imported sugar from the Caribbean and Mexico that have guaranteed higher sugar prices. This action jeopardizes the future profits of sugar producers and means that they have to optimize crop quality. Finally, various special interest groups have pressured sugar companies to be more conscious of what they are doing to the physical environment. Some environmental groups are interested in protecting plants and animals. Others have turned to the South Florida Water Management District for help in preserving the quality of drinking water.

Such forces act to some degree on all companies, both domestically and internationally. Some external forces actually create opportunities for organizations. For example, the system of ponds for filtering wastewater before it is discharged into the canals also may provide an opportunity for U.S. Sugar to raise catfish commercially for restaurants. Other external forces create threats to an organization's future. If the profits on growing sugar continue to be threatened, U.S. Sugar may decide to switch to another crop or move to another location with a less fragile ecosystem. Managers are challenged to monitor these forces constantly and to use their critical thinking skills to respond effectively.

At U.S. Sugar Company, the complexities of external forces combined with decisions made by the company's managers created problems that have high costs, both economically and in terms of the company's reputation. In extreme cases of environmental insensitivity, a company can even be forced to shut down. Phelps Dodge Copper Smelting in Douglas, Arizona, is a prime example. For many years, the company emitted sulphur dioxide into the air as a byproduct of copper smelting. Alternative technology for this process was available but was water-based and required new equipment. Eventually, the U.S. Environmental Protection Agency (EPA) told the company that it had to purchase and install the new equipment or close the facility.

Other external changes generate new products and create new organizations to produce and sell them. Soft contact lenses are a result of a burn-treatment material developed to provide a moist healing environment during the Vietnam War. The removal of FDA approval for silicon and dacron products for repair and replacement surgery has created a market for a small high-technology company named Corvita, a manufacturer of an FDA-approved surgical grafting material.

How can managers best deal with their environment? Although there are no simple answers to this question, managers can pursue two basic approaches:

1. position the organization so that its own capabilities provide the best *defense* against an environmental threat. U.S. Sugar did so by experimenting with wastewater filtration;
2. take the *offensive* by attempting to change or take advantage of the environment. U.S. Sugar is doing so by encouraging the public to visit its sugar-cane operations, including state-of-the-art housing accommodations for almost 40,000 Jamaican migrant workers.

In brief, managers must develop both strong reactive (defensive) and strong proactive (offensive) strategies for taking advantage of environmental opportunities and reducing environmental threats.

We were selective in choosing environmental forces to address in this chapter. For example, the international arena is certainly a key part of most managers' environments—today more than ever. However, we mention international forces here only briefly because Chapter 4 is devoted to this topic. Also, various groups are pressing for new forms and higher levels of ethical behavior by managers and for increased social responsibility by organizations. We allude to these forces here, but cover them in detail in Chapter 7. Throughout this book, we discuss environmental forces and their management wherever they are relevant to the topic being considered.

We begin this chapter by introducing the basic features of the general organizational environment. We then present a framework for diagnosing various types of task environments to add to your growing toolkit of managerial skills. We devote most of the chapter to four types of environmental forces that managers must monitor and diagnose because of their direct or indirect importance: cultural, political-legal, technological, and competitive.

The General Environment

The **general environment,** sometimes called the *macroenvironment,* includes the external factors that usually affect all or most organizations. As depicted in Figure 3.1, the

FIGURE 3.1

The General Environment and Environmental Forces Affecting Organizations

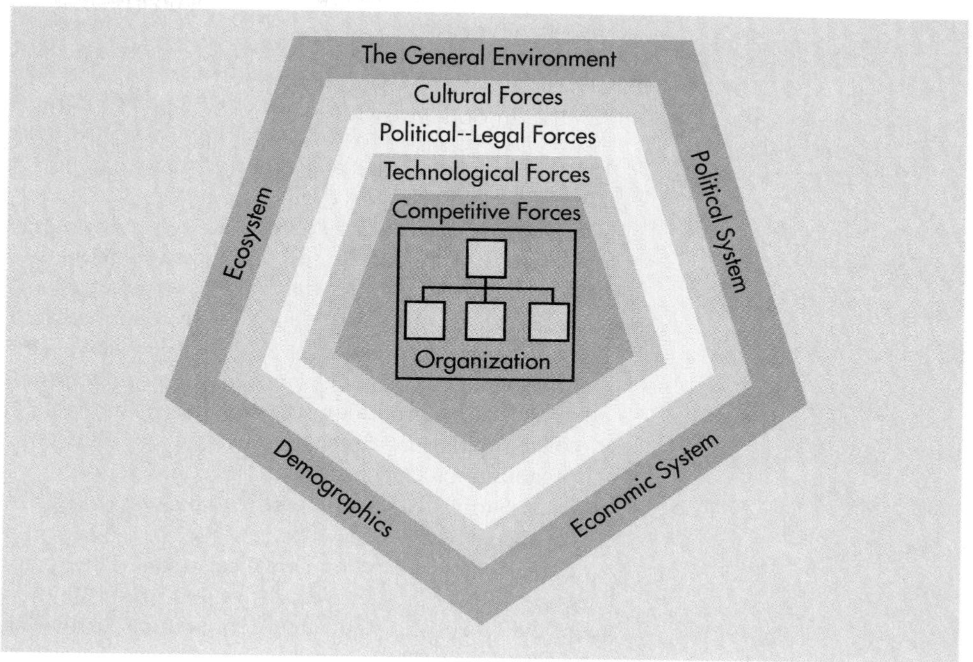

general environment includes the type of economic system (e.g., free enterprise, socialist, or planned demand) and economic conditions (expansionary and recessionary cycles and the general standard of living); type of political system (democracy, dictatorship, or monarchy); condition of the ecosystem (extent of land, water, and air pollution); demographics (age, gender, race, ethnic origin, and education level of the population); and cultural background (values, beliefs, language, and religious influences). Those aspects of the general environment spawn the cultural, competitive, technological, and political-legal forces that impinge on organizations.

Although we treat each force separately, they are linked. Consider, for example, the impact of the North American Free Trade Agreement (NAFTA) on the U.S., Mexican, and Canadian political systems and businesses. Both U.S. and Mexican companies must now meet tighter controls regarding waste disposal and pollution emissions. In general, NAFTA created proactive (offensive) opportunities in terms of new markets for companies such as Ford and Wal-Mart. At the same time it created reactive (defensive) threats to the same companies in terms of having to improve their waste disposal practices.[2]

Economic and Political Systems

The United States has an economic system in which privately controlled markets based on supply and demand prevail over governmental control of production and prices. Free market competition, private contracts, profit incentives, technological advancement, and labor with collective bargaining rights are essential elements in this system. The government (part of the political system) acts as a watchdog over business, providing direction in antitrust, monetary policy, human rights, defense, and environmental matters. Government ownership of enterprises is the exception to the rule, rather than the norm. There is no centrally planned economy as in North Korea or the People's Republic of China. Particularly challenging economic and political conditions may include fluctuating inflation, unemployment, and tax and interest rates; environmental regulations; and safety regulations covering both the workplace and goods produced.

The Ecosystem

Political and economic conditions in the United States have led to a renewed environmentalism. A 1981 *New York Times*/CBS poll found that only 4 percent of the U.S. population agreed that "environmental improvements must be made regardless of cost." In 1994, 80 percent of the population strongly agreed.[3] As a result, national environmental groups are becoming even more active. The Audubon Society has broadened its efforts from protection of wildlife to actively monitoring business practices that affect native plants and animals. In the U.S. Sugar situation, the Audubon Society was the first to propose legal agreements that called for removal of significant amounts of phosphate from the water that had been used to refine sugar. The National Resources Defense Council has abandoned some of its earlier views—considered by some to be "fanatic and utopian"—and has displayed a greater understanding of the trade-offs that have to be made. The organization has shown a greater willingness to move from confrontation to collaboration in order to improve the environment. Nonetheless, some environmental organizations, such as Wise Use, continue to press legislatures to adopt stricter laws and regulatory boards that enforce land use and waste disposal regulations to tighten their procedures.

This renewed environmentalism poses numerous challenges to business. With the passage of the U.S. Clean Air Act of 1990 and NAFTA, organizations' responses now are more than a choice—they are a requirement. Increasingly, organizations are making environmental considerations part of their decision making from the beginning. They must now think long term, even though profits may suffer in the short term. The following are a few of the steps organizations can take in heeding the call of renewed environmentalism.

Ask Students
Are any operations on campus obviously environmentally unsafe? (Examples: medical school waste or scientific and engineering lab waste.)

Cut Back on Environmentally Unsafe Operations. U.S. Sugar created both smoke and water pollution by burning sugar cane and dumping toxic effluents into the water supply. The damage to the company's reputation opens opportunities for Caribbean growers to export more cane to the United States at lower prices.

Compensate for Environmentally Risky Endeavors. Applied Energy Services, a power plant management firm, donated $2 million in 1988 for tree planting in Guatemala to compensate for a coal-fired plant it was building in Connecticut. Oxygen generated by the trees is meant to offset carbon dioxide and carbon monoxide emissions that might lead to global warming.

Avoid Confrontation with State and Federal Pollution Control Agencies. W. R. Grace failed in this respect and is currently making expensive and time-consuming restitution for asbestos disposal. Browning-Ferris, Waste Management, and Louisiana-Pacific abused local landfill requirements. In the future, when they bid for city, township, and county refuse collection and disposal contracts, their service plans will come under much tighter review.

Comply Early with Government Regulations. Because compliance costs increase over time, organizations that act early will have lower costs. Thus they will be able to increase their market share, profits, and competitive advantage. For example, 3M's goal is to meet government requirements for replacing or improving underground storage tanks by 1993 instead of 1998, the deadline. Both GE and Carrier have created CFC-free cooling compressors for refrigeration and air-conditioners in advance of a 1995 deadline.

Promote New Manufacturing Technologies. In light of the problems with the earth's ozone layer, Motorola and other microprocessor manufacturers have switched from clorofluorocarbon (CFC) chemicals, such as Freon, to a substance made from the skin of oranges, called turpene, to clean their chips. New companies will emerge to satisfy the demand for turpene.

Environmental concerns have changed the way producers and consumers think about products, the raw materials used to make them, and the byproducts from manufacturing processes. This GM Hughes technician is monitoring electronic cards being cleaned with an environmentally friendly solution, instead of one containing CFCs.

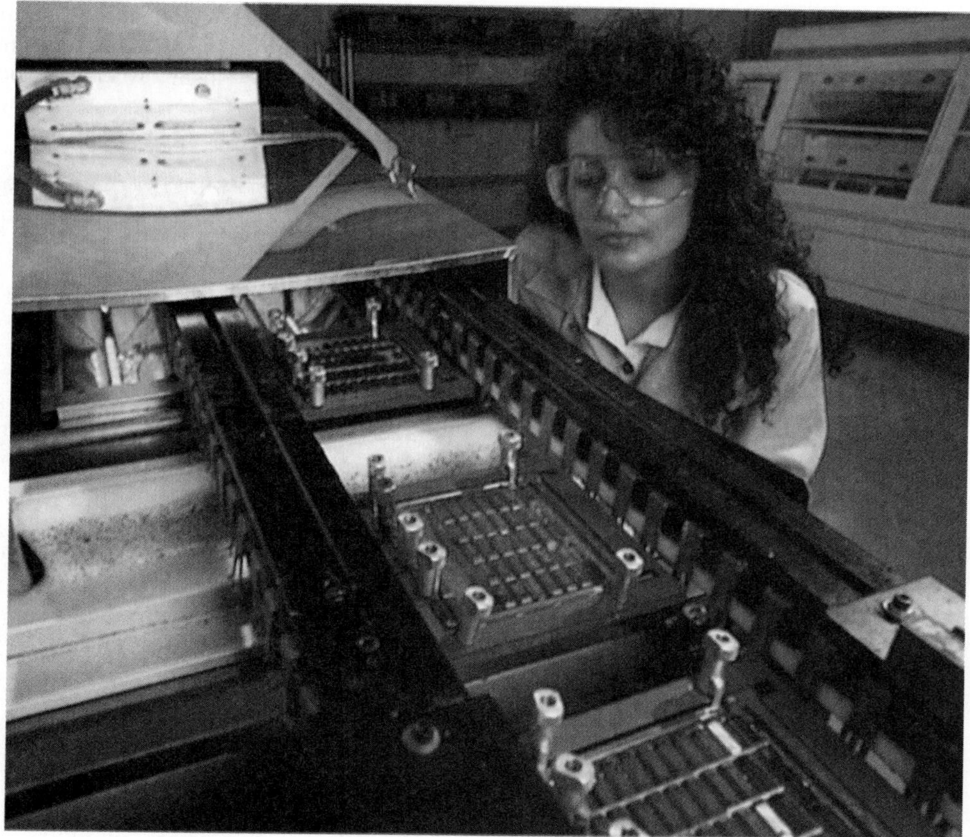

Teaching Tip
Have students do a minirecycling audit of the university. Divide the class into groups to look at different parts of the university to determine how much recycling each unit does. If the school newspaper has run stories or editorials on recycling, use it as a resource. Perhaps the students could publish the results of their audit in the campus paper.

Recycle Wastes. The 3M Company is recycling and reusing solvents it once spewed into the atmosphere. Other firms with active recycling programs are Safety-Kleen (solvents and motor oil), Wellman (plastics), Jefferson Smurfit (paper), and Nucor (steel). Polyfoam Packers, a styrofoam manufacturer, has initiated a recycling process that reuses styrofoam beads.[4]

Summary of Steps. Managers can take the following steps to respond to environmental concerns.

- Give a senior-level person well-defined environmental responsibilities. This approach makes environmental concerns a top-down issue.
- Measure everything: waste, energy use, travel by personal vehicles, and the like. Set measurable goals and target dates for environmental improvements. Monitor progress.
- Consider reformulating products in order to use less toxic chemicals in the manufacturing process and cleanup. Try to use materials that won't harm the environment when the consumer eventually discards the product.
- Consider business opportunities from recycling or disposing of your products, including having your customer bring them back to you when they have reached the end of their useful lives.
- Recognize that environmental regulations are here to stay and that they are likely to become more restrictive. Environmental awareness and behavior ("green behavior") will have a lot to do with a firm's reputation in the future. Plan for the future by taking that into account today.

Environmental concerns have changed the way producers and consumers alike think about products, the raw materials used to make them, and the by-products from

Discussion Question 1
How have changes in the economic and political system affected task environments of organizations?

manufacturing processes. In fact, a whole new generation of successful products has been developed in response to the Clean Air Act and reuse and recycling regulations. For example, Louisiana-Pacific now makes wood products out of milling scraps.

Demographics

Demographics are the characteristics of work group, organization, specific market, or national populations, such as individuals between the ages of 18 and 25.[5] Demographics—and in particular, changes in demographics—play an important role in marketing, human resources management, finance, and other aspects of business. Let's consider a few of the broad demographic changes that have occurred in the United States recently and that are expected to continue through the end of this century.

From 1985 to 2000, the Hispanic and Asian populations each will have grown by 48 percent. The African-American population will have grown by 28 percent, and the Anglo population by 5.6 percent. As a result, the proportion of non-Hispanic whites will have fallen from 78 to 73 percent of the total population by 2000.

Women have dramatically increased their representation in occupations and industries from which they were once excluded (or at least not encouraged to enter), such as business, engineering, medicine, and law. Women will constitute 47 percent of the work force in 2000, up from about 44 percent in 1986. Many professional schools, such as business and engineering schools, have up to 50 percent female students. They represented only about 25 percent of enrollment ten years ago. By 2000, the number and percentage of women in middle and top management positions is expected to rise dramatically.[6]

Finally, the U.S. work force is aging. The projected population increase for those aged 45 and over is 30 percent, but it's only 2 percent for the 18–44 age group. The average age of workers will jump from 32 in 1990 to about 40 by the turn of the century. At that point, nearly half the labor force will come under the protection of the Age Discrimination in Employment Act. This act provides protection against age discrimination in employment for those aged 40 and older.[7]

Employers are likely to face new pressures from an increasingly diverse work force. They need to recognize this trend and learn how to *manage diversity*. Some organizations are providing training to help employees be more tolerant of language, age, race, and ethnic differences; to identify and reject racial and gender preferences in hiring and promotion; and to be responsive to the handicapped. Management no longer can impose an "Anglo-male" organizational culture.[8] For example, six of the fourteen executives at American Airlines in the Research Triangle Park, North Carolina, are women, and 20 percent of the management positions just below the executive level are held by nonwhite women.[9]

Real-World Example
Black men and women held 7 percent of the U.S. economy's white-collar jobs in 1992 (*Wall Street Journal*, March 8, 1994, A1, A12).

In New York City's bus and subway systems, a growing number of ads for familiar products are in Spanish as well as English, and all safety instructions are in both English and Spanish. Hispanic food has become popular in Chicago, Detroit, and other major cities, where a variety of restaurants—Mexican, Cuban, Salvadoran, and others—reflect large Hispanic communities. Mexican food tops the list. In the United States, 38 million households eat Mexican food, sales of which rose 60 percent between 1982 and 1990. Kraft's Velveeta cheese now comes in a spicy Mexican version, and jalapeño-flavored potato chips are sold nationally. Farmers in New Mexico report doubling their crops of chiles between 1977 and 1990. Salsa is a staple in many households and now outsells ketchup. Burritos are popular substitutes for sandwiches in many college and university student centers.

Of course, efforts to target any market can have pitfalls. Borden advertised ice cream using the Mexican slang word *nieve,* which literally means "snow." The campaign worked fine in California and Texas, where there is a large Mexican-American population. But Cubans and Puerto Ricans in the East, unfamiliar with Mexican slang, thought that the company actually was selling snow because they call ice cream *helado*. Throughout the United States, the Latin community and many others recognize *snow* as being slang for cocaine.

Real-World Example
Minorities make up less than 10 percent of the managerial ranks in the United States (U.S. Department of Labor, 1992).

Univision, the largest Spanish language television network, reaches an estimated 17 million Hispanics, with at least 5 million regular viewers. Formerly known as the Spanish International Network, it has been joined by a second Spanish network, Telemundo, with more than 3.3 million regular viewers.[10] In most cities, Spanish radio stations air talk shows and traffic reports in a local Spanish dialect. However, these stations are having some communication problems because of different dialects and slang terms used by the Hispanic listening audience.

The blending of Anglo and Latin terms is being fueled by NAFTA. Although the agreement also covers Canada, much of the attention has been focused on business activity involving the United States and Mexico. The following Diversity Insight indicates how NAFTA has permitted U.S. companies to form joint ventures with Mexican companies, capitalizing on similarities rather than differences.

Diversity *Insight*

All of Your Favorite Things—with a Mexican Spin

The largest emerging middle-class market in the world shares a 1,900-mile border with the United States. For years, the prevalence of Mexican food, beer, and music has emphasized the presence of these 90 million neighbors. But NAFTA is pushing the mixing of the two cultures through joint ventures of U.S. companies who can deliver their goods and technologies promptly to Mexican consumers and Mexican companies who have access to increasingly skilled but low-paid workers. Cifra is but one example. It is a large discount department store that resembles Wal-Mart in the 1970s. In small and medium-sized cities, Cifra has operated discount type stores with some limited success. With the signing of NAFTA, however, Cifra has implemented a joint venture with Wal-Mart to operate Wal-Mart and Sam's Discount Centers in nearly 20 cities. Similarly, Cinemark Theaters, a large chain of U.S. movie theaters, is building movie multiplexes in Monterrey and other large cities.

But the direction of business activity isn't one way. During the early 1990s, a group of Mexican investors, including major fruit and vegetable growers, purchased Del Monte. Vitro and Cemex purchased U.S. companies. And the United States, Canada, and Mexico have the potential to be the new automobile manufacturing corridor of the world in the next few years.

As companies and management teams blend, work-force diversity will increase. So the challenges of understanding the workplace and consumer issues associated with successful free trade are likely to increase with further collaboration.

Free trade offers many opportunities for expansion of U.S., Canadian, and Mexican markets and business opportunities. Joint ventures and free trade also have the potential to diminish cultural barriers by familiarizing customers and employees with new products and with each other.[11]

Cultural Forces

Underlying a society and surrounding an organization are various cultural forces, which often are not as visible as other general environmental forces. **Culture** can be defined as the shared characteristics (e.g., language, religion, and heritage) and values that distinguish the members of one group of people from those of another.[12] A *value* is a basic belief about a condition that has considerable importance and meaning to individuals and is relatively stable over time.[13] A **value system** comprises multiple beliefs that are compatible and supportive of one another. For example, beliefs in private enterprise and individual rights are mutually supportive.

Managers need to appreciate the significance of values and value systems, both their own and those of others.[14] Values can greatly affect how a manager:

- *Views other people and groups, thus influencing interpersonal relationships.* One male manager might believe that women are inferior, belong in the home, and should simply follow orders. Another might view women as equals who should be recognized, consulted, and promoted because of their abilities and contributions.
- *Perceives situations and problems.* One manager might believe that conflict and competition can be managed and used constructively. Another might think that they should be avoided.
- *Goes about solving problems.* One manager might believe that team decision making can be effective. Another might believe that individuals should make decisions.
- *Determines what is and is not ethical behavior.* One manager might believe that ethics means doing only what is absolutely required by law. Another might view ethics as going well beyond minimum legal requirements to do what is morally right.
- *Leads and controls employees.* One manager might believe in sharing information and using controls based on mutual trust. Another might think that subordinates are not to be trusted and that controls should emphasize impersonal rules, close supervision, and a rigid chain of command.[15]

Teaching Tip
Remind students that, in intercultural communication, there is no right or wrong—only differences. Ask them to explain how judgments about right and wrong can get them into trouble.

By diagnosing a culture's values, managers and employees can understand and predict others' expectations and avoid some cultural pitfalls. Otherwise, they risk inadvertently antagonizing fellow employees, customers, or other groups by breaking a sacred taboo (e.g., showing the bottom of a person's shoe to a Saudi) or ignoring a time-honored custom (e.g., preventing an employee from attending an important religious ceremony in Indonesia).

The framework of work-related values outlined here and expanded on in Chapter 4 has been used in numerous studies of cultural differences among employees. It was developed by Geert Hofstede, Director of the Institute for Research on Intercultural Cooperation in the Netherlands, while he was an organizational researcher at IBM.[16] The data reported here are based on his surveys of thousands of IBM employees in fifty countries. Hofstede's project uncovered some intriguing differences among countries in terms of four value dimensions: power distance, uncertainty avoidance, individualism (versus collectivism), and masculinity (versus femininity).[17]

Ask Students
What are some other value dimensions?

The following discussion focuses primarily on Hofstede's ranking of four nations—Canada, France, Mexico, and the United States—with respect to each dimension. These rankings are based on the *dominant* value orientation in each country, with a ranking of 1 for the lowest and 50 for the highest position (relative to all fifty countries in the survey) on each value dimension. Figure 3.2 shows the rankings for Canada, France, Mexico, and the United States.

Power Distance. The degree to which influence and control are unequally distributed among individuals and institutions within a particular culture is the measure of its **power distance.** If most people in a society support an unequal distribution, the nation is ranked high. In societies ranked high (e.g., Mexico, France, India, and the Philippines), membership in a particular class or caste is crucial to an individual's opportunity for advancement. Societies ranked lower play down inequality. Individuals in the United States, Canada, Sweden, and Austria can achieve prestige, wealth, and social status, regardless of family background.

Managers operating in countries ranked low in power distance are expected to be generally supportive of equal rights and equal opportunity. For example, managers in Canada and the United States typically support participative management. In contrast, managers in Mexico, France, and India do not value the U.S. and Canadian style of participative management. Managers in the United States and Canada try not to set themselves too much apart from subordinates by appearing to be superior or unique. In

Ask Students
What would likely happen if you personally had high power distance and were hired to manage in a low power distance culture?

FIGURE 3.2

Relative Ranking of Four Countries on Four Value Dimensions

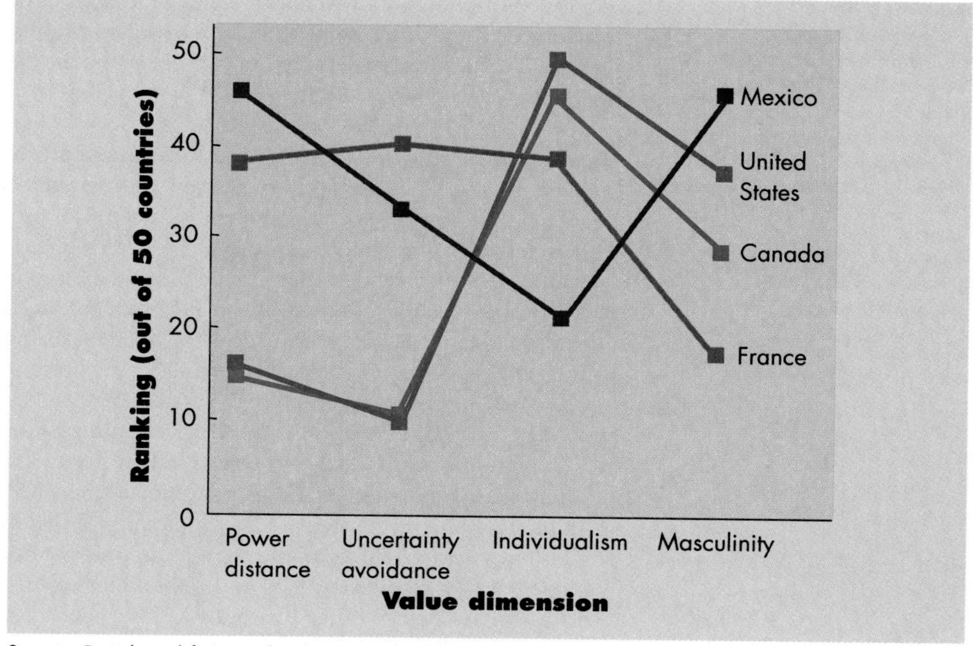

Source: Developed from Hofstede, G. *Culture's Consequences: International Differences in Work-Related Values.* Beverly Hills, Calif.: Sage, 1980.

countries with high power distance, however, a more autocratic management style not only is more common but is expected by employees.

Uncertainty Avoidance. The degree to which members of a society attempt to avoid ambiguity, riskiness, and the indefiniteness of the future is the measure of its **uncertainty avoidance.** Individuals in cultures ranked low on this dimension generally are secure and don't expend a great deal of energy trying to avoid or minimize ambiguous situations. In cultures with high uncertainty avoidance, individuals often try to make the future more predictable by establishing procedures and rules that foster job security. In organizations, high uncertainty avoidance is often associated with built-in career stability (job security), numerous rules governing behavior, intolerance of deviant ideas and behavior, belief in absolute truths, and overreliance on expertise.

In the United States and Canada, employees and managers ranked low on uncertainty avoidance, sharing a relatively high tolerance for uncertainty compared with workers and managers in France and Mexico. Thus Canadian and U.S. managers are more likely to be receptive to changing rules, open competition, and new ideas.

Teaching Tip
Remind students that these are generalizations that may not apply to everyone in a culture. How would making the generalization that all Mexican and French people have a low tolerance for uncertainty get someone into trouble?

Individualism. A combination of the degree to which society expects people to take care of themselves and their immediate families and the degree to which individuals believe they are masters of their own destiny is its measure of **individualism.** The opposite of individualism is **collectivism,** which refers to a tight social framework in which group (family, clan, organization, and nation) members focus on the common welfare and feel strong loyalty toward one another.

In the United States and Canada, employees ranked high on individualism, a result that agrees with the frequent characterization of these two countries as "I" societies rather than "we" societies. A strong sense of individualism supports and maintains a competitive market-based economic system. High individualism also is consistent with the individual merit and incentive pay systems favored in the United States and Canada. Conversely, group incentives and strong seniority systems are likely to exist in countries with low individualism (high collectivism), such as Mexico and Japan. Managers and

Ask Students
Is conflict more likely in a multicultural work force in which there are relatively equal numbers of individualistically and collectively oriented employees than in a homogeneous work force? Why or why not?

employees in a high-individualism culture move from organization to organization more frequently. They don't believe that their organizations are solely responsible for their welfare, nor do they expect that group decisions are better than decisions made by individuals.

Masculinity. In Hofstede's framework, **masculinity** is the degree to which assertiveness and the acquisition of money and material things are valued, as well as the degree of indifference to others' quality of life. The opposite of the masculinity dimension is **femininity,** a more nurturing, people-oriented dimension. Masculinity also reflects the division of labor among men and women in a society. Canada and the United States probably rank lower today on the masculinity dimension than they would have twenty years ago, largely because of the societal changes that have been taking place in role expectations for males and females. In recent years significant social pressures have begun to change stereotyped notions that men should be assertive and women should be nurturing or that gender roles should be clearly differentiated.

In high-masculinity cultures (e.g., Mexico, Japan, Austria, and Italy), women still do not hold many managerial jobs. Men dominate most settings, and an organization's right to influence the private lives of its employees is widely accepted. One researcher observed that Mexico, for example, rigidly defines gender-role expectations: The woman is expected to be supportive of and dependent on men—not to do for herself, but to yield to the wishes of others, caring for their needs before her own. A common belief in Muslim countries is that women are the inferior gender and should be subordinates instead of managers.[18]

Discussion Question 5
What advice would you give to a manager who was being transferred to a facility in Mexico for two years? To France? How did the cultural values in each country influence your answer?

Applying Hofstede's Dimensions. In later chapters we use the four work-related value dimensions discussed here to address differences and similarities in cultures. We also apply these value dimensions to understanding and managing diverse groups of employees in a single work setting.

Discussion Question 2
How do cultural values influence a manager's decision making?

2
Define the role of the task environment and how it changes.

THE TASK ENVIRONMENT

In contrast to the general environment with its relatively indirect influences, the **task environment** includes those external forces and groups that *directly* influence an organization's growth, success, and survival.[19] It normally includes an organization's customers or clients, competitors, suppliers, shareholders, government regulators, pressure groups, employees, and labor unions (if unionized). For the U.S. Sugar Corporation, the task environment includes the migrant workers from Jamaica, the Audubon Society and other environmental groups, the EPA, and the South Florida Water Management District. With so many groups putting pressure on the company, its managers probably would characterize the task environment as somewhat turbulent.

Everyone in organizations—from the manager and checkout clerk at the local supermarket to the postmaster and mail carrier at the U.S. Postal Service—is finding that focusing on groups in the task environment is essential. Hence managers need to spend a lot of time and effort diagnosing the changing needs and expectations of these external groups in order to meet them. For example, Hertz, Alamo, and other car rental agencies permit their agents to meet competitors' prices—or to take whatever other action is needed—on the spot to satisfy a customer. At Alamo, these changes have resulted in explosive growth and a 20 percent increase in sales revenues.

Ask Students
The task environment changes in the car rental example have forced employees to take more responsibility in helping their employers adapt to change. What do you need to do to prepare yourself for taking on such responsibility?

The task environment encompasses the competitive and technological forces shown in Figure 3.1. Although we treat political-legal forces as part of the task environment, we recognize that they can be viewed as part of the general environment, depending on the situation and the perspective taken. For example, labor unions may be part of an organization's task or general environment. The United Auto Workers (UAW) is part of the task environment for, and *directly* affect, Ford, General Motors, and Chrysler. (In turn, the management of these firms *directly* affects the UAW.) But unions are not part

Ask Students

What forces are in your university's competitive and technological environment?

of the task environment for nonunion firms such as IBM, Hewlett-Packard, and Alamo Rent-A-Car. Unions *indirectly* affect them, however, as part of the general environment. Indirect effects might include successful union efforts to obtain legislation benefiting all workers, union and nonunion alike.

Managers must constantly evaluate the task environment as they diagnose issues and weigh decisions. The task environment has an important bearing on organizational planning, organizational structure, human resources management, and control decisions. But monitoring the complexities of environmental forces can be difficult for managers because of their numerous day-to-day responsibilities. Hoechst Celanese, Southwest Airlines, Frito-Lay, and other organizations have special positions or departments (e.g., marketing research, strategic planning, and public affairs) with primary responsibility for helping managers keep track of environmental forces. One of the unintended benefits of total quality management programs has been closer contact with suppliers in the external environment. The reason is that work teams now frequently include supplier and key customer representatives. In the Motorola example in Chapter 1, the wristwatch pager that is marketed in Japan came from work teams that included representatives of major department stores in Japan. Through this process Motorola also learned that the U.S. market would not be interested in such a device.

Types of Task Environments

Figure 3.3 shows an uncomplicated way to diagnose and classify the task environment. This framework has two dimensions: simple-complex and stable-changing.[20]

FIGURE 3.3

Basic Types of Task Environments

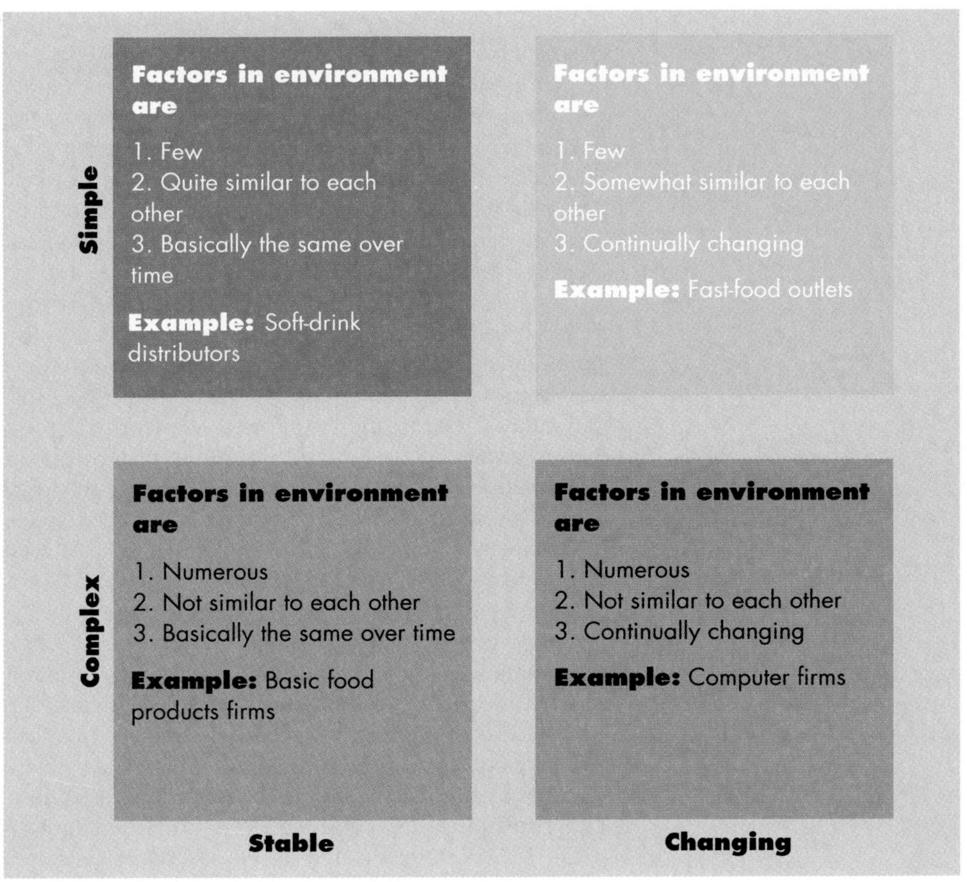

Source: Adapted from Duncan, R. What is the right organization structure: Decision tree analysis provides the answer. *Organizational Dynamics,* Winter 1979, 63.

The *simple-complex dimension* refers to whether the factors in the task environment are few and similar or numerous and different. A construction firm that builds standardized low-income residential housing would have a relatively simple environment. In contrast, a firm that builds customized homes, office buildings, and shopping centers is likely to face a more complex environment. The home builder is affected primarily by local economic cycles, the availability of raw materials, and local building codes. However, the commercial builder must respond to the same forces as the residential builder *and* deal with scheduling crews (e.g., electricians, plasterers, plumbers, and roofers) for multiple building sites, bank regulators who influence lending practices, and changes in the general economy.

The *stable-changing dimension* refers to whether the factors in the task environment remain the same or vary over time. For both types of builders, the task environment may remain stable for long periods of time. But it also may change rapidly. Consider, for example, the impact of natural disasters such as Hurricane Andrew in 1992, the Mississippi River floods of 1993, and the Los Angeles earthquake of 1994 on the building industry. These events changed the task environment radically for all builders. Building materials became more expensive and scarce. Local building codes were changed to minimize loss of life and property in the future.

Ask Students
Do sororities and fraternities have a stable or changing environment? Explain.

Regulatory changes also affect the stability of the task environment. The Regional Bell Operating Companies that came into being as a result of the AT&T breakup in 1984 were permitted to provide local telephone service as a monopoly. For example, Illinois Bell was the vendor of local telephone service to Chicago, Champaign, and Springfield. But changes in federal law in 1993 permitted other companies to provide telephone service. Thus the environment of the "Baby Bell" companies has become more complex as they anticipate competition from cellular telephone companies and cable operators who are now permitted to deliver the same type of service.

Four basic types of task environments—simple/stable, simple/changing, complex/stable, and complex/changing—are derived from classifying a firm's environmental factors along the simple-complex and stable-changing dimensions. An example of organizations facing a simple/stable environment are local soft-drink bottlers. Soft-drink bottlers have many customers, but the services they typically provide are standardized: delivering the right number of cases of soft drinks to each customer. Most soft-drink bottlers deal with national firms, such as Pepsi or Coca-Cola. Local bottlers also undertake most marketing campaigns, such as annual spring-break parties. Thus the task environment for such organizations is relatively simple and stable over time.

The simple/changing and complex/stable environments fall between the two extremes. Local fast-food outlets, such as Rally's and Burger King, operate in a simple/changing environment. They offer limited menus and have standardized and simple procedures for preparing and serving the food. Their customers do not expect and cannot receive much personal service. However, they constantly tinker with the menus, restaurant decor, and marketing tactics to adjust to changes in consumer preferences and to keep up with the competition. In contrast, Heinz, Campbell's, and other basic food products firms operate in a complex/stable environment. For example, the basic line of Campbell's soups—chicken noodle, tomato, and cream of mushroom—hasn't changed for decades. However, the production and distribution processes for getting these soups onto grocery store shelves are quite complex. They require meeting the demands of many suppliers and customers and conforming to various governmental regulations. Recently, the health consciousness of many consumers has put added pressure on prepared food manufacturers to reduce sodium and fat content. Thus the stability of the environment for these companies may be changing.

Ask Students
Does the campus cafeteria operate in a simple or changing environment? Has it adapted its menu to changing consumer tastes?

Obviously, organizations in a simple/stable environment face the least amount of uncertainty, and those in a complex/changing environment face the most. **Environmental uncertainty** refers to the ambiguity and unpredictability of some external factors. Organizations such as computer chip manufacturers (lower right-hand corner of Figure 3.3) face a **turbulent environment,** one that is complex, is constantly changing, and is both ambiguous and unpredictable. In his book *Managing in*

Turbulent Times, author and management consultant Peter Drucker concluded: "Some time during the 1970s, the longest period of continuity in economic history came to an end. At some time during the last ten years, we moved into turbulence."[21]

Ask Students
What type of task environment does your university operate in? Explain.

Turbulent environments aren't limited to large corporations. Consider the competitive, regulatory, and technological changes faced by dentists who run their own practices. Their task environment has changed rapidly and become very complex over the past ten years, as the following Small Business Insight illustrates.

Small Business *Insight*

Dentist Wears Space Garb to Clean Teeth!

The practice of dentistry has changed dramatically in the past ten years: Dentists now wear space suits! Well, they aren't actually space suits; they simply are protection against infectious disease. Sally Marx is no exception. She has been practicing family dentistry in Louisville, Kentucky, since 1963. At that time, the typical dentist graduated from an accredited college of dentistry, established an office, and waited for patients to come. Those who did show up paid for their own dental work. The population was growing rapidly at that time and the water supplies of most communities did not contain fluoride, so finding patients with dental needs wasn't difficult.

But practicing dentistry isn't so simple for Dr. Marx in the mid-1990s. The simple/stable environment has been replaced with a complex/dynamic environment, and it shows no sign of settling down. Let's look at these differences. In 1960, the environment was stable: The supply of patients was ample, loan money to buy new equipment was fairly inexpensive, and regulation, beyond getting a license and observing continuing education requirements, was virtually nonexistent. The environment was simple: Compliance with legal requirements and awareness of changing technology were all that were necessary to be successful.

In the 1990s, however, the environment is complex: AIDS, hepatitis, and other serious infectious diseases threaten dentists and their patients; the Occupational Safety Hazards Act (OSHA) requires that the dentists provide proper attire for themselves and all patient-care personnel, in addition to proper dental equipment and supply cleaning and disposal. Revenues come from many sources, including insurance companies and health maintenance organizations (HMOs)that pay the dentist a fixed fee for each patient assigned to his or her practice. In addition to complexity, the environment is dynamic. Competition has increased. Advancements in prosthetic devices and plastics technologies continually introduce new procedures. Patients move from dentist to dentist as their insurance coverages change, often because of employment changes.

When Dr. Marx appears before her patients now, she wears a face mask, gloves, goggles, and long sleeves. Her office appears the same but behind closed doors is a fax machine and a computer with a modem to transmit insurance forms. Every workroom has a container with a skull and crossbones to indicate environmental hazardous waste. And she has ultraviolet lights to harden plastics and ceramics for use in restoring teeth to their natural appearance with crowns and plates. Has the basic work of a dentist changed? Not much. They still preserve, protect, and defend teeth. Has the practice of dentistry changed? Just ask Dr. Marx.[22]

Obviously, several environmental forces have changed the "business" of dentistry. One is the change in payment practices, as insurance companies and HMOs have replaced personal payment. Another is the emergence of two catastrophic diseases over the past fifteen years: autoimmune deficiency syndrome (AIDS) and virulent forms of hepatitis, a liver disease.

Moreover, relatively powerless dentists usually are forced to agree to the fee constraints imposed by company-purchased or other types of dental plans. Agreeing to each new constraint is preferable to the possible loss of patients and income for noncompliance. In addition, OSHA inspectors have increased their observation of dental practices to protect dentists, their patients, and dental assistants and hygienists.

Even more uncertainty faces physicians who, thirty years ago, had a paternalistic relationship with patients and the task environment. Between 1960 and 1990, the number of physicians in the United States more than doubled, from 259,000 to more than 550,000. The U.S. population, however, hasn't increased proportionately. Competitive organizations providing health care also are proliferating. They include HMOs, independent practice associations (IPAs), ambulatory care centers, outpatient clinics, and large group practices.

Ask Students

Did you think that being a physician or dentist involved so many environmental change variables? Is there similar environment in the profession you want to enter?

Turbulence in the physicians' environment is compounded by fewer total patient visits (both at offices and during hospital rounds), more group practices, and less real income for physicians in small general practices. Also, the technology affecting the provision of health care (new drugs, new diagnostic procedures, new specialties, and new cures) has grown and changed explosively. And, if all of this weren't enough, the constant threat from lawsuits and liability claims from patients (customers) has caused malpractice insurance costs to skyrocket. Clearly, the present task environment of dentists and physicians is turbulent.[23]

In the remainder of this chapter we address the three major forces in the task environment that organizations must continually monitor, diagnose, and manage. We begin with the innermost ring of Figure 3.1 and move outward—from competitive forces to technological forces to political-legal forces—in terms of domestic operations. In Chapter 4 we address the same forces in terms of international operations. Competitive forces have the greatest day-to-day impact on organizations. Most middle-level and top managers (as well as professionals such as market researchers, planning analysts, purchasing agents, and sales representatives) spend considerable time and energy monitoring, diagnosing, and figuring out how to deal with competitive forces.

3

Identify the five competitive forces that directly affect organizations in an industry.

COMPETITIVE FORCES IN THE TASK ENVIRONMENT

Organizations in any industry are directly affected by at least five competitive forces: competitors, new entrants, substitute goods and services, customers, and suppliers. The combined strength of these forces affects long-term profitability, as shown in Figure 3.4.[24] Managers must therefore monitor and diagnose each one, as well as their combined strength, before making decisions about future courses of action.

FIGURE 3.4

Competitive Forces in the Task Environment

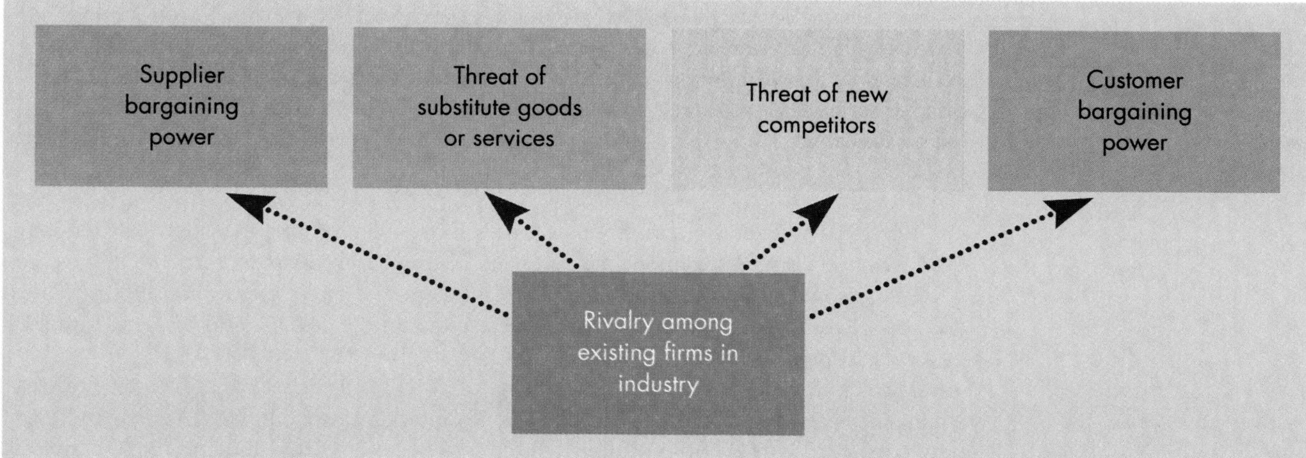

Source: Based on Porter, Michael E. *Competitive Strategy: Techniques for Analyzing Industries and Competitors.* New York: Free Press, 1980, 4.

Competitors

Aside from customers, competitors are the single most important day-to-day force facing organizations. Bruce D. Henderson, founder and chairman of the Boston Consulting Group, comments: "For virtually all organizations the critical environment constraint is their actions in relation to competitors. Therefore any change in the environment that affects any competitor will have consequences that require some degree of adaptation. This requires continual change and adaptation by all competitors merely to maintain relative position."[25]

Ethics
What ethical problems might competition cause for managers? Compare rivalry as described in the text to rivalry for grades and ethical problems in school that could result from such competition.

Rivalry among competitors produces strategies such as price cutting, advertising promotions, enhanced customer service or warranties, and improvements in product or service quality. Competitors use these strategies to try to improve their relative positions in an industry or to respond to actions by others. For example, in the airline industry when one firm cuts prices, other firms often quickly follow. All may end up worse off in the short term because lower profits or even losses may result. In the long run, though, price-cutting may increase demand for their product and leave the industry as a whole better off. Also, in the airline industry, numerous regional carriers began service following deregulation, but some larger airlines, such as People Express, Western Airlines, and Piedmont, have gone out of business.

As organizations attempt to gain market share through advertising, claims may be made about the product and/or service that are difficult to prove. For example, Procter & Gamble recently filed a truth-in-advertising complaint with the National Advertising Review Board against Arm & Hammer baking soda toothpaste for claiming that "two out of three dentists and hygienists recommend baking soda for healthier teeth and gums." Procter & Gamble argued that the statement had no scientific basis. The following Ethics Insight highlights some of the ethical challenges facing European companies who target children as customers for their products.

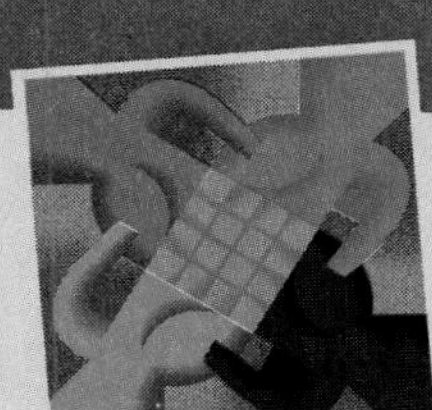

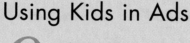

Ethics *Insight*

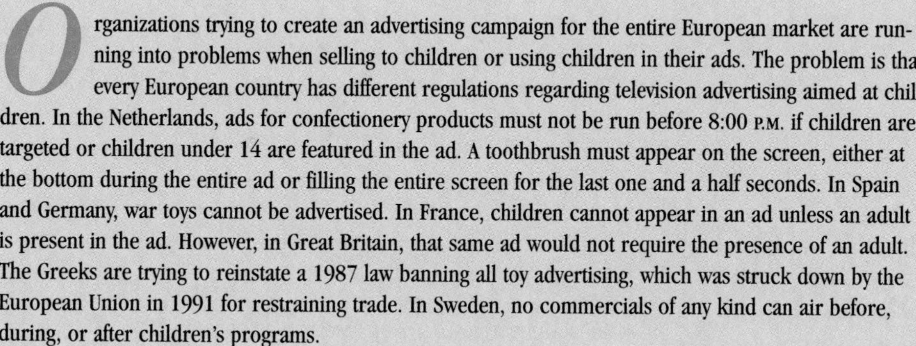

Using Kids in Ads

Organizations trying to create an advertising campaign for the entire European market are running into problems when selling to children or using children in their ads. The problem is that every European country has different regulations regarding television advertising aimed at children. In the Netherlands, ads for confectionery products must not be run before 8:00 P.M. if children are targeted or children under 14 are featured in the ad. A toothbrush must appear on the screen, either at the bottom during the entire ad or filling the entire screen for the last one and a half seconds. In Spain and Germany, war toys cannot be advertised. In France, children cannot appear in an ad unless an adult is present in the ad. However, in Great Britain, that same ad would not require the presence of an adult. The Greeks are trying to reinstate a 1987 law banning all toy advertising, which was struck down by the European Union in 1991 for restraining trade. In Sweden, no commercials of any kind can air before, during, or after children's programs.

By endorsing self-regulation, members of the European Association of Advertising might be restricting some organizations' ability to enter a market and make a profit. With the diversity of European countries and their regulations, what ethical problems might organizations face when trying to reach kids with their product advertising on TV?[26]

New Entrants

The threat or reality of increased competition in an industry depends on the relative ease with which new firms can compete with established firms. In an industry with low barriers to entry (e.g., the photocopy industry or the fast-food industry) competition will be fierce. The airline industry is a particularly interesting case because it has had both high and low barriers to entry during the past ten years. Economies of scale, product differentiation, capital requirements, and government regulation are four common factors that need to be diagnosed in assessing barriers to entry. Let's see how they have affected airline competition.

Ask Students
Would increasing class size at universities gain economies of scale?

Ask Students
How can you use product differentiation in your search for a job? How can you differentiate yourself from all the others graduating in your field from this and other universities at the same time? Write down your unique selling points and share them with another student in the class. Give each other feedback as to whether the differentiation is substantial.

Economies of scale refer to decreases in per unit costs as the volume of goods and services produced by a firm increases. The potential for economies of scale in the airline industry is substantial. For example, the McDonnell Douglas MD-11 is a jumbo jet with relatively high fixed costs to fly (e.g., cost of the aircraft and maintenance, fuel costs, landing fees, and crew costs). Even when every passenger seat is filled and all the passengers bring extra baggage, the bottom portion of the plane contains an enormous amount of unused space. Therefore, when American Airlines loads freight in addition to passengers on its Dallas-Tokyo flights, it takes advantage of the economies of scale made possible by the MD-11.

Product differentiation is uniqueness in quality, price, design, brand image, or customer service that gives one firm's product an edge over another firm's. Its frequent-flyer program is one way American Airlines tried to differentiate its service from Delta, USAir, and other airlines. Members qualify for free tickets after flying a certain number of miles. In addition, frequent fliers receive hotel and car rental discounts and other travel-related benefits. But other airlines copied American's AAdvantage Frequent Flyer Program, eliminating this aspect of product differentiation as a way to gain a competitive advantage. In addition to frequent flyer programs, Southwest Airlines offers its Friends Fly Free program and unlimited free beverages to its passengers. TWA provides more leg room between seats on its planes.[27]

Capital requirements are the dollars needed to finance equipment, supplies, advertising, research and development, and the like. The capital requirements for starting an airline run into the tens of millions of dollars. Recently, however, some new airlines, such as Comair Air and Kiwi Airlines, have entered the marketplace by hiring an air charter service to provide passenger service. Their start-up investment was only a monthly fee-for-service.

Government regulation is a barrier to entry if it bars or severely restricts potential new entrants to an industry. Before deregulation of the airline industry in 1978, the interstate airlines comprised a cartel regulated by the Civil Aeronautics Board (CAB), which set fares and controlled routes. From 1945 to 1975 the air-carrier industry grew three times faster than the economy in general, yet no new trunk carriers entered the industry nor did any existing carriers file for bankruptcy.[28] After deregulation, fourteen new nonunion airlines emerged. With their lower labor, maintenance, and capital costs, these new airlines immediately began to compete with the eleven established trunk airlines (including American, TWA, and Delta) by cutting prices. The price wars and other forms of competition stimulated by deregulation were followed by a number of airline failures (Braniff) and mergers (People Express and New York Air into Continental). The decline in the number of domestic trunk airlines has led some politicians and consumer groups to call for reregulation of the airlines.

Substitute Goods and Services

In a general sense, all competitors produce **substitute goods or services,** or goods or services that can easily replace their own. For example, the introduction of desktop publishing systems by IBM, Apple, and Dell has enabled graphic design companies to use personal computers to design and typeset brochures, catalogs, flyers, and even books. Desktop publishing or typesetting *software* thus substitutes for the services of typesetting firms at a fraction of their cost. Many organizations (e.g., Westinghouse, Xerox, and the U.S. State Department) commonly use fax, e-mail, or overnight delivery services as a substitute for the U.S. Postal Service. Electronic surveillance systems, such as those produced by Sensormatic, have drastically reduced the need for retail personnel to monitor continuously all parts of a store and the behavior of customers. Electronic systems thus substitute for observation by salesclerks, managers, and security guards.

Customers

Customers for goods or services naturally try to force down prices, obtain more or higher quality products (while holding price constant), and increase competition among sellers by playing one against the other. Customer bargaining power is likely to be relatively great under the following circumstances.

- *The customer purchases a large volume relative to the supplier's total sales.* J.C. Penney, Kmart, and Wal-Mart have clout because their large-volume purchases account for a sizable percentage of some suppliers' total sales.
- *The product or service represents a significant expenditure by the customer.* Customers generally are motivated to cut a cost that constitutes a large portion of their total costs. An individual will spend much more time and effort to obtain a rock-bottom price on a new car than on a car wash, a cheeseburger, or a paperback book.
- *Large customers pose a threat of backward integration.* **Backward integration** is when a company enters the business of its suppliers, usually to ensure component quality, on-time delivery, or stable prices. McDonald's threatened to bake its own bread, grow its own potatoes, and raise its own cattle to get lower prices and better quality from suppliers.
- *Customers have readily available alternatives for the same services or products.* For example, a consumer may not have a strong preference between Wendy's and McDonald's, a Ford truck and a Chevrolet truck, or *VISA* and American Express. The Quality Insight that follows demonstrates how Barnes and Noble differentiates itself from Waldenbooks, Borders Books and Music, and Taylors by providing quality service.

Teaching Tip
Have students divide into groups of 5. Ask each group to list the four circumstances under which customers have relatively greater power than the seller. Then ask them to identify the relative power of students, fast-food customers, and the U.S. Department of Defense. Discuss each circumstance and type of customer to determine which customer is the most powerful under which circumstance.

Quality *Insight*

Books and Coffee for an Evening of Entertainment

Barnes and Noble is known to many college students as the company that operates the campus bookstore. To people from New York, it is remembered as a small, not very exciting bookstore in Manhattan. But today, Barnes and Noble is a 975-outlet chain of bookstores that provide a wide selection of books, comfortable seating, and cappuccino. This merchandising success stems from several insights on the part of CEO Leonard Riggio. His first insight was that *shopping is a form of entertainment.* In fact, shopping apparently is an alternative to movies, theater, and party-going for dual career families who are struggling to manage time and enjoy the social ambiance of malls. His second insight was that *books are consumer products.* However, this insight wasn't unique to Barnes and Noble. Waldenbooks and the other chains already knew that books were consumer products, and they also knew that people would probably buy audiotapes, books, magazines, and software at the same outlet. So Riggio differentiated his stores with posters, wall decorations, attractive furniture, and fancy logo-imprinted bags.

Recently, Barnes and Noble created superstores. In these large outlets, people can spend a Saturday evening eating pastry, drinking fancy coffees, reading trendy books, and, of course, buying some of the books at competitive prices. In Ann Arbor, Michigan, the Barnes and Noble bookstore is a date location. It is open until midnight and serves food until 11:00 P.M. Single people can spend their evenings in the bookstore without feeling uncomfortable.

Riggio thus converted a commodity into a differentiated product while maintaining a competitive price structure. In doing so, he gained a competitive advantage. But look out. In every major city and many college towns, other entrepreneurs are doing the same thing. So the advantage won't last forever![29]

The Barnes and Noble example shows how the characteristics of product differentiation and price-sensitive customers can combine to provide a competitive edge in a crowded industry. Barnes and Noble's size also makes it a strong customer of publishing companies on many college campuses.

Suppliers

The bargaining power of suppliers often controls how much they can raise prices above their costs or reduce the quality of goods and services they provide before losing customers. Book publishers used to be able to dictate the net selling prices of books to merchants. However, large volume purchasers such as Barnes and Noble, Waldenbooks, and Borders Books and Music have demanded price breaks for large lots to enable them to sell at discounts to compete with Sam's, Target, and Kmart. Thus book publishers have become less able to dictate prices to such merchants.

In aircraft manufacturing, Boeing dominates the commercial aircraft market. It holds 54 percent of the world market because of its reputation for quality, not because of low price. Its supplier power comes primarily from technological leadership, high quality, and excellent service. Of course, Boeing's prices probably are lower than they would be without competition from two major rivals: Airbus Industrie and McDonnell Douglas Corporation.[30]

Ask Students
How powerful are film studios as suppliers? Why?

All businesses play the role of supplier and customer in their competitive environments. In these sometimes conflicting roles, they may not have equal power.[31] For example, in its role as customer, Boeing now combines orders for similar parts for various models of jet aircraft to get prices from suppliers that are more competitive than those given when it bought the items separately. In its role as supplier, Boeing used to have to fill 600 or more requests from commercial airline customers for alterations to basic specifications. Now that it has an established reputation, its bargaining power with airlines is considerably greater, and customers have less of a free hand in designing their planes. As an accommodation, Boeing has a catalog from which customers may select some option packages.[32] Barnes and Noble is a strong customer of publishing houses owing to the size of its retailer network. However, it faces stiff competition as a supplier because customers may patronize other bookstores, department stores, and discount stores.

Copyrights and patents generally increase supplier strength over defined periods of time. The prices of movie tickets and videos of popular films are higher than they might otherwise be because of copyright protection. This protection prevents suppliers from copying and distributing a film or video without permission from and payment of a royalty to the original producer. In general, high supplier strength in unrestricted markets tends to be short-lived, as demonstrated by the personal computer industry. The PC manufacturers know that their innovations will be copied quickly. Toshiba and Texas Instrument notebook computers, for example, commanded high prices for about a year. With numerous brands of similar products now available, prices have fallen, eroding the profit margin for the manufacturers.

Ethics
Bootlegging reduces the advantage of a supplier's copyright. How ethical is bootlegging? Should something be done to prevent it? If so, what?

Supplier-Customer Alliances. Some total quality programs have increased the strength of suppliers by qualifying them as the single-source supplier for a large company. Asahi Glass Company, for example, is the sole supplier to the Toyota Camry factory in Georgetown, Kentucky, as well as to Honda in Marysville, Ohio. Rohm and Haas is the sole supplier of certain resins to Ford for use in the paints and interiors of its cars. And Johnson Control's Globe Battery company is the sole supplier of car batteries to Nissan. These companies have driven off the competition by agreeing to close collaboration and management control by these large customers.[33]

Discussion Question 3
What are the five competitive forces in an industry? How have these forces affected competition in higher education?

4

Explain why technological forces have become increasingly important in strategic planning.

TECHNOLOGICAL FORCES AND INFORMATION TECHNOLOGY

In Chapter 2 we defined the transformation process as the technology that changes organizational inputs into outputs. **Technology** is the knowledge, tools, techniques, and actions used to transform materials, information, and other inputs into finished goods and services.[34] A technology may be as simple as making coffee at a restaurant or as complicated as the engineering transformations in manufacturing autuomobiles.

Impact of Technology

Technological forces play an increasingly pivotal role in creating and changing an organization's task environment. Technological change eliminates the present and helps create the future. New technologies force organizations to reconsider their purposes and methods of operation or face extinction.[35] The United States and several other industrial societies have become information societies. This shift was made possible by the explosion in computer-based and telecommunication technologies. One example is the personal computer and its integration with mainframe computers and telecommunications systems to form supernets. Through them, organizations can collect, process, and transmit vast amounts of data quickly and economically. For instance, Kodak now supplies photographic dealers with a microcomputer and software system that enables the dealers to order Kodak products directly rather than through wholesalers. The management of information technology is woven into various chapters of this book, and all of Chapter 19 is devoted to this topic.

Role in Strategy. Computer-based information technologies are now essential in most organizations, which is one reason for including technological forces as part of the task environment. Inadequate information technologies can severely limit strategic options for both manufacturing and service organizations. For example, a large bank couldn't provide account balances on line to customers because of limitations in its computer software. A large, urban public library couldn't accept fines and check in a book at the same workstation, causing it to hire extra personnel. A brokerage company could not satisfy its clients' repeated requests for an integrated picture of its holdings because the information from its equity, bond, and commodity account management systems couldn't be easily combined. Because of weaknesses in its inventory management systems, a large truck manufacturer was losing track of cabs costing $100,000 that had been taken off the production line for rework.[36]

Information technology creates options, including the following, that simply weren't feasible with older technologies.

- Computer-aided design linked to versatile, computer-controlled machines permits short production runs of custom designs with economies of scale approaching those of traditional large-scale manufacturing facilities.
- Consumers can shop via home computers and "electronic shopping malls" more easily than using the Yellow Pages and telephones.
- With on-line, real-time financial management systems, managers can determine profit and loss positions daily, which was impossible with manual methods and earlier stages of computer technology.
- Retail banking customers can perform numerous banking functions from remote locations, including ATMs in shopping centers, apartment building lobbies, corporate offices, and out-of-state banks, and in homes with personal computers.[36]

Teaching Tip
Tell students that previous generations had to type their papers manually instead of on computers with word processing software, and use paper card catalogs instead of online library reference systems.

Today, the building of an international information highway extends far beyond simple message systems and bulletin boards. Satellites, cellular towers, and fiber optic telephone cables allow individuals and companies to exchange voice, data, and graphic messages in real time. Futurists speculate that within five to ten years everyone will have personal numbers for all the telecommunication devices they use; that wireless technology will replace twisted pair, coaxial, and fiber optics cable; and that telephone, fax, and computing will be integrated in hand-held devices. There is reason to be optimistic about these projections. In Sweden, Erikkson telephone customers already have personal cards that can be slipped into any device so that they can receive calls anywhere in their calling areas. Mexico is considering skipping wired systems in favor of cellular

Teaching Tip
Impress upon students that computer literacy is crucial to their careers. Encourage them to be computer literate and to stay abreast of the latest in hardware and software.

Teaching Tip
Some MBA programs supply their students with laptops so that professors, students, and staffs can communicate easily with one another.

technologies. And personal communicators made by an AT&T/IBM joint venture will permit phone, fax, and computing with a pen input screen.[37]

As a result, organizations will change the way they conduct business, and new companies that have developed and manufactured such devices will become household words like AT&T and IBM. The following Global Insight describes how some companies are gambling that access to the information highway will control the future of information technology.

Global *Insight*

Traveling the Information Superhighway

While the politicians try to decide what it is, the information superhighway is being put together by entrepreneurs, corporations, and universities around the world. This superhighway, unlike the Interstate Highway System begun in the 1950s, is an invisible web of machines, software, data, and graphics that interconnects users from throughout the world. This superhighway offers vast opportunities to those who design and develop its component parts and to those who use it to speed up organizational activities. Let's look at some of the organizations competing in this industry.

Oracle is a $1.6 billion Silicon Valley company that hasn't yet become a household word. The company is the number one producer of database software used by large corporations today. But CEO and part owner Larry Ellison isn't satisfied with his company's successes. He sees its database technology expanding to include multimedia databases so that global merchandising bazaars can bring together such diverse sellers and customers as a borrower in Iowa and a lender in Germany, or a bronze manufacturer in Korea with a vase buyer in Minneapolis.

But that database is a only small piece of the whole. To access the database, both industrial and end user consumers will have to use an array of digital signal processing (DSP) methods—a U.S. created and dominated technology. Digital signals drive new generations of displays called high-definition television (HDTV), new generations of cellular technology, and new generations of wired telephone connections. The use of DSP permits compression, so that much larger amounts of data, particularly graphics, can be transferred around the world instantaneously.

Although relatively new U.S. companies, such as Sprint, have been leaders in the global effort to create the information superhighway, older, more established players are not out of the race. Microsoft has invested nearly 25 percent of its $400 million annual research and development budget in developing operating systems that make user access to the information superhighway appealing to even the most unsophisticated user. Deregulated European and Latin American telephone companies also are racing to update their equipment so that their customers will not defect to the communications companies of other countries.

The information superhighway represents a change in technology for all companies. Like the computer-driven engineering technologies that revitalized manufacturing, the information superhighway has the ability to change the basic ways in which people communicate at work and home. Consider the International Cargo Management System. With this information system, Seal and other cargo carriers can send an electronic guard with cargo that will let the shipper visually inspect the location, condition, and environment of the product. When the container is on land, the signal is sent via cellular carrier. When the cargo is at sea, ship-to-shore or global communication satellite program (GPS) can track the cargo. It is more than a cute gadget because theft is a major cost for shippers; more than $5 billion in losses are reported annually in the United States alone.

Joining the information superhighway is the wave of the future. It presents unparalleled opportunities for those firms who do and can lead to demise for those firms who don't.[38]

The information superhighway will affect every organization in the years ahead. Because it represents new technology, this element of the task environment undoubtedly will create turbulence in the political-legal environment as customers and managers struggle with the problem of having confidential information travel around the world and the problems of equipment and operator safety.

5

Describe the principal political strategies used by managers to cope with external political-legal forces

POLITICAL-LEGAL FORCES

Societies try to resolve conflicts over values and beliefs through their legal and political systems. For instance, in the United States and Canada the concepts of individual freedom, freedom of the press, property rights, and private enterprise are widely accepted. But these countries' legislative bodies, regulatory agencies, interest groups, and courts operate—often in conflict with one another—to define the meaning and influence the day-to-day interpretation of these values.

Many political and legal forces directly affect the way organizations operate. Changes in political forces have been especially significant during the past twenty-five years and will continue to affect organizations in the future. To achieve organizational goals, managers must accurately diagnose these forces and find useful ways to anticipate, respond to, or avoid the disturbances they cause.

For many organizations (e.g., telephone companies, banks, and public utilities), government regulation is a central aspect of the task environment. Consider how two of the five federal credit laws affect customers and creditors each time they do business in the United States.

Ethics

Few people realize that credit reports are largely unprotected by rules, laws, or codes of ethics. Companies are free to pore over, analyze, sell, and pair credit information with other data to obtain a profile of consumers' habits. Is this practice ethical?

- The *Equal Credit Opportunity Act* entitles the customer to be considered for credit without regard to race, color, age, sex, or marital status. Although the act doesn't guarantee that the customer will get credit, it does ensure that the credit grantor applies tests of credit-worthiness fairly and impartially.
- The *Truth in Lending Act* says that credit grantors must reveal the "true" cost of using credit—for instance, the annual interest rate the customer will be paying. In the case of a revolving charge account, the customer must also be told the monthly interest rate and the minimum monthly payment.

Political-legal forces operating on an organization extend beyond laws and government institutions. They encompass the entire range of task environment components—individuals, groups, and institutions—that have the power to affect the organization's future. Competitors, customers, shareholders, labor unions, consumer groups, minority groups, environmental groups, and foreign governments—all can and do directly influence managers' decisions. Conversely, managers' decisions can and do influence those groups.

As shown in Figure 3.5, managers use five basic political strategies to cope with the political-legal forces operating in their environments: negotiation, lobbying, alliance, representation, and socialization. These strategies are not mutually exclusive, are usually used in some combination, and often contain elements of the others. Negotiation probably is the most important political strategy because each of the other four strategies contains some degree of negotiation.

Negotiation is the process by which two or more individuals or groups having both common and conflicting goals present and discuss proposals in an attempt to reach an agreement.[39] Negotiation can take place only when the two parties believe that some form of agreement is possible and mutually beneficial. Recall that, in the U.S. Sugar Company example at the beginning of the chapter, the outcome was based on negotiations between the company and various regulatory agencies. However, some of the environmental groups continue to press for tighter standards and more phosphate cleanup, so the issues haven't been completely resolved.

Lobbying is an attempt to influence government decisions by providing officials with information on the anticipated effects of legislation or regulatory rulings. The U.S. Congress and regulatory agencies, such as the Securities and Exchange Commission (SEC), the Federal Communications Commission (FCC), and the Interstate Commerce

FIGURE 3.5

Managerial Political Strategies

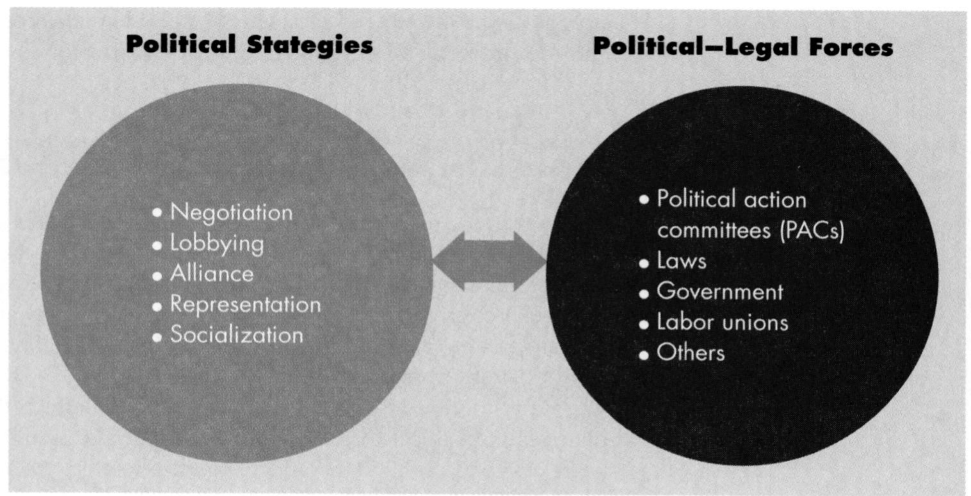

Commission (ICC), are the targets of continual lobbying efforts by organizations affected by their decisions.[40] Organizations whose stability, growth, and survival are directly affected by government decisions typically use their top managers to lobby for them. Postmaster General Anthony Frank personally lobbies Congress on legislation affecting the U.S. Postal Service. Of course, major users of the U.S. Postal Service also lobby Anthony Frank and Congress to obtain more favorable postal regulations or to ward off proposed changes that would be unfavorable to those users.

Only the largest organizations (e.g., Brown and Williamson Tobacco Company, NBC, AT&T, and Exxon) can afford to lobby for themselves. The most common form of lobbying is by associations, representing the interests of groups of individuals or organizations.[41] Approximately 4,000 national lobbying organizations maintain staffs in Washington, D.C. An additional 75,000 state and local associations and organizations occasionally lobby Washington's decision makers. Two of the largest associations representing business interests are the National Chamber of Commerce, with about 36,000 business and organizational members, and the National Association of Manufacturers, with about 12,500 member corporations.[42] The American Association of Retired Persons (AARP), with more than 33 million members, is the largest U.S. association representing individual interests. The AARP lobbies on behalf of U.S. citizens aged 50 and over and has a paid staff of 1,300, with headquarters in the heart of the nation's capital.[43]

Ethics
Is hiring lobbyists and public relations firms to influence legislation and public attitudes ethical? Does taking a public official out to dinner or inviting a client to play golf at your club count as corruption—or is it simply a display of hospitality and appreciation?

An **alliance** is a unified effort involving two or more organizations, groups, or individuals to achieve common goals with respect to a particular issue.[44] Alliances, especially those created to influence government actions, typically form around issues of economic self-interest.[45] Economic issues that motivate the formation of alliances include government policy (e.g., the control of raw materials or taxes), foreign relations (e.g., the control of foreign sales or investment in overseas plants), and labor relations (e.g., the control of industrywide salaries and benefits, as within the construction industry or the National Football League). Alliances often are used for the following purposes.

- Oppose or support legislation, nomination of heads of regulatory agencies, and regulations issued by such agencies.
- Improve competitiveness of two or more organizations through collaboration. Corning Glass uses its twenty-three joint ventures with foreign partners such as Siemens (Germany), Samsung (Korea), Asahi Chemical (Japan), and Vitro (Mexico) to penetrate and thrive in a growing number of glass markets.
- Promote particular products or services, such as oranges, computers, and electricity. For example, the Edison Electric Institute promotes both the use and conservation of electrical energy.

- Construct facilities beyond the resources of any one organization, such as a new super chip plant. IBM, Toshiba, and Siemens have dedicated $750 million to develop jointly a new 256 megabit chip.
- Represent the interests of specific groups, such as women, the elderly, minorities, and particular industries. The National Association of Manufacturers (NAM) lobbies the U.S. Congress to pass legislation favorable to its members, including restricting imports on foreign goods, such as shoes and automobiles, and trying to open new markets in foreign countries, such as rice, in Japan.

An alliance both broadens and limits managerial power. When an alliance makes possible the attainment of goals that a single individual or organization would be unable to attain, it broadens managerial power. When an alliance requires a commitment to making certain decisions jointly in the future, it limits managerial power. Members of OPEC periodically negotiate production levels and the price to be charged for oil. These agreements are intended to broaden OPEC's power by generating more revenue for its members. However, to be successful in this endeavor, OPEC members must abide by the limits on production agreed to.

Ask Students
Why and how might fraternities and sororities cooperate for mutual self-interest in a joint venture?

A *joint venture,* which typically involves two or more firms becoming partners to form a separate entity, is a common example of an alliance.[46] Each partner benefits from the others' competence, which allows them to achieve their goals more quickly and efficiently. For example, CBS formed several joint ventures in the 1980s: with IBM and Sears to develop and market Prodigy on-line services; with Twentieth Century-Fox to develop videotapes; and with Columbia Pictures (Coca-Cola) and Home Box Office (Time, Inc.) to develop motion pictures. BellSouth recently formed an alliance with IBM to obtain access to multimedia technologies.

Teaching Tip
Tell students how many professional associations you belong to and what they're for.

Representation refers to membership in an outside organization to serve the interests of the member's organization or group. Representation strategy often is subtle and indirect. School administrators, for example, often receive paid time off and the use of school resources to participate in voluntary community associations that might sup-

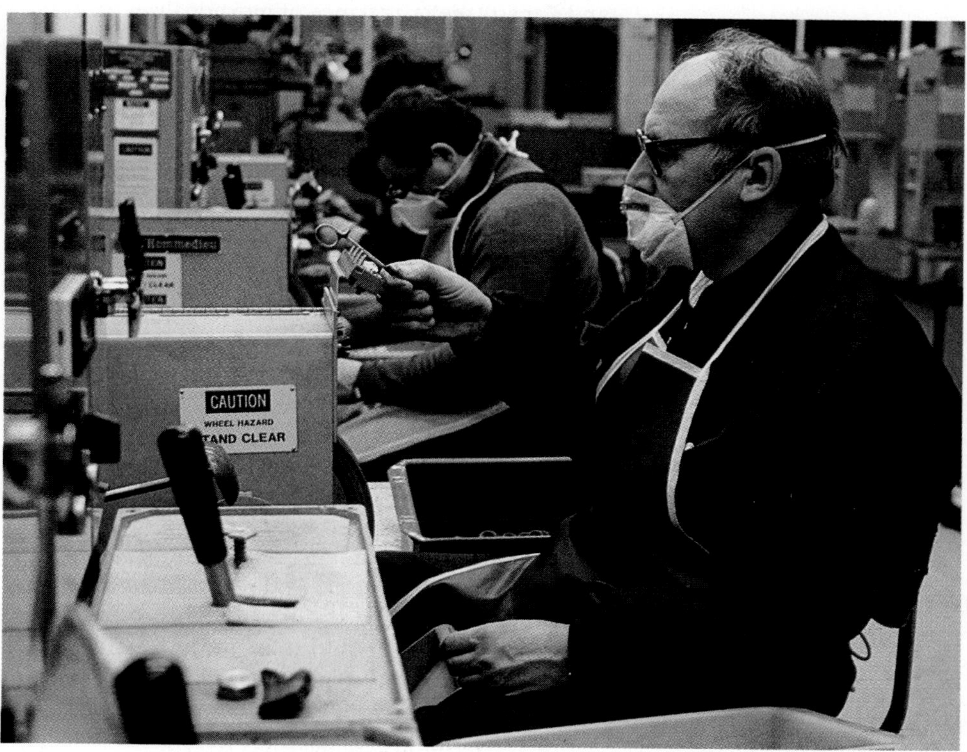

A joint venture typically involves two or more firms becoming partners to form a separate entity. Baxter International has a joint venture in this Russian surgical instrument plant.

port the school system, such as the PTA, Chamber of Commerce, Elks, Kiwanis, Moose, Rotary, and United Way. A more direct form of representation, often based on some legal requirement, occurs when a specific group selects representatives to give it a voice in an organization's decisions. For example, union members elect officers to represent them in dealing with management.

Corporate boards of directors, the top-level policy-making groups in firms, are elected by and legally required to represent shareholders' interests. The National Association of Corporate Directors, however, suggests a much broader role for board members: Board members should ensure that long-term strategic goals and plans are established; that a proper management structure (organization, systems, and people) is in place to achieve these goals; and that the organization acts to maintain its integrity, reputation, and responsibility to its various constituencies.[47] The board's responsibility to monitor and control the actions of the chief executive officer and other top officers is essential to its representing the interests of the shareholders.[48]

Socialization is the process by which people learn the values held by an organization or the broader society. The assumption is that people who accept and act in accordance with these basic values are less likely to sympathize with positions that threaten the organization or the political system. The so-called American business creed stresses the idea that a decentralized, privately owned, and competitive system in which price is the major regulator, should be continued and that citizens should oppose government actions interfering with or threatening this system. Most U.S. and Canadian businesspeople subscribe to these beliefs and act on them.

Socialization includes formal and informal attempts by organizations to mold new employees to accept certain desired attitudes and ways of dealing with others and their jobs. At its headquarters in Crotonville, New York, General Electric introduces thousands of its managers to the company's values and philosophy.[49] These values include identifying and eliminating unproductive work in order to energize employees and to encourage creativity and feelings of ownership at all levels. Xerox uses its training facility in Leesburg, Virginia, to influence the attitudes of new managers. Of course, top management's attempts may be offset or reinforced by the expectations of and pressures exerted by fellow workers or other groups within the organization.

Discussion Question 4
What are some of the political tactics that managers can use to increase their influence in their environment?

The political strategies discussed are subject to cultural forces. In the United States and Canada the importance of individualism limits the extent to which organizations can use the socialization strategy. Too much or what may be seen as the "wrong kind" of socialization is likely to be met with resistance and charges of invasion of privacy or violation of individual rights.

CHAPTER SUMMARY

The purpose of this chapter was to help develop your diagnostic and monitoring skills with respect to the external environment. We discussed and gave examples of various reactive and proactive approaches that organizations can use in coping with general environmental forces (culture) and task environmental forces (competition, technology, and political-legal forces). Such forces create both opportunities and threats and will challenge all the skills and competencies you acquire.

1 ***Describe the main forces in the external business environment and how they influence organizations.***

The general environment includes the external factors that usually affect organizations, either directly or indirectly. It encompasses the type of economic system and current economic conditions, type of political system, natural resources, demographics of the population, and the ecosystem. Cultural forces, primarily working through value systems, shape the viewpoints and decision-making processes of managers and other employees. Hofstede's work-related value framework has four dimensions: power distance, uncertainty avoidance, individualism, and masculinity.

2 ***Define the role of the task environment and how it changes.***
The task environment includes all the external factors and groups—customers, competitors, technology, regulatory agencies, laws, and the like—that *directly* influence an organization's growth, success, and survival. Environmental forces are increasingly turbulent and global, requiring managers to monitor and diagnose constantly the type of task environment they face.

3 ***Identify the five competitive forces that directly affect organizations in an industry.***
Managers must assess and respond to five competitive forces in the task environment: competitors, new entrants, substitute goods and services, customers, and suppliers.

4 ***Explain why technological forces have become increasingly important in strategic planning.***
Technological forces in the task environment are rapidly changing the specific knowledge, tools, and techniques used to transform materials, information, and other inputs into particular goods or services. Usable technologies include four interconnecting elements: hardware, software, communications linkages, and brainware.

5 ***Describe the principal political strategies used by managers to cope with external forces.***
Political-legal forces, which used to be in the background, now often directly influence the way organizations operate. Five political strategies that managers use in coping with political-legal forces in the task environment are negotiation, lobbying, alliances, representation, and socialization.

QUESTIONS FOR DISCUSSION

1. How have changes in the economic and political systems affected task environments of organizations?
2. How do cultural values influence a manager's decision making?
3. What are the five competitive forces in an industry? How have these forces affected competition in higher education?
4. What are some of the political tactics that managers can use to increase their influence in their environment?
5. What advice would you give to a manager who was being transferred to a facility in Mexico for two years? To France? How did the cultural values in each country influence your answers?

FROM WHERE YOU SIT

1. Describe an office that uses the new information superhighway. How could you use these new tools to assist in you selling Procter & Gamble (e.g., Tide or Crest toothpaste) products to grocers?
2. What new job opportunities might be available to you as a result of changes in the general business environment?
3. How have the five competitive forces affected your local bank's operations?
4. Are there any ethical considerations for companies that attempt to overcome threats from new entrants? Do these considerations vary from country to country? If so, cite two examples.
5. You are transferring a Mexican national manager from your company's plant in Mexico to a two-year assignment in the United States. Develop a cultural description of the new environment that this individual will confront, based on Hofstede's four dimensions of culture.

SKILL-BUILDING EXERCISE

Assessing Tolerance for Ambiguity

Intolerance for ambiguity is defined as the tendency to perceive ambiguous situations as threatening. Conversely, tolerance for ambiguity is the tendency to perceive ambiguous situations as acceptable or desirable. Ambiguity arises from novelty, complexity, or problems that have no obvious solutions. Complex/changing task environments usually possess these characteristics. The following statements will permit you to assess your own tolerance for ambiguity. Answer the following questions *yes* if you agree or *no* if you disagree with the statement.

1. An expert who doesn't come up with a definite answer probably doesn't know too much. _______
2. There is really no such thing as a problem that can't be solved. _______
3. A good job is one where what is to be done and how it is to be done are always clear. _______
4. In the long run, more can get done by tackling small, simple problems rather than large complicated problems. _______
5. What we are used to is always preferable to what is unfamiliar. _______
6. A person who leads an even, regular life in which few surprises or unexpected happenings arise really has a lot to be grateful for. _______
7. I like parties where I know most of the people more than parties where all or most of the people are strangers. _______
8. The sooner we all acquire similar values and ideals, the better. _______
9. I would like to live in a foreign country for a while. _______
10. People who fit their lives into a schedule probably miss most of the joy of living. _______
11. Tackling a complicated problem is more fun than solving a simple one. _______
12. Often the most interesting and stimulating people are those who don't mind being original or different. _______
13. People who insist on a yes or no answer just don't know how complicated things really are. _______
14. Many of our most important decisions are based on insufficient information. _______
15. Teachers or supervisors who hand out vague assignments give you a chance to show initiative and originality. _______
16. A good teacher is one who makes you wonder about your way of looking at things. _______

Scoring

For items 1–8, give yourself 5 points for every *No* and 1 point for every *Yes.*
For items 9–16, give yourself 5 points for every *Yes* and 1 point for every *No.*
Add the total score. The higher your score, the more comfortable you might be with ambiguity and ambiguous situations.
Now, using the same scoring system, add up your points for items 1, 2, and 14. This score indicates your tolerance for situations that cannot be solved. Add up your points for items 3, 4, 8, 10, 11, 12, 13, 15, and 16. This score indicates your tolerance for ambiguity caused by the complexity of the situation. Add items 5, 6, 7, and 9. This score indicates your tolerance for ambiguity caused by the novelty of the situation.[50]

CRITICAL THINKING CASE

Ford *Had* a Better Idea . . . Who Will Have It Next?

The future of Detroit as the center of automaking depends to some degree on the ability of U.S. companies to develop a generation of ultraclean, ultraefficient vehicles. The industry has been in turmoil for nearly two decades. The first sign of trouble came in the mid-1970s with the OPEC oil embargo and a sudden perception of the doubtful future of fossil fuels. Chrysler, Ford, and GM were forced to take notice of the smaller Japanese imports that were outselling their larger, gas-guzzling vehicles. As consumers continued to buy Japanese cars, they became aware of the much higher defect rates of U.S. vehicles.

At first, U.S. automobile manufacturers were puzzled by how the Japanese could produce high-quality, fuel-efficient, and (at the time) cheaper cars. They soon discovered that Japanese car companies were using a totally different type of technology to design and manufacture their vehicles. Known as Design for Flexible Manufacturing Systems (DFMS), or concurrent engineering, all cars designs were based on feedback from many sources in addition to the input of designers and plant engineers. No part of the vehicle was considered sacred, and all assemblies and components were redesigned by function. In the process, Toyota reduced the number of parts in a brake assembly from 14 to 5. New information technologies permitted inventory reductions. This change from a sequential, mass-assembly technology was fundamental and affected the entire industry.

Each U.S. auto manufacturer responded with an "experiment." Ford was the first to try to reproduce the qualities of the Japanese cars by combining defect-free vehicles with many features at a moderate price. The Team Taurus experiment created the best-selling vehicle of the early 1990s. Chrysler attempted a series of experiments that failed before it finally introduced its "cab forward" line, also known as the Intrepid, Concord, and Vision models. These vehicles—designed by combining customers' desires, Chrysler's profit goals, and its car designers' dreams—have received acclaim from car buffs as well as the Canadian auto-workers at the newly refurbished plant near Windsor, Ontario. General Motors designed and built its Saturn plant differently from all its other facilities. The Saturn, which has had some profit problems, has nevertheless been a consumer success.

With auto quality problems barely solved, the U.S. economy went into decline, causing a slowdown in sales and forcing U.S. car manufacturers to lay off workers. The recovery from this recession was different from that of previous recessions. A full recovery and return to high-wage work did not occur. Automakers were forced to rethink their product lines and the ways in which cars were purchased. This rethinking led to a trimming of product lines and promotion of leasing as an option to buying. The General Motors Acceptance Corporation is the most profitable of GM's businesses at present.

But the pressures for change have not let up. The problem of the 1990s is pressure from the regulatory environment. California has passed legislation mandating that 20 percent of the vehicles driven there be powered by electricity by 1998. Concurrently, the federal government initiated a $1 billion program to create an affordable family sedan with three times the fuel efficiency of today's average car. Undoubtedly, the future holds more regulation for auto manufacturers.

Entrepreneurs are already busy trying to meet the mandates and proposed mandates. In Palm Bay, Florida, near Cape Canaveral, Renaissance Cars has created an electric car that sells for $12,500 and can go about 40 miles at 60 miles per hour. CalStart, a California-based group of alternative vehicle companies, supports these efforts. Some pessimists even believe that the auto of the future may be designed and built outside the United States, while political factions here argue about how to allocate the money.[51]

Questions

1. Imagine that you are the CEO of Ford. Where would you look for opportunities? Threats? Suppose that you were the Dean of an engineering school. Would your programs be enhanced or jeopardized by the potential mandated changes in autos?
2. Can any of the big three automakers respond to the new clean air and efficiency rules? Why or why not?
3. Does an efficient and clean auto have to be powered by electricity? What other options exist?
4. Describe the auto of the future (year 2004, according to federal guidelines). Who might build it?

VIDEO CASE

Glaxo Gets Ready for a New Health Care System

Ulcers, headaches, asthma, and upset stomachs are common complaints of the 1990s. However, Glaxo Pharmaceuticals, the U.S. division of Britain's Glaxo holdings, has products to treat these ailments. Glaxo is best known for its Zantac ulcer treatment product. In addition, the pharmaceutical giant with facilities in the Research Triangle Park, North Carolina, also makes Imitrex for treating migraine headaches, Ventolin for asthma, and Zofran for counteracting nausea.

Until recently, Glaxo has maintained a product line of expensive prescription drugs with the support of reimbursement from health care plans. Several recent developments threaten Glaxo's prosperity, however.

The first is the change in the regulatory environment for health care. Large purchasing blocks responsible for delivering less expensive services are balking at the high price of some patent-protected drugs, such as Zantac. This drug currently provides about 40 percent of U.S. revenues for the company. Although Zantac is patent-protected until 2002, health care providers are pressing for a less expensive alternative. Access to this global $8.4 billion market is shaping up to be the biggest, costliest scramble for market share in drug industry history. Already, Glaxo's largest competitor, SmithKline Beecham PLC, has felt its effects. On May 17, 1994, SmithKline's anti-ulcer blockbuster, Tagamet, lost its patent protection in the United States, unleashing a flood of cheaper generics onto the American market. Already, SmithKline is offering price cuts of up to 80 percent to protect Tagamet's $1 billion in sales, two-thirds of it in the United States, from ten generic rivals expected to enter the fray. Novopharm, a generic drug company in Ontario, Canada, has a nearly identical product that sells for about half the price. The Canadian company has been attempting to get a U.S. court ruling saying that Zantac is no longer a proprietary drug. The new competition will cut deeply into corporate earnings, but it should prove to be a windfall for customers.

The second threat comes from changes in how pharmaceuticals are purchased. Until the mid-1990s, most of the attention was directed at physicians, who made the medication decisions. As the health care system changes, however, insurers are limiting doctors to lists of eligible pharmaceuticals. These lists typically include substitutes and generics for the more expensive patented, or "name-brand," products. In a survey of 288 U.S. drug buyers, Goldman, Sachs, & Co. found that most plan to reduce their use of Zantac or negotiate larger discounts when generic Tagamet becomes available at less than one-tenth the price. A Goldman, Sachs analyst says that Zantac's $2 billion in U.S. sales could drop by 10 percent a year starting in 1996, when generic competition begins in earnest.

The third threat comes for pharmaceutical dispensers such as drug stores and mail-order pharmacies. Most of these outlets currently advise their customers of lower priced alternatives. At the same time, they provide the lower priced options to third-party payers. So companies such as Glaxo, Merck, and SmithKline are being forced to reconsider the type of products they produce, as well as the mechanisms by which they distribute them.

How is Glaxo responding to these threats? The first change is an increase in sales training. Glaxo is spending about 2 percent of its revenues to educate and train its salespeople so that they can build long-term relationships with physicians. One of the techniques they are taught is how to condense information about the products and their attributes to arm busy physicians with concise information about the drug and its proper uses.

The second change is one of leadership at corporate headquarters. Robert Ingram, an experienced insider, has been promoted to president and put in charge of operations. This frees Charles Sanders, Glaxo's chairman and CEO, to take a more public role and act as a statesman for the industry. In Washington, Sanders has been busy lobbying against price controls. Unhappy with President Clinton's health care plan, Sanders believes that the industry can avoid the worst case by keeping its head low and restraining price increases.

The third change is the creation of a joint venture between Glaxo's parent company and Warner-Lambert. Warner-Lambert is one of the world's largest vendors of products for the home medicine chest, such as Listerine mouthwash and Efferdent denture cleaners. The first product is expected to be a nonprescription version of Zantac. For consumers, that will mean access to medication that formerly required a physician's prescription. For Glaxo, it means the ability to generate new life for products that don't appear on the physicians' prescription lists, yet keep the revenues for these products rather than letting them go to rivals who make generic drugs. For Glaxo, that's more than enough reason to cause serious heartburn.[52]

Questions

1. What other forces might affect a company such as Glaxo?
2. Does use of the chairman as a politician offset pressures from the business environment? Why or why not?
3. Develop another response that Glaxo could use to counteract the pressures of regulation, competition, and substitute products.

Chapter *4*

Strategic Management: Global Forces

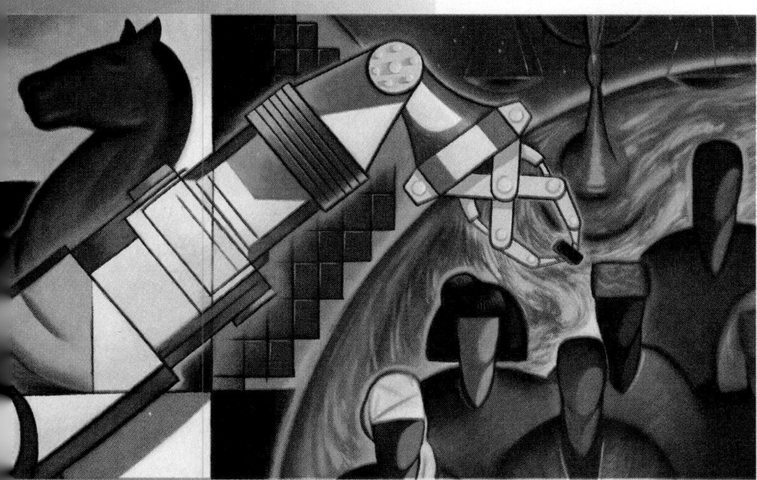

Learning *Objectives*

After studying this chapter, you should be able to:

1. Describe the growing global economy.
2. Identify five ways of organizing for international operations.
3. Describe the main strategies for international operations.
4. Explain how international political-legal forces affect organizations.
5. Identify the competitive forces fostered by the recent major trade agreements.
6. Describe how cultural factors affect international management.

Chapter *Outline*

Preview *Insight*

Telmex in Mexico

Anyone who visited Mexico as recently as 1991 knows that making a phone call, particularly long distance or international, was frustrating and required patience. Even more recently, Rogelio Ramirez noted that his home phone hadn't worked for three months before a repairman showed up. Customers of Teléfonos de México (Telmex), the telephone monopoly, used to stand in line for hours to resolve disputes over a few pesos. Telmex ranked eighty-third worldwide in telephone customer service. There were only seven telephone lines for every thousand residents. However, busy circuits and sudden disconnections are becoming less common.

Carlos Slim, a multibillionaire and former mathematics professor in Mexico, saw a great opportunity when the Mexican government decided to privatize the telephone company. In 1990, Slim's Grupo Carso acquired 20 percent of Telmex as did each of its partners, namely, Southwestern Bell and France Telecom. A five-year, $13 billion investment program was launched, including the addition of numerous repair trucks and new maintenance centers. The firm is installing fiber-optic cable and state-of-the-art switches to automate and speed up Mexico's communication links with the world. As of 1996, all telephone lines in Mexico's five major cities will be digital. Telmex has reduced the waiting time for a new line from three years to six months and has eliminated the bribery that often was necessary to speed up the installation of a line.

The infusion of capital and technological sophistication is only part of turning Telmex around. The partners are modifying the company's culture by changing the attitudes and practices of its fifty thousand employees. Customer orientation and high-quality service were new concepts for this previously government-owned monopoly. Such changes in attitudes and practices has been as important to Telmex as the introduction of technology from France and the United States.

Since 1988, the government of Mexico has been committed to catapulting the country into the global economy. The 1994 elections suggest that the trend toward market-based competition and more open markets to global competition will continue. As more U.S., Canadian, Asian, and European businesses enter Mexico, the role of Telmex in providing global communication networks is crucial. In 1994 alone, foreign investment in Mexico totaled approximately $16 billion. Telmex is only one of many firms in Mexico and worldwide that must increasingly compete in the global marketplace and economy.[1]

1

Describe the growing global economy.

THE GROWING GLOBAL ECONOMY

The growing global economy creates new imperatives for an increasing number of firms to expand internationally. We consider a few of the indicators of that growth in this section. The other sections in this chapter focus on a range of issues and strategies for international operations. Obviously, the levels of international involvement of firms in a country and between countries vary. For example, the Preview Case illustrates how competitive, cultural, political, and technological forces—both domestic and global—are influencing the dramatic changes in Telmex.

Global economic activity is shifting both qualitatively and quantitatively. During the past two decades, trade has grown faster than the economies of most countries. Some one-fifth of the $20 trillion of world output is now traded. Twenty or so years ago it was an eighth. (One trillion is a thousand billions). Moreover, the range of what is traded is expanding rapidly.[2] Services now account for one-fifth of world trade. International telephone calls to and from the United States went from about 500 million in 1981 to 1.5 billion in 1989 to 2.5 billion in 1993.[3] Finally, the nature of trade is changing dramatically. Increasingly, trade is between different parts of the same corporation or through alliances (joint ventures). Asking whether a product—computer, car, or shirt—has been "Made in the USA" or "Made in Canada" has become almost meaningless. The produc-

Teaching Tip
Tell students that learning international business will expand their employability by opening up more job and career options.

tion of components for products is increasingly scattered around the world. Sales by overseas subsidiaries of U.S. and Canadian corporations are about three times greater than the value of their exports from their home countries.[4]

One driving force in the expanding global economy is the rapidly growing number of middle-class consumers in many countries. The Third World, which has 80 percent of the world's population, now accounts for about 45 percent of the global economy. The Third World includes countries in Latin America, Eastern Europe, and Asia (except Japan, Korea, and Hong Kong). The economies in these regions are expected to average 5 percent per year growth compared to 2 percent growth for the advanced industrialized countries.[5]

A second driving force in global activity is the development of new information technologies that permit instantaneous worldwide communication.[6] A major challenge for Telmex is to meet the increasing demand by its customers for high-quality and reliable international telephone service. In addition, computer-based information technologies enable firms to respond quickly to changing consumer demand worldwide. Benetton, the Italian-based clothing manufacturer, obtains timely information on sales around the world through its computer linkages. Benetton's network provides the data needed to adjust production and distribution daily to respond to consumer demand, including the provision of new supplies of "hot" selling items.[7]

We discuss other forces that are driving and restraining the global economy throughout this chapter. Before going on, however, let's consider briefly the international quality standards program ISO 9000, presented in the following Quality Insight. This program is viewed by some as a catalyst to international trade and the global economy.

Quality *Insight*

ISO 9000

The ISO 9000 quality standards were created in 1987 by the International Organization for Standardization (ISO), in Geneva, Switzerland. To date, ninety-five countries have approved those standards for voluntary application in both the manufacturing and service sectors. Approximately 40,000 certificates have been issued worldwide with about 2,000 going to U.S. firms.

Although the ISO in Geneva issues the standards, it does not regulate the program internationally; that is left to national accreditation organizations like the U.S. Registrar Accreditation Board. This and other such boards authorize the ISO to issue ISO 9000 certificates. ISO 9000 certification does not testify as to the quality of a company's products or services. Rather, it signifies that a company has fully adopted and documented a quality system within the framework of ISO and is abiding by it. It's theoretically possible that a company could, while meeting the ISO 9000 standards, turn out inferior products; but this is not likely.

ISO 9000 is a set of worldwide standards that establish requirements for the management of quality. Unlike *product* standards, these standards are for *quality* in product design, process control, inspection and testing, purchasing, after-sales service, and training. The standards are being used by many European nations to provide a universal framework for quality assurance—primarily through a system of internal and external audits. The goal is to ensure that a certified firm has a quality system in place that will enable it to meet its published quality standards. The ISO standards are general in that they apply to all functions and all industries, from banking to automobile manufacturing. This is also a source of criticism by managers in some firms.

One example of the impact of ISO 9000 is reflected in the requirements on suppliers to Siemens, the global German electronics firm. The company mandates ISO compliance in 50 percent of its contracts with suppliers and is pressing all others to conform. A major justification for this action is that it eliminates the need for Siemens to test parts, which saves time and money and establishes common requirements for all suppliers around the world.

Tim Barry, training and continuous-improvement process manager at American Saw in East Longmeadow, Massachusetts, says that, for his company, "the process of achieving ISO 9000 has improved in-house communication and created a major drop-off in employee accidents." He's witnessed fewer product defects and increasingly satisfied customers. Although ISO 9000 is a certificate program in transition, it is likely to have an increasing impact on how firms worldwide address quality issues and standards.[8]

2

Identify five ways of organizing for international operations.

Ask Students
Is your employer or the university involved in global operations? Is your employer's or the university's competitors involved in global operations? Generally describe those operations.

ORGANIZING FOR INTERNATIONAL OPERATIONS

Chances are that the organization you will work for and your job will be strongly affected by global forces. Although they are being felt around the world, the relative importance of these forces to specific industries and firms varies widely. Their impact depends on the level of direct international business done by an industry or firm. An ice cream manufacturer (e.g., Blue Bell Ice Cream in Texas) has little, if any, direct international involvement. However, a huge bank (e.g., Citicorp, headquartered in New York) is truly global in its outlook and operations. For example, an automated teller machine (ATM) customer can use a Citibank machine in Hong Kong to exchange U.S. dollars for Hong Kong dollars at a favorable exchange rate. If this person is a Citibank customer, no transaction fee is charged.

Figure 4.1 shows the relative degree of complexity (vertical axis) and the relative degree of resource commitment (horizontal axis) by firms engaged in international busi-

FIGURE 4.1

Organizing for International Operations

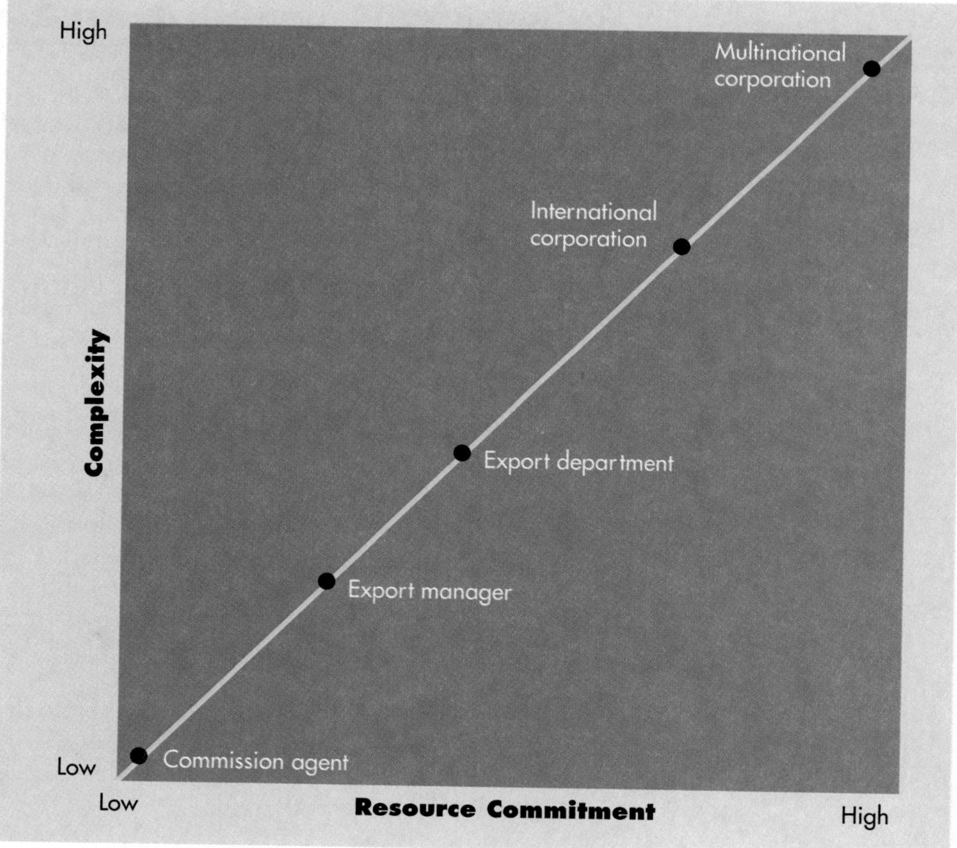

ness. By *resource commitment,* we mean the dedication of assets that cannot be redeployed to other uses without cost. Resources could be tangible, such as offices and plants located abroad, or intangible, such as managers and other employees who have the knowledge and skills (or can learn them) needed for international operations.[9] Figure 4.1 also shows how a firm might organize internationally over time, starting with hiring a commission agent to represent the company in international transactions. The process can eventually lead to a firm's becoming a full-fledged multinational corporation. A firm's degree of internationalization (DOI) has three general attributes: *performance* (what goes on abroad), *resources* (what assets are abroad), and *attitudinal* (what is the international orientation of key personnel). Other DOI measures include foreign sales as a percentage of total sales, export sales as a percentage of total sales, foreign profits as a percentage of total profits, foreign assets as a percentage of total assets, and top managers' international experience.[10]

Ask Students
How much international experience do you and the people you work with or go to school with have?

The competitive forces acting on a firm, as well as its stated goals, will influence its organizational structure. Let's briefly explore the five primary ways of organizing for international business—from the simplest to the most complex and from the least to the greatest resource commitment. In Chapters 10 and 11 we address the issues of organizational design in greater detail.

Commission Agent

Real-World Example
Amway, Mary Kay Cosmetics, and multilevel marketing companies use commission agents.

A firm's first step toward international operations might be to retain one or more commission agents to handle an inquiry from a potential foreign customer or to look into a possible opportunity to sell its products abroad. A **commission agent** is a person or firm who represents businesses in foreign transactions in return for a negotiated percentage of each transaction's value (a commission). An agent is likely to represent more than one firm and will usually carry catalogs of their products and attempt to sell them to customers abroad. The use of commission agents is the simplest way to enter international business. The firm may not even need to create new positions or departments—a top or middle manager may simply be assigned the added responsibility of working with the agent. Hence firms with limited resources may find the use of commission agent to be advantageous initially. However, use of commission agents in international trade need not be limited to small scale firms, as the following Insight on Nu Skin International demonstrates.

Teaching Tip
Becoming a commissioned agent is a good way to get into international business. There are opportunities for inexperienced people as commissioned agents.

Insight

Nu Skin International

Nu Skin International is a Utah-based direct-sales company. It uses a computer network and special software to help its 300,000 independent distributors sell personal care and health products in any of eight countries where the company has a sales license.

The company uses a multilevel marketing approach. Distributors receive commissions on their own sales, as well as a share of the commissions generated by the salespeople they recruit and by the salespeople later recruited by their enlistees. But no matter how complex or how international the distributors' "trees" of commissions, they get paid instantly. Renn Patch, international vice-president, gives an example. If a sales trainee recruited by a distributor in California moves to Canada and sets up her own sales force, the Californian gets commissions on the Canadian sales. If a recruited Canadian distributor then moves to Mexico to help open the Mexican market, a share of the Mexican commissions winds its way back to California, too, by way of Canada.[11]

Export Manager

As its exports increase, a firm may hire an export manager to take over from the commission agent or to work with commission agents in some countries and handle transactions directly with customers in other countries. Much like a commission agent, an **export manager** actively searches out foreign markets for the firm's goods or services. Unlike most commission agents, an export manager represents only one firm. The export manager typically has a small staff—possibly only a secretary—and travels abroad extensively. A firm having a relatively small export sales volume is likely to limit itself to commission agents or an export manager.[12]

Hiring an export manager means that a firm must incur some new ongoing costs. These costs include, at a minimum, the export manager's salary and benefits, office space, travel expenses, and secretarial support. Regardless of the amount of sales generated by the export manager, which may be quite small initially, these costs could easily amount to $150,000 or more per year. In contrast, commission agents receive only a percentage of the dollar value of the goods sold.

Export Department

As export activities and sales increase, the export manager may have to form an export department. This unit may consist of only a few people in addition to the export manager. An **export department** often (1) represents the interests of foreign customers to the firm's other departments and to top management, (2) meets the increasing demand for services by foreign customers, (3) makes special arrangements for customs clearance and international shipping, (4) assists foreign customers with financing of the goods they are purchasing, and (5) arranges for the collection of accounts receivable from foreign customers. An export department might also establish branches abroad to handle sales and promotional tasks.

A firm's interest in exporting often develops in stages and may even begin quite accidentally in small firms. In the United States, both public and private agencies help businesses identify countries and customers who may be interested in their products or services. These agencies include the U.S. Department of Commerce's Trade Information Center, the United States Chamber of Commerce, and the U.S. Small Business Administration. However, being a small firm doesn't always mean that exports are a small percentage of the firm's total sales, as indicated in the following Small Business Insight.

Small Business *Insight*

DMT Goes International

DMT Corporation manufactures backup electrical generators and controls in Waukesha, Wisconsin. In 1990, over 50 percent of its sales were from exports. More recently, 65 percent of its approximate $30 million in sales were from export sales.

Most of the company's recent growth has been from exports to developing industrial markets in the Far East and Central and South America. DMT doesn't export to highly industrialized Western Europe, but it is interested in Eastern Europe and the newly independent states of the former Soviet Union.

DMT sees so much potential for small businesses in international trade that it has created DMT World Trade, a subsidiary company designed to serve as an international distributor for other small companies. The secret of DMT's success in exporting is its commitment, says Tom Repp, product sales manager for DMT World Trade. "Our domestic sales have grown, but we see a greater potential in international markets."[13]

Discussion Question 2
If entrepreneur Juanita Jain wanted to expand her car dealership business to include Monterrey, a large city in northern Mexico, how might she begin the process?

Some of the factors that move an organization well beyond the export department level include (1) growth in international sales and production capacity equal to 15 percent or more of domestic division growth, (2) diversification in product lines to serve a variety of customers, and (3) difficulties in coordinating between domestic and international operations.

International Corporation

An **international corporation** has significant business interests that cut across national boundaries, often focuses on importing and exporting goods or services, and operates production and marketing units in other countries. One approach is to create an international division with offices or manufacturing operations for major regions—or even countries—of the world. Units might be created for the Americas (Canada, Mexico, the United States, and Central and South America), Europe (France, Germany, the United Kingdom, and others), and the Pacific Rim (Australia, Japan, Hong Kong, and others). The nature of the units would depend on market size and the scope of the international manufacturing and service operations.[14]

The international units represent their country or regional interests and operate as semi-independent units. Coordination between country or regional units usually is limited, and what does occur is handled by the company's top management. Coleman, Briggs & Stratton, Rubbermaid, and the Thomson Corporation are but a few of the major international corporations.

Figure 4.2 shows a portion of the organizational structure of the Thomson Corporation, which is headquartered in Toronto, Ontario. Its principal activities are specialized information and publishing, newspaper publishing, and leisure travel. The International Thomson Publishing group provides specialized information services and produces publications around the world. It is organized primarily as subsidiary companies within particular world regions or countries. South-Western College Publishing, headquartered in Cincinnati, Ohio, and the publisher of this textbook is one of those companies. This subsidiary focuses on the U.S. and Canadian markets. Of course, any of South-Western's products may be sold through the distribution offices of International Thomson Publishing. For example, the distribution office in London, England, serves the United Kingdom, Europe, the Middle East, and Africa.

Diversified corporations may even establish separate international divisions for each major product line. Thus top managers of those lines may have both domestic and international responsibilities. Procter & Gamble, Sara Lee, and H.J. Heinz are representative of such international corporations. As the following Global Insight indicates, Morton International, a company best known in the United States for its salt products, is an international corporation known in other countries for its automobile parts.

Global *Insight*

Morton's Nonsalt Products

Many people are familiar with the Morton Salt logo of a young girl spilling a trail of salt on a rainy day to accompany its motto "When It Rains, It Pours." Less well-known is the fact that Morton obtains only about 22 percent of its $2.5 billion in revenues from the sale of salt products. A larger portion of its sales come from automotive specialty products, especially airbags.

Airbags have a short history in the United States. The industry has evolved rapidly since 1989 when Chrysler put an airbag on the driver's side of all its vehicles. The U.S. airbag industry is fueled by the government requirement that 95 percent of all cars must have both driver- and passenger-side airbags by 1996. The United States isn't the only country to respond to calls for automobile safety. Morton

International has been selling airbags to Mercedes Benz since 1985 and has about 60 percent of an expanding global market. TRW is Morton's primary international competitor. Nissan started using Morton airbags in 1995 for cars sold in Japan, and Volkswagen will start offering Morton airbags in 1996.

With a significant portion of sales to foreign companies, it made sense for Morton to be closer to those companies. As a start, Morton built a $30 million airbag assembly plant in Braunschweig, Germany. In addition, the company formed a joint venture, United Airbags Systems, with Robert Bosch. The joint venture will develop and market new intelligent airbag system. This new type of airbag is targeted at the upscale market occupied by firms such as Mercedes Benz. The alliance with Bosch and the German location permits Morton to work closely with more of its customers. It also gives Morton better access to new customers in other markets.[15]

Multinational Corporation

A **multinational corporation** (MNC) features a worldwide approach to markets (customers), services, and products and has a global philosophy of doing business. An MNC emerges when (1) management assesses problems and opportunities in global terms, (2) one or more subsidiaries operate in several countries, (3) management seeks to make sales, obtain resources, and produce goods throughout the world, (4) some of the key

FIGURE 4.2

Portion of Thomson's Corporate Structure

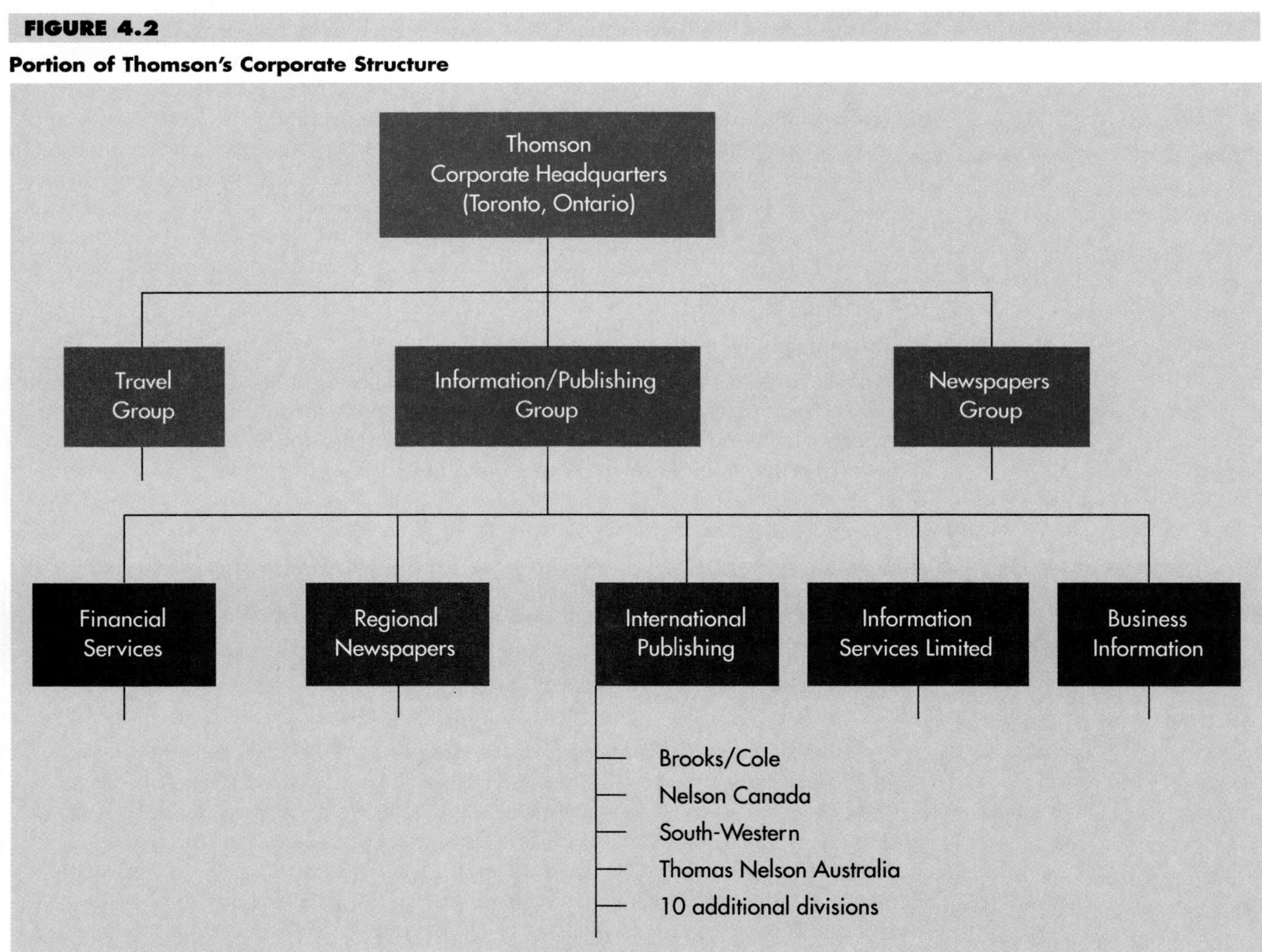

Source: Adapted from *The Thomson Corporation 1993 Annual Report.* Toronto, Ontario, Canada, 1994.

managers at corporate headquarters are from operations around the world, not just from the country where the corporate headquarters is located, and (5) most of the key managers of *foreign* operations are from the countries or regions in which the operations are located. The features that most distinguish a multinational corporation from an international corporation are its integrated philosophy and view of the entire world as its market.[16] A few of the firms that operate as multinational corporations are Caterpillar, IBM, Shell, Honda, General Electric, and Imperial Chemical. At least seventeen major foreign-based MNCs earn 20 percent or more of their revenues in North America.[17]

Coca-Cola is a multinational corporation that obtains over 70 percent of its operating income from outside the United States. Its management team considers a geographic focus to be the fundamental way of organizing. As Figure 4.3 shows, the basic functional units—marketing, operations, and bottlers—are represented in each geographic region. Coca-Cola operates in 185 markets, has 650,000 employees, and serves more than 5 billion customers. One of the company's core values is to "think globally, but act locally." The geographic units focus on day-to-day marketing, operations, and distribution. Corporate headquarters focuses on broad issues such as new international markets and new or improved product lines. For example, Coca-Cola moved aggressively into eastern Germany after the fall of the Berlin Wall.[18] In Chapter 11 we explore multinational organization design in greater detail.

A multinational corporation often competes directly with a small number of other multinationals in each world market. Again, these firms view the entire world (or its major regions) as a single entity. Each company seeks to respond to local market needs while maintaining efficiency in its worldwide system. More than 100 industries are represented by companies that are or will soon become multinationals with worldwide systems. These

FIGURE 4.3

Portion of Coca-Cola's Multinational Structure

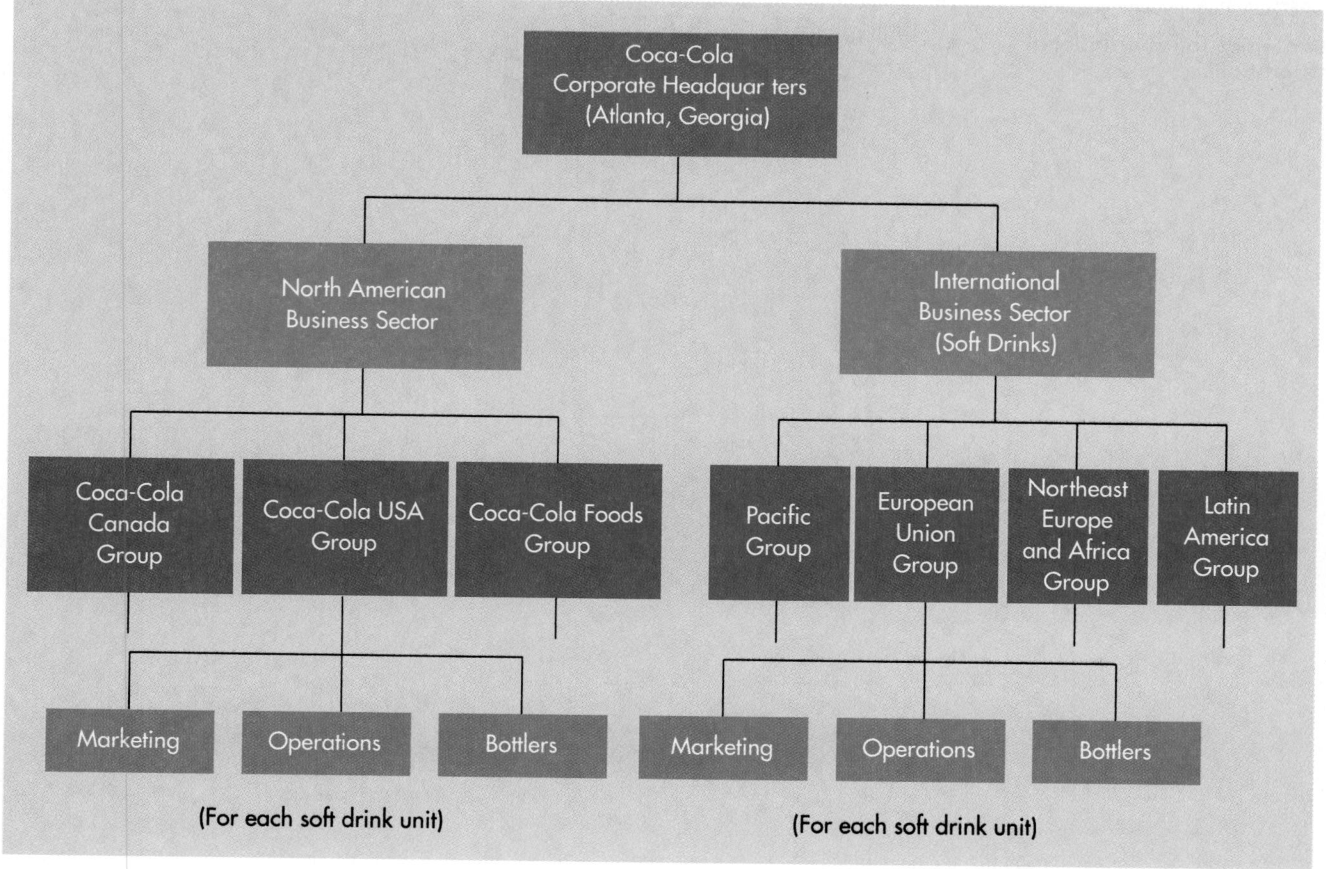

industries produce goods and services that vary from accounting, autos, banking, consumer electronics, and entertainment to pharmaceuticals, travel services, washing machines, and zippers.[19] To be competitive, firms in these industries must manufacture, conduct research, raise capital, and buy supplies wherever they can gain a competitive advantage. They must stay on top of technological and market trends worldwide.

3

Describe the main strategies for international operations.

STRATEGIES FOR INTERNATIONAL OPERATIONS

The ways that firms organize for international operations are influenced by their choice of international strategies.[20] In this section we present six strategies, also ranging from low to high in complexity and low to high in resource commitment, as shown in Figure 4.4. An organization may use one or more of these strategies at the same time. These strategies are only a few examples of the vast range of choices available.

Exporting Strategy

The **exporting strategy** involves maintaining facilities within a home country and transferring goods and services abroad, for sale in foreign markets. For many firms, it is the major strategy of international operations. Exports from the United States were about $500 billion and imports (exports from foreign countries) were about $600 billion as of 1995.[21] Harley-Davidson is one company that uses an exporting strategy. It produces heavyweight motorcycles at its manufacturing facilities in Pennsylvania and Wisconsin. In 1994, some 20,000 motorcycles were exported and some 64,000 units were sold domestically. Japan, Germany, Canada, and France, in that order, currently represent Harley-Davidson's largest export markets and account for about 63 percent of its export

FIGURE 4.4

Strategies for International Operations

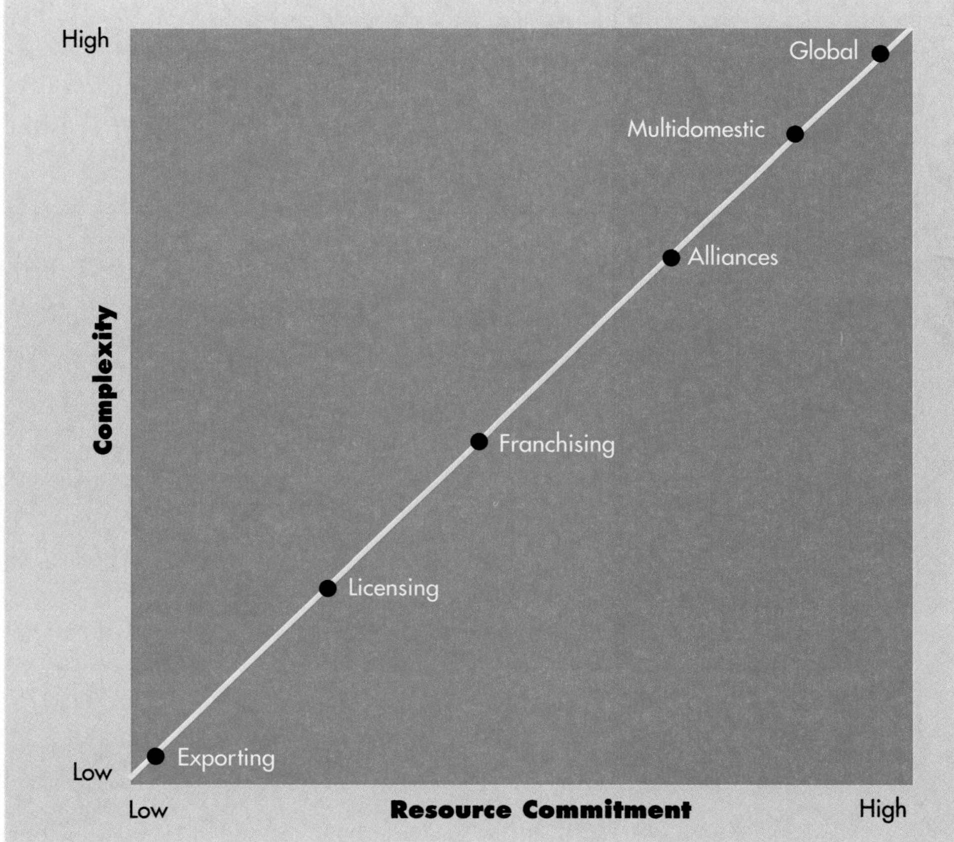

sales. Top management sees tremendous potential for increased export sales in the years ahead.[22]

A variation on exporting (or importing) is **counter trade,** an arrangement in which the export sale of goods and services by a producer is linked to an import purchase of other goods and services.[23] This form of exporting is sometimes called *bartering* and may occur when the currency of the importing company cannot be traded in the international currency exchange. The best known example of counter trade is PepsiCo's exporting of syrup and related soft drink items to Russia in exchange for vodka.

Licensing Strategy

A **licensing strategy** involves a firm (the *licensor*) in one country giving other domestic or foreign firms (*licensees*) the right to use a patent, trademark, technology, production process, or product in return for the payment of a royalty or fee. This contractual arrangement also may involve the licensor in providing manufacturing, technical, or marketing expertise to the licensees.[24] A simple licensing arrangement occurs when U.S. and Canadian book publishers give foreign publishers the right to translate a book into another language and then publish, market, and distribute the translated book. The licensor doesn't have to worry about making major capital investments abroad or becoming involved in the daily production, technical, marketing, or management details of the international operation.

Real-World Example
The United States licenses fighter jet technology to Israel. Some U.S. officials have accused Israel of violating the license by selling the technology to China (*Los Angeles Times*, December 27, 1994, A1).

Technological and market forces are stimulating the use of the licensing strategy. The reason is that licenses can be used to disseminate new technologies rapidly to new markets. In the computer industry, some firms license their technologies to potential users in an attempt to broaden their customer base. In late 1994, Apple Computer changed course by adopting a licensing strategy—both in the United States and abroad—for its Power Macintosh line. Apple hopes to have licensees worldwide producing more than a million Mac clones a year by 1997. Critics claim that Apple's unwillingness to license the Mac and its operating system in the 1980s was one of the greatest strategic blunders of all time. This failure allowed Microsoft to establish what analysts at the time called an inferior system (Windows) as the standard for the personal computer industry.[25]

Franchising Strategy

In a **franchising strategy,** a parent organization (the *franchiser*) grants other companies or individuals (*franchisees*) the rights to use its trademarked name and to produce and sell its goods or services. The franchiser provides franchisees with a complete assortment of materials and services for a fee. The franchiser usually is actively involved in training, monitoring, and controlling the actions of the franchisee to make sure that it conforms to the franchise agreement. Alamo Rent-A-Car, Holiday Inns, TGI Friday's, and McDonald's are but a few examples of global franchisers. The more than 3,000 franchising companies headquartered in Canada and the United States operate about 50,000 outlets in international markets.[26]

Ask Students
Does your university run its own food services or franchise name brand fast foods?

Wallace Doolin, president and CEO of TGI Friday's, made the following comments on its use of the franchising strategy.

> *To transplant your personal identity into a foreign setting, it usually is advisable to take on a development partner—in our case, a franchisee—who knows how to conduct business in Europe, Asia or whichever market you want to enter. A strong partner can help you negotiate government obstacles, labor unions, hiring practices and other hurdles that are unique to various parts of the world. . . . Opening businesses abroad takes two to three times longer than you would expect. Finding the right locations and securing development permits are only part of it. Training also takes longer, partly because of language barriers, but mainly because our way of doing business is literally foreign to most people outside the U.S.*[27]

Real-World Example
Alliances also are used between nations. The Gulf War and restoring democracy to Haiti are but two examples of recent transnational alliances. In high-tech industries, alliances are used to offset the high research and development costs that are too great for one company alone to bear.

Alliance Strategy

An **alliance strategy** involves agreeing with other companies to pool physical and human resources to achieve common goals. International business alliances take many forms, from straightforward marketing agreements to joint ventures (ownership) of worldwide operations. Interestingly, the first Chinese-foreign joint venture was formed in 1979. Today, *more than 50,000 Chinese-foreign joint ventures are operating in China.*[28]

The formation of alliances, especially joint ventures, has been stimulated by the following needs and desires.

- The need to share and lower the costs of high-risk, technologically intensive development projects, such as computer-based information systems. Inmarsat, a joint venture with 65 partners from various countries, operates telecommunications satellites. The partners are simultaneously *owners* investing capital, *customers* routing calls through the satellites, and *suppliers* of technology to the venture.
- The desire to lower costs by sharing the large fixed-cost investments for manufacturing plants in some locations and in industries such as autos, steel, and appliances. To reduce manufacturing costs, Ford and Volkswagen recently formed a joint venture to make four-wheel-drive vehicles in Portugal.
- The desire to learn another firm's technology and special processes or to gain access to customers and distribution channels. Samsung entered into a joint venture with GE to produce microwave ovens and later became a competitor of GE's in the full line of household appliances.
- The desire to participate in the evolution of competitive activity in growing global industries. Royal Crown Company signed a joint venture agreement with Consorcio Aga in 1994. Royal Crown hopes that this bottler will help it boost sales in Mexico from $18 million in 1994 to $180 million by the end of 1997. In addition to licensing its brands, Royal Crown will provide advertising, promotional, and technical support to Consorcio Aga.[29]

Ask Students
What are some of the potential problems of alliances? (Examples: egos, power struggles, unequal inputs, unfairly sharing the work, inequitable distribution of profits.)

Alliances provide entry into markets that are risky because of strict political requirements or great economic uncertainty. For example, China doesn't permit foreign

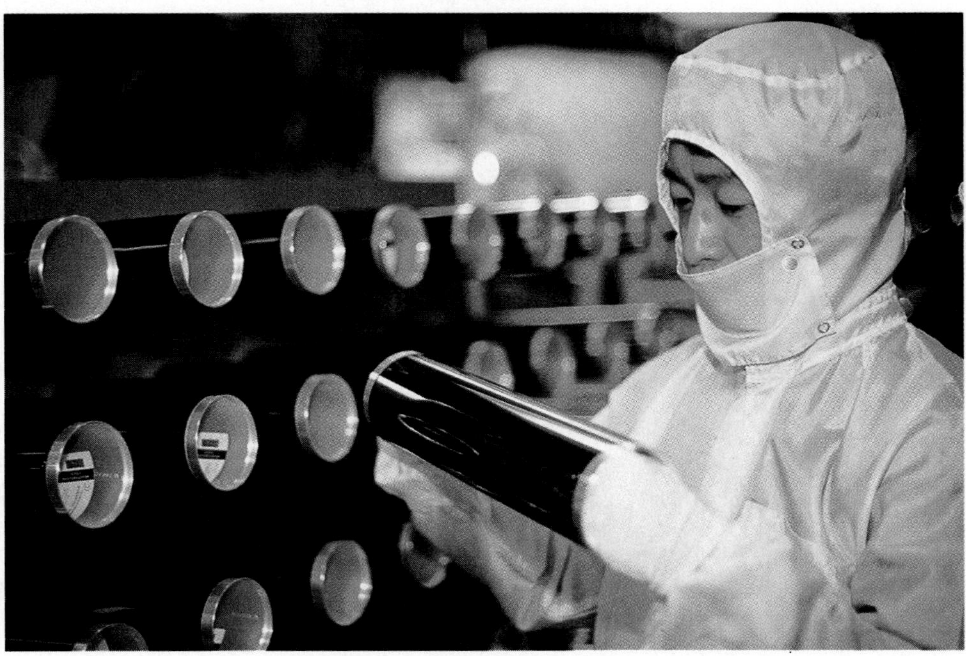

In an alliance strategy, companies pool physical and human resources to achieve common goals. Here a Chinese worker performs quality control at the Xerox Corporation. Today, there are more than 50,000 joint ventures operating in China.

corporations to establish solely owned subsidiaries there—they must form some sort of alliance with Chinese participants. Finally, domestic partners are likely to have a deeper understanding of how to deal with severe political and great economic uncertainty in countries such as China and Russia.

Multidomestic Strategy

A **multidomestic strategy** involves adjusting products, services, and practices to individual countries or regions (for example, Pacific Rim versus Western Europe versus North America). This strategy is driven by pressures for local customizing to respond to the differences in customer desires, distribution channels, host government demands, and/or employee needs. The multidomestic strategy is based on the assumption that the benefits of local response will outweigh the extra costs of customizing.[30] Companies that have followed a multidomestic strategy successfully include Honeywell (process controls), Alcoa (aluminum), and Campbell Foods (food products). These companies view the world as a whole of unique parts and deal with each part individually.

Under a multidomestic strategy, each major overseas subsidiary usually is somewhat independent. Often each is a profit center and contributes earnings and growth in line with its market opportunity. A **profit center** is an organizational unit that is accountable for both the revenues generated by its activities and the costs of those activities. Its managers are responsible for generating the revenues and minimizing the costs necessary to achieve the expected profit for the unit. For example, Coca-Cola has more than 200 profit centers worldwide.[31] The company's world headquarters maintains financial controls and coordinates broad marketing (including product line) policies worldwide. A multidomestic strategy also means that some research and development, and even production, may be handled in the home country. But the specific marketing and transportation operations usually are delegated to managers in each region or nation.

Campbell Soup uses a multidomestic strategy and has a goal of earning half its revenues outside the United States by the year 2000. The company has introduced eight varieties of condensed soup in Poland, including a local peppery tripe soup. In part of China, Campbell offers duck-gizzard soup, radish and carrot soup, and pork fig and date soup. In Hong Kong, Campbell opened a special kitchen and taste-testing facility in 1991. It is being used to create new products for Asian consumers, including scallop and ham soups, among other products.[32]

Global Strategy

Teaching Tip
Tell students that some firms have a global strategy that ensures uniform food taste the world over. Other firms have a multidomestic strategy in which they adjust the taste of the food to suit local preferences. Ask whether any of them have gone to a familiar American brand fast-food outlet in a foreign country and discovered that the food tastes differently from what they expected?

A **global strategy** stresses operating with worldwide consistency, standardization, and low relative cost. Subsidiaries in various countries are highly interdependent in terms of goals, practices, and operations. As much as possible, top managers focus on coordination and mutual support of the firm's worldwide activities. For example, a Black & Decker subsidiary in one country manufactures parts of products, such as power drills, and exchanges components with subsidiaries in other countries to complete the products. Profit targets vary for each subsidiary, depending on the impact of its operations on the effectiveness of the company's total system.[33]

Pressures from the evolution of global industries drive this strategy,[34] which have global customers and distribution channels. The customers (e.g., purchasers of personal computers) have needs that are relatively similar in many countries. Thus primary marketing strategies are highly transferable across national boundaries. For example, the marketing of Intel's Pentium chips to computer manufacturers in various countries has many similarities.[35] Customers' technical standards are relatively compatible, and, for the most part, governments don't regulate production and sales practices.

Discussion Question 1
What approach might a company such as Frito-Lay use to begin doing business in India? In Russia? In Mexico?

An increasing number of multinational corporations use global strategies. They include Caterpillar and Komatsu (heavy construction equipment); Timex, Seiko, and Citizen (watches); and Texas Instruments, Intel, Mitsubishi, Hitachi, and Motorola (semiconductors). As indicated previously, telecommunications also has become a global industry.[36] Thus firms such as Telmex (Mexico), AT&T (United States), Telecom Italia (Italy), Deutsche Telekon (Germany), Motorola (United States), and Nokia (Finland) had to adopt global strategies. The following Global Insight describes Nokia's presence in the global cellular phone business.

Global *Insight*

Nokia's Cellular Strategies

Since 1981, 35 million cellular phones have been sold worldwide. Although you may not have heard of Nokia, it is the number two manufacturer of cellular phones after Motorola. The company has sold more than 5 million of them and currently has a 20 percent share of the world market. In the United States, its phones usually are sold under the cellular carriers' names—the Bell companies, AT&T, McCaw Cellular, and GTE.

Nokia's switches and base stations are used in cellular systems throughout Europe and Asia. After Sweden's Ericsson, Nokia is the second largest maker of cellular equipment based on the so-called GSM digital standard, which has taken hold throughout much of the world. Nokia got its break in the late 1970s when the telecommunications authorities of Sweden, Denmark, Norway, and Finland decided to build the world's first international cellular system. "Some of the big telecommunications companies thought wireless was a pretty small market niche," says Sari Baldauf, head of Nokia's cellular systems division. "But we saw it as an opportunity."

When the Scandinavian cellular system was switched on in 1981, Nokia was there with both equipment and phones. In the United States, commercial cellular service was turned on two years later, and Nokia was ready to supply phones. But it faced a major problem. How was a Finnish company with no name recognition outside Scandinavia going to break into the U.S. market? "We didn't have the money to do it all ourselves," recalls Kari-Pekka Wilska, head of Nokia's U.S. operations. Nokia's solution was to team up with Tandy Corporation and build a jointly owned cellular phone factory in Korea in 1985. In one fell swoop, Nokia got its cellular phones into more than 6,000 Radio Shack stores under the Tandy brand. As the number of U.S. cellular subscribers took off, Nokia and Tandy built another factory in Fort Worth, Texas, seven years later. Nokia has since bought out Tandy's interests in both factories but still produces Tandy phones. In the 1990s, big cellular service carriers—McCaw Cellular and the Bells—were marketing phones bundled with talking time on the cellular system. Motorola relentlessly cut phone prices to gain market share. The president of the mobile phones division gave Nokia's U.S. management authority to counter Motorola at every turn. The results were impressive: In the exploding U.S. market for cellular phones, Nokia's market share went from 10 percent in 1990 to 20 percent by 1995.[37]

Various ingredients are needed for a multinational's global strategy to be successful. The following are six such ingredients.

1. The firm needs to be a significant competitor in the world's most important regional markets—North America, Europe, and Asia.
2. Most new goods and services need to be developed for the whole world—such as Nokia's and Motorola's cellular phones.
3. Profit targets should be based on product lines—such as Black and Decker's line of hand-held power drills—rather than countries or regions of the world.
4. Decisions about products, capital investment, research and development, and production should be based on global considerations—such as Nokia's strategically located plants for producing cellular phones in Finland (home country), South Korea, and the United States.
5. Narrow-minded attitudes—such as "this isn't how we operate here"—must be overcome. Some ways to change attitudes include training employees to think globally,

sending them to various countries for first-hand exposure, and giving them the latest information technology.

6. Foreign managers need to be promoted into senior ranks at corporate headquarters.[38]

4

Explain how international political-legal forces affect organizations.

POLITICAL-LEGAL FORCES

Organizations that engage in international operations encounter a web of political and legal forces. Only if these forces are diagnosed accurately can management understand the risks and uncertainties associated with international operations. Recall from Chapter 3 that managers may use one or more of five political strategies—negotiation, lobbying, alliance, representation, and socialization—to reduce political risk. **Political risk** is the probability that political decisions or events in a country will negatively affect the long-term profitability of an investment.[39] Of concern to all international and multinational corporations is the political risk associated with resource commitments in foreign countries.

Assessing Political Risk

Political risk factors may be grouped into four principal categories: domestic instability, foreign conflict, political climate, and economic climate. As Figure 4.5 shows, managers may estimate the seriousness of the political risk associated with conducting business in a country by assessing various factors in each category.

Ask Students
Raise your hand if you would take a big promotion even if it meant going to a country where your company's plant had been bombed? Why?

Domestic instability is the amount of subversion, revolution, assassinations, guerrilla warfare, and government crisis in a country. Haiti's long history of domestic instability has generally discouraged foreign investment in Haiti.

Foreign conflict is the degree of hostility one nation shows toward others. Such hostility can range from the expulsion of diplomats to outright war. The invasion of Kuwait by Iraq is one of the more dramatic recent examples. In August 1990, then President George Bush determined that the actions of the government of Iraq were an unusual and extraordinary threat to the national security and foreign policy of the United States. Under authority granted by the U.S. Export Administration Act of 1979, the government imposed a total ban on trade with Iraq, which directly affected many

FIGURE 4.5
Assessing Political Risk

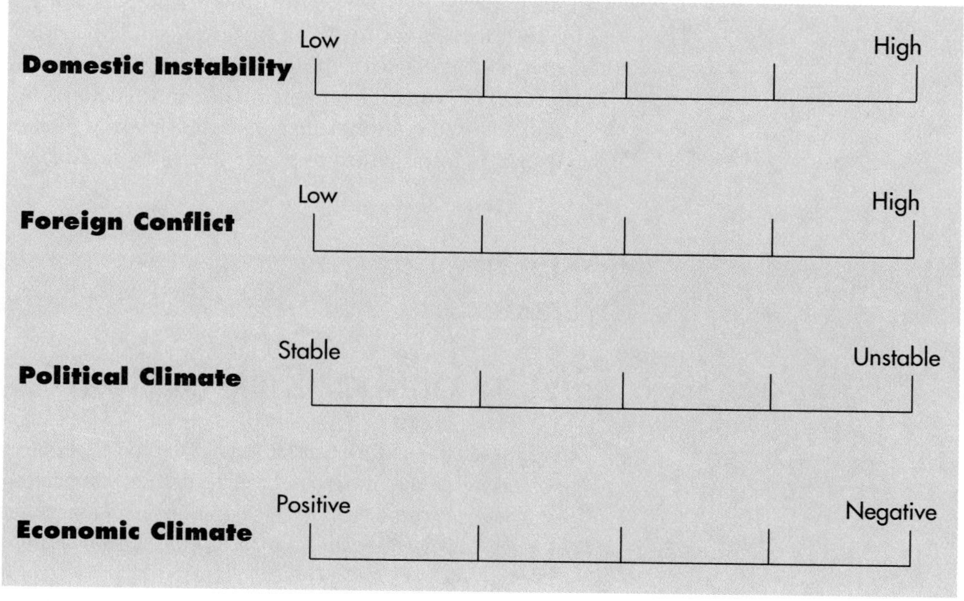

firms. This ban continues even though Iraq—in an effort to force lifting of the ban—again threatened military action against Kuwait in 1994. In one composite rating of political risk for 1994, Iraq's risk rating was high: 31 out of 100 points (the lower the number the higher the risk on this scale). The lowest risk ratings were for Luxemburg (91 points) and Switzerland (90 points). The United States ranked eleventh with 85 points and Canada ranked fourteenth with 83 points. Iraq ranked 126th (high risk) out of the 130 countries evaluated, and Somalia ranked 130th (highest) with a rating of 19.[40]

Ask Students
What are some high-risk countries that have been in the news recently?

Political climate is the likelihood that a government will swing to the far left or far right politically. Managers may evaluate such variables as the number and size of political parties, the number of factions in the legislature, role of the military in the political process, amount of corruption in government, effectiveness of political leadership, influence of organized religion in politics, extent of racial and nationality tensions, and quality of the governmental bureaucracy. Currently, Russia is considered to have a risky political climate because of the instability of the Yeltsin government and the opposing political forces that are trying to retreat to a planned economy.[41] In the ratings noted previously, Russia had a composite political risk rating of 60 and a relative ranking of 90 out of the 130 countries evaluated.

Ask Students
What are some countries that have been in the news recently that seem to be politically unstable?

The **economic climate** reflects the extent of government control of markets and financial investments, as well as government support services and capabilities. Variables in this category are government regulatory and economic control policies (wages, prices, imports, and exports), government ability to manage its own economic affairs (inflation, budget surpluses or deficits, and amount of debt), and government provision of support services and capabilities (roads, airports, electricity, water, and refuse and sewage disposal), often referred to as *infrastructure,* and capabilities in general.

Ask Students
What are some economically unstable countries that have been in the news recently?

The U.S. government has had a greater tendency than most other governments to impose export controls unilaterally as a way to advance its foreign policy. Unilateral U.S. export controls cost U.S. businesses an estimated $25 billion per year in sales.[42] The current export controls system—covered in 1,500 pages of federal regulations—is an "absolute disaster," said John Murphy, chief executive of Dresser Industries, a Dallas oilfield supplier. "The theory is everybody else in the world will follow our lead," Murphy continued. "They have not, and they continue to export a lot of things." The system is so complex that some small and medium-sized companies don't even try to export their products, according to David Richardson, an economist who studies U.S. government impediments for exporters. For example, Boeing wanted to sell jetliners to Iran. The government said *no* because of Iran's support of terrorism. Airbus Industries obtained the sale. AT&T wanted to sell fiber-optic transmission equipment to China. The government said *no* because eavesdropping on fiber-optic lines is more difficult. Israel got the sale. Commerce Secretary Ron Brown said that the export control system has become "a major impediment to doing business" and should be relaxed as much as possible.[43] Relaxation is likely with the passage in 1994 of the General Agreement on Tariffs and Trade (GATT), which we explain later in this chapter.

Discussion Question 4
Suppose that Texas Instruments (TI), a large microprocessor manufacturer, wants to open four new plants overseas. Name four countries that might represent a high degree of risk for such operations. Would it be better off to export to those countries? Why or why not?

The following Global Insight describes how General Motors forecasts political risk and uses this information to make decisions regarding the location of new plants.

Global *Insight*

GM's Political Risk System

The centerpiece of the General Motors (GM) political assessment system is the Political Risk Index—an annual comparison of the political environment for U.S. automakers in sixty-four countries around the world. The company assesses nine factors in measuring the level of political risk in any country: three are macropolitical factors; two measure the policy-making process; and four reflect key regulatory issues. Each factor is assigned a weight indicative of its relative importance to GM's business overseas; the total weight of the factors is 100. The variables are defined (and weighted) as follows.

- Macropolitical Factors

1. ***Leadership* (15 points):** The degree to which a government is favorably disposed toward foreign investment, including the auto industry, and has political institutions and processes that are adaptable and reasonably reliable.
2. ***Social cohesion* (10 points):** The degree to which a society is reasonably free from ideological, religious, class, regional, tribal, and/or ethnic conflicts.
3. ***External involvement* (10 points):** The degree to which the country is free from involvement with outside powers, movements, organizations, and/or institutions.

- Policy Factors

4. ***Development* (10 points):** The capability of national policy-makers and administrative processes to encourage the necessary changes in the economy in the long run, as it moves from one stage of development to another, and the expected impact of those changes on foreign investors in the automotive industry.
5. ***Economic management* (10 points):** The capability of governmental policymakers and processes to minimize the adverse effects of cyclical economic fluctuations.

- Regulatory Factors

6. ***Finance* (10 points):** The degree to which regulations restrict financial aspects of an investment, such as taking profits out of the country, foreign exchange rates, taxes, or price and credit controls.
7. ***Energy* (10 points):** The degree to which a motor vehicle operation will not be hurt by energy policies concerning availability and security of supply, control of demand, or fuel consumption.
8. ***Labor* (10 points):** The degree to which a motor vehicle investment will not be adversely affected by policies toward labor, such as regulations of unemployment, unionization, bargaining, or arbitration.
9. ***Automotive* (15 points):** The degree to which the overall management of an investment by a foreign automotive producer will not be seriously distorted by local content requirements, import restrictions, export incentives, domestication of management or ownership, functional spin-off requirements, non-auto transportation requirements, or restrictions on the ownership of cars and trucks.

Policy and regulatory factors together represent 65 percent of the total weighting, and macropolitical factors account for 35 percent. These weights reflect the specific risks faced by the auto industry. Factors and their relative importance would differ for companies in other industries, such as Exxon in the oil industry or Citicorp in the banking industry.[44]

Political Mechanisms

Governments and businesses utilize a variety of political strategies, as discussed in Chapter 3, to cope with political and legal forces. In this section we go beyond those strategies to describe two significant categories of international political practices: (1) protectionism and (2) bribery and extortion. We do so to alert you to actual practices that you are bound to encounter someday in international operations.

Ethics
Some people say that, although protectionism may be legal, it is at the very least unsparing, if not unethical. They argue that it protects U.S. goods through legal means rather than by letting the market force U.S. firms to make superior products at competitive prices. (A case in point: U.S. automakers used protectionism against higher quality Japanese imports.) What do you think?

Protectionism. Various mechanisms designed to help a home-based industry or firms avoid (or reduce) potential (or actual) competitive or political threats from abroad are called **protectionism.** Four widely used protectionism mechanisms are tariffs, quotas, subsidies, and cartels.

A **tariff** is a government tax on goods or services entering the country. Its purpose is to raise the price of imported goods or services. As a result, domestic goods and services gain a relative price advantage. Consider a few of the problems that Mark Thimmig faces in running Trinity Motors, the General Motors Corporation dealership in Moscow. When Trinity opened its U.S.-style showroom in 1992, imported cars were exempt from Russian tariffs. Since then, tariffs and other taxes have climbed to a combined 166% of the base car price. A Chevrolet Caprice that retails for $24,000 in the United States sells in Moscow for $58,000. Thimmig recognizes that Russia's duties are meant to protect the country's domestic carmakers, which produced about 1 million passenger cars in 1994.[45]

A **quota** is a restriction on the quantity of a country's imports (or sometimes, on its exports). Import quotas generally are intended to guarantee home-country manufacturers access to a certain percentage of the domestic market. For example, U.S. sugar import quotas have existed for more than fifty years. The intent is to preserve about half the domestic market for U.S. sugar producers. Domestic sugar cane and sugar beet growers are guaranteed about $0.215 a pound. Hence U.S. consumers pay an estimated $3 billion per year in extra food costs because of sugar quotas.[46] Most experts agree that, if protectionism is politically unavoidable, tariffs are preferable to quotas. The reason is that quotas fix the levels of imports entering a country and thus freeze markets. Domestic producers then are under less pressure to become more productive and efficient. Quotas are a hidden tax on consumers, whereas tariffs are a more obvious tax.

A **subsidy** is a direct or indirect payment by a government to its country's firms to make selling or investing abroad cheaper for them—and thus more profitable. For example, the Overseas Private Investment Corporation (OPIC) is a self-sustaining agency of the U.S. government that helps qualified U.S. investors establish commercial projects in developing countries. The agency has programs that offer reinvestment assistance and financing. It also insures eligible projects against losses from political risks, including government seizure of assets, nonconvertibility of local currency into U.S. dollars, and damage caused by war, revolution, insurrection, or strife.[47] Many countries provide subsidies to farmers whose products are then able to compete on price in global markets.

A **cartel** is an alliance of producers engaged in the same type of business, formed to limit or eliminate competition.[48] Tariffs, subsidies, and quotas are implemented through government regulations. In contrast, cartels are negotiated agreements between firms or governments, as in the case of the Organization of Petroleum Exporting Countries (OPEC). A primary objective of any cartel is to protect its members' revenues and profits by controlling output and therefore prices. International cartels currently exist in oil, copper, aluminum, natural rubber, and other raw products. The best-known cartel is OPEC, which was formed in 1960. As evidenced by the recent history of the oil industry and OPEC, cartels often have roller-coaster lives. In recent years, OPEC hasn't been very effective in controlling oil production by member countries. Members often cannot agree on prices or quantities to be produced. By law, U.S. firms are forbidden to form or participate directly in cartels because their purpose is at odds with preserving competitive markets and individual rights based on private property.

Protectionism has both strong advocates and opponents. Generally, it works against consumers' interests by raising prices. Advocates claim that it protects home-country industries and jobs against unfair competition from countries with subsistence wages and special subsidies. Therefore whether companies, business associations, and employee groups favor or oppose protectionism depends on how they interpret a particular measure in their own interests.[49]

Bribery and Extortion. A **bribe** is an improper payment made to induce the recipient to do something for the payer. Bribes are illegal in Canada, the U.S., and many other countries, but they are not illegal in some countries. By offering a bribe, the payer

Ethics
Americans doing business in a foreign country may consider offering a payment to an official a "bribe." To local officials, the so-called "bribe" is a time-honored tradition. Are Americans imposing their moral judgments on others who have a right to live any way they choose in their own countries? What do you think?

hopes to obtain a special favor in exchange for something of value (money, a trip, a car, or the like). In recent years, the growing moral revulsion against bribery and other forms of corruption has swept politicians out of office in Brazil, Italy, and Japan. In Italy, state prosecutors exposed an elaborate web of relationships among the Mafia, politicians, and business executives. Bids for highways, sewers, and other public projects now come in at up to 40 percent below the past bids for comparable projects.[50]

Extortion is a payment made to ensure that the recipient does not harm the payer in some way. The purpose of extortion is to obtain something of value by threatening harm to the payer.[51] Coca-Cola refused to respond to extortion efforts by the Russian Mafia. In retaliation, the Mafia launched a bazooka attack on the bottling plant that Coca-Cola was building in Moscow. In addition, the Mafia has intimidated many of the company's distributors in Russia.[52]

Bribery and extortion are practiced throughout the world. They occur frequently in Algeria, Iraq, Saudi Arabia, Bolivia, Kenya, Indonesia, Nigeria, and several other countries. In fact, some countries culturally define certain forms of bribery and extortion as an acceptable, appropriate, and expected form of gift giving.[53]

The U.S. Foreign Corrupt Practices Act of 1977 makes it a crime for U.S. corporations to offer or make payments to officials of foreign governments or companies for the purpose of obtaining or retaining business. The act established specific record-keeping requirements for publicly held corporations, making difficult the concealment of political payments prohibited by the act. Violators—both corporations and individuals—face stiff penalties. A company may be fined up to $1 million, and a manager who directly participates in or has knowledge of any violations of the act faces up to five years in prison and/or $10,000 in fines.[54] Furthermore, the act prohibits corporations from paying any fines imposed on their directors, managers, employees, or agents.

Ethics
Where do you draw the monetary line between a "grease payment" and a "bribe"? Is a bottle of wine a bribe or grease? How about a case of wine? What if a case of wine were given to the official's cousin instead of directly to the official?

The act does not prohibit grease payments to employees of foreign governments whose duties are primarily procedural or clerical. **Grease payments** are small payments—almost gratuities—used to get lower level government employees to speed up required paperwork. Such payments may be required to persuade employees to perform their normal duties. Prohibiting grease payments would put U.S. firms at an extreme competitive disadvantage when conducting business abroad. Such a prohibition also would be very difficult to enforce. For example, Paul Gimona of Rome, Italy, is a manufacturer's representative and sole distributor of a high-tech Swedish oil flow detector. His territory includes the United Arab Emirates, Egypt, and other Mideast oil countries. To get his company's device installed in pipelines as they are built, he must pay an unofficial fee to local inspection officials who then give approval to the project.[55]

5
Identify the competitive forces fostered by the recent major trade agreements.

COMPETITIVE FORCES

We discussed five key competitive forces in Chapter 3: competitors, new entrants, substitute goods and services, customers, and suppliers. These forces must be diagnosed and interpreted by management whether the firm competes locally (say, in the Seattle, Washington, area), nationally (say, in Canada), regionally (say, in North America), or worldwide. In this section we briefly review three major agreements, resulting from various political forces, that directly affect one or more of the five competitive forces. These agreements, when implemented as intended, will heighten the market-based competitive pressures on firms.

General Agreement on Tariffs and Trade

The General Agreement on Tariffs and Trade (GATT) represents a series of negotiated understandings regarding trade and related issues among the participating countries. The first GATT was signed by 23 countries in 1947, and seven rounds of negotiations have followed. The most recent round, called the *Uruguay Round,* began in 1986 and continued through the end of 1993.[56] At the end of 1994, the legislatures of only 24 of the 123 participating nations have ratified the new accords. The U.S. Congress was the latest to do so, ratifying late in 1994 the provisions that the Clinton administration had agreed to.

The new GATT proposes to cut tariffs on 8,000 categories of manufactured goods. It also attempts to strengthen copyright and patent protections and extends world trade rules to services. It sets up a new World Trade Organization (WTO), which replaces GATT. Under GATT, the United States and other nations have been able to block adverse rulings by arbitration panels but could not do so under the new WTO. Some experts forecast that this latest agreement could boost world output by $270 billion a year by 2005 and create millions of jobs in the United States and Canada over the next decade.[57]

Three concepts have been fundamental to the various rounds of GATT negotiations. The *most forward nation concept* means that when country A grants a tariff concession to country B, the same concession automatically applies to all other countries that are members of GATT. The *reciprocity concept* ensures each member country that it will not be forced to reduce tariffs unilaterally. A tariff concession is made only in return for comparable concessions from the other countries. The *transparency concept* establishes that any tariffs be readily visible to all countries. In theory, tariffs are the only permitted form of restriction. Thus GATT doesn't allow internal taxes and regulations to be applied to imported goods if they are not equally applied to domestic goods. However, GATT provides for exceptions to these concepts. For example, the *escape clause* provides that, if a product is being imported into a country in such increased quantities that it causes or threatens to cause serious injury to domestic producers of that product, the importing country may temporarily increase the tariff.[58] The following Global Insight describes U.S. producers' response to rising honey imports from China.

Global *Insight*

Honey Imports from China

The U.S. honey-producing industry filed an antidumping petition against China in 1994. This action was taken to stem a rising tide of cheap imported honey that has devastated U.S. producers. Honey imports from the People's Republic of China increased from about 25 million pounds in 1990 to some 77 million pounds in 1993 and were estimated to be at the same level or higher in 1994.

The petition claims that China is selling honey in the United States for as little as $0.30 a pound—exclusive of freight, duties, assessments, and insurance—although actual production and packaging costs are about $0.83 per pound.

The Chinese bee industry is subsidized by its government, claims Richard Adee, president of the American Honey Producers. For example, Adee claims that Chinese producers can buy pesticide strips used to control mites on bees for $0.05 each but that U.S. producers must pay $1.65 each for the same strips.

In late 1994, the International Trade Commission, an arm of the U.S. government, was considering recommending to the president imposition of a 170 percent tariff on Chinese honey.[59]

Under GATT, trade negotiations also may take place directly between two or more countries. For example, the United States and Japan have engaged in grueling negotiations to further open Japanese markets to U.S. exports and investments. An agreement was reached in late 1994 that provides some opening in the areas of government purchasing practices, insurance, medical equipment, window glass, and telecommunications equipment. Formulas also were established to measure the rate of progress in opening Japan's markets.[60]

North American Free Trade Agreement[61]

The North American Free Trade Agreement (NAFTA) went into effect on January 1, 1994. It created a U.S., Canadian, and Mexican trade zone of 8.2 million square miles, 364 million consumers, and $7 trillion in economic activity. NAFTA represents an extension of the Canada-United States Free Trade Agreement, which went into effect on January 1, 1989.[62]

Actually, NAFTA didn't create free trade, but it certainly liberalizes trade. Over a fifteen-year period, NAFTA initially is intended to reduce and eliminate all tariffs and most nontariff barriers between Canada, Mexico, and the United States. Although full elimination of tariffs will take fifteen years, about 68 percent of the goods imported from Mexico may now enter the United States without tariffs. At the same time, 50 percent of U.S. exports to Mexico are now tariff-free. The agreement also realizes long-held goals of liberalizing trade in services and foreign investment rules abroad, and it tightens the protection of intellectual property (copyrights and patents, in particular).

Ethics
On the Mexican side of the U.S.-Mexico border American, Japanese, and European firms have set up manufacturing operations, called *maquiladoras*. These jobs used to be done by American workers. Some critics say that the maquiladoras are exploiting Mexican workers by paying them a fraction of what U.S. workers get and that they are ruining the environment because Mexico has such lenient antipollution laws. The firms argue that they are helping Mexicans who used to have high unemployment and poor working conditions. What do you think?

Although NAFTA further opens Canadian and U.S. markets, the most significant liberalization applies to Mexico. NAFTA expands Canadian and U.S. companies' ability to establish or purchase a business in Mexico and facilitates their ability to sell if they want to leave. NAFTA also loosens previous restrictions on expanding operations for such companies, and it removes restrictions on transferring profits to other countries.

Despite much liberalization, NAFTA retains protectionist elements, some of which may persist indefinitely. NAFTA protects sensitive sectors (e.g., agriculture, minerals, banking, textiles, and apparel) by stretching out the phase-in time, but this protection is temporary. NAFTA also contains other types of protection that not only are permanent but appear to raise trade barriers above pre-NAFTA levels. In some sectors—notably automobiles, textiles, and apparel—NAFTA imposes higher North American content rules. Under the previous Canada-United States Free Trade Agreement, for example, automobiles could be imported duty-free if they contained at least 50 percent Canadian-U.S. inputs. For auto imports to receive NAFTA benefits, the North American rule is now 62.5 percent. For textiles or apparel to qualify for "free" trade under NAFTA, all components—beginning with the yarn or fiber—must be made in North America.

The services that received the most attention in the NAFTA negotiations were finance, insurance, transportation, and telecommunications. NAFTA doesn't change requirements for foreign banks' entry into the United States and Canada. But the opening of the Mexican financial system is among the agreement's most significant achievements. Requirements for entry into brokerage, bonding, insurance, leasing, and warehousing are even more liberal than for banking.

Teaching Tip
GATT and NAFTA have been controversial. For extra credit, have students take a poll of ten people they do not know, asking them whether GATT and NAFTA have helped or hurt their pocketbooks. Ask the students to report back to the next class session.

NAFTA and GATT do not eliminate all trade problems among the member countries. But they do provide frameworks through which these problems can be resolved. The less restricted trade resulting from these agreements increases the competitive forces on firms. The ultimate intent is to achieve greater efficiency and consumer satisfaction. GATT and NAFTA are political documents that attempt to cope with competing economic and cultural interests among countries. As such, they contain loopholes and exceptions that will be tested over the decades to come. The provisions of these agreements no doubt will be welcomed or resisted, depending on their effect on a particular country and industry.[63]

European Union

The European Union (EU), called the European Community (EC) until 1994, has twelve members: Belgium, Denmark, France, Germany, Greece, Ireland, Italy, Luxemburg, the Netherlands, Portugal, Spain, and the United Kingdom. These countries contain some 350 million consumers. Austria, Finland, Norway, and Sweden are expected to join the

Discussion Question 3
Is Russia likely to be permitted to join the European Union in the foreseeable future? Why or why not?

EU sometime in 1995 or 1996. These four countries plus Turkey and Iceland have been members of the European Free Trade Association (EFTA) for about thirty years. The second group of additional countries expected to join the EU are Hungary, Poland, and the Czech Republic. The potential membership of other countries (Turkey, Slovakia, Estonia, Latvia, Lithuania, and the other newly independent countries from the former Soviet Union) remains to be determined.[64]

The goals of the European Union include the creation of a single market among the member countries through the removal of trade barriers (such as tariffs) and establishing the free movement of goods, people, services, and investment capital. The implementation of these and other goals officially began at the end of 1992. In addition, the changes go beyond economic interests to include social changes as well.[65] Educational degrees have already been affected. The EU Council of Ministers issued a directive that recognizes diplomas of higher education across national boundaries. This action makes it easier for professionals to work in different countries. Most member countries have developed master's degree programs in business administration that are compatible with each others' and those in the United States.

The EU clearly is more than an economic union: It is a state of mind and a political force. At the same time, it should lead to less government interference in economic activities. Uniform standards of quality through ISO, worker safety, and environmental controls will be expected of all companies who trade in the EU.

A major stage of the EU program is to complete formation of the common internal market. That involves eliminating

1. *physical barriers* at each country's borders, which prevent the free flow of goods and persons;
2. *technical barriers,* which prevent goods produced or traded in one member nation from being sold in others;
3. *fiscal barriers,* such as red tape and the different national tax systems, which hinder cross-border trade; and
4. *financial barriers,* which prevent the free movement of investment capital.

The EU also intends to introduce a common currency no later than 1999. Owing to nationalistic and other economic factors, most analysts are skeptical that this goal will be achieved.[66]

The European Commission is the EU's executive body and sole initiator of legislation. The commission claims that 95 percent of the legislature measures set out in the 1992 program have been adopted and only 17 remain to be acted on as of 1995. However, the toughest issues were not included in the 1992 program, including agreement on a common immigration policy. Some member nations are concerned that they'll be flooded with immigrants if an open door policy is adopted.

The EU has already increased market opportunities, fostered competition, and encouraged competition from the outside. The removal of transnational trade restrictions and the relaxation of border controls have had a considerable impact on U.S. and Canadian companies. For example, NBC, with no previous global experience, took control of Europe's Super Channel in 1994. It is now beaming its programs to about 60 million homes and hotels across Europe.[67]

Others continue to be concerned that the supposedly free market of Europe will be anything but free to outsiders. The EU Commission has pressured U.S. and Japanese firms to conduct more research and production in Europe or face the risk of increased tariffs and other barriers. Restrictions still apply to non-EU banks and security firms unless foreign countries (e.g., the United States, Canada, and Japan) grant reciprocal rights. These restrictions range from limiting the right to acquire banks in EU countries to special taxes on foreign banks operating there.[68]

Various alternative strategies are available to U.S. and Canadian enterprises. One is to export goods and services to the EU. In general, North American firms have had only limited success with this strategy. The most successful strategy has been setting up sub-

One of the goals of the EU program is to form a common internal market. This will involve removing physical barriers at each country's borders. Here there is a delay in crossing the border from Germany into the Czech Republic, which is not a member of the EU.

sidiaries or branches in one or more of the EU countries. The advantages of subsidiaries has been demonstrated by well-established companies such as Opel (a subsidiary of GM in Germany), Ford, and IBM. Some companies have consolidated their previous positions in Europe. For example, United Parcel Service (UPS) purchased eleven companies in EU nations to strengthen its market position. Whirlpool, one of the largest U.S. manufacturers of appliances, formed a joint venture with the Dutch electronics firm N.V. Philips. They are making major appliances under the Philips name for sale in the EU.[69]

6

Describe how cultural factors affect international management.

CULTURAL FORCES

The cultural forces discussed in Chapter 3 underlie the day-to-day competitive and political forces operating within and among nations. Four aspects of a culture that have direct implications for international management are views of social change, time orientation, language, and value systems.

Views of Social Change

Ask Students

Would you expect non-Western countries or Western countries to have a faster new product development cycle? Explain.

Different views of the need for and pace of social change can have a significant impact on an organization's plans for international operations. The people of many non-Western cultures, such as those of India, Saudi Arabia, and China, view change as a slow and natural progression. For them change is part of the evolution of human beings and the universe, guided by a Supreme Being, and the attitude toward it tends to be passive or reactive. In contrast, the people of Western cultures tend to view change differently. For them change can be shaped and controlled to achieve their own objectives and destinies, and the attitude tends to be proactive. Therefore Western managers assigned to non-Western countries often run into difficulty when trying to introduce innovations too rapidly. In cultures that hold a passive/reactive view of change, new ways of doing things often must go hand in hand with a painstaking concern for their effect on interpersonal relationships. People in nations such as India, Italy, and Turkey that are characterized by high uncertainty avoidance also are likely to resist or react cautiously to social change. Managers plunged into these cultures have to recognize this viewpoint, plan for it, and manage change accordingly.[70]

Time Orientation

Many people in the United States and Canada think of time as an extremely scarce commodity. They often say that "time is money," or that "there is too little time." Several popular books on time management show an almost frenetic concern with how managers should plan their days. The need to set and stick to tight deadlines for accomplishing tasks is a basic tenet of this style of management. Other books, such as *Fast Cycle Time,* go on to suggest that the future belongs to the time-based competitors.[71]

In some cultures, however, time is viewed as an unlimited and unending resource. For example, Hindus believe that time does not begin at birth or end at death. The Hindu belief in reincarnation gives life a nontemporal, everlasting dimension. Because of such attitudes, employees, customers, and suppliers in some cultures are quite casual about keeping appointments and meeting deadlines—an indifference that can be highly frustrating to Canadian and U.S. managers who have to deal with them.

Traditionally, the Mexican attitude toward time could best be summed up in the word *mañana,* meaning "not today"—but not necessarily tomorrow either! A manager in Mexico might have said, "Yes, your shipment will be ready on Tuesday." You would arrive on Tuesday to pick it up but find that it wasn't ready. No one was upset or embarrassed; they would say politely that the paperwork had not been processed yet or offer some other explanation. Time commitments were considered desirable but not binding promises. This attitude toward time is changing among Mexican businesspeople and professionals. As life-styles become more complex and pressures for greater productivity increase, more people in Mexico are paying increased attention to punctuality and meeting time commitments.[72]

Ask Students
How do you feel about time? Does this belief fit with the type of job and the type of employer you want?

Real-World Example
Chevy's Nova is pronounced "no va" in Italian, which means "doesn't go." Coca-Cola means "bite the head of a dead tadpole" when translated into Chinese.

Language

Language serves to bind as well as to separate cultures. Fluency in another language can give an international manager a competitive edge in understanding and gaining the acceptance of people from the host culture. However, the ability to speak a language correctly isn't enough: A manager must also be able to recognize and interpret the nuances of phrases, sayings, and nonverbal gestures.

The story is told of several U.S. executives who were trying to negotiate with their Japanese counterparts. The American head negotiator made a proposal. The Japanese head negotiator was silent. His silence meant that he was considering the offer. The American, however, took his silence to mean that the offer was not good enough. So the American raised the offer! Again the Japanese considered in silence, and again the silence prompted the American negotiator to raise the offer. Finally the American reached his limit, and an agreement was struck. The Japanese head negotiator had obtained several concessions simply because the American negotiator has misread his silence.[73] The following Diversity Insight provides additional perspective on the need to be sensitive to unique patterns of language and communication with those from another culture.

Teaching Tip
Many students view their foreign language requirements as just another roadblock to getting their degrees. Tell students that learning a business-related second language will help them find a better job.

Real-World Example
Nonverbal communication also differs among cultures. In most European countries, not having both hands on the table at a business meeting is considered to be impolite.

Diversity *Insight*

Face of Honor

The public image, the face of honor, is carefully observed in Mexico. Putting on a good appearance is tremendously important at all levels of society. A child may quit school because his or her family can't afford good shoes. A new salesperson's first purchase may be a proper-looking gold watch. Employees will quit in outrage if criticized in public by their bosses.

Maintaining face and minding that of others is one of the reasons for what appears to be excessive flattery and flowery language. Similarly, status considerations lie behind the custom of calling people by their titles, rather than by their surnames—much less their first names. Thus, showing respect in a business setting involves keeping a proper distance; that is, being formal rather than friendly, casual, and intimate.

An American manager in a casting plant in Chihuahua, Mexico, habitually wore jeans and rumpled sports shirts. He insisted that everyone call him Jim and addressed all the Mexican managers by their first names. He felt that he was doing a good job of reducing the visible economic and status gap between himself and the Mexicans. Thus he was amazed to hear through the grapevine that the local employees and staff considered him uncultured and boorish. In Mexico, a manager's level in the hierarchy is to be reflected in appropriate appearance and language.[74]

Value Systems

In Chapter 3 we discussed the importance of value systems and described four value dimensions: power distance, uncertainty avoidance, individualism (versus collectivism) and masculinity (versus femininity). Differences in cultural values naturally affect how managers and professionals function in international operations. However, an organization's ethical values do not have to be abandoned abroad, as illustrated in the following Ethics Insight on Levi Strauss, the world's largest manufacturer of apparel.

Ethics *Insight*

Levi Strauss's Global Values

Levi Strauss, headquartered in San Francisco, got a jolt in 1991. One of its suppliers in the U.S. territory of Saipan was accused of keeping some imported Chinese women as virtual slaves. After finding that the workers were being paid below the island's legal minimum, Levi fired the contractor. It then formed a committee of top managers to review the way it monitored contractors. In early 1992, it became the first multinational corporation to adopt a wide-ranging set of guidelines for its supplier factories, covering the treatment of workers and the environmental impact of production. The company even inspects supplier factories and will cancel contracts with those that violate its standards. Levi Strauss also was concerned with its image among customers. "Anyone seeking to protect their brand and company reputation will realize these policies make business sense," says Robert Dunn, who helped design the company's human rights plan. "The alternative is to put ourselves at risk."

Citing human rights violations of its global sourcing guidelines, the company in May of 1993 announced that it was pulling all its contracting operations out of China. The guidelines include health and safety, human rights, and environmental standards, which the company believes are basic to ethical business operations. On the question of human rights, the document notes: "We should not initiate or renew contractual relationships in countries where there are pervasive violations of basic human rights."

After sending investigators to the more than forty countries in which the company has contractors, chairman and CEO Robert Haas said China (and Burma) just didn't measure up. About thirty contractors were affected. However, the company continues to buy fabric in China and sell its clothes there. The decision sparked fiery debate within the company. An internal committee recommended that it continue to do business with the Chinese factories that were seeking to reform their operations, rather than punish them. Some observers say that the move will only benefit Levi Strauss's competition as more manufacturers are drawn to China for its cheap labor.[75]

Because of continuing interest in the competitive challenge of Japanese firms, let's look at some of the differences in Japanese and U.S. values and a few of the management implications of these differences.

Teaching Tip
Divide the class into groups of 3. Have one student volunteer to tell a story of a values conflict that she or he had with someone from another culture. Ask the second student to be an interviewer. Tell the interviewer to make sure to elicit the underlying values. The third student shouldn't say anything until the other two have finished. This person should ask any questions the interviewer missed.

U.S. and Japanese Societies. Collectivism means that people identify strongly with the groups to which they belong—from the family unit to the society as a whole. It emphasizes group goals and dependence on others. Groups are not thought of as collections of individuals.[76] Rather, the group exists first and absorbs the individual into it. Consequently the individual is governed by the norms (rules) of each group. The Japanese form of collectivism leads to group cohesion. The short-term sacrifice of the individual's wants for the benefit of the group is commonly accepted. As a result, Japan's high levels of achievement tend to be group-oriented. Furthermore, because Japan's value system is less diverse than that of the United States, severe conflicts caused by underlying differences in values occur less frequently.

In contrast, much (but not all) of the population in the United States—as well as countries such as Canada, Australia, and Great Britain—is relatively individualistic. James Hodgson, former U.S. ambassador to Japan, explains the basic difference between U.S. and Japanese societies:

> *American society is first and foremost underpinned by that venerable Judeo-Christian objective of individual justice. The Japanese, however, spurn individual justice as a priority goal. Instead, they seek something in many ways the opposite; they seek group harmony. We American justice-seekers speak proudly of our rights. The harmony-minded Japanese stress not rights but relations. They reject our emphasis on individual rights as being divisive and disruptive.*
>
> *Americans make our national policy decisions and settle our many differences largely through adversary proceedings—we compete, we sue, and we vote. In Japan "adversaries" is out. Consensus is in, and it has been for centuries. The Japanese do not consider 51 percent a "majority," at least not a workable majority. The distinction that emerges from all this may be capsulized simply. In American life, the individual strives to stand out. The Japanese citizen, however, seeks to fit in. And fit in he does—into his family, his schools, his company, his union, his nation. Japan is a nation where the parts fit.*[77]

U.S. and Japanese Organizations. The fundamental societal differences that we have been discussing are reflected in some very basic differences between U.S. and Japanese organizations. Does this mean that U.S. managers cannot transfer to their organization *any* of the ideas that have worked so well in Japan? Not at all. In fact, several Japanese management practices—such as the use of team management—have been successfully adapted to U.S. operations.[78]

In identifying differences between the two nations' organizations and management practices, we are painting with a broad brush. Moreover, the differences in values and philosophies among U.S. firms and managers are much greater than the differences among Japanese firms and managers. Table 4.1 broadly characterizes and compares U.S. and Japanese organizations based on six dimensions that are strongly influenced by the contrasting values of the two nations. The themes of individualism in the United States and collectivism in Japan are readily apparent. For many Japanese, the company isn't just a place to work. It is a sharing and caring group, which treats the employee like a family member. Japanese employees are proud of their company's success and frequently identify with their firm—an employee becomes Mr. Yamada of Sony, Mr. Tanaka of Toyota, Ms. Ogawa of Honda, and so on.[79]

Discussion Question 5
Which portions of the Japanese management system might be applied successfully to a U.S. car manufacturer? Could the Japanese system be applied successfully to Roadway Trucking Company? Explain.

Changing Landscape. Exceptions to the traditional patterns in Japanese organizations suggested in Table 4.1 are becoming more numerous. Highly capable and assertive individuals do leave their organizations and start businesses of their own or join smaller organizations. In the past, firms started by such individualistic entrepreneurs included

TABLE 4.1

Characteristics of Many U.S. and Japanese Organizations

Dimensions	Many (not all) Major U.S. Organizations	Many (not all) Major Japanese Organizations
Employment	Short term on average, but varies widely; unstable and insecure	Long term for males (decline in lifetime employment) moderately secure and stable
Salary and promotion	Merit pay based on individual contribution; rapid promotion in career	Seniority-based early in career; more merit pay later; slow promotion; group-based bonuses
Attitude toward work	Individual responsibilities	Collective responsibilities; group loyalty, duty-oriented
Decision making	Individual-oriented; relative top-down emphasis	Consultation oriented; bottom-up inputs
Relationship with employees	Depersonalized; emphasis on formal contacts; employee resents organizational interference into his or her personal life	Personalized; employee treated as family member; paternalism; employee expects organization to show concern for personal affairs
Competition	Relatively free and open among individuals	Low among individuals within groups; high among groups

Source: Adapted from Keys, J.B., Denton, L.T., and Miller, T.R. The Japanese management theory jungle—Revisited. *Journal of Management,* 1994, 20, 373–402; Ouchi, W.G., and Jaeger, A.M. Type Z organization: Stability in the midst of mobility. *Academy of Management Review,* 1978, 3, 305–314.

Honda, Sony, and Matsushita. Small Japanese enterprises (300 or fewer employees) can't afford to offer extensive fringe benefits as do the giant corporations. Small firms also are able to offer less job security because they are less secure in their markets. Owing to the recent recession in Japan, even large corporations, such as Toyota, have found it necessary to create a new category of temporary (contract) professional workers.[80]

Some young Japanese workers are not as devoted as the preceding generation to long hours of hard work. Many young Japanese have realized that some aspects of the Western life-style are preferable to their own. Some have accepted the concept of "flexible individualism"—not the rugged American variety but a simple desire for self-expression in their work, life-styles, and possessions.[81]

Child rearing and other household duties, once relegated completely to the woman, are sometimes shared by husband and wife. Materialism is leading some families to have two wage earners.[82] These trends in Japan appear to be a result of its increasingly global economic participation, which is modifying its once homogeneous culture.

CHAPTER SUMMARY

1 ***Describe the growing global economy.***

Various indicators show the rapid growth of the global economy. One-fifth of world output is now traded, and middle-class consumers are emerging throughout the world. Corporations are locating operations in many countries to serve growing consumer demand. New information technologies are helping create the *global village*. Quality expectations increasingly cut across national boundaries, as illustrated by the ISO 9000 quality standards.

2 ***Identify five ways of organizing for international operations.***
Approaches to international operations continue to evolve. Basically, involvement in international business begins with a commission agent and culminates in a multinational corporation, which views issues and opportunities from a worldwide perspective. Intervening steps are the export manager, export department, and international corporation approaches. These organizational approaches increase in relative complexity and relative resource commitments required.

3 ***Describe the main strategies for international operations.***
The strategies include exporting, licensing, franchising, alliances, multidomestic, and global. They also vary in both relative complexity and relative resource commitments required.

4 ***Explain how international political-forces affect organizations.***
International operations create new complexities, risks, and uncertainties. Four broad categories of political-legal issues are domestic instability, foreign conflict, political climate, and economic climate. GM's political risk assessment system was presented as one of many possible approaches. Political mechanisms utilized in international business include tariffs, quotas, subsidies, cartels, bribes, and extortion.

5 ***Identify the competitive forces fostered by three recent major trade agreements.***
The General Agreement on Tariffs and Trade (GATT) is intended to open markets and reduce barriers (such as tariffs) among its 123 member nations. The North American Free Trade Agreement (NAFTA) is intended to further reduce barriers, encourage investment, and stimulate trade among Canada, Mexico, and the United States. The European Union (EU) is an organization of 12 member countries. Its primary goals are to create a single market and allow the free movement of goods, services, people, and capital among its member countries. All of these agreements have the ultimate goal of improving the standard of living and quality of life for the citizens of the member countries.

6 ***Describe how cultural factors affect international management.***
The four cultural factors that can influence how an organization is managed include views of social change (passive or active), time (scarce or unlimited), language (verbal and nonverbal differences), and value systems (such as individualism versus collectivism). Special attention is given to understanding how cultural issues have led to differences in the management system in Japan and the United States.

QUESTIONS FOR DISCUSSION

1. What approach might a company such as Frito-Lay use to begin doing business in India? In Russia? In Mexico?
2. If entrepreneur Juanita Jain wanted to expand her car dealership business to include Monterrey, a large city in northern Mexico, how might she begin the process?
3. Is Russia likely to be permitted to join the European Union in the foreseeable future? Why or why not?
4. Suppose that Texas Instruments (TI), a large microprocessor manufacturer, wants to open four new plants overseas. Name four countries that might represent a high degree of risk for such operations. Would TI be better off exporting to those countries? Why or why not?
5. Which portions of the Japanese management system might be applied successfully to a U.S. car manufacturer? Could the Japanese system be applied successfully to Roadway Trucking Company? Explain.

FROM WHERE YOU SIT

1. Osh-Kosh Clothing Company has hired you as a service representative in Japan. What recommendations would you make to the management of Osh-Kosh to ensure your success in Japan?
2. Your high-tech employer assigns you to a project team to begin a manufacturing operation in Mexico. What issues will your team have to resolve to be effective?
3. Select a country of interest to you. Describe how you would go about entering that country's market for wood products. Would your approach be different if you worked for one of the Bell operating companies?
4. How important is it to speak the native language of a country to which you have been assigned? How would you prepare yourself for the assignment?
5. Should business school students have more formal education in international business? Why or why not?

Cultural Traits and Preferences[83]

Ten pairs of statements are presented. Pick the statement in each pair that best represents your personal attitudes and preferences. There are no correct or incorrect choices.

1. a. Family has priority.
   b. Family is usually second to work or school.

2. a. I have a fatalistic outlook.
   b. I have a master-of-my-life outlook.

3. a. I am sensitive to differences of opinion.
   b. Sensitivity is a weakness.

4. a. Title and position are more important than money.
   b. Money is a main status indicator and is a reward for achievement.

5. a. I work to live.
   b. I live to work.

6. a. Deadlines and commitments are flexible.
   b. Deadlines and commitments are firm.

7. a. Promotions should be based more heavily on loyalty to my superior.
   b. Promotions should be based more heavily on my performance.

8. a. Truth is a relative concept.
   b. Truth is an absolute value.

9. a. I shun confrontation.
   b. I put up a tough business front.

10. a. Money is for enjoying life.
    b. Money is an end in itself.

Interpretation

Count the number of (a) responses; they are considered to be stereotypical attitudes of traditional Mexican society and managers. Count the number of (b) responses; they are considered to be stereotypical attitudes of traditional U.S. society and managers.

Questions

1. Based on your self-description, what challenges would you expect to face in negotiating with a Mexican manager who represents the stereotypical profile of (a) responses?

2. What precautions should you take in interpreting these profiles?

CRITICAL THINKING CASE

All Shave in Saudi Arabia

Mike Lacey lay on his bed and watched as the fan went around. He felt whipped and did not really know what to do next. All week he had been trying to influence Mustafa Almin. He had had no more effect than the fan was having on the heat of Riyadh (Saudi Arabia).

Until three years ago, the All Shave Company, of which Lacey was Middle Eastern Manager, had been very successful in exporting razors and blades to Saudi Arabia. Then, in the face of possible import restrictions, the company had sold its business to a new company financed by the Almin family. The family was an impressive collection of leading Saudi industrialists who had made a fortune producing steel products but was interested in diversifying. All Shave received a minority interest in the new business in return for its trade name and technical aid.

The contract with the Almin family specified that the new owners would "actively promote All Shave products." Lacey thought that the Almins clearly understood what this type of promotion meant: continuing All Shave's aggressive program that had built the company's sales in the 1970s from nothing to a high level. Under Almin management, however, All Shave sales dropped steadily. It soon became evident that the Almins were not pushing sales. In visits and correspondence, the company applied increasing pressure on the Almins for more activity.

When nothing happened, Lacey finally decided he would go to Saudi Arabia and stay until he could find a way to get the Almins moving. That was over six weeks ago. He had spent the first month in the field and had found that All Shave products were being sold from Almin warehouses with virtually no sales effort. Promotion was limited to a few newspaper ads and a scattering of posters distributed by the company's regular salesmen. No additional sales personnel had been hired to handle All Shave accounts. The selling activity fell far short of All Shave's former program and that of its leading competitor. Lacey worked up a detailed program designed to reestablish All Shave's market position.

For the past week he had argued in vain with Mustafa Almin, the 60-year-old head of the family, to adopt the program. Lacey pointed to the low sales volume and to the Almins' limited program, which he asserted did not meet the agreement's terms. In particular, he demonstrated that All Shave's previous success and the present results achieved by the competition proved the benefits of strong promotion.

Mustafa Almin expressed appreciation for Lacey's interest and efforts but agreed to nothing. He explained that a sales drop was inevitable with the change to the Saudi manufacturer. Though sales were lower, the company was making a reasonable profit. Almin said that he had fulfilled the contract's terms by advertising in the newspaper, even though he did not believe in it and its blatant character hurt the Almin family's image.

Almin believed that a good product was its own best advertisement and, on that basis, the Almin family had built a great business. He observed that the closest competitor sold a higher quality blade than All Shave. He said that it was quite likely that quality, rather than promotion, accounted for the competitor's success. He also pointed to several British firms in related fields who did very little advertising. Since they had been around for many years, Almin felt that their marketing approach must be sound.

Lacey found it hard to rebut these arguments. He was sure he was right and equally sure that Almin was a competent businessman, who should be able to see the logic of his proposal. Lacey greatly respected and liked Almin. Lacey believed that once Almin grasped the value of promotion, he would do great things for All Shave in Saudi Arabia. But how could he convince Almin?

Mustafa Almin settled himself to relax before the evening meal and reflected for a moment on the events of the past week. He had spent a great deal of time with the young man from the United States. Lacey was full of energy and ideas, but he drove so hard. And for what? This whole arrangement with All Shave had turned out differently from what the Almins had expected. The product was good. Left to themselves, the Almins could develop a good business, as they had with the rest of their operations. But they were not left to themselves. Instead, they had been constantly pushed and argued with. These people from the United States never seemed to be satisfied with anything. Now they sent out this young man who scarcely knew the Saudis to tell the Almins how to run their business. It was not pleasant at all. He hoped the young man would give up soon.[84]

Questions

1. What should Mike Lacey do?
2. What should the All Shave company do?
3. What alternative strategies might All Shave have used in doing business in Saudi Arabia?

VIDEO CASE

Doing Business with China

China is the sleeping giant of the twentieth century and is beginning to wake up. Since the United States first granted most-favored nation (MFN) trading status to China in the 1970s, many companies have attempted to open new markets in China and take advantage of its low-wage work force. China has managed to hold on to its MFN status despite resistance from groups alleging human rights abuses.

Compared to industrialized nations in the West and in other parts of Asia, China appears to be economically disadvantaged. For example, the Chinese Gross Domestic Product (GDP) per person was about $1,700 compared to $22,000 in the United States. However, China's annual growth averages 9.4 percent compared to the U.S. rate of 2.7 percent. The annual inflation rate has been 8 percent, which is relatively low compared to rates in other developing nations, such as Russia, that have inflation rates in excess of 50 percent. Pollution emissions remain low at slightly over two tons per capita, probably because few automobiles are used as personal transportation. Finally, there was only 1 telephone line per 1,000 people compared to 40-60 lines in most industrialized nations.

Data regarding cultural and social environments reveal similar contrasts. China has few television sets, movie theaters, and newspapers per 1,000 people compared to the industrialized world. The divorce rate and alcohol consumption are low. Unfortunately, the education level, life expectancy, and access to medical care also are low, and infant mortality is somewhat high at 38 deaths per 1,000 live births (compared to the United States, with 9 deaths per 1,000 live births).

This environment poses both threats and opportunities. Although the market doesn't seem ready for specialty consumer products, many opportunities exist to help China build the necessary business infrastructure, particularly roads, power plants, and telecommunications. In fact, China's ability to sustain high economic growth is largely contingent on its capacity to upgrade its infrastructure. The country's dearth of good highways and its antiquated railroad and aviation systems hamper trade and industrial growth at every turn. Electricity blackouts and a technology-starved telecommunications network further constrain Chinese economic growth. According to a recent survey conducted by Hong Kong-based Peregrine Brokerage, Ltd., China will need at least $233 billion from 1994-2000 to modernize its transport, power, and telecommunications systems. Clearly, Beijing will not have to provide such vast sums itself. China's success in developing its infrastructure will depend in large part on its ability to attract foreign investment to finance key projects.

As evidence of this, many large U.S. companies (e.g., Boeing, GE, Westinghouse Electric, Caterpillar, Du Pont, Motorola, and Eastman Kodak) have opened manufacturing operations there. Some analysts estimate that China will need to double its output of electricity by early in the twenty-first century. Westinghouse gets one-third of its revenues from steam turbines that help convert coal into power. General Electric chose to target China as a customer of medical equipment, locomotives, home appliances, and high-tech plastics for construction. GE also gets a boost from Boeing in China by supplying jet engines for the 62 airplanes recently ordered by Chinese airlines.

Motorola is helping China leap into the cellular age, believing that the country cannot get wired fast enough to provide adequate service for business growth. As evidence of its success, sales of cellular phones and pagers in China were approximately 5 percent of worldwide revenues from these products.

Consumer products such as toothpaste, chewing gum, and soft drinks also are increasing. Coca-Cola entered China in 1979 and has the best chance for success in this market as disposable income continues to rise. Similarly, Colgate generated some brand loyalty early in post-Cultural Revolution China by distributing toothpaste and toothbrushes to elementary school students. And Avon, using its masses-to-masses selling strategy, deploys 25,000 Avon salespersons (generally female) in southern China alone, calling China its number one investment priority for growth.

Among the high-tech products entering the Chinese market are personal computers (PCs). AST Research, a U.S. manufacturer of personal computers, is the PC leader in China with a 26 percent market share. As in other transition economies, AST works through resellers who have access not only to privatized businesses but also to state-owned businesses and governmental agencies.

Not all companies have been as successful as AST. Bill Gates, CEO and Chairman of Microsoft, has been banned from China because he initially ran his Chinese operations from Taiwan. The computer chief of China's technology ministry warned Microsoft that it must conform to Beijing's technology standards. Many firms find that they can enter China only as part of joint ventures. For example, Hewlett-Packard made over $200 million in sales in a joint venture to sell workstations and testing and measuring equipment.

China will continue to pose opportunities for globalization. But companies who venture into this new, complex society must recognize that cultural and social differences will pose difficulties for market entry, management practices, product acceptance, and product use.[85]

Questions

1. Identify four consumer products that probably would be accepted enthusiastically in China. What strategy of international operations would you suggest for each one?
2. What is the single biggest threat to a U.S. company that opens a new production operation in China?
3. If you were going to enter an untapped market in China, how would you choose to organize? Why?

Chapter 5

Strategic Management: Planning and Strategy Formation

Learning *Objectives*

After studying this chapter, you should be able to:

1. Explain why planning may help achieve organizational effectiveness.
2. State the characteristics of strategic and tactical planning.
3. Differentiate the corporate, business, and functional levels of planning and strategies.
4. Explain the eight tasks of the strategic planning process.
5. Use models of business-level strategy to develop competitive strategies.

Chapter *Outline*

Preview *Insight*

Southwest Airlines

The U.S. airline industry has experienced financial losses from 1990 through 1994. Large airlines, such as American Airlines and United Airlines, have tried various strategies to return to profitability. These strategies include cutting costs (primarily through employee layoffs), cutting ticket prices to spur customer demand or meet the price cuts of competitors, reducing the number of daily flights and cities served, and canceling orders for new aircraft. After deregulation of the airline industry in 1978, most large airlines adopted the ***hub-and-spoke route system.*** It flies passengers to a central hub where they change planes and then fly from the hub to their destinations. In contrast, Southwest Airlines uses a point(city)-to-point(city) system. Let's take a look at how Southwest, headquartered in Dallas, and Herb Kelleher, its CEO, have successfully applied unique strategies and practices.

Southwest Airlines stands by itself in the airline industry with an overall low-cost strategy based on (1) relatively short flights (the longest as of 1994 is a three-hour nonstop flight between Phoenix, Arizona, and Nashville, Tennessee), (2) frequent flights between paired cities (minimum of ten per day), (3) no-frills service (no assigned seat, no food, and passenger-handled baggage), (4) rapid turnaround between flights (standard of 20 minutes or less for moving a plane in and out of a gate compared to one hour for larger carriers), and (5) a fleet of only Boeing 737s (cuts maintenance, inventory, and training costs compared to other airlines with many different types of planes). Southwest views automobile travel as a major source of competition.

Southwest's strategies and values are reinforced and promoted by its CEO, Herb Kelleher. The three core values or "pillars of belief at Southwest Airlines" are: (1) work should be fun . . . it can be play . . . enjoy it; (2) work is important . . . don't spoil it with seriousness; and (3) people are important . . . each one makes a difference. Kelleher declares that "Fun is a stimulant to people. They enjoy their work more and work more productively." His humor and energy have been transmitted to employees who even engage in spontaneous entertainment, such as gate agents awarding a prize to the passenger with the largest hole in a sock. The humor has a serious purpose, as Kelleher explains: "What's important is that a customer should get off the airplane feeling: 'I didn't just get from A to B. I had one of the most pleasant experiences I ever had and I'll be back for that reason.' "

Southwest remains unique in the airline industry by satisfying customers with high value at a low price. Kelleher states: "We deliver more for less, not less for less."[1]

Southwest Airlines developed competitive strategies that are supported by a set of values and practices to create a profitable and efficient firm in a turbulent industry. Throughout this chapter, we refer to this Preview Insight and provide additional information on Southwest's planning and strategies.

1

Explain why planning may help achieve organizational effectiveness.

WHY PLAN?

Planning is the most basic managerial function. When done properly, it sets the direction for the organizing, leading, and controlling functions. In Chapter 1, we stated that planning involves defining goals and objectives for future performance and deciding how to reach them. Now we need a more comprehensive definition. **Planning** is the formal process of (1) choosing an organizational mission and overall goals for both the short run and long run, (2) devising divisional, departmental, and even individual goals based on organizational goals, (3) choosing strategies and tactics to achieve those goals, and (4) allocating resources (people, money, equipment, and facilities) to achieve the various goals, strategies, and tactics.[2]

Teaching Tip

An important lesson from the Southwest case is "staying the course." Sometimes managers change plans at the first sign of difficulty, whereas the plan could have worked if given reasonable time and resources. Ask students if they have ever reacted in this way.

The successes at Southwest have occurred, in part, because it followed well-developed plans that called for using a single type of aircraft, flying short-haul routes, maintaining stringent cost controls, controlling growth to avoid too much debt, and so on.

Adapting to Change

Organizations survive only if they can simultaneously manage change, maintain a degree of stability, minimize confusion, and establish a sense of direction. Organizations that effectively accomplish this feat are more likely to progress and grow. As the rate of change and degree of complexity in the business world increase, managers and other employees must find better ways to anticipate and respond to change.

If undertaken properly, planning will assist in (1) identifying future opportunities, (2) anticipating and avoiding future problems, and (3) developing courses of action (strategies and tactics).[3] Thus the organization will have a better chance of achieving its general goals. These goals include adapting and innovating in order to create desirable change, improving productivity, and maintaining organizational stability. Achieving these general goals should enable the organization to reach its ultimate goals—long-term growth, profitability, and survival. In sum, planning at its best creates organizationwide learning. It creates a process for discovering key issues and options.

Facilitating Entrepreneurship

Effective planning should facilitate entrepreneurship. In Chapter 1, we defined the *entrepreneur role* as designing and starting a new project or enterprise. Entrepreneurs such as Herb Kelleher have the drive and ability to envision and create new ventures and new businesses and to bring about major change. In the process they focus their energy and intellect on initiating, doing, and achieving—that is, on building an organization. Similarly, effective planning stimulates new ideas and encourages doing the right things (as opposed to just doing things right).

To encourage entrepreneurship, there is a need for a middle ground between planning paralysis and no planning at all. Compared to some typical large corporation planning practices, the entrepreneurial planning approach is characterized by the following critical elements.[4]

1. Opportunities are screened quickly to weed out unpromising ventures. Thus judgment and reflection, not stacks of studies and data, are encouraged.
2. The focus is on a few important issues. As revealed in the Preview Insight, Herb Kelleher and the other top managers at Southwest Airlines demonstrated great conceptual skills in identifying the key issues for competing profitably in the airline industry.
3. Analysis is quickly integrated with action. There is no need to wait for all the answers as with more comprehensive planning. Also, there is a readiness to change based on signals from customers and competitors. In May 1994, three of the major airline reservation systems removed Southwest's fares and schedules from their lists. They said that they would no longer provide their services to airlines that do not pay them booking fees. Southwest had never paid booking fees, which average about $2.50 per round trip, except to American Airlines. In August 1994 (only three months later), Southwest was testing a "ticketless" system among its corporate travelers and frequent flyers in four of the forty-one cities it serves. Passengers can make reservations, check luggage, and board their flights without a ticket. They receive a confirmation number when making reservations and state the number for a boarding pass when they reach the gate.[5]

Managing Risk and Uncertainty

Effective planning helps reduce risk and uncertainty or, at least, it improves the understanding of the risks and uncertainties associated with decisions. Unfortunately, even the most effective planning can't eliminate risk and uncertainty. As one manager notes, "No amount of sophistication is going to dismiss the fact that all our knowledge is about the past and all of our decisions are about the future."[6] In Chapters 3 and 4, we discussed a wide range of competitive, political-legal, and cultural forces and issues that create opportunities and threats for organizations. Whether managers deal with them *reactively* or *proactively*, these forces are sources of risk and uncertainty. Planning gives managers a better chance to understand these forces as issues that create tensions by pulling an organization in different directions at the same time. For example, if IBM views declining sales for mainframe computers as a threat, a promotional plan designed to increase sales of its PCs might be a likely response. However, IBM may view this same issue (e.g., declining sales) as an opportunity to explore new markets for the product or to develop new products.[7] An even more fundamental issue in planning is the tension between: Where are we are now? and Where do we want to be? Two of the questions raised by this tension are: (1) What are the alternative strategies for closing this gap? and (2) What are the risks or uncertainties of losses or gains associated with each of the strategies?

Maintaining Perspective

Planning works well only when managers and other employees keep in mind that it is a *means*—not an *end*.[8] As a result, managers sometimes approach planning from one of two extremes that are ineffective. One of these extremes is the *extinction-by-instinct* approach: Managers and other employees are so concerned with solving immediate problems and making quick decisions that they neglect to monitor or scan for opportunities and threats. Firms in simple, stable environments (e.g., producing baked goods or canned foods) may use this approach for years without loss in profitability. However, firms in complex and changing environments (e.g., airlines, autos, and computers) are more likely to fail or to grow slowly if they use this approach.[9] The other extreme is the *paralysis-by-analysis* approach: Managers get so bogged down in planning every detail and for every eventuality that they neglect to make the really important decisions or even fail to recognize the important issues. In this approach, strategic planning becomes bureaucratic (e.g., by having lots of planning forms that must be filled in properly) and too quantitative (e.g., by requiring dollars-and-cents justification for everything).

One of the sharpest attacks on the *practice* and *concept* of strategic planning is provided by Henry Mintzberg.[10] We provide a brief look at some of his criticisms. One major pitfall is the assumption that top management and planners take charge, centralizing and isolating the planning process from the people whose commitment is needed to carry out the plans. The process is detached and analytical when, instead, a deep commitment to change is needed. This type of planning favors incremental change rather than sweeping change. It works best when strategy is firmly in place, not when significant change affecting the planning process itself is needed. Mintzberg strips away the pretensions of planners who fuss with perfecting their plans and processes, rather than testing the waters by acting. One fallacy in their thinking is that analysis can provide synthesis, that the strategy-making process can be programmed by using systems, and that systems, not people, think and create strategy. Another fallacy is that conditions will stay relatively stable after the analysis has been completed and plans have been made, allowing the strategic plans to unfold logically and neatly.[11]

Ask Students
Because of the complexity of change, how useful can planning really be? Explain.

2

State the characteristics of strategic and tactical planning.

TYPES OF PLANNING

Both strategic and tactical planning are concerned with developing courses of action, improving effectiveness and productivity, and ensuring profits. There are many types of planning, but for now we divide them into two basic categories: strategic planning and tactical planning.

Strategic Planning

Teaching Tip
Ask a senior university administrator to come to class to discuss the university's strategic plan.

Strategic planning is the process of developing and analyzing the organization's mission and vision, overall goals, and general strategies and allocating resources. In developing strategic plans, managers take an organizationwide approach. The overall purpose of strategic planning is to deal effectively with environmental opportunities and threats as they relate to the organization's strengths and weaknesses.[12]

In some organizations, such as Royal Dutch Shell, the strategic planning process includes **contingency planning,** or preparation for unexpected and rapid changes (positive or negative) in the environment that will have a large impact on the organization and that will require a quick response. A contingency plan could be developed for a disaster response (e.g., an earthquake, flood, or fire destroying the company's largest production facility) or for managing a crisis (e.g., a strike at a busy facility). A positive dramatic event might be how to respond if customer demand for products (goods and/or services) overwhelms the firm's current capacity. Generally, no more than five potentially critical events should be emphasized in contingency planning; too many events can make the process unmanageable. Contingency planning forces managers to be aware of possibilities and prethink strategies to respond to them. In brief, it supports orderly and speedy adaptation, in contrast to paniclike reactions, to external events beyond the organization's direct control.[13]

Teaching Tip
Invite a disaster preparedness official (e.g. Red Cross, FEMA, Fire Department, or Campus Police) to class to discuss scenarios and contingency plans.

Let's now consider briefly the major issues addressed in strategic planning: mission and vision, goals, strategies, and resource allocation.

Mission and Vision. There are no uniform definitions or uses of the terms *mission* and *vision*. Basically, the **mission** is the organization's purpose or reason for existing. A statement of mission may answer basic questions such as: (1) What business are we in? (2) Who are we? and (3) What are we about?[14] It may describe the organization in terms of the customer needs it aims to satisfy, the goods or services it supplies, and the markets it is currently pursuing or intends to pursue in the future. The following statements illustrate how four organizations define their missions.

- *Southwest Airlines*: Dedication to the highest quality of Customer Service delivered with a sense of warmth, friendliness, individual pride, and Company Spirit. We are committed to provide our employees a stable work environment with equal opportunity for learning and personal growth. Creativity and innovation are encouraged for improving the effectiveness of Southwest Airlines. Above all, employees will be provided the same concern, respect, and caring attitude within the organization that they are expected to share externally with every Southwest Customer.[15]
- *AT&T*: Dedicated to being the world's best at bringing people together—giving them easy access to each other and to the information and services they want and need—anytime, anywhere.[16]
- *Cupertino National Bancorp*: To build a growing and profitable business by providing financial services to middle market and emerging-growth commercial and technology companies, real estate firms, executives, and professionals in the [San Francisco] Bay Area.[17]
- *Reader's Digest Association*: The legacy of service and quality lives on—timeless ideas guiding us in our mission: to profitably develop, produce and market high-quality, profitable products that enrich, inform, inspire and entertain people all over the world. Today our company is a global publisher of magazines, books, music and video collections, and one of the world's leading direct mail marketers.[18]

A mission statement has meaning only if it serves as a unifying and driving force for guiding strategic planning and achieving the organization's long-term goals. The mission statement should stimulate those in an organization to think and act strategically—not just once a year but every day.

Some organizations develop a statement of vision different from their mission statement. A **vision** expresses an organization's fundamental aspirations and values, usually by appealing to its members' hearts and minds.[19] A vision statement adds "soul" to a mission statement if it lacks one. The following statements represent the visions of three organizations.

Ethics
Ethics should be part of both the mission and vision development process and written into those statements.

NYNEX Corporation's mission is to be a world-class leader in helping people communicate using information networks and services. NYNEX provides wireline and wireless telecommunications services to 12 million customers in the U.S., and offers these services in selected markets around the world. In 1993, NYNEX began construction of a $1.6 billion "information superhighway" that will serve the northwest region of the U.K.

Teaching Tip
Group students by their extracurricular affiliations. Place the remaining students in a separate group. Have those involved in extracurricular activities draw up mission and vision statements for their activities. Have the nonaffiliated group draw up statements for the university.

Teaching Tip
Have students visit different types of local businesses to learn about their missions and goals and report their findings to the class.

- *Southwest Airlines*: We dignify the CUSTOMER. [The company insists on capitalizing the word *customer* wherever it is used—in ads, brochures, and even the annual report].[20]
- *AT&T*: We intend to lead as providers of communications and information systems that make businesses more productive and enhance people's personal lives.[21]
- *General Motors (GM)*: Our vision is for GM to be the world leader in transportation products and services. We will know we have achieved the vision when we have the most satisfied and enthusiastic customers in all market segments where we compete.[22]

Goals. An organization's **goals** are what it is committed to achieving. Goals may be expressed both qualitatively and quantitatively (what is to be achieved, how much, and by when).

A qualitative goal at Southwest Airlines is to earn a profit associated with expanding into a city within six months. Two of its quantitative goals are (1) to turn each plane around within twenty minutes from the time of arrival at an airport gate, and (2) to maintain costs per available seat mile at least $0.01 below the nearest competitor.[23] Organizational goals at Reader's Digest include: (1) to grow our current product lines by increasing our customer base in countries where we do business, (2) to develop new products to sell to our existing customers, and (3) to expand current product lines into new countries.[24] AT&T has a corporate goal of at least a 10 percent growth in earnings per year.

Strategies. The major courses of action that an organization takes to achieve its goals are called **strategies.**[25] In Chapters 3 and 4, we presented various competitive and political strategies that organizations use to cope with threats or take advantage of opportunities. Throughout this chapter, we present additional general and firm-specific strategies. Southwest Airlines partly achieves its goal of turning flights around within twenty minutes of gate arrival by having flight attendants clean the planes' cabins as soon as passengers have disembarked rather than waiting for a contract service or a ground crew—part of its cross-training strategy. Recall from the Preview Insight that three other Southwest strategies are: one type of aircraft, flights between paired cities to avoid the costs of a hub, and frequent flights between paired cities.

Ethics
Ethics should be applied to the resource allocation process.

Resource Allocation. When an organization allocates resources, it assigns money, people, facilities and equipment, land, and other resources to various functions and tasks. As part of the strategic planning process, **resource allocation** generally means the earmarking of money, through budgets, to various purposes.[26] When an organization announces a **downsizing strategy,** it signals its intent to rely on fewer resources—primarily human—to accomplish its goals. Organizations often implement this strategy through layoffs, early retirement programs, not filling vacant positions, reassignment of personnel, and the like. For example, to cut the financial resources allocated to personnel, IBM has reduced (downsized) its work force from about 410,000 employees in 1984 to some 210,000 employees in 1995.[27]

Teaching Tip
Have students write a goals statement, develop strategies, and allocate resources for completing their degree requirements. Ask several students to share them with the class.

In response to Southwest Airline's tough new competition (e.g., Continental Lite) that emerged in 1994, Herb Kelleher said that "we are . . . going to be very aggressive."[28] For example, it is adding eighteen jets in 1995, sixteen of which will be new Boeing 737–300s and the other two will be leased 737s. Originally, Southwest had planned to add only twelve jets in 1995. These purchases and leases represent a significant allocation of resources by Southwest to help maintain its competitive position.

Tactical Planning

Teaching Tip
To help introduce the topic of planning, ask students to identify their own strategic and tactical plans for building a career.

The process of making detailed decisions about what to do, who will do it, and how to do it—with a normal time horizon of one year or less—is called **tactical planning.** Middle and first-line managers, along with other employees, often are heavily involved in tactical planning. The process generally includes the following tasks:

- choosing specific goals and the means of implementing the organization's strategic plan,
- deciding on courses of action for improving current operations, and
- developing budgets for each department, division, and project.

Discussion Question 1
What are the key differences between strategic planning and tactical planning?

Departmental managers and employees develop tactical plans to anticipate or cope with the actions of competitors, to coordinate with other departments, customers, and suppliers, and to implement strategic plans. Tactical planning differs from strategic planning primarily in terms of shorter time frames and level of detail, as Table 5.1 shows. Despite their differences, they are closely linked in a well-designed planning system.

TABLE 5.1
General Profile of Strategic and Tactical Planning

Dimension	Strategic Planning	Tactical Planning
Intended purpose	Ensure long-term effectiveness and growth	Means of implementing strategic plans
Nature of issues addressed	How to survive and compete	How to accomplish specific goals
Time horizon	Long term (usually two years or more)	Short term (usually one year or less)
How often done	Every one to three years	Every six months to one year
Condition under which decision making occurs	Uncertainty and risk	Low to moderate risk
Where plans are primarily developed	Middle to top management	Employees, up to middle management
Level of detail	Low to moderate	High

The following Small Business Insight shows how a small specialty foods company links strategy, tactics, and feedback to help its employees understand how well its strategies are working. It also identifies the links needed between the planning function and the control function (presented in Chapter 18).

Small Business *Insight*

Rhino Foods

Ted Castle, former hockey coach at the University of Vermont, uses a "game" to run his specialty bakery company. Employees at Rhino Foods play the game every day as they create brownie batter for Ben & Jerry's Ice Cream, as well as other baked goods sold to restaurant wholesalers. Castle fostered a strategic game mentality in Rhino Foods' employees. The key to his strategies game is to know the "enemy." For example, one strategic issue is "expenses as the enemy."

To address this strategic issue, Castle concluded that he had to open the company books to his employees. "Imagine," he says, "having a team play touch football for two hours. I am sitting there the whole time with a book. All of a sudden I blow the whistle and say okay, that's it. Everybody go home." But he also recognized that a set of numbers could be confusing for the untrained. So he developed an in-house game that covers four-week sessions. A scorecard is at the center of the game. It is updated and posted daily. This scorecard actually is a brief profit and loss statement for both the day and the year-to-date. Tolerances (overall goals) are clearly stated. For example, on a day-to-day basis, the company has a goal of 6 percent profit after taxes. Any amount over that is distributed to the employees as profit sharing (strategy). An overall scale is posted every day that represents an individual bonus to be distributed at the end of each four-week game. The individual bonus is a tactic used to reach the goal of six percent.

This game incorporates strategic and tactical planning in a unique way. First, all employees share in company goals. Second, all employees are responsible for implementing strategies. And finally, the employees are involved in the tactics that determine success and failure.

Would this same "game" work in all situations? Not likely. Rhino Foods produces baked goods in response to customer orders. Thus revenues are known, which means little uncertainty about the actual profit margin as long as the expense "enemy" is controlled.[29]

Teaching Tip
Get students to brainstorm about barriers to effective planning in organizations. (Examples: resistance to change, expense, and inappropriate goals.)

The following business proverbs capture the need for properly undertaken strategic and tactical planning.

- Any organization that does not plan for its future is not likely to have one.
- The most effective way to cope with change is to help create it.
- When you do not know where you are going, any road will get you there.

3

Differentiate the corporate, business, and functional levels of planning and strategies.

LEVELS OF STRATEGY AND PLANNING

The scope of strategic planning varies from organization to organization. It depends substantially on the organization's level of diversification and on the levels within the organization at which the planning is done.

Diversification Level

The variety of goods and/or services produced and the number of different markets served constitutes an organization's level of **diversification.**[30] A firm's diversification level may be single business, dominant business, related businesses, or unrelated businesses. As Figure 5.1 indicates, diversification and scope of strategic planning are directly related. A firm that produces varied goods or services for unrelated markets often must have a broadly based planning process. A firm involved in a single product line or service needs a less elaborate planning process.

A **single-business firm** provides a limited number of goods or services to one segment of a particular market. Southwest Airlines provides one type of transportation service to travelers seeking high value for a low price.

A **dominant-business firm** serves various segments of a particular market. Continental Airlines has introduced a new no-frills service called Continental Lite, which it provides between paired airports to compete directly with Southwest Airlines. Continental also offers a mainstream passenger airline service with economy and business classes, a commuter service, and a reservation system that is used by many travel agents.

A **related-businesses firm** provides a variety of similar goods and/or services. Its divisions generally compete in the same markets, use similar technologies, or share common distribution channels. PepsiCo is one example of this type of firm. In addition to its soft drink business, PepsiCo owns several fast-food chains, including Pizza Hut and KFC (Kentucky Fried Chicken). This strategy permits PepsiCo to own some of the outlets (distribution channels) at which its soft drink products are sold. General Motors (GM) is also a related-businesses firm. It acquired Electronic Data Systems (EDS) and Hughes Electronic Systems in the 1980s because these firms possessed technological ca-

FIGURE 5.1

Planning and level of diversification

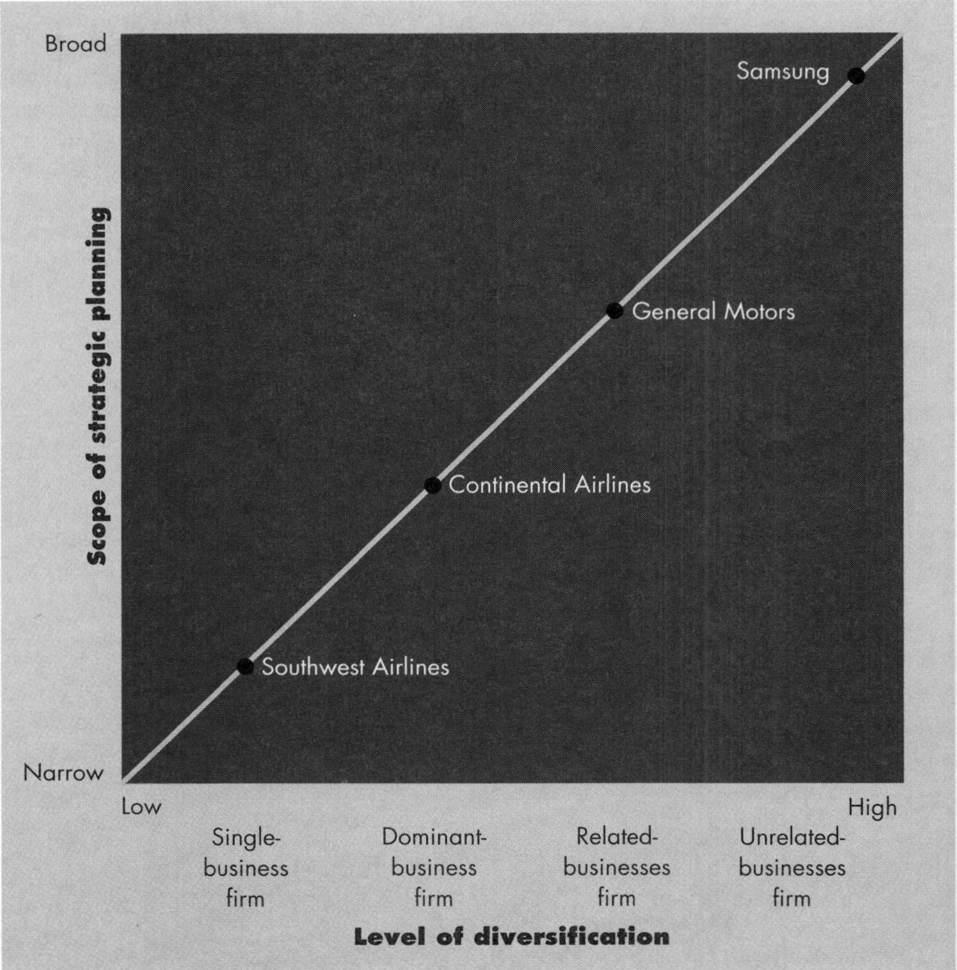

pabilities that were crucial to GM's other divisions. Its auto and truck loans and insurance subsidiary, General Motors Acceptance Corporation (GMAC), moved into mortgage banking and life and homeowner's insurance coverage.[31]

An **unrelated-businesses firm** provides diverse products (goods and/or services) to many different markets. Often referred to as a conglomerate, such a firm usually consists of distinct companies that have no relation to each other. During the past ten years, many North American firms have backed away from unrelated diversification by selling off unrelated businesses. For the most part, these unrelated-businesses firms were extremely difficult to lead. The volume and diversity of information needed to manage them was overwhelming. As a result, their top managers often reverted to financial data and controls that usually focused on the past and near-term for making strategic decisions. Many other types of problems also arose, such as too little investment in long-term R&D. Research shows a strong connection between extensive diversification and a decline in a firm's competitiveness.[32]

Textron is a dramatic example of an unrelated-businesses firm. It has sold 24 businesses, from foundries to flatware, since 1985 and is deemphasizing financial services to concentrate on manufacturing. But Textron is still very diversified, with businesses ranging from helicopter to pleasure and executive aircraft (Cessna Aircraft) to auto parts to golf carts. Another example is ITT, which has sold 240 companies since 1979. Although still an unrelated-businesses firm, ITT has reduced its unrelatedness to four broad lines: manufactured products, insurance and financial, forest products, and hotels.[33] The following Global Insight about Samsung illustrates that the special problems of unrelated-businesses firms are not limited to those in North America.

Ask Students
What type of diversification strategy does your university have? How does it compare with the diversification strategies of other types of universities?

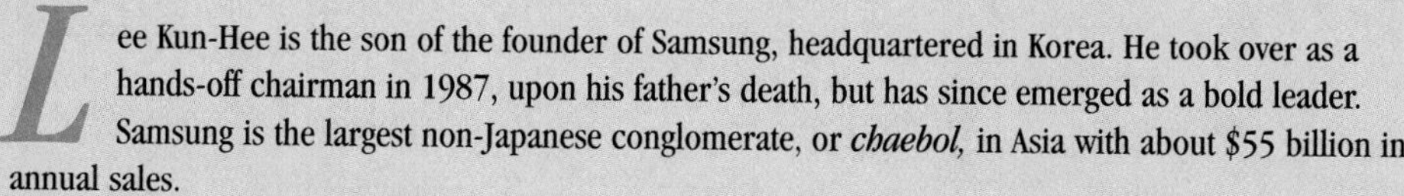

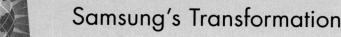

Samsung's Transformation

Lee Kun-Hee is the son of the founder of Samsung, headquartered in Korea. He took over as a hands-off chairman in 1987, upon his father's death, but has since emerged as a bold leader. Samsung is the largest non-Japanese conglomerate, or *chaebol,* in Asia with about $55 billion in annual sales.

Samsung struggled with its high degree of unrelated-businesses diversification. From its 30 companies in many lines of business in 1991 it has cut back to 24. One of Samsung's goals by the year 2000 is to make 75 percent of its sales in three core businesses: electronics (four companies), machinery (three companies), and chemicals (three companies).

Lee vows that Samsung's days of emphasizing growth and size over quality are behind it. Today "we must specialize," says Lee. "If we don't move into more capital- and technology-intensive industries, our very survival will be at stake." Lee has shaken up management by decentralizing decision making and changed investment priorities. Today, Samsung's spending on R&D, 8.6 percent of manufacturing sales, is far higher than the average of 2.2 percent spent by other Korean *chaebols.*

Samsung has to compete against world leaders in its markets. Lee's mission is to bring Samsung into the new age of quality concerns. He is challenging employees to be innovative. Lee tells Samsung's 180,000 employees, "Change everything but your spouses and children." The gist of his speeches is that Samsung needs a "quality-first management" that can show results fast. If curtailing production to ensure quality caused a Samsung company to lose money, he said he would make up the difference out of his own pocket. He also promised to donate 70 to 80 percent of his personal fortune (a figure he won't disclose) to a foundation benefiting Samsung employees if the effort brings tangible results by 1997. Otherwise, he added, he would resign as chairman and keep his money. As Lee puts it, "I have staked my honor, my life, and my assets on these changes."[34]

Corporate Level

Dominant-business, related-businesses, and unrelated-businesses firms often develop plans and strategies at three levels: corporate, business, and functional. Figure 5.2 shows these levels for Dick Clark Productions, Inc., a related-businesses firm.

Core Focus. At the top, **corporate-level strategy** guides the overall direction of firms having more than one line of business. Diversification is a key issue in corporate-level planning and strategy. The top corporate managers determine the role of each separate business within the organization. Corporate strategies focus on the types of businesses the firm wants to engage in, ways to acquire or divest businesses, allocation of resources among the businesses, and ways to develop synergy or learning among the businesses.[35]

Dick Clark Productions' corporate strategy is to utilize the strength of its trademarks, goodwill, and related assets from its television business in order to capitalize on other entertainment-related businesses. These other businesses are intended to complement the core television business, contribute to each other's development, and support the company's growth as a whole.[36]

FIGURE 5.2

Dick Clark Production, Inc., Strategy Levels

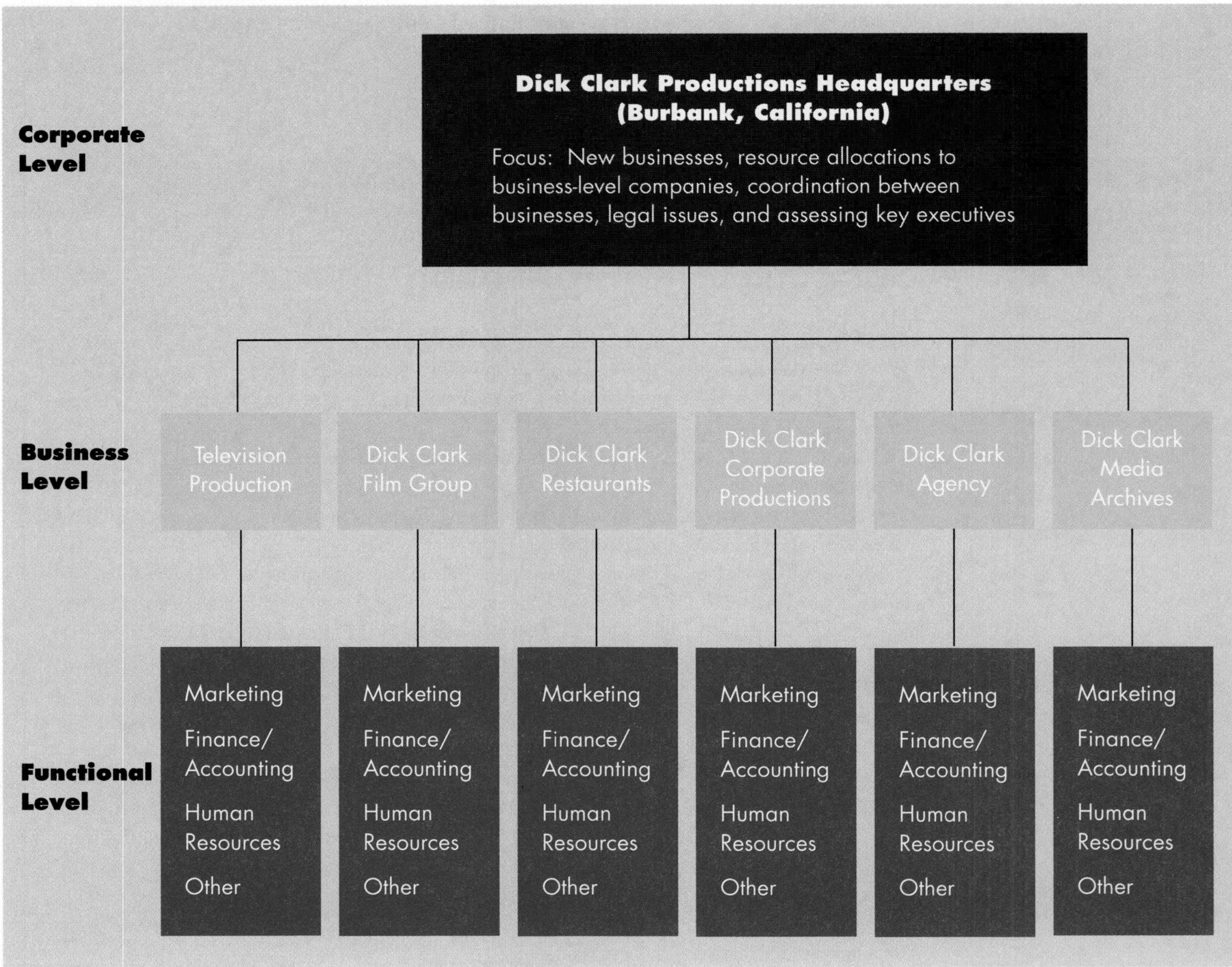

Source: Developed from *Dick Clark Productions, Inc., 1993 Annual Report.*

The corporate-level management provides guidance and reviews entities at the business level, often called strategic business units. A **strategic business unit (SBU)** is a division or subsidiary of a firm that provides a distinct product or service and often has its own mission and goals. An SBU may have a well-defined set of customers and/or cover a specific geographic area. An SBU is usually evaluated on the basis of its own income statement and balance sheet. The top managers of each SBU are responsible for developing a strategic plan for their unit. This strategic plan normally is submitted to corporate headquarters for review. Top corporate management is heavily involved in determining which SBUs to form, acquire or divest. Corporate-level management also decides whether to allocate the same, less, or more capital and human resources to the various SBUs. Figure 5.2 shows six of the strategic business units (there are others) at Dick Clark Productions. Television Production, the core SBU, has a strategy of focusing on programming that has the potential both to be profitable in the first year of release and to be renewed year after year. The television unit is cautious in developing situation comedies and dramatic programs. The reason is that they require substantial development and production financing and have a greater risk of not being profitable, which would divert resources from other promising ventures.[37]

Real World Example
"Most mergers don't live up to expectations," says Merck CEO P. Roy Hughes (*Harvard Business Review,* November-December 1994, 113).

Common Growth Strategies. Five common corporate-level growth strategies are forward integration, backward integration, horizontal integration, concentric diversification, and conglomerate diversification. **Forward integration** occurs when a company enters the businesses of its customers, moving it closer to the ultimate consumer. For example, in 1993, Merck & Co., the world's preeminent pharmaceutical company, acquired Medco Containment Services, a successful mail-order distributor of discount prescription drugs, for more than $6 billion.[38]

Backward integration occurs when a company enters the businesses of its suppliers, usually to control component quality, on-time delivery, or stable prices. This strategy is implemented by acquiring suppliers or by creating new businesses that provide the same goods or services as suppliers. In 1989, Dick Clark Productions established the Dick Clark Agency as a talent-booking personal appearance agency for musical artists. This SBU was a natural extension of the corporation's business and talent relationships throughout the music world.

Real-World Example
Saks Fifth Avenue recently purchased I. Magnin. Both California HMOs, FHP and Foundation Health, want to buy out their rival, Health Net (*Los Angeles Times,* December 31, 1994, D2).

Horizontal integration occurs when a company acquires a competitor to consolidate and extend its market share. In 1994, Federated Department Stores paid about $4 billion for R.H. Macy to create the largest department store company in the United States. Union Pacific Corp. bid about $4 billion to acquire the Santa Fe Pacific Railroad. Horizontal mergers and acquisitions were commonplace in the early and mid-1980s and have again emerged as a primary strategy in the past several years as firms strive to improve their competitive positions.[39] In the United States, increasing concern is being expressed that the new wave of horizontal mergers may reduce competition and violate antitrust laws. For example, the purchase of McCaw Cellular Communications by AT&T in 1993 is being contested.

The *alliance strategy,* as through joint ventures, is an alternative to traditional forms of backward, forward, and horizontal integration. For example, Chrysler formed a joint venture, Eurostar, with Steyr (a German firm) to assemble the Jeep Grand Cherokee and minivans in Austria beginning in 1994.[40]

Concentric diversification, sometimes called *related diversification,* occurs when a firm acquires or starts a business related to the firm's existing business in terms of technology, markets, or products. Generally, a related-businesses firm acquires another company or starts a new venture. Some common thread must link the two firms, such as the same general set of customers, similar technology, overlapping distribution channels, compatible managerial skills, or similar goods or services. In 1991, AT&T acquired NCR, a computer company, for $7.5 billion in stock. It operates as a strategic business unit of AT&T and is now known as AT&T Global Information Solutions. It provides information technology and services required by global customers who rely on vast amounts of business information.[41]

Flight Safety's aquisition of the VITAL product line of visual simulation systems is a good example of concentric, or related, diversification. The simulation systems create full daylight, dusk, and night views, which are used to train airline pilots.

Conglomerate diversification occurs when a firm adds unrelated goods or services to its line of businesses. Generally one company acquires another company or starts a venture in a totally new field. Firms operating in the unrelated-businesses stage of diversification most often use this strategy. One of the more successful unrelated acquisitions was the purchase of MCA, the U.S. entertainment company, by Matsushita Electric Industrial Co. Ltd., the Japanese electronics giant, for $6 billion in 1990.[42] However, as discussed previously, this corporate-level strategy increasingly is being viewed with skepticism.

Business Level

Once it agrees on a corporate-level strategy (or strategies) and plans, top management can turn its attention to business-level strategy and plans. **Business-level strategy** is a guide for the operations of a single business and answers questions such as "How do we compete?" A single-business firm or an SBU provides a particular line of goods or services to a specific industry or market segment. Its top managers are constantly involved with planning for (1) how the firm or SBU can maintain a competitive edge, (2) how each key functional area (production, human resources, marketing, finance) can contribute to the firm's or SBU's overall effectiveness, and (3) how resources should be allocated among the functions within the firm or SBU.

The Preview Insight and follow-up comments on Southwest Airlines illustrate various issues involved in developing business-level strategy.[43] The following Insight presents Southwest's business-level growth strategy.

Insight

Southwest's Growth Strategy

Most of Southwest Airline's growth is from internal expansion rather than the acquisition of other firms. An exception is the purchase of Morris Air (horizontal integration) in late 1993, which enabled Southwest to expand more rapidly into the Chicago market. Morris Air provided Southwest with gates at Midway Airport which had no other gates to lease at the time.

Before adding flights at a new city, Southwest begins with a simple formula to estimate its potential traffic on a short-haul route between that city and one already served. It looks at the existing number of flights serving the route, the average fare, the distance, and the cities' populations. Southwest's CEO Herb Kelleher comments: "We suppose that Southwest goes in and doubles the number of flights and reduces the average fare by 60 percent, then estimates how much traffic would be in the market based on prior experience. It is very accurate. "We knew going into the Kansas City-to-St. Louis route that air fares were $295 one way, more than if you hired a cab," he said. "We didn't need anybody to tell us that a heck of a lot of people were driving."

Another key to Southwest's expansion strategy is its controlled, moderate pace. The airline tries to grow at 10 to 15 percent a year. Kelleher cites two main reasons for controlling growth. First, the airline stays financially strong by not becoming overextended with debt in an industry prone to seasonal declines, recessions, and fuel price hikes. Second, it preserves the company's values. "We are pleased with the relations people have with one another and their dedication to the company. That culture would be impaired by hiring too many new employees too fast," he said. Kelleher vows that he will not lose his focus on Southwest's short-haul niche, despite the hints that it might challenge United on some longer routes.[44]

Functional Level

Discussion Question 3
What are the main differences between corporate-level, business-level, and functional level strategies? Give an example of each level for a company that you know.

Functional-level strategy is a guide for managing a firm's functional areas, such as manufacturing, marketing, human resources, and finance. Functional-level strategies and plans should be designed to complement business-level strategies and plans. Functional-level strategies often involve a combination of tactical and strategic planning. Table 5.2 provides a few examples of the issues that management in various types of firms usually addresses in developing functional-level strategies.

TABLE 5.2

Examples of Issues Addressed in Developing Functional Strategies

Sample Functions	Sample Key Issues
Human resources	• What kind of reward system is needed? • How should the performance of employees be reviewed? • What approach should be used to recruit qualified personnel? • How is affirmative and fair treatment ensured for women, minorities, and the disabled?
Finance	• What is the desired mixture of borrowed funds versus equity funds? • What portion of profits should be reinvested and what portion paid out as dividends? • What criteria should be used in allocating financial and human resources to projects? • What should be the criteria for issuing credit to customers?
Marketing	• What products or services should be emphasized? • How should products be distributed (e.g., direct selling, wholesalers, retailers, etc.)? • Should competition be primarily on price or on other factors? • What image and features should be emphasized to customers?
Manufacturing	• What should be the level of commitment to total quality? • How should suppliers be selected? • Should the focus be on production runs for inventory or producing primarily in response to customer orders? • What production operations should be changed (e.g., automated or laid out differently) to improve productivity?

The following Ethics Insight explores Southwest Airlines' human resource values and strategies. They strongly emphasize the kinds of ethical behaviors expected of employees when dealing with customers. Organizations increasingly are recognizing the essential role of ethics and human resource strategies and systems in sustaining a competitive advantage in the marketplace.[45]

Ethics *Insight*

Southwest's Human Resources Values and Strategies

Recall that one part of Southwest Airlines' mission statement addresses employees and states several important ethical values.

Southwest looks for people with a certain attitude (an approach to life, a way of living, or a set of values) that isn't narrow, rigid, tightly defined, or restrictive. As Herb Kelleher puts it, "Tolerance for human beings, their peculiarities or eccentricities, and their differences is very important." This does not mean that Southwest has no limits in tolerating unusual behaviors. The company won't hesitate to fire someone who fails to treat fellow employees as they should be treated. Kelleher comments: "We can train people to do things where skills are concerned. But there is one capability we do not have and that is to change a person's attitude. So, we prefer an unskilled person with a good attitude rather than a highly skilled person with a bad attitude."

Passengers help maintain the customer-driven culture: Frequent fliers sit in with human resource staff to interview and evaluate prospective flight attendants. They also participate in focus groups to help gauge response to new services or solicit ideas for improving old ones.

From the start, Southwest has been leanly staffed. It does not, for example, hire extravagantly when times are good and lay off people when times get tough. "We don't furlough anybody, so we have to be lean all the time," says Kelleher. That loyalty is returned.

Unlike many of the airlines that sprang up under deregulation, Southwest's employees are unionized. Its edge isn't in lower pay because wages average about the same as those paid by American and United. However, by not having an antagonistic relationship with the unions, Southwest has negotiated flexible work rules. Southwest also offers generous profit sharing, with about 15 percent of net profits returned to the workers. It will match up to 100 percent of employee contributions to 401(k) plans, depending on union contract provisions. As a result, Southwest employees are far more productive than those at other carriers, allowing Southwest to fly more planes and serve more passengers with fewer workers than its rivals.[46]

4

Explain the eight tasks of the strategic planning process.

STRATEGIC PLANNING PROCESS

We have presented various concepts and issues involved in planning and strategy formation. In this section, we expand on some of those concepts and issues and present them as a process of strategic planning. We focus on business-level planning, with some consideration of functional-level planning. Considerably more attention is given to functional-level issues and planning in Chapters 6 (Planning Aids and Implementing), 10 (Fundamentals of Organizing), 12 (Human Resources Management), and 20 (Operations Management).

We present the process of strategic planning for single-business firms (or SBUs) as a sequence of eight core tasks as summarized in Figure 5.3. Keep in mind, however, that managers and others involved in business-level strategic planning may jump back and forth between tasks, or even skip tasks, as they develop strategic plans.[47] Moreover,

FIGURE 5.3

Basic Strategic Planning Process

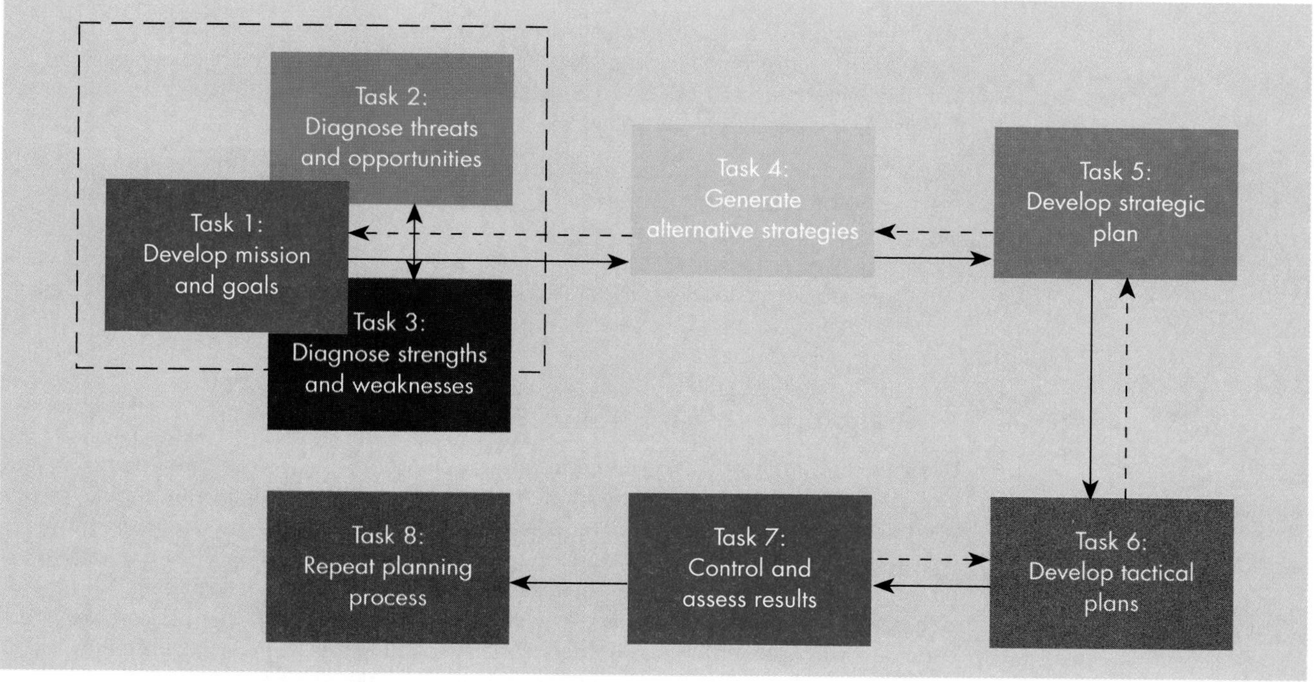

Teaching Tip
Students often believe—erroneously—that every business person plans methodically. Let them know that the process they are about to learn will help them become better planners than many business people are.

a proposed strategy may be abandoned if it can't be implemented for some reason that was not apparent at first.

Task 1: Develop Mission and Goals

As noted previously, the organizational mission and goals are developed by answering questions such as: What business are we in? What are we committed to? What results do we want to achieve? General goals provide broad direction for decision making and may not change from year to year. The mission and goals are not developed in isolation. As suggested by the two-way arrows in Figure 5.3, they are influenced by a diagnosis of environmental threats and opportunities (task 2) and a diagnosis of the organization's strengths and weaknesses (task 3).

The following Quality Insight suggests how one of AT&T's strategic business units—AT&T Global Business Communications Systems—used quality as a common thread in developing its vision, mission, values, and goals. This discussion is from the SBU's 1993 strategic plan, which is intended to establish a three- to five-year direction.

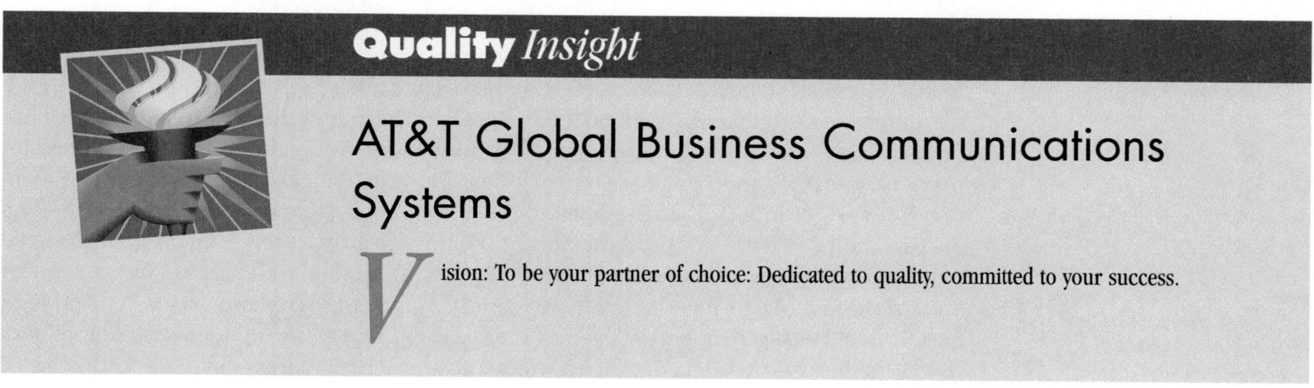

Quality *Insight*

AT&T Global Business Communications Systems

Vision: To be your partner of choice: Dedicated to quality, committed to your success.

Mission: To be the worldwide leader in providing the highest quality business communications products, services, and solutions.

Values: Seven values were developed to guide decisions and behavior. They represent how this SBU and its employees (referred to as "associates") are to treat customers, suppliers, and each other. In summary form, they are (1) respect for individuals, (2) dedication to helping customers, (3) highest standards of integrity, (4) innovation, (5) teamwork, (6) accountability, and (7) excellence.

Sample Goals: One of the goals related to associates is to increase the percentage of "extremely" and "very" satisfied associates from 56 percent in 1992 to world-class levels (80 percent or higher) by 1995 and in future years. Two of the goals related to customers are to increase customers' willingness to repurchase by 10 percent annually and to achieve "best in class quality" levels by 1995. One of the goals related to shareholders is to achieve at least 10 percent earnings growth per year.[48]

Task 2: Diagnose Threats and Opportunities

Teaching Tip
Ask students to identify threats and opportunities for their place of employment. Making a list of responses on a transparency or chalkboard will help students recognize the diversity of threats and opportunities that organizations face.

In Chapters 3 and 4, we presented important environmental forces, both domestic and global, that can affect an organization. These forces represent significant threats or opportunities for an organization. Strategic planning takes these threats and opportunities into account in developing the mission, goals, and strategies. Political forces and stakeholders within and outside the organization play a key role in determining the organization's current mission and goals, as well as possible changes in them.[49] Top managers negotiate with powerful stakeholders (boards of directors, banks, government, major customers, and suppliers) in an attempt to influence those forces.

The task environment exerts the most direct influence on an organization's strategic planning process. In Chapter 3, we reviewed the framework suggested by Michael Porter for diagnosing the immediate competitive forces confronting a firm at any particular time.[50] Recall that this framework (see Figure 3.4 and related discussion) includes five competitive forces: threat of new competitors, customer bargaining power, supplier bargaining power, threat of substitute products, and rivalry among existing firms in the industry. The combined strength of these forces affect the long-run profit potential in an industry. That, in turn, affects each individual firm's (or SBU's) overall profit potential, growth prospects, and even likelihood of survival. To be effective, strategic planning must include a careful diagnosis of these forces. Several specific variables affect the strength of each force, but a review of all of them is beyond the scope of this book. Here, we simply review each force and highlight its potential impact on a firm's strategic planning.

Ask Students
How often should management analyze strengths, weaknesses, opportunities, and threats (a SWOT analysis)?

Ethics
Ethical boundaries for dealing with new competitors should be included in strategic plans. Tactics such as driving them out of business unfairly should be identified and prohibited.

Threat of New Competitors. The entry of new competitors often is a response to high profits earned by established firms and/or rapid growth in an industry. The difficulties new competitors face depend mainly on the barriers to entry and the reactions of established competitors. Barriers to entry are factors that make entering an industry relatively easy or relatively difficult. Two important barriers are economies of scale (lower costs as volumes increase) and capital requirements.

In 1955, Chrysler, Ford, and General Motors made 95 percent of the cars sold in North America.[51] The economies of scale associated with high-volume production and the enormous capital requirements of the auto industry had thrown up significant barriers to entry, effectively limiting competition for these automakers. Then, the competitive landscape began to change—first with the introduction of the Volkswagen Beetle in the 1950s—to eliminate barriers to entry as a protection from competition for the "Big 3." Not until the mid 1980s did the "Big 3" begin seriously to revise their strategies, especially with respect to product quality.[52] Today, 12 foreign automakers have assembly and other manufacturing operations in North America. For twenty years, critics suggested that the Big 3 essentially were blind to the threat of these new competitors and didn't "wake up" until faced with enormous financial and market share losses.[53]

Ask Students
How might the continual threat of new competitors be good for businesses? Explain your reasoning. (New competitors can be used as a change force to increase quality, develop new products, improve productivity, and so on.)

Ask Students
Have you ever had high customer bargaining power so that you could play off one seller against another? How can you achieve this type of power?

Customer Bargaining Power. The bargaining power of customers depends on their relative ability to play one firm off against another in order to force down prices, obtain higher quality, or buy more goods or services for the same price. For example, GM is able to press for lower prices and better quality from suppliers because it is such a large-volume customer. The bargaining power of customers is likely to be high in the following situations.

- A small number of customers purchase relatively large volumes from the seller.
- Customers purchase standard and undifferentiated goods or services.
- Customers can easily switch from one seller to another.[54]

Ethics
Ethical boundaries for dealing with customers should be included in strategic plans.

The bargaining power of auto industry customers was relatively low until the mid-1970s. It has increased substantially since that time because more competitors have gained entry to the auto industry. Customers can choose from vastly increased numbers of makes and models, dealers, and financing plans. Many automakers and dealers have introduced special financing and rebate programs and have extended the length of coverage of their warranties. These strategies are intended to attract and retain customers.

Supplier Bargaining Power. The bargaining power of suppliers increases when they can raise prices or eliminate certain features of their goods or services with little fear of losing customers. The situations that tend to make suppliers more powerful are similar to those that make customers more powerful. The bargaining power of suppliers is likely to be high in the following situations.

Ethics
Ethical boundaries for dealing with suppliers should be included in strategic plans.

- A small number of suppliers sell to a large number of customers in an industry.
- Suppliers don't have to worry about substitute goods or services that their customers can readily buy.
- Suppliers' goods or services are differentiated.[55]

Compaq Computer attempts to achieve supplier power through product and technological leadership. As one of hundreds of PC manufacturers, Compaq states its strategic challenge as a question: "How to rise above the clatter and communicate to the world that we have the leadership products at competitive prices with the best customer support programs?"[56] Even if the claims implied by this question are exaggerated, Compaq clearly is striving to differentiate its products and services from other suppliers.

Threat of Substitute Goods or Services. The seriousness of the threat of substitute goods or services depends on the ability and willingness of customers to change their buying habits. Substitutes limit the price that firms in a particular industry can charge for their products without risking a loss in sales. Southwest Airlines is attempting to be a substitute for autos on trips of about 100 to 700 miles. Paul O. Neil, the CEO of Aluminum Company of America (ALCOA), is on a mission to persuade automakers worldwide of the benefits of lightweight, fuel-efficient aluminum versus steel cars. The initial strategy of ALCOA is to expand the use of aluminum wheels, engine blocks, and other parts. Aluminum weighs 40 percent less than steel but costs about three time as much. The first model of an aluminum car—the Audi 8, which sells for about $46,000—has recently been developed for the European market, where gasoline prices are two to three times higher than in North America.[57]

Rivalry among Existing Firms. The rivalry among existing firms in an industry varies with top management's view of threats or opportunities, strategies the firm pursues, and competitors' reactions to those strategies. These strategies and reactions include price increases or decreases, advertising campaigns, introduction of improved or new goods, changes in customer service, and so on. Three of the variables affecting the strength of rivalry with an industry are the number of firms, the rate of industry growth, and level of fixed costs. These variables have been important to the increased intensity of competition among airline firms, as revealed in the following Insight.

Insight

Airline Competition

Except for Southwest Airlines, U.S. and Canadian airlines experienced an overall growth in traffic (measured by the number of passenger-miles) that averaged about 1 percent annually from 1987 through 1994. This low rate of growth occurred even though in many cases tickets were sold at below costs of operations in order to attract passengers. The airline industry's total loss between 1990 and 1994 is estimated at more than $12 billion.

Having survived two energy crises (1973 and 1979), the carriers started cutting costs again in the early 1980s. Deregulation in 1978 led to increased competition (including new competitors) and lower air fares. Productivity improved, but the cost of new aircraft (a fixed cost) are generally up. In fact, the cost per seat, one indicator of new aircraft costs, has been rising steadily since 1985. Many of the new aircraft require only two people to fly the plane but otherwise aren't much more productive than the planes they are replacing—they go no faster, carry only a few more people, and are only a bit more fuel efficient. On the demand side, the airline industry faces accelerated competition from electronics in the form of video conferencing, fax machines and electronic mail. Widely forecast as a competitor (substitute service) to air travel over the long run, electronics has arrived earlier than expected. Historically, a little over half of all air travel was by business people. As of 1995, it is about 45 percent and continues to decline.

American, Northwest, and other airlines have taken steps to deal with slow-growth. For example, American has pulled back from hubs where it can't compete successfully. This cutback often meant dropping service at airports where American faced Southwest head-to-head.[58]

Discussion Question 4
What are the primary forces driving industry and market competition for companies in the airline industry?

Southwest Airlines even experienced new direct competition on short-haul routes in 1994. For example, Continental established its low-fare Continental Lite service and United Airlines has done the same with its U2 service.[59]

Task 3: Diagnose Strengths and Weaknesses

The diagnosis of internal strengths and weaknesses enables managers to identify an organization's core competencies and to determine which need to be improved. This diagnosis covers factors such as the organization's relative competitive position, ability to adapt and innovate, human resources skills, technological capabilities, financial resources, managerial depth, and the values and background of its key employees.

Core competencies are the complementary strengths that make a company distinctive and presumably more competitive by providing unique value to its customers.[60] Let's consider just three of the ways that core competencies may strengthen the competitiveness of a firm.[61] First, core competencies may provide access to more markets. Honda's core competencies in engines and power trains enables it to make not only cars, but also snowmobiles, jet skis, gasoline-powered lawn mowers, and motor scooters. Second, core competencies may make a major contribution to customers' perceived benefits from the good or service. Clearly, Honda's engine expertise meets this requirement: its large financial commitment to formula one auto racing. Third, a firm's core competencies may make simple imitation difficult if that firm is highly successful. Honda's commitment to designing and manufacturing quality engines and power trains helped create a culture of quality throughout the organization.[62].

Teaching Tip
To illustrate the difficulty managers often have with identifying organizational weaknesses, ask students: How do you respond when a job interviewer asks you to identify your weaknesses? Can these weaknesses actually be strengths?

Most individuals find that diagnosing strengths is easier than diagnosing weaknesses. Weaknesses often are blamed on management and employees. As a result, they may perceive statements of organizational weaknesses as personal threats to their positions, influence, and self-esteem. But weaknesses are not self-correcting and are likely to become worse if not openly dealt with in the strategic planning process. As noted previously, the Big 3 automakers—Chrysler, Ford, and General Motors—failed to address in any meaningful way their internal weaknesses, in responding to raised customer expectations and foreign competitors. At GM, these weaknesses were widespread: a culture of separated and fighting divisions, poor financial and operating controls, lack of commitment to quality processes and standards, bureaucratic and slow decision making, detached and arrogant top leaders, and so on. Jack Smith, who became CEO of General Motors in 1992, is literally leading a transformation of GM in an effort to address these and other weaknesses.[63]

Table 5.3 shows a basic framework for diagnosing some business-level and functional-level strengths and weaknesses. This framework is best suited to a single-business firm or an SBU. In some companies, top, middle, and first-level managers are required to develop statements of opportunities, threats, strengths, and weaknesses for their areas of responsibility. The specific issues identified by middle-level plant managers may be different from those raised by top managers. Plant managers may focus on manufacturing opportunities, threats, strengths, and weaknesses, whereas top managers are more likely to focus on current and potential competitors, legislation and government regulations, societal trends, and the like. Ideally, the key issues raised, regardless of their source, are addressed in the strategic plan.

TABLE 5.3

Basic Framework for Diagnosing Strengths and Weaknesses

Instructions: Evaluate each issue on the basis of the following scale.

A = Superior to most competitors (top 10%).

B = Better than average. Good performance. No immediate problems.

C = Average. Equal to most competitors.

D = Problems here. Not as good as it should be. Deteriorating. Must be improved.

F = Major cause for concern. Crisis. Take immediate action to improve.

		Scale				
Category	**Issue**	**A**	**B**	**C**	**D**	**F**
Human resources	Employee skills	___	___	___	___	___
	Reward systems	___	___	___	___	___
	Quality of managers	___	___	___	___	___
	Team orientation	___	___	___	___	___
	Other	___	___	___	___	___
Marketing	Share of market	___	___	___	___	___
	Channels of distribution	___	___	___	___	___
	Advertising effectiveness	___	___	___	___	___
	Customer satisfaction	___	___	___	___	___
	Other	___	___	___	___	___
Finance	Ability to obtain loans	___	___	___	___	___
	Debt-equity relationship	___	___	___	___	___
	Inventory turnover	___	___	___	___	___
	Usefulness of financial reports	___	___	___	___	___
	Other	___	___	___	___	___
Manufacturing	Per unit cost	___	___	___	___	___
	Inventory control	___	___	___	___	___
	Flexibility	___	___	___	___	___
	Quality process	___	___	___	___	___
	Other	___	___	___	___	___

Task 4: Generate Alternative Strategies

The diagnosis process and development of organizational goals are closely linked to generating alternative strategies for the organization. These potential strategies, in turn, must be evaluated in terms of (1) environmental forces, (2) the organization's strengths and weaknesses, and (3) the strategies' likelihood of helping the organization achieve its mission and goals.[64]

To simplify the discussion, we consider the task of generating and evaluating alternative strategies only for a single-business firm or an SBU. Firms such as Samsung, GM, and AT&T have many strategic business units. Thus the task of generating and evaluating alternative strategies for such firms is very complex.

Previously, we discussed five corporate-level strategies. Here, we highlight three growth strategies common to business-level strategy and planning.[65] In the last section of this chapter we present additional alternative business-level strategies.

Teaching Tip
Market leaders in desirable markets face stiff competition. Have students name Honda Accord's competitors. Market leaders in declining markets have fewer competitors because the market is undesirable (e.g., firms didn't want to enter the typewriter market after the personal computer was introduced).

A **market penetration strategy** involves seeking growth in current markets with current products. A firm might increase market share by increasing the use of the product (e.g., getting its current customers to use AT&T'S long distance service more often), attracting competitors' customers (e.g., getting United Airlines' customers to fly Southwest Airlines), or buying a competitor (e.g., Ford's buying Jaguar). Market penetration also may be achieved by increasing the total size of the market by converting nonusers into current users (e.g., providing a financing package that enables college seniors to buy new cars).

Teaching Tip
Tell students that they can use the market development strategy by considering other markets for their talents (e.g., perhaps moving to another city, another country, and/or another industry).

The **market development strategy** involves seeking new markets for current products. The principal ways to do so are (1) finding new geographic markets (e.g., Southwest Airlines continuing to expand by adding air service between pairs of cities), (2) finding new target markets (e.g., Reader's Digest continuing to add foreign-language versions of its magazine, including a new Czech Republic edition in 1994), and (3) finding new uses for current products and facilities (e.g., AT&T's using its regular phone lines to carry new multimedia products and services, such as videoconferencing).

Ethics
The ethics of not serving people and communities that can't afford the organization's products should be addressed in strategic plans.

Teaching Tip
The x4 CD-ROM is an example of product development strategy based on earlier editions. Have students name other examples of product development strategy.

A **product development strategy** involves developing new or improved goods or services for current markets. Approaches that can be used to develop improved products include: improve features (e.g., multiple-disk CD players in cars), improve quality in terms of reliability, speed, efficiency, or durability (e.g., Compaq Computer's steady introduction of new lines of PCs), enhance aesthetic appeal (e.g., universal remote controls for consumer electronics), or introduce new models (e.g., Gillette's 1994 introduction of the Sensor Excell Shaving System, an upgrading of its twin-bladed Sensor razor introduced in 1989).

Real-World Example
A study in the *Harvard Business Review* (November–December 1994, 53) indicated that managers prefer product-line extensions on their existing products over developing entirely new products because the former is a low-cost, low-risk way to meet the needs of various market segments.

Task 5: Develop a Strategic Plan

After generating and selecting from alternative strategies, management is ready to develop a strategic plan. It should specify the primary actions (strategies) to be taken to achieve the organization's mission and goals. A strategic plan contains: (1) organizational mission and goals, (2) strategies for obtaining and utilizing the necessary technological, marketing, financial, and human resources, (3) strategies for manufacturing processes and conducting R&D, and (4) strategies developing and utilizing organizational and employee competencies. The strategic plan may also include a summary of the diagnosis of external opportunities and threats and internal strengths and weaknesses.

However, strategic plans rarely unfold in a sequential and orderly process. Consider the crisis conditions that faced the leadership of AT&T and the political turmoil surrounding its new strategic plan for managing diversity described in the following Diversity Insight.

Diversity *Insight*

AT&T's Diversity Crisis and Plan

AT&T faced a crisis from an incident in the fall of 1993 that made headlines. The company's employee magazine featured a cartoon of customers on various continents making phone calls. The caller in Africa was depicted as an animal.

Letters and calls poured in from irate employees, customers, civil rights groups, and members of Congress. Tackling the situation head on, the company apologized in the press for the "racist" illustration, which had been drawn by a freelancer. AT&T Chairman Robert E. Allen wrote a letter of apology to the employees, sat down with the Congressional Black Caucus, and vowed to "turn this ugly incident" into an opportunity to accelerate the pace of work-force diversity at AT&T. He immediately set up a hotline for employees and assigned four senior managers to lead diverse, cross-functional teams charged with devising a strategic plan to improve AT&T's efforts in managing diversity.

"I regret that some of these actions are being driven by a crisis," Allen stated at the annual meeting of the Alliance of Black Telecommunications Employees, the oldest and largest employee caucus group at AT&T. "One of the mistakes we have made is to manage diversity at the edges and not in the mainstream of our operations," he stated.

In January 1994, the accelerated diversity plan appeared, with the mission to "create a work environment that sets the world-class standard for valuing diversity." Although timetables and numerical goals are not included, the six-page plan recommends several actions. Among them: All thirteen top officers should increase their direct interaction with employee caucus groups. The absence of specific goals has set off another round of letter writing and anger. Allen responded: "We're putting an aggressive diversity strategy in place, but we must take care to assure that whatever goals and objectives we establish are credible and achievable." Do you agree or disagree with the decision not to include numerical goals and timetables in AT&T's diversity plan? Why or why not?[66]

Task 6: Develop Tactical Plans

Teaching Tip
These last three tasks often are done inadequately or ignored altogether by managers. Caution students to be extra careful here.

The purpose of tactical plans is to help implement strategic plans. As indicated in Figure 5.3, middle and first-line managers and employee teams normally base tactical plans on the organization's strategic plan.

Task 7: Control and Assess Results

Strategic and tactical planning must be accompanied by controls to ensure implementation of the plans and evaluation of their results. If the plans haven't produced the desired results, managers and teams may need to change the controls, mission, goals, or strategies, or the plans themselves. Earlier in this chapter, we noted how the lack of planning can lead to extinction by instinct and how poor planning can lead to paralysis by analysis. A thorough assessment of the results of planning should reveal whether either of these conditions exists.

Task 8: Repeat the Planning Process

Discussion Question 6
What difficulties might arise in following the sequence of the eight core tasks of the strategic planning process?

The forces that affect organizations are constantly changing. Sometimes these changes are gradual and foreseeable. At other times they are abrupt and unpredictable. Whatever the nature of change, managers and other employees need to be ready to adapt or innovate by repeating the planning process. Hence planning is an ongoing process—it is always a *means,* never an *end* in itself.

5

Use models of business-level strategy to develop competitive strategies.

MODELS OF BUSINESS-LEVEL STRATEGY

In this section we describe two models of business-level strategy: the product life cycle model and the generic strategies model. Each provides a different way to generate and evaluate alternative strategies (task 4 in Figure 5.3). In combination, these models can be powerful aids in the business-level planning and management process.

Product Life Cycle Model

Teaching Tip
Students enjoy sharing their knowledge of the product life cycle. Divide the class into groups to identify examples of products in the introduction, growth, maturity, decline, and termination phases. (Example of termination: the 8-track tape.)

The **product life cycle model** identifies the market phases that many products go through during their lifetimes. Figure 5.4 shows one version of a product life cycle that has five phases: introduction, growth, maturity, decline, and termination. The vertical axis shows whether market demand (sales volume) for the product is increasing, stable, or decreasing. The horizontal axis shows time. For fad products, such as the *Lion King* and its related items, the time span for all five phases often is two years or less. In contrast, automobiles have been on the market for more than seventy-five years. This industry now appears to be in the maturity phase, which usually means that the total number of units sold in the industry is constant or is increasing by no more than 3 percent per year. However, automakers are hoping for a new stage of growth as a result of forecasted increases in income levels in many countries (e.g., Brazil, Mexico, Poland, China, Thailand, and Turkey).

Strategic planning for each good or service is influenced by its life cycle and the phase of that cycle the product is in. However, management can sometimes intervene in the cycle through new strategies, shifting a mature or declining good or service into a new growth stage. For example, several years ago Japanese manufacturers, unlike U.S. manufacturers who believed that motorcycles and radios were entering the decline stage, developed new markets (reentered a growth stage) for motor scooters, all-terrain vehicles (ATVs), and Walkman radios.[67] According to this model, the emphasis on strategies and functional areas (e.g., marketing, production, R&D, and finance) needs to change for different phases of the product life cycle.[68]

During the introduction phase, the dominant strategic concerns are with product development (R&D), finding customers (marketing), and financing start-up, expansion,

FIGURE 5.4
Product Life Cycle Model

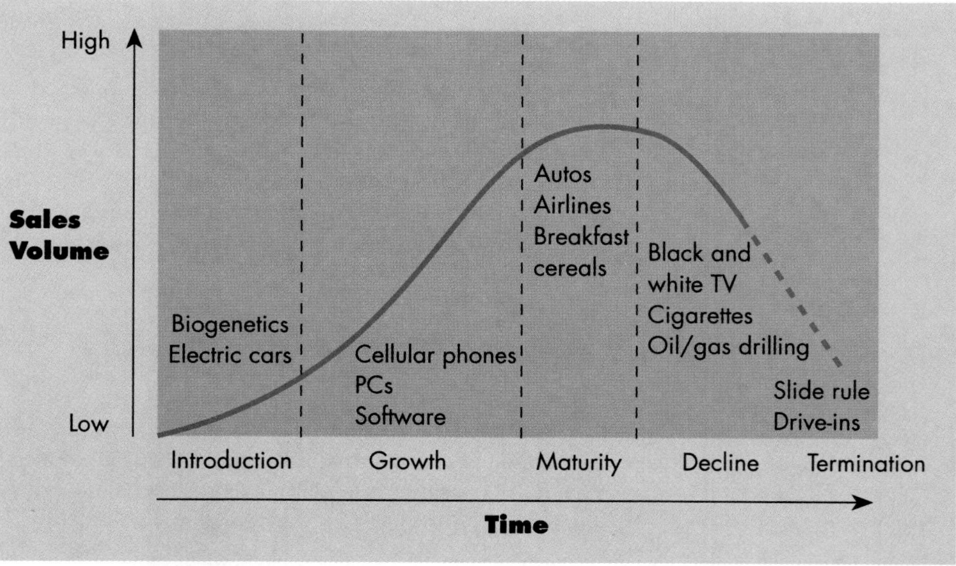

and marketing costs (finance). Few versions of the good or service exist as competitors struggle to build volume to a break-even level. Marketing often is aimed at educating potential customers about the product rather than pointing out product differences or building identity for the firm's product. Risk and the possibility of failure are great in this initial phase for a single-business firm or SBU.

In the growth phase, new distribution channels are sought (e.g., getting Wal-Mart to carry the product) and marketing activity tends to remain at a high level. However, the nature of marketing changes from educating consumers to an emphasis on product differences and brand identity (e.g., the strategies being used by Compaq Computer). One competitor's sales growth doesn't have to come at the expense of other and new competitors. However, as a business's sales increase, the market share of any one competitor is likely to decline. In the later growth phase, some firms may seek a competitive advantage by lowering prices (e.g., as PC manufacturers have done).[69] Significant price cuts may further stimulate product demand, as with PCs.

During the maturity stage of a good or service, a major strategic issue is the need to reduce per unit costs. Cost cutting may involve closing plants or eliminating the provision of services at unprofitable locations, laying off employees, reducing levels of management, and automating. Automakers and airlines are among the industries that have used such measures extensively to cut per unit costs. Another strategy is to maintain, or even try to increase, market share at the expense of competitors. Again the airlines and automakers are among those who have used this strategy. Further cost reductions may be made by reducing the number of product lines to achieve efficiency. General Motors is cutting the number of platforms for its various lines of cars from twelve to five. Pricing also is likely to be more competitive. The horizontal integration strategy (mergers between direct competitors) becomes a more common method of eliminating direct price competition, achieving greater efficiency in marketing and management, and protecting market share. Distribution to a large number and a wide range of customers may be crucial during the maturity stage. This need is especially true if a competitive advantage is difficult to achieve through either lower per unit costs or product differentiation.

During the decline phase of a product's life cycle, the strategic emphasis on efficiency (reduced costs per unit) continues to be strong. This effort may be associated with reducing capital investment, rather than holding it steady (or increasing it to achieve substantial improvements in efficiency), as in the maturity phase. Product options and variations often are standardized and their number reduced. Efforts are also made to improve marketing efficiency. Mergers or acquisitions and many failures among competing firms occur because of overcapacity. For example, over the past ten years, many firms providing services related to oil and gas drilling have either failed or merged. Cutthroat price competition may occur as firms try to increase their capacity utilization and drive competitors from the industry.

Discussion Question 2
At which level of diversification is Southwest Airlines? Where does this firm's services seem to fall in the product life cycle model? What are the primary implications of these answers for the firm?

In the termination phase, product availability is reduced sharply, and the product may even be eliminated altogether. Drive-in theaters throughout North America have closed during the past two decades, as the popularity of television, VCRs, and other home electronics products has exploded.

Generic Strategies Model

The **generic strategies model** comprises a framework of three basic business-level strategies that can be applied to a variety of organizations in diverse industries.[70] This model is called *generic* because all types of organizations can use it, whether they are involved in manufacturing, distribution, or services. Figure 5.5 shows the basic parts of this model. The strategic target dimension (vertical axis) indicates how widely the good or service is intended to compete: throughout the industry or within a particular part of the industry. The source of advantage dimension (horizontal axis) indicates the basis on which the good or service is intended to compete: uniqueness as perceived by the customer or low cost (price) to the customer. The various combinations of these two variables—strategic target and source of advantage—suggest three different generic strategies: differentiation strategy, cost leadership strategy, and focus strategy.

Ask Students
Name a clothing store that uses a differentiation strategy.

Differentiation Strategy. The **differentiation strategy** emphasizes competing with all other firms in the industry by offering a product that customers perceive to be unique. This strategy is dominant in the auto industry. Most automakers attempt to create unique value (benefits) by influencing customer perceptions and/or providing real differences. Various approaches are associated with the differentiation strategy. They may include, among others, innovative product design (BMW), high quality (Ford's theme of "Quality is Job 1"), unique brand image (Mercedes-Benz), technological leadership (Honda's four-wheel steering), customer service leadership (GM's Mr. Goodwrench), an extensive dealer network (Ford and GM), and product warranty (Mazda's bumper-to-bumper warranty). The long-term effectiveness of the differentiation strategy depends on how easily competitors can imitate the unique benefits provided by the firm. As soon as most or all competitors imitate the offering (such as a bumper-to-bumper car warranty), it no longer is an effective means of differentiation.

Ask Students
Name a clothing store that uses a cost-leadership strategy.

Cost Leadership Strategy. The **cost leadership strategy** emphasizes competing in the industry by providing a product at a price as low as or lower than competitors. This strategy requires a constant concern with efficiency (reduction in per unit costs). Autos produced and marketed primarily under the cost leadership strategy include the Chrysler Neon, Pontiac Grand Am, Hyundai, Ford Escort, and Honda Civic. Southwest

FIGURE 5.5
Generic Strategies Model

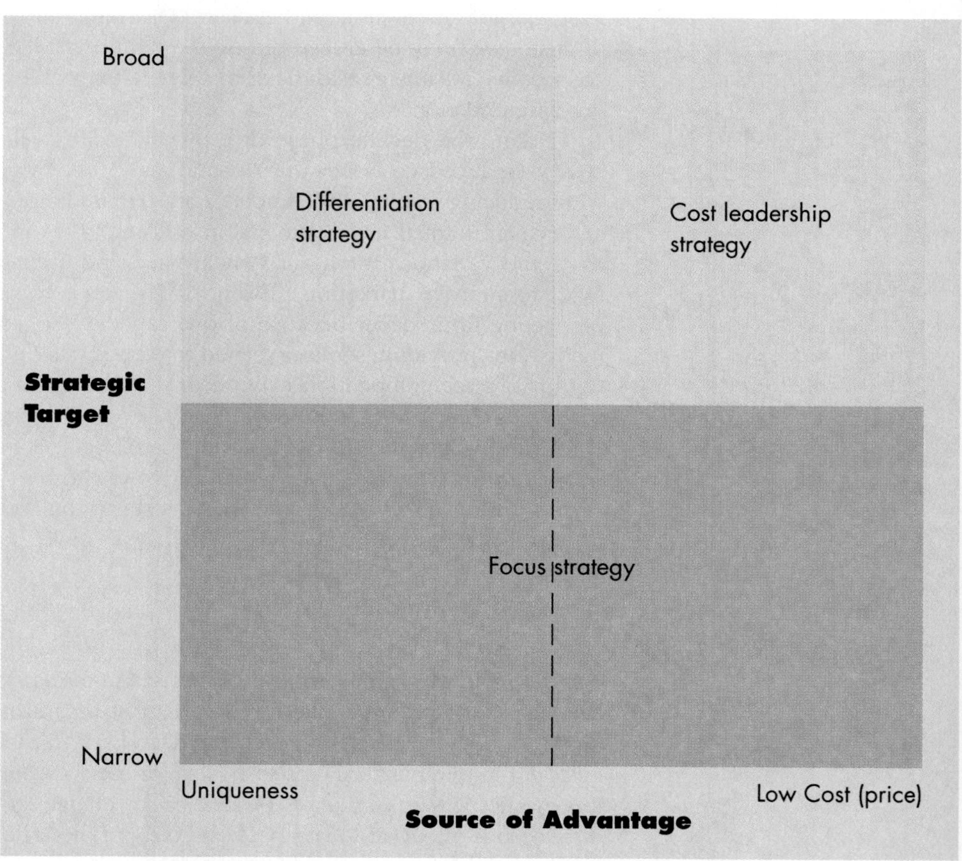

Source: Adapted with permission of The Free Press, a Division of Simon & Schuster, Inc. from Competitive Strategy: Techniques for Analyzing Industries and Competitors (p. 39) by Michael E. Porter, Copyright © 1980 by The Free Press.

Airlines, Motel 6, and Wal-Mart also use a cost (price) leadership strategy. Several essential actions are associated with a cost leadership strategy: (1) utilizing facilities or equipment that yield high economies of scale; (2) constantly striving to reduce per unit overhead , manufacturing, marketing, and follow-up service costs; (3) minimizing labor-intensive personal service and sales forces; and (4) avoiding customers whose demands would result in high personal selling or service costs. High volume and/or rapid growth often are needed for profitability with the cost leadership strategy.

Real-World Example
Technol beat out industry leaders 3M and J&J to gain a 60 percent market share by making a cheaper surgical mask (*Business Week,* December 5, 1994, 66).

Ask Students
Name a clothing store that uses a focus strategy.

Focus Strategy. The **focus strategy** emphasizes competing in a specific industry niche by directing efforts to the unique needs of certain customers or a narrowly defined geographic market.[71] A *niche* is a narrowly defined market segment that competitors may overlook, ignore, or have difficulty serving (e.g., a specific geographical area) or a specialized group of customers (e.g., teenagers, physicians, or retirees). Organizations attempt to create a unique image for their products by catering to the specific demands of the selected niche, ignoring other potential customers.

Strategic actions associated with the focus strategy are adaptations of those associated with differentiation and cost leadership strategies but are applied to a specific market niche. Autos produced and marketed under the focus strategy with a differentiation emphasis include Porsche, Lexus LS500, Rolls-Royce, BMW 735i, Mercedes-Benz S-600, Cadillac STS, Ferrari, and Maserati. Only a small percent of car buyers can afford these cars, as their sticker prices start at about $40,000 and go on up from there. Oshkosh Truck, in contrast, utilizes a cost leadership strategy for a specific market niche in the production of heavy-duty military vehicles.

Discussion Question 5
To compete effectively in the 1990s, should firms select one of the generic strategies—differentiation, cost leadership, or focus—and stick with it? Explain.

Smaller firms with limited resources often choose one of the two versions of the focus strategy, that is, cost leadership or differentiation applied within a specific niche. Larger firms with substantial resources and a broad product line often use various combinations of these three generic strategies. For example, the products of Ford's Lincoln-Mercury Division range from low-cost autos (the basic Topaz) to autos with unique characteristics for special customer niches (Lincoln Continental and Lincoln Town Car). Table 5.4 summarizes the key features of the generic strategies model and gives further examples of organizations that have successfully used them.

TABLE 5.4

Overview of the Generic Strategies Model

Business-Level Strategy	Feature	Company Examples
Differentiation	Premium quality	Coleman—camping equipment
	Brand image	Compaq—PCs
	Technological leadership	Gillette—razors
	Customer service	Maytag—appliances
		NIKE—sports shoes
Cost leadership	Tight cost controls	Discount Tires—tire replacement
	Efficient scale of facilities	Motel 6—travel accommodations
	Efficient service, sales force, and advertising	Wal-Mart—retailing
	Competitive pricing	UPS—package delivery
Focus	Careful identification of target market (niche)	Nieman Marcus—elite retailing
	Cost leadership emphasis or differentiation emphasis	Oshkosh Truck—heavy-duty military trucks
	Constant review of customer demand in niche	Polo—clothing
		Rolex—watches

CHAPTER SUMMARY

In this chapter, we presented an overview of how firms may develop and use strategies. Strategic planning may be characterized as a complex decision-making process with two major branches: corporate-level planning and business-level planning. Strategic plans are further refined by tactical planning and implemented through action plans.

1 ***Explain why planning may help achieve organizational effectiveness.***

Planning is the most fundamental managerial function. Effective planning will help an organization adapt to change by (1) identifying future opportunities, (2) anticipating future problems, and (3) developing appropriate strategies and tactics. Effective planning also facilitates entrepreneurship and helps employees deal with risk and uncertainty.

2 ***State the characteristics of strategic and tactical planning.***

Strategic planning focuses on the development of an organization's mission and vision, goals, general strategies, and major resource allocations. Tactical planning is concerned with shorter term detailed decisions regarding what to do, who will do it, and how to do it. Tactical planning provides the specific ideas for implementing strategic plans.

3 ***Differentiate the corporate, business, and functional levels of planning and strategies.***

The four major levels of diversification are: (1) single-business firm, (2) dominant-business firm, (3) related-businesses firm, and (4) unrelated-businesses firm. At each higher level, the range of the organization's goods, services, and markets increases which, in turn, increases the scope and complexity of its strategic planning. Corporate-level strategy guides the activities of various businesses (or product lines) within a parent organization. Corporate-level growth strategies include forward integration, backward integration, horizontal integration, concentric diversification, and conglomerate diversification. Business-level strategy directs the operations and performance of a single business-firm or strategic business unit (SBU). It addresses issues such as "How do we compete?" Functional-level strategy creates guidelines and tactics for managing each functional area and specifies how each will contribute to the organization's business-level strategies and goals.

4 ***Explain the eight tasks of the strategic planning process.***

The strategic planning process comprises eight interrelated core tasks: (1) develop the mission and goals, (2) diagnose threats and opportunities, (3) diagnose strengths and weaknesses, (4) generate alternative strategies (e.g., market penetration strategy, market development strategy, or product development strategy), (5) develop a strategic plan, (6) develop tactical plans, (7) control and assess the results of both strategic and tactical plans, and (8) repeat the planning process.

5 ***Use models of business-level strategy to develop competitive strategies.***

The product life cycle model emphasizes planning and strategies according to the life cycles that many products go through—introduction, growth, maturity, decline, and termination. The generic strategies model provides a framework of three basic business-level strategies (differentiation, cost leadership, and focus) that are applicable to a variety of organizations in diverse industries.

QUESTIONS FOR DISCUSSION

1. What are the key differences between strategic planning and tactical planning?
2. At which level of diversification is Southwest Airlines? Where does this firm's services seem to fall in the product life cycle model? What are the primary implications of these answers for the firm?
3. What are the main differences between corporate-level, business-level, and functional-level strategies? Give an example of each level for a company that you know.

4. What are the primary forces driving industry and market competition for companies in the airline industry?
5. To compete effectively in the 1990s, should firms select one of the generic strategies—differentiation, cost (price) leadership, or focus—and stick with it? Explain.
6. What difficulties might arise in following the sequence of the eight core tasks of the strategic planning process?

FROM WHERE YOU SIT

1. Which strategic planning concepts can you apply to your career development? Using these ideas, write a brief strategic career plan for yourself.
2. Identify two companies that have recently changed their missions or their most important goals. What factors probably influenced these changes?
3. What are three opportunities and three threats facing the college (university) in which you are enrolled?
4. Should diversity be stated as a formal and quantitative strategic goal? Would this affect your decision to work for a company? Why or why not?
5. Select a company that you are familiar with. Write three functional goals for that company.
6. Based on what you learned in this chapter, what issues would you consider if you were interviewing for a managerial position at (1) Southwest Airlines, (2) AT&T, and (3) General Motors?

SKILL-BUILDING EXERCISE

Marzilli's Fine Italian Foods

Introduction. This exercise can be undertaken by you alone, the class as a whole, or groups of five to eight class members. Study the description of this situation, then answer the two questions about it, following the guidelines for strategic thinking that are given.

The Situation. Marzilli's Fine Italian Foods is a grocery store founded in 1945 by Gino Marzilli and his wife, Maria. Gino and Maria were immigrants. In its early years the business provided Italian specialty grocery items to the residents of an Italian immigrant neighborhood in the center-city area. Gino's family ran a grocery store in Milan, Italy, and his own store had much of the flavor of Milan.

Over the years the business has been quite successful. In 1962 Gino and Maria bought a large building not far from the original store. The building was remodeled and provided them with a much larger store area plus an apartment to live in. In 1970 they began producing homemade pasta and a series of high-quality sauces to be used with Italian foods. The recipes were developed by Maria, and the products, sold exclusively at the store, have continued to be quite popular.

Gino and Maria retired to Florida in 1982, turning the business over to their only child, Jim Marzilli. Jim has been involved in the business all of his life. He is married, but his wife has not been involved in the business. They and their four children live in a southern suburb of the city.

Although the business remained very successful in the early 1990s, recently the sales revenues have shown a steady decline. Jim attributes this decline to several factors. Most important is the fact that most of the old Italian population has moved from the center-city area to the suburbs. These people are dispersed in five or six southwestern suburbs that are a forty- to sixty-minute drive from the old neighborhood. Thus many of the store "regulars" shop infrequently at Marzilli's, although the store is crowded on Fridays and Saturdays, particularly before holidays and feast days. A related factor is that the center-city neighborhood where the store is located is now populated by young professionals. Although some of them patronize the store, they purchase only a limited number of items, such as bread and certain sauces. Jim feels that this is because their knowledge of Italian cuisine is limited, although many seem to be interested in Italian cooking. Over the past year the business has been barely at the break-even point, and Jim feels it is time to do something about the situation. He would like the store to be the busy meeting place for Italians that it was through the mid-1970s but realizes that times have changed. He is 52 years old and does not want to retire or sell the business. Three of his four children now live out of town and are not interested in the business, but his youngest son Dom has expressed some interest. Dom lives in an apartment above the store and works downtown for a market research firm. His wife June is a teacher and has helped in the store during rush times. Although June is not Italian, Jim says that she is almost as great an Italian cook as he and his mother. Dom and June have no children.

At this point, Jim sees two basic alternative strategies:

1. *Maintain the same line of products, but cut back on the number of employees and store hours.* He now has six full-time employees and thinks he could get along with four. And since much of the business comes from old customers who come on Fridays and Saturdays, Jim feels that he could maintain the same level of sales be being open only Tuesday through Saturday. The cutback of employees and shorter hours will cut costs; if sales remain at about the same level, Jim thinks the business will be profitable in the coming years.

2. *Start adding "American" foods to attract more of the current neighborhood residents.* Marzilli's would thus become a neighborhood grocery store rather than an Italian specialty food store. Jim would retain some Italian foods to serve his old customers, but the store would gradually evolve into a neighborhood grocery store. There are no grocery stores within a four- or five-block radius, and Jim feels that he could pick up a lot of neighborhood trade.[72]

Questions

1. What are the apparent opportunities and threats for this business?

2. How would you diagnose the strengths and weaknesses of Marzilli's Fine Italian Foods?

3. What planning process can you recommend that would allow Jim Marzilli to make a wise decision about the future of the business?

4. If required to choose, which of the two strategies being considered by Marzilli would you recommend to him? Why? Should another strategy be considered? Explain.

CRITICAL THINKING CASE

Carnival Cruise Lines

Carnival Cruise Lines, whose vessels are registered under Bahamian and other foreign flags, is one of the largest and most popular cruise lines in the world. They originally began by offering fun cruises for twenty-something travelers. They now provide a wide range of services, including many that appeal to more mature and more affluent travelers. Carnival has built its own fleet and has acquired two well-known companies: Holland America, a vendor of luxury cruises, and Windstar, a company specializing in Windjammer trips. In addition, it has acquired a casino operation in Nassau, Bahamas, and has started an airline to complement the cruise operations. Carnival might be characterized as a related-businesses firm. In acknowledgment of its diverse structure and to accommodate the array of its related-businesses, Carnival recently changed its name to the Carnival Corporation.

The cruise line, as do all cruise lines, operates in a highly competitive and turbulent environment. The industry has grown at a steadily increasing rate—from handling 500,000 passengers in 1970 to a projected 5.5 million passengers by the year 2000. This growth has enticed many new entrants. Carnival's three companies have the largest market share in the industry (27 percent). Royal Caribbean, Princess, and Norwegian Cruise Lines have a combined market share of about 37 percent. Carnival competes directly with these firms and with thirteen other cruise lines operating from various parts of North America. Cruises also compete with "land" packages such as those offered by Delta Dream and American FlyAway vacations to similar destinations.

There have been many opportunities for growth over the past twenty years. This growth has been fueled by economic growth in the United States, Europe, and Asia and by the failures of smaller cruise companies. By positioning itself to capture leisure dollars, Carnival has been able to take advantage of new markets created by the opening of a port near Disney World in Orlando and to explore niche cruises for targeted populations. Two examples are the S.V. Fantasy positioned in Port Canaveral for day cruises that appeal to Disney patrons and the Fiesta Marina designed in a Latin motif to attract the large Latin population in the United States. Carnival also is experimenting with family cruises designed to attract vacationing families with small children and moderate incomes. If Cuba is opened to U.S. travelers, Carnival is positioned to open cruise operations to Cuba quickly. Many tourism experts consider Cuba to be a sleeping giant destination; European travelers are already enjoying Cuba as a destination alone or in combination with Florida packages.

All is not smooth on the horizon, however. Two bills in the U.S. Congress have serious implications for all cruise lines. The first, the Clay Bill, extends some labor laws including the right to organize and the right to receive minimum wages by employees on foreign ships that call at U.S. ports. These changes would alter Carnival's costs because many ship employees are paid by tips only. Also, Carnival uses local labor from the countries in which they dock. The Shipbuilding Trade Reform Act of 1993 also is threatening to erode profitability. This legislation, known as the Gibbons Bill, provides for sanctions to companies that accept subsidies from foreign countries to build ships in those countries. Carnival and the other cruise lines operating in the Caribbean also are monitoring the governmental proposals in the Caribbean nations. The Jamaican Prime Minister has recommended that the island governments create a licensing authority to regulate cruise activity in the region.

Cruise lines have also come under the scrutiny of environmental agencies. Based on some evidence that marine life is being destroyed in the Caribbean, pressure is being exerted on governments to exercise greater controls on garbage and oil dumping and anchoring activities. A Norwegian Cruise Line crew was videotaped dumping plastic bags of garbage into the ocean—a practice common to all ship companies. As a result of the adverse publicity, the United States and the Caribbean nations are pressuring all shipping companies, including the cruise lines, to modify garbage disposal, deep water anchorage, and oil containment methods.

Carnival Corporation clearly has some strengths that have permitted it to grow over the years. It was the first cruise company to issue new stock on the New York Stock Exchange. That stock issue gave it the capital needed to acquire new ships when the industry was first expanding. Coupled with an image of being a fun cruise line, Carnival has been a trend setter with the introduction of the first three- and four-day cruises. Carnival also established a price structure to accommodate discounting, as evidenced by its early implementation of Super Saver cruise rates. Large market penetration and a flexible price structure gave Carnival a comfort zone as industry capacity expanded at a seemingly uncontrolled rate in the early 1990s.

Another company strength is the wide range of cruise services that it has acquired and developed. Although Carnival's original products were mid-priced cruises, the acquisition of Holland American and Windstar provided a wider customer appeal. The addition of several superliners, the Fantasy and the Ecstasy, permitted the company to compete with others that featured large ships.

Explosive growth and expanding markets can be troublesome to a company. Some analysts express concern over increasing capacity in the cruise industry to the point of excess and the increasing debt burden of Carnival Corporation. Both developments could erode profitability. In addition, the lackluster performance of the Casino in Nassau is causing Carnival to reconsider that diversification attempt. However, the hotel and casino business as a whole in the Bahamas is not robust, and Carnival may have difficulty selling the property. Carnival's entry into the airline industry creates some uncertainty because of the nature of that industry.[73]

Questions

1. What are the most significant industry forces that affect Carnival's ability to compete?
2. What are the benefits of Carnival's diversification into hotels and an airline? What are the perils of this strategy?
3. Write a mission statement for Carnival Corporation. Based on that mission, evaluate the company's strategies and present at least three recommendations for modifying those strategies.

VIDEO CASE

Allied-Signal's Radical Changes

What does a company do when its primary customers are from three industries that have been in turmoil? If the company is Allied-Signal, it hires Lawrence Bossidy, former vice-chairman of General Electric. Allied-Signal is not a household word. As an industrial supplier, it provides component parts to the aerospace, automotive, and other industries that make manufactured durable goods. Some brands such as Fram filters and Autolite spark plugs are recognized by end-user consumers. But the largest part of its revenues, 42 percent, comes from supplying turbines, auxiliary power units, environmental control systems and other essential but unglamorous components for space modules.

Allied-Signal, like other mergers of failing companies (e.g., Unisys), was created from the old Allied Chemical Company, Bendix, and Signal Companies. Each of the constituents was weak when they were merged into a corporate entity, and the whole was synergistically less than the sum of its parts. The single largest problem facing Allied-Signal as Bossidy took over in 1991 was a negative cash flow of $435 million. He began with three goals: to make targeted financial indicators, to make total quality management (TQM) more than a slogan, and to make Allied-Signal into a unified company. These were difficult goals to meet; however, the people at Allied-Signal knew they were on a sinking platform and the only way to go was up.

What strategies did Allied Signal use to tackle each of these difficult problems? The first goal, to meet the numbers, required strategies targeted at increasing revenues while controlling costs and restructuring the debt inherited from the mergers of the 1980s. Control of cash was the first target. Management started by divesting eight small businesses that were underperforming or did not fit with the general lines of businesses in the diversified company. But careful cost control also became an important issue. Allied-Signal started using working capital turnover as a gauge of cash flow that was universal across all divisions. Allied-Signal's target was to achieve 5.2 turns of working capital annually. At the current level of sales at Allied-Signal, that would generate about $500 million of new cash annually. Other financial goals were to increase sales revenues by 8 percent annually. Unfortunately, cutbacks in aerospace programs and the banning of fluorocarbons have prevented this sales objective from being met. When Bossidy revealed his strategy for growth, Wall Street reported that the stock jumped from $2.50 in 1991 to $71.375 on the day he spoke in August 1993. The same day the company reported a second-quarter profit of $170 million. Bossidy promises annual earnings growth of 13 to 17 percent through 1995. Much of the bottom line improvement driving the stock price came from a companywide restructuring, initiated in 1991 with a massive downsizing. A daunting challenge was to motivate the pared-down work force of 88,000 employees to embrace new management and manufacturing approaches in an organization long criticized for lacking vision and paying scant attention to costs and customers.

What has caused the increase in profits in the face of somewhat flat revenues? The second goal, making TQM a reality, has contributed significantly to the bottom line. Bossidy treated nothing as sacred. This approach required a culture change and the use of extensive four-day training for all employees, ranging from plant managers to janitors. In that unique training program, workers attended in groups and brought real problems for discussion. For example, in Tempe, Arizona, an aerospace team raised their concern that hand-finishing of hardware was being subcontracted to outside vendors for $25,000 per month. During the four-day session they learned that the poor quality of their in-house work came from the use of antiquated machines that did a poor job prepping the material for its final finishing. With a thorough understanding of the problem, they were able to convince the management to buy new tumblers for $60,000, which were projected to save the company $24,000 per year. Another component of the TQM program is materials management. Like other companies, Allied Signal quickly realized that not all productivity gains could come from reduction of supplier costs—that lead times and quality also had to improve. The company informed all suppliers that they were to reduce prices by 10 to 15 percent and improve lead times by 30 percent while continuously improving their quality standards for materials and components. Materials management was improved internally. For example, two weeks were required to move supplies from the receiving docks to storerooms. During this time, the company was incurring the cost of a part that was essentially unusable. The time has been reduced to 2-3 hours. Similar gains also were achieved in order processing.

Both the focus on numbers and the attention to TQM have led naturally to accomplishment of the third goal, to unify the company. By using standardized formulas for computing gains and by controlling relationships with suppliers, diverse businesses are learning to be "mindful" of common issues and problems. Commodity teams have been formed across functional and divisional lines to purchase products used throughout the company. This change has improved company cohesiveness and has given the company the ability to negotiate volume discounts. Moreover, human resources has become a corporate function. Thus all employees now are subject to similar policies so that no division can accuse corporate management of giving preferential treatment to other divisions. Since coming to Allied-Signal, Bossidy, reflecting his GE background, has been urging a move from being "internally focused" to "customer focused," from a "vertically organized" to a "horizontally organized" structure in which people with different duties work as a team, and from managing employees to leading and motivating them.

Has Allied-Signal dug out yet? It's too soon to tell how its strategies will work in the long run. One overall concern is its continued presence in industries that are still unstable. A second concern stems from the continued presence in chemical products that are under scrutiny by environmentalists. But the company now has about $6 billion in cash and credits to fund research and buy attractive acquisitions in the global arena as the opportunity arises.[74]

Questions

1. What type of diversification does Allied-Signal exhibit?
2. Does Allied-Signal have a mission and a well-stated vision? If so, what are they?
3. Allied-Signal is operating in three different product sectors: aerospace, automotive parts, and chemicals. What is another line of business that could help the company reduce the dangers inherent in those three sectors? Explain.

Chapter 6

Strategic Management: Planning Aids and Implementation

Learning *Objectives*

After studying this chapter, you should be able to:

1. Describe the essentials of the scenario, Delphi technique, and simulation forecasting aids.
2. Apply dialectical inquiry and devil's advocacy to reveal and diagnose assumptions.
3. Explain the phases of team-based management by goals.
4. Describe benchmarking and the Deming Cycle, two planning aids specifically designed to improve quality.
5. Define project management and describe how the program evaluation and review technique (PERT) is applied in project management.

Chapter *Outline*

Preview *Insight*

Planning at Emerson Electric

Headquartered in St. Louis, Missouri, Emerson Electric makes refrigerator compressors, temperature sensors, pressure gauges, motors, In-Sink-Erator garbage disposals, and similar components used by other manufacturers. Emerson's markets are so competitive that it has operated without significant price increases since the mid-1980s. Yet, this firm has maintained an unbroken string of increased earnings over the past thirty-six years.

Charles Knight is the longtime chairman and CEO of Emerson. At the beginning of 1993, he brought together fifteen Emerson executives and asked them to tell him what he was doing wrong. They told him that Emerson needed an environment that would encourage both revenue growth and profit margins. Knight responded by stating: "We are shifting gears to growth." The executives immediately changed Emerson's planning process. Emerson's exceptionally detailed planning is a classic of its kind. It seeks to identify problems before they emerge and start doing something about them at once.

Planning at Emerson involves every aspect of the business. For example, every two years each of its 70,000 employees is asked to fill out lengthy opinion surveys, which ask questions such as: "Is the plant manager competent and doing a good job?" and "If you were starting over, would you go to work for this plant again?" If more than a third of the responses to the questions are negative, the division manager must come up with a proposal for corrective action. If the thoughts and feelings of the workers count heavily in Emerson's planning process, so do those of managers at all levels. Knight goes to great lengths to get to know them personally and obtain their inputs.

An important part of the planning process is forecasting. The forecasts presented to Knight by the fifteen executives helped guide the switch from an efficiency-is-all strategy to a growth strategy. The forecasts suggested that further gains from cost cutting would be marginal. To keep the profit line climbing, Emerson would have to maintain operating margins but generate larger sales volumes.

Knight spends 60 percent of his time attending planning sessions, many held at Emerson's rural Winfield conference center outside of St. Louis. Scores of managers from Emerson's fifty divisions shed their suits and ties and arrive there lugging thick binders of charts and graphs. Standing before Knight, who is often accompanied by his right-hand man, senior vice-chairman Al Suter, the managers present multiyear business analyses, budgets, and forecasts.

Those attending know one thing: No matter how strong their arguments, Knight and Suter are going to challenge them. "The concept is to disagree with the thesis being presented, irrespective of the thesis," explains Robert Staley, vice-chairman and chief administrative officer. Says Knight, "People who do the planning present it to the people who do the approvals. There are no levels of bureaucracy." If the manager making the forecast can stand up to the withering analysis from Knight and Sutra, the plan becomes the operating blueprint for that strategic business unit.

Until the summer of 1993, at least half of the time spent in planning sessions focused on costs, margins, and profits. To make sure the message got through that Emerson has refocused toward growth, Knight established a new rule. Planning sessions now focus exclusively on sales, new product development, overseas expansion, and so on. Discussion of profits are held separately with James Bergs, an executive vice-president. Emerson's management compensation formula also was changed to increase the rewards for meeting growth goals and coming up with new products, acquisitions, and ideas for international expansion.[1]

1

Describe the essentials of the scenario, Delphi technique, and simulation forecasting aids.

FORECASTING AIDS

One recent study identified forty-nine planning aids and techniques and reviewed thirty of them.[2] Rather than review all those methods, we begin by discussing the basics and limitations of forecasting and the essentials of three commonly used forecasting techniques: scenarios, the Delphi technique, and simulation. Because planning is always

Teaching Tip
To introduce planning aids, read the following quote and ask students to discuss it: "As more line managers are given primary responsibility for planning, there is an urgent need to acquaint them with the spectrum of potent tools and techniques for developing and focusing strategy."

Teaching Tip
Forecasts are a common part of daily life. Weather forecasts are the most familiar type. Ask students to name some types forecasts they make regularly.

Ask Students
Name an event from which you made an extrapolation but were proved incorrect when the future didn't turn out to be like the past.

based on assumptions, we next look at aids for identifying and challenging those assumptions. Then we describe the phases of team-based management by goals, an approach used both to develop and to carry out plans. We consider two aids that help bridge strategic and tactical issues in planning for improved quality: benchmarking and the Deming cycle. Finally, we discuss project management as a process for implementing specific plans and strategies.

Forecasting involves predicting, projecting, or estimating future events or conditions in an organization's environment. As an important part of the planning process, forecasting is concerned primarily with external events or conditions (beyond management's control) that are important to a firm's survival and growth. As noted in the Preview Insight, forecasting is fundamental to the planning process at Emerson Electric. Forecasts suggested that further gains from cost cutting would be marginal. They led Emerson's management to switch from an efficiency-is-all strategy to a growth strategy.

Most forecasting is based on extrapolation. **Extrapolation** is the projection of some tendency from the past or present into the future.[3] The simplest, and at times most misleading, form of extrapolation is a linear, or straight-line, projection of a past trend into the future.[4] In the mid-1980s, IBM began to experience serious sales and profitability problems. In part, these problems were the result of projecting a steady increase in the demand for large mainframe computers and continuing to be overly preoccupied with the company's traditional way of doing things. Unfortunately, these projections (forecasts) were out of touch with massive changes in the marketplace.[5] A new generation of PCs made by Apple, NEC, Canon, Compaq, Dell, and many other manufacturers, the advances in microchips and processors developed and produced by Intel and others, and the massive introduction of new user-friendly software made by Microsoft and others, gave PC users enormous computer power right at their desks.

Even though forecasting is uncertain, it's still necessary. Managers have to use whatever is available to them in anticipating future events and conditions. Three forecasting aids—scenarios, the Delphi technique, and simulation—are often used in strategic planning. Because all of them focus on understanding possible futures, they are not mutually exclusive.

Discussion Question 2
It is January 2000, and the Joneses have settled down for an evening of television. Joe Jones aims his remote control at a 3-by-5 screen across the room and taps in a three-digit code to call up the fifth rerun of his all-time favorite flick, *Rambo XIII*. The family doesn't drive to a videocassette rental store for a movie any more, and the number of such outlets is shrinking. Of course, network TV is free, but nothing much there grabs the Joneses tonight. It is time for a rerun of *Rambo*, or almost anything else on film the Joneses can think of. The shows are all there—thousands of shows—ready to be punched up by computer. Welcome to the impending age of fiber-optic TV. Welcome to the fast-developing wonders of electronic switching systems. Watch out, investors in cable systems. Be alert, those of you who use TV for marketing purposes. Technology is about to change your worlds.[52] Do you agree with this scenario? Why or why not?

Scenarios

A **scenario** is a written description of a possible future. *Scenario* became a popular business term in 1967, with the publication of Herman Kahn and Anthony Weiner's book, *The Year 2000*. **Multiple scenarios** are simply written descriptions of several possible futures. Planners use scenarios to address questions such as: What future environment might exist for the organization? How could some potential (hypothetical) situation come about? What types of strategies might be useful in preventing, diverting, encouraging, or dealing with these futures?[6] Thus scenarios are intended to

- provide a wide range of possibilities against which to evaluate strategies,
- provide a broader vision of possible events,
- assist in the identification of events that warrant the development of contingency plans, and
- help managers and others identify broad patterns, generalizations, and interrelationships.[7]

Scenarios are quite useful in forcing those involved in planning to evaluate preliminary plans against future possibilities. Royal Dutch/Shell, which has been doing scenario planning for twenty-five years, developed two twenty-year scenarios.[7] The first, called "Sustainable World," predicts increased concern about global warming trends and greater emphasis on conservation, recycling, and emission controls. The second, entitled "Mercantilist World," suggests an increase in protectionism, a slump in world growth, and a deemphasis of environmentalism. Shell management realizes that these two scenarios do not cover everything that might happen in the future and that neither

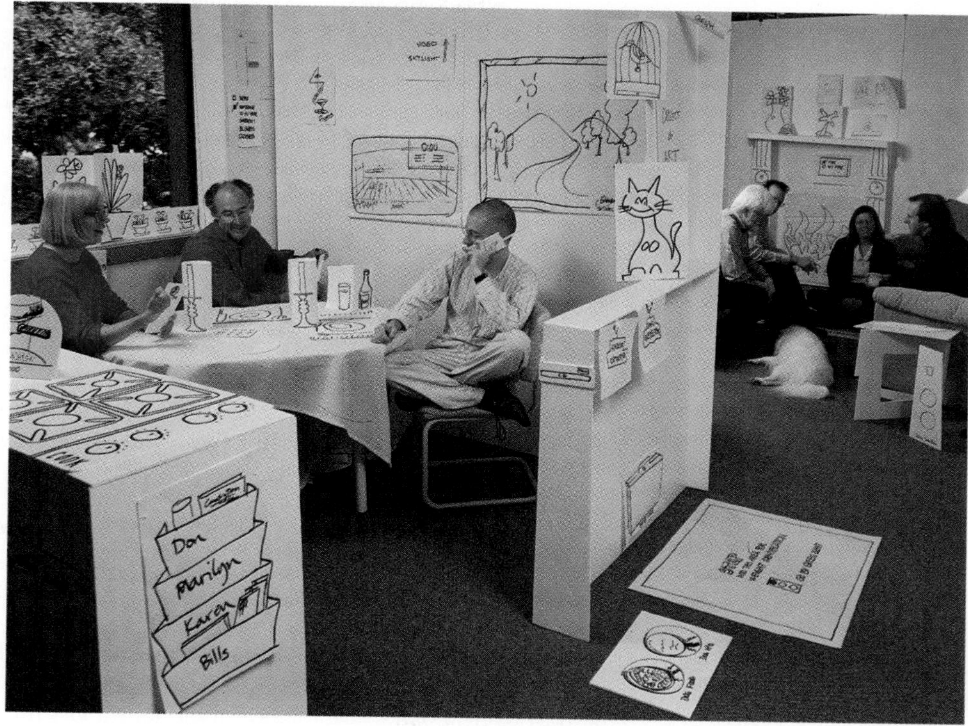

Scenarios are one type of forecasting aid used in strategic planning. Here researchers at Interval Research created a kitchen and living room scenario to act out imagined electronic futures.

is a perfect predictor. Group planning coordinator Peter Hadfield points out that the scenarios are there to help the organization to think more deeply about the future.[8]

Hadfield also believes that scenario planning has helped Shell be better prepared than its competitors for external shocks. In the early 1980s, for example, while most forecasters were predicting a steadily increasing price for crude oil, Shell, in one of its scenarios, had considered the possibility that the price would slide to $15 a barrel. As a hedge against such an eventuality, the company began looking into cost-saving exploration technologies. When the slump hit, Shell was able to sustain a higher level of drilling activity than many of its competitors.

Scenarios are usually developed for possible futures that are five to twenty years ahead. To keep the process manageable, three scenarios are usually sufficient: the most probable scenario, a pessimistic scenario, and an optimistic scenario.

Ethics
Ethical issues should be written into scenarios. (Example: With the global warming trend in a scenario, ethical considerations—among other issues—for an oil company would be whether the company is contributing to the problem and what it can do to help solve the problem.)

Teaching Tip
Have each student write a scenario involving an earthquake hitting the university while they are in class. Discuss the various scenarios and how they differ.

Delphi Technique

Named after an ancient Greek oracle, the **Delphi technique** is a forecasting aid based on a consensus of a panel of experts.[9] The experts refine their opinions, step by step, until they reach a consensus. Because the technique relies on opinions, it obviously isn't foolproof. But the consensus arrived at tends to be much more accurate than a single expert's opinion.[10] The method was developed by the Rand Corporation in the early 1950s to obtain expert judgments on how many Soviet atomic bombs would be required to do a specific amount of damage to the United States. The Delphi technique is now recognized as an important aid to strategic planning.

Basic Steps. The Delphi technique involves three basic steps.

1. ***A questionnaire is sent to a group of experts.*** These experts remain unknown to one another. The questionnaire requests numerical estimates of specific technological or market possibilities. It also asks for expected dates and an assignment of probabilities to each of these possibilities.

2. ***A summary of the first round is prepared.*** This report may show the average, medium, and quartile ranges of responses. The report, along with a revised questionnaire, is sent to those who completed the first questionnaire. They are asked to revise their earlier estimates, if appropriate, or to justify their original opinions.
3. ***A summary of the second round is prepared.*** This report often shows that a consensus is developing. The experts are then asked in a third questionnaire to indicate whether they support this emerging consensus and the explanations that accompany it. To avoid blind agreement, they are encouraged to find reasons for *not* joining the consensus.[11]

Three rounds generally are recommended. Although more rounds could be used, the experts often begin dropping out after the third round because of other time commitments. The number of participating experts may range from only a few to more than 100, depending on the results desired. A range of fifteen to twenty is recommended for a fairly narrow issue. As the sample size (number of experts) increases, the amount of coordination required also increases, as do costs.

Delphi Questionnaires. The heart of the Delphi technique is the series of questionnaires. The first questionnaire may include broadly worded questions. In later rounds the questions become more specific because they are built on responses to the preceding questionnaires.

Teaching Tip
Select a current controversy as reported in the media. Apply the Delphi technique by designing a simple questionnaire and giving it to experts in various disciplines at the university to respond to. Go over the results, noting, comparing, and contrasting these opinions.

Table 6.1 shows a Delphi technique questionnaire developed for student and classroom use. It is concerned with possible developments in typical U.S. business firms over the next twenty years. You might want to take a few minutes now to answer these questions.

TRW, a major advanced-technology firm, began using the Delphi technique in 1960 to forecast developments in such diverse fields as space, transportation, and housing. Goodyear Tire and Rubber Company now uses the method to plan tire research and other company activities. In recent years the Delphi technique has been effectively applied to help identify and solve problems and set goals and priorities in the areas of environmental consequences of business strategies, urban redevelopment, energy conservation, pollution control, and housing.[12]

Simulation

A **simulation** is a representation of a real system. The simulation model usually describes the behavior of the real system (or some aspect of it) in quantitative and/or qualitative terms. For example, an organization simulation may show how changes in external variables (e.g., inflation rate, competitors' price changes, and unemployment rate) may affect a firm's sales, profits, and losses.

Computers often are used in simulation. For example, Abbot Laboratories, a major diversified health care company, uses SIMPLAN, a general software modeling language that can be learned easily by people who have no prior experience with a computer. It actually comprises three models that simulate the relationships among marketing, production, and finance at Abbot from data entered into the computer by the employee. The marketing model simulates pricing that is driven by a simulated market demand. The production model converts these sales volumes into raw materials and inventory requirements. These results are inputs for the financial model. The end result is a set of reports that contain sales projections, materials and labor requirements, and projected income statements for alternative scenarios.[13]

Teaching Tip
Do a simulation in class from the *Journal of Management Education.*

Simulation often is used to forecast the effects of environmental changes and internal management decisions on an organization, department, or SBU. The goal of simulation is to reproduce or test reality without actually experiencing it. Most simulations are intended to let management ask numerous "what if" questions. For example, "What profits can we anticipate next year if inflation is 8 percent and we continue current pric-

TABLE 6.1

Delphi Questionnaire: Future Developments in North American Businesses

The ten questions here are concerned with future possible developments in the typical North American business firm within the next twenty years or so. In addition to giving your answer to each question, you are asked to rank the questions from 1 to 10. The ranking 1 means you think that you have the best chance of making an accurate projection for this question relative to the others. The ranking 10 means you regard your answer as least probable relative to other years identified. Please rank all questions, using every number from 1 to 10 only once. "Never" is also an acceptable answer.

RANK (1–10)		QUESTIONS	YEAR
______	1.	In what year will women serve as presidents of at least fifty of the *Fortune* 500 Corporations?	______
______	2.	In what year will most boards of directors of publicly held corporations contain members who represent primarily the consumer rather than the shareholders?	______
______	3.	In what year will managers regularly be paid for working a thirty-five-hour week?	______
______	4.	By what year will business have effectively reduced its pollution of the environment to a nondangerous level?	______
______	5.	By what year will the average company become smaller, employing fewer people?	______
______	6.	By what year will the use of mind-stimulating drugs be employed by 10 percent of top-level managers as an aid in determining corporate policy alternatives?	______
______	7.	In what year will alternative energy sources be greater than the use of oil, gas, and coal?	______
______	8.	By what year will an MBA degree be a minimum requirement for entry into the management training programs of most corporations?	______
______	9.	In what year will at least 30 percent of employees of firms work mostly at their homes?	______
______	10.	In what year will most corporations' financial statements reflect a significant level of accounting for social costs and assets (e.g., pollution, welfare, and human resources)?	______

Source: Adapted from personal correspondence with Dr. Harvey Nussbaum, School of Business Administration, Wayne State University, Detroit. Used with permission.

ing policies?" or "What profits can we expect next year if inflation is 12 percent and we open two new plants?" To answer such questions, analysts often develop complex equations and use computers to perform many of the step-by-step computations required. Such models can be used to simulate virtually any area of concern (e.g., profits, sales, and earnings per share) for which a forecast is needed.

Typical Questions and Variables. A simulation can help planners deal with three common strategic questions.

1. What general effect will certain changes in the economy (e.g., an increase in interest rates from 6 to 10 percent) have on the firm if its primary strategies remain unchanged?
2. What will be the specific effects on the firm if a particular strategy (e.g., low cost, focus, or differentiation) is selected in anticipation of those changes in the economy?
3. Are there any particular combinations of strategies that will enable the firm to gain a competitive advantage over its competitors?

Types of environmental variables used in a simulation might include inflation rate, short-term interest rate, tax rate, and unemployment level. Strategies used in a simulation could affect price, sales, dividends, cash flow, depreciation, or production capacity. The performance measure used to present the outcome of a simulation model might be an income statement, a financial ratio (e.g., debt-to-equity ratio, return on equity, or earnings per share), or a balance sheet (assets and liabilities).

Manufacturing processes have been studied using computer simulation. In the past, simulations of manufacturing systems were performed mainly by mathematical experts who believed in the results. However, managers often did not believe in them because the results were presented in the form of hard-to-interpret computer printouts. Simulation of manufacturing systems now utilizes a new technology—computer graphics—that is much clearer and easier to understand. Using graphic displays, the simulation evolves step by step on the screen for the user and others to see. As a result, many managers are gaining confidence in simulation results.[14]

Discussion Question 4
What are the similarities and differences between the Delphi technique and simulation? Explain.

Ask Students
Has anyone ever tried virtual reality? Ask a volunteer to describe it briefly.

Virtual Reality. A new technology, **virtual reality,** is a surrogate environment created by communications and computer systems.[15] The term denotes a simulated environment into which a user "enters," moves around, and interacts with objects. Virtual reality fulfills the sensory requirements of human beings for sight, sound, and movement. One of the earliest practical uses of virtual reality was the training of pilots in flight simulators. Its entertainment uses are becoming increasingly common in video games. Some dentists are even using it to relax their patients while performing oral surgery.

The advantage of virtual reality as a planning aid is the freedom it allows for experimentation. The pace of action may be slowed down or speeded up. Processes that occur very rapidly can be slowed down for more careful study. Processes that extend over very long periods of time can be speeded up to reveal more clearly the consequences of particular actions. Actions that cannot be replayed in the real world can be

A Caterpillar engineer tests an electronic prototype of a wheel loader using virtual reality—a surrogate environment created by communications and computer systems.

Discussion Question 3
Are there any potential ethical concerns with an increasing use and application of virtual reality? Explain.

redone countless times. Complexity can be simplified by uncoupling variables that are interlocked in reality.[16] The following Insight describes some applications of virtual reality as a planning aid.

Insight

Virtual Reality Comes to Planning

Virtual reality can be as simple as a representation of an architect's sketchpad. The architect can draw and talk through moves in a spatial-action language, leaving traces that represent the forms of buildings on a site. Because the drawing reveals qualities and relations unimagined beforehand, moves can function as experiments—for example, discovering that building shapes do not fit the slope of the land or that classrooms are too small.

In some systems, a viewer wearing a sensor-laden glove manipulates objects in the computer as the person would naturally. In others, images on the screen or a viewer's perspective are manipulated with a mouse or joystick. At IBM's Watson Labs in Hawthorne, New York, for instance, an engineer seated in front of a projection screen looking at a sleek, beige dashboard becomes a test driver in a 1997 Chrysler. Wearing 3-D glasses and a glove with sensors, she turns the steering wheel and reaches for buttons as though in a real car. Chrysler Corporation is developing the system in cooperation with IBM in an attempt to cut months off the three- to five-year car-design process by letting engineers spot inconveniently positioned knobs and other problems before they surface in expensive prototypes. In medicine, virtual reality tools are being used to create 3-D X-rays to help surgeons plan procedures or assist in surgery.

Engineers at the Northrup Corporation are using a virtual reality system to help redesign the Air Force's F-18 jet fighter plane. They model air-intake ducts on computers to make sure they fit through bulkheads, rather than building expensive physical models. An operator wearing wraparound goggles moves parts around with a type of mouse, making sure that they fit together in virtual space. The software even simulates resistance, so engineers know when parts "bump" against each other. Project Engineer Robert E. Joy loves the flexibility: "It's like reaching into the workstation and grabbing the part," he says.[17]

2

Apply dialectical inquiry and devil's advocacy to reveal and diagnose assumptions.

Ask Students
Have you had a conflict recently with someone in which you both "saw what you wanted to and heard what you wanted to"? Was the situation resolved? If so, how? If not, how could it have been resolved? Describe this incident to the person next to you.

Discussion Question 1
Reread the Preview Insight. Charles Knight, Emerson's CEO, still isn't convinced that he and Al Suter are doing everything possible to get managers to reveal the assumptions in their proposed plans. What would you recommend to him? How could this recommendation be implemented?

DIAGNOSING ASSUMPTIONS

One of the critical thinking skills required in the planning process is the diagnosis of assumptions. **Assumptions** are the underlying thoughts and feelings of one or more individuals that are taken for granted and believed to be true. The expression, "We see what we want to see and hear what we want to hear," is a reflection of how our assumptions affect perceptions, which, in turn, influence decisions and actions.[18]

A plan can never be better than the assumptions on which it is based. Recall the Preview Insight on Emerson Electric and Charles Knight, its CEO. The fifteen executives successfully challenged Knight's assumption that the best strategy for Emerson was to focus on increasing profit margins through increased efficiency. Forecasts influenced the change in this assumption and the development of a planning process based on a growth strategy. Of course, the view that Emerson's new growth strategy will be in the best long-term interests of the firm is, itself, an assumption.

The diagnosis of assumptions in planning involves three basic activities. First, the assumptions must be identified. Second, the assumptions must be displayed so that all who are involved may see them. Third, the validity of the assumptions must be tested.

In effect, an individual or team must "suspend" their beliefs in presumed facts or truths so that the validity and usefulness of those assumptions may be diagnosed.[19] The following Global Insight reveals how the underlying values and related assumptions of Chinese expatriates influence their choice of strategies, planning process, and management practices.

Global *Insight*

The Overseas Chinese

Among the champions of economic development during the past thirty years are three countries populated mainly by Chinese living outside the Chinese mainland: Taiwan, Hong Kong, and Singapore. Moreover, overseas Chinese play an important role in the economies of Indonesia, Malaysia, the Philippines, and Thailand.

Many overseas Chinese enterprises are family-owned, cooperate with others through networks based on personal relations, and differ from Western organizations in various ways. There is no distinction between ownership and management, which is typical in the West, Japan, and Korea. A firm normally focuses on one product or market, with growth through opportunistic diversification, in which it usually is extremely flexible. Decision making is centralized in the hands of one dominant family member. But, other family members may be given new ventures on which they try their skills. Overseas Chinese maintain a low profile and are extremely cost conscious. The assumed lack of loyalty of nonfamily employees keeps their firms comparatively small. If outside employees are any good, the family assumes that the employees will just save until they can start their own family business.

Regardless of where they live or how rich they are, the overseas Chinese share an abiding belief in hard work, strong family ties, frugality, and education. These attributes are not musty relics from their culture's past; they are compelling rules to live by. Overseas Chinese are wary of great debt. The most treasured asset of any ethnic Chinese businessman, whether a billionaire or a small manufacturer with a one-room workshop, is *xinyong.* It means having both a good reputation and a solid credit rating.

Many overseas Chinese prefer economic activities such as commodity trading, real estate, and finance. They employ few professional managers, except their sons (and sometimes daughters) who have been sent to prestigious business schools abroad, but who upon return continue to run the family business the Chinese way. The overseas Chinese also have adapted their traditional way of doing business in countries where they are an ethnic minority. As a minority group that has long suffered persecution and discrimination—problems that still flare up from time to time—most overseas Chinese shy away from publicity and cling to their own communities. Even the public companies they run are merely parts of family-controlled conglomerates that rarely reveal the full details of their finances or ownership structure.[20]

Real-World Example
Alfred Sloan of General Motors was said not to have made any decision until his executives could tell him its downside. Gavin Rawl, CEO of Exxon, encourages "healthy disrespect." Scott McNealy of Sun Microsystems wanted noisy, table-pounding meetings that included dissent and opinion as part of a system of "controlled chaos" (*The Executive,* February 1990, 69).

Dialectical inquiry and devil's advocacy are two useful aids for identifying and evaluating assumptions that may underlie current or proposed plans, strategies, and practices. The assumptions revealed and challenged aren't necessarily flawed or invalid, but they could be. For example, this process is likely to expose any political (hidden) agendas to manipulate outcomes for personal gain.

Dialectical Inquiry

The **dialectical inquiry method** is a process for systematically examining issues from two or more opposing points of view.[21] Let's consider this method first in general terms and then apply it to the testing of assumptions. Dialectical inquiry is especially useful with problems that require innovative solutions and is most effective in situations that have one or more of the following characteristics.

- Individuals can't agree on a process for developing a plan and strategies.
- Individuals don't know and can't agree on a clear definition of goals, the factors under their control, or the factors beyond their control.
- Individuals must deal with two or more stakeholders (such as shareholders, suppliers, customers, employees, and government agencies) with vested and potentially conflicting interests.
- Individuals face risky and uncertain situations.[22]

Teaching Tip
Pick a controversial current topic at the university (e.g., tuition hikes, increasing graduation requirements, or multicultural curriculum) and apply the dialectical inquiry method to it.

As indicated in Figure 6.1, the dialectical inquiry method consists of four phases: identification phase, dialectical phase, consolidation phase, and strategy creation phase. Generally a group of from twelve to thirty people participate in the process. During part of each phase all the participants meet as a single group. Most of the activities, however, are undertaken by teams of three to five people. Each team member has a different area of responsibility, such as a product line, an organization function (marketing, finance, production, or human resources), or types of customers served.[23]

Identification Phase. The identification phase is intended to reveal the participants' hidden or informal assumptions. Remember, assumptions are underlying thoughts or beliefs about issues, problems, or the future. The employees of an electric utility company who believe that their firm is a monopoly and in the business of providing electricity are likely to view problems and generate strategies quite differently from the employees at the same utility who believe that the firm has many competitors and is in the energy business. The following sequence of tasks should get participants to reveal their assumptions.

1. State the proposed (or current) plan or strategy for dealing with the problem.
2. Identify any information that supports the plan, strategy, or definition of the problem.
3. Identify the underlying assumptions on which the plan, strategy, or definition of the problem is based.

A *detailed* list of underlying assumptions should be developed to ensure that nothing is being left out. This list also should include organizational and stakeholder goals.

Dialectical Phase. The purpose of the dialectical phase is to identify *opposing* goals, strategies, problems, or potential solutions. If necessary, the issue itself may be redefined during this phase. The following sequence of tasks should be undertaken.

1. Engage in assumption negation; that is, challenge with an opposing assumption each assumption on which the goal, strategy, or plan was based.
2. Drop from consideration any opposing assumption that is unreasonable.
3. Search for data to support the remaining opposing assumptions. These assumptions can serve as a basis for developing one or more entirely new set of goals, strategies, or plans.

FIGURE 6.1

Phases in the Dialectical Inquiry Method

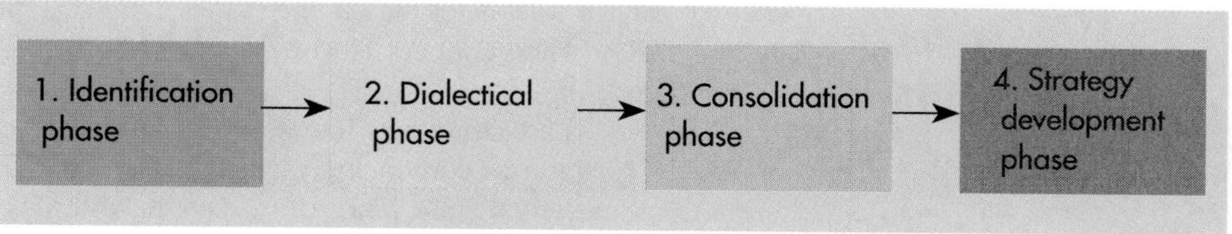

The dialectical phase ends when the participants conclude that they cannot identify any more plausible opposing assumptions.

Ethics
The dialectical inquiry method phase of the course is an ideal time to argue ethics.

Consolidation Phase. The consolidation phase focuses on bringing together the diverse sets of assumptions generated in the first and second phases. A consolidated set of acceptable assumptions won't always emerge from this phase. If power is balanced among the participating stakeholders, the result could be a standoff. Or the most powerful decision makers might impose their will. In most cases, the following sequence of tasks can eventually lead to agreement.

1. If various stakeholders are participating in the process, form teams representing the major stakeholders.
2. Each stakeholder team ranks the sets of assumptions on two criteria: the relative importance of each assumption to the team and the relative certainty of each assumption.
3. Each stakeholder team discusses the assumptions considered important but uncertain.
4. Each team is asked to modify its assumptions to the extent possible in order to arrive at a consensus.

Eventually, agreement on a set of assumptions (usually a set of compromise assumptions) can be achieved. The need to compromise and base decisions on a new set of assumptions—which are likely to be quite different from those developed in the first place—makes this the most difficult phase.

Strategy Creation Phase. When an acceptable set of assumptions has been developed, the strategy-creating phase proceeds step by step, as with the other phases in the strategic planning process (see Figure 5.3). That is, state the mission and goals, diagnose threats and opportunities, and so on.

Assessment of Dialectical Inquiry. Only a few well-designed studies of the effectiveness of the dialectical inquiry method have been made. Although the method appears promising, its automatic use in many organizations is premature. It is designed to promote healthy conflict among participants in order to sharpen alternative points of view. If the individuals involved are already engaged in power struggles and distrust each other, the dialectical inquiry method could deepen rather than resolve conflict. As with any planning aid, the use of the dialectical inquiry method should be governed by the situation. This method is most likely to be effective in those situations involving a high degree of uncertainty but basic agreement on the organization's mission, as discussed in Chapter 5.[24]

Devil's Advocacy

Real-World Example
Steve Huse, Chairman and CEO of Huse Food Group, wants to avoid costly mistakes by identifying pitfalls instead of rushing to agreement too quickly (*The Executive,* February 1990, 72).

The **devil's advocacy method** involves the selection of one person in a decision-making group (the devil's advocate) to critique a preferred plan or strategy. The process is much simpler than that of the dialectical inquiry approach. The purpose, however, is the same—to stimulate constructive controversy as a means of revealing and challenging assumptions.[25] Recall the Preview Insight on Emerson Electric. Knight and Suter play the role of devil's advocates when the other managers present their plans. According to Robert Staley, "The concept is to disagree with the thesis being presented, irrespective of the thesis."

Ethics
Devil's advocacy is an ideal technique for arguing ethics.

The devil's advocate acts like a good trial lawyer, presenting arguments against the proposed position as convincingly as possible. She or he tries to punch holes in the assumptions underlying the plan, draw out the internal inconsistencies in the proposed course of action, and reveal problems that may lead to its failure. Rather than have one person play the role of devil's advocate, another option is to form a team to play that role. The individual or team should remain sensitive to unpopular views and present the most reasonable case possible for alternative viewpoints and plans.

The Gould Company uses a version of this approach in evaluating companies to acquire. Each company it considers is analyzed by two teams, a green team and a red team. The green team argues for acquisition; the red team argues against it. The divergent results of their analyses are then presented to top management as inputs to a final decision.[26] No effort is made to have the two teams meet and resolve their differing perspectives. A third team—top management—does that.

Teaching Tip
Allow students to brainstorm about how small businesses might be able to use dialectical inquiry and devil's advocacy. (Students may differentiate small business forecasting from that of large business.)

The assessment of the dialectical inquiry method also applies, for the most part, to the devil's advocacy method. Both approaches have been used effectively to improve planning and decision making. However, both may backfire if power struggles and distrust dominate relations among the participants.

3

Explain the phases of team-based management by goals.

TEAM-BASED MANAGEMENT BY GOALS

Teaching Tip
Involve students in brainstorming the purposes of setting goals. List them on the board or a transparency.

Team-based management by goals is both a philosophy of and approach to management that helps integrate strategic and tactical planning. More specifically, it provides a way to translate key organizational goals and strategies into tactical goals and plans, as illustrated in Figure 6.2.[27] Portions of this discussion are adapted from a management approach known as **management by objectives,** which typically emphasizes the development of objectives (goals) for organizational units and individual employees and the review of performance against these objectives.[28] We discuss individual goal (objective) setting and the review of individual performance based on goals in Chapter 12 (Human Resources Management) and Chapter 13 (Motivating for Performance).

There are five main reasons for utilizing the team-based management by goals approach:

Ask Students
Is team or individual goal setting better? Explain.

1. to emphasize that there is *no single goal* for the organization, departments, teams, or individual employees;
2. to stress that setting goals and making trade-offs among them *involves risk and uncertainty;*
3. to clarify goals and their relative *priorities;*
4. to enhance the *relationships* among organizational, departmental, team, and individual job goals; and
5. to *focus* organizational resources and employees' energies and expenditures of time.

FIGURE 6.2

Team-Based Management by Goals

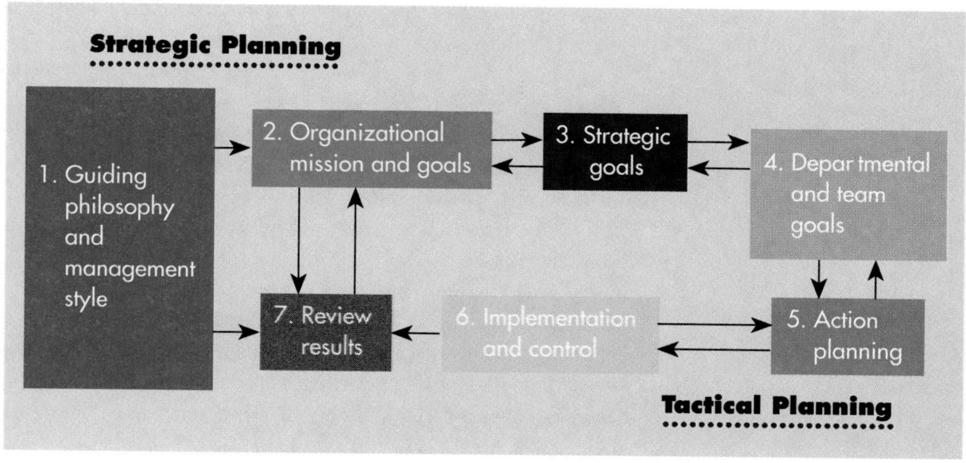

Philosophy and Management Style

Team-based management by goals reflects a positive philosophy about people and a participative management style. In Figure 6.2, it is phase 1 and provides the foundation for all subsequent planning and implementation actions. It has the following attributes.

- Mutual problem solving by individuals and teams across departmental lines and at different organizational levels.
- Trusting and open communication.
- Emphasis on win-win relationships in which all parties can benefit through cooperation.
- Rewards and promotions based directly on job- and team-related performance and achievement.
- Minimal use of political games, fear, and/or force.
- A positive, proactive, and challenging organizational culture.

This philosophy and management style fosters broad participation by teams and individuals in the development and review of goals and plans. However, some goals have to come from the top. For example, the U.S. Environmental Protection Agency (EPA) has required companies to achieve environmental goals within a specified period of time or pay stiff fines. Consequently, top management may require managers and teams to set departmental goals to reduce environmental hazards.

As suggested in the following Diversity Insight, strong leadership may be crucial in providing the spark to develop goals and plans on difficult and sensitive issues. It emphasizes the essential role that participation, teams, and incentives played in implementing Hoechst Celanese's diversity plan.

Diversity *Insight*

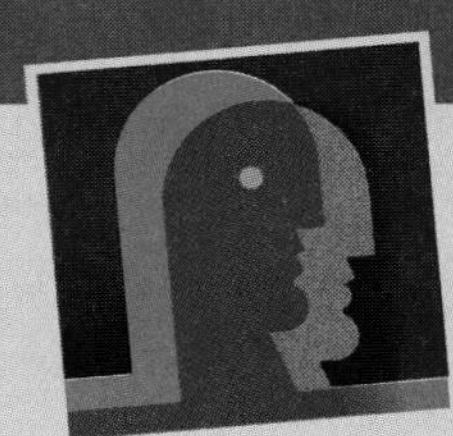

Hoechst Celanese Diversity Plan

Ernest H. Drew, the CEO of Hoechst Celanese, the chemical giant, remembers exactly when he became an advocate of a more diverse work force. He was attending a 1990 conference for Hoechst's top 125 officers. They were mostly white men, who were joined by 50 or so lower level women and members of minority groups. The group split into problem-solving teams; some were mixed by race and gender, but others were all white and male. The main issue was how the corporate culture affected the business and what changes might be made to improve results. When the teams presented their findings, a light clicked on for Drew. "It was so obvious that the diverse teams had the broader solutions," he recalls. "They had ideas I hadn't even thought of. For the first time, we realized that diversity is a strength as it relates to problem solving. Before, we just thought of diversity as the total number of minorities and women in the company, like affirmative action. Now we knew we needed diversity at every level of the company where decisions are made."

Under Drew's direction, work-force diversity is one of four performance criteria equally weighted in determining managers' salaries and bonuses. The other three are financial success, customer satisfaction, and environmental and safety improvements. Hoechst Celanese's diversity goal is specific: at least 34 percent representation of women and minorities at all levels of the company by the year 2001. This top-to-bottom target, which Drew refers to as reaching "vertical parity," mirrors the company's future work force—the percentage of women and minorities graduating with relevant majors from colleges where the company recruits.

The diversity plan includes a comprehensive set of strategies and proposed actions. One strategy is the requirement that the top twenty-six officers join two organizations in which they are a minority. Drew is a board member of the African-American Hampton University and of SER-Jobs for Progress, a Hispanic association. He explains why management put this policy in place: "The only way to break out of comfort zones is to be exposed to other people. When we are, it becomes clear that all people are similar."[29]

Setting and Linking Goals

Teaching Tip
Invite a local city planner to talk about the necessity of setting and linking goals.

The distinguishing feature of this management approach is the setting and linking of organizational, divisional and SBU, departmental, and team goals. These goals state the quality and quantity of results expected within a specific period of time. Phases 2 through 4 in Figure 6.2 should provide clear answers to two basic questions: "Why are we here?" and "If this is why we are here, what should we accomplish?" These phases should include the efforts of managers, teams, and individual employees across functional areas and at different organizational levels.

Teaching Tip
Draw up a sample mission statement and strategic goals for your university, strategic goals for your school and department, and your professional goals.

Teaching Tip
Have students visit the library to obtain the mission statement of a large organization or interview the dean of their college about its mission.

Organizational Mission and Goals. In phase 2, the organization's mission and broad goals are set, usually by top management and the board of directors. They express what the organization is and what it is trying to become. This phase corresponds to the "develop mission and goals" task in the strategic planning process discussed in Chapter 5. Recall that organizational goals often are broad, general statements that change little, if at all, from one year to the next. Since its founding in 1961, a key organizational goal of Mylan Laboratories, Inc., is to be a leader in generic pharmaceuticals. Mylan sells most of the drugs it produces to large pharmaceutical companies, such as Parke-Davis, who sell them to retailers.

Strategic Goals. Managers and teams develop strategic goals in phase 3. Strategic goals often are more quantitative than general goals and specify a time period for accomplishment. For example, a strategic goal of Mylan Laboratories might be to market five new generic drugs between 1995 and 1998. Another strategic goal within this time period may be to form three strategic alliances with foreign pharmaceutical firms—in Germany, Great Britain, and Russia. However, strategic goals are likely to be revised over time as conditions change.

Departmental and Team Goals. Middle and first-line managers, with participation by their employees, develop tactical goals for their departments and teams. Teams may even develop some of their own goals without direct managerial involvement. These goals should support the organizational strategic goals. For example, one tactical goal of the production department might be to reduce electrical consumption by 10 percent over the next twelve months to help meet an overall company goal of a 5 percent reduction in operating costs.

Ask Students
What are some specific goals you have had in a previous job or your current job?

Criteria for Setting Goals. Goals provide standards against which effectiveness can be measured. For example, a sales team's quantitative goals for the year might be to increase sales by 5 percent, maintain private-label sales at 7 percent of total sales, and hold advertising expenses at last year's level. All are clear, specific quantitative standards against which performance can be measured. The sales team's qualitative goals for the year might be to (1) work with the credit team to develop improved criteria and a process for evaluating the credit worthiness of sales prospects, and (2) create a new sales presentation that more clearly indicates the quality features of the company's product line. Although not as precise as the quantitative goals, these goals also are indicators against which results can be compared.

Setting goals includes identifying specific areas of team or job responsibility and standards of performance.[30] When setting goals, participants should consider the following points.

- Goals should be specific enough to have significance for the department, team, and employee. A poor goal would be "to maximize the welfare of the firm and of society." A better goal would be for the sales team "to achieve an 8 percent sales increase for 1997, while maintaining the gross profit margin at 40 percent on all sales."
- Goals normally should be broad enough to keep teams or employees from having to concentrate on dozens of day-to-day goals.
- Planning efforts shouldn't get so embroiled in political power struggles and conflicts

Goals provide standards against which effectiveness can be measured. At L. L. Bean in Freeport, Maine, employees work together to increase annual sales and fill orders in an efficient and timely manner.

that attempts to set clear goals become futile. For example, using the dialectical inquiry method when a power struggle is going on may actually increase rather than help resolve conflict.

Action Planning

In phase 5 managers and teams develop action plans for accomplishing departmental and team goals. For example, a goal of the marketing department might be to increase sales volume by 10 percent within twelve months. To achieve this goal, the marketing manager might develop the following action plan with her subordinates.

1. Release new product A, developed to supplement the product line, within six months.
2. Evaluate the feasibility of a price reduction to stimulate demand for products B and C within three months.
3. Increase the specific sales volume targets of sales teams in Los Angeles, Dallas, and New York by 10 percent.
4. Increase the on-time delivery for products B and C by 5 percent within four months.[31]

The type of participation by employees in developing an action plan may vary. Developing a departmental action plan might involve discussions by a team consisting of the departmental managers and most of the department's employees.[32] In contrast, an action plan to achieve an individual's job goals might be developed by the employee and discussed with his or her superior for review and comment.

Implementation and Control

The translation of tactical plans into day-to-day actions that will lead to the attainment of the stated goals occurs in phase 6. Team-based management by goals allows individuals and teams freedom in performing their tasks. Managers should be available to coach and counsel teams and subordinates to help them reach goals but should not control ("micromanage") their every activity. Teams and individuals must be trusted to work effectively toward agreed-on goals. At the same time, they must feel free to discuss problems with their superiors or others who can help them.

Review Results

The last phase in this process calls for a review of results to measure progress, identify and resolve problems, and revise (drop or add) goals or even the core mission. If these reviews are conducted properly, managers, teams, and individual employees can learn significant lessons from the immediate past and apply those lessons to future planning and actions.[33] Recall from the Preview Insight about Emerson Electric that James Berges, an executive vice-president, holds discussions on profit results with the key managers from Emerson's fifty divisions.

Goals and strategies are the basis of the review process. Managers and teams must review their own results and actively participate in evaluating them. Ideally, the review of results is a mutual problem-solving process involving managers and teams. Managers encourage the teams to identify obstacles or problems that affected the achievement of their goals and to suggest ways to improve performance. These reviews provide feedback to both managers and teams, letting them know how well they are achieving agreed-on goals. Knowledge of results is essential to maintaining and increasing effectiveness and the development of new plans.

Discussion Question 5
What problems might be anticipated if the top leaders of an organization decided to adopt the team-based management by the goals approach?

Team-based management by goals calls on superiors to shift from being judgmental and critical to being helpful and willing to engage in mutual problem solving.[34] Some managers wrongly interpret this type of review process as "soft." People may be demoted, dismissed, and otherwise held fully accountable under this approach. However, the bases for such actions are less subjective. As a result, making well-founded demotion or dismissal decisions, when corrective actions have failed, should be easier. Moreover, this process should reduce the need for such decisions.[35]

4

Describe benchmarking and the Deming cycle, two planning aids specifically designed to improve quality.

Ask Students
Which of these definitions of quality do you agree with as a consumer? Put yourself in the position of the seller. Would your definition change? Why or why not?

Teaching Tip
Have the students divide into teams of 5 to 8. Ask each team to make a presentation, benchmarking typical U.S. college students with their counterparts in Canada, Japan, and Germany. Be sure that they compare high school and college graduation and placement rates, income, and scores on standardized tests. Ask them to present their findings to the class.

PLANNING FOR QUALITY

Many issues and methods must be considered in planning for total quality. We have already addressed some of them in the Quality Insights and the text of Chapters 1–5. Here and in the remaining chapters we present additional concepts, techniques, and examples for achieving total quality in an organization.

Planning for quality starts with the recognition that there is no single indicator of quality. **Quality** has variously been defined as value (linking different grades of products and price), conformance to established specifications or standards, excellence (providing the best), and meeting and/or exceeding customers' expectations. The most common definition of quality is the extent to which a good or service meets and/or exceeds customers' expectations.[36] Consumers often apply the value definition of quality when making purchasing decisions. *Consumer Reports* magazine ranks products and services on both quality and price to arrive at recommendations of "best-buys." Thus alternative perspectives of quality are appropriate in different circumstances.[37]

Let's now turn to two planning aids that focus specifically on enhancing quality: benchmarking and the Deming cycle. Both may be used effectively in the team-based management by goals approach.

Benchmarking

Benchmarking is the continuous process of comparing an organization's strategies, products, or processes with those of *best-in-class* organizations. It is intended to help employees learn how such organizations achieved excellence and then set out to match or exceed them.[38] Benchmarking may be used to assess virtually any aspect of an organization. It identifies and assesses the "best" that is occurring elsewhere to aid a firm in developing its own strategic or tactical plans and processes to reach that level.

Basic Steps. As noted in Figure 6.3, the benchmarking process includes seven basic steps.[39] Step 1 involves *defining the domain* to be benchmarked. This step includes a careful study of the organization's own products and processes that are to be compared to benchmark products and processes. For example, in the advertising for the 1995 Chrysler Cirrus (a new model) the company claimed that more than 300 different aspects of the car were targeted to meet or exceed current benchmarks in automotive design. They included 10 aspects of the feel and operation of the turn signals.

Functional areas such as manufacturing, finance, marketing, inventory management, transportation, accounting, legal services, human resources, and management may be benchmarked. In addition, various processes in functional areas may be benchmarked. Each function or process may be broken down into more specific processes and categories for that purpose. For example, benchmarking in human resources may include the processes of recruiting, diversity enhancement, training, compensation, performance appraisal, recognition programs, and job design.

Benchmarking can be an expensive and time-consuming process. Thus some people recommend that benchmarking be directed at the specific issues and processes that are likely to yield the greatest competitive advantage (e.g., new employee motivation, capabilities, and reduced costs).[40] Others suggest that benchmarking be applied to all functions and processes to instill total quality in the organization's mission and goals.

Step 2 involves *identifying the best performers,* or best-in-class, for each function, process, and product to be benchmarked. They may include organizations in the firm's own industry or in other industries. For example, Xerox compared its warehousing and distribution process with that of L.L. Bean, the catalog sales company, because of its excellent reputation in this domain. In addition, Xerox compared itself with American Hospital Supply for automated inventory control, American Express for billing and collection, Proctor & Gamble for marketing, Toyota for quality management, and so on.

Step 3 involves *collecting and analyzing data to identify gaps,* if any, between the organization's function, product, or process being evaluated and that of the best-in-class organizations. The data collected needs to focus on specific methods utilized, not simply on the results obtained. It is one thing to know that Wal-Mart has a superb warehouse distribution system. It is another thing to learn how Wal-Mart has achieved this level of excellence. There are many sources of information for learning about best-in-class organizations. They include customers, suppliers, distributors, trade journals, company publications, newspapers, books on total quality, consultants, presentations at professional meetings, and even on-site interviews with people at the best-in-class organizations. This last source usually is easier to tap if the organizations aren't direct competitors.[41]

The remaining steps are consistent with the typical planning phases: Step 4 involves *setting improvement goals;* step 5, *developing and implementing plans to close gaps;* step 6, *evaluating results;* and step 7, *repeating the evaluations as necessary.* Step 7 suggests

FIGURE 6.3

The Benchmarking Process

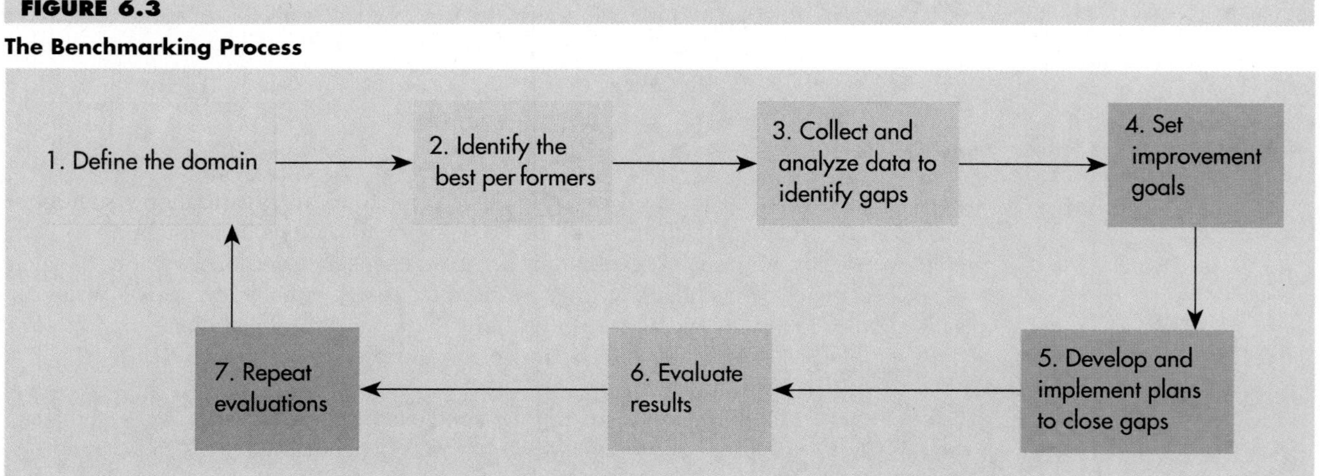

Ethics

Executives may benchmark their company against companies that they can easily outperform to make themselves and their company look good. Many of these executives are given large financial incentives based on the company's performance. Is this practice ethical?

that benchmarking needs to be an ongoing process. Over time, the domains benchmarked may remain the same or need to be revised. Revisions may include dropping and/or adding domains as issues, conditions, technology, and processes change. In addition, the organizations identified as the best performers in a particular domain may change over time. For example, the new-product development process at Chrysler that was viewed as weak ten years ago is now rated as one of the best in the automotive industry.[42]

Limitations. Benchmarking should be linked to other sources of information, such as changing customer expectations and preferences. By definition, benchmarking always looks at the present in terms of how some domain is being handled by others. This approach may not be adequate for determining what should be done in the future or whether an organization should retain a function or process or contract it out. For example, an organization could contract out its computer operations to Electronic Data Systems (EDS) or some other firm. When used simply to copy the best-in-class competitors, benchmarking may lead only to short-term competitive advantage. Finally, benchmarking needs to be used to complement and aid, not to substitute for, the creative and innovative efforts of the organization's own employees.[43]

Depending on an organization's management style (e.g., participative decision making) and goals, benchmarking may be applied and used in a variety of ways. The following Quality Insight on Mellon Bank, a major financial organization headquartered in Pittsburgh, describes its initial, focused use of benchmarking.

Quality *Insight*

Mellon Bank Benchmarks

Mellon started benchmarking in 1991 and felt the benefits in less than one year. For its initial target, Mellon picked credit card billing disputes. Poor service generally sends more upset customers off to look for another bank than any other factor. Mellon appointed a team of eight people from different departments, including four who ordinarily handle such disputes, and gave it the power to make changes. The highest ranking member was Lina Edmonds, a section manager, one rung below vice-president.

The team worked part time on the problem and met once a week. It benchmarked seven companies: five credit card operations, one airline, and one competing bank. The team visited three of these firms and talked to representatives of the other four on the phone. Its members learned several things about solving disputes quickly.

When a customer called with a complaint, for example, a Mellon clerk had to look in several places for the relevant documents. Sometimes, this search took three to four days. Equipped with better software, the other companies' customer service agents could call up and view all the documents on their computer terminals. They could quickly bounce a complaint to a "help" desk staffed by an experienced employee who could tell the customer precisely where a dispute stood. After adopting these and other improvements, Mellon cut complaints outstanding from month to month from 5,200 to 2,200 in less than a year. Also, complaints, on average, were resolved in twenty-five days rather than the forty-five days required prior to benchmarking. The study took five months, and the changes were begun immediately.[44]

Deming Cycle

In Chapter 2, we provided some information on W. Edwards Deming, considered by some to be the "godfather" of the quality movement. One of the aids he advocates for improving quality is commonly known as the Deming cycle. It was originally developed by Walter Shewhart and is known to some as the Shewart cycle. Others refer to it as the

FIGURE 6.4
The Deming Cycle

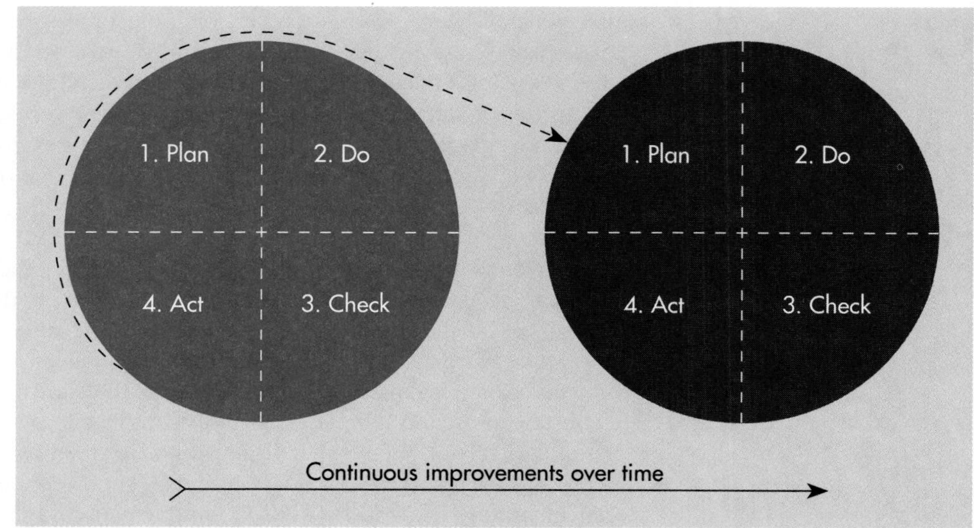

PDCA cycle because it involves the four stages of plan (P), do (D), check (C), and act (A). As Figure 6.4 suggests, these stages unfold in sequence and continuously. Thus the **Deming cycle** comprises four stages—plan, do, check, and act—that should be repeated over time to ensure continuous improvements in a function, product, or process.[45]

Teaching Tip
Have students use the Deming cycle to help improve their grades in a class they are having difficulties in. Ask several students to share their plans with the class.

Three questions should be answered during the *plan* stage of the Deming cycle: (1) What are we trying to accomplish? (2) What changes can we make that will result in improvement? (3) How will we know that a change is an improvement? Most of the effort involves analyzing the current situation, gathering data, and developing ways to make improvements. The *do* stage involves testing the plan experimentally in a laboratory, establishing a pilot production process, or trying it out with a small number of customers. The *check* stage determines whether the trial plan is working as intended, any revisions are needed, or it should be scrapped. The *act* stage involves implementing the final plan within the organization or with all its customers and suppliers.[46] Benchmarking may be one of the aids used in the plan stage. Other tools that may be used to support the Deming cycle include the program evaluation and review technique presented in the next section. The following Quality Insight shows how the owner of the Deluxe Diner applied the Deming cycle to reduce the problem of long lines.

Discussion Question 6
What are the primary similarities and differences between benchmarking and the Deming cycle?

Quality *Insight*

Long Lines at Deluxe Diner

The owner of Deluxe Diner, Kim Bravenec, decided to do something about the long lines that occurred every day. One process in the Plan stage involved several team meetings with her employees. They identified four main aspects of this problem: (1) customers were waiting in line for up to fifteen minutes, (2) usually, tables were available, (3) many of the customers were regulars, and (4) people taking orders and preparing food were getting in each others' way.

The employees offered various ideas. Bravenec developed a plan that involved the following changes: (1) allow customers to fax their orders in ahead of time (rent a fax machine for one month), (2) construct a preparation table for fax orders in the kitchen where there was ample room, and (3) devote one of their two cash registers to handling fax orders. To assess improvements with these changes, Bravenec decided to collect data on the number of customers in line, the number of empty tables, and the delay before customers are served. The length of the line and the number of empty tables would be measured every fifteen minutes during the lunch hour. When the fifteen-minute line check was done, she would note the last person in line and note the time until that person was served.

Next, the results of the three measures were observed for three weeks. Three improvements were detected in the Check stage. Time in line dropped from fifteen minutes to five minutes on average. The line length was cut to a peak average of twelve people, and the number of empty tables declined slightly. Bravenac held another team meeting with her employees to discuss the results. They decided to purchase the fax machine, fill the fax orders, and use both cash registers to handle walk-up and fax orders. Kim Bravenec thought that the Deming cycle was very helpful in resolving the problem and intends to use it again.[47]

5

Define project management and describe how the program evaluation and review technique (PERT) is applied in project management.

PROJECT MANAGEMENT

A **project** is a one-time activity with a well-defined set of desired results. Other characteristics of a project include a definite start and finish, a time frame for completion, uniqueness, involvement of people on a temporary basis, a limited set of resources (people, money, and time), and a sequence of activities and phases. **Project management** consists of the principles, methods, and techniques used to establish and implement a project and achieve its goals. The essentials of project management can be applied to projects as simple as developing a thirty-page business plan in an entrepreneurship course or as complex as constructing a sixty-story office tower.[48] As suggested in the following Ethics Insight, project management has become a professional field with its own body of knowledge, journals, professional association, and code of ethics.

Ethics *Insight*

Ethics in Project Management

Like many other professional areas, project management has been concerned with ethical behaviors and decisions in recent years. Much of this attention has been directed through the Project Management Institute, a nonprofit professional organization dedicated to advancing the state of the art in project management. It publishes *Project Management Journal* and the *PM Network.*

The association champions a code of ethics for the project management profession. The following is an excerpt from the code. According to this code of ethics, project management professionals shall:

- Provide the necessary project leadership to promote maximum productivity while striving to minimize costs.
- Apply state-of-the-art project management tools and techniques to ensure that quality, costs, and time objectives, as set forth in the project plan, are met.
- Treat fairly all project team members, colleagues, and co-workers, regardless of race, religion, sex, age, or national origin.
- Protect project team members from physical and mental harm.
- Seek, accept, and offer honest criticism of work and properly credit the contribution of others.
- Assist project team members, colleagues, and co-workers in their professional development.

These ethical standards, for the most part, apply to team leaders of any type of project, including student group projects.[49]

Program Evaluation and Review Technique (PERT)

Teaching Tip
Remind students that their class groups intend to be project teams that are formed temporarily to do a project and then disband.

The **program evaluation and review technique (PERT)** is a method of scheduling the sequence of activities and events required to complete a project, estimating their costs, and controlling their progress. It is one of the most useful aids in project management. In its first major application in 1958, PERT was used in the U.S. Navy's ballistic missile program, more popularly known as the Polaris missile program. The Navy's prime contractor cited PERT as a major reason for completing the program two years ahead of the original schedule. Several government agencies now require companies with which they have contracts to use PERT.

The technique normally is used for one-of-a-kind projects (such as Disney World and Epcot Center), projects that involve a new production process (such as a robotic automobile plant), or projects that require interlocking building processes (such as an apartment complex). Project managers use PERT to analyze and specify in detail what is to be done, when it is to be done, and the likelihood of achieving the goal on time. As commonly used in practice, PERT consists of four major elements: (1) a network, (2) a critical path, (3) resource allocations, and (4) cost and time estimates.[50]

Network. A **PERT network** is a diagram showing the sequence and relationships of the activities and events needed to complete a project. As shown in Figure 6.5, events (the boxes) are points where decisions are made or activities are completed. Activities (the arrows) are the physical or mental tasks performed in order to move from one event to another.

Teaching Tip
Stress that event 3 can't happen unless A, B, and C have been completed. Impress on them the concept of interdependency and underscore the need for cooperation and teamwork. Students are used to working alone and being rewarded for individual performance.

The network is the basis of the PERT approach. To build one, the project team must identify key project activities, determine their sequence, decide who will be responsible for each activity, and calculate the amount of time needed to accomplish each. The network diagram identifies the relationship among the sequence of events and the activities. For example, the arrows in Figure 6.6 show that event 3 cannot occur until activities A, B, and C have been accomplished. A PERT network clearly shows how the different managers and teams responsible for the various activities must coordinate their work.

FIGURE 6.5
A Basic PERT Network

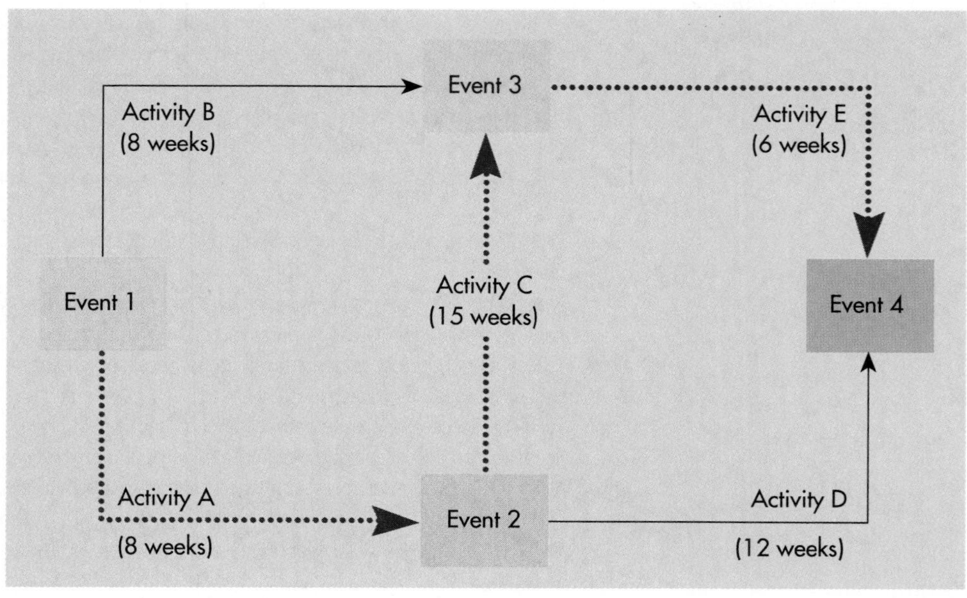

Critical Path. Every project follows paths, or sequences of events and activities. The **critical path** is the path with the longest elapsed time, which determines the length of the project. To shorten the time for project completion, the project team must give the most attention to activities along the critical path. Of course, a delay in any other path that exceeds the time for the critical path would also delay the completion date. A complex project like the construction of Disney World and the new Denver International Airport consists of thousands of activities and hundreds of paths. Work goes on concurrently along each separate path, and in the case of such huge projects, a master PERT network and individual PERT networks for each path are common.

The wide-band arrows in Figure 6.5 identify the critical path, which requires a total elapsed time of twenty-nine weeks. It equals the sum of the times required to complete the activities between events 1 and 2, events 2 and 3, and events 3 and 4. Any delay in activity completion along the critical path will delay project completion.

Resource Allocation. In order to undertake their assigned activities, project teams require a variety of resources. Resource availability greatly influences the length of time between events and the costs associated with each activity. Project leaders must estimate types and amounts of required materials, equipment, facilities, and human resources as accurately as possible. For example, the first major activity in constructing a house without a basement is excavating and pouring footings. A contractor would estimate that this activity will require one backhoe, one backhoe operator, and three laborers for four days, as well as specific amounts of sand for fill, wood for concrete forms, steel reinforcing rods, and concrete.

Cost and Time Estimates. Of value to management is PERT's ability to help reduce project costs and time. The project team prepares cost estimates for each activity (task), such as excavating and pouring footings for a house. Similarly, the team estimates the amount of time needed for each activity. For example, Figure 6.5 shows that activity A *should* take eight weeks.

Four time estimates often are made for each activity. The *most likely time* is the estimated time required to complete an activity, taking into consideration normal problems and interruptions. The *optimistic time* is the estimated time required to complete an activity if everything goes right. The *pessimistic time* is the estimated time required to complete an activity if unusual problems and interruptions occur. Given Murphy's

FIGURE 6.6

A Simplified PERT Diagram for Constructing a House

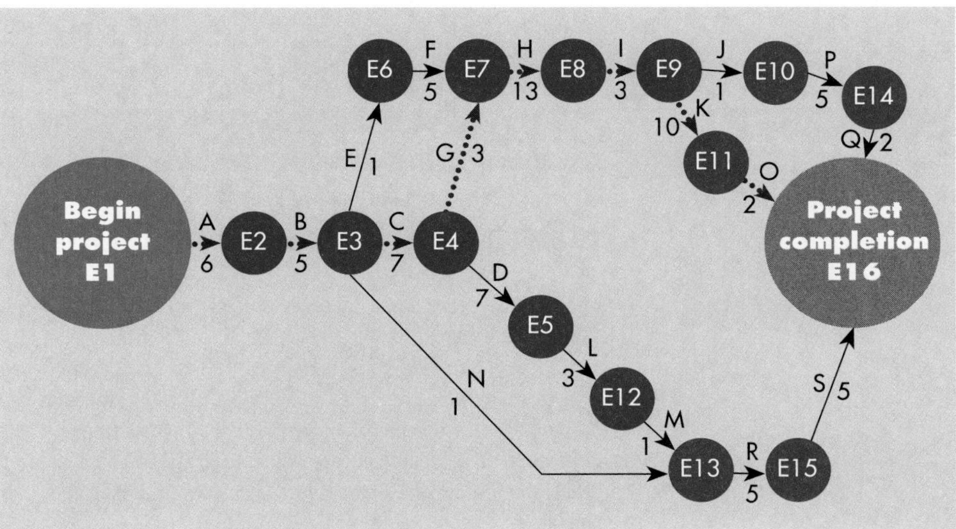

law, the assumption is that serious problems may arise, although even the pessimistic estimate normally doesn't take into account rare, catastrophic events, such as fires, tornadoes, floods, and war. The *expected time* represents a weighted average of the most likely, optimistic, and pessimistic time estimates.

By developing alternative time estimates, the project team can anticipate and react quickly to problems or opportunities. If an activity is running behind schedule, having people work overtime or hiring additional people might be advantageous. If an activity is ahead of schedule, the project leader might speed up deliveries of supplies that are needed for later activities. Without a PERT network, project managers might not perceive that further action is required.

After a project is underway, PERT becomes a control mechanism. Using PERT's reporting procedures, a project team can monitor differences between actual and planned times and costs for each activity.

Assessment of PERT

Most useful when projects are complex and require tight coordination, PERT helps reduce project time and costs under the following conditions.

- The project consists of a well-defined collection of job or team activities.
- The job or team activities may be started and stopped independently of one another. Continuous-flow processes, such as oil refining, where jobs or operations follow each other in a strict time sequence day after day, do not lend themselves to the use of PERT.
- The job or team activities are ordered; that is, they must be performed in a particular sequence or often in multiple simultaneous sequences that create complex networks. For instance, the foundation of a house must be laid before the walls are erected.[51]

Various PC and mainframe software systems are available for PERT and other project management aids. For example, Open Plan, provided by Welcom Software Technology, enables the user to handle projects with up to 100,000 activities. Open Plan creates easy-to-read graphics and can provide as many as 256 calendar schedules per project. Open Plan and similar project management software systems also offer many other features, such as cost scheduling and control aids.

The following Small Business Insight describes a simplified version of PERT for the construction of a modest single-story house with no basement. The builder, Jody Fry, is a small business general contractor.

Small Business *Insight*

Using PERT in House Construction

Jody Fry is a home builder in Corpus Christi, Texas, who builds homes on customers' properties for under $100,000. In planning the construction of a house, Fry has to determine (1) the major activities to be performed, (2) the time required for each activity, (3) the sequence in which the activities must be completed, and (4) the manpower needed for each activity. Table 6.2 shows Fry's estimates for a house. The list of nineteen major activities is presented roughly in the sequence required for project completion. Each activity could be broken down further if Fry wanted more detail. The total expected time shown is in working days; that is, it doesn't include weekends and legal holidays.

TABLE 6.2

PERT Activities and Times for Constructing a House

Job Activity	Description of Activity	Immediate Preceding Activity	Expected Work Time (Days)	Expected Slack Time (Days)	Total Expected Time (Days)	Labor Needed
A	Excavate, pour footings	—	4	2	6	1 backhoe operator, 2 laborers
B	Pour concrete foundation	A	2	3	5	1 carpenter, 2 laborers
C	Erect frame and roof	B	4	3	7	5 carpenters, 5 laborers
D	Lay brickwork	C	6	1	7	3 masons, 2 laborers
E	Install drains	B	1	0	1	2 plumbers, 1 laborer
F	Install plumbing	E	3	2	5	2 plumbers, 1 laborer
G	Install wiring	C	2	1	3	3 electricians
H	Fasten plaster and plasterboard	F, G	10	3	13	2 laborers, 1 finisher
I	Lay finished flooring	H	3	0	3	2 carpenters
J	Install kitchen equipment	I	1	0	1	2 carpenters
K	Finish carpentry	I	7	3	10	2 carpenters
L	Finish roofing and flashing	D	2	1	3	4 roofers
M	Fasten gutters and downspouts	L	1	0	1	2 laborers
N	Lay storm drains	B	1	0	1	1 backhoe operator, 4 laborers
O	Sand and varnish floors	K	2	0	2	1 painter
P	Paint	J	3	2	5	2 painters
Q	Finish electrical work	P	2	0	2	2 electricians
R	Finish grading	M, N	2	3	5	3 laborers
S	Pour walks; landscape	R	5	0	5	1 landscape gardener, 2 laborers

Source: Wiest/Levy, *A MANAGEMENT GUIDE TO PERT/CPM*, © 1969, 16–20. Adapted by permission of Prentice-Hall, Inc., Englewood Cliffs, N.J.

A PERT network based on Table 6.2 is shown in Figure 6.6. This network contains the major job activities (A, B, C, . . . , S), the sequence of those activities, and the expected number of days between the beginning of one job activity and the next. The circles designate events. Circle E1 represents the project beginning, circle E2 represents completion of excavation and footings, and so on to circle E16, which represents project completion.

The wide arrows in the figure indicate the critical path, which totals forty-nine working days:

$$A(6) + B(5) + C(7) + G(3) + H(13) + I(3) + K(10) + O(2) = 49.$$

Thus completing the house will take about 10 weeks, or 2.5 months, plus weekends and holidays. If Fry wants to reduce overall construction time, he must reduce the amount of time required for activities along the critical path.

CHAPTER SUMMARY

1 ***Describe the essentials of the scenario, Delphi technique, and simulation forecasting aids.***

An important early part of planning, forecasting is the process of estimating future events and conditions in an organization's environment. Scenarios are written descriptions of possible futures. The Delphi technique is a process of consensus building among experts to arrive at estimates of future events and conditions. Simulation involves the use of models of real systems that permit the testing of alternatives, often on a computer.

2 ***Apply dialectical inquiry and devil's advocacy to reveal and diagnose assumptions.***

The dialectical inquiry method is a team process that involves systematically examining issues and assumptions from opposing points of view. The devil's advocacy method involves a critique of a preferred plan, strategy, or assumptions by one person or a team.

3 ***Explain the phases of team-based management by goals.***

Team-based management by goals is both a philosophy of and an approach to management. It guides and implements the planning process through seven basic phases: (1) establish a positive philosophy about people and a participative management style, (2) develop the organization's mission and broad goals, (3) develop strategic goals, (4) develop more specific departmental and team goals that support the strategic goals, (5) create action plans to achieve the desired goals, (6) implement and control day-to-day actions taken to attain the desired goals, and (7) review the results to measure progress.

4 ***Describe benchmarking and the Deming cycle, two planning aids specifically designed to improve quality.***

Benchmarking is the continuous process of comparing an organization's functions, products, or processes with those of *best-in-class* organizations. The process includes a sequence of seven steps, as shown in Figure 6.3. The Deming cycle includes four stages—plan, do, check, and act—that should be repeated over time to ensure continuous improvement in functions, products, and processes.

5 ***Define project management and describe how the program evaluation and review technique (PERT) is applied in project management.***

Project management refers to the principles, methods, and techniques used to establish and implement a project. PERT has four main elements: (1) network, (2) critical path, (3) resource allocation, and (4) cost and time estimates. It is a valuable tool for planning and implementing one-of-a-kind and extremely large or complex projects.

QUESTIONS FOR DISCUSSION

1. Reread the Preview Insight. Charles Knight, Emerson's CEO, still isn't convinced that he and Al Suter are doing everything possible to get managers to reveal the assumptions in their proposed plans. What would you recommend to him? How could this recommendation be implemented?
2. It is January 2000, and the Joneses have settled down for an evening of television. Joe Jones aims his remote control at a 3-by-5 screen across the room and taps in a three-digit code to call up the fifth rerun of his all-time favorite flick, *Rambo XIII*. The family doesn't drive to a videocassette rental store for a movie anymore, and the number of such outlets is shrinking. Of course, network TV is free, but nothing much there grabs the Joneses tonight. It is time for a rerun of *Rambo*. Or almost anything else on film the Joneses can think of. The shows are all there—thousands

of them—ready to be punched up by computer. Welcome to the impending age of fiber-optic TV. Welcome to the fast-developing wonders of electronic switching systems. Watch out, investors in cable systems. Be alert, those of you who use TV for marketing purposes. Technology is about to change your worlds.[52] Do you agree with this scenario? Why or why not?

3. Are there any potential ethical concerns with the increasing use and applications of virtual reality? Explain.
4. What are the similarities and differences between the Delphi technique and simulation? Explain.
5. What problems might be anticipated if the top leaders of an organization decided to adopt the team-based management by goals approach?
6. What are the primary similarities and differences between benchmarking and the Deming cycle?

FROM WHERE YOU SIT

1. Describe the most likely scenario of your life in the year 2010.
2. Identify a team situation you have been in within the past year that might have benefited from the use of the devil's advocacy method or the dialectical inquiry method. How would you have implemented either of these methods?
3. How might the team-based management by goals approach have made a difference in your last job? Which phases would you likely have been involved in?
4. Describe how benchmarking could be used to help plan improvements in one service or process (such as registration, advising, or financial aid) at your college or university.
5. Use the program evaluation and review technique (PERT) to develop an action plan for your successful completion of the next academic year.

Total Quality Management (TQM) Inventory

Introduction

This instrument is based on the Federal Quality Institute's *Federal Total Quality Management Handbook 2: Criteria and Scoring Guidelines for the President's Award for Quality and Productivity Improvement,* Washington, DC: Office of Personnel Management, 1990. A necessary first step in learning about and implementing TQM is to assess the emphasis that an organization places on the eight basic criteria in the questionnaire. The Total Quality Management (TQM) Inventory is designed for use as a diagnostic tool rather than as a rigorous data-gathering instrument. Applied in this manner, the inventory has demonstrated a high level of face validity when used with audiences ranging from executive managers to nonmanagement personnel.

Instructions. Please read carefully the six statements listed under each criterion. Select the statement that best describes how that criterion applied to an organization for which you now work or have previously worked. Write the letter of that statement in the blank to the left of each criterion. Another approach is to interview experienced individuals in that organization by asking them to respond to this instrument. Choices range from exceptionally strong commitment to the absence of performance for each criterion.

Inventory Items

_____ *Criterion 1: Top-Management Leadership and Support*

A. Top managers are directly and actively involved in activities that foster quality.
B. Top managers participate in activities that foster quality.
C. Most top managers support activities that foster quality.
D. Some top managers are supportive of and interested in quality improvement.
E. A few top managers are tentatively beginning to support activities that foster quality.
F. No top management support exists for activities involving quality.

_____ *Criterion 2: Strategic Planning*

A. Long-term goals for quality improvements have been established across the organization as part of the overall strategic planning process.
B. Long-term goals for quality improvement have been established across most of the organization.
C. Long-term goals for quality improvement have been established in key parts of the organization.
D. Short-term goals for quality improvement have been established in parts of the organization.
E. The general goals of the organization contain elements of quality improvement.
F. No quality improvement goals have been established anywhere in the organization.

_____ *Criterion 3: Focus on the Customer*

A. A variety of effective and innovative methods are used to obtain customer feedback on all organizational functions.
B. Effective systems are used to obtain feedback from all customers of major functions.
C. Systems are in place to solicit customer feedback on a regular basis.
D. Customer needs are determined through random processes rather than by using systematic methods.
E. Complaints are the primary methods used to obtain customer feedback.
F. No customer focus is evident.

_____ *Criterion 4: Employee Training and Recognition*

A. The organization is implementing a systematic employee training and recognition plan that is fully integrated into the overall strategic quality planning process.
B. The organization is assessing what employee training and recognition is needed, and the results of that assessment are being evaluated periodically.
C. An employee training and recognition plan is beginning to be implemented.
D. An employee training and recognition plan is under active development.
E. The organization has plans to increase employee training and recognition.
F. There is no employee training and there are no systems for recognizing employees.

_____ *Criterion 5: Employee Empowerment and Teamwork*

A. Innovative, effective employee empowerment and teamwork approaches are used.
B. Many natural work groups are empowered to constitute quality improvement teams.
C. A majority of managers support employee empowerment and teamwork.
D. Many managers support employee empowerment and teamwork.
E. Some managers support employee empowerment and teamwork.
F. There is no support for employee empowerment and teamwork.

_____ *Criterion 6: Quality Measurement and Analysis*

A. Information about quality and timeliness of all products and services is collected from internal and external customers and from suppliers.
B. Information about quality and timeliness is collected from most internal and external customers and from most suppliers.
C. Information about quality and timeliness is collected from major internal and external customers and from major suppliers.
D. Information about quality and timeliness is collected from some internal and external customers.
E. Information about quality and timeliness is collected from one or two external customers.
F. There is no system for measuring and analyzing quality.

_____ *Criterion 7: Quality Assurance*

A. All goods, services, and processes are designed, reviewed, verified, and controlled to meet the needs and expectations of internal and external customers.
B. A majority of goods, services, and processes are designed, reviewed, verified, and controlled to meet the needs and expectations of internal and external customers.
C. Key products, services, and processes are designed, reviewed, verified, and controlled to meet the needs and expectations of internal and external customers.
D. A few goods and services are designed, reviewed, and controlled to meet the needs of internal and external customers.
E. Goods and services are controlled to meet internally developed specifications that may or may not include customer input.
F. There is no quality assurance in this organization.

_____ *Criterion 8: Quality and Productivity Improvement Results*

A. Most significant performance indicators demonstrate exceptional improvements in quality and productivity over the past five years.
B. Most significant performance indicators demonstrate excellent improvement in quality and productivity over the past five years.
C. Most significant performance indicators demonstrate good improvement in quality and productivity.
D. Most significant performance indicators demonstrate improving quality and productivity in several areas.
E. There is evidence of some quality and productivity improvement in one or more areas.
F. There is no evidence of quality and productivity improvements in any areas.

Scoring

To determine your scores on the inventory, complete the following three steps:

1. For each of the *Total Quality Management Criteria* listed in the left column, find the letter under the heading labeled *Response Categories/Points* that corresponds to the one you chose on the questionnaire.

2. Then circle the one- or two-digit *point* number that corresponds to the letter you chose.

3. Finally add the points circled for all eight criteria to determine your *overall* score.

The numbers you are about to circle correspond to the relative weights attached to individual Quality/Productivity Criteria in the President's Award guidelines. Therefore, in addition to helping to score your responses, the points also identify the categories that are more significant than others. For example, scores on Criterion 8 (Quality and Productivity Improvement Results) are better indicators of an organization's orientation toward quality and productivity than are its scores on Criterion 4 (Employee Training and Recognition).

Total Quality Management Criteria	**Response Categories/Points**					
	A	**B**	**C**	**D**	**E**	**F**
1. Top-Management Leadership and Support	20	16	12	8	4	0
2. Strategic Planning	15	12	9	6	3	0
3. Focus on the Customer	40	32	24	16	8	0
4. Employee Training and Recognition	15	12	9	6	3	0
5. Employee Empowerment and Teamwork	15	12	9	6	3	0
6. Quality Measurement and Analysis	15	12	9	6	3	0
7. Quality Assurance	30	24	18	12	6	0
8. Quality and Productivity Improvement Results	50	40	30	20	10	0
SCORES FOR CHOICE CATEGORIES	___	___	___	___	___	___
OVERALL SCORE:	___ (range: 0–200)					

Interpretation of Scores

160–200 points: An overall score in this range indicates a "world-class" organization with a deep, long-term, and active commitment to improving quality and productivity. At this level, goals should focus on the challenge of maintaining gains as well as seeking ways to attain even higher levels of quality and productivity.

120–159 points: An overall score in this range indicates that an organization with a sound, well-organized philosophy of quality and productivity improvement is beginning to emerge. At this level, goals should focus on fully implementing a sound TQM effort while continuing to build on current levels of excellence.

80–119 points: An overall score in this range indicates an organization that is starting to learn about and plan quality and productivity improvements. At this level, goals should focus on moving from the planning stages to actually implementing a TQM effort in order to gain the necessary hands-on experience.

40–79 points: An overall score in this range indicates an organization that is vaguely aware of quality and productivity improvement but has no plans to learn about or implement such activity. Scores at this level approach the danger point; if long-term organizational viability is sought, progress must be made quickly. Goals should focus on strongly encouraging top managers to learn more about TQM while reexamining their assumptions about possible contributions that the process can make to the health of their organization.

0–39 points: An overall score in this range indicates an organization that currently has neither an awareness of nor an involvement with quality and productivity improvement programs. Unless an organization has an absolute, invulnerable monopoly on extremely valuable goods or services, this level represents a de facto decision to go out of business. Goals should focus on an emergency turnaround. Learning about total quality management must occur at an accelerated rate, and plans to bring quality and productivity consciousness to the organization must be implemented immediately.[53]

CRITICAL THINKING CASE

Metropol of Canada

Vandalism, theft, and terrorism are bad news. Bad news, that is, for everyone except those in the security business, which is a growth industry. The market for security guards and security hardware is worth about $900 million in Canada, with 60,000 people earning a living as guards or investigators. The third-largest security company, with an estimated 7 percent of the national Canadian market, is Winnipeg's Metropol Base-Fort Security Group. In the past few years, Metropol has expanded rapidly and earned a reputation for high quality—a rarity in the security business.

As spring arrives in Winnipeg, Metropol President Pat Haney is worried about the company's future. Competition, especially from large multinationals, such as Pinkerton's, Inc., is increasing, which may reduce already low profit margins. Haney is also concerned that Metropol's services are not sufficiently diversified: Security guards account for fully 90 percent of the company's revenues. Haney needs to make some key decisions about the company's future, including how to differentiate Metropol's services from those of its competitors.

Metropol was founded in 1955 by George Whitbread, a former Royal Canadian Mounted Police officer. In 1979, Whitbread sold it to former Manitoba premier Duff Roblin. Haney came aboard in 1980 to run the Winnipeg operation, which at the time accounted for 80 percent of Metropol's business. In the mid-1980s Metropol expanded into Saskatchewan and Alberta. In 1987, it took over the leading Alberta security firm, Base-Fort Security Group, Inc. Of Metropol's $40 million in sales in 1994, 70 percent were in western Canada. The company has offices in all four western provinces, the Northwest Territories, Quebec, and Newfoundland.

Anyone can enter the security business simply by opening an office. Start-up costs are low, and neither the company nor its employees needs any accreditation or specialized training. Thus Metropol has hundreds of competitors, ranging in size from a couple of ex-cops operating out of a basement to big multinationals. Vendors of security hardware—such as alarms, fences, locks, safes, electronic surveillance devices (ESDs), and monitoring equipment—also compete with providers of guards.

Most customers don't understand the difference in services provided by various companies. As a result, business often goes to the cheapest suppliers. Customers have the upper hand and don't hesitate to switch if they think they have found a better deal. Government agencies and firms that place a low priority on security usually choose the lowest bidder. Moreover, customers find it a simple matter to bring the security function in-house if they see a chance to cut costs. Most security companies earn average pretax profits of only 4 percent on gross sales. Thus there is little room for price cutting.

Although the primary basis of competition is price, Haney believes it possible to succeed by offering superior service. "We have attempted to provide greater value to our customers than our competitors," he says. For example, Metropol has a 24-hour dispatch service at a cost of $125,000 a year. Many of the other firms use answering services. Haney says some customers, who at first say that price is their only consideration, find that they like the extra service and are willing to pay for it. Metropol also gives its guards special training in reacting to emergencies such as bomb threats, hostage taking, and fires.

Despite offering a high level of service, Metropol manages to keep costs as low as its competitors', partly because its size allows economies of scale when buying such items as uniforms. Cost control is a key to success in a low-margin business. Metropol analyzes every expense activity for every job, looking for deviations from budget.

Of Metropol's 2000 employees, 1900 are security guards and the remainder are administrative personnel. Like other security firms, Metropol experiences an annual turnover of about 100 percent, probably because pay is low and the work usually is boring. Haney's favorite clients are those who are concerned about the high turnover and are willing to pay extra to ensure that guards assigned to them earn more than the minimum wage.

Haney is considering five strategies for the future: (1) continuing the company's current course, (2) expanding geographically, (3) expanding the range of goods and services offered, (4) diversifying into other service areas, and (5) serving the home-security market.

If he decided to stay with the current strategy, Haney would try to make Metropol the fastest-growing security guard company in western Canada, with the highest profits, the lowest employee turnover rate, and the most satisfied customers. This strategy would require a formal marketing program, even tighter cost controls, and better employee motivation.

The geographic expansion strategy would involve an attempt to make Metropol a national Canadian company. Following this strategy, Haney's first priority would be to establish the company in the Toronto area, because that is where most national companies make their decisions about security. Southern Ontario itself offers substantial business. Metropol could buy a local firm, merge with another company, or bid on contracts and open an office once a contract had been obtained.

The strategy of expanding the company's line of security goods and services would enable Metropol to satisfy customers who dislike having

Cooper Tire & Rubber Company

The Cooper Corporation began operations in 1920, and distributed its tires through its own wholesale business. The corporation's founder, Ira J. Cooper, emphasized three principles: good merchandise, fair play, and a square deal. This so-called Cooper creed remains a well-known corporate doctrine.

In 1930, Giant Tire & Rubber and the Cooper Corporation merged with the Falls Rubber Company to form the Master Tire & Rubber Company. Within a year, the combined production of the three plants totaled 2,850 tires per day. In 1946, the firm's name was changed to Cooper Tire & Rubber Company, in recognition of Ira J. Cooper's contribution.

In 1960, the company went public with a listing on the New York Stock Exchange, and its sale of shares facilitated another decade of growth. Cooper's strong financial condition has enabled it to expand capacity while most of the industry has been contracting. Since the late 1970s, tire producers have closed thirty-five plants in the United States, giving Cooper the chance to acquire existing facilities and modernize them. By 1983, Cooper had made the Fortune 500 list of America's largest industrial companies, and the following year its net income exceeded $24 million on sales of more than $500 million. In 1985, Cooper made its first foreign acquisition, a manufacturer of inner tubes, in Mexico. In the same year, Cooper was named one of the "101 Best Performing Companies in America."

Since 1981, the U.S. tire market has grown by just 29 percent, whereas Cooper's production has increased by 238 percent, its earnings by 465 percent, and its stock value by 3,800 percent. And with a per share price of 14 times earnings, Cooper has been safe from takeover threats.

Overview of the Industry

The tire industry comprises two major markets: (1) the original equipment (OE) market, and (2) the replacement market. The demand for OE tires is determined by the number of vehicles produced. Over the past several years, worldwide production of motor vehicles has remained steady at about 48 million units per year. But the demand for replacement tires depends on the average age of a vehicle, the durability of tire treads, the number of vehicles in use, the average number of miles driven, and gasoline prices. Statistics show that the market for replacement tires is three times larger than the one for OE market.

Vehicle manufacturers buy tires in large quantities and, because the number of buyers is low, they can usually negotiate low prices. As a result, the OE tire market has become low margin relative to the replacement tire market. And with the demand for vehicles having remained relatively flat in recent years, the market for OE tires has shrunk, making tire competition fiercer in the replacement market. Thus many tire producers have dumped entire inventories into the replacement market, lowering prices and making profit margins even leaner. So the most successful companies will be the low-cost producers.

Competition

Competition in the replacement tire market has centered mainly on two variables: price and tire performance. As of 1995, tire production capacity exceeded annual shipments by about 20 percent, and tire prices remained at 1985 levels. Overall, tire quality and performance have improved. The longer tread life of OE and replacement tires threatened to reduce radically the number of sets of replacement tires needed per vehicle in service. As of 1994, the ten largest tire manufacturers accounted for almost 82 percent of the world's $60.4 billion in tire sales, with $3.5 billion in profits. As of 1995, Cooper's major competitors in the replacement tire market were Goodyear, Michelin, and Bridgestone.

Goodyear leads the U.S. tire market but ranks second in the world market. Its market share accounted for 28.6 percent of North America's $18 billion tire sales in 1993. During the past decade, Goodyear and its subsidiaries have increased their share of the U.S. replacement tire market from about 15.5 percent to about 31 percent. Its North American market share in the passenger car replacement tire market was 16 percent in 1993. The company made $1.16 billion in profits in 1993 on corporatewide sales of $11.6 billion. Goodyear's reputation for tire quality has been good to excellent, generally on a par with Michelin and slightly ahead of Bridgestone. Over the years, the company has been among the top fifty national advertisers in promoting its tires. Goodyear employed approximately 92,000 people as of 1994. Its R&D expenditures for 1993 were $320 million, with a capital investment of $432 million.

Michelin, a French tire producer, is the acknowledged leader in radial tire technology. Michelin brand tires appeal mainly to quality-

Source: This case was prepared by Javad Karger, with the research assistance of Richard A. Mofor, North Carolina Central University.

sensitive buyers who drive relatively expensive cars. Michelin operates seventy tire plants in fifteen countries in Europe, the United States, Africa, and Asia. Its total market share accounted for about 2 percent of North American tire sales as of 1994. However, its North American market share in passenger car replacement tires was 15 percent in the same year. Michelin is represented by nearly 8,000 U.S. dealers. The Michelin name is well known and widely advertised. As of 1993, North American market share in passenger car replacement tires was about 8 percent, which was much smaller than its share in the OE market. The company made $354 million in 1993 on sales of $11.2 billion. Michelin employs about 120,000 people. The company's R&D expenditures for 1993 were $560 million, with a capital investment of $489 million.

Bridgestone dominated the Japanese tire market, ranked third in the U.S. market, and was the second top producer worldwide as of 1994, with sales of $9.5 billion and profits of $1.15 billion. Of its 20.5 percent share of the North American market in 1993, about 12 percent was in the replacement tire market. Bridgestone's R&D budget for 1993 was $380 million, with a capital investment of $1.1 billion. The company employs about 88,000 people.

Overview of the Company

Corporate Structure and Top Management

Ivan W. Gorr, a CPA, joined Cooper in 1972. He held the positions of controller, treasurer, and executive vice-president during the company's most intense decade of expansion and modernization and is widely credited for the company's success. To meet the challenge posed by global competition, Cooper's management has emphasized four corporate goals: (1) improving productivity through advanced systems technology, (2) involving employees in the attainment of production objectives, (3) expanding and modernizing production facilities, and (4) developing new tires and industrial rubber products.

A high level of free-flowing communication has been developed among all employees concerning company strategies and goals. Top management deeply believes that the success of the organization is based on the success of its individual members, and vice versa. Cooper emphasizes a strong commitment to customer service and quality, both of which demand a high degree of loyalty and an integrated effort. To foster this integration, Cooper maintains few hierarchical levels. The bureaucratic layering is so thin that finding anyone who bears the title of "assistant" is difficult.

Human Resource Management

Cooper employed approximately 7,600 people in 1993. Its management has long recognized that the performance of dedicated employees can make a difference where competitors sell basically undifferentiated products. Therefore Cooper always is seeking motivated employees who are team players, good communicators, and have the right attitude toward their jobs. Not surprisingly, potential employees undergo an exhaustive hiring process, which seems to pay off. Monthly meetings are held in each department to update workers on new developments, to identify problems, and to solicit suggestions.

For staff and management alike, a long tenure with the company is the norm. At age 63, Gorr himself ranks as a newcomer, having only 21 years with the company. President Patrick W. Rooney has been with Cooper for 38 years, and even Alec Reinhardt—the most junior member of the top management team—joined the company almost 18 years ago. Cooper has extremely low turnover and absenteeism rates of 3.1 and 0.1 percent, respectively.

An innovative system of paid incentives is tied as closely as possible to individual performance and contribution to productivity. Executive compensation, also tied to performance, provides for cuts as well as raises of up to 30 percent. Profit-sharing opportunities and paid incentives also augment the paychecks of Cooper's blue-collar and clerical workers. Hourly workers get paid extra for producing more, and salaried employees can earn bonuses of up to 7.5 percent on the returns on assets they handle. Interestingly, the strategy that produced the enviable growth is not a growth strategy. In fact, although incentive programs are offered to every Cooper employee, none are based on market share. According to Reinhardt, "Market share is not something that drives our company at all. We are very oriented to return on assets. It is more success breeds success rather than any concerted effort for growth."

Most Cooper employees grew up in and around the rural areas where the company's four tire plants are located. Analysts say that Cooper's small-town locations permit it to pay lower salaries and to achieve other savings over companies in urban areas. All of Cooper's managers are substantial shareholders, as are many workers.

Production and Products

Cooper specializes in the manufacturing and marketing of consumer and industrial rubber products. These products include automobile and truck tires, inner tubes, vibration control products, hose and tubing, automobile body sealing products, and specialty sealing components.

The company maintains two production divisions: the tire division and the engineered rubber products division. Tire products represent about 85 percent of the company's production and sales.

Cooper is a superefficient, cost-conscious producer in the industry. Some analysts believe that Cooper builds tires with 5 to 6 percent more efficiency than the industry average. Cooper runs its plants at 100 percent capacity. In a capital intensive industry, that creates a lot of leverage.

Although Cooper is the fourth largest tire producer in the United States, it manufactures exclusively for the replacement tire market. Therefore the company doesn't emphasize R&D. Instead, it waits two to three years to measure acceptance of the latest tire designs, then copies the winners and competes in the after-market on price. In 1994, Cooper spent $15.1 million on R&D. This amount represents about 1.3 percent of 1994 sales, compared to about 2.8 percent for Goodyear and Bridgestone, and 4.0 percent for Michelin. In 1994, 203 million replacement tires were sold in the United States, and Cooper made about 11 percent of them. Cooper's foreign sales represent only 5 percent of its total business.

Cooper's quality control policies and procedures are managed by specific staff, but a great deal of the responsibility for quality rests with the individual employee, who is trained to do his or her own quality assurance checks. Employees receive as many as 900 hours of training, and signs bearing such slogans as "Quantity is Important, but Quality is MORE Important" hang from factory walls. As part of its quality control efforts, each tire carries not only a brand name, but also a sticker identifying the worker who built it.

Cooper's innovative application of advanced computer technology provides it with a competitive advantage in bringing high-quality products to market quickly.

Marketing and Distribution

Cooper's primary channels of distribution—independent dealers and distributors—remain crucial to the company's success. Rather than selling through its own retail chains as Goodyear and Bridgestone do, Cooper distributes half its production as private label merchandise. The other half of Cooper's production is marketed under its own brand names and is distributed entirely through independent tire dealers, who command two-thirds of the U.S. market. Many dealers are loyal to Cooper for a couple of reasons. First, they make good money on Cooper tires, with an average margin of 33 percent versus a 28 percent margin on comparable brands. Second, dealers like the company because, unlike Goodyear or Bridgestone/Firestone, Cooper doesn't compete with them by operating its own outlets. Cooper focuses its relatively modest marketing budget on supporting its independent dealers, mainly by providing superior service and delivery and by offering a value-priced product that the dealers generally make relatively large profits on.

Financial Performance

Over the past decade, Cooper has demonstrated that a company doesn't have to lead its industry to generate enormous wealth for its owners. The company has posted impressive profits as other tire producers have been struggling to regain profitability. Its average return on equity between 1988 and 1994 was 22.1 percent. In 1994, its net operating profit was $102.2 million, down from $108 million in 1992, but up from $79 million in 1991. Cooper's net income, expressed as a percentage of net sales, in 1994, 1993, and 1992 was 9.2, 8.6, and 7.9 percent, respectively. Between 1988 and 1992, earnings per share have grown at a rate of 27 percent annually. Its long-term debt-to-equity ratio was 1:14 in 1994.

Company's Future

Gorr's management team positioned Cooper as the profit leader in the replacement tire market. Cooper anticipates a continued strong demand for tire products. The number of vehicles in use and the number of miles driven annually continue to increase.

Gorr knows that he will be faced with some interesting and difficult new challenges. One is that longer warranties of 60,000 to 80,000 miles are likely to present an intermediate-term demand problem. Therefore Cooper might be hard-pressed to maintain its past growth rate. Cooper has always operated under a "price umbrella" created by the OEMs; as that umbrella rose, so did Cooper's profitability. However, increased competition is posing a threat. Goodyear, for example, recently introduced a new tire aimed directly at the replacement market. Cooper won't have the luxury of watching how it performs for two or three years before deciding whether to copy it. Now the challenge is to hold market share in the replacement tire market, implement quality strategies, and even position itself for growth.

Questions

1. How would you use Porter's five forces model to diagnose Cooper Tire & Rubber Company?
2. What are the key global issues confronting the firm?
3. What specific business-level strategies would you recommend to Gorr?
4. What is the basis of Cooper's competitive advantage? How might it lose that advantage?

Part *Three*

Decision Making

Chapter 7

Ethics and Social Responsibility

Learning *Objectives*

After studying this chapter, you should be able to:

1. State the importance of ethics for organizations and their employees.
2. Describe how the societal, legal, organizational, and individual levels of ethics influence decisions and behavior.
3. Discuss the standards and principles of utilitarian, moral rights, and justice models of ethics.
4. Explain how the traditional, stakeholder, and affirmative social responsibility concepts are related to the three models of ethics.

Chapter *Outline*

Preview *Insight*

Martin Marietta's Ethics Program

Martin Marietta Corporation, a U.S. aerospace and defense contractor, created an ethics program in 1985. At the time, the defense industry in general was under attack for fraud and mismanagement. Martin Marietta specifically was under investigation for improper travel billings. Managers knew that they needed a better form of self-governance, but most doubted that an ethics program could influence behavior. "Back then people asked, 'Do you really need an ethics program to be ethical?' " recalls President Thomas Young. "Ethics was something personal. Either you had it, or you didn't."

The corporate legal counsel initially played a key role because legal compliance was a crucial objective. It was implemented as a companywide initiative aimed at creating and maintaining a *do-it-right* climate. In its initial form, the program emphasized core values, such as honesty and fair play in dealing with suppliers, customers, and governments. Over time, management expanded it to include quality and environmental responsibility.

Today the program consists of a code of conduct, an ethics training program, and procedures for reporting and investigating ethical concerns within the company. In place is a system for disclosing violations of federal procurement laws to the government. A corporate ethics office manages the program, and ethics representatives are stationed at major manufacturing plants. An ethics steering committee, made up of Martin Marietta's president, senior executives, and two rotating members selected from field operations, oversee the ethics office. The audit and ethics committee of the board of directors oversees the steering committee.

The ethics office is responsible for responding to questions and concerns from the company's employees. Its network of representatives serves as a sounding board, a source of guidance, and a channel for raising issues. These issues vary from allegations of wrongdoing to complaints about poor management, unfair supervision, and company policies and practices. Martin Marietta's ethics network accepts anonymous complaints. The ethics office also works closely with the human resources, legal, audit, communications, and security departments to respond to employee concerns.

The program has helped change employees' perceptions and priorities. Many employees compare their new ways of thinking about ethics to the way they understand quality. They more carefully evaluate how situations will be perceived by others, the possible long-term consequences of decisions, and the need for continuous improvement. Norman Augustine, CEO, states: "Ten years ago, people would have said that there were no ethical issues in business. Today employees think their number-one objective is to be thought of as decent people doing quality work."[1]

1

State the importance of ethics for organizations and their employees.

IMPORTANCE OF ETHICS

The thumbnail sketch of Martin Marietta's total ethics program represents a proactive strategy designed to go beyond the minimum standards of integrity imposed by government laws and regulations. The program is based on the assumption that managers and other employees are guided by more than economic self-interest. Martin Marietta's ethics program is based on the assumption that individuals are guided by personal values and ideals, their peers, societal values, and the organization's culture. The day-to-day decisions and actions of employees at various levels of an organization make real its culture of ethics.

Ask Students

What do you think about Martin Marietta's proactive ethics program? Explain.

When a Martin Marietta employee alleged that the company had retaliated against him for voicing safety concerns about his plant on CBS news, top management commissioned an investigation by an outside law firm. Although failing to support the allegations, the investigation found that employees at the plant feared retaliation when raising health, safety, or environmental complaints. The company redoubled its efforts to identify and discipline those employees taking retaliatory action and stressed the desir-

In today's world of increasing competition for customers, being in step with society's expectations can be beneficial in the long run. In the aftermath of Hurricane Andrew, Home Depot's Southeast Florida stores sold storm-related building materials at cost plus freight. The stores lost short-term profits but gained a strengthened, long-term bond with customers.

ability of an open work environment in its ethics training and company communications.[2]

Teaching Tip
Students constantly face ethical dilemmas. Have them generate a list of some they face daily. (Examples: plagiarism, calling in sick at work when they aren't sick, copying software, and copying cassette tapes.)

The ethical issues facing managers and other employees have grown in significance in recent years. This concern is fueled by stakeholders' attention to the effects of internal decisions on them.[3] In addition to higher standards of right and wrong, economic rivalry also has pushed organizations to address issues of ethical and moral conduct. Some individuals still think that businesses and their managers cannot be highly ethical and earn a profit at the same time. We disagree with this simplistic attitude. In a world of increasing local and global competition for customers, being in step with society's expectations can be beneficial to all parties over the long run. Customers remember those companies that don't take advantage of them and those that do.

Ask Students
Do you think this is a simplistic or realistic attitude?

Teaching Tip
Allow students to debate the question of whether ethics can be taught.

In the aftermath of Hurricane Andrew, Home Depot's nineteen Southeast Florida stores sold storm-related building materials, such as plywood and roofing shingles, at cost plus freight. Home Depot's policy contrasted strikingly to the widespread price gouging occurring in the area at the time. By forsaking short-term profits derived from the tragedy of the storm, Home Depot strengthened its long-term bond with customers. As one Home Depot customer said to the *New York Times*: "If they had spent $50 million on advertising, they couldn't have bought the goodwill they got by doing this."[4] This example represents the *enlightened self-interest* view of why organizations should strive to be ethical.[5] As we discuss in this chapter, there are many other reasons for ethical decisions and behavior.

Teaching Tip
Ask students to write a definition of ethics and an example of an ethical management practice. Compare the responses in class.

In this chapter we focus on the complex ethical and social responsibilities facing organizations, managers, and employees alike. We begin by outlining four system levels—societal, legal, organizational, and individual—that both influence and define ethical and unethical decisions and behavior. The potential conflicts inherent in organizational ethics become even more evident when we review the utilitarian, moral rights, and justice ethical models. Finally, we present three concepts of organizational social responsibility: traditional, stakeholder, and affirmative.

2
Describe how the societal, legal, organizational, and individual levels of ethics influence decisions and behavior.

LEVELS OF ETHICS

In the most elementary sense, **ethics** is a set of values and rules that define right and wrong conduct. They indicate when behavior is acceptable and when it is unacceptable.

In a broader sense, ethics includes (1) distinguishing between fact and belief, (2) defining issues in moral terms, and (3) applying moral principles to a situation.

Moral principles prescribe general rules of acceptable behavior that are intended to be impartial. They are of great importance to a society and cannot be established or changed by the decisions of powerful individuals alone; nor are they established as "true" solely by appeals to consensus or tradition.[6] Moral principles and the values they represent are fundamental to ethics. As you will learn in this chapter, some moral principles concerning managerial and employee behavior are widely shared, but others are not.[7]

Teaching Tip
Religion plays a major role in defining morality.

What is considered ethical may depend on the level of an ethical system at which ethical issues are considered. Figure 7.1 identifies four levels for diagnosing and considering ethical issues within a system of ethical values and decisions. Rarely can the ethical implications of any single decision or behavior be understood by looking at a single level, such as the legal level, of what is defined as right or wrong. Thus ethical decisions and behavior need to be evaluated within a wider context—the systems viewpoint. In this section we first describe each of the levels shown in Figure 7.1 somewhat independently of the others. We then describe the interplay of those levels in terms of a system of ethical decisions and behavior.

Societal Level

A large part of any view of what is considered ethical comes from the society in which the behavior occurs. The results of various public opinion surveys suggest a growing disenchantment with the degree of ethical behavior in general and with managerial ethics in particular. Do you agree or disagree with the following statements?

1. The ethical standard of business managers and executives is only fair or poor.
2. White-collar crime is common or somewhat common.
3. The lack of ethics in business people is contributing to crumbling moral standards.
4. People are less honest today than they were ten years ago.
5. Business people harm the environment to maintain profits.
6. Executives and managers put workers' health and safety at risk to maintain profits.

FIGURE 7.1

Levels of Ethical Behavior and Decisions

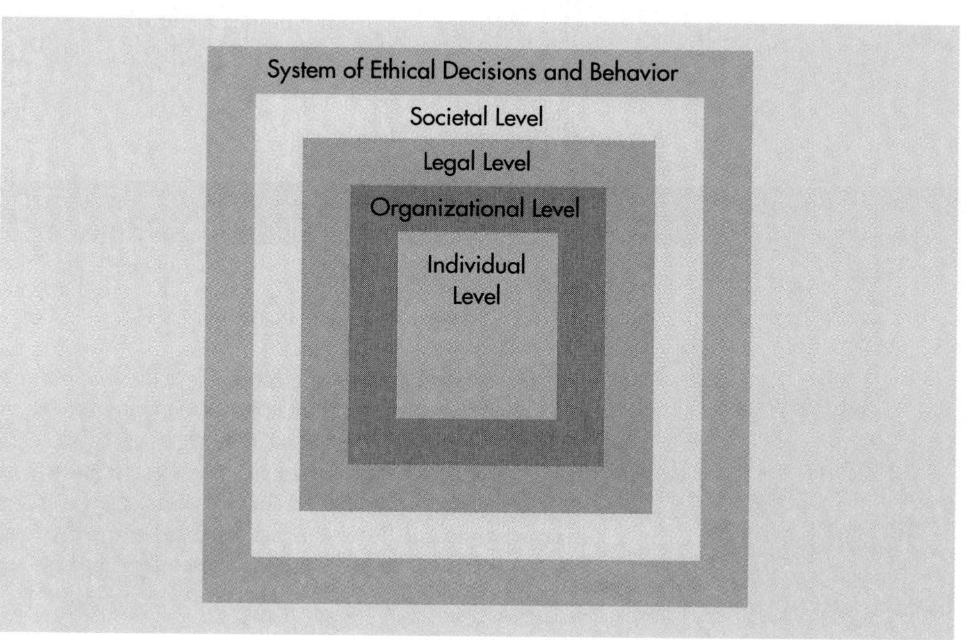

These statements were submitted to adults in several surveys. The following percentages of those surveyed *agreed* with the statements: 1, 58 percent; 2, 90 percent; 3, 76 percent; 4, 54 percent; 5, 47 percent; and 6, 42 percent.[8]

Ask Students
How do you explain this discrepancy between top management and lower levels of management?

In contrast to these relatively negative survey results, a comprehensive survey of managers revealed that 80 percent thought that their organizations were "guided by highly ethical standards."[9] The lower level managers responding to the survey were more likely than top managers to say that their organizations were *not* guided by highly ethical standards. In another study of honesty and trustworthiness in business, one anonymous entrepreneur attributed his longevity to his reputation for trustworthiness:

> *The most important reason for our success is the quality of my [product] line. But we wouldn't have survived without my integrity because our lines weren't always very successful. There are parabola curves in all businesses, and people still supported me, even though we had a low, because they believed in me.*[10]

Teaching Tip
Even if it could be fully known, "reality" may not be particularly relevant to managers. Most people assume that their perceptions are "reality," and they act on them. To discount people's perceptions is foolish.

A lack of research prevents us from concluding either that *perceptions* of business ethics reflect *reality* or that business ethics have improved or declined over the past ten years. Regardless of the reality, the survey results suggest that the general public perceives serious ethical problems in the way that business is conducted, whereas managers of organizations tend to see serious ethical problems in business as the exceptions that grab headlines.

In general, however, managers are under increasing pressure to make decisions on the basis of stricter standards of ethical behavior than in the past. Managers and other employees work in more of a fishbowl than ever before. Decisions and behavior are exposed by the media, with decisions and actions judged publicly by many different interest groups.[11] For example, auto manufacturers were judged by Ralph Nader and other consumer advocates as unethical for not doing everything possible to maximize the safety of autos, such as immediately installing stronger side panels and dual air-bags in all cars. The automakers countered that they weren't being unethical; rather, customers didn't want to pay for this additional safety, which the manufacturers claimed was marginal. The issue was resolved by government regulations that required stronger side panels in cars. Most shareholders want management to move cautiously to avoid driving the price of new cars up so much that demand drops off, leading to lower profits and dividends.

For organizations with operations in other societies, ethical decisions and behavior are even more complex.[12] The following Global Insight illustrates how societal views of ethical behavior vary from culture to culture.

Global *Insight*

Tax Returns Italian Style

An American manager was confronted with the ***Italian style*** of submitting tax returns. It involves understating taxes, hiring a ***commercialista*** to meet with a tax authority, and negotiating a tax for the company. The amount of tax agreed upon depends in part on the size of a ***bustarella*** (bribe) given to the tax authority. The American manager was disturbed both by lying on the tax return and by the apparent bribery of the tax official. He submitted an ***American style*** tax return and refused to hire a ***commercialista.*** He was eventually forced to meet with tax officials and his bank was made to pay taxes approximately three times the amount that would have been required if he had ***played the game—Italian style.***

How would you have handled this situation? Why? One suggestion for diagnosing and handling this situation follows. In this case, both honesty and the corruption of government officials seems to reflect societal norms. In Italy, submitting a false and favorable tax return isn't seen as deceptive. The tax authorities expect returns to show taxes owing at between 30 percent and 70 percent of actual amounts due. In fact, an accurate return is defined as deceptive, suggesting to tax authorities much higher than actual corporate profits. Although submitting accurate tax returns has value, it may be not be nearly as important as avoiding the perception of deception. For the American manager to adjust to the Italian style of handling tax matters probably is reasonable.

However, the issue of bribery can't be handled so easily. The American understandably was uncomfortable with the payment of *bustarella.* A compromise strategy might involve understating taxes but refusing to pay *bustarella.* The company probably would pay more than its fair share of taxes but would avoid the extreme taxes paid by the American bank in this case. Another compromise may be to pay some *bustarella* but attempt to estimate what is required to get fair and reasonable treatment from the tax authority. Paying only this amount avoids getting special favorable treatment and thus paying less than the taxes fairly owed. These actions preserve the manager's (and home country's) values of fairness of results, even though he will still be uneasy with the process. (Of course, the manager would have to determine whether payment of such *bustarella* is illegal under the U.S. Foreign Corrupt Practices Act.) What do you think of the diagnosis and suggestions for handling this situation?[13]

Even in the same society the view of what is ethical and legal changes over time. For example, during prohibition (1919–1932), buying and drinking alcohol was illegal. Throughout the chapter, we present examples of how changing societal views of ethical behavior eventually result in new legal requirements, as well as voluntary changes in behavior by organizations and their managers.

Legal Level

What a society interprets as ethical or unethical frequently ends up being expressed through court decisions and the passage of laws within that society. **Laws** are simply society's values and standards that are enforceable in the courts.[14] However, the idea of operating strictly according to the law as a basis for ethical decisions and behavior often is inadequate. The legality of actions and decisions doesn't necessarily make them ethical. At one time, for example, Canadian and U.S. organizations could legally discriminate against women and minorities in hiring and promotions. As these countries came to recognize that these practices were unethical, laws were passed in an attempt to stop the practices.

Teaching Tip
Have students pick a current event reported in the media in which an action was legal but about which some ethical questions remain.

Teaching Tip
Americans tend to have more consumer protection than do people in other countries. In many Asian countries (except Japan), for most products, "once you buy it, it's yours forever—no refund, no exchanges."

Dealing with behavior that is clearly both unethical and illegal (e.g., theft) is easy. In this case societal values and standards of behavior are clearly understood and reinforced by the law. But what about behavior that the courts interpret as legal but that society comes to see as unethical? Or, vice versa? The classic legal concept of *caveat emptor*—"let the buyer beware"—used to be the defense for a variety of shady business practices. During the 1950s and 1960s, an increasingly aware public in both Canada and the United States began to challenge the ethics of such a position. Shifting societal attitudes and values concerning *appropriate* behavior by businesses led to a flood of U.S. consumer legislation during the late 1960s and early 1970s, which substantially diminished the concept of *caveat emptor.* Moreover, in the past, banks, loan companies, and other lenders commonly concealed the actual annual rates of interest charged on consumer loans. The public eventually realized that this behavior was unethical and socially irresponsible. Laws now require a clear statement of the true annual rate of interest on all loan agreements in Canada and the United States.

Ask Students
Would you want to work under the "employment-at-will" arrangement?

Even without specific legislation defining certain behaviors as legal, the courts may rule on what constitutes ethical decisions and behavior. Consider the concept of employment-at-will. **Employment-at-will** is a traditional common-law concept holding that employers are free to discharge employees for any reason at any time and that employees are free to quit their jobs for any reason at any time. Many employees, especially those in managerial positions, have been dismissed without explanation (at will) by their employers. Over the past twenty-five years, courts have modified the free-wheeling notion that employees can be fired for any reason. For example, employers have been held liable for firing employees who refused to lie before a legislative hearing, who blew the whistle about illegal conduct by their employers, or who filed workers' compensation claims. One way to sum up these cases is to say that employees can now recover damages from an employer if they are fired for reasons that violate an important public policy.[15]

Discussion Question 1
What is the difference between judging a decision from an individual level and a legal level in a system of ethics?

Finally, certain business practices that are ruled illegal may be viewed by most people as ethical. In addition to formal laws and the courts, regulatory agencies—such as the Occupational Safety and Health Administration and the Equal Employment Opportunity Commission—play a major role in defining and enforcing what is considered to be legal or illegal. As suggested by the following Small Business Insight, some actions may be defined as a violation of a *legal* rule by a regulatory agency but not be considered unethical by the broader society.

Small Business *Insight*

Philatron's Nightmare

Phil Ramos, president and founder of Philatron International, has talked freely about his firm's regulatory nightmare. It forced him to lay off forty of the firm's eighty-five employees in 1992 and 1993. Philatron makes electrical wire and cable products at a plant in Santa Fe Springs, California, near Los Angeles.

The regulatory issue involves a coiled air-brake hose used on tractor-trailer rigs between the cab and the trailer. Standard hoses are made of stiff nylon. Philatron's, made of a rubbery proprietary material, is softer and springier. It has several advantages over conventional hose, says Ramos. The main advantage is that it neither sags as it ages nor kinks when stretched taut. This is potentially an important safety benefit, as a kink in the hose could shut off the air supply needed to operate a trailer's brakes.

Philatron began producing the hoses early in 1991 and sold 45,000 in the first few months. Then the National Highway Traffic Safety Administration called the product unsafe, told Ramos to stop selling it, and ordered a recall. The safety issue: The hoses could not survive a 72-hour immersion in 212°F. engine oil, which was designed to simulate long-term stress. Ramos was stunned. He knew the hoses didn't meet that requirement. He had told the agency so himself. That old regulation didn't make any sense for modern trucks because coiled air hoses don't get bathed in oil.

Ramos hired a lawyer, began lining up support from Congressmen and Small Business Administration officials, and asked for an exemption from the recall. He argued that there was no safety issue. After several months the agency agreed and rescinded its order. But it said that he still couldn't sell the hoses, even though they are safe. He'll have to wait until the regulation is changed—a process that has dragged on with no end in sight.[16]

Ask Students
Should management be responsible for establishing ethical norms? Why or why not?

Teaching Tip
In general, organizations get what they reward for. Rewarding unethical people will encourage others to do the same.

Organizational Level

The organization itself can determine whether behavior by its employees and agents is ethical or unethical.[17] The most fundamental organizational influence is top management's commitment to ethical conduct. It may communicate this commitment through directives, policy statements, codes of ethics, speeches, publications, and—most important—its actions. Recall the Preview Insight on Martin Marietta's ethics program. The top managers there used all these means to communicate *and* demonstrate a commitment to ethical conduct.

Real-World Example
At American Honda, former Senior VP James Cardiges solicited $10,000 in bribes from dealers in exchange for franchises and allotments of popular models of new cars. Dealers bribed VP John Billmeyer, who received $19,000 to build a pool and spa and $8,000 for a down payment on his Palm Springs vacation home. Seven former Honda executives and two Honda dealers have been indicted (*Los Angeles Times,* January 6, 1994, D1).

Teaching Tip
Encourage students to visit a company and ask about its code of ethics. Have them report their findings to the class.

Organizations take different approaches to establishing principles of organizational ethical conduct. The approach that is most common and that is growing in popularity is presenting expectations for the entire organization in written documents, which may include a code of ethics. Even if managers and professionals work for organizations that don't have a code of ethics, their management and professional associations probably have one.

Codes and standards clearly communicate expectations. But organizations have learned that even more is needed: Vigorous implementation is essential, as demonstrated by Martin Marietta's experience. Implementation mechanisms include:

- management involvement and oversight down the line;
- attention to values and ethics in day-to-day recruiting, hiring, and promotion decisions (e.g., don't distort the reality of job expectations when recruiting an employee);
- emphasis on corporate ethics in training and development programs (e.g., let employees know that all will have an equal opportunity for training and development);
- alternative ways for employees to report questionable actions of peers and superiors (e.g., let employees know and demonstrate that whistleblowers will not be punished for reporting ethical misconduct directly to superiors, the human resources department, or some other entity outside the direct chain of command); and
- auditing and enforcement procedures that contain stiff disciplinary and dismissal procedures.

The nature of an organization's culture, leadership, reward systems, and practices can work for or against ethical conduct.[18] Two researchers have developed a questionnaire to help managers evaluate the extent to which employees perceive that organizational factors work for or against ethical decisions and behavior.[19] Sample questions from that questionnaire are shown in Table 7.1. Respond to these sample questions in terms of

TABLE 7.1

Ethical Climate Questionnaire

We would like to ask you some questions about the general climate in your company. Please answer the following in terms of how it really is in your company, not how you would prefer it to be. Please be as candid as possible; remember, all your responses will remain strictly anonymous.

Please indicate whether you agree or disagree with each of the following statements about your company. Please use the scale below and write the number which best represents your answer in the space next to each item.

To what extent are the following statements true about your company?

COMPLETELY FALSE	MOSTLY FALSE	SOMEWHAT FALSE	SOMEWHAT TRUE	MOSTLY TRUE	COMPLETELY TRUE
0	1	2	3	4	5

____ 1. In this company, people are expected to follow their own personal and moral beliefs.

____ 2. People are expected to do anything to further the company's interests.

____ 3. In this company, people look out for each other's good.

____ 4. It is very important here to follow strictly the company's rules and procedures.

____ 5. In this company, people protect their own interests above other considerations.

____ 6. The first consideration is whether a decision violates any law.

____ 7. Everyone is expected to stick by company rules and procedures.

____ 8. The most efficient way is what is best for everyone in the company.

____ 9. Our major consideration is what is best for everyone in the company.

____ 10. In this company, the law or ethical code of the profession is the major consideration.

____ 11. It is expected at this company that employees will always do what is right for the customer and the public.

Source: Ethical Climate Questionnaire. Copyright © 1986. Victor, B. (University of North Carolina at Chapel Hill) and Cullen, J.B. (University of Rhode Island).

Discussion Question 2
Can the ethical climate of an organization be improved? If so, how?

an organization for which you have worked. Based on your responses, characterize the ethical climate of that organization.

The following Ethics Insight demonstrates how the *Kansas City Star* and others in the newspaper industry are attempting to address issues of ethical conduct and overall ethical climate.

Ethics *Insight*

Kansas City Star

The *Kansas City Star* got a hot tip: Municipal employees were selling city-owned asphalt mix to a privately owned gas station. The *Star* sent a reporter to the scene. A municipal employee asked the reporter (thinking it was the station operator) for $30 to cover the payment. The reporter agreed and the asphalt was dumped. Once the city was notified, it quickly picked up the asphalt mix and later fired two employees. In journalistic terms, it was a slam dunk. But the story was never written. The *Star*'s editors considered the reporter's decision to provide cash a serious ethical mistake. "At this moment, the *Star* became a part of the story it was there to report," Editor and Vice-President Arthur S. Brisbane wrote in a column. "It is our job to witness and publish—not to participate in the making of the news."

After that incident and another involving a conflict of interest, the Star's editors decided to take a close look at the various guidelines used by departments in the newsroom and merge them into one set of guidelines. "It surprised us that some things we thought were common knowledge weren't," stated Mark Zieman, the managing editor. The *Star* is not alone. From the tiny *Napa Valley Register* in California, which doesn't have formal written ethical guidelines, to the *Hartford Courant,* which is updating its seven-year-old code, newspaper editors are talking about ethics. Should they have a written code like doctors, lawyers and a growing number of businesses?

Few newspapers are vehemently opposed to written codes. Yet less than 100 newspapers have them, according to a survey by the Associated Press Managing Editors (APME). More editors now believe that written codes—not just broadly stated principles—are necessary and are writing or considering their own. Many say that a strong ethics code will enhance credibility in an industry that has been losing public confidence. They say that reporters need to know the ground rules and that a code should be written down and discussed. Editors can't just assume that reporters—who change jobs relatively often—will know the guidelines.[20]

Individual Level

Despite prevailing societal, legal, and organizational interpretations of what is ethical, we all have our own values and a sense of what is right or wrong. Because some individuals may not be predisposed to ethical decisions and behavior on the job, managers of both large and small organizations need to pay close attention to values and ethics in recruiting, hiring, and promotion.

Discussion Question 3
What percentage of the adult population (eighteen years old and older) do you estimate is at each of Kohlberg's stages of moral development? What is the basis for your estimate?

Lawrence Kohlberg (1927–1987) probably is the best-known scholar in the field of the psychology of ethical decision making and behavior. Kohlberg's model of moral development is useful for exploring questions about how members of an organization regard ethical dilemmas, including how they determine what is right or wrong in a particular situation.[21] Kohlberg held that people develop morally, much as they do physically, from early childhood to adulthood. As they develop, their ethical criteria and patterns of moral reasoning go through six stages. Figure 7.2 shows these stages of moral development, ranging from the lowest (obedience-and-punishment orientation) to the highest (universal ethical principles). (We use somewhat simpler labels for some of these stages than those used by Kohlberg.) Kohlberg did not assume that all individuals progress through all stages. For example, an adult criminal could be stuck in the first stage.

FIGURE 7.2

Kohlberg's Stages of Moral Development

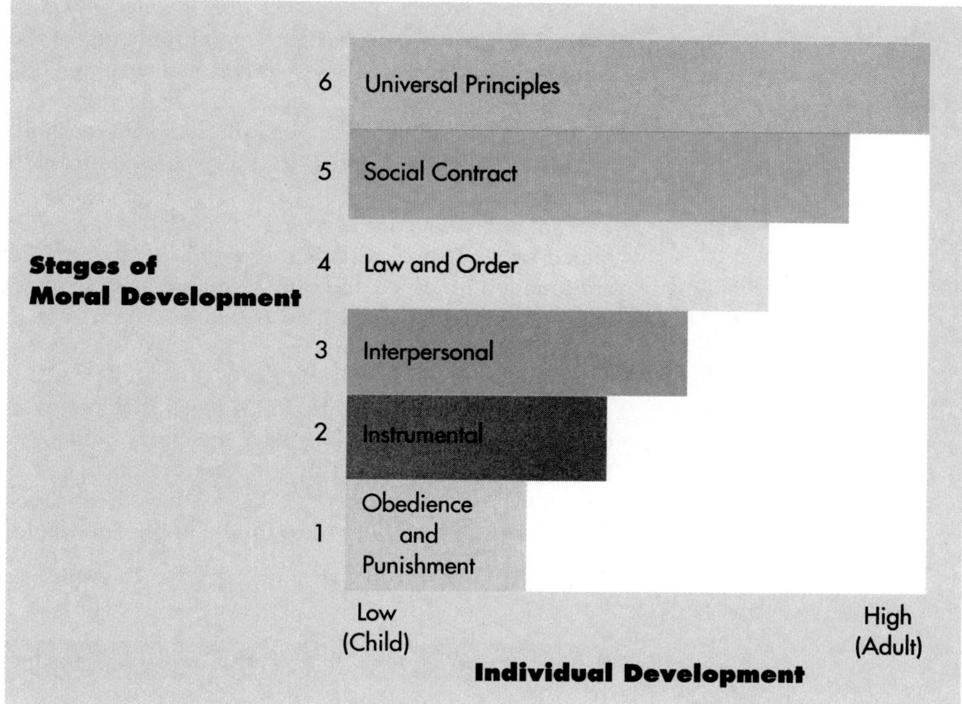

Ask Students
At which of Kohlberg's stages are you? At which stage is your best friend? At which stage is a close relative (e.g., brother, sister, father, or mother)? At which stage is your manager at work?

The individual at the *obedience and punishment stage* (presumably a young child) does the right thing mainly to avoid punishment or to obtain approval.[22] Such a person has little sense of the needs of others; only the immediate consequences of an action determine its goodness or badness. An employee stuck at this stage might think that the only reason not to steal money from an employer is the certainty of getting caught and then fired or even arrested. Obviously, organizations would not want to employ such an individual.

The individual at the *instrumental stage* (presumably an older child) becomes aware that others also have needs and begins to defer to them to get what the individual wants. Right behavior is what satisfies the person's self-interest. Right is what is judged to be fair from the perspective of the individual—an "equal" exchange, or a deal. An employee at this stage might be willing to take fewer than the allotted number of paid sick days only if paid extra to reduce absences.

The individual at the *interpersonal stage* considers appropriate behavior as what pleases, helps, or is approved by friends or family. Right behavior exhibits conformity to conventional expectations, often of the majority. At this stage, being seen as a "good person" with basically good motives, is important. An employee at this stage might focus on the importance of being a loyal follower who is always friendly and who avoids or smoothes conflict.

The individual at the *law and order stage* recognizes that ethical behavior is not determined only by reference to friends, family, co-workers, or others whose opinions the individual might value. Right behavior consists of doing a person's duty, showing respect for authority, and maintaining the social order for its own sake. Loyalty to the nation and its laws are paramount. The person sees other people as individuals and also as parts of the larger social system that gives them their roles and obligations. An employee at this stage may rigidly adhere to organizational rules and regulations and legitimate orders from superiors. The employee is likely to resist or criticize the efforts of co-workers or superiors to bend or break the rules—for example, by taking paid sick days when they are not actually ill.

The individual at the *social contract stage* is aware that people hold a variety of conflicting personal views that go beyond the letter of the law. A person at this stage understands that, although rules and laws may be agreed upon and for the most part must be impersonally followed, they can be changed if necessary. Some absolute values, such as life and liberty, are held regardless of different individuals' values or even majority opinion. "The greatest good for the greatest number" is the characteristic ethical norm at this stage.[23]

The individual at the *universal principles stage* views appropriate conduct as determined by a person's conscience, based on universal ethical principles. These principles are founded in justice, the public welfare, the equality of human rights, and respect for the dignity of individual human beings. When formal rules or laws are at odds with these principles, the individual at this stage is likely to act in accordance with the principles rather than the rules or laws.

Just as determining any individual's stage of moral development is difficult, so is discovering the ethics motivating managers' and other employees' decisions and behavior. To do so requires considering the impact of the societal, legal, organizational, and individual levels of ethics that we have been discussing.[24] Three ethical models of decision making and behavior can be applied to the four system levels of ethics to ease that task.

3

Discuss the standards and principles of the utilitarian, moral rights, and justice models of ethics.

ETHICAL MODELS

We may interpret what is ethical by comparing individual decision making and behavior with three important ethical models.[25]

- The **utilitarian model** judges the effect of decisions and behavior on others, with the primary goal of providing the greatest good for the greatest number of people.
- The **moral rights model** judges decisions and behavior by their consistency with fundamental personal and group liberties and privileges.
- The **justice model** judges decisions and behavior by their consistency with an equitable, fair, and impartial distribution of benefits (rewards) and costs among individuals and groups.

Teaching Tip
Find a current ethical controversy in *The Wall Street Journal* or business magazine that students can relate to. Divide the class into groups of 3 or 4. Assign each group an ethical model. Have the groups research the case and argue for their perspective being the most ethical. Ask the groups to make their presentations in class next week.

Each model provides a different but somewhat related set of principles or standards for judging the right or wrong of managerial and employee decisions and behavior. As suggested by Figure 7.3, all three ethical models can, at times, reinforce and support a particular pattern of decisions and behavior. At other times, decisions and behavior can be defined as ethical from the perspective of only one particular ethical model. All three models may be applied to issues that involve ethical questions. In general, a proposed course of action that is supported by all three models is probably the ideal solution. However, in complex decision-making situations with conflicting individual and group interests, the ability to find such an ideal solution may be more the exception than the rule.

Utilitarian Model

The utilitarian model focuses on *actions* (behaviors), not on the *motives* for such actions.[26] It is most consistent with Kohlberg's social contract stage. A manager or employee guided by this model considers the potential effects of alternative actions on all involved. The alternative chosen is supposed to benefit the greatest number of people, although such benefit may come at the expense of the few or those with little power. In other words, this alternative may help some individuals but harm others. As long as potentially positive results outweigh potentially negative ones, the decision maker considers the decision to be both good and ethical.

Merit pay is a system that rewards different employees with different rates of pay

FIGURE 7.3

Models of Ethics for Decision Making

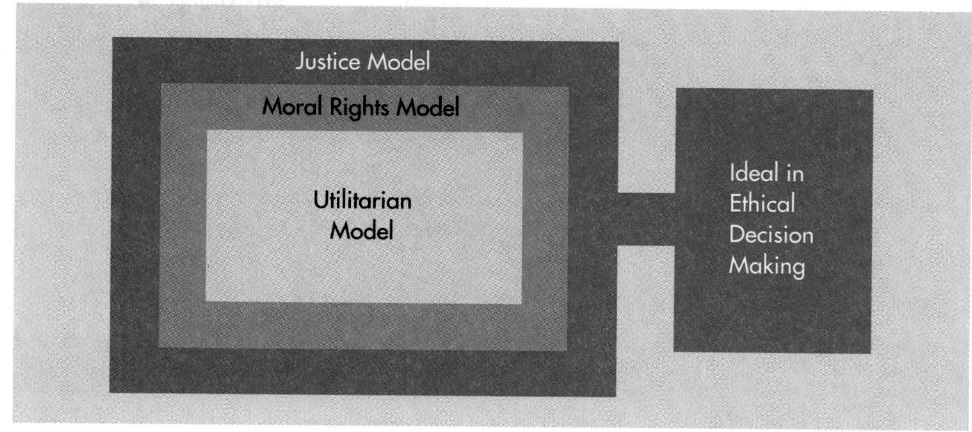

Ask Students
Is it ethical under the utilitarian model for older assembly-line workers to get paid more than younger workers who work just as fast and produce as much? Why or why not?

based on their performance. The ethical aspect of this system is justified under the utilitarian approach: Those who perform best should receive the greatest reward. Also, in an economy based on competitive markets, the successful actions of one firm (i.e., the one that performs best) may cause other firms to suffer financial loss or bankruptcy. This result is justified ethically under the utilitarian approach by the belief that, of the recognized economic systems, capitalistic private enterprise offers consumers the highest quality products (goods and/or services) at the lowest prices. Thus a competitive market economy provides the greatest good for the greatest number. The utilitarian model views bankruptcy and loss of jobs as necessary consequences of market competition.

Ethical Standards. The utilitarian model prescribes ethical standards for managers and employees in the areas of organizational goals, efficiency, and conflict of interest.[27]

1. ***Organizational Goals.*** Managers should attempt to satisfy the needs of customers, suppliers, lenders, employees, and shareholders. Providing the greatest good for the greatest number in a competitive market system means focusing on maximizing profits. Achieving high profits is thought to result in the highest quality products and the lowest prices for consumers. Profits are seen as the reward for satisfying consumers. If profits get too high, new competitors will enter the market, thereby increasing the supply of high-quality goods and pushing prices back down.
2. ***Efficiency.*** Managers and other employees should try to attain organizational goals as efficiently as possible. Efficiency is achieved by minimizing both inputs (e.g., labor, land, and capital) and external costs to society (e.g., air and water pollution and use of nonrenewable resources).
3. ***Conflicts of Interest.*** Managers and other employees should not have personal interests that conflict with the organization's achievement of its goals. A purchasing agent having a significant financial interest in one of the firm's major suppliers faces a potential conflict of interest. The purchasing agent may be motivated to purchase from that supplier, even when the price or quality isn't the best available.

Teaching Tip
At most universities, the policy toward students is based on rule utilitarianism, or the greatest good for the greatest number, through strict adherence to impersonal rules. Could granting an exception to the deadline policy in your class for one person without changing the rules for everyone else be justified? If so, under what conditions?

Act and Rule Utilitarianism. The utilitarian model has two major branches. **Act utilitarianism** emphasizes the consequences of providing the greatest good for the greatest number; that is, the end justifies the means. **Rule utilitarianism** relies primarily on following predefined rules or standards to obtain the greatest good for the greatest number. Individuals often have difficulty anticipating *all* the consequences of their decisions and behavior, as required under act utilitarianism. However, employees can usually tell whether they are following a rule, as required under rule utilitarianism—a distinction that may be helpful in ambiguous situations. Under act utilitarianism, a manager might agree to pay a bribe because it is necessary in order to get a job done that benefits the entire organization. Under rule utilitarianism, any idea of bribery may be rejected if it is against the rules of the organization or against the law.

The utilitarian model is consistent with strong values of individualism, acceptance of uncertainty, and masculinity, as defined in Chapter 3. These values support profit maximization, self-interest, rewards based on abilities and achievements, sacrifice and hard work, and competition.[28] Supported by the utilitarian approach, many firms are increasingly attempting to capitalize on the growing diversity of the U.S. population to improve profits. Consider the recent actions of Kmart in the following Diversity Insight.

Diversity *Insight*

Kmart Goes Ethnic

The Kmart store near Watts in Los Angeles is stocked with products geared toward African-American customers: African-style clothing and imported jewelry, Malcolm X merchandise, greeting cards, and hair care items. "It's a market that's just beginning to open," said Kmart Manager Bob Dito. "Only recently has Kmart gotten into it and it's been very successful." Kmart is joining other major retailers in developing the growing ethnic market.

"We realize that 24 percent of Americans today are ethnic," said Ed Francis, Kmart director of ethnic merchandising for the fashions division. "It's slated to grow to 48 percent by 2050." In 1992, he said, only five Kmart stores had distinctly ethnic products. In 1993, 300 Kmart stores out of 2,400 across the country had multicultural goods. Some 700 Kmart stores serve areas in which more than 20 percent of their customers are ethnic. Apparel made in West Africa priced under $50 tested successfully in 17 stores and is now found in 50 Kmart outlets, the company said.

"Historically, we've tended to ignore ethnic minorities. The assumption was they will amalgamate with the rest and will want mainstream products," said David Stewart, a University of Southern California marketing professor. "Where else in the U.S. are you looking to grow? Populations that you haven't served," Stewart said, adding that minority middle classes are getting more affluent. "Here you've got an underserved market that's growing and becoming increasingly affluent. It's a natural target."[29]

Over the past twenty-five years, utilitarian ethics have been increasingly challenged and tempered by the moral rights and justice models.

Moral Rights Model

The moral rights model holds that decisions should be consistent with fundamental rights and privileges (e.g., life, freedom, health, privacy, and property), as set forth in the first ten amendments to the U.S. Constitution—the Bill of Rights—and the United Nations' Declaration of Human Rights, for instance.[30] This model is consistent with Kohlberg's universal principles stage of moral development. According to the moral rights model, decisions and behaviors should preserve the following six moral rights.[31] Several U.S. and Canadian laws enacted during the past twenty-five years require managers and other employees to consider these rights as guides for their decision making and behavior.

Life and Safety. Employees, customers, and the general public have the right *not* to have their lives and safety unknowingly and unnecessarily endangered. This moral right in large part justifies the U.S. Occupational Safety and Health Act (OSHA) of 1970. It contains many requirements designed to increase the safety and healthfulness of work environments that organizations must meet. For example, OSHA and its implementing regulations restrict the use of asbestos, lead-based paint, and various toxic chemicals in the workplace.

Truthfulness. Employees, customers, and the general public have the right *not* to be intentionally deceived on matters about which they should be informed.[32] For example, critics claimed in 1994 that code sharing on computer screens by airlines was highly deceptive. Code sharing wasn't just a computer gimmick. Under such an arrangement between airlines, one of the carriers involved operated the flight, but both partners sold tickets on it. Code sharing allowed a partner to affix its two-letter computer code (such as DL for Delta and CO for Continental) to flights actually operated by another partner. If you lived in Houston, Texas, and wanted to fly to Rio de Janeiro, Brazil, agents' computer screens displayed no nonstop flights from Houston. But near the top of the list they showed a Continental Airlines' flight to Miami that connected with a Delta Air Lines flight to Rio. But if you assumed that this flight was operated by Delta, you were wrong. Actually, this leg was operated by Varig, a Brazilian carrier with which Delta had an alliance. An asterisk next to the item indicated that it was a code-sharing flight, but the asterisk was so subtle that travel experts said that it was easy to miss. And, even then busy agents had to take extra time to look up which airline actually was flying the route.[33] As a result of government and public pressure, code sharing was made obvious to agents and customers in late 1994.

Real-World Example
The Educational Film Center commissioned a survey on employee privacy and found that four out of ten U.S. workers believe that their employers failed to respect their off-hour privacy. Eleven percent suspect their employers of collecting or abusing personal information. Eight percent said that employers collected inappropriate health or life-style information. Four percent said that employers improperly disclosed medical information to co-workers (*Los Angeles Times,* August 19, 1994, D1-D2).

Privacy. Citizens have the right to control access to and use of personal information about themselves by government agencies, employers, and others. This moral right was the basis for the U.S. Privacy Act of 1974. The act restricts the use of certain kinds of information by the federal government and limits those to whom this information can be released. This act allows individuals to (1) find out what personal information the government has collected, recorded, maintained, and used; (2) review relevant records and have inaccuracies corrected; (3) prevent certain uses of such records by the federal government; and (4) bring suit for damages against those who intentionally violate their rights, as specified in the act. A more recent act designed to protect privacy is the 1988 Video Privacy Protection Act, which forbids retailers from disclosing video rental records without the customer's consent or a court order. For example, a customer who rents exercise videos need not worry about getting on mailing lists for exercise equipment catalogues, fitness magazines, and the like.

With the availability of a whole array of new information technologies (especially computers and videos), there is enormous concern with invasions of privacy at the societal, legal, organizational, and individual levels.[34] A few of these privacy issues include drug testing, honesty testing, confidentiality of medical and psychological counseling records, managerial monitoring of e-mail and work performed on computers, surveillance through videos, and access to credit records. One of many examples of the invasions of privacy is provided in the following Ethics Insight.

Ethics *Insight*

Dunkin' Donuts' Snooping

At some Dunkin' Donuts shops, the walls had ears, although the owners of those franchises insist that they weren't being nosy. They claimed that it is just another way to increase security and keep employees on their toes.

"Knowing this, I would never have a conversation in here," said customer Frank Bowser, a private investigator who was discussing a case with a partner. "I think the general public would be in an uproar to know that every time they come in for a cup of coffee and a doughnut they could be heard." Thalia Hondrogen, a customer, said: "It's like spying. It sounds like Nazism or the KGB. It's not American. Many times you say things to close friends you don't want overheard." The systems also were unwelcome news in 1994 at Dunkin' Donuts' corporate headquarters in Randolph, Massachusetts. Any systems powerful enough to record customers' conversations would be "highly inappropriate" and a violation of company policy, spokesman Bill Chiccarelli said. Still, store owners are using them. Security systems dealer Jeff Meuse told the *Concord Monitor* that he has installed systems in 500 Dunkin' Donuts shops in Massachusetts in the last five years and 300 had audio monitoring. Shops that have the monitoring systems display small stickers on their doors saying, "Audio monitoring on the premises."

Use of concealed video recorders to deter crime is widespread at fast-food restaurants, convenience stores, and other businesses, according to one company that sells them. But, unlike antishoplifting mirrors and surveillance cameras, hidden microphones are news to most of the public. Lewis Weiss, CEO of Louroe Electronics, Inc., of Van Nuys, California, said that his company's systems can pick up conversations within thirty feet. "Unfortunately, this is going to be the future until we get to the point where there is minimal crime in this country," Weiss said. "Until then, store owners are going to have to have these devices to protect their employees and their customers."

The American Civil Liberties Union grudgingly accepts surveillance cameras and audio equipment at store and restaurant cash registers (not tables, booths, or counters), providing customers and staff are notified. "We would prefer not to see them at all, but if and when it does happen, we would strongly (want) there to be actual and functional notification," ACLU spokesman Milind Shah said in New York. "Often a sign on the door is not enough." Federal law requires stores to post signs informing customers that they might be monitored, and customers should take notice, Weiss said. "There is no invasion of privacy in a public store like a Circle K or a Dunkin' Donuts because you can't carry on a private conversation there," he said. Do you agree with this statement by Weiss?[35]

Ask Students
What do you think of this case? Why?

Ask Students
Even though your right to criticize your employer's ethics or the legality of its actions is protected under the law, would doing so be wise? Explain.

Teaching Tip
Too often, whistleblower protection laws are enforced by the system in which the whistleblower originated his or her charges. Have students discuss what is needed to successfully challenge bureaucratic tendencies to cover up mistakes.

Real-World Example
Sometimes whistleblowers are publicly vindicated. John Moorlach lost with 39 percent of the vote in his bid for County Treasurer Orange County, California. Incumbent Robert Citron won with 61 percent of the vote, despite Moorlach's warnings that Citron was taking excessive risks with the county's investment portfolio. After the election it was revealed that Citron lost about 25 percent of the $2 billion in investments, owing to his incorrect belief that interest rates would go

(continues)

Freedom of Conscience. Individuals have the right to refrain from carrying out orders that violate their moral or religious beliefs. An Oregon court ruled in favor of a woman who had been fired because she insisted on serving as a juror. Her boss had ordered her not to serve, knowing that she could get out of jury duty because of her young children.[36] The woman felt that she had a moral obligation as a citizen to accept jury duty.

Free Speech. Employees and others have the right to criticize the ethics or legality of their employers' actions. This right holds only if the criticisms are conscientious and truthful and do not violate the rights of others within or outside the organization. Virtually all U.S. federal legislation passed concerning occupational safety, pollution, and health contained provisions designed to protect employees who report violations of laws by their employers.[37]

Employees who report unethical or illegal actions of their employers to external stakeholders are often referred to as **whistleblowers.** Michigan passed a Whistleblowers' Protection Act. This act came about because of the actions of a chemical company that sold farmers animal feed accidentally contaminated with a fire retardant. The company compounded its error by issuing a gag order forbidding employees to report this information to government investigators.

Research indicates clearly, however, that the legal approach is inadequate to encourage whistleblowing.[38] It needs to be strongly addressed at the organizational level to increase the probability that employees will report wrongdoing. Patricia Werhane, editor of *Business Ethics Quarterly* comments: "Whistleblowers often are blackballed for not being team players. Companies should be proactive and portray these people as heroes."[39] Whistleblowers have been labeled "snitches," "rats," "stoolies," and "tattle-tales." Many whistleblowers have been harassed, denied raises or promotions, and even dismissed. The actions or judgments of managers often are being questioned by whistleblowers, and the managers retaliate. Unless an employee sues for wrongful dismissal or makes the case public in a dramatic way, the employer usually has the upper hand.[40]

The Conference Board, an industry think tank, has proposed the following elements for a model whistleblowing policy.

- *Shout it from the rooftops.* Aggressively publicize a reporting policy that encourages employees to bring forward valid complaints of wrongdoing.

down despite a steady upward trend. After Moorlach had been proved right, his critics either are declining to comment or are now praising him. Moorlach is being encouraged to run for the State Senate or again for County Treasurer (*Los Angeles Times*, December, 1994, A1, A30).

Ethics
If you know a secret about your employer that, if revealed, would prevent others from getting hurt and yet you do not blow the whistle, are you being ethical?

Ethics
Is whistleblowing by informing a professor of known cheating ethical? Should the professor tell the cheater who the informant was? If cheating occurred, is penalizing the entire class ethical?

Ask Students
Some argue that seniority isn't a relevant principle and that merit is the primary relevant principle. What do you think?

- *Face the fear factor.* Defuse fear by directing complaints to someone outside the whistleblower's chain of command.
- *Get right on it.* An independent group, either in or out of the company, should investigate the complaint immediately.
- *Go public.* Show employees that complaints are taken seriously by publicizing the outcome of investigations whenever possible.[41]

Private Property. The legal and value systems of the United States, Canada, Great Britain, Germany, Japan, and other societies recognize the individual's right to private property. This right allows people to acquire, use, and dispose of shelter and have life's basic necessities. British philosopher John Locke (1632–1704) believed that human beings by nature have rights to life, political equality, and property. The extension of that belief is that the state should not interfere with these rights because of people's partial and biased nature. However, the state needs to protect those rights.[42] Thomas Jefferson and other founding fathers of the United States were influenced by Locke's view of private property:

> *The great and chief end . . . of men uniting into commonwealths, and putting themselves under government, is the preservation of their property: to which in the state of Nature there are many things wanting.*[43]

During the past twenty-five years, other moral rights have served as justification for numerous laws and court rulings that limit, define, and redirect the rights of individuals in the use of their private property. The enactment of zoning codes by many municipalities, which restrict the types of structures that the owner can place on a piece of property, is but one example.

Justice Model

The justice model evaluates decisions and behavior on how equitably they distribute benefits and costs among individuals and groups.[44] It is consistent with Kohlberg's universal principles stage. The concepts of fairness, equity, and impartiality are supported by three implementing principles: the distributive justice principle, the fairness principle, and the natural duty principle.

Distributive Justice Principle. The **distributive justice principle** morally requires that individuals not be treated differently on the basis of arbitrarily defined characteristics. The distributive justice principle holds that (1) individuals who are similar in relevant respects should be treated similarly, and (2) individuals who differ in relevant respects should be treated differently in proportion to the differences between them. On this basis the U.S. Equal Pay Act of 1963 made illegal the payment of different wages to women and men when their jobs require equal skill, effort, and responsibility and are performed under similar working conditions. The act does allow wage differentials if they are based on a seniority system, a merit system, a system that measures earnings by production quantity or quality, or other nonbiasing factors such as market demand.[45] Similarly, Title VII of the U.S. Civil Rights Act of 1964 forbids employers from considering personal characteristics such as race, gender, religion, or national origin in decisions to recruit, hire, promote, or fire employees.

Fairness Principle. The **fairness principle** morally requires employees to support the rules of the organization when two conditions are met: (1) the organization is just (or fair); and (2) employees have voluntarily accepted benefits provided by the organization or have taken advantage of opportunities offered in order to further their own interests.[46] Employees are then expected to follow the organization's rules, even though those rules might restrict their individual choices. Rules requiring employees to be present and on time would be defined as fair because excessive absenteeism and tardiness can negatively affect fellow workers and the organization as a whole.

An organization and its employees have obligations (responsibilities) under the fairness principle. These mutual obligations should satisfy the following criteria.

1. ***They should be a result of voluntary acts.*** Employees cannot be forced to work for a particular organization, and employers cannot arbitrarily be forced to hire a particular person.
2. ***They should be spelled out in clearly stated rules.*** These rules should specify what both the employee and the organization are required to do.
3. ***They are owed between individuals who are cooperating for mutual benefit.*** The employees and managers share a common interest in the survival of the organization.[47]

The following Insight suggests how Marshall Industries, an electronics distributor in El Monte, California, changed its compensation system to address issues of fairness.

Insight

Marshall Industries Compensation System

Marshall Industries was clear about its goals when it overhauled its commission-based compensation system. The old way, says CEO Robert Rodin, pitted people against each other and ultimately hurt business. "It was Detroit vs. Chicago instead of Marshall vs. the world. We used to have people shipping ahead of schedule just to make a number or win a prize. In this day of quality, you can imagine our customers were not too happy getting product early."

The commissions and every other such incentive are gone: no more cars, bicycles, VCRs, or trips to Hawaii for top performers. Instead, Marshall's 600 salespeople, who in 1993 sold $650 million worth of parts, earn salaries plus bonuses. Pay varies according to seniority and responsibility. In addition, everyone stands to receive the same percentage bonus—up to 20 percent of annual salary—based on pretax corporate profits. Though the new pay system is costing Marshall 15 percent more than the old, Rodin says sales in 1994 are up $250 million from 1990 levels.

Selling a skeptical sales force on such a radical idea wasn't easy. "We talked to every single person in this company during the conversion," Rodin says. "It took great patience, and a lot of sleepless nights. I was scared to death about making the changes." Denise Stoll, one of Marshall's stars, says she prefers the predictability of a salary. Under the old commission system, her $26 million in sales in 1993 would have netted her roughly $400,000, well over twice her current salary. But her shipments in 1994, she says, were half what they were in 1993. Stoll, 38, still works the same ten-hour day she always did. With two young children, she finds the current compensation arrangement far less stressful.[48]

Natural Duty Principle. The **natural duty principle** morally requires that decisions and behavior be based on a variety of universal obligations: (1) to help others who are in need or in jeopardy, provided that the help can be given without excessive personal risk or loss; (2) not to harm or injure another; (3) not to cause unnecessary suffering; and (4) to support and comply with just institutions. With respect to the last obligation, justice model advocates tend to frown on employee dismissals inconsistent with the purpose and ideals of the legal system. For example, in one landmark case, the courts supported a Teamster Union member's claim that he was fired for refusing to lie in court about certain activities of the union and a trucking firm.[49]

In this discussion of the justice model, we highlighted only some of the main principles for ethical decision making and behavior. We did not examine the numerous problems that managers and employees face in attempting to apply the justice model in conjunction with the utilitarian and moral rights models when making a decision.

Assessment of Ethical Models

Discussion Question 4
Assume that you have 100 points to allocate among the utilitarian, moral rights, and justice models of ethics. How would you allocate those points to convey the relative emphasis that managers probably place on each model? Explain. How would you allocate those 100 points for nonmanagerial employees? Explain.

Each of the three ethical models—utilitarian, moral rights, and justice—has strengths and weaknesses, which are summarized in Table 7.2. Utilitarian views are most compatible with the goals of efficiency, productivity, and profit maximization, all strong managerial values in Canada and the United States. Managers in many organizations overwhelmingly value this ethical model. The moral rights and justice models emphasize individual rights and the need to distribute benefits and burdens fairly among individuals. If managers relied exclusively on the moral rights and justice approaches, they probably would be less innovative, less receptive to technological change, less willing to take risks, and less efficient. These models give greater weight to employee welfare than to organizational efficiency. At times, for instance, organizational efficiency may require the dismissal, layoff, or early retirement of employees.

As noted previously, individuals who attempt to reach the *ideal* in making ethical decisions face many difficulties.[50] But when used in combination to the greatest extent possible, these three models increase the probability that individuals will make decisions and behavior ethically—and will be so judged by others. Decisions and behavior won't always be absolutely ethical or absolutely unethical. Many decisions fall into a gray area, especially those that are complex, involve many groups and individuals, and are con-

TABLE 7.2
Assessment of Models of Ethics

Model	Strengths	Weaknesses
Utilitarian The greatest good for the greatest number	1. Encourages efficiency and productivity 2. Consistent with profit maximization; is easiest for managers to understand 3. Encourages looking beyond the individual to assess impact of decisions on all who might be affected	1. Virtually impossible to quantify all important variables 2. Can result in biased allocations of resources, particularly when some who are affected lack representation or voice 3. Can result in ignoring rights of some who are affected, to achieve utilitarian outcomes
Moral rights Individual's rights to be protected	1. Protects the individual from injury; consistent with rights to freedom and privacy 2. Consistent with accepted standard of social behavior, independent of outcomes	1. Can imply individualistic selfish behavior that, if misinterpreted, may result in anarchy 2. Can foster personal liberties that may create obstacles to productivity and efficiency
Justice Fair distribution of benefits and burdens	1. Attempts to allocate resources and costs fairly 2. Is the democratic approach 3. Protects the interests of those affected who may be underrepresented or lack power	1. Can encourage a sense of entitlement that reduces risk, innovation, and productivity 2. Can result in reducing rights of some in order to accommodate rules of justice

Source: Adapted by permission of the publisher, from "Organizational Statesmanship and Dirty Politics: Ethical Guidelines for the Organizational Politician," by Velasquez, M., Moberg, D.V., and Cavanagh, G.E., from *Organizational Dynamics*. Autumn 1983.

troversial. The natural tensions created for managers by business ethics have been summed up this way:

> *Rest assured that business ethics exists. But, like all ethics, it is under fire. Because it exists in the sphere of aspiration, where one's reach exceeds one's grasp, it is condemned to play the role of the critic. It lives in the gap between what is and what ought to be. To create awareness of this breach is to create discomfort.*[51]

CONCEPTS OF SOCIAL RESPONSIBILITY

4 Explain how the traditional, stakeholder, and affirmative social responsibility concepts are related to the three models of ethics.

Struggles over various concepts of organizations' social responsibility reflect the conflicts created by the three ethical models just discussed. Managers and other employees have no single, agreed upon concept of social responsibility to guide them. With the diverse values and ethical models of societies around the world, this lack of agreement isn't surprising.

Three commonly accepted views of social responsibility are the traditional, stakeholder, and affirmative concepts. Each places a different relative emphasis on the utilitarian, moral rights, and justice models. Figure 7.4 indicates that the traditional social responsibility concept is based primarily on the utilitarian model. In contrast, the affirmative social responsibility concept draws heavily on the justice and moral rights models. The arrows cutting across the figure roughly indicate the relative emphasis of each concept on each of the ethical models. Note that the degree of an organization's obligations is relatively limited under the traditional social responsibility concept. Obligations broaden under the stakeholder concept and become substantial under the affirmative concept.

Within the United States and Canada, the traditional concept emerged in the 1880s as large corporations developed. The stakeholder concept emerged in the 1930s as large government developed to fight the ravages of the Great Depression. The affirmative concept emerged in the 1960s as social unrest and societal dissatisfaction with business increased.

FIGURE 7.4

Social Responsibility Concepts and Models of Ethics

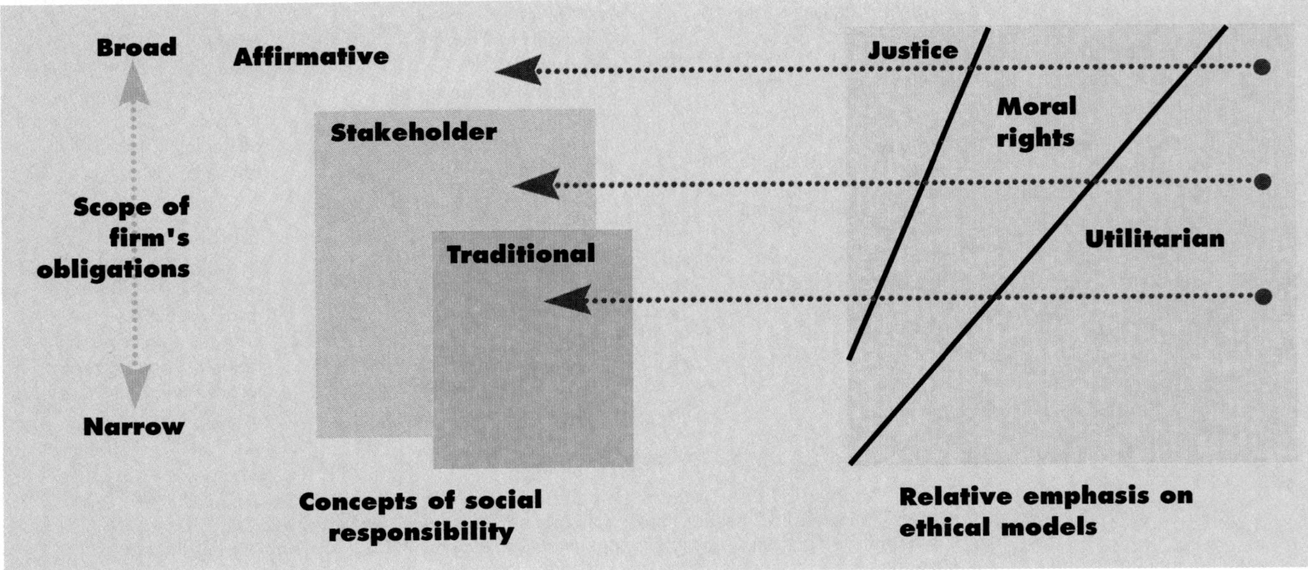

Traditional Social Responsibility

The **traditional social responsibility** concept holds that organizations should serve the interests of shareholders. In other words, the overriding managerial obligation is to maximize shareholders' profits and their long-term interests. Nobel Prize-winning economist Milton Friedman is probably the best-known advocate of the traditional social responsibility concept.[52] Friedman asserts that using resources in ways that do not clearly maximize shareholder interests amounts to spending the owners' money without their consent. In other words, managerial actions should be limited by their companies' economic needs, profit is the bottom line, and managers should not risk profitability by involving their firms in social tasks that aren't legally required of them. This viewpoint holds that government—not business—is the institution best suited for solving social problems. According to Friedman, "there is one and only one social responsibility of business—to use its resources and engage in activities designed to increase its profits so long as it stays within the rules of the game, which is to say, engages in open and free competition without deception or fraud."[53]

Ethics
Is Friedman being ethical? Do you agree with Friedman? Why or why not?

For example, according to Friedman, no firm *unilaterally* should go beyond what the law requires for the sake of the environment. Doing so would only decrease that firm's market share and profits and would do nothing to eliminate the pollution caused by its competitors. They would obtain a greater share of the market and profits because of lower costs and thus lower prices. Friedman contends that the government is responsible for protecting the environment. That is, the government should pass environmental laws and regulations that apply to *all* companies.

Friedman presents two utilitarian arguments for the concept of traditional social responsibility. First, he questions the competence of business leaders (or any other individuals) to determine and directly promote the general good. Second, he argues that the market itself is the best mechanism by which to promote the public good. He believes that firms best promote the general good, not by aiming at it directly, but by pursuing their own individual interests.[54] Thus Friedman's views parallel those of Adam Smith. Although it appears to be highly valued among many executives and shareholders, the traditional concept receives less support among the general public. Individuals and stakeholders often challenge management's rights under the traditional social responsibility concept, especially the rights to discipline and fire employees.[55]

Stakeholder Social Responsibility

The **stakeholder social responsibility** concept holds that managers and other employees have obligations to identifiable groups that are affected by or can affect the achievement of an organization's goals.[56] As indicated in Figure 7.4, the scope of stakeholder obligations is greater than with traditional social responsibility. **Stakeholders** are groups having potential or real power to influence an organization's decisions and actions. Stakeholders commonly include shareholders, customers, competitors, government agencies, unions, employees, debt holders (e.g., banks and pension funds), trade associations, suppliers, and consumer groups.

Under the stakeholder concept, the management of a firm deciding to close down a manufacturing plant should inform the employees and the community well in advance of the sixty days required by U.S. law. Also, the firm should expend resources to reduce both the short-term and long-term adverse impacts on these stakeholders. The vast majority of managers who accept the stakeholder concept probably endorse Peter Drucker's interpretation of a firm's obligation:

Discussion Question 5
What arguments support Peter Drucker's statement that the first "social responsibility" of business is to make enough profit to defray future costs? What arguments oppose that statement?

> *The first "social responsibility" of business is to make enough profit to cover the costs of the future. If this "social responsibility" is not met, no other "social responsibility" can be met. Decaying businesses in a decaying economy are unlikely to be good neighbors, good employers, or "socially responsible" in any way. When the demand for capital grows rapidly, surplus business revenues available for noneconomic purposes, especially for "philanthropy," cannot possibly go up. They are almost certain to shrink.*[57]

Teaching Tip
Have students prepare a list of local organizations they would like to work for after graduation. Form groups of 5 to 8 students. Assign each group to do a social audit of one of those organizations. Have the groups make an oral presentation next week.

Three primary reasons often are suggested for embracing the stakeholder social responsibility concept: (1) enlightened self-interest, (2) sound investment, and (3) interference avoidance.[58] Under the rationale of enlightened self-interest, management uses social responsibility to justify numerous decisions and actions. The general idea is that a better society creates a better environment for business. Under the rationale of sound investment, management believes that social responsibility has a positive effect on a company's net worth. Socially responsible firms claim that their stocks sell at higher prices than those of less socially responsible firms. Higher stock prices, in turn, reduce the cost (interest rate) of capital and increase earnings. As you might expect, this view is highly controversial.[59] Under the rationale of interference avoidance, management aims to minimize control of company decisions by powerful stakeholders, such as government agencies and pressure groups. Industry self-regulation often is justified on the basis of interference avoidance.

Although there is virtually no research on the subject, we suspect that the stakeholder concept is the concept most widely supported by the general public and many managers. More and more organizations are likely to apply the stakeholder concept proactively in the future when considering complex issues and alternative courses of action. The following Quality Insight reviews AT&T's application of the stakeholder concept in improving environmental quality. It illustrates that multiple stakeholders—environmental groups, governmental agencies, the general public, and shareholders—can be winners through lower costs.

Quality *Insight*

AT&T Goes Green

American Telephone & Telegraph (AT&T) established goals for reducing air emissions, CFCs, solid waste, and hazardous waste in 1990. Under the direction of David R. Chittick, AT&T's vice-president of environment and safety, the company has either surpassed its goals or been ahead of schedule in meeting them. To engineer ozone-depleting emissions out of its operations, AT&T invested $25 million to develop an array of alternative technologies. One, called low solids spray fluxer, eliminates the need for CFC solvents to clean excess flux from electronic circuit boards. AT&T is now selling this technology to some twenty-five other companies, among them IBM. AT&T even gives its ideas away at times. Engineers developed an alternative for 1,1,1-tricholroethane, another ozone-depleting solvent used to clean circuit boards. AT&T managed to eliminate virtually all its ozone-depleting substances a year and a half before the company's goal, and 2fi years ahead of the worldwide ban.

Now AT&T doesn't have to worry about the new U.S. law that requires companies to put warning labels on all goods that contain or are manufactured with ozone-depleting substances. The company figures that the cost of tracking and labeling all the tiny components and switching systems that it once manufactured with CFCs would add up to hundreds of thousands of dollars. The early phaseout also will save AT&T $25 million annually in supply costs because taxes on CFCs have helped boost its price from about $0.80 per pound in 1986 to more than $11 per pound in 1993. The substitutes developed for CFCs average $0.50 per pound.

In addition, AT&T embraced total quality management (TQM) principles to solve the universal office pollution problem of too much paper. First, the company established a corporate paper reduction goal of 15 percent by 1995; then it created a corporate TQM team to figure out how to meet it. Following classic TQM techniques, the team identified AT&T's heaviest paper users, called "fat rabbits." The fat rabbits in turn formed TQM teams to help meet the companywide goal. The internal information management unit, fat bunny No. 2 behind copying centers, accounted for about a quarter of AT&T's total paper use for such things as marketing and financial reports. The department's TQM teams suggested simple ways to decrease paper consumption, such as eliminating cover pages and using electronic rather than printed media. The department was consuming 22 percent less paper within a year.[60]

Affirmative Social Responsibility

The **affirmative social responsibility** concept holds that managers and other employees are obligated to (1) avoid problems by anticipating changes in their environment, rather than simply reacting to them; (2) blend the organization's goals with those of stakeholders and the general public; and (3) take concrete, positive steps to promote the mutual interests of the organization, its stakeholders, and the general public.[61]

As noted earlier, this concept draws heavily on the justice and moral rights ethical models. If it had been operating under affirmative social responsibility, McDonald's would have initiated changes in cooking ingredients and posted nutritional information long before external pressures forced it to make changes or face the possibility of lawsuits, new legislation, and the loss of business. It might even have marketed healthier menu items and launched a campaign to convince customers to eat its nutritionally sound foods.[62]

Obligations. Affirmative social responsibility is the most difficult, complex, and expensive concept for organizations to implement. It includes the core obligations of the stakeholders concept, all of which suggest the need for ongoing communication among managers, stakeholders, and the general public. The following are five categories of obligations and examples of actions under affirmative social responsibility.[63]

1. ***Broader Performance Criteria.*** Managers and other employees must consider and accept broader criteria for measuring the organization's performance and social role than those required by law and the marketplace. Anita Roddick is the founder and CEO of The Body Shop. It has grown from one outlet in Brighton, England, in 1976 to outlets in the United Kingdom, Canada, United States, and numerous other countries. These shops sell only skin-, body-, and hair-care products that are biodegradable and environmentally safe. The firm actively promotes recycling. It even pays employees while they donate half a day a week to a social cause of their choice. Roddick comments: "The purpose of business isn't just to generate profits, to create an ever-larger empire. It's to have the power to affect social change, to help make the world a better place."[64]

Anita Roddick is founder and CEO of The Body Shop, which sells only skin-, body-, and hair-care products that are biodegradable and environmentally safe. Roddick's philosophy is that profits aren't everything; a business also can contribute to "making the world a better place."

2. ***Ethical Norms.*** Managers and other employees must take definite stands on issues of public concern. They must advocate ethical norms for all in the organization, the industry, and business in general. These ethical norms are advocated even when they seem detrimental to the immediate profits of the organization or are contrary to prevailing industry practices. Roddick, of The Body Shop, makes it a point not to use styrofoam and other chlorofluorocarbon-based packing material. The Body Shop also avoids the use of animal-derived products and wood from tropical rain forests. The company contributes hundreds of thousands of dollars a year to environmental causes, ranging from Greenpeace to Friends of the Earth.
3. ***Operating Strategy.*** Managers and other employees should maintain or improve the current standards of the physical and social environment. Organizations must compensate victims of pollution and other organization-related hazards, even in the absence of clearly established legal grounds. Managers and other employees need to evaluate possible negative effects of the organization's plan on other stakeholders and then attempt to eliminate or substantially reduce such negative effects prior to implementing the plan. Again, at The Body Shop, products are packaged in simple plastic containers designed for refill. Purchases go into paper sacks bearing a variety of environmental messages.
4. ***Response to Social Pressures.*** Managers and other employees should accept responsibility for solving current problems. They need to be willing to discuss activities with outside groups and make information freely available to them. They also need to be receptive to formal and informal inputs from outside stakeholders in decision making.
5. ***Legislative and Political Activities.*** Managers must show a willingness to work with outside stakeholders for enactment of, for example, environmental protection laws. They must promote honesty and openness in government and in their own organization's lobbying activities.

Teaching Tip
"The long-term value of conducting business in a socially responsible manner far outweighs short-term costs." Ask students to discuss the implications of this statement for businesses today.

Social Audit. An organization run under the stakeholder or affirmative social responsibility concepts may undertake a social audit. A **social audit** is an attempt to identify, measure, evaluate, report on, and monitor the effects the organization is having on its stakeholders and society as a whole—information not covered in traditional financial reports.[65] In contrast to a financial audit, a social audit focuses on social actions rather than fiscal accountability. A social audit measures achievement under the affirmative social responsibility concept. Conducting such an audit is typically viewed as an optional activity under the stakeholder concept. A few of the firms that undertake social audits include AT&T, The Body Shop, McDonald's, and Johnson & Johnson.

The obligations identified under the affirmative social responsibility concept could provide a framework for the development of a social audit. Objective narrative statements should be used when quantitative measurements are unavailable. The social audit should provide a reasonable profile of an organization's performance in environmental, cultural, and economic areas without having to put a dollar sign on every activity and achievement. Although there will always be measurement problems, an organization can develop a reasonable profile and assessment of its level of social responsibility.

Some large organizations report their social responsibility accomplishments in their annual reports, which are distributed to stakeholders—especially to shareholders, in the case of corporations. However, critics have suggested that relatively few of these corporate reports rate very high in terms of the desired criteria and in terms of the expectations raised by research. They claim that much of what is reported is selective and that some of it is self-serving.[66] Table 7.3 provides an example of the environmental policies and actions that might be reflected in a social audit under the affirmative social responsibility concept.

The affirmative social responsibility concept isn't widely accepted or practiced by business organizations in the United States, Canada, and most other countries. Societal pressures for adoption of the stakeholder social responsibility concept seem to be much stronger than pressures for the affirmative concept. In fact, with increasing pressures

TABLE 7.3

Examples of Affirmative Environmental Policies and Actions

Area	Policies and Actions
Accidents	• Openly disclose accidents. • Use same safety standards worldwide. • Exhibit extra cooperative attitudes in case of accidents. • Establish a crisis management system.
Routine pollution	• Provide incentives within and outside firm to reduce pollution. • Set up "green teams" to involve employees and external stakeholders.
Waste disposal	• Actively minimize waste. • Take back customers' waste. • Offer waste disposal services.
Products	• Seek out and use environmentally safer substitutes. • Actively prevent abuse of products. • Impose own higher standards on suppliers.
Packaging	• Minimize unnecessary packaging. • Take packaging back from customers. • Use environmentally safe packaging.

Source: Adapted from Corbett, C.J., and Van Wassenhove, L.N. The green fee: Internalizing and operationalizing environmental issues. *California Management Review,* Fall 1993, 116–135.

Discussion Question 6
Which of the social responsibility concepts—traditional, stakeholder, and affirmative—do most employees likely favor for their organizations? Explain.

from domestic and global competition, expectations that organizations apply the affirmative concepts' broader set of organizational obligations to their decisions and actions may diminish. Further, there seems to be no reason to expect this situation to change in the near future. However, one thing is certain: All significant managerial and employee decisions and behavior need to be assessed continually in terms of ethics and social responsibility.

CHAPTER SUMMARY

1 ***State the importance of ethics for organizations and their employees.***
An explicit concern with ethical issues and guidelines represents a positive strategy to minimize ethical problems and to react quickly and effectively when they do occur. Stakeholders, such as customers, are increasingly holding organizations responsible for ethical decision making and conduct. However, as this chapter revealed, there are conflicting perspectives on what being *ethical* and *socially responsible* means.

2 ***Describe how the societal, legal, organizational, and individual levels of ethics influence decisions and behavior.***
The ethics of any decision or behavior can rarely be understood by looking at a single ethical level. The potential influences of all four levels of an ethical system must be considered. The societal level includes shared values and how they affect individuals' and groups' standards for acceptable behavior. The legal level includes the enactment of new laws and interpretation of current laws that define ethical behavior. The organizational level includes decisions and actions going beyond those mandated by law that demonstrate the ethical standards of the organization. The individual level includes values and behavior that reflect a person's stage of moral development: obedience and punishment, instrumental, interpersonal, law and order, social contract, or universal principles.

3 ***Discuss the standards and principles of the utilitarian, moral rights, and justice models of ethics.***

Managers and other employees commonly rely on one or some combination of three ethical models to guide decision making and behavior. The utilitarian model focuses on actions rather than motives and has two branches: act utilitarianism and rule utilitarianism. The moral rights model upholds the six fundamental rights to life and safety, truthfulness, privacy, freedom of conscience, free speech, and private property. The justice model advocates impartial, equitable distribution of benefits and costs among individuals and groups, according to three principles: distributive justice, fairness, and natural duty.

4 ***Explain how the traditional, stakeholder, and affirmative social responsibility concepts are related to the three models of ethics.***

The diverse values and ethical approaches prevalent in advanced economies have given rise to three different concepts of an organization's social responsibility. The traditional concept is based primarily on the utilitarian ethical approach. Management simply seeks to maximize profits, and the focus of the organization's social responsibilities is narrow. The stakeholder concept broadens the focus by reflecting to some extent the moral rights and justice models of ethics. Managers and other employees have obligations to stakeholders of the organization. The affirmative concept draws heavily on the moral rights and justice models of ethics. It obligates the organization and its employees to the broadest focus of social responsibility: utilizing organizational resources to anticipate and meet stakeholders' needs.

QUESTIONS FOR DISCUSSION

1. What is the difference between judging a decision from an individual level and a legal level in a system of ethics?
2. Can the ethical climate of an organization be improved? If so, how?
3. What percentage of the adult population (eighteen years old and older) do you estimate is at each of Kohlberg's stages of moral development? What is the basis for your estimate?
4. Assume that you have 100 points to allocate among the utilitarian, moral rights, and justice models of ethics. How would you allocate those points to convey the relative emphasis that managers probably place on each model? Explain. How would you allocate those 100 points for nonmanagerial employees? Explain.
5. What arguments support Peter Drucker's statement that the first "social responsibility" of business is to make enough profit to defray future costs? What arguments oppose that statement?
6. Which of the social responsibility concepts—traditional, stakeholder, and affirmative—do most employees likely favor for their organizations? Explain.

FROM WHERE YOU SIT

1. Do you prefer the utilitarian model or the moral rights model as a guide for decisions and behavior? Explain. What personal decisions and actions within the past three months can you point to that illustrate your personal preference?
2. What personal and organizational factors would you consider in deciding to engage in whistleblowing?
3. From your college booklet on rules and regulations for students, identify, if possible, one example of each model of ethics.
4. Several years ago *Time* magazine expressed this bottom-line view of the U.S. ethical climate: "Large sections of the nation's ethical roofing have been sagging badly,

from the White House to churches, schools, industries, medical centers, law firms and stock brokerages—pressing down on the institutions and enterprises that make up the body and blood of America."[67] Based on what you learned in this chapter, present a case in support of this view and in opposition to it. Do you personally agree or disagree with this view? Explain.

5. Think of the last significant disagreement that you had with a manager, co-worker, friend, or family member. What ethical concepts and issues were implicit or explicit in this conflict? How did they influence the conversation and outcome?

SKILL-BUILDING EXERCISE

What Is Your Diagnosis?[68]

Scenario 1: The U.S. Patent Office recently issued a patent to Tiger Automotive for a device that has been proven to increase the average car's gas mileage by 45 percent. Given that Tiger is protected from direct competition by this patent, it has decided to price the new product at $45 to auto parts dealers. The device costs less that $1 to produce and distribute.

How would you rate this action on the following five-point scale?

1	2	3	4	5
Strongly Disapprove	**Disapprove**	**Neutral**	**Approve**	**Strongly Approve**

What ethical and social responsibility concepts are the basis of your rating for scenario 1?

Scenario 2: A friend of yours is the president of a company in a highly competitive industry. Your friend learns that a competitor has made an important scientific discovery that will give the competitor an advantage and will substantially reduce (but not eliminate) the profits of your friend's company for about a year. Your friend learns that there is a possibility of hiring one of this competitor's employees who knows the details of the discovery and proceeds to do so.

How would you rate this action on the following five-point scale?

1	2	3	4	5
Strongly Disapprove	**Disapprove**	**Neutral**	**Approve**	**Strongly Approve**

What ethical and social responsibility concepts are the basis of your rating for scenario 2?

Scenario 3: Jack Ward works in product development for an auto parts contractor. Last summer Ward's firm won a big contract to manufacture transaxles for use in a new line of front-wheel-drive cars to be introduced by a major auto manufacturer in the near future. Winning the contract was very important to the firm. Just before getting the contract, the firm had scheduled half its employees, including Ward, for an indefinite layoff.

Final testing of the assemblies ended last Friday, and the first shipments are scheduled to be made in three weeks. The manufacturer's specifications call for the transaxle to carry 30 percent more than its rated capacity without failing. While examining the test reports, Ward discovers that the transaxle tended to fail when loaded to more than 20 percent over rated capacity and subjected to strong torsion forces. Such a condition could occur with a heavily loaded car braking hard for a curve while going down a mountain road. The consequences would be disastrous. Ward shows the test results to his supervisor and the company president, who both indicate that they are aware of the problem but have decided to ignore the report. Chances of transaxle failure in ordinary driving are low, and there isn't enough time to redesign the assembly. If the company doesn't deliver the assemblies on time, it will lose the contract. Ward decides not to show the test results to the auto manufacturer.

How would you rate this action on the following five-point scale for scenario 3?

1	2	3	4	5
Strongly Disapprove	**Disapprove**	**Neutral**	**Approve**	**Strongly Approve**

What ethical and social responsibility concepts serve as the basis of your rating?

Interpretations

Scenario 1: *Strongly disapprove or disapprove*—reflects the justice model and affirmative social responsibility concept. *Strongly approve or approve*—reflects the utilitarian ethical model and traditional social responsibility concept. *Neutral*—reflects no preference.

Scenario 2: *Strongly disapprove or disapprove*—reflects the moral rights model of ethics and the stakeholder or affirmative social responsibility concepts. *Strongly approve or approve*—reflects the utilitarian model of ethics (especially act utilitarianism) and the traditional social responsibility concept. *Neutral*—reflects no preference.

Scenario 3: *Strongly disapprove or disapprove*—could reflect the utilitarian, moral rights, or justice model of ethics; could reflect the traditional social responsibility concept and most certainly the stakeholder or affirmative concept. *Strongly approve or approve*—might reflect rule utilitarianism (Ward has no responsibility beyond telling his supervisor or the president) or act utilitarianism (the risk of death or injury is too low to hold up the sale), along with a minimal form of the traditional social responsibility concept. *Neutral*—reflects no preference.

CRITICAL THINKING CASE

Durable Vehicle Industries[69]

Durable Vehicle Industries (DVI), a subsidiary of Mogul Corporation, is the world's leading manufacturer of tow and hauling vehicles and other equipment used at airport facilities to handle luggage and move airplanes. Although DVI has a superb reputation for quality and safety, it has suffered revenue declines of 20 and 35 percent in the last two years. The reason is sagging demand and new competition from Niko, an aggressive Japanese company. Last year, revenues were at a ten-year low of $90 million, and the company lost $11 million. The company's management is committed to a budget requiring a 10 percent increase in revenue and a 15 percent decrease in costs.

Allen Brent, DVI's plant manager, instructed Jermaine Smoot, his assistant, to "streamline" the manufacturing process of its basic Model 1200 tow vehicle by eliminating certain built-in safety features and several quality control procedures. The vehicle will otherwise be the same, but it will have different graphics and will be called the "Model 1250." It will be described in the company literature only as the "new, updated replacement of the 1200 series."

Smoot is a 19-year veteran of the company (she is eligible for a generous pension in another year). She tells Brent: "Our customers expect a certain kind of product from DVI and, in effect, they will be 'defrauded' by substituting the new, less safe and less durable version, especially if they are not told that the company has changed its specifications. In addition, 30 percent of our business is with Airco, and the old specs are part of the contracts. Besides, we have always preached quality and pride to our work force; this will make us look like hypocrites."

Brent responds: "Look, lots of jobs depend on our ability to be creative, flexible, and aggressive. We must cut costs and that means we have to reexamine our assumptions. Our new '1250' series will still be better and safer than Niko's model and it's what the market wants. Don't come at me with unrealistic and sanctimonious talk about tradition and quality. I'm as concerned with this company and its reputation as you are. We won't jeopardize the essential quality of the product; we're just removing some frills in tough times. If you can't do what is necessary, I'll find someone who can." Smoot is convinced that Brent's policies will seriously compromise the quality and the safety of the product and undermine morale and a concern for quality in other aspects of manufacturing.

Questions

1. What ethical concepts are involved in this case?
2. Who are DVI's stakeholders and how are they likely to view this situation?
3. What are Smoot's options? What are the strengths and weaknesses of each option?
4. What should Smoot do? Why?

VIDEO CASE

The Body Shop: Trade Not Aid

In less than a generation, since opening the first Body Shop in 1976, Anita and Gordon Roddick have build the company into a global brand by claiming to sell natural, environmentally friendly cosmetics. The company has approximately 1,100 franchised shops in forty-five countries. They stocked their first store, in Brighton, England, with fifteen different products, all manufactured by third parties. In 1983, The Body Shop began making some of its own products and today makes a broad line of naturally based skin and hair care products.

From its humble beginnings, the company has grown rapidly and received numerous awards. Anita Roddick was chosen Businesswoman-of-the-Year in 1985. The Body Shop was chosen Company-of-the-Year in 1987 and Retailer-of-the-Year in 1989, and it received the Queen's Award for Export in 1990.

With company sales in excess of $650 million annually, The Body Shop has been known as environmentally oriented from its conception. The company uses a simple approach, selling most products in reusable bottles along with refill services for many of its high-volume product lines. It has supported recycling efforts with notices on all its packages. The company has opposed animal testing, embraced fair trading practices with indigenous groups, and encouraged liberal activism among its employees and franchisees. One example of the firm's applying its principles is a dusty village in northeast Mexico, where Indians are exporting loofahs (sponges) for The Body Shop.

Direct trading links are set up with producer communities in less-developed countries so that social development and environmental protection go hand in hand. The Body Shop philosophy is not to change the culture but rather the environment. This philosophy supports the belief that if communities can finance their economic and social development through fair-trade prices obtained through their own efforts, donor agencies can direct their dollars toward more humanitarian ends.

The more ambitious a company's social agenda, the more elusive success may be. The Body Shop considers "changing the world" its charter. However, 1994 saw a storm in a bubble bath when bad publicity knocked 15 percent off Body Shop's share price. Attacks appeared in *Business Ethics,* a Minneapolis magazine, with critics stating that the company policy of not selling products that have been tested on animals is less firm than that of some of its competitors. Further, critics complain that The Body Shop's "trade not aid" scheme of sourcing from indigenous people accounts for less sales than it claims. Some claim that The Body Shop played down the scale of shampoo spills at an American factory and that the company mistreated American franchisees. The Body Shop claims to have been the victim of an "obsessive campaign of vilification" by Jon Entine, an American journalist. After Entine's alligations, 95 percent of the U.S. franchisees signed a letter repudiating the accusations.

While leftists protest that the company has done too little, those on the right complain that the company proselytizes too much. The Roddicks believe that their business must live with admirable goals year after year and settle for only incremental success. Instead of declaring the elimination of third-world poverty a corporate goal, the goal may be stated as ". . .to make a difference in the lives of a few hundred people at a time." The Roddicks believe that, when a business is pledged to profound social change, it will either (a) fail or (b) not fail entirely—it never flat-out succeeds.

Enemies have failed to prove that The Body Shop engages in mendacious profiteering. The company claims that the accusations haven't perturbed customers. Although the company was vindicated by the courts in a libel case it litigated in 1994, Roddick states, "You have to expect you'll be held up for rigorous examination. This is not for the chickenhearted."[70]

Questions

1. Explain the benefits of "trade not aid."
2. A potentially large threat to The Body Shop is from competitors that have entered the natural products market. In the United States alone, The Body Shop—whose offerings include the likes of Peppermint Foot Lotion, Passion Fruit skin cleansers, and White Musk Shower Gel—estimates that at least twenty stores have copied its products and shop format. The difficulty is that natural products can't be patented. Ethically speaking, should other firms be able to copy The Body Shop's products and shop format?
3. Do consumers really care about environmental issues when they purchase a product such as a skin cleanser? Why or why not?

Chapter *8*

Fundamentals of Decision Making

Learning *Objectives*

After studying this chapter, you should be able to:

1. Define decision making.
2. State four preconditions for meaningful decision making.
3. Explain the conditions of certainty, risk, and uncertainty under which decisions are made.
4. Describe a framework for understanding the three primary categories of decisions.
5. Apply goals to decision making.
6. Describe the rational, bounded rationality, and political models of decision making.

Chapter *Outline*

Preview *Insight*

Motel Bandits

Tom Shaffer, the manager of a local Holiday Inn, heard a news story that's every motel manager's nightmare come true: A violent criminal gang, dubbed by the media "the Motel Bandits," was working its way through his metropolitan area. The thieves' mode of operation involved assaulting and robbing motel guests as they entered or left their rooms.

The local sheriff soon contacted Shaffer to ask if he had made any special arrangements for security. The sheriff even offered to work as a security guard when off duty, a security measure that the local motel had used in the past. Shaffer wasn't authorized to make this decision alone and phoned his supervisor, Barbara Abelson. After reviewing his request, Abelson expressed concerns about cost, public perception, and corporate policy.

For the past year this motel had barely been breaking even. Any additional expenditures would push it into the red. Twenty-four-hour security, even with the employment of the off-duty sheriff, would cost about $400 a day. Shaffer and Abelson discussed fencing the property, but that would cost $5,500, clearly out of the question as far as Abelson was concerned. Moreover, Holiday Inn had been promoting a family image, Abelson was concerned about making the motel look and feel like an armed camp.

Abelson was familiar with Holiday Inn's corporate loss-prevention manual, which encourages additional security when a risk is perceived. However, no one in the organization had emphasized this policy. Instead, her supervisor had stressed meeting quarterly budget projections.

The bottom line from Abelson's viewpoint was that no one at Holiday Inn had ever been promoted for making a motel safer—just for making it more profitable. She decided to live with the risk and instructed Shaffer not to provide any extra security measures. She feared the career risk of an operating loss, created by the additional costs of providing security, more than she feared the security risk. She thought that additional security probably wouldn't stop the bandits anyway.[1]

The following evening Bob and Elaine Smith checked into Shaffer's Holiday Inn. As they entered their room, two armed men forced their way in and beat, bound, and gagged Bob. The men pushed Elaine down and demanded her money and jewelry. When she told them that her wedding ring wouldn't come off, one of the men put a gun to her head and threatened to "blow her brains out." She finally removed the ring and gave it to them. They then bound, beat, and gagged her before fleeing. The Smiths sued Holiday Inn. The jury returned verdicts in their favor, finding that the criminal acts were reasonably foreseeable by Holiday Inn's managers. The jury found the defendants, including Holiday Inn, negligent in not providing adequate security. The jury concluded that this negligence caused the Smiths' injuries and awarded Elaine $400,000 and Bob $100,000 in compensatory damages. An appellate court upheld the awards.[2]

1

Define decision making.

WHAT IS DECISION MAKING?

Under less dramatic conditions, managers and other employees make decisions every day as Barbara Abelson did, using a process that contains the same basic elements. They define the problem (e.g., the risk of robbery), gather information (e.g., asking Shaffer about the robbers' methods), identify and assess the alternatives (e.g., hire guards, fence the motel, do both, or do nothing), and decide what to do. Abelson's decision was to do nothing other than to encourage employees to "keep their eyes out" for individuals on the motel property who didn't appear to be motel guests. She was under heavy pressure to move the motel into a stronger financial position and let that be the determining factor in her decision. Fortunately, relatively few individuals face outcomes as extreme as the one in this case when they make decisions on the job, but most do encounter a wide range of decision-making situations.

Teaching Tip
Bring in a copy of yesterday's *Wall Street Journal* and select an example of flawed decision making. Tell students how training in decision making could have averted the error.

In this chapter, we present the fundamentals of **decision making,** which include defining problems, gathering information, generating alternatives, and choosing a course of action. We demonstrate how managers and other employees can systematically approach various types of decisions based on the nature of problem to be solved, the possible solutions available, and the degree of risk involved.

Recall that successful management involves the meshing of the planning, organizing, leading, and controlling functions to achieve organizational goals. Issues of ethics and social responsibility are embedded in these functions and in fundamental decision-making processes. In turn, decision-making processes are basic to all managerial functions. Sometimes those functions are implemented with the assistance of decision-making aids (Chapter 9) that can be adapted to a variety of situations.

2

State four preconditions for meaningful decision making.

PRECONDITIONS FOR DECISION MAKING

The fundamentals of decision making come into play whenever anyone in an organization plans, organizes, leads, or controls. However, certain preconditions need to exist before a decision-making process can be called complete. Those preconditions are met if all four of the following questions can be answered with a *yes*.[3]

1. ***Is there a gap (or a difference) between the present situation and desired goals?*** At first this gap may be only a vague sense of dissatisfaction—vague, but still worth paying attention to—or the gap may be obvious or multiple gaps may surface, as in the Preview Insight. The situation in that case was increased risk created by the violent criminal gang. Initially, the desired goals were customer safety, profitability, and maintaining the Holiday Inn image (one gap). However, Barbara Abelson soon saw another gap being created—between her current position and the situation's potential effect on her desired career progress.
2. ***Is the decision maker aware of the significance of the gap?*** Abelson seemed to be aware of the potential significance of the gap. In the end, though, she rationalized that additional security would not be effective in stopping the gang if it did strike.
3. ***Is the decision maker motivated to act to close the gap?*** Abelson was not motivated to act on the gap between the normal risk for customer safety and the increased risk created by the gang's activities. Instead, she concluded that her career would be adversely affected by a strong response to provide more security, further weakening the inn's shaky financial position.
4. ***Does the decision maker have the resources (e.g., ability and money) to act to close the gap?*** Abelson had the resources to close the gap of increased safety risk. However, she wasn't motivated to do so because of the perceived risks to profitability and her career.

Ask Students
What type of training (if any) might help managers fulfill the preconditions for decision making?

Barbara Abelson implicitly answered *yes* to questions 1, 2, and 4 but answered *no* to question 3. Because of her misplaced emphasis on career concerns, she wasn't motivated to act on the key gap in the case—increased risk to customer safety.

Most individuals have to assess these four preconditions in a variety of situations daily. They often make these assessments so fast that they may not be consciously aware of doing so. The relative ease or difficulty of analyzing these preconditions varies with the conditions involved in the decision-making situation.

3

Explain the conditions of certainty, risk, and uncertainty under which decisions are made.

CONDITIONS UNDER WHICH DECISIONS ARE MADE

The conditions under which individuals in an organization make decisions reflect the environmental forces (developments and events) that those individuals cannot control but that may in the future influence the outcomes of their decisions.[4] The discussion of general and global environmental forces in Chapters 3 and 4 introduced many of the forces that managers and other employees often confront. These forces can range from new technologies or the entrance of new competitors into a market to new laws or political turmoil. Besides attempting to identify and measure the magnitude of these forces, managers must estimate their potential impact. For example, in early 1994, hardly anyone in the world recognized the possibility that more than a million people would flee Rwanda for Zaire and exert enormous pressures on Zaire's economy and the resources of international relief agencies.

Ask Students
What important current events could not have been easily foreseen and accounted for in the decision-making process.

The impact of such events always is felt in the future, either sooner or later. Managers and others involved in forecasting and planning may be hard-pressed to identify those events and their impacts, especially when they may not occur until years later. More often than not, people have to base their decisions on limited, available information. Hence the amount and accuracy of information and the level of individuals' conceptual skills (see Chapter 1) are crucial to sound decision making.

We can broadly classify the conditions under which decisions are made as certainty, risk, and uncertainty.[5] Figure 8.1 shows these conditions as a continuum. When individuals can identify developments and events and their potential impact with great confidence, they make decisions under the condition of certainty. As information dwindles and becomes ambiguous, the condition of risk enters into decision making. Individuals begin to base their decisions on either objective (clear) or subjective probabilities (intuition and judgment). The condition of uncertainty occurs when individuals have little or no information about developments and events on which to base a decision. Because of that uncertainty, the decision makers may be able to make only a reasonable guess rather than an informed decision.

Certainty

Certainty is the condition under which individuals are fully informed about a problem, alternative solutions are obvious, and the likely results of each solution are clear. Under the condition of certainty, people can at least anticipate (if not control) events and their outcomes. This condition means that both the problem and alternative solutions are known and well defined. Once an individual identifies alternative solutions and their expected results, making the decision is relatively easy. The decision maker simply chooses the solution with the best potential outcome. For example, a purchasing agent for a printer is expected to order standard-grade paper from the supplier who offers the lowest price and the best service. Of course, the decision-making process usually isn't that simple. A problem may have many possible solutions, and calculating the expected outcomes for all of them might be extremely time-consuming and expensive.

Ask Students
Did you make a decision earlier today that you are certain will lead to an occurrence after this class is over? (Example: You are certain you will find your car where you parked it.)

Decision making under the condition of certainty is the exception for most managers and other professionals. However, first-line managers make day-to-day decisions under conditions of or near certainty. For example, a tight production schedule may cause a first-line manager to ask ten employees to work four hours of overtime. The

FIGURE 8.1

Conditions Under Which Decisions Are Made

Certainty ◀·· **Risk** ··▶ **Uncertainty**

Objective probabilities | Subjective probabilities

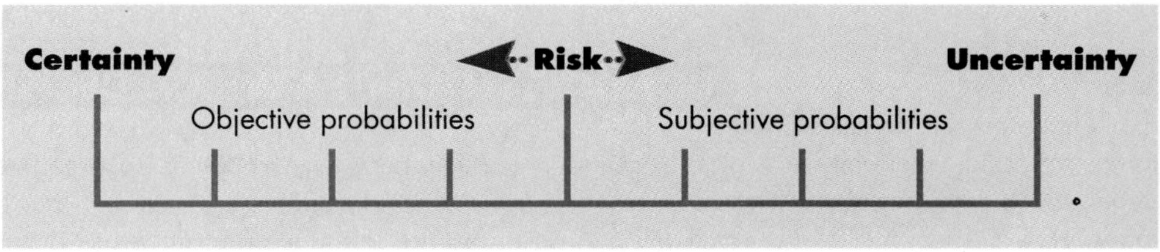

manager can determine the cost of the overtime with certainty. The manager also can anticipate with near certainty the number of additional units that will be produced. Thus the labor costs for the extra units can be figured with near certainty before the overtime is scheduled.

Risk

Real-World Example
Estimates of risk can be affected by cultural factors. For example, Americans are accustomed to taking risks; the British aren't.

Ask Students
Have you recently made a decision under the condition of risk? If so describe it and its outcome.

Risk is the condition under which individuals can define a problem, specify the probability of certain events, identify alternative solutions, and state the probability of each solution leading to the desired results.[6] Risk generally means that the problem and the alternative solutions fall somewhere between the extremes of being known and well defined and being unusual and ambiguous.

Probability is the percentage of times that a specific outcome would occur if an individual were to make a particular decision a large number of times. The most commonly used example of probability is that of tossing a coin: With enough tosses of the coin, heads will show up 50 percent of the time and tails the other 50 percent. Another example is the federal regulation that requires all new cars to be equipped with dual air bags by 1997 to protect the driver and the front-seat passenger. The National Highway Traffic Safety Administration concluded that the probability of a seat-belted driver's death in an accident is reduced by 50 percent in a car equipped with a driver's-side air bag. In contrast, the probability of death in an accident for a seat-belted driver with no air bag is reduced by 45 percent.[7]

The amount and quality of information available to an individual about the relevant decision-making condition can vary widely—as can the individual's estimates of risk. The type, amount, and reliability of information influence the level of risk and whether the decision maker can use objective or subjective probability in estimating the outcome (see Figure 8.1).

Discussion Question 2
Identify three issues or problems that are likely to involve the use of objective probabilities by a decision maker. Explain the basis for your selection.

Objective Probability. The likelihood that a specific outcome will occur, based on hard facts and numbers, is known as **objective probability.** Sometimes an individual can determine the likely outcome of a decision by examining past records. For example, although life insurance companies can't determine the year in which each policyholder will die, they can calculate objective probabilities that specific numbers of policyholders, in various age categories, will die in a particular year. These objective probabilities are based on the expectation that past death rates will be repeated in the future.

Discussion Question 3
Identify three issues or problems that are likely to involve the use of subjective probabilities by a decision maker. Explain the basis for your selection.

Real World Example
In Miami, drivers run red lights and don't stop after being involved in traffic accidents. The police, district attorneys, and judges often let these people break the law because they are otherwise law-abiding citizens scared by a wave of car jackings (*Houston Chronicle*, October 2, 1993, 8A).

Subjective Probability. The likelihood that a specific outcome will occur, based on personal judgment and beliefs, is known as **subjective probability.** Such judgments vary among individuals, depending on their intuition, previous experience with similar situations, expertise, and personality traits (e.g., preference for risk taking or risk avoidance). Recall Barbara Abelson's analysis of probabilities in the Preview Insight. She assigned a low subjective probability to motel customers' being attacked and a high subjective probability to expenditures for additional security cutting deeply into profits and hurting her career.

A change in the condition under which decisions are made can alter expectations and practices. Such a change may shift the basis for judging the likelihood of an outcome from objective probability to subjective probability or even to uncertainty. Consider how the decisions of some motorists have changed as a result of objective and perceived changes in highway driving conditions. Sandy Stubbs, a Delta flight attendant, runs red lights driving home from the airport late at night. Patti Cantwell, a doctor, didn't stop recently when her Jeep was bumped by a truck early in the morning. Both drivers broke the law, according to the Florida Driver's Handbook. But following the well-publicized murders of several tourists on the state's highways, some drivers say they'd rather break the law than risk their lives. In this climate of fear, driving rules are being ignored. Obeying the old rules—stop for red lights, stop for accidents, or pull over and nap if you get sleepy driving at night—can now be very risky at certain times and in certain locations. The conditions under which drivers make such decisions, especially at night, has changed. "Years ago they'd tell you to pull over and take forty winks if you were tired," Judge Harvey Baxter said. "I won't do that any more."[8]

Uncertainty

Ethics
Having well-understood ethical codes under conditions of uncertainty is important. How can inventors and scientists get into ethical difficulties as they deal with conditions of uncertainty? (Example: In the movie *Jurassic Park,* scientists invented a process that recreated dinosaurs from DNA. As was said in the movie, they were too busy thinking about whether they could do this and didn't consider whether they should do this.)

Uncertainty is the condition under which an individual doesn't have the necessary information to assign probabilities to the outcomes of alternative solutions. In fact, the individual may not even be able to define the problem, much less identify alternative solutions and possible outcomes. Uncertainty often suggests that the problem and the alternative solutions are both ambiguous and highly unusual.[9]

Dealing with uncertainty is an important facet of the jobs of many managers and various professionals, such as research and development engineers, market researchers, and strategic planners.[10] Organizations face uncertainty when they enter new markets or launch significantly different products requiring the use of novel technologies. Uncertainty is present even when organizations do considerable research and planning before committing resources to projects. "The impossibility of total prediction is clearly illustrated by the principle that if we had tomorrow's newspaper today, a good deal of [the events reported] would not happen."[11] Yet at times individuals must make decisions under the condition of uncertainty. They may base these decisions on a combination of research, experience, and hunches that they hope will lead to desirable results.[12]

The following Global Insight provides a sense of the uncertainties experienced by Whirlpool management in the process of deciding to become a global corporation.

Dealing with uncertainty is an important facet of the jobs of many managers and other professionals, including research and development engineers. Organizations face uncertainty when they create products using novel technologies. Here, a Westinghouse R&D engineer demonstrates a pyroplasma torch.

Ask Students
Have you made a decision recently under conditions of uncertainty? If so, describe it and its outcome.

Whirlpool had been primarily a North American company. Today it has manufacturing operations in eleven countries, with facilities in the United States, Europe, and Latin America. Whirlpool markets products in more than 120 locations as diverse as Thailand, Hungary, and Argentina. This Insight presents a snapshot of the self-diagnosis that Whirlpool's management undertook in confronting the firm's uncertainties and that led to the eventual decision to go global.

Global *Insight*

Whirlpool's Self-Diagnosis

Whirlpool's senior management started with the knowledge that, if the company continued down the path it was on, the future would be neither pleasant nor profitable. Even though Whirlpool had dramatically lowered costs and improved product quality, profit margins in North America had been declining because everyone in the industry was pursuing the same course and the domestic market was mature. The four main players—Whirlpool, General Electric, Maytag, and White Consolidated, which had been acquired by Electrolux—were beating one another up every day on price and service warranties.

Whirlpool's senior management explored several strategies. One was to restructure the company financially and pay large dividends to the shareholders. Another was to diversify into other businesses. If the appliance industry didn't offer growth, were there other industries that did (e.g., other durable goods)? Other alternatives considered were horizontal expansion (buying other appliance makers) and vertical expansion (buying suppliers). In the process of examining alternatives, it became clear to management that the basics of managing the business were the same in Europe, North America, Asia, and Latin America. Whirlpool was already very good at what it did. What it needed was to enter appliance markets in other parts of the world and learn how to satisfy different kinds of customers.

Previously, Whirlpool's management hadn't identified the potential power of its existing capabilities in global marketing. Whirlpool had been limiting its definition of the appliance market to the United States and Canada. Whirlpool's eight months of analysis turned up a great deal of evidence that, over time, the industry would become global, whether Whirlpool chose to become global or not. Thus Whirlpool faced three choices. It could ignore the inevitable—a decision that would have condemned Whirlpool to a slow death. It could wait for globalization to begin and then try to react, which would have forced Whirlpool to play catch up, technologically and organizationally. Or Whirlpool could control its own destiny and try to shape the very nature of globalization in the industry.[13] Whirlpool chose the latter.

4

Describe a framework for understanding the three main categories of decisions.

FRAMEWORK FOR DECISION MAKING

Managers and other employees must make decisions in a variety of situations, and no single decision-making method will cover all of them. In general, though, the decision maker should begin by defining accurately the problem at hand, move on to evaluating alternative solutions, and—finally—make a decision.

The conditions under which decisions are made—certainty, risk, and uncertainty—provide a foundation for a comprehensive framework for decision making. Decisions may be classified as routine, adaptive, or innovative. These categories reflect the type of problem encountered and the type of solutions considered. Figure 8.2 illustrates the different combinations of problem types (vertical axis) and solution types (horizontal axis) that result in the three decision-making categories. In addition, the conditions of certainty, risk, and uncertainty appear along the diagonal line from lower left to upper right.

Discussion Question 1
Recall the Global Insight on the Whirlpool Corporation. What were the preconditions for whirlpool's decision to go global?

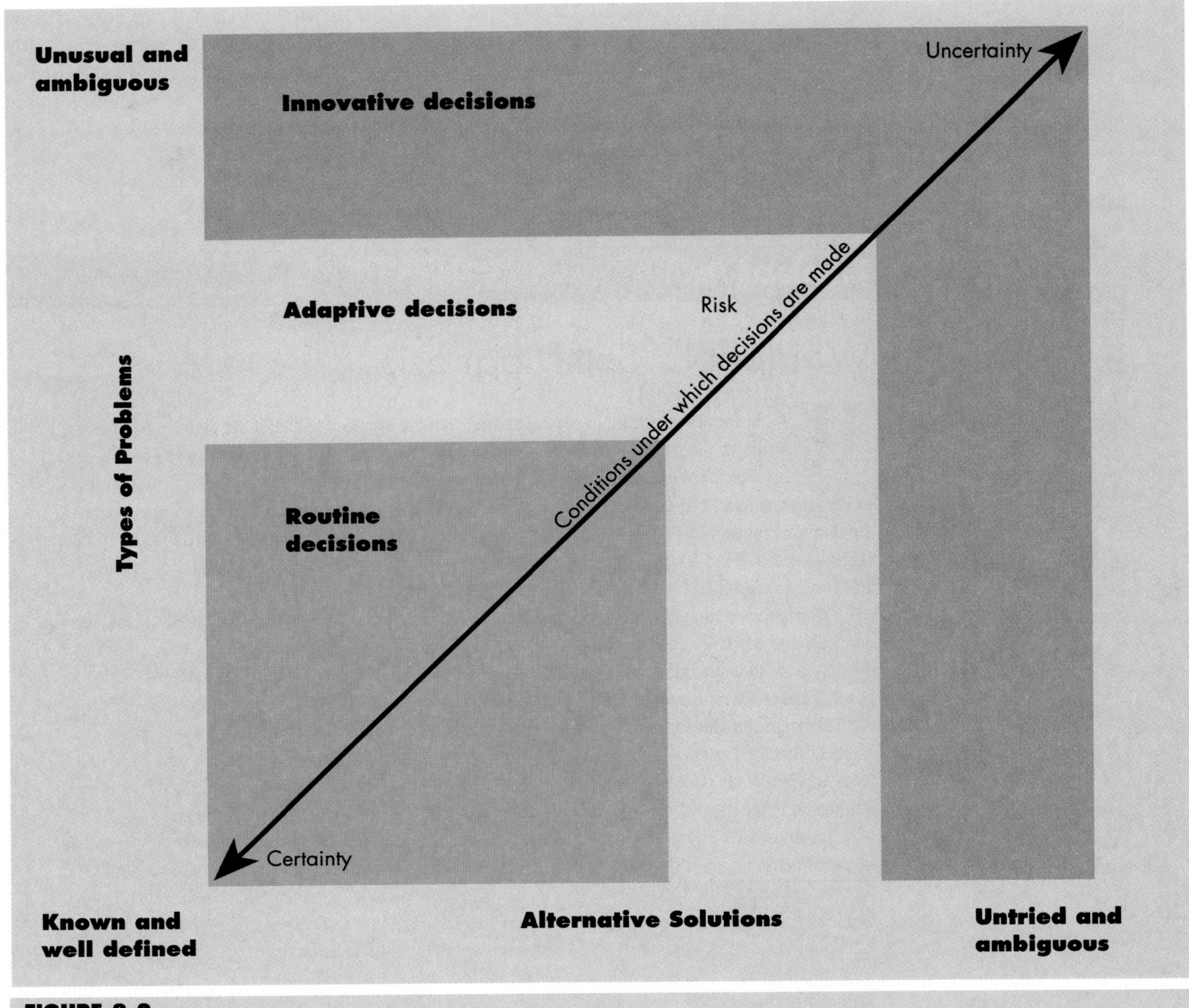

FIGURE 8.2

Framework for Decision Making

Types of Problems

The *types of problems* that managers and other employees deal with range from the known and well defined to the unusual and ambiguous. The bank teller with an out-of-balance cash drawer at the end of the day faces a known and well-defined problem. In contrast, the problem of women and minorities not moving faster into management positions is ambiguous: Some people maintain that it is caused by both overt and hidden forms of discrimination, whereas others believe that women and minorities just need more time in the management pipeline and that gender and/or racial discrimination no longer has anything to do with the problem.[14]

Types of Solutions

The *alternative solutions* available also range from the known and well defined to the untried and ambiguous. The bank teller with an out-of-balance cash drawer follows a specific, well-defined procedure—check all deposit slips against deposit receipts and cash tickets and recount all the cash.

In contrast, several years ago the Boeing Company faced the daunting task of finding a permanent solution to the serious problem of engines falling off its 747s. Boeing finally was able to announce that exhaustive engineering work and trillions of supercomputer calculations had produced an answer. Evidence pointed to the failure of a hollow steel "fuse pin," slightly smaller than a soda can, that attaches an engine to a wing. It was supposed to sever only in a crash (to reduce the risk to passengers) but instead broke while planes were aloft. The company tried to fix the problem by introducing a new generation of fuse pins in 1980. But they also proved susceptible to failure. The company moved to a third generation of pins—plus an extra steel brace should the pins fail—which Boeing expects to work. In the original design, even the untimely breakage of a fuse pin was not supposed to cause a 747 to crash. The company believed that, if the pins did break in flight, the engine would fall away cleanly and the plane would fly on the remaining three. But Boeing discovered that, if an inboard engine breaks away, it can knock off the same wing's outboard engine—as happened in both the Taiwan and the Netherlands crashes.[15]

Routine Decisions

Routine decisions are standard choices made in response to relatively well-defined and well-known problems and alternative solutions. Employees often find a solution in established rules or standard operating procedures (discussed in more depth in Chapter 9) or, increasingly, in computer software, such as computerized airline reservation systems. Cleaning buildings, processing payroll vouchers, packing and shipping customers' orders, and making travel arrangements are but a few examples of tasks requiring routine decisions.

Ask Students
Describe a situation in which you made a routine decision when an adaptive decision was called for. What was the outcome?

Employees need to guard against the tendency to make routine decisions when a problem actually calls for an adaptive or innovative decision.[16] At a meeting a manager says, "Let's spend more on TV advertising. When we did that in 1994, sales jumped." But this form of routine thinking can be based on faulty logic. The implication is that, because sales increased after an increase in advertising expenditures, the ad increases caused sales to rise. In fact, the sales may have gone up for any number of reasons, including blind luck. The proposal for increasing advertising requires firmer proof, and the causes of lagging sales require deeper analysis. At a minimum, in this case the need for adaptive decision making exists.

Adaptive Decisions

Ask Students
Describe an adaptive decision you made recently. What was the outcome?

Teaching Tip
Point out that continuous improvement requires a belief that the worker can affect the outcome. For example, a student engaged in continuous improvement would look at his or her errors on quizzes and the midterm exam and decide to improve through more intensive study.

Adaptive decisions are choices made in response to a combination of moderately unusual and only partially known problems and alternative solutions. Adaptive decisions often involve modifying and improving upon past routine decisions and practices. In fact, the concept of continuous improvement is a key to total quality management.

Continuous improvement involves streams of adaptive decisions made over time in an organization that result in a large number of small incremental improvements year after year. Continuous improvement requires a commitment to constant diagnosis of technical, organizational, and managerial processes in search of improvements.[17] In part the process resembles the wheel in a hamster cage—a ladder wrapped into a cylinder, with no beginning and no end. Each turn of the wheel improves an existing product and/or its production methods. Year after year the organization's products keep getting better, more reliable, and less expensive. John P. McTague, research vice-president at Ford Motor Company, asserts: "The accumulation of a large number of small improvements is the surest path, in most industries, to increasing your competitive advantage."[18]

Continuous improvement is driven by the goals of providing better quality, improving efficiency, and being responsive to customers. Accordingly, improvements typically serve to:

1. enhance value to the customer through improved and new products and services;
2. reduce errors, defects, and waste;
3. increase responsiveness to customer changes and expectations; and
4. elevate productivity and effectiveness in the use of all resources.[19]

Continuous improvement is a cornerstone to Rubbermaid's value system and strategy. The firm is consistently viewed as one of the most admired, adaptive, and innovative corporations in the Corporate Reputations Survey conducted each year by *Fortune* magazine.[20] The following Quality Insight provides some examples of the adaptive process and decisions at Rubbermaid.

Quality *Insight*

Rubbermaid Adapts

Rubbermaid's success depends on making small improvements to some 5,000 unspectacular products: mailboxes, window boxes, storage boxes, toys, mops, dust mitts, spatulas, snap-together furniture, desk organizers, step stools, wall coverings, playhouses, drink coasters, lint brushes, ice cube trays, stadium seats, garbage pails, bath mats, sporting goods, dinnerware, playground equipment, laundry hampers, dish drainers, and more. For example, the company took a mop bucket, added an *antimicrobial* agent to its plastic, and it became the only antimicrobial mop bucket on the market at the time.

Rubbermaid profits by taking seriously the basic products that others dismiss as trivial. For example, a team at Rubbermaid focused on ways to improve the common mailbox. The team developed a new model with a double-wide floor that lets magazines lie flat and a little flag that pops up, automatically, to show homeowners that their mail has arrived. Another "household" product Rubbermaid improved is the lunch box. To ensure that the lunch box (known as Sidekick) keeps food well insulated, Rubbermaid engineers adapted the design from its existing line of plastic coolers, which feature high-density polyethylene liners.

In product development, Rubbermaid makes extensive use of focus groups (small groups of customers that meet face-to-face with company personnel to discuss products). No customer gripe is too small to consider. When focus group participants complained of puddles in their dish drainers, Rubbermaid responded with a drain tray made a bit higher in back to help water flow into the sink.

However, most ideas for improved and new products flow from teams. Twenty teams, each made up of five to seven people (one each from marketing, manufacturing, R&D, finance, and other departments), focus on specific product lines, such as bathroom accessories. Also innovative, Rubbermaid introduces about 350 new products each year. The company typically spends 14 percent of profits on research and development. A competitor in the cookware business states: "They're in a class by themselves."[21]

Innovative Decisions

Real-World Example
Innovative decisions aren't always successful. Coca-Cola made a poor decision when it changed its formula several years ago and dropped the original formula. After customer protest, the original formula was brought to market as Coca-Cola Classic.

Innovative decisions are choices based on the discovery, identification, and diagnosis of unusual and ambiguous problems and/or the development of unique or creative alternative solutions. The solutions frequently involve a series of small, interrelated decisions made over a period of months or even years. In particular leading-edge innovations may take years to develop and involve numerous professional specialists and teams. Because innovative decisions normally represent a sharp break with the past, they normally don't happen in a logical, orderly sequence. In fact, they may be made before problems are fully understood. To be effective, decision makers therefore must be especially careful to define the right problem. They also must recognize that earlier actions can significantly affect current decisions.[22]

Over the past twenty years, Hanover Insurance has gone from the bottom of the property and liability industry to a position among the top 25 percent of such companies in the United States. It is viewed as a major innovator in this sector of the insurance industry. William O'Brien, the CEO of Hanover, shared a few of his thoughts on innovation as anything but a logical, orderly sequence:

> *We had to get beyond mechanical, linear thinking. The essence of our jobs as managers is to deal with "divergent" problems—problems that have no simple answer. "Convergent" problems—problems that have a "right" answer—should be solved linearly. Yet we are deeply conditioned to see the world in terms of convergent problems. Most managers try to force-fit simplistic solutions and undermine the potential for learning when divergent problems arise. Since everyone handles the linear issues fairly well, companies that learn how to handle divergent issues will have a great advantage.*
>
> *The next basic stage in our progression was coming to understand inquiry and advocacy. We learned that real openness is rooted in people's ability to continually inquire into their own thinking. This requires exposing yourself to being wrong—not something that most employees are rewarded for. But learning is very difficult if you cannot look for errors or incompleteness in your own ideas.*[23]

Defining unusual and ambiguous problems in an organization will remain an evolutionary process, affected by many points of view, vested interests, and bits and pieces of information that become available at different times. Pressures from interest groups will ebb and flow, which requires shifting attention from one unusual and ambiguous problem to another and changing definitions to involve or exclude various individuals. Sometimes the real problem doesn't materialize until well into the decision-making process, perhaps even after some action has been taken.[24]

Whirlpool's decision to go global represented a major innovative decision that spawned the need for many other innovative decisions and behaviors. One innovation involved finding ways to get employees at all levels to accept the vision of Whirlpool as a worldwide company. David Whitwam, Whirlpool's CEO, commented:

> *You must create an organization whose people are comfortable at exchanging ideas, processes, and systems across borders; people who are absolutely free of the* not-invented-here *syndrome; people who are constantly working together to identify the best global opportunities and the biggest global problems facing the organization.*[25]

Innovative decisions often are made on the basis of incomplete and rapidly changing information. Hence the conditions of Whirlpool's task environment continues to be uncertain, unstable, and ambiguous.

5

Apply goals to decision making.

GOALS AND DECISION MAKING

Decision making in organizations under the conditions of risk and uncertainty are coupled directly with goals in one of two ways: (1) the decision-making process is triggered by a search for better ways to achieve established goals; or (2) the decision-making process is triggered by an effort to discover new goals, revise current goals, or drop goals. Let's return to Whirlpool. David Whitwam stated that Whirlpool's overall goal now is to achieve "world-class performance in terms of delivering shareholder value, which we define as being in the top 25 percent of publicly held companies in total returns through a given economic cycle."[26]

Goals are crucial in giving employees, managers, and organizations a sense of order, direction, and meaning. In fact, the four core managerial functions—planning, organizing, leading, and controlling—would be merely random activities if they were not based on goals. Setting goals is especially important in adaptive and innovative decision making. As suggested in Chapter 6, the planning process is vitally concerned with identifying possible new goals, revising goals, and finding better ways to accomplish existing goals.

What Are Goals?

Ask Students
What are your postgraduation goals, either qualitative or quantitative?

Goals are results to be attained. They indicate the direction in which decisions and actions should be aimed. Clear goals also specify the quality or quantity of the desired results. In the Preview Insight, Barbara Abelson considered three basic goals: safety of motel customers, profitability of the motel, and her career progress. Many goals guide people's behavior without their giving them much thought. For example, most drivers automatically go through the motions of driving—observing the speed limit, looking out for other cars and pedestrians, using seat belts, and so on—when pursuing the goal of getting to and from work or school safely. When individuals deliberately choose to modify or change goals, they often engage in a conscious, full-blown decision-making process.

Teaching Tip
Go through the business section of the newspaper and pick out examples of organizational goals.

Goals also are called objectives, ends, purposes, standards, deadlines, targets, and quotas.[27] Whatever they are called, goals specify results and outcomes that someone believes to be desirable and worth achieving. The goal chosen, however, doesn't always ensure an organization's or person's well-being. Many banks and savings and loan associations (S&Ls) established high-growth goals during the 1980s. To achieve this growth, those institutions had to make high-risk loans and engage in other questionable practices. Those high-growth goals had devastating consequences, resulting in the S&L and banking crisis. Congress was forced to establish the Resolution Trust Corporation and appropriate tens of billions of dollars to "bail out" failing S&Ls, banks, and investors, many of whom still lost large sums.

Ethics
In setting goals, managers should consider ethical concerns relating to the various choices. Ask students to identify some of these ethical considerations.

Goals can cover the long run (years) or the short run (minutes, hours, days, or months). Long-range, or general, organizational goals such as survival, growth, and profitability often remain stable. However, the development of specific, short-range goals for departments and projects requires constant managerial and employee attention. Specific production, human resource, marketing, and financing goals usually change from year to year or even quarter to quarter.

Why Set Goals?

Setting goals can yield several benefits, which are the same whether the goals apply to an entire organization, a specific department or division, a team, or an individual em-

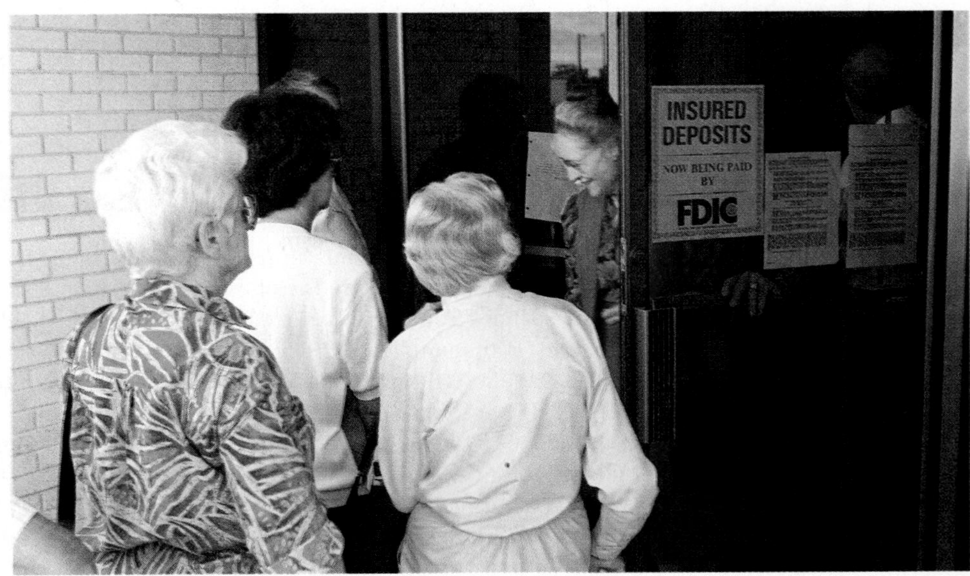

Many banks and savings and loans established high-growth goals during the 1980s. To reach their goals, they made high-risk loans and engaged in other questionable practices. The result was the S&L and banking crisis and a bail-out by Congress.

ployee. First, goals serve to focus individual and organizational decisions and efforts. Ken Thuerbach, the successful founder and CEO of Alpine Log Homes, Inc., of Victor, Montana, states: "Every successful person is an obsessive goal setter. Once you have goals, you have a pattern of opportunity. You can't hit a target that you can't see. You must have focus."[28] In terms of the organization, goals provide a set of stated expectations that everyone can understand and work to achieve. Second, goals aid the planning process, as discussed in Chapters 5 and 6. After diagnosing problems and the competition, managers usually establish goals as a part of their planning efforts. Third, goals motivate people and stimulate better performance. Clear and specific goals often raise productivity and improve the quality of work.[29] Fourth, goals assist in performance evaluation and control. To modify an old saying, "If you don't know where you're going, you'll never know when you get there."

Teaching Tip
Tell students that the popular phrase "go for it" is really about setting high goals, not just any goals.

Employees in organizations aren't the only ones who can benefit from setting goals in terms of evaluation and control. For example, let's say that your goal is to get a B in this course but that you get a D on the first exam. This feedback should serve as a powerful incentive to assess your efforts so far and determine how to avoid the same result on the next exam. This type of assessment, and acting on it, is a self-controlling way of working toward your goal.

General and Operational Goals

General goals provide broad direction for decision making in qualitative terms. For example, one of the general goals of the Smithsonian Library in Washington, D.C., is to serve as an educational resource for the people of the United States and the rest of the world. **Operational goals** state what is to be achieved in quantitative terms, for whom, and within what time period. A simple operational goal might be "to reduce my weight by ten pounds within three months." It specifies what in quantitative terms (lose ten pounds), for whom (me), and a measurable time period (three months).

Ask Students
What should be the general goals for your major department and what should be its operational goals?

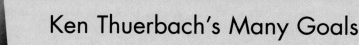

The following Small Business Insight indicates how general goals provide both a sense of direction and criteria for the development of operational goals and decisions. It also illustrates the ideal situation of integrating individual and organizational goals.

Small Business *Insight*

Ken Thuerbach's Many Goals

Ken Thuerbach set out in search of an opportunity that would match what he wanted out of life and not just meet a short-term goal. "You can go through life, or you can design one," he says. "If you have a plan, if you have a goal, then opportunities pop out in front of you. And if you've got the criteria, you'll know the right opportunity when you see it." Thuerbach believes that his decision to form Alpine Log Homes was a natural match with eight core general goals he had developed for forming a business. The business needed to (1) have relatively low capital requirements, (2) be labor intensive, (3) require no accounts receivable, (4) be in front of a trend, (5) be an exciting, new business, (6) sell a product exciting for the purchaser, (7) allow him to live in the Rocky Mountains with a casual lifestyle, and (8) be one that he could build up and make a profit.

Taken together these general goals functioned like a compass, allowing Thuerbach to pursue his personal desires while staying on a sound entrepreneurial course. Goals 1, 2, and 3, for example, are *financial* necessities for a relatively low capitalized start-up. "I was out of debt, but had no money," Thuerbach says. Goals 4, 5, and 6 are *strategic,* with growth potential as the common denominator. "It's much easier to be in front of a trend than to try to catch up to one," he says. Far from being an afterthought, the personal goal (goal 7) directed Thuerbach's search. "I wasn't a hippie or anything, but I wanted to live in the mountains," he says.

Under the traditional system of building log homes, builders worked on-site and traveled from job to job. Thuerbach's idea was to centralize the building and then distribute: "If we could build houses in one location, dismantle and then ship homes to customers, we could open the whole world as a market." This meant reinventing how log houses were built. With borrowed funds, he sunk thousands of dollars into equipment design: machine-powered hammers and chisels, a compact crane that would allow a single person to pick up and maneuver a 60-foot log weighing 800 pounds. A system for numbering logs was developed so that the houses could be reassembled quickly and easily.

Thuerbach claims that most people "don't do the daily disciplines that it takes to be successful, whether it's reading a book a week or writing down their goals." But he cautions against goals as an end in themselves. "It's the process of meeting them that matters." And he distinguishes between what he defines as good and unworthy goals: "To do anything just for money is instant failure."[30]

Hierarchy of Goals

Ask Students
What would a hierarchy of goals for your school in the university consist of?

Management usually tries to *link* goals—from one organizational level to another and among departments, teams, and employees. This task isn't easy and can be the source of conflict. A **hierarchy of goals** represents the formal linking of goals between organizational levels so that meeting the goals of the lowest level units helps achieve goals at the next higher level, and so on, until the goals of the organization as a whole are attained.

Figure 8.3 presents a simplified hierarchy of operational goals for an organization with five levels. Note that goals for the lower level units are more detailed, narrower in scope, and easier to measure than those for the higher level units. The arrows pointing in both directions indicate that setting and reaching goals involves a two-way flow of information and decisions between organizational levels. We deliberately kept Figure 8.3 simple by not including all the performance goals found at each organization level or the interaction between departments, teams, or individuals at the same level (such as production and marketing). The figure doesn't reflect the influence of various stakeholders—unions, shareholders, and the government—in setting goals. Moreover, whenever possible, management shouldn't unilaterally set goals and impose them on the rest of the organization. Goal setting should be a participative process.

Role of Stakeholders

Teaching Tip
Have students identify their university's stakeholders. Diagram their relationships on the board. What demands, constraints, and choices do these stakeholders impose?

Goals aren't set in a vacuum. As mentioned in earlier chapters, various stakeholders (e.g., customers, shareholders, suppliers, and government agencies) have an impact on an organization and its employees. This impact is felt in the goal setting and revision process. As suggested in Figure 8.4, stakeholders play a crucial role in shaping the demands, constraints, and choices of alternatives that managers and other employees face when setting goals.[31]

Demands are the desires expressed by powerful stakeholders that an organization make certain decisions and achieve particular goals.[32] Even stakeholders within an organization don't always agree with the goals of their departments, divisions, or organization as a whole—or the means for achieving them. When William Norris was the CEO of Control Data Corporation, some board members disagreed with him over the high priority given to affirmative social responsibility goals and the corporate resources devoted to achieving them.[33] When profits declined, the board, with the support of the shareholders, encouraged Norris to retire. Norris's retirement was quickly followed by a reduction in the resources allotted to social responsibility goals.

Constraints limit the types of goals set, the decisions made, and the actions taken. Two important constraints are laws and ethics. A salesperson facing declining sales could not legally obtain a government contract by giving the contracting officer a kickback. Likewise, for a salesperson to promise customers a product that cannot be delivered at the quoted price is unethical.

FIGURE 8.3

A Simplified Hierarchy of Goals

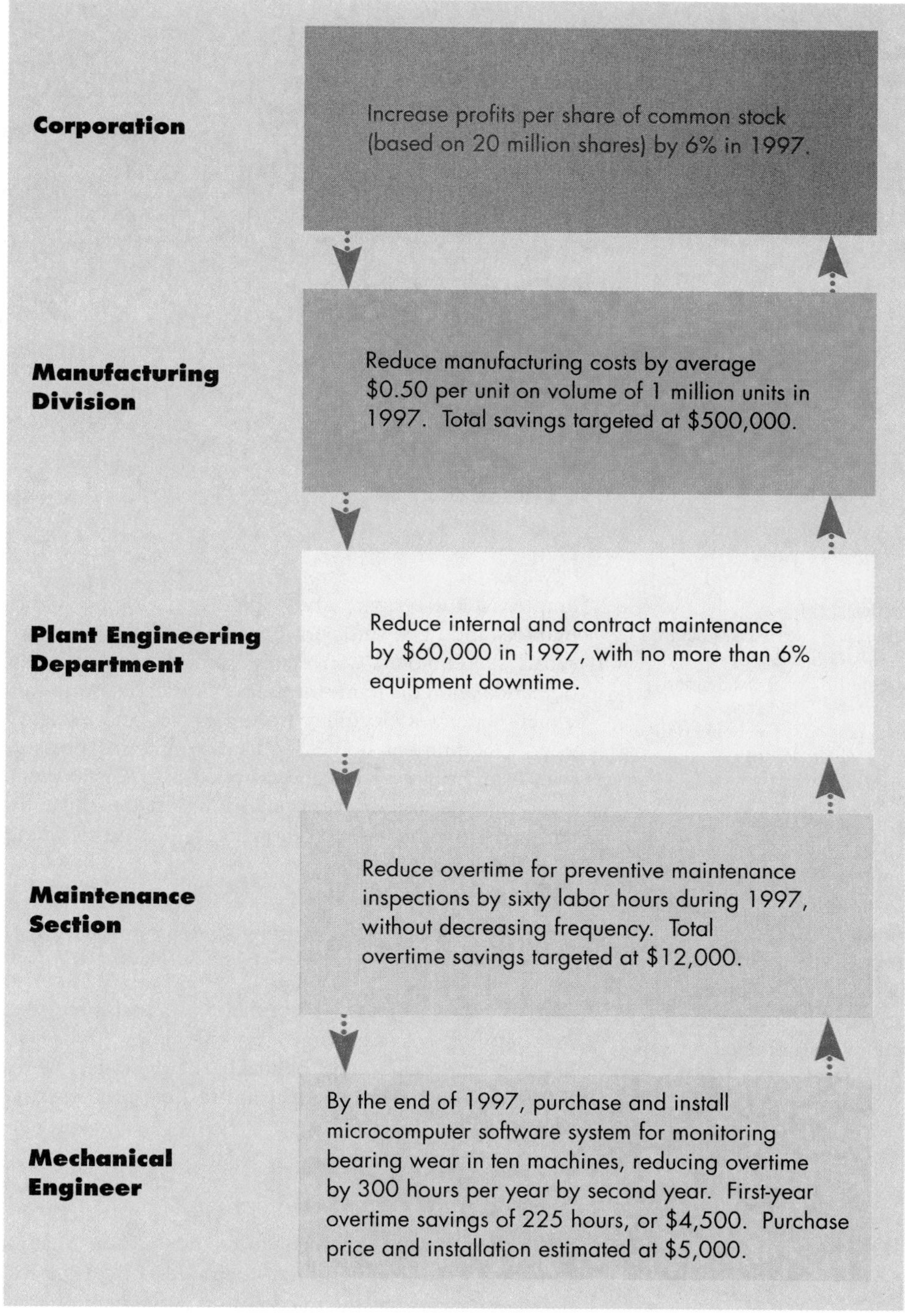

Corporation
Increase profits per share of common stock (based on 20 million shares) by 6% in 1997.
Manufacturing Division
Reduce manufacturing costs by average $0.50 per unit on volume of 1 million units in 1997. Total savings targeted at $500,000.
Plant Engineering Department
Reduce internal and contract maintenance by $60,000 in 1997, with no more than 6% equipment downtime.
Maintenance Section
Reduce overtime for preventive maintenance inspections by sixty labor hours during 1997, without decreasing frequency. Total overtime savings targeted at $12,000.
Mechanical Engineer
By the end of 1997, purchase and install microcomputer software system for monitoring bearing wear in ten machines, reducing overtime by 300 hours per year by second year. First-year overtime savings of 225 hours, or $4,500. Purchase price and installation estimated at $5,000.

Choices are goals and alternatives that organizations and individuals are free to select, but don't have to. As demonstrated in the previous Small Business Insight, Ken Thuerbach had the choice of matching his personal goal (live in the Rocky Mountains with a casual lifestyle) with the establishment of a business—Alpine Log Homes—which, in turn, satisfied his other general goals.

The relative range of choices that organizations have in setting goals varies greatly, depending on the magnitude of stakeholder power. Organizations can have many choices in setting goals when external stakeholder power is relatively low, as, for ex-

FIGURE 8.4

Stakeholders, Alternatives, and Goals

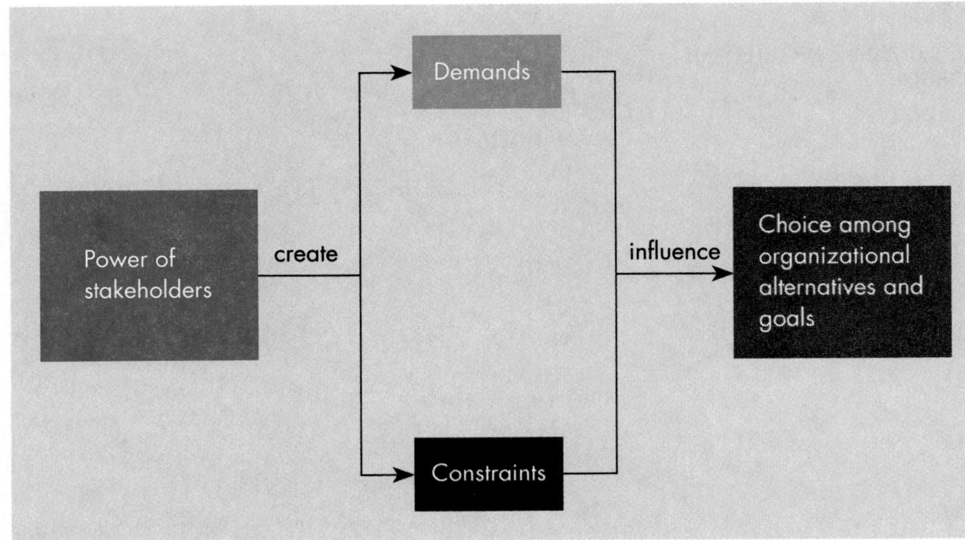

Ethics
The range of choice should be clearly and consciously constrained by ethical boundaries. (Example: Businesses that have insufficient parking should deal with the problem to ensure that nearby residents can park in front of their own homes and to avoid excessive traffic on neighborhood streets.)

ample, at Rubbermaid and Alpine Log Homes. They are leading competitors in their markets and have sufficient human, technological, and financial resources to shape and satisfy stakeholders. Conversely, some organizations face powerful external stakeholder demands and constraints and have few choices in setting goals. Commonwealth Edison, which generates electricity from coal, oil, and nuclear energy, seems to be in this category. Government bodies and environmental pressure groups have made strong demands and placed strict constraints (governmental regulations) on where the utility can build nuclear and conventional power plants, how these power plants are to be constructed, how they are to be operated, how nuclear and other wastes are to be disposed of, and so on.

6

Describe the rational, bounded rationality, and political models of decision making.

DECISION-MAKING MODELS

Our discussion of the preconditions to and circumstances surrounding most decision making has set the stage for examining three decision-making models: rational, bounded rationality, and political. These models were developed by management theorists to describe various decision-making processes. Goals are important in all of three models.

Rational Model

Teaching Tip
Choose a major policy problem from the newspaper that President Clinton will have to make a decision on. Divide the class into teams of 5 to 8 each. Assign one of the three models to each team. Have each team base its decision on its decision-making model and report to the class.

The **rational model** prescribes a series of steps that individuals or teams should follow to increase the likelihood that their decisions will be logical and well founded. A rational decision permits the maximum achievement of goals within the limitations of the situation. This definition addresses the rationality of means (how to best achieve a goal) and not of ends (i.e., goals). For example, the goal of many public utility companies is to generate electricity at the lowest possible cost. One way to achieve this goal is to minimize the cost of the fuel used to power the generators. Thus some power plants are designed to permit easy switching from one type of fuel to another. The plant manager can choose among natural gas, oil, or coal, depending on their relative costs at any particular time. If the cost of natural gal skyrockets relative to the cost of oil and coal, the rational decision would be to shift to oil or coal. The continued use of natural gas under those circumstances would be an irrational decision.

Figure 8.5 shows the rational decision-making model as a seven-step process. It begins with defining and diagnosing the problem and moves through the succeeding steps

FIGURE 8.5

Rational Decision-Making Model

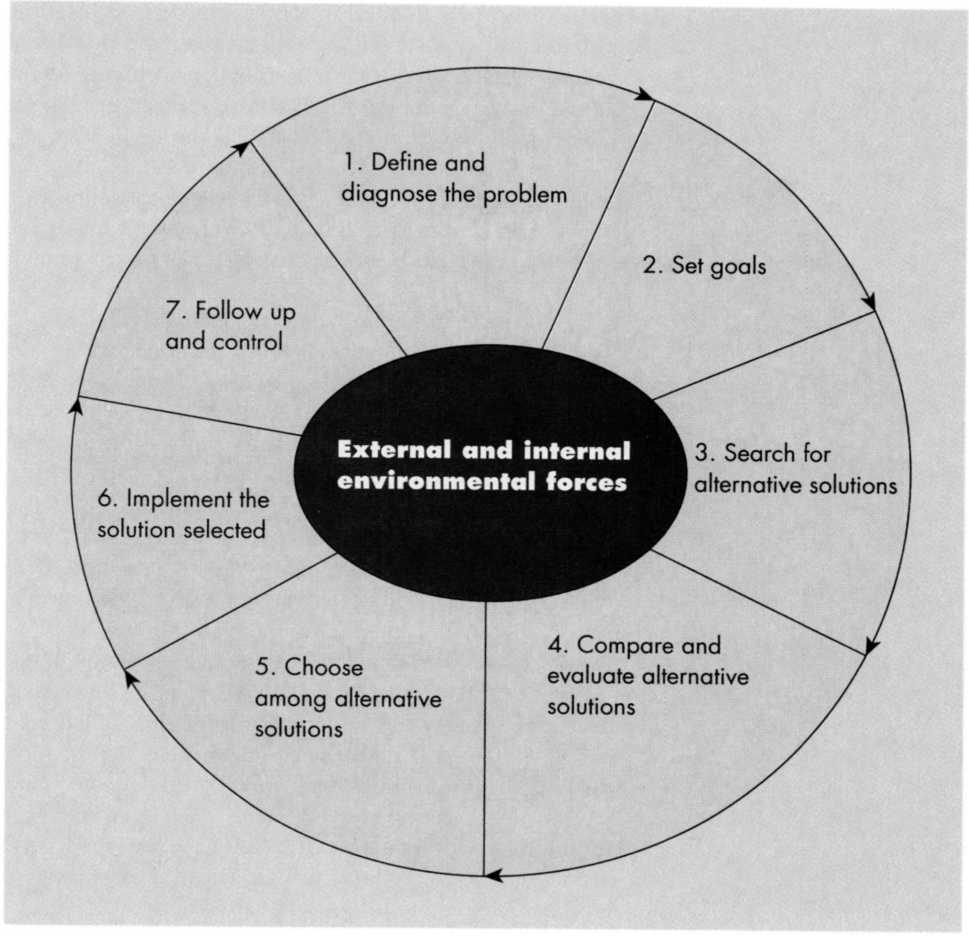

to following up and controlling. When making routine decisions, individuals can follow these steps easily. In addition, people are more likely to utilize this process in situations involving conditions of near certainty or low risk when they can assign objective probabilities to outcomes. Routine decisions under conditions that approximate certainty obviously don't require using all the steps in the model. For example, if a particular problem tends to recur, decisions (solutions) may be written as standard operating procedures or rules. Moreover, individuals or teams rarely follow these seven steps sequentially when making adaptive or innovative decisions.[34]

Real-World Example
American forces shot down two friendly helicopters in Iraq after they incorrectly identified the choppers as enemy aircraft.

Step 1: Define and Diagnose the Problem. If managers, teams, or individual employees are unaware of the true problems and their possible causes, no effective decision making can occur.[35] Problem definition and diagnosis involves three conceptual skills: noticing, interpreting, and incorporating. *Noticing* involves identifying and monitoring numerous external and internal environmental forces and deciding which ones are contributing to the problem or problems. *Interpreting* involves assessing the forces noticed and determining which are causes, not merely symptoms, of the real problem. Finally, *incorporating* involves relating those interpretations to the current or desired goals (step 2) of the department or organization.[36] If noticing, interpreting, and incorporating are done incorrectly, the individual or team eventually is likely to choose a poor solution.

Let's consider two examples of the need for sound problem definition and diagnosis. Taking aspirin for headaches may do the trick in the short run, but headaches usually are a symptom, not the problem. The problem underlying the symptom could be physiological (e.g., eyestrain) or psychological (e.g., stress). Also, problems are sometimes incorrectly defined in terms of proposed solutions. For example, the members of a marketing department may assert that "the problem is that our department is understaffed." Acting on this definition of the problem, department members focus on the obvious goal of obtaining funds for new positions. The more basic problem may be that the firm's selling strategies have become ineffective as a result of competitors' actions.

Fundamental to problem definition and diagnosis is asking numerous probing questions. Stop for a moment. How would you define the word *question*? Our use of the word goes beyond the dictionary definition: an act or instance of asking. We like the following multiple meanings expressed by two creativity experts.

- *A question is an invitation to creativity.*
- *A question is an unsettled and unsettling issue.*
- *A question is a beginning of adventure.*
- *A question is a disguised answer.*
- *A question pokes and prods that which has not yet been poked and prodded.*
- *A question is a point of departure.*
- *A question has no end and no beginning.*[37]

By asking a variety of *who, when, where, how,* and *why* questions, individuals and teams will improve the odds of effective problem definition and diagnosis.

Step 2: Set Goals. After individuals or teams have defined a problem, they can set specific goals for eliminating it. For example, let's say that top management has defined excessive manufacturing costs as a problem, which actually is but a symptom of the real problem. The real problem could be defective materials (inputs) getting into the production process, production workers' inadequate quality control (inspection) skills, or any of numerous other possibilities. However, management could convert the *seeming* problem into a hierarchy of goals for the various levels in the organization, from the division level to the lathe operator. These goals would spell out the desired results: what is to be achieved and by what date (see Figure 8.3).

Under the condition of uncertainty, setting precise goals can be extremely difficult. Individuals or teams may have to identify alternative goals, compare and evaluate them, and choose among them. For example, a business career might be your overall goal, but you could be uncertain about which specific path to follow. Should you become an accountant or a sales representative or choose one of many other occupations that can lead to a satisfying career in business? To arrive at an answer, you'll have to consider the alternative paths for achieving your general goal.

Ethics
Is it ethical for managers not to conduct an exhaustive search after a minimally acceptable alternative has been identified?

Step 3: Search for Alternative Solutions. Individuals or teams must look for alternative ways to achieve a goal. This step might involve seeking additional information, thinking creatively, consulting experts, undertaking research, and similar actions. However, when there seems to be no feasible solution for reaching a goal, there may be a need to modify the goal. For example, some people set impossible goals for themselves and then try harder and harder to achieve them, often without success. The solution selected might be to work longer and longer hours, literally seven days a week. The ultimate result could be high levels of stress and dissatisfaction that eventually force these individuals to reexamine their goals and decide which ones are really important. As indicated in the previous Small Business Insight, Ken Thuerbach expressed the importance of matching long-term personal goals with achievable professional goals.

Step 4: Compare and Evaluate Alternative Solutions. After individuals or teams have identified alternative solutions, they must compare and evaluate these alternatives. This step emphasizes expected results and determining the relative cost of each alternative.[38] In Chapter 9, we present several aids for rationally comparing and evaluating alternative solutions.

Step 5: Choose among Alternative Solutions. Decision making is commonly associated with having made a final choice. Choosing a solution, however, is only one step in the rational decision-making process. Many managers complain that when recent college graduates receive a project assignment, they tend to present and discuss only one solution. Instead of being able to compare and evaluate several alternatives, a manager can only accept or reject the choice being presented. Although choosing among alternative solutions might appear to be straightforward, it may prove difficult when the problem is complex and ambiguous and involves high degrees of risk or uncertainty.[39]

Step 6: Implement the Solution Selected. A well-chosen solution isn't always successful. A technically correct decision has to be accepted and supported by those responsible for implementing it if the decision is to be acted on effectively. If the selected solution can't be implemented for some reason, another one should be considered. We explore the importance of participation in making a decision by those charged with implementing it in Chapters 14 and 16.

Step 7: Follow Up and Control. Implementing the preferred solution won't automatically achieve the desired goal. Individuals or teams must control implementation activities and follow up by evaluating results. If implementation isn't producing satisfactory results, corrective action will be needed. Because environmental forces affecting decisions change continually, follow up and control may indicate a need to redefine the problem or review the original goal. Feedback from this step could even suggest the need to start over and repeat the entire decision-making process. That's what Boeing did in responding to the problem of engines falling off some 747s. Eventually, Boeing totally redesigned and replaced the engine mounts on the 747s and issued new maintenance procedures to airlines.

You might think of the rational model as an ideal, nudging individuals or teams closer to rationality in making decisions. At best, though, human decision making only approximates this ideal. When dealing with some types of problems, people don't even attempt to follow the rational model's seven steps.[40] Instead, they may apply the bounded rationality or political models, which are based on observations of actual decision processes in organizations. Such observations suggest that individuals modify or even ignore the rational model, especially when faced with making certain types of adaptive and innovative decisions.[41]

Teaching Tip
Public sector organizations typically operate under bounded rationality while claiming to use full rationality. They often cannot hire the best candidate because of below-market pay levels. They often limit their search for alternatives by announcing job vacancies through their own publications rather than advertising in commercial newspapers. They may not be able to control the choice of key personnel, for a centralized politically appointed personnel board may make the final selection from choices provided by the organization.

Bounded Rationality Model

The **bounded rationality model** refers to an individual's tendencies (1) to select less than the best goal or alternative solution (i.e., to *satisfice*), (2) to engage in a limited search for alternative solutions, and (3) to have inadequate information and control over external and internal environmental forces influencing the outcomes of decisions.[42] Herbert Simon, a management scholar, introduced this model in the mid-1950s. It contributed significantly to the Swedish Academy of Sciences' decision to award him the 1978 Nobel Prize in economics for his "pioneering research into the decision making process within economic organizations." The bounded rationality model is particularly useful because it emphasizes the limitations of rationality and thus provides a better picture of the day-to-day decision-making processes used by most people. This model partially explains why different individuals make different decisions when they have exactly the same information.

Ask Students
Did you consider every college in the country before applying here, or did you stop at the first acceptable choice that would admit you?

Satisficing. The practice of selecting an *acceptable* goal or alternative solution is called **satisficing.** An acceptable goal might be easier to identify and achieve, less controversial, or otherwise safer than the best available goal. For example, quality improvement goals often are quantified. A quality goal might be an error rate of no more than 40,000 per million parts for the coming year. During the current year, the firm might have had an actual error rate of 60,000 per million parts. The 40,000 or less error rate goal might be viewed as satisficing because it might not be the maximum attainable. In fact, such goals may represent little more than the decision maker's subjective judgment of reasonable goals, that is, goals that are challenging but not impossible to achieve.[43]

In an interview almost thirty-five years after introducing the bounded rationality model, Herbert Simon described satisficing for a management audience:

> *Satisficing is intended to be used in contrast to the classical economist's idea that in making decisions in business or anywhere in real life, you somehow pick, or somebody gives you, a set of alternatives from which you select the best one—maximize. The satisficing idea is that first of all, you don't have the alternatives, you've got to go out and scratch for them—and that you have mighty shaky ways of evaluating them when you do find them. So you look for alternatives until you get one from which, in terms of your experience and in terms of what you have reason to expect, you will get a reasonable result.*
>
> *But satisficing doesn't necessarily mean that managers have to be satisfied with what alternative pops up first in their minds or in their computers and let it go at that. The level of satisficing can be raised—by personal determination, setting higher individual or organizational standards [goals], and by use of an increasing range of sophisticated management science and computer-based decision-making and problem-solving techniques. As time goes on, you obtain more information about what's feasible and what you can aim at. Not only do you get more information, but in many, if not most, companies there are procedures for setting targets, including procedures for trying to raise individuals' aspiration levels [goals]. This is a major responsibility of top management.*[44]

Teaching Tip
How often do you say something like, "This is good enough. I don't have to call every car battery retailer in the phone book to find a battery."? This is an example of satisficing.

Limited Search. People usually make only a limited search for possible goals or alternative solutions to a problem, considering options until they find one that seems adequate. For example, when trying to choose the "best" job, college seniors can't evaluate every available job in their field and probably would reach retirement age before obtaining all the information available. In the bounded rationality model, individuals stop searching for alternatives as soon as they hit on an acceptable one. Even the rational decision-making model recognizes that identifying and assessing alternative solutions costs time, energy, and money.

Inadequate or Misinterpreted Information. Bounded rationality also recognizes that individuals frequently have inadequate information about problems and that events that they can't control will influence the results of their decisions.[45] For example, management might decide to purchase automatic stamping machines to make disc brakes for automobiles. By reducing labor costs, the machines could pay for themselves within two years. But management might fail to anticipate either union resistance to automation or declining automobile sales. In those cases the machines couldn't be used as effectively as expected, and thus the payout time for the machines could more than double.

Discussion Question 4
Why can individuals, whose rationality is limited according to the bounded rationality model, be expected to make reasonably rational decision at times?

The following Diversity Insight demonstrates the process of bounded rationality decision making used by the officers of Raveneaux Country Club in Houston, Texas, in modifying its policy on tee times.

Diversity *Insight*

Tee Times

Yolanda Marimon and several of her clients teed off at 9:30 A.M. at Raveneaux Country Club one Saturday for the first time in mid-1994. "I've been battling Raveneaux for a whole year," Marimon said. "I usually play golf with a group of career women, and we can't tee off until noon on Saturdays. I have clients who would like to play, but certainly not in the afternoon or on Sunday. "They want to get out there Saturday morning. And I couldn't do that."

Raveneaux, like many private golf and country clubs in the United States, restricted Saturday morning tee times to men. It was a long-standing practice, rationalized by the attitude that most men who play golf at country clubs work all week; most women who play at country clubs have their weekdays free. The thinking was women could play any time all week long, so the men should have at least one morning to call their own. But as Marimon sees it, times had changed. Marimon is the owner of Marimon Business Machines in Houston. She can't get to the course during the week, so Saturday is her day to relax on the golf course. "I pay the same dues as the men," Marimon said. "I have the same type of membership. I should have the same rights." Marimon is not alone in her views. Female executives and businesswomen across the country are taking private clubs to task—and to court—to rescind the practice of men-only Saturday morning tee times. Despite the growing number of businesswomen who are taking up golf, several private clubs in the Houston area were standing by their men-only Saturday tee times as of 1995.

Randy Lowry, president of Raveneaux Country Club, and its board of directors drafted and approved a modified policy to help ease the Saturday morning restrictions for their female members such as Marimon. "It will allow more access on Saturdays," Lowry said. "Women will be able to tee off just after 9 A.M. with a limited number of tee times. If we find we need more time than what we're allowing, we can adjust that later." In the past, Lowry said, the club has tried to make arrangements when a female member wanted to bring clients on a Saturday morning. "It was always considered a special favor," he said. "Now the women don't want to feel like they're asking for a favor to be allowed to play on Saturdays. I think it will work fine."[46]

Information-Processing Biases. Consistent with the bounded rationality model, individuals often fall prey to some information processing biases when they engage in bounded rationality decision making. The following are five of these biases.[47]

Teaching Tip
Pick an incident from the newspaper in which two parties to a situation both used selective perception. Ask students whether they have ever been in this situation? What problems does it cause? How can they prevent it from happening?

1. The **availability bias** means that a person who easily recalls specific instances of an event may overestimate how frequently the event occurs. People who have been in serious automobile accidents often overestimate the frequency of such accidents.
2. The **selective perception bias** means that what people expect to see often is what they do see. People seek information consistent with their own views and downplay conflicting information. Some people eagerly leap from a tower 100 feet above the ground with only a bungee cord between them and certain death. Yet these same bungee jumpers may not be willing to live near a closed plant that has been declared a superfund cleanup site.[48]
3. The **concrete information bias** means that vivid, direct experience usually prevails over abstract information. A single personal experience can outweigh statistical evidence. An initial bad experience on the job may lead a worker to conclude that most managers can't be trusted and are simply out to exploit their subordinates.
4. The **law of small numbers bias** means that a few incidents or cases may be viewed as representative of a larger population (i.e., a few cases "prove the rule") even when they aren't. A number of Arab-Americans experienced hostility from some non-Arabs after the invasion of Kuwait by Iraqi forces. Apparently the non-Arabs incorrectly attributed the unsavory characteristics of Saddam Hussein (sample of 1) to Arab-Americans in general.
5. The **gambler's fallacy bias** means that seeing an unexpected number of similar events can lead to the conviction that an event not seen will occur. For example, after observing nine successive reds turn up on a roulette wheel, a player might incorrectly believe that chances for a black on the next spin are greater than 50/50. They aren't!

Political Model

Teaching Tip
Ask students for examples from their own lives of politics being involved in decision making.

The **political model** describes the decision-making process in terms of the particular interests and goals of powerful external and internal stakeholders. Before considering this model, however, we need to define power. **Power** is the ability to influence or control individual, departmental, team, or organizational decisions and goals.[49] To have power is to be able to influence or control (1) the definition of the problem, (2) the choice of the goal, (3) the consideration of alternative solutions, (4) the selection of the alternative to be implemented, and, ultimately (5) the actions and success of the organization. Political processes are most likely to occur when decisions involve uncertainty, disagreement, and/or poor information.[50]

Problem Definition. In the political model, internal and external stakeholders try to define problems for their own advantage. The U.S. Surgeon General's Office and the American Cancer Society have defined cigarette smoking as a major health hazard. The U.S. tobacco industry has consistently argued that tobacco products do not represent a significant health problem and have lobbied Congress against restrictive legislation and regulations. Cigarettes have not been taken off the market, but an agreement was reached in the 1960s that tobacco companies would put health warnings on each cigarette package and discontinue advertising cigarettes on television. In this situation, problem definition was subject to negotiation between powerful opposing stakeholders. Although the influence of U.S. tobacco companies has declined in the United States, it remains strong in much of the rest of the world.

When things go wrong within politically based or oriented organizations, one or more individuals may be singled out as the cause of the problem. This finger pointing is called **scapegoating,** which refers to the process of casting blame for problems or shortcomings on an innocent or only partially responsible individual, team, or department. Individuals or units may use scapegoating to preserve a position of power or maintain a positive impression of themselves.[51] Scapegoating is a form of unethical behavior—even if it isn't recognized as such by the individuals who are engaged in its use.

Real-World Example
After the Democrats lost control of Congress in 1995, they blamed their political consultants for the failure.

Choice of Goals. The political model recognizes the likelihood of conflicting goals among stakeholders. The choice of goals will be influenced strongly by the relative power of stakeholders. Often no clear "winner" will emerge, but if power is concentrated in one stakeholder, the organization's major goals will likely reflect that stakeholder's goals. When H. Ross Perot was CEO and principal owner of Electronic Data Systems (EDS), a computer services firm, the company reflected his personal power and goals. After selling EDS to General Motors, Perot lost much of that power. His inability to influence GM's board led Perot to sell his stock in GM for a reported $750 million and to step down from its board of directors.

Teaching Tip
The phrase "dark horse" refers to a candidate whose chances of winning are uncertain at best.

In contrast a balance of power among several stakeholders may lead to negotiation and compromise in the decision-making process. It's then characterized by the push and pull of the stakeholders who have both power and conflicting goals.[52] Although a balance of power may lead to compromise, as in most union-management negotiations, it also may lead to a stalemate, as in the case of the players' union and club owners of major league baseball in 1994–1995. Recall that a common political strategy is to form a coalition (alliance) when no one person, group, or organization has sufficient power to select or implement its preferred goal. Many health-related organizations and associations—such as the American Cancer Society, American Heart Association, and the American Medical Association—have formed an informal coalition with the U.S. Surgeon General to fight smoking.

Search for Alternative Solutions. Some goals or the means used to achieve them may be perceived as a win-lose situation: My gain is your loss, and your gain is my loss. The 1994–1995 baseball strike is an example. In such a situation, stakeholders (owners and players) often distort and selectively withhold information in order to further their own interests. Such actions can severely limit the ability to make adaptive and innova-

Ask Students
Have you been involved in a win-lose situation recently? How might searching for alternative solutions have made it a win-win proposition?

TABLE 8.1

Checklist for Identifying Ethical Decisions

	Yes	No
1. Does my decision treat me as an exception to a standard that I would expect others to follow?	___	___
2. Would I offend customers by telling them of this decision?	___	___
3. Would I offend qualified job applicants by telling them of this decision?	___	___
4. Is my decision biased in anyone's favor?	___	___
5. Will I have to pull rank (use coercion) to implement this decision?	___	___
6. Would I prefer to avoid the consequences of this decision?	___	___
7. Did I avoid any of the above questions by telling myself that I could get away with it?	___	___

Source: Adapted from Hyman, M.R., Skipper, R., and Tansey, R. Ethical codes are not enough. *Business Horizons,* March–April 1990, 17.

tive decisions, which, by definition, require utilizing all relevant information, as well as exploring a full range of alternative solutions.[53]

Stakeholders within the organization often view information as a major source of power and use it accordingly. The rational decision-making model calls for all employees to present all relevant information openly. However, employees operating under the political model would view free disclosure as naive and as making achievement of their personal, team, or departmental goals more difficult. To complicate the picture, information often is (1) piecemeal and based on informal communication ("Did you know that . . . ?"); (2) subjective rather than based on hard facts ("Those computer printouts don't really matter around here."); and (3) defined by what powerful stakeholders consider to be important ("What does the boss think?" or "How will the board respond?").[54]

Real-World Example
Student radicals of the 1960s often were coopted by college administrators who made the radicals part of the "establishment" they were fighting by giving them administrative jobs.

One of the common political strategies used by stakeholders to achieve their goals is **co-optation.** Co-optation involves bringing new stakeholder representatives into the strategic decision-making process as a means of averting threats to an organization's stability or existence.[55] An example is placing a banker on a firm's board of directors when the firm needs to borrow money. Also, some organizations have created *junior* executive committees as a way of involving middle managers in selected strategic issues to gain their support in implementing a chosen course of action.

The political model of decision making sometimes reflects the pursuit of short-term and narrowly defined self-interests. In this situation, an individual or organization is prone to behave in ethically questionable ways. Table 8.1 provides a short checklist of questions that can be used to help you decide whether a proposed course of action is ethically questionable. The following Ethics Insight reveals how the producers of CBS TV's news program "60 Minutes" lost their ethical compass in pursuit of a cause that they viewed as noble.

Ethics *Insight*

"60 Minutes's" Deception

Several years ago, the producers of "60 Minutes" investigated the controversial use of polygraph tests by private employers. This investigation took place prior to the passage of legislation that sharply curtailed such use. The "60 Minutes" staff designed a demonstration of the use of polygraph tests. What resulted was an elaborate but deceptive experiment.

Using the CBS-owned *Popular Photography* magazine as a front, "60 Minutes" hired several polygraphers to identify the culprit in an alleged theft. CBS randomly selected four polygraph examiners from the telephone directory and had each one examine four suspects. The polygraphers were contacted initially by a manager at the magazine. This manager told them that more than $500 of camera equipment had been stolen, almost definitely by someone on the inside. None of the polygraphers knew that other examiners had been engaged, and they conducted their examinations in a *Popular Photography* office. Unbeknownst to the polygraphers, the office had been modified to enable secret filming. When the polygraphers arrived at the office, each was told that all of the suspects had access to the stolen camera. However, one of the four was probably the guilty party. A different person was "fingered" for each polygrapher.

Not surprising to polygraph critics, each examiner found the person who had been fingered to be deceptive. Each examiner tried hard to get the person who had been "fingered" to confess. No one, of course, had stolen anything. The four "employees" were confederates, paid $50 if they could convince the polygrapher of their innocence. With dramatic flair, CBS demonstrated that polygraphers do not necessarily use psycho-physiological information to make their diagnoses of deception.

The demonstration was very clever, but dishonest. The "60 Minutes" staff had lied to the polygraphers. The four polygraphers unwittingly starred in a television drama viewed by millions. The "60 Minutes" staff were gleeful at the success of the deception and the clarity of the outcome of the demonstration. No doubt, some polygraph critics also were pleased.[56]

Discussion Question 5
What elements of the decision-making process are affected by ethical concepts and issues? Give an example of how an ethical concept or issue affects each element identified.

We presume that the producers justified their actions by the ethical concept of the "means are justified by the end" or the "greatest good for the greatest number." Recall that this concept is called *act utilitarianism*. However, the "experiment" violated the *moral rights* model of ethics, particularly its aspects of truthfulness and privacy. Recall also that in the Preview Insight Barbara Abelson applied the utilitarian approach to decision making. If she had used the moral rights approach, she would have felt a stronger obligation to protect the safety and property of the motel's customers. The $500,000 award to Bob and Elaine Smith indicates that the jury and several judges who heard the case thought that the moral rights approach should have been given greater weight in this situation.

CHAPTER SUMMARY

1 ***Define decision making.***

Decision making involves identifying problems, gathering information, and choosing a course of action from the alternatives generated.

2 ***State four preconditions for meaningful decision making.***

The preconditions required for the full-blown decision-making process to occur are (1) the existence of a gap between the current situation and desired goals, (2) awareness of the significance of the gap, (3) motivation to close the gap, and (4) access to the resources needed to act effectively.

3 ***Explain the conditions of certainty, risk, and uncertainty under which decisions are made.***

Decisions are made under conditions that reflect the likelihood that developments and events will occur over which the decision maker has no control but which may influence the outcomes of decisions. These conditions may be characterized as a continuum from certainty to risk to uncertainty. The greater the risk and uncertainty of future events, the more difficult and challenging is decision making.

4 ***Describe a framework for understanding the three main categories of decisions.***

Combinations of various types of problems and alternative solutions yield three general categories of decisions: (1) routine, (2) adaptive, and (3) innovative. Routine decisions involve relatively well-defined and well-known problems and solutions. Adaptive decisions involve somewhat unusual problems and/or solutions of low to moderate risk. Innovative decisions involve very unusual and ambiguous problems and/or solutions of high risk or uncertainty.

5 ***Apply goals to decision making.***

Goals indicate the direction that decisions and actions should take and the quality or quantity of the results desired. Four benefits derived from setting goals are (1) focusing decisions and efforts, (2) aiding the planning process, (3) motivating people and stimulating performance, and (4) assisting performance evaluation and control. In an organization the formal linking of lower level and higher level goals produces a hierarchy of goals. Stakeholders are crucial in the selection or change of organizational goals.

6 ***Describe the rational, bounded rationality, and political models of decision making.***

The rational model is a sequence of seven steps for making decisions: (1) define and diagnose the problem, (2) set goals, (3) seek alternative solutions, (4) compare and evaluate alternative solutions, (5) choose among alternative solutions, (6) implement the solution selected, and (7) follow up and control the results. The three constraints of the bounded rationality model are (1) satisficing, (2) limited search, and (3) inadequate or misinterpreted information. This model recognizes the practical limitations on individuals' decision making. The political model emphasizes the role of powerful stakeholders in decision making. In particular, political clout tends to influence decision making in terms of identifying problems, setting goals, generating alternative solutions, and even choosing which solution to implement.

QUESTIONS FOR DISCUSSION

1. Recall the Global Insight on the Whirlpool corporation. What were the preconditions for Whirlpool's decision to go global?
2. Identify three issues or problems that are likely to involve the use of objective probabilities by a decision maker. Explain the basis for your selection.
3. Identify three issues or problems that are likely to involve the use of subjective probabilities by a decision maker. Explain the basis for your selection.
4. Why can individuals, whose rationality is limited according to the bounded rationality model, be expected to make reasonably rational decisions at times?
5. What elements of the decision-making process are affected by ethical concepts and issues? Give an example of how an ethical concept or issue could affect each of the elements identified.

FROM WHERE YOU SIT

1. Did your decision to enroll in this course involve certainty, risk, or uncertainty? What is the basis of your answer?
2. Identify ten routine decisions that you have made within the past two days.
3. Identify three adaptive or innovative decisions that you have made within the past six months.
4. Evaluate the *process* you used to make one of the decisions identified in Question 3 in terms of the rational model's seven steps of decision making.
5. What does your hierarchy of goals include? Begin with passing this course as one of your most specific goals.
6. Have you ever observed the political model of decision making in action? Describe the situation.

SKILL-BUILDING EXERCISE

On the Spot[57]

Instructions: For each incident below, indicate your degree of approval of each course of action by assigning any number of points from 0 to 100. Total points assigned for all six alternatives *must* equal 100.

1. You are the manager of a team of workers. Unfortunately, your philosophy and the company's philosophy conflict, and your influence with upper management is limited. Your team is dissatisfied with company policy. Would you ask employees:

______ a. To fall in line.
______ b. To make up their minds.
______ c. To follow the majority decision of all members.
______ d. To follow your position on issues.
______ e. To communicate their concern to management.
______ f. Not to fall in line.

2. A group of your employees develops an improved tool capable of increasing productivity by 50 percent. Actual productivity increases 10 percent, and quality improves as well. The group withholds information about the tool from the methods engineer. Would you:

______ a. Tell the methods engineer.
______ b. Attempt to convince the employees to divulge the information.
______ c. Be satisfied with the 10 percent increase from the use of the tool.
______ d. Speak to each worker individually to assess the situation.
______ e. Ask the workers to increase their output.
______ f. Not tell the methods engineer.

3. You are a manager in the production department of your firm. The firm has stringent regulations against the consumption of alcohol on business premises. One hot afternoon you find an "old timer" drinking a bottle of beer. Would you:

______ a. Report the person.
______ b. Reprimand the person and give a warning.
______ c. Ask for an explanation of the behavior.
______ d. Lay off the person as allowed in the union contract.
______ e. Overlook the incident after making certain that the person sees you.
______ f. Not report the person.

4. You find out that a shipper has been "working a deal" with the majority of your best salespeople, whereby they all gain financially at the expense of the organization. The amounts are not large, but the practice is widespread. You are the sales manager. Would you:

______ a. Fire all the guilty parties.
______ b. Fire the shipper and keep the salespeople.
______ c. Call a meeting to tell them you know what they are doing but not fire anyone.
______ d. Overlook the situation, assuming it to be a "bonus."
______ e. Try to catch them in the act.
______ f. Not fire all guilty parties.

5. Due to rapid expansion of your organization, your "open door" policy is taking up a disproportionate amount of your time. People constantly drop in to chat. Would you:

______ a. Close the door.
______ b. Try to have your secretary screen employees before they reach you.
______ c. Institute a formal communication system, such as a company newsletter.
______ d. Work after hours so as to maintain your close relationship with employees.
______ e. Set up an appointment book.
______ f. Not close the door.

6. A new production process will increase profits by an estimated 10 percent. It will also significantly pollute a large river running through a nearby town. Government regulations do not affect your firm. Would you:

______	a.	Introduce the process.
______	b.	Introduce the process only if profits are lower than usual.
______	c.	Introduce the process only if your competitor does.
______	d.	Not introduce the process unless pressured by upper management.
______	e.	Not introduce the process if residents of the town complain.
______	f.	Not introduce the process.

7. A friend is having difficulty at work with subordinates. Informally you have heard it said that your friend is too autocratic and disorganized. The friend has asked you for your opinion of why problems exist. Would you:

______	a.	Tell your friend what you have heard.
______	b.	Tell your friend that he/she is too autocratic but not discuss the issue of organizational ability.
______	c.	Tell your friend that he/she is disorganized but not discuss his/her autocratic behavior.
______	d.	Tell your friend that what he/she does at work is his/her own business.
______	e.	Ask your friend what he/she thinks the problem is.
______	f.	Not tell your friend what you have heard.

8. As manager of a radio station, you are faced with a dilemma. Your program manager works a twelve-hour day, but the popularity of the station is declining, and it is losing money. The program manager has worked for your organization for five years. Would you:

______	a.	Fire the program manager.
______	b.	Replace the person and give him/her another job.
______	c.	Take over some of the program manager's duties yourself.
______	d.	Ask the person to look for another job but continue to employ him/her.
______	e.	Try to determine the person' weaknesses so that you can help.
______	f.	Not fire the program manager.

9. Your best salesperson has difficulty relating to peers. The position of sales manager is open, and this salesperson has told you that he/she plans to leave if not promoted. Would you:

______	a.	Give the person the job.
______	b.	Tell the person that he/she needs more management training.
______	c.	Tell the person that you hate to lose a great salesperson to gain a questionable sales manager.
______	d.	Ask the person what qualities he/she has to do a good job.
______	e.	Tell the person to prove he/she can get along with others first.
______	f.	Not give the person the job.

10. A bright young scientist joined your research team a few months ago. The scientist has come to you with a letter from a competing firm offering a job with a 25 percent salary increase. Would you:

______	a.	Offer an equal salary.
______	b.	Ask why he/she is showing you the letter.
______	c.	Try to sell the advantages of your firm.
______	d.	Tell the scientist that he/she can make as much at your firm after a time.
______	e.	Tell the person that loyalty should count for something.
______	f.	Not offer to increase the salary.

SCORING

Transfer your raw scores form the questionnaire to the S columns in the following grid. Using the conversion table below the grid, convert each raw score in each S column to an AS score, and enter the converted score in the AS column. Total the AS columns vertically. Then total all the AS sums horizontally. Divide the total by 10 (the number of incidents). Round up if the result contains a decimal part of 0.5 or more. Note whether your score falls within the low, medium, or high range.

	1		**2**		**3**		**4**		**5**		**6**		**7**		**8**		**9**		**10**	
	S	AS	S	AS	S	AS	S	AS	S	AS	S	AS	S	AS	S	AS	S	AS	S	AS
a																				
b																				
c																				
d																				
e																				
f																				
Total			+		+		+		+		+		+		+		+		+	

Sum of totals _____ ÷ 10 = _____ Total Score

Conversion Table

S	0	1–3	4–6	7–11	12–20	21–30	31–40	41–60	61–80	81–90	91–100
AS	1	7	13	19	26	30	32	29	21	7	0

Range	Low	Medium	High
	0	76	96
Total Score	75	95	156

INTERPRETATION

Low scores. Scores of 0–75 indicate a self-reported intolerance for ambiguity. Despite complex or contradictory cues, you say you are able to make clear-cut, unambiguous decisions. Those with this style often appear to be able to "cut through the smoke" and recommend a clear-cut course of action when others are unwilling to move. One of the disadvantages of this style is that you may appear to be abrupt and perhaps even bullheaded.

Medium scores. Scores of 75–95 indicate a self-reported moderate tolerance for ambiguity. When the cues in a situation are complex or contradictory, you try to sort them out and narrow the alternative so that you have identified feasible courses of action. One of the advantages of this style is that you may be seen as a sensitive, understanding person who can see many sides of a problem. One of the disadvantages of this style is that you may be seen as opportunistic or self-serving.

High scores. Scores of 96–156 indicate a self-reported high tolerance for ambiguity. You will find it easy to postpone a decision when the cues for decision making are ambiguous or not clear-cut. One of the advantages of this style is that you may often appear wise and unwilling to rush into complex or novel situations. One of the disadvantages of this style is that you may appear "wishy-washy" and indecisive, surrendering your power to others.

1. How does your score match with your self-perception of your tolerance for ambiguity? You can also check this perception with friends and family.

2. How does your score fit with the level of tolerance for ambiguity required for your job?

CRITICAL THINKING CASE

A Risk of Disclosure?

The coffee cascaded from the machine, but before it had run its course, Sophia pulled the cup away, splashing some of it into the saucer. Moving toward her friend, Sara Grimsley, she frowned and said, "I guess I'm really more upset about this problem than I thought." She found a comfortable place on the other end of the blue wool couch and started into the story. As Sara listened intently, focusing on the implications of what Sophia was saying, she wondered when to introduce the word "fraud." What her friend was describing, left unchecked, could move close to the edge of that cliff.

Sophia Benson worked as the comptroller for a small firm, Bentley Moldings. It had been founded ten years ago by Steve Bentley, an entrepreneur who had a great idea, a big heart, and very little capital. The company manufactured specialized plastic tools. It was highly leveraged and maintained a $2 million line of credit with River City Bank. This line of credit was secured with corporate assets as well as with Steve's personal assets. Over the years, Bentley Moldings had grown to $6 million in annual sales, and was marginally profitable. Steve acted as chairman of the board. A year ago he brought Jane Robinson on as president.

The "problem," as Sophia described it, had surfaced about a year ago when a vendor, RCH (owned by a friend of Steve's) was about to go belly up. Steve had co-signed a $300,000 note to help his friend, and when RCH went under, he ended up with his friend's company and nearly $300,000 of debt.

Bentley Moldings provided corporate financial statements monthly and personal financial statements semiannually to reflect any changes in financial strength. "The first red flag was the monthly financial statement for May," Sophia lamented to her friend. "It showed that we posted a loss for the first time in over eighteen months. The increase in costs for one of our key ingredients was cited as the reason for the decline. But the problem continued, and by July it caught the eye of people down at River City Bank. Sara, you know that for over three years I've been working my tail off to manage the cash flow problems of the company, so when Jane informed me we were absorbing RCH into our company, I was amazed. She told me that it was Steve's call and tried to reassure me by saying that the disclosure issue with the bank was not my responsibility. When I contacted our CPA firm, I was told the same thing."

By this time, Sara noticed that Sophia was hugging herself, as if there was a chill in the air. "I couldn't help feeling a certain obligation to our bank since I was the bank's main contact," she continued. "The questions from its president became more intense. I finally contacted Steve. After all, the bank was within its rights to pull our loan and foreclose on us. Steve told me that Jane had planned this course of action, and I was to let her call the shots. I felt that if we leveled with the bank, perhaps they could help us; but if they accidentally discovered what we were doing, they would show no mercy. I'm concerned about the loss of my professional integrity. I think that we have an obligation to be aboveboard. I really believe this company has a good product and some wonderful people."

Sophia was hoping that, as an executive with a financial services organization, Sara might help her gain perspective. But instead of setting her mind at ease, Sara had impressed her with the gravity of the situation. Sophia filled both of their cups again, and they settled down to discuss what she should do.[58]

Questions

1. Does this situation involve routine, adaptive, or innovative decision making?
2. Use the bounded rationality model to analyze this situation.
3. Use the political model to analyze this situation.
4. What would you do? Why?

VIDEO CASE

General Tire

General Tire, based in Akron, Ohio, had 1994 revenues of approximately $1.4 billion and an 8 percent share of the U.S. tire market. The company is a subsidiary of Continental AG of Germany and was purchased in 1987. Since then, a weak U.S. dollar enabled foreign manufacturers to buy U.S. tire production facilities and combine operations within these existing U.S. plants to capitalize on economies of scale. The growth rate in the tire industry is relatively slow at 1 to 2 percent per year. New technology that enables manufacturers to produce longer lasting tires accounts for much of this slow growth. The development of the steel-belted radial tire has been the single most important innovation and today accounts for 95 percent of all passenger car tire sales. Every new car comes equipped with steel-belted radial tires.

Market research indicates that consumers have very little brand loyalty with regard to buying tires. Rather than having loyalty to a brand of tires, the research conducted by General Tire suggests that consumers are more loyal to the dealer who sells tires. However, to some extent, consumers initially compare the original tires with other brands in the market before making a tire purchase.

In the decision-making process consumers identify with both individual and social factors. The process begins with a stimulus—perhaps a balding tire—followed by problem recognition. Next comes an information search and then an evaluation of alternatives, such as comparing General Tire, Goodyear, Michelin, and Firestone tires. The result is a purchase, or outcome, and postpurchase behavior. In this process, the individual factors may include perception, motivation, learning, values, personality, and lifestyle. The social factors may include reference groups, opinion leaders, family status, social class, and culture.

General Tire competes head to head with Goodyear and Michelin. In particular, high-performance tires are one of the most attractive segments of the consumer tire market. These tires are designed to fit sports cars and performance sedans and give the car better handling characteristics at relatively high speeds. High-performance tires wear faster, prompting more frequent replacement. A premium-priced tire offers a higher profit margin to the manufacturer. Also, this segment is one of the fastest growing in the tire market. Consumers interested in performance tires look for a variety of product features when selecting replacement tires for their cars. These include features such as speed rating, traction, temperature rating, and appearance.[59]

Questions

1. What decision-making process do people generally use when buying high-performance tires? Describe it.
2. What problems might General Tire have in competing with Goodyear and Michelin in the high-performance tire market? What possible solutions might General Tire come up with?
3. Discuss how General Tire helps facilitate the purchase of its products.

Chapter 9

Decision-Making Aids

Learning *Objectives*

After studying this chapter, you should be able to:

1. State the benefits and limitations of normative decision making.
2. Discuss rules and standard operating procedures and artificial intelligence as aids to routine decision making.
3. Explain break-even analysis, the payoff matrix, and Pareto analysis as aids to adaptive decision making.
4. Describe Osborn's creativity model and the cause and effect diagram as aids to innovative decision making.

Chapter *Outline*

Preview *Insight*

Andersen's Window of Knowledge

Andersen Windows, Inc., of Baypoint, Minnesota, makes windows in various shapes and sizes. They include made-to-order units designed for diverse home and office needs. Multimedia software called *Window of Knowledge* provides Andersen dealers with an interactive, on-line tool that they can use to demonstrate and design customized window systems. The same software provides specifications for Andersen products and information about competitors' products. It also supports a full range of administrative and sales tasks. These tasks include creating proposals, pricing installations, calculating the energy efficiency of designs, placing and tracking orders, and managing accounts.

Dave Coraccio of Harvey Industries, Inc., a supplier to building contractors in Woburn, Massachusetts, is a big fan of the *Window of Knowledge* system. "The system has enabled me to work with customers faster, more accurately and with more professional-looking results," Coraccio says. A customer recently posed the problem of how to redesign a room around a painting. Using the *Window of Knowledge* at his desktop computer, Coraccio was able to work with her, demonstrating on the PC how different window styles and placements would work with the picture. The system also allowed him to quote a price quickly for the installation they had worked together to design. "A quote like that used to take an hour and a half," Coraccio states. "Now I can do it in 10 minutes or less."[1]

1

State the benefits and limitations of normative decision making.

NORMATIVE DECISION MAKING

Andersen's *Window of Knowledge* computer software is one of hundreds of examples of decision-making and planning aids. Thus, of necessity, we had to be selective in choosing the aids to be presented in this chapter. The seven aids selected for discussion represent a range of decision-making aids that are widely used to help managers and other employees analyze various problems. These problems arise in virtually every department of an organization, including accounting, data processing, finance, marketing, human resources, and manufacturing.

Before describing the specific decision-making aids, we need to put them in perspective. **Normative decision making** is any step-by-step process that individuals use to help them make choices.[2] The rational model described in Chapter 8 (see Figure 8.5) is an example of normative decision making. Recall that that model includes seven prescribed steps: (1) define and diagnose the problem, (2) set goals, (3) search for alternative solutions, (4) compare and evaluate alternative solutions, (5) choose among alternative solutions, (6) implement the solution selected, and (7) follow up and control. In contrast, the bounded rationality and political models, also presented in Chapter 8, are descriptive models (representations of how individuals actually make decisions). Normative decision making is based on the following assumptions.

- The goals can be stated and agreed upon.
- The nature of the problem can be defined and agreed upon.
- Some information about the problem is available.
- The state of nature affecting the problem ranges from certainty to risk to uncertainty.[3]

Real-World Example
The "bail-bond con" is a common bunco scheme. The con artist calls the victim in the middle of the night when she or he isn't alert enough to ask for details. The con artist claims to be a relative by saying something like, "Aunt Mildred, this is your niece. I've been arrested by mistake. I need bail money. My girlfriend Louise lives around the corner and will be there in ten minutes." Aunt Mildred doesn't use normative decision making. She thinks that the caller is a real niece and hands over the money. Had Aunt Mildred used normative decision making, she would have asked the caller to give her name, asked to speak to a jailer, and/or called her lawyer, discovering the deception in the process (*Money*, April–May, 1991, 42–44).

As you will see in this chapter, normative decision-making aids offer the following potential benefits.

- Hidden assumptions and their implications are likely to be brought into the open and clarified. Most step-by-step decision-making processes require that assumptions be identified and alternatives be assessed.

- The reasoning underlying a decision may be communicated to others effectively. Laying out all the assumptions, alternatives, and probabilities makes the basis for a solid decision easier to see.
- Defining the true nature of problems, collecting relevant information, and quantifying data where possible increases the likelihood of making a decision based on sound judgment.
- Decision makers may become more aware of powerful emotional forces, such as the fear of financial loss, when choosing among alternatives.
- Common biases affecting individual or team decision making can be reduced.[4]

In this chapter we present several aids for each type of decision discussed in Chapter 8: routine, adaptive, and innovative (see Figure 8.2). First, we discuss the use of rules and standard operating procedures and artificial intelligence. These techniques are especially useful to people making routine decisions. Second, we present three aids for helping individuals make adaptive decisions: break-even analysis, payoff matrix, and Pareto analysis, which is an important tool in total quality management efforts. Third, we review the fundamentals of creativity and innovation. The two aids discussed here also are used in total quality management programs—namely, Osborn's creativity model and cause and effect diagrams.

2

Discuss rules and standard operating procedures and artificial intelligence as aids to routine decision making.

ROUTINE DECISION MAKING

Recall that *routine decisions* are standard choices made in response to relatively well-defined and well-known problems and solutions. Numerous aids are available to help employees make routine decisions. Increasingly, these aids are available in the form of computer software, such as Andersen's *Window of Knowledge* software, Lotus 1-2-3, and others. Rules and standard operating procedures provide solutions to a wide range of routine problems. Although it may seem rather esoteric, artificial intelligence is still in its infancy and, to date, has most often been used as an aid in making complex but routine decisions.[5]

Ask Students
What are some examples of routine decisions you made today? (Example: whether to take the car, a bus, bike, or walk to school.)

Rules and Standard Operating Procedures

Rules and standard operating procedures (SOPs) specify actions or steps to be taken to prevent or correct (eliminate) a particular well-defined problem. Public and private organizations alike typically have rules and SOPs to guide employees in making routine decisions. The larger and more bureaucratic an organization is, the more extensive are its rules and SOPs.

Ask Students
Are you currently following one or more SOPs? If so describe one. (Example: The university catalog is an SOP that all students must follow in a certain sequence to earn a degree.)

A **rule** specifies a course of action that must be followed in dealing with a particular problem. Rules help to establish uniformity in decision making. A **standard operating procedure** is a series of rules that employees must follow in a particular sequence when dealing with a certain type of problem. In other words, SOPs prescribe not only how employees should make certain decisions but also what their decisions should be.[6]

Ethics
SOPs are a good place to institutionalize ethics. Have students bring the university catalog to class and check it to see how many places ethics are mentioned. Write on the board how many times and where in the catalog ethics are mentioned.

Organizational rules and SOPs affect employees in their daily work. For example, as a result of federal laws (such as the 1992 Americans with Disabilities Act), most U.S. organizations must follow comprehensive rules and SOPs for individuals with disabilities. For example, Texas A&M University published a thirty-three page handbook entitled *Partners in Learning: Guidelines for Working With Students With Disabilities at Texas A&M University*.[7] Most colleges and universities now have such handbooks for faculty and staff. Based on laws, court decisions, and the institution's own policies, these handbooks present the rules and standard operating procedures that faculty and staff—and students with disabilities—are expected to follow.

Ethics
Name an SOP that you follow that relates to ethics.

These rules and SOPs specify that all colleges and universities must routinely make the following accommodations and adjustments for those with disabilities: (1) extend

Teaching Tip
Have students read an SOP by which they are governed and identify three things that they didn't know before and that are useful for them to know. Ask the students to write up this exercise and hand it in.

Teaching Tip
Involve students in a discussion of how and why the proliferation of rules can adversely affect employee morale.

the time permitted for the student to earn a degree, (2) modify examination formats, (3) develop course substitutions or waivers, and (4) permit the use of such learning aids as tape recorders, word processors, calculators, lap-top computers and spell-checkers. In addition, colleges and universities may *not* (1) limit the number of students with disabilities admitted, (2) make preadmission inquiries regarding an applicant's disability, (3) use admission tests or criteria that inadequately measure the academic level of applicants with a disability because special provisions were not made for them, (4) exclude a student from a course of study, (5) counsel a student with a disability toward a more restrictive career, (6) measure student achievement using methods that adversely discriminate against the student with a disability, and (7) institute prohibitive rules that may adversely affect students with disabilities.[8]

Codes of ethics and standards of conduct often are rules and SOPs for routinely handling sensitive issues. As suggested in the following Ethics Insight, however, such rules and SOPs may still require individuals to make assessments and judgments in each situation.

Ethics *Insight*

The Golden Rule

As is commonly known, the **Golden Rule** states: "Do unto others as you would have them do unto you." Sometimes called the "rule of reciprocity," this rule for behavior has a long history. Versions of it can be found in ancient Chinese and Greek philosophy, as well as in the Bible. The Golden Rule requires us to place ourselves in the position of those who will be helped or harmed by our decisions and behavior. We then need to treat others as we would want to be treated in a similar situation. If you don't want to be lied to or deceived, do not lie to or deceive others. If you want others to keep their commitments to you, keep your commitments to them. The Golden Rule isn't easy to practice. It requires personal restraint, self-discipline, and even sacrifice.

Some individuals believe that the Golden Rule will work when applied only to a small circle of family and friends. To survive, they claim that they must: "Do unto others, *before* they can do unto you." This philosophy and attitude, of course, becomes a self-fulfilling prophecy, which breeds the "everyone for themselves" attitude.

The Golden Rule is a guide to which decisions and actions are ethical and which are not. The main problem with this rule is that it is not adequate in situations that involve many stakeholders, all of whom may be affected in different ways. Nor does the Golden Rule help management rank order the competing interests of shareholders, employees, suppliers, customers, and the community at large.[9]

Ethics
Is the use of artificial intelligence to put human beings out of work ethical?

Teaching Tip
Have students brainstorm the opportunities and risks associated with artificial intelligence.

Teaching Tip
Have students interview managers to determine whether their organizations use artificial intelligence in decision making. If so, find out how they use AI.

Artificial Intelligence

Artificial intelligence (AI) is the ability of a properly programmed computer system to perform functions normally associated with human intelligence, such as comprehending spoken language, making judgments, and even learning.[10] In recent years, computer software representing the first steps toward AI has been developed. Most business applications of AI involve what is called an expert system.

Expert Systems. An **expert system** is a computer program based on the decision-making processes of human experts that stores, retrieves, and manipulates data, diagnoses problems, and makes limited decisions based on detailed information about a specific problem.[11] It helps users find solutions by posing a series of questions about a specific situation and then offering solutions based on the information it receives in response. The primary characteristics of an expert system include the following.

- It is programmed to use factual knowledge, if-then rules, and specific procedures to solve certain complex problems. If-then rules are logical steps of progression toward a solution.
- It is based on the decision-making process used by effective managers or specialists when they search among possible alternatives for a "good enough" solution.
- It provides programmed explanations, so the user can follow the assumptions, line of reasoning, and process leading to the recommended alternative.[12]

Discussion Question 1
What are the key differences between rules and SOPs and artificial intelligence (AI)?

The following Insight describes one of the expert systems that Nynex uses.

Insight

Nynex's Expert System

Harry Bolton, a buyer at Nynex, the New York City telecommunications firm, uses an expert system to help make dozens of purchases of wire cable—about $13 million worth annually. Despite the amount of money at stake, when Bolton negotiates with suppliers, he drafts his own custom purchase agreements without even consulting an attorney.

He uses Nynex's Contract Drafting System. First, he selects the type of legal document he wants to create from a menu of more than twenty choices. Then, questions begin to appear on his computer screen: What is the name of the supplier? How long will the contract last? Will there be an option to extend the agreement? Will Nynex receive "most favored customer" pricing?

A half-hour and twenty-five to thirty-five questions later (depending upon the complexity of the contract), Bolton can print out a comprehensive fourteen-page agreement tailored to the transaction. Before Nynex installed this expert system in 1992, it would have taken at least four hours of Bolton's time, four hours of a word processor's time, and two hours of an attorney's time to produce an equally sophisticated and correct document.[13]

Real-World Example
Neural networks are programs that imitate the functions of the human brain. They can discern patterns and trends that are too subtle for human beings to recognize. This technology has a wide range of commercial applications. Using a neural net program professional racehorse gambler Don Emmons picked eleven of twenty-two winners recently. John Deere & Company investment analyst Dr. James Hall uses it to manage his company's $100 million pension fund. The U.S. Army uses it to experiment with driverless vehicles, such as ambulances, to function under hostile fire (*Fortune*, September 6, 1993, 96).

Nynex's Contract Drafting System belongs to a new breed of expert systems. They are enabling people who aren't attorneys to create legal documents that once were prepared exclusively by attorneys. The software gathers the factual information from the user. The preprogrammed "expertise" of the system then plugs it into a highly developed decision tree that can include hundreds of variations on the document being created. Commercial packages are now available to produce wills, trusts, simple employment contracts, incorporation documents, and regulatory compliance forms. As you might expect, some attorneys have reservations about such expert systems. Some of these concerns may be legitimate, but others may be self-serving.

Assessment of AI. Evaluations of AI range from claims that it is on the verge of transforming the way managers and employees make decisions (i.e., machines will make them) to extreme skepticism. Most commercial uses of AI are highly specialized business and industrial applications ranging from financial advising to robot control. One of the most enthusiastic assessments of the future of AI is expressed by Edward Rosenfeld, publisher of the newsletter *Intelligence: The Future of Computing*. He states: "Neural networks (an advanced branch of AI) provide an adaptive human-style intelligence that will enable future computers to fly planes, run factories, hear, speak, see, understand, and discover."[14]

Ethics
Critics of expert systems say that some experts may rely on them too much and thereby try to evade their professional responsibilities. How can this situation be prevented?

At present, most successful AI applications involve complex and routine (repetitive) decision situations. However, as demonstrated by Nynex's Contract Drafting System, it also can help employees make better adaptive decisions. With continued advances in computer technology and software, AI is at the threshold of even helping managers and employees to make innovative decisions.[15]

3

Explain break-even analysis, the payoff matrix, and Pareto analysis as aids to adaptive decision making.

ADAPTIVE DECISION MAKING

Adaptive decisions involve a combination of moderately ambiguous problems and alternative solutions. Break-even analysis, the payoff matrix, and Pareto charts are three particularly helpful aids for diagnosing problems and making adaptive decisions. A variety of software packages for personal computers (PCs) make using all these aids relatively easy. In addition, numerous other aids are available for making adaptive decisions, including those presented in Chapter 6 for making adaptive and innovative decisions during the planning process.

Break-Even Analysis

Break-even analysis examines the various relationships among sales (revenues) and costs in order to determine the point where total sales equal total costs. It shows basic relationships among units produced (output), sales revenue, costs, and profits for a firm or a product line. This information is needed as a basis for projecting profits, controlling expenses, determining prices, and, most important, helping employees to choose among alternatives. The numbers used in the analysis can be developed from historical data. Dr Pepper/7-Up uses break-even analysis to make year-by-year comparisons of product-line (e.g., diet versus regular) profits. Break-even analysis helps employees probe moderately ambiguous problems, such as why total sales are below total costs, and stimulates the need to search for new alternatives. It can help answer questions such as: At what point should a particular product be discontinued? How much will the company lose or gain with each combination of sales, costs, and units of goods or services produced? What will happen if fixed costs rise 8 percent and sales don't change?

Variables and Relationships. The following seven variables are used in break-even analysis.

Teaching Tip
Have students do a break-even analysis of their educational investment.

Ethics
Social responsibility costs can be included in break-even analysis.

Discussion Question 4
By the time coffee arrived, Zita Thurman and Tom Namura were deeply involved in an after-dinner discussion about problems at work. Thurman, manager of the small-parts division of a manufacturing company, had just taken a management science course. Namura, human resource director of the same company, had not. "I tell you," Thurman claimed, "chances are you cannot make a decision without having your emotions color it. Answer this for me. You have two options: A, a 100 percent chance to win $3,000; and B, an 80 percent chance to win $4,000. Which would you take?" Namura thought for a few seconds and chose option A, the guaranteed $3,000. Was Tom Namura correct? Why or why not?[44]

- *Fixed costs* are those costs that remain constant over a specific period of time, regardless of the number of units produced (e.g., insurance premiums, real estate taxes, administrative expenses, and interest).
- *Variable costs* are those costs that tend to vary with changes in the number of units produced but not necessarily in proportion to each additional unit of output (e.g., direct labor, electricity, raw materials, packaging, and transportation).
- *Total costs* are the sum of all fixed and variable costs.
- *Total revenue* represents the total dollars received from sales.
- *Profit* is the excess of total revenue over total costs.
- *Loss* is the excess of total costs over total revenue.
- *Break-even point* is the point at which total costs equal total revenue.

Figure 9.1 illustrates the relationships among these variables for a hypothetical firm. Monthly costs (fixed and variable costs) and monthly revenues are plotted versus monthly units produced in order to determine profit, loss, and the break-even point. When monthly production and sales go above that point, the firm sells more than it spends and makes a profit. Below that point, costs exceed sales and the firm suffers a monthly loss.

Assessment. Break-even analysis has proven very useful to employees making financial, marketing, and other types of decisions. However, it has several limitations. First, expecting profits to depend only on the quantities of units sold is incorrect. Profits are also influenced by changes in the price or quality of competing products, improvement in production processes, and increases in marketing effectiveness. Second, general economic conditions may cause the relationships among the variables to shift. For example, a surge in general business activity might rapidly drive up the cost of certain raw materials (a variable cost). Third, quantifying all the variables can be difficult.

FIGURE 9.1

Monthly Break-Even Analysis

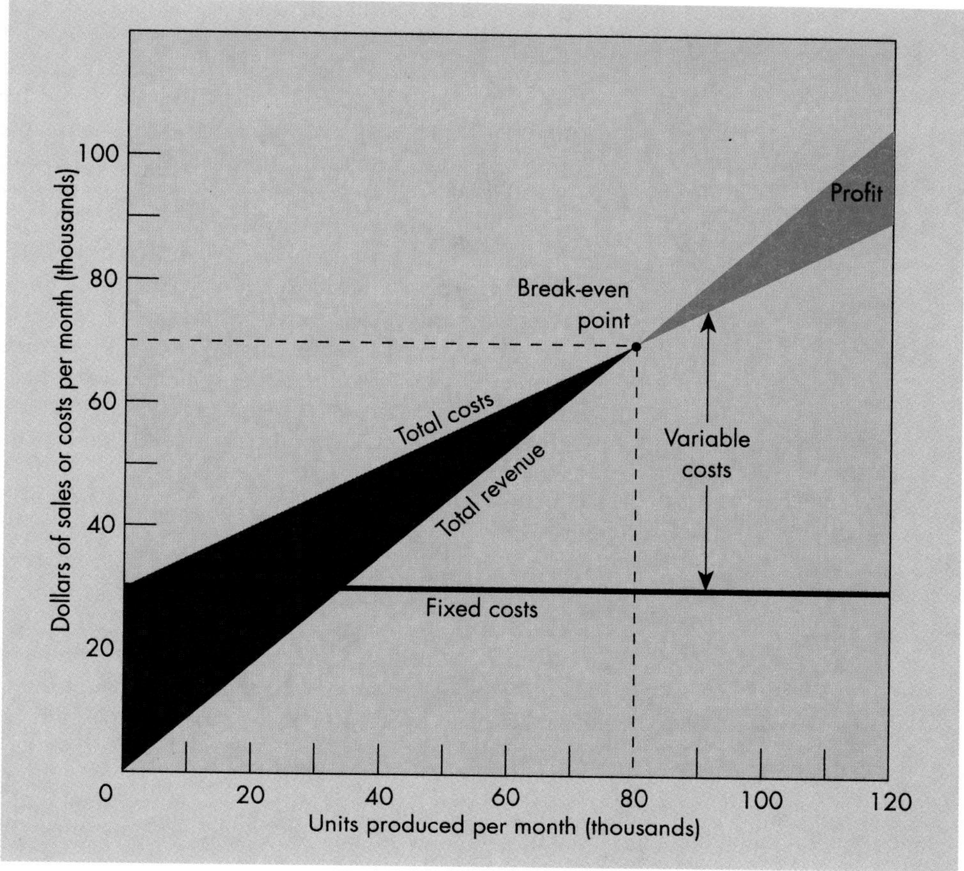

An analyst can partially overcome these limitations by doing several break-even analyses, basing each one on different assumptions and estimates.[16] However, the analyst may still need to consider factors other than the seven variables used in break-even analysis. We discuss several of these additional factors in connection with the payoff matrix.

Payoff Matrix

A **payoff matrix** is a table of figures or symbols used to identify the possible states of nature, probabilities, and outcomes (payoffs) associated with alternative strategies.[17] The payoff matrix is based on the assumption that decision makers are able to identify desired goals and specify alternative strategies to reach them. Managers can use the payoff matrix to help make a variety of adaptive decisions, such as whether to open a new branch store, whether to increase (or decrease) the price of a product, and whether to rent or buy an office building.

Variables and Relationships. The payoff matrix includes four variables, as shown in Table 9.1.

1. *Strategies* are the feasible alternatives that have been identified. In Table 9.1 they are $S_1, S_2, S_3, \ldots, S_n$.
2. The *states of nature* are the anticipated specific conditions of certainty, risk, or uncertainty under which the decision is to be made. In Table 9.1 they are $N_1, N_2, N_3, \ldots, N_m$.

3. *Probability* is the likelihood that each state of nature will occur. In Table 9.1, the probabilities are $P_1, P_2, P_3, \ldots, P_m$. The sum of all the probabilities in the payoff matrix must equal 1.0. At least one of the specified states of nature is expected to occur. A matrix with four states of nature could have probabilities of 0.1, 0.2, 0.2, and 0.5 (which sum to 1.0) for those states of nature. Because it embodies so many possible strategies to which probabilities can be assigned, the payoff matrix of Table 9.1 indicates that the decision is being made under the condition of risk. If the condition were certain, the payoff matrix would show only one state of nature. Under a condition of uncertainty, a payoff matrix would not be as useful. The reason is that the analyst would have no data available on which to base probabilities.
4. An *outcome* is the expected payoff (profit or loss) for each combination of a strategy and a state of nature. In Table 9.1 the outcomes are O_{11} through O_{nm}. For example, O_{11} in Table 9.1 is the outcome if the first strategy (S_1) is chosen and the first state of nature (N_1) occurs. Each outcome in a payoff matrix is called a **conditional value (CV)** because it is based on a particular state of nature and a specific strategy.

Expected Values. The payoff matrix is useful only when the decision maker can assign probabilities to states of nature. In order to work toward a decision when the matrix consists of two or more states of nature, the expected value for each strategy must be calculated. Thus the **expected value (EV)** is the weighted-average outcome for each strategy. That is, the expected value is the sum of the conditional values after each has been multiplied by its probability. For example, we can present each of the expected values for the payoff matrix in Table 9.1 as follows:

$$EV_1 = P_1O_{11} + P_2O_{12} + P_3O_{13} + \cdots + P_mO_{1m}$$

$$EV_2 = P_1O_{21} + P_2O_{22} + P_3O_{23} + \cdots + P_mO_{2m}$$

$$EV_3 = P_1O_{31} + P_3O_{32} + P_3O_{33} + \cdots + P_mO_{3m}$$

.

.

.

$$EV_n = P_1O_{n1} + P_3O_{n2} + P_3O_{n3} + \cdots + P_mO_{nm}$$

Discussion Question 3
What are the similarities between break-even analysis and the payoff matrix?

In the Insight on the next page we apply the payoff matrix to a specific situation.

TABLE 9.1

Payoff Matrix

	Possible State of Nature				
	N_1	N_2	N_3	. . .	N_m
Strategy (Alternative)	**Probability That Each State of Nature Will Occur**				
	P_1	P_2	P_3	. . .	P_m
	Outcome of Strategy				
S_1	O_{11}	O_{12}	O_{13}	. . .	O_{1m}
S_2	O_{21}	O_{22}	O_{23}	. . .	O_{2m}
S_3	O_{31}	O_{32}	O_{33}	. . .	O_{3m}
.	.	.	.	.	.
.	.	.	.	.	.
.	.	.	.	.	.
S_n	O_{n1}	O_{n2}	O_{n3}	. . .	O_{nm}

Insight

The Stadium Decision

A university president is trying to decide how many seats to add to the football stadium. The available information and the assumptions being made are as follows.

1. Most of the games during the past two years have been sold out. If more seats had been available, additional tickets could have been sold for those games.
2. The president and administrative staff believe that the football team will be good, if not excellent, during the next three years. The squad has a large number of sophomores and juniors, and an excellent group of first-year players has been recruited.
3. A modular seating system has been chosen because of its low cost, excellent quality, and ease of installation. The system comes in units of 4,000 seats.
4. Moderate increases (4 percent per year) are anticipated in the current student enrollment of 30,000 and the local town population of 100,000. The town is thirty miles from a major metropolitan area.

The president and staff have decided to consider four alternative strategies. They also have developed subjective probabilities for four levels of additional seating demand (states of nature).

Seating Demand	*Probability of This Level of Demand*
4,000	0.50
8,000	0.30
12,000	0.15
16,000	0.05
	1.00

The president and staff have assumed that there is a 50 percent probability that 4,000 added seats will be sold out. They also have assumed that there is only a 5 percent probability that 16,000 added seats will be sold out.

The conditional values (CV) in this case show what would happen if each state of nature (seating demand) and strategy (seat expansion) were to occur. A conditional value can be determined for each combination of a strategy and a state of nature by using the following equation:

$$CV = RQ_d - CQ_{c'}$$

where CV = conditional value, R = revenue per seat, Q_d = quantity of seats demanded, C = total costs per seat, and Q_c = quantity of seats constructed.

For the 4,000-seat strategy, the costs of each seat will be $30 per year over the payback period. The maximum potential revenue per season will be $80 per seat. Thus, if 4,000 seats were demanded (O_d) and 4,000 seats were constructed (O_c),

$$\begin{aligned} CV &= (\$80 \times 4{,}000) - (\$30 \times 4{,}000) \\ &= \$320{,}000 - \$120{,}000 \\ &= \$200{,}000 \text{ (profit)} \end{aligned}$$

The conditional values (outcomes) for the four strategies under each of the four states of nature are shown in the following table. Note, however, that the probabilities associated with different seating demands (states of nature) have not yet been considered.

CONDITIONAL VALUES FOR STADIUM EXPANSION DECISION (IN THOUSANDS OF DOLLARS)

Seats Constructed (Strategies)	*Seating Demand (States of Nature)*			
	4,000	*8,000*	*12,000*	*16,000*
4,000	$200	$200	$200	$200
8,000	80	400	400	400
12,000	−40	280	600	600
16,000	−160	160	480	800

From the information in the table and the probabilities listed earlier, the president and staff can develop the expected values. The first step in calculating the expected values is to multiply each conditional value by the probability of occurrence assigned to each state of nature. For example, the expected value for constructing 4,000 stadium seats and having a demand of 4,000 seats is

$$\begin{aligned} EV &= CV(P) \\ &= \$200{,}000(0.50) \\ &= \$100{,}000. \end{aligned}$$

The following table shows the expected values for each probability of demand. The results indicate that the university should expand the stadium by 8,000 seats because this number of added seats would lead to the highest total expected value.

EXPECTED VALUES FOR STADIUM EXPANSION DECISION (IN THOUSANDS OF DOLLARS)

	Seating Demand				
	4,000	8,000	12,000	16,000	
Seats Constructed (Strategies)	*Probability of Demand*				*Total Expected Value*
	0.50	*0.30*	*0.15*	*0.05*	
4,000	$100	$ 60	$30	$10	$200
8,000	40	120	60	20	240
12,000	−20	84	90	30	184
16,000	−80	48	72	40	120

Teaching Tip
Have students prepare a payoff matrix on the decision to get a job after graduation or go straight to graduate school.

Three of the four decision-making aids that we have presented so far (excluding rules and standard procedures) require the exercise of individual or team judgment. Judgment is required in setting goals, defining problems, making assumptions, and assigning probabilities. The following aid is more limited in scope because it focuses on diagnosing problems.

Pareto Analysis

Pareto analysis focuses on the sources and relative priorities of the causes of problems. It is frequently used to assess the causes of quality problems in TQM programs. The **Pareto principle** states that a small number of causes (usually 20 percent of the total) accounts for most of the problems (usually 80 percent of the total) in any situation. It is based on research done by a nineteenth century Italian economist, Vilfredo

Pareto and often is referred to as the "80/20 Rule." Pareto analysis separates the "vital few" from the "trivial many." Thus it improves the analyst's chances of getting the greatest results for the least amount of time and effort.[18]

Pareto Diagram. One of the tools of Pareto analysis is the **Pareto diagram,** which is a chart used to determine the relative priorities of issues or problems. The issues or problems are arranged in descending order of magnitude or importance, indicating which problems to address first. Pareto diagrams also can be used to highlight the before and after results of projects by comparing multiple diagrams. The following Quality Insight describes one application of Pareto analysis at Oregon State University.

Teaching Tip
Identify a problem facing your university, school, or department. Have students draw a Pareto diagram for the problem.

Quality *Insight*

Complaints in Building Remodeling

As part of a larger total quality management program, the Physical Plant Department at Oregon State University sought feedback from their customers—that is, other units throughout the campus—on what they thought of its remodeling services. The units were asked to respond to six questions on a six-point scale from 1 (excellent) to 6 (needs major improvement). The questions were: (1) Was the cost reasonable? (2) Was there a timely response to your request? (3) Was work completed to your satisfaction? (4) Were you kept current on the status of work? (5) Was the job site left clean? (6) Is there anything we could do to improve our service? Question six was open-ended to encourage written responses.

The Physical Plant team developed the Pareto diagram shown in Figure 9.2 from the raw data to help determine which concerns were most serious. The team developed the diagram by

1. separating the data collected into categories of complaints,
2. summing the number of complaints in each category and calculating its percentage of the total,
3. listing the categories on the horizontal axis in descending order of magnitude from left to right,
4. dividing the vertical axis on the left by numbering it from 0 to 36, the total number of responses,
5. drawing bars for all of the categories, the height of each representing the number of responses for that category,
6. dividing the vertical axis on the right and numbering it from 0 to 100 percent,
7. placing the cumulative percentage for each category above its bar and next to a dot referenced to the vertical axis (0% to 100%),
8. connecting the dots with a curve and marking the cumulative 80 percent point.

A properly constructed diagram suggests that an individual or team should start by addressing the concern stated most often (the one on the far left of the chart) and then proceed to each lesser concern (moving to the right). In this case, the first category represents 28 percent of all the complaints, and the second represents 25 percent of total complaints. Thus the cumulative percentage for the second category is 53 percent.

According to the Pareto principle, the vertical dotted line indicates that the categories *Not Timely, Status Unclear,* and *High Cost* account for nearly 80 percent of all the complaints. Hence the team should concentrate on addressing those problems to get the greatest return for their efforts.[19]

Discussion Question 5
Which of the following alternatives should Lois Garcia choose: (1) a 100 percent chance to lose $3,000, or (2) an 80 percent chance to lose $4,000 with a 20 percent chance to lose nothing?[45] Why?

Assessment. The preceding Quality Insight shows that the 80/20 rule doesn't always hold absolutely in practice. According to Figure 9.2, three of the seven identified categories accounted for 72 percent of the complaints. For the 80/20 rule to hold exactly, 80 percent of the complaints would need to be reflected in one out of five or two out of ten categories.

FIGURE 9.2

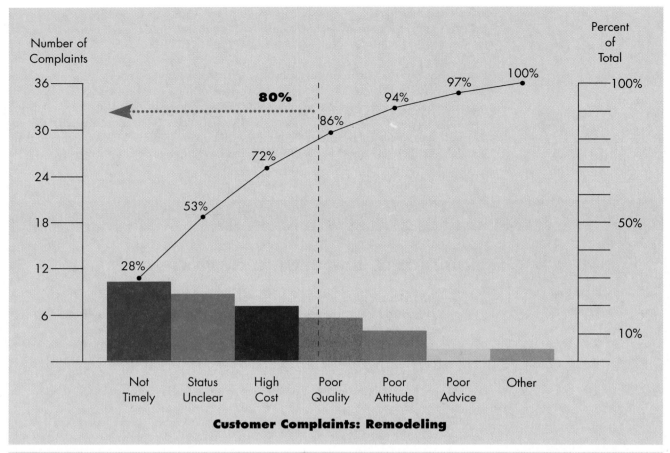

Pareto Diagram of Customer Complaints on Remodeling
Source: Howard, N.L. (ed.). *Total Quality Management: Facilitator and Team Leader Training.* Corvallis: Oregon State University, Department of Human Resources, 1991, 50.

Discussion Question 6
What are two limitations to the use of the Pareto diagram?

Thus analysts must use good judgment when interpreting a Pareto diagram. For example, the complaints of two major customers that account for 40 percent of sales in an infrequently mentioned category may be more important than a particular complaint mentioned by 20 customers who account for just 2 percent of sales. Also, the initial broad categories of identified problems often need to be analyzed further to verify that specific categories of problems, not just symptoms, are being considered. Generally, two or three Pareto analyses must be developed before the process of identifying alternative solutions can begin.

Describe Osborn's creativity model and the cause and effect diagram as aids to innovative decision making

INNOVATIVE DECISION MAKING

Innovative decisions are based on the discovery, identification, and diagnosis of unusual and ambiguous problems and/or the development of unique or creative alternative solutions. Underlying innovative decision making is the creative process and a creative climate. The two aids presented in this section for facilitating innovative decision making involve creativity. Their application can help individuals think more openly and systematically about goals, problems, and alternatives.[20]

Ask Students
The hardest part of coming up with new solutions is said to be knowing where and how to start looking for them. Do you agree? Why or why not?

Real-World Example
Jukus are cram schools in Japan. Several Japanese firms use them to train managers and employees to be more creative. Electronic control maker Omron Corporation gets its mid-level employees out of their routine decision-making patterns by asking them to plan and think as if they were nineteenth century warlords, private detectives, or Formula One race car drivers. Fuji Film has its top managers study topics as diverse as the history of Venice and the sociology of apes (*Fortune,* April 19, 1993, 129).

Ask Students
Can personal or cultural perceptions block managers' creativity? If so, how?

Creative Process

Before discussing two of the many aids for innovative decision making, we need to discuss a few fundamentals of the creative process and the creative climate.[21] **Creativity** is the ability to visualize, foresee, generate, and implement new ideas. Creative thinking increases the quality of solutions to many types of problems, helps stimulate innovation, revitalizes motivation and commitment by challenging individual skills, and serves as a catalyst for effective team performance. Creativity is no longer optional—it is imperative. In particular, for TQM initiatives to succeed, managers and employees need creative thinking skills. A supportive organizational culture is essential for the development and application of such skills.[22]

The creative process comprises five interconnected stages: preparation, concentration, incubation, illumination, and verification.

Preparation means that a thorough investigation must be made to identify and ensure that all parts of a problem are understood. This stage involves searching for and collecting facts and ideas.

Concentration occurs when energies and resources are focused on identifying and solving a problem. A commitment must be made in this stage to defining the problem and implementing a solution.

Incubation involves an internal and unconscious ordering of gathered information. This stage may involve an unconscious personal conflict between what is currently accepted as reality and what may be possible. Relaxing, sometimes distancing oneself from the issue, and allowing the subconscious to search for possible problems and solutions is important. A successful incubation stage yields fresh ideas and new ways of thinking about the nature of the problem and possible alternatives.

Science fiction writer Ray Bradbury once said that he often had flashes about good material during the half-awake state before real sleep. Often he forced himself completely awake to make notes on these ideas. In fact, you can coach yourself to receive dream images by telling your unconscious, "Give me a dream about [the issue or problem you are working on]. Wake me as soon as the dream is over." (With practice, you will be able to dream and awaken like this.) As soon as you are awake, *do not* open your eyes but do review your dream. Then open your eyes and, using the pad and pencil you have left by your bedside, quickly write down the main elements of the dream.[23]

Novelty, an original approach to a problem, involves seeing a possibility before anyone else does. Sally Fox, founder of Natural Cotton Colours, was working for a California cotton breeder when she found a paper bag of brown cotton seeds and lint. This gave her the idea that weavers and other hobbyists would buy undyed brown cotton. After years of experimentation, she started a mail-order business. The first year she sold less than $1,000 of cotton. Then she decided to go after the commercial market. Three Japanese firms bid on her 12-acre crop. The winning bid was $5 per pound for 2,000 pounds of brown and green cotton. (Ordinary cotton sells for 70 cents per pound.)

The *Illumination* stage is the moment of discovery, the instant of recognition, as when a "light" seems to be turned on mentally. The mind instantly connects a problem with a solution through an observation or occurrence. Ray Jones, the research lab director for a chemical firm, describes the illumination stage in this way:

> *Somebody came to me recently with the problem of making silicon nitride powders. We can make silicon nitride fibers, but could we make very fine powders? We came up with some solutions that we thought could do it, but neither of us was satisfied with them. About a month later an idea popped into my head which I think solves the entire thing.*[24]

Verification refers to testing the created solution or idea. In this stage, the individual seeks confirmation and acceptance of the new approach.

These five interconnected elements apply to various types of creativity. One type is *novelty,* or an original approach to a problem. Novelty involves seeing a possibility before anyone else does. Arthur Fry, a researcher at 3M, was the first to use Post-It-Notes to mark pages on his church hymnal. He then realized the tremendous variety of applications for Post-It-Notes. A second type of creativity is *synthesis,* or the combining of existing ideas from various sources into a new whole. Many organizations have expanded their markets by synthesizing new services to complement existing product lines. Ben & Jerry's Homemade Ice Cream expanded its line into fat-free desserts to complement its ice cream products. A third type of creativity is *extension,* which involves extending an idea to another application. The following Small Business Insight demonstrates Pamela Coker's use of *synthesis* and *extension* in the development of her business.

Small Business *Insight*

Pamela Coker

Pamela Coker founded Acucobol, headquartered in San Diego, with a $200,000 investment, in 1988. As of 1995, Acucobol had more than $12 million in annual sales, with half of it coming from international sales.

Acucobol's services are software programs that modernize business applications written in COBOL (common business-oriented language). When Coker started her business, experts generally thought that COBOL was an out-of-date software language. However, Coker recognized that there are millions of COBOL programs in use. In some places—including Brazil, India, and Italy—COBOL is still Number 1. The language is effective at handling high-volume, repetitive business tasks such as invoicing. Acucobol replaced the old and difficult user interface with a new one that features user friendly, colorful screens. Acucobol's software also lets customers use their old programs with any modern operating systems, including Windows and Unix. Currently, it is running 300,000 business programs worldwide.

Coker thought that there might be a large market for Acucobol's services overseas and headed for Europe a year after the company started selling software. She attended trade shows and looked for potential partners. She started by licensing the Acucobol name to an entrepreneur in Germany and took a 20 percent equity stake in his company—"so he would know we were supporting him, and so I would have a board seat and know what was going on." Coker entered into similar minority partnerships in Italy, Great Britain, and Scandinavia.

Coker also adapted what had worked in the United States, especially in marketing. Take telephone sales for example: "The Germans told us we would never sell anything unless we made personal visits to everyone," says Coker. "We said, 'You'll never make money if you do that. You really need to sell it over the phone.' Our guy tried it and it worked. He was surprised that he was able to do it all over the phone."

Acucobol now has about 120 employees, and its export strategies have broadened. The firm now sells large software packages directly to major corporations such as Chrysler in the United States, Daimler-Benz in Germany, and Saab in Brazil. To do that, Coker says, "You need a direct sales force and a lot more handholding." As a result, Acucobol has set up wholly owned subsidiaries in new key target markets: Hong Kong, Japan, and England.[25]

Creative Climate

In the Broadway musical *Fiddler on the Roof,* a beautiful song entitled "Tradition" extols the virtues of having strong cultural traditions. Many benefits to families, organizations, and societies are derived from tradition-based holidays, rituals, and ceremonies. But "we have always done it this way" is a major reason why creativity cannot even get a toehold in some organizations. In Chapter 2, we discussed bureaucratic management, an organizational system that relies on rigid rules and procedures, a set and strict hierarchy, and a narrow division of labor, and one in which employees are expected to perform only prescribed duties. That type of organizational system and climate usually is alien and hostile to creative thinking.

A creative climate often is encouraged under less bureaucratic management and positive leadership. In brief, a creative climate usually consists of the following attributes.[26]

Teaching Tip
Have students brainstorm elements of a creative climate that comprise the acronym CREATIVE. (Example: Collaboration, Rewards, etc.)

- Trust, so that people can try and fail without prejudice.
- An effective system of internal and external communication, so that everyone concerned is fully aware of the organization's needs and goals.
- A variety of personality types within the organization and on its teams.
- A process that ensures the survival of and ultimately the reward for potentially useful ideas.
- A merit system that is based, at least in part, on the generation and implementation of innovative ideas.
- Flexibility in organizational design and financial and accounting systems, so that new approaches can survive.

Hewlett-Packard fosters a creative environment by keeping its labs open to engineers around the clock. It encourages its 965 researchers to devote 10 percent of company time to exploring their own ideas.

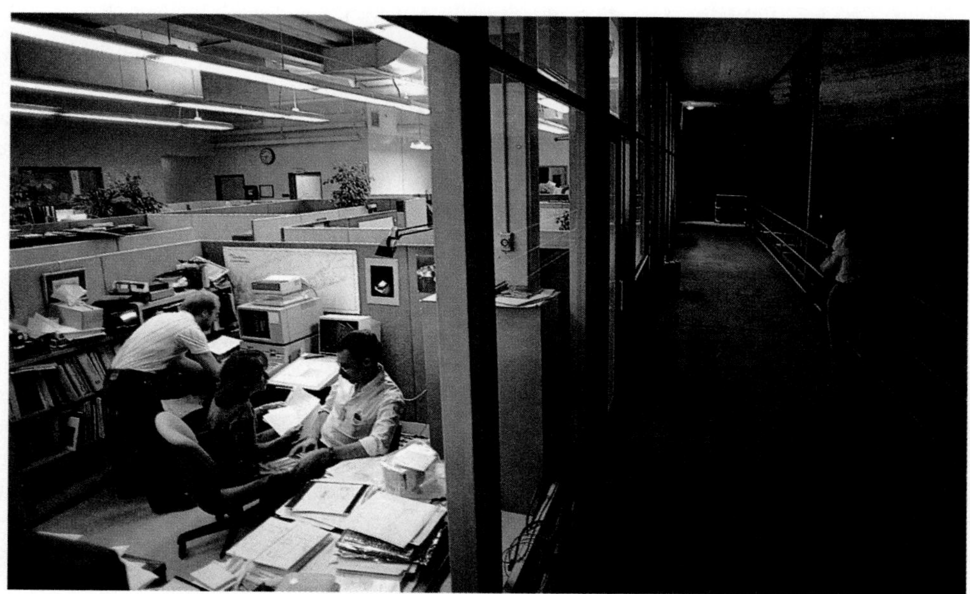

The following Global Insight describes a few of the efforts by one Japanese organization to stimulate creativity by modifying its rigid organizational system and climate of excessive consensus management.

Global *Insight*

Fostering Creativity at Shiseido

Shiseido, Japan's largest cosmetics maker, is encouraging more creativity by its managers and employees. In one creativity program, twenty of Shiseido's division heads were brought into a conference room to find goldfish in bowls on tables. The leader of the session announces: "This goldfish is Shiseido." He asks the managers to analyze the creature and its role in the world, and to draw parallels with their company. Some ask for magnifying glasses. All of the managers jot down notes. Later they look for other Shiseido corporate characteristics by poking and pulling at an Alaskan king crab.

After dinner, the session leader leads a free-wheeling discussion of the parallels between companies and living systems, starting with the goldfish. He asks everyone to keep Shiseido in mind while he asks a series of questions: Why is the goldfish in water? Why is it symmetrical? Why is its head so large? Why does it have so many scales? What does it hope to achieve? What is its function? Most conclude that the goldfish is an efficient company, as long as it operates in the safe surroundings of water.

Next, the leader directs the group's attention to the crab. The managers identify some merits of a crab. It can see 360 degrees. It has a solid infrastructure. It is rugged and can survive after losing a leg. As for the negatives, the ungainly crab is definitely in need of downsizing. It moves too slowly and only from side to side. It has an image problem—nobody wants to be a crab. Which is a better model for Shiseido? Masami Hamaguchi, who works in international operations, comments: "Maybe if it was still in a period of high economic growth, Shiseido would do well to be a goldfish. But in these times, we should be a crab with a strong corporate philosophy as our shell."

The long-term effects of Shiseido's various programs to stimulate innovation and creativity are yet to be completely determined. However, Shiseido has managed to remain profitable and annually increase sales modestly to about $5 billion as of 1995. This achievement contrasts sharply with Japan's deep recession and losses for most Japanese firms.[27]

The Skill-Building Exercise at the end of this chapter provides a way for you to assess your own barriers to creative thought and innovative action. Part five of his book contains many ideas for developing a creative organizational climate. For now, we present A.F. Osborn's creativity model and the cause and effect diagram as aids for fostering innovation and creativity in organizations.

Osborn's Creativity Model

Osborn's creativity model is a three-phase decision making process that involves finding facts, ideas, and solutions. It is designed to help overcome blockages to creativity and innovation, which may occur for a variety of reasons. It is intended to stimulate cooperation and freewheeling thinking that lead to innovative team decisions.[28] It can be used with all types of groups (e.g., a manager and subordinates or a team of employees). Sufficient time and freedom must be allowed for the model to work well, and some degree of external pressure and self-generated tension are helpful. However, too much pressure or too many threats from the wrong sources (e.g., an order from top management to determine within ten days why quality has deteriorated) can easily undermine the process.

In contrast to the decision-making aids discussed so far in this chapter, which tend to focus on step-by-step analysis, Osborn's creativity model stimulates novel ideas and curiosity. It is one of several aids for finding new ways of identifying and considering problems and generating solutions.[29] The model has three phases: fact finding, idea finding, and solution finding.

Fact-Finding Phase. Fact finding involves defining the problem and gathering and analyzing important data. Although the Osborn creativity model provides some fact-finding procedures, they are not nearly as well developed as the idea-finding procedures.[30] One way to improve fact finding is to begin with a broad view of the issue or problem and then proceed to define subproblems. This phase requires making a distinction between a symptom of a problem and an actual problem. For example, a manager might claim that negative employee attitudes constitute a problem. A deeper investigation might reveal that negative employee attitudes are only symptoms. The real problem may be a lack of information from superiors.

Idea-Finding Phase. Idea finding starts by generating tentative ideas and possible leads. Then, the most likely of these ideas are modified, combined, and added to, if necessary. Osborn maintains that individuals can generate more good ideas by following two principles. First, defer judgment: individuals can think up almost twice as many good ideas in the same length of time if they defer judgment on any idea until after creating a list of possible leads to a solution. Second, quantity breeds quality: The more ideas individuals think up, the more likely they are to arrive at the potentially best leads to a solution.[31]

To encourage uninhibited thinking and generate lots of ideas, Osborn developed seventy-five questions to use when brainstorming a problem. **Brainstorming** is an unrestrained flow of ideas in a group with all critical judgments suspended. The group leader must decide which of the seventy-five questions are most appropriate to the problem. Moreover, the group leader isn't expected to use all of them in one session. Examples of questions that could be used in a brainstorming sessions are:

Ask Students
Is creativity better described as brainstorming ideas or as a work style?

- How can this issue, idea, or thing be put to other uses?
- How can it be modified?
- How can it be substituted for something else, or can something else be substituted for part of it?
- How could it be reversed?
- How could it be combined with other things?[32]

A brainstorming session should follow four basic rules:

1. ***Criticism is ruled out.*** Participants must withhold critical judgment of ideas until later.
2. ***Freewheeling is welcomed.*** The wilder the idea, the better; taming down an idea is easier than thinking up new ones.
3. ***Quantity is wanted.*** The greater the number of ideas, the greater is the likelihood that some will be useful.
4. ***Combination and improvement are sought.*** In addition to contributing ideas of their own, participants should suggest how ideas of others can be turned into better ideas, or how two or more ideas can be merged into still another idea.[33]

These rules are intended to separate creative imagination from judgment. The two are incompatible and relate to different aspects of the decision-making process.[34] The leader of one brainstorming group put it this way: "If you try to get hot or cold water out of the same faucet at the same time, you will get only lukewarm water. And if you try to criticize and create at the same time, you [will not do either very well]. So let us stick solely to *ideas*—let us cut out *all* criticism during this session."[35]

A brainstorming session should have from five to twelve participants in order to generate diverse ideas. This size range permits each member to maintain a sense of identification and involvement with the group. A session should normally run not less than twenty minutes nor more than an hour. However, brainstorming could consist of several idea-generating sessions. For example, subsequent sessions could address individually each of the ideas previously identified. Guidelines for leading a brainstorming session are presented in Table 9.2.

Solution-Finding Phase. Solution finding involves identifying and evaluating tentative courses of action and deciding how to implement the chosen course of action. The solution-finding phase relies on judgment, analysis, and criticism. A variety of decision-making aids—such as those presented earlier in this chapter—can be used. To initiate this phase, the leader could ask the group to identify from one to five of the most important ideas generated. The participants might be asked to jot down these ideas individually on a piece of paper and evaluate them on a five-point scale. An extremely important idea would get 5 points; a not-so-important idea would get 2 or 3 points; and an unimportant idea would get 1 point. The highest combined scores should indicate the actions or ideas to be investigated further.

Teaching Tip
Pick a current issue from the business section of the newspaper. Divide the class into groups of 5 to 8 and have them apply Osborn's creativity model to the issue. Have the groups report back with their solutions.

Osborn's creativity model has been modified often and applied in a variety of ways. The following Quality Insight reveals how Airo Industrial Gases, a premier supplier of gas products headquartered in Lisle, Illinois, uses a modified version of Osborn's creativity model and other creativity aids in its TQM program.

TABLE 9.2

Guidelines for Leading a Brainstorming Session

Basic leadership role	• Make a brief statement of the four basic rules. • State the time limit for the session. • Read the problem and/or related question to be discussed and ask, "What are your ideas?" • When an idea is given, summarize it by using the speaker's words insofar as possible. Have the idea recorded by a participant or on an audiotape machine. Follow your summary with the single word "Next." • Say little else. Whenever the leader participates as a brainstormer, group productivity usually falls.
Handling problems	• When someone talks too long, wait until he or she takes a breath (everyone must stop to inhale sometime), break into the monologue, summarize what was said for the recorder, point to another participant, and say "Next." • When someone becomes judgmental or starts to argue, stop him or her. Say, for example, "That will cost you one coffee or soda for each member of the group." • When the discussion stops, relax and let the silence continue. Say nothing. The pause should be broken by the group and not the leader. This period of silence is called the "mental pause" because it is a change in thinking. All the obvious ideas are exhausted; the participants are now forced to rely on their creativity to produce new ideas. • When someone states a problem rather than an idea, repeat the problem, raise your hand with five fingers extended, and say, "Let's have five ideas on this problem." You may get only one or you may get ten, but you're back in the business of creative thinking.

Source: Adapted from Osborn, A.F. *Applied Imagination,* 3rd rev. ed. New York: Charles Scribner's Sons, 1963, 166–196.

Quality *Insight*

Quality through Creativity at Airco

Creativity techniques such as freewheeling, the round-robin technique, and the nominal group procedure are used as part of Airco's total quality management program.

Freewheeling involves establishing a typical brainstorming atmosphere that fosters creative notions for finding or solving a particular problem. Using freewheeling, participants continually build upon one another's ideas. The *round-robin technique* provides all participants with an equal opportunity to express and convey their ideas so that no one person dominates the session. Finally, the *nominal group procedure* calls for each participant secretly to write a list of general problem areas or potential solutions to a problem. Because this approach provides anonymity, it allows sensitive topics to surface. The nominal group procedure has been used effectively with very large groups.

A team of Airco's employees gathered in Omaha, Nebraska, to generate new ideas regarding modular freezer equipment. The team consisted of engineering managers, engineers, designers, fabrication managers, and technicians. Customers also were represented. The company used the round-robin technique to encourage all ideas and input and to avoid curtailing the creative process. All ideas were written out, and subteams were selected to evaluate the potential benefits of each. Later, the entire team reconvened to discuss the implications of each new idea and recommend a set of changes, which were subsequently implemented. Another round-robin meeting was held sometime later so the company could continue to meet the demands of its customers.

Airco's new modular tunnel has been one of the most successful recent additions to the cryogenic food business. Airco introduced the cryogenic spiral to the industry about thirty years ago and continues to lead with technical improvements. These include menu-driven control screens, improved methods of construction that result in less heat leakage, and variable internal circulating fan speeds that allow for different product sizes and weights.

The creative methods used at Airco have helped it to develop totally new technologies and to update its customers' current processes and equipment.[36]

Assessment. A basic assumption of the Osborn creativity model and adaptations of it is that most people have the potential for greater creativity and innovation in decision making than they use. However, a considerable amount of research suggests that the same number of individuals working alone generate more ideas and more creative ideas than do groups.[37] However, most of this research was conducted with students rather than employee teams on the job. Unlike employees who have diverse knowledge and skills and who are brought together to brainstorm problems that have serious long-term consequences (as at Airco), student groups are relatively homogeneous. Most students have a limited range of knowledge of the problems given to them and limited skills to apply to their solution. Because students do not have to be concerned with real-world consequences, they may have less than a full commitment to the process. Thus whether group brainstorming in a work setting is less effective than individuals working alone to generate ideas that require innovative decisions remains and open question.

However, there is growing evidence that in work settings electronic brainstorming may often be a better way to generate ideas than traditional face-to-face brainstorming.[38] **Electronic brainstorming** makes use of technology to input and automatically disseminate ideas in real time over a computer network to all team members, each of whom may be stimulated to generate other ideas. For example, GroupSystems has a software tool called *Electronic Brainstorming*. Individuals input their ideas as they think of them. Every time an idea is entered, the team's ideas appear in random order on each person's screen. An individual can continue to see new sets of ideas in random order by pressing the appropriate key.[39] The random order format prevents the system's users from identifying who generates each idea.

Cause and Effect Diagram

The **cause and effect diagram** helps team members display, categorize, and evaluate all the possible causes of an effect, which is generally expressed as a problem.[40] Kaoru Ishikawa proposed this type of analysis. Hence the cause and effect diagram is also called an *Ishikawa diagram*. It also is called a *fishbone diagram* because of its appearance. Figure 9.3 shows the general framework of a cause and effect diagram, the construction of which usually involves four steps.[41]

- *Step 1:* The team needs to begin by agreeing on the "effect," which should be stated in terms of the problem (e.g., files out of place, late delivery of merchandise to a customer, or job cost above estimate). Sometimes, brainstorming or other techniques are needed if the team isn't able to begin with a clear, common view of the nature of the problem. The problem, or effect, is then shown on the right side of the diagram, as in Figure 9.3.
- *Step 2:* The team identifies all the general factors or categories that contribute to the problem, which will help the team organize the specific causes. Figure 9.3 shows the four commonly used categories of people, equipment, methods, and materials. These categories are only suggestions, and the team may use any categories that aids creative thinking. The assumption is that for every effect there are likely to be several major categories of causes. These are the main "bones of the fish." Sometimes this step isn't taken until all the possible causes have been brainstormed. At that time, they are placed in major categories.
- *Step 3:* The team may also use brainstorming or other techniques to generate all the possible causes that contribute to the problem (or effect) in that category. The session leader or members repeatedly ask, "What causes this cause?" In theory, the team will ask this question five times as it moves from "surface" causes to "root" causes.
- *Step 4:* This step involves reaching agreement on the top three to five root (critical) causes in each major category. These are written on the diagram and connected to the appropriate main category with arrows.

FIGURE 9.3

General Framework of Cause and Effect Diagram

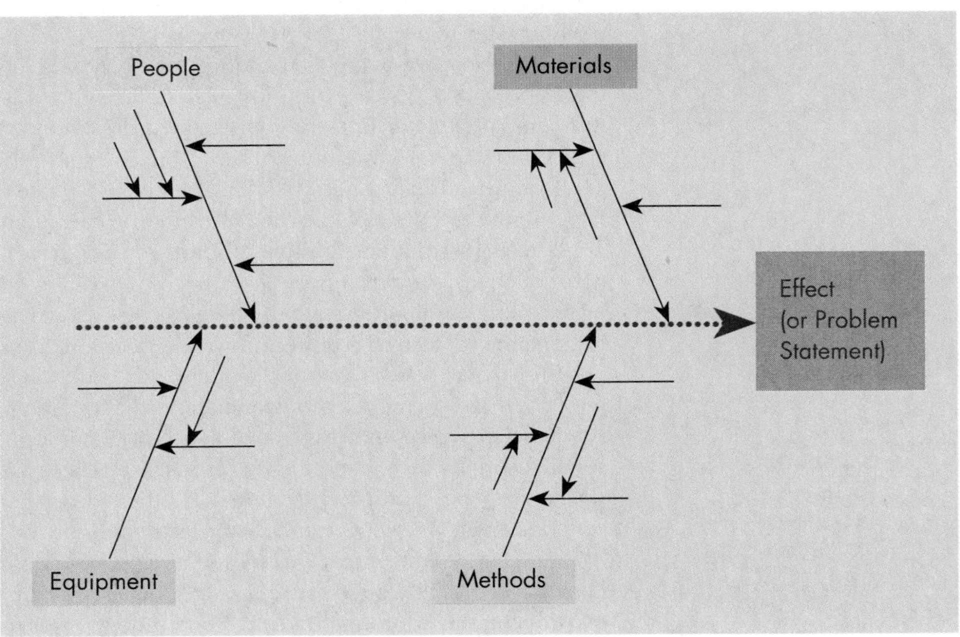

Using this diagram, the team can then focus its efforts on collecting additional data to determine whether the relationships between the assumed causes and effect are valid. Team members' hunches and perceptions about what causes the problem will be either supported or refuted by the data. Solutions can then be developed to eliminate genuine causes.

The following Quality Insight suggests how one team at a community college used the cause and effect diagram to address the problem of calls lost during the phone registration period.

Quality *Insight*

Phone Registration Project

The problem confronting the Phone Project team stemmed from a course registration system that encouraged nondegree students taking one or two courses to register by phone. The college hadn't anticipated the overwhelming effect on its telephone operations. The purposes of phone registration are to ease registration for the large number of part-time students who find it difficult to register in person and to reduce the long lines associated with "field house" registration. The phone registration system, however, created a new problem. Prospective students calling the admissions office for information, catalogues, or other purposes often could not get through. A multiline phone console operated by the receptionist in the admissions office routed most calls. The result was a major bottleneck; callers experienced endless busy signals or indefinite holds.

To understand better why callers couldn't get through and why calls were lost, the team brainstormed possible causes and developed a cause and effect diagram, as shown is Figure 9.4. Analysis of the diagram led the team to believe that the distribution of calls probably was the greatest cause of the problem. The team members then analyzed the incoming phone traffic. First, they listed the kinds of calls that come into the admissions office and traced their routes. The results confirmed the suspected problem. Almost all incoming calls were routed through extension 5050, the admissions receptionist's phone console.

At this point team members felt confident that they had focused on the major problem. To verify their opinion and to learn more about the nature of the problem, they developed a data collection plan. They collected data to determine the types and frequency of calls, times when lines were full, number of technical problems, adequacy of staffing coverage, number of lost calls, and the like. Analysis of the data enabled the team to develop several strategies for improving the system.[42]

Discussion Question 7
How does Osborn's creativity model differ from the cause and effect diagram?

Assessment. The cause and effect diagram, Osborn model, or any other aid intended to stimulate creativity can't guarantee innovative outcomes. However, the proper use of such aids in supportive organizations usually increases the likelihood of innovative decisions. As noted previously, such aids often are used to stimulate creativity in total quality management programs where innovation is needed.[43] Use of the cause and effect diagram encourages individuals and teams to spend more time searching for root causes. This effort reduces the people's tendency to identify symptoms as causes. If the process is successful, resources will not be spent on exploring or correcting the wrong things (e.g., symptoms or superficial causes).

FIGURE 9.4

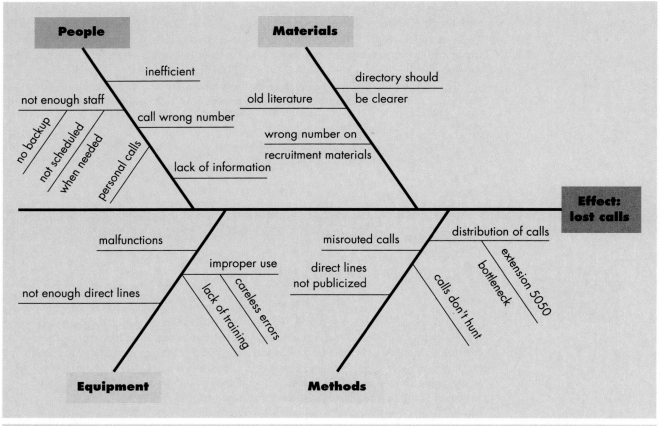

Cause and Effect Diagram for Phone Project

Source: DeCosmo, Richard D., Parker, Jerome S., and Haverly, Mary Ann. "Total Quality Management Goes to Community College," from p. 18. In L.A. Sherr and D.J. Teeter (eds.), *Total Quality Management in Higher Education,* no. 71. Copyright 1991 Jossey-Bass Inc., Publishers.

CHAPTER SUMMARY

1 ***State the benefits and limitations of normative decision making.***
Normative decision-making aids provide step-by-step procedures for helping individuals make effective decisions. Their purpose is to reveal hidden assumptions, clarify underlying reasoning processes, improve judgments, increase awareness of emotional responses, and reduce judgmental biases. They are limited by the impossibility of eliminating all emotional and attitudinal biases, of foreseeing all future events, and of acquiring complete data.

2 ***Discuss rules and standard operating procedures and artificial intelligence as aids to routine decision making.***
Rules and standard operating procedures (SOPs) prescribe specific ways of solving organizational problems and making decisions. Artificial intelligence (AI) refers to a wide range of computer systems programmed to manipulate data and make limited humanlike judgments based on information that users enter into the systems.

3 ***Explain break-even analysis, the payoff matrix, and Pareto analysis as aids to adaptive decision making.***
Break-even analysis shows graphically the relationships between sales (revenues) and costs and identifies the break-even point where revenues and costs are equal. The payoff matrix helps decision makers mathematically evaluate alternative solutions after goals have been set and alternative strategies specified. The alternatives

and goals are displayed visually in a table. The Pareto diagram is a graph that helps individuals or teams to determine which problems should be solved and in what order. The Pareto diagram is frequently used in total management quality programs to establish priorities for quality-related problems.

4 ***Describe Osborn's creativity model and the cause and effect diagram as aids to innovative decision making.***

Osborn's creativity model and the cause and effect diagram help decision makers solve unstructured and ambiguous problems, which often call for unique and innovative decisions. The creative process as a whole includes five interconnected elements: preparation, concentration, incubation, illumination, and verification. For innovation to flourish in organizations, a creative climate is needed. Such a climate generally includes attributes such as trust, open communication, and diversity. Osborn's creativity model is designed to stimulate and reduce blocks to creativity and innovation. The cause and effect diagram provides a process for getting at the root causes of a problem (an effect).

QUESTIONS FOR DISCUSSION

1. What are the key differences between rules and SOPs and artificial intelligence (AI)?
2. Review the Preview Insight. How might Andersen's *Window of Knowledge* be adapted to provide additional services to prospective or current customers? What are some potential problems that Andersen must avoid in using this system?
3. What are the similarities between break-even analysis and the payoff matrix?
4. By the time coffee arrived, Zita Thurman and Tom Namura were deeply involved in an after-dinner discussion about a problem at work. Thurman, manager of the small-parts division of a manufacturing company, had just taken a management science course. Namura, human resource director of the same company, had not. "I tell you," Thurman claimed, "chances are you *cannot* make a decision without having your emotions color it. Answer this for me. You have two options: A, a 100 percent chance to win $3,000; and B, an 80 percent chance to win $4,000. Which one would you take?" Namura thought for a few seconds and chose option A, the guaranteed $3,000. Was Tom Namura correct? Why?[44]
5. Which of the following alternatives should Lois Garcia choose: (a) a 100 percent chance to lose $3,000, or (b) an 80 percent chance to lose $4,000 with a 20 percent chance to lose nothing?[45] Why?
6. What are two limitations to the use of the Pareto diagram?
7. How does Osborn's creativity model differ from the cause and effect diagram?

FROM WHERE YOU SIT

1. Describe one way in which you have been affected personally by an application of AI.
2. Apply a normative decision-making aid to your studying practices.
3. Develop a cause and effect diagram for one personal problem, such as getting a grade in a course or an overall grade point average lower than you desire.
4. You should do this activity in a discussion group with four to six other students. Each person should take five minutes and write down the five things that irritated them most while eating at local restaurants during the past three months. From this data, the group should develop a Pareto diagram. Does it offer any clues for needed changes to restaurant operators in the area?
5. Develop a preliminary cause and effect diagram related to one problem that you have experienced at your college or university. This task may require some speculation on your part. You may also undertake this assignment with four to six other students in this class.
6. Describe a personal situation that occurred within the past six months for which Osborn's creativity model would have been useful. Why would it have been?

Personal Barriers to Creativity[46]

Instructions: For each of the statements in this inventory, please refer to the following scale and decide which number best corresponds to your level of agreement of disagreement with the statement. Write that number in the blank to the left of each statement. Please do not skip any statements.

1	2	3	4	5
Strongly Agree	**Agree Somewhat**	**Agree**	**Disagree**	**Strongly Disagree**

_____ 1. I evaluate criticism to determine how it can be useful to me.

_____ 2. When solving problems, I attempt to apply new concepts or methods.

_____ 3. I can shift gears or change emphasis in what I am doing.

_____ 4. I get enthusiastic about problems outside of my specialized area of concentration.

_____ 5. I always give a problem my best effort, even if it seems trivial or fails to arouse enthusiasm.

_____ 6. I set aside periods of time without interruptions.

_____ 7. It is not difficult for me to have my ideas criticized.

_____ 8. In the past, I have taken calculated risks and I would do so again.

_____ 9. I dream, daydream, and fantasize easily.

_____ 10. I know how to simplify and organize my observations.

_____ 11. Occasionally, I try a so-called unworkable answer in hopes that it will prove to be workable.

_____ 12. I can and do consistently guard my personal periods of privacy.

_____ 13. I feel at ease with peers even when my ideas or plans meet with public criticism or rejection.

_____ 14. I frequently read opinions contrary to my own to learn what the opposition is thinking.

_____ 15. I translate symbols into concrete ideas or action steps.

_____ 16. I seek many ideas because I enjoy having alternative possibilities.

_____ 17. In the idea-formulation stage of a project, I withhold critical judgment.

_____ 18. I determine whether an imposed limitation is reasonable or unreasonable.

_____ 19. I would modify an idea, plan, or design, even if doing so would meet with opposition.

_____ 20. I feel comfortable in expressing my ideas even if they are in the minority.

_____ 21. I enjoy participating in nonverbal, symbolic, or visual activities.

_____ 22. I feel the excitement and challenge of finding a solution to problems.

_____ 23. I keep a file of discarded ideas.

_____ 24. I make reasonable demands for good physical facilities and surroundings.

_____ 25. I would feel no serious loss of status or prestige if management publicly rejected my plan.

_____ 26. I frequently question the policies, goals, values, or ideas of an organization.

_____ 27. I deliberately exercise my visual and symbolic skills in order to strengthen them.

_____ 28. I can accept my thinking when it seems illogical.

_____ 29. I seldom reject ambiguous ideas that are not directly related to the problem.

_____ 30. I distinguish between trivial and important physical distractions.

_____ 31. I feel uncomfortable making waves for a worthwhile idea if it threatens the inner harmony of the team.

_____ 32. I am willing to present a truly original approach even if there is a chance it could fail.

_____ 33. I can recognize the times when symbolism or visualization would work best for me.

_____ 34. I try to make an uninteresting problem stimulating.

_____ 35. I consciously attempt to use new approaches toward routine tasks.

_____ 36. In the past, I have determined when to leave an undesirable environment and when to stay and change the environment (including self-growth).

Scoring Instructions: Transfer your inventory responses to the blanks provided below. Then add the numbers in each column, and record the column totals.

	A	B	C	D	E	F
	1.____	2.____	3.____	4.____	5.____	6.____
	7.____	8.____	9.____	10.____	11.____	12.____
	13.____	14.____	15.____	16.____	17.____	18.____
	19.____	20.____	21.____	22.____	23.____	24.____
	25.____	26.____	27.____	28.____	29.____	30.____
	31.____	32.____	33.____	34.____	35.____	36.____
Column Totals:	____	____	____	____	____	____

Profile Instruction: Plot the scores from your scoring sheet onto the following graph. The vertical axis, which represents your numbered scores, ranges from 5 to 30. The horizontal axis represents the columns on your scoring sheet and ranges from A to F. The *Key to Barriers* at the end of this exercise identifies the category of barriers in each column. Connect the points you have plotted with a line. The high points represent your personal barriers as you see them.

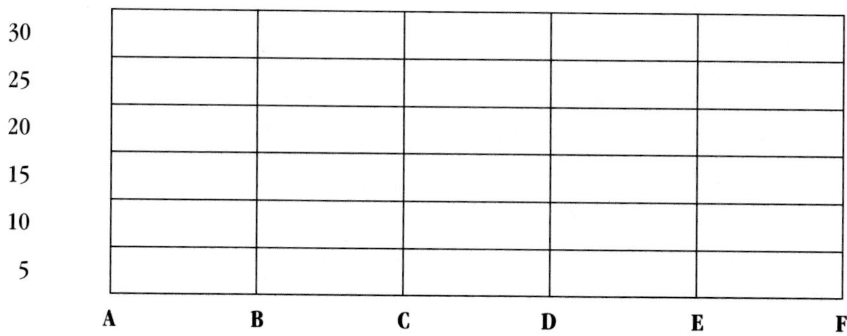

Key to Barriers

A = Barriers related to self-confidence and risk taking
B = Barriers related to need for conformity
C = Barriers related to use of the abstract
D = Barriers related to use of systematic analysis
E = Barriers related to task achievement
F = Barriers related to physical environment

CRITICAL THINKING CASE

Raytech, Inc.[47]

Raytech, Inc., is a small successful business. For twelve years, it has been producing various components to be used in IBM-compatible personal computers. Trevor Hansen is the original and current president of Raytech. He has always made it his personal goal to pursue ways to improve the quality of the company's products. Hansen has been particularly active in that effort in the past few years of increasing competition. For the past four years, the company has been fortunate to have an extremely capable and assertive vice-president of marketing. As a result of its exceptional combination of quality products and assertive selling, the company has established a reputation for producing high-quality parts and has benefited from steadily increasing sales.

Key Concerns

The company's management team has been very pleased with Raytech's performance. However, the increasing volume of business has created the usual concerns that accompany a rapidly expanding business—concerns such as human resource and plant capacity constraints. Hansen is aware that these concerns could become serious problems in the future and has been discussing them with the management team. But the most recent report from Leo Dodge, vice-president for production, indicates that the capacity problem has intensified more quickly than expected. The sales demand for the most profitable product will soon exceed Raytech's current maximum production capacity. This situation will have to be addressed within the next three weeks.

The product of concern is a disk drive that Raytech sells at $30.00 per unit. Raytech's production policy is one of practical capacity: It produces only what it sells. In essence, yearly production equals yearly sales. At the present time, Raytech operates one eight-hour production shift a day, six days a week. The company's present maximum capacity is 300,000 units per year, which had been sufficient to meet demand. In fact, with increasing production volumes, the system has become highly efficient. The capacity problem has suddenly become crucial because of a recent large-volume sales order from a new customer. Jan Link, vice-president of marketing at Raytech, has estimated that, with the additional orders her sales force is likely to generate, the current production capacity will be exceeded within the next month or so. Link has always fostered an assertive and effective sales department. Thus there is every reason to expect that it will generate the estimated number of orders.

Alternatives Considered

Link reported to Dodge the new large-volume sales order and the potential for orders to exceed capacity within the next month. Dodge immediately notified Hansen, who called a meeting of the management team to discuss possible solutions. Everyone agreed that the expected production problem would occur if the new customer account order was accepted. They also agreed that the potential for increasing business for this disk drive during the next few years was very realistic because of their company's high-quality product and the weaker competition. They considered the alternative of remaining a high-quality, but small, business undesirable and unacceptable. Thus the solution to the company's problem meant having to produce at a higher capacity. The management team asked Dodge to submit a proposal for increased production. Its members were to receive copies of the proposal for their examination. A meeting to discuss proposal was scheduled in three weeks.

Dodge's Proposal

Dodge's proposal recommended operating a second eight-hour production shift a day. Doing so should double the production capacity to 600,000 parts per year. The proposal included the following report of the current manufacturing and nonmanufacturing costs provided in a management committee meeting the previous month by Jay Ellis, the Controller at Raytech:

Direct materials per unit	$12.00
Direct labor per unit	$6.00
Variable manufacturing overhead per unit	$3.00
Variable marketing and administrative expense per unit	$4.00
Fixed manufacturing overhead per unit	$100,000
Fixed marketing and administrative expense per unit	$50,000

Dodge estimated that the proposed second shift would result in an increase of $1.00 per unit in direct labor costs, owing to a shift premium that would be paid to those employees. Having conferred with Ellis, the controller, Dodge also indicated that the fixed manufacturing overhead costs would increase if the additional shift were added. Raytech would need to install new equipment and hire more workers to meet the increased demand. Dodge estimated the increase in fixed manufacturing costs at $50,000 per year for the addition of a second shift.

Questions

1. If 300,000 units per year is, in fact, the maximum number of units Raytech can produce during a day shift, what is the maximum profit that can be generated in one shift each year?
2. If Raytech adds a second shift, what will be the maximum profit?
3. If Raytech adds a second shift, what will be the profit if it produces and sells 400,000 parts?
4. What is Raytech's break-even point in unit sales if it operates only one shift?
5. If Raytech adds a second shift, how many units would it have to produce and sell in order to make a profit equal to the one determined in Question 1?
6. What might be the negative effects on Raytech if Trevor Hansen decides not to add a second shift?
7. Are there any other ways to increase production besides adding a second shift? What about overtime, part-time workers , or subcontracting? Describe how Raytech's costs would be different if the company subcontracts manufacturing to all demand in excess of 300,000 units.
8. Would adding a second shift be justified if the expected business didn't materialize?
9. If you were the president of Raytech, Inc., what would your decision be?

Meyers & Morrison: A Question of Professional Ethics

Michael Morrison, partner in the accounting firm of Meyers & Morrison, didn't know what to think after the telephone conversation with one of his firm's oldest clients. The client had stated that he had received a letter from Stephen Adams, an associate with Meyers & Morrison, asking the client to switch to a new firm that he, Adams, was about to start. Morrison remarked to his partner, Phillip Meyers, "I can't believe that Adams would actually do this. He hasn't even left the firm yet. I thought he was going to wait to see what we could offer him to stay with the company." Meyers responded, "This isn't what I expected from someone in this office. We've always treated everyone like family here. This isn't a big impersonal, public accounting firm. I thought we all got along pretty well. This doesn't make a lot of sense."

Morrison paused, looked back at Meyers, and asked, "What do we do now?"

Background

Phillip Meyers had started his own small certified public accounting firm thirty years earlier in the seacoast town of Portsmouth, New Hampshire. For several years, he worked independently, establishing a small, but loyal, customer base. As his business continued to grow, he realized that he needed to hire additional employees to capitalize on his firm's excellent reputation.

Thus, after ten years on his own, Meyers hired Michael Morrison, the son of one of his largest clients. Morrison was a graduate of the MBA program at Boston University and had worked for five years for KPMG Peat Marwick in its Boston office. However, he had indicated that he wanted to move back to the Portsmouth area. He also had mentioned that he preferred the style and pace of a small firm to that of a branch of a Big Eight accounting firm. Together, Meyers and Morrison continued to expand the firm's client list by emphasizing customer service. They focused on small business and professional clients such as Morrison's father.

Through the years the firm continued to grow. Morrison was rewarded for his effort and dedication with a partnership in the firm, now called Meyers & Morrison. The partners gradually expanded the staff until it comprised ten employees, including a computer operator, payroll specialist, staff accountants, and clerical personnel. Only Meyers and Morrison were CPAs, however.

A few years after Morrison became a partner, however, the firm encountered some minor setbacks. One of its clients, which was responsible for over 40 percent of the firm's revenues, went bankrupt. The two partners were forced to lay off some of their employees to keep the firm profitable. After this incident, they vowed never again to become dependent on any one firm or client for a significant portion of their business.

Owing to the combined efforts of the partners and the remaining employees, Meyers & Morrison regained the profitability it had once enjoyed. Eventually the firm was able to expand the staff to its previous level. Then, as a result of continued expansion, the partners decided to hire an additional CPA. Morrison stated, "Our intent was to find someone who was like us and would be able to share some of this increased auditing and tax load. We also wanted someone who would help us to continue our expansion. Besides, my partner wanted to start withdrawing from active involvement with the firm." As a result the partners hired Stephen Adams, who was in his early thirties. He had an undergraduate degree in business from a local business school with a concentration in accounting. Hoping that Adams would prove his ability, the partners offered him a position that could lead to a partnership in the firm. Morrison stated that "the process of bringing Adams in was somewhat loose and informal, much the way we do everything around here." The partners believed that the offer, which included an extremely generous salary and benefits package, compared to those of associates in other small firms in the area. They admitted that they hadn't done a full salary analysis of the local market, however.

Stephen Adams came to Meyers & Morrison from another small public accounting firm in Massachusetts. He was married but had no children. His adjustment to the firm appeared to go well, according to Morrison. He stated that "Adams was looked upon favorably by the office staff. He worked long hours serving the needs of his clients and spent additional hours recruiting new business." Morrison added that "after the first twelve months, all in all, we were very happy with Stephen Adams's performance. Everyone in the office seemed to be getting along well."

Adams's first tax season came during his first nine months with the firm. That gave him a chance to become fully acclimated to the area and to the firm's policies and procedures, according to Michael Morrison. His responsibilities increased until, by the end of his second year with the firm, he was accountable for almost a quarter of the firm's clients. Most of these clients were new, and he had brought their business into the firm. Morrison noted that Adams felt very confident during his first year with the firm but that his wife was having trouble making the adjustment. Morrison later recalled that Adams had said that his wife was miserable in the area and wasn't making new friends to ease the transition. Adams told Morrison that she spent her time shopping and renovating the house that the couple had purchased. Adams occasionally joked that she was trying to drive him into poverty but added that this was nothing new.

The partners stated that they had been pleased with his performance, but began noticing small changes in Adams's behavior during his second year with the firm. Morrison remarked that "he became impatient with his progress within the firm. This was difficult for us to understand, as he was only in his early thirties and had a very promising future with the firm. We estimated that he would make partner within the next couple of years."

Staff members in the firm reported to Morrison that Adams also had begun having difficulties handling crisis situations by the end of his second year. Later they said that they had noticed him chewing on his fingers until they bled consistently. The other employees stated that they were uncomfortable looking at his fingers. They were worried that clients might feel slightly disgusted having to shake hands with him. They told Morrison that, when they questioned Adams about this, he told them that he bit his fingers to deal with the pressures of daily life. Morrison stated that "he didn't seem to have any pressure" during his first year at the firm. The partners wondered what had changed.

Local Competition

Small to medium-sized firms comprised the accounting industry in the Portsmouth, New Hampshire, area. Some thirty-five accounting firms or independent accountants were listed in the area as certified public accountants. No major national firms operated in the immediate area, although several of the local firms had offices in other parts of the state. The closest national firm was based in Manchester, the state's largest city, 45 miles west of Portsmouth.

Industry Norms

Industry sources noted that a firm the size of Meyers & Morrison commonly sought a third professional as the number of clients increased. There were no industry standards for the amount of time with a firm that might be required for a senior associate to be offered a position as partner. However, in a small firm it typically was within three years, especially if the associate had held a senior position previously with another firm. The decision to offer an associate a partnership would depend not only on the results demonstrated, but also on the associate's people-oriented skills. In a small firm, interpersonal skills were a crucial element in a decision to elevate an associate to partner.

Nor were there any specific standards concerning the amount of time that an associate was expected to spend with a firm before leaving. However, an associate leaving a firm was expected to stay long enough to acquaint someone else in the firm with the needs of all the clients with whom the associate was working.

No specific restrictions covered who retains clients when an associate leaves a firm. Clients brought into a firm by an associate probably would want to stay with that person rather than the firm. The reason is that the accountant–client relationship is based on personal as much as professional interaction. The American Institute of Certified Public Accountants (AICPA) Code of Conduct does restrict advertising, however. Solicitation of clients while working for a firm would have to be handled very carefully to avoid violating the advertising prohibition. A summary of the code is presented in Exhibit A.

Company Philosophy

Meyers & Morrison was considered a small local firm by industry standards. Because of its previous bad experience with losing a large client, the firm worked hard to ensure a varied client base. Through these efforts, the firm became one of the most successful in the area. Some of its accountants had waiting lists of potential clients. This fact was astonishing, as the firm didn't advertise or otherwise promote itself. It relied solely on word of mouth from satisfied clients to expand its client base.

The firm followed a mid-range pricing policy, with average fees being slightly higher than those of most private firms in the area. The partners stated that they didn't want to have a cost-conscious client base. They were more interested in doing complicated corporate returns than simple personal returns. Jokingly, these personal returns were referred to by Michael Morrison as the "H&R Blockers." Also, the partners' philosophy was: If no one was complaining, the prices must be too low; if everyone was complaining, the prices must be too high. The partners felt that somewhere in the middle was just right.

The Confrontation

One day just before the end of tax season, Stephen Adams asked for a meeting with the partners. He began by stating that he wanted to give notice. He then presented a formal letter of resignation. He said that he would be available only for two more weeks, or just to the end of the tax season. Morrison responded that "while this may be customary for most industries, it is rather short notice for the accounting profession."

The partners were shocked. Adams had been well liked and respected. Morrison stated that "he had been given every advantage, with the hope that eventually he would become a partner." In fact, the partners said that they probably would have offered him a partnership within the year. That would have brought both greater responsibility and compensation. Basically, he would have been sharing, on an agreed upon basis, in the profits of the firm. Typically, a financial commitment on his part to buy into the partnership would have been required. However, Morrison noted that some form of long-term financial arrangement could have been worked out, allowing him to pay for his partnership from his expected higher earnings. The partners then asked Adams to explain why he was leaving the firm.

Adams stated that "the decision finally came down to one of money." He added that "he liked working at Meyers & Morrison but that he just couldn't afford to anymore." He said that his wife was spending money faster than he could make it. He also stated that he had become frustrated because he hadn't been offered a partnership in the firm. Morrison noted that "Adams said that he was not sure that he would be able to afford waiting much longer. However, he said that if we (the partners) would give him a sizable raise and a partnership he would be willing to stay. We told him that we needed some time to think over this proposition."

Adams didn't tell the partners what he intended to do after he left the firm. After learning that Adams planned to leave the firm, everyone wanted to ask, but felt that, if he had wanted people to know, he would have told them. Morrison noted that the staff had learned of the resignation from his secretary, when he asked her to file Adams's resignation letter. The people in the office weren't sure what the partners would do about Adams's request.

While the partners were considering their options a few days after the meeting with Adams, Morrison received the phone call from his client. Morrison stated that "the client had received a letter in the mail from Stephen Adams and was upset about the contents" (reproduced in Exhibit B). He went on to say that "I should look it over immediately and agreed to forward it by fax." Morrison continued, "After contacting a few of our other most trusted clients, we realized that Adams probably had sent a similar letter to all of our clients. At that point, we felt that some kind of quick action was needed to be able to minimize the impact of the situation."

EXHIBIT A
SUMMARY OF AICPA CODE OF CONDUCT

Responsibilities
In carrying out their responsibilities as professionals, members should exercise sensitive professional and moral judgments in all their activities.

The Public Interest
Members should accept the obligation to act in a way that will serve the public interest, honor the public trust, and demonstrate commitment to professionalism.

Integrity
To maintain and broaden public confidence, members should perform all professional responsibilities with the highest sense of integrity.

Objectivity and Independence
A member should maintain objectivity and be free of conflicts of interest in discharging professional responsibilities. A member in public practice should be independent in fact and appearance when providing auditing and other attestation services.

Due Care
A member should observe the profession's technical and ethical standards, strive continually to improve competence and the quality of services, and discharge professional responsibility to the best of the member's ability.

Scope and Nature of Services
A member in public practice should observe the Principles of the Code of Professional Conduct in determining the scope and nature of services to be provided.

Rule 502: Advertising and Other Forms of Solicitation

A member in public practice shall not seek to obtain clients by advertising or other forms of solicitation in a manner that is false, misleading, or deceptive. Solicitation by the use of coercion, over-reaching, or harassing conduct is prohibited.

EXHIBIT B

Following is a copy of the letter that Stephen Adams sent to the client of Meyers & Morrison.

> *Dear Client:*
>
> *I am writing this letter to inform you of my impending departure from the accounting firm of Meyers & Morrison. Upon resignation, I will be starting my own practice in Dover, N.H. The services that I will be offering include:*
>
> 1. *Preparation of individual tax returns—My rate is $100.00 minimum with a charge of $50.00 per hour. Meyers & Morrison have a $150.00 minimum with a charge of $80.00.*
> 2. *Estate planning—My rate will be contingent solely on my hourly rate stated above. This is true at Meyers & Morrison also.*
> 3. *Corporate tax returns—My rate will be a $500.00 minimum. Meyers & Morrison charge a $750.00 minimum.*
>
> *At the present time I am not equipped to provide any auditing services. I hope to be adding them in the very near future. As you can see, my rates are much more affordable than those of Meyers & Morrison. In addition, it is my belief that you will find my services to be much more efficient and of higher caliber than the services provided at Meyers & Morrison. I would like to emphasize how pleasurable it has been to do business with you over the past three years. It is my hope and intention that you will follow my lead and bring your future business to my new office.*
>
> *Sincerely,*
>
> */s/Stephen Adams, C.P.A.*

Questions

1. Analyze the symptoms presented in the case and the underlying problems relating to those symptoms.
2. Develop a stakeholder analysis of the Meyers & Morrison firm.
3. Discuss the ethical considerations of the actions taken by Stephen Adams.
4. What alternatives are available to Meyers & Morrison?
5. Based on those alternatives, what actions should Meyers & Morrison take?

Part *Four*

Organizing

Chapter *10*

Traditional Organization Designs

Learning *Objectives*

After studying this chapter, you should be able to:

1. Describe the main elements of organizational structure and how they're shown on an organization chart.
2. Discuss the most common types of departmentalization.
3. State the basic principles of coordination.
4. Describe the authority structure of an organization.
5. Explain the factors that affect the centralization or decentralization of decision making.
6. State the differences between line and staff authority.

Chapter *Outline*

Preview *Insight*

Taco Bell

For more than forty years, fast-food restaurants successfully followed a model based on the principles of mass-production manufacturing. The rewards for this approach were enormous. But times have changed. In the early 1990s, for the first time ever, the sales and operating income of many fast-food chains began to fall. Customers were attracted to restaurants that offered varied menus, lower prices, and service quality. In order to attract and retain customers, the fast-food chains reorganized their business practices to serve their customer's needs and expectations better.

Taco Bell, a division of PepsiCo, grew its fast-food restaurants from a regional chain with 1,500 outlets and $700 million in annual sales into a $3.9 billion multinational food delivery company with more than 15,000 outlets or "points of access." What is a point of access? It's a place where people can meet to munch—an airport, a supermarket, a school cafeteria, or a college student union building. Taco Bell changed the way it thinks about doing business from a company that prepared food to a company that serves food. Making this change necessitated reorganizing its outlets.

Taco Bell outlets no longer prepare food—crushing beans, dicing cheese, and preparing beef. Instead, they buy food prepared by outside suppliers. This allows Taco Bell to keep prices low and use up to 40 percent more of an outlet's space for customer service. Like most fast-food chains, Taco Bell previously used a traditional top-down management system. Employees did routine jobs just like people working on an assembly line. The manager's job was to control the employees.

Today, many Taco Bell points of access operate with no manager on the premises. Self-directed teams manage inventory, schedule work, order supplies, and train employees. These outlets have lower employee turnover and higher customer satisfaction than conventionally run outlets. Managers, now business school graduates, oversee as many as 30 outlets each. They see themselves as entrepreneurs managing a multimillion dollar company with as many as 250 employees. Managers who formerly made about $25,000 now earn as much as $100,000, depending on sales and customer satisfaction scores.[1]

1

Describe the main elements of organizational structure and how they're shown on an organization chart.

ORGANIZATIONAL STRUCTURE

Charging managers with increasing productivity has emphasized their role as resource allocators. Total quality programs and downsizing require that managers adjust their organization's structure to make it more flexible for today and into the future. Managers often have been too far removed from the day-to-day operations of their organizations to structure them properly. A dramatic turn of events, such as plunging sales and/or profits, may be required to motivate managers to identify and deal with problems of organizational structure.

In this chapter we focus on organizational structure, or the formal system that enables managers to allocate work, coordinate tasks, and delegate authority and responsibility in order to achieve organizational goals efficiently. First, we examine elements of an organization's structure and various types of departmentalization that allow managers to determine who should perform which activities. Then, after discussing how managers or teams allocate work and coordinate tasks, we look at lines of authority that affect the flow of real decisions in an organization. In doing so we consider the need to relate responsibility, authority, and accountability. We then explore delegation and questions of centralized versus decentralized authority. Finally, we examine the roles of line and staff authority. Many aspects of this chapter revisit concepts based on the traditional views of management introduced in Chapter 2.

Teaching Tip
Students, and most people for that matter, have too literal and simplistic an understanding of organizational structure. They think that organizational structure refers only to pyramidal hierarchies. You should start to debunk this misconception at the beginning of this chapter.

Organizational structure is a formal system of working relationships that both separates and integrates tasks. Separation of tasks makes clear who should do what, and integration of tasks indicates how efforts should be meshed. Organizational structure helps employees work together effectively by

1. assigning human and other resources to tasks;
2. clarifying employees' responsibilities and how their efforts should mesh with job descriptions, organization charts, and lines of authority;
3. letting employees know what is expected of them through rules, operating procedures, and performance standards; and
4. establishing procedures for collecting and evaluating information to help managers make decisions and solve problems.

Teaching Tip
Have students apply and write down the elements of organizational design at their workplace or at the university. Discuss their analyses in class.

Elements of Organizational Structure

For our purposes, organizational structure includes four basic elements: specialization, standardization, coordination, and authority.[2]

Specialization is the process of identifying particular tasks and assigning them to individuals or teams who have been trained to do them. At Hoechst Celanese, for example, middle managers are responsible for directing the work of teams in production, quality control, and energy. Functional managers usually supervise a particular department, such as marketing, accounting, or human resources. First-line managers usually are in charge of a specific area of work, such as printing, medical records, or data processing. Thus one person can specialize in any of a number of different management jobs. Later in this chapter we describe how the principle of specialization is applied in terms of different forms of departmentalization.

Ethics
Is standardization dehumanizing and unethical? Is the standardization provided in organizations justified?

Standardization refers to the uniform and consistent procedures that employees are to follow in performing their jobs. Written procedures, job descriptions, instructions, rules, and regulations are used to standardize the routine aspects of jobs. Standards permit managers to measure an employee's performance against some criteria. Job descriptions and application forms standardize the selection of employees. On-the-job training programs develop standardized skills and reinforce values important to the organization's success. This approach may seem mechanical, but if jobs weren't standardized, many organizations couldn't achieve their goals. Just walk into any McDonald's, Wendy's or Burger King, where every person has a job with well-defined standards: from how long a customer may be kept waiting for service to the length of time food stays on the warming trays to the amount of French fries that go into an order of "regular fries."

Coordination comprises the formal and informal procedures that integrate the activities performed by separate individuals, teams, and departments. In bureaucratic organizations, such as United Parcel Service (UPS), written rules are enough to link such activities. In less structured organizations, such as the San Diego Zoo, coordination requires managerial sensitivity to companywide problems, willingness to share responsibility, and effective interpersonal communication. Later in this chapter we examine some specific principles of coordination.

Ethics
Are there circumstances in which one person has the right ethically to decide how others will act?

Authority is basically the right to decide and act. Various organizations distribute authority differently. In a centralized organization, such as Pier 1, top managers make decisions about what merchandise to buy and where to locate a new store—and communicate these decisions to lower level managers. In a decentralized organization, such as Taco Bell, decision-making authority is given to lower level managers and employees working in teams. Firms often combine the two approaches by centralizing certain functions (e.g., accounting and purchasing) and decentralizing others (e.g., marketing and human resources). We also discuss authority in more detail later in this chapter.

Teaching Tip
Bring a copy of *The Wall Street Journal* to class. Find a story in it about corporate reorganization. Have students draw the old and new organization charts.

The Organization Chart

One way to visualize the interrelationships of these four basic elements of organizational structure is to create an **organization chart.** It is a diagram showing the reporting relationships of functions, departments, and individual positions within an organization. Figure 10.1 is the organization chart for FedEx, a market leader in the small-package de-

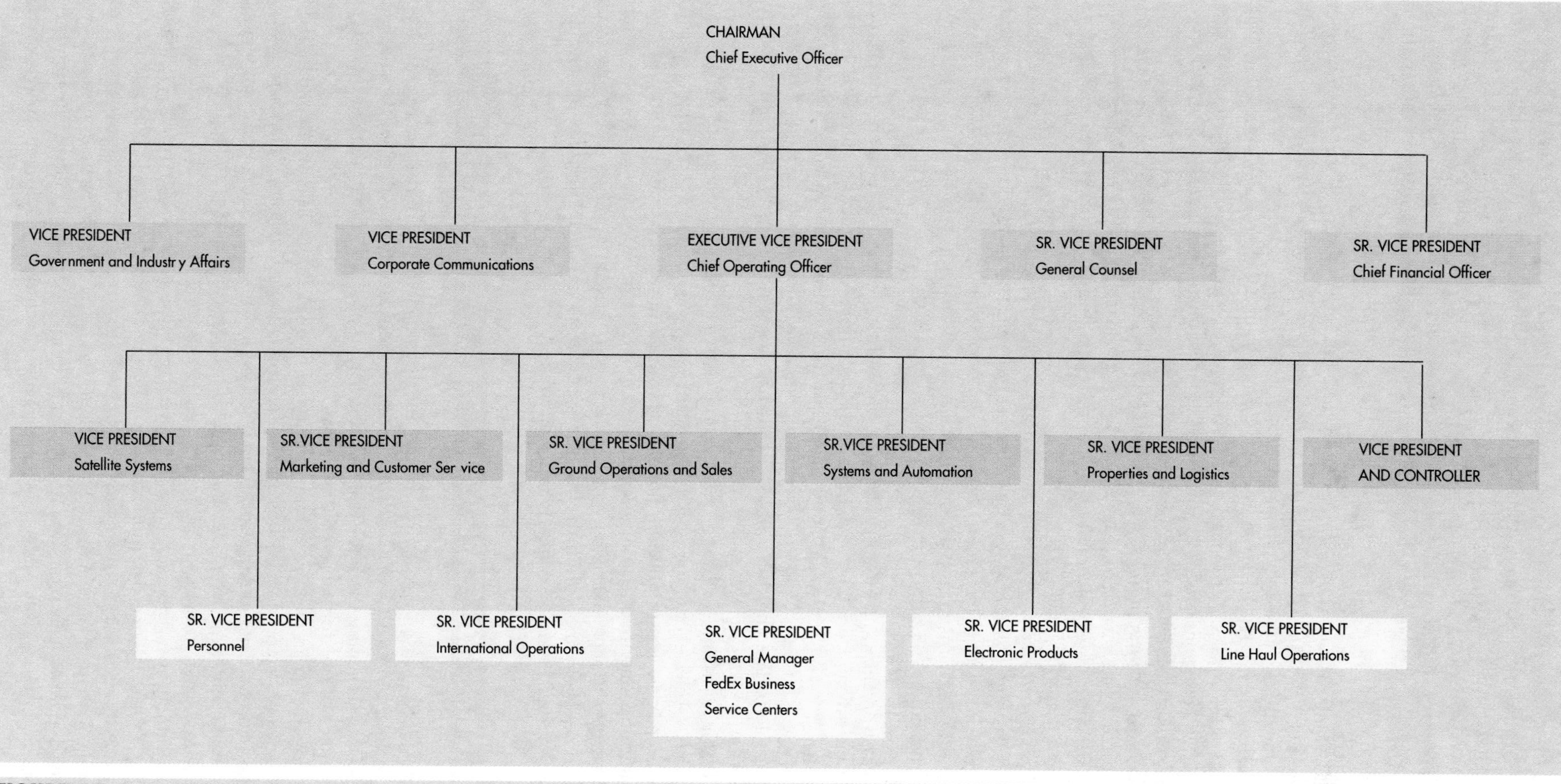

FIGURE 10.1

Organizational Structure of FedEx

Source: *1994 Annual Report,* FedEx.

Teaching Tip
Ask each student to visit a local business or other organization (e.g., public library) and ask for a copy of its organization chart. Use the charts as the basis for a discussion about differences in organizational structure.

Teaching Tip
Have each student bring in or draw an organization chart of an organization he or she is familiar with. Divide the class into groups of 5–8. Ask them to share their charts with their group. What similarities and dissimilarities are apparent? Why? Does the industry the organization is in, the type of customers served, or the type of technology used make any difference?

Ask Students
How do the organization charts of nonprofit and for-profit organizations differ?

livery service industry. The chart could be expanded to show even greater detail by including the titles of departmental managers and identifying work teams within the departments according to the specific tasks they perform. For example, various departments, such as express products, retail marketing, cooperate marketing, marketing and customer service, report to the senior vice-president of marketing and customer service.

In general, an organization chart provides four major pieces of information about an organization's structure:

1. ***Tasks.*** The chart shows the range of different tasks within the organization. For instance, tasks at FedEx range from personnel to properties and logistics to satellite systems to line haul operations.
2. ***Subdivisions.*** Each box represents a subdivision of the organization that is responsible for tasks. For example, the senior vice-president for line haul operations at FedEx is responsible for maintenance services, quality programs, flight operations and support, and aircraft acquisition and sales.
3. ***Levels of management.*** The chart shows the management hierarchy from the chairman of the board to the various divisional managers. All those directly subordinate to the same individual usually appear at the same management level and report to that individual.
4. ***Lines of authority.*** Vertical lines connecting the boxes on the chart show which positions have authority over others. At FedEx, the executive vice-president reports to the president. The senior vice-presidents of marketing and customer service, ground operations and sales, properties and logistics, and international operations, among others, report to the executive vice-president.

The advantages and disadvantages of organization charts have been debated for years.[3] One advantage is that such a chart shows employees how the pieces of the entire organization fit together. That is, it indicates how their own specialized tasks relate to the whole. Thus everyone knows who reports to whom and where to go with a particular problem. The chart also may help management detect gaps in authority or duplication of tasks.

A major disadvantage of the organization chart is that it's just a piece of paper; it simply can't show everything about an organization's structure. For example, it can't show who has the most political influence or where the vital informal channels of communication operate. In addition, employees may incorrectly read status and power into their jobs, based on the proximity of their boxes to that of the CEO. These disadvantages can be overcome only if the chart is used for its intended purpose—to illustrate the basic, formal structure of the entire organization.

2
Discuss the most common types of departmentalization.

DEPARTMENTALIZATION

Departmentalization addresses two of the four basic elements of organizational structure: *specialization and standardization.* **Departmentalization** is defined as subdividing tasks and assigning them to specialized groups within an organization and devising standards for the performance of those tasks.

Management can use any of four basic types of departmentalization: by function, by place (location), by product (goods and/or services), and by customer. Division of work is the first step in departmentalization, but *how* people are grouped depends on the goals of the organization. At Taco Bell, employees now work in self-directed teams. Many of the daily tasks they previously performed, such as dicing or preparing ingredients, are now performed by outside suppliers, who prepare these items to Taco Bell's standards.

The key to effective departmentalization lies in organizing people and activities in such a way that decisions easily flow throughout the organization. Large, complex organizations, such as J.C. Penney, NationsBank, and Levi Strauss, actually use different forms of departmentalization at various organizational levels to facilitate this flow. Levi Strauss, for instance, has eight product divisions, including Jeanswear, Womenswear,

Large, complex organizations such as Levi Strauss use different forms or departmentalization at various organization levels to facilitate decision flow. One form is by location. The photograph shows pants production at a plant in Blue Ridge, Georgia.

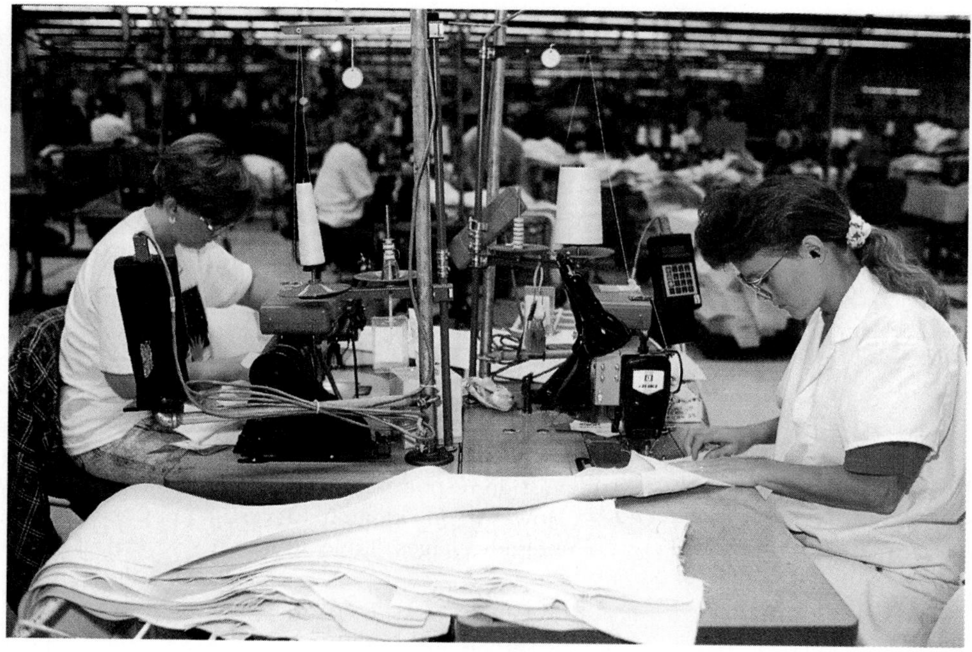

and Menswear, that reflect a product structure. Each division is then broken down into functional departments (e.g., accounting, production, and marketing) that support the division's products.

Functional Departmentalization

Recall that functions are the groups, or sets, of tasks that an organization performs, such as production, marketing, and finance. **Functional departmentalization** groups employees according to their areas of expertise and the resources they draw on to perform a common set of tasks. Functional grouping is the most widely used and accepted form of departmentalization.[4]

Teaching Tip
Have students list five major products they use every day. (Examples: computer, car or bus, bed, toothpaste, blue jeans.) Ask them to determine how the organizations that make these products are departmentalized. Suggest looking in the business section of the newspaper or in *The Wall Street Journal,* or calling its 800 customer service line. Have the students submit their results next week in class.

Functions vary widely, depending on the nature of the organization. For example, hospitals don't have product development departments, but they do have admitting, emergency room, and nursing departments. Churches don't have production departments, but they do have youth, education, and choir departments. Delta Airlines has operations, traffic, and finance departments. Toys "R" Us and other large retail chains have general merchandising, physical distribution, and support services departments (e.g., legal, human resources, and accounting). The following Small Business Insight illustrates how Nan Napier, owner of Tres Mariposas of El Paso, Texas, uses functional departmentalization to operate her upscale women's specialty store.

Small Business *Insight*

Tres Mariposas

When Nan Napier and her husband opened their 6,000 square foot women's specialty store, they performed all the tasks themselves and put in long hours to build the business. When they divorced five years later, Napier decided that she needed to reorganize the store to achieve her goals of providing customers with innovative, upscale women's apparel. She chose the functional structure shown in Figure 10.2. She hired people to staff each of the three functions: sales management, finance, and buying. A retail consultant helped her identify specific duties for the employees to enable them to carry out their tasks efficiently. The consultant also provided a seminar that helped the employees develop their communication skills. Napier also discovered that her own responsibilities weren't clearly identified and that she needed to outline them if she were to run the store efficiently.[5]

Discussion Question 1
As it grows, what problems is Tres Mariposas likely to face because of the way it is organized?

Grouping tasks and employees by function can be both efficient and economical. It is efficient, particularly for small organizations making a single product because it creates a clear hierarchy of authority and decision making. At PETsMART, a leading operator of 115 superstores specializing in pet food, supplies, and services operating in twenty states, key decisions are made by the chairman of the board and the president. PETsMART employs more than 3,000 people and is organized by function: real estate, finance, general merchandise, and store operations. Large firms organized by function often assign responsibility and authority for several departments to one senior manager.

However, in addition to certain advantages, functional departmentalization has some disadvantages. Table 10.1 shows several of each.

Advantages of Functional Departmentalization. Departmentalization by function is economical because it results in a simple structure. It is often the best form for organizations that sell a narrow range of goods and/or services mainly in one market (product and geographic). Management creates one department for each primary task to be performed (e.g., engineering, sales, and research and development). This structure keeps administrative expenses low because everyone in a department shares training, experience, and resources. Job satisfaction may increase if employees can improve their specialized skills by working with others in the same functional area. Employees can see clearly defined career paths within their own departments. As a result, the organization can more easily hire and promote personnel who have or develop good problem-solving skills in each area of specialization.

Disadvantages of Functional Departmentalization. The disadvantages of functional departmentalization become obvious when an organization has diversified products or markets. For instance, J.C. Penney offers a variety of products, ranging from life insurance to women's clothing. Making decisions quickly becomes difficult when employees have to work their way through layers of structure for approvals. In addition,

FIGURE 10.2

Tres Mariposas' Functional Departmentalization

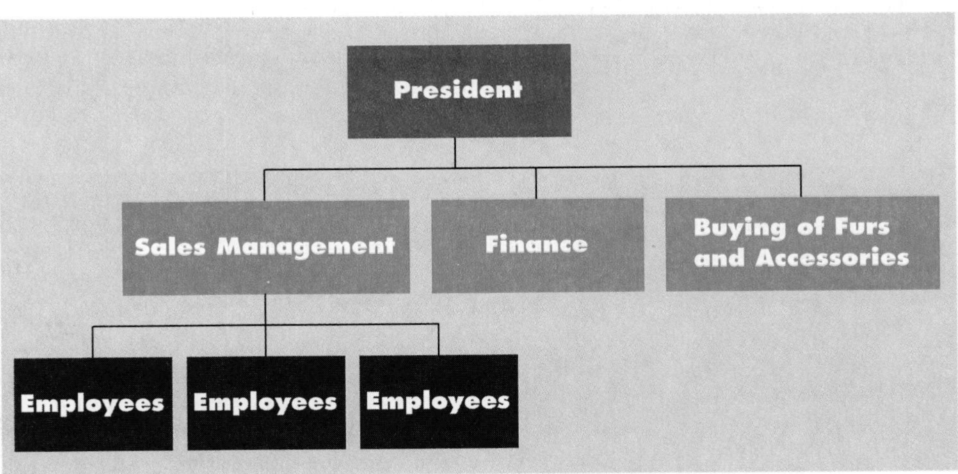

Source: Adapted from Napier, N. Change is big even for a little guy. *Arthur Andersen Retailing Issues Letter*, May 1994.

TABLE 10.1

Advantages and Disadvantages of Functional Departmentalization

Advantages	• Promotes skill specialization.
	• Reduces duplication of resources and increases coordination within the functional area.
	• Enhances career development and training within the department.
	• Allows superiors and subordinates to share common expertise.
	• Promotes high-quality technical problem solving.
	• Centralizes decision making.
Disadvantages	• Emphasizes routine tasks.
	• Reduces communication between departments.
	• May create conflict over product priorities.
	• May make interdepartmental scheduling difficult.
	• Focuses on departmental rather than organizational issues and goals.
	• Develops managers who are experts in narrow fields.

when there's friction between departments, managers have to spend time resolving the problems. For example, a sales representative may lose a good account because she has to wait for the sales manager to get the production manager to make a scheduling decision. Pinpointing the accountability and performance levels of employees who are performing separate functions may be difficult. In other words, a top manager may not be able to determine easily which department is responsible for declining profits: production, sales, or credit.

Another disadvantage is that top management may have a hard time coordinating the activities of employees in different departments. Functional departmentalization tends to de-emphasize the goals of the entire organization. Employees may focus on departmental goals, such as meeting their own budgets and schedules, and lose sight of the big picture. Moreover, when functional employees begin to worry about their own areas of expertise, they may have trouble seeing others' points of view. Employees develop a loyalty to their own department, which in turn may erect barriers instead of encouraging employees to identify and coordinate with their counterparts in other departments.

Place Departmentalization

Real-World Example
Police and fire agencies use place departmentalization to station their personnel and equipment in areas where they are needed.

Place departmentalization groups all functions for a geographic area at one location under one manager, rather than dividing functions among different managers or grouping all tasks in one central office. It is commonly used by organizations with operations in many different locations. Many large companies, including IBM, Sony, and Colgate-Palmolive, have set up regional and district offices. Similarly, federal agencies such as the IRS, the Federal Reserve Board, and the U.S. Postal Service use place departmentalization to provide nationwide services. And multinational firms often use this form of departmentalization to address cultural and legal differences in various countries, as well as the lack of uniformity among geographic markets.[6]

The following Insight highlights how Broadcasting Partners uses place departmentalization to coordinate the activities of its five FM and two AM stations in New York, Chicago, Detroit, Charlotte, and Dallas. The stations owned and operated by this firm are diverse in terms of format, target audience, and geographical location. This strategy helps insulate the company from downturns in specific markets and changes in listening preferences.

Insight

Broadcasting Partners

The company's mission is to earn a profit by meeting the needs of listeners and advertisers. The company has approximately 160 full-time and 50 part-time employees and is headquartered in New York City. However, the manager of each station is responsible for its profitability. Figure 10.3 shows the company's organization chart.

The station in each market targets a different audience. In New York, FM station WYNY has a country music format and targets adults between the ages of twenty-five and fifty-four. In Chicago, FM station WVAZ has a black adult music format and targets women in the same age range. In Dallas, AM station KSKY plays inspirational music and targets middle-aged conservative listeners.

Each radio station manager determines the station's music format and the number of advertisements to be played and when to play them. Most advertising contracts run for only a few weeks, so the station can adjust its pricing effectively. To ensure consistent customer service by all five stations, the company has guidelines for task performance ranging from research to pricing to sales training. Headquarters management also devotes significant resources to recruiting, training, and retraining employees to manage each station's operations.[7]

Advantages of Place Departmentalization. The advantages of place departmentalization, as summarized in Table 10.2, are primarily those of efficiency. If each unit is relatively small and in direct contact with its customers, it can adapt more readily to market demands. For production, place departmentalization might mean locating near raw materials or suppliers. In addition, because their attention is more focused, managers are more likely to remain sensitive to changes in consumer demand and to adapt their products quickly to meet those changes.

FIGURE 10.3

Broadcasting Partners, Inc.'s, Place Departmentalization

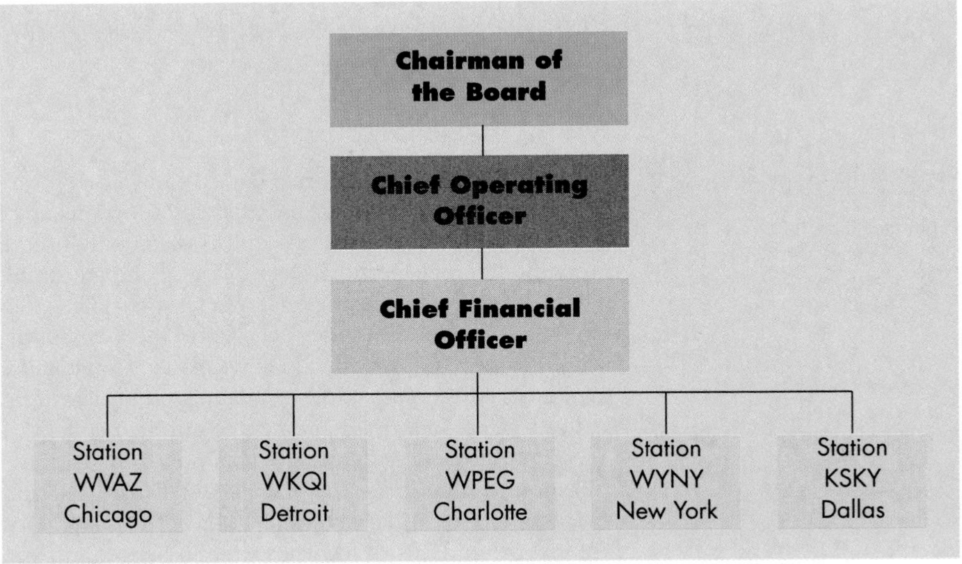

Source: Abridged from *1993 Annual Report* and *Form 10-K, Broadcasting Partners, Inc.*

A distinctive competence for KSKY in Dallas is its ability to format its music to appeal to a statewide, rather than local, listening market. Therefore it doesn't sell advertising to local firms, but rather to firms that have customers throughout the state. In contrast, station WVAZ in Chicago sponsors local events such as "An Expo for Today's Black Woman" that appeal to its target audience.

Disadvantages of Place Departmentalization. Table 10.2 also shows some disadvantages of place departmentalization. Organizing by location clearly increases problems of control and coordination for top management, which often is far away. To ensure uniformity and coordination, organizations that use place departmentalization—such as Blockbuster Video, Southland (7-Eleven stores), Enterprise Rent-A-Car, Air Canada, and Hilton Hotels—make extensive use of rules that apply to all locations. One reason for doing so is to guarantee a standard level of quality regardless of location, which would be difficult if units in various locations went their own separate ways. Also, employees may emphasize their own units' goals or focus only on problems that occur within their own geographic areas without some direction from headquarters. Because most of an organization's functional departments must be duplicated at each location, costs are higher than for an organization that has a more centralized operation.

Real-World Example
The disadvantage of place departmentalization for police and fire agencies is that, in the event of an unexpected, large-scale need for resources (e.g., a riot or refinery fire), resources may be too far away to respond in time.

Product Departmentalization

As an organization grows, the weaknesses of functional and place departmentalization begin to overshadow their strengths. This fact becomes particularly clear when the organization expands its product lines and attracts diverse customers. In response, top management often turns to product departmentalization. **Product departmentalization** divides the organization into self-contained units, each capable of designing, producing and marketing its own goods and/or services.

Organizations that have worldwide operations often use this form of departmentalization. Large multiproduct companies such as Sanyo, Matsushita, Quaker Oats, Arthur Andersen, CitiCorp, and Samsung also use this approach. Each of these companies started with a combination of functional and place departmentalization, but growth and an increasing inability to serve the needs of particular customers made those structures unworkable or uneconomical.

Harrisons & Crosfield operates manufacturing facilities around the world. The following Global Insight highlights how it uses place and product departmentalization as organizing strategies to serve its diverse group of customers.

TABLE 10.2

Advantages and Disadvantages of Place Departmentalization

Advantages	• Equipment used for products is all in one place, saving time and costs. • Managers develop expertise in solving problems unique to one location. • Managers know customers' problems. • Method is suited to multinational organizations.
Disadvantages	• All functions—accounting, purchasing, manufacturing, customer service—are duplicated at each location. • May cause conflicts between each location's goals and corporate goals. • May require extensive rules and regulations to coordinate and ensure uniformity of quality among locations.

Global *Insight*

Harrisons & Crosfield

Based in London, Harrisons & Crosfield has divisions in many parts of the world. Figure 10.4 illustrates how it uses place and product departmentalization to achieve its success. It owns rubber, cocoa, coffee, and tea plantations in Indonesia and New Guinea. The commodities produced on those plantations are marketed through division headquarters in Singapore. Weather and labor unrest are the primary problems that this division faces.

The chemicals and industrials division manufactures chrome chemicals, zinc products, and numerous organic chemicals. It has manufacturing plants and offices in Europe, the United Kingdom, and the United States. Waste, pollution, energy use, and accident frequency are the main problems that this division faces.

The foods and agriculture division produces animal feed, pet foods, malt, flour, and other consumer foods for people living in the United Kingdom. Stiff competition from other global companies who sell consumer products in the United Kingdom is the toughest problem that this division faces.[8]

Discussion Question 3
Why do global organizations such as Harrisons & Crosfield organize by product and place?

The advantages and disadvantages of product departmentalization are shown in Table 10.3.

Advantages of Product Departmentalization. Increased specialization allows managers and employees to concentrate on a particular product line. Management also can pinpoint costs, profits, problems, and successes more accurately for each product line. Moreover, management can develop a distinctive competence, or strategic advantage, for each product line. Other potential gains include lower costs for materials, freight rates, and labor. For marketing, locating near customers can mean better service for them. Salespeople can spend more time selling and less time traveling. Being closer

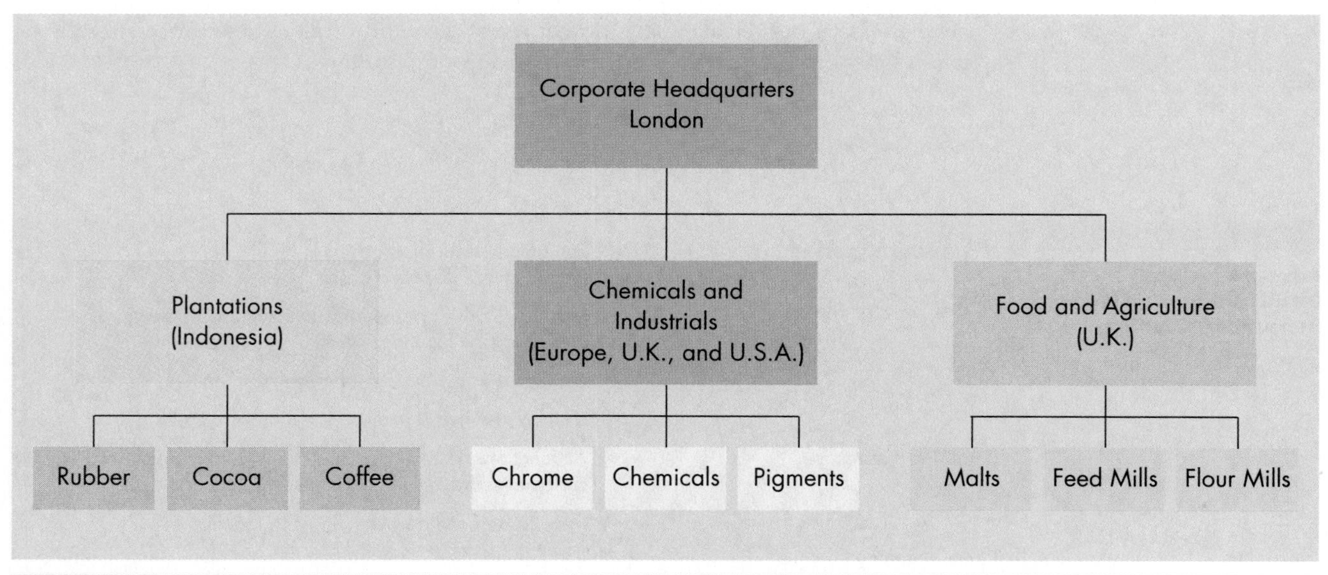

FIGURE 10.4

Harrisons & Crosfield's Place and Product Departmentalization

Source: Abridged from *1993 Annual Report, Harrisons & Crosfield,* and a conversation with Irma Caballero, June 1994.

TABLE 10.3

Advantages and Disadvantages of Product Departmentalization

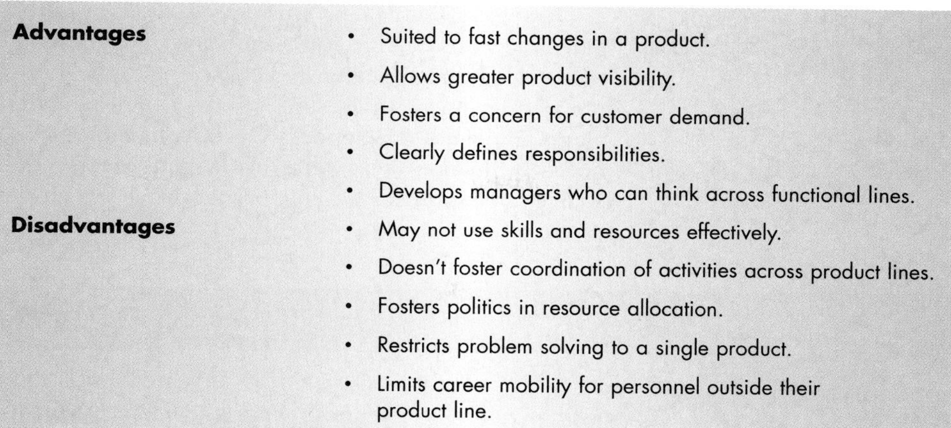

Advantages	• Suited to fast changes in a product. • Allows greater product visibility. • Fosters a concern for customer demand. • Clearly defines responsibilities. • Develops managers who can think across functional lines.
Disadvantages	• May not use skills and resources effectively. • Doesn't foster coordination of activities across product lines. • Fosters politics in resource allocation. • Restricts problem solving to a single product. • Limits career mobility for personnel outside their product line.

to customers also can help sales managers pinpoint the marketing tactics most likely to succeed in a particular region.

Disadvantages of Product Departmentalization. Because functions are duplicated for each product line (i.e., each business), resource utilization is relatively inefficient. In addition, products with seasonal highs and lows in sales volumes may result in high personnel costs. For example, Jostens has high demand for high school yearbooks in the spring but low demand the rest of the year, so fewer workers are needed much of the year. Hence the company faces the choice of transferring employees to other product lines or laying them off. Either solution means higher personnel costs than if product demand were less seasonal.

Coordination across product lines usually is difficult. Employees tend to focus on the goals for their particular product, rather than on broader company goals. This situation often creates unhealthy competition within an organization for scarce resources. For example, at Harrisons & Crosfield, discussions might range from the acquisition of a new sugar cane plantation in Indonesia to building a new malt plant in the United Kingdom. The debate over which project should be undertaken may revolve around what each division manager believes would be best for that product line, not what might be best for the company as a whole.

Career mobility is restricted when employees develop skills that are relevant only to a particular product line. Specialization doesn't allow people to develop the skills needed to move up in the organization's hierarchy or into its other businesses.

Discussion Question 2
When is product departmentalization preferable to functional departmentalization?

Top management may set common profit standards for *all* product lines, which may not be realistic for the industries in which some of them have to compete. For example, PepsiCo's managers have put tremendous pressures on the company's Kentucky Fried Chicken (KFC) subsidiary to earn profits that are standard in the beverage industry but simply can't be attained in the fast-food industry.

Customer Departmentalization

Customer departmentalization involves organizing around the type of customer served. It is used when management wants to ensure a focus on the customer's needs rather than on the organization's skills (functional) or the brands it produces and sells (product). In the increasingly service-oriented U.S. economy, the customer form of departmentalization is becoming more and more common.[9] Customer departmentalization is commonly used to differentiate products and offer different terms to different customers (production of different models and volume discounts to large customers and not-for-profit customers, etc.). This form of departmentalization indicates that management is sensitive to the needs of each customer segment and that it has identified segments that have substantial sales potential.

The following Insight illustrates how Fluor Corporation, a global international engineering, construction, and maintenance organization with 20,000 employees, uses customer departmentalization to organize its operations. Fluor offers its customers a full range of technical services that allows it to respond to customer needs anywhere in the world. Fluor has developed a global communications network that identifies customer needs by market area. With this system, Fluor can allocate human and financial resources to customer opportunities that have the greatest potential.

Insight

Fluor Corporation

The decision to use customer departmentalization begins with top management's belief that Fluor has the most skilled people available to solve customers' technical problems. Each client has specific needs, and therefore Fluor should be organized to listen to the client and deliver services at the most cost-effective price. Fluor has identified five types of customers—hydrocarbon, industrial, government, process, and power—as shown in Figure 10.5. In the industrial area, Fluor made the site selection studies for the new Mercedes-Benz plant in Tuscaloosa, Alabama. It also designed a new plant at the Pernis Refinery in the Netherlands for Shell. In the power area, it operates A.T. Massey, a coal company that produces high-quality, low-sulfur coal for the electric generating and steel industries.[10]

Discussion Question 4
What conditions should be present before an organization adopts customer departmentalization? Could this structure be used in your business school? If so, explain how the school might be organized?

Advantages and Disadvantages of Customer Departmentalization. Table 10.4 shows the advantages and disadvantages of customer departmentalization. One of the primary advantages of this form is that the organization can focus on customers' needs. Various customers have specialized needs, and this form of departmentalization helps the organization cater to those needs.

However, customer departmentalization can lead to pressure on the organization to meet too many specialized customer demands. Attempting to do so can overly complicate production scheduling and result in short, expensive production runs.

FIGURE 10.5

Fluor Corporation's Customer Departmentalization

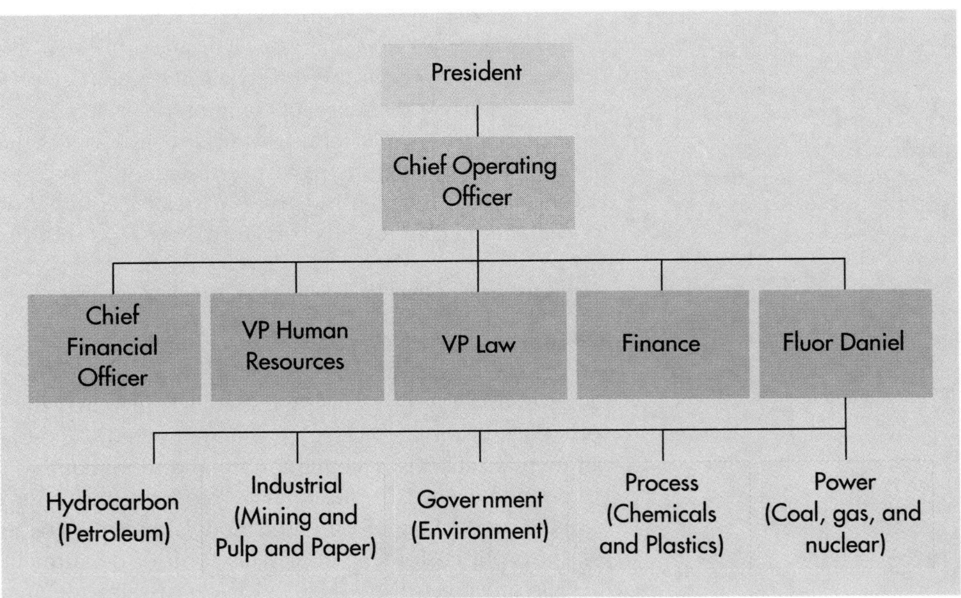

Source: Adapted from *1994 Annual Report* and Form 10-K, Fluor Corporation.

TABLE 10.4

Advantages and Disadvantages of Customer Departmentalization

Advantages	• Allows greater customer focus. • Clearly identifies key customers. • Suited to understanding customer needs. • Develops managers who become customer advocates.
Disadvantages	• Doesn't foster coordination between customers. • Fosters politics in resource allocation. • Employees feel pressure from customers to give them privileges. • Restricts problem solving to a single type of customer.

Selecting an Organizational Structure

Teaching Tip
Go around the room and ask students how their or their parents' employing organization is departmentalized.

Teaching Tip
Lead students in a discussion of the advantages and disadvantages of the four types of departmentalization.

Ask Students
If you had a choice, which type of organizational structure would you prefer to work in?

No particular type of departmentalization—functional, place, product, or customer—is best in all circumstances. Managers must select the organizational structure that matches the firm's specific needs.[11] Table 10.5 lists characteristics that can help managers decide which structure is best for their situations.

Alphagraphics, Sir Speedy and other quick-printing firms, and other small organizations that have standard products and diverse customers, probably would find functional departmentalization the best. Procter & Gamble and other organizations with large and diverse product lines probably would find product departmentalization most useful. Merck and other organizations in the pharmaceutical business with a number of complex technologies probably would find product and customer departmentalization most appropriate. American Airlines and other organizations that operate in numerous national and international regions probably would benefit from place departmentalization.

Clearly, the choice depends on the situation.[12] Some organizations even use all four types of departmentalization. For example, Rhone-Poulenc Rorer is a global pharmaceutical company headquartered in Paris with 22,000 employees throughout the world. Because of cultural and product line differences, it is organized by country (France, United States, Canada, and Australia), product line (prescription pharmaceuticals, plasma products, and consumer pharmaceuticals), function (research and development, marketing, and finance), and customer (hospitals and other institutions).[13]

TABLE 10.5

Organizational Characteristics and Type of Departmentalization

Organizational Characteristic	Type of Departmentalization Favored
Small size	Functional
Global or national scope	Place
Depends on customer needs	Customer
Essential to use scarce resources appropriately	Customer
Customer base is	
Diverse	Product
Stable	Functional or customer
Makes use of specialized equipment	Product
Requires skill specialization	Functional
High transportation costs for raw materials	Place or customer

State the basic principles of coordination.

Ask Students
What trouble did lack of coordination in a nonprofit or for-profit organization cause, as reported in a recent news story?

COORDINATION

Departmentalization divides the organization's work and allows for specialization and standardization of activities. However, to achieve organizational goals, people, projects, and tasks have to be coordinated. Without coordination, people's efforts are likely to end in delay, frustration, and waste. For precisely that reason, it is one of the basic elements of organizational design.

Many managers believe that good people can make any organizational design work. Although this may be overstating the case, people who work well together are an extremely valuable asset. A good analogy is football, where teamwork is of the essence. During practice sessions, coaches try to transform the individual players into one smoothly functioning team. Players learn their functions as part of a cooperative effort, see how each task relates to every other task, and relate these tasks to the whole. Coordination is required as the players execute their functions, particularly when they are called on to innovate or adjust to the unexpected in a game situation. Similarly, managers have to encourage employees to subordinate their individual interests to the organization's broader goals.

In this section we present three basic principles of coordination: the unity of command principle, the scalar principle, and the span of control principle. All are valuable additions to your bundle of management skills.

Unity of Command Principle

Ask Students
Have you worked in an organization that applied unity of command? What are the strengths and weaknesses of this approach?

The **unity of command principle** states that an employee should have only one boss. Every employee is supposed to know who is giving direction and to whom he or she reports. According to this principle, managers must minimize any confusion over who makes decisions and who implements them because uncertainty in this area can lead to serious productivity and morale problems.

Scalar Principle

Ask Students
Are informal relationships an important part of an organizational structure? If so, why do so many companies use the scalar principle?

The **scalar principle** states that a clear and unbroken chain of command should link every person in the organization with someone a level higher, all the way to the top of the organization chart. Tasks should be delegated clearly, with no overlapping or splitting of assignments. This principle is illustrated in Figure 10.6, which shows part of Comair Holdings, Inc.'s, organization chart. Headquartered in Cincinnati, Comair has six product divisions. Its Comair, Inc., division offers 600 weekly flights to seventy-eight cities in twenty-seven states and three countries. Within that division are various functional vice-presidents. Reporting to the vice-president for flight operations are employees who work at two major hubs (cities) served by Comair. Application of the scalar principle means that managers at the Orlando hub are responsible for the company's employees in Key West, Tampa, Miami, and other cities served from the Orlando hub.[14]

Teaching Tip
Communication overload occurs for many managers because of the scalar principle. They don't have time to absorb or are unable to comprehend all the information that comes to them. As a result, a communication and decision-making bottleneck occurs. Point out to students that the situation underscores lack of coordination and that it causes stress.

If followed rigidly, the scalar principle would require that all job-related communications between employees in different product departments at the same level (e.g., the aviation academy division and the services division at Comair Holdings) be approved by their respective superiors. Obviously, strict adherence to this principle would waste time and money—and be extremely frustrating. In practice, informal relationships across departmental lines spring up to facilitate problem solving and communication within the organization.

Span of Control Principle

The **span of control principle** states that the number of people reporting directly to any one manager must be limited because one manager can't effectively supervise a large number of subordinates. Span of control is a concept as old as organizations. In

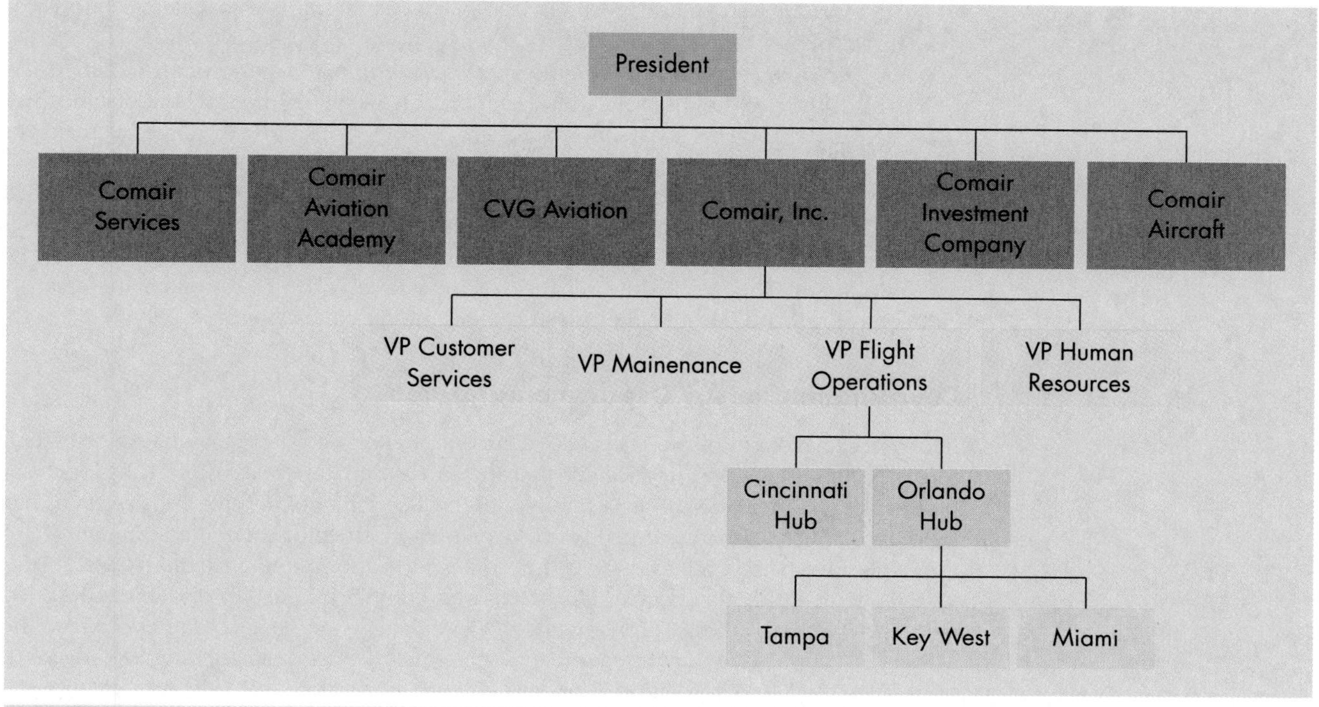

FIGURE 10.6

Comair Holdings, Inc., Organization Chart

Source: *1994 Annual Report*, Comair Holdings, Inc.

fact, it began with Roman military commanders' belief that narrow spans of control were effective in combat. The traditional viewpoint of management (Chapter 2) holds that the ideal number of subordinates reporting to any one manager should be no fewer than four and no more than twelve.

For the most part, successful organizations in the future century will have flat structures—that is, few levels of management. Many companies (Gillette, Firestone, and Pacific Bell, among others) already have flattened their structures by reducing the number of management layers between the CEO and first-line managers. This approach broadens the span of control, with a much larger number of people reporting to each manager. For example, when Victor Kiam bought Remington Razors, the company had only 480 employees. He ran the business with six senior executives in key functional areas (e.g., production, sales, and engineering). Less than ten years later Remington had more than 2,000 employees and eight senior managers with clearly defined authority and responsibilities. As he could not directly oversee more than 2,000 people, Kiam delegated decision making to those managers. Each of them has clear goals and assignments that can be divided into manageable parts.[15]

Ask Students
Why is there no "correct" number of subordinates that a manager can supervise effectively?

There is no "correct" number of subordinates that a manager can supervise effectively.[16] However, four key factors determine the best span of management for any situation:

1. ***The competence of both the manager and the employees.*** If a manger and/or employees are new to a task, they obviously require more supervision than knowledgeable veteran managers and employees do. The less experienced the manager and/or employees, the narrower the span of control should be.
2. ***The similarity or dissimilarity of tasks being supervised.*** A process focus means widely varying products and tasks, whereas a product focus means more standardization. For example, at Fluor Corporation, the span of control in the power area is broad because all managers can focus on one product: power plant services.

The more numerous and dissimilar the products, the narrower the span of control should be.

3. ***The incidence of new problems in the manager's department.*** A manager should know enough about the operations of the department to understand precisely the problems that subordinates are likely to face. The more the manager knows about these factors, the broader the span of control can be.
4. ***The extent of clear operating standards and rules.*** Clear rules and standard operating procedures leave little to chance and lessen the need for adaptive decisions. For example, at McDonald's extensive rules govern the tasks and behavior of employees. The greater the reliance on rules and SOPs, the broader the span of control may be because the rules do much of the controlling.[17]

Coordination versus Departmentalization

In any organization tension exists between coordination and departmentalization. When forces for coordination are stronger than those for departmentalization, functional departmentalization works best. Pep Boys, the self-service automotive repair chain, has kept pace with the changing needs of car owners by stocking a large assortment of automotive tires, parts, and accessories for domestic and imported cars and trucks. It provides speedy, efficient service to customers by smooth coordination of departmental activities. In general, when a problem arises, top managers must be able to coordinate the actions of various functional departments (e.g., merchandising, marketing, and distribution) quickly to find a solution. Under such conditions, functional departmentalization helps ensure the necessary degree of coordination.

When forces for coordination and departmentalization are equal, a customer form of departmentalization works best. The customer structure addresses the conflict between, say, the product manager's need to satisfy a customer and the functional department's need to provide technical help. Employees move from customer to customer, depending on the customer's needs. At Fluor Corporation, engineers could work on a power plant for Enron in the Philippines and an oil refinery in Thailand for Rayong Refinery Company. Additionally, some of these same employees may be assigned to work on building a 250-mile trans-Andean crude oil pipeline from Argentina to Chile.

A customer form of departmentalization works best when forces for coordination and departmentalization are equal. Employees move from customer to customer, depending on the customer's needs. At Fluor Corporation, engineers could work on a power plant for Enron in the Philippines (pictured) and an oil refinery in Thailand for Rayong.

When forces for departmentalization are stronger than those for coordination, place or product departmentalization is best. Managers decide what is appropriate for only their product, and they decide without having to consider the impact of their decisions on other product lines. Each radio station manager at Broadcasting Partners faces audiences that require unique programming. Because each market is unique, coordinating programming activities between stations isn't needed. However, some coordination might be necessary in terms of requiring the use of the same or similar reporting methods for financial, accounting, or audience market share information, so that the corporate level receives comparable data from all five stations.

For multinational companies (e.g., Texas Instruments, Kraft Foods, and Motorola), the use of several types of departmentalization and methods of coordination is common. In such organizations there is no single best way to balance the tension between coordination and departmentalization. Recall that Comair Holdings is organized into six product groups, or divisions. Comair, Inc., is further departmentalized by function and then by place. The methods of coordination vary for each division, depending on its circumstances. In some of the functional departments, the scalar principle and narrow spans of control will be effective. In departments that reflect place departmentalization, violation of the scalar principle is common, and wide spans of control are effective.

4

Describe the authority structure of an organization.

AUTHORITY

As discussed earlier, *authority,* the fourth element of organizational structure, is the right to make a decision and act. Authority is exercised, for instance, when a board of directors authorizes a bond issue to raise capital, when an executive approves a new advertising campaign, when a sales manager signs a contract with a client, when a production manager promotes a worker to first-line manager, and when a supervisor fires someone. In short, authority is the glue of organizational structure.

Ask Students

How does the zone of indifference apply to grades? Give an example.

As we pointed out in Chapter 2, Chester Barnard, president of New Jersey Bell Telephone Company from 1927 to 1948, held a somewhat different view of authority.[18] He maintained that authority flows from the bottom up, rather than from the top down. This view is known as the *acceptance theory of authority.* Barnard didn't think that an employee should analyze and judge every decision made by an immediate superior before either accepting or rejecting it. Rather, he thought that most decisions or orders fall within the subordinate's **zone of indifference,** which means that the subordinate will accept or obey them without serious question. If a decision or directive falls outside that zone, however, the subordinate will question whether to accept or reject it. For example, a manager's request that a secretary type a report probably falls within the secretary's zone of indifference—it's a part of the job description. But the manager's request that the secretary work on Sunday probably falls outside that zone, and the secretary may refuse.

Authority implies responsibility and accountability. That is, by exercising authority, managers accept the responsibility for acting and are willing to be held accountable for success or failure. Furthermore, when delegating tasks to others, managers should take care to match the responsibility they confer with authority and then insist on accountability for results.

Responsibility

Responsibility is an employee's obligation to perform assigned tasks. The employee acquires this obligation upon accepting a job or a specific assignment. A manager is responsible not only for carrying out certain tasks but also for the actions of subordinates. Joyce Herlihy is director of worldwide employee relations at American Express Travel Related Services (TRS). She is responsible for developing policies relating to diversity issues in that division. The TRS division employs more than 50,000 people worldwide and has a net income of more than $800 million annually. She felt that it was important that

TRS develop programs that would enable it to attract and retain employees in the face of increasing diversity with respect to values, expectations, lifestyles and family responsibilities. The following Diversity Insight highlights some of the programs she is responsible for at TRS.

Diversity *Insight*

Travel Related Services of American Express

Diversity is defined broadly at American Express's TRS division with respect to lifestyles, values, and family obligations. Over 70 percent of TRS's employees are women, almost 50 percent are in dual-career marriages, and over 40 percent have dependent children. The majority of these employees hold customer service jobs, such as answering phones, handling billing questions, providing credit authorization, or entering data.

In an effort to develop diversity programs for all employees, Herlihy asked senior managers for their suggestions on managing this type of work force. She then drafted a "think tank" report that summarized their suggestions. She held a two-day conference to make top managers aware of the changing demographics of the work force and how they would affect TRS. Based on suggestions offered during the two-day conference and those made by other employees, she recommended that TRS develop four programs:

1. child care subsidies that would provide partial reimbursement for the cost of child care;
2. improved part-time benefits, including medical and dental coverage, group life insurance, and short- and long-term disability insurance;
3. sabbaticals for employees with more than ten years of service, allowing them to deal with personal problems or engage in community service; and
4. flexible work arrangements that would let people share jobs, work compressed work weeks (ten hours a day for four days), and gradually return to work after a sickness.

Although local managers could be flexible in how these programs were phased in, Herlihy was responsible to the president of the TRS division for overall implementation in the division. She will also be held accountable for program results.[19]

Accountability

Accountability is the expectation that each employee will accept credit or blame for results achieved in performing assigned tasks. Employees are expected to report the results of their work. This feedback enables management to determine whether effective decisions are being made and whether tasks are being performed properly. No supervisor can check everything an employee does. Therefore guidelines are established within which responsibilities are carried out. The employee is accountable for performance within these limits. Thus, unlike authority, accountability *always* flows from the bottom up. The news assistant of a newspaper is accountable to the senior reporter, the senior reporter is accountable to the editor, the editor is accountable to the publisher, and so on.

Accountability is the point at which authority and responsibility meet. It is essential for obtaining effective performance. For example, the state grants you the authority to drive an automobile and assigns you the responsibility for obeying traffic laws. You are then held accountable for your behavior while driving a car. When either authority or responsibility are lacking, managers cannot judge a subordinate's accomplishments fairly. And when managers are reluctant to hold subordinates accountable for their tasks, subordinates can easily pass the buck for nonperformance.

Discussion Question 5
How can organizations create an authority system that makes ethical problems like those found in the Churning Accounts Ethics Insight less likely to happen?

The following Ethics Insight highlights the problem when accountability and responsibility break down and control and discipline within the organization are lost. Managers sometimes don't enforce accountability because that isn't easy. It involves monitoring tasks and confronting employees who are poor performers. This was the problem at Prudential Bache's Dallas, Texas, office. As a result, it has been sued by investors for more than $371 million.

Ethics *Insight*

Churning Accounts

Charles Grose, a manager in the Prudential Bache Securities Branch in Dallas, noticed that a broker was rapidly buying and selling securities that brought clients less than $200 in profits but generated more than $1,000 in sales commissions for the broker. The broker was preying on old women who didn't understand the mechanics of buying and selling stocks. Prudential had an honor code: No broker should just trade for commissions. But why did these abuses occur? Grose wrote a confidential memo to the regional director. The regional director, rather than discipline the broker, had another idea: destroy the memo.

At the core of the regional director's decision to destroy the memo was the fact that he didn't want to confront a broker who brought the firm more than $700,000 in commissions during the year. If the broker left the firm, the Dallas branch couldn't reach its revenue goals. Prudential stockbrokers also traded customers' shares without authorization, forged customers' signatures, and put customers in questionable investments. With money pouring into the firm and to brokers, everyone benefited except the customers.

After the mismanagement was brought to the attention of senior managers at headquarters by irate customers and government agencies, Prudential has tried to clean up its practices. New employees were hired, and Prudential is cooperating with numerous federal agencies in an attempt to pay back customers. Accountability and responsibility for brokers' actions have now been clearly defined.[20]

Delegation of Authority

Delegation of authority is the process by which managers assign the right to act and make decisions in certain areas to subordinates. Thus, in addition to assigning a task to a subordinate, the manager also gives the subordinate adequate decision-making power to carry out the task effectively. Delegation starts when the structure of the organization is being established and tasks are divided. It continues as new tasks are added during day-to-day operations.

Teaching Tip
Have students describe situations in which they worked under someone who was afraid to delegate.

Delegation of authority occurs in conjunction with the assignment of responsibilities, as when a company president assigns to an executive assistant the task of preparing a formal statement for presentation to a congressional committee, or when the head of a computer department instructs a programmer to debug a new management reporting system. In each case a manager gives decision-making power to a subordinate.

The basic components of the delegation process are determining expected results, assigning tasks and the authority needed to accomplish them, and holding those to whom the tasks were assigned accountable for results achieved. These components shouldn't be separated. If they are, problems like those faced by Prudential Bache Securities can arise.

Improving Delegation. The following six principles are useful for improving delegation of authority.

1. ***Establish goals and standards.*** Subordinates should participate in developing the goals that they will be expected to meet. They should also agree to the standards that will be used to measure their performance.
2. ***Define authority and responsibility.*** Subordinates should clearly understand the work delegated to them, recognize the scope of their authority, and accept their accountability for results.
3. ***Involve subordinates.*** The challenge of the work itself won't always encourage subordinates to accept and perform delegated tasks well. Managers can motivate subordinates by involving them in decision making, by keeping them informed, and by helping them improve their skills and abilities.
4. ***Require completed work.*** Subordinates should be required to carry a task through to completion. The manager's job is to provide guidance, help, and information—not to finish the job.
5. ***Provide training.*** Delegation can be only as effective as the ability of people to perform the work and make the necessary decisions. Managers should continually appraise delegated responsibilities and provide training aimed at building on strengths and overcoming deficiencies.
6. ***Establish adequate controls.*** Timely, accurate reports should be provided to subordinates so that they may compare their performance to agreed-upon standards and correct their deficiencies.[21]

Barriers to Delegation. Delegation can be only as effective as the ability of people to delegate.[22] Table 10.6 lists excuses managers make for not delegating. The greatest psychological barrier to delegation is fear. A manager may be afraid that if subordinates don't do the job properly, the manager's own reputation will suffer. "I can do it better myself." "My subordinates are not capable enough." "It takes too much time to explain what I want done." In addition, managers also may be reluctant to delegate because they fear that subordinates will do the work their own way, do it too well, and outshine the boss!

Discussion Question 6
Why do some managers find delegating decision-making powers to subordinates to be difficult?

Failing to delegate can be justified only if subordinates are untrained or poorly motivated. However, it is the manager's responsibility to overcome such deficiencies. Gabrielle Bush, owner of a small computer software company, had to delegate responsibility and authority to others when she realized that she couldn't directly manage all thirty-two employees in three functional departments. She had to overcome her fear of delegating if her organization was to grow and prosper.

Among the organizational barriers that may block delegation is a failure to define authority and responsibility clearly. If managers themselves don't know what is expected or what to do, they can't properly delegate authority to others. The *Challenger* space shuttle disaster in January 1986 has been blamed on the combined failure of NASA and Morton Thiokol (NASA's principal contractor for booster rockets) to define authority and responsibility clearly. A presidential commission found that NASA engineers had

TABLE 10.6

Excuses Managers Make for Not Delegating

- Employees lack experience.
- It takes more time to explain than to do the job myself.
- A mistake by an employee could be costly.
- Employees are already too busy.
- Delegating is terrifying to me.

Source: Adapted from Nelson, R.B. *Empowering Employees Through Delegation.* Burr Ridge, Ill.: Irwin Professional Publishing, 1994, 20–26.

TABLE 10.7

The Art of Delegation

- Delegate strategically by measuring employees' successes against jointly set goals.
- Treat delegation as a career-building tool that provides employees with the needed experiences to prepare them for greater responsibility.
- Find the right person for the task.
- Let employees establish their own plan(s) of action.
- Make sure you stay on top of things and hold employees accountable.

Source: Ayres-Williams, R. Mastering the fine art of delegation. *Black Enterprise.* April 1992, 91–93.

sufficient information about the O-rings prior to the flight to cancel it but that this information didn't reach the people with authority to do so. NASA managers failed to delegate decision-making authority and responsibility to those (the engineers) who knew that the crew would be in serious danger. Failure to delegate in that case cost seven lives and demoralized NASA employees.[23]

Overcoming Barriers to Delegation. Table 10.7 lists five factors that can help managers become better delegators. Effective delegation requires that employees be given some freedom to accomplish assigned tasks. Managers must accept that there are several ways to deal with problems and that their own ways of solving them aren't necessarily those their subordinates will choose. Of course, subordinates will make errors. Whenever possible, they should be allowed to develop their own solutions to problems and learn from their mistakes. This approach is very difficult for many managers, but unless they follow it, they won't be able to delegate effectively. They will be so busy with minor tasks or with checking on subordinates that they will fail to complete their own important assignments. Managers must keep in mind that the advantages of delegation justify giving subordinates freedom of action, even at the risk of letting mistakes occur.

Improved communication between managers and subordinates also can overcome barriers to delegation. Managers who make it a point to learn the strengths, weaknesses, and preferences of their subordinates can more effectively decide which tasks can be delegated to whom. Such knowledge will give them greater confidence in their delegation decisions. In addition, subordinates who are encouraged to use their abilities and who feel that their managers will back them up are likely to accept responsibility eagerly.

5

Explain the factors that affect the centralization or decentralization of decision making

Teaching Tip

If the maturity of workers is high and they can work without close supervision, fewer managers and controls are needed, thus enabling decentralization.

CENTRALIZATION AND DECENTRALIZATION OF AUTHORITY

Centralization and decentralization of authority are basic, overall management philosophies of delegation, that is, of where decisions are to be made.[24] **Centralization of authority** is the concentration of authority at the top of an organization or department. **Decentralization of authority** is a high degree of delegated authority throughout an organization or department. Decentralization is an approach that requires managers to decide what and when to delegate, to select and train personnel carefully, and to formulate adequate controls.

Advantages of Decentralization

Decentralization has several potential advantages.

1. It frees top managers to develop organizational plans and strategies. Lower level managers and employees handle routine, day-to-day decisions.

Real-World Example
DuPont decentralized by cutting seven layers of management. The U.S. Naval Air Maintenance in California replaced its 600-page manual with a 4-page document (*Business Horizons*, September–October, 1994, 36).

2. It develops lower level managers' conceptual skills. According to Jack Welch, president of GE, decentralization prepares managers for positions requiring greater judgment and increased responsibility.[25]
3. Because subordinates often are closer to the action than higher level managers, they may have a better grasp of all the facts. This knowledge may enable them to make sound decisions quickly. Valuable time can be lost when a subordinate must check everything with the boss.
4. Decentralization fosters a healthy, achievement-oriented atmosphere among employees.

Neither centralization nor decentralization is absolute in an organization. No one manager makes all the decisions, even in a highly centralized setting. Total delegation would end the need for middle and first-line managers. Thus there are only degrees of centralization and decentralization. In most organizations some tasks are relatively centralized (e.g., payroll systems, purchasing, and human resource policies), and others are relatively decentralized (e.g., marketing and production).

General Mills manufactures food products such as Cheerios, Gold Medal flour, and Betty Crocker cake mixes and operates the Red Lobster and Olive Garden restaurant chains. Each vice-president at General Mills has the authority to delegate production and marketing decisions to subordinates. According to CEO Bruce Atwater, delegating these decisions is necessary to stay in tune with customer tastes, be innovative, and stay ahead of the competition. However, General Mills centralizes purchasing decisions, enabling the company to use its vast buying power to get all managers a good prices from suppliers.

Factors Affecting Centralization and Decentralization

Ask Students
Is this university's administrative staff centralized or decentralized?

Several factors can affect management's decision to centralize or decentralize decision-making responsibilities. Let's briefly consider six of these factors.

Costliness of Decisions. Cost is perhaps the most important factor in determining the extent of centralization. As a general rule, the more costly the decision is to the organization, the more likely it is that top management will make it. For instance, the General Mills decision to sell off Izod apparel, Parker Toys, and Eddie Bauer retail outlets was made by CEO Atwater and his staff. Costs may be measured in dollars or in intangibles such as the company's reputation in the community, social responsibilities, or employee morale.

Uniformity of Policy. Managers who value consistency favor centralization of authority. These managers may want to assure customers that everyone is treated equally in terms of quality, price, credit, delivery, and service. At Home Depot, a nationwide home improvement retailer, sales promotion on paint requires that all stores charge the same price.

Uniform policies have definite advantages for cost accounting, production, and financial departments. They also enable managers to compare the relative efficiencies of various departments. In organizations with unions, such as General Motors and American Airlines, uniform policies also aid in the administration of labor agreements regarding wages, promotions, fringe benefits, and other personnel matters.

Corporate Culture. A firm's culture will play a large part in determining whether authority will be centralized. **Corporate culture** comprises the norms, values, and practices that characterize a particular organization.[26] Caring about its employees and serving its customers are the dominant values in J.C. Penney's corporate culture. Management actions have reinforced these values ever since founder James Cash Penney laid down the seven guiding principles called the "Penney Idea." For instance, one store manager was warned by a top manager for making too much profit—it was unfair to customers. Customers can return merchandise with no questions asked. Everyone within the company is treated as an individual. Employees are encouraged to participate in decisions that will affect them, and layoffs are avoided at all costs. Long-term employee loyalty is especially valued. Decision making at Penney's is decentralized in merchandising but centralized in finance

PepsiCo has a very different corporate culture, reflecting its desire to overtake Coca-Cola's share of the soft drink market. Managers compete fiercely against one another to gain market share, to squeeze more profit from a product line, and to work harder. Employees who don't succeed are fired. Even the company picnic is characterized by intensely competitive games, which teams strive to win at all costs. Everyone knows the corporate culture and either thrives on the creative tension it creates or leaves. At PepsiCo each brand manager is responsible for his or her decisions. Decentralizing decision making to those closest to the customer clearly establishes accountability.[27]

Availability of Managers. Many organizations work hard to ensure an adequate supply of competent managers and employees—an absolute necessity for decentralization. These organizations believe that practical experience is the best training for developing managerial potential. They are willing to permit employees to make mistakes involving small cost.

Control Mechanisms. Even the most avid proponents of decentralization, such as DuPont, GE, and Marriott insist on controls and procedures to determine whether actual events are meeting expectations. Each hotel in the Marriott chain collects certain key data, including number of beds occupied, employee turnover, number of meals served, and the average amount that guests spend on food and beverages. Analysis of the data helps the manager control important aspects of the motel's operation and compare it against the performance of others in the chain. If a motel's operations are not within certain guidelines, top management can undertake a diagnosis of the situation.[28]

Teaching Tip
The Virgin Group, the parent company of Virgin Records, Virgin Superstores, and Virgin-Atlantic Airlines, has no central headquarters and no central staff. How is this possible? (Functions are located in the operating divisions. CEO Richard Branson has a high-delegation, nonhierarchical style.)

Environmental Influences. External factors (e.g., unions, federal and state regulatory agencies, and tax policies) affect the degree of centralization in a firm. Government policy on the employment of minorities, for example, makes decentralizing hiring authority difficult for a company. Moreover, local managers can't establish hours and wages that violate government limits on number of hours worked and the minimum wage.

Unions with long-term contracts also exert a centralizing influence on many organizations. When unions bargain on behalf of the employees of an entire organization, such as Ford or Delta Airlines, top management can't risk decentralizing labor negotiations. But when small local or regional unions represent employees in various departments, top management may delegate the authority to negotiate the terms of labor contracts to departmental managers.

Discussion Question 7
What factors suggest that Taco Bell is relatively decentralized?

6

State the differences between line and staff authority.

LINE AND STAFF AUTHORITY

Line authority belongs to managers who have the right to direct and control the activities of subordinates who perform tasks essential to achieving organizational goals. Line authority thus flows down the organization through the primary chain of command, according to the scalar principle. In contrast, those with **staff authority** direct and control subordinates who support line functions through advice, recommendations, research, technical expertise and specialized services.

Line functions are closely tied to organizational goals and processes. These functions differ from one type of organization to another. For example, Figure 10.7 shows an abridged version of the Toys "R" Us organization chart. In this case, line departments perform tasks such as marketing, store merchandising, and physical distribution. Staff departments provide specialized information and services to the line departments, in-

Teaching Tip
Divide the class into two teams representing line and staff departments and ask them to debate the importance of their roles to the organization.

cluding finance and administration, real estate, and management information systems. The line departments follow the line of authority from the office of CEO to the vice-presidents for divisional merchandising, and so on. All staff departments at Toys "R" Us exist at the corporate level and support the line managers in the performance of their tasks.

Location of Staff Departments

Usually, the location of staff departments within an organization is determined by the differences between generalized and specialized functions.[29] If staff services are used extensively throughout an organization, staff departments may need to be located relatively high up in the hierarchy. In fact, most large organizations centralize general staff functions at the top. In Toys "R" Us, for instance, the corporate staff consists of offices that handle finance and administration, real estate, management information systems, and treasury functions, and the corporate legal staff. The vice-presidents who manage these staff functions usually are in corporate policy-making positions. For example, the vice-president for real estate at Toys "R" Us is responsible for developing store locations companywide.

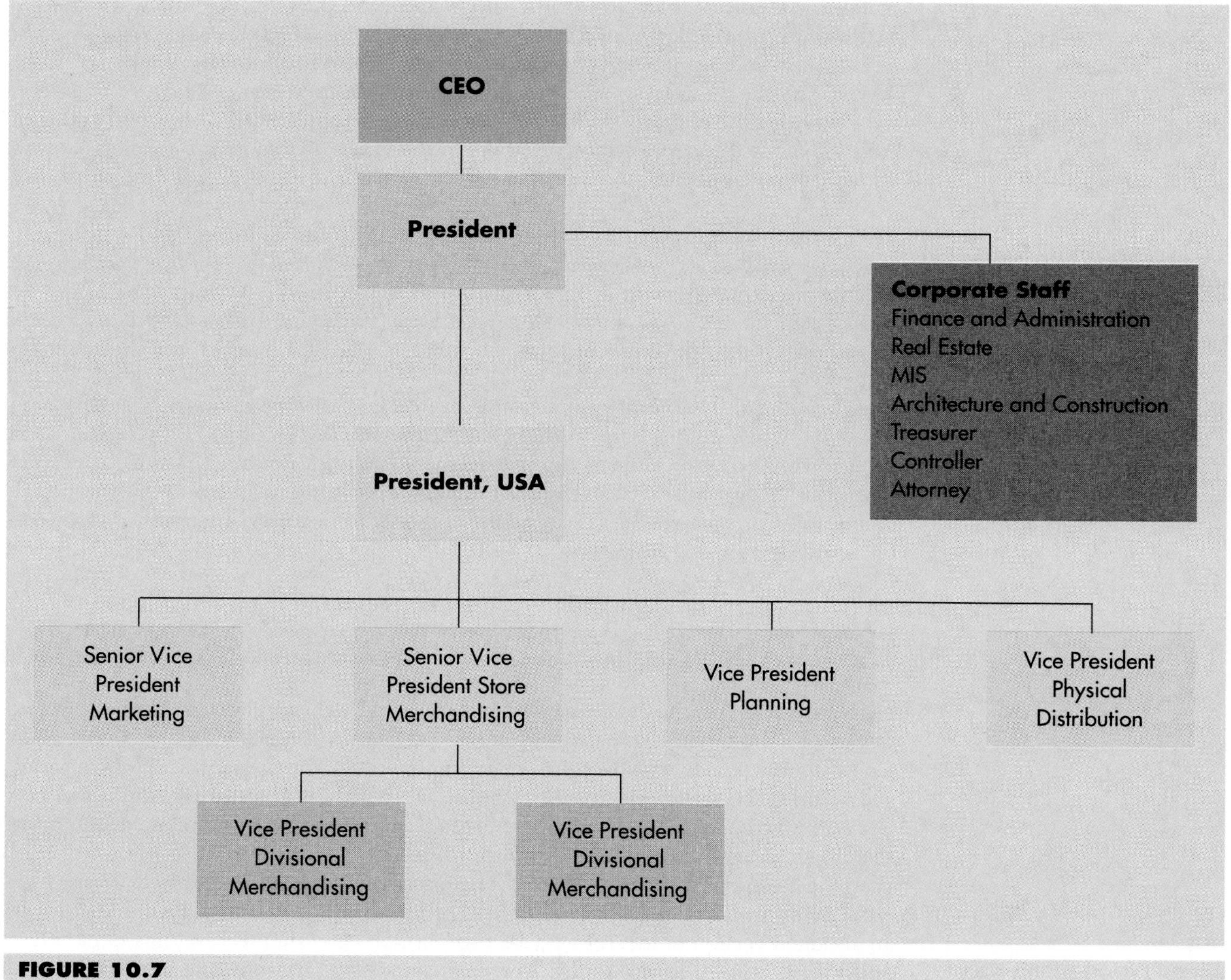

FIGURE 10.7

Line and Staff Structure at Toys "R" Us

Teaching Tip
Asea Brown Boveri (ABB), a Zurich-based $28.9 billion diversified manufacturing company, has 150 central staffers and three layers of management. How can ABB run with so few central staffers?

If a staff department provides necessary services to a specific line function, it should be located near that function both physically and in terms of managerial authority. A staff specialist who performs some support functions that a line manager would otherwise have to perform usually reports directly to that line manager.

CHAPTER SUMMARY

In this chapter we highlighted the traditional ways of structuring organizations. As organizations get more involved in global activities, incorporate new information technology, compete for customers, and respond to new employee expectations, the need will be to fundamentally rethink organizational structure.

1 ***Describe the main elements of organizational structure and how they're shown on an organization chart.***
The four basic elements of organizational structure are specialization, or the process of identifying tasks and assigning them to individuals or teams trained specifically to perform them; standardization, or the process of developing the procedures by which the organization promotes uniform and consistent performance; coordination, or the formal and informal procedures that integrate tasks performed by separate groups; and authority, or the right to make decisions and take action. An organization chart shows the interrelationships among these four elements.

2 ***Discuss the most common types of departmentalization.***
The four primary types of departmentalization are functional departmentalization, which groups employees according to common tasks to be performed; place departmentalization, which groups functions and employees by geographic location; product or service departmentalization, which groups employees in self-contained units, each responsible for its own product or service; and customer departmentalization, when management wants to focus on specific customer needs.

3 ***State the basic principles of coordination.***
Three principles can be used in coordinating employee activities: the unity of command principle, which states that each employee should report to only one boss; the scalar principle, which states that a clear, unbroken chain of command should link every person in the organization with his or her superior; and the span of management principle, which states that the number of subordinates who report directly to a particular manager should be limited.

4 ***Describe the authority structure of an organization.***
Three factors comprise the authority structure of an organization: authority, or the right to make decisions and take action; responsibility, or the obligation to perform assigned tasks; and accountability, or the expectation that each employee will accept credit or blame for the results of his or her performance. Delegation is the assignment of authority to employees.

5 ***Explain the factors that affect the centralization or decentralization of decision making.***
Six factors affect managers' decisions to centralize or decentralize authority: costliness of decisions, uniformity of policy, corporate culture, availability of talented employees and managers, control mechanisms, and environmental influences.

6 ***State the differences between line and staff authority.***
Line authority flows through the primary chain of command, according to the scalar principle, and is held by those managers whose activities are essential to achieving organizational goals. Staff authority is held by managers whose offices support line activities by providing specialized information and services.

QUESTIONS FOR DISCUSSION

1. As it grows, what problems is Tres Mariposas likely to face because of the way it is organized?
2. When is product departmentalization preferable to functional departmentalization?
3. Why do global organizations, such as Harrisons & Crosfield, organize by product and place?
4. What conditions should be present before an organization adopts customer departmentalization? Could this structure be used in your business school? If so, explain how the school might be organized.
5. How can organizations create an authority system that makes ethical problems like those found in the Churning Accounts Ethics Insight less likely to happen?
6. Why do some managers find delegating decision-making powers to subordinates to be difficult?
7. What factors suggest that Taco Bell is relatively decentralized?

FROM WHERE YOU SIT

1. How might your career advancement differ in an organization using functional departmentalization and one using product departmentalization?
2. Describe the types of departmentalization used by your university or employer.
3. Identify line and staff employees in your organization or university. On what basis did you make this classification?
4. If you were the manager, how might you structure your department to increase your employees' awareness of diversity issues?
5. Describe the authority structure for some organization with which you are familiar. Explain why you believe that the authority structure is as you described it.
6. You have been hired as a consultant by a firm specializing in manufacturing and marketing novelties for college fraternities and sororities in Canada and the United States. In a memo to the president of the firm, describe a form of departmentalization that would be most appropriate for that organization.

Centralization or Decentralization: What's Your Choice?

People differ in their organizational and work-setting preferences. Debates on how the organization should be run consume untold hours around the water cooler. Such debates often involve specific personalities and policies, but they also tend to reflect the general biases or preferences of the individuals involved. The following inventory is designed to help you survey your own preferences. There are no right or wrong answers. Instead, the inventory is designed to stimulate your thoughts about working in a centralized or decentralized organization.

Instructions: Your preferences are to be expressed by checking one of the following responses for each statement: Your first reaction to each statement is probably the best. Spending too much time debating your feelings with yourself will only leave you undecided.

I prefer to work in an organization where:	Strongly Agree (SA)	Agree Somewhat (A)	Undecided (U)	Disagree Somewhat (D)	Strongly Disagree (SD)
1. Goals are assigned by senior managers.	____	____	____	____	____
2. Methods and procedures for achieving goals are specified for me.	____	____	____	____	____
3. Top management makes important decisions.	____	____	____	____	____
4. My loyalty counts as much as my ability to do the job.	____	____	____	____	____
5. Clear lines of authority and responsibility are established.	____	____	____	____	____
6. Top management is decisive and firm.	____	____	____	____	____
7. My career is pretty well planned out for me.	____	____	____	____	____
8. I can specialize.	____	____	____	____	____
9. My length of service is almost as important as my level of performance.	____	____	____	____	____
10. Management is able to provide the information I need to do my job well.	____	____	____	____	____
11. A chain of command is well established.	____	____	____	____	____
12. Rules and procedures are adhered to equally by everyone.	____	____	____	____	____
13. People accept the authority of the leader's position.	____	____	____	____	____
14. People are loyal to their boss.	____	____	____	____	____
15. People do as they have been instructed.	____	____	____	____	____
16. People clear things with their boss before going over his or her head.	____	____	____	____	____

Scoring

Each question attempts to assess your preference for either a centralized or a decentralized organization. The more you agree with each statement, the more you prefer decision making to be centralized. By assigning a 5 to each SA response, a 4 to each A response, and so on down to a 1 for each SD response, you can score the strength of your preferences.

head of merchandising and brought in an outsider, Arthur C. Martinez, vice-chairman of Saks Fifth Avenue.

Martinez shook up the Merchandise Group by shutting down 112 unprofitable retail outlets, cutting 50,000 jobs and bringing in outsiders at every level of management. The 112 stores affected by Sears' restructuring accounted for 1.8 percent of net revenues and about 4 percent of Sears' total retail space. The restructuring left Sears with some 800 stores.

Another significant aspect of the effort was restructuring of the catalog division, costing the company more than $3 billion in lost revenues. However, the retail outlet and catalog division cuts were expected to improve the Merchandise Group's income by more than $200 million. The catalog division restructuring affected thousands of people in the distribution, trucking, and modeling industries. It received an enormous amount of publicity because the Sears catalog had been an American institution for decades and, in fact, was the company's original business. Many people were unhappy with the decision because they had vivid memories of doing their shopping through the catalog and, especially as children, making their Christmas wish lists from it. The restructuring was, to say the least, an emotional one. Between 250 and 500 of the 2,000 catalog stores were retained to capitalize on their strengths: selling appliances, electronics, and hardware.

Sears also ended an era during which it tried to be all things to all customers. Martinez has stated that the company has for the first time decided to focus on a target customer: the working woman between 25 and 54 years in age, with an annual household income of between $16,000 and $45,000. John Costello, senior executive vice-president in charge of marketing and advertising, says that the Sears' targeted working woman is the chief purchasing agent for her household, shops in malls, and is looking for superior value in everything. The main thrust of the new Sears is low-priced, but fashionable, apparel—touted in ads as the softer side of Sears. Studies have indicated that 70 percent of women's apparel and 60 percent of men's apparel are sold in malls. Focusing on customer departmentalization, Sears will continue to offer more lines of goods than other stores in malls, making it the only full-line department store left, according to Martinez. Sears intends to spend $5 billion to remodel its 800 stores and improve the presentation of its apparel lines. Only about 250 to 300 stores had been remodeled by the end of 1994, but customers are streaming back to Sears anyway.

Has the restructuring helped? According to Martinez, the first quarter of 1994 was good and the month of May, which is typically a tough month for retailers, was a double-digit growth month for Sears. Total domestic store sales for the four weeks ending May 28 were $1.89 billion, or 10.5 percent above the $1.72 billion reported for 1993. For the thirteen weeks ending April 30, the Merchandise Group reported gross revenues of $7.53 billion, or 12.9 percent above the $6.67 billion reported for 1993.

Meanwhile 1993 proved to be the most profitable year in Sears' 107-year history, with record earnings of $2.37 billion, compared with the $3.9 billion loss reported in 1992. The restructuring has been credited for the remarkable turnaround. Martinez says that the plan's success ultimately will depend on how well Sears' workers and managers can continue to adopt and implement "new thinking for new times."[32]

Questions

1. How can Sears reposition its hard goods lines to compete with stores such as Circuit City and Home Depot that consistently have beaten Sears' prices?
2. What type(s) of departmentalization does Sears have? What are the major advantages and disadvantages of organizational structure?
3. Rumors circulated in the investment community during 1992 that Sears Chairman, Edward Brennan, had been given an ultimatum to improve Sears's performance quickly—or else. The alleged ultimatum supposedly was similar to one believed to have been delivered by the board of General Motors to former Chairman Robert Stempel, who was ousted in October 1992 after he failed to move quickly enough to turn GM around. Does this type of restructuring ultimatum hurt or hinder a company's growth? Why?

Chapter 11

Contemporary Organization Designs

Chapter *Outline*

Learning *Objectives*

After studying this chapter, you should be able to:

1. Define organization design.
2. Explain how different environments influence organization design.
3. Describe the differences between mechanistic and organic organizational structures.
4. Discuss the effects of technology on the design of manufacturing and service organizations.
5. Explain how environment and technology combine to determine the amount of information an organization must process.
6. Describe the factors that affect the organization design.

Preview *Insight*

In Search of Tomorrow's Organization

Lawrence Bossidy, CEO of Allied Signal, predicts a revolution as organizations search for ways to redesign themselves to face the competitive challenges of the twenty-first century. Although Bossidy doesn't know what Allied Signal will look like in the future, he knows that Allied will have to be structured differently if it is to survive. Organizations as diverse as the San Diego Zoo, Kodak, Hallmark Cards, and General Electric are facing three challenges. How organizations respond to each of them will greatly affect the design of each organization's structure. What are these challenges?

1. Give employees jobs with meaning in which they can make important decisions.

Labeled "high-involvement workplaces," highly participative organizations have proven that they can deliver greater productivity, higher quality, and more job satisfaction than traditional organizations. These workplaces provide employees with the power and incentive to get things done without checking with a supervisor. The goal is to create organizations with clearly defined customers, markets, and measures of success.

2. Organize work by business processes (materials handling, billing, and customer service) rather than by functional departments (purchasing, manufacturing, and finance).

Employees and teams who actually carry out the organization's tasks will be involved in these business processes. Whoever is needed to work in a process will be assigned to it. For example, process teams will work with customers and suppliers to share information and satisfy their needs, whether for low cost or fast service. Many organizations traditionally organized by product, customer, function, or location have found that these structures don't adequately serve customers because information doesn't flow freely. The goal is to create organizations with few internal boundaries. In essence, customer needs will influence structure by grouping employees into the processes necessary to serve them.

3. Move information directly to where it's needed, unfiltered by the hierarchy.

At Wal-Mart, for example, each day the electric cash registers in each store inform warehouses and manufacturers (e.g., Procter & Gamble, to ship new boxes of Tide to replace those just bought by customers). Employees and managers can spend more time serving customers because the purchasing process is automated. At Hoechst Celanese, employees log onto their PCs to read their e-mail. While visiting suppliers in Singapore, Karen Jones used her PC to solve problems in her Dallas, Texas, office. Her PC gave her information that she could use at a moment's notice. Building computer networks on an information superhighway can transmit data almost instantaneously to employees performing each business process, dramatically reducing the need for departments and hierarchies as we have known them.[1]

Define organization design.

WHAT IS ORGANIZATION DESIGN?

Organization design is the process of determining the structure and authority relationships for an entire organization as a means of implementing the strategies and plans that embody the organization's goals (see Chapter 5). For example, Hallmark Cards has redesigned the way it makes cards. It has done away with functional departments and created teams for particular holidays, such as Valentine's Day. A team of artists, writers, lithographers, operations personnel, merchandisers, and accountants are assigned to each holiday. Team members work together at Hallmark's Kansas City plant until the cards or groups of cards have been produced.

The practice of matching organization design to a firm's strategy isn't new. In his landmark study of seventy large organizations, Alfred Chandler found that organization design follows strategy.[2] The choice of organization design makes a difference because not all forms of design support a particular strategy equally well. This structure-follows-strategy theory is based on the idea that, like a plan, an organization's design should be a means to an end, not an end in itself. Thus there are few hard and fast rules for designing or redesigning an organization. Every firm's organization design is the result of many decisions and historical circumstances.

Teaching Tip
Emphasize this point to students. They tend to think that all organizations are the same and that we only teach them the obvious.

To some extent managers and other employees make design decisions all the time—not just during major upheavals, such as expansions or reorganizations. In any organization, every time a new department is formed, new methods of coordination are tried, or a task is assigned to a different department, the organization design is being tested or tinkered with. This type of change isn't necessarily bad. In fact, you might think of design features as tools with which managers work, just as sailors use the sails, rigging, and rudder as tools to steer their boats. Sailors frequently "fine-tune" their boats, even when sailing a relatively steady course. The effective manager also constantly fine-tunes the organization's design in light of changes in the environment and technology.

Teaching Tip
Students may have the misconception that organizations are eternal. Let them know that organizations are reproduced or reinforced in everyday decisions. Organizations always are evolving.

Organization design is no more than the sum of managerial decisions for implementing a strategy and, ultimately, achieving the organization's goals. Hence the design of the organization acts both as a "harness," helping people pull together in the performance of their diverse tasks, and as a means of coordinating the various tasks in ways that promote the attainment of the firm's goals. When we talk about organization design, then, we are talking about managers' decisions concerning the organization's very nature, shape, and other features.[3]

Figure 11.1 shows the key factors that affect organization design. We discuss the environment, technology, and information processing in depth in this chapter. We discussed strategy in Chapters 3, 4, and 5, and refer to these chapters as appropriate.

2
Explain how different environments influence an organization's design.

ENVIRONMENT AND ORGANIZATION DESIGN

In a sense, everything outside the organization comprises its external environment (Figure 11.2). In Chapters 3, 4, and 5 we discussed many of the forces that shape the environment within which an organization operates. In this section we concentrate on how environmental stability or change influences an organization's design—that is, shapes its departments, coordination mechanisms, and control systems.

An organization that provides goods and/or services in an environment with slow technological innovation and relatively few competitors has problems that are different from those of an organization in a growing, changing, highly competitive market. The first environment is stable; the second, changing and uncertain. Recall that the relative stability of an organization's environment has major implications for its strategy and structure. The competitive forces—customers, competitors, suppliers, new entrants, and substitute goods and services—influence the type and amount of information managers need in order to make decisions. Most firms, however, operate in both stable and changing environments. As a result, some functions may undergo little structural change, but others may change considerably.

Stable Environment

A **stable environment** is characterized by few changes, and the changes that do occur have minimal impact on the organization's internal operations. A stable environment has several main features:

Teaching Tip
Have students identify five organizations in different industries, including the public sector, that are consistent with these features.

- products that haven't changed much in recent years,
- little technological innovation,
- a fixed set of competitors, customers, and other stakeholders, and
- consistent government policies.

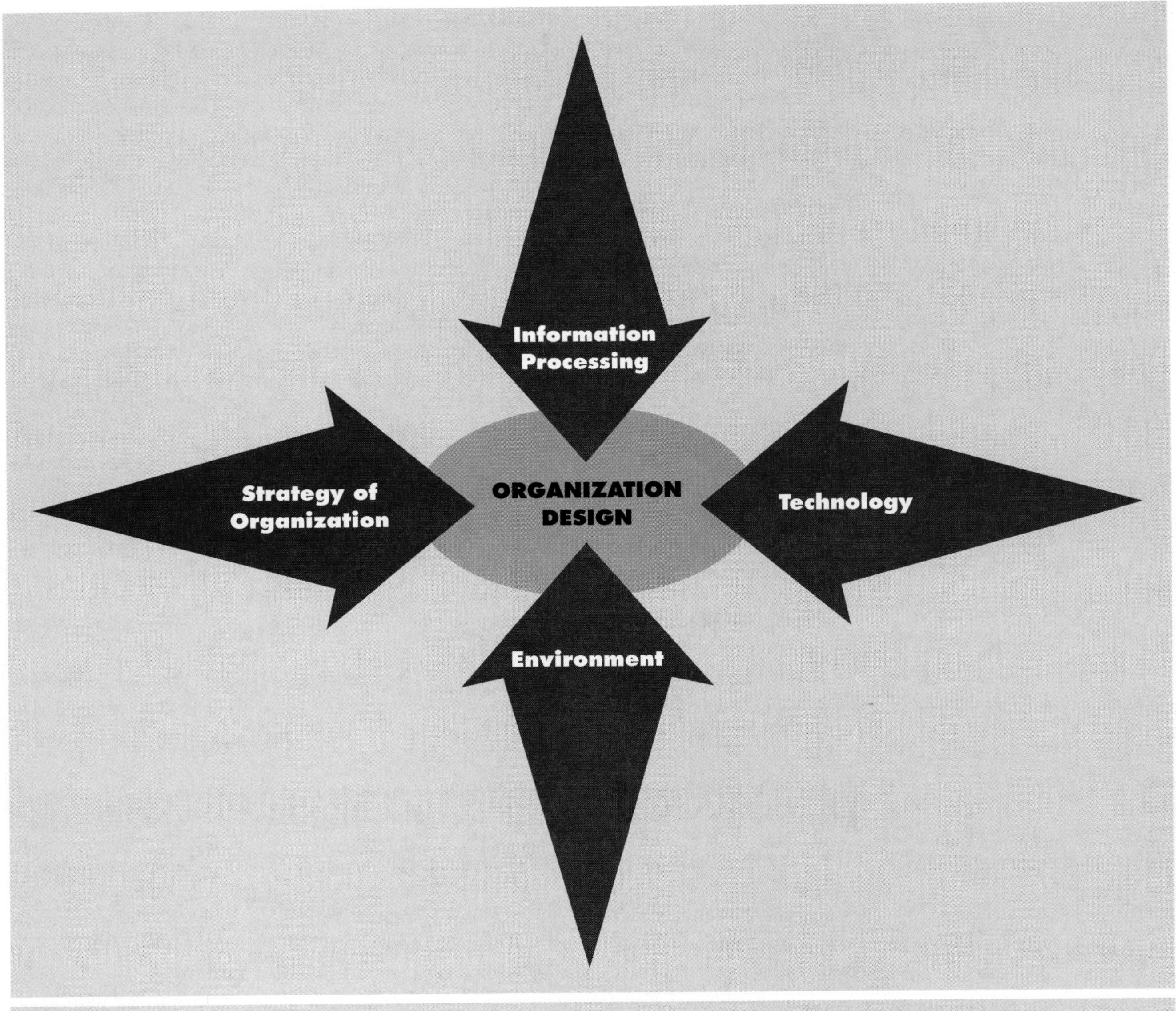

FIGURE 11.1

Overall Factors Affecting Organization Design

In a stable environment, top management can easily keep track of what is going on. For example, companies in the brewing, ice cream, fast-food, glass container, farm equipment, and industrial tools industries operate in relatively stable technological environments. Although companies in these industries may make slight changes in their products, the changes can be incorporated easily into their existing manufacturing processes. Changes in the quantity of the product produced and sold, rather than the quality of the product, are likely to occur in a stable environment. Such changes usually have little impact on the organization's design. Because the product itself doesn't change significantly from year to year, production managers don't have to alter entire manufacturing processes. Firms in highly stable environments are likely to develop extensive distribution systems and invest heavily in capital equipment. These firms adapt to fluctuations in demand by changing the size of their work forces, not by introducing a new product line or changing production methods.

One industry that has remained relatively stable over the past twenty-five years is the ice cream industry. Americans ate more than 925 million gallons of ice cream in 1994, or about 18.5 quarts each, which was the same as the previous year. In 1970, the

FIGURE 11.2

Forces That Affect an Organization's Design

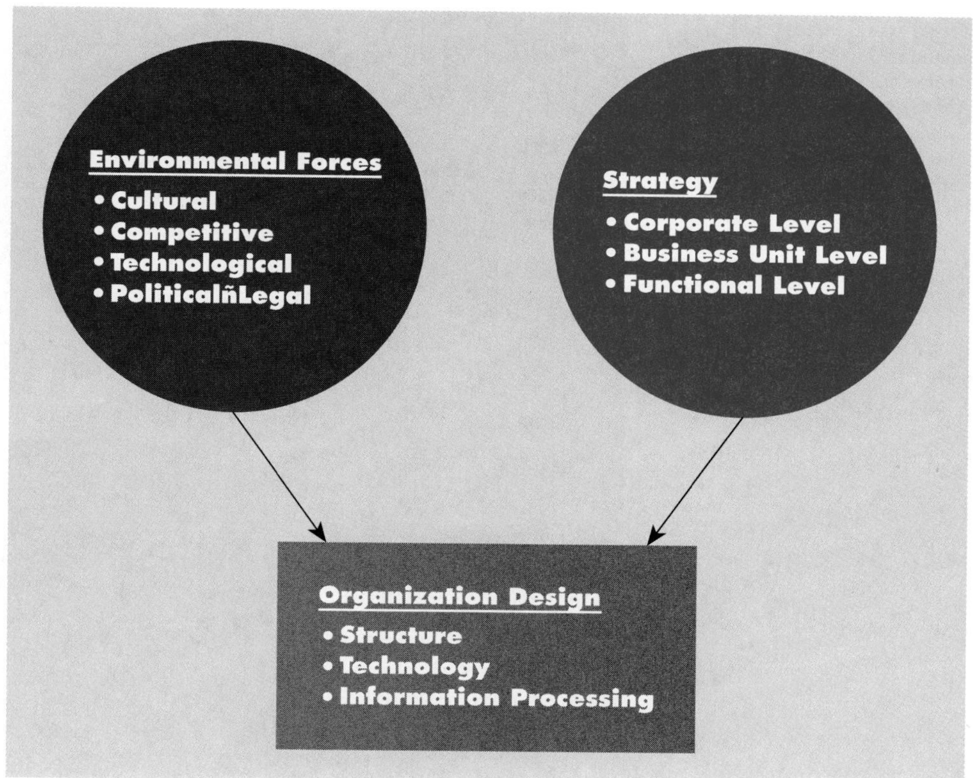

per capita consumption of ice cream was 15 quarts. The per capita consumption of ice cream varies between 21 quarts in the Pacific Northwest to a low of 10 quarts in the Mountain States. Ninety-four percent of all households bought ice cream, and families with young children and people over 55 years of age ate the most. Ice cream consumption isn't as seasonal as you might suspect, with summer months accounting for only 30 percent of annual consumption. Major manufacturers include Ben & Jerry's, Kraft, Dreyer's, and Unilever. Unilever makes Sealtest, Borden's, and Good Humor and is the largest ice cream maker in Europe. Hundreds of ice cream makers, such as Blue Bell in the Southwest, compete for regional customers. The largest manufacturer is Unilever's, which has about a 15 percent share of the ice cream market.[4]

A stable environment means a relatively high level of sales predictability. Firms operating in this type of environment can base planning and sales efforts on the information provided by common business indicators. For instance, the U.S. Department of Commerce prepares annual output projections for various industries based on changes that occurred during the preceding ten years. Firms operating in stable environments use these indexes to forecast market changes and sales trends.

Although the ice cream industry is relatively stable, some consumer buying habits have changed. The low-fat frozen dessert manufacturers are offering alternatives for health-conscious customers in the form of low-calorie and low-fat frozen desserts. Since 1987, annual industry sales have grown from almost nothing to $8 billion. To capture part of this market, many of the nationwide ice cream makers have started to manufacture low-fat frozen desserts. These companies still can use their same types of machinery, sales forces, and methods of distribution—supermarkets and convenience stores. The point is that, even in industries where changes occur gradually, they can "sneak up" on an organization and cause it to lose market share.[5] In the ice cream industry, adaptation to production of low-fat substitutes was easy for most manufacturers because they could use the same basic production and distribution systems and advertising agencies.

The following Insight focuses on McDonald's, an example of a firm operating in the relatively stable fast-food environment. Over the past three years the fast-food industry

The ice cream industry has remained relatively stable over the past twenty-five years. Any changes made in the product can be incorporated easily into existing manufacturing processes and machinery.

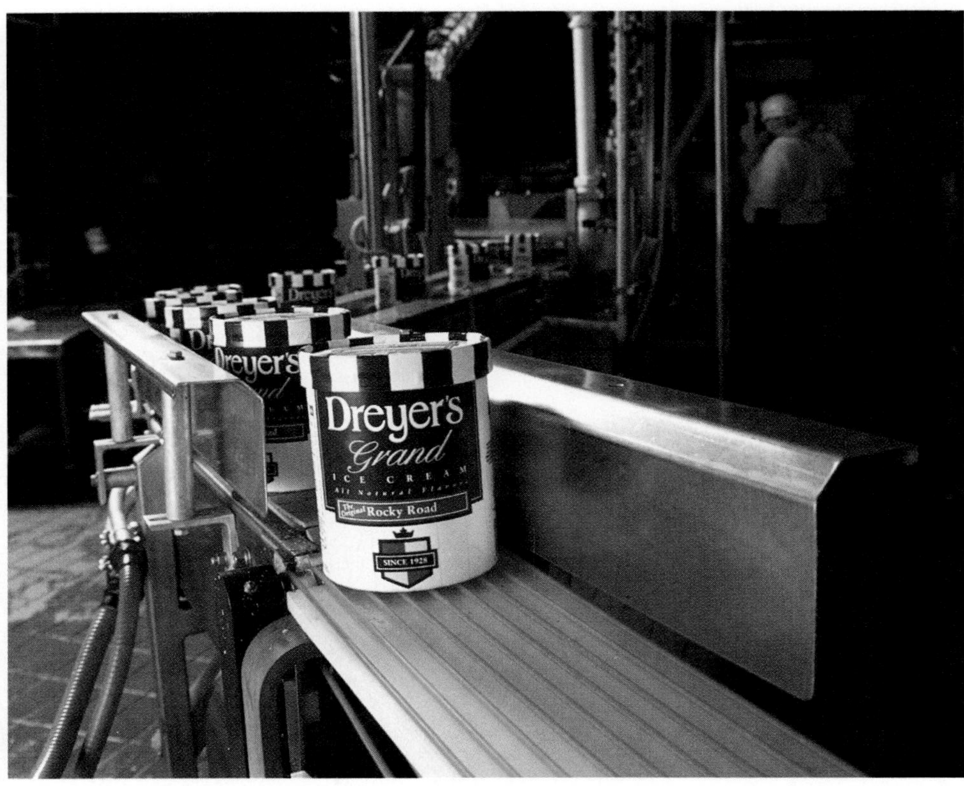

Discussion Question 2
How does the environment affect the way fast-food organizations are designed?

has grown at an average rate of 4.5 percent. Hamburger chains dominate the fast-food industry with 18.5 percent of total sales. In 1994, McDonald's had 14,124 restaurants, and during that year it opened 900 restaurants worldwide—576 outside the United States and Canada. Its worldwide sales were more than $23 billion, up slightly from 1993. Its overseas sales were nearly 40 percent of its total sales.

Insight

Will McDonald's Take Over the World?

McDonald's operates in a relatively stable environment; for instance, fast-food technology has remained fairly constant over the past decade or so. Despite the stability of the technological environment, the fast-food industry is fiercely competitive. Two of McDonald's chief competitors, Burger King and Wendy's, are continually upping the ante. Nevertheless, McDonald's has grown to become the largest fast-food restaurant chain in the world. It opens a restaurant somewhere in the world every seventeen hours and is the largest commercial owner of real estate in the United States. How does McDonald's make it work?

To begin with, new McDonald's managers must attend an intensive ten-day training program at Hamburger University, the company's management training center in Elk Grove, Illinois. (McDonald's even trained there the employees who would be responsible for operating the former Soviet Union's first McDonald's, in Moscow's Pushkin Square.) The curriculum includes hands-on experience in a McDonald's restaurant, as well as intensive classroom study. Subjects range from day-to-day restaurant management to more general courses in business management, accounting, marketing, personnel management, and community relations.

Trainees learn quickly that McDonald's standards are important in maintaining effectiveness. Analysts have broken down every job into its smallest steps and then automated the entire process. For example, the process of cooking and bagging fries consists of nineteen steps. The videotape introducing new employees to preparing French fries starts with boxes of frozen fries rolling off a delivery truck. Employees are then instructed to stack them in the freezer six boxes high, leaving one inch between stacks and two inches between stacks and freezer wall. Specially designed scoops determine the precise number of fries in each pouch. French fries are kept under the warming light for only seven minutes.

The basic hamburger patty must be a machine-cut, 1.6-ounce chunk of pure beef—no lung, heart, cereal, soybean, or other fillers—with no more than 19 percent fat content. Hamburger buns must have 13.3 percent sugar in them. A flashing light cues the cook at the exact moment the hamburger patties have to be flipped. Although the standardization of work reduces employee freedom of action it provides product uniformity and consistency for consumers.

McDonald's also has developed management coordination mechanisms that include a detailed organizational structure and the provision by corporate staff of operating, public relations, and advertising services to restaurant managers. In addition, area field consultants regularly visit all restaurants to ensure that each franchise conforms to McDonald's rules and regulations.

McDonald's operating manual is a 385-page book covering the most minute details of running a restaurant. In foreign countries, however, McDonald's operators sometimes need to take the initiative. For example, shortly after U.S. planes bombed Libya in 1986, a mob gathered in front of a McDonald's in Barcelona, Spain, to protest. The company manual didn't have instructions on how to handle the situation, so the owner simply shut down the store and "got the hell out of there." That night the restaurant was firebombed.

Finally, McDonald's has a stable and consistent promotional strategy embodied in the persona of Ronald McDonald, who despite his international celebrity remains the same fun-loving clown that Ray Kroc introduced in 1963. A company survey indicated that 96 percent of all American children can identify Ronald McDonald, who is second only to Santa Claus in recognition level.[6]

Changing Environment

A **changing environment** is unpredictable because of frequent shifts in products, technology, competitors, markets, or political forces. This type of environment also has certain characteristics:

- products that are continuously changing or evolving,
- significant technological innovations that make production processes or equipment obsolete,
- sets and/or actions of competitors, customers, or other stakeholders that change continually, and
- government actions that reflect the current level of political clout wielded by various interest groups for consumer protection, product safety, pollution control, and civil rights.[7]

Teaching Tip
Have students identify five examples of organizations in changing environments.

Teaching Tip
Have students brainstorm the impact of external environmental factors on their lives. Ask them whether they have a stable or changing environment.

Firms operating in a changing environment usually experience *constant* pressure to adapt their products to meet new customer preferences and demands—and they often do so. Organizations in the telecommunications, computer hardware and software, electronics, and fashion industries operate in rapidly changing environments.

When a technology is changing, organizations dependent on it must be able to respond quickly, generating new ideas that can affect either the product itself or the way it is manufactured. In the electronics industry, breakthroughs in integrated circuits and miniaturization significantly affected the nature of other products. For example, the introduction of electronic digital watches produced a revolution in the market dominated for centuries by Swiss-made mechanical watches. Swiss firms had always stressed the craftsmanship that went into each hand-wound timepiece. However, they were unable to compete with this technological innovation. As a result, many Swiss watch manufacturers suffered declining sales and revenue. In the same industry, Timex also lost its market share when it failed to pursue new electronic technologies. Timex's failure is spectacular because only two decades ago, one of every two watches sold in the United States was a Timex. Today Timex's market share is about 5 percent, badly lagging behind Citizen, Seiko, and Casio.

Technological advances also have transformed the personal computer, motorcycle, microwave, and computer communications industries. Computer communications used to be simple. A company simply leased a few phone lines from AT&T and bought some modems from a supply house. It then began sending data between its home office and its branches. If service failed, the company just called the modem supplier or AT&T. Today data communications is a whole new world. There are many more service and equipment providers, including local phone companies, satellite suppliers, microwave vendors, and local-area networking companies. And corporate computer networks are far more complex, often containing analog and digital links of all types, as well as intermixed voice, data, and video traffic.

Network management systems, which allow trained personnel to monitor performance, identify problems, and take remedial action, now make up a computer communications market worth some $295 million, soon to be worth $500 million annually. Products designed to assist network management range from simple, self-diagnostic features packaged within each system to full-blown command centers that provide a single point of control over the entire operation. Different products monitor different parameters and offer varying capabilities for taking corrective action automatically.[8]

Discussion Question 1
What are the main features of stable and changing environments?

Discussion Question 4
How does the environment influence a manager's choice of structure?

The following Small Business Insight illustrates the environmental changes facing Malden Mills and how it designed its organization structure to keep abreast of the latest changes in the marketplace. The company was formed in 1906 in the heart of the Lawrence, Massachusetts, textile mills. During the past several decades, many U.S. textile manufacturers have gone out of business because they were unable to compete successfully with high-tech European and low-cost Asian manufacturers. Moreover, many were slow to develop manufacturing processes to deliver smaller quantities of more varied clothing styles within weeks, not months.

Small Business *Insight*

Malden Mills: Breaking All the Rules

When Aaron Feuerstein took over the family business from his father in the mid-1980s, it was near bankruptcy. His father had heavily invested in the fur market, but with the rise of anti-animal killing sentiments in the United States, the demand for fur coats almost disappeared. Interest rates were almost 20 percent, which meant that new capital for manufacturing was scarce.

Since the mid-1980s, Malden Mills has undergone a radical transformation. It refocused from manufacturing to marketing and from fashion to high-tech. Instead of trying to be a low-cost manufacturer of many textile products, it now has only two major product lines: apparel and upholstery. The entire company was reorganized around these two lines. In so doing, it carved out market niches with little competition. It created a name brand—Polartec—that keeps skiers, hikers, and others warm, dry, and free to move about. Many top garment makers buy from Malden, including L.L. Bean and Ralph Lauren, because of its superior quality and product innovation. To guard against imitators, Malden Mills has designed most of its own machinery and developed its brand name so that customers could ask for that name from retailers. Feuerstein plans to open a factory in Western Europe to serve its growing European customer base more quickly and economically. Customers will not wait ten days for material as it crosses the Atlantic on a ship and then pay import duties. Customers want goods within twenty-four hours after placing an order. Employees in the company's marketing department are able to communicate with customers in six languages to achieve faster and more accurate order filling.

Feuerstein has also reorganized workers into self-managed teams. There are few hierarchical levels and all employees may come right to him with their problems. Most other textile manufacturers hire low-cost laborers and control employees by the extensive use of rules and regulations established long ago through time and motion studies (see Chapter 2). Employee loyalty and commitment are high at Malden Mills because employees participate in decisions that affect their jobs. Employees are constantly striving to improve customer service and find innovative ways of satisfying customers' demands. Job security is high because Feuerstein doesn't believe in layoffs as a way to cut costs. Instead, he focuses on new products as a way to increase sales.[9]

In changing environments, managers should constantly seek to modify their organization designs to satisfy the needs of customers whose demands and needs are changing. Success in changing markets depends on the organization's being able to anticipate market trends and respond to them quickly. To do so may mean redesigning the organization substantially or entirely.

3

Describe the differences between mechanistic and organic organizational structures.

MATCHING STRUCTURE AND ENVIRONMENT

Firms operating effectively in stable environments tend to choose organizational structures that differ from those chosen by firms operating in changing environments. Researchers Tom Burns and Gene Stalker labeled these contrasting structures *mechanistic* and *organic,* respectively. Table 11.1 highlights the differences between the two.

A **mechanistic structure** is one in which management breaks activities down into separate, specialized tasks.[10] Tasks, authority, responsibility, and accountability for both managers and subordinates are defined by level in the organization. Firms using this structure resemble bureaucratic organizations. Decision making is centralized at the top. Top management decides what is important and how to share this information with others. Its objective is to train employees to work efficiently. When one employee leaves, another can slip into the empty spot—like interchangeable machine parts. Thus the mechanistic structure seems best suited to firms operating in stable environments, such as the IRS, McDonald's, UPS, and Coors. In such environments, where employees tend to perform the same tasks over and over, job specialization and standardization are par-

TABLE 11.1

Differences Between Mechanistic and Organic Structures

MECHANISTIC	ORGANIC
• Tasks are highly specialized.	• Tasks tend to be interdependent.
• Tasks tend to remain rigidly defined unless changed by top management.	• Tasks are continually adjusted and are defined through interaction.
• Specific roles (rights, obligations, and technical methods) are prescribed for each employee.	• Generalized roles (responsibility for task accomplishment beyond specific role definition) are accepted.
• Structure of control, authority, and communication is hierarchical.	• Structure of control, authority, and communication is a network.
• Communication is primarily vertical, between superior and subordinate.	• Communication is both vertical and horizontal, depending on where needed information resides.
• Communication primarily takes the form of instructions and decisions issued by superiors and of information and requests for decisions supplied by subordinates.	• Communication primarily takes the form of information and advice among all levels.

Source: Adapted from Burns, T., and Stalker, G.M. *The Management of Innovation.* London: Tavistock, 1961, 119–122.

FIGURE 11.3

Matches and Mismatches of Structure and Environment

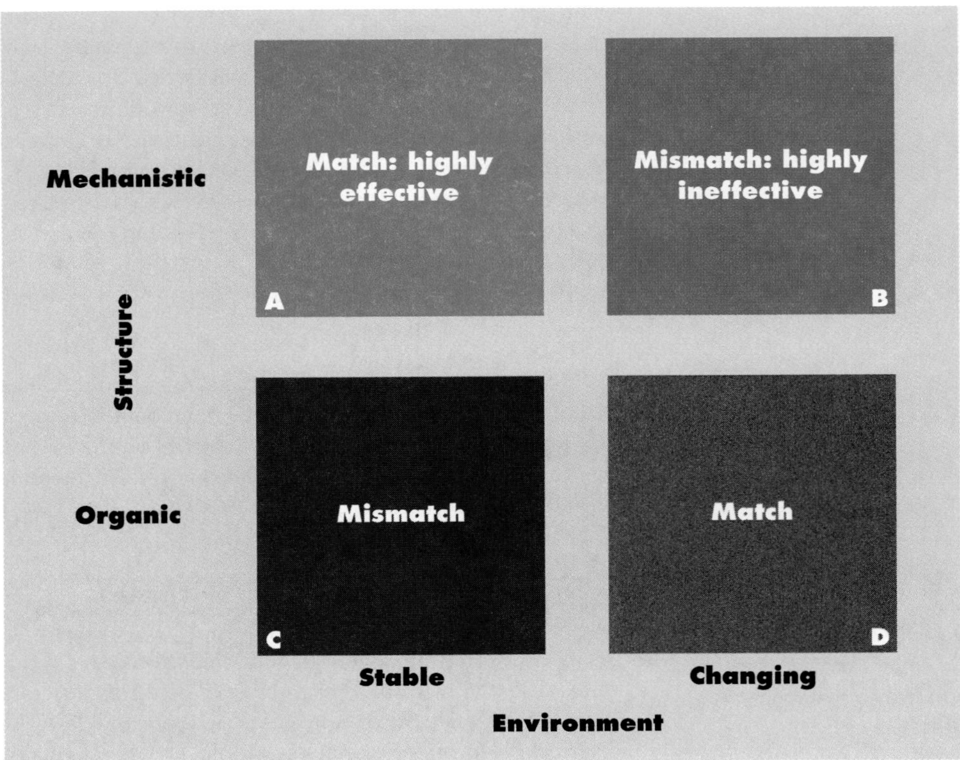

ticularly appropriate to drive the cost of training down. In Figure 11.3, block A shows the match between an organization's stable environment and mechanistic structure.

An **organic structure** places less emphasis on giving and taking orders and more on encouraging managers and subordinates to work together in teams and to communicate openly with each other. In fact, employees are encouraged to communicate with anyone who might help them solve a problem. Decision making is decentralized. Authority, responsibility, and accountability flow to employees with the expertise required to solve problems. An organic organizational structure is well suited to a changing environment. In Figure 11.3, block D shows this relationship.

Ethics
Some people argue that the organic structure is more humane and therefore more ethical than the mechanistic structure. Others say that both types of organization have their place in the economy no matter how well they treat their employees and customers. What do you say?

Aaron Feuerstein organized Malden Mills along organic lines so that it could move swiftly into new markets. To do so, employees' tasks had to be changed and employees had to be skilled at solving a variety of problems. Phil Knight, NIKE's CEO, also organized the company along organic lines. He encourages people to take risks, delegates employees the authority to make a decision, holds them accountable for results, and has few levels of management.[11] Why are Feuerstein's and Knight's structures effective?

Teaching Tip
In a copy of a recent newspaper, highlight each organization mentioned in the business and news sections. Bring it to class and list the organizations on the board. Have students identify which are mechanistic and which are organic.

In changing environments, the organization needs to respond quickly to changing markets and/or create new markets for its products. For NIKE, it was the decision to advertise Michael Jordan as "AIR JORDAN" before he was a superstar. Once Jordan became a superstar, NIKE quickly developed a line of shoes and athletic apparel to capture a large share of these markets. Because employees need to respond to environmental changes quickly, job descriptions are broad rather than narrow, and teams (not managers) make decisions.

Teaching Tip
To create a greater awareness of mechanistic and organic structures, engage students in role-playing interviews between human resources managers and prospective employees in each type of organization.

Differentiation and Integration. Burns and Stalker's findings were supported and extended by Paul Lawrence and Jay Lorsch, who examined the organization designs of three departments—production, research and development (R&D), and marketing—in ten different companies.[12] They found that departments in companies operating in stable environments, such as can manufacturing companies, were designed differently than the same departments in companies operating in unstable environments, such as plas-

Ask Students
What are some advantages and disadvantages of working for an organization with an organic structure versus working for one with a mechanistic structure?

Teaching Tip
When top managers and workers switch jobs for a day, they are integrating by learning about areas of the organization different from their own.

tics manufacturing firms. They also found that all three departments in the same company would not be affected to the same extent by the firm's environment. That is, employees in R&D departments in the can companies viewed their environment as more unstable than did employees in production departments in the same companies.

The researchers found that the key to organization design for a manager was to structure the department to match the challenges posed by its external environment. Production departments in both stable and unstable environments were structured more mechanistically than R&D departments were. Departments designed to fit their environments were more effective than those that had been misdesigned. To describe the character of design differences between departments, Lawrence and Lorsch used the terms *differentiation* and *integration*.

Differentiation is the measure of the differences among various departments with respect to structure, tasks, and goals. If departments have different structures, tasks, and goals, an organization can be classified as highly differentiated. For example, a production manager at Bally Engineered Structures is concerned about reducing costs, meeting daily production quotas, and following rules that ensure efficient production of walk-in coolers and refrigerated rooms. In contrast, Bally's marketing manager is concerned about increasing volume, introducing innovative products, and making last-minute changes to satisfy an important customer.

Liz Claiborne, a manufacturer of men's and women's clothing, is a highly differentiated organization. Marketing department employees try to stay abreast of the latest fashion trends. They attend trade shows and ask customers for their design preferences. Their goal is to be in the forefront with the latest styles. However, once a decision is made to produce a certain item, it is communicated to the production department. Employees in that department are concerned with meeting production quotas in order to supply the more than 3,500 Liz Claiborne clothing outlets around the world. Changes in style at the production level are expensive and must be avoided if at all possible.

Teaching Tip
Students often have a preference between differentiation and integration. They need to understand that one isn't better than the other. These are not concepts of right and wrong. Rather, they are complementary—like day and night. Both are needed, but at different times and in different circumstances.

Integration is the measure of coordination among departments with respect to structure, tasks, and goals. If departments have similar goals, are organized similarly, and work together as a team to accomplish organizational goals, an organization is highly integrated. The three important principles of integration—unity of command, scalar principle, and span of control—apply especially in integrated organizations. In contrast, organizations that are highly differentiated require a greater number of integrating devices and tactics to achieve a coordinated effort because, internally, their goals and structures vary.

Lawrence and Lorsch's results confirmed their expectations. For example, the production department of a plastics firm operating in a *changing environment* would retain long-standing production processes and would be organized along formal, mechanistic lines because production lines need to be stable to be efficient. However, the R&D department in the same firm would face constant demand for *new ways to make and use* plastics and, as a result, would be organized more organically.

Research thus supports the importance of designing an organization's structure to fit its environment. It also emphasizes the importance of integration. Depending on the situation, successful firms use a variety of integrative tools. In stable environments, following the chain of command is most effective. In unstable environments, the use of task forces greatly improves coordination among departments. Moreover, the presence of a mechanistic structure in certain departments and an organic structure in others doesn't necessarily reduce the firm's overall effectiveness. In fact, that approach could very well enhance the firm's effectiveness.

The following Global Insight explores how Black & Decker has restructured itself to go global in a changing environment. It uses different types of differentiation and integration to achieve its goals. Recall that a *global corporation* looks at the entire world as its market. It manufactures, conducts research, raises capital, and buys supplies wherever it can get the best results. It keeps in touch with technology and market trends around the world. National boundaries and differences tend to be irrelevant, and corporate headquarters might be anywhere.

Global *Insight*

Black & Decker: Where the Sun Never Sets

Black & Decker (B&D), manufacturer of power tools for home and professional users, had manufacturing plants in ten countries and sold its products in more than ninety in the 1990s. Design centers, manufacturing plants, and marketing programs were focusing on making and selling products worldwide. But it wasn't always that way.

In 1981, earnings had begun to slip, and a worldwide recession caused a significant downturn in the power tools segment of B&D's business, its bread and butter. However, B&D's problems were partly a result of its own strategy. By 1982, B&D operated twenty-five manufacturing plants in thirteen countries on six continents. It had three operating groups and a headquarters group, in Maryland. Each group had its own staff, which led to duplication and overstaffing. In addition, individual B&D companies, such as B&D of West Germany, operated autonomously in each of the more than fifty countries where B&D sold its products. The company's philosophy had been to let each country company adapt products and product lines to fit the unique characteristics of each market. The Italian firm produced power tools for Italians, the U.K. subsidiary made power tools for Britons, and so on.

As a result, these companies didn't communicate well with each other. Successful products in one country often took years to introduce in others. For example, the highly successful Dustbuster, introduced in the United States in the late 1970s, wasn't introduced in Australia until 1983. When efforts were made to introduce B&D home products into European markets, the European managers refused to comply. They felt that home appliances and products were uniquely American and wouldn't do well outside the United States.

Because of the tailor-made specifications for different markets, design centers were not being used efficiently. At one point, eight design centers around the world were producing 260 different motors, even though market research had revealed that the firm needed fewer than ten different models. Plant utilization was quite low, employment levels were high, and output per employee was unacceptably low.

As B&D moved into the mid-1980s, management realized that something had to be done. One area in which the Japanese had not made significant inroads was housewares and small appliances. So B&D acquired the small appliances division of General Electric in 1984 to give itself more shelf space in housewares and also a large enough line of products to provide economies of scale in manufacturing.

To gain some efficiencies from being a global corporation, starting in 1987, B&D tried to match staffing requirements with sales and limited the number of motors it was going to market around the world. Standardizing motors allowed B&D to develop a global product strategy. It allows B&D to change features for local market tastes but retain a product's essential design. Presently, B&D organizes its business around product lines. These product lines (e.g., vacuum cleaners) have common distribution channels, technologies, customers, competitors, or geographic markets. Product line managers are responsible for all functions, such as manufacturing, advertising, and sales, for their product lines.[13]

Discuss the effects of technology on the design of manufacturing and service organizations.

TECHNOLOGY

In Chapter 2 we noted that technology is a major contingency variable that affects the design of an organization. Recall that, in general, technology is the process that transforms information and raw materials into finished products. Most people associate it only with the machinery used in manufacturing plants, but technology greatly influences all types of organizations and their products. Schools, banks, hospitals, governments, and retail stores all now rely heavily on technology. Therefore we can analyze the impact of technology on organization design in a variety of settings, and its importance cannot be overstated.

Technological Interdependence

A firm's technology has a significant impact on its organization design because different types of technologies generate various types of internal interdependence. **Technological interdependence** is the degree of coordination required between individuals and departments to transform information and raw materials into finished products.[14] There are three types of technological interdependence: pooled, sequential, and reciprocal. Figure 11.4 shows how they operate to coordinate the efforts of employees in order to achieve desired results.

Pooled interdependence, illustrated in Figure 11.4(a), involves little sharing of information or resources among individuals within a department or among departments. Although the various departments contribute to overall organizational efforts, they work on their own specialized tasks. At NationsBank, for example, the savings, loan, and real estate departments work independently of one another. NationsBank achieves coordination by requiring each department to meet certain standards and follow certain rules. These rules are consistent for all of its banks in various states and apply to all routine situations, such as check cashing and receiving deposits. There are few exceptions.

Sequential interdependence, illustrated in Figure 11.4(b), serializes the flow of information and resources between individuals within the same department or between departments. That is, the output from department A becomes the input for department B, the output from department B becomes the input for department C, and so on. A typical example of sequential interdependence is an automobile assembly line. To ensure coordination of its departments (or workstations), managers must carefully schedule when parts arrive and leave each department (workstation).

Teaching Tip
Poll the class to find out what types of technological interdependence they have had on their current or a previously held job. Have a representative for each type briefly describe the job.

Reciprocal interdependence, illustrated in Figure 11.4(c), encourages every individual and department to work with every other individual and department; information and resources flow back and forth freely until the task is completed. For example, hospitals use resources from several departments (e.g., x-ray, nursing, surgery, and physical therapy) to restore a patient's health. Each specialist and department supplies some of the resources needed to assist the patient. Doctors and professionals from each spe-

FIGURE 11.4

Three Types of Technological Interdependence

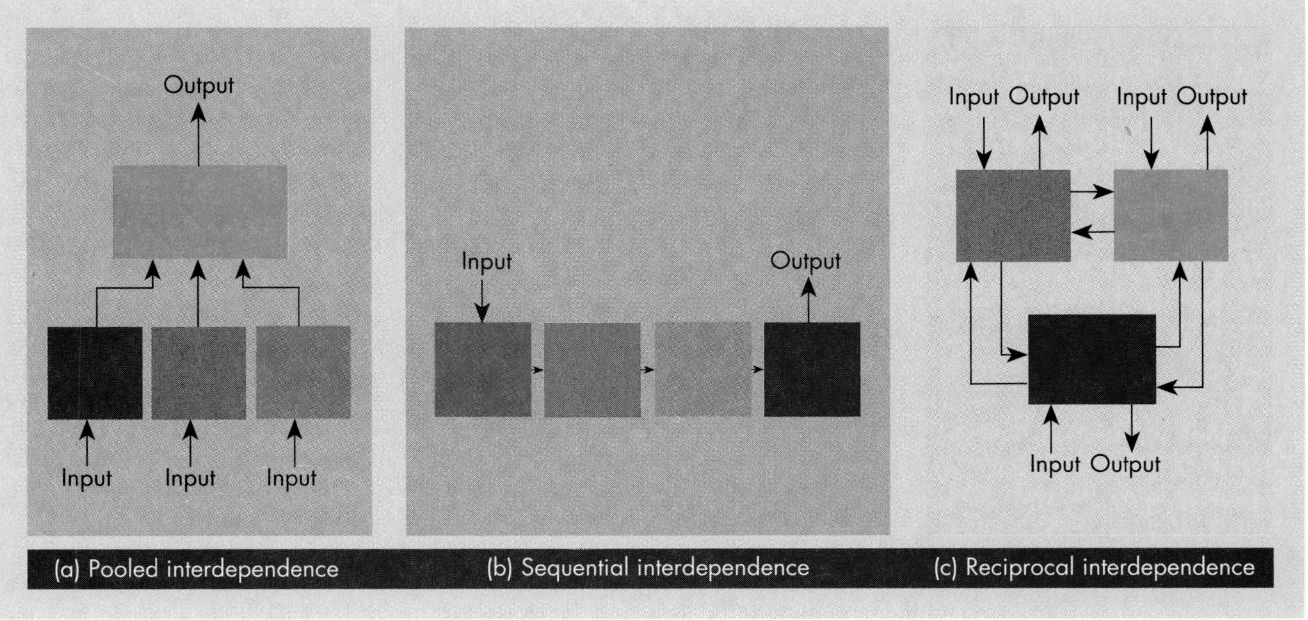

cialized area meet to discuss the patient's recovery. The method of coordination is mutual adjustment, achieved through group meetings.

Designing an organization to handle reciprocal interdependence and then managing it is very challenging. The structure of the organization must allow for frequent communication among departments, and planning is essential. Because management can't easily anticipate all customer demands or solve all problems, managers must continually communicate face to face to make sure that they understand the nature and scope of issues and problems—and devise solutions.

Galoob Toys markets Micro Machines and depends on independent inventors and entertainment companies to dream up most of its products. Outside specialists do most of the design and engineering work. After the basic design and engineering decisions have been made, the potential product goes back to the inventor for final approval. Galoob farms out manufacturing and packaging to firms in Hong Kong. When the toys arrive in the United States, Galoob distributes and sells them nationwide through commissioned manufacturers' representatives. It employs Commercial Credit Corporation to collect the sales revenue from these representatives. Robert and David Galoob, the owners of the company, spend most of their time coordinating the various parts of their company. Phones, fax machines, and telexes are in constant use as schedules are revised and adjusted to accommodate design modifications, shortages of raw materials, customer order changes, and the like.[15]

Discussion Question 6
What problems might the use of multiple forms of technological interdependence create for managers?

Service Technologies

Technological interdependence is fairly obvious in a manufacturing firm's assembly line. But what is technology's role in the design of service organizations? The service sector of the U.S. economy now employs far more people than manufacturing. In fact services now account for 74 percent of the nation's total employment and more than 71 percent of its gross domestic product. Service organizations have grown so rapidly in number and size that they account for nearly 90 percent of all new, nonfarm jobs created in the United States since 1953. Some are quite large: Southland Corporation (operator of 7-Eleven stores) has 32,400 employees, J.C. Penney has more than 193,000 employees, and AMR Corporation (including American Airlines and Sabre) employs more than 119,00 people.

Ask Students
What service technologies have experienced increased demand during the past decade owing to the ever-increasing number of women in the work force? (Examples: day care centers, clothing outlets, and restaurants.)

Two distinguishing characteristics differentiate service organizations from manufacturing organizations:

- *Intangibility.* The output of a service firm is intangible and thus cannot be stored. The output must be used immediately or lost forever. Holding seats on a plane or train in inventory is impossible. If these seats aren't sold prior to departure, the revenue is lost forever. Manufactured goods, such as cars, TVs, and computers, can be stored and sold at some later time.
- *Closeness of the customer.* Direct customer contact is involved in the provision of most services. In a very real sense, the employees of a travel agency are simultaneously producing and selling a service to their customers. Service employees dispense output directly to customers, but production employees in manufacturing firms are separated from their customers.[16]

Real-World Example
Waiters, waitresses, actors, actresses, and salespeople have their outputs consumed directly by the customer.

These two features have an important implication for managers: The simultaneous production and consumption of services means that quality control cannot be achieved by the inspect-and-reject method traditionally used in manufacturing plants. Instead, quality control must occur at the point of service delivery. The service provider is responsible for ensuring quality of service during each interaction with the client.

Types of Service Technologies. There are two basic types of service technologies: routine and nonroutine. **Routine service technologies** are methods used by organiza-

Teaching Tip
For extra credit have a team of three students contact (either in person, or via an ordering phone line) an organization that provides a routine service. One person should ask for a nonstandard item (e.g., ask for a custom-made hamburger at a fast-food outlet or call an airline and insist on having a pet monkey ride in first-class). The second person should take notes. The third person should observe. What happens when nonroutine service is asked for? Why? Have the team write up and turn in a three-page paper on the project.

Ask Students
What opportunities and threats face fast-growing firms that use nonroutine service technologies?

tions operating in relatively stable environments and serving customers who are relatively sure of their needs. Organizations such as retail stores, fast-food restaurants, banks, travel agencies, gas stations, and bookstores utilize routine service technologies to serve their customers. These organizations aren't so much involved with producing the service as with dispensing it. The information being exchanged is simple, and the tasks are standardized. The demand on the service provider is fairly precise, and thus employees interact with customers for only short periods of time. For example, the interaction between a bank teller and a customer who wants to make a deposit has all these qualities.

Nonroutine service technologies are methods used by organizations operating in complex and changing environments and serving customers or clients who are unsure of their needs or imprecise about their problems. Moreover, these customers or clients usually don't know how to go about solving their problems even when they are able to identify them. In this context, service providers—usually professionals—continually encounter new problems, and variety is the norm, not the exception. Consequently, creativity and novelty are essential as the service provider tries to come up with techniques to fit the situation at hand. The types of service firms using nonroutine technologies include legal, accounting, brokerage, marketing and advertising, medical, and architectural firms. The focus is on meetings between the service provider and the client, and on the tasks and skills needed to serve the client's needs. Each meeting between the client and the provider lasts a relatively long time. The outcome depends on the client's willingness to give the service provider the information needed to develop a solution satisfactory to the client.

Organization Design and Service Technology. Selected organization design features (specialization, standardization, coordination, and authority) and their relationships with the two types of service technologies are shown in Table 11.2. Firms using nonroutine service technologies tend to be organic. They are organized informally, and decision making is decentralized. Because problems facing such a firm are unique, reciprocal interdependence among employees is common. However, firms utilizing routine service technologies can be designed along more mechanistic lines. Specialization is low and standards are common because customers' needs are known. Decision making is centralized in top management. Pooled technological interdependence, which stresses routine tasks and standardization, ensures efficiency.

We can further examine not only how a service technology affects the design of an organization, but also what the role of the customer is in the service production process.

TABLE 11.2

Matching Design Features and Service Technologies

	Service Technology	
Design Feature	**Routine**	**Nonroutine**
Needs of client	Known	Unknown
Structural characteristics		
Specialization	Low	High
Standardization of activities	High	Low
Span of management	Wide	Moderate
Authority	Centralized	Decentralized
Organizational structure	Mechanistic	Organic
Environment	Stable	Changing
Technological interdependence	Pooled and/or sequential	Reciprocal
Examples	Banks, retail stores, fast-food chains, hotels and motels	Law firms, brokerage houses, marketing and advertising firms, accounting firms

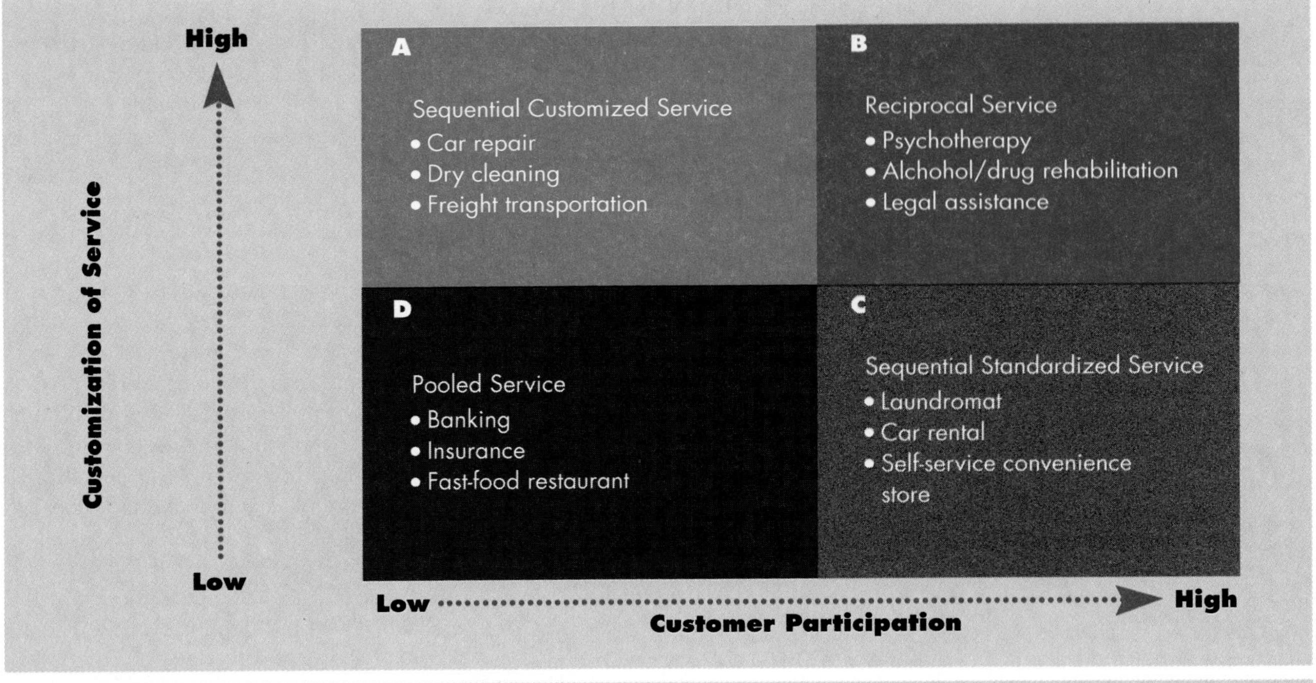

FIGURE 11.5

Service Technology

Source: Adapted from Larsson, R., and Bowen, D.E. Organization and customer: Managing design and coordination of services. *Academy of Management Review,* 1989, 14, 213–233.

Figure 11.5 illustrates the amount of customer participation in the process and the degree to which the organization tries to customize its offerings to satisfy unique customer needs.[17] Each combination presents the organization with different choices of technology. Let's explore the organization design implications for several different types of service.

In quadrant A, customers simply need to tell employees what they want. Employees can routinely adjust their behavior to satisfy customers' needs. Organizations that provide services for a variety of customers who desire to have a home cleaned, lawn mowed, or car repaired would be examples. Customers are price sensitive, and in many instances they could provide the service for themselves. They usually don't observe the actual performance of the work. Rather, they inspect the final product for quality. Sequential task interdependence permits standardization of tasks, and extensive rules and regulations govern employee behavior. The customer initially calls on the organization for service and then turns the process over to it.

If customers have complex and unique problems, they are typically less price sensitive, less able to provide the service themselves, and will want the organization to provide customized solutions to their problems. Quadrant B of Figure 11.5, indicates that the client's problems require an organization's complex services, as in psychotherapy or legal advice. The client must actively participate by providing highly sensitive information before a method of treatment can be selected. As the service provider learns more and more about the client's problem, various treatments are offered. As the client's behavior changes, he or she monitors the effects of the treatment and communicates these changes back to the provider. This type of exchange leads to reciprocal interdependence between the client and the service provider. In such cases, the provider should have multiple skills for helping the client address his or her problems face to face. Through conversations with the client, the service provider gains immediate feedback, which can help avoid costly and embarrassing misunderstandings.

Many services are purchased for mere convenience, and are delivered using sequential standardized service technology. Quadrant C in Figure 11.5 represents situations in which an employee greets the customer to find out what the customer wants. The employee notes the customer's desires on a document (e.g., a work order) and then passes it on to other employees to handle. Jiffy Lube, Midas Muffler Shops, and Enterprise Rent-A-Car are examples of firms that use sequential standardized service technology to satisfy customers demand. The customer evaluates the organization's quality against known standards, such as time, cost, store hours, availability, and accessibility.

Banks, insurance companies, movie theaters, and fast-food restaurants represent organizations in quadrant D of Figure 11.5. The interdependence between the customer and the organization is pooled. Customers don't participate in the process after their initial request for service. The organization uses standard procedures to achieve low-cost mass production.

An example of an organization design that matches a low customization of its services and requires low customer participation is PETsMART, a retailer of pet products. PETsMART estimates that U.S. households currently spend more than $11.5 billion on pet food and related pet items. More than 54 million households own at least one pet, with 40 percent owning more than one type of pet. PETsMART targets middle- to upper middle-income households with children aged five to nineteen. The primary shoppers are women. To capture a share of this market, PETsMART currently operates 103 superstores in twenty states. Its goal is to offer the pet owner a complete assortment of pet products, at prices that are typically 10 to 20 percent below those offered by supermarkets and other traditional pet food and pet supply stores. How is PETsMART structured to achieve these results? The following Insight highlights how it uses a pooled service organization design to achieve its results.

Discussion Question 3
What are the differences between a mechanistic and an organic structure? How would you classify PETsMART's structure? Why?

Insight

PETsMART: A Super Pet Store

All PETsMART stores occupy 25,000 square feet and carry approximately 7,000 pet-related items. To attract customers and maintain customer loyalty, it offers innovative marketing programs and merchandising techniques for the pet owner. For example, it offers on-site professional grooming services, conducts periodic vaccination clinics and obedience classes, and distributes monthly newsletters.

All stores are designed to use a hybrid retail-warehouse format (similar to Wal-Mart or Sam's) that reinforces its image of warehouse shopping at discount prices. The company buys its pet supplies directly from manufacturers and obtains significant volume discounts on most products. It uses a computerized "plan-o-gram" system that links each store's sales directly to its distribution centers. Merchandise is shipped immediately to the store to replace items sold. To respond to changing prices, it uses replaceable price signs on shelves instead of one on each item, which saves on the labor required to mark each item. Bar coding enables electronic cash registers to charge each customer the correct price.

PETsMART has standardized many key aspects of its operations, such as accounting, store layouts, merchandise displays, purchasing, advertising, and pricing. Doing so ensures that all stores look similar and that all operations are consistent throughout the chain. Each store manager is responsible for all store operations, including hiring, work scheduling, and maintenance activities. The company prefers to hire individuals who have proven experience in high-volume retail stores such as Sam's or Home Depot. Once hired, employees are required to go through an extensive training program that gives them the knowledge they need to answer customers' questions. The company views the quality of its customer service as essential to its success.[18]

5

Explain how environment and technology combine to determine the amount of information an organization must process.

INFORMATION PROCESSING STRATEGIES

Part of technology's impact is that it determines an organization's information needs. Information is important because nearly every activity in an organization involves information processing. Managers spend nearly 80 percent of their time actively exchanging information as they, along with other employees, attend meetings, talk on the telephone, receive reports, read computer printouts, and so on. Information is the glue that holds the organization together.

The design of an information processing system is *contingent* on the stability of an organization's environment and its technology.[19] The basic effect of rapid changes (or instability) in an organization's environment and technology is to create uncertainty. With respect to organization design, *uncertainty* refers to the gap between the amount of information needed to perform a task and the amount of information available.

Uncertainty limits managers' ability to plan for the effects of change. Three factors contribute to uncertainty: (1) the diversity of the organization's outputs, (2) the number of different technical specialists on a project, and (3) the level of difficulty involved in achieving objectives. The greater the diversity of high-quality products and the number of different technical specialists utilized, the greater the number of factors a manager must assess prior to making a decision.

Discussion Question 7
How do environmental and technological factors influence the selection of the most effective information processing strategy?

Although the organization's design should ensure the provision of the information needed for decision making, sometimes it fails to do so. To solve this problem, managers can turn to one of two general approaches: (1) increase the organization's ability to process information, or (2) reduce the need to process information. These two general approaches and specific strategies for implementing them are shown in Table 11.3.

Increasing the Ability to Process Information

Managers can increase their organization's ability to process information by creating vertical information systems or lateral relations.[20] Both strategies enable the organization to manage better the information it needs to process. These strategies are especially useful when the people or departments involved are either sequentially or reciprocally interdependent.

Vertical Information Systems. A **vertical information system** is an information processing strategy that managers can use to send information efficiently up the organization. With such a system the organization can constantly update rapidly changing information, giving managers the right information at the right time for planning and coordinating. By bringing information up to top management, vertical information systems support centralized decision making.

The types of businesses that have effectively invested in vertical information systems include Ticketmaster outlets, airline reservation departments, off-track betting parlors, and supermarkets. Most of these information systems are computerized. For example, many supermarkets now use optical scanners at their checkout counters. As purchases pass over the eye of the scanner, the cost, item type, and related data are read

TABLE 11.3
Information Processing Strategies

GENERAL APPROACH	STRATEGY
Increase the organization's ability to process information	1. Create vertical information systems 2. Create lateral relations
Reduce the organization's need to process information	1. Create slack resources 2. Create self-contained tasks or departments

Source: Adapted from Galbraith, J.R. *Designing Complex Organizations.* Reading, Mass.: Addison-Wesley, 1973, 15. Reprinted with permission.

directly from the universal product code (UPC) into a computer. When the store manager wants to know how a special coupon affected a product's sales volume, the computer readily provides the information. The manager also can determine the percentage of sales from each department (e.g., produce, meat, and dairy). Finally, these systems process information faster than manual keying and reduce checkers' errors.

One of the largest and most successful catalogue stores in the world uses a vertical information system to improve customer service and quality. The following Quality Insight illustrates how L.L. Bean of Freeport, Maine, moves more than 10 million items yearly by its ability to process efficiently its customers' orders from anywhere around the world.

Quality *Insight*

L.L. Bean Keeps Items Moving

Beth Lucas never thought that she'd be using her newly learned Japanese language skills to sell Wicked Good Slippers, but she did. To serve international customers, L.L. Bean sales representatives speak fourteen different languages. This capability ensures that almost all customers—no matter what language they speak or where they are calling from—can have their orders promptly and properly handled. Being able to speak the customer's language conveys calm and competence. Lucas works on the second shift at L.L. Bean where she's a phone representative. Once during her shift a customer in Osaka, Japan, bought more than $3,000 worth of merchandise over the phone. Lucas handled the entire sale in Japanese. The next caller, from Franklin, Massachusetts, ordered five items and wanted each placed in an appropriate gift box and shipped to five different addresses.

In December each year, when 25 percent of the year's $900 million business at L.L. Bean is done, some 3,000 phone representatives handle more than 150,000 calls a day. To handle such volume, all sales representatives use the same equipment: headsets and terminals. All are connected to a large mainframe computer that constantly updates inventory levels on every item that L.L. Bean sells. If an item falls below a predetermined inventory level, the computer automatically notifies a supplier that additional stock is needed. The hum of hundreds of fax machines is constant, as nearly 35 percent of all international business is done by fax.

After orders have been taken, the computer transmits them to the employees in Bean's 625,000 square foot distribution center. During the holiday season, 5 million orders will be filled and shipped the day they are received. A computer system tracks each order, and more than 200 packages per minute stream off the conveyor belts. Gift wrappers wrap each gift, prepare an address label, and send it on a conveyor belt to the mail center. FedEx, L.L. Bean's primary delivery company, then delivers the merchandise to the buyer.[21]

Lateral Relations. Another information processing strategy, **lateral relations,** cuts through the chain of command by placing decision making in the hands of those who have access to the information needed to make the decision. In contrast to vertical information systems, which centralize decisions by bringing information up to top managers, lateral relations tend to decentralize decision making. The two methods of implementing this strategy are to (1) establish direct contact between employees or departments, or (2) create a new position to integrate information.

Teaching Tip
This solution does violate the scalar principle discussed in Chapter 10 but nevertheless is efficient.

The simplest form of lateral relations is to allow direct contact between two employees or departments that share the need to solve a common problem, in order to facilitate joint decision making. Figure 11.6 illustrates lateral relations. If department A is falling behind in its production of parts needed by department D, the manager of A would contact the manager of D directly, instead of referring the problem up through the managers of E and G and back down to the manager of D through the manager of

FIGURE 11.6

Lateral Relations in Organizations

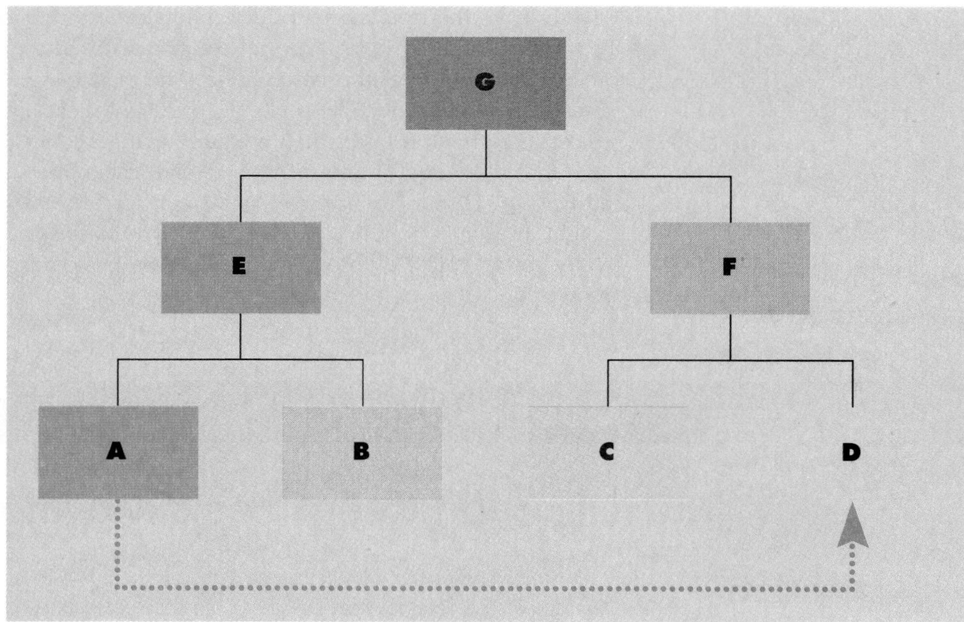

F. If the managers of A and D can arrive at a mutually agreeable solution, the number of problems flowing through the hierarchy is reduced. This process also frees more managers to deal actively with environmental change. Top managers can devote more of their attention to problems that lower level managers can't solve.

Real-World Example
Aerospace firms often employ matrix designs because they need a high degree of interdisciplinary coordination to build new, nonroutine, complex products.

Real-World Example
Matrixes were once thought to be a dead fad from the 1970s. Today, matrixes are back but are called "empowered teams," such as Ford's Team Taurus, and Chrysler's Viper Team (*Business Horizons,* November–December, 1994, 8).

Matrix Organization. Yet another alternative is to create a matrix organization. A **matrix organization** is a design that combines the advantages of functional and product structures to increase the ability of managers and other employees to process information. In a matrix organization, functional managers (e.g., engineering, manufacturing, and sales) and product managers (individual product lines) report to a matrix manager. The matrix manager's job is to coordinate the activities of the functional and product managers. Instead of reporting to separate higher level managers, they report to one general matrix manager who consolidates and integrates their activities.

A matrix design integrates activities and holds down costs by eliminating duplication of key functional activities for each product line. The functional manager's responsibility is to identify the resources needed to perform a job, and the product manager's responsibility is to identify products that the organization can make to satisfy customer's needs. The matrix manager's job is to achieve an overall balance by coordinating the organization's functional and product activities to ensure delivery of the product on time and within budget. Figure 11.7 illustrates this balance. The functional and product managers need to work closely with each other (reciprocal interdependence) to make the matrix design work well.

Matrix organizations require that managers demonstrate high levels of trust and communication, teamwork, and negotiating skills. Often, human resource managers work with managers and employees to help them learn how to make decisions *organically* rather than *mechanistically.* That is, they need to base decisions on expertise and persuasion rather than on rules, SOPs, formal roles and hierarchical position. Disagreements must be dealt with through confrontation and problem solving rather than getting passed "upstairs." Coordination is achieved through extensive formal and informal meetings or in one-to-one conversations. Teams consisting of both product and functional managers and other employees decide who will do what and when.

The following Global Insight illustrates how Philips, the global electronics organization based in the Netherlands, uses a matrix design to succeed in the highly competitive electronics industry. The company has more than eight product divisions that op-

High

Relative Influence

Low

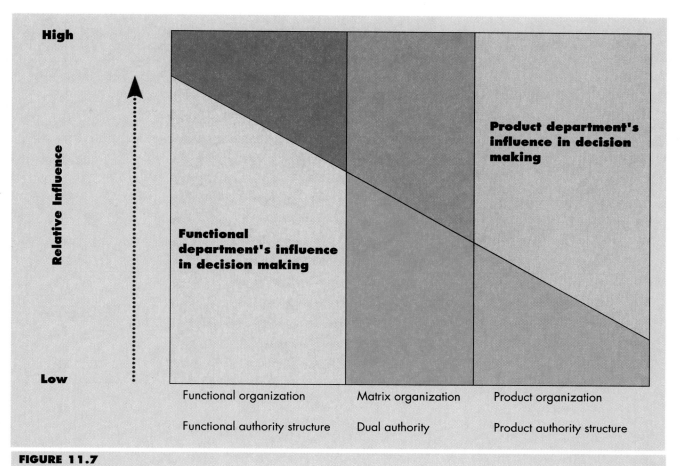

Product department's influence in decision making

Functional department's influence in decision making

Functional organization | Matrix organization | Product organization

Functional authority structure | Dual authority | Product authority structure

FIGURE 11.7

Matrix Organization Design

erate in more than sixty countries around the world. We highlight Philips's use of a matrix in its lighting division. In addition to development of lighting systems, the lighting division also sells control systems that allow lighting, heating, alarm, and ventilation systems to communicate.

Global *Insight*

Let There Be Light

The lighting division of Philips Electronics manufactures four different types of products: lamps, luminaries, car lights, and specialty lighting, as shown in Figure 8 on page 352.

The lamp product line includes light bulbs, energy-efficient fluorescent bulbs for table lamps, and bulbs for lamps used by dentists and doctors. The luminary product line includes lights for sports arenas and floodlighting for dams, highways, and parking lots and garages. These lights are waterproof for outdoor use. The division's engineers have developed a new technique to transport light in special tubes. This technique makes it possible to accentuate building contours, as with the NationsBank building in Dallas.

Engineers for the car lamp product line developed a lamp filled with neon gas that produces the red light for the brake and tail lights and the amber central lights of cars. The specialty product line includes decorative lighting for special events such as for the Olympic Games of 2000. The division will light the Sydney Opera House with the colors of the Olympiad rings. It has also lighted the Acropolis in Athens, Shenzhen stadium in China, and the Grand Louvre in Paris.

Employees who are assigned to various product lines come from the various functional departments shown in Figure 11.8. Depending on the functional expertise required, these employees may work on various products. For example, R&D employees were assigned to design the lighted Olympiad rings for the Sydney Opera House. After this activity had been completed, many of these employees were assigned to activities in the luminaries product line. The general matrix manager assigns functional employees to each product line when and where their expertise is needed most.[22]

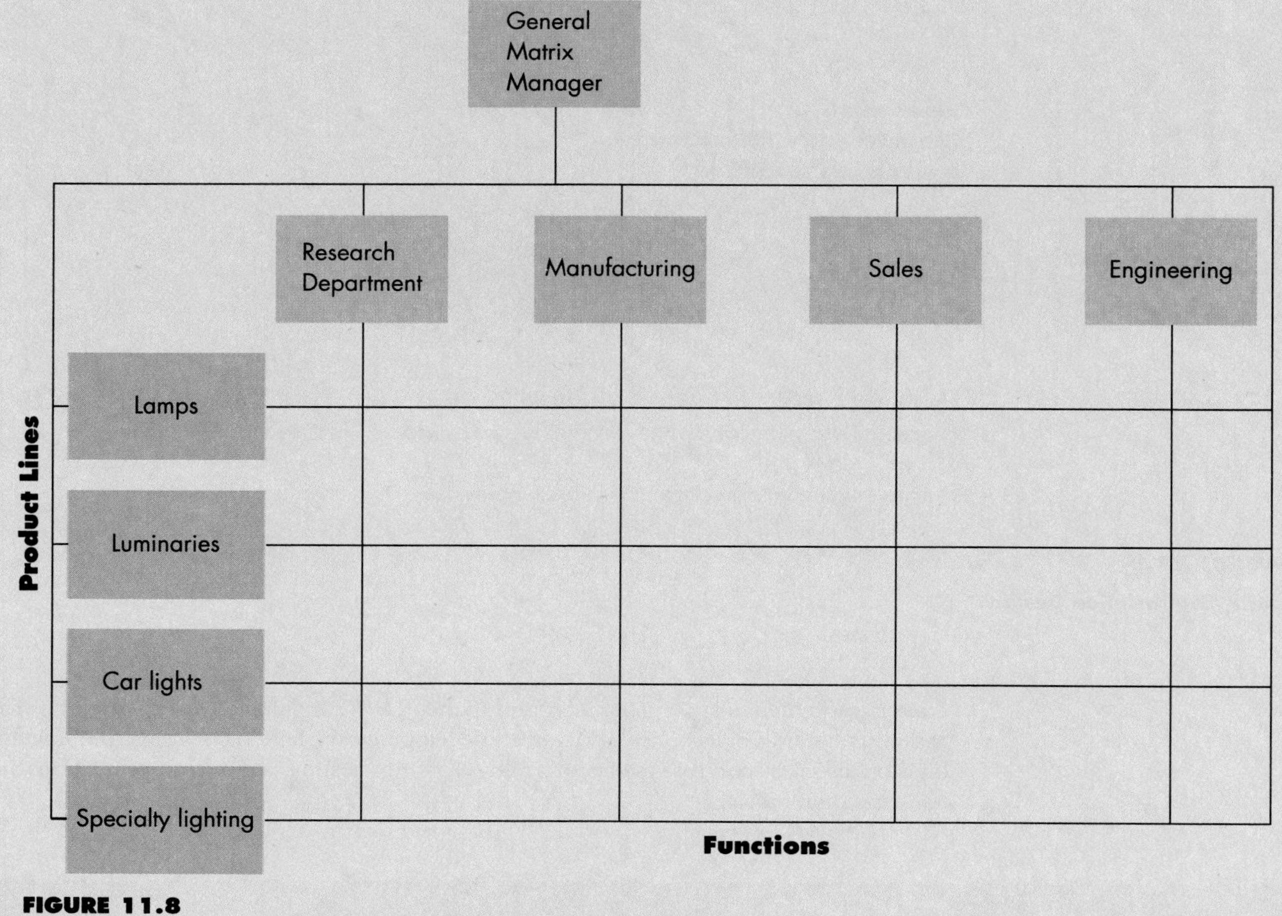

FIGURE 11.8

Philips Electronics, N.V.'s Matrix Design

Source: Adapted from McAra, A., and Vorstenbos, P. *Expertise in Electronics*. Eindhoven, Netherlands: Philips, 1994.

Advantages of a Matrix Design. The advantages of a matrix design are highlighted in Table 11.4.[23] Basically, a matrix design permits the flexible sharing of employees across product lines. The job of the matrix manager is to assess new products, obtain resources for the entire division, and integrate the efforts of product and functional personnel.

Disadvantages of a Matrix Design. The disadvantages associated with the matrix design include the reality that the maintenance of two management hierarchies (functional and product) is expensive. Further, the "matrixed" employees typically have two

TABLE 11.4

Advantages and Disadvantages of Matrix Design

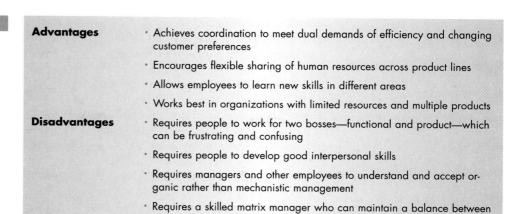

Advantages	• Achieves coordination to meet dual demands of efficiency and changing customer preferences • Encourages flexible sharing of human resources across product lines • Allows employees to learn new skills in different areas • Works best in organizations with limited resources and multiple products
Disadvantages	• Requires people to work for two bosses—functional and product—which can be frustrating and confusing • Requires people to develop good interpersonal skills • Requires managers and other employees to understand and accept organic rather than mechanistic management • Requires a skilled matrix manager who can maintain a balance between functional and product interests

bosses: a functional boss and product boss. Who should they listen to? This often creates confusion and ambiguity for the employee. What happens when the product is delivered and there are no new products to work on? Massive layoffs then usually occur. Therefore employees sometimes tend to drag out their activities to keep their jobs. Finally, the expense of training employees to behave as coaches and facilitators and not bosses should not be overlooked. Many employees and managers simply cannot give up assumptions about clear lines of authority and accountability and thus are unable to function effectively in a matrix design.

Reducing the Need to Process Information

Managers can reduce the need to process information by either reducing the number of exceptions (problems) that occur or reducing the number of factors to be considered when exceptions do occur. Two strategies used to implement this approach are slack resources and self-containment.

Slack Resources. **Slack resources** are extra resources—materials, funds, and time—that organizations stockpile in order to be prepared to respond to environmental changes. Slack resources can reduce the need to process information by minimizing the problems that are likely to arise. One form of slack resources is an organization's ability to lengthen production and delivery schedules or increase lead times. When an organization overestimates the length of time needed to complete a project, it creates slack—extra time—in the schedule that can be used for dealing with unexpected difficulties. The student who writes a term paper well in advance of the due date builds slack into his or her schedule—extra time that can be used for editing and typing or for something else entirely.

One effect of slack resources is to reduce departmental interdependence. For example, Eljer Industries, manufacturers of plumbing, heating, and ventilation products, maintains extra inventory of plumbing and ventilation products to meet unexpected demand. Less communication is needed among the purchasing, production, and sales departments because of this extra inventory. However, if purchasing keeps only a minimal amount of inventory on hand (no slack), the three departments must coordinate activities closely to avoid creating an unmanageable backorder situation. If backorders pile up, customer satisfaction drops because customers must wait for what they ordered.

Real-World Example
University departments that own their own copiers, faxes, and VCRs/TVs have created slack resources so that they do not have to coordinate and cooperate with other departments.

Creating slack resources also has negative cost and customer relations implications.[24] Increasing manufacturing lead time generates inventories that cost money to store. At Eljer Industries, this extra cost is reflected in warehousing expenses, such as building construction or leasing costs, additional employees, and energy costs to maintain the buildings. The money thus tied up could have been used for other purposes.

Moreover, extending time horizons for planning, budgeting, and scheduling may lead to lower performance expectations. Moreover, some customers may not be able to live with extended schedules because of their own plans or commitments.

Self-Contained Tasks or Departments. The second strategy for reducing the need to process information is to assign *all* activities concerning a specific product, project, or geographic region to one group. This approach effectively reduces the number of factors to be dealt with when exceptions, or problems, arise. The self-contained strategy involves choosing product or place rather than functional departmentalization. Recall that some organizations choose a product form of departmentalization because they are having problems with their functional organization. In a firm organized around products (e.g., Procter & Gamble, General Foods, and PepsiCo) each product group has its own resources for the functional areas of accounting, marketing, manufacturing, personnel, and finance. That is, each product line contains all the resources needed to satisfy its customers needs.

Teaching Tip
This approach is akin to creating minicompanies.

Organization by product lines enables a company to achieve flexibility and adaptability. It also reduces the amount of information a manager needs to process, in two ways. First, product departmentalization reduces the number of products and consumers that each group deals with; that is, managers deal with limited product and customer demand. And within the organization, managers have little need to share information concerning manufacturing costs, delivery schedules, distribution channels, and the like with managers in other groups. One manager's concerns aren't relevant to another's. Second, specialization across product lines is reduced. In functional departmentalization, an accountant must know something about all the organization's products; in product departmentalization, an accountant needs to know something about only one product line. Thus uncertainty is reduced because all necessary information will pertain only to a limited set of product problems.

Real-World Example
Calyxx & Corrola (C&C) sell flowers by catalog. Customers choose flowers from the catalog and then call in an order to C&C. It transmits the order to one of its more than twenty-five growers. The growers cut and pack the order and FedEx it to the customer (*Business Horizons,* November–December, 1994).

Network Organizations

Another form of organization design called the network organization has been created to permit the processing of information more effectively and efficiently. The **network organization** subcontracts some or all of its operating functions to other firms to per-

Michael Cohl, CEO of the Rolling Stones' 1994–95 *Voodoo Lounge* tour, created a "virtual corporation" with 250 full-time employees and potential worldwide revenues of $300 million. He ran the tour via fax, computer, and telephone. At the end of the tour, the corporation dissolved.

form and coordinates their activities through managers and other personnel at its headquarters.[25] The traditional functions of sales, accounting, and manufacturing are no longer under one roof, but are provided by separate organizations connected by computer to headquarters. Contacts and working relationships in the network are maintained by electronic means, not personal meetings. Communications on the information superhighway permit managers quickly to locate suppliers, designers, manufacturers, and others through on-line clearinghouses.

Network organizations cannot operate effectively unless they have the ability to communicate quickly, accurately, and over great distances. This capability permits managers to

- search globally for opportunities and resources;
- maximize use of all resources for a business, whether owned by the organization or not;
- perform only those functions for which the organization has or can develop expertise;
- outsource those activities that can be performed more quickly and at a lower cost by others.

Ethics
Unions accuse companies that switch to the network design as wanting to break the union and utilized cheap nonunionized labor by outsourcing here at home or overseas. To stay in the same industry, unionized workers may have to go to work for an outsourcer at a much lower wage. Managers claim that the network design is the most efficient and is necessary for the survival of many companies. What do you think?

This design means that subcontractors flow into and out of an organization's orbit as they are needed. Subcontractors in the network are added or dropped with the flexibility of switching parts in a child's Lego set. Figure 11.9 illustrates the use of this design by Galoob Toys. Subcontractors are hired only temporarily to perform a specific task.

Organizations in the fashion, toy, publishing, motion picture, and software industries have used this design effectively. Virtually all large retailers have limited the amount of capital invested in plant and equipment and manufacturing operations by outsourcing these functions to subcontractors. At Kmart, Wal-Mart, J.C. Penney, and other large retailers, corporate headquarters aggregates the day's sales each night as reported by each store over the electronic cash register point-of-sale information system. The system breaks product-line sales into item, cut, size, material, color, style and number sold. That data is then transmitted from corporate headquarters to subcontractors around the world. Within a few days, replacement merchandise is on the shelves.

FIGURE 11.9

Galoob Toys's Network Design

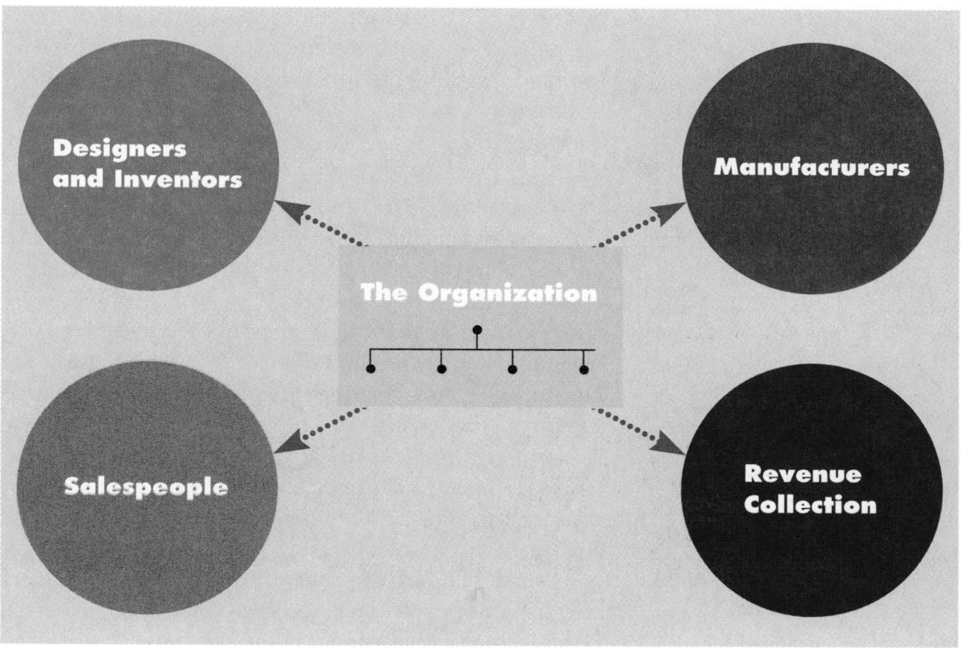

An example of a network organization is NIKE. With sales of more than $3.4 billion and a 29 percent share in the sports shoe-leisure apparel market, NIKE employs few people at its Beaverton, Oregon, headquarters. The heart of the company's success lies in its ability to design technologically advanced athletic shoes and get them to the market quickly. Designers and market researchers at headquarters introduce new models. A small plant at headquarters makes prototype shoes, which are worn and tested by employees and athletes. Once the design has been finalized, it is faxed to suppliers in the Pan-Pacific region for mass production. NIKE then distributes them to retailers throughout the world from its huge distribution warehouse in Memphis, Tennessee, home of FedEx.[26]

Implications for Global Organizations. The evolution of global organizations has been characterized by a growing need to balance several conflicting goals: meeting requirements for economic survival, adjusting to demands from host countries, and integrating company operations throughout the world.[27] Some companies have extensive manufacturing operations in several countries and must integrate their operations through the use of a network design.

As mentioned previously, Galoob Toys is one global organization that uses a network design (see Figure 11.10). Only 100 employees in California run the entire operation. Galoob uses subcontractors to perform all its operations functions. Independent inventors and entertainment companies conceive most of Galoob's toys, and outside specialists do most of the design and engineering work. Galoob subcontracts manufacturing and packaging to firms in Hong Kong, who in turn subcontract most of the labor-intensive work to factories in China. When the toys arrive in the United States, Galoob distributes them through commissioned sales representatives. Galoob doesn't even collect its own money. Commercial Credit Corporation collects from these salespeople, charges Galoob a fee, and then remits the rest to Galoob. In short, Galoob is simply a broker for all these subcontractors.

Advantages of a Network Design. A network design has several advantages. First, the structure is unbelievably lean. There are very few employees on the payroll because most activities are contracted for and coordinated by means of vertical information processing systems. Moreover, work-force flexibility and challenge are high because employees are subcontractors who respond to changing tasks and new demands. In addition, some networks preserve highly specialized teams and always use them. For example, NIKE has found it to its advantage to use the same suppliers in Korea, Taiwan, and other Pan-Pacific countries because these suppliers know its quality and production standards. Finally, the brokering organization has the freedom to choose subcontractors from anywhere in the world where electronic information systems can be set up and maintained.

Disadvantages of a Network Design. This unusual organization design also has some disadvantages.[28] For one thing, there is little hands-on control. Operations are not under one roof, and managers must adjust to relying on independent subcontractors to do the work.

Second, the network organization runs the risk of a subcontractor's dropping the ball and not reporting it. For example, when Intel worried about not being able to make the necessary financial commitment to introduce a new line of chips, it enlisted two subcontractors to manufacture its flash chips. NMB Semiconductors had trouble getting its manufacturing process up and running just as the demand for the chips was exploding. As a result, Intel couldn't get nearly enough chips and lost market share to competitors who didn't outsource their manufacturing. According to Andy Grove, Intel's chairman, the network design is a "meaningless buzz phrase."

Third, defining the organization is difficult because it changes rapidly. As subcontractors change, new relationships need to be formed and these take time to develop. Finally, employee commitment to the organization is low because employees tend to be

Discussion Question 5
What are the strengths and limitations associated with the network design of global corporation such as Black & Decker?

committed to the subcontractor that employs them, not to the brokering firm. They realize that they may be dismissed at any time if the brokering firm decides to use a different contractor.

Describe the factors that affect the design of an organization.

FITTING AN ORGANIZATION WITH A DESIGN

Teaching Tip
Use the university as an example as you go through this concluding section.

To conclude, let's look at how the key factors we've discussed in this chapter affect the design of some of the organizations highlighted in previous chapters and this one. We've said that an organization's design should reflect its environment, strategy, technology, and information processing needs. No single design is going to be appropriate for an organization all the time. Rather, managers choose a design that fits the organization's needs at a particular time, and as these needs change, so must the design. An organization design is a blueprint to help an organization achieve its goals; it's not an end in itself.

In any organization, some activities and skills are always more crucial to success than others. For instance, L.L. Bean is trying to provide its customers with a high-quality product in a very competitive, but somewhat stable, market. Its business strategy is to differentiate itself from other catalogue retailers, such as Eddie Bauer or J.C. Penney, by providing customers with extraordinary service and a wide variety of name brand products. Bean's managers have chosen a routine service technology and a vertical information system to implement this strategy. This choice of design enables employees to monitor the sales of each item, the number of times a customer has called, type of payment, and other relevant information.

For McDonald's, Burger King, and Hardee's, the environment is stable, and competitors are well-known and established. These firms have chosen a low-cost business strategy to attract and maintain customers. Customers can shop around to find the best price and quality. These organizations also have fit their design to a routine service technology. This service technology is appropriate because many of the jobs performed by employees are routine, such as processing customers' orders. A mechanistic structure fits the needs of their technology and the conditions of their environments.

Grouping and Coordinating Activities

We have indicated that managers can put in place one of four types of departmentalization, or a mixture of them, to achieve their organization's goals. A functional form of departmentalization is appropriate when the organization is small. For example, Nan Napier used this design at Tres Mariposa, the dress store we discussed in Chapter 10. Information could be processed easily within each function. She coordinated the various decisions made by the functional managers. This pooled interdependence supported functional departmentalization.

The place departmentalization utilized by Harrisons & Crosfield is appropriate when the organization is large, mature, and operates in various locations around the world. To coordinate its various divisions, Harrisons & Crosfield uses pooled interdependence. It allows each division to focus on the customers buying a particular product and to minimize the communication required between product lines. Key activities can be grouped by product line, each being self-contained, with its own engineers, accountants, manufacturing processes, marketing campaigns, and other functions. Top managers rely on rules, regulations, and standards to coordinate activities among divisions.

If the organization operates in several geographical areas, each with its own special needs, place departmentalization also is appropriate. Broadcasting Partners uses this form effectively. Each station is treated as a self-contained business. American Airlines also organized geographically, but uses vertical information systems extensively to transmit information simultaneously to everyone concerned with changes in flight schedules, weather, and so on. The company has chosen a routine service technology to deliver products to its customers. This type of service technology relies extensively on rules and standard procedures that dictate the way in which employees are to perform their tasks.

Philips Electronics implemented a matrix design to gain the benefits of both functional employees' expertise and the need to change its products constantly to appeal to its customers. Reciprocal interdependence serves members of a matrix best because it promotes the integration of both functional and product managers' activities. The stage of the project becomes the basis for the type of interdependence and the assignment of employees. In the engineering design stage Philips uses reciprocal interdependence with the matrix. Employees from engineering, marketing, and manufacturing are brought together to discuss the financial implications of a new product. After the product has been designed and approved for production, employees in the manufacturing department actually produce it. Mass production relies on sequential technological interdependence to coordinate employees' efforts. Finally, employees and their managers in the sales department jointly set sales goals. If all the salespeople achieve their goals, Philips will achieve its goal.

The network form of design allows an organization to use subcontractors to perform many of its functions, such as design, manufacturing, sales, finance, and the like. The advantage is that the organization itself doesn't have to maintain all these functions and can select contractors who have the expertise needed to solve problems for the organization. An extensive vertical information processing system links various subcontractors to the firm.

Determining the Authority Structure

Determining how much authority and freedom employees should have to make decisions is an integral part of choosing a design. In the case of Tres Mariposa, most key decisions are made by Nan Napier, the owner. To ensure that she has the needed information, she talks with employees. In larger firms that are organized by function, such as Toys "R" Us, a vertical information system efficiently transmits information up the chain of command. A mechanistic structure supports the centralization of decision making.

Place departmentalization divides the organization by location. Often this is a function of the product marketed and the difficulty of transporting it over large distances, as in construction and meat packing. Global organizations also recognize the trade-offs between centralized control and the complexity of operating in different environments. Authority to commit the organization's resources resides with employees within each geographical region. Local management is closer to the customers and can satisfy their specialized needs better than can some manager far away.

The product form of structure places the authority to make decisions with those individuals in charge of a "business." At Harrisons & Crosfield, divisional managers are totally responsible for their own businesses, including finding raw materials, financing new plants, manufacturing, distribution, marketing, and sales. They have the authority to organize their divisions in the most appropriate manner for the environments they operate in.

Departmentalization by customer is used when managers want to focus on customers' needs rather than on producing a product (functional) or products to sell (product). Managers have the authority to make decisions regarding their customers. Pillowtex, a manufacturer of pillows and other bedding products, quotes different prices for the same goods to different types of customers, such as discount stores and small retailers. It offers volume discounts to large customers. This practice signals that management is sensitive to the needs of its customer segments and can make decisions to satisfy the needs of various types of customers.

In a matrix structure, decisions should be delegated to the managers closest to the action. The crucial administrative skill is selecting managers to head up each project and delegating enough authority to them to carry out the necessary tasks. At Philips, decision making is delegated to each matrix manager in the division. An organic, as opposed to a mechanistic, structure supports the project manager's role in this matrix. To increase the manager's ability to process information, matrix structures rely on lateral relations, which allow product and functional managers to coordinate their tasks. Reciprocal interdependence characterizes the relationships among managers.

Authority is centralized in the network form of design. The organization's use of temporary workers and other organizations dictates that most major decisions are made at headquarters. Subcontractors simply implement these decisions within the guidelines established by the organization.

CHAPTER SUMMARY

1 ***Define organization design.***
Organization design is the process of determining the structure and authority relationships for an entire organization. It is undertaken only after a firm's strategy and goals have been established.

2 ***Explain how different environments influence an organization's design.***
Organizations operate in relatively stable or changing environments. A stable environment is characterized by few product changes, little technological innovation, a fixed set of competitors and customers, and consistent government policies. A changing environment is characterized by continuous product changes, major technological innovation, an ever-changing set of competitors and customers, unpredictable government policies, and rapid changes in individual values and expectations.

3 ***Describe the differences between mechanistic and organic organizational structures.***
Firms operating in stable and changing environments tend to choose mechanistic and organic organizational structures, respectively. In a mechanistic structure management concentrates on specialization, standardization, and centralized authority. The organization tends to be highly differentiated. In an organic structure management concentrates on teamwork, communication, constant job redefinition, and decentralized authority. The organization tends to be well integrated.

4 ***Discuss the effects of technology on the design of manufacturing and service organizations.***
Three types of technological interdependence affect organizational structure: pooled, sequential, and reciprocal. Pooled interdependence requires little sharing of information and other resources by departments. Individuals work on specialized tasks. Sequential interdependence serializes the flow of information and other resources between individuals and departments to accomplish tasks. Reciprocal interdependence encourages the flow of information and other resources back and forth between individuals and departments to accomplish tasks.

5 ***Explain how environment and technology combine to determine the amount of information an organization must process.***
In a stable environment, technological interdependence is likely to be pooled or sequential. There is relatively little need to share information internally or to process greatly varying amounts of externally generated information. In a changing environment, technological interdependence more often is reciprocal, with great need for sharing information internally and also for processing large amounts of externally generated information. To deal with uncertainty, firms can either increase their ability to process information by creating vertical information systems or lateral relations, or reduce their need to process information by utilizing slack resources or forming self-contained tasks or departments. To be effective, matrix and network designs require vertical information systems.

6 ***Describe the factors that affect the design of an organization.***
Designing an organization is a complex task. The manager must consider environmental forces and the organization's goals and strategies before choosing a design. Choosing a design requires selecting a type of departmentalization and technology. Different combinations of these two design features affect the amount of information an organization can process.

QUESTIONS FOR DISCUSSION

1. What are the main features of stable and changing environments?
2. How does the environment affect the way fast-food organizations are designed?
3. What are the differences between a mechanistic and an organic structure? How would you classify PETsMART's structure? Why?
4. How does the environment influence a manager's choice of structure?
5. What are the strengths and limitations associated with the network design of a global corporation such as Black & Decker?
6. What problems might the use of multiple forms of technological interdependence create for managers?
7. How do environmental and technological factors influence the selection of the most effective information processing strategy?

FROM WHERE YOU SIT

1. Develop an organization chart in sufficient detail that all employees know to whom they report and how they fit into the total picture. What type(s) of organization might use this structure? Why?
2. Describe the global forces that you have observed in your local business community and how these might influence the design of a local retail store.
3. Visit a service organization and analyze its structure. What design principles did it use to meet customer demand?
4. What types of technological interdependence do various sports teams use? What analogies can you draw for other types of organizations that may use the same types of interdependence?
5. Identify some organizations that use mechanistic and organic management systems. Are they equally successful? If so, why?
6. What are the advantages and disadvantages for your management career if you work in an organization using a network design?

SKILL-BUILDING EXERCISE

Is Your Organization Mechanistic or Organic?[29]

INSTRUCTIONS: In this questionnaire you are to focus on either an organization you are currently working for or one that you have worked for in the past. Please check the box on the scale indicating the degree to which you agree or disagree with each statement. There is no "right" answer. Please respond according to how you see your organization being managed.

Describe the extent to which each of the following 10 statements is true of or accurately characterizes the organization in question.

	To a Very Great Extent	To a Considerable Extent	To a Moderate Extent	To a Slight Extent	To Almost No Extent
1. This organization has clear rules and regulations that everyone is expected to follow closely.	___	___	___	___	___
2. Policies in this organization are reviewed by the people they affect before being implemented.	___	___	___	___	___
3. In this organization a major concern is that everyone be allowed to develop their talents and abilities.	___	___	___	___	___
4. Everyone in this organization knows who their immediate supervisor is; reporting relationships are clearly defined.	___	___	___	___	___
5. Jobs in this organization are clearly defined; everyone knows exactly what is expected of a person in any specific job position.	___	___	___	___	___
6. Work groups are typically temporary and change often in this organization.	___	___	___	___	___
7. All decisions in this organization must be reviewed and approved by upper level management.	___	___	___	___	___
8. In this organization the emphasis is on adapting effectively to constant environmental change.	___	___	___	___	___
9. Jobs in this organization are usually broken down into highly specialized, smaller tasks.	___	___	___	___	___
10. Standard activities in this organization are always covered by clearly outlined procedures that define the sequence of actions that everyone is expected to follow.	___	___	___	___	___

Scoring: On the scoring grid, circle the numbers that correspond to your response to each of the 10 questions. Enter the numbers in the boxes, then add up all the numbers in boxes. This is your ORG MECH score

	Q1	Q2	Q3	Q4	Q5	Q6	Q7	Q8	Q9	Q10
Great	5	5	1	5	5	1	5	1	5	5
Considerable	4	4	2	4	4	2	4	2	4	4
Moderate	3	3	3	3	3	3	3	3	3	3
Slight	2	2	4	2	2	4	2	4	2	2
No	1	1	5	1	1	5	1	5	1	1
	—	—	—	—	—	—	—	—	—	—

Total Score ____

Interpretation: High scores indicate high degrees of mechanistic/bureaucratic organizational characteristics. Low scores are associated with adaptive/organic organizational characteristics.

10	20	30	40	50
Highly Organic		Mixed		Highly Mechanistic

CRITICAL THINKING CASE

Bally Engineering Structures[30]

Several years ago when Tom Pietrocini became president of Bally, he and his top management team decided that Bally had to become a mass customizer to survive. They concluded that Bally had to change from a company that made specific products, such as refrigerated rooms and walk-in coolers used in hotels and restaurants, to one that could make a growing range of products tailored to individual customers' needs but at the prices of mass-produced goods. Ideally, customers would indicate the products they desired, and Bally would use its technology to satisfy them.

With the market for Bally's products depressed and competition fierce, price wars were rampant. Bally had positioned itself as a "quality" manufacturer and was charging premium prices. This strategy was not being accepted in the marketplace. Salespeople were having trouble persuading customers to pay increasingly high premiums for marginally better mass-produced products.

Realizing that Bally's strategy and functional organization design weren't working, Pietrocini and his top management team started turning Bally into a lean, cost-efficient manufacturer that could grow by gaining market share. He hoped to achieve this goal by reducing the number of defects, the time required to fill customers' orders, and seeking new markets, such as cool, clean rooms for pharmaceutical companies. Barriers between functions, especially marketing and production, had to be broken down and quality teams needed to be formed. For years, information had been passed up to managers by employees who waited to be told what to do. Employees were viewed as cogs in the machine. As cogs, their jobs were standardized and narrowly defined. Because people were relatively costly, replacing them with technology was the logical solution. However, it had the effect of reducing their numbers and their skill levels.

Pietrocini needed to create a vision that would capture the enthusiasm of employees and customers alike. Employees needed to believe that part of their job was to figure out better ways to do it. He held meetings with all employees and challenged them to find ways that Bally could become the best walk-in refrigerator company in the market. He encouraged employees to listen to and learn from every customer, not just depend on customer reported defects or periodic customer satisfaction surveys for feedback, as had always been done. Employee training programs were begun to supplement employees' knowledge and skills because they would now have to possess multiple skills.

Bally's structure needed to change to make mass customization work. Before Pietrocini joined Bally, it had been producing components (such as walls and motors) that theoretically should have enabled it to customize individual orders. But the organization's structure was so rigid that doing so was difficult. Customers had to choose from a set of standard product offerings in a catalog. Then, because of the bureaucratic way the company processed orders, weeks often passed before they got to the shop floor. In addition, manufacturing processes were organized in sequence, which left no room for modifications.

Bally has now not only broken up its tightly integrated set of manufacturing processes but also has greatly expanded them. In the past, when an order finally reached the factory floor, the foam panels, metal skins, corners, floors, ceilings, doors, and refrigeration units needed to cool the unit were built in that sequence. Now, the number of customer options has soared from 12 to more than 10,000. Different modules can be used to make up each specific order easily and quickly.

Bally's information processing system allowed these changes to occur. Bally created a database record for each customer. This information gave salespeople data on industry trends, past purchases, and complaints from each customer at their finger tips. A sales representative can custom design each order in the customer's office on a laptop computer connected to Bally's mainframe via a modem. The customer's unique product requirements are quickly translated, oftentimes with the salesperson still in the customer's office, into the set of manufacturing processes needed to create the product. The computer electronically stores all the information generated so that every employee who needs it can access it.

The information processing system connects everyone in the company, as well as independent sales reps, suppliers, and customers. The mainframe contains nearly all the information Bally uses, including such things as leads, price quotes, designs, purchase orders, and the skills and experience of all Bally employees. This information is accessible to anyone authorized to access it without their having to contend with functional boundaries. When an order is received, the information system identifies the right employees and brings them together to work on that customer's order. Thus employees who have never worked together immediately form an effective multiskilled team. It's an almost frictionless and seamless system. The system also enables everyone to find quickly the employees who have worked with the customer in the past and are knowledgeable about that particular customer's unique problems.

Questions

1. How has the environment influenced the Bally's organization design?
2. How did information processing affect Bally's organization design?
3. What type(s) of interdependence operate at Bally? To what extent did Bally's mass production technology fit a mechanistic design?

VIDEO CASE

L.L. Bean: A Commitment to Customer Service

Is customer service truly an integral component of organization design? Obviously, yes when you look closely at L.L. Bean, a Maine-based mail-order company that has a reputation for superior customer service. Its reputation dates back to 1912 when L.L. Bean marketed the legendary waterproof Maine hunting shoe for $3.95. When 90 of the first 100 pairs were returned because faulty stitching caused them to leak, L.L. Bean borrowed money to send out refunds. This corporate philosophy has continued over the years. With sales now surpassing $900 million annually, L.L. Bean publishes its guarantee of "100 percent satisfaction in every way." Fewer than 2 percent of returns each year are regarded as abuses of the guarantee system. L.L. Bean received the 1994 Silver Award for its 1994 Home & Camp Catalog, featuring housewares, linens, and furniture, many of which are "Made in Maine" products. The icon appears frequently in the eighty-eight-page catalog, giving merchandise the stamp of authenticity and reinforcing the company's New England values. The company's personality shines in L.L. Bean's products, including a vast assortment of furniture for the living room, bedroom, dining room, and den, as well as lamps, rugs, decorating accessories, and folk-art collectibles. It also offers a wide choice of sleepwear and a special "Back to Basics" collection of untreated, undyed, and unbleached apparel and bedding.

The Malcolm Baldrige National Quality Award committee made a site visit to L.L. Bean, which prompted the company to embark on a total quality management process that would lead it first through changes in people management and later through revisions of processes. Robert Peixotto, vice-president of total quality and human resources, states: "We really pioneered the no-questions-asked guarantee," which resulted in L.L. Bean gaining the reputation of being a "world-class" company.

The company demonstrated its commitment to customer service when a representative in Freeport once strapped a canoe on his car and delivered it to a customer in New York who had ordered one for a hunting trip that was to begin the next morning. L.L. Bean prides itself on employee involvement. One way the company encourages that involvement is by conducting attitude and work climate surveys to obtain employee views.

Until 1994, L.L. Bean saw itself as a fairly traditional hierarchical organization in which decision making occurred at a high level. The company then decided to implement recommendations of the Malcolm Baldrige National Quality Award Committee. Its new attitude became: "Total quality involves managing an enterprise to maximize customer satisfaction in the most efficient and effective way possible by totally involving people in improving the way work is done." As Robert Peixotto expressed it, "Quality for us doesn't happen on a production line, but every time you call up one of our phone centers and talk to a customer representative, which is where quality really happens for L.L. Bean."

L.L. Bean even determined to slow its growth rate in order to pay attention to quality. The majority of L.L. Bean's 4,000 company employees have spent approximately ten months familiarizing themselves with total quality and what it means to L.L. Bean. All salaried employees have received three days of total quality training, and all hourly employees have received one day's training. Peixotto stated that "we started with the senior level and we rolled the training on down through the organization so that each level within the company was well versed and able to support total quality as the next level learned about it."

L.L. Bean enlisted nearly seventy people within the organization to begin putting their knowledge into action. It created seven quality teams, comprising eight to ten workers each from various levels and functions in the organization. The teams work simultaneously on projects to bring about change and draw on each other's work. Another cross-level, cross-functional quality action team incorporated the total quality definition into the management learning program.

Based on a survey conducted by Thomas Rand, president of Management Research Group, L.L. Bean identified the characteristics of successful managers in the company. They were creative, open to change, strategic-minded, provided feedback, and addressed conflict. They were more persuasive than less efficient managers and often served as advocates for ideas and change. Bean managers also have moved toward creating an empowered work force.

People involvement—both customer and employee—has been crucial to L.L. Bean's success in achieving total quality. The company continues to add to its list of satisfied customers. Job satisfaction, as measured by the feedback for improvement process, is up 12fi percent. Because of the company's emphasis on total quality, use of its no-questions-asked guarantee is becoming less and less frequent.

Questions

1. What type of environment does L.L. Bean operate within?
2. What type of organizational structure does L.L. Bean have? Does this type of structure work effectively for the organization? Why or why not?
3. Based on the video and the Quality Insight "L.L. Bean Keeps Items Moving," explain the type of information system that L.L. Bean is currently using.

Chapter *12*

Human Resources Management

Learning *Objectives*

After studying this chapter, you should be able to:

1. Define human resources management and describe its role in an organization's strategy.
2. Discuss how human resources management is affected by changes in the work force and government regulations.
3. Describe the phases of the staffing process and the staffing tools and techniques used by organizations.
4. Explain the components of a total compensation package.
5. Discuss several methods of appraising performance and problems arising from the subjective nature of the process.
6. Explain how training and development programs can improve employee performance.

Chapter *Outline*

Preview *Insight*

Human Resources Management at Cadillac

At the Cadillac division of General Motors, the human resources department has a partnership with the other functional areas of the organization. ***People-strategy teams*** of salaried and hourly workers are responsible for ensuring that the company's ***people strategy*** fits with its ***product strategy*** and ***business strategy***. Within this broad context, each people-strategy team has different responsibilities. One team is researching employee development opportunities. A second team is examining the best human resources management (HRM) practices in other organizations. A third team is researching ways of improving communication with employees. A fourth team is looking at how Cadillac can become a more socially responsible company.

Cadillac does other things to ensure that its people strategy fits with its product and business strategies. The performance appraisal system emphasizes employee development. Extensive training is provided in quality management, health and safety issues, and leadership skills. A profit sharing plan supports Cadillac's team efforts.

All of Cadillac's HRM policies and programs also are designed to fit with the organization's product and business strategies. The HRM policies and programs are crucial elements in Cadillac's efforts to achieve its strategic goals.[1]

1

Define human resources management and describe its role in an organization's strategy.

WHAT IS HUMAN RESOURCES MANAGEMENT?

Human resources management (HRM) is concerned with the philosophies, policies, programs, practices, and decisions that affect the people who work for an organization.[2] Human resources management activities are aimed at securing, retaining, and directing the people in an organization to achieve its strategic goals.[3] For example, Wal-Mart's use of thousands of part-time employees helps keep its payroll costs low by eliminating fringe benefits. This approach, in turn, helps keep its overall costs low, thus enabling it to pass on these savings to customers by offering them low prices.

Human resources philosophies, policies, programs, practices, and decisions should be consistent with other systems and activities of the organization.[4] For example, if an organization uses a total quality management (TQM) approach, staffing, compensation and benefits, performance review and evaluation, and training and development all should support the TQM effort. That is, the organization should be staffed with people who can solve problems and perform the analyses demanded by TQM techniques such as statistical process control (SPC) and Pareto diagrams. In addition, extensive training in problem solving is needed. Organizations that use team problem-solving processes also need to train their employees in team processes and decision making. Performance appraisal methods and incentive pay then need to reflect team rather than individual achievements. Compensation practices in general shift from paying people for the job they hold to paying them for the results of their skills and knowledge. Rather than reinforcing status differences within the organizational hierarchy, perks such as parking spaces, dining areas, and benefit plans are eliminated or provided equally throughout the organization to reinforce collective responsibility.[5] These are the types of actions that Cadillac took in linking its people, product, and business strategies.

Ethics
If employee theft is a problem, HRM policy must support management's loss-prevention efforts by using selection methods that detect potential thieves, providing training to reduce theft, and giving rewards to discourage theft and encourage whistleblowers to come forward.

Discussion Question 1
How does Cadillac link its human resources practices to its business strategy?

In this chapter we consider the major human resources management challenges. We begin by examining the environment in which human resources management takes place. Then, we present the essentials of the staffing process as a whole—from planning and recruiting to selection and orientation. Next, we explain the components of

This chapter was contributed by Michael K. McCuddy, Professor of Human Resource Management, College of Business Administration, Valparaiso University, Valparaiso, Indiana.

the total compensation package and how it can help an organization attract, motivate, and retain capable people. Then, we explore the performance appraisal process: what it is, why it is necessary, and how various organizations use it. Finally, we review how organizations can help their employees grow further, through training and development.

2

Discuss how human resources management is affected by changes in the work force and government regulations.

THE ENVIRONMENT OF HUMAN RESOURCES MANAGEMENT

Human resources management activities are influenced by certain features of the organization's external environment. We discuss two of them in this chapter: (1) global and domestic work-force trends, and (2) regulatory influences.

Global and Domestic Work-Force Trends

Teaching Tip
Poll the class to determine what jobs the students want. Identify a pattern, if any, of gender preference wherein the men want traditionally male-dominated occupations and the women want traditionally female-dominated occupations. Engage the class in a discussion of gender segregation.

Dramatic changes are taking place in work forces in the United States and throughout the world. In some parts of the world—for instance, Pakistan, Indonesia, Brazil, and Spain—women haven't been absorbed into the work force in large numbers and represent a huge untapped resource. In other countries—for instance, Canada, the United States, France, Japan, Sweden, the United Kingdom, and Italy—women represent a significant percentage of the work force.[6] Although labor shortages have been forecast for many industrialized nations, the world's work force is growing fast but unevenly. The vast majority of new employees will join the work forces in developing countries (e.g., Mexico, India, and the Philippines).

Some developing countries—Honduras and Pakistan, among others—rely heavily on child labor. The conditions of employment often are appalling. Children as young as kindergarten age work twelve-hour days, sometimes for as little as $0.05 per hour and often are beaten if they don't work fast enough.[7] Condoned by their governments, many employers in developing nations use such practices in order to be price competitive in the global marketplace. These practices probably will continue despite the attempts of some international human rights organizations and industrialized nations to change them.

Ethics
Have students state the age at which they believe child labor would be ethical. Ask them to explain their reasoning.

International trade agreements, such as the North American Free Trade Agreement (NAFTA) and the General Agreement on Tariffs and Trade (GATT), will affect not only regional and global trade but the size and perhaps even the composition of work forces. One of the concerns about NAFTA was that manufacturers would shift jobs from the United States to Mexico to take advantage of lower labor costs.[8] In fact, the United States has become a service-oriented economy, partly as a result of companies' moving production jobs offshore. This shift in economic orientation requires a different mix of skills in the work force.

Skills at accessing and using computers and databases are becoming increasingly important in the information technology revolution that is part of this economic shift. The technical, interpersonal, conceptual, communication, and critical thinking skills important for managers in the past are becoming essential for success. In particular, interpersonal and communication skills are vital today not only for managers, but also for an increasing number of nonmanagerial employees. Being able to work independently and in small teams also are skills increasingly needed by all employees.[9] All highlight the evolving skills mix needed by those in the work forces in Canada, the United States, and other countries.

The U.S. work force also is becoming increasingly diverse. For example, as shown in Table 12.1, the average annual growth rate in the U.S. work force is expected to be just slightly smaller from 1992 to 2005 than it was from 1980 to 1992. However, dramatic changes are taking place in its *composition*. The number of people in minority groups entering the work force has grown about two and a half times faster than that of Caucasians. It will continue at more than two times the growth rate for Caucasians for the foreseeable future. Moreover, the number of women entering the work force will

TABLE 12.1

Percentage Changes in the Average Annual Growth Rate of the U.S. Work Force

	1980–1992	1992–2005
Total work force	+1.57%	+1.43%
Caucasians	+1.32	+1.23
Minorities	+3.33	+2.61
Female	+2.25	+1.81
Male	+1.04	+1.12
Under 25	−1.62	+1.39
25 to 44	+1.67	+0.16
45 and over	21.04	18.29

Source: Adapted from U.S. Bureau of the Census, *Statistical Abstract of the United States: 1993*, 113th ed., Washington, D.C., 1993, 393, Table 622.

continue to grow more rapidly than the number of men. The proportion of the youngest and oldest workers actually declined from 1980 to 1992, but those groups will provide the growth in the labor force between 1992 and 2005, with most of it being older workers.

These changes will bring an increasingly diverse mix of talents, abilities, perspectives, skills, and interests to organizations. Effectively utilizing this diversity is one of the major challenges for human resources management in the years ahead. Organizations in general are attempting to develop employees that are more tolerant of language and cultural differences, that identify and reject racial and sexual prejudices, that accommodate the handicapped, and that appreciate and can capitalize on the contributions that a diverse work force can make. The following Diversity Insight describes how Hewlett-Packard is responding to this challenge for managing diversity.

Discussion Question 2
How might changes in the composition of the work force affect human resources management policies and programs?

Diversity *Insight*

Managing Diversity at Hewlett-Packard

Hewlett-Packard developed a multifaceted diversity management program in response to results from an employee attitude survey indicating that minority employees felt more negative than nonminority employees about pay, benefits, the work environment, and promotional opportunities. The five-part diversity management program at HP consists of training, employee communication, accountability, development programs, and employee networks.

Diversity training involves nine modules that focus on awareness, legal issues, diversity objectives, management responsibilities, and practical applications. Regular ***employee communication*** provides information about H-P's commitment to diversity. H-P emphasizes ***accountability*** by including the achievement of diversity goals in the appraisal of managers' job performance. ***Development programs*** are used to help a more diverse range of employees advance in the company. ***Employee networks*** address the needs of specific employees.

Hewlett-Packard's diversity management program has helped to slow turnover. It also has brought more women and minorities into the organization at all levels. In addition, H-P now encourages and values different approaches and the people who introduce them.[10]

Regulatory Influences

In the United States, Canada, and several other countries, governments have determined that equal opportunity in all aspects of employment is a worthy and just goal. As a result, executive orders, laws, and court rulings specify acceptable and unacceptable human resources actions. These legal requirements affect not only recruitment, selec-

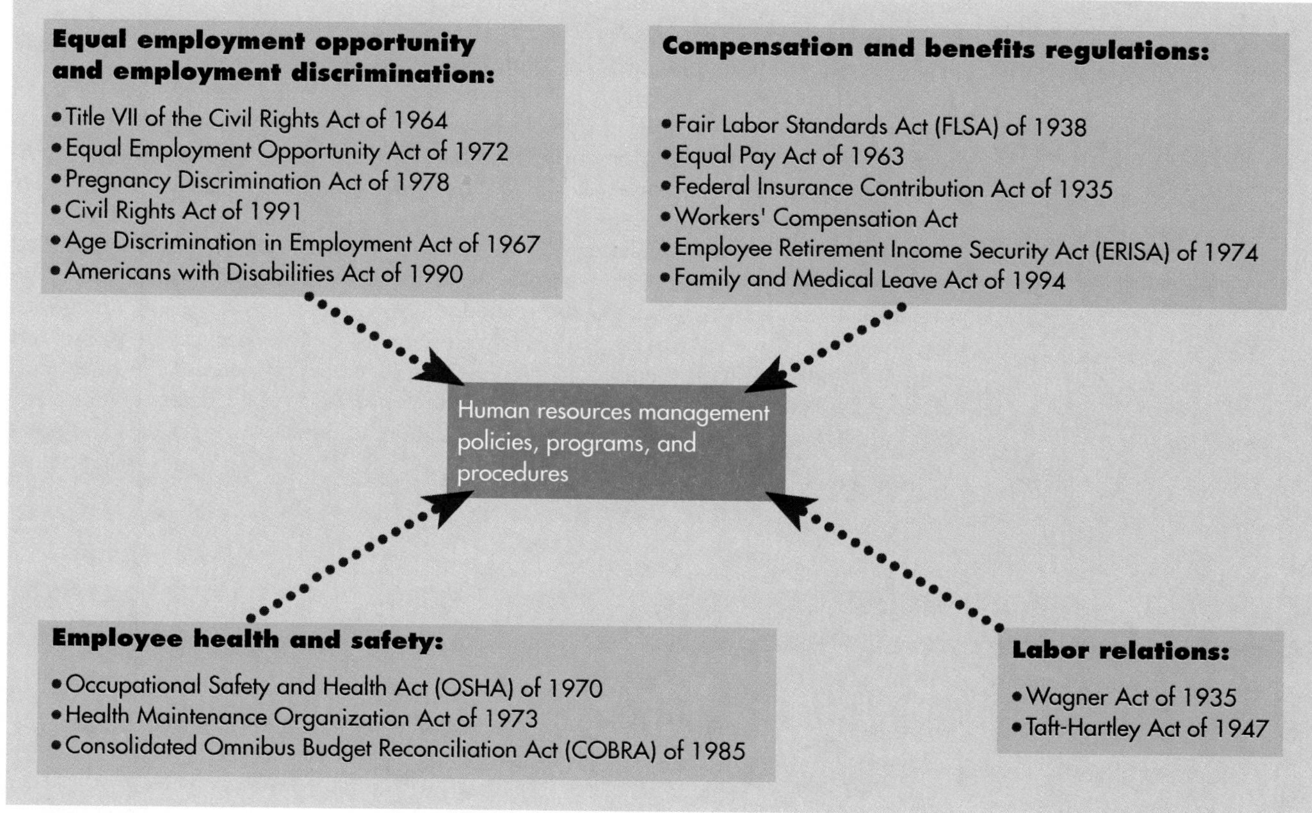

FIGURE 12.1

Major Regulatory Influences on Human Resources Management in the United States

tion, and placement, but also pay plans, benefits, penalties, and terminations. Let's briefly consider the primary regulatory influences shown in Figure 12.1 for the United States before examining specific HRM activities in more detail.[11]

Equal Employment Opportunity and Employment Discrimination. The most important legislation pertaining to equal employment opportunity and employment discrimination is Title VII of the Civil Rights Act of 1964, as amended by the Equal Employment Opportunity Act of 1972, the Pregnancy Discrimination Act of 1978, and the Civil Rights Act of 1991. *Title VII of the Civil Rights Act of 1964* prohibits discrimination in all phases of employment on the basis of race, color, religion, sex, or national origin. However, there are some exceptions to these general provisions. If any of these factors is a valid occupational qualification, it can be used in making employment decisions. For instance, religious discrimination is permitted in filling certain key administrative positions in religiously affiliated colleges and universities. Moreover, elected public officials and their staff members aren't covered by Title VII. Compliance with Title VII is monitored by the Equal Employment Opportunity Commission (EEOC) and enforced by the Justice Department.

Ethics
Ask the campus Affirmative Action Officer for a summary of an EEO case that was filed on campus and resolved. Discuss this case with the students to show them that real issues are being grappled with right around them.

Additional legislation modified and extended the impact of Title VII. The *Equal Employment Opportunity Act of 1972* gave the EEOC the power to sue employers in federal court on behalf of an aggrieved individual or class of people. The *Pregnancy Discrimination Act of 1978* requires employers to treat pregnant women as they would any other employee. Employers cannot use pregnancy, childbirth, or related medical conditions to justify differential treatment if the employee can perform the job. Finally, a major feature of the *Civil Rights Act of 1991* permits the awarding of both compensatory damages—for the loss of income or emotional pain and suffering—and punitive damages to aggrieved employees. Prior to passage of this act, only compensatory damages were allowed.

Other important employment discrimination regulations cover age and disabilities. The *Age Discrimination in Employment Act of 1967,* as amended, protects people aged forty or over against discrimination because of age. These workers are protected with regard to recruiting, hiring, promotion, termination, and most other terms and conditions of employment. The *Americans with Disabilities Act of 1990* prohibits employers with more than fifteen employees from discriminating against disabled individuals.

Ethics
Is protecting only these groups ethical? Do past injustices against these groups justify their protection now? If so, how long should they be protected?

Collectively, the laws regulating equal employment opportunity (EEO) are intended to do away with discrimination in employment. In other words, employees are to be judged solely on characteristics that are related to the performance of the job. Categories of existing and prospective employees covered by EEO laws are called **protected groups.** Nondiscriminatory employment policies and practices increase the likelihood that an organization can capitalize on the unique contributions of a diverse work force and ultimately succeed in meeting its goals. The failure to pursue such policies and practices can foster significant organizational problems, as the following Ethics Insight illustrates.

Ethics *Insight*

Gender Discrimination at Jenny Craig

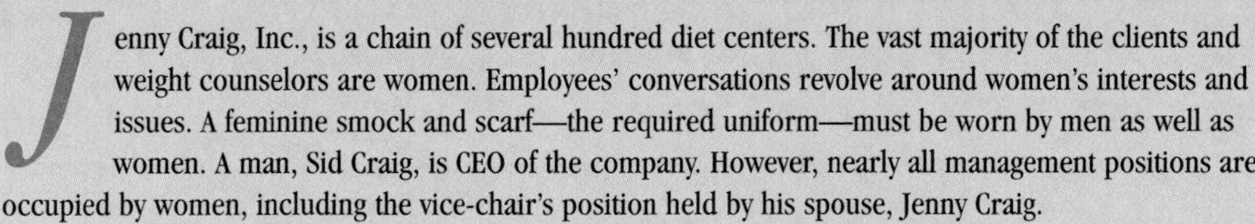

Jenny Craig, Inc., is a chain of several hundred diet centers. The vast majority of the clients and weight counselors are women. Employees' conversations revolve around women's interests and issues. A feminine smock and scarf—the required uniform—must be worn by men as well as women. A man, Sid Craig, is CEO of the company. However, nearly all management positions are occupied by women, including the vice-chair's position held by his spouse, Jenny Craig.

Eight male employees in the Boston, Massachusetts, area have alleged they are victims of sexual discrimination and harassment at work. They complain about humiliating remarks made by women employees and about being given demeaning tasks and unfavorable sales assignments. One man reports that a female supervisor asked him to fix her car and that another female supervisor discussed having erotic dreams involving him. Female co-workers reportedly commented on his physique. Other complainants describe a pattern of men-bashing at the company.

Most of these eight men allege they were passed over for promotion even though they were well qualified. One man, who was among the top sales producers in the region, was denied a promotion and another man was even demoted. A female supervisor allegedly told one of the men seeking promotion that the only way a man "could be promoted was if he got a sex-change operation or wore a push-up bra." Corporate headquarters for the company declined to discuss the complaints or the employment circumstances of the eight men.[12]

Ethics
Do you believe these men? Are women incapable of being harassers in a company in which they are the majority? Discuss the historical pattern of sexual harassment against women and how it might be changing.

Compensation and Benefits Regulations. Of the several laws that influence an organization's compensation and benefits practices. the primary one is the *Fair Labor Standards Act (FLSA) of 1938.* The FLSA specifies a minimum wage and required payment for overtime work by covered employees. As of 1995, the minimum hourly wage was $4.25. Employers are required to pay one and one-half the regular hourly pay rate for any work over forty hours per week. Employers, either voluntarily or through union negotiations, may provide a higher rate or require fewer hours before paying overtime rates.

Not all employees are covered by the FSLA. The act distinguishes between **nonexempt employees**—those covered by the act—and **exempt employees**—those not covered by the act.

Ethics
Organized labor says that the current minimum wage is too low. Management, especially small-business owners, say that they can't afford to pay more. Are ethics involved in either position? Explain.

Ethics
Is the historical pattern of women earning less than men for similar work ethical? Why or why not?

Exempt employees include, among others, outside salespeople, and executive, administrative, and professional personnel. These employees usually are compensated at rates far above the minimum wage. Employers are obligated to pay at least the minimum wage to nonexempt employees.

Another regulatory influence on compensation practices is the *Equal Pay Act of 1963*. This act requires men and women to be paid equally when they are doing equal work (in terms of skill, effort, responsibility, and working conditions) in the same organization.

Some legislation mandates that employers provide employees with certain benefits. This category includes the following laws.

- The *Federal Insurance Contribution Act (FICA) of 1935* and later amendments require most employers to make social security contributions on behalf of their employees. The act also requires employers to participate in an unemployment compensation system.
- The *Workers' Compensation Act* requires employers to pay into a fund to be used to compensate people for work-related injuries or diseases.

We discuss these laws more fully later in the chapter when we consider management of the total compensation package.

Ethics
Although illegal, organizations have fired or laid off workers just before they were to become vested in a pension plan and never recalled them. Is this practice ethical? Explain.

Retirement plans, a benefit provided voluntarily by employers, are regulated by the *Employee Retirement Income Security Act (ERISA) of 1974*. This act influences the management of retirement plans in two main ways: participation eligibility and vesting. Under ERISA, employees who are twenty-one years of age and have completed one year of service must be allowed to participate in a company's retirement plan if it has one. **Vesting** refers to the employee's right to receive specified benefits from the company's retirement plan. The act specifies that employees who stay with a company for ten years are entitled to 50 percent of the employer's retirement plan contribution even if the employee leaves the organization. After fifteen years of service, the employee is entitled to 100 percent of the employer's pension contribution.

Employee Health and Safety. Employee health and safety is influenced by both state and federal law. The primary federal law is the *Occupational Safety and Health Act*

Employees at OshKosh B'Gosh in Wisconsin were beseiged by cumulative trauma disorders, such as carpal tunnel syndrome, when the company received a citation from OSHA in 1990. The company inspected every aspect of production and discovered that the injuries are primarily caused by awkward, repetitious movements. One of the solutions was to give sewing machine operators a pulley system that allows them to sew with their arms at rest.

(OSHA) of 1970. This act requires that employers provide a safe and healthful workplace by arranging for adequate protection against hazards that are likely to cause serious physical impairment or death. These hazards could be dangerous equipment, unsafe production processes, exposure to noxious chemicals, and so on.

However, many jobs (e.g., construction, foundry work, metal stamping, spray painting, and coal mining) are inherently dangerous but must be performed. In such cases, OSHA calls for the use of all appropriate safety precautions. In metal stamping, for instance, safety devices must be used so that the operator's limbs are in a safe zone before the machine can be operated. Spray painters commonly wear respirators to protect themselves from paint fumes. Sometimes a ventilated spray booth is used to control exposure to paint mists and fumes. No matter how risky the job, the intent of OSHA is to ensure that employers do not expose employees to unsafe practices, thereby endangering their physical well-being.

Real-World Example
Coors gets a return of $6.15 for each dollar it spends on worksite health promotion. Coors offers aerobics, strength training, cardiovascular monitoring, and an indoor running track to its employees (*Business Horizons*, November-December, 1994, 75).

In addition to OSHA, the *Health Maintenance Organization (HMO) Act of 1973* and the *Consolidated Omnibus Budget Reconciliation Act (COBRA) of 1985* address employee health concerns. The former requires companies with at least twenty-five employees to provide an HMO alternative to regular group insurance if an HMO is available in the locality. The latter requires employers with twenty or more employees to provide extended health care insurance to terminated employees for as long as eighteen months, usually at the employees' expense.

Labor Relations. The right to unionize and bargain collectively is an important part of the regulatory aspect of human resources management. Different laws govern labor relations for public sector (federal, state, and local government workers) and private sector employees. In our discussion we focus on those covering the private sector, primarily the Wagner Act of 1935 and the Taft-Hartley Act of 1947.

The *Wagner Act* (also known as the *National Labor Relations Act*) gave employees the right to form or join labor unions, to bargain collectively, and to strike in order to secure better economic and/or working conditions. The NLRA also prohibited employers from engaging in unfair labor practices such as

- interfering with or threatening employees who exercise their rights as guaranteed by labor law;
- discriminating against employees because of their union activities;
- refusing to bargain in good faith with union representatives concerning employees' wages, hours, and terms and conditions of employment; and
- attempting to control or interfere with union affairs.

The NLRA did not prohibit unfair labor practices by unions. However, the *Taft-Hartley Act*, which amended the NLRA, was enacted to counteract union abuses. Under Taft-Hartley, unions cannot

- refuse to bargain in good faith;
- threaten or restrain employees in exercising their rights to join or not join a union;
- charge discriminatory dues or entrance fees; and
- force employers to discriminate against employees who are not union members.

Implications for Organizations

Increasingly, organizations need to address issues of diversity—issues such as sexual harassment, promotional opportunities for women and minorities, and hiring disabled workers, to name a few. Organizations may need to change their compensation and benefit packages and alter their training and development programs to meet the various needs of an increasingly diverse work force.

The human resources department normally is responsible for ensuring compliance with laws affecting employers' relationships with employees. These laws affect all orga-

Discussion Question 3
Discuss the major regulatory influences on human resources management.

nizations because they influence the pool of applicants and the procedures that must be followed after a person has been hired. Professionals in the human resources department must educate and train others in the organization with respect to these laws and their implications.

3

Describe the phases of the staffing process and the staffing tools and techniques used by organizations.

Teaching Tip
College recruitment and matriculation is a part of the selection process at your university.

THE STAFFING PROCESS

Staffing is the process by which organizations meet their human resources needs, including forecasting future needs, recruiting and selecting candidates, and orienting new employees.[13] Some organizations deliberately seek to attract, hire, and retain certain types of people—resulting in the image of a stereotypical employee. For example, PepsiCo hires college graduates who are assertive overachievers, who are risk takers, and who respond positively to intense pressure to reach sales and cost goals.[14] At Loral Vought Systems, where most of the work is defense related, the preference is to hire people with military experience.

The staffing process involves much more than simply hiring people. It also includes easing employees' entrance into an organization, as well as their movement through (promotion, job rotation, transfer) and out of (termination, retirement) it. Figure 12.2 highlights the components of the staffing process:

- ***Planning.*** Before hiring anyone, the organization needs to forecast its human resource requirements. By doing so, it can determine the number of employees to hire and the types of skills they will need. Moreover, management will be able to determine when it will need these employees.
- ***Recruitment.*** The organization next develops a pool of job candidates from which to select qualified employees. Candidates are recruited, for example, by running ads, contacting employment agencies, and visiting college campuses.
- ***Selection and hiring.*** After recruiting candidates for available positions, the organization selects and hires those people who are most likely to perform well on the job.
- ***Orientation.*** After employees have been hired, they must be oriented to their jobs and to the organization in general. Effective orientation programs familiarize new employees with company policies, safety rules, and work expectations. They also include explanations of compensation and employee benefits.
- ***Movement.*** After completing the orientation process, an employee continues to participate in the staffing process. Promotions, demotions, transfers, and training are all part of the process that spans an employee's career.

Teaching Tip
First-year student orientation is a type of organizational orientation program.

FIGURE 12.2
The Staffing Process

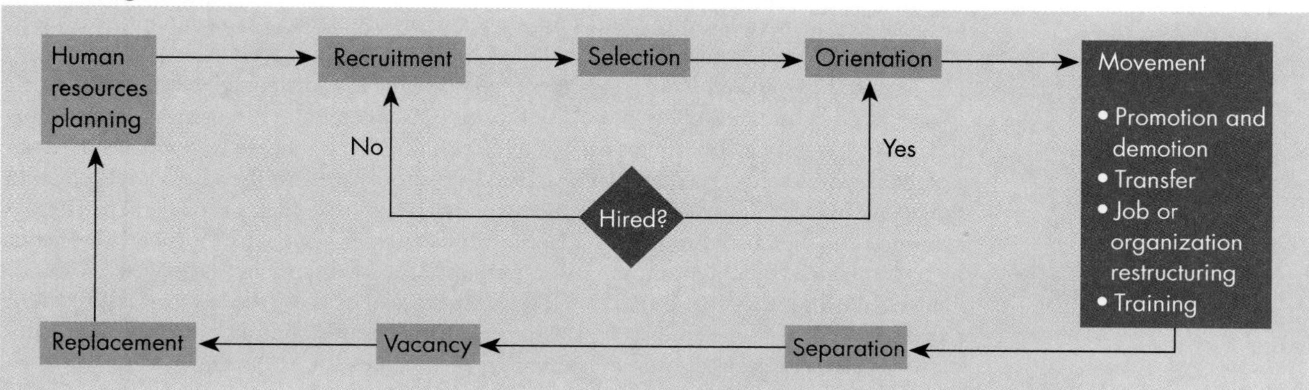

- ***Separation.*** The final stage is separation of the employee from the organization. Separation can occur as a result of the employee's finding a new job, retiring, becoming disabled, or being fired or laid off.

Human Resources Planning

The first stage of the staffing process, **human resources planning,** involves forecasting the organization's human resource needs and developing the steps to be taken to meet them. It consists of setting and implementing goals and actions needed to ensure that the right number and type of individuals are available at the appropriate time and place to fulfill organizational needs.[15] Human resources planning is tied directly to strategic planning (see Chapter 5).

Teaching Tip
Invite to class an alum who works as a human resources manager. Ask the alum to bring an HR plan to discuss with the class.

Determining an organization's human resources needs is the foundation of human resources planning. Let's consider some of the tools and techniques used for planning and forecasting these needs: skills inventories, job analyses, replacement charts, and expert forecasts.

Skills Inventory. A **skills inventory** is a detailed file maintained for each employee that lists his or her level of education, training, experience, length of service, current job title and salary, performance history, and personal characteristics such as age, gender, race, and marital status. Many organizations use computerized human resources information systems for storage and easy retrieval of such vital job-related information. For example, Texas Instruments (TI) maintains such files on its thousands of employees. These files help the firm's top managers spot human resources gaps. They also help TI demonstrate that it followed legal requirements when filling a job or taking some other type of personnel action.

Job Analysis. A **job analysis** is a breakdown of the tasks for a specific job and the personal characteristics necessary for their successful performance. A thorough job analysis has two parts: a description and a specification. A **job description** is a detailed outline of a position's essential tasks and responsibilities. A **job specification** is a listing of the personal characteristics, skills, and experience a worker needs to carry out a job's tasks and assume its responsibilities. Figure 12.3 reproduces part of a job description and part of a job specification for a sales associate position at Pier I Corporation.

The job specification helps human resources professionals and department managers identify the right person for the job. Job descriptions are used most often to develop sound and fair compensation and performance appraisal systems. However, job descriptions also allow recruiters to give potential candidates realistic descriptions of vacant positions.

Teaching Tip
Draw a replacement chart on the board for the president of your university. Discuss who might logically replace the president and why.

Replacement Chart. A **replacement chart** is a diagram showing each management position in the organization, along with the name of the person occupying each position and the names of candidates eligible to replace that person. These charts, which are usually confidential, provide a simple means of forecasting management needs and identifying internal availability of candidates.

Figure 12.4 illustrates a replacement chart covering four management positions. It gives the position titles, the name of each position's incumbent, the names of likely candidates for each position, their years of tenure in the department, and their promotional potential. Sometimes, holders of lower level positions may not be considered suitable replacements for higher level jobs. In that event, gaps in a firm's replacement chart—positions for which there are no suitable replacements—point to the need for better management development programs or, perhaps, outside recruiting. Jack Welch, CEO of General Electric, says that one of his assessment practices is to have each vice-president name a potential replacement. He believes that a vice-president who can't name a successor hasn't spent enough time grooming subordinates for advancement.

FIGURE 12.3

Job Description and Job Specification Statement

JOB TITLE

Sales Associate

Job Description

Primarily responsible for selling merchandise to customers who enter the store. Additional responsibilities include certain merchandising and housekeeping duties. Examples of duties required include:

- Handles repairs, including providing estimates, maintaining repair records, sending merchandise to repair shop, and following up on overdue repairs.
- Straightens and cleans display and understock merchandise, cases, and windows; sets up merchandise displays; and otherwise maintains store appearance.
- Asks questions of customer to determine what he or she is looking for in terms of merchandise type, style, cost, etc.
- Makes suggestions on how to mix methods of payment in financing a purchase.
- Attempts to close a sale several times.

Job Specifications

Personal characteristics impor tant to success include:

- Previous sales experience.
- Maturity.
- Well-groomed and neat appearance.
- Assertive and persistent demeanor .
- High school education.

Expert Forecasts. A variety of expert forecasting methods—some simple, some complex—can be used to determine an organization's demand for human resources. The forecasting method used depends on the time horizon, the type, size, and strategy of the organization, and the accuracy of the information available. More than 60 percent of all large firms utilize some type of expert forecasting to project HR needs.

Recruitment

Teaching Tip
Show students a position announcement for a faculty opening at your university. Find out who the candidates are.

When there aren't enough obvious candidates among current employees to meet the demand that human resources planning predicts, the organization must recruit people to fill those jobs. **Recruitment** is the process of searching, both inside and outside the organization, for people to fill vacant positions. Recruitment also should be concerned with identifying potential employees' needs. In this way recruitment not only attracts in-

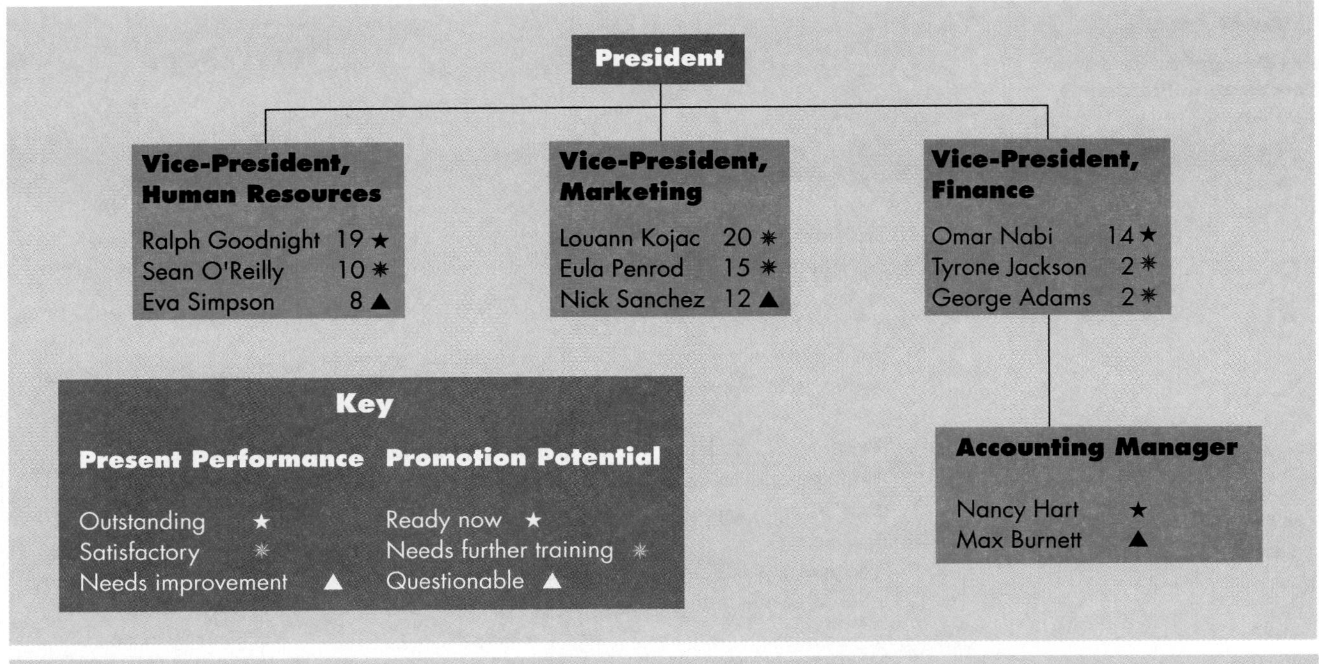

FIGURE 12.4

Management Replacement Chart

dividuals to the organization, but also increases the chances of retaining them once they're hired.

Factors Affecting Recruiting. In addition to the human resources planning activities we've discussed, the organization must consider its external environment in developing a recruiting program. Three external factors affect the recruiting process: government regulations, labor unions, and the labor market.

Teaching Tip
Pass around the class an affirmative action survey form that is sent to potential hires by your university.

- ***Government Regulations.*** An organization's recruiting policies and practices are influenced heavily by laws and regulations. The EEOC requires employers to maintain records on the number of openings in various job groups and the number of applicants for them, broken down by race, ethnicity, gender, and other characteristics. An affirmative action program may require an organization's work force to reflect the composition of the relevant labor market. **Affirmative action programs** are efforts intended to ensure that a firm's hiring practices and procedures guarantee equal employment opportunity, as specified by law. A company's **relevant labor market** is the geographic and skill areas in which an employer usually recruits to fill its positions. Thus, if the racial composition of the relevant labor market is 60 percent white, 30 percent black, and 10 percent other, an organization's work force should at least equal the percentages for minority workers. When, in the EEOC's opinion, a company underemploys members of a designated minority, the agency may require the company to engage in special recruiting efforts.
- ***Labor Unions.*** About three-fifths of the states permit a union shop provision in management-labor contracts. A **union shop** is an organization whose agreement with a union stipulates that, as a condition of continued employment, all employees covered by the contract must already be or must become union members within a specified period of time—usually 60 or 90 days.[16] This practice prevents a company from diluting union influence by hiring only employees who are against unions. The UAW, for example, has made union security a key issue in its negotia-

TABLE 12.2

Usual Sources for Recruitment of Job Candidates

Source	Comment
Educational institutions	High schools can be an excellent source for office, clerical, and secretarial employees. Trade and vocational schools provide many machinists, mechanics, and paraprofessionals. Colleges and universities provide most management trainees and professionals.
Public employment services	Many states and the federal government provide employment services at no charge. Such services list primarily the unemployed and to a lesser extent those seeking a job change. The military also provides some placement assistance for veterans.
Private employment services	These services differ according to who pays for them. Search consultants, or "headhunters," are paid by the organization and tend to focus on upper-level professionals and managers. In contrast, employment agencies collect their fees from job seekers.
Unsolicited applications	Many jobs are filled by walk-in or write-in candidates. Walk-ins tend to seek lower level jobs, but many professionals mail in unsolicited résumés.
Employee referrals	One of the best and most consistently used sources of new employees is referral of candidates by current employees. However, reliance on employee referrals may perpetuate past discrimination, if the work force is homogeneous. A predominantly white male work force may refer mostly white males, thereby inviting an EEOC investigation.
Advertisements	Newspapers carry many help-wanted ads, particularly in their Sunday editions. Available professional positions that require specialized backgrounds are advertised in many professional journals.

tions with GM, Ford, and Chrysler. (In states with right-to-work laws, however, employees cannot be forced to join a union.)

Teaching Tip
Invite three recent graduates to class. Have them discuss the local labor market in their respective fields.

- ***Labor Market.*** The labor market itself greatly influences recruiting efforts. If the local supply of qualified employees in a job category exceeds local demand, wages will be depressed and recruitment will be relatively easy. But when the local supply of qualified employees is limited, recruiting efforts intensify and wages may rise. For instance, Meijer, a Great Lakes area chain of one-stop shopping department and grocery stores, faced an extremely tight local labor market for retail employees when it opened two new outlets in northern Indiana in early 1995. Seeking to hire about 800 people for all those stores, Meijer had to recruit aggressively and offer highly competitive wages and benefits to attract enough full-time and part-time employees.[17]

Sources of Recruitment. Faced with the cost of recruiting, organizations try to identify and attract qualified employees who will stay with them. Typically, a department manager submits a personnel requisition to the human resources department. The requisition details the department in which the opening exists, job title, salary range, and so on. Most importantly, the requisition usually contains a job specification outlining the qualifications required to perform the job.

Teaching Tip
Have students contact five recent alums and ask them how they got their jobs. Use the results to illustrate the different sources of recruitment used.

Using such requisitions, a recruiter searches for candidates, either inside or outside the organization. Table 12.2 lists several of the more common recruitment sources. Some, such as unsolicited applications, are relatively inexpensive. Others, such as executive search firms, can be quite expensive. Which source a recruiter turns to is usually determined by the type of job to be filled. For example, a position at Ernst & Young or Arthur Andersen specifying an undergraduate accounting degree will be more readily filled through on-campus recruiting efforts or an ad in a professional journal than through a classified ad in the Sunday paper.

TABLE 12.3

Sources of Information That Aid Selection Decisions

- Résumés
- Reference checks
- Job applications
- Realistic job previews
- Interviews
- Tests
- Assessment centers

Selection and Hiring

The next step in the staffing process is actually filling the vacant position. Table 12.3 lists seven information sources available to managers making selection decisions. Many organizations, such as Marriott Hotels, use a combination of information sources.

Teaching Tip
Many students have no résumé or a very poor one. Have them write résumés that contain these six features and hand them in. Mix the résumés up and hand them back, making sure that no one gets his or her own. Have the recipients suggest improvements. Have the students take their own résumés home, redo them, and turn in final versions for credit.

Résumés. A well-written résumé is clear, concise, and easy to read and understand. It gives (1) personal data (name, address, and telephone number); (2) career objectives; (3) education (including grade point average, degree, and major and minor fields of study); (4) work experience, highlighting special skills and responsibilities; (5) other skills, activities, and personal information; and (6) references, with their addresses and telephone number. The *How To Pack Your Career Parachute* supplement to this textbook offers some useful tips on résumé preparation.

Teaching Tip
Although many former employers do not make evaluations when called on for a reference check, many others do. Have students list three references and hand them in. Mix them up and hand the lists back, making sure that no one gets her or his own. Have the recipients call the people listed to check the references. They are to ask the former employers: "Would you hire this person again? Why or why not?" Have them report back to the students who made the lists. Tell them that the assignment will not be graded or collected—that the purpose of the assignment is developmental, not valuative.

Reference Checks. Because résumés can be falsified easily, managers should request references and conduct reference checks. Many human resources professionals routinely check educational qualifications, including schools attended, major areas of study, degrees awarded, and dates. An applicant's work experience is more difficult to check because employers often are reluctant to provide evaluations of former employees. Their concern stems from cases in which reference givers have been successfully sued by former employees who were given bad references. In fact, by law, organizations are required to provide only the job title and dates of employment of a former employee.

Teaching Tip
Ask students to obtain copies of job applications from local businesses. In class, compare the types of information requested.

Job Applications. Most organizations require candidates to fill out a job application. In many cases this application serves the same purpose as a résumé. Employers also can use it to gather information for EEOC reports. A common misconception is that questioning applicants about their race, age, marital status, and national origin is illegal. In reality, employers are sometimes required by the government to ask such questions. During the recruitment phase, for instance, an organization may need to record demographic data in order to analyze and defend its recruitment techniques. However, using such information in a discriminatory way *is* against the law. To guard against charges of discrimination, organizations usually ask an applicant to give this type of information only voluntarily. Table 12.4 lists subjects that fall into this category. The EEOC calls questions that may raise suspicions of discrimination "problem questions" in its affirmative action literature.

TABLE 12.4

Potentially Sensitive Job Application Questions

Subject of Question	Possible Type of Selection Bias
Height or weight	May indicate sexual bias.
Eye or hair color	May indicate racial bias.
Birthplace	May indicate national-origin bias.
Marital status	May be used to discriminate against women planning to have children.
Birth date	May be used to discriminate on the basis of age.
Child-care plans	May be used to discriminate against women.

Teaching Tip
Have students identify a local business that has an affirmative action program and interview a management representative about the company's utilization analysis.

Discussion Question 4
Which recruitment sources are likely to be most effective for filling (a) secretarial jobs, (b) positions in skilled trades, and (c) professional and managerial posts?

Teaching Tip
Engage students in role playing some realistic job previews based on jobs they have held.

Teaching Tip
Have the class members describe the pluses and minuses of being a student. Have them write an RJP based on this information. Ask them to give the RJP to younger siblings or friends to help prepare them for college.

Ask Students
Why are interviews relatively poor predictors of on-the-job performance?

Teaching Tip
Conduct mock job interviews in class. This role playing will allow students to practice answering common questions such as, "What are your strengths and weaknesses?"

Ask Students
If interviewers rely heavily on first impressions, how can you make a good first impression?

Teaching Tip
Invite a human resources manager from a local business to discuss job interviewing skills with the class.

Ask Students
Have you ever taken any tests like these? If so, what were the tests like? What type of job were you applying for?

Ask Students
Why aren't personality tests generally very useful in employee selection?

Realistic Job Previews. A screening technique gaining in popularity is the **realistic job preview,** which clearly shows candidates a job's tasks or requirements, thus pointing out its good and bad aspects. American Airlines has one of the industry's best realistic job previews. Potential flight attendants are shown a variety of tasks that they would be required to learn and perform, such as safety procedures and serving techniques. In a full-sized cabin mockup at the Dallas-Fort Worth Learning Center, they get a realistic look at the job.

Interviews. In making a final selection, most human resources professionals rely on a combination of interviews and tests. Although commonly used, interviews vary in their ability to predict on-the-job performance accurately. Situational interviews that probe what the applicant would do in different situations are better predictors of performance than job-related interviews that focus on past work behavior and job-related information. In turn, job-related interviews are more valid than psychologically based interviews that assess personal traits.[18]

Additionally, an interview can be manipulated because most people can remain alert and pleasant for a thirty-minute interview. However, their behavior during the interview session may not accurately indicate how well they'll perform or relate to coworkers eight hours a day, day in and day out. Furthermore, research indicates that interviewers tend to decide about a person early in the interview and spend the rest of the time seeking information to support that decision.[19]

Interviewers are likely to make three types of errors in judgment. A **contrast error** occurs when an interviewee's rating of particularly good or bad is based on a comparison with the preceding interviewee. A **similarity error** occurs when the interviewer forms a bias in favor of candidates who look or act like the interviewer. The **halo effect** occurs when the interviewer judges the candidate's overall potential on the basis of a single characteristic (e.g., how well the candidate dresses or talks or where she or he attended college), allowing it to overshadow the candidate's other characteristics.

Despite its potential drawbacks, an interview does serve some useful purposes. It allows interviewer and applicant to learn what each has to offer the other. Although it may not determine whether someone will perform well, an interview may indicate how well an applicant will fit in with other members of the work group. Finally, human nature is such that most people simply won't hire someone they haven't met. The book, *How to Pack Your Career Parachute* that accompanies the text, lists some do's and don'ts of interviewing that should enable you to conduct useful interviews.

When you first enter the world of work, you probably will be interviewed many times before you're in a position to conduct interviews yourself. Typically, college graduates go through three types of interviews: on-campus, plant or office, and final selection. Also, you should be aware that the interviewer's approach can affect how you conduct yourself during the interview.[20] An aloof approach may stifle your responses, but a gregarious interviewer might get you to open up and be more expressive.

Tests. Many organizations use tests in addition to interviews to screen and select candidates. Tests may be oral, written, or performance based. A common type of written test, the **cognitive ability test,** measures general intelligence, verbal ability, numerical ability, reasoning ability, and so on. Such tests have proved relatively successful in predicting which applicants are qualified for certain jobs. Another type of test commonly used in industry is the performance test. A **performance test** requires a candidate to perform simulated actual job tasks. Two examples would be a typing test for secretarial candidates and a code-writing test for computer programmers.

Unlike cognitive ability and performance tests, personality tests have no right or wrong answers. **Personality** refers to the unique blend of characteristics that define an individual. Although personality sometimes plays a role in job success or failure, personality tests generally aren't considered very useful for employee selection.[21]

Drug testing is now done routinely by many organizations. Testing positive for drugs usually keeps an applicant from being hired. Penalties for existing employees who test positive depend on the organization's policies and procedures. For example, Warner Plumbing, a residential and industrial plumbing contractor in Washington, D.C., fires employees with positive test results. However, the company counsels them to give up drugs and offers them the option of reapplying for employment after remaining drug-free for six months.[22] Other organizations fire such employees without any option of re-hiring. Still other organizations provide counseling and treatment programs for employees who test positive.

Once a hotly contested issue, particularly the random testing of existing employees, drug testing is now more widely accepted as a way of organizational life. It's often accepted because of the benefits of a drug-free workplace, including reduced insurance premiums, lower turnover, and fewer workers' compensation claims.[23] Additionally, substance abuse can lower workplace productivity. Although the full extent of the impact is uncertain, workplace substance abuse is estimated to cost American businesses about $120 billion annually.[24]

Ethics
Some people believe that personality, drug, and honesty tests are an invasion of privacy. Find out what students think about such tests.

As part of the selection process, honesty tests are becoming more common because employee theft costs American businesses an estimated $40 billion annually.[25] An **honesty test** is a specialized paper-and-pencil measure that attempts to gauge a person's tendency to behave dishonestly. Some honesty tests also attempt to predict the likelihood that people will break rules, abuse sick leave privileges, or use drugs at work.[26] Honesty tests, like any other test, are subject to concerns about reliability and validity.

Test Reliability and Validity. All tests should be judged on two basic criteria: reliability and validity.[27] **Reliability** measures the degree to which a test provides consistent scores. For example, if you stepped on a bathroom scale and it read 150 pounds and a minute later you reweighed yourself and it read 140 pounds, the scale wouldn't be too reliable. **Validity** measures the degree to which a test measures what it's supposed to measure. For example, a valid test to measure an electrical engineer's knowledge wouldn't contain questions about financial statements or the history of the creative arts.

Unless a test is both reliable and valid, the organization using it won't receive a good return on its investment and may face legal action. Using invalid and/or unreliable tests to discriminate against a minority group is indefensible. Any test that is not job-related but serves to reject a disproportionate number of a protected class (African-Americans, veterans, people forty years of age and older) is discriminatory.

Teaching Tip
Many people believe that assessment centers are used only for selecting upper level managers. However, their use is quite common in filling various types of positions. (Examples: sales, police officer, and fire fighter jobs.)

Assessment Centers. An **assessment center** simulates job situations in order to assess potential employees' performance.[28] One common situational test is the in-basket exercise. Job candidates receive a stack of letters, notes, memos, telephone messages, faxes, and other items and are told to imagine that they have been promoted to a new position. They are given a specific amount of time to deal appropriately with these communications. In most cases they will have the opportunity to explain or discuss their decisions in a follow-up interview with a counselor.[29]

Orientation

Upon completion of the selection and hiring process, the employee enters orientation. **Orientation** is either a formal or an informal program that introduces new employees to their job responsibilities, their co-workers, and the organization's policies. It typically lasts one to two days.

Formal orientation programs serve two purposes. First, they inform new employees about benefits, organizational procedures, and other routine matters. Second, and more important, they orient new employees socially, by fine-tuning their job-related expectations, identifying reporting relationships, and setting a tone for their work.

Ask Students
Did your first-year student orientation program cover all of these points?

Teaching Tip
Have students generate a list of elements they feel are essential to an effective orientation program. You can help by asking them to recall things that a previous employer failed to cover.

When formal orientation programs are effective, both the newly hired employees and the organization benefit in several ways. An effective formal orientation program:

- ***Promotes realistic job expectations.*** Even experienced employees must gain a fundamental understanding of their new organization and "how things really work" because every organization has unique norms, networks of co-workers, and ways of getting things done.
- ***Promotes functional work behavior.*** Properly oriented employees can become effective quickly because they know which behaviors are valued and which are not.
- ***Reduces time and effort.*** Formal orientation programs reduce the time and effort required by managers and other professionals to train new employees. In addition, a formal orientation program ensures systematic coverage of key points.
- ***Reduces employee turnover.*** Properly oriented new employees are eased into their jobs and therefore, feeling reassured, are more apt to stay than employees thrust hurriedly into their new jobs with little orientation.

Implications for Organizations

When all phases of the staffing process operate effectively, an organization will be able to recruit and retain employees with needed skills and competencies. In addition, effective staffing also should help (1) socialize employees to the organization's culture; (2) minimize job-related performance and behavioral problems (e.g., absenteeism, turnover, and poor workmanship); (3) decrease the likelihood of discriminatory human resources actions; and (4) capitalize on the talents and perspectives of a diverse work force. In short, effective staffing enables an organization to acquire the human resources that it needs to achieve its strategic goals, as the following Quality Insight demonstrates.

Quality *Insight*

The Staffing Process at Marriott Hotels

Quality of service in the hotel industry depends on the quality and competency of the organization's employees. Recognizing this, Marriott Hotels uses a staffing process designed to provide the organization with the best qualified, dedicated, and enthusiastic work force it can find. What's its staffing process like? Let's consider a typical hotel in the Marriott chain.

At Marriott's hotel in Denver, Colorado, applicants respond to a self-administered test on a personal computer. The computer program asks questions such as: Why did you leave your last job? How well do you get along with co-workers? How well do you get along with superiors? How frequently do you get frustrated at work? How would you rate your organizational skills? Do other people think you are adaptable? The applicant responds to each question with a multiple-choice answer.

The computer program is designed to analyze the applicant's test responses and prepare a list of questions to be used by a manager in conducting a later interview. The computer analysis also reports the questions on which the applicant paused longer than normal—viewed as a potential red flag that the applicant may not be telling the complete truth.

The test responses and the interview are used to select employees who fit Marriott's needs and who are likely to remain with the company for a reasonable period of time. This selection process has contributed to a steady decline in Marriott's turnover rate. Previously, about 40 percent of new employees left during the first ninety days on the job.

Marriott also emphasizes orientation. It begins with a formal eight-hour training program. During the next ninety days each new employee is assigned a mentor for guidance. Each new employee attends refresher training sessions at the end of the first and second months. When each class of new employees completes the ninety-day orientation period, the hotel treats them to a banquet.[30]

4

Explain the components of a total compensation package.

Teaching Tip

Take a poll of the class. Ask the students if they would rather have more direct compensation and less indirect compensation or less direct compensation and more indirect compensation? Younger students tend to prefer more direct compensation and less indirect compensation because they tend to be healthier and less concerned about retirement.

MANAGING TOTAL COMPENSATION

The purpose of any compensation system is to reward employees equitably, to provide the means to attract potential new employees, and to motivate and retain good employees. As shown in Figure 12.5, a total compensation system has two major components: direct compensation and indirect compensation. **Direct compensation** is a person's base wage or salary and any incentive pay received. **Indirect compensation** is benefits required by law (e.g., social security contributions and unemployment compensation) and those provided voluntarily by the employer (e.g., medical insurance, retirement plans, and life insurance).

Base Wage or Salary

The two main approaches to establishing the base wage or salary for employees are job-based pay and skill-based pay. With **job-based pay,** compensation is linked to the specific tasks a person performs. To establish the pay level, a **job evaluation** is done to determine the monetary worth of the job's important characteristics. Job-based pay has been widely used in the past, but it presents some serious problems for organizations. In particular, job-based pay

- reinforces an organizational culture that emphasizes hierarchy and centralized decision making and control, and limits employee participation;
- creates status differentials that can foster competition rather than cooperation among people; and
- may fail to reward the work behavior that is necessary for organizations to adapt and survive in a rapidly changing environment.[31]

FIGURE 12.5

Components of a Total Compensation System

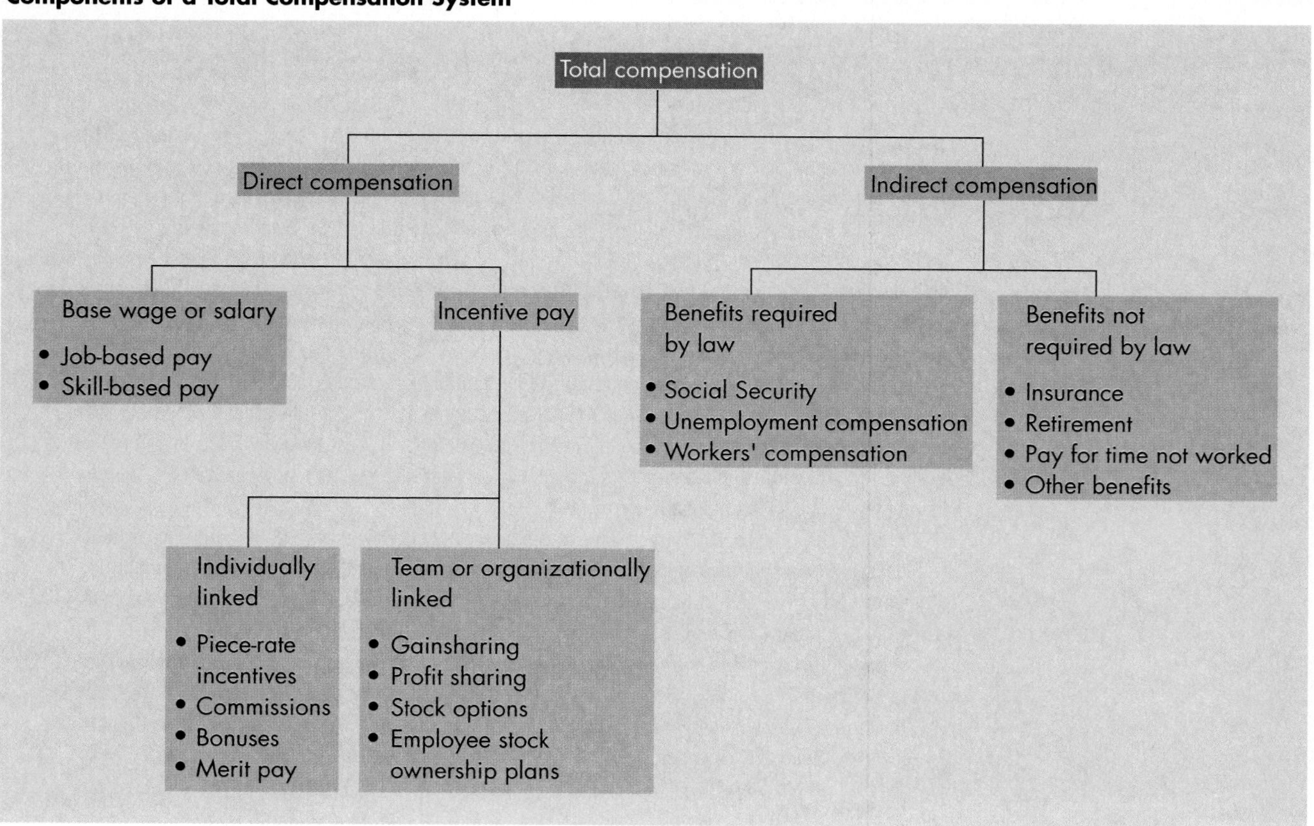

Skill-based pay links compensation to people's skills and knowledge. Employees with more skills and knowledge receive higher pay than those with less skills and knowledge. Skill-based pay encourages employees to learn additional skills, thereby becoming more valuable to the organization. As a result, the organization is more flexible and adaptable to changing demands. With a more flexible work force, the organization may need fewer employees and thus reduce human resources costs. Also, productivity and product or service quality may be enhanced.

Whether an organization uses job-based pay or skill-based pay for establishing the base wage or salary, it should strive for equity in its compensation system. Equity, which concerns fairness, can dramatically affect employee work motivation and job performance. (We discuss the motivational basis of equity in Chapter 13.) When the compensation system is equitable, employees are more likely to do their jobs well and to be committed to the organization than when employees perceive the compensation system to be inequitable. Inequitable pay can result in a variety of counterproductive employee behaviors.[32]

Sometimes a company will establish a reward system with the best of intentions only to discover that it creates perceptions of inequity—and thus is ineffective. Only by changing the reward system can inequity be resolved, as the following Small Business Insight illustrates.

Small Business *Insight*

Inequity and Equity at Modern of Marshfield

Modern of Marshfield, a furniture manufacturer with 100 employees in Marshfield, Wisconsin, tried two different reward systems to motivate employees to submit cost-saving suggestions. Initially, Bill Mork, Modern's CEO, implemented a reward system that was run by management and relied on recognition. After reviewing all employee suggestions that had been implemented during the month, the company's managers selected a "colleague of the month." This person didn't receive any cash but was honored with a special parking place and a handshake in front of the assembled employees. The results of the reward program were disappointing—very few suggestions were offered, and winners were called "brown-nosers" by their co-workers.

Mork decided to change the reward system. Now, whenever the company implements an employee suggestion, he or she gets a cash award of 10 percent of the estimated savings. An additional 10 percent of the estimated savings goes into a fund, the proceeds of which are distributed annually to all employees who have made useful suggestions. Employees who have had their suggestions implemented participate in monthly drawings for prizes ranging from T-shirts to televisions. A colleague of the month is still selected, but now it is done by a panel of the six previous winners. The employee selected as colleague of the year wins an expenses-paid trip for two to an exotic location.

Employees are now submitting about 1,200 suggestions a year— approximately one per employee per month. Employees' attitudes changed when they saw people getting checks. The winners weren't perceived as brown-nosers any longer. As Mork says, "Suddenly, the winner became someone who could buy a round of beer."[33]

The employees of Modern of Marshfield probably were unmotivated by the first reward system because they perceived it to be inequitable. Employees whose suggestions were implemented didn't perceive the reward to be enough in relation to those not making suggestions. This situation of perceived inequity changed with the second reward system. Employees then perceived that they were being rewarded more fairly for their suggestions.

Incentive Pay

Incentive pay (or pay for performance) is intended to link at least a portion of pay to job performance to encourage superior performance. According to W. Edwards Deming, one of the most influential persons in the field of quality, incentives are essential for a business to change and survive.[34] But incentives must be used properly to encourage and reward employee behaviors that help achieve the organization's goals.

Incentive pay has several advantages and disadvantages. The benefits of incentive pay include:

- ***Motivation.*** Linking pay to performance increases employee motivation to perform. Superior performance is encouraged and inferior performance is discouraged.
- ***Retention.*** High performers are more motivated to stay with an organization when they are rewarded more generously than poor performers.
- ***Productivity.*** Because incentive pay encourages superior performance and discourages inferior performance, an organization's productivity can be improved.
- ***Cost savings.*** Cost savings result from productivity improvements and from the organization's ability to match compensation costs and performance levels better.
- ***Organizational goals.*** Incentive pay helps in aligning individual goals with organizational goals.[35]

Although incentive pay is an attractive compensation option for organizations, it isn't problem free. In particular, managers need to be aware of problems of trust, time consumption, and union opposition:

- ***Trust.*** The organization must have an effective performance appraisal system, and employees must trust management to use the system equitably.
- ***Time consumption.*** Successfully administering a pay-for-performance system is more time-consuming than using a base wage or salary system with periodic across-the-board increases.
- ***Union opposition.*** Many unions tend to oppose pay-for-performance systems based on individual performance or demand strict rules to guide their use. But they are more receptive to systems that are based on team, plant, or companywide performance.[36]

Individually Linked Incentive Pay. As indicated in Figure 12.5, individually based incentive pay includes piece-rate incentives, commissions, bonuses, and merit pay. **Piece-rate incentives** involve the adjustment of a fixed amount of money paid for each unit of output produced when the number of units produced exceeds a standard output rate.[37] The more an employee exceeds the standard output, the greater is the rate of incentive pay. Piece-rate incentives tend to focus employees on those aspects of the job that increase their own output. Other useful activities such as machine maintenance or the training of new employees may be neglected.

Ethics
Some people argue that pay based on a piece rate discriminates against older workers who tend to be slower than younger workers. Is an ethical issue involved? If so, what is it?

Typically used with salespeople, **commissions** are compensation based on a percentage of total sales. Some salespeople work on a base salary plus commission. Others work on a straight commission basis, with all their direct compensation being incentive pay. Unfortunately, this creates a temptation for some individuals to use high-pressure sales tactics or to behave unethically in order to generate income. For example, stockbrokers at Prudential Bache's Dallas office made unauthorized trades for clients just to generate commissions. After paying a huge fine, Prudential Bache stopped this practice.

Ethics
Has anyone in the class worked on commission? Are there any ethical problems with this system?

Bonuses are lump-sum payments given for achieving a particular performance goal. Bonuses may be one-time payments linked to nonrepetitive goals. For instance, the Lawrence, Kansas, plant of Quaker Oats bases part of its annual lump sum payouts on the achievement of goals, such as completing plant training on schedule, maintaining employee participation levels, and developing departmental mission statements.[38] Bonuses also may be linked to the annual achievement of continuing performance goals. At Duke Power Company, cash awards to employees in thirty different business units are based on the company's achieving its targeted return on equity and the business unit's realizing its specific goals.[39]

Merit pay is a permanent increase in base pay linked to an individual's performance during the preceding year. Annual pay raises for faculty members at many colleges and universities are linked to their performance in (1) teaching, (2) research and scholarship, and (3) professional, university, and community service during the preceding academic or calendar year.

Ask Students
What potential problems might arise with merit pay plans?

Team- or Organizationally Linked Incentive Pay. Figure 12.5 identified three types of team or organizationally linked incentive pay: gainsharing, profit sharing, and stock ownership (either stock options or employee stock ownership plans). In a **gainsharing reward system,** teams of employees share in the gains (or cost savings) realized by measurable improvements in productivity. Typically, the amount of the reward varies from team to team because of differences in their amount of improvement. In one hospital, for instance, departments (e.g., cardiac care, intensive care, and medical management) that substantially exceeded their productivity improvement targets received a larger share of the gain than departments (e.g., dietary, rehabilitation, and home health care) that just met their goals. Departments that didn't meet their productivity improvement goals did not receive a reward under the gainsharing system.[40] Recent research indicates that about 2,000 companies—including Bell & Howell, Champion Spark Plug, Adolph Coors, Hooker Chemical, Weyerhaeuser, and many others—use gainsharing programs to help them achieve their goals.[41]

Unlike gainsharing, profit sharing isn't linked to measurable productivity improvements that teams of employees can control.[42] Rather, **profit sharing** is based on the actual profits a business earns and rewards employees with a share of those profits. The link between individual performance and an organization's profits may be relatively weak; thus profit sharing may not have as much effect on individual performance as a gainsharing system. Profit sharing may be restricted to managers and/or key executives, or it may involve all employees.

Like profit sharing, stock ownership may be restricted to certain people or made available to all employees. Stock ownership may take the form of stock options or an employee stock ownership plan. **Stock options** give employees the right to buy the company's stock at a specified price. Traditionally, stock options have been limited to key managers, but companies now are making stock options available to most, if not all, of their employees. Companies such as Rockwell International, Kroger, and AT&T use **employee stock ownership plans (ESOPs)** to provide employees throughout the organization with shares of their stock. A company with an ESOP either contributes shares of its stock or cash to purchase shares on the open market. The shares owned by the ESOP are then allocated among individual employee accounts. Employees become shareholders just as like anyone else who invests in the company. Stock ownership may increase motivation and commitment but not unless employees perceive a clear linkage between individual and organizational performance.[43]

Benefits Required by Law

Teaching Tip
Bring in a pay stub and show students what these deductions mean and amount to.

Employers are obligated by law to provide certain benefits for their employees. These legally mandated benefits include social security, unemployment compensation, workers' compensation, and family and medical leave.

Social Security. Under the *Federal Insurance Contribution Act (FICA) of 1935* (commonly called the Social Security Act) and subsequent amendments, most employers are required to contribute financially to the *social security* of their employees. The Social Security system provides retirement income, disability income, survivors' benefits, and Medicare coverage to employees and their dependents—if they meet certain eligibility criteria. In 1995, employers' FICA contributions for each employee amounted to 7.65 percent of the employee's earnings up to a maximum of $61,200.

Unemployment Compensation. As a benefit for employees, unemployment compensation is intended to offset lost income during involuntary unemployment and to help unemployed workers secure new jobs. Employers must contribute to this program, though not all employers contribute equally. The rate that employers pay varies from state to state, as does the amount of employee earnings upon which the unemployment compensation tax is paid. Additionally, within each state the amount of tax an employer pays is influenced by the employer's history of layoffs. Companies with a history of periodically laying off a large percentage of their work force pay more unemployment tax than organizations with a history of fewer layoffs.

Workers' Compensation. As specified by the *Workers' Compensation Act,* this benefit is designed to compensate people for work-related injuries or diseases. The benefits that employees could receive include disability income, medical care, rehabilitative services, and death benefits for their families. Like unemployment compensation, the cost of workers' compensation varies by state and the organization's record.

Family and Medical Leave. The *Family and Medical Leave Act of 1993* requires employers with fifty or more employees to grant up to twelve weeks unpaid leave annually for the birth or adoption of a child, to care for a spouse or an immediate member of the family with a serious health condition, or when the employee is unable to work because of a serious health condition. Employers are required to maintain preexisting health coverage during the leave period and, once the leave is concluded, to reinstate the employee to the same or an equivalent job. To be eligible, employees must have worked at the organization for at least one year.

Teaching Tip
Give each student the same amount of play money and allow them to choose their own package of benefits from a list that includes prices. Ask them to discuss their choices.

Benefits Not Required by Law

A variety of benefits are provided voluntarily by employers or as a result of union negotiations. These benefits fall into four broad categories: insurance, retirement, pay for time not worked, and other.

Insurance. Health insurance is probably the type of insurance most often included in a benefits package. All or part of the insurance premium is paid by the employer. Coverage of major medical costs and hospitalization is the most common component of health insurance. In addition, many employers' insurance plans provide dental, vision, and/or psychiatric coverage.[44]

In addition to health insurance, employers may provide group life insurance, accidental death and dismemberment insurance, and/or disability insurance as part of the benefits package. These insurance plans provide financial compensation to the employee or the employees' family in the event of the employee's death or inability to work.

Retirement. In addition to the retirement benefits provided by Social Security, many companies sponsor retirement plans for their employees. A **defined benefit retirement plan** is funded by the employer and relies on some type of formula for specifying participant benefits. Each plan participant might receive, say, a monthly benefit of $30 for each year of service. In a **defined contribution retirement plan,** each participant has a retirement account that is funded by contributions by the employer, the employee, or both. Most companies with pension plans use a defined contribution plan.[45]

Pay for Time Not Worked. Pay for time not worked includes holidays, vacation, sick leave, bereavement leave, and paid personal days. Some employers even provide paid leaves immediately before or after the birth of a child.

Other Benefits. Employers frequently provide benefits other than insurance coverage, retirement programs, and pay for time not worked. For example, J.C. Penney pro-

A variety of benefits may be provided voluntarily or as a result of union negotiations. For example, Bethlehem Steel provides employees with an in-house health care clinic.

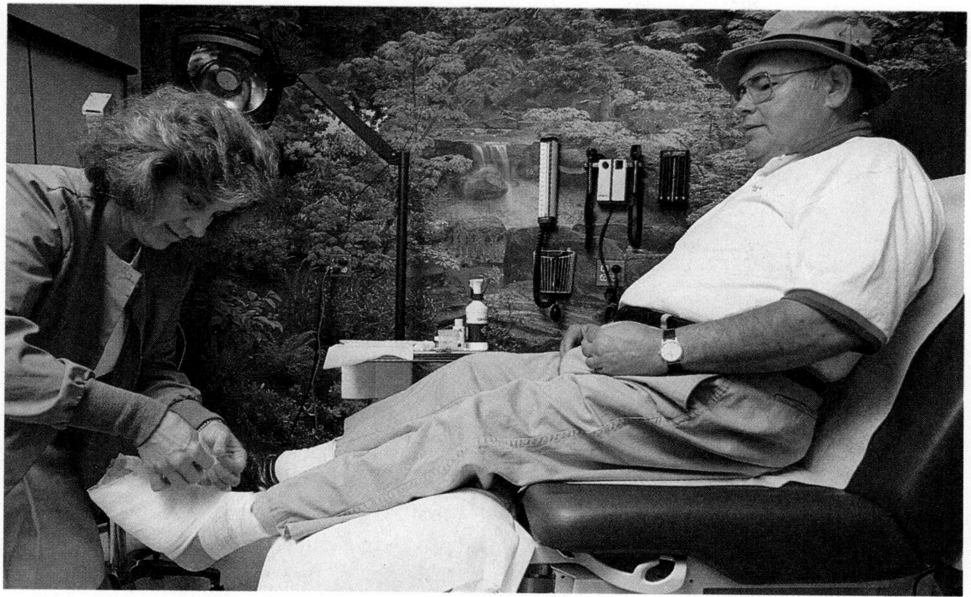

vides educational assistance and child or elder care assistance to employees throughout the organization. Extra benefits provided for managers and executives are known as **perquisites** (perks). Among the more common perks are company cars, country club memberships, professional or trade association memberships, financial planning advice, and expense accounts.

Implications for Organizations

An organization's compensation system can dramatically affect employee behavior. Thus incentive programs should be designed and administered to reward employees for performance-related behaviors that contribute to the organization's success. However, an incentive pay system may reward employees for unethical behavior. Recall the Sears Auto Service debacle presented in Chapter 1. Sears established a sales quota and incentive system that prompted employees to sell unnecessary auto repairs to customers. Subsequently, Sears changed its incentive system to eliminate the problem.

Discussion Question 5
Describe the options that an organization has in designing its total compensation system. What advantages and disadvantages do they have for employer and employee alike.

A total compensation plan should be used to reinforce and support other organizational systems and procedures. Job-based pay and individualized incentives can be used effectively in organizations having a traditional culture that emphasizes top-down decision making, narrowly defined jobs, direct supervision, limited employee involvement, and the like. Skill-based pay and group or organizationwide incentives are more appropriate for organizations having a high commitment-high performance culture that stresses teamwork, participation, and self- and peer supervision.[46]

5
Discuss several methods of appraising performance and problems arising from the subjective nature of the process.

PERFORMANCE APPRAISALS

One of the chief responsibilities of managers is to assess their employees' performance. Their evaluations influence who is promoted, demoted, transferred, and dismissed, and the size of the raise each employee receives. Managers usually have to explain ratings to their subordinates, who may—in fact, probably will—disagree with them in at least some respects.[47]

Performance appraisal is the process of systematically evaluating each employee's job-related strengths, developmental needs, and progress toward achieving goals, and then determining ways to improve the employee's job performance. This function is essential if the organization is to reward fairly the efforts of good perform-

Teaching Tip
Get students who have had a performance appraisal at work describe how it was structured. Have them state whether they felt the appraisal was fair and effective and why or why not.

Teaching Tip
Have each student set a performance goal for this term in general and this class in particular. Discuss some of these goals.

ers, redirect the efforts of struggling performers, and know when to let inadequate performers go. However, performance appraisal continues to be a challenging human resources management issue.

Relation to Goal Setting

An important part of performance appraisal involves an assessment of each employee's progress toward achieving his or her goals. Goals should have two primary attributes if they are to be effective in motivating people to perform in a superior manner.

- Goals should be clear and specific so that an employee knows what is to be achieved. Unclear and nonspecific goals force employees to guess at performance expectations and how their performance will be reviewed.
- Goals should be challenging for people, yet be within their reach if they work hard and use their abilities and skills.[48]

Being committed to a goal enhances motivation. Consider, for example, your experiences with student project teams. You probably observed that students who were committed to the goal of receiving an "A" for the team project were highly motivated and worked hard. In contrast, students who weren't committed to the goal probably did as little work as possible, being willing to settle for whatever grade the other members' work produced.

Feedback also is essential for the goal-setting process to be effective. Regular assessment of progress toward attaining goals helps employees remain motivated and solve any problems that might arise. Regular feedback also helps the individual to focus on skill development needs. One innovative way to provide employees with feedback is the **360-degree appraisal system** that gathers feedback from an employee's colleagues inside the company and people outside the organization with whom the employee does business.[49] Finally, regular feedback encourages periodic reexamination of goals to determine whether they should be adjusted. Goals may need to be made clearer or more specific, or they made need to be made more difficult to challenge a fast-track employee.

Uses of Performance Appraisals

Performance appraisals can be invaluable aids for making many human resources management decisions. A particularly important use is to help managers distinguish between good and poor performers.

Reward Decisions. We've already indicated that many organizations try to motivate employees by basing pay, bonuses, and other financial rewards on performance. To do so, organizations must have a method for accurately measuring employee performance. (We discuss performance measurement methods later in this chapter.)

Personnel Movement. Performance appraisal information also helps guide decisions about personnel movement. Who should receive a promotion? Who should be transferred, demoted, or terminated? All such personnel movements should be based on performance-related factors, not gender, race, age, or other unrelated factors. Using any of these other factors as the basis for promotion, demotion, transfer, or termination decisions would constitute employment discrimination.

Feedback on Performance. A primary purpose of any performance appraisal system is to improve job performance. Performance reviews should provide employees with feedback about their specific strengths and developmental needs. They also should provide guidelines for building on those strengths and addressing those developmental needs.

Training Needs. Identifying areas of inadequate performance allows the manager to suggest training programs to improve certain skills. Training programs may range from classes that teach specific tasks—such as how to operate a forklift—to those designed to develop proficiency in a skill such as communications.

Problems with Performance Appraisals

Most people who have given or received a performance appraisal would agree that a major problem is its subjective nature. Let's briefly examine four errors commonly made when giving performance appraisals.

Rater Characteristics. Characteristics of the rater exert a subtle and often indirect influence on performance appraisals. Younger and less experienced managers, who may have received low evaluations themselves, tend to rate others more strictly than do older, more experienced managers. Managers who have high self-esteem, low anxiety, good social skills, and emotional stability give more accurate performance appraisals than managers with the opposite personality traits.[50]

Leniency. **Leniency** occurs when an individual rates all employees in a group higher than they deserve. Leniency is particularly likely to occur when there are no organizational norms against high ratings and when rewards aren't tied to performance appraisals. Tying rewards to appraisals places a natural limit on the number of high ratings a manager can give and the organization can afford.

Ask Students
How could a manager in a small organization avoid the halo effect when appraising subordinates' performance?

Halo Effect. The halo effect occurs in rating when the rater's knowledge of an employee's performance on one dimension colors the rating on all others. In some cases an equal rating on all dimensions doesn't reflect an error in judgment—an employee may actually perform all tasks equally well or equally poorly. However, most people do some tasks better than other tasks, so their ratings should vary from one performance dimension to another.

Ask Students
Have you ever been a victim of any of these four biases? Explain.

Real-World Example
Forty-nine-year-old Lt. Commander Mary C. Murphy, Ph.D., a U.S. Navy reservist, was in a performance appraisal interview in the Pentagon with her immediate supervisor, Captain Charles C. Chadborn III on July 25, 1993. He allegedly told her that "the only performance I will rank you on is in bed." Later he is said to have added, "If you don't give me what I want, I'll destroy your career." He lowered her fitness report and changed his recommendation for promotion to against promotion after learning that she had told others of his alleged proposition. He denied the allegations. The Navy's two investigations have not resulted in a conclusion. As it launched a third investigation, Captain Chadborn was given a new command (*Los Angeles Times,* March 1, 1995, E1-E2).

Central Tendency. **Central tendency** is a rating error that occurs when a manager rates all employees "average," even when their performance varies. Managers with broad spans of control and little opportunity to observe behavior are likely to play it safe by rating most of their subordinates in the middle of the scale rather than high or low.

Political Issues in Performance Appraisal

Any realistic discussion of performance appraisal must recognize that organizations are more or less political places. Office politics may play a role in deciding who gets what raise, promotion, or demotion. Research reveals that political considerations nearly always influence performance appraisal because

- a formal written document is generated,
- interpersonal relationships with subordinates may be affected, and
- subordinates' advancement and careers may be affected.[51]

If politics play too large a role in performance appraisal, the consequences may be serious. Organizational goals and performance may be undermined. The link between performance and pay may be weakened. Political manipulation of other organizational systems and processes may be encouraged. The organization may be subject to litigation for employment discrimination, particularly in the case of terminations. Organizations can minimize the politicization of the appraisal process by developing and communicating clear and specific goals and standards, linking performance to results, and providing employees with periodic, accurate feedback on their performance.[52]

Ask Students
Can politics ever be removed from the performance appraisal process?

Fit with Total Quality Management

Throughout this chapter we have suggested that human resources management policies and programs should fit the organization's overall strategy, tactics, policies, and procedures that it uses to achieve its goals. Although performance appraisal long has been an important HRM activity, some advocates of total quality management (TQM) suggest that traditional performance appraisals are incompatible with TQM in several respects:

- ***Assessment orientation.*** Traditional performance appraisal focuses on individual goals and performance standards. TQM focuses on the process and the system, emphasizing team, departmental, and organizational performance.
- ***Promotion of teamwork.*** Being individually oriented, traditional performance appraisal undermines teamwork. Being systems oriented, TQM promotes teamwork.
- ***Responsibility for failure.*** Traditional performance appraisal places responsibility for failure on the individual. Many TQM experts attribute up to 90 percent of all performance problems to management practices, such as poor selection and inadequate training.
- ***System variability.*** Traditional performance appraisal does not account for the normal variability inherent in any system. TQM recognizes normal system variability and tries to reduce it.
- ***Pursuit of excellence.*** Traditional performance appraisal may encourage establishing safe goals, thereby fostering mediocrity. TQM encourages continuing improvement throughout the organization.
- ***Personal versus collective gain.*** Traditional performance appraisal may encourage some people to manipulate or avoid the system for personal gain. TQM focuses on improving the system for collective gain.[53]

Do these conflicts between traditional performance appraisal and total quality management mean that companies adopting a TQM approach no longer assess individual performance? Not at all. The following Quality Insight describes how Ensoniq Corporation considers individual performance in the context of its TQM approach.

Quality *Insight*

Performance Reviews at Ensoniq Corporation

Ensoniq Corporation began business as a low-cost producer of electronic keyboards for musicians. Later it adopted a total quality management approach in order to compete effectively in the global market for electronic keyboards. As the business grew, Ensoniq developed a line of computer-programmable hearing aids. In adopting TQM, Ensoniq followed W. Edwards Deming's philosophy that the ratings typically used in traditional performance appraisal can hurt motivation, morale, and performance. Comparisons of individual performance means that about half the employees will be rated as performing below average and about half above average. When such ratings are used in making compensation decisions, some employees may perceive inequity and their motivation, morale, and performance might suffer. Consequently, Ensoniq doesn't use traditional performance appraisals. Instead, it uses performance reviews to promote employee development and keeps the reviews completely separate from compensation decisions.

At Ensoniq, the purpose of the performance review is to encourage dialogue between employee and manager regarding ways to enhance performance. Reviews, which occur every four months, focus on an employee's total effectiveness in terms of communication skills, leadership, adaptability, and initiative. Emphasis is placed on both the employee's achievements and developmental needs. The performance reviews are qualitative rather than quantitative. Quantitative measures of performance aren't needed in Ensoniq's review system because the company's TQM system provides immediate and direct quantitative feedback to employees.

Although Ensoniq doesn't use a traditional performance appraisal system, it still assesses individual performance. However, it is designed to promote the teamwork behaviors that contribute to TQM's effectiveness.[54]

Methods of Performance Appraisal

The problems that we've discussed highlight the difficulties encountered in assessing employee performance objectively. Most attempts to solve these problems have focused on devising new methods of appraising performance. As a result, many different types of rating formats and evaluation techniques are used. Here we focus on three general types: the ranking, graphic rating, and behavioral rating methods.

Ranking. The **ranking method** appraises performance by comparing employees doing the same or similar work. In simple ranking, the rater lists employees from best to worst. A variation of this method, alternation ranking, requires the rater to select the best and worst employees, then the second best, the second worst, and so on.

Teaching Tip
Discuss with the students the advantages and disadvantages of the ranking method.

Teaching Tip
The quality of students' high schools may have affected their decisions about which colleges they applied to.

The ranking method is easy to use. It also reduces the effects of leniency because the rater can't give everyone a high evaluation. Rankings are especially useful for making defensible promotion decisions or reducing the size of the work force. The manager can simply select names from the top down on the list until all promotion vacancies are filled—or from the bottom up until all necessary work-force reductions are made.

The ranking method has several disadvantages, though, which limit its usefulness for certain appraisal purposes. Because rankings tend to be based on overall performance, they aren't very useful in providing specific feedback. For an employee to know that she is ranked fourth out of ten people, for example, doesn't tell her what she needs to do to become the top-ranked employee, or even number two. Furthermore, rankings indicate that one person is performing better than another, but not by how much or in what ways. Thus the ranking method is of limited use in making pay decisions. Determining equitable pay raises requires knowledge about the degree of difference among those who are evaluated. Another disadvantage of the ranking method is that raters must be familiar with the performance of all employees being ranked, which effectively limits the number of employees who can be evaluated by each rater.

Graphic Rating. The **graphic rating method** of performance appraisal evaluates employees on a series of performance dimensions, usually along a five- or seven-point scale. Such scales are the most widely used form of performance evaluation. A typical rating scale may be from 1 to 5, with 1 representing poor performance and 5 representing outstanding performance. Figure 12.6 illustrates four common rating scales that could be used to evaluate a salesperson's sales volume. The more clearly and specifically the scales and the performance dimensions are defined, the better.

Teaching Tip
Have students break into groups of 5–8 and design a BARS for the job of student in this class. Observe the groups and help them write behavioral descriptions. When they have finished, have them discuss how difficult measuring performance is.

Behavioral Rating. A **behaviorally anchored rating scale (BARS)** describes specific job behaviors along a continuum of intensity. It is similar to the graphic rating method in that a numerical scale typically is used to measure a range of performance. However, BARS differs from graphic rating in terms of the level of descriptive detail for each point on the scale. An example of a behaviorally anchored rating scale that can be used to assess student oral presentations is shown in Figure 12.7.

Ask Students
Can a graphic rating method of performance appraisal be objective? Why or why not?

The specificity of BARS is both an advantage and a disadvantage. The advantage is that performance-related behaviors are described carefully and in detail. Therefore it is useful in providing specific performance feedback to the person being evaluated. The disadvantage is that developing a behavioral scale can be time-consuming and costly because of the precise observable descriptions of behaviors that are required.

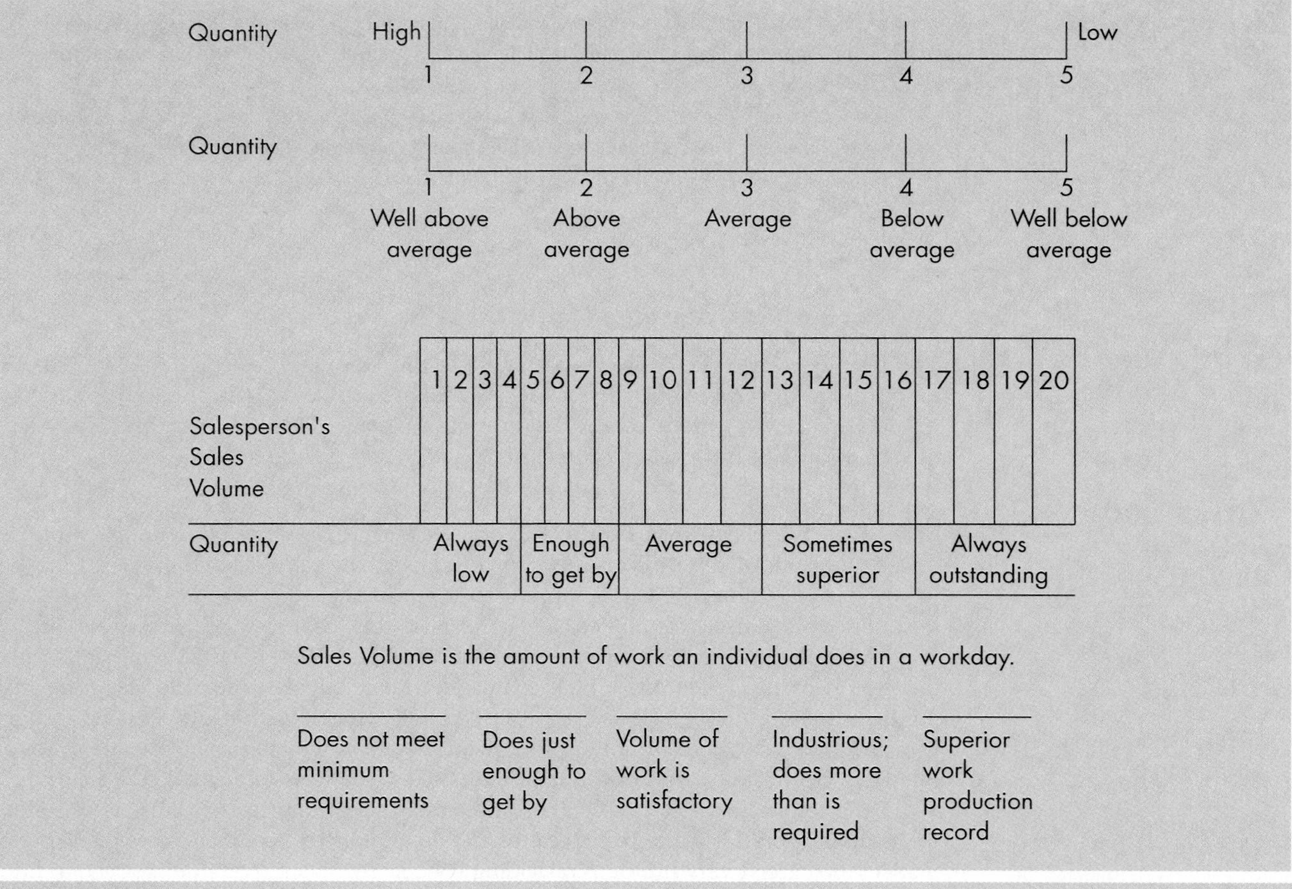

FIGURE 12.6

Samples of Rating Scale Formats

Source: Adapted from Schuler, R.S., and Huber, V.L. *Personnel and Human Resource Management,* 5th ed., St. Paul, Minn.: West, 1995, 297.

Performance Appraisal Interviews

Performance appraisal isn't a single act or a particular form used to evaluate job behavior. After using one of the forms to evaluate an employee, the manager must communicate his or her performance appraisal judgments to the employee. The manager usually does so in a performance appraisal interview.

During the interview, the manager and the employee should exchange information about the employee's strengths and developmental needs. Managers often keep a diary to record actual events that illustrate effective and ineffective behaviors of the employee. Allowing the employee to respond to these observations makes the session meaningful to both the manager and employee. When the manager listens carefully and responds to the employee, the employee receives positive reinforcement. The focus should be on job-related performance, not on personality, habits, or mannerisms, that don't affect job performance. Finally, the manager and employee should mutually agree on goals for improvement.

After conducting appraisal interviews, managers should follow subordinates' progress and reward them for performance improvements. Communicating about performance is as important after the interview as it is before. By making valued rewards—such as merit pay raises and praise—contingent on accomplishing goals, managers can motivate subordinates to succeed.

FIGURE 12.7

Sample of a Behaviorally Anchored Rating Scale (BARS)

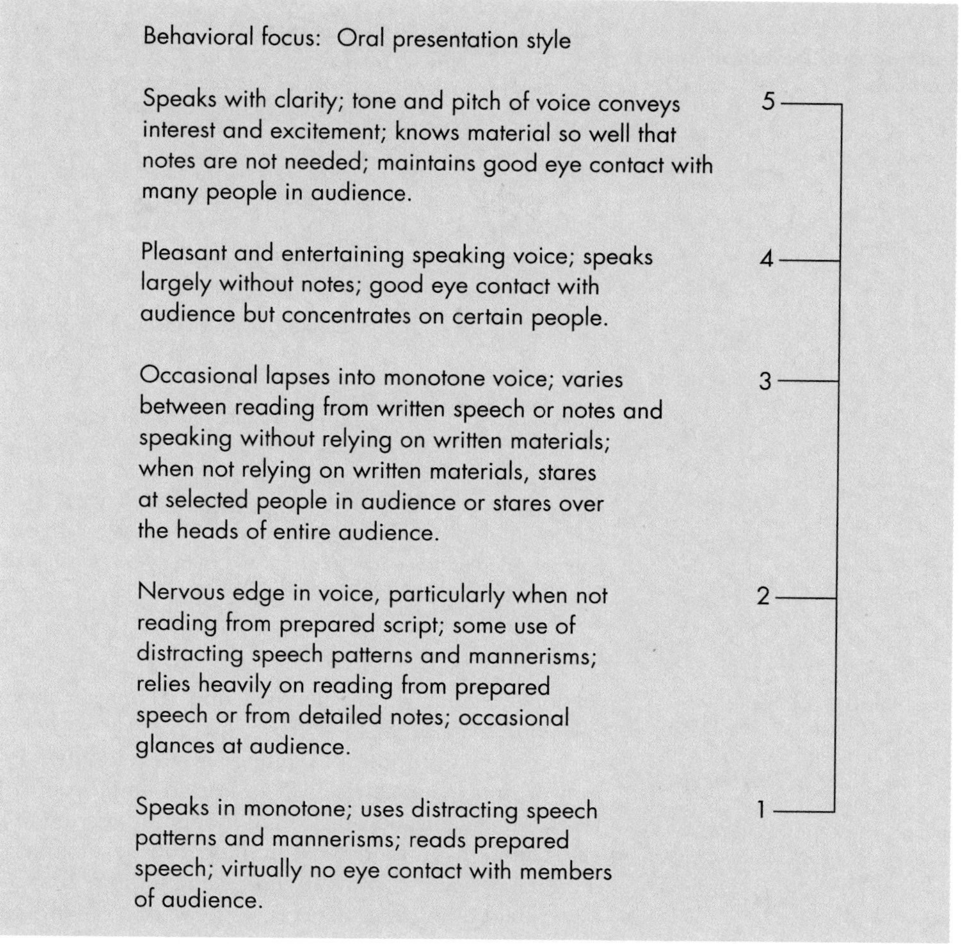

Behavioral focus: Oral presentation style
Speaks with clarity; tone and pitch of voice conveys interest and excitement; knows material so well that notes are not needed; maintains good eye contact with many people in audience.
5
Pleasant and entertaining speaking voice; speaks largely without notes; good eye contact with audience but concentrates on certain people.
4
Occasional lapses into monotone voice; varies between reading from written speech or notes and speaking without relying on written materials; when not relying on written materials, stares at selected people in audience or stares over the heads of entire audience.
3
Nervous edge in voice, particularly when not reading from prepared script; some use of distracting speech patterns and mannerisms; relies heavily on reading from prepared speech or from detailed notes; occasional glances at audience.
2
Speaks in monotone; uses distracting speech patterns and mannerisms; reads prepared speech; virtually no eye contact with members of audience.
1

Implications for Organizations

Like all the other human resources management activities, the review of employee performance should be consistent with and support the organization's strategic goals, culture, and operating systems and procedures. For example, in organizations having a low-cost strategy, such as Wal-Mart, ways to increase employee's efficiency should be stressed. Extensive use of part-time help is needed and those employees must be capable for performing routine jobs with little training. In organizations pursuing a differentiated strategy based on outstanding customer service, such as Nordstrom or Arthur Anderson, employees must be able to work in teams, solve customer problems collaboratively, and work without direct supervision. In each type of organization, the performance appraisal system should foster the behaviors that are needed to remain competitive. If employees lack certain skills, training and development activities should be offered to help those employees grow in the job.

6

Explain how training and development programs can improve employee performance.

TRAINING AND DEVELOPMENT

In the United States, organizations spend tens of billions of dollars every year on formal training and development programs to improve employees' knowledge and skills. These training programs encompass a variety of basic skills; customer relations; customer service or field service; executive education; environmental health and safety; equal employment opportunity issues; specific job skills; management and supervisory skills; pro-

TABLE 12.5

Training and Development Methods

Method	Advantage(s)	Disadvantage(s)
Job rotation	Provides exposure to many jobs; real learning experience	Doesn't convey full sense of responsibility; time on each job is too short
Programmed instruction	Provides individualized learning and feedback	Time-consuming to develop; cost-effective only for large groups
Videotape	Conveys consistent information to all employees	Doesn't provide for individual feedback
Simulation	Creates lifelike situations to teach interpersonal skills	Can't always duplicate real situations; costly to design and run
Role playing	Gives insights into others' jobs; focuses on interpersonal skills	Can't create real situations
Interactive video	Self-paced learning with computer feedback	Costly to develop and requires staff to implement

Source: Adapted from Schuler, R.S., and Huber, V.L. *Personnel and Human Resource Management,* 5th ed. St. Paul, Minn.: West, 1995, 522.

Real-World Example
Fortune 1000 firms recently have reduced training budgets by 54 percent, according to a survey conducted by the American Society for Training and Development (*The Wall Street Journal,* February 20, 1995, A3).

fessional, scientific, engineering, and technical skills; quality management skills; and sales and marketing skills.[55]

The main purpose of training and development is to overcome the limitations, current or anticipated, that are causing an employee to perform at less than the desired level. An organization may save money by recruiting trained individuals, but many organizations have found that training and development programs are preferable to hiring experienced employees. For example, EDS has found that hiring "green" recruits is better than hiring experienced workers from other organizations because it doesn't have to *retrain* the new employees to do things its way. Because training and development are so important and so costly, organizations want them carried out as effectively as possible.

Training for the Job

Training refers to improving an employee's skills to the point where he or she can do the current job. Training methods often used by organizations are listed in Table 12.5, along with their primary advantages and disadvantages. Although training is important in all organizations, it is essential in organizations that provide a standardized service to their customers.

Ethics
Many executives complain that the cost of providing remedial education to workers is driving up the costs of their products and making them uncompetitively higher than foreign-produced goods. Ethically, who is responsible for ensuring that workers have basic skills?

Many organizations (General Dynamics, Delta Wire, and Collins & Aikman, among others) provide basic skills training for employees who are unable to read, write, do arithmetic, or solve problems well enough to perform even simple tasks. These employees cannot write letters to customers, read warning labels on chemical containers, or understand machine operating symbols. Consequently, many organizations spend large sums of money on remedial training programs for employees. These organizations believe that if employees can master certain basic skills, they can perform a wider variety of jobs and better deal with new technologies.[56]

Development Programs

The intent of **development programs** is to improve an employee's conceptual and human skills in preparation for future jobs. With the increasingly complex demands placed on managers and other professionals, many organizations invest a great deal of time and money in development programs. Before sending an employee to a development program, a needs analysis is made to identify that person's particular strengths and developmental needs. These developmental needs usually include the lack of ability to set goals with others, negotiate interpersonal conflicts, and conduct performance appraisal reviews.[57]

On-the-Job Programs. On-the-job development programs are tailored to fit the individual's specific needs. For example, Hoechst Celanese requires all of its managers to attend at least forty hours of management development programs each year at one of its development centers. Such programs help managers gain insight into how the organization operates, upgrade specific managerial skills, learn team building processes, and become familiar with TQM methods.

Teaching Tip
Bring in a brochure on a university-based executive program and pass it around the class.

[**Discussion Question 6**
What are the advantages of on-the-job training and development programs? Do such programs eliminate the need for off-the-job training? Why or why not?

Off-the-Job Programs. Off-the-job development programs remove employees from the stress and daily routines of their jobs, enabling them to focus on the learning experience. Because employees from various organizations attend such programs, participants learn not only from the instructor but also from their peers.

Some organizations send selected employees to university-sponsored management development programs. Penn State, Duke, Northwestern, Dartmouth, Harvard, and Stanford, among others, offer such programs, which run from two to sixteen weeks. Many managers who attend such programs are slated for either a promotion or assignment to a different division or department. The organization wants to broaden these managers' perspectives and prepare them for general (as opposed to functional) management positions.

Training and Development for Global Assignments

One of the increasingly important challenges for organizations is preparing people to be **expatriate employees** working in a nation other than their home country. Without this preparation, such employees may not be able to take on and successfully complete an overseas assignment. Table 12.6 identifies some of the issues that organizations must address in preparing their employees for a foreign assignment.

TABLE 12.6

Typical Issues Facing Expatriate Employees

- What is the host country's business culture like? What is its management style? How do managers handle relationships with employees? How do they go about getting things done?
- What role does work play in people's lives in the host country?
- What skills qualify the employee for this assignment? What other job skills will the employee need to develop?
- How will this assignment affect the employee's career?
- What is the country like? What are its customs? Can the employee adjust to the culture? Can the employee's family adjust to it?
- How does the climate and weather differ from what the employee is used to?
- Will the employee have to learn a new language in order to communicate effectively? Will the employee's family need to learn a new language?
- How do the employee and the employee's family arrange for a place to live? Open a bank account? Obtain health care?
- Will the employee's spouse be able to find work?
- What recreational activities will be available in the host country?

Source: Adapted from Solomon, M. Success abroad depends on more than job skills. *Personnel Journal,* April 1994, 51–59; Harvey, M. Repatriation of corporate executives: An empirical study. *Journal of International Business Studies,* 1989, 20(1), 131–143; Harvey, M. The impact of the dual-career family on international relocation. Unpublished manuscript, University of Oklahoma, Norman, 1995.

One important aspect of this effort is **cross-cultural training,** which includes cultural awareness, language instruction, and practical assistance with daily matters.[58] Cultural awareness should create a sensitivity to and appreciation for the host country's culture. Language training improves an expatriate employee's ability to communicate and negotiate. Practical assistance with daily matters helps employees and their families adjust to life in the new environment.

The need for cross-cultural training isn't limited to Americans who are headed for overseas assignments. Citizens of any country who are preparing for job assignments in a different nation should receive cross-cultural training. As the following Global Insight shows, Colgate-Palmolive is one organization that effectively prepares employees throughout the world for job assignments in other countries.

Global *Insight*

Developing Global Employees at Colgate-Palmolive

New York-based Colgate-Palmolive Company operates in more than 170 countries and derives more than 70 percent of its $7 billion of revenue from overseas markets. Colgate-Palmolive's success is due in part to its global human resources strategy of selecting and preparing people for job assignments around the world. And it's not just Americans who are being prepared for overseas assignments—it's people from around the world being prepared for assignments somewhere other than their homelands. About 60 percent of Colgate's expatriate employees are from countries other than the United States.

In preparing its employees for global assignments, Colgate-Palmolive considers both the needs of the company and the needs of its employees. HRM professionals help determine the skills and qualifications that employees will need to meet Colgate's business goals. HRM professionals also help identify and develop employees who have what the company calls *global talent.* These are people who are interested in the global environment, want the challenge of a global assignment, and are motivated to work toward the company's global business goals. They also are people who would contribute to the country in which they live and be likely to experience personal growth from the assignment.

In developing global talent, Colgate-Palmolive focuses on three levels of competencies. First, development focuses on acquiring the necessary skills to be effective in a functional or technical area. Second, a managerial/planning focus emphasizes presentation skills, planning, and execution. Third, a leadership/strategic focus stresses strategy, vision, teamwork, and long-range planning.[59]

Implications for Organizations

In our discussion of work-force trends early in this chapter, we identified some profound changes that are taking place in work-force demographics. In turn, these changes are having dramatic effects on organizations' training and development activities. Increasingly, basic training is needed to bring people up to functional literacy levels. Others need to acquire more sophisticated skills, ranging from teamwork skills to interpersonal skills to technical skills to advanced analytical and problem-solving skills. All organizations must be concerned about preparing their employees for the future. To remain competitive and be successful, organizations must have skilled people when they are needed and in the numbers needed in order to meet their goals.

CHAPTER SUMMARY

1 ***Define human resources management and describe its role in an organization's strategy.***

Human resources management (HRM) is concerned with the philosophies, policies, programs, practices, and decisions that affect the people who work for an organization. The various HRM functions should help the organization achieve its strategic goals. HRM philosophies, programs, and practices also need to be compatible with other systems and activities of the organization.

2 ***Discuss how human resources management is affected by changes in the work force and government regulations.***

The work forces of Canada, the United States, and other countries are changing rapidly. They are becoming more diverse and are acquiring the skills needed to perform effectively in today's technological workplace. Both attracting and retaining competent people with the needed skills and dealing with and capitalizing on the contributions that a diverse work force can make represent a big challenge to human resources professionals. Compensation and performance appraisal practices may be affected by changing skill levels, skill mixes, and team approaches to work. Training and development are addressing the need for basic skills and the need for developing technical and teamwork skills, among others.

The regulatory aspect of human resources management encompasses equal employment opportunity and employment discrimination, compensation and benefits, employee safety and health, and labor relations. Although their most pervasive impact is on the staffing and compensation functions, government regulations also influence performance appraisals and training and development activities.

3 ***Describe the phases of the staffing process and the staffing tools and techniques used by organizations.***

The staffing process normally includes six phases: (1) planning and forecasting human resource needs, (2) recruitment, (3) selection, (4) orientation, (5) movement, and (6) separation. The primary tools and techniques used to plan and forecast human resource needs are the skills inventory, job analysis, a replacement chart, and expert forecasts.

4 ***Explain the components of a total compensation package.***

The compensation package is used to attract, motivate, and retain qualified employees. Total compensation includes both direct compensation and indirect compensation. Direct compensation consists of the base wage or salary and incentive pay. Job-based pay and skill-based pay are two methods of determining the base wage. Incentive pay is designed to link at least part of employee pay to job performance. Incentive pay can be linked to individual, team, department, or organizationwide performance. Indirect compensation includes benefits that are mandated by law and those that employers provide voluntarily or as a result of contract negotiations with unions. Social Security, unemployment compensation, and workers' compensation are benefits that employers must provide. Insurance, retirement, pay for time not worked, and a variety of other benefits are not required by law, although some legislation does regulate how these benefits are managed if they are provided.

5 ***Discuss several methods of appraising performance and problems arising from the subjective nature of the process.***

Four important uses of performance appraisals are (1) to make reward decisions (raises, bonuses, and other rewards), (2) to make personnel movement decisions (promotions, demotions, transfers, and layoffs), (3) to give subordinates constructive feedback on their performance over a specified period of time, and (4) to identify training and development needs. The performance appraisal methods most commonly used are ranking, graphic rating, and behavioral rating. Performance appraisals often are affected by the rater's subjectivity and by organizational politics.

6 ***Explain how training and development programs can improve employee performance.***
The purpose of training programs is to maintain and improve current job performance. The intent of development programs is to teach skills and behaviors that employees will need in the future. Both training and development can be conducted on or off the job. Two of the greatest challenges facing organizations are remedial skills training and grooming people for global job assignments.

QUESTIONS FOR DISCUSSION

1. How does Cadillac link its human resources practices to its business strategy?
2. How might changes in the composition of the work force affect human resources management policies and programs?
3. Discuss the major regulatory influences on human resources management.
4. Which recruitment sources are likely to be most effective for filling (a) secretarial jobs, (b) positions in skilled trades, and (c) professional and managerial posts?
5. Describe the options that an organization has in designing its total compensation system. What advantages and disadvantages do they have for employer and employee alike?
6. What are the advantages of on-the-job training and development programs? Do such programs eliminate the need for off-the-job training? Why or why not?

FROM WHERE YOU SIT

1. How do you feel about an organization's hiring only certain types of people? What drawbacks might this sort of policy have?
2. Suppose that as a condition of employment you would have to take both a drug test and an honesty test? How would you feel about being required to do this?
3. Soon you will be entering the job market as a college graduate. What types of direct and indirect compensation would you like to receive? Why?
4. A manager once said: "Let's just say that there are a lot of factors that tug at you and play on your mind that cause you to soften the ratings you give. It may not have a great impact all the time, but when you know a 5 will create problems and a 6 will not, many managers give a 6." Why do managers inflate performance appraisals?
5. Teachers often contend that students should not evaluate their teaching performance. Conversely, administrators support the position that student evaluations should be used. Which of the performance appraisal errors are students most likely to commit? How can they be minimized?
6. Arrange for an interview with a professional in the human resources department of a local organization. Ask this individual to describe the training and development programs used. What strengths and limitations do you see in these programs?
7. Should organizations invest resources in training people in basic reading, writing, math, and problem-solving skills? Explain your answer.

SKILL-BUILDING EXERCISE

What Questions Can You Ask During an Employment Interview?[60]

Read each of the ten questions. Place a check mark in the appropriate column to indicate whether the question is legal or illegal (and therefore should not be asked).

	Legal	Illegal
1. How old are you?	_____	_____
2. Have you ever been arrested?	_____	_____
3. Do any of your relatives work for this organization?	_____	_____
4. Do you have children, and if you do, what kind of child care arrangements do you have?	_____	_____
5. Do you have any handicaps?	_____	_____
6. Are you married?	_____	_____
7. Where were you born?	_____	_____
8. What organizations do you belong to?	_____	_____
9. Do you get along well with other men [or women]?	_____	_____
10. What languages can you speak and/or write fluently?	_____	_____

Answers

The following evaluations provide clarification rather than strict legal interpretation. Employment laws are constantly changing.

1. *How old are you?*

This question is legal but inadvisable. An applicant's date of birth or age can be asked, but telling the applicant that federal and state laws prohibit age discrimination is essential. Avoid focusing on age, unless an occupation requires extraordinary physical ability or training and a valid age-related rule is in effect.

2. *Have you ever been arrested?*

This question is illegal unless an inquiry about arrests is justified by the specific nature of the organization—for instance, law enforcement or handling controlled substances. Questions about arrests generally are considered to be suspect because they may tend to disqualify some groups. Convictions should be the basis for rejection of an applicant only if their number, nature, or recent occurrence renders the applicant unsuitable. In that case the question(s) should be specific. For example: Have you ever been convicted for theft? Have you been convicted within the past year on drug-related charges?

3. *Do any of your relatives work for this organization?*

This question is legal if the intent is to discover nepotism.

4. *Do you have children, and if you do, what kind of child-care arrangements do you have?*

Both parts of this question are currently illegal; they should not be asked in any form because the answers would not be job-related. In addition, they might imply gender discrimination.

5. *Do you have any handicaps?*
This question is illegal as phrased here. An applicant does not have to divulge handicaps or health conditions that do not relate reasonably to his or her fitness to perform the job.

6. *Are you married?*
This question is legal, but may be discriminatory. Marriage has nothing directly to do with job performance.

7. *Where were you born?*
This question is legal, but it might indicate discrimination on the basis of national origin.

8. *What organizations do you belong to?*
As stated, this question is legal; it is permissible to ask about organizational membership in a general sense. It is illegal to ask about membership in a specific organization when the name of that organization would indicate the race, color, creed, gender, marital status, religion, or national origin or ancestry of its members.

9. *Do you get along well with other men [or women]?*
This question is illegal; it seems to perpetuate sexism.

10. *What languages can you speak and/or write fluently?*
Although this question is legal, it might be perceived as a roundabout way of determining an individual's national origin. It is not permissible to ask how any given language was learned.

CRITICAL THINKING CASE

Human Resources Management at AT&T[61]

When AT&T lost its monopoly in 1984 through the court-ordered breakup of the Bell System, the company didn't roll over and die. Instead, the company transformed itself and has emerged as a worthy and enviable global competitor. How did AT&T do this? Part of the credit for transforming AT&T into a world-class company goes to the organization's human resources policies and programs. According to Harold Burlingame, AT&T's senior vice-president of human resources, its selection and development of people, training and education programs, performance standards, and compensation system all played a vital role in helping AT&T to transform itself and achieve its strategic goals.

AT&T's business strategy and daily operations are guided by a value system that it calls its *Common Bond.* The principles of this value system are respect for individuals, dedication to helping customers, highest standards of integrity, innovation, and teamwork.

With 300,000 employees worldwide, AT&T now comprises twenty-six business units organized into four major customer service groups. Let's look at how one of these business units—AT&T Universal Card Services—links its human resources policies and programs to the business unit's strategic objectives.

AT&T Universal Card Services (UCS), a business unit launched in March 1990, received the Malcolm Baldrige National Quality Award just two years later. It relies on a set of seven guiding principles: continuous improvement, customer delight, teamwork, commitment, trust and integrity, mutual respect, and sense of urgency. UCS has learned that satisfying employees (called associates) is as important as satisfying customers. The UCS approach to satisfying associates contains four elements.

- *Involve every associate in continuous improvement.* Associates are encouraged to submit ideas for improvement, and they receive cash or gifts for those that are implemented. Beginning with the first day of training, employees "are empowered to do whatever it takes to delight the customer."
- *Provide a comprehensive system of training and development.* Training and development activities are formulated in the context of the UCS strategic plan and focus on both current and future needs of associates as well as UCS. Training and development activities cover basic job skills, career-based skills, quality training, and personal development.

- *Link performance and recognition systems to quality and financial goals.* Performance objectives are jointly set by associates and their managers. Performance is evaluated by managers, peers, and subordinates. This feedback is used for personal improvement. Associates receive bonuses based on the number of days that UCS meets it quality performance standards. Managers are rewarded both for achieving financial goals and on the basis of their individual performance. Many other rewards are used to encourage and reinforce exceptional quality and performance by individuals and teams.
- *Foster employee wellness and morale.* Physical well-being is encouraged through employer provided fitness centers. Other perks include employer subsidized child care, on-site dry cleaning and shoe repair services, a gift shop, a restaurant, among others. Associates' morale is measured periodically with opinion surveys, and action is taken on issues raised in the survey results.

Questions

1. How could the values expressed in AT&T's Common Bond influence human resources policies and programs?
2. How does AT&T Universal Card Services use the staffing, total compensation, performance appraisal, and training and development functions to support the achievement of their strategic goals?
3. Referring to Question 2, what are the advantages and disadvantages of the human resources policies and programs used by UCS?

VIDEO CASE

360 Degrees of Evaluation

The revision of performance appraisal measures is rapidly becoming a prerequisite to improving productivity, competitiveness, and profitability in U.S. businesses. Even after making strong efforts to raise morale and use teams, many managers still must rank their subordinates both individually and critically, often being forced to use a standardized system that doesn't accurately reflect the realities of the workplace.

W. Edwards Deming, a total quality management expert, states, "The annual review of people is a major culprit generating fear and wreaking havoc in our corporations and on our people. Companies suffer untold loss because of the annual review. People emerge from their reviews shaken and destroyed, unable to function properly for months." Further, the traditional standardized appraisal system causes many employees to dismiss criticism or praise as one person's opinion. Feedback has much more impact when peers, customers, and managers rate employees and give them direct feedback.

This relatively new approach, known as 360-degree feedback, is being used by companies ranging from Alcoa and Du Pont to Levi Strauss and UPS. Rather than judging employees solely on the evaluations of their immediate supervisors, these companies also ask business contacts and customers to evaluate employees.

Workers today often desire the approval of their colleagues even more than the praise of their bosses. This desire often transforms underachievers into corporate stars. With the strong cultural emphasis today on total quality management, managers and subordinates are existing in a partnership that focuses on the ultimate judge of performance: the customer. This process involves meeting customers' expectations 100 percent of the time.

How can companies involve the employee's peers, the employee's manager, and the employee's customers in positive three-way feedback? The process requires written documentation of the customer's expectations and measures, which in turn result in customer-generated performance ratings. Then, the customer determines whether the expectations were met. How is this process different from the traditional standardized appraisal system? First, the focus is on performance at the end of the process and not on the process itself. The thought is that defects are being inspected rather than prevented. Second, the traditional standardized appraisal system emphasizes short-term individual accomplishment rather than long-term thinking and effective teamwork. Finally, the traditional approach is manager centered rather than customer focused.

How can companies implement this system? Knowledge Systems, a Cary, North Carolina, software and training company, instituted a program of peer reviews of its fifty employees. Every twelve months, when an employee is due for a review, surveys are distributed to ten to twelve employees who work directly with that employee on a regular basis. The survey contains about forty-five positive statements, such as "I like the way Sandra handles herself in meetings." Each co-worker indicates whether he or she agrees, agrees strongly, disagrees, disagrees strongly, or cannot judge each statement.

Work teams then decide, together with their managers, which statements best measure performance. Approximately half the statements deal with interpersonal skills and are common to all the surveys. The rest of the statements deal with job-specific skills. Too many weak responses to a statement indicate that the statement is either unclear or not observable and needs to be rewritten. The managers receive copies of individual responses and past survey scores, but the person being reviewed sees only aggregate scores, which tend to eliminate biased judgments.

The peer review process began at General Electric in the early 1980s to allow employees to participate in handling their problems. One vice-president of human resources for GE states, "To us, peer review is a fundamental foundation piece. Organizations need to allow leaders to lead and allow people to manage themselves. Peer review supports this. It supports a teaming concept, whether you're looking at quality improvement teams, self-directed work teams, or any kind of teaming effort."[62]

What value does the 360-degree process have? Ideally, it serves several purposes: to motivate work performance, to inform team members about job performance, to clarify the job to be done, to encourage increased competence and growth, to enhance and improve communication, to improve discipline and correct problem behavior and performance, to measure performance for salary action, to develop backup data for management decisions on promotions, demotions, and discharges, and to encourage ownership and responsibility.

The cost of designing and implementing a 360-degree process varies with the size of the program, the degree of customization desired, and the amount of outside consulting involved. A standard evaluation instrument may run about $225 per person, plus the costs of training and staff and consulting time.

Companies that have implemented the 360-degree process have found it to be both efficient and effective. William Hodgetts, director of management development for Fidelity Investments, states, "In flatter organizations with less hierarchy, managers have many more direct reports than ever before. Now a manager may have a dozen or more people to evaluate. This is too many for anyone to keep track of in detail, and 360 delegates the task of gaining information."

However, experts warn that highly competitive situations can bring out the worst in a 360-degree process and that the feedback may be brutal. The majority of those using 360s make sure that the feedback is useful and accurate, instead of merely antagonistic, by focusing evaluation synopses on core patterns of behavior.

How do employees feel about the process? One user put it well: "Each of us is tooling along for years, thinking we are doing okay, though we all harbor a secret fear. Maybe I think I am not very good at making decisions. But I just go on, pushing down that nagging anxiety. Suddenly, with 360, it's all out on the table, and I'm relieved rather than threatened. Now I can talk to people about what I'm weak at and do something about it."

Questions

1. Despite the shortcomings of traditional performance measures, many people are comfortable with them and usually are reluctant to give them up. Why?
2. What are some of the drawbacks of peer review?
3. Linda Kane, vice-president of human resources development at Stride Rite has said, "Personally, I think 360 is more useful for employee development. It's not just about strengths and weaknesses and what we must pay you for your current level of performance. It's about how we can make your strengths much stronger." Do you agree with this statement? Why or why not?
4. Some experts have said that 360s should be used for management development and coaching but that other techniques, such as management by objectives, should be used for salary determination. Do you agree? Why or why not?

Starbucks Coffee Company: The Blend for Success

Company Overview

Starbucks Coffee Company has a relatively short history. It began in Washington state in 1971 when three young entrepreneurs began to sell coffee at Pike Place Market I Seattle. The original Starbucks' store was named after the first mate in Moby Dick. The organization itself is modeled after what President and CEO Howard Schultz considers to be four very successful companies: Nordstrom's, Home Depot, Microsoft, and Ben & Jerry's. Starbucks is the largest specialty coffee retailer and roaster in North America with more than 425 company-owned stores. On average, they handle over 1,000,000 customer transactions per week. Starbucks prides itself on selling only the best coffee drinks and whole bean coffees. The stores sell coffee beans, beverages, coffee-making equipment, pastries, and accessories. Starbucks likes to position its stores in very visible high-traffic locations. Starbucks is vertically integrated and controls its coffee sources, roasting, and retail sales to ensure adherence to its strict principles. Eighty-seven percent of its sales come from retail store operations and the remainder from catalog operations. Starbucks doesn't franchise its stores, and it has never paid a cash dividend.

Howard Schultz, CEO, believes that the quality of Starbucks' coffee will one day "alter how everyday Americans conduct their lives." He recently was named one of the top five entrepreneurs of the year, and Starbucks was rated among the 100 fastest growing companies in the United States by *INC.* magazine. The success of the company is attributed to its 6,500 employees. The turnover rate at Starbucks is only 60 percent compared to the retail average of 150 to 300 percent.

Howard Schultz, CEO

In 1985, Howard Schultz was asked to manage retail sales and marketing for Starbucks. On a buying trip to Italy a year later he was overcome with a new vision for the company: to open stores in the United States based on the Italian coffee bar model. However, the CEO at that time was doubtful, so Schultz left Starbucks with his vision and wrote a business plan for a new company. He went back to Italy to further develop his ideas and brought them back to the United States. Again he faced rejection—this time by more than 200 people he had approached to invest in his vision. He managed to raise $1.7 million on his own and opened his first coffee bar in Seattle. It was an instant success. The next year he made an offer to buy out his old bosses at Starbucks for $4 million. The rest is history.

Retail Stores

The actual Starbucks' stores vary in size from 300 to 1,200 square feet, depending on their location. Average sales are $746 per square foot. To open a Starbucks' store during 1994 cost an average of $279,000. The number of Starbucks stores has been increasing steadily over the years, as the following table shows.

Total Retail Store Count by Year

Year	Count
1990	84
1991	116
1992	165
1993	272
1994	425

Coffee Roasting

Dave Olsen is the person responsible for overseeing the company's roasting room. Only nineteen individuals have qualified to roast the coffee beans in all its years of operation. "Learning to roast is a tremendous privilege," according to Olsen. "It is considered an art form." Starbucks purchases only top quality green arbica coffee beans from coffee producing regions throughout the world. The bean searchers will go wherever they must to find the highest quality coffee beans. They do many taste tests before deciding whether the beans are good enough to become Starbucks coffee.

The coffee beans are roasted in small batches to the "exacting Starbucks Roast™ standard." Each batch (600 pounds of coffee) is roasted for approximately 15 minutes in a powerful gas oven. The coffee beans make sounds similar to that of popcorn when they are "precisely" done. Qualified roasters then test the color of the beans in a blood-cell analyzer. If the beans are not perfect the entire batch will be discarded. Beans have a life of seven days at Starbucks, in which time they have to be served or sold. The actual coffee that is served at the stores has a pot life of one hour and ten minutes.

Source: This case was prepared by Jodi Suttor and Helen LaVan of DePaul University. Adapted and used with permission of the authors, 1995.

Sales

As the number of people who drink coffee continues to decline, the gourmet coffee industry is thriving (measured by its profits Starbucks' sales have increased almost sevenfold since 1989 and in 1994 exceeded $284.9 million, as shown in the following table). By the end of the decade, Starbucks expects its sales to reach $1 billion.

Net Sales (in millions)	
1990	$42.3
1991	65.3
1992	103.2
1993	176.5
1994	284.9

Currently 87 percent of the company's sales come from its retail operations. The remainder comes from catalog operations and specialty sales. Starbucks' sales are subject to seasonal and quarterly fluctuations, with the majority of sales occurring during the winter months. Sales figures also are affected by the opening of new stores.

Ownership

Current outstanding shares	28,756,595
Number of shareholders	5,245
Net earnings per share	$0.34
Share price (4/1/95)	$24.00

Employee Development, Compensation, and Recognition

Starbucks' employees are considered *baristas,* Italian for bar person. Each employee receives at least 25 hours of formal training. The classes cover customer service, cash register operation, coffee brewing methods, and how to scoop coffee beans correctly. The most important is customer service. A team spirit is conveyed at Starbucks through companywide meetings, incentive programs, and joint decision making. A companywide program, called the Bravo Award, had been initiated. It identifies employees who have done something exceptional and what they have done. Bean Stock is the official name for the stock option plan offered unilaterally to all employees. The plan is intended to give employees a stake in Starbucks' future. The vast majority of the workers at Starbucks are in their mid-twenties and at least partially college educated.

Full-time and part-time employees alike are eligible for medical, vision, and dental insurance benefits. Employees receive them after working at least twenty hours or more a week for ninety days. Each employee is paid $6.00 an hour, but enrolled employees pay only $100 a year for health insurance. It pays for 80 percent of their medical costs up to $1,250 and 100 percent of all charges above that amount. Dental insurance is provided at no extra charge, as is vision coverage, which allows employees up to $70 per year in new contact lenses and new eyeglass frames every other year. Life insurance and disability insurance also are included in this package. Employees receive one free pound of coffee a week for their personal use. A 401(k) plan is available to employees after one full year of employment. Employee contributions are matched at the rate of $1.00 for every $4.00.

Howard Schultz believes that every dollar invested in the employee helps the bottom line. That's why he offers such a liberal benefits package to employees. These benefits are an important recruiting tool and also help keep employees once they are hired.

Catalog operations

Since catalog operations began in 1988, they have grown by over 1,000 percent. Starbucks currently has catalog customers in every state. The company is anticipating that this division will be one of its major growth areas in the future. The products that the catalog carries are coffee makers, espresso and cappuccino makers, grinders, cups, and—its core product—coffee beans. Starbucks believes the catalog operations have generated a devoted group of coffee drinkers who make recurring purchases. A main advantage of Starbucks as a catalog operator is that the products are affordable and are consumed regularly.

Geographic Locations

Over the past six years, Starbucks has opened new stores at the rate of one per week. Starbucks currently has stores in and around Seattle, Portland, Vancouver (British Columbia), San Francisco, Los Angeles, San Diego, Orange County (California), Chicago, Denver, and Washington, D.C. The company opened 159 new stores in 1994 and plans to open at least 200 more in 1995. Starbucks recently announced plans to expand further into eastern and midwestern markets, including cities such as Boston, New York, and Minneapolis.

Guiding Values

- Establish Starbucks as the premier purveyor of the finest coffee in the world.
- Provide a great work environment and treat each other with respect and dignity.
- Apply the highest standards of excellence to the purchasing, roasting, and fresh delivery of Starbucks coffee.
- Develop enthusiastic satisfied customers all of the time.

- Provide a superior level of customer service.
- Engender a high degree of customer loyalty.
- Contribute positively to the community and the environment.
- Recognize that profitability is essential to future success.
- Become the leading specialty coffee retailer in each of the target markets.

President's Letter

To Our Shareholders:

Much has transpired since June of 1992 when Starbucks became the first publicly-owned specialty coffee company in North America. With 156 stores and 1,600 employees, we set out to become the leading retailer and brand of specialty coffee in North America. We began with what was second nature to us: an unparalleled commitment to roasting the finest quality coffee, hiring talented people and pursuing excellence in all aspects of our operations.

Two years later, we still have the same commitment to our values, the same passion for our product, the same dedicated employees—just more of them. With 425 company-owned stores, 26 licensed airport stores, and over 6,500 employees, we've made our dream a reality. At the conclusion of another very successful year, we are pleased to announce our belief that Starbucks has fulfilled its original promise of becoming the industry leader. Although this is no small achievement, we are excited to realize that the majority of our challenges and accomplishments still lie before us.

With our eyes on the goal of 1,500 stores in North America by the year 2000, our partners have a renewed commitment to our vision. We realize it is more important now than ever to execute flawlessly, to recognize and respond to opportunities in a disciplined and strategic manner, and most of all, to exceed our customers' expectations. In fiscal 1994, our dedicated team opened 159 new stores, surpassing our original goal of 125 stores. By the end of the fourth quarter, our expertly-trained retail partners were serving over two million customers each week, and we successfully entered the new markets of New York, Boston, Minneapolis and Atlanta. Our fiscal 1995 plans call for opening at least 200 new stores, including those just opened in the new markets of Dallas and Houston, and those we plan to open in Philadelphia and Las Vegas in the second quarter.

In fiscal 1995 and beyond, we will continue to reinforce our brand and market leadership position, with the long-term goal of becoming the most recognized and respected brand of coffee in the world. With fiscal 1994 net revenues at approximately $285 million, an increase of 61% over 1993, we feel fortunate to have experienced what some might call extraordinary growth and success. We are proud to know that while many would view this as a sign that we have been doing everything right, our partners prefer to see it as a challenge to do everything better.

We realize that our people are the cornerstone of our success, and we know that their ideas, commitment and connection to our customers are truly the essential elements in the Starbucks experience. Therefore, we are extremely pleased that we were able to grant eligible full and part-time partners stock options under our Bean Stock program in fiscal 1994. Based upon the input of our partners, we also refined our nationally recognized healthcare and benefits programs to reflect the changing needs of our diverse workforce.

At this time, we are poised for many exciting new business opportunities, a position we know is made possible by the way our people have embraced our guiding principles. Our mail order department increased their core continuity business by 170%, and our specialty sales and marketing team added ITT Sheraton Hotels and Delta Airline's Shuttle to their ever expanding list of national accounts. We entered into a 50/50 joint venture partnership with the Pepsi-Cola Company to create, bottle and distribute an innovative new beverage that we believe will potentially expand the reach of the Starbucks brand.

We continue to be strongly committed to developing our infrastructure ahead of our growth. In August, we completed negotiations to build what we expect will ultimately be a one million square foot roasting and distribution facility in York, Pennsylvania. We promoted two of our top executives: Orin Smith to the position of president and chief operating officer, and Howard Behar to president, Starbucks International. We completed the acquisition of The Coffee Connection, Inc., a highly-regarded Boston-based company, which greatly accelerated our entrance into the all-important East Coast markets.

We also realize our successes would not be possible without the support of our surrounding communities, which is why we make every effort to contribute positively to our neighbors and the environment. Through the world-wide relief organization CARE, we are able to financially assist people in the coffee-producing countries where we do business. Starbucks-sponsored assistance programs have made a difference in more than 1.3 million lives to date, and we are proud to be the largest annual corporate donor to CARE in North America.

Making a difference is truly what Starbucks is all about. From our people to our coffee to our stores, we seek to offer a singular Starbucks Experience.

For all of you who touch Starbucks in any way, I would like to thank you for your ongoing support.

Warm regards,

/s/Howard Schultz
chairman and chief executive officer
1/24/95

Questions

1. How would you assess the human resources practices at Starbucks?
2. What bases of departmentalization are being used?
3. If Starbucks continues to grow, what organization design would you recommend?

Part *Five*

Leading

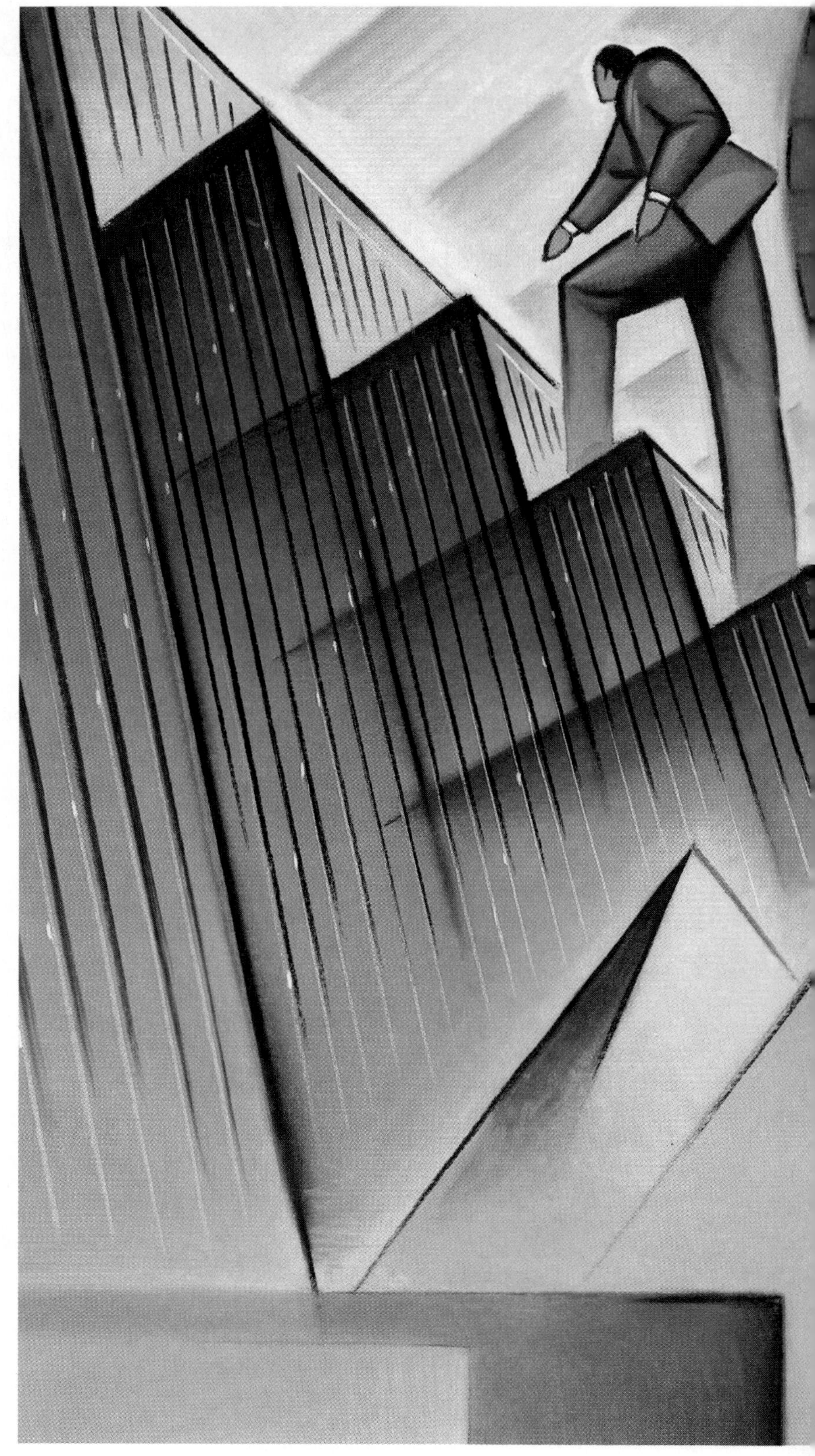

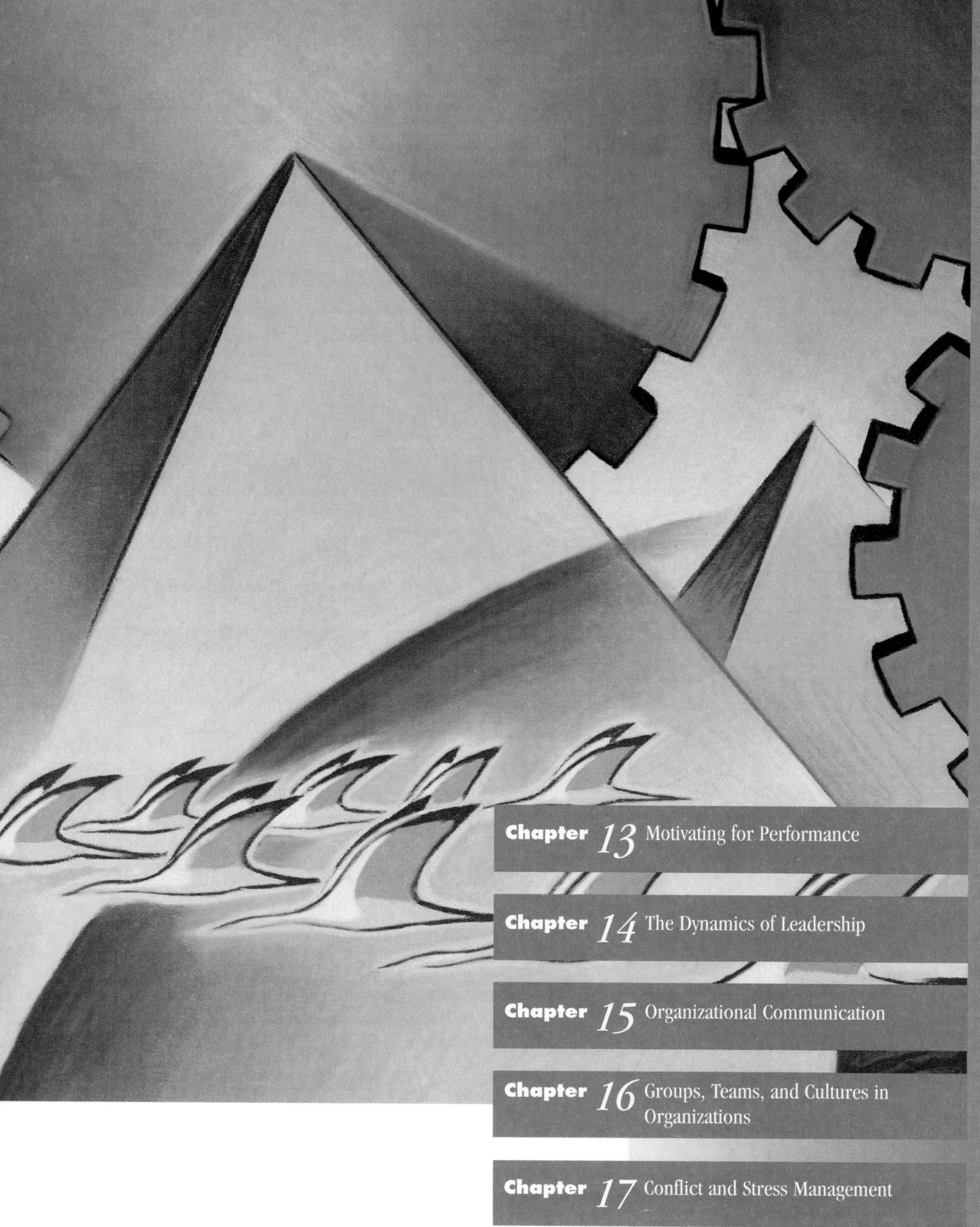

Chapter *13*

Motivating for Performance

Learning *Objectives*

After studying this chapter you should be able to:

1. State the main factors that affect work motivation.
2. Identify the primary approaches to work motivation.
3. Use the needs hierarchy to describe how individuals' needs motivate them to perform their jobs.
4. Use the ERG model to describe how need satisfaction and need frustration affect motivation.
5. Discuss how achievement, affiliation, and power influence work motivation.
6. Describe the characteristics of work and the work environment that affect job satisfaction and performance.
7. Explain how job enrichment affects people's motivation at work.
8. Discuss the basic assumptions and concepts underlying the expectancy model of motivation.
9. Describe how perceptions of equity and inequity arise and how they affect motivation.
10. State how rewards and punishments may be used to influence employees in organizations.

Chapter *Outline*

Preview *Insight*

Motivation at Covenant House

Darrell Mell, vice-president of telemarketing at Covenant House, a nonprofit organization that provides shelter and comprehensive services for tens of thousands of runaway and abused youths, says that business organizations can learn much about employee motivation by studying nonprofit organizations. Mell says that he's learned more about employee motivation in his five years at Covenant House than in fourteen years as a sales and marketing manager for AT&T's Bell System. Let's take a look at what Darrell Mell has learned.

Employees of nonprofit organizations are paid, on average, about 70 percent of the salaries they would make in the private sector. Yet, they typically work very hard because they are dedicated. Why? Because they are actively involved in the organization's decision-making process. Through their input, they gain a sense of ownership in the decisions and become committed to carrying them out.

Telemarketing employees at Covenant House also believe that their work makes a significant contribution to society above and beyond raising funds to support the organization's charitable programs. They recognize that their work helps provide food, clothing, shelter, and medical care to youth who have become disconnected from their families. They recognize too that their work helps "street kids" reconnect to their families or to caring relatives.

Covenant House telemarketing employees also know how their jobs affect the organization's financial stability. They have goals to meet in making solicitation calls and processing donations. Progress toward goals is reviewed regularly, and positive feedback is provided.

But perhaps most important, employees in nonprofit organizations such as Covenant House are motivated by the organization's mission "to encounter, welcome and care for street kids." Employees at Covenant House identify with and believe in the mission of caring for runaway and abused youth and protecting and safeguarding all children. This mission keeps Covenant House employees clearly focused on the purpose and meaning of their jobs.

Darrell Mell has discovered some of the secrets of motivating Covenant House employees to perform well. He has learned something about what motivates people. And he has learned something about how and why people become motivated.[1]

1

State the main factors that affect work motivation.

Real-World Example
Peter Drucker, author and management expert, has stated: "You must manage under the assumption that you need the employees more than they need you."

Ask Students
Can a manager really motivate a worker, or can the manager only provide conditions that most workers will find motivating?

Ask Students
How can a manager "demotivate" employees?

FACTORS AFFECTING MOTIVATION

Motivation is any influence that brings out, directs, or maintains people's goal-directed behavior. This chapter is about motivated performance, like that of the people at Covenant House. As a manager, you'll be responsible for helping employees perform their jobs effectively and efficiently. But you can't fulfill this responsibility until you understand what motivates both them and you. In this chapter, we introduce you to various factors that trigger and maintain employee behaviors. We also explore ways that managers and employee teams can use rewards to enhance everyone's performance.

To provide a basic understanding of motivation, let's focus for a moment on three sets of the many factors that influence motivation: individual differences, job characteristics, and organizational practices. Figure 13.1 depicts these three sets of variables. To develop an effective motivation program, managers must consider how these factors interact to affect employee job performance. Of course, some factors that affect an employee's job performance may be beyond a manager's control. For instance, worrying about a sick child in the day care center or the need to help parents financially is bound to affect an employee's performance, but neither factor is within a manager's control.

This chapter was contributed by Michael K. McCuddy, Professor of Human Resource Management, College of Business Administration, Valparaiso University, Valparaiso, Indiana.

FIGURE 13.1

Motivational Variables

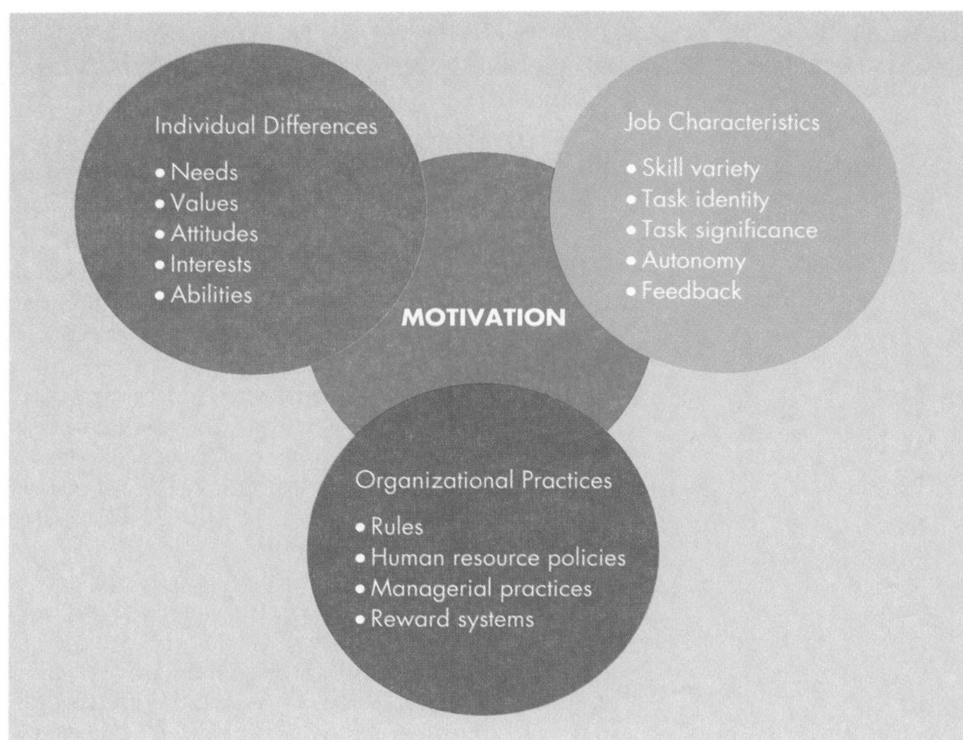

Teaching Tip
Have students brainstorm about factors that have affected their motivation in a current or past job. List the suggested factors on the board or an overhead transparency.

Ethics
Some people argue that everyone is unique and that organizations have an ethical responsibility to accommodate their differences. Others argue that individuals are lucky to have a job and should conform to the organization's wishes because they are being paid to do so. Discuss these different viewpoints with the students.

Ask Students
What motivates you? List the responses on the board to determine whether any patterns emerge.

Ask Students
How many of these characteristics are present in your job or in your role as a student?

Individual Differences

Every person is unique. **Individual differences** are the personal needs, values, attitudes, interests, and abilities that people bring to their jobs. Because these characteristics vary from person to person, so does what motivates people. One employee may be motivated by money and go for a job paying a high salary. Another may be motivated by security and accept a lower paying job that involves few risks of unemployment.[2] Still another may thrive on challenges and seek a position that stretches the employee's abilities to the limit. For example, an overseas assignment can give an employee a chance to tackle something new and challenging. Learning to handle such a job gives an employee an advantage in today's increasingly global organizations. In Chapters 1 and 12 we highlighted the changing nature of the work force and discussed how organizations go about attracting, motivating, and retaining a diverse work force.

Job Characteristics

Job characteristics are the aspects of the position that determine its limitations and challenges. These characteristics include (1) the variety of skills required to do the job, (2) the degree to which the employee can do the entire task from start to finish (task identity), (3) the personal significance attributed to the job, (4) autonomy, and (5) the type and extent of performance feedback that the employee receives. Different jobs may rate high on some characteristics and low on others. For example, the job of a telemarketer at Covenant House requires performing a repetitive and scripted, but nonetheless important, task. It would rate low on autonomy and skill variety but high on significance and task identity. The telemarketer also gets quick and clear feedback (pledges or refusals) from potential donors. In contrast, Darrell Mell's job as vice-president of telemarketing probably rates relatively high on all five job characteristics. As many organizations have found, an employee who derives satisfaction from the job and its particular characteristics will be more motivated to perform well than one who doesn't.

Organizational Practices

Organizational practices are the rules, human resources policies, managerial practices, and reward systems of an organization. Policies defining fringe benefits (e.g., paid vacations, insurance, and child or elder care) and rewards (e.g., bonuses and/or commissions) can attract new employees and keep existing employees happy. Rewards can motivate employees, but if they are to do so effectively, they must be administered fairly and based on performance. For example, Duke Power Company had an incentive program that emphasized corporate goals, which were difficult for individual employees to influence. To make the system fairer and to have a greater impact on employees job behavior, Duke Power revamped its system to reward employees with cash bonuses for attaining individual and team performance goals.[3]

Teaching Tip
Ask students to interview two or more managers about organizational practices. Use the results as a basis for class discussion to compare the effectiveness of different rewards as motivators.

Interaction of Factors

The three sets of factors we've described interact to influence an employee's motivation. Essentially this interaction involves (1) the personal qualities the employee brings to the workplace, (2) the tasks the employee performs in the work situation, and (3) the organizational systems that affect the employee in the workplace. In working with employees on motivation, managers need to consider all three factors. Darrell Mell at Covenant House pays attention to all three factors, and that contributes to the success of the nonprofit organization and its employees.

Paying attention to all three factors is more complicated than it sounds. Because of individual differences, people may respond in vastly different ways to their jobs and their employer's practices. Perhaps this is nowhere more evident than in seasoned managers' efforts to motivate members of the so-called baby bust generation, or the twentysomethings. The following Diversity Insight provides a useful perspective on this problem.

Diversity *Insight*

Motivating the Twentysomethings

Managers from the baby boom generation (people born from 1946–1969) may have difficulty understanding the baby busters because they are so diverse. Michael Woodruff, president of a management training firm, says that twentysomethings (the baby busters) "are so diverse that trying to understand them is a lot like trying to nail jello to a tree." Some twentysomethings are realistic and pragmatic like people who are considerably older. Others act like they are still adolescents who are in no hurry to go out into the *real world.* Perhaps the only thing that unites the twentysomethings is their view of the baby boomers' approach to work. Twentysomethings feel that boomers don't do enough work, are technologically outdated, and stand in the way of their own advancement. The boomers, however, believe that they have advanced by being loyal to an organization, being sensitive to organizational politics, and waiting for promotions to come. Consequently, the boomers expect the twentysomethings to respect authority, be loyal to the organization, and wait their turn for promotions.

Interestingly, boomers are often the ones who are responsible for designing jobs and administering organizational practices that affect the twentysomethings. Boomers need to approach these activities in terms of the way twentysomethings are, not in terms of how they would like twentysomethings to be. Moreover, to the extent possible, flexibility will need to be designed into jobs and organizational practices to help motivate the diverse generation of twentysomethings.[4]

2

Identify the primary approaches to work motivation.

OVERVIEW OF APPROACHES TO MOTIVATION

Motivating for performance may be best understood through both the content approach and the process approach. The **content approach** addresses the question: What motivates behavior? The answers are based on the assumption that individuals are motivated by the desire to fulfill inner needs. For example, someone who has a strong need to belong may be more highly motivated to join an organization than to start a business at home. Employees with a strong need for self-esteem might be motivated to produce high-quality products because that enhances their pride. Abraham Maslow's hierarchy of needs, Clay Alderfer's ERG model, David McClelland's learned needs model, and Frederick Herzberg's two-factor model are content theories that we examine here.

Teaching Tip
Divide the class into three groups to brainstorm answers to the following questions: (1) What needs do people seek to satisfy at work? (2) Why do people choose certain behaviors to meet their goals? (3) How do past outcomes influence employees' future actions?

Discussion Question 1
What are the main similarities among the different content models of motivation?

Discussion Question 2
What are the main similarities among the different process models of motivation?

Both the hierarchy of needs and the ERG model suggest that people's motivation is affected by certain desires or needs that are arranged in a hierarchy of importance. The learned needs model identifies three needs that are important for understanding work motivation. The two-factor model uses the nature of work and the context in which work occurs to explain motivation, satisfaction, and performance.

The **process approach** to motivation emphasizes how and why people choose certain behaviors in order to meet their personal goals. For example, individuals may perceive a strong possibility of receiving some desired reward—such as a promotion or a salary increase—if they perform in a certain way, such as working hard. In other words, the prospect of the reward motivates them to work hard. We discuss three process approaches—the expectancy model, the equity model, and the reinforcement model—in this chapter.

The expectancy model suggests that motivation, performance, and job satisfaction all depend on the belief that the effort expended will lead to desired results. The equity model emphasizes that people are motivated to seek reward equality with other employees for their performance. The reinforcement model indicates that people behave as they do because they have learned through experience that certain behaviors are associated with certain outcomes.

Content models do not ignore questions of *why* or *how,* and process models do not ignore questions of *what*. Rather, it is a matter of emphasis. Content models emphasize the *what* of employee motivation, and process models emphasize the *how* and *why*.

3

Use the needs hierarchy to describe how individuals' needs motivate them to perform their jobs.

MASLOW'S HIERARCHY OF NEEDS: A CONTENT APPROACH

As we've said, content approaches hold that motivation springs from a desire to satisfy a need. A **need** is a strong feeling of deficiency in some aspect of a person's life that creates an uncomfortable tension. The individual strives to reduce that tension, usually by taking some action to satisfy the need. Some people are driven by a need to succeed; others by the need to be well liked, to gain power and/or wealth, or to feel secure in their jobs. If an individual succeeds in reducing the sense of deficiency, the intensity of the motivating force also is reduced. The role of needs in motivating people is illustrated in Figure 13.2.

Teaching Tip
Brainstorm a list of needs with the students. Classify each need according to Maslow's theory.

The most widely known content approach to motivation probably is psychologist Abraham Maslow's **hierarchy of needs model.**[5] He believed that people have a complex set of five categories of needs, which he arranged in order of primacy (see Figure 13.3): physiological (at the base), security, affiliation, esteem, and self-actualization (at the top). He suggested that, as a person satisfies each level of needs, motivation shifts to satisfying the next higher level of needs.

Physiological needs are those for food, clothing, and shelter. As the most basic human needs, they occupy the first level in Maslow's hierarchy. People try to satisfy physiological needs before all others. For example, the primary motivation of a hungry person is to obtain food rather than, say, gain recognition of achievements.

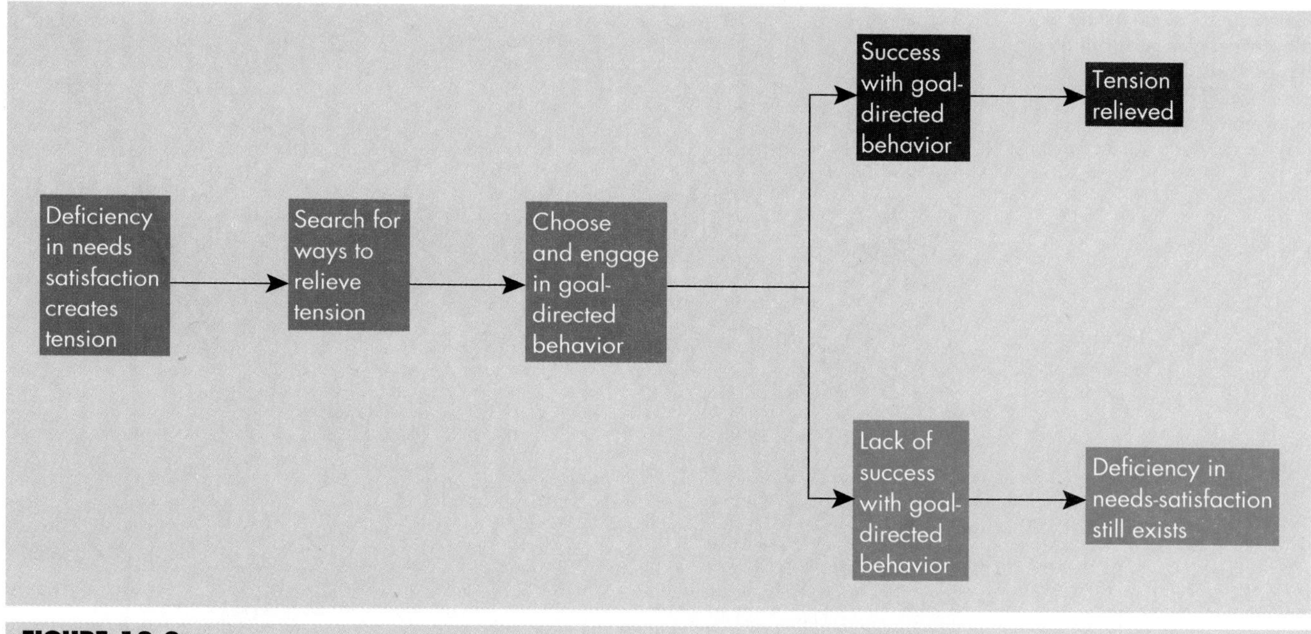

FIGURE 13.2

The Role of Needs in Motivation

Ask Students
Pay has been identified as a basic physiological need. Is money a motivator? Why or why not?

Security needs include the desires for safety and stability, and the absence of pain, threat, and illness. People deprived of the means to satisfy security needs become preoccupied with obtaining them. Many workers express their security needs as a desire for a stable job with medical, unemployment, and retirement benefits. In an era of layoffs and downsizing (e.g., the early 1990s), job security becomes a powerful motivator. Lack of job security stifles innovation and risk taking while prompting caution.

FIGURE 13.3

Maslow's Hierarchy of Needs

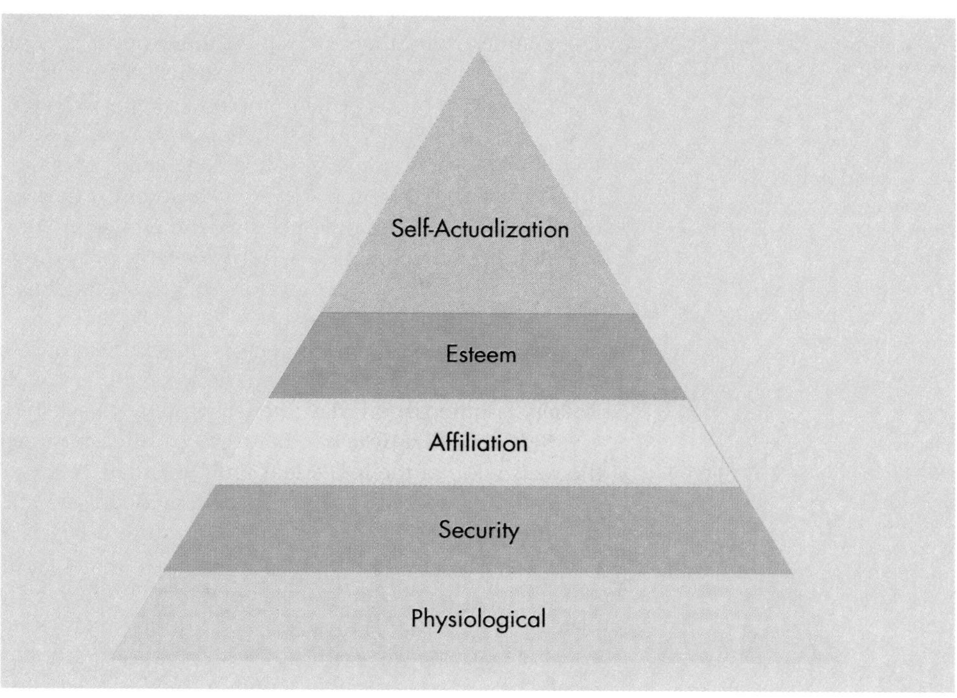

Companies can meet their employees' esteem needs in a number of ways. One is to provide public rewards and recognition, as demonstrated by this Mary Kay Cosmetics award ceremony.

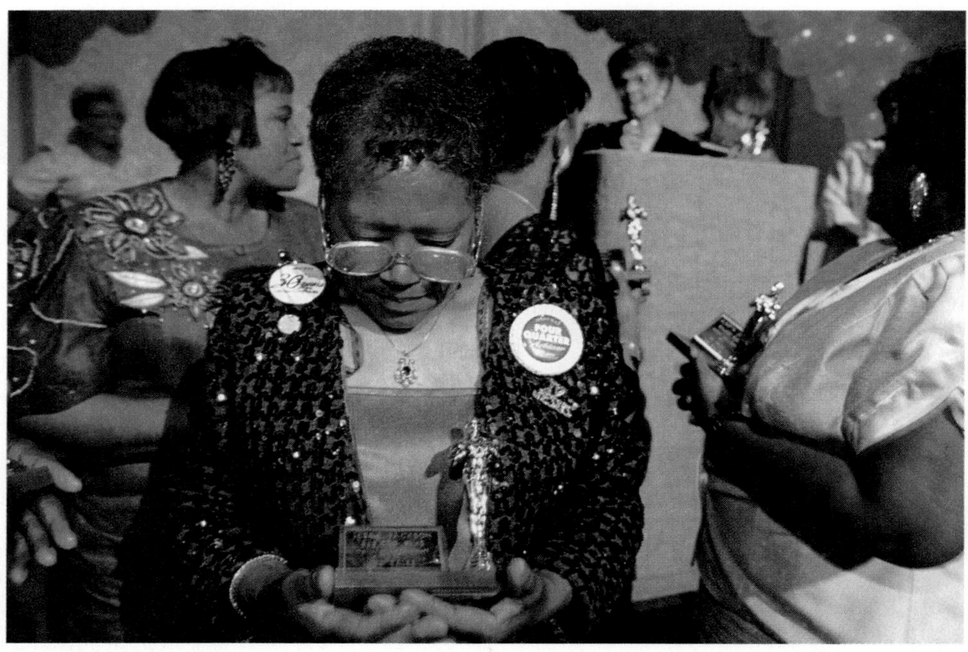

Affiliation needs are the desires for friendship, love, and belonging. This level in Maslow's hierarchy represents a clear step up from the truly basic physiological and security needs. Employees with high affiliation needs enjoy working closely with others. Employees with low affiliation needs may be content to work on tasks by themselves. When an organization doesn't meet affiliation needs, an employee's dissatisfaction may be expressed in terms of frequent absenteeism, low productivity, stress-related behaviors, and even emotional breakdown. Managers who recognize that subordinates are striving to satisfy affiliation needs should act supportively. They might encourage co-workers to cooperate more closely and participate in the organization's social activities.

Ask Students
Does anyone ever reach true self-actualization? Why or why not?

Esteem needs are desires for self-respect, a sense of personal achievement, and recognition from others. To satisfy these needs, people seek opportunities for achievement, promotion, prestige, and status—to reinforce their competence and worth. Managers who perceive that employees are motivated by esteem needs emphasize the hard work and finely honed skills that are required for success. They may publicly reward achievement with published achievement lists, bonuses, praise, lapel pins, and articles in the organization's paper. These and other forms of recognition help to build employee pride. When the need for esteem is dominant, managers can promote job satisfaction and high-quality performance by providing opportunities for exciting, challenging work and recognition of accomplishment. Battelle Pacific Northwest Laboratories and SRI International, among others, use royalty compensation systems to motivate its scientists and inventors.[6] Giving scientists and inventors "a piece of the action" encourages creativity and productivity, as well as contributing to self-esteem. Royalty compensation may even contribute to satisfying physiological needs.

Ask Students
Where do you think you are on Maslow's hierarchy of needs? Explain.

Ethics
Is there an ethical imperative for management to provide employees with what they need to satisfy a certain level of needs? Why or why not? If so, what should that level be?

Self-actualization needs are the desires for personal growth, self-fulfillment, and the realization of the individual's full potential. A self-actualized person accepts both the self and others. Traits commonly exhibited include initiative, spontaneity, and problem-solving ability. Managers who recognize this level of motivation in employees can help them discover the growth opportunities inherent in their jobs. For example, managers can create a motivating environment by involving employees in the decision-making process, restructuring their jobs, or offering them special assignments that call for special skills. At Merck, scientists can attend law school and become patent attorneys; at Hewlett-Packard, a parallel technical ladder has been established so that scientists can earn higher salaries without taking on management tasks.

Core Assumptions

Maslow's hierarchy of needs rests on four basic assumptions.

- A satisfied need isn't a motivator. Once a need is satisfied, another emerges to take its place. Thus people are always striving to satisfy some higher need.
- The needs network for most people is complex. That is, various needs affect a person's behavior at the same time.
- In general, lower level needs must be satisfied before higher level needs become strong enough to stimulate behavior.
- There are many more ways to satisfy higher level needs than there are to satisfy lower level needs.

Application in Organizations

Maslow never claimed that his hierarchy was a fixed, rigid order that applied to all people. He believed that people are motivated to satisfy the needs that are foremost at specific times in their lives. The strength of a specific need depends on the extent to which it and all lower level needs have been satisfied. Thus Maslow's model predicts a dynamic, step-by-step process in which a continuously evolving set of needs motivates behavior. Physiological needs are the most basic and must be satisfied first. Self-actualization needs are fulfilled last and least often by individuals.

Research supports Maslow's view that, until basic needs are satisfied, people won't be concerned with higher level needs.[7] However, little evidence supports the view that people must meet their needs in the sequence defined by Maslow's hierarchy (Figure 13.3). For example, not everyone satisfies social needs (aspects of Maslow's affiliation and esteem needs) before moving on to satisfy self-actualization needs. Some people pay little attention to social needs as long as they are free to do what they do best (e.g., playing chess, participating in sports, doing handicrafts, or solving computer-programming problems).

In fact, research shows that a two-part hierarchy—with physiological and security needs at the bottom and affiliation, esteem, and self-actualization needs at the top—is more realistic. Unless an organization helps employees satisfy the two lower level needs, addressing the three higher level needs won't influence on-the-job behavior. Moreover, if an employee's lower level needs appear to be threatened, they will take on even greater importance. For instance, when Jostens Learning Corporation, a producer of educational software, downsized its work force by just over 10 percent, many survivors of the layoff became frightened about their futures with the company. They wondered whether they too would lose their jobs. Some worked harder than ever to try to ensure their survival. Others were consumed by depression and worry that they would be the next victims of a rumored new round of layoffs and had trouble concentrating on their work.[8]

The implication of a two-part hierarchy is that, once basic needs have been satisfied, no single other need is likely to emerge as the best candidate for motivating subordinates. In other words, managers will have to address more than one need simultaneously. Therefore they must continually reevaluate *what* motivates their subordinates and *how* to motivate them.

Teaching Tip
After discussing Maslow's hierarchy of needs, have students identify ways in which organizations can satisfy each kind of need. Examples include salary (physiological), pension plan (security), friendships made at work (affiliation), job title (esteem), and challenging work (self-actualization).

Ask Students
What practical value does Maslow's hierarchy of needs have for managers?

Trying to understand what motivates another person is never easy. And when a manager is working with subordinates from another culture, the task becomes even more difficult. Many books and articles have been written on how to motivate people from different cultures, raising questions about the usefulness of U.S. management practices abroad. For example, a recent study in a Russian cotton mill showed that extrinsic rewards such as valued merchandise was a greater motivator and raised performance more than did recognition and praise. In turn, recognition and praise influenced employee motivation and performance more than the opportunity to participate in making decisions about how to improve productivity.[9] Motivational programs that satisfy higher level needs probably are less meaningful to most Russian employees because their lower level needs haven't been adequately satisfied.

4

Use the ERG model to describe how need satisfaction and need frustration affect motivation.

ALDERFER'S ERG MODEL: A CONTENT APPROACH

Like Maslow, Clay Alderfer looks at motivation from a hierarchy of needs perspective. Instead of five categories of needs, however, his **ERG model** specifies a hierarchy of three needs categories: existence, relatedness, and growth.[10] **Existence needs** are the desires for material and physical well-being that are satisfied through food, water, air, shelter, working conditions, pay, fringe benefits, and the like. **Relatedness needs** are the desires to establish and maintain interpersonal relationships with other people, including family, friends, supervisors, subordinates, and co-workers. **Growth needs** are the desires to be creative, to make useful and productive contributions, and to have opportunities for personal development.

Ask Students
Do you agree with this hypothesis?

A key feature of Maslow's need hierarchy is the **satisfaction-progression hypothesis,** or the idea that a lower level need must be reasonably satisfied before the next higher level need emerges as a motivator of behavior. The ERG model recognizes the satisfaction-progression hypothesis, but it also contains a frustration-regression hypothesis. The **frustration-regression** hypothesis holds that when individuals are frustrated in meeting higher level needs, the next lower level needs reemerge. For example, a finish carpenter who does highly creative trim work in houses may work for a contractor who builds a limited number of floor plans with few trim work options. Because the job doesn't provide a creative outlet, the carpenter may stop pursuing satisfaction of growth needs at work and instead focus on socializing with other construction workers.

Figure 13.4 illustrates the satisfaction-progression and frustration-regression components of the ERG model. The right-hand side of the figure shows the satisfaction-progression hypothesis and the left-hand side demonstrates the frustration-regression hypothesis. Even though an individual has regressed to seeking satisfaction of a lower level need, the higher level need may reemerge as an important motivator of behavior. When that happens, the person will progress to the next higher level need, seeking again to satisfy that need, though perhaps in a different way.

Let's illustrate this result by going back to the preceding example. The finish carpenter has been frustrated in satisfying the growth needs in his present job and has coped by socializing with other construction workers. However, he still feels the creative urges tugging at him and seeks employment with a builder of higher priced, custom-designed homes where he can express his creativity. As the carpenter satisfies his growth needs in this new job, those needs will likely increase in importance.

Application in Organizations

Several studies support the three categories of needs identified by Alderfer, and some research indicates that individuals move among the three needs levels, as Alderfer proposed. Also, the research suggests that growth needs increase in importance when they are satisfied.[11] Intuitively, managers can easily grasp the ideas of existence, relatedness, and growth needs as they attempt to understand employee motivation. This classification provides a useful way for describing *what* motivates people's behavior. Movement among the three levels begins to address questions of *how* and *why* people become motivated, yet the answers are incomplete. More complete answers regarding the how and why of employee motivation are provided in our discussion of process approaches later in this chapter.

Perhaps the most important implication of the ERG model is the contribution of the frustration-regression hypothesis to how managers can approach employee motivation.

FIGURE 13.4

ERG Model of Motivation

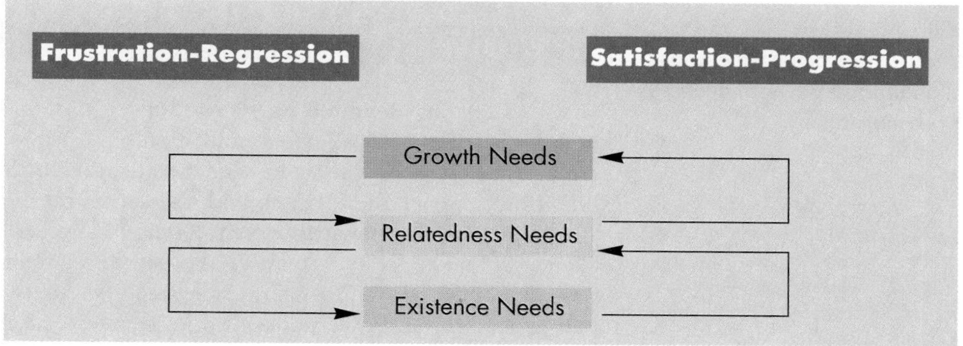

When employees are frustrated in fulfilling their needs, managers should try to determine the cause of the frustration and, if possible, work to remove blockages to need satisfaction. If blockages can't be removed, managers should try to redirect the employees' behavior toward satisfying a lower level need. For example, a company's production technology may limit the growth opportunities for people in their jobs. If employees are frustrated because they cannot be creative or cannot develop new skills, they could be encouraged to focus on developing meaningful relationships with their co-workers.

Sometimes need satisfaction is blocked for some employees by organizational actions such as corporate downsizing. Employees whose jobs are eliminated may cope with their needs frustration in many different ways. Some of them do so by going into business for themselves, as the following Small Business Insight indicates.

Small Business *Insight*

How Do Victims of Downsizing Cope?

Managers and other employees who lose their jobs as a result of downsizing may be traumatized by the experience. Typically, they have been fairly successful in their careers but have become victims of their organization's efforts to cut costs and become more productive with fewer people. Companies eliminate hundreds or even thousands of jobs as entire departments or entire layers of management are phased out. Whatever the scenario, the out-of-work people often are frustrated because they no longer have the challenge of their work, are no longer part of a structure, don't interact with associates as they formerly did, and often have trouble meeting financial obligations, particularly if they are unemployed very long.

Some victims of downsizing respond by hiding in their homes during normal business hours, afraid that their neighbors will find out that they are unemployed. Some actively seek other full-time employment. Some seek part-time employment.

More and more displaced workers respond by going into business for themselves. Some test their entrepreneurial abilities by opening small businesses—possibly converting a hobby into a business venture. Some become consultants working out of their homes. Others seek franchise opportunities or buy an existing small business. Whatever self-employment avenue they choose, these victims of downsizing tend to share a common perspective: They don't want to be victims again, and they view the autonomy of self-employment as an advantage. In terms of motivation, they view self-employment as a way to satisfy needs that were frustrated when they were let go.[12]

Discuss how achievement, affiliation, and power influence work motivation.

MCCLELLAND'S LEARNED NEEDS MODEL: A CONTENT APPROACH

David McClelland's **learned needs model** specifies that people acquire three important needs or motives—achievement, affiliation, and power—through interaction with their surrounding environments.[13] In other words, the social contexts in which people live and work influence the learning and strength of these motives.

Ask Students
What occupation might a person with high achievement needs try?

Ask Students
What occupation might a person with high affiliation needs try?

Ask Students
What occupation might a person with high power needs try?

The **achievement motive** is the desire to succeed relative to some standard of excellence or in competitive situations. People with a high need for achievement often like to assume personal responsibility for setting their goals, prefer to pursue moderately difficult goals, and desire immediate and concrete feedback. The **affiliation motive** is a person's desire to develop and maintain close, mutually satisfying interpersonal relationships with others. Individuals with a strong affiliation motive tend to seek approval and reassurance from others and conform to group norms. The **power motive** is an individual's desire to influence and control others and the social environment. The power motive manifests itself in two ways: as *personal power* and as *socialized power*.[14] With personal power, people try to influence and control others merely to assert their dominance. With socialized power, individuals use their power to solve organizational problems and help the organization reach its goals.

Application in Organizations

All three acquired motives are important to people who desire to function effectively in an organization. They need to be achievement oriented in order to succeed in an increasingly competitive world and as they deal with the challenges of corporate downsizing and reorganization. If people aren't achievement oriented, they may well be let go when their organizations eliminate positions, departments, and/or layers of management.

Increasingly, organizations are using teams of managers and other employees to solve problems and meet goals. The affiliation motive affects people's willingness to work together in teams. People who dislike interacting with others won't be able to function effectively in a team environment. The power motive also may affect how employees react to team operations, particularly with regard to self-managed work teams. **Self-managed work teams** comprise groups of employees who must work together daily to produce a product (or major component) and who perform various managerial tasks (e.g., setting team goals, scheduling work assignments, ordering materials, and hiring replacement personnel) regarding their operations. To manage themselves successfully, employees need to have a socialized power orientation rather than a personal power orientation.

Discussion Question 3
Using Maslow's needs hierarchy and McClelland's learned needs model, analyze the motivational approach at the Covenant House. What needs did this nonprofit organization satisfy?

Describe the characteristics of work and the work environment that affect job satisfaction and performance.

HERZBERG'S TWO-FACTOR MODEL: A CONTENT APPROACH

The content approaches just discussed focus on individual differences. In contrast, Herzberg's two-factor model stresses job characteristics and organizational practices in addressing the question of what motivates behavior.[15] Herzberg initially examined the relationship between job satisfaction and productivity for 200 accountants and engineers. In carrying out their research, Herzberg and his associates asked participants to describe job experiences that produced good and bad feelings about their jobs. The researchers discovered that the presence of a particular job characteristic, such as responsibility, might increase job satisfaction. However, the lack of that same characteristic didn't necessarily produce dissatisfaction. Conversely, if lack of a characteristic, such as job security, produced dissatisfaction, high job security didn't necessarily lead to satisfaction. As shown in Figure 13.5, traditional thinking was that satisfaction and dissatisfaction were at opposite ends of a single continuum and that employees were in var-

FIGURE 13.5

Views of Job Satisfaction

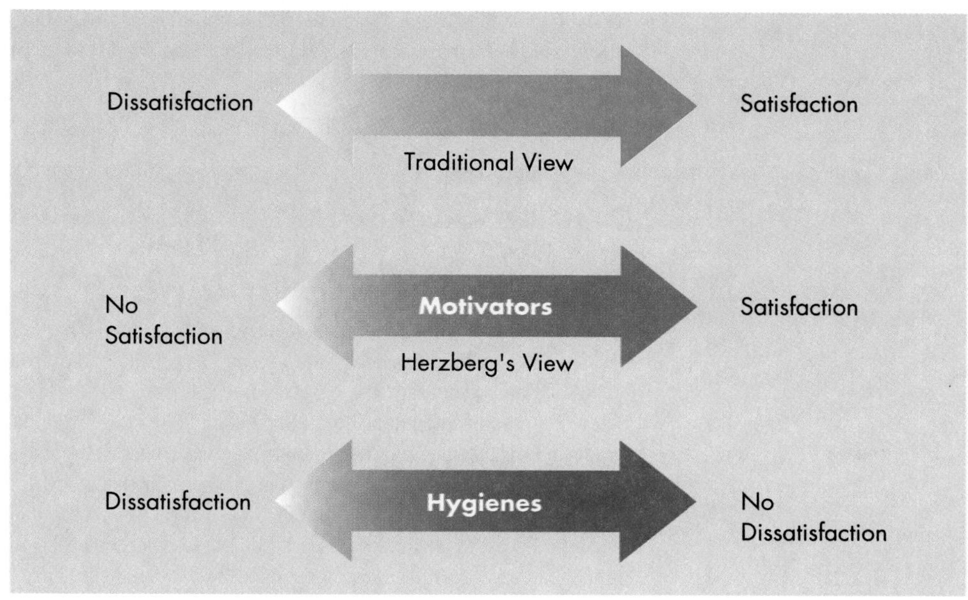

ious stages along it. Herzberg and his associates suggested that there are really two continuums: one ranging from no satisfaction to satisfaction and the other ranging from dissatisfaction to no dissatisfaction.

The study's results led Herzberg to conclude that two separate and distinct kinds of experiences produced job satisfaction and job dissatisfaction, which came to be known as the **two-factor model.** The factors associated with positive feelings about the job are called motivator factors. Those associated with feelings of dissatisfaction are called hygiene factors. Table 13.1 lists the primary motivator and hygiene factors.

Motivator factors are job characteristics (challenge of the work itself, responsibility, recognition, achievement, and advancement and growth) that, when present should create high levels of motivation. These factors determine whether a job is exciting and rewarding. However, they lead to superior performance *only* if no dissatisfiers are present.

Dissatisfiers are found among the hygiene factors. **Hygiene factors** are characteristics of the work environment outside the job (working conditions, company policies, supervision, co-workers, salary, formal status, and job security) that, when positive, maintain a reasonable level of job motivation but don't necessarily increase it. Let's assume that an organization provides free parking and that employees receive fringe benefits in the form of health and life insurance, a retirement plan, and time off for child or elder care. Will these employees be more highly motivated to perform than if those benefits weren't provided? According to Herzberg, the answer is *no*! Herzberg suggested that, although positive environmental factors are needed to maintain job satisfaction,

Teaching Tip
Make a list of the different jobs students have had, including the job of student itself. Analyze the motivators and hygiene factors for some of those jobs.

Ask Students
A Dallas manager claims that "workers won't carry the hatchet too much longer. I think they realize they've got a job and a pretty good job, and they know it's going to be there tomorrow. What more could they want?" Relate this claim to Herzberg's two-factor model.

TABLE 13.1

Examples of Motivator and Hygiene Factors

MOTIVATOR FACTORS (SOURCES OF JOB SATISFACTION)	HYGIENE FACTORS (SOURCES OF JOB DISSATISFACTION)
Challenge of the work itself	Working conditions
Responsibility	Company policies
Recognition	Supervision
Achievement	Co-workers
Advancement and growth	Salary, status, and job security

only motivators will increase the level of job satisfaction. The following Global Insight illustrates what can happen when hygiene factors are present but motivating factors are not.

Global *Insight*

Window Sitting in Japan

Until recently, Japanese human resources policies and practices were based on an expected lifetime relationship between employee and employer. People are recruited not for their creativity or ambition, but for how well they will fit into the corporate culture. Extensive orientation programs indoctrinate new employees to the organization's corporate culture. Extensive management development occurs through job rotation. This exposure, in turn, helps to develop the interpersonal relationships that foster information exchange among managers—a crucial element in consensus decision making. Successful Japanese managers cultivate interpersonal relationships and the ability to focus on the group. The pay system is based on seniority.

But what happened when Japanese companies no longer needed all of their employees, yet were constrained by a culture of lifetime employment and laws that restricted termination of employees? A common practice was to give unwanted employees a "window seat," in hopes that they would eventually quit because they no longer had satisfying work to do. Yasuhiko Ushiba, a middle-aged former employee of Japan's Mitsubishi Corporation, was given a window seat. During the last ten years of his employment with Mitsubishi he was given a dead-end job with no specific task assignments. Mitsubishi undercut any effort he made at developing projects. Eventually he spent his working hours at the zoo and the movies, still drawing an annual salary of approximately $85,000. Later Ushiba left the company to start his own consulting practice.

The window seat was a form of corporate welfare in Japan whereby senior employees were kept on the payroll but given little or nothing to do. They might spend their time in mind-numbing make-work activities. Or their work might amount to little more than twiddling their thumbs. Or they may do things that are totally unrelated to work. Yet they still got paid and had job security. Many Japanese view the window seat as an entitlement—their reward for years of loyalty. Employees in the window seat still have essential hygiene factors met, but motivating factors aren't present. Window sitters aren't satisfied, and that is what their employers hope will eventually cause them to quit their jobs.[16]

Application in Organizations

For many years, some organizations required employees to perform routine, assembly-line tasks. They were then plagued with human resources problems such as high turnover, absenteeism, grievances, and low productivity. These organizations generally relied on hygiene factors alone to motivate employees. According to Herzberg and others, hygiene factors do not stimulate performance; therefore management should focus on motivator factors to solve this problem. However, hygiene factors shouldn't be ignored when the content of a job is changed. When the environmental elements outside a job are favorable, changes in job content will more likely have positive outcomes.[17]

Discussion Question 4
What are the managerial implications of Herzberg's two-factor model?

The two-factor model has been criticized because of flaws in its research methodology and the failure to consider differences in individuals' needs. However, many people in HRM accept the two-factor model for at least two reasons. First, it's easy to understand: Individuals can easily identify motivator and hygiene factors. Second, the actions required to improve employee performance are straightforward:

- give employees challenging jobs;
- allow employees to make suggestions on ways to improve their jobs; and
- focus on the job itself and not just on the physical work environment.

7

Explain how job enrichment affects people's motivation at work.

JOB ENRICHMENT: EXTENDING THE TWO-FACTOR MODEL

Job-enrichment models focus on changing specific job characteristics in order to motivate employees and promote job satisfaction[18] addressing employees' higher level needs. The most popular and extensively tested job-enrichment model was developed by J. Richard Hackman and Greg Oldham (see Figure 13.6).[19]

As shown in Figure 13.6, the Hackman-Oldham model indicates that three crucial psychological states—experienced meaningfulness, experienced responsibility, and knowledge of results—affect motivation in the workplace. The nature of each of these psychological states is described in Table 13.2. When any are low, employee motivation is low.

We can illustrate the concepts represented by these psychological states with an analogy to the game of golf. Players hit the ball and follow its flight. They receive immediate feedback in the form of their scores on each hole, which tells the golfers how well they are playing against a standard (par). Personal responsibility for performance is high even though golfers may make excuses for poor performance. Experienced meaningfulness also may be high when golfers see their efforts translated at once into scores that can be compared to par and to the scores of their playing partners. Because all three psychological states usually are high among regular players, motivation usually is high. In fact, some golfers exhibit motivated behavior rarely seen at work: getting up before dawn, playing in rain and snow, feeling despair or joy (depending on how the round went), and even aggression (throwing a club after a muffed shot).

FIGURE 13.6

Hackman-Oldham Job-Enrichment Model

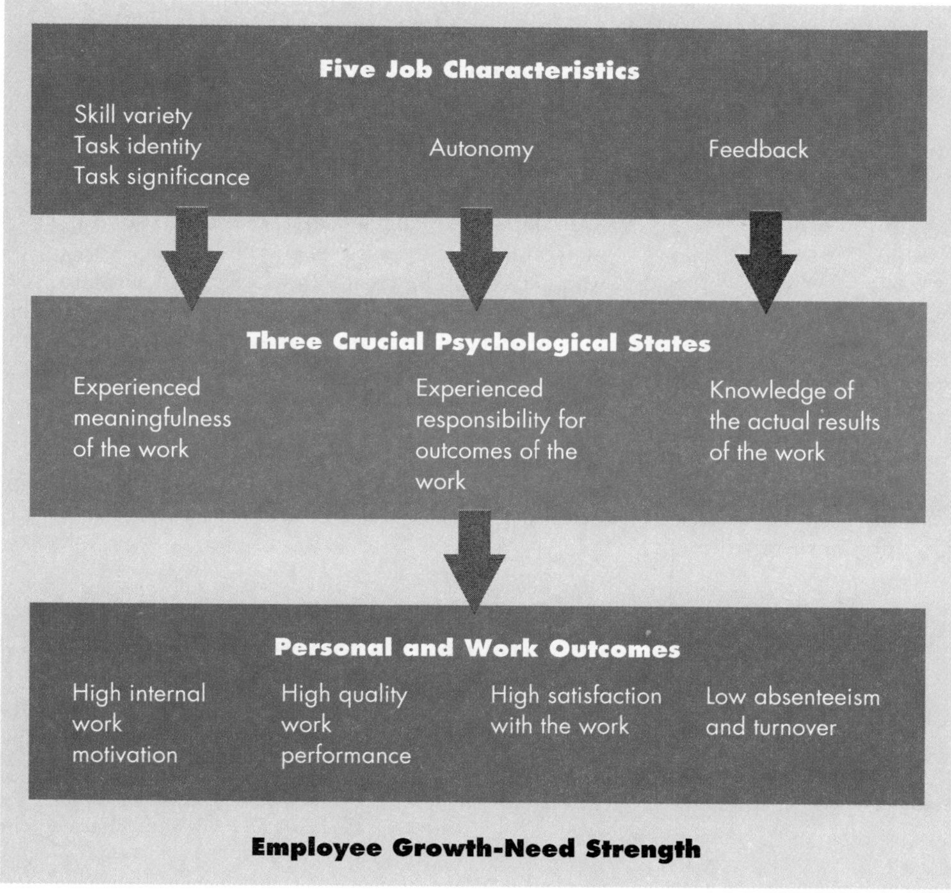

Source: Hackman, J.R., and Oldham, G.R. *Work Redesign,* Reading, Mass.: Addison-Wesley, 1980, 83. Reprinted with permission.

TABLE 13.2

Crucial Psychological States

Experienced meaningfulness	The degree to which employees perceive their work as valuable and worthwhile.
Experienced responsibility	The extent to which employees feel personally responsible for the quality of their work.
Knowledge of results	The extent to which employees receive feedback about how well they are doing the job.

Source: Adapted from Hackman, J.R., and Oldham, G.R. *Work Redesign,* Reading, Mass.: Addison-Wesley, 1980, 72–73. Reprinted with permission.

Real-World Example

According to Michael Hammer co-author of the best-selling book *Reengineering the Corporation,* in traditional organizations the characteristics of the job offer little satisfaction for they are designed in a piecemeal manner. Workers do not have a sense of the whole process and lack a sense of closure and competition. Do you agree with Hammer's view?

Figure 13.6 also shows that the crucial psychological states that employees experience are affected by five key characteristics of their jobs: skill variety, task identity, task significance, autonomy, and feedback. We identified these job characteristics earlier in this chapter (see Figure 13.1) and now define them in Table 13.3. As Figure 13.6 shows, skill variety, task identity, and task significance all contribute to the experienced meaningfulness of work. Jobs lacking these characteristics seem trivial and worthless. To offset feelings of meaninglessness, employees sometimes play mental games. For example, taxi cab drivers and long-distance truck drivers say that they occasionally play license-plate poker in their heads. Autonomy fosters feelings of personal responsibility. When jobs provide autonomy, employees will relate performance directly to their own efforts and decisions. When autonomy isn't possible, employees are less likely to see a strong, direct link between performance and their own efforts. In this case, feedback should be used to help employees see the linkage between their job behaviors and their job performance.

Additionally, Figure 13.6 indicates that certain moderator variables influence the relationships between both job characteristics and crucial psychological states and work motivation. In other words, these moderator variables influence how different people will respond to having their jobs enriched. Individuals with a strong desire for personal challenges, a sense of accomplishment, and learning—that is, high **growth-need strength**—are likely to respond positively to job-enrichment programs. People also will respond positively to job enrichment when they have the knowledge and skills to perform the job and are satisfied with contextual variables such as pay, job security, working conditions, supervisors, and co-workers. However, if an individual has weak growth needs, lacks the requisite knowledge and skills, or isn't satisfied with contextual factors, attempts at job enrichment may only increase stress and job dissatisfaction.

Teaching Tip

Compile a list of jobs students currently hold and a second list of jobs they would like. Select a few jobs from each list and use Hackman and Oldham's model to compare them.

Individuals bring different attributes to the job, so various employees will respond to the same job in different ways. What may be a good job for one person will be bad for someone else. The job-enrichment model demonstrates this concept by showing that

TABLE 13.3

Key Job Characteristics

Skill variety	The degree to which the job involves a variety of different work activities or requires the use of a number of skills and talents.
Task identity	The degree to which the job requires completing an identifiable piece of work, that is, doing a job with a visible beginning and outcome.
Task significance	The degree to which the job has a substantial impact on the goals or work of others in the company.
Autonomy	The degree to which the job provides substantial freedom, independence, and discretion to the individual in scheduling work and determining the procedures to be used in carrying out tasks.
Feedback	The degree to which carrying out work activities required by the job results in the individual's obtaining direct and clear information about his or her performance.

Source: Adapted from Hackman, J.R., and Oldham, G.R. *Work Redesign,* Reading, Mass.: Addison-Wesley, 1980, 78–80. Reprinted with permission.

a person's need for growth, knowledge and skills, and contextual satisfaction define the relationship of job characteristics to performance and/or satisfaction.

Application in Organizations

The Hackman-Oldham job-enrichment model suggests that employees' jobs should be studied to identify core job characteristics that can be changed.[20] For example, an effort to increase the skill variety of a job could overload an employee who is already working on numerous complex tasks. By also understanding employees' personal needs for growth and achievement or their knowledge and skills, more realistic decisions can be made about redesigning jobs to improve performance and job satisfaction.

Ethics
Forcing everyone into an enriched job is no more ethical than forcing everyone into a boring job. What management techniques would you use to help people find out what type of job they want and place them in it? What would you do if they want one kind of job but the jobs they now have pay better? Is either forcing them to change jobs or redesigning the job ethical?

For employees who don't want to grow on the job, enrichment programs may be frustrating and dissatisfying. This point is illustrated by a study in which autoworkers from Detroit worked in Sweden as engine assemblers in a SAAB plant. These jobs allowed them a great deal of freedom and responsibility in performing their jobs. After one month, however, 75 percent of the Americans reported that they preferred their traditional assembly-line jobs. As one worker said, "If I've got to bust my a__ to have a meaningful job, forget it; I'd rather be monotonous."[21] Clearly, enriched jobs aren't for everyone.

In addition, some union members and managers have resisted job-enrichment programs. To quote one AFL-CIO leader, "If you want to enrich the job, enrich the paycheck . . . that's the kind of job enrichment unions believe in." And managers have trouble assessing the results of job enrichment in dollars and cents. For example, what is the cost of a poor decision or a redundant inspection? Will these costs be lowered by introducing a job-enrichment program? Without answers to such questions, determining whether a job-enrichment program will pay off can be difficult.

The potential value of job enrichment, even in a unionized company, is illustrated by the contrast between the approaches General Motors and Ford have used to improve productivity. General Motors spent billions of dollars on highly automated machinery to replace employees. Ford used an employee involvement program that not only encouraged employee input in problem solving but made the employees feel like important and valued contributors. Peter Petillo, a human resources executive at Ford Motor Company, says "GM was determined to minimize the role of the hourly people." "Our goal was to maximize the contribution of the hourly people."[22] This is what job enrichment is all about. It helps identify how jobs can be designed to give employees feelings of being important, contributing members of the organization.

One way in which employees' jobs can be enriched is through the use of self-managed teams. In Chapter 16 we describe in detail how job enrichment concepts can be applied to self-managed teams. For now, the following Small Business Insight illustrates how a small newsletter publishing company enriched employees' jobs through the use of self-managed teams.

Small Business *Insight*

Self-Managed Teams at Published Image

Plagued by poor employee morale, high turnover, poor product quality, and limited customer retention, Published Image, a Boston-based newsletter publisher with 26 employees, adopted self-managed work teams as a way to solve its problems. Accustomed to narrowly defined jobs, "employees believed their job was to please their boss instead of the customer." Eric Gershman, founder and president of Published Image, radically changed how employees' jobs are done. Now, they operate as members of four self-managed work teams—each a cohesive, integrated unit that sets its own schedules, prepares its own budgets, and receives team bonuses based on its performance. Each team has its own clients and its own staff of sales, editorial, and production employees. Team members know what is going on with each client's job, and they share responsibility for the entire job. Team members perform a broader range of tasks than they formerly did. For instance, Shelley Danse functions primarily as an account executive but also does research for writers, helps with art layouts, and proofreads copy.

Have self-managed teams solved the problems of poor employee morale, high turnover, poor product quality, and limited customer retention? Gershman says that they have. Turnover is virtually nonexistent, compared to the previous 50 percent annual rate. Published Image now is losing less than 5 percent of its customers annually, in contrast to about 33 percent before. The company's profit margin increased from 3 percent to 20 percent. Redesigning jobs through self-managed teams seems to have worked very well for this organization.[23]

8

Discuss the basic assumptions and concepts underlying the expectancy model of motivation.

EXPECTANCY MODEL: A PROCESS APPROACH

Our discussion of motivation so far has focused on the different needs that employees bring to their jobs and how organizational practices and characteristics of the job itself can influence their behavior. However, none of the content approaches to motivation adequately explain how people become motivated or why people behave in so many different ways as they seek to fulfill their needs and achieve their goals. Expectancy models of motivation try to account for the differences in human behavior by tracing each step in the motivation process—from the initial decision to exert effort to the ultimate reward.

Vroom's Expectancy Model

One of the most widely accepted models for explaining how people make such decisions is Victor Vroom's expectancy model. The **expectancy model** suggests that people choose among alternative behaviors because they anticipate that particular behaviors will lead to one or more desired outcomes (e.g., recognition, or new challenges) and that other behaviors will lead to undesirable outcomes.[24] This model also suggests that employees will be motivated to improve performance if they know that they are capable of the desired behavior, believe that satisfactory performance will result in the desired outcome, and value that outcome highly. Vroom's expectancy model rests on three basic assumptions.

Ask Students
Is this statement always true? Why or why not?

Teaching Tip
Have students identify behaviors that they can make conscious decisions about and guide the potential outcomes of.

- *Forces within individuals and in their job situations combine to motivate and determine behavior.* As Maslow stated, people seek to satisfy different needs. Forces in the job situation influence how they go about doing so.
- *People make conscious decisions about their own behavior.* For example, an individual decides whether to accept a job with the organization, come to work or call in sick, put in overtime, strive for a promotion, and so on.
- *Selecting a course of action depends on the expectation that a certain behavior will lead to one or more desired outcomes instead of undesired outcomes.* In essence, individuals tend to behave in ways that they believe will help them achieve their objectives (such as a promotion or job security) and avoid behaving in ways that will lead to undesirable consequences (such as a demotion or criticism).

Ask Students
State an expectancy.

Ask Students
State a first-order outcome.

Figure 13.7 illustrates the relationships among the key concepts of Vroom's expectancy model. Let's consider each concept in more detail.

Expectancy. Before acting, the individual must assess the chance that expending the required effort will lead to achievement of the desired behavior. **Expectancy** is the belief that effort will lead to first-order outcomes, and it is usually expressed as a probability. A **first-order outcome** is any work-related behavior (e.g., satisfactory perfor-

FIGURE 13.7

Key Concepts of Vroom's Expectancy Model

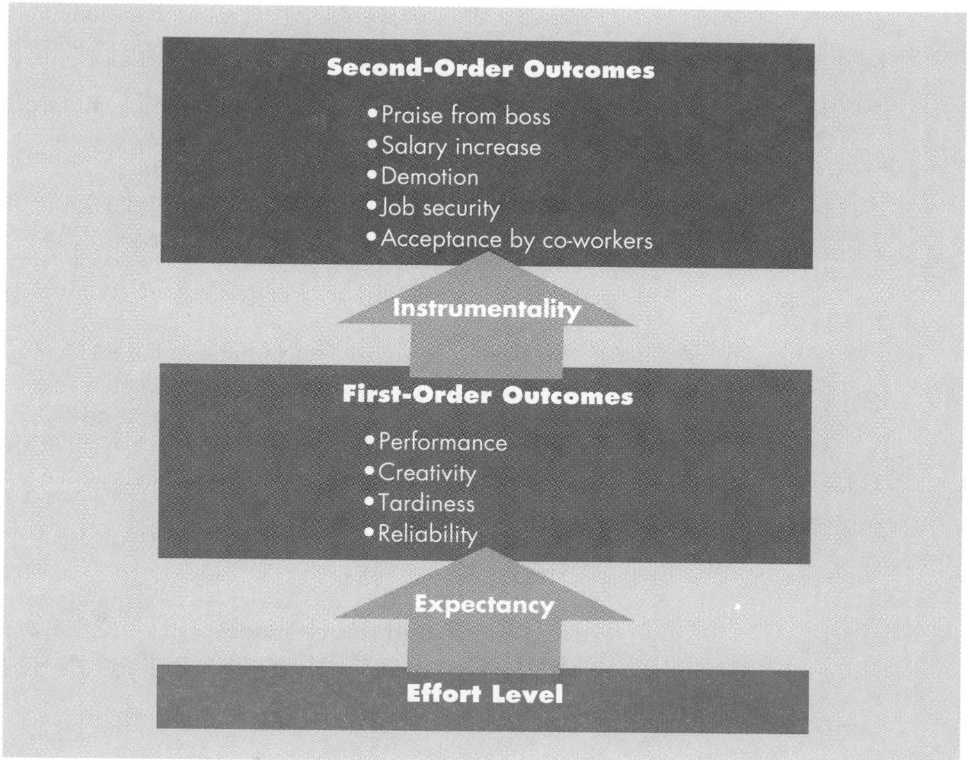

mance, creativity, reliability, or habitual tardiness) that is the direct result of the effort an employee expends on a job.

Ask Students
State an instrumental relationship.

Instrumentality. **Instrumentality** is the perceived relationship between first-order outcomes and the attainment of second-order outcomes. The individual must believe that certain work-related behaviors will lead to desired outcomes. This relationship typically is expressed as a correlation; thus high performance, for instance, could result in avoiding outcomes as well as attaining outcomes. If you achieve an A in this course, you expect your grade to increase the likelihood of your receiving your parents' approval, graduating from college, and getting a better job—your desired second-order outcomes. A **second-order outcome** is the result, good or bad (e.g., a raise, promotion, demotion, acceptance by co-workers, or job security), brought about by a first-order outcome, or behavior.

Ask Students
State a second-order outcome.

The motivational process that links expectancy and instrumentality is illustrated by the performance appraisal and reward system used at Johnsonville Foods, Inc., in Sheboygan, Wisconsin. Employees rate themselves and fellow employees on seventeen performance dimensions that are grouped into three categories: quality and quantity of work, teamwork, and personal development. All final scores, with names deleted, are then passed to a profit-sharing group that carves out five categories of performance: superior, better-than-average, average, below-average, and poor. Employees expect that if they work hard they'll be rated as superior performers by their fellow employees. This superior rating means a larger share of the profit-sharing money paid to employees quarterly by the company.[25]

Ask Students
State a valence.

Valence. Tthe value or weight that an individual attaches to a first- or second-order outcome is called its **valence,** which can motivate behavior and influence decisions. Valences are subjective, so the same outcome may have a high valence for one person and a low valence for another. For example, a promotion to the higher paying position of museum director would appeal more to an individual who values (places a high valence on) financial gain and increased responsibility than to an individual who values creativity and independence as a curator.

The valence of a first-order outcome, such as performance, depends on the valences assigned to second-order outcomes and on the instrumentalities between first- and second-order outcomes. Let's continue with the Johnsonville Foods example. Getting a superior performance rating from fellow workers will mean a lot to someone who values money. However, if the person receiving a superior performance rating then receives the "cold shoulder" from fellow workers, she might reevaluate whether such performance and the money it brought are worth being given the silent treatment by co-workers.

Motivation therefore is determined by individual beliefs about the relationship between effort and behaviors and the expectation that certain behaviors (first-order outcomes) will produce the desired results (second-order outcomes). Simply put, the theory holds that people choose to behave in ways that are highly likely to enable them to realize desirable outcomes and to avoid undesirable outcomes.

Porter-Lawler Expectancy Model

Lyman Porter and Edward Lawler have extended the basic expectancy model. The **Porter-Lawler expectancy model** states that satisfaction is the result rather than a cause of performance.[26] Different levels of performance lead to different rewards. The

FIGURE 13.8

Porter-Lawler Expectancy Model

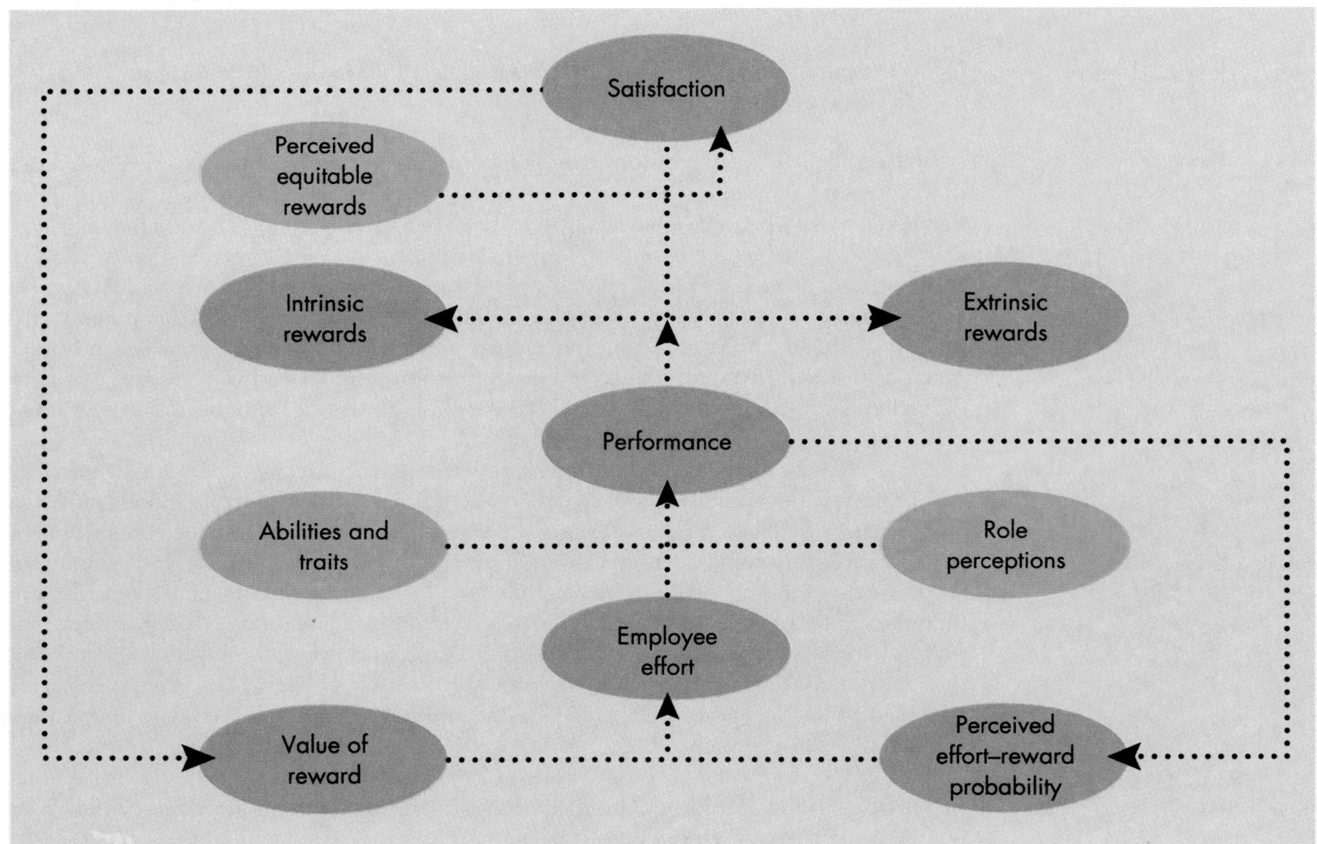

Source: From Porter, L.W., and Lawler, E.E. III. *Managerial Attitudes and Performance,* Homewood, Ill.: Irwin, 1968, 165. Used with permission.

rewards, in turn, produce different levels of job satisfaction. Figure 13.8 shows the complete Porter-Lawler expectancy model, which draws on personal, job, and organizational characteristics to explain motivation.

The **value of reward** is the importance that a person places on benefits to be obtained from a job (e.g., friendship of co-workers, promotion, a good salary, or a feeling of accomplishment). Some workers might prize the friendship of co-workers; others might value money more highly.

Ethics
Bryan Monday, a former DJ who is now a clothing salesman, claims: "There doesn't seem to be the appreciation for the work ethic anymore. It seems to be 'Can a person make my cash register ring?' And as you do, the demand just grows. But the reward doesn't." Can an organization justify this kind of performance expectation? What can an employee do about it?

The **perceived effort-reward probability** is a person's perception of the linkage between expending effort and obtaining certain rewards. Suppose that a manager wants to transfer from the Midwest to the Northeast. She might feel that chances of getting the transfer have little to do with performance but rather depend on other factors (e.g., luck, "pull," or the state of the economy). Under such conditions the manager would perceive a low effort-reward probability.

Employee effort is the amount of physical and/or mental energy exerted to perform a task. In other words, how hard is the employee trying? In baseball, a shortstop's attempt to throw the runner out at first base is an example of effort. Whether the effort results in an out is a measure of performance. Effort refers solely to the energy expended—not to how successful it is. The amount of effort applied depends on the interaction between the value of the reward and the effort-reward probability.

Of course, employee effort isn't the only variable that affects performance; abilities, traits, and role perceptions also influence performance. **Ability** refers to an individual's mastery of the skills (e.g., technical, interpersonal, conceptual, communication, and critical thinking) required to do a job. **Traits** are individual personality characteristics (e.g., the strength of various needs) that can affect a person's job performance. Thus abilities and traits are relatively independent of the work situation. Although employees can learn new skills by practicing on the job, they generally acquire basic abilities and traits before beginning work.

Teaching Tip
Have students identify some situations in which they were highly motivated to perform because they expected to perform well. Then have them identify some situations in which they did not pursue a goal because they felt there was no chance of success. Relate these experiences to expectancy theory.

Role perceptions refer to the employee's belief that certain tasks should be performed (i.e., certain roles played) in order to do a job successfully. Role perceptions determine how employees define their jobs and the types of efforts they believe are essential to effective performance.

Performance is the level of the individual's work achievement that comes only after effort has been exerted. It depends not only on the amount of effort exerted, but also on the individual's abilities and role perceptions. An employee who exerts a great amount of effort but has little ability or has inaccurately assessed what it takes to succeed in the organization may perform poorly. To perform well, an individual must not only put forth the effort (or want to do the job) but also must know what should be done and be able to do it. The following Quality Insight shows how the Ritz-Carlton Hotel chain deals with each of the factors that affect performance in the expectancy model.

Teaching Tip
Have students apply expectancy theory to their own performance in this class.

Quality *Insight*

Motivation at the Ritz-Carlton

The Ritz-Carlton Hotel chain, a winner of the Malcolm Baldrige National Quality Award, is noted for providing exceptional service to its customers. How does the Ritz achieve this high level of quality? It uses motivational methods that are consistent with the Porter-Lawler expectancy model of motivation. Hotel management tries to influence employee effort by providing rewards that are valued by employees and are contingent on their performance, thereby strengthening the employees' perceived effort-reward probabilities. The company uses 5 *Star Awards* to recognize superior performers who have been nominated by their peers and managers. Each hotel has five quarterly award winners,

FIGURE 13.9

Reinforcement Process

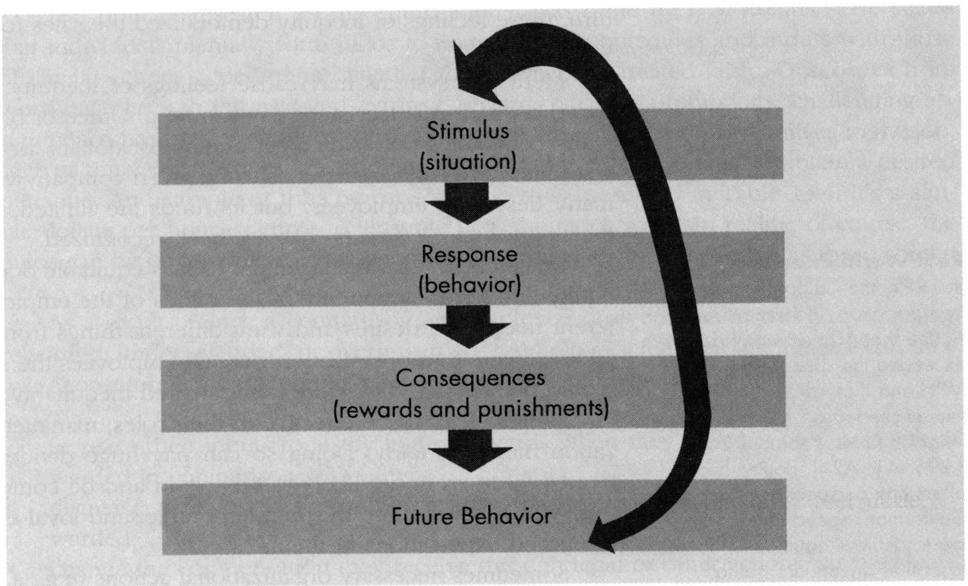

staff meeting with a proposed style sheet for all diagrams created for user manuals, much like the existing style sheets for text. If your manager praises your initiative and creativity, your behavior is rewarded. You probably will be motivated to come up with other innovations. However, if your manager gives you a disapproving look and says that the firm is perfectly happy with the existing conditions, your behavior isn't rewarded. You probably will conclude that new ideas lead to unpleasant consequences and that the best way to earn a reward is just to follow orders.

A manager who wants to change an employee's behavior must also change the specific consequences of that behavior. For example, to encourage ridesharing among its employees, Farmers Insurance Group's regional office in Simi Valley, California, instituted a program whereby employees earned points that they could redeem for merchandise. Rewarding employees for changing their driving habits enabled the regional office to comply with the provision of the Clean Air Act that required employers with 100 or more employees to reduce the number of vehicles driven to their facilities.[40]

Behavior modification relies on three basic principles: (1) measurable behavior, (2) types of consequences, and (3) schedules of reinforcement and punishment.[41]

Measurable Behavior

Measurable behavior is work-related action that can be observed and expressed in terms of quantity (e.g., number of units produced, percentage of defective units, number of meals served, or number of students taught). Thoughts and feelings are not considered to be part of measurable behavior because they are difficult to observe and quantify.

Teaching Tip
Focusing on measurable (quantifiable) behaviors may be at odds with obtaining quality.

Measurable behavior is a key element of the gainsharing programs that some companies, such as Boeing and Lennox, have instituted. Recall that in gainsharing programs all employees in a department or team get a bonus when it exceeds predetermined performance goals, such as high productivity or courteous customer service. The advantages of measurable performance goals include better coordination and teamwork among employees, expanded employee knowledge about the business and focus on goals, and improved employee work habits. The main disadvantage is that performance goals focus only on measurable actions. Thus employees may ignore other important goals—such as interdepartmental cooperation, quality, and the training of new employ-

All companies in a department benefit when it exceeds predetermined productivity goals. By equipping every truck with a pallet jack, loading and unloading time has been cut by about 30 percent at O. M. Scott & Sons.

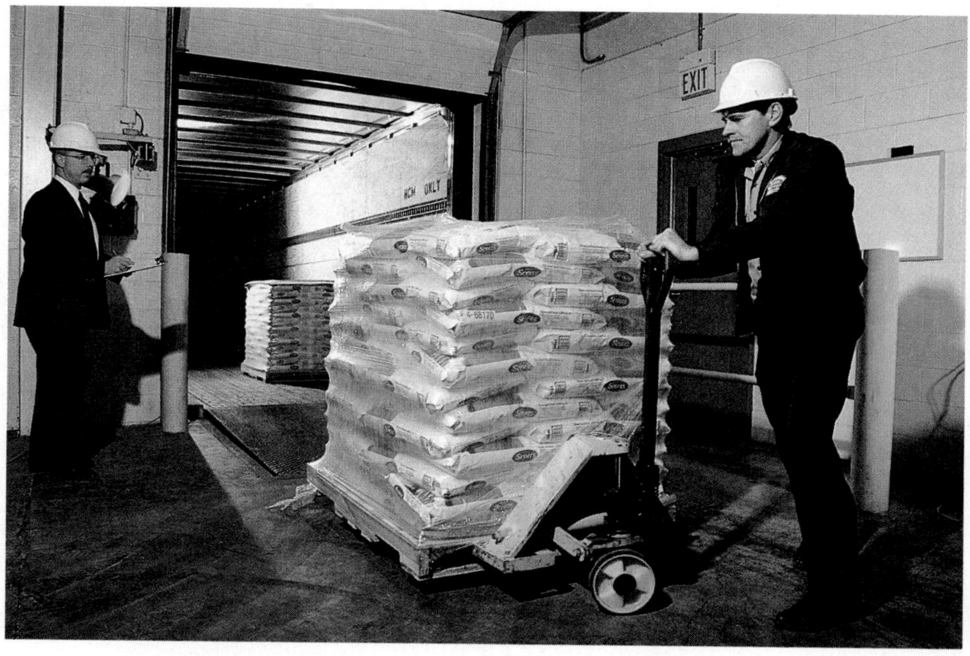

ees—that can't be quantified as easily. Only behaviors that can be observed and measured are relevant to behavior modification.

Types of Consequences

Consequences are either pleasant or unpleasant, which is determined by two factors: the action that follows the behavior and the nature of the outcome. Actions that follow behavior consist of removing an outcome or presenting an outcome. Outcomes are either rewarding (positive) or aversive (negative). Figure 13.10 shows how these two factors combine to differentiate among four types of consequences that can modify behavior: positive reinforcement, negative reinforcement, punishment, and extinction. The first two types, positive reinforcement and negative reinforcement, are consequences that strengthen or maintain behaviors. The second two, punishment and extinction, are consequences that reduce or stop behaviors.

FIGURE 13.10

Differentiating Among Types of Consequences

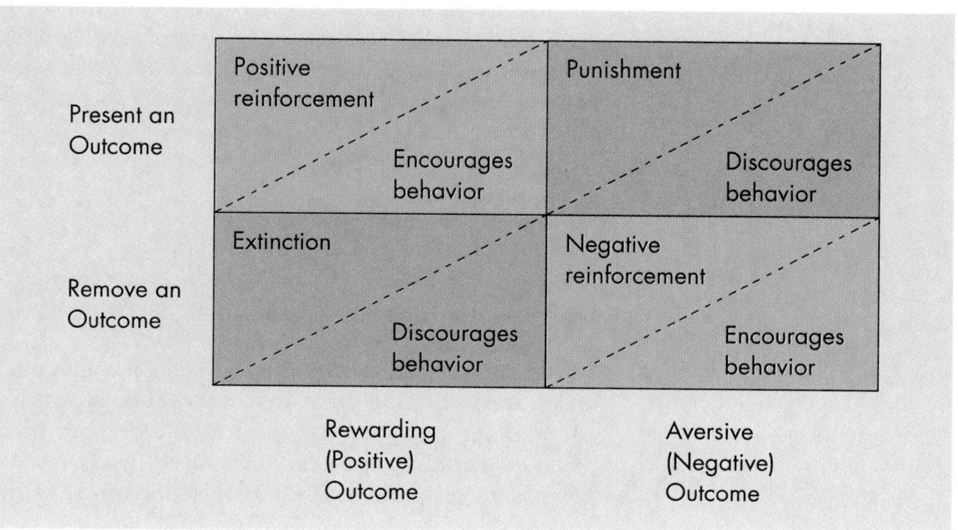

A common misconception is that reinforcement, either positive or negative, is linked only to desired (functional) behavior, whereas punishment and extinction are used only with undesired (dysfunctional) behavior. In reality, each of the four types of consequences can be used with either functional or dysfunctional behavior. For example, some team members may not carry their fair share of the burden on a project, but the boss compliments the entire team on the project's success. In this instance, the dysfunctional behavior of the loafing team member's behavior has been reinforced—either intentionally or accidentally—thereby strengthening it. Another example concerns the employee who takes on additional tasks without being asked and then is chastised by the manager for overstepping his responsibilities. Here, functional behavior has been punished, and the probability of its future occurrence has been weakened.

According to behavioral psychologists, dysfunctional behavior persists because it is being maintained by reinforcement. Moreover, functional behavior is sometimes suppressed, if not eliminated, because it results in unpleasant consequences. To avoid such unfortunate occurrences, individuals should carefully and deliberately apply pleasant consequences only to desired behaviors and unpleasant consequences only to undesired behaviors. The following Ethics Insight demonstrates what can happen when people are rewarded for doing the wrong things.

Ethics *Insight*

Sales Practices at Met Life's Tampa Office

The Tampa Office of Metropolitan Life Insurance Company became the biggest seller of life insurance in the United States. According to Florida's insurance regulators, Met Life's Tampa office became number one by misleading registered nurses about the product they were buying. The nurses were led to believe that they were buying retirement accounts when in fact they were purchasing life insurance. Agents were directed by their managers not to mention that they were selling life insurance and to substitute the word "deposit" for the word "premium." Rick Urso, head of the Tampa office, told agents they had the company's approval to use "misrepresentations, fraud and other unlawful means" to sell insurance.

The Tampa office had a strict sales formula. Promotional materials were sent to registered nurses throughout the nation. Requests for additional information led to a sales appointment, at which an agent presented a standard sales pitch from memory. It was misleading because it concealed the fact that the agent actually was selling life insurance. Yet, Met Life agents garnered most of the more than $4 million in sales commissions in a recent year from such sales.

However, when some Met Life employees "blew the whistle" on the Tampa office's sales practices, they were dismissed. Met Life said that the dismissals were for cause; the employees said that they were dismissed because they blew the whistle. Some filed lawsuits against the company, and Florida insurance regulators investigated the questionable sales practices. Subsequently, Met Life offered refunds to approximately 60,000 policyholders.[42]

Discussion Question 6
What does the reinforcement model suggest for improving employees' performance? What happens when the consequences of behavior are incorrectly applied?

The Tampa office of Metropolitan Life rewarded agents for behavior that actually was dysfunctional for the organization. As a consequence, Met Life strengthened the behavior until some employees realized that the behavior was unethical, if not illegal, and objected to it.

Positive reinforcement creates a pleasant consequence by using rewards to increase the likelihood that a behavior will be repeated. Any rewarding outcome that encourages an individual to repeat a behavior can be classified as a positive reinforcer. Some common positive reinforcers used by organizations are praise, recognition of accomplishment, promotion, and salary increases. Many people regard these reinforcers as desirable.

Ethics
Is negative reinforcement ethically justifiable? What are the arguments for and against this method?

Negative reinforcement occurs when a person engages in behavior to avoid impending unpleasant consequences or to escape from existing unpleasant consequences. Some students may come to class on time to avoid a reprimand from the instructor. Similarly, most employees follow coffee break and lunch hour guidelines to avoid incurring the disapproval of managers or co-workers. In both cases, these individuals are acting to avoid unpleasant results. Unlike the other three types of consequences, negative reinforcement is applied by the employee, not by others in the organization.

Teaching Tip
Learning often extinguishes after students leave school. Ask students how they can reinforce their learning and make it a lifelong endeavor.

Punishment is an attempt to discourage a target behavior by the application of negative outcomes whenever it does occur. The purpose of punishment is to reduce the likelihood that an individual will repeat the target behavior. For example, disciplinary actions may be taken against an employee who comes to work late, neglects to clean up the work area, or turns out too many defective parts. The disciplinary action might take the form of a verbal reprimand, a monetary fine, a demotion, or, if the employee persists, a suspension—all with the intention of discouraging the behavior. Whatever form it takes, punishment should match the nature of the infraction and should be consistent with what other employees have received.[43]

Extinction is the absence of any reinforcement, either positive or negative, following the occurrence of a target behavior. Usually, extinction occurs when the positive reinforcement that once normally resulted from the behavior is removed. Because the behavior no longer produces reinforcement, the behavior will be weakened. Extinction may occur when disruptive behavior that has been maintained by social attention is simply ignored. For example, the pedestrian who ignores the heckling of disruptive adolescents by walking past them, rather than arguing with them, is trying to stop the undesired behavior (heckling) through extinction. Arguing with them may merely provide the attention they seek and serve to strengthen the undesired behavior.

Schedules of Reinforcement and Punishment

The effectiveness of consequences for motivating employees depends not only on the type of consequence, but also on the frequency with which the consequence is provided. Table 13.5 lists the five most commonly used schedules of reinforcement and punishment: fixed interval, variable interval, fixed ratio, continuous, and variable ratio. Depending on the circumstances, some will be more effective than others.

Reinforcement Schedules. The **fixed interval reinforcement schedule** provides reinforcement at fixed intervals of time—for example, a weekly, twice-monthly, or monthly paycheck. This type of reinforcement schedule provides the least immediate incentive for performing well. Employees know that they will be paid for a minimal level of desired behavior during that time interval.

Teaching Tip
Pop quizzes are an example of variable interval schedules.

A **variable interval reinforcement schedule** provides reinforcement at irregular intervals of time. Inspection crews work on this type of schedule. Not knowing when an inspection is going to occur may help maintain a reasonably high level of desired behavior.

TABLE 13.5

Schedules of Reinforcement and Punishment

TYPE	DESCRIPTION
Fixed Interval	Reinforcement or punishment given at fixed times, regardless of behavior.
Variable Interval	Reinforcement or punishment given at variable times, regardless of behavior.
Fixed Ratio	Reinforcement or punishment given after a fixed number of target behaviors, regardless of time.
Continuous	Reinforcement or punishment given after every behavior.
Variable Ratio	Reinforcement or punishment given after a variable number of target behaviors, regardless of time.

A **fixed ratio reinforcement schedule** provides reinforcement after a fixed number of target behaviors have occurred. Salespeople on commissions and employees on piece-rate systems operate under this type of schedule. Motivation usually is high as employees approach the point at which reinforcement is next due.

A **continuous reinforcement schedule** is a special type of fixed ratio schedule in which the ratio of reinforcement to number of responses is 1:1. In other words, every target behavior results in reinforcement. Initial levels of motivation and performance tend to be high with this type of schedule. However, employees may become satisfied quickly with a specific reinforcer because they receive it so frequently. When satiation sets in, the reinforcer loses it power to motivate behavior.

A **variable ratio reinforcement schedule** provides reinforcement after a varying number of target behaviors has occurred, regardless of the amount of elapsed time. It is the most powerful type of reinforcement schedule for maintaining desired behaviors. Except for promotions, it also is the most difficult for organizations to use effectively. Employees paid under this schedule wouldn't know when to expect the reinforcement (paycheck). They would have difficulty paying bills on time or planning a trip because paychecks of various sizes would arrive at different times during the year. A manager who praises a salesperson after getting the third, fifth, tenth, and seventeenth orders is using a variable ratio schedule by varying the number of desired behaviors needed for reinforcement. (State lotteries and gambling casinos use this reinforcement system to keep people betting.)

Punishment Schedules. Punishment schedules refer to the frequency with which punishment occurs. Each of the reinforcement schedules that we discussed has a corresponding punishment schedule. Each of the schedules is defined similarly, except that punishment, rather than reinforcement, results from the behavior. Thus a **fixed interval punishment schedule** provides punishment at fixed time intervals, whereas a **variable interval punishment schedule** provides punishment at irregular intervals of time. A **fixed ratio punishment schedule** provides punishment after a fixed number of target behaviors has occurred, and a **variable ratio punishment schedule** provides punishment after a varying number of target behaviors has occurred. A **continuous punishment schedule** is a special type of fixed ratio schedule in which the ratio of punishment to number of target responses is 1:1.

Ethics
Is punishment ethically justifiable? What are the arguments for and against this view?

A continuous punishment schedule tends to be more effective than any of the other four punishment schedules for suppressing the target behavior. When punishment is administered after every occurrence of an undesired behavior, the employee quickly learns that the behavior is inappropriate. However, if punishment is discontinued, reoccurrence of the undesired behavior tends to be greater with punishment delivered continuously than with punishment provided intermittently.[44]

Application in Organizations

Positive reinforcement is the preferred approach for influencing work behavior. However, an effectively designed and administered disciplinary system often is necessary in organizations. By following certain guidelines, managers can use positive reinforcement or punishment most effectively.

- Link the reinforcer directly to the performance of desired behavior (principle of contingent reinforcement).
- Administer the reinforcer immediately after the desired behavior occurs (principle of immediate reinforcement).
- Provide a larger rather than a smaller amount of the reinforcer (principle of reinforcement size).
- Limit access to the reinforcer (principle of reinforcement deprivation).[45]
- Link the punishment directly to the performance of undesired behavior (principle of contingent punishment).

Teaching Tip
An Army general pinning medals on troops after a battle is an example of immediate reinforcement.

TABLE 13.6

Six Guidelines for Using Reinforcement Theory

GUIDELINE	COMMENT
Don't reward all individuals equally.	To be effective reinforcers, rewards should be based on performance. Rewarding everyone equally in effect reinforces poor or average performance and ignores high performance.
Failure to respond can also modify behavior.	Managers influence their subordinates by what they do not do as well as by what they do. For example, failing to praise deserving subordinates may cause them to perform poorly the next time.
Tell individuals what they can do to receive reinforcement.	Setting performance standards lets individuals know what they should do to be rewarded; they can then adjust their work patterns to get these rewards.
Tell individuals what they are doing wrong.	If managers withhold rewards from subordinates without indicating why they are not being rewarded, the subordinates may be confused about what behaviors the manager finds undesirable. The subordinates may also feel that they are being manipulated.
Don't punish in front of others.	Reprimanding subordinates might sometimes be a useful way of eliminating an undesirable behavior. Public reprimand, however, humiliates subordinates and may cause all the members of the work group to resent the manager.
Be fair.	The consequences of a behavior should be appropriate for the behavior. Subordinates should be given the rewards they deserve. Failure to reward subordinates properly or overrewarding undeserving subordinates reduces the reinforcing effect of rewards.

Source: Adapted from Hamner, W. Clay. Reinforcement theory and contingency management in organizational settings. In Henry L. Tosi and W. Clay Hamner (eds.), *Organizational Behavior and Management: A Contingency Approach,* rev. ed. New York: John Wiley & Sons, 1977, 93–112.

- Administer the punishment immediately after the undesired behavior occurs (principle of immediate punishment).
- Provide a larger rather than a smaller amount of the punishment (principle of punishment size).[46]

Additionally, W. Clay Hamner suggests six guidelines to follow when using the reinforcement model. Table 13.6 lists these guidelines along with comments on each one. Use of these principles can improve efficiency, cut costs, increase attendance, and raise productivity.

Although the reinforcement model has many positive features, it also has some drawbacks.[47] First, the model may oversimplify behavior by not recognizing individual characteristics, such as needs and values. Second, it may unduly emphasize manipulating and controlling subordinates. Finally, with its heavy emphasis on external rewards, the model tends to ignore the fact that an increasing number of employees are motivated by the job itself.

CHAPTER SUMMARY

State the main factors that affect work motivation.

Three key variables that affect motivation are individual differences, job characteristics, and organizational practices. These variables interact to determine an employee's motivation.

2 ***Identify the primary approaches to work motivation.***
Two general approaches to motivation are content approaches and process approaches. Content approaches try to determine *what* needs people want to satisfy at work. Process approaches emphasize *how* and *why* people choose certain behaviors to meet their personal goals.

3 ***Use the needs hierarchy to describe how individuals' needs motivate them to perform their jobs.***
Maslow's hierarchy of needs identifies five categories of individual needs: physiological, security, affiliation, esteem, and self-actualization. People are motivated to satisfy these needs according to their importance at specific times in their lives.

4 ***Use the ERG model to describe how need satisfaction and need frustration affect motivation.***
Alderfer's ERG model identifies three, rather than five, categories of needs: existence, relatedness, and growth. Alderfer's model describes a satisfaction-progression phenomena and a frustration-regression phenomena.

5 ***Discuss how achievement, affiliation, and power influence work motivation.***
McClelland's learned needs model suggests that people acquire three motives—achievement, affiliation, and power—by interacting with their social environment. These motives have implications for what people want from their work experiences and how they interact with others, especially in a team-oriented environment.

6 ***Describe the characteristics of work and the work environment that affect job satisfaction and performance.***
Herzberg's two-factor model states that factors in the work situation strongly influence satisfaction and performance. Motivator factors—including the challenge of the work itself, responsibility, recognition, achievement, and advancement and growth—reflect the nature of the job and can create high levels of motivation and satisfaction. Hygiene factors—such as reasonable working conditions, company policies, and benefits—involve the context in which the job occurs and relate to feelings of dissatisfaction. Hygiene factors can hurt employee performance if not present but don't necessarily increase it when present.

7 ***Explain how job enrichment affects people's motivation at work.***
The job-enrichment model states that three critical psychological states—experienced meaningfulness, experienced responsibility, and knowledge of results—lead to high motivation and job satisfaction. In turn, five job characteristics—skill variety, task identity and significance, autonomy, and feedback—influence crucial psychological states. Individuals with strong growth needs and the necessary knowledge and skills to perform the job (and who are satisfied with contextual variables) are more likely to respond positively to job-enrichment programs than individuals who do not have these characteristics.

8 ***Discuss the basic assumptions and concepts underlying the expectancy model of motivation.***
The expectancy model is a process approach to motivation that suggests that people make conscious decisions about their own behavior and select a course of action because they expect a certain behavior to lead to a desired outcome. The Porter-Lawler expectancy model explains the motivational process in terms of value of reward, perceived effort-reward probability, effort, abilities and traits, role perceptions, performance, rewards, perceived equitable reward, and satisfaction.

9 ***Describe how perceptions of equity and inequity arise and how they affect motivation.***
The equity model, also a process approach to motivation, is based on the assumption that people want to be treated fairly. A fair or equitable situation is one in which people with similar inputs experience similar outcomes. When inequities exist, people aren't satisfied, performance drops, and they then choose one of six actions to reduce their inequity.

10 ***State how rewards and punishments may be used to influence employees in organizations.***

The reinforcement model suggests that behavior is a function of its consequences. There are four types of consequences: positive reinforcement, negative reinforcement, punishment, and extinction. Positive reinforcement provides rewards to increase the probability of a behavior occurring. Negative reinforcement occurs when an employee engages in a behavior to avoid or escape from unpleasant outcomes. Punishment applies negative outcomes to discourage repetition of a behavior. Extinction withdraws the reinforcement that previously had been applied to a behavior. Positive and negative reinforcement should be used to encourage desired work behaviors, whereas punishment and extinction should be applied to discourage undesired work behaviors. The effectiveness of reinforcement and punishment is influenced by the schedule (or frequency) with which reinforcement and punishment are given. Additionally, several guidelines (e.g., principles of contingent reinforcement and punishment and principles of immediate reinforcement and punishment) exist for enhancing the effectiveness of reinforcement and punishment.

QUESTIONS FOR DISCUSSION

1. What are the main similarities and differences among the different content models of motivation?
2. What are the main similarities and differences among the different process models of motivation?
3. Using Maslow's needs hierarchy and McClelland's learned needs model, analyze the motivational approach at the Covenant House. What needs did this nonprofit organization satisfy?
4. What are the managerial implications of Herzberg's two-factor model?
5. What does the Porter-Lawler expectancy model recommend to improve people's performance?
6. What does the reinforcement model suggest for improving employees' performance? What happens when the consequences of behavior are incorrectly applied?

FROM WHERE YOU SIT

1. Think about a job that you have held. Did the organization attempt to motivate you to achieve maximum performance? Explain.
2. If you realize that the existence needs in Alderfer's ERG model are motivating you, what implications does that have for your behavior on the job?
3. How could you apply the Hackman-Oldham job-enrichment model to motivating college students?
4. Explain how you can use the equity model to determine your level of satisfaction with your grade in this course.
5. Visit a local fast-food restaurant and find out how rewards and punishments are used to motivate its employees.
6. What model of motivation seems to explain best your own motivation over the past month? Explain your answer.

Work Motivation Questionnaire

This questionnaire is designed to assess the types of needs that are important to you. There are no right or wrong answers. The best response to any item is simply the one that best reflects your feelings—either as you have experienced them or as you anticipate you would experience them—in a work situation. Respond to the twenty statements by indicating the degree to which each is true for you. Use the following key and circle the number that best indicates how true and accurate the statement is.

1 = Not true and accurate
2 = Slightly true and accurate
3 = Partly true and accurate
4 = Mostly true and accurate
5 = Completely true

1.	I believe that the real rewards for working are good pay, working conditions, and the like.	1	2	3	4	5
2.	The most important thing to me in evaluating a job is whether it gives me job security and employee benefits.	1	2	3	4	5
3.	I would not want a job in which I had no co-workers to talk and share work stories with.	1	2	3	4	5
4.	I want a job that allows rapid advancement based on my own achievements.	1	2	3	4	5
5.	Searching for what will make me happy is most important in my life.	1	2	3	4	5
6	Working conditions (office space, equipment, and basic physical necessities) are important to me.	1	2	3	4	5
7.	I would not want a job if the equipment was poor or I was without adequate protection against layoffs.	1	2	3	4	5
8.	Whether the people I was going to work with were compatible would affect my decision about whether or not to take a promotion.	1	2	3	4	5
9.	A job should offer tangible rewards and recognition for a person's performance.	1	2	3	4	5
10.	I want a job that is challenging and stimulating and has meaningful activities.	1	2	3	4	5
11.	If I took a job in which there were strong pressures to rush and little time for lunch, coffee breaks, and the like, my motivation would suffer.	1	2	3	4	5
12.	My motivation would suffer if my fellow employees were cold or held grudges toward me.	1	2	3	4	5
13.	Being a valued member of the team and enjoying the social aspects of work are important to me.	1	2	3	4	5
14.	I'm likely to work hardest in a situation that offers tangible rewards and recognition for performance.	1	2	3	4	5
15.	Going as far as I can, using my skills and capabilities, and exploring new ideas are what really drive me.	1	2	3	4	5
16.	An important factor for me is that my job pays well enough to satisfy the needs of my family and me.	1	2	3	4	5
17.	Fringe benefits, such as hospitalization insurance, retirement plans, and dental programs, are important to me.	1	2	3	4	5
18.	I would likely work hardest in a job where a group of employees discuss and plan their work as a team.	1	2	3	4	5
19.	My accomplishments give me an important sense of self-respect.	1	2	3	4	5
20.	I would work the hardest in a job where I could see the returns of my work from the standpoint of personal interest and growth.	1	2	3	4	5

Scoring

Directions: In the following table, insert the number you circled for each of the twenty statements. Then add each column to get your summary scores.

1. ___	2. ___	3. ___	4. ___	5. ___
6. ___	7. ___	8. ___	9. ___	10. ___

	11. ___	12. ___	13. ___	14. ___	15. ___
	16. ___	17. ___	18. ___	19. ___	20. ___
Totals	___	___	___	___	___
Motives	Basic creature comfort	Safety	Social or affiliation	Self-esteem	Self-actualization

INTERPRETATION

For each of the five motives, there is a minimum of 4 and a maximum of 20 points. Scores of 18 or more are quite high and suggest that the motives measured by that scale are very important to you. Scores from 13 to 17 suggest that the motives measured are moderately important to you. Scores from 9 to 12 suggest that the motives are not especially important to you. Scores below 9 are quite low and suggest that the motives measured are not at all important to you.

CRITICAL THINKING CASE

The "Cult of Bill" at Microsoft Corporation[48]

Microsoft Corporation, the industry leader in the software market with a 30 percent share, sells more than its three top competitors combined. In the early 1990s, sales rose by 50 percent to $3 billion in just four quarters. Future prospects are for continued, though less explosive, growth in sales and profits.

How did Microsoft become so successful? In part, the company's success is the result of an aggressive strategy for developing and marketing software products. In part, Microsoft's success stems from the culture that Bill Gates, Microsoft's founder and CEO, has fostered. Known as the "Cult of Bill," the Microsoft culture is intense and action-packed, yet fun.

Bill Gates believes in empowering people so that everyone can have a positive impact on and make a real difference for the company. Typically, employees such as programmers and product managers get a lot of responsibility early in their careers with Microsoft.

Because Microsoft is a relatively flat organization with fewer layers of management than most, Bill Gates' presence is felt in unique ways. For instance, Gates often becomes actively involved in recruiting prospective employees. Interviews are intense, but Gates goes to extraordinary lengths to persuade talented, creative people to join the company. He will call undecided candidates himself to discuss the situation and talk them through their decision.

New employees participate in an intensive two-week training program during which they learn the fundamentals of Microsoft's business and begin to build alliances with other new employees. Annual sales meetings also are intense and action-packed. Conducted at attractive locales, the sales meetings are filled with lots of different sessions and team-building activities. Neither spouses nor significant others are allowed to attend. The pace is one of breakneck speed with little scheduled free time.

Daily work activities are equally intense and demanding. Microsoft's headquarters, where most of the software development is done, is known as the "Velvet Sweatshop" because it's a fun place to be but the work is so demanding. The atmosphere is relaxed and casual, to appeal to creative people. Software developers, for example, don't have scheduled work hours as long as they produce. Microsoft's physical facilities are like a college campus, yet in meetings managers are challenged and questioned by fellow managers and a demanding boss. Called "Bill meetings," these sessions with Gates reveal that he "demands that his colleagues be remarkably well-informed, logical, vocal, and thick-skinned."

Still, Microsoft employees have fun at work. People like what they do. Not only are they challenged to be creative but they also are provided with ample opportunities to be creative and contribute. Being creative is fun, but Microsoft employees also have fun in other zany ways.

One employee decorates the ceiling of his office with "dead mice" (the computer variety) that customers have sent in. Another hangs a plastic chicken from his desk. Still another shoots sponge arrows at people in a courtyard of the company's campuslike facilities.

The "Cult of Bill" works. Why does it work?

Questions

1. Using Maslow's hierarchy of needs theory and Alderfer's ERG theory, analyze the motivational system that Bill Gates uses at Microsoft.
2. How does Bill Gates use the Hackman-Oldham job enrichment model to motivate his employees?
3. How can the Porter-Lawler expectancy model be used to explain the motivation of Microsoft's employees?
4. If you could, would you like to work for at Microsoft? Why or why not?

VIDEO CASE

Morale Crisis

Even though restructuring seems to be an unavoidable and inevitable part of doing business today, have companies learned to motivate their employees effectively during downsizing? Or is a morale crisis pervading corporate America?

According to a survey conducted by the American Management Association in 1993, 60 percent of the companies undergoing downsizing experienced no productivity gain, 44 percent experienced rising costs, and 20 percent experienced declining earnings. The Wyatt Company's 1992 Survey of Corporate Restructuring showed that downsizing was causing even more morale problems than it had two years earlier. The survey reported that only 46 percent of the companies undergoing downsizing had achieved their profit goals and that only 32 percent had become more competitive. Fifty-one percent of the companies surveyed said that the restructuring they did during the 1980s adversely affected employee morale. A similar question about restructuring was posed in the Wyatt Company's 1993 survey: This time, even more respondents—53 percent—said that employee morale posed problems. Similarly, a cost management study conducted by Kempner-Tregoe, Inc., revealed a 50 percent decline in the quantity of work following downsizing. A study by Mitchell & Company showed that the stock of downsized companies trailed competitors by 26 percent.

It has been said that, next to the death of a relative or friend, nothing is as traumatic as losing a job. Corporate cutbacks threaten the job security and self-esteem of survivors and victims alike. Turmoil and shattered morale pervade downsized organizations. Management seems to have underestimated the costs of eliminating workers and the impact that cutbacks have on the morale of the survivors.

Companies appear to be in danger of making themselves too thin, with managers treating slimming down as an end in itself rather than as a means to corporate renewal. Downsizing, or the fear of downsizing, can have a devastating impact on company morale and on its ability to handle growth in demand. A study conducted by the Roffey Park Management Institute in 1994 revealed a high degree of cynicism among employees after downsizing had occurred. Fifty-three percent of senior human resources managers believed that morale had fallen since downsizing had been implemented, whereas 89 percent of junior-level staff believed that morale had fallen.

Is downsizing a panacea for poor management? The answer overwhelmingly is "no." Companies that hastily downsize send a demoralizing message to employees. Other alternatives, including shorter work weeks, wage and hiring freezes, and cutbacks in executive perks should be explored first.

What other tactics are companies using to support restructuring and enhance employee morale? According to a survey by the Wyatt

Company, the following tactics are being used to support restructuring:

1.	TQM initiative	68%
2.	Companywide training	64%
3.	Task forces and committees	60%
4.	Restructuring process teams	56%
5.	Employee focus groups	49%
6.	Cross-training	46%
7.	Retraining for new work	45%
8.	"Town hall" meetings	42%
9.	Self-directed work teams	41%
10.	Employee opinion surveys	39%

What else can be done to heal the wounds of downsizing? Management inevitably must change its basic orientation toward employees. Promises to employees that, if they work hard, they will always have a job must cease. The impression that good work equals job security only increases the problems of downsizing. Management must remember those employees who haven't been laid off are filled with anxiety about being next. The epithet of "doing more with less" creates organizational incompetence. A counterproductive work ethic prevails, whereby employees redirect their creativity, energy, and commitment from organizational goals and toward retaliation and self-protection. This reorientation helps them deal with their anger and fear.

Companies also should pay attention to those who are leaving. They can offer seminars on early retirement, résumé writing and job hunting, and career planning. Some companies allow employees paid time off to job hunt; others offer outplacement support and even counseling to help employees deal with the stress of being laid off or fired. The key is *communication.* Accurate, timely, and honest communication with employees will go a long way toward easing the adjustment process.

Whether an organization refers to it as downsizing, layoffs, rightsizing, realignment, or reorganization, the end results are the same. Employees, supervisors, and managers share a sense of inequity in carrying the burden of more work for the same pay. They have a heightened sense of fear that the next reorganization will affect them. Seemingly, nothing will ever eliminate the pervading "survivors' syndrome."[49]

Questions

1. Because of excessive downsizing, U.S. companies may be facing labor shortages. What types of problems will that cause?
2. Relate the problems of downsizing—insecurity and distrust of management—to Maslow's hierarchy of needs.
3. In an era of downsizing, job insecurity, and distrust of management, what can organizations to motivate employees?

Chapter *14*

The Dynamics of Leadership

Learning *Objectives*

After studying this chapter, you should be able to:

1. Describe the basics of leadership.
2. State the contributions of the traits models of leadership.
3. Describe the primary behavioral models of leadership.
4. Explain the principal contingency models of leadership and the situational factors that determine a leader's effectiveness.
5. State the unique behaviors of transformational leaders and their impact on followers.

Chapter *Outline*

Preview *Insight*

Ricardo Semler of Semco

When Ricardo Semler took over the family business in 1979, Semco looked much like many other Brazilian companies. Leaders used fear as the governing principle. Armed guards patrolled the factory floor, timed employees' trips to rest rooms, and frisked employees for contraband when they left the building. Employees who broke equipment had their paychecks docked to replace it. Revenues from the manufacture of industrial pumps, mixers, and other products averaged $10,800 per employee.

Semler's autocratic style worked until he collapsed one day on the factory floor. Doctors told Semler that his relentless work pace and need for control were killing him. Unless Semler changed his behavior, he would die.

After that experience, Semler decided to change his leadership behavior—to replace fear with trust and freedom. He reduced the organization's hierarchy from eight levels to three. The new levels were designed as concentric circles. One tiny circle contains the six people who develop business strategies and coordinate the activities of the company as a whole. The second circle contains the heads of the divisions. The third circle contains all the other employees.

Employees are called associates. Associates make most day-to-day decisions, dress as they want, choose their own supervisors, and have no time clocks. All associates attend classes to learn how to read and understand financial statements. A union leader teaches the course. Every month, each associate gets a balance sheet, a profit-and-loss analysis, and a cash flow statement for his or her division. Almost a third of the associates set their own salaries.

Associates also evaluate their supervisors. These evaluations are posted for everyone to see. If a manager's evaluation is consistently low, that manager steps down. Senior managers in the tiny central circle also are graded by their subordinates. Semler's grades average 80, which he says is okay. People tell him that he needs to make more decisions and provide more direction. However, he's resisting their suggestions. Even though Semler's family still owns the company, his vote on decisions carries no more weight than anyone else's. Six people share duties as CEO, rotating through the job every six months.

Initially, many Semco executives were alarmed by these changes. They were afraid that workers would take too much control. Managers who couldn't make the transition were fired.

What are the results? In 1994, on sales of $30 million, $278,000 was set aside for profit sharing. Employees decide on who gets what because they know the numbers and who is contributing to profits. Sales per employee are $135,000, more than four times Semco's competitors. Semco gets 1,000 job applications for every job opening.[1]

1

Describe the basics of leadership.

Discussion Question 4
Harvard Business Review ran a cover story entitled "Essential Leader Behaviors" in its January–February 1995 issue. The nine essential leader behaviors it identified are (1) clarify the mission of your employees; (2) describe assignments clearly; (3) listen to your employees; (4) make sure the resources necessary to carry

(cont.)

BASICS OF LEADERSHIP

The basics of leadership include core leader competencies, a follower or followers, and a specific situation. **Leadership** involves influencing others to act toward the attainment of a goal.[2] As Ricardo Semler discovered, over the long run, a leader can't simply threaten or coerce people into complying. The exchange between leader and follower must satisfy both. In other words, leadership focuses on interpersonal processes, not administrative activities and directives. One of the reasons for Semco's success is that Semler realized this truth.

Quite a bit can be learned about the conditions for successful leadership from the experiences of Ricardo Semler, Fred Smith, CEO of FedEx, Anita Roddick, CEO of The Body Shop, and others. First, mutual trust must be established. Giving employees more freedom to act autonomously and make decisions is a necessary first step. Second, leaders must do their homework. Others will follow more willingly if they believe that the leader knows at least as much as they do. Third, effective leaders encourage others to

out the assignment are available; (5) make clear the standards by which you will evaluate their performance; (6) ensure that rewards make it worthwhile for your employees to try hard; (8) merit your employees' trust; and (9) make decisions that are yours to make. Using these criteria, evaluate Ricardo Semler's leadership as presented in the Preview Insight.

Teaching Tip
Have several students give a one-minute definition of leadership. Encourage the class to discuss the various definitions.

Ask Students
What is the long-term problem with leadership by threat or coercion?

Ethics
Is leading by threat or coercion ethical? Why or why not?

Teaching Tip
Ask students to brainstorm about the primary skills that effective leaders should have. List these skills on the board or by using a transparency.

take risks. A project failure shouldn't derail a person's career. According to Frederick Smith, founder of FedEx, "Fear of failure must never be a reason not to try something different."

Core Leader Competencies

Leaders come from many different backgrounds, and successful organizations don't always wait for leaders to come along. They seek out people with leadership potential and expose them to experiences designed to develop their competencies. If you're aware of the basic competencies that organizations look for in leaders, you can start developing them in this course. Figure 14.1 shows five core competencies possessed by effective leaders: (1) empowerment, (2) intuition, (3) self-understanding, (4) vision, and (5) value congruence.[3] In Chapter 1 we suggested that conceptual, interpersonal, technical, and communication skills were essential for managing. However, these skills alone aren't sufficient for effective leadership; they simply provide the foundation for obtaining the core competencies needed.

Empowerment. Traditionally, leaders have been reluctant to share power with followers. That is changing, and **empowerment** occurs when a leader shares influence and control with followers. In doing so, the leader involves employees (individually or in teams) in deciding how to achieve the organization's goals, thus giving them a sense of commitment and self-control. Empowerment helps to satisfy the basic human needs for achievement, a sense of belonging, and self-esteem. When employees have positive feelings about their work, the work itself becomes stimulating and interesting, and the leader has done a good job.

FIGURE 14.1
Leadership Competencies

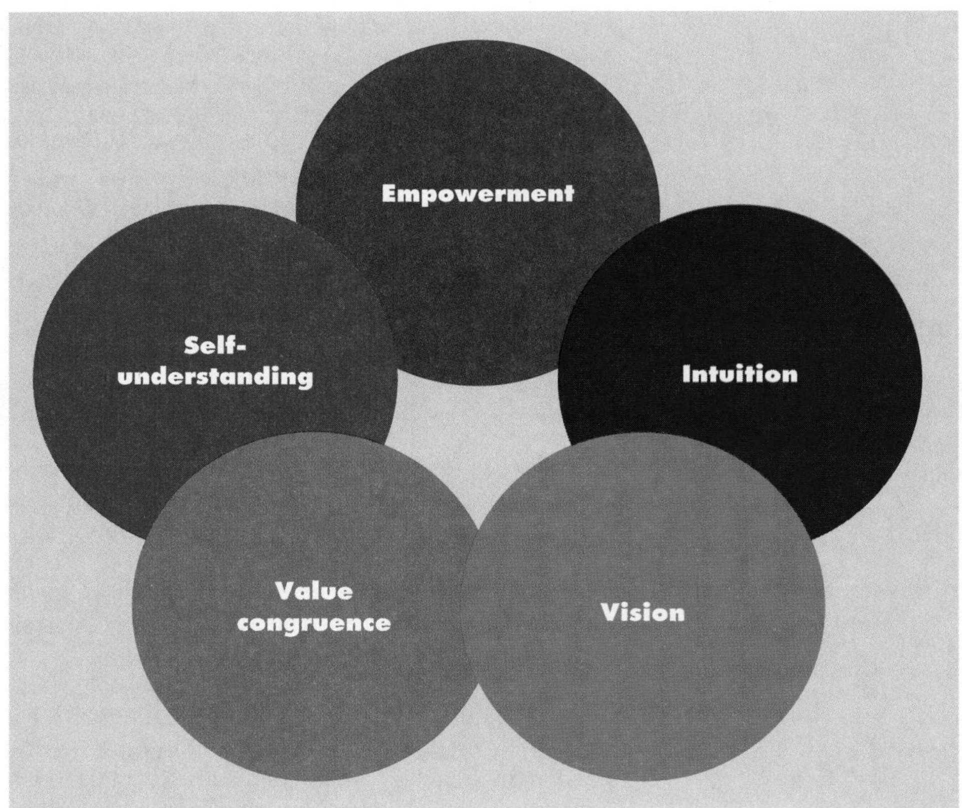

Teaching Tip
Have students think about how they can start developing these competencies now and write their ideas down. Break the students into small groups. Have them take turns sharing their ideas.

Ask Students
Have you worked in an organization where influence and control were shared? How did this sharing affect employees' feelings about their work?

Ask Students
Which needs theories covered in Chapter 13 does empowerment fulfill? (Answer: McClelland's learned needs model, and Maslow's hierarchy of needs theory.)

Teaching Tip
Have students write down one thing that they have recently come to understand about themselves. Have them go up to someone on the other side of the room and share this insight. Ask them to return to their seats and state how they felt about disclosing themselves to a stranger. Tell them that as leaders they must be able to admit their shortcomings and mistakes as they occur rather than cover them up and deny that they exist. If they aren't comfortable with being forthcoming in a relatively safe environment such as this class, suggest that they work on being so. Have them write a development plan for increasing self-understanding and turn it in for credit.

Ask Students
What is your vision?

Teaching Tip
Get students to interview the top managers of an organization to learn what their visions are.

Teaching Tip
Draw two columns on the board, one for students' values and the other for the university's values. Ask the students: How do these two sets of values differ and how can they be reconciled?

Real-World Example
According to Michael Hammer, coauthor of the best-selling book
(cont.)

Intuition. The abilities to scan a situation, anticipate changes, take risks, and build trust are aspects of **intuition.** Competent leaders have an intuitive feel for changes that will occur around them. They move quickly to serve new customers, find new competitive advantages, and exploit organizational strengths. Ricardo Semler, despite being questioned by other Semco executives, used his intuition in making innovative changes in his leadership and the firm's management systems.

Self-Understanding. The ability to recognize a person's own strengths and weaknesses is known as **self-understanding.** Corporations that have done a good job at developing leaders (e.g., Johnson & Johnson, 3M, and General Electric) emphasize creating challenging opportunities for young employees with management potential. These opportunities stretch and develop the competencies and self-understanding they need to become better leaders. According to Steve Kerr, vice-president for corporate development at General Electric, "Leaders are developed by challenges." Employees at GE receive peer performance appraisals that provide feedback concerning the ability to delegate and set clear priorities. This feedback becomes the basis for developing self-understanding.[4]

Vision. The ability to imagine different and better conditions and ways to achieve them is called **vision.** Having vision doesn't always mean coming up with a striking, original goal or method. Vision may involve a simple, realistic corporate strategy that serves the interests of customers, employees, and shareholders. McDonald's founder Ray Kroc incorporated vision in his company motto: "quality, service, cleanliness & value." He repeated this motto to employees for the rest of his life. Its impact is in its simplicity—a vision that management and employees alike can identify with and implement.

Value Congruence. Recall that employees bring various values with them to the job and that these values don't always coincide with the organization's. **Value congruence** is the ability to understand the organization's guiding principles and employees' values and reconcile the two. Beth Randolph, manager of the reservations center at Choice Inns, loves the hospitality industry and wanted a job "away" from it all. When Choice Inns decided to relocate its reservations center to Minot, North Dakota, she took the job. She interviews all employees and negotiates contracts for office equipment, cleaning supplies, and even the food for the kitchens. Top managers at Choice Inns want managers at all levels to be creative and solve problems rather than kick lackluster performers upstairs.[5]

Types of Power

Possessing the core leadership competencies won't necessarily produce a leader. In addition, leaders must have power in order to obtain compliance from followers.[6] **Power** is the ability to influence the behavior of others. Leadership is the exercise of that power and an effective leader knows how to use it wisely. The types of power used by a leader reveal a great deal about why others follow that individual. One of the most useful frameworks for understanding the power of leaders was developed by John French and Bertram Raven.[7] They identified five types of power: legitimate, reward, coercive, referent, and expert.

Legitimate Power. Influence based on the leader's formal position in the organization's hierarchy is **legitimate power.** In deciding on new directions for the Fort Worth Museum of Science and History, Director Don Otto has greater legitimate power than the museum's curator of science. Otto has the authority to allocate funds for capital expenditures, schedule overtime, and purchase equipment within financial guidelines.

Reengineering the Corporation, there are three types of new managers: (1) process owner—a work engineer who manages work order and product design flows; (2) coach—a teacher who is a developer of people; and (3) leader—a motivator who creates an environment in which things get done (*The Wall Street Journal,* February 21, 1995, B1).

Ask Students
How do you define power?

Teaching Tip
Have students recount personal experiences with leader power. Lead a class discussion about these experiences.

Ask Students
Have you ever exercised power over someone else? Has someone ever exercised power over you? Describe the situation(s) and how you felt.

Ask Students
Give an example of your being the holder of legitimate power and an example of being the object of legitimate power.

Ask Students
Give an example of your being the holder of reward power and an example of being the object of reward power.

Ask Students
Give an example of your being *(cont.)*

Reward Power. The influence stemming from a leader's ability to satisfy followers' needs is **reward power.** In other words, employees follow their supervisor's requests in the belief that their behaviors will be rewarded. The supervisor may be able to reward them with favorable job assignments, preferred vacation schedules, promotions, and/or raises. The success of Semco, as illustrated in the Preview Insight, was determined in part by Semler's ability to use his reward power to satisfy employees' needs for self-actualization and esteem.

Coercive Power. The ability of a leader to obtain compliance through fear or punishment is **coercive power.** Punishment may take the form of official reprimands, less desirable work assignments, pay cuts, demotions, suspensions, or even termination. A manager who says "I want these appliances shipped by June fifteenth or heads will roll" is using coercion. Coercive power usually is less effective than, say, reward power for the same reasons that punishment has a limited effect as a motivator (see Chapter 13). Employees have been known to respond to coercion by falsifying performance reports, stealing company property, and exhibiting similar negative behavior, rather than improving their performance.

Referent Power. Influence based on followers' personal identification with the leader is **referent power.** The followers are apt to like, admire, and want to emulate the leader. Referent power usually is possessed by leaders who have admirable personal characteristics, charisma, and/or excellent reputations.

Expert Power. A leader's specialized knowledge grants that person **expert power.** It is a key source of power for managers at the present time and will continue to be so in the future. When a leader has this type of power, subordinates go along with recommendations because of the leader's knowledge. Employees often are promoted because their experiences in the organization help them gain this source of power.

Effective leaders may find it necessary to use all five types of power at different times. As Ricardo Semler discovered, his effectiveness as a leader comes from knowing which type(s) of power to use and how to use that power wisely. His use of reward and expert power—combined with a major reduction in coercive power—was instrumental in turning Semco around.

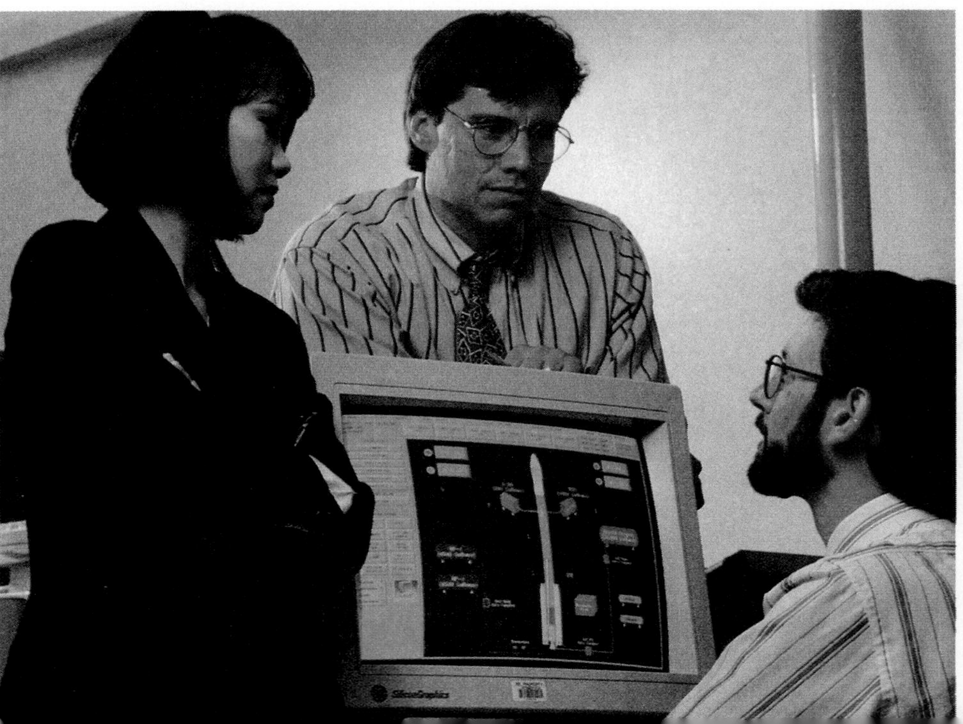

Expert power comes from a leader's specialized knowledge. It is a key source of power for managers and is often a prime reason for employee promotion.

the holder of coercive power and an example of being the object of coercive power.

Ethics
Discuss with the class a situation in which the use of coercive power would be ethical.

Ask Students
Does the use of coercive power always result in dysfunction?

Ask Students
Give an example of your being the holder of referent power and an example of being the object of referent power.

Ask Students
Give an example of your being the holder of expert power and an example of being the object of expert power.

Discussion Question 1
How do the types of a leader's power influence followers' behaviors?

Ask Students
What advantages and disadvantages are closely associated with the use of clout?

Ethics
What uses of clout, if any, can you justify ethically?

Ask Students
What types of clout do you possess?

Ask Students
Give an example of commitment, compliance, and resistance resulting from the use of power in a team, group, or organization that you belong to or have belonged to in the past.

Using Power Effectively

Access to resources, information, and key decision makers gives some leaders an edge in influencing events and passing on information and rewards to subordinates.[8] Such leaders are said to have clout. **Clout** is someone's pull or political influence within an organization. Clout can

- get a good job for a talented employee,
- obtain approval for expenditures beyond the budget,
- get above-average salary increases for subordinates,
- provide easy access to top people in the company, and
- ensure knowing early about important decisions and policy shifts.

Power is most easily gained when a leader's job includes the freedom to make decisions, results in recognition (visibility and notice), and is relevant (central to major organizational problems and issues). Ygnacio Dominiguez, a business development manager at IBM, is a leader with clout. He has gotten his subordinates better-than-average raises and has been assigned to important task forces that report to a senior vice-president. Power also is strengthened through peer networks, which provide information faster than formal channels of communication.

The leader's use of different types of power or clout can lead to one of three types of behavior in followers: commitment, compliance, or resistance. *Committed* subordinates are enthusiastic about meeting their leader's expectations and strive to do so. Subordinates who merely *comply* with their leader's requests will do only what has to be done—usually without much enthusiasm. In most cases, *resistance* by subordinates will be expressed as appearing to respond to their leader's requests while not actually doing so or even intentionally delaying or sabotaging plans.[9]

As Table 14.1 shows, expert and referent power tend to result in subordinate commitment, legitimate and reward power tend to result in compliance, and coercive power tends to result in resistance. Referent power usually leads to high levels of performance. Hence effective leaders are likely to rely on expert, referent, and reward power. They use legitimate and coercive sources of power only minimally. Legitimate power is effective when a manager simply requires an employee to perform a task that is within the employee's capabilities and job description. In some situations coercive power may be effective in getting subordinates to comply with rules, as indicated in Chapter 13. In general, however, when leaders threaten or punish, the response is a lot of anger.

Power is changing within organizations because the design of organizations is changing. Employees in the so-called knowledge-based organizations (such as AT&T, MCI, IBM, NEC, and Xerox) will not put up with just being told what to do. Managers in these organizations have found that real power comes from inspiring commitment. Commitment is gained when managers encourage employees to participate in decisions, strive to build consensus, and rely more on two-way than top-down communication.

TABLE 14.1

Types of Leader Power and Resulting Behavior of Subordinates

POWER TYPE	COMMITMENT	COMPLIANCE	RESISTANCE
Legitimate	Possible	Likely	Possible
Reward	Possible	Likely	Possible
Coercive	Unlikely	Possible	Likely
Referent	Likely	Possible	Possible
Expert	Likely	Possible	Possible

Source: Adapted from Yukl, G.A. *Leadership in Organizations,* 2nd ed. Englewood Cliffs, N.J.: Prentice-Hall, 1989, 44.

Ethics
Discuss the ethics of an employee's resisting the use of power on the job when its use isn't justified.

Empowering those in a position to make things happen engenders commitment. One person who took empowerment to heart is Gabriel Battista, CEO of Cable & Wireless based in Vienna, Virginia. Cable & Wireless pins its success on choosing customers it can serve best—small to medium-sized businesses. These firms are too small to hire their own telecommunication consultants and rely on Cable & Wireless for its expertise. The following Quality Insight illustrates how he operates at Cable & Wireless.

Quality *Insight*

Gabriel Battista of Cable & Wireless

The company attributes its 20 percent annual growth rate in number of long-distance customer minutes to its striving continuously to best its bigger competitors (e.g., MCI, Sprint, and AT&T) in customer service. In fact, the company differentiates itself by providing the best customer service in the industry. To do so, salespeople are empowered to make decisions to improve the quality of customers' businesses.

What quality features does CEO Gabriel Battista stress?

1. An obsession with helping the customer understand exactly what's needed and being sure that the solution gets implemented.
2. Hiring employees who like to make decisions.
3. Empowering employees to make decisions.
4. A culture that thrives on deep and lasting client relationships.

Salespeople are empowered to make decisions to satisfy a customer. They keep their sales managers informed of decisions but have the authority to quote prices and commit the organization to provide services right in the customer's office. Local sales managers allocate money for trade shows, promotions, and advertising as they deem necessary. They also go over each salesperson's monthly activities to identify errors and help them learn from those errors. Salespeople are paid on customer retention, so they don't hesitate to suggest that customers switch to more appropriate services, even if doing so brings in less revenue. The result is extremely high customer retention rates; Cable & Wireless loses only 2 percent of long-distance minutes billed each month versus the industry average of 3 to 5 percent. Obviously, the result is more satisfied and loyal customers.[10]

Ask Students
Why don't "knowledge workers" like being told what to do?

Ask Students
Do all leaders share certain traits? If so, what are they?

Several different models describe how leaders integrate their competencies and power to influence others. There is no single or simple answer to which style of leadership works best, although numerous research articles and books have been written on the subject. Here, we have grouped the results of this research into four categories of models: traits, behavioral, contingency, and transformational. Each category is based on a different set of factors that describe leadership styles and indicate which are most effective in various situations.

2

State the contributions of the traits models of leadership.

TRAITS MODELS

Many early studies of leadership were directed at identifying the personal traits of leaders. **Traits models** are based on the assumption that certain physical, social, and personal characteristics are inherent in leaders.[11] According to this view, the presence or absence of these characteristics distinguishes leaders from nonleaders. Some of the key traits are:

Teaching Tip
Have each student identify a leader who has had a major impact on his or her life. Have the student analyze the essential traits of this leader.

Ask Students
Do you believe that people are born leaders? If so and you want to be a leader but weren't "born a leader," where does that leave you? Are you wasting time trying to improve yourself in school? Explain.

Teaching Tip
Take a poll of the class to determine how many class members believe that they possess each trait. Discuss the results. Remind the students that this is a self-rating exercise and that others' ratings of them may differ.

Discussion Question 2
What are the three most useful traits for a leader? Do they vary by the situation?

- ***Physical:*** young to middle-aged, energetic, striking appearance, tall, slender
- ***Social background:*** educated at the "right" schools, socially prominent or upwardly mobile
- ***Personality:*** adaptable, aggressive, emotionally stable, dominant, self-confident
- ***Social characteristics:*** charming, tactful, popular, cooperative, diplomatic, sociable
- ***Task-related characteristics:*** driven to excel, accepting of responsibility, full of initiative, results-oriented

There is some common-sense support for the notion that effective leaders have certain interests, interpersonal skills, and personality traits. However, traits models generally aren't very helpful in understanding leadership. Research hasn't proved that traits consistently separate potential leaders from nonleaders. This lack of proof doesn't mean that certain traits have nothing to do with effective leadership. It simply means that traits must be evaluated in relation to other factors, such as the situation and the followers' needs.

Limitations

Traits models are flawed because they focus almost exclusively on physical and personality characteristics. Physical characteristics do not correlate with successful leadership; they relate only to *perceived* leadership ability. Physical characteristics still may be helpful in the performance of some manual-labor jobs, but effective leadership rarely depends on a person's height, strength, or weight. For example, personality traits found to relate to a sales manager's effectiveness include gregariousness, risk taking, impulsiveness, exhibitionism, and egocentrism. However, these traits aren't common to successful coaches of sports teams. Their personality traits usually include self-assertion, self-assurance, a strong need for power, and a low need for security. Besides, many successful sales managers and coaches have personality profiles completely different from those mentioned.

Significance for Practice

Despite these limitations, traits models shouldn't be dismissed too hastily. For one thing, leadership often depends heavily on social characteristics. Leaders are likely to have highly developed communication, problem-solving, and negotiation skills. That is, they are socially assertive but in a positive way. They tend to have more energy than others and are a little smarter, but not geniuses. Although none of these traits is absolutely necessary, each can help individuals perform in leadership roles.[12]

3
Describe the primary behavioral models of leadership.

BEHAVIORAL MODELS

After discovering that leaders do not have a uniform set of personal traits, researchers turned their attention to isolating behaviors that are characteristic of effective leaders. **Behavioral models** of leadership focus on differences in the actions of effective and ineffective leaders. In other words, they look at what effective and ineffective leaders actually do: how they delegate tasks to subordinates, where and when they communicate to others, how they perform their roles, and so on. Unlike traits, behaviors can be seen and learned. Because behaviors can be learned, individuals can be trained to lead more effectively.

Theory X and Theory Y

Ask Students
How many of you believe these assumptions to be valid?

Assumptions and beliefs about individuals and how to motivate them often influence a leader's behavior. Table 14.2 lists two contrasting sets of assumptions held by leaders about their subordinates. These sets of assumptions are called Theory X and Theory Y.

TABLE 14.2

Comparison of Theory X and Theory Y Assumptions

Assumptions of Theory X		Assumptions of Theory Y
The typical employee dislikes work and will avoid it if possible		People like to work.
Employees want direction whenever possible.	versus	Employees who are committed to the company's objectives will exercise self-direction and self-control.
Managers must coerce employees (threaten them with punishment) to get them to work.		Employees learn to accept and even seek responsibility at work.

Ask Students
How many of you believe these assumptions to be valid?

Teaching Tip
Get students to share personal experiences with a Theory X or Theory Y leader. Have students brainstorm about situations in which a Theory X or Theory Y style would be effective.

Ethics
Is one of these theories more ethical than the other? Explain.

Ask Students
Have you ever had such a boss?

Ask Students
If people are often relieved to be fired, wouldn't quitting before being fired be more intelligent? Why would someone "stick it out"? Would you? Explain.

Managers who believe that people are motivated mainly by money, are lazy and uncooperative, and have poor work habits will treat them accordingly. Such managers tend to use a directive leadership style: They tell people what to do. They lead by telling their subordinates what's expected of them, instructing them in how to perform their jobs, insisting that they meet certain standards, and making sure that everyone knows who's boss. Douglas McGregor, author of *The Human Side of the Enterprise,* labeled this leadership style **Theory X.**[13]

In contrast, leaders who believe that their people work hard, cooperate, and have positive attitudes will treat them accordingly. Such leaders use a participative leadership style: They act by consulting their subordinates, seeking their opinions, and encouraging them to take part in planning and decision making. According to McGregor, these leaders practice **Theory Y.** By and large, employees clearly prefer Theory Y because of the opportunities afforded them for getting involved in the decision-making process.

Since 1980, *Fortune* magazine has conducted a poll to determine who are America's toughest bosses. The "toughest" boss is defined as the leader who is demanding, unrelenting, stubborn, impatient, and generally hard to please. An effective tough boss pushes subordinates to their limits to achieve significant results. An ineffective tough boss pushes them to achieve minor results; people often find that being fired by such a leader is a relief.

The following bosses made a recent *Fortune* magazine's list: T.J. Rogers of Cypress Semiconductor, Steven Jobs of NeXT Computer, Linda Wachner of Warnco, Herbert Haft of Dart, and John Connors of Hill Holliday. The following Insight highlights Wachner and Connors. What do you think it would be like to work for them?

Insight

Tough Bosses

Linda Wachner is the only female CEO of a Fortune 500 industrial company. Employees describe her as a person who's so impatient to achieve results that she will do almost anything, including humiliating employees in front of others. Employees carry notebooks to meetings with the words DO IT NOW! inscribed on the front cover. She regularly arrives at work early and often holds meetings until 1:00 A.M. Over one Thanksgiving holiday, she called a manager 31 times to ask him questions. She also asked a newly hired vice-president, "Have you fired anyone yet?" He replied, "No." "Well," she said, "you'd better start firing people so they'll understand you're serious." She tells people, "If you don't like it, leave. It's not a prison."

John Connors has two styles. One style is warm and outgoing. The other style is cold, calculating, and mean. The Dr. Jekyll and Mr. Hyde split permitted him to hire and fire the same employee four times. His outbursts in the office are called "Jack Attacks" by employees. He has been known to try to kick the chair out from under an employee while the employee was sitting on it. On another occasion he gradually stripped the authority away from an employee and then fired her because she wasn't doing enough. These attacks reveal him as a manager who takes perverse pleasure in seeing others twist in the wind. The theme of all Jack Attacks is "I do everything, and no one else does anything around the office."[14]

Ohio State University and University of Michigan Models

Researchers at Ohio State University took another approach to studying leadership styles. They asked employees to describe the behaviors of their supervisors. Based on the responses, the researchers identified two leadership styles: considerate and initiating-structure.[15]

A **consideration leadership style** is characterized by concern for employees' well-being, status, and comfort. A considerate leader seeks to create a friendly and pleasant working climate. Such a leader assumes that subordinates want to do their best and that his or her job is to make it easier for them to do theirs. A considerate leader seeks acceptance by treating subordinates with respect and dignity and tends to downplay the use of both legitimate power and coercive power. Typical behaviors of a considerate leader include

Ask Students
Is this your style?

Ask Students
Just because subordinates like this style, does that make it effective? Why or why not?

Ask Students
How many of you would prefer to work for someone with an initiating-structure style?

- expressing appreciation when employees do a good job,
- not demanding more than employees can achieve,
- helping employees with their personal problems,
- being friendly and accessible, and
- rewarding employees for jobs well done.

Not surprisingly, the considerate leadership style usually is readily accepted by subordinates. Advocates contend that this style of leadership generates good will and leads to job satisfaction for subordinates. Other positive outcomes include closer cooperation between leader and subordinates, increased motivation of subordinates, more productive work groups, and low turnover and grievance rates.

The **initiating-structure leadership style** is characterized by active planning, organizing, controlling, and coordinating subordinates' activities. In addition to accepting the assumptions of Theory X, both Linda Wachner and John Connors use this style of leadership. Typical behaviors of an initiating-structure leader include

Ask Students
Is this your style?

- assigning employees to particular tasks,
- establishing standards of job performance,
- informing employees of job requirements,
- scheduling work to be done by employees, and
- encouraging the use of uniform procedures.

A forceful initiating-structure leadership style causes higher employee grievance and turnover rates and lower employee satisfaction than does a strong considerate leadership style. However, research suggests that effective leaders may exhibit both considerate and initiating-structure behaviors.[16] Employees' reactions to initiating-structure leaders depended on whether they also believe that the leaders were considerate. If so, their leader's behavior is viewed as effective. However, if employees believe a leader to be inconsiderate, they tend to view the leader's behavior as "watching over employees' shoulders" or "micromanaging."

Similar studies of leadership behavior were undertaken by researchers at the University of Michigan. They classified leaders' behaviors as either production-centered or employee-centered. Leaders who utilize a **production-centered leadership style** set standards, organize and pay close attention to employees' work, keep production schedules, and stress results. Those who have an **employee-centered leadership style** en-

Discussion Question 3
Describe the basic elements in the Ohio State University and University of Michigan leadership models. How can these concepts help you to become a more effective leader?

courage employees to participate in making decisions and make sure they are satisfied with their work. This type of leader's primary concern is with employees' welfare. The researchers found that employee-centered leaders were more likely to be in charge of high-performance teams than were production-centered managers. More effective leaders were those who had supportive relationships with their team members and encouraged them to set and achieve their own goals.[17]

Managerial Grid Model

The **managerial grid model,** developed by Robert Blake and Jane Mouton, identifies five leadership styles that combine different proportions of concern for production (similar to the initiating-structure and production-centered styles) and concern for people (similar to the consideration and employee-centered styles).[18] These styles are plotted on a grid in Figure 14.2.

At the lower left-hand corner of the grid, point (1, 1), is the *impoverished style,* characterized by low concern for both people and production. The primary objective of managers who use this style is to stay out of trouble. They pass orders along to employees, go with the flow, and make sure that they can't be held accountable for mistakes. They exert the minimum effort required to get the work done and avoid being fired or demoted.

Ask Students
Name a leader and an organization that use this style.

At the upper left-hand corner, point (1, 9), is the *country club style,* identified as a high concern for people and a *low* concern for production. Managers who use this style try to create a secure and comfortable atmosphere and trust that their subordinates will respond positively. Attention to the need for satisfying relationships leads to a friendly, if not necessarily productive, atmosphere and work tempo.

Ask Students
Name a leader and an organization that use this style.

FIGURE 14.2
The Managerial Grid Model

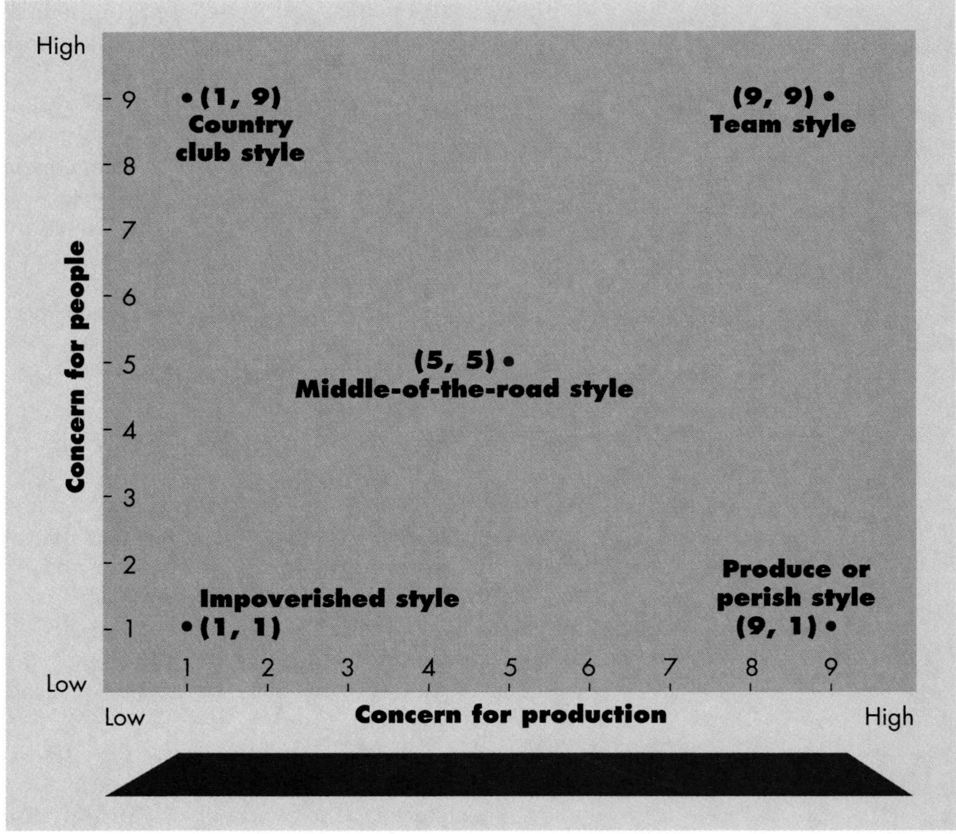

Source: Blake, R.R., Mouton, J.S., and Greiner, L.E. Breakthrough in organization development. *Harvard Business Review.* November-December 1964.

Leaders who use a team style of management show high levels of concern for both people and production. This style fosters cohesion and commitment among workers.

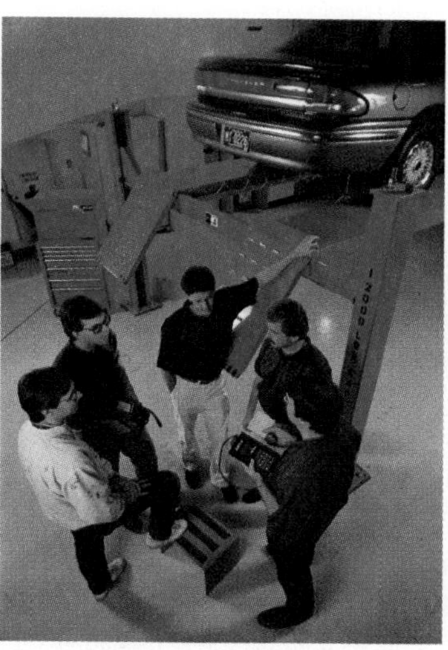

Ask Students
Name a leader and an organization that use this style.

Ask Students
Name a leader and an organization that use this style.

Ask Students
Name a leader and an organization that use this style.

Teaching Tip
Have students describe personal experiences with the managerial styles identified in the managerial grid model. Divide the class into groups to debate the advantages and disadvantages of each style.

A high concern for production and a low concern for people are reflected at point (9, 1) in the lower right-hand corner. This is the *produce or perish style*. Leaders who use this style don't consider employees' personal needs to be relevant to achieving the organization's objectives. They use their legitimate and coercive powers to pressure subordinates to meet production quotas. They believe that operational efficiency results from arranging the work so that employees merely have to follow orders. Ricardo Semler of Semco started out using this style.

In the middle of the grid, point (5, 5) indicates the *middle-of-the-road style*. Leaders who use this style seek a balance between workers' needs and the organization's productivity goals. Adequate performance is obtained by maintaining employee morale at a level sufficient to get the work done.

In the upper right-hand corner, at point (9, 9), is the *team style*, which shows high levels of concern for both people and production. Leaders who use this style attempt to establish cohesion and foster feelings of commitment among workers. Ricardo Semler chose this leadership style after his health crisis. As a result, both production and job satisfaction improved markedly. By introducing a "common stake" in the organization's purposes, the leader builds relationships of trust and respect.

Significance for Practice

Behavioral models have added greatly to the understanding of leadership. The focus shifted from who leaders are (traits) toward what leaders do (behaviors). However, leadership behaviors that are appropriate in one situation aren't necessarily appropriate in another. Steven Jobs's considerate leadership style effectively motivated skilled and creative people when Apple Computers first started. But when Compaq, Tandy, Dell, and others began to encroach on Apple's market share, the company needed a leader who had a more initiating-structure (production-centered) style. Jobs was replaced by John Sculley, who had the initiating-structure leadership style needed to address the demands of a highly competitive marketplace. Whether Jobs's style will prove effective at NeXT, his new computer company, remains to be seen.

4

Explain the principal contingency models of leadership and the situational factors that determine a leader's effectiveness.

CONTINGENCY MODELS

Because the behavioral models failed to uncover leadership styles that were consistently appropriate to all situations, other models of leadership were devised. The next step in the evolution of knowledge about leadership was the creation of contingency or situa-

FIGURE 14.3

Situational Factors Influencing a Leader's Effectiveness

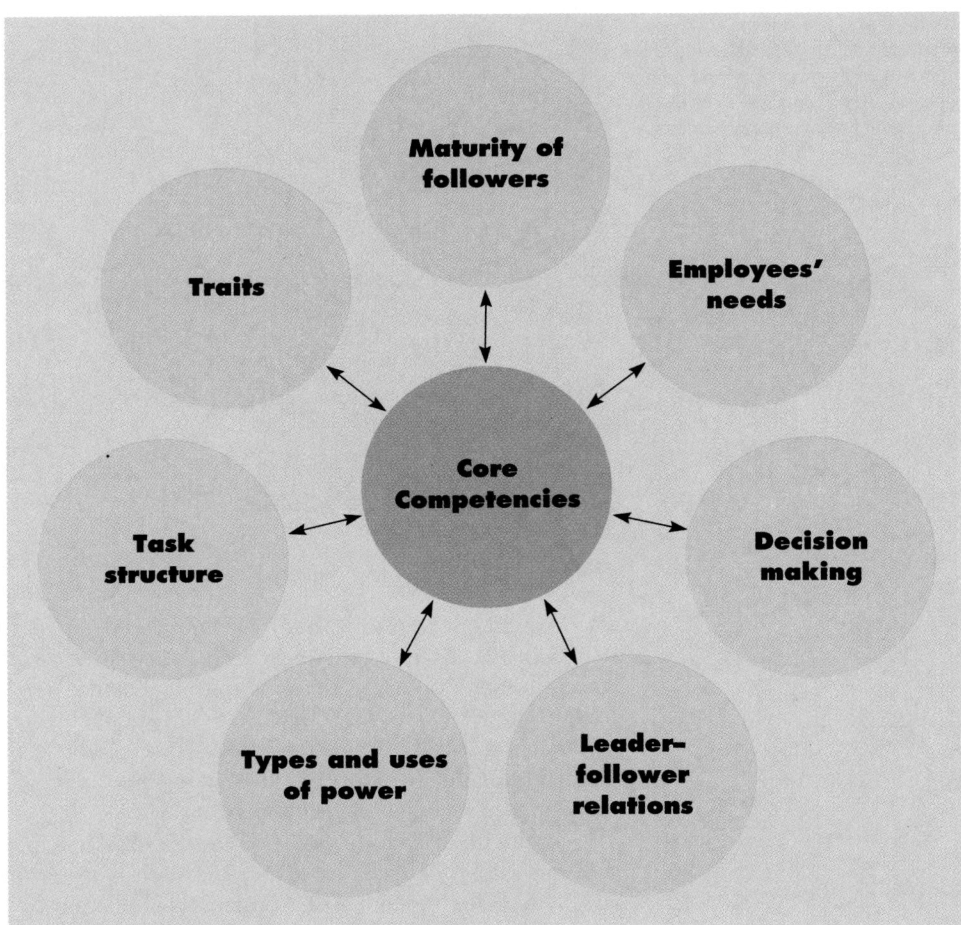

Discussion Question 8
Is a person's leadership style fixed or flexible? Why or why not?

Ethics
The previous approaches imply that there is one best way to manage. They also imply that the "one best way" is the most ethical. Now look at situational factors.

tional models. According to **contingency models** of leadership, the situation determines the best style to use.[19] The situational factors contained in these models are shown in Figure 14.3. However, no single contingency model encompasses all these factors. The four most influential contingency models of leadership are Fiedler's contingency model, Hersey and Blanchard's situational model, House's path-goal model, and the leader-participation model.

Fiedler's Contingency Model

The first contingency model was developed by Fred Fiedler and his associates.[20] **Fiedler's contingency model** suggests that successful leadership depends on matching a leader's style to a situation's demands. In other words, each leadership style is most effective when it is used in the right situation. According to this model, the manager has to understand his or her own leadership style, diagnose the particular situation, and then match style and situation. That may mean either changing the situation to match the manager's style or giving the leadership role to someone whose style does match the situation.

Leadership Styles. What differentiates this model from others is the method of characterizing a leader's style. It is considered to be a trait and thus is difficult to change. To determine his or her leadership style, the manager is asked to describe his or her **least preferred co-worker (LPC),** the employee with whom the manager can work least well. The descriptions used are sixteen bipolar adjectives, including the following:

open	___|___|___|___|___|___|___	guarded
gloomy	___|___|___|___|___|___|___	cheerful
friendly	___|___|___|___|___|___|___	unfriendly
relaxed	___|___|___|___|___|___|___	tense
close	___|___|___|___|___|___|___	distant

Ask Students
Which one of these is you?

Teaching Tip
Have students state whether they would prefer to work with a relationship-oriented leader or a task-oriented leader and why.

A high-LPC leader describes the least preferred co-worker using positive adjectives. A leader who recognizes the importance of developing strong and positive emotional ties with followers is called a **relationship-oriented leader.** This type of leader is similar to the leader who uses a considerate or an employee-centered style. A leader who describes the least preferred co-worker with negative adjectives is a low-LPC leader. Called a **task-oriented leader,** this type of person structures the job for employees and closely watches their behavior. Such a leader simply wants to get the job done and places greater value on tasks than people.

Situational Variables. Fiedler identified three variables in the work situation that help determine which leadership style will be effective: leader-member relations, task structure, and the leader's position power. Each can be described as either favorable or unfavorable for the leader.

Leader-member relations is the extent to which the leader is accepted by followers. It is the most important determinant of a leader's effectiveness. A leader who gets along well with employees and whose expertise and ability to get things done are respected may not have to rely much on formal authority. However, a leader who is disliked, isn't trusted, and appears to lack clout in the organization has to rely on legitimate and coercive power to get others to perform their tasks.

Ask Students
What problems, if any, might be associated with a high degree of task structure?

Task structure is the degree to which a job is routine. Recall that a simple and routine job has clearly defined performance standards (e.g., making a pizza in twelve minutes) and detailed instructions on how to do the work. When giving directions, the leader can refer to standard operating procedures. In contrast, a complex and nonroutine job presents a leader and subordinates with many alternatives for getting it done; there are no clear guidelines for how to do the job. Under these conditions the leader has to guide and direct employees.

Ask Students
What personal characteristics might affect leader-member relations?

Leader position power is the extent to which a leader has legitimate, coercive, and reward power. Having strong position power simplifies a leader's ability to influence subordinates. Low position power makes the leader's task difficult because she or he has to rely on personal, rather than organizational, sources of influence.

Ask Students
What do you believe President Clinton's leader position power to be currently? Compare it with when he first took office.

Figure 14.4 illustrates Fiedler's contingency model of leadership. The basic situational variables are shown on the far left. The numbered columns represent possible combinations of the three variables and are arranged from the most favorable situation (1) to the least favorable situation (8) for the leader. The leadership style best suited to each combination of variables is indicated in the bottom row of boxes.

Obviously, the more pleasant the leader-member relations, the more structured the task, and the stronger the leader's position power, the more favorable the situation is for the leader. Thus a leader will have the most control and influence in situations represented by column 1. A leader will have somewhat less control and influence in situations represented by column 2. Here, the leader is accepted and the tasks are structured, but the leader has little position power. In column 8 a leader's control and influence are quite limited. Here, the leader isn't accepted and has little position power, and the tasks are unstructured.

Effective Leadership Styles. As suggested in Figure 14.4, task-oriented leaders perform most effectively in the most favorable situations (columns 1, 2, and 3) and in the least favorable situation (column 8). In the most favorable situations the leader is well respected, has freedom to reward and punish subordinates, and subordinates' activities

FIGURE 14.4

Fiedler's Contingency Model

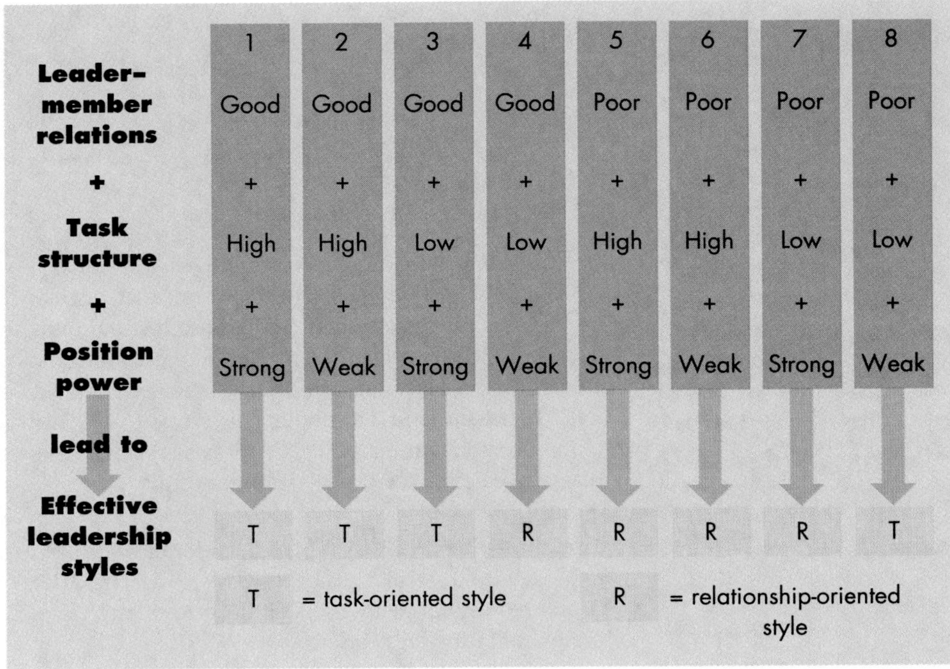

are clear and specific (as in payroll, data entry, and maintenance). In the least favorable situation (column 8), tasks are unstructured, group support is lacking, and leader's position power is low. The unpopular president of a school PTA or Red Cross fund-raising drive is an example. In such a case, the only hope for achieving any results appears to be task-oriented leadership.

1 2 3 4 5 6 7 8
Leader-member relations
Good Good Good Good Poor Poor Poor Poor
+
Task structure
High High Low Low High High Low Low
+
Position power
Strong Weak Strong Weak Strong Weak Strong Weak
lead to
Effective leadership styles
T T T R R R R T
T = task-oriented style
R = relationship-oriented style

Discussion Question 5
Describe Fiedler's three situational variables and his contingency approach to leadership.

Relationship-oriented leaders are generally most effective in moderately favorable situations. In these situations, tasks are structured but the leader is disliked, or vice versa. Regardless of the situation, the leader must depend on employees' willingness and creativity to accomplish the tasks.

Fitting the leader's style to the task can yield big dividends, as the following Small Business Insight reveals. What style of leadership do you think Dan England, CEO of this organization, practices?

Small Business *Insight*

Dan England of C.R. England

In the long-haul refrigerator trucking business, often the differences between success and failure are measured in cents per mile and employee turnover. According to Dan England, "We want to run this place like the cockpit of a jetliner, where you have hundreds of different instruments before you at all times and you know exactly where you are." England believes that if you can measure something, you can manage it.

All C.R. England employees receive feedback weekly and are graded from A to F. A computer system at headquarters in Salt Lake City, Utah, gives truckers data on the time needed to wash their trucks, fuel consumption, tire wear, the time required to complete a bill, and how well they treated their customers. England had tracking devices placed in each truck and installed a $12 million satellite system that permits managers to know the location and speed of each truck at all times. The company ties bonuses and extra vacation days to reaching performance targets. Truckers can earn up to $9,000 a year extra if they meet safety and fuel consumption goals.[21]

Clearly, Dan England's leadership style is task-oriented, which matches the situational variables at C.R. England. Leader-member relations appear to be good, tasks are highly structured, and Dan England's power position is strong (see Figure 14.4).

Limitations. Fiedler's model, like any other, has its limitations.[22] First, the situational variables are complex and difficult to assess. Measurement of actual leader-member relations, task structure, and position power must necessarily be subjective. Second, the model pays little attention to the characteristics of subordinates. Whether they are highly skilled professionals or unskilled laborers could make a big difference in determining the appropriate leadership style. Third, the model is based on the assumption that the leader has the skills (see Figure 14.1) needed to direct subordinates' efforts competently. But if the leader lacks these core leadership skills, others aren't likely to respect the leader or trust his or her judgment, negating the situational variables. Finally, the logic underlying the LPC scale is open to question. Fiedler asserts that LPC measures a fixed trait and that a leader cannot easily change his or her leadership style to fit a situation. When a leader's style and the situation do not match, he argues, the situation, *not* the leader, should be changed to fit the leader's style. This often isn't practical. For example, many jobs at Texas Instruments are performed by engineers and scientists. Because of the content and scope of these jobs, restructuring them to fit a leader's style would be difficult.

Significance for Practice. Both relationship-oriented and task-oriented leaders perform well in some but not all situations. For example, an outstanding team leader who is promoted to quality control manager may fail because his or her task-oriented leadership style doesn't match the demands of the new situation. As tasks become more complex and nonroutine, different leadership styles must be used to motivate others and direct their work.

Even though it remains controversial, Fiedler's contingency model is an interesting approach to understanding leadership and one that many managers find appealing. Its greatest contribution may be its redirection of research in the field, rather than provision of any firm answers. Researchers started to examine a situation more closely before attempting to find the leadership style that is most appropriate to it. Fiedler pointed out that a leader cannot be labeled good or poor. Rather, the leader may perform well in one situation but not in others. In other words, leadership effectiveness depends more on situational variables than on leadership style. Top management might mistakenly attempt to change a leader's style when making the situation more favorable or shifting the leader to a situation that better matches her or his style might be easier and better.[23]

Hersey and Blanchard's Situational Leadership Model

Hersey and Blanchard's situational leadership model suggests that the levels of directive (similar to initiating-structure and production-centered) and supportive (similar to considerate and employee-centered) leader behaviors should be based on the level of readiness of the followers.[24]

Directive behavior occurs when a leader relies on one-way communication, spelling out duties and telling followers what to do and where, when, and how to do it. Directive leaders structure, control, and supervise subordinates. **Supportive behavior** occurs when a leader relies on two-way communication, listening, encouraging, and involving followers in decision making.

Discussion Question 6
Explain how Hersey and Blanchard's situational leadership model relates to the readiness of followers.

Readiness is a subordinate's ability to set high but attainable task-related goals and a willingness to accept responsibility for reaching them. Readiness is related to the task and not to the person's age. People have varying degrees of readiness, depending on their backgrounds and specific task they are trying to accomplish. This model prescribes different combinations of directive and supportive leader behaviors for different levels of subordinates' readiness. In contrast to Fiedler, who believes that a leader's style is rel-

FIGURE 14.5

Hersey and Blanchard's Situational Leadership Model

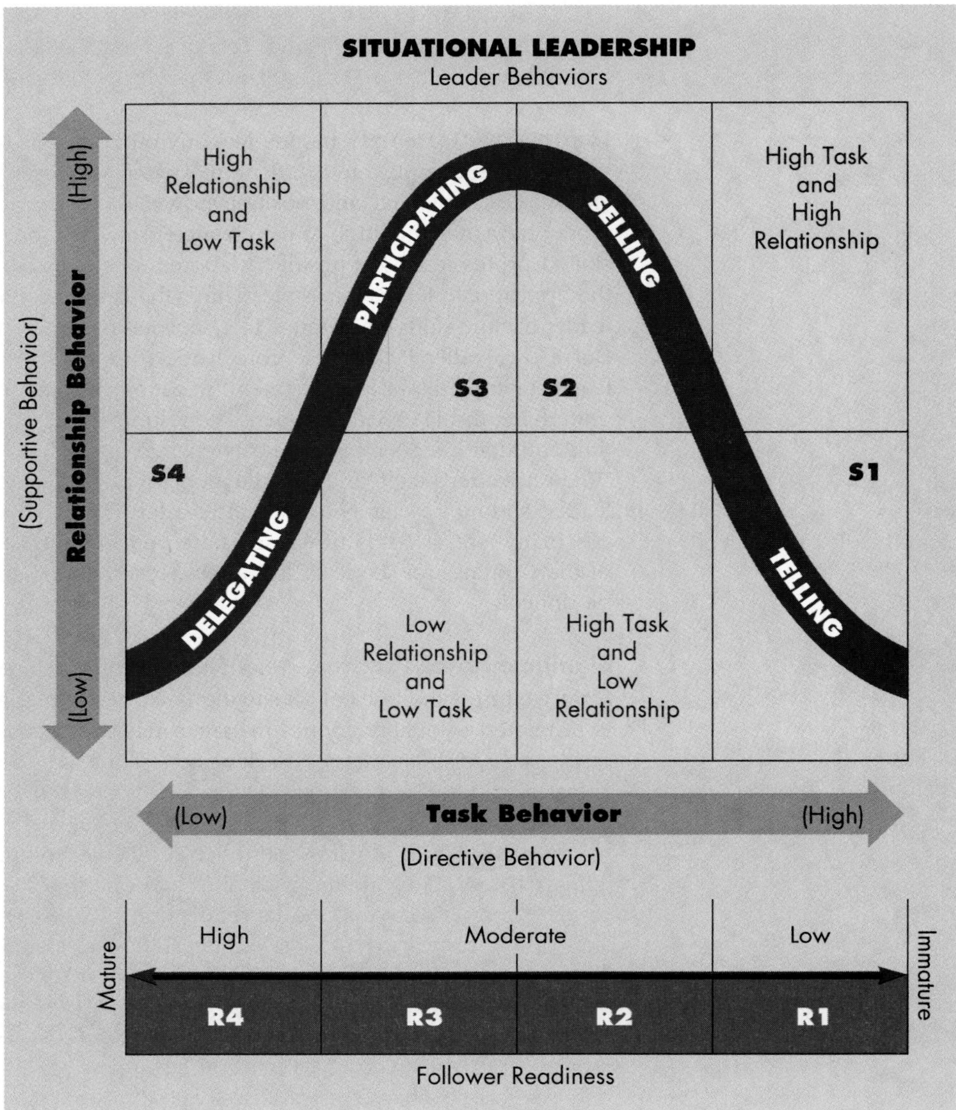

Source: Hersey, P., and Blanchard, K.H. *Management of Organizational Behavior: Utilizing Human Resources,* 6th ed. Englewood Cliffs, N.J.: Prentice-Hall, 1993. Used by permission from Ronald Campbell, President, Leadership Studies, Escondido, California, 1995.

atively rigid, Hersey and Blanchard emphasize a leader's flexibility to adapt to changing situations.

Figure 14.5 portrays the relationship between Hersey and Blanchard's leadership styles and levels of follower readiness. The curve running through the four leadership quadrants (S4–S1) indicates the level of directive and/or supportive behavior that characterizes each style. The readiness level of the individual or team being supervised ranges from low to high.

A leader with a **telling style** (lower right-hand quadrant) provides clear instructions and specific direction. When an employee first enters the organization, directive leadership style is most appropriate. Newcomers usually are committed, enthusiastic, and energetic. They are anxious to get started and learn. As commitment is high, a lot of support from the leader isn't needed or appropriate.

Ask Students
With what type of employee would this style work best?

As employees learn their jobs, a telling style is still important because the employees aren't yet ready to assume total responsibility for doing the job. At this point, however, a leader needs to begin using supportive behavior in order to build employees' confidence and maintain their enthusiasm, called the **selling style.** It encourages two-

Ask Students
With what type of employee would this style work best?

way communication and helps build confidence and motivation on the part of the employee, although the leader still has responsibility and controls decision making.

When followers feel confident performing their tasks, the leader no longer needs to be directive. However, the leader does need to open up communication by actively listening and to support subordinates' efforts to use the skills they have learned. In the **participating style,** the leader and followers share decision making and no longer need or expect the relationship to be directive.

The **delegating style** is appropriate for a leader whose followers are ready to accomplish a particular task and are both competent and motivated to take full responsibility for it. Even though the leader may still identify problems, the responsibility for carrying out plans is given to experienced followers. They are permitted to run the show and decide how, when, and where the task is to be done.

Ask Students
With what type of employee would this style work best?

Ask Students
With what type of employee would this style work best?

What happens when a leader misreads the readiness of subordinates and chooses the wrong style? This happened at the American Automobile Association (AAA) when the Board of Directors selected Paul Verkuil to become CEO of its 127 motor clubs in 1992. The AAA was losing money, its technology lagged behind competitors, and it was inefficient. On August 30, 1994, the Board of Directors fired Verkuil. What happened? The following Insight highlights the bumpy road Verkuil followed as he tried to bring about change. After reading this insight, you should be able to identify Verkuil's leadership style and assess the readiness of the club's members.

Insight

A Leadership Failure at AAA

The American Automobile Association (AAA) has long been revered as the motorists' Red Cross because its name is associated with emergency road service, Triptik guides, and dependability. The organization found its market share slipping because new competitors were offering similar services at lower prices. American Express, the American Association of Retired Persons (AARP), and most major oil companies started offering services that only AAA traditionally had provided. The AAA is organized by clubs, which are loosely affiliated with the organization's headquarters. The clubs are run as independent ventures, with membership fees ranging from $17 to $50. As a result, AAA has no central computer, no national publications, and no Michelin-style guide. The role of the national AAA has been to support and accredit clubs. Some of the smaller clubs have chosen to merge with larger ones to survive.

The clubs' independence helped them cater to their members' unique needs. However, this approach resulted in few common or coordinated efforts. Verkuil changed that without much input from the clubs. He pressed for uniform new quality standards that AAA clubs must meet for accreditation, such as a twenty-four-hour-a-day answering service for stranded club members and arranging towing contracts with selected tow services. He wanted to publish a glossy dining and hotel guide that would be made available to all members. Many clubs weren't interested in such a guide and joined forces to stop him. In 1994, AAA began advertising its travel business on cable TV. It also selected tour operators, rental car agencies, and cruise lines as preferred suppliers.

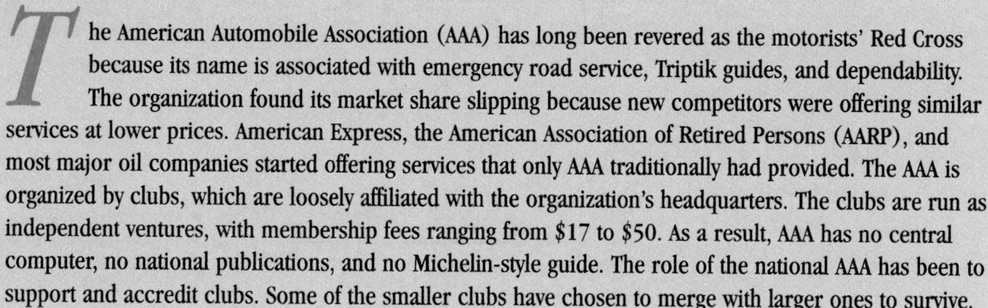

Verkuil's priorities also clashed with members' expectations. He flew to Paris and Geneva frequently to represent AAA in international travel discussions instead of spending that time on domestic travel problems. He redecorated his office and hired a gourmet chef. Such amenities raised Verkuil's profile but didn't solve the clubs' problems of declining membership and revenues.[25]

Verkuil's leadership style was telling, and he assumed that the AAA clubs' members were at a low readiness stage. This assumption clashed with the clubs' perceived high readiness level. They wanted a leader who used a participating style.

Limitations. The Hersey and Blanchard model also has some limitations. First, can leaders actually choose a leadership style when faced with a new situation? The answer to this question has important implications for management selection, placement, and promotion. As AAA club members found out, Paul Verkuil's leadership style appeared to be inflexible. Some people can read situations better and adapt their leadership style more effectively than others. For those who can't, what are the costs of training them to be able to do so? Do these costs exceed the potential benefits? Second, the model ignores many factors (e.g., the leader's personality traits and power base) that could influence a leader's choice of style. Third, different employees are likely to be at different levels of readiness. Under this condition, what is the best style? Finally, the model does not distinguish among types of tasks and the reasons for low readiness. That is, are tasks routine or varied, simple or complex? Does lack of readiness reflect a lack of motivation, a lack of ability, or some combination of both?[26]

Ask Students
Which style of the situational leadership model would you adopt when beginning a new job after five years with another organization?

Significance for Practice. Hersey and Blanchard's situational leadership model has generated a lot of interest.[27] The idea that leaders should be flexible with respect to the leadership style they use is appealing to many. However, the leader must constantly monitor the maturity level of followers in order to determine the combination of directive and supportive behaviors that is most appropriate. An inexperienced (immature) employee may perform as well as an experienced employee if properly directed and closely supervised. If the leader's style is appropriate, it should also help followers become more mature. Thus as a leader helps followers evolve, his or her leadership style also needs to evolve.

House's Path-Goal Model

Another contingency model was developed by Robert House.[28] **House's path-goal model** indicates that effective leaders, clearly specify the task, reduce roadblocks to task achievement, and increase opportunities for task-related satisfaction, thereby clarifying the paths, or means, by which employees can attain job satisfaction and improve per-

FIGURE 14.6
House's Path-Goal Model

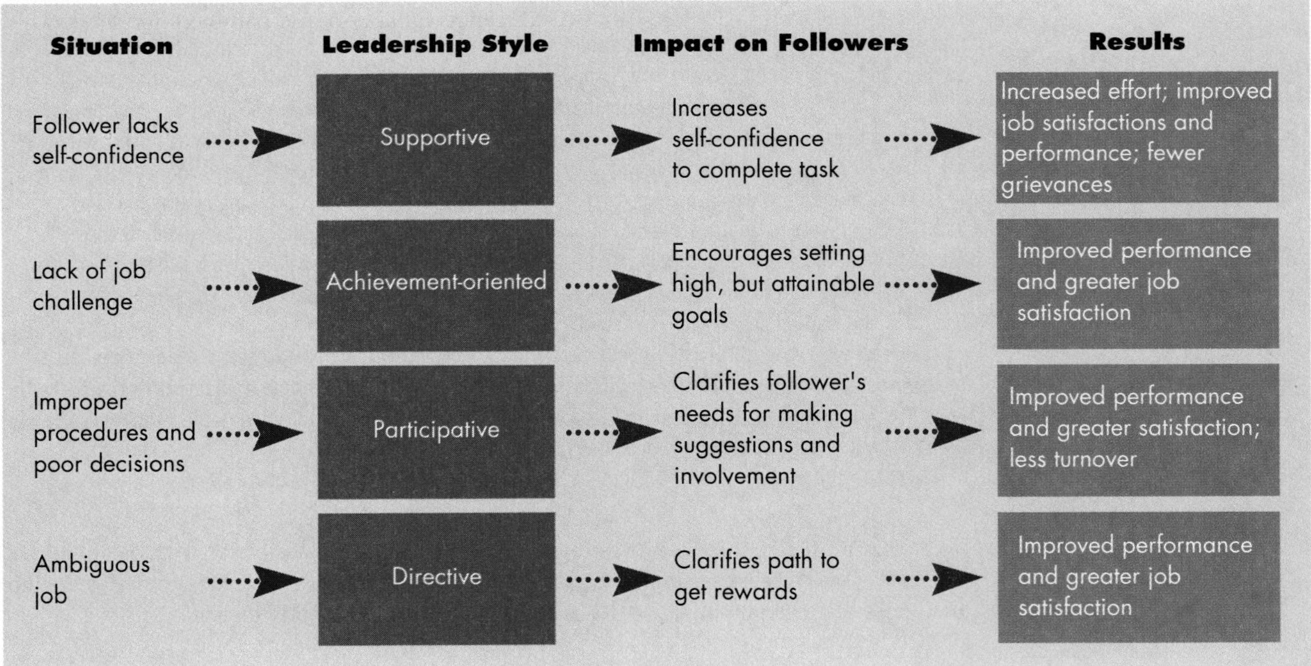

formance. The leader's function is to motivate subordinates and help them reach their highly valued, job-related objectives. The specific style of leader behavior exhibited should be determined by two contingency variables: employee characteristics and task characteristics. A version of the path-goal model is shown in Figure 14.6.

Like the other two contingency models, the path-goal model doesn't provide a single formula for the best way to lead. Instead it stresses that, to be effective, a leader should select the style most appropriate to a particular situation and the followers' needs. The model identifies four styles of leadership.

Achievement-oriented leadership is setting challenging goals, expecting followers to perform at their highest level, and showing confidence that they will meet this expectation.

Directive leadership is letting followers know what's expected of them and telling them how to perform their tasks. This style is similar to the initiating-structure and production-centered styles.

Participative leadership is consulting with followers and asking for their suggestions before making a decision.

Supportive leadership is being friendly and approachable and showing concern for followers' psychological well-being. This style is much like the considerate and employee-centered styles.

Ask Students
Which style do you use? Which one would you like for your boss to use? Is there a difference? Why or why not?

Employee Characteristics. House's first contingency variable is employee characteristics. The model suggests that employees will accept a particular leadership style if they perceive it to be an immediate source of job satisfaction or to be necessary for future job satisfaction. For example, employees who have strong needs for self-esteem and affiliation may readily accept supportive leadership. Employees who have strong needs for autonomy, responsibility, and achievement are more likely to accept and be motivated by achievement-oriented leadership. Beth Pritchard, who heads the Johnson's Wax Insect Control Division, set a radical course when she took over. She changed the formulas of successful products, revamped packaging, and assigned a person to each region of the United States to focus on the needs of customers there. She accomplished her goals by using an achievement-oriented leadership style—her support team could handle responsibility and make decisions without constantly seeking her advice.

Task Characteristics. The other contingency variable of the path-goal model is task characteristics. When tasks are routine and simple, employees will regard directions as unnecessary. Directive leadership may increase performance by preventing "goofing off," but it may also decrease job satisfaction. Participative or supportive leadership is likely to increase satisfaction with the leader and with company policies even though the tasks are unsatisfying. However, when tasks are nonroutine and complex, directive or achievement-oriented leadership is more appropriate than supportive leadership. Subordinates appreciate the leader who clarifies the paths to their objectives.

When Stanley Gault took over as CEO of Rubbermaid in 1980, the producer of household items was in financial trouble. Gault immediately told his management team that he was aiming for a 15 percent average annual growth in sales and a billion dollars in sales by 1990. The sales goal was achieved, but the growth rate goal was met later than Gault had hoped. Rubbermaid's 1994 sales finally topped the $2 billion mark and surpassed 15 percent annual growth. He clarified how the organization would achieve these goals—by selling off unprofitable divisions and introducing more than 1,000 new products. He said that as a leader you must define objectives and strategies and show others what you expect from them. Recognition came when a panel of experts surveyed by *Fortune* magazine's editors rated Rubbermaid as America's most admired corporation in 1994 and 1995.

Ask Students
What benefits would you gain from having a leader who clarified paths, or means, for you?

The following Insight highlights how Chris Sullivan, Robert Basham, and Timothy Gannon used various leadership styles to create a new business in an industry in which everything has been tried.

Insight

Outback Steak House

As owners and founders of Outback Steakhouse, Sullivan, Basham, and Gannon started out with modest ambitions in 1987. Eight years later, 210 Outback restaurants are generating sales of more than $750 million. The owners plan to open another 140 steak houses by 1996. In 1995, the organization earned more than $25 million in profits and had more than 8,500 employees.

During their years of working in the food industry, Sullivan, Basham, and Cannon had discovered that most managers were working long hours and were well paid but wanted a piece of the action. With that in mind, they crafted a plan that would require each restaurant manager to invest $25,000 in the firm's stock. Starting at a base salary of $45,000, managers can earn more than $80,000 a year if the restaurant does an average volume ($3.2 million). With the restaurant managers having a direct stake in the company's success, they strive to make good decisions. The ability of the restaurant manager to operate as a partner and share in the store's profits is a strong motivator.

The plan has paid off in several ways. First, restaurant manager turnover averages only 5.4 percent, compared to an industrywide norm of 40 percent. The managers know their jobs better and are making better decisions locally than staff at headquarters could. Second, managers are establishing roots in their communities by hosting local charity events and running special promotions to attract families. Each restaurant manager is encouraged to take an active part in the community. Third, there is only one layer of management between the founders and the restaurant manager. The industry norm is four or five layers for comparable chains. The only decisions made at headquarters concern floor plans and location. Every restaurant is designed so that a server should be setting the customer's steak on the table within twelve minutes after the order was placed. Fourth, there is no human resources department at corporate headquarters, which has only fifty-five people, because hiring decisions are made locally. Basham, Gannon, and Sullivan base their selection of restaurant managers on their past successes and commitment to quality. Fifth, restaurant managers buy beef, salad dressings, breads, vegetables, and other food stocks from suppliers approved by headquarters management. This approach allows local managers to obtain volume discounts and lock in prices. By carefully controlling costs, restaurant managers have the opportunity to earn even more income.[29]

The founders of Outback demonstrated all four leadership styles. Their achievement-oriented style was used when they created the concept and asked others to join them as shareholders. Restaurant managers are empowered to manage their restaurant as they see fit within the chain's general guidelines, demonstrating the founders participative and supportive leadership styles. The owners use a directive style when deciding on the location of a new restaurant and its decor.

Ask Students
Would individuals respond differently than teams? State your reasoning.

Significance for Practice. Employees performing routine and simple tasks have reported greater job satisfaction when leaders provide supportive rather than directive leadership. Employees performing nonroutine and complex tasks have reported higher productivity when leaders provided directive leadership, but they haven't necessarily reported greater job satisfaction. Like Fiedler's and Hersey and Blanchard's models, House's model indicates that participative leadership styles aren't always effective. A participatory style is needed most when employees' acceptance of the decision is important, when the leader doesn't have some of the information needed to make a decision, and when the problem is unstructured. Directive or task-oriented leadership seems to work better when employees don't share the manager's and/or organization's goals, when the production schedule is tight, and when employees are receptive to top-down decisions.[30]

Leader-Participation Model

One of the more recent contributions to the contingency approach is the leader-participation model proposed by Victor Vroom and Philip Yetton and revised by Arthur Jago in 1988.[31] The **leader-participation model** provides a set of rules to determine the amount and form of participative decision making that should be encouraged in different situations. Recognizing that a task can be structured or unstructured, these researchers suggest that the leader adjust her or his behavior to the task's structure. This model provides a sequence of rules for a leader to follow in determining the form and amount of employee participation in decision making.

Teaching Tip
Select an issue from the newspaper headlines. Have the students play President Clinton, your state's governor, or some other policymaker and relate the eight contingency questions to resolution of the issue.

The model suggests that the effectiveness of a decision is gauged by both its quality and its acceptance. According to the model, to arrive at the best decision a leader needs to analyze the situation and then choose one of five decision-making styles. These styles are summarized in Table 14.3. There are two autocratic styles (AI and AII), two consultative styles (CI and CII), and one group style (GII). The leader's analysis is guided by eight contingency questions, which must be answered in the following order.

- ***QR—Quality Requirement:*** How important is the technical quality of this decision?
- ***CR—Commitment Requirement:*** How important is subordinate commitment to the decision?
- ***LI—Leader's Information:*** Do you have sufficient information to make a high-quality decision?
- ***ST—Problem Structure:*** Is the problem well structured?
- ***CP—Commitment Probability:*** If you were to make the decision yourself, are you reasonably certain that your subordinates would be committed to the decision?
- ***GC—Goal Congruence:*** Do subordinates share the organizational goals to be attained in solving this problem?
- ***CO—Subordinate Conflict:*** Is conflict among subordinates over preferred solutions likely?
- ***SI—Subordinate Information:*** Do subordinates have sufficient information to make a high-quality decision?

The leader-participation model, containing the eight contingency questions and the five leadership styles, is diagrammed in Figure 14.7. To use this model, the leader starts on the left-hand side and asks the first question: "How important is the technical quality of this decision?" The answer, high or low, determines the path to the second question: "How important is subordinate commitment to the decision?" After answering that

TABLE 14.3

Decision-Making Styles According to the Leader-Participation Model

Decision Style	Definition
AI	Leader makes the decision alone.
AII	Leader asks for information from team members but makes the decision alone. Team members may or may not be informed as to what the situation is.
CI	Leader shares the situation with each team member and asks for information and evaluation. Team members do not meet as a team, and the leader alone makes the decision.
CII	Leader and team members meet as a team to discuss the situation, but the leader makes the decision.
GII	Leader and team members meet as a team to discuss the situation, and the team makes the decision.

Note: A = autocratic; C = consultative; G = group.

Source: Vroom, V.H., and Yetton, P.W. Leadership and Decision-making. Pittsburgh: University of Pittsburgh Press, 1973. Reprinted by permission of the University of Pittsburgh Press.

question, either high or low, the leader goes to the next question, and so on until the eighth question is asked and answered and an appropriate leadership style is determined. The leadership style should then lead to a high-quality decision that will be accepted by subordinates. The following Diversity Insight illustrates how to use the leader-participation model.

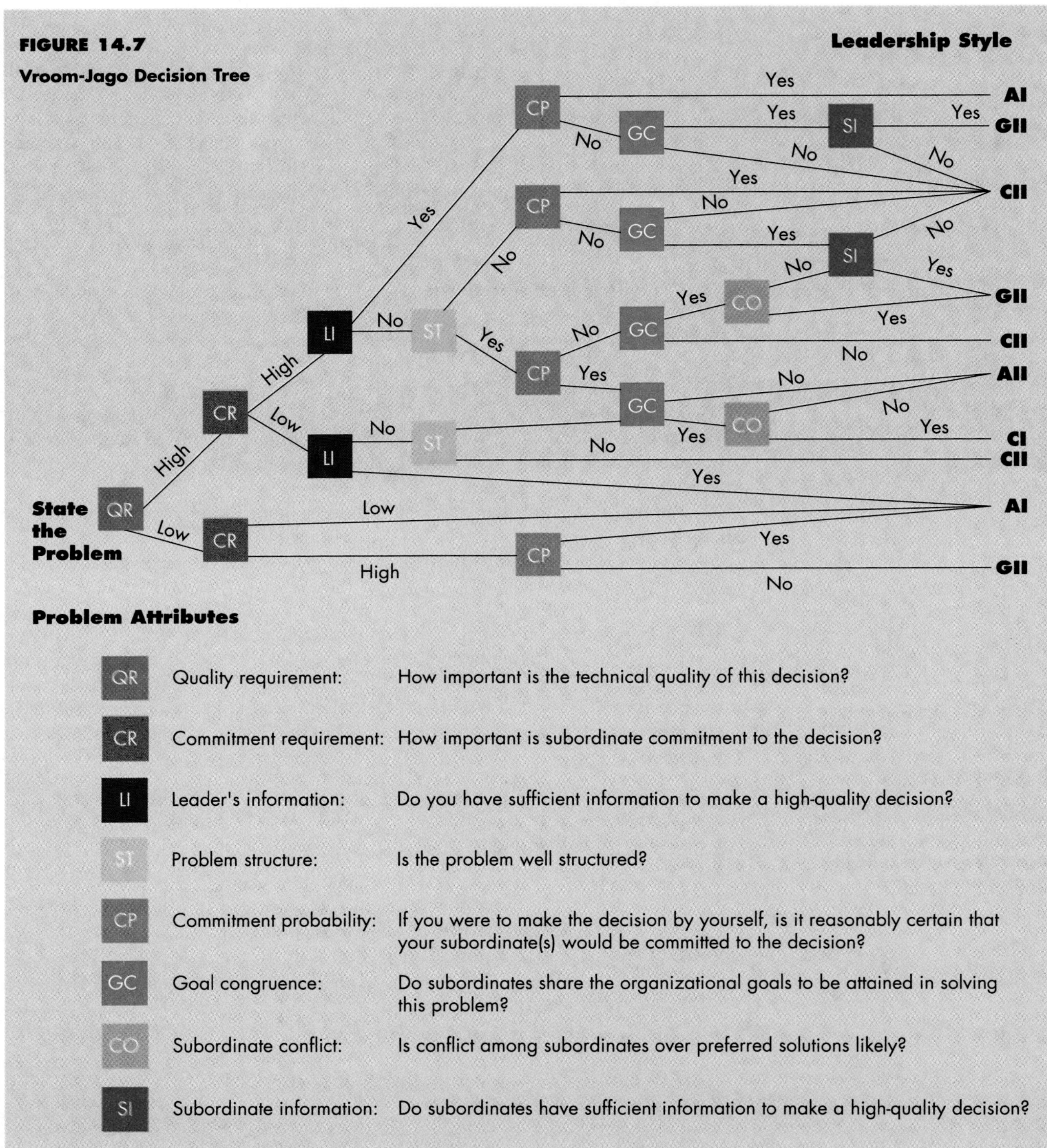

Leadership Style
State the Problem
QR
CR
LI
ST
CP
GC
CO
SI
High
Low
Yes
No
AI
GII
CII
GII
CII
AII
CI
CII
AI
GII
Problem Attributes
QR Quality requirement: How important is the technical quality of this decision?
CR Commitment requirement: How important is subordinate commitment to the decision?
LI Leader's information: Do you have sufficient information to make a high-quality decision?
ST Problem structure: Is the problem well structured?
CP Commitment probability: If you were to make the decision by yourself, is it reasonably certain that your subordinate(s) would be committed to the decision?
GC Goal congruence: Do subordinates share the organizational goals to be attained in solving this problem?
CO Subordinate conflict: Is conflict among subordinates over preferred solutions likely?
SI Subordinate information: Do subordinates have sufficient information to make a high-quality decision?

FIGURE 14.7
Vroom-Jago Decision Tree

Source: Reprinted from *The New Leadership: Managing Participation in Organizations* by Victor H. Vroom and Arthur G. Jago, 1988, Englewood Cliffs, N.J.: Prentice Hall. Copyright 1987 by V. H. Vroom and A. G. Jago. Used with permission of the authors.

Diversity *Insight*

Angelita Guajardo of Telex Aerospace

Angelita Guajardo is vice-president of operations at Telex Aerospace, a large aerospace company in Tulsa, Oklahoma. The company has been under competitive pressure to reduce costs and increase efficiency. Several months ago the manufacturing manager requested funds for new machines. Guajardo gave her permission to buy and install them, but much to her surprise, productivity has *not* increased, and employee turnover *has* increased.

She believes that nothing is wrong with the machines and that they were installed properly. Other companies in Tulsa have similar machines and haven't reported declines in productivity. Representatives of the Dallas company that manufactured the machines have checked their installation and told Guajardo that the machines were installed properly and should operate "just fine."

She suspects that changes in the ways people are required to work might be the problem. However, this view isn't widely shared by the other vice-presidents, the manufacturing manager, and the first-line managers. Those managers believe that production has declined because of poor training, lack of adequate financial incentives to increase production, time needed to train new employees to replace those who have left the firm, and low morale. Clearly, these are issues that affect the operation of the entire plant and over which Guajardo and the others might disagree.

The president calls Guajardo into her office. She is displeased with the production figures for the last three months because both the quality and quantity of work have fallen off since the new machines were installed. She wants Guajardo to "get to the bottom of this problem quickly" and indicates that the problem is Guajardo's to solve. She gives Guajardo four days to come up with a solution. Guajardo shares the president's concern about the decline in productivity and knows that the manufacturing manager and her first-line managers are upset. Her problem is to decide what to do to correct the situation.

If you were Guajardo, and were applying the leader-participation model, what leadership style would you choose? Start at the left-hand side of Figure 14.7. The first box to the right is QR (quality requirement). You must make a decision about whether the importance of quality requirements is high or low. After you make that decision, go to the next box, or CR (commitment required). Again, you must make a decision about the importance of having subordinates committed to the final decision. After you have made that decision, you face another decision and then another. As you make each decision, follow the appropriate line to the next box. Eventually, at the far right-hand side of Figure 14.7, you will arrive at the best style of leadership to use, based on your eight answers. To determine whether you've arrived at the correct style, review the following analysis.

Contingency Questions	*Answers*
• *QR— Quality Requirement*	High
• *CR— Commitment Requirement*	High
• *LI — Leader Information*	No
• *ST — Problem Structure*	No
• *CP— Commitment Probability*	No
• *GC— Goal Congruence*	Yes
• *CO— Subordinate Conflict*	Yes
• *S — Subordinate Information*	Yes

The answer is GII. Guajardo should choose the GII leader-participation style in this situation.

Organizational Implications. The leader-participation model provides an excellent guide for determining the type and degree of subordinate participation in decision making. It confirms the findings of other research—that leaders use participation when the quality of the decision is important, when it's important that subordinates accept the decision and it's unlikely that they'll do so unless they're allowed to have some say in it, and when subordinates can be trusted to strive for organizational rather than individual goals.[32]

This model also stresses that the situation—not the leader— should receive attention. Along with Hersey and Blanchard's and House's models, the leader-participation model states that a leader can adopt different styles of leadership to meet the demands of different situations. But, before choosing a leadership style, the leader must assess the situation. However, not all leaders can do what's suggested by the model. Although they may know how they *should* behave, they may lack the core leadership skills to tailor their behavior to meet the specific situation.

Comparing Contingency Models

To recap, leaders need to be able to direct and motivate others to achieve both high productivity and greater job satisfaction. The four contingency models just discussed offer somewhat different advice about choosing an effective leadership style. Table 14.4 compares the elements of these models. The following Insight illustrates and compares these approaches in terms of choosing a leadership style for a team project.

Insight

Choosing a Leadership Style

David Lei, a professor at Southern Methodist University, teaches a course in business policy and strategy. Every semester he divides the class into teams of four to six students, each of whom is given different responsibilities (marketing research, finance, production, human resources, accounting, and customer services). The teams are responsible for developing detailed business plans for a client's organization. Three teams are assigned to each client. At the end of the semester, managers from those organizations attend class and listen to the analyses of their firms. They critique the presentations and then choose the best plans for their firms. The presentation and final choice heavily influence each student's grade for the course.

Suppose that you're elected to lead one of the student teams preparing a business plan for Murata Business Machines, a company that makes fax machines and other telecommunications equipment. Your objective is to best the other two Murata teams and have your plan adopted. What leadership style should you choose?

According to *Fiedler's contingency model,* your effectiveness depends on the match between the situation and your particular leadership style. The three situational variables to be considered are leader-member relations, task structure, and position power. You and your team members probably have good leader-member relations. You were chosen because others in the team perceived you to be trustworthy and easy to work with. Your team's task is relatively unstructured, and you have no formal power to make team members work on their assignments. Under these conditions, what style of leadership does the Fiedler model recommend? In Figure 14.4 find the column for contingency variable ratings of good, low, and weak, respectively. This model says that a relationship-oriented leadership style is likely to work best in this situation.

According to *Hersey and Blanchard's situational leadership model,* you must assess the readiness level of those on your team to determine the appropriate leadership style to use. If members of your team have set low goals and appear unwilling to take responsibility for the project (low readiness), a telling style of leadership is most likely to lead to high performance. If you want to improve the readiness level of your group members so that they will assume more responsibility, your best bet is to reduce your telling behavior a little by giving members opportunities to assume increased responsibility for their part of the project. If improved performance follows, increase your supportive behaviors until you've adopted a selling, or even participating, style. If team members initially show a willingness to take their responsibilities seriously and have the knowledge to perform the necessary tasks, you may need to provide little direction and help. A delegating style is then appropriate.

According to *House's path-goal model,* a leader's major function is to provide a path by which people can increase their job satisfaction and productivity. You can do so by clarifying the nature of the project, increasing the opportunities for team member satisfaction, and helping members complete the project. The project is somewhat unstructured, but the team needs to perform well so that it will win the competition and each member will receive a high grade. Under these conditions, House's model supports a directive leadership style because it will enable you to give specific directions about what is supposed to be done when, where, by whom, and at what level of performance.

According to the *leader-participation model,* your assessment of the situation is the key. Using the eight contingency questions in Figure 14.7 will help you choose a leadership style that produces the highest quality decisions and team member commitment. The following are answers to the questions.

Contingency Question	*Answer*
QR — Quality requirement	High
CR — Commitment Requirement	High
LI — Leader Information	No
ST — Problem Structure	No
CP — Commitment Probability	No
GC — Goal Congruence	Yes
CO — Subordinate Conflict	Yes
SI — Subordinate Information	Yes

Based on these answers, which style of leadership should you choose? Follow the path in Figure 14.7 to find the correct answer. The paths point to GII style of leadership. You should meet with your team members to generate alternatives and help them to reach a consensus on what solution is best.

TABLE 14.4

A Comparison of Four Contingency Models

	Hersey and Fiedler's Contingency Model	**Blanchard's Situational Model**	**House's Path-Goal Model**	**Leader-Participation Model**
Key situational variables	Task structure Leader-member relations Leader position power	Level of followers' readiness	Task characteristics Employee characteristics	Eight diagnostic questions concerning time, quality, and acceptance
Leadership styles	Task-oriented Relationship-oriented	Telling Selling Participating Delegating	Achievement Directive Participative Supportive	Autocratic I and II Consultative I & II Group II
Implications	Leader's style is matched to situation or situation is changed to fit leader's style. High or low control situations favor task-oriented leader. Moderate control situ–ations favor relationship-oriented leader.	Effective leaders choose a style to match the maturity level of their followers.	If tasks are routine and simple, supportive or participative leadership is best for team members who want their social needs satisfied. If tasks are nonroutine and complex, directive or achievement-oriented leadership is best for team members who want to self-actualize on the job.	Effective leaders analyze the situation by answering the eight contingency questions, then choose among the five styles, depending on the answers.

Teaching Tip
Ask several students to give a one-minute presentation on how a leader can motivate team members.

Significance for Practice

The preceding Insight emphasizes the complexity involved in choosing a leadership style. All the models demonstrate the importance of followers to a leader and how followers make a difference in the leadership style a leader chooses. Thus leadership is a two-way street. Successful leaders are adept at recognizing the requirements of the situation and the needs of their followers and then adjusting their own behavior (or the situation) accordingly.

5

State the unique behaviors of transformational leaders and their impact on followers.

TRANSFORMATIONAL LEADERSHIP

The leadership models presented clearly don't agree on how leaders can best influence followers. Early models focused on personality traits, and most of the later ones look at leader behaviors as determined by contingency or situational factors. In the past few years, many top managers around the world have realized that they will have to make major changes in the ways they do things in order for their organizations to survive. A new look at traits theories has resulted. Many now believe that the type of leadership needed by top managers for tomorrow's organizations is what has been labeled *transformational*.[33]

Teaching Tip
Students often think that transformational leaders do grand things that will be recorded in history books. Ask them whether they know any transformational leaders who are just plain folks.

Quite simply, **transformational leadership** is leading by motivating. Transformational leaders provide extraordinary motivation by appealing to followers' ideals and moral values and inspiring them to think about problems in new ways.[34] Joan of Arc, Abraham Lincoln, Franklin D. Roosevelt, John F. Kennedy, and Martin Luther King, among others, have transformed entire societies through their words and by their actions. Followers of these leaders feel trust, admiration, loyalty, and respect for them and are motivated to do more than they thought they could, or *would,* do. A leader can motivate followers by making them more aware of the importance and value of their task and the need to place it ahead of their own self-interests. Transformational leaders' influence rests on their ability to inspire others through their words, visions, and actions. In essence, transformational leaders make tomorrow's dreams a reality for their followers.

Real-World Example
Visionary companies like Colgate, Douglas Aircraft, Pfizer, TI, Westinghouse, and Zenith did not need leaders with charisma (*California Management Review,* Winter 1995, 30).

When Lee Iacocca took over as president of Chrysler, he refused to believe that it was a dead company. Instead, he launched a campaign to unite the company's employees behind his vision and lobbied Congress to approve the loans necessary for Chrysler to continue its operation. Cutting his salary to $1, he urged all employees to sacrifice for the good of the company. Chrysler survived and again is a profitable U.S. automaker.

What methods do transformational leaders use to affect their followers profoundly and generate this type of response? Transformational leaders exhibit three behaviors: vision, framing, and impression management.[35] Figure 14.8 shows these behaviors and followers' reactions.

Vision

Perhaps the most important behavior that transformational leaders have developed is their ability to create a *vision* that binds people to each other. Dr. Martin Luther King's famous speech "I Have A Dream" galvanized a generation of people to support the civil rights movement in the United States. Lee Iacocca used similar emotional language in his appeal to Congress when he said, "Would you rather have people on welfare or working at Chrysler? The choice is yours." But both leaders had more than just a vision: They also had a road map for attaining it. What is important is that followers "buy into" that vision and that the leader have a plan to energize people to reach it.

Teaching Tip
Show the video of the "I Have a Dream" speech in class.

Framing

When changes in the environment are slow, many top managers fail to recognize them as threats to their organizations. To make members of an organization aware of envi-

FIGURE 14.8

Transformational Leadership Model

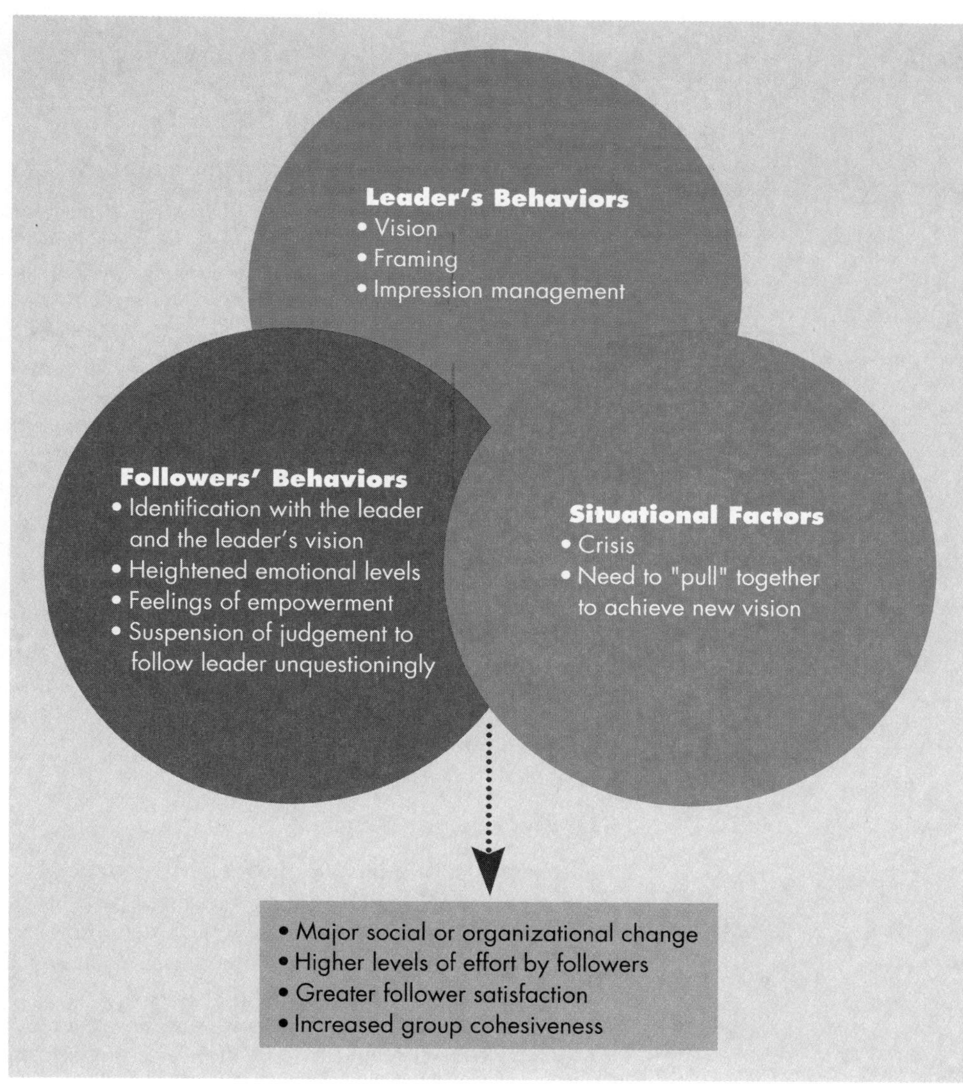

Real-World Example
Sam Walton, founder of Wal-Mart, is an example of the visionary who put the company before himself. He once said, "I have concentrated all along on building the finest retail company that we possibly could. Period. Creating a huge personal fortune was never particularly a goal of mine" (*California Management Review,* Winter 1995, 30).

ronmental changes, transformational leaders often *frame* their vision by giving employees a new purpose for working. **Framing** is a process whereby leaders define the purpose of their movement (or organization) in highly meaningful terms for their followers. Ben Cohen, co-founder of Ben & Jerry's Ice Cream, has been able to use success in business to show other leaders and employees that they could both maximize profits *and* have a positive impact on society. Cohen framed the overall strategy of the company to create a higher moral standard for others to follow.

Impression Management

Impression management is a leader's attempt to control the impressions that others form about the leader through practicing behaviors that make the leader more attractive and appealing to others. Anita Roddick, CEO of The Body Shop, uses slogans and advertising campaigns to inspire others to follow her beliefs about environmentalism, animal testing, and women's rights.

Discussion Question 7
What behaviors would you look for in a transformational leader?

The following Global Insight illustrates how Paolo Cantarella, CEO of Fiat, used his transformational style of leadership to turn that company's financial fortunes around. In 1993, Fiat lost more than $1.1 billion; in 1994, it made $600 million.

Global *Insight*

Paolo Canteralla of Fiat

In 1989, Canteralla was head of Fiat Auto's supplies and distribution. He cut the number of main suppliers from 500 to 120 and encouraged large vendors to integrate their operations with Fiat. He also persuaded Fiat's engineers to codesign parts with suppliers instead of developing them exclusively in-house. As a result, Fiat was able to cut costs by 15 percent.

When he became CEO in 1991, he told employees of his vision for Fiat: recapture Italy's market share by reducing costs, dramatically improve quality, and bring new cars to market faster. Fiat's market share in Italy had slipped from 60 percent to 45 percent because of poor quality, inefficient service, and high costs. He immediately slashed the layers of management that separated plant management and employees. He asked all employees to take a wage freeze, promised labor peace, and took a pay cut himself. In return, he pledged to turn Fiat around, train employees, and save their jobs.

Fiat spent $64 million of quality training for employees and restructured employees jobs by placing them in small teams. Now, thirty-one teams oversee car assembly from start to finish. Such innovations have helped cut the time Fiat takes to get new models to market from sixty months in 1989 to thirty-six months. That's the fastest time in Europe. As a result, nine new models have hit the market since 1992, giving Fiat a fresher look than its rivals.[36]

Significance for Practice

Transformational leaders are most effective when an organization is new or when its survival is threatened. The poorly structured problems that face these organizations call for leaders with vision, confidence, and determination. These leaders must influence others to assert themselves, to join enthusiastically in team efforts, and arouse their feelings about what they are attempting to do.

However, transformational leadership has several drawbacks. First, overzealous followers can become blind to conditions surrounding the leader and the movement—a bit like the children who followed the Pied Piper of Hamelin. Such leaders emotionally manipulate followers and so can create visions for their own self-aggrandizement. Sometimes these visions can wreck havoc with the rest of the world (e.g., Attila the Hun or Adolph Hitler). Second, because followers and movements become dependent on the transformational leader, the danger is that these leaders surround themselves with "yes people" and fail to receive information that might challenge their decisions intended to help realize their vision. Finally, some transformational leaders are known for their autocratic style of leadership, (e.g., David Koresh, the Branch Davidian cult leader who died along with his followers in a fiery farmhouse outside Waco, Texas, in 1993).[37]

Real-World Example
Agee was fired on February 9, 1995 by his board of directors, who were under pressure to do so by lenders. The company's stock price went up in response. Agee's proteges, Stephen Hanks and Robert Tinstman, became acting CEO and acting COO, respectively. Morrison is behind schedule on its contracts and is about to post a $150M fourth quarter loss for 1994 (*The Wall Street Journal*, February 13, 1995, B1).

In 1980, William Agee and Mary Cunningham were playing leading roles at Bendix Corporation. He was the CEO and she was his young, smart, and charming executive assistant with an MBA from Harvard Business School. In two years, she rose to executive vice-president but was forced to leave the company when she became Mrs. Agee. After a takeover attempt by Martin Marietta Corporation, Agee lost his job. In 1988, he became CEO of Morrison Knudsen Corporation, a giant construction and rail-equipment company headquartered in Boise, Idaho. After some early success, his transformational leadership style couldn't overcome serious problems there. The following Ethics Insight illustrates how these transformational leaders sought goals that satisfied their immediate self-interests to the detriment of employees and shareholders and almost bankrupted Morrison Knudsen.

Ethics *Insight*

Celebrity Boss Exiled

Upon arriving in Boise, Idaho, in 1988, the Agees were lightning rods in the town and at its largest employer, the Morrison Knudsen Corporation. Mary was brilliant, charming, and gracious. In this small city where everyone knew everyone else, the lavish parties and Agees' friends astounded people. William Agree had maintained his contacts from his days at Bendix and was able to have Peter Ueberroth, former baseball commissioner and 1984 Olympic Games Chairman, among others, put Knudsen's name in front of people who could direct business to the company. He and Mary Cunningham commanded full support of the board of directors with their charisma, track records, and vision of huge contracts to turn the company around. By securing some small contracts and immediately selling off businesses, Agee improved the company's financial picture.

Initially, these decisions paid off. The company's stock rose from $15 to $29 in three years. But, by 1991, its financial fortunes started slipping. Managers questioned Cunningham's use of company operations for her personal benefit (e.g., making life-sized unicorns for an Agee birthday party and rushing orders for her causes through the print shop while company business had to wait or be done outside). Agee defended his wife's actions by stating that organizations should encourage employees to extend philanthropy to their communities. When his chief financial officer politely tried to tell Agee that his lavish life-style, personal use of the corporate jet, and $2.2 million dollar salary were excessive, he was reassigned. When Agee informed employees not to leak information to the press about internal morale problems, he had security employees wire-tap employees' phones. When bad news eventually got out, he identified who was leaking it to the press and fired them. When employees found out about it, morale dropped to an all-time low.

As troubles mounted, Agee became more remote and ultimately moved the company's headquarters to his seaside estate in Pebble Beach, California, and ran the company by fax, phone, and weekly briefings from executives. His use of the company jet for personal trips was so blatant that the IRS questioned the company's tax deductions. When he tried to sell off the company's start-up locomotive and maintenance operation, he was more concerned about how the sale would affect his compensation than whether the sale was good for the company. As investors became worried about Knudsen's financial stability, he replaced experienced managers with inexperienced people who wouldn't question his decisions. Without adequate engineering support on big projects, Knudsen lost contracts. Because of all these problems, in February 1995 the company's share price had fallen to its all-time low of less than $10.[38]

CHAPTER SUMMARY

1 ***Describe the basics of leadership.***
An understanding of leadership begins with the five competencies that leaders use to influence others: empowerment, intuition, self-understanding, vision, and value congruence. Leaders also rely on five types of power: legitimate, reward, coercive, referent, and expert.

2 ***State the contributions of the traits models of leadership.***
Traits models of leadership were early attempts to identify the personal characteristics that make a leader successful. The characteristics studied included physical, social background, personality, and task-related.

3 ***Describe the primary behavioral models of leadership.***
Behavioral models of leadership provide a way of identifying effective leaders by their actions. The primary behavioral models are Theory X and Theory Y, which represent two quite different ways that leaders view their subordinates and thus

manage them; the Ohio State University and University of Michigan models, which identify two leadership styles (considerate and initiating structure—Ohio State) and two types of leader behaviors (production-centered and employee-centered—Michigan); and the managerial grid model, which identifies various combinations of concern for people and production.

4 ***Explain the principal contingency models of leadership and the situational factors that determine a leader's effectiveness.***

The principal contingency leadership models are Fiedler's contingency model, which suggests that successful leadership depends on matching the demands of the situation to the leadership style; Hersey and Blanchard's situational leadership model, which indicates that leaders must adapt their leadership style to the readiness level of their followers; House's path-goal model, which holds that effective leaders clarify the paths, or means, by which subordinates can attain job satisfaction and perform well; and the leader-participation model, which suggests that leaders can choose one of five leadership-decision styles, depending on the situation.

5 ***State the unique behaviors of transformation leaders and their impact on followers.***

Transformational leadership involves inspiring, and thereby motivating, individuals to reach the leader's highest goals. Leaders influence others by creating a vision that appeals to subordinates' emotions, framing the problem in ways that others can easily understand, and using impression tactics to increase their attractiveness to followers.

QUESTIONS FOR DISCUSSION

1. How do the types of a leader's power influence followers' behaviors?
2. What are the three most useful traits for a leader? Do they vary by the situation?
3. Describe the basic elements in the Ohio State University and University of Michigan leadership models. How can these concepts help you to become a more effective leader?
4. *Harvard Business Review* ran a cover story entitled "Essential Leader Behaviors" in the January-February 1995, issue. The nine essential leader behaviors it identified are (1) clarify the mission of your employees; (2) describe assignments clearly; (3) listen to your employees; (4) make sure the resources necessary to carry out the assignment are available; (5) make clear the standards by which you will evaluate their performance; (6) ensure that rewards make it worthwhile for your employees to try hard; (7) give prompt feedback on employees' performance; (8) merit your employees' trust, and (9) make decisions that are yours to make. Using these criteria, evaluate Ricardo Semler's leadership as presented in the Preview Insight.
5. Describe Fiedler's three situational variables and his contingency approach to leadership.
6. Explain how Hersey and Blanchard's situational leadership model relates to the readiness of followers.
7. What behaviors would you look for in a transformational leader?
8. Is a person's leadership style fixed or flexible? Why or why not?

FROM WHERE YOU SIT

1. Set up an interview with the dean of your school to discuss diversity issues on your campus. What style of leadership did the dean display while talking with you?
2. Describe how you could apply Hersey and Blanchard's situational model to a class project you and others are doing this semester.

3. Consider a student leader at your school. What style of leadership does that person use? When is that style most and least effective? Why?
4. How would you know whether a transformational leader is present in your class? What behaviors and skills might she or he show to others?
5. Peter Drucker, noted management consultant, said, "Whenever anything is being accomplished it is being done by a monomaniac with a mission." In light of what you have learned about leadership, evaluate that statement.
6. How would you like working for one of America's toughest bosses? Why do people work for them?

What's Your Leadership Style?[39]

The following questions analyze your leadership style. Read each item carefully. Think about how you usually behave when you are the leader. Then, using the following key, circle the letter that most closely describes your style. Circle only one choice per question.

A = Always   O = Often   ? = Sometimes   S = Seldom   N = Never

1.	I take time to explain how a job should be carried out.	A	O	?	S	N
2.	I explain the part that members are to play in the team.	A	O	?	S	N
3.	I make clear the rules and procedures for others to follow in detail.	A	O	?	S	N
4.	I organize my own work activities.	A	O	?	S	N
5.	I let people know how well they are doing.	A	O	?	S	N
6.	I let people know what is expected of them.	A	O	?	S	N
7.	I encourage the use of uniform procedures to get things accomplished.	A	O	?	S	N
8.	I make my attitudes clear to others.	A	O	?	S	N
9.	I assign others to particular tasks.	A	O	?	S	N
10.	I make sure that others understand their part in the group.	A	O	?	S	N
11.	I schedule the work that I want others to do.	A	O	?	S	N
12.	I ask that others follow standard rules and regulations.	A	O	?	S	N
13.	I make working on the job more pleasant.	A	O	?	S	N
14.	I go out of my way to be helpful to others.	A	O	?	S	N
15.	I respect others' feelings and opinions.	A	O	?	S	N
16.	I am thoughtful and considerate of others.	A	O	?	S	N
17.	I maintain a friendly atmosphere in the team.	A	O	?	S	N
18.	I do little things to make it pleasant for others to be a member of my team.	A	O	?	S	N
19.	I treat others as equals.	A	O	?	S	N
20.	I give others advance notice of change and explain how it will affect them.	A	O	?	S	N
21.	I look out for others' personal welfare.	A	O	?	S	N
22.	I am approachable and friendly toward others.	A	O	?	S	N

Scoring Form

The following list entries are numbered to correspond to the questionnaire items. In each box, circle the number next to the letter of the response you picked. Add the numbers you circled in each of the columns.

COLUMN 1

1.	A = 5 O = 4 ? = 3 S = 2 N = 1	2.	A = 5 O = 4 ? = 3 S = 2 N = 1
3.	A = 5 O = 4 ? = 3 S = 2 N = 1	4.	A = 5 O = 4 ? = 3 S = 2 N = 1
5.	A = 5 O = 4 ? = 3 S = 2 N = 1	6.	A = 5 O = 4 ? = 3 S = 2 N = 1
7.	A = 5 O = 4 ? = 3 S = 2 N = 1	8.	A = 5 O = 4 ? = 3 S = 2 N = 1
9.	A = 5 O = 4 ? = 3 S = 2 N = 1	10.	A = 5 O = 4 ? = 3 S = 2 N = 1
11.	A = 5 O = 4 ? = 3 S = 2 N = 1	12.	A = 5 O = 4 ? = 3 S = 2 N = 1

TOTAL COLUMN 1 _____

COLUMN 2

13.	A = 5 O = 4 ? = 3 S = 2 N = 1	14.	A = 5 B = 4 ? = 3 S = 2 N = 1
15.	A = 5 O = 4 ? = 3 S = 2 N = 1	16.	A = 5 B = 4 ? = 3 S = 2 N = 1
17.	A = 5 O = 4 ? = 3 S = 2 N = 1	18.	A = 5 B = 4 ? = 3 S = 2 N = 1
19.	A = 5 O = 4 ? = 3 S = 2 N = 1	20.	A = 5 B = 4 ? = 3 S = 2 N = 1
21.	A = 5 O = 4 ? = 3 S = 2 N = 1	22.	A = 5 B = 4 ? = 3 S = 2 N = 1

TOTAL COLUMN 2 ______

Interpretation

The questions scored in Column 1 reflect an initiating-structure leadership style. A score of greater than 47 would indicate that you describe your leadership style as high on initiating structure. You plan, organize, direct, and control the work of others.

The questions scored in Column 2 reflect a considerate style. A total score of greater than 40 indicates that you are a considerate leader. A considerate leader is one who is concerned with the comfort, well-being, and contributions of others.

In general, managers rated high on initiating structure and moderate on consideration tended to be in charge of higher producing groups than those whose leadership styles are the reverse.

CRITICAL THINKING CASE

Cheryl Womack, CEO of VCW, Inc.

People who don't give 110 percent to their jobs don't last long at VCW. Perhaps they aren't willing to come in early and leave late during a crunch, or they can't get along with other people. They are provided a written warning by their department manager and receive specific deadlines for improving. The few who can't are urged to leave. Tough, yes. But for those who make the grade, Womack promises them a ride of their life.

VCW sells a full-range of insurance policies—workers' compensation, life, truck—to long-haul truck drivers. During the past ten years, the organization has grown from a one-woman company to a company with revenues of more than $25 million and over 8,600 policyholders. Salaries are on par with other companies in the Kansas City area. Fringe benefits include full health insurance, profit sharing, spot bonuses for extraordinary results, and onsite day care.

Womack believes that her organization can grow only if her seventy employees have a real sense of purpose and grow personally. Working at VCW, she says, "is like having a loving parent with strict rules." She hires people because of their passion for work, the excitement they bring to the job, and their flexibility.

All employees write goal statements, which they are asked to review annually. They check their progress and make sure their goals mesh with VCW's. Teamwork is important, and fellow employees are the first to confront an employee who isn't pulling his or her weight. Most people who can't rise to the teamwork challenge leave within the first month; turnover after the first month is low—5 to 7 percent a year.

Employees are empowered to make decisions and be innovative. They develop policies and handle all claims. Ninety-five percent of new product innovations come from employees. When their innovations are approved, they are rewarded with extra vacation time, money, or some combination of the two. VCW also offers its truckers newsletters and audiotapes to help them with their personal problems, and a drug testing service to make meeting federal requirements easier.[40]

Questions

1. What leadership competencies does Cheryl Womack demonstrate?
2. Choose a model and diagnose her leadership style. Why is it effective?
3. Under what conditions might this style not be effective?

VIDEO CASE

Dow Chemical's CEO Frank Popoff—View from the Top

In a decade of tightening regulations, a lackluster economy, and intense global competition, the chemical industry has been dealing with a poor public image. Dow Chemical is the sixth largest chemical company in the world, and its chairman and CEO Frank Popoff has guided his company through many recent changes. Popoff estimates that nearly half his time is spent resolving various types of issues.

Although the chemical industry traditionally has been very cyclical, Dow has attempted to diversify into higher margin chemical-based pharmaceutical, agricultural, and other consumer product specialities. Brand names include Saran Wrap and Ziploc plastic bags. At one time 80 percent of Dow's production comprised basic chemicals, but the company now is aiming to diversify in equal thirds: consumer specialties, basic chemicals, and industrial specialties.

Popoff's plans for Dow's growth called for increasing capital spending in the basic chemicals business. Overall, capital spending for 1994 was flat at the 1993 level of $1.4 billion. The industrial specialties need to grow through research and development and product line extensions. Consumer specialties need to grow through agricultural products. Popoff's main goal is to focus on individual markets while maintaining the company's integrated strength.

Even with diversity, though, the downturn in sales and overcapacity in the chemical industry is forcing Dow to cut costs in the hope of reversing thinning profit margins. Contrary to his original plans, Popoff has had to cut total capital spending while trying not to touch research spending. In addition, he has been closing the gaps on overdue research.

Popoff states, "I don't like business interruptions for any reason and I sure don't like them when they're self-inflicted." Recent interruptions included management restructuring in which Dow's chemicals and plastics businesses reduced their work forces by a total of 3,500 jobs worldwide. In North America the company has cut 4,300 jobs in the past three years.

Many of Popoff's critics argue that he is missing out on the opportunities in Asia and the Pacific Rim. He denies those charges, saying that Dow has been very aggressive in building new facilities and investing substantial amounts of money in those areas. However, the Pacific Rim currently accounts for less than 10 percent of corporate sales. Popoff hopes to raise that to 20 to 25 percent and expects to add $1 billion of sales in the region. Popoff argues that, because Europe is the largest chemical market and the largest value added market for his industry, he is driving the majority of the company's business there.

For Popoff, the chemical industry has a strong record in R&D, product and market development, global trade, total quality management, and leadership on environmental issues. Popoff combined the commercial company Merell Dow with the research company Marianne Laboratories. He believes that this merger of research and development pipelines can infuse the product mix and better serve changing customer needs.

Have Popoff's strategies paid off? He was the 1994 recipient of the *Societe de Chimie Industrielle's Palladium* medal. Popoff's standing as perhaps the preeminent leader in the industry was recognized when newly elected President Clinton invited him to the Little Rock summit in 1992. Dow's business is picking up, but not exponentially.

Popoff doesn't see too many clouds on the horizon for Dow that say "yes, but." In fact, at a press reception in November 1994, Popoff said that he sees "our business very good through 1997." By then, Popoff believes that a key determinant will be whether the industry "will have built an inordinate amount of new capacity." Popoff claims that "the industry overall will do very well if we take our medicine and continue the reengineering, at the same time balancing productivity improvement and growth."

Dow has a strong cash flow, and Popoff is satisfied with the company's diversification efforts. Popoff's leadership style is reflected in his thought: "Now the template is, whatever business adds shareholder value, we have to support."

This philosophy, which involves redesign, requires top-level commitment. Popoff states, "Many redesigners follow a 'field of dreams' approach: If process redesign isn't driven and supported by top management, it won't attract the commitment required for implementation."

Dow's business is demand driven, and Popoff is convinced that the slide has been arrested, the bottom is behind Dow, and it now has to define the slope of the curve up. However, Popoff still follows the attitude of never getting too satisfied with success: You can always do better.

Questions

1. What leadership style best describes Dow CEO Frank Popoff?
2. The statement, "Good management controls complexity; effective leadership produces useful change," is insightful. Does this statement apply to Popoff? Why or why not?
3. Has Popoff adequately recognized and addressed the changes and threats to Dow in the external environment? What successful visions has Popoff implemented?

Chapter 15

Organizational Communication

Learning *Objectives*

After studying this chapter, you should be able to:

1 Define the main elements of the communication process.

2 Describe the importance of information technology in the communication process.

3 Define barriers to communication and describe ways to overcome them.

4 State the guidelines for effective communication.

Chapter *Outline*

Preview *Insight*

Empowering Charles Chaser

Puzzled, Charles Chaser scanned the inventory reports from one of his company's distribution centers one Wednesday morning. According to the computer printouts, stocks of Rose Awakening Cutex nail polish were down to a three-day supply, well below the three-and-a-half-week supply Cheesebrough-Ponds, Inc., tries to keep on hand. But Chaser knew that his plant had shipped 346 dozen bottles of the nail polish just two days before. Chaser turned to his computer terminal and typed instructions for the production department to produce 400 dozen more bottles Thursday morning.

All in a night's work for a scheduling manager except that Chaser isn't a manager. He's a "line coordinator," or one of hundreds of employees who routinely tap the plant's computer network to track shipments, schedule their own workloads, and perform functions that supervisors ordinarily performed. As the information age spreads, the chain of command between workers and managers is being broken. Workers now have information to make decisions that once were reserved for managers. Information technology is changing the entire communication system. Workers now are expected to do and think more than ever. They are being asked to analyze and make decisions that once were parceled out to them by management.[1]

1

Define the main elements of the communication process.

THE COMMUNICATION PROCESS

Whether in a school district, bank, transportation system, or manufacturing plant, effective communication is essential. Communication is to an organization as the bloodstream is to a person. Just as a person can develop hardening of the arteries, which impairs physical efficiency, an organization can develop blockages of communication channels, which impair its effectiveness. And just as heart bypass surgery may be necessary to save a person's life, an organization may have to revamp its communication system to survive.

Communication affects how people in an organization relate to each other. Without *effective* communication, managers can accomplish very little. Recall that in Chapter 1 we discussed the work of Henry Mintzberg, who described the manager's job in terms of three categories of roles (interpersonal, informational, and decisional). Communication plays a vital part in each, as Figure 15.1 illustrates.

FIGURE 15.1

Management Roles in Communication

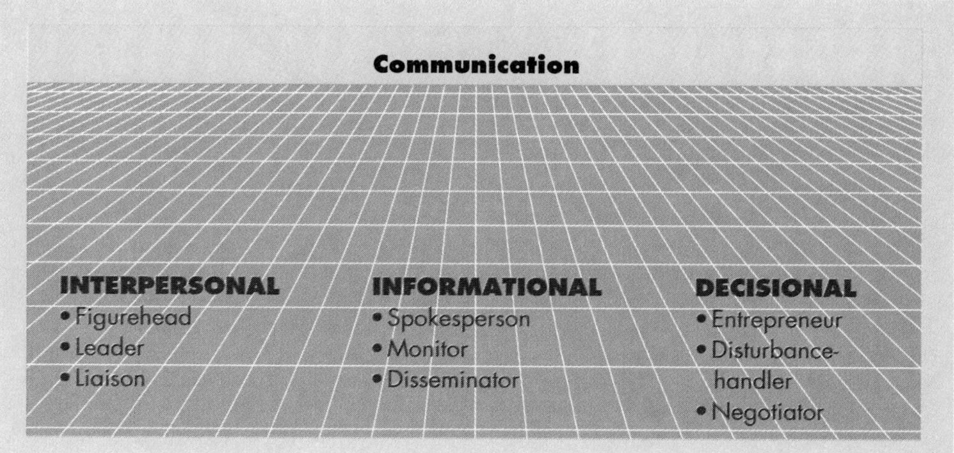

In their interpersonal roles, managers act as figureheads and leaders of their organizations. Top managers spend about 45 percent of their contact time with peers, about 45 percent with people outside the company, and only about 10 percent with superiors.[2]

Teaching Tip
Information workers (e.g., professors, scientists, and inventors) tend to have large information networks and emphasize the informational managerial role.

Effective employees and managers build networks of contacts through the "informational" role. Because of these contacts, employees can become the nerve center of an organization. That is, much like radar units, they scan their environment for changes that could affect the organization, share this information with others, and talk to others outside the organization about industry trends.

In their decisional (decision-making) roles, managers decide whether to undertake new projects, how to handle disturbances, and how to distribute resources. Although some managerial decisions may be reached privately, many are based on information that others provide.

Teaching Tip
Ask students to write a one-minute paper defining *communication.* Call on various students to share their definitions.

In Chapter 1 we also pointed out that communication may be verbal or nonverbal and may take many forms, including face-to-face interactions, phone calls, faxes, e-mail, notes posted on bulletin boards, letters, memos, reports, and oral presentations. In this chapter, we examine how communication takes place, identify some barriers to communication, and explore ways of improving communication in organizations.

Communication is the transfer and exchange of information and understanding from one person to another through meaningful symbols. It is a way of exchanging and sharing ideas, attitudes, values, opinions, and facts. Significantly, communication is a process that requires both a sender, who begins the process, and a receiver, who completes the communication link. When the receiver understands the communication, the cycle is complete.

Ask Students
How do managers depend on the communication process to carry out their four functions (planning, organizing, leading, and controlling)?

Within the organization, managers use the communication process to carry out their four functions (planning, organizing, leading, and controlling) and to play their three roles. A manager must have access to relevant information in order to make sound decisions. However, until a manager effectively communicates these decisions to others, they cannot be carried out. For example, Delta Airlines posted a sign on employee bulletin boards that read, "NO SMOKING HERE." Delta Airlines managers thought they had communicated a message not to smoke in that area. However, the sign was only the start of the communication process. Until employees actually read and understood the

FIGURE 15.2

Elements in the Communication Process

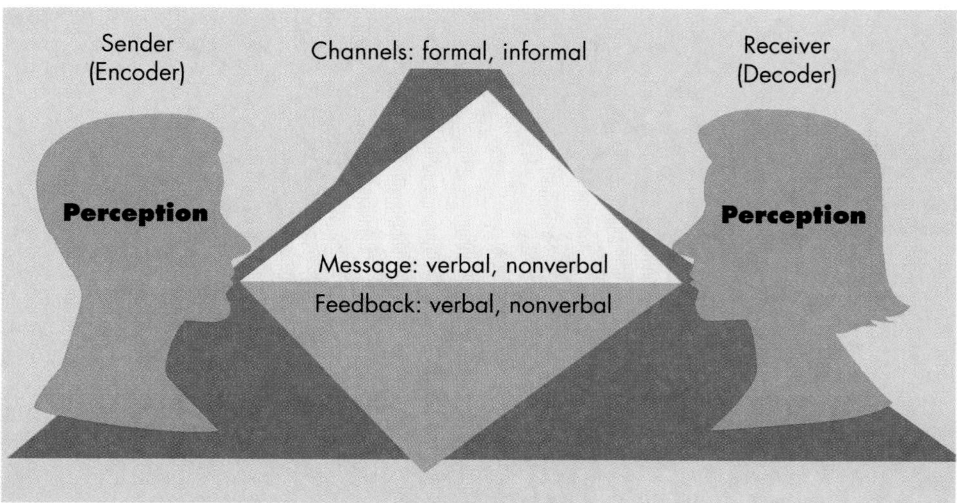

Source: Adapted from Huseman, R.C., Lahiff, J.M., and Penrose, J.M., Jr. *Business Communication: Strategies and Skills,* 3rd ed., 1988, P. 38. The Dryden Press. Copyright © 1988 by CBS College Publishing. Reprinted by permission of Holt, Rinehart & Winston.

"NO SMOKING HERE" sign, communication had not taken place. To make sure that employees understood the sign, Delta had it translated into 15 languages, representing the different countries Delta flies to.

Few employees spend most of their time alone. Many spend a large part of their working day communicating with superiors, peers, customers and others; writing memos, letters, and reports; and talking to others on the phone. In doing so, they are engaged in the communication process, which involves six basic elements:

1. sender (encoder),
2. receiver (decoder),
3. message,
4. channels,
5. feedback, and
6. perception.

Figure 15.2 shows how these elements interact during the communication process.[3] Managers and employees who are concerned with improving their communication skills need to be aware of these elements and how they contribute to successful communication. We discuss the roles of the sender and the receiver first because they are the actors in the process.

Sender (Encoder)

Ask Students
How many times a day are you a sender and how many times are you a receiver? Is this number different for you at school, at work, in extracurricular activities, and in your social life? If so, what do these differences tell you?

Ethics
Sometimes people intentionally send ambiguous messages because they don't want to be the "bearer of bad news" or because they want to avoid responsibility. Have you ever done so? Why? Is this type of action ethical?

The **sender** is the source of information and the initiator of the communication process. The sender tries to choose the type of message and the channel that will be most effective. The sender then encodes the message.

Encoding translates thoughts or feelings into a medium—written, visual, or spoken—that conveys the meaning intended. Imagine that you are planning to apply for a summer job. You will get the best response by phoning first to find out whether an opening exists, then writing a letter, and then phoning again to confirm that your letter was received. You will want your letter to convey certain ideas and impressions. For example, you should explain why you are interested in that company. You also need to provide background information about your qualifications for the job and explain how you believe the job will further your career. When you transfer these ideas to paper, you are encoding your message.

Five principles of increasing encoding accuracy—relevancy, simplicity, organization, repetition, and focus—apply to all forms of communication.

1. ***Relevancy.*** Make the message meaningful and significant, carefully selecting the words, symbols, or gestures to be used.
2. ***Simplicity.*** Put the message in the simplest possible terms, reducing the number of words, symbols, and/or gestures used to communicate the intended thoughts and feelings.
3. ***Organization.*** Arrange the message as a series of points to facilitate understanding. Complete each point in a message before proceeding to the next.
4. ***Repetition.*** Restate key points of the message at least twice. Repetition is particularly important in spoken communication, because words may not be clearly heard or fully understood the first time.
5. ***Focus.*** Focus on the essential aspects, or key points, of the message. Make the message clear and avoid unnecessary detail. In spoken communication, emphasize significant points by changing your tone of voice, pausing, gesturing, or using appropriate facial expressions. In written communication, underline key sentences, phrases, or words.

Ask Students
Are you aware of any encoding errors you made within the last week? If so, which of these five principles could have helped you avoid making the errors?

CIBA-GEIGY, the giant multinational Swiss pharmaceutical and chemical firm, recently revamped its corporate logo to communicate more clearly its strategy to various stakeholders. The following Quality Insight illustrates how CIBA-GEIGY used the five principles of encoding accuracy to design its new corporate logo.

Quality *Insight*

What's in a Logo?

CIBA-GEIGY's new corporate logo is a circle divided into three equal wedges. Each wedge contains a symbol or symbols that reflect a major aspect of CIBA-GEIGY's businesses and its responsibilities.

One wedge has a chemical flask and a gear wheel, symbolic of CIBA-GEIGY's traditional business leadership and the fact that it has to make profits in order to survive. Another wedge contains an icon of people, symbolic of the basic responsibility that CIBA-GEIGY has toward its employees, their families, and the larger human community. The third wedge contains an icon representing trees, symbolic of the company's responsibility toward the environment.

The new logo was displayed when CIBA-GEIGY held an international working conference at its headquarters in Zurich, Switzerland. The purpose of the conference was to formulate strategies for communicating its new corporate logo and, more important, the new corporate philosophy upon which it was based. Because CIBA-GEIGY has thousands of employees and stockholders around the world, management felt that it needed a simple symbol that would reflect its philosophy and strategy.

At this meeting, managers debated questions such as, "How can we get our pharmaceutical drugs to those who are in desperate need of them and not merely to those who can afford to pay for them?"

After much debate, CIBA-GEIGY's management decided to sell its drugs in Africa even though it would make a profit of only 1 or 2 percent, substantially below its usual rate of return. Management justified the decision to shareholders by noting that, if the company sold drugs in Africa, its reputation as a company that cares about providing less fortunate people with a higher quality of life would be enhanced worldwide. Pointing to the logo, the president reminded all stakeholders what CIBA-GEIGY stood for.[4]

Receiver (Decoder)

Ask Students
If you received a piece of junk mail and threw it away without opening it, at what stage did you interrupt the communication process?

The **receiver** is the person who receives and decodes (or interprets) the sender's message. **Decoding** translates messages into a form that has meaning to the receiver. The person who receives your letter about a summer job reacts to it first on the basis of whether there are any jobs open. If there aren't, the receiver probably won't pay much attention to it. If there are jobs to be filled, the receiver probably will compare what you wrote about yourself with the type of person the organization wants to hire.

One of the major requirements of the receiver is the ability to listen. **Listening** involves *paying attention to* the message, not merely hearing it. Of the 75 percent or more of their time that managers spend in communicating, about half is spent listening to others.[5] Becoming a better listener is an important way for people to improve their communication skills. Studies have shown that most people can recall immediately only about 50 percent of what someone tells them. Two months later, they can recall only about 25 percent. That's why effective communicators often use several media, such as newsletters, e-mail, and the telephone. For example, after Nokia, Inc., a Finnish telecommunications conglomerate, decided to build a cellular telephone manufacturing plant in Fort Worth, Texas, it had to announce its plans to thousands of employees working in forty countries, and hundreds of suppliers. To accomplish this feat, Nokia explained the changes in a thirty-two-page report, written simply. The company's senior

TABLE 15.1

Guidelines For Effective Listening

- Stop talking! You can't listen if you're talking.
- Show a talker that you want to listen. Paraphrase what's been said to show that you understand.
- Remove distractions.
- Try to see the other person's point of view.
- Go easy on argument and criticism, which put people on the defensive and may make them "clam up" or become angry.
- Before each person leaves, confirm what has been said.

managers also met with Fort Worth's mayor, Kay Granger, to explore ways that Nokia managers could become a part of local civic organizations and use local employment agencies to fill its 200 jobs. Because it wanted to hire local employees to work in the distribution center, Nokia managers needed to communicate the skills and talents it was looking for in its employees.[6]

Six guidelines for effective listening are presented in Table 15.1. Try using them the next time you are trying to communicate with someone else. You'll be surprised how your listening improves the communication process.

Message

Ask Students
What are some of the reasons that employers and employees often are not *effective* listeners?

The **message** contains the verbal (spoken and written) symbols and nonverbal cues that represent the information the sender wants to convey to the receiver. Like a coin, a message has two sides, and the message sent and the message received aren't necessarily the same. Why? First, encoding and decoding of the message may vary because of differences between the sender's and the receiver's backgrounds and viewpoints. Second, the sender may be sending more than one message. When you prepared your résumé for the summer job inquiry, did you type it or write it out in longhand? Was it neat or sloppy? If it was sloppy and contained misspelled words, that in itself sends a clear message to the receiver: The job really isn't important to you; you don't care enough about it to take the trouble to be neat and correct.

Managers and other employees use three types of messages: nonverbal, verbal, and written. The use of nonverbal messages is extremely important, although many individuals don't recognize this fact. Accordingly, we discuss nonverbal messages at greater length than the other two types.

Ask Students
Why is body language important in the communication process?

Ask Students
What are some examples of nonverbal communication that stand out in your mind as a student? As an employee?

Ask Students
Have you recently misread a nonverbal message because you and the sender came from different cultures, genders, or classes? Describe the situation.

Nonverbal Messages. All messages not spoken or written constitute nonverbal messages. **Nonverbal messages** involve the use of facial expressions, body movement, gestures, and physical contact (often called *body language*) to convey meaning. When people communicate in person, as much as 60 percent of the content of the message is transmitted through facial expressions and body movement.

When talking with someone, individuals can effectively reinforce or supplement their words with nonverbal messages. Let's look at three of the many kinds of nonverbal messages that you should be aware of and be able to use effectively: use of space, personal appearance, and body language.

Space. How close you are to another person, where you sit or stand, and how you arrange your office can have a real impact on communication. The term **proxemics** refers to the study of ways people use physical space to convey a message about themselves. Think of how you would feel if you walked into class midway through the term and someone was sitting in "your" seat. You'd probably feel angry because your space, or territory, had been invaded. Space and the use of space have communicative importance. (To test how important your territory is to you, complete the questionnaire shown in Figure 15.3.)

Status or power also is often communicated through spatial arrangements in corporate offices in North America. Top managers have larger offices, windows with bet-

FIGURE 15.3

How Territorial Are You?

Instructions: Circle one number to answer each question as follows: 1 = strongly agree, 2 = agree, 3 = not sure, 4 = disagree, and 5 = strongly disagree.

1. If I arrive at my apartment (room) and find my roomate sitting in my chair, I am annoyed if he/she doesn't at least offer to get up immediately.

   1 2 3 4 5

2. I do not like anyone to remove anything from my desk without asking me first.

   1 2 3 4 5

3. If a stranger puts a hand on my shoulder when talking to me I feel uncomfortable.

   1 2 3 4 5

4. If my suit jacket is lying on the back of a chair and another student comes in and chooses to sit in that chair, I feel that he or she should ask to move my jacket or choose another chair.

   1 2 3 4 5

5. If I enter a classroom and "reserve" a chair with a notebook, I am annoyed or offended upon my return to find my book moved and someone sitting in "my seat."

   1 2 3 4 5

6. If a person who is not a close friend of mine gets within a foot from my face to talk to me, I will back off or uncomfortably stand my ground.

   1 2 3 4 5

7. I do not like strangers walking into my room (apartment).

   1 2 3 4 5

8. If I lived in a apartment, I would not want the landlord to enter for any reason without my permission.

   1 2 3 4 5

9. I do not like my friends or family borrowing my clothes without asking me first.

   1 2 3 4 5

10. If I notice someone staring at me in a restaurant I become annoyed or uncomfortable.

    1 2 3 4 5

Add the numbers that you circle for all 10 statements. Then compare your total with the following definitions.

10-25 points: *Highly territorial.* Your instincts for staking out and protecting what you consider yours are high. You believe strongly in your territorial rights.
26-39 points: *Ambiguous about territory.* You may act territorial in some circumstances but not in others. You are somewhat unsure about how you feel about the use of space.
40-50 points: *Not territorial.* You disagree with the entire concept of territoriality. You dislike possessiveness, protectiveness, and jealousy. The concept of private ownership is not central to your philosophy of life.

Teaching Tip
Have students pair up and ask one student in each pair to place his or her partner physically at a comfortable standing distance away. Would the distance change because of the type of relationship between the partners? Explain.

ter views, plusher carpeting, and higher quality furnishings than middle managers. Meriting a personal secretary, a head of the table seat at meetings, a chauffeured limousine, use of a private dining room, and the ability to summon employees for discussion—all send messages via the use of space. The following Insight illustrates how managers use space when designing corporate headquarters to convey messages to employees and customers about the organization.[7]

Insight

Offices at Pier 1

Various elements of office design influence attitudes, behaviors, and (through symbolic messages) impressions. Senior managers at Pier 1, a 550-store retailing chain, chose not to move into the top floor of the company's new office building but instead moved into the middle floor. This location sent employees the message that job titles were not overly important and that senior managers really wanted employees to drop by to talk informally. Clark Johnson, Pier 1's CEO, and his vice-presidents keep a pot of coffee brewing and invite employees to drop in to chat about issues and problems.

Management also found that chair placement affects communication. People seated face-to-face are more likely to argue than people seated at right angles. Placing chairs directly next to each other often inhibits communication among those seated, and placing chairs back-to-back results (not surprisingly) in no communication at all. When Pier 1 redecorated its corporate boardroom, changing the design from one in which the board members directly faced senior management to one in which everybody shared a U-shaped table resulted in greater participation.

Finally, management discovered that office decor sends strong messages. Anyone entering Pier 1's corporate headquarters, immediately sees plants and flowers. They convey warmth and friendliness. Decorating the walls are certificates, trophies, and plaques commemorating Pier 1's contributions to the communities in which they have stores and how they have contributed to the community. Such items suggest that the organization values good performance. Flags, logos, seals, and pictures of the organization's leaders communicate that the organization values commitment to its employees and the communities in which it operates.

Teaching Tip
Have the students break up into teams of 5–8. Ask each team to select an academic department on campus with which it is familiar. Then have each team do the following: Get a copy of the catalog or go to the building roster and determine the ranks of the faculty members in that department; find each faculty member's office; note the location and size of the office, number and sizes of windows, and whether two or more people share the office; note the type of furniture and whether the office is carpeted; and determine whether the office has its own secretary. Finally, have each team determine whether these factors relate to the ranks of the people who occupy those offices and present their findings orally to the class.

Personal Appearance. Undoubtedly, you have heard the expression, "Clothes make the person." Style consultants for major corporations believe that the way a person dresses definitely communicates something to others. You should ask yourself: Is the way I'm dressed going to hurt or help my business? Like it or not, people still judge you partly on the basis of how you look. If you are dressed appropriately, customers and others may see you as a more effective person than someone who dresses inappropriately.

Body Language. The body and its movements—particularly those of the face and eyes, which are very expressive—tell other people a lot about you. As much as 50 percent of the content of a message may be communicated by facial expression and body posture; another 30 percent by inflection and the tone of the speech. The words themselves may account for only 20 percent of the content of the message.[8]

The ability to interpret facial expressions is an important part of communication. Eye contact is a direct and powerful way of communicating nonverbally. In the United States, social rules suggest that in most situations, brief eye contact is appropriate. We often interpret prolonged eye contact as either a threat or a sign of romantic interest, depending on the context.

Teaching Tip
Have students conduct a field experiment in teams of 3. One person is to dress shabbily, go to a department store, and try to get waited on. Later in the week, the same person is to return to the store well dressed. The second team member is to observe, and the third person is to take notes each time. Note whether the salesperson approaches or ignores the team member trying to get waited on. Is the salesperson more polite when the subject is well dressed?

Posture also communicates meaning by signaling a person's degree of self-confidence or interest in what is being discussed. The more interested you are, the more likely you are to lean toward the person who is talking. Conversely, leaning away may communicate a lack of interest. A good poker player watches the eyes of the other players as new cards are dealt. Pupil dilation often betrays whether the card(s) just dealt improved the player's hand. Similarly, tension and anxiety typically show in a person's legs and feet. People often are able to hide tension from the waist up but may give themselves away by crossing their legs tightly and tapping their feet.

The following Global Insight focuses on how nonverbal messages can help or hinder you in communicating with Mexican managers. Note especially how some practices that U.S. and Canadian businesspeople believe to be acceptable can lead to communication problems.

Global *Insight*

Doing Business in Mexico

Doing business in Mexico is different from doing business in the United States, Canada, and Europe. Although most Mexican businesspeople speak English, if you are to avoid making serious blunders in nonverbal communication, you need to remember several customs regarding dress, use of time, negotiations and physical contact.

1. ***Dress.*** Businesspeople in Mexico dress quite formally and conservatively, especially in Mexico City. Suits should be worn with long-sleeved shirts and shoes should be well shined. For women, hose should always be worn.
2. ***Time.*** Most businesses in Mexico are open five days a week and operate between 9:00 A.M. and 6:00 P.M. Senior managers usually start their day at about 9:30 A.M. and take a long lunch. Dinner usually is served quite late, between 9:00 and 10:00 P.M. Visitors usually are kept waiting 30 minutes or longer, but they are expected to be punctual.
3. ***Negotiations.*** Before formal negotiations take place, a representative from the company should determine whether the Mexican manager is fluent in English. Since most negotiations involve some bargaining, you must have a "walk away" point prior to the start and also decide which points can be compromised. Suggesting highly inflated prices that are expected to be bargained down isn't wise. Mexican business-people aren't accustomed to this approach and may be offended, contrary to the experience of individuals who are used to bargaining with retailers in border towns.
4. ***Physical contact.*** Mexicans are prone to have close physical interaction with people they consider friends. The distance that people stand from each other is closer than in the United States. Women often kiss on both cheeks when greeting someone of either gender, and men do the same when greeting women.[9]

Teaching Tip
Have students conduct a field experiment in teams of 3. One team member is go to a department store and never make eye contact as the salesperson tries to wait on him or her. Later in the week, the same person is to come back dressed differently and stare down the salesperson in another service encounter. The second team member is to observe, and the third team member is to take

Verbal Messages. Employees communicate verbally (speaking and writing) more often than in any other way. Spoken communication takes place face-to-face and over the telephone. Most people prefer face-to-face communication because nonverbal messages are an important part of it. To get their meaning across on the telephone, they must choose their words and tone of voice carefully.

Effective verbal communication requires the sender to (1) encode the message in words (and nonverbal cues) that will convey it accurately to the receiver, (2) convey the message in a well-organized manner, and (3) try to eliminate distractions.

Written Messages. People usually prefer spoken to written messages because spoken communication is quicker and the sender and receiver can interact. However, or-

notes. The team is to report on how the salesperson reacts to the subject.

Discussion Question 2
What are some of the communication problems that arise in doing business in a foreign country?

Ask Students
Why do some managers prefer written communication to verbal communication?

ganizations use many forms of written messages (e.g., reports, memoranda, letters, and newsletters). Such messages are most appropriate when information has to be distributed to many people at scattered locations and when keeping a record of what was sent is necessary. The following are some guidelines for good written messages.

1. The message should be drafted with the receiver clearly in mind.
2. The contents of the message should be well thought out ahead of time.
3. The message should be as brief as possible, without extraneous words and ideas. Important messages should be prepared in draft form first and then polished. If the message has to be long, include a brief summary on the first page. This summary should clarify the main points and contain page references to details on each item.
4. The message should be carefully organized. State the most important point first, then the next most important point, and so on. This way, even if the receiver reads only the first few points, the essentials of the message will get across. Make the subject clear by giving the message a title. Make the message more readable by using simple words and short, clear sentences.

Channels

The **channel** is the path a message follows from the sender to the receiver. **Information richness** is the information carrying capacity of the channel.[10] Not all channels can carry the same richness of information. Some are highly informative for both sender and receiver; others provide little information. Channels low in richness are considered to be *lean* because they are effective mainly for sending specific data and facts.

As Figure 15.4 indicates, face-to-face is the richest channel. It conveys several cues simultaneously, including spoken and nonverbal information. Face-to-face also provides immediate feedback so that understanding can be checked and misinterpretations corrected. The telephone is somewhat less rich than face-to-face. Immediate feedback is possible, but visual cues are lacking. Written communications are less rich, because feedback is slow and only the information written down is received. Numbers tend to be used to describe simple data, such as absenteeism, turnover, checkbook balances, number of grievances, and the like.

Teaching Tip
Most people have a channel preference. Take a poll in the class to determine the students' preferences. Have those who prefer each channel explain to the class why they prefer their choice. Tell them the channel you would like for them to use in communicating with you.

For sending routine cost figures to employees in the production department, Amy Forsberg, a senior diagnostic engineer at Convex Computer Corporation, uses a simple budget report—a lean channel. In contrast, Chavonne Yee, manager of total quality management at AT&T Power Systems, regularly schedules face-to-face meetings with AT&T personnel to obtain information on total quality management and to communicate ways of continuously improving AT&T's quality. She has chosen a rich channel for sending this information.

In addition to selecting a level of information richness, individuals must choose among four *types* of channels to communicate with others. These types are downward, upward, and horizontal formal channels and the informal grapevine.

Teaching Tip
Divide the class into four brainstorming groups and ask each group to identify the various advantages and disadvantages of one of the four channels of organizational communication: downward, upward, horizontal, and grapevine.

Downward Channels. Managers use **downward channels** to send messages to employees. For instance, L.L. Bean mail-order headquarters in Freeport, Maine, receives more than 165,000 phone calls a day during the holiday season for items ranging from socks to flannel shirts to hunting bows to tents.[11] To communicate effectively with L.L. Bean's 3,000 employees, its managers use downward channels to communicate

- how to handle special promotional items;
- job descriptions detailing duties and responsibilities;
- policies and procedures explaining what is expected of employees, and the organization's rules and employee benefits;
- feedback about an individual's job performance; and
- news of activities and events that management believes employees should participate in (charitable organizations, blood drives, and the like).

FIGURE 15.4

Information Richness of Channels

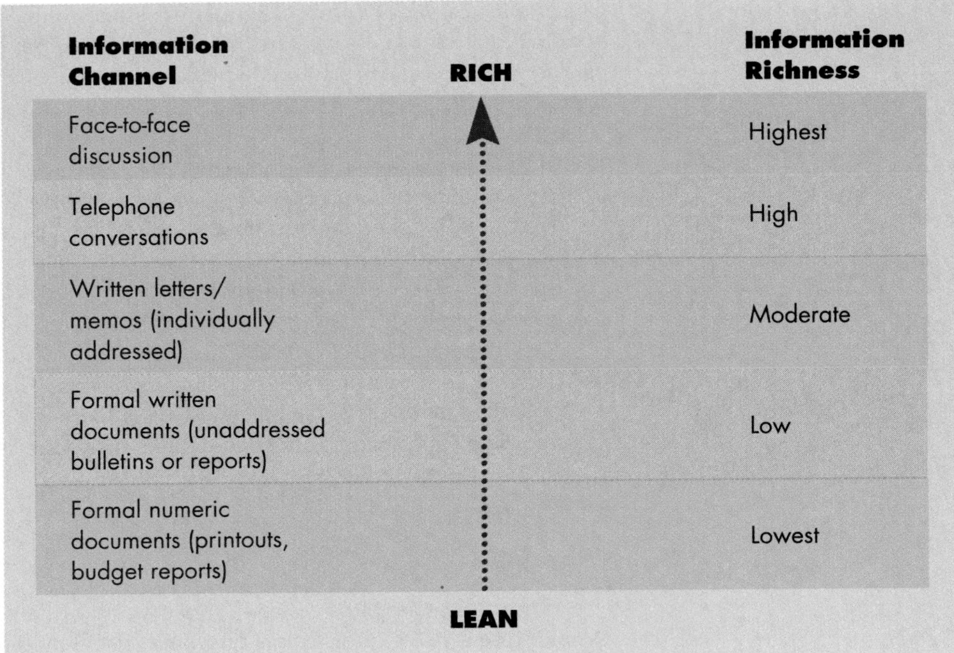

Information Channel
RICH
Information Richness
Face-to-face discussion
Highest
Telephone conversations
High
Written letters/ memos (individually addressed)
Moderate
Formal written documents (unaddressed bulletins or reports)
Low
Formal numeric documents (printouts, budget reports)
Lowest
LEAN

Source: Adapted from Daft, Richard L., and Lengel, Robert H. Information richness: A new approach to managerial behavior and organization design. In Barry M. Staw and Larry L. Cummings (eds.), *Research in Organizational Behavior,* vol. 6. Greenwich, Conn.: JAI Press, 1984, 191–233.

Managers frequently use downward communication as a channel. Doug Key, president of Medstar Ambulance, devotes nearly 50 percent of his time to communicating with employees through meetings, policy directives, and memos to explain Medstar's goals, strategic plans, and activities. The downward channel also may be the most misused because it provides little opportunity for employees to respond. In fact, the fundamental problem with downward communication is that it is too often one-way: It's a lean channel that doesn't encourage feedback from those on the receiving end. To correct this problem, managers should urge employees to use upward channels.

Upward Channels. Some managers do not see the value of encouraging employees to participate in setting goals, planning, and formulating policies. The result is a failure to provide upward channels of communication. Subordinates use **upward channels** to send messages to superiors. Such channels may be the only formal means that employees have for communicating with managers and managers with higher level managers in the organization. As noted in the Pier 1 Insight, managers are finding innovative ways to increase upward communication in their organizations. When you complete an evaluation survey at the end of a course—rating the course, book, and instructor—you are using an upward channel of communication.

Teaching Tip
Show students the upward channel they have in the university catalog's grievance procedures.

Upward communication provides feedback on how well employees understand the messages they have received. Moreover, it enables employees to voice their opinions and ideas. If effective, upward communication can provide an emotional release and, at the same time, give employees a chance to participate, the feeling they are being listened to, and a sense of personal worth. Most important, they often have excellent suggestions for improving efficiency and effectiveness.

Managers should be aware of the problems that can plague upward communication. First, few employees want their superiors to learn anything negative about them, so they may screen out bad news. Most employees try to impress their superiors by emphasizing their contributions to the company. Some may even try to make themselves look better by putting others down. Second, an employee's personal anxieties, aspirations, and attitudes almost always color what is communicated. How many of you would tell a potential employer of the bad things you have heard about the organization? If you really wanted the job, you probably wouldn't be so bold. Finally, the employee may be competing for the manager's job and thus be willing to remain silent and let the manager stumble.

Horizontal Channels. Managers and other employees use a **horizontal channel** when communicating across departmental lines, with suppliers, or with customers. This type of channel is especially important in network organizations (see Chapter 11). Essential to the success of a network organization is maintaining effective communication among customers, suppliers, and employees in various divisions or functions. For example, as NIKE continues to outsource the manufacturing of its athletic shoes and apparel to manufacturers throughout the world, it needs an effective horizontal communication channel to link suppliers and market demand for the purposes of scheduling production and shipping.

Horizontal channels are formal if they follow formal organizational paths.[12] However, they also may be informal. They frequently connect people on the same level in the company. Messages communicated horizontally usually are related to coordinating activities, sharing information, and solving problems. Horizontal channels are extremely important in today's hi-tech organizations. For example, at Rizzuti Marketing & Media Group, seven employees use horizontal channels to effectively communicate among themselves to solve their clients' business problems as the following Small Business Insight details.

Discussion Question 1
What are the three most commonly used information channels in organizations? When is each channel most effective?

Small Business *Insight*

Rizzuti Marketing & Media Group

A paper sign taped to the door of John Rizzuti's small bedroom in Dallas identifies the headquarters of this organization. A half-inch of faxes and e-mail messages greet the president. The director of client services for a firm in Frisco, Texas, wants to know whether she can buy the list of vendors attending the big computer show in the Dallas Convention Center. Another client in Vancouver, British Columbia, is riled because a phone company is using an ad similar to one his software company is running and he wants it stopped.

The six other people who work for the company all live in different parts of Dallas and are linked by high-speed fax-modems, mega-memory computers, e-mail and cellular phones to serve clients in Texas, California, Washington, and Canada. They never meet at the office because they don't have one. They go days, even weeks, without seeing each other. When they do get together, it may be at a client's place of business, a restaurant, or a rock concert. They have no secretaries and no clerical help. Because the firm doesn't have fancy mahogany conference tables and offices, they charge clients less for their services but offer the same high quality of services as their competitors.

Offbeat? Certainly. But Price Waterhouse, IBM, Kodak, and other firms are using some version of Rizzuti's organization. With effective horizontal communication channels, Rizzuti's employees all enjoy the freedom of working at home or wherever. Office politics are minimized because no managers are watching and controlling—or need to be impressed by—the day-to-day activities of Rizzuti's employees. Clients' demands and requests dictate what needs to get done by whom and when.[13]

Informal Channels. So far we have concentrated on formal channels of communication. However, do not underestimate the importance of informal channels of communication. The **grapevine** is an organization's informal communication system. The term comes from a Civil War practice of hanging telegraph lines loosely from tree to

Ethics
The grapevine often carries rumors. Is starting, spreading, or even listening to rumors ethical? Do rumors hurt their subjects? Why or why not?

tree, like a grapevine. The grapevine functions to ease communication problems between managers and/or employees. The path that messages follow along the grapevine is based on social interaction. American Airlines has recognized the importance of this channel to the extent of maintaining a "grapevine file" in the computer's online systems. This file enables employees to ask managers and other employees questions, offer compliments and suggestions, and verify rumors.

Networking. Managers and other employees also spend considerable time meeting with peers and others outside the organization. They attend the meetings of professional associations, trade shows, and other gatherings. As a result, they may develop various close, informal relationships with talented and useful people outside the organization. People use these networks to help each other, trading favors and calling on each other's resources for career advancement or other types of information and support.

Teaching Tip
Advise students to start networking now. They never know who can be helpful or be a barrier in the future. Remind them that good human relations is vital to networking. Combined, those in the class have a large number of contacts.

A recent survey of more than 1,000 organizations found that 86 percent had reduced their managerial ranks during the past five years.[14] Fierce global competition and heavy corporate debt loads have forced many large organizations to cut their work forces. Downsizing has cut loose a number of employees from senior vice-president to shop-floor employees. Drake, Beam and Morin, the nation's largest outplacement firm, has found that most people who have been let go find their next job through contacts with friends and others whom they met in the course of doing their jobs. In addition, the business schools at Stanford, Northwestern, and other universities have started outplacement services for their alumni who need counseling. These services and informal networks help out-of-work graduates of their schools find new jobs.

Feedback

Feedback is the receiver's response to the sender's message. It is the best way to show that a message has been received and to indicate whether it has been understood. You shouldn't assume that everything you say or write will be understood exactly as you intend it to be. If you don't encourage feedback, you are likely to misjudge how much others understand you. Thus you will be less effective than those who encourage feedback.

Teaching Tip
Feedback can be a sign of politeness and acknowledgment of the individual sending the message. Feedback also can build informal relationships and foster effective communication.

Whenever a message is sent, the actions of the sender affect the reactions of the receiver. The reactions of the receiver, in turn, affect the later actions of the sender. If the sender receives no response, the message was never received or the receiver chose not to respond. In either case, the sender is alerted to the need to find out why the receiver didn't respond. Upon receiving rewarding feedback, the sender continues to produce the same kind of message. When feedback is *not* rewarding, the sender eventually changes the type of message.

Receiver reactions also tell the sender how well objectives or tasks are being accomplished. However, in this case the receiver exerts control over the sender by the type of feedback provided. The sender must rely on the receiver for an indication of whether the message was received and understood. Such feedback assures the sender that things are going as planned or brings to light problems that have to be solved.

Procter & Gamble, 3M, IBM, and other companies have set up guidelines to encourage effective feedback.[15] According to these guidelines, feedback should have the following characteristics.

Teaching Tip
Judging others creates defensiveness. Ask several students to tell of a recent communication breakdown in which being judgmental caused unnecessary conflict.

1. ***It should be helpful.*** If the receiver of the message provides feedback that adds to the sender's information, the feedback is likely to be helpful.
2. ***It should be descriptive rather than evaluative.*** If the receiver responds to the message in a descriptive manner, the feedback is likely to be effective. If the receiver is evaluative (or judgmental), the feedback is likely to be ineffective or even cause a breakdown in communication.

3. ***It should be specific rather than general.*** The receiver should respond specifically to points raised and questions asked in the message. If the receiver responds in generalities, the feedback may indicate evasion or lack of understanding.
4. ***It should be well timed.*** The reception—and thus the effectiveness—of feedback is affected by the context in which it occurs. Giving performance feedback to a person during halftime of a football game or at a luncheon is different from giving the same person feedback in the office. Informal settings usually are reserved for social as opposed to performance-based feedback.
5. ***It should not overwhelm.*** Spoken communication depends heavily on memory. Accordingly, when large amounts of information are involved, spoken feedback is less effective than written feedback. People tend to "tune in and out" of conversations. They may fail to grasp what the speaker is saying if the message is too long and complex.

Perception

Teaching Tip
Perceptions are the "reality" that many people act on and try to get others, who may see things entirely differently, to do the same. Managers must recognize that different people perceive events differently and pay attention to those differences.

Perception is the meaning ascribed to a message by either sender or receiver (see Figure 15.1). Perceptions are influenced by what people see, by the ways they organize these elements in memory, and by the meanings they attach to them. The ability to perceive varies from person to person. Some people, having entered a room only once, can later describe it in detail, whereas others can barely remember anything about it. Thus the mental ability to notice and remember differences is important. How people interpret what they perceive is affected by their past. A clenched fist raised in the air by an employee on strike and walking the picket line could be interpreted as both an angry threat to the organization or as an expression of union solidarity and accomplishment. The attitudes people bring to a situation color their perception of it.

Ask Students
How have you used *selective perception* as a student? Give some examples.

Some problems in communication can be traced to two problems of perception: selective perception and stereotyping. **Selective perception** is the process of screening out information that a person wants or needs to avoid. Many "tune out" TV commercials. Most everyone has been accused of listening only to what they want to hear. Both are examples of selective perception. In organizations, employees sometimes do the same thing. Manufacturing employees pay close attention to manufacturing problems, whereas accounting employees pay close attention to debits and credits. These employees filter out information about other areas of the organization and focus on information that is directly related to their own jobs.[16]

Ask Students
Give examples of how you have used stereotyping as a student. How has doing so affected your ability to communicate? (You can help students think about stereotyping and communication by noting that an instructor usually enters class on the first day wearing professional attire instead of jeans or sweats. Why?)

Stereotyping is the process of making assumptions about individuals solely on the basis of their belonging to a certain gender, race, age, or other group. Stereotyping distorts reality by suggesting that all people in a category have all the same characteristics, which simply isn't true. Some organizations, such as Corning Glass Works and Arthur Andersen, have classes to teach employees about managing a diverse work force and to demonstrate how stereotyping can lead to inefficiency and turnover.

Karen Kallow conducts sessions for Arthur Andersen employees on gender issues.[17] She points out that successful women are often stereotyped as having to (1) take more risks and be consistently more outstanding than men; (2) be tough, but not macho; (3) be ambitious but not expect equal treatment; and (4) take responsibility but follow the advice of others. These stereotypes place unrealistic expectations on women, even though mounting evidence suggests that when careers are matched, women are remarkably similar to men in their characteristics, abilities, and motives.

Ask Students
Have you been stereotyped recently by someone else? How did you feel?

Oftentimes gender or racial stereotyping is difficult to overcome. Coopers & Lybrand has undertaken a communications program designed to attract and retain women and minorities in their firm. Currently, women and minorities hold 50 percent of the entry-level staff jobs in the firm, a dramatic increase from 14 percent just a decade ago. Coopers & Lybrand also established a program to assist in managing work-force diversity. The following Diversity Insight outlines its program.

Diversity *Insight*

Grass-Roots Approach at Coopers & Lybrand

Coopers & Lybrand considered two approaches to meet its diversity challenge. First, it considered special programs for women and minority members. It decided not to introduce any because these particular professionals and other staff might resist; many of them would not want to stress those differences. Besides, child care, elder care, and the balance of work and home life were not just women's and minorities' issues. Therefore any approach to work-force diversity had to address issues for everyone in the firm.

Coopers & Lybrand established a grass-roots communication program at each local office. At the invitation of the regional human resources officer and others, a one-day meeting was held at each office to discuss its diversity issues. Afterward, each office designed communication programs to address its own diversity issues.

After six months, employees were asked to evaluate the lessons learned from and the effectiveness of each program. Finally, after a communication program had shown promise at one office, other offices addressing similar issues were contacted. Coopers & Lybrand management was aware that the "not-invented here" syndrome traditionally hampers communication between offices. To overcome such resistance, employees who actually designed the communication programs visited the other interested offices and told them about their successes and failures. Using this approach helped overcome the stereotype of management telling employees what to do.[18]

In brief, then, encoding and decoding skills are based on a person's ability to perceive a message and situation accurately. This ability may vary widely. The message sent, the channel of communication used, and the ability to respond all depend on a person's perceptions.

2

Describe the importance of information technology in the communication process.

IMPACT OF INFORMATION TECHNOLOGY

Ask Students
How has technology affected the communication process in the last ten to fifteen years?

Real-World Example
Nu Skin International, a Provo, Utah, maker of skin products, uses live satellite broadcasts to solicit new distributors around the world (*Success*, December 1994).

New information technologies are rapidly changing the methods of communication available to managers and other employees—and thus the channels of communication. As indicated in the Preview Insight, information technology is changing the manner in which employees communicate with each other and make decisions. Telephone answering machines (voice-mail), fax machines, teleconferencing, closed-circuit television systems, computerized report preparation, and videotaping are examples of communication methods developed during the past twenty-five years. Here, we review two of the most widely used new information technologies: electronic mail (e-mail) and the Internet.

Electronic Mail

At Bank of America, Boeing, Memorex, Manufacturer's Hanover Trust, and Cummins Engine Company, among others, managers and other employees are using advanced methods of communicating with each other. **Electronic mail (e-mail)** uses computer text-editing to send and receive written information quickly, inexpensively, and efficiently.[19] In seconds, messages are transmitted from the sender's computer to the receiver's. They are read at the receiver's convenience. Senders and receivers usually process their own e-mail. They don't have to give messages to, or receive messages from, secretaries or telephone operators. Messages appear on (and disappear from) video screens with no hard copies produced, unless one is specifically desired.

Discussion Question 3
How does information technology affect Charles Chaser's job, as described in the Preview Insight?

Electronic mail has become popular with managers for several reasons. First, a manager doesn't have to wait "maybe a week" for a response because information usually can be sent, returned, and recalled in moments. Second, e-mail is relatively inexpensive because it can "piggyback" on computers and other equipment that companies already have in place. Third, it increases productivity by eliminating the need for the paper-handling steps required in traditional interoffice or intercompany communication systems. Mort Meyerson, CEO of Perot Systems, sends and receives more than 7,000 e-mail messages a month. In some months, IBM employees exchange more than 580,000 messages with outside suppliers and customers because staying in touch with these people with e-mail is easier and faster than by using the traditional written communication medium—letters.[20] One significant disadvantage has been observed in companies that use e-mail extensively. Employees who might never confront a co-worker face to face are less hesitant to explode at others via e-mail, a phenomenon called *flaming*. The following account describes the benefits of using e-mail at Intel—without flaming.

Ethics
E-mail should be used cautiously because it isn't private and has even been used in court cases as evidence. Is viewing, repeating, and otherwise using someone else's e-mail ethical?

Global *Insight*

E-Mail at Intel Corporation

Intel Corporation began using electronic mail more than a decade ago. Today thousands of PCs connect Intel's more than 29,500 employees at locations throughout the world, along with its more than 2,000 customers. The system covers the United States and plants in more than twelve foreign countries.

To illustrate how e-mail works, consider the options available to President Andrew Grove for communicating with a manager in Tsukuba, Japan. Grove can use traditional mail but may not get a reply for weeks. He can send a message via a telex center. To do so, he must dictate a letter containing the message, which has to be retyped at the telex center. The telex message may not arrive in Japan for up to eight hours. (The same procedure, in the opposite direction, must be followed for Grove to receive a reply.) Of course, Grove can call Tsukuba. However, 5:00 P.M. in California is equivalent to 4:00 A.M. in Tsukuba, so timing (as well as cost) make the telephone a less-than-optimal method. E-mail enables Grove to send a message before leaving work in the evening and to have an answer waiting on his computer when he arrives for work the next morning. In terms of cost, e-mail is 90 percent less expensive than overseas calls and letters and 75 percent less costly than telex.

Grove estimates that e-mail and other automated office techniques, such as ProShare©—a system that provides users with video-conferencing capabilities—have had a positive effect on research and development at Intel. Producing state-of-the-art products and services at affordable prices requires that everyone in the organization have access to global information that could affect their efforts.[21]

Internet

The **Internet** is a loosely configured, rapidly growing web of 25,000 corporate, educational, and research computer networks around the world.[22] It was created by the Defense Department in 1969 and designed to survive a nuclear war. Rather than route messages through central computers, the Internet makes use of thousands of computers linked by thousands of different paths. Each message sent bears an address code that lets any computer in the Internet forward it toward its destination. Messages usually arrive in seconds; only on rare occasions do they vanish into cyberspace. The Internet is like any other communications device in that a user can get a busy signal. With thousands of Internet groups and e-mail lists, sometimes the traffic is heavy and a user might have to wait. Also, there is no privacy. The information on the Internet is available to anyone.

Using personal computers connected over the Internet and America Online, Wendy Rickard of Rickard Associates and her employees work together as if they were in the same office. The company, which produces magazines and marketing materials, has an art director in Arizona and editors in Florida, Georgia, Michigan and the District of Columbia.

Who manages it? There is no Internet, Inc. The closest thing to a managing group is the Internet Society of Reston, Virginia. It is a volunteer organization with more than 2,000 individual and 84 organization members who promote the use of the Internet. Anybody with a computer and modem can get on the Net for a monthly fee of $20, plus phone charges, by subscribing to a company such as the World in Boston. The following Insight indicates how some organizations use the Internet system to speed communications with other organizations around the world.

Insight

Life on the Internet

Glenn Trewitt is a supplier of science fiction and fantasy books, posters, pottery, and related items. When he decided to open his store in Palo Alto, California, he put the store opening announcement on the Internet. Between 12 and 15 percent of his sales now come from people ordering items from his store on the Internet.

By using the Internet, people can gather information on numerous subjects. There are chemical engineering, Middle East politics, semiconductor manufacturing, pets, sex, cooking, humor, and many other groups. Last year, Nicholas Graham, president of Joe Boxer underwear, wrote the following message for his company's advertising campaign on Internet: "Contact us in underwear cyberspace" and gave the company's Internet address: joeboxer@jboxer.com. The company permits people to specify the type of underwear they like and even put their names on the Internet to establish a Joe Boxer dating club.

With economic barriers falling and Mexican organizations facing stiff competition for the first time, their managers need to catch on quickly to international ways of doing business. In remote areas of Mexico, employees at Panamerican Beverages, Inc., a Mexican soft-drink bottling company, are experimenting with Internet bulletin boards to keep employees up-to-date on important events. This company also is experimenting with having its more than 180,000 truck drivers keep track of store inventories by using hand-held computers and putting the data on the Internet.

Clearly, a risk is involved in linking a corporate network to the public world of the Internet. Panamerican Beverages, among other Internet users, has taken steps to buffer its messages from competitors and others who might gain from this information. They do so by creating firewalls. **Firewalls** are workstations with special software that screen incoming messages to ensure that an outsider is authorized to access a certain computer in the company and doesn't leave confidential information on the Internet. At Silicon Graphics and Digital, Internet users are issued smart cards that identify them to the firewall. Once they are recognized as legitimate Internet users, they can access certain of those companies' computers.[23]

TABLE 15.2

How Information Technology Affects an Organization

CUSTOMER RELATIONS	No longer simply an "order entry" job, customer-service representatives are tapping into companywide databases to solve callers' demands instantly, from simple changes of address to billing adjustments.
QUALITY	Manufacturers are using information technology to shrink cycle times, reduce defects, and cut waste. Likewise, service firms are using electronic data interchange to streamline ordering and communication with suppliers and customers.
ORGANIZATION	New electronic systems are breaking down old departmental barriers, allowing critical information to be shared instantly across functional departments or product teams—and even with teams on the factory floor.
STAFFING	New systems and processes have eliminated management layers and cut employment levels. Less costly computers and communication devices are used to create "virtual offices" from workers in far-flung locations.
NEW PRODUCTS	The information "feedback loop" is collapsing development cycles. Companies are electronically feeding customer and marketing comments to product-development teams so that they can rejuvenate product lines and target specific consumers.

Source: Adapted from: Sager, Ira. The great equalizer, *Business Week Information Technology Special Issue 1994;* Quinn, J.B., and Baily, M.N. Technology: Increasing productivity in services. *Academy of Management Executive,* 1994, 8(3), 28–51.

Real-World Example
Representative Newt Gingrich (R, Georgia), the Speaker of the U.S. House of Representatives, wants to use Internet as a national town hall meeting. What do you think of the idea? You can respond to him via his mailbox georgia@hr.house.gov (*Business Week,* December 5, 1994, 38).

Table 15.2 illustrates how information technology is affecting organizations in terms of customer relations, product quality, organization, staffing, and new products. Forced to do more with less, organizations are rethinking how they do business and encouraging information sharing among once separate people and functions. As organizations depend more on collecting, analyzing, and sharing information their employees need new skills. At Motorola, for example, all factory employees must have math and basic computer skills in order to run computer programmed equipment or use statistical control processes to monitor the product quality during production.

3

Define barriers to communication and describe ways to overcome them.

BARRIERS TO EFFECTIVE COMMUNICATION

One of the first steps in communicating more successfully is to identify barriers to the process. These barriers hinder the sending and receiving of messages by distorting, or sometimes even completely blocking, intended meanings. We divided these impediments into organizational and individual barriers—although there is obviously some overlapping—and listed them in Table 15.3.

TABLE 15.3

Barriers to Communication

ORGANIZATIONAL

- Structure of the organization
- Specialization of task functions by members
- Different goals
- Status relationships among members

INDIVIDUAL

- Conflicting assumptions
- Semantics
- Emotions
- Communication skills

Teaching Tip
Ask students to identify their perceived barriers to effective communication. List the responses on the board or display them by using an overhead transparency.

Teaching Tip
Most students are familiar with the game *Telephone,* which effectively demonstrates how messages can easily be misunderstood. Start a message at each end of the class, and have each student whisper the message to the next student. Compare the final versions of the message with the original, noting any changes in both tone and content.

Ask Students
Have you ever been afraid to talk to someone in authority? Did your reluctance cause any problems for you personally, the other person, or an organization of which you were a member?

Teaching Tip
Have students watch police dramas on TV for the next week and turn in a list of fifteen examples of police jargon.

Organizational Barriers

Channels of communication, both formal and informal, are largely determined by organizational design. The degree of specialization present in the organization also may affect clear communication.

Authority Levels. Whenever one person holds a higher position than another, communication problems are likely to occur. The more levels in the organization, and the farther the receiver is from the sender, the more difficult effective communication becomes.

Figure 15.5 illustrates the loss of understanding as messages are sent downward through a formal communication channel. To help reduce this problem, top managers increasingly are using live video presentations or videotapes that deliver the same message to all employees at various locations. In doing so, these managers use both verbal and nonverbal messages and cut out intervening receivers and senders in order to increase the probability that their original message will be received intact. Many organizations use videotapes when trying to move managers to new locations. The presentations can reinforce the reason(s) for the relocation and the need for employee cooperation during the changeover.

Specialization. As knowledge becomes more specialized, professionals in many fields develop their own jargon, or shorthand, to simplify communication among themselves. That often makes communication with people outside the field difficult. For example, a tax accountant and a marketing research manager might have trouble communicating successfully. Moreover, in an attempt to make themselves indispensable, some people intentionally use the language of specialization to obscure what is going on. Employees often use specialized language when trying to "snow" others. A plumber recently wrote to the U.S. Department of Housing and Urban Development (HUD) to

FIGURE 15.5

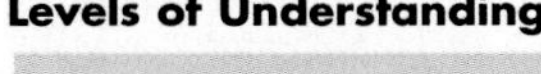
Levels of Understanding

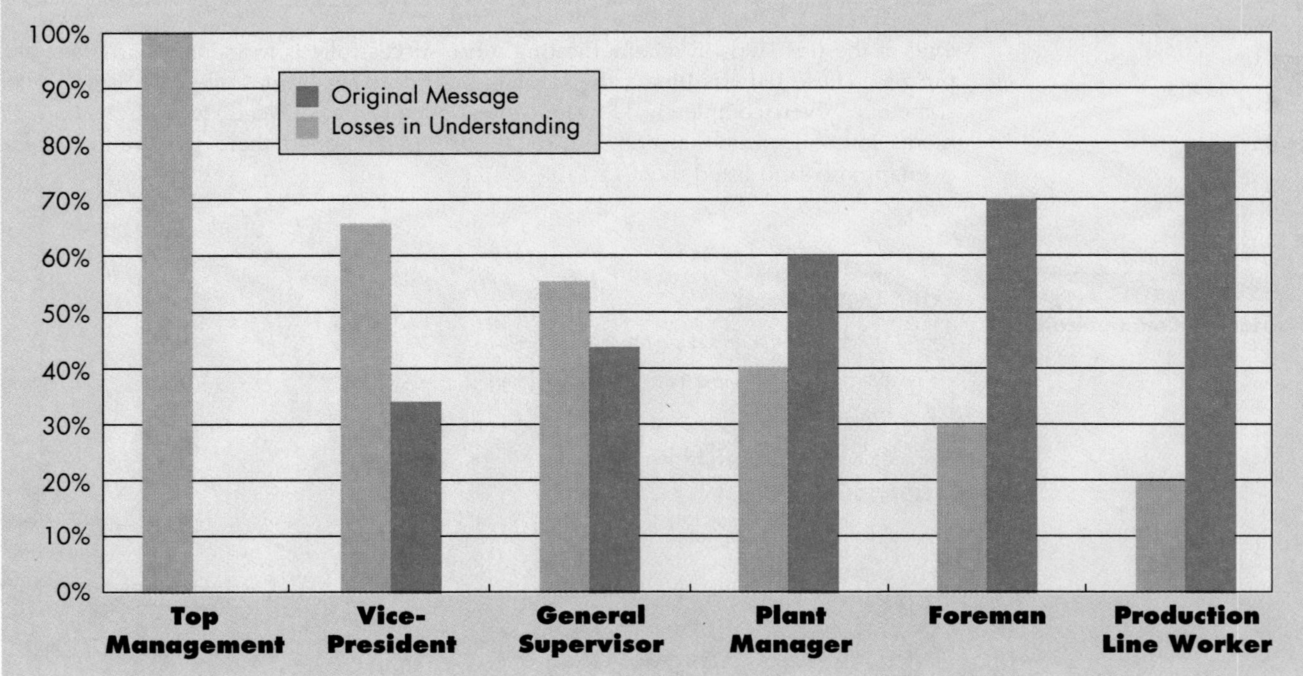

Through an intense training session at the Center for Creative Leadership at Greensboro, N.C., managers can learn to improve their communication skills. The Center estimates that 50 percent of all managers and 30 percent of all top managers have some problems with communication.

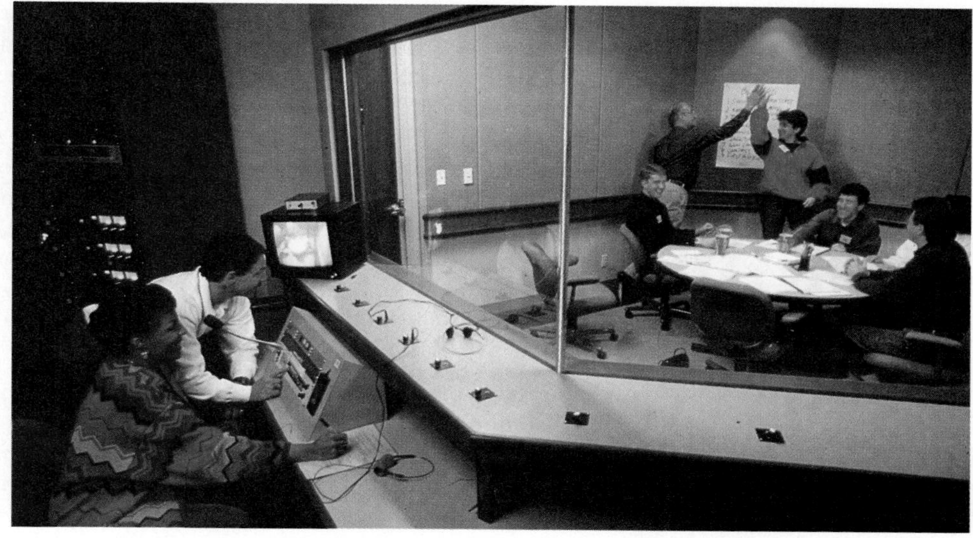

Ask Students
What are some examples of the jargon you as a student use in communicating? What problems can jargon cause in attempts to communicate?

find out whether using hydrochloric acid to unclog drains was safe. A HUD bureaucrat wrote back: "The efficacy of hydrochloric acid is indisputable, but corrosive acid is incompatible with metallic permanence." The plumber wrote back saying he agreed and was using it. A fax message from the bureaucrat arrived immediately at the plumber's shop. It read: "Don't use hydrochloric acid. It eats the hell out of pipes." Then the plumber understood.

Different Goals. When AT&T decided to close its plant in Winston-Salem, North Carolina, different goals surfaced. AT&T chose to close this plant because it was the company's smallest. The company assumed that the work and employees from the plant could easily be absorbed by its larger plants. However, many workers felt that the plant closing was unjustified and didn't want to relocate for various reasons. Some took a substantial cut in pay, in addition to losing company-paid fringe benefits, just to stay in the area while their children finished school or to be close to friends and relatives.[24]

Ask Students
What are some examples of status?

Discussion Question 5
Why do communication difficulties arise in organizations?

Status Relationships. **Status** is a person's social rank in a group. We reviewed some typical symbols of status, such as spacious offices and special privileges, earlier in this chapter. These symbols usually are visible, external things that attach to a person or job and are evidence of social rank. They emerge most clearly at different levels of management. Each higher level usually has the authority to give itself additional perquisites (perks).

Status may be a significant barrier to effective communication because (1) it often is used to insulate managers from things they don't want to hear, and (2) it influences the amount and kinds of information that subordinates channel upward.

Individual Barriers

The Center for Creative Leadership at Greensboro, North Carolina, estimates that half of all managers and 30 percent of top managers have some difficulty in communicating with others. The center also has found that some managers are aloof and are poor communicators.[25] Through an intense training session at the center, managers can learn how to improve their communication skills. The center's staff works with participants who think that their messages are clear and effective when, in fact, they aren't. Their words, phrases, and references may be clear to some individuals, puzzling to others, and obscure to still others. This type of problem can be caused by conflicting assumptions, semantics, emotions, and/or poor communication skills.

Conflicting Assumptions. The sender assumes that the receiver will interpret the message as the sender intends. But a key word or phrase may mean one thing to the sender and something else to the receiver. For example, Brad Williams, a sales representative at Banctec, phoned in a special order for Bank of America, asking that it be shipped "as soon as possible." Five days later, Williams got a call from an irate Bank of America employee wanting to know when the order would be delivered. Upon checking with the shipping department, Williams found that the order was being shipped that day. "I thought I told you to ship it as soon as possible," shouted Williams. "That's just what we're doing," yelled the shipping manager. To Williams, "as soon as possible" meant now. To the shipping department, which often received that kind of order from sales reps, it meant something totally different.

Teaching Tip
Have students cite examples of how misinterpretation of meaning can affect the communication process negatively.

Semantics. The study of the way words are used and the meanings they convey is called **semantics.** Misinterpretation of word meanings can play a large role in communication failure. Most words in the dictionary have several meanings; some common words have as many as eighteen. One example of a common word with many meanings is *charge:*

Real-World Example
The 500 most common English words have an average of twenty-eight meanings each!

- Please charge the battery.
- Charge it.
- You are charged with running a red light.
- The charge for this service is $25.00.
- Let's charge ahead on this new plan.

When two people attribute different meanings to the same words but don't realize it, a barrier exists. Faculty members who say, "This is an easy test," can mislead students who don't know the faculty member's definition of *easy.*

Teaching Tip
In a bureaucracy (Chapter 2), emotions aren't supposed to be displayed. Give some examples of bureaucratic workers who are supposed to be impersonal and indifferent. (Examples: police officers, 911 operators, and ER hospital workers.)

Emotions. An **emotion** is a subjective reaction or feeling. Remembering experiences, an individual recalls not only events but also the feelings that accompanied them. Thus when people communicate, they convey emotions as well as facts and opinions. The sender's feelings influence encoding of the message and may or may not be apparent to the receiver. If they are clear, then both the sender's and the receiver's feelings affect decoding of the message and the nature of the response.

Communication Skills. The ability to communicate varies from person to person. Articulate, persuasive, and confident people communicate more effectively than those who are less so. Some differences in communication skills result from culture, education, and training, whereas others stem from basic cultural learning. For instance, compared to U.S. businesspeople, their Japanese counterparts speak little because they prefer to wait and listen. The higher the position of Japanese managers, the more they listen. Hiroyoshi Takanaka, general manager of Honda Motors' China Division, says that Japanese have a saying: "He who speaks first at a meeting is a dumb ass."

Some people are naturally better listeners than others—or have trained themselves to be. Anxious people may be too preoccupied with personal problems or with what they are going to say next to pay close attention to what other people are saying. People under considerable stress also may be unable to listen properly.

Teaching Tip
Firing, laying off, telling people they didn't get raises and promotions, and other negative news often are timed for a Friday afternoon to avoid or minimize conflict and emotional outbursts during work hours.

In addition, communication effectiveness is influenced by the timing of messages. Managers who relay important instructions to employees on the Friday afternoon before a Monday holiday show poor timing. The employees' attention has already shifted from work to their plans for the long weekend. In contrast, the department manager who asks for a budget increase after the company has achieved its financial objectives for the year shows good timing. Under these circumstances, the department manager's superior is likely to listen to the request.

Overcoming Barriers

The good news is that you can overcome barriers to effective communication. You must first be aware that they exist and can cause serious organizational problems. Then you must be willing to invest the effort and time necessary to overcome the barriers. Several ways of overcoming barriers to communication are presented in Table 15.4.[26]

Discussion Question 6
The world is a busy and confusing place, and people are constantly bombarded by multiple messages. How do people simplify these messages in order to handle the confusion?

Teaching Tip
Tell students that, when they want to encourage feedback, they should be sure that body language doesn't contradict what they're saying. (Example: Some may see crossed arms as a defensive gesture, indicating that the other person don't really want to listen).

Regulate the Flow of Information. If you receive too much information you will suffer from information overload. You should set up a system that identifies priority messages for immediate attention. One way of doing so is to ask others to bring you information only when significant deviations from goals and plans occur (known as *exception reporting*). When everything is going as planned, you don't need a report. In addition, messages should be condensed. Procter & Gamble recommends that all messages be limited to a page or less. Key assumptions usually get lost and loose logic may be camouflaged in a ten-page proposal. Not so on a single page.

Encourage Feedback. You should follow up to determine whether important messages have been understood. Feedback lets you know whether the other person understands the message accurately. Feedback doesn't have to be verbal; in fact, actions often speak louder than words. The sales manager who describes desired changes in the monthly sales planning report receives feedback from the report itself when it is turned in. If it contains the proper changes, the manager knows that the message was received and understood. Similarly, when you talk to a group of people, look for nonverbal feedback that will tell you whether you are getting through to them.

Simplify the Language of the Message. Because language can be a barrier, you should choose words that others will understand. Your sentences should be concise, and you should avoid jargon that others won't understand or that may be misleading. In general, understanding is improved by simplifying the language used—consistently, of course, with the nature of your intended audience.

Listen Actively. You need to become a good listener as well as a good message sender. Recently, several organizations have developed training programs to improve employee listening. For example, at a Loral Vought Systems Middle Management Program taught in Grand Prairie, Texas, the content includes awareness training in "active listening" to what others have to say, reducing "noise" to improve communication, and developing better communication skills through role playing and team presentations.

Restrain Negative Emotions. Like everyone else, you convey emotions when communicating, but negative emotions can distort the content of the message. When emotionally upset, you are more likely than at other times to phrase the message poorly.

TABLE 15.4

Overcoming Barriers to Communication

- Regulate the flow of information.
- Encourage feedback.
- Simplify the language used in the message.
- Listen actively.
- Restrain negative emotions.
- Use nonverbal cues.
- Use the grapevine.

When emotionally upset, both manager and subordinate are likely to misinterpret a message. The simplest answer in such a situation is to call a halt until the people involved can restrain their emotions—that is, until they can be more descriptive than evaluative.

Use Nonverbal Cues. You should use nonverbal cues to emphasize points and express feelings. Recall the methods of nonverbal communication that we presented. You need to make sure that your actions reinforce your words so that they don't send mixed messages.

Discussion Question 4
What are the primary barriers to communication and how can individuals overcome them?

Ask Students
Have you had a business transaction recently—such as trying to order a meal in a restaurant or purchase something at a store—in which the language barrier prevented effective communication? If so, describe the incident.

Use the Grapevine. As a manager you couldn't get rid of the grapevine in an organization even if you tried, so you should use it to send information rapidly, test reactions before announcing a final decision, and obtain valuable feedback. Also, the grapevine frequently carries destructive rumors, reducing employee morale and organizational effectiveness. By being "plugged into" the grapevine you can partially counteract this negative effect by making sure that relevant, accurate, meaningful, and timely information gets to others.

As hard as you try to communicate your messages to others effectively, you may often fail. Communicating with others in foreign countries poses even more problems. Mistakes in translation can lead to some embarrassing blunders as revealed in the following Global Insight.

Global *Insight*

Lost in the Translation

Translation errors cause many blunders in international business. In fact, the largest number of blunders in advertising promotions in foreign countries is caused by faulty translation. These blunders fall into three categories: carelessness, multiple meanings, and idioms.

Carelessness. Consider the experience that Otis Engineering Corporation had when it participated in an exhibition held in Moscow. Initially, the company's representatives couldn't understand why its display was laughed at and scorned. Much to their embarrassment, they discovered that a translator had labeled their product as "equipment for orgasms" rather than "completed equipment."

An American auto manufacturer advertised its battery as "highly rated." Unfortunately, when the company introduced its car in Venezuela, the translation described the battery as "highly overrated."

Multiple Meanings. Translated messages also can convey more than one meaning. Consider the trials and tribulations of Parker Pen Company. In ads destined for Latin America, Parker wanted to use the word *bola* to describe its ballpoint pen. However, the firm soon discovered that the word has various meanings in different Latin American countries. In some, *bola* conveys the intended meaning of "ball," but in another it means "revolution." It is used as an obscenity in yet another country and means "lie" in still another. Fortunately, the company recognized this problem before forging ahead. However, a few years later, Parker decided to use its slogan "Avoid embarrassment—use Parker Pens" in Latin America. The slogan was intended to show that Parker pocket pens wouldn't leak when put in a shirt pocket. But anticipated sales never materialized. Why? The Spanish word for "embarrassment" also indicates pregnancy, so the Parker Pen Company was unknowingly promoting its pens as contraceptives!

Idioms. Everyone in the United States probably has heard the advertisement for Pepsi-Cola, "Come alive with Pepsi." When the ad campaign was introduced in Germany, the company was forced to revise the ad because it discovered that its translation of "come alive" into German conveyed "come out of the grave."

In China, a kitchen equipment manufacturer in Hangzhou tried several names for a product line, including Red Star, Treasure, and Prosperity, but couldn't find one that helped sales. Finally the maker tried Boss, and sales rose dramatically. A survey of customers revealed that many customers asked for the Boss brand because it implied good fortune and promised robustness that other names did not.[27]

According to management consultant Bob Rasberry, companies should routinely have translated messages translated back to the original language to ensure the accuracy of the translation.

4

State the guidelines for effective communication.

GUIDELINES FOR EFFECTIVE COMMUNICATION

To be an effective communicator, you must understand not merely the roles presented in Figure 15.1 but also the guidelines for effective communication. These guidelines, as presented throughout the chapter, are summarized in the following list. We have expressed them in terms of the American Management Association's eight guidelines that you can use to improve your communication skills.[28]

- ***Clarify your ideas before communicating.*** Analyze the topic or problem to clarify it in your mind before sending a message. Communication often is ineffective because the message is inadequately planned. Part of good message planning is considering the goals and attitudes of those who will receive the message.
- ***Examine the true purpose of the communication.*** Before you send a message, ask yourself what you really want to accomplish with it. Decide whether you want to obtain information, convey a decision, or persuade someone to take action.
- ***Consider the setting in which the communication will take place.*** You convey meanings and intent by more than words alone. Trying to communicate with a person in another location is more difficult than doing so face-to-face.
- ***Consult with others, when appropriate, in planning communications.*** Encourage the participation of those who will be affected by the message. They can often provide a viewpoint that you might not have considered.
- ***Be mindful of the nonverbal messages you send.*** Tone of voice, facial expression, eye contact, personal appearance, and physical surroundings all influence the communication process. The receiver considers both the words and the nonverbal cues that make up your message.
- ***Take the opportunity to convey something helpful to the receiver.*** Considering the other person's interests and needs often presents opportunities to the sender. You can make your message clearer by imagining yourself in the other's position. Effective communicators really try to see the message from the listener's point of view.
- ***Follow up the communication.*** Your best efforts at communication can be wasted unless you succeed in getting your message across. You should follow up and ask for feedback to find out whether you succeeded. You cannot assume that the receiver understands; feedback in some form is necessary.
- ***Be sure your actions support your communication.*** The most effective communication is not in what you say but in what you do. Actions speak louder than words.

In terms of ethics, the job of effective communication is never quite finished. As William Adams, chairman and president of Armstrong World Industries knows, he and his managers must constantly communicate Armstrong's ethical standards to all 22,000 people employees in seventeen states and ten foreign countries. As you read how Armstrong communicates its ethical standards in the following Ethics Insight, recall the practices suggested in this chapter.

Ethics *Insight*

Armstrong World, Inc.

Armstrong has a statement of ethical principles that it circulates to all its employees and customers. These principles are further communicated through the use of four business practices.

First, when new employees join the firm, they receive pep talks on ethics. The orientation program makes clear which behaviors are acceptable and which are unacceptable. Adams leads these pep talks himself.

Second, inspirational stories about employees who acted with high ethical principles with customers are circulated throughout the company. One such story involves Ralph Williams, a quality assurance employee, who discovered that carpets being sold by Armstrong were flammable, a violation of its business principles and practices. He insisted that the company manufacturing them for Armstrong replace them and that all such carpets already installed be replaced by the manufacturer without charge to Armstrong's customers. Several Armstrong employees were shocked by Williams's request, fearing that Armstrong would lose a manufacturer. When Adams visited the plant one day he said, "I've heard what Ralph Williams has done. If anyone doesn't agree with that kind of action, it is probably time for that person to resign."

Third, employees and managers practice what they preach. All employees throughout the company are treated fairly and are trusted. Newly hired employees are coached by senior managers on the impact of the organization's ethical climate on performance so that everybody can learn from these experiences.

Fourth, along with the first three methods, which serve to clarify and promote ethical standards, all employees have access to senior managers and are encouraged to speak out on questions of fairness and integrity. When employees encounter an ethical problem, they are encouraged to go to others to straighten it out. Employees are not restricted to talking to just their immediate supervisors.[29]

CHAPTER SUMMARY

1 ***Define the main elements of the communication process.***

The communication process comprises six elements: the sender (encoder), the receiver (decoder), the message, channels, feedback, and perception. Of the many possible forms of nonverbal communication, managers should be particularly aware of—and able to use effectively—space, physical appearance, and body language. Channels of communication are both formal and informal. Formal channels are downward, upward, and horizontal. Managers most frequently use downward channels to send messages to the various levels of the organization. Upward channels allow employee participation in decision making and provide feedback to management. Horizontal channels are used between peers in different departments and are especially important in network organizations. Informal channels—the grapevine—often are as important as formal channels of communication. Managers can never eliminate the grapevine and thus should learn to use it to send messages and receive feedback.

2 ***Describe the importance of information technology in the communication process.***

Information technology now permits communication that enables employees to make decisions traditionally reserved for managers. E-mail and the Internet are two means by which information technology affects the communication process in organizations.

3 ***Define barriers to communication and describe ways to overcome them.***

Barriers to communication hinder the sending and receiving of messages by distorting or even blocking intended meanings. Barriers can be either organizational or individual. Organizational barriers may result from the design of the organization itself, from the jargon that often grows up around highly specialized tasks, from differing departmental goals, and from the insulating effects of differences in status. Individual barriers may result from conflicting assumptions on the part of the sender and receiver, from misinterpretation of meaning, from emotional blockage, and from communication skills.

4 ***State the guidelines for effective communication.***
Guidelines for effective communication include clarifying your ideas, examining your purpose in communicating, considering the setting, consulting with others, being mindful of nonverbal messages, taking the opportunity to convey something helpful to the receiver, following up, and being sure your actions support your communication.

QUESTIONS FOR DISCUSSION

1. What are the three most commonly used information channels in organizations? When is each channel most effective?
2. What are some of the communication problems that arise in doing business in a foreign country?
3. How does information technology affect Charles Chaser's job, as described in the Preview Insight?
4. What are the primary barriers to communication and how can individuals overcome them?
5. Why do communication difficulties arise in organizations?
6. The world is a busy and confusing place, and people are constantly bombarded by multiple messages. How do people simplify these messages in order to handle the confusion?

FROM WHERE YOU SIT

1. Invite classmates from other countries to describe communication and cultural differences and similarities between the United States and their countries.
2. Visit the president's office at a local bank. What nonverbal messages does the office convey? How did these messages affect your communication with the president?
3. How might the Internet affect your communication in the future? What are some potential ethical issues that you will face?
4. Describe a recent communication situation that you were part of that involved an encoding or decoding error. What could you have done to avoid it?
5. As information technologies continue to blur the lines between white- and blue-collar jobs, a manager's job is becoming more one of supporting employees who manage themselves. What implications does this change have for the design of organizations?

Communication Skills Survey[30]

The purpose of this exercise is to help you gain insights into your communication skills. Think back to a work or other organizational experience you have had, and respond to each statement by circling the response that best fits your attitude and behavior. Remember, there are no right or wrong answers.

Statement		Strongly Agree	Slightly Agree	Not Sure	Slightly Disagree	Strongly Disagree
1.	When responding, I try to use specific details or examples.	5	4	3	2	1
2.	I tend to talk more than others do.	1	2	3	4	5
3.	If the other person seems not to understand me, I try to speak more slowly and more distinctly.	5	4	3	2	1
4.	I tend to forget that some words have many meanings.	1	2	3	4	5
5.	When I give feedback, I respond to the facts and keep the feelings out of it.	1	2	3	4	5
6.	I am not embarrassed by periods of silence when I'm talking to someone.	5	4	3	2	1
7.	I concentrate hard to avoid distracting nonverbal cues.	5	4	3	2	1
8.	Listening and hearing are the same things.	1	2	3	4	5
9.	I make sure that the person wants feedback before I give it.	5	4	3	2	1
10.	I avoid saying "Good," "Go on," etc., while the other person is speaking.	5	4	3	2	1
11.	I try to delay giving feedback so that I can have more time to think it through.	1	2	3	4	5
12.	I enjoy using slang and quaint local expressions.	1	2	3	4	5
13.	My feedback focuses on how the other person can use my ideas.	5	4	3	2	1
14.	Body language is important for speakers, not listeners.	1	2	3	4	5
15.	I use technical jargon only when talking to experts.	5	4	3	2	1
16.	When someone is wrong, I make sure that she or he knows it.	1	2	3	4	5
17.	I try to express my ideas in general, overall terms.	1	2	3	4	5
18.	When I'm listening, I try not to be evaluative.	5	4	3	2	1

Communication Skills Survey Scoring Sheet

Transfer your numeric responses from the survey onto this scoring sheet, sum the categories, and obtain the total. For instance, your Feedback Skill score is the sum of your responses to statements 1, 5, 9, 11, 13, and 16.

	Feedback Skill	Listening Skill	Oral Skill
	1 _____	2 _____	3 _____
	5 _____	6 _____	4 _____
	9 _____	8 _____	7 _____
	11 _____	10 _____	12 _____
	13 _____	14 _____	15 _____
	16 _____	18 _____	17 _____
Subtotals	_____	_____	_____
Total	_____		

Place an X on each of the three category continuums to mark your subtotals.

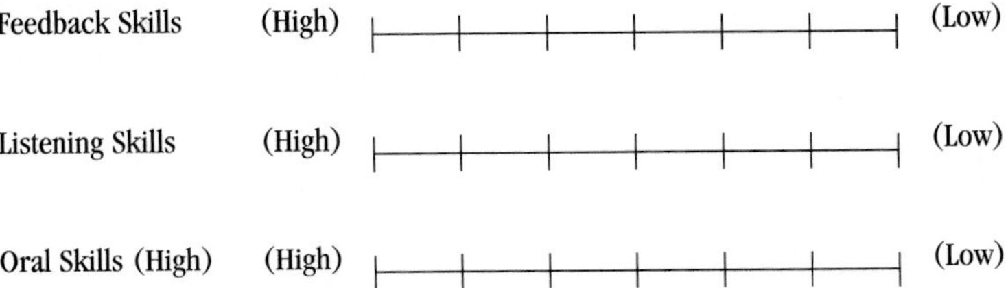

Place an X on the overall continuum to mark your total score.

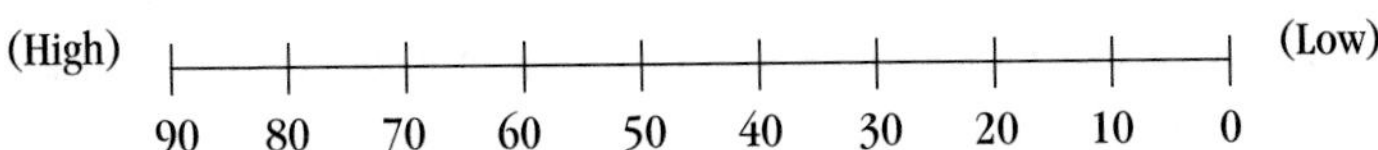

CRITICAL THINKING CASE

Anita Winsor

Anita Winsor, project leader for the Grupo Azeteca, had fourteen computer programmers reporting to her. These programmers were developing three large information systems for Panamerican Beverages, Inc., a major distributor of soft drinks in Mexico. Each programmer was assigned to one of three teams, and each team was responsible for one of the information systems. Winsor decided that she could control the projects better, and free more time for her administrative responsibilities, by assigning team leaders to each project. The team leaders, she decided, would be called "lead programmers." Before announcing her decision to all the programmers, however, she decided to discuss it privately with each of the three prospective lead programmers. She wanted to be sure that they understood the project and were willing to accept this new responsibility.

Winsor called Judith Rodriquez into the office and told her that she would like Rodriquez to be the lead programmer on projects related to the billing and pricing systems. She carefully explained to Rodriquez that this position carried the authority to direct the project-related activities of the people assigned to the project. These people were Flores Zaher, Ramon Barrios, and Arrendadora Nimex. Winsor clearly explained how project-related activities were distinguished from areas of administrative authority, which she would retain. Judith Rodriquez accepted the new position and, as she was leaving the office, asked Winsor to announce and explain the new position to the other programmers. Winsor assured Rodriquez that she would do so the next day, but the day got away from her and she didn't. The following week Anita Winsor began her annual vacation.

One morning while Winsor was still on vacation, Judith Rodriquez asked Arrendadora Nimex to prepare the computer operator procedure for a system test that had to be run that night. Later that day, Rodriquez asked Nimex whether the test procedure was ready; Nimex replied that it wasn't.

Rodriquez asked, "Why not, didn't you have enough time?"

"No," Nimex replied, "I had enough time, but where I worked before, that task was the responsibility of the project's systems analyst."

Rodriquez was upset. "Fortunately or unfortunately, it is a programming responsibility here; I explained that to you earlier. I'm the lead programmer on this project; now why didn't you do as I asked?"

"You're the lead programmer?" Nimex seemed surprised. "To my knowledge, we don't have a lead programmer on this project."

Questions

1. What caused the communication breakdown?
2. What barriers affected the effort to communicate?
3. If you were Rodriquez, what would you do?

VIDEO CASE

Unraveling the Tragedy at Bhopal

In the early hours of Monday, December 3, 1984, a toxic cloud of methyl isocyanate (MIC) gas enveloped the hundreds of shanties and huts surrounding a pesticide plant in Bhopal, India. Later, as the deadly cloud slowly drifted in the cool night air through the surrounding sections, sleeping residents awoke, coughing, choking, and rubbing painfully stinging eyes. By the time the gas cleared at dawn, many were dead or injured. Four months after the tragedy, the Indian government reported to Parliament that 1,430 people had died. In 1991 the official Indian government panel charged with tabulating deaths and injuries updated the count to more than 3,800 dead and approximately 11,000 with disabilities.

Although not known at the time, the gas formed when a disgruntled plant employee, apparently bent on spoiling a batch of methyl isocyanate, added water to a storage tank. The water caused a reaction that built up heat and pressure in the tank, quickly transforming the chemical compound into a lethal gas that escaped into the air.

The plant was operated by Union Carbide of India, Ltd. (UCIL), just over 50 percent of which was owned by Union Carbide Corporation. The first report of the disaster reached Union Carbide executives in the United States more than twelve hours after the incident. By 6:00 A.M. in the United States, executives were meeting with technical, legal, and communications staff at the company's Danbury, Connecticut, headquarters. Information was sparse but, as casualty estimates quickly climbed, management soon recognized it as a massive industrial disaster.

The first press inquiry in the United States came at 4:30 A.M., marking the beginning of a deluge that, at its peak, reach 500 calls a day for several weeks. The scope of the Bhopal tragedy made it "page one" material in the weeks and months that followed. And, as its legal, political, technological, and—above all—human aspects were explored, it became a persistent headline into the 1990s.

In those frustrating first few days, as the dimensions of the tragedy gradually were learned, some vital decisions were made.

- A Union Carbide facility in West Virginia was quickly closed because it manufactured methyl isocyanate. It remained closed until safety measures were reexamined and more light had been shed on the cause of the Bhopal tragedy.
- A management task force, headed by Chairman Warren M. Anderson, was set up to deal with the crisis. President and Chief Operating Officer Alec Flamm took over running the company's day-to-day business. That decision by Anderson permitted his Bhopal team to concentrate on the facts of the tragedy and its aftermath.
- Anderson, seeking to underscore Union Carbide's concern, decency, and humaneness in the face of the terrible tragedy, accepted

moral responsibility for the incident at the December 4 news conference and announced that he would travel at once to India to offer relief to the victims, including an immediate $1 million in aid. UCIL also pledged the Indian equivalent of $840,000.

- A medical and technical team was dispatched to Bhopal within 24 hours after the disaster occurred. Its tasks were to help arrange immediate and long-term relief; to assist in the safe disposal of remaining methyl isocyanate supplies at the plant; and to investigate the incident.

These decisive early actions gave Union Carbide an answer to the press question, "What is Carbide doing about this?" But the company didn't have answers to such basic questions as, "What caused the disaster?" or even, "What happened?" During the information vacuum, Union Carbide reaffirmed a standing procedure—no speculation. It took courage to say, "We don't have the information. We'll have to get back on that," especially in the face of the obvious question, "Why don't you know?" The company shared what information it had and stressed its determination to find the cause of the Bhopal tragedy and apply the lessons learned.

From the very first day, top management knew that communication resources had to be committed, on a high-priority basis, to informing Union Carbide employees. On December 3 and the days following, corporate offices were marked by individual and collective shock. As fatality estimates rose, many employees were emotionally devastated. Some wept openly at their desks.

Great care was taken to include employees in the overall communication effort. The policy of open and early release of factual information covered both internal and external communication. Employees received information at the same time the press received it. Existing channels of communication—news bulletins, regular publications, and special videotapes in which senior executives appeared—were used to provide a consistent body of knowledge to all 90,000 employees.

In January, *UC Word* magazine, which is mailed regularly to employees and retirees at their homes, dedicated its front page to coverage of the Bhopal incident. Later, the company videotape series, *What's Going On,* shown in cafeterias and at employee meetings, reviewed the Bhopal tragedy from the perspective of media coverage.

In early February, Anderson met with employees in Charleston, West Virginia, where the petrochemical business started in the 1920s and not far from the company's only other methyl isocyanate-producing plant in Institute. He reassured them of the company's continuing commitment to employee and community safety and, specifically, to reaffirm the safety measures in place at that facility. The appearance was videotaped, and highlights of the meeting were circulated to company and affiliated sites throughout the world. A measure of the personal concern and compassion of Union Carbide employees was their spontaneous establishment of a Carbide Employees Bhopal Relief Fund that collected more than $100,000 to aid the tragedy's victims.

By mid-December, Union Carbide's communications system on the Bhopal incident was solidly in place. Danbury was the contact point for the media. Within the team at Danbury, rotating assignments helped management cope with the stress and fatigue generated by nonstop inquiries and the task of communicating simultaneously with company employees and others.

As the tragedy unfolded, the Union Carbide team made technical and legal investigators available to field inquiries from the press and other professional groups, reinforcing the company's policy of open communication. But underlying this rationale was a clear understanding that, whatever the cause, a disaster had occurred and the company was obligated to help ensure that it would not happen again.[31]

Questions

1. How effective were Union Carbide's channels of communication?
2. What were the barriers to communication following the Bhopal tragedy, and what did Union Carbide do to overcome these barriers?
3. With an obvious company commitment toward open communication, why would an employee become disgruntled to the point of sabotage?

Chapter 16

Groups, Teams, and Cultures in Organizations

Learning *Objectives*

After studying this chapter, you should be able to:

1. Describe the basic types of groups, their importance, and developmental stages.
2. Explain the use of the model of group process to describe and diagnose informal and formal groups.
3. Discuss the key issues—empowerment, types of teams, decision making, and leadership—in the establishment and use of teams.
4. Describe the core elements of organizational cultures and the basic types of cultures.

Chapter *Outline*

Preview *Insight*

Jostens Goes Teamwork

Jostens is a world-class manufacturer of a variety of products, the most well known being quality class rings. Its principal facility is located in Denton, Texas.

In 1990, Jostens employees were producing sixteen rings per employee per day. The process, on average, took thirty calendar days from receipt of the work order to shipping the rings. After the entire facility switched to self-managing teams, the employees produced twenty-five rings per person per day. The process was reduced to ten calendar days from receipt of work order to shipping. Indirect benefits from self-managing teams included lower turnover and higher satisfaction, resulting from greater task variety.

Jostens now has thirty-five self-managing teams. Most are made up of three to ten members. After establishing the teams, the company stopped keeping individual performance and quota records. A plantwide gainsharing plan (see Chapter 12) was begun. Now, team recognition for performance is emphasized.

Jostens employees developed a self-managing team certification process outlined in a *Team Certification Manual.* Certification is considered important for defining specific short-term goals for teams, providing structure, describing desirable team behaviors, and motivating progress in small steps. The manual helps teams recognize the stages they can expect to go through as they move from a traditional work environment to a work culture that supports self-managing teams. After self-managing teams were established throughout the facility, an advisory resource team was formally created. It includes the plant manager, production manager, training manager, a team facilitator, and three hourly employees. Facilitywide issues are discussed by this team. Also, it reviews the self-managing teams for certification.

Every Monday morning all plant employees meet for a short time to discuss the current status of the year's progress, scheduling, results from the week before, recognition of safety awareness, and team performance. Every day team leaders meet for ten to twenty minutes to discuss what they did the day before and the current day's goals. The leaders then share this information with their respective team members.[1]

1

Describe the basic types of groups, their importance, and developmental stages.

INTRODUCTION TO GROUPS

Importance of Groups

Jostens is only one of many organizations that are using teams to improve productivity. Many other organizations (e.g., AT&T, Compaq Computer, Ford, and General Electric) are making use of teams. Teams provide a forum for making decisions, sharing information, improving coordination, building trust, smoothing interpersonal relations, and achieving performance goals.[2] Teams create vital communication links between individuals, departments, and organizational levels.

In this chapter we introduce and discuss groups, teams, and organizational cultures—and describe how they can be effective. We consider organizational cultures because the way teams evolve, make decisions, and operate are affected by the presence or lack of a strong organizational culture. Of course, the influence of organizational culture on groups and teams isn't just one-way. Groups can be messengers and enforcers of organizational values, norms, and ways of operating. They can also be the trigger points and facilitators of changing ineffective organizational cultures. Jostens' introduction of a team system is central to making its organizational culture more responsive to customers and its competitive environment. But teams and informal groups also can be cells of resistance or even opposition to efforts to create or maintain an organizational culture. We develop the intricate relationships between groups and teams and organizational culture in this chapter.

Types of Groups

Ask Students
How many groups do you belong to? What are some of them?

On average, people belong to six or more groups, some at work, some in the community, some formally organized, and some informal and social in nature. A **group** is two or more individuals who come into personal and meaningful contact on a continuing basis.[3] If five individuals play basketball together just to pass the time, they don't constitute a group. If five individuals play basketball together every Saturday, share a common goal of winning games, and communicate freely among themselves, they are a group. They may even think of themselves as a team. In the work setting, teams comprise employees who must collaborate to achieve team goals, which are linked with departmental, divisional, and organizational goals.

Ask Students
How many formal groups do you belong to? Name them.

Teaching Tip
Ask students to interview a member of a formal group about its organizational goals. Have students report their findings to the class.

There are two types of groups within an organization: formal and informal. A **formal group** consists of people who jointly have and work toward goals that relate directly to the achievement of organizational goals. Formal groups generally perform specific tasks, pass along and share information, train people, gain commitment, and help make decisions. Formal groups are an organization's departments, sections, task forces, self-managing teams, project groups, cross-functional teams, committees, and board of directors.[4] Some formal groups, such as the self-managing teams and advisory resource team at Jostens, exist over an extended period of time. Other formal groups, such as a task force formed to handle a specific issue (like moving a department from one location to another) have short lives.

An **informal group** consists of a small number of individuals—usually three to twelve—who jointly participate in activities frequently, otherwise interact, and share sentiments for the purpose of meeting their mutual needs. They may support, oppose, or have no interest in organizational goals, rules, or higher authority. A social group is one of the most common types of informal groups, within or outside organizations.

An organization's design often influences the development of informal groups. It does so by the physical layout of work space, departmental structure, and type of technology used. For example, the use of rigid assembly-line technology along with autocratic managers often results in employee dissatisfaction, high turnover, and the formation of hostile informal groups.[5] These groups may attempt to slow production by agreeing to work at a reduced pace and taking time to socialize. Or a new manager might tell subordinates to "shape up or ship out," motivating them to form an informal group united against the manager.[6]

Ask Students
What groups have you helped form?

Several recent surveys suggest continuing tensions and difficulties between managerial and nonmanagerial employees in the United States and Canada. For example, nearly two of three managers say that their companies do a good job involving employees in decisions that affect them. But only one of four production workers agree. Most managers say that the greatest barrier to change within their companies is their employees. Most employees say that the main problem is their managers' lack of skills and support.[7]

Stages of Group Development

Researchers have developed at least nine different models in an attempt to explain how groups develop.[8] Because many of these models overlap, we review only one of them, which is outlined in Figure 16.1. The vertical axis indicates that groups develop on a *continuum of maturity,* which ranges from immature (e.g., inefficient and ineffective) to mature (e.g., efficient and effective). The horizontal axis represents a *continuum of time together,* which ranges from *start* (e.g., the first group encounter) to *end* (e.g., the point at which the group adjourns).

No particular period of time is needed for a group to progress from one stage to the next on the development line in Figure 16.1. For example, a group whose members have effective interpersonal skills and high initial commitment to the group's goals could move rapidly to the performing stage. In contrast, an informal group may never make much progress and quickly disband voluntarily if its members aren't satisfied with it. A formal group may be discontinued in a variety of ways. It may simply stop meeting and

FIGURE 16.1

Stages of Group Development

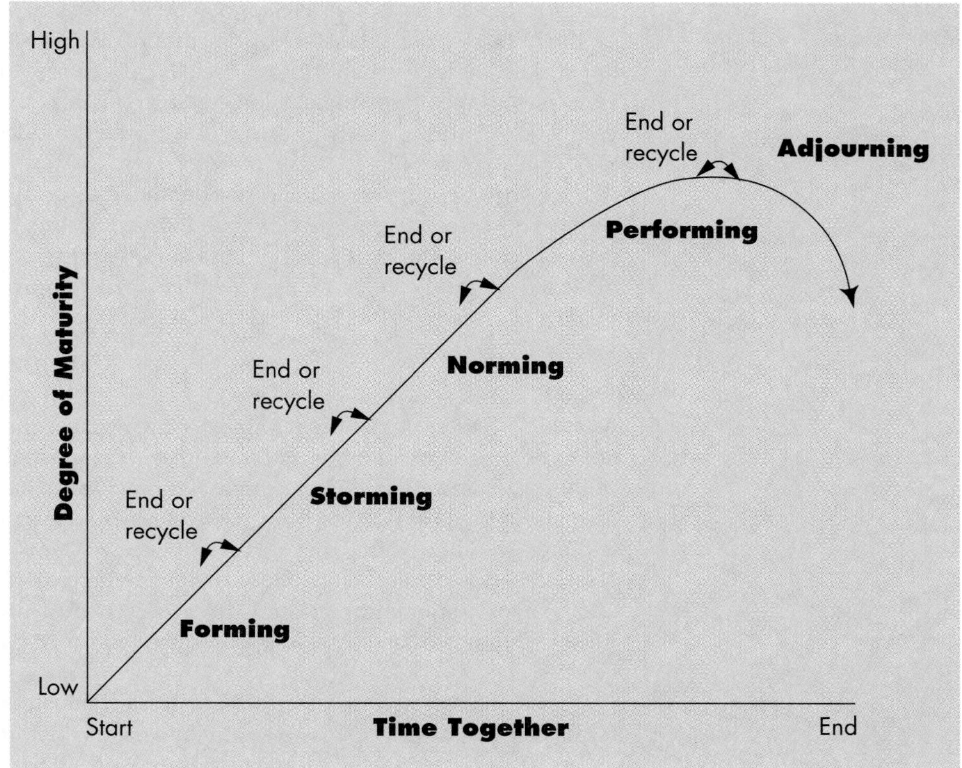

Source: Adapted and modified from Tuckman, B.W., and Jensen, M.A.C. Stages of small-group development revisited. *Group and Organization Studies, 1977,* 2, 419–442; Tuckman, B.W. Developmental sequence in small groups. *Psychological Bulletin,* 1965, 63, 384–389.

continue to exist only on paper. It may meet rarely and only engage in routine tasks. Its membership may change (e.g. adding, losing, or changing members), weakening its purpose or commitment. It may be terminated officially by the authority that created it.

Figure 16.1 also shows the possibility of a group ending at each stage or recycling to a previous stage. For example, a mature formal group, such as the seven-person advisory resource team at Jostens, could lose the majority of its members in a short period of time to promotions, retirements, and/or rotation of membership. With so many new members, the group may recycle to an earlier stage of development. Thus the stages identified represent general tendencies, and groups may develop by going through repeatable cycles rather than linearly, as shown. Also, each stage simply reveals the *primary* issues facing group members. Behaviors from other stages may occur at times within each stage.[9] Let's now examine each stage of group development.

Ask Students
What is your opinion? Explain.

Teaching Tip
The importance of the forming stage often is overlooked. Discuss your approach to forming this class with the students.

Forming Stage. A group focuses on orientation—to its goals and procedures—in the forming stage. The amount of information available and the manner in which it is presented are crucial to group development. Most members may be anxious about what the group and they, as individual members, are supposed to do. Testing and resolving coordination issues between members are the principal relationship behaviors. Task relationships often are guarded, cautious, and noncommittal. Understanding leadership roles and getting acquainted with other group members facilitate development. Group members might think: "How can there be conflicts when we are all busy keeping our distance from one another? We just don't interact enough to generate conflict."

Storming Stage. The second stage begins when competitive or strained behaviors emerge. Initially, the storming process may involve resistance and impatience with the lack of progress. A few dominant members may begin to force an agenda without re-

Teaching Tip
Most people are taught to avoid unpleasant emotions. They dislike the conflict stage and try to suppress it. Have students state whether they have ever tried to suppress conflict and give an example.

Ethics
Is it ethical for an individual to avoid unpleasant emotions if doing so prevents the group from developing by suppressing the conflict stage?

gard for the needs of other group members. Group members may challenge the leader, or they may isolate themselves from group discussion. If conflict spreads, frustration, anger, and defensive behavior (especially self-serving "look out for yourself") may appear. Group members might think: "Our problem is that we don't want to resolve our conflicts. We thrive on them. It may be counterproductive, but conflict seems to be a way of life for now."

If conflict is suppressed and not permitted to occur, resentment and bitterness may result. This can lead to apathy or abandonment. Although conflict resolution often is the goal of groups during the storming stage, conflict management generally is what is achieved. In fact, conflict management is a more appropriate goal because maintaining conflict at a manageable level is a desirable way to encourage a group's growth and development.

Norming Stage. At the beginning of this stage, the dominant view might be: "We are in this together, like it or not. Let's make the most of it." If the group gets to the end of this stage, most members may like their involvement. They become increasingly positive about the group as a whole, the other members as individuals, and what the group is doing. In other words, they begin to develop a sense of belonging and commitment. Task-related and role behaviors of members increasingly are resolved through cooperation, open communication, and the acceptance of mutual influence. **Norms,** or the rules of behavior that are widely shared and enforced by the members of the group, develop.

Sometimes, however, the group focuses too much on "we-ness," harmony, and conformity. When that happens, group members may avoid task-related conflicts that need to be resolved to achieve optimal performance. That in turn may cause the quality and/or quantity of performance to slip.

Performing Stage. Although some groups never reach their performance potential, regardless of how long they exist, by the performing stage, members usually have come to trust and accept each other. To accomplish tasks, diversity of viewpoints (rather than we-ness) is supported and encouraged. Members are willing to risk presenting "wild" ideas without fear of being put down by the group. Careful listening and giving accurate feedback to others focus on the group's tasks and goals. That reinforces a sense of clear and shared goals. Leadership within the group is flexible and may shift among members in terms of who is most capable of solving a particular problem. In terms of relationship behaviors, the group accepts the reality of differences and disagreements and works on them cooperatively and enthusiastically. The group tries to reach consensus on important issues and to avoid internal politics. Hence the following core characteristics lead to high levels of group or team performance.

- Members direct their energies toward the twin goals of getting things done (task behaviors) and building constructive interpersonal ties and processes (relationship behaviors).
- Members have adopted procedures for making decisions, including how to share leadership.
- Members have achieved trust and openness among themselves.
- Members have learned to receive help from and give help to one another.
- Members experience a sense of freedom to be themselves while feeling a sense of belonging with others.
- Members have learned to accept and deal with conflicts.
- Members know how to diagnose and improve their own functioning.[10]

Teaching Tip
The importance of adjournment often is ignored in group life. Have the students plan a class adjournment at the end of the term.

The degree to which one or more of these characteristics is absent determines the extent to which groups or teams are likely to be ineffective. Later in this chapter, we present additional suggestions for making teams effective and efficient.

Teaching Tip
Have students pair off. Ask them to tell each other about a group they have been in. Have them describe how the group went through (or failed to go through) each stage.

Discussion Question 1
What are the stages of group development? Which stage is most crucial?

Adjourning Stage. The adjourning stage involves terminating task behaviors and disengaging from relationships. This stage isn't always planned and may be rather abrupt. However, a planned group conclusion often involves recognition for participation and achievement and an opportunity for members to say personal good-byes. Adjournment of a group charged with a particular task should be set for a specific time and have a recognizable ending point. Of course, many formal groups (e.g., the executive committee of an organization's board of directors) are ongoing. As members turn over, some recycling through earlier stages rather than adjournment may occur. Staggered terms of appointment can minimize the amount of recycling required.

As suggested in the following Small Business Insight, even small businesses are finding the use of formal groups (e.g., committees and teams) helpful in making decisions and achieving high quality and output goals.

Small Business *Insight*

Better Bags

Rafael Alvarado is president of Better Bags, a manufacturer of plastic bags in Houston, Texas. Alvarado often discusses how this plastic bagmaker's sole purpose is to please its supermarket customers. "It sounds like PR but it's not," Alvarado insists. "You ask anybody and they will share that with you." All Better Bags' employees have been taught that the customer is the boss.

The message seems to have worked. Better Bags has grown to sixty-four employees from eight in 1989. The firm bought its first equipment in 1989 to make plastic bags used in supermarket produce and deli departments. Before that, it sold bags made by other companies.

In 1991, an ex-manager convinced the company to adopt the total quality principles of the late W. Edwards Deming and other quality management experts. Better Bags' management has since taken TQM to heart, training every employee, hiring consultants, and sending managers to seminars. Management emphasizes worker involvement, teams, goal setting, and communication within the company—as opposed to competition among workers and rigid management control. "We have to invest (in training) just as we invested in equipment," Alvarado says.

To deepen the effort, Alvarado, who along with Vice-President Ilsa Pena owns the company, has empowered employees. In 1995, Better Bags installed a six-person executive steering committee to help run the business. "I think our diversity is one of our strengths," says Kim Burnett, a marketing manager and member of the steering committee. He notes that the company's eleven-member administrative staff includes people from seven different countries, including Guatemala, Argentina, and Mexico. In what is becoming increasingly common at Better Bags, a team was formed to reorganize the warehouse and figure out the best way to organize the work. The latest inventory took one employee only five hours, compared to earlier inventories that took several employees three days.

A team analyzed buying patterns of its largest customers and came up with a method of anticipating repeat orders, which represent about 75 percent of the business. Now, Better Bags produces some bags in advance, rather than waiting for a purchase order. This approach has improved service, reduced costs, and cut equipment setup times.[11]

2

Explain the use of the model of group process to describe and diagnose informal and formal groups.

MODEL OF GROUP PROCESS

Our general model of group process is adapted from the one developed by George Homans.[12] This model helps explain why people act as they do within groups, provides a way to diagnose group processes, identifies key contingency factors that are likely to affect group processes and outputs, and notes how groups are likely to develop and change over time. As suggested in Figure 16.2, this model of group process consists of two interrelated parts: the internal system and the external system.

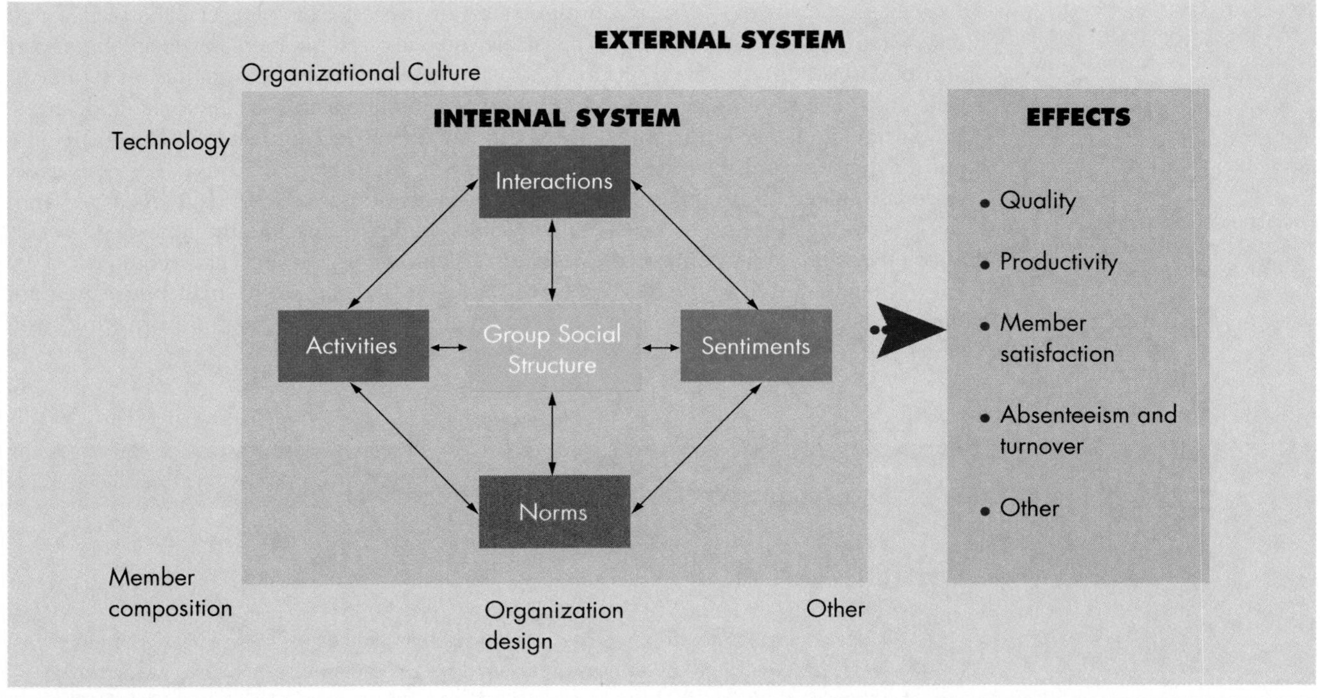

FIGURE 16.2

Model of Group Process

Internal System

The **internal system** includes the activities (tasks), interactions, sentiments, norms, and social structure that group members develop over time. As shown in Figure 16.2, these variables are interrelated: A change in one may result in a change in others. The activities, interactions, and sentiments grow beyond merely what is required to do the job; they lead to a social structure, norms, and commitment. Thus a group should be thought of as a system, not simply the sum of individual members' behaviors.

The way members interact influences their effectiveness as a group. Freedom to develop the group's internal system leads to fulfillment of members' needs to belong, achieve satisfaction, and commit themselves to the task. It also helps create and maintain group morale, which is one of the reasons for the success of many self-managing teams. Informal groups also may achieve the same results.

Activities. Activities of formal groups include many types of task behaviors: analyzing problems, evaluating alternatives, making decisions, operating a machine, or writing a memo. In an organizational team, task-related activities usually take up most of the employees' time. For professionals and managers, task activities, rather than social behaviors, are likely to be of primary interest. Activities of an informal group with social goals might include playing cards, telling jokes, or discussing politics and sports at mealtime and breaks.

Interactions. Interactions are communications between two or more people. The type and amount of interaction can be identified by answering the following questions.

Teaching Tip
Have students pair off and take turns answering these questions about a group they are currently in.

- With whom do the members communicate?
- How often do they communicate with one another?
- How long do they communicate?
- Who starts the communication?

Interactions involve both task-oriented behaviors and relationship behaviors.[13] Recall from the Preview Insight that Jostens now has thirty-five self-managing teams and an advisory resource team. The interactions of these teams are likely to focus on task behaviors. For the teams to be effective, however, important relationship behaviors also must be present: warmth, praise, and acceptance of others; encouragement of participation by all members; and resolution of team conflicts and tensions.[14] These ideas are consistent with the performing stage of group development. By assigning tasks, management often has some influence over the interactions that develop within a team, task force, committee, or department. Such influence doesn't extend to informal groups of employees who lunch together regularly or play golf with each other every week. Their interaction patterns emerge over time and are influenced more by the social needs and sentiments of the individual members than by tasks and organizational goals.

Ask Students
What emotions were you not allowed to display as a member of a work group?

Ask Students
How can day-to-day sentiments affect the life of business?

Teaching Tip
Have students pair off and take turns telling each other why these statements do or do not match a group they are in.

Sentiments. Sentiments include the emotions of anger, happiness, and sadness and deeper feelings of trust or distrust. Sentiments reflect the emotional climate of a group. The four sentiments most likely to influence team effectiveness and productivity are the feelings of trust, openness, freedom, and interdependence. The more these sentiments are present, the more likely the work team will be effective and the members will experience satisfaction.[15] These sentiments probably are present in a formal or informal group to which you belong if you agree with the following statements.

- *Trust:* Members have confidence in each other.
- *Openness:* Members are really interested in what others have to say.
- *Freedom:* Members do what they do out of a sense of responsibility to the group, not because of a lot of pressure from others.
- *Interdependence:* Members coordinate and work together to achieve common goals.

The greater the degree to which the four sentiments are present, the higher is the level of group cohesiveness. **Cohesiveness** is the strength of members' desires to remain in the group and their commitment to it. Cohesiveness cannot be dictated by managers or other group members. It is a reflection of the members' sentiments toward one another and the group as a whole. A cohesive group can work effectively for or against organizational goals.[16] For example, a cohesive group with negative sentiments toward the organization may promote performance standards that limit productivity and pressure individual members to conform to them. In contrast, a cohesive group with positive sentiments toward the organization may support and reinforce high quality and productivity.

Ask Students
What are some of the norms of an extracurricular group you are in?

Ask Students
What norms influence your behavior in class with respect to seating, getting involved in classroom discussion, and so on?

Ethics
Norms can foster ethical behavior or anti-ethical behavior. How can you set norms favor ethical behavior?

Norms. Recall that norms are the informal rules of behavior that are widely shared and enforced by the members of a group. They set standards for members' behaviors under specific circumstances. Their main function is to regulate and standardize the behaviors viewed as important by group members.[17] Norms may specify how much members should do, how customers should be treated, the importance that should be assigned to quality, what members should wear, what kinds of jokes are acceptable, how members should feel about the organization, how they should deal with their managers, and so on.

A group norm exists when three criteria have been met.[18] First, there is a standard of appropriate behavior for group members. For example, there may be a standard for the lower and upper limits of production for the group as a whole and individual members. Second, members must generally agree on the standard. That doesn't mean that all group members need to agree. But, if most members have widely varying opinions about how much work is enough, for example, the group doesn't have a productivity norm. Third, the members must be aware that the group supports the particular standard through a system of rewards and punishments—rewards for compliance and punishments for violations. For example, a member who produces more integrated circuit boards per day than the group norm may get the silent treatment until he or she complies with that norm. Of course, someone who doesn't care about the group and its sanctions may continue to violate the group productivity norm.[19]

Ask Students
Have you ever had a *free rider* in a student group (other than this class) you were in? What did you do about it?

In contrast, a group member could engage in **free riding,** which means not contributing fully to group performance because she or he can share in group rewards despite making less effort than the others.[20] An example of free riding is the individual on a six-person team in a class who contributes much less than others in producing a term paper or case analysis, yet all members receive the same grade.

Figure 16.3 indicates that most norms develop as the result of one or more of four factors.[21] Superiors or co-workers may make an *explicit statement* with respect to the rules of behavior to enable the group or team to meet it goals. For example, management at Mobil bans smoking (except in designated areas) at its refineries for safety reasons. If team leaders and members accept and help enforce this prohibition, it becomes a team norm as well as a formal rule of the organization. *Critical events* in a group's history may lead to the development of norms. Group members may view a whistle-blower with scorn, thus establishing a norm for what may and may not be communicated to outsiders. The *first behaviors* in new groups or teams may emerge as norms, setting future expectations and standards. For example, the seating arrangement at a group's first meeting may lead to norms dictating where each group or team member is to sit. Seating arrangements also influence who talks to whom. The carryover of norms from *past experiences* also influences the formation of norms in a new situation. Students and professors do not have to create new norms about acceptable classroom behavior as they go from class to class; they simply carry them over.

Group Social Structure. As suggested in Figure 16.2, the formation of a relatively consistent pattern of activities, interactions, sentiments, and norms creates **group social structure.** It is determined primarily by members' contributions to achieving the group's goals, acceptance of the group's norms, and personal characteristics. At a minimum, the group's social structure can be determined by analyzing the patterns of group leadership (e.g., a single leader or shared leadership), communication network (e.g., through one or two members or wide open among members), and member status (e.g., differential ranking or relatively equal among members).[22] The following statements illustrate one possible pattern of the relationships in a group's social structure.

- A member of higher status more often initiates interaction with a person of lower status than vice versa.
- The higher a member's status, the wider is his or her range of interaction both within and external to the group.

FIGURE 16.3

Development of Group Norms

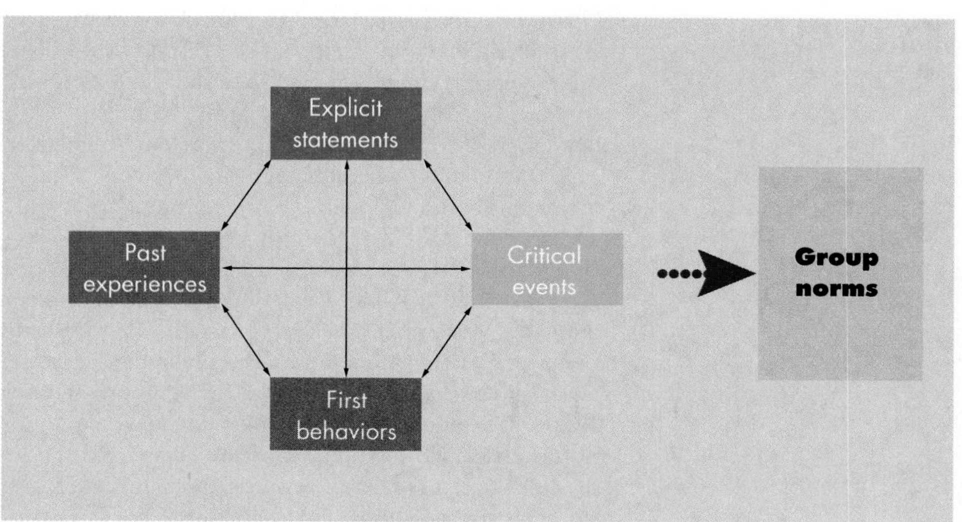

- The group leader's sentiments carry greater weight than do those of the followers. For example, a leader's demonstration of trust, openness, freedom, and interdependence would have greater influence than a member who tends to free ride and simply mouths such sentiments.
- The higher the status of a group member, the closer the member's activities will conform to the group's norms.[23]

Ask Students
Can male managers be taught to identify and overcome the ways they unconsciously treat women unfairly? If so, how?

The social structure of groups in organizations have traditionally discriminated against women and minorities. Stereotyping by some groups still may prevent women or minorities from having a fair chance to demonstrate their abilities. Increasingly, organizations are taking concrete steps to diversify their work groups and teams. Some examples of the special challenges experienced by women moving into management are presented in the following Diversity Insight.

Diversity *Insight*

Women in Management

Women often have their comments ignored, particularly in management team situations. During a leadership conference at Du Pont, Marcia Coleman, a laboratory director, confronted a male colleague, Vice-President Anthony J. Cardinal. "Did you notice what happened in the meeting whenever a woman offered a thought?" asked Coleman. Cardinal replied that he hadn't. "Pay attention tomorrow," she suggested. The next day Cardinal noticed that whenever a woman brought up an idea, the conversation swept past her. "I had never appreciated the problem before. I started to get an inkling of what women go through every day," Cardinal said.

Like a growing number of companies, Du Pont is training male managers to help them identify and overcome the ways they may unconsciously treat women unfairly. "Men have to understand that their behavior can exclude women in a variety of ways," says Elsie Y. Cross. Cross is a consultant who conducts training on race and gender bias for Johnson & Johnson, Exxon, and others.

Honeywell managers were intrigued by an employee survey in which women cited personal relationships as the key element in upward mobility. Men said personal relationships were least important. To get women into the management loop, Honeywell is trying to influence the way workplace relationships are established. The company started teaming promising young women and minorities with more experienced executives. The experienced "coaches" give advice on career strategies and corporate politics; that is, the ropes to skip and the ropes to know.

During a gender awareness workshop at Corning, women managers complained that their male colleagues never invited them to lunch. The women felt that they were missing out on useful informal communications. That could include news of someone being transferred, which would mean that a job had opened up. Or it could be a comment about higher management's interest in a new product category. Tidbits like these often are the root of one element of success—the one that managers usually call being in the right place at the right time.[24]

External System

The second part of the model of group process (see Figure 16.2) is the **external system,** which comprises outside conditions and influences that exist before and after the group is formed. These external influences may include organizational culture, technology, member composition (age, race, and gender), organization design, and so on. Because of our extensive discussion previously of forces that could affect the dynamics of any formal or informal group, here we only briefly discuss the external system. The conditions encountered in this system often continue even if the group or team ceases to function.

The organizational culture, especially whether the values support or oppose participation by lower level employees, is likely to influence whether informal groups form to embrace organizational goals and authority relations or undermine them.[25] For example, a rigid assembly-line technology is likely to hinder the development of informal groups and thus increase employees' feelings of isolation and job dissatisfaction. Member composition (similarity versus diversity) may influence group dynamics. Contrary to the popular view, diversity can enhance a group's performance.[26] Also, individuals who value collectivism, as the Japanese do, are very comfortable working in groups. In contrast, forming effective work teams among people who value individualism is more of a challenge. However, when such individuals are empowered through self-managing teams, they gain more control and influence over their work. This result is consistent with their valuing individualism—and thus may increase their satisfaction.[27]

Organization design directly influences the formation and functioning of groups. Recall the adoption of the TQM philosophy and system at Better Bags. The system eventually spawned an executive committee and employee teams to deal with problems that had been handled by the owners—Rafael Alvarado and Ilsa Pena. The company changed from a centralized decision-making design to a cross-functional, decentralized, and participative design.

Changes in the group's external system can generate changes in its internal system. The external system may even impose the conditions of the group's or team's survival. For instance, a reduction in the work force could create havoc for established informal or formal groups by removing many of their members. The internal system, in turn, directly affects quality, productivity, member satisfaction, absenteeism and turnover.[28] If employees believe that a reduction in force was handled unfairly, it may motivate the formation of informal groups with negative sentiments. Such groups may develop norms and processes that attempt to further productivity improvements because their members fear additional layoffs. Positive sentiments, including a strong sense of interdependence, are likely to help increase satisfaction and decrease absenteeism and turnover. Sentiments of trust and openness, as well as achievement-based norms, are likely to promote higher levels of quality and productivity. These effects eventually provide feedback to both the internal and external systems, which may result in action to modify the internal system. For example, low productivity or quality by a team might lead management (part of the team's external system) to diagnose the source of the problem and intervene to improve the situation.

Organizational Implications

The primary implications of the model of group process are in the areas of individual and team empowerment, internal and external systems diagnosis, and constructive norms.

Teams may make more of an effort to achieve organizational goals if members are empowered (given authority and responsibility) to do their jobs. Conversely, if their authority and responsibility are restricted, team members may well reduce their level of commitment. They might continue to perform satisfactorily but with little enthusiasm for improving quality and productivity.

Understanding and anticipating group actions is aided by a diagnosis of its internal and external systems. The model of group process (Figure 16.2) provides guidance in making such a diagnosis. The group's sentiments, interactions, activities, and norms define the group's social structure, which has various effects. For example, a manager or team leader who issues an order that is inconsistent with team norms, such as radically changing productivity standards, could face a team united in demanding a change in the order. Or a manager trying to change or eliminate established communication patterns in an informal group may face consequences ranging from complaints to increased absenteeism and turnover.

Instead, managers and team leaders should encourage the establishment of norms that support organizational (the external system's) goals. Where there is mutual interdependence among employees (e.g., on a project team), the use of team or combined team and individual rewards often is effective. These rewards could be in the form of praise and recognition of the team as a whole or even a compensation system based, in part, on team effectiveness.

The following Quality Insight describes the dynamics between the internal system and the external system (including the broader society's cultural values held by employees) resulting from the introduction of teams in the workplace to improve quality and productivity.

Quality *Insight*

Shelby Die Casting

Shelby Die Casting makes automobile parts and is located in Shelby, Mississippi. The firm has about 400 employees. In late 1992, it began reorganizing into workplace teams in an effort to save the plant, which was scheduled to close. The quantity and quality of performance is now up. For example, scrap is down to 12 percent from 40 percent in 1992.

Getting employees to accept their new roles as members of teams with decision-making authority was a challenge. According to Lois McMurchy, training coordinator, the Mississippi Delta culture perpetuates the notion that employees shouldn't make decisions or even think. It started during the time of slavery, she says. Since then, generations of employees have been conditioned by their employers that management knows best. "Now, we are telling them it is okay to think and respond to business challenges," she says. "Believe me, it takes time to make this kind of cultural and societal change."

The road to empowerment has been a rocky one. Employees were reluctant to express their opinions to supervisors, who never had listened before. As a result, top management substantially cut the number of supervisors and saved $250,000 in the process. The employees were given greater authority to run their own teams. To be effective, team members required training in group dynamics, communication, problem solving, and brainstorming. Slowly, the employees began to understand the company's goals and are becoming more involved in setting them. "We are teaching employees how to be empowered," McMurchy says. She believes that all the teams should be fully self-managing by 1997.[29]

3

Discuss the key issues—empowerment, types of teams, decision making, and leadership—in the establishment and use of teams.

TEAMS IN ORGANIZATIONS

We have discussed and illustrated workplace teams as one type of formal group. We now offer a formal definition of this term. A **team** is a small number of employees who are organizationally empowered to establish some or all of a team's goals, to make decisions about how to achieve those goals, to undertake the tasks required to meet them, and to be individually and mutually accountable for their results. "The essence of a team is common commitment. Without it, groups perform as individuals; with it, they become a powerful unit of collective performance."[30]

Team Empowerment

Empowerment is the delegation of authority, responsibility, and discretion to an individual or team. Figure 16.4 shows a wide range of tasks that could be assigned to teams in a manufacturing plant. The vertical axis indicates the degree of empowerment (i.e., authority, responsibility, and general decision-making discretion) for tasks. The horizontal axis indicates the amount and range of skills required by team members for handling the increasing number and complexity of tasks.

Ask Students
How many of the "teams" you are a member of are truly teams?

The empowerment options shown for teams in manufacturing plants illustrate a broader point. Management often rushes to form the wrong types of teams with the

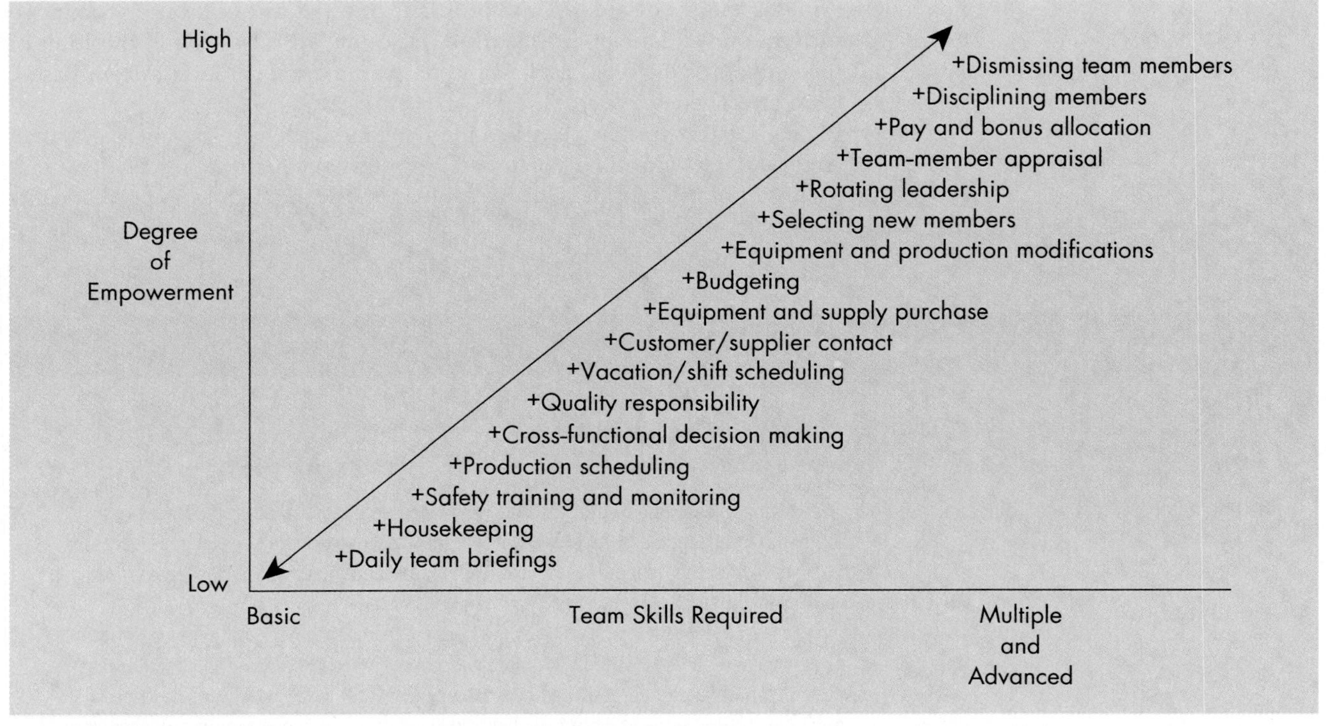

FIGURE 16.4

Examples of Empowerment Options for Teams in a Manufacturing Plant

Source: Adapted from Holpp, L. Applied empowerment. *Training,* February 1994, 39–44; Bakersfield, D.M. Why business loves work-teams. *Black Enterprise,* April 1993, 85–90.

Real-World Example
Stanford University Head Football Coach Bill Walsh says that ego is a major threat to teamwork. He defines ego as a distraction with one's own importance (*Harvard Business Review,* January-February, 1993, 112). Have students state whether they agree.

wrong amounts of empowerment for the tasks to be performed. To compound this problem, the teams may be launched in a vacuum. Team members may have received little or no training to ensure that they have the skills to perform the required tasks and achieve the goals set.[31] Or, the teams may be launched in an organizational culture that doesn't support shared decision making and open communication.[32] The following Insight describes the rocky road traveled by Allina, which runs seventeen nonprofit hospitals in Minnesota, toward the use of teams.

Insight

Allina's Rocky Road

Allina tried to form teams during the 1980s but failed each time. There were hostile relations with the labor unions representing nurses and several other employee groups. A nurses' strike basically shut down a hospital for six weeks. Some Allina managers had never even met a union official. The unions were not blameless either. A worker remembers being taught by union officials that all you need to know is that boss spelled backward is *double SOB*. Jack Dobier, Allina's labor-management coordinator states: "You will fail with teams if you do not change people's attitudes."

Allina began the process of changing hostile attitudes by forming a team of management and union officials. It was empowered to make a difference. For instance, the team found a way to close one of Allina's hospitals without leaving employees stranded. The team set up an employment center that placed 95 percent of the closing hospital's employees elsewhere in Allina or in other organizations. This gesture raised morale generally and saved the company $8 million in severance costs. More important, it showed that management was serious about working with labor.

Allina has since created worker-management teams in eleven of its seventeen hospitals, with great results. One of these problem-solving teams saved the company $200,000 a year by suggesting that maintenance on some hospital equipment, such as emergency electrical generators and operating room lights, be done by the hospital's own staff.[33]

Types of Teams

There are many ways to categorize and label teams. Teams may differ in terms of their general goals, duration, and membership.[34] The differing *goals* of teams may focus on product development, quality improvement, or problem solving. The *duration* of teams may vary from short term (e.g., a four-month project team) to permanent (e.g., a functional department team). The *membership* of teams may vary from functional (employees in the same department) to cross-functional (employees from various functions and even suppliers and customers). Let's consider four of the most common types of organizational teams: functional, problem solving, cross-functional, and self-managing.

Functional Team. A **functional team** includes a manager and subordinates, who consider issues and solve problems common to their area of responsibility and expertise for which they are interdependent. The amount of empowerment available to the team often depends on the leadership style of the manager and the specific issue or problem being dealt with.[35] For example, a functional team could be as simple as a purchasing manager and the purchasing agents who report to this person. They need to coordinate their activities constantly and share information on price changes, new products, and the output of the manufacturing department.

Problem-Solving Team. A **problem-solving team** usually consists of five to twenty hourly and salaried employees from different areas of a department who consider how something can be done better. Such a team may meet one or two hours a week (or as needed) to discuss ways to improve quality, safety, productivity or diversity. The empowerment of a problem-solving team to implement its ideas may range from none to limited. Although these teams can improve quality and reduce costs, they do not fundamentally reorganize work or change the role of managers.[36] For example, they usually do not discuss issues such as wages and salaries, personality clashes, hiring or firing, disciplinary actions, or major resource allocations.

Ask Students
How many of you have ever been involved in a quality circle? Describe the situation and the outcome.

One form of problem-solving team is the **quality circle.** A quality circle is a group of employees from the same work area, or who perform similar tasks, who voluntarily meet regularly to identify, analyze, and propose solutions to problems in the workplace. Meetings usually lasting an hour or so are held once every week or two during or after regular working hours. Members often are given overtime pay if the quality circle meets after work. They normally receive eight or more hours of formal training in decision-making and team processes, which they apply in their meetings. Quality circles normally don't have the authority to implement their proposed solutions. These solutions are presented to management for further consideration.[37] Quality circles were an organizational fad in the 1980s, but are being replaced by teams that are empowered to decide and act. Such empowerment speeds up decision making, reduces the need for as many managers, and creates greater commitment to the team and a deeper sense of accountability for results.

Teaching Tip
Give extra credit to students who form a quality circle, meet outside class weekly, and report the results.

Discussion Question 3
What are the primary differences between funtional teams and cross-functional teams?

Cross-Functional Team. A **cross-functional team** may consist of five to thirty employees from various functions and sometimes two organizational levels who collectively have specific goal-oriented tasks. These tasks may include designing and introducing work reforms and new technology, meeting with customers and suppliers to

Much of the design of the Bell-Boeing V-22 TiltRotor aircraft utilizes cross-functional teams consisting of employees from manufacturing, engineering, tooling, and othe disciplines. This reduces manufacturing costs and aircraft weight.

improve quality, developing new products, linking separate functions (marketing, finance, manufacturing, and human resources) to increase product innovations, and/or improving links among tactical and strategic decisions and plans. These teams usually operate with a much greater degree of empowerment than problem-solving teams. Their use is spreading rapidly, even into unionized companies.[38]

Discussion Question 2
Gail Stevens described her workplace as "...friendly, just great. All the people get along together, and we bowl and play softball after work." However, quality and production records show Gail's team to be one of the least productive in the plant. Why might this be?

A cross-functional team may be permanent or temporary, depending on its tasks and goals. A **quality improvement team** has members from interrelated functions and meets regularly to improve continuously the product or process for which it is responsible. In contrast, a **product development team** exists only for the period of time required to bring a product to market, which could vary from a couple of months to several years. Chrysler and Boeing, among many other firms, are using product development teams extensively.

Cross-functional teams provide several important competitive advantages if they are properly formed and managed. We consider three of these potential advantages: speed, customer focus, and creativity.[39] First, *speed* is vital in product development and customer service. In product development, cross-functional teams reduce time by replacing serial development with parallel development. In the past, the development process involved one function (e.g., basic research) completing its task and then forwarding it to the next function (e.g., prototyping), and so on until all of the functions completed their tasks in sequence. With parallel development, many tasks are done at the same time and are closely coordinated between the functions. This method cuts the time spent in the development cycle, or what is often called *time to market*. Second, cross-functional teams are more likely to bring a *customer focus* to bear on the tasks at the beginning of the process. At times, customers may even serve on the cross-functional team. Also, a customer focus becomes the common bond among the functions throughout the project.[40] Third, *creativity* is increased by bringing together people having a variety of experiences and expertise to address a common problem or task.

Boeing decided to use a hierarchy of teams in the design and development of its new 777 jet liner. This project involved 10,000 employees and 500 suppliers working in more than 200 cross-functional teams. Each team was made up of people from engineering, manufacturing, finance, and other departments, depending on its task. At the top of the hierarchy was a management team of the five or six top managers from each discipline. It had the responsibility for the plane being built correctly and on time.

Below this management team was a large group of the fifty or so team leaders—half each from engineering and operations. They were set up in 25 to 30 two-person teams and oversee the more than 200 operational cross-functional teams that had responsibility for producing specific parts of the plane. These work teams typically include five to fifteen workers, such as a wing team, a flap team, and a tail team.[41]

Discussion Question 4
What are the main differences between problem-solving teams and self-managing teams?

Self-Managing Team. A **self-managing team** normally consists of five to fifteen employees who work together daily to produce an entire good (or major identifiable component) or service. These teams often perform various managerial tasks, including scheduling their members' work and vacations, rotating job tasks and assignments among members, ordering materials, deciding on team leadership (which may rotate among members), and setting production goals. As suggested in Figure 16.4, they are empowered to control how they perform their jobs. Self-managing teams that are highly empowered are sometimes called *high-performance teams.*

Frequently, each member learns the multiple skills required by all the tasks that have to be performed by the team. The use of these teams fundamentally changes how work is organized, and the impact can be enormous. Self-managing teams have raised productivity in some cases 30 percent or more and have increased quality substantially. Typically, one or more managerial levels are eliminated with the introduction of these teams, thereby creating a flatter organization. The result has been downsizing at many of these organizations, including the dismissal of many middle managers. Self-managing teams began to spread rapidly in the early 1990s in response to customer demands for higher quality and lower prices.[42]

As revealed in the following Global Insight, a single organization may use different types of teams to meet various needs and goals.

Global *Insight*

TI Malaysia's Quality Teams

Texas Instruments Malaysia (TIM) produces about three million high-volume integrated circuits per day, many of which are shipped to companies in Japan. This operation employs 2,600 people, almost all Malaysian nationals.

At TIM, the use of quality improvement teams (QITs) started in the management and engineering offices. Mohd Azmi, a key manager, explains: "Why did we not start at the grass roots level? Because, according to Dr. [Joseph] Juran [a quality expert], 80 percent or more of problems are management-controllable problems. For example, many systems, design, and other problems are not operator-controllable." The first QITs were cross-functional, consisting of managers and professionals from different departments. Following the success of QITs at the management and professional support levels, effectiveness teams (similar to quality circles) were created among employees.

TIM managers went on to begin implementing what they called the flexible organization. Plant manager Jerry Lee explains that operator self-control, though a step in this direction, didn't fully meet the goal of empowering all employees. The design of the flexible organization involved three components: a *quality steering team* (Jerry Lee and his reports), a *process management team* (middle managers and engineers who provide guidance and expertise), and *self-managing teams* (employees who manufactured the circuits).

The company now uses self-managing teams as an integral part of its evolution into a TQM culture. Mohd Azmi says, "All quality activities here are aimed at trying to satisfy customers. Customers look at quality, cost, service, and so forth. But at TIM, people development shares equal priority with customer satisfaction. Why? If our people are not developed and trained to deliver, you cannot have customer satisfaction. Personnel development is the cause and customer satisfaction is the effect or result."

The self-managing teams have taken on many tasks previously performed by supervisors. They perform the daily operations of marking attendance, doing setups, controlling materials use and quality, monitoring cycle time, fostering safety, and making line audits. The team members also are expected to detect deviations and take corrective action, making improvements in their work areas by using problem-solving techniques and quality control tools.[43]

Team Decision Making

Some individuals believe that team decision making is a waste of time and should be used only when the politics of the situation demand it. Others view it as superior to individual decision making and believe that it should be used whenever possible. As suggested in Figure 16.5, team decision making has the potential for either positive or negative results.[44]

Ask Students
Under what circumstances should a team be used to make decisions?

Ethics
Is it ethical for a company always to encourage team decision-making processes when some decisions could be made better by an individual working alone? Explain.

Ask Students
How would you handle a team member who is so enthusiastic about one alternative that he or she loses sight of finding the best solution?

Positive Results. There are four potential positive results to team decision making: greater knowledge, more approaches, increased acceptance, and better understanding.

A team's information and knowledge should be and usually are greater than those of any one member. If the group's members have various skills and sources of information about the task, each should be able to fill gaps in the knowledge of others. For example, when Chrysler decided to produce the new Cirrus, it formed a product development team. This cross-functional team had members from key departments, including marketing, engineering, production, accounting, human resources, and legal. The team's purpose was to solve the problems of designing, making, and marketing the Cirrus at a competitive price.

Individuals tend to develop tunnel vision, regarding only their part of the problem as important. When individuals on a team share a problem, their discussion can stimulate the search for a variety of approaches. By challenging one another's thinking, team members may arrive at a decision that recognizes all viewpoints and reaches a consensus or a workable compromise.[45]

A person who is given a chance to influence a team's decision may be more committed to the decision and accept more responsibility for making it work than someone who is just told what to do. A high-quality solution handed down by a superior may not be carried out as effectively as a low-quality solution developed by or with the team. Thus effectiveness relates not only to the quality of the solution, but also to the team's power to resist or implement it.

Someone who solves a problem alone usually has the additional tasks of persuading others to implement the solution. As a result, further problems often are caused by

FIGURE 16.5

Potential Results with Team Decision Making

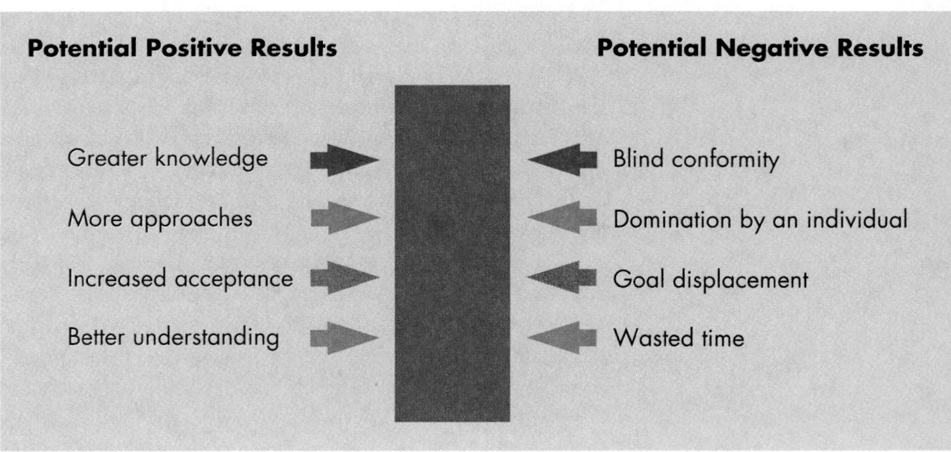

subordinates' or co-workers' inadequate understanding of the solution. If those who must implement a decision have helped to make it, communication failure isn't as likely—they already know how and why the decision was made.[46]

Negative Results. The potential positive results of team decision making are not guaranteed. There are four potential negative results: blind conformity, domination by an individual, goal displacement, and wasted time.[47]

Social pressures to maintain friendships and avoid disagreements can lead to blind conformity whereby group members unquestioningly accept a decision. This problem is especially acute when a solution is based more on personal feelings than on facts and analysis. Moreover, team acceptance of a decision isn't necessarily related to the quality of that decision. When decision-making teams are cohesive and conform blindly, a condition called groupthink can develop. **Groupthink** is an agreement-at-any-cost mentality that results in ineffective team decision making and possibly poor solutions. The fundamental problem underlying groupthink is pressure on members to concede and accept what other members think. The likelihood of groupthink increases when four conditions are present: peer pressure to conform is great, a highly directive leader presses for a particular interpretation of the problem and course of action, the need to process a complex and unstructured issue under crisis conditions exists, and the group is isolated.[48]

Ask Students
Have you ever participated in a meeting where one individual could be characterized as a "meeting robber" or in a class where one student tried to dominate class discussion? If so, how did you feel toward this individual, and how would you have suggested handling the situation?

Team effectiveness can be reduced if one individual, such as the team leader, dominates the discussion by talking too much or being closed to other points of view. Some team leaders try to control the team and provide most of the input to decisions, not the actions of good problem solvers. Team leaders need to be aware of their potential for dominating the team and the negative effects such domination can have. Even the brightest team members can't upgrade team decisions if they aren't permitted—much less encouraged—to contribute.

One primary goal of team decision making is to solve a problem effectively.[49] Team members need to take time to consider possible causes of the problem and various alternative solutions to it. Some members, though, may become so enthusiastic about and involved in winning support for one alternative that they lose sight of the goal—to find the best solution. Obviously this goal displacement can lower the quality of the decision. When it occurs, the team should go back to the beginning, generate new alternatives, and avoid evaluating them for the time being. If evaluation is clouded by a lack of facts—or controversy over the facts—the group session can be stopped until the facts can be supplemented and clarified.

Real-World Example
Use the example of a jury in a current or recent high-profile case as an example of team decision making. (Examples: the trials of O.J. Simpson, Rodney King, and William French Kennedy Smith.)

Time costs money, so a waste of time becomes a disadvantage if a decision made by a group could have been made just as effectively by an individual working alone. If the cost of a middle manager's time is $40 per hour, a two-hour meeting attended by ten middle managers costs the organization $800. The results may well be worth this cost, but not if nine of those managers could have better spent their time on other tasks.

Task Type. One of the most important factors to consider in determining whether an individual or team approach to decision making should be used is the type of task involved. We developed this point previously in this chapter and in the contingency models of leadership presented in Chapter 14. Some form of team process is desirable when one or more of the following forms of task interdependence exist.

- Various bits of information must be brought together to produce a good solution, as in an attempt to develop a new product, improve quality, or increase productivity.
- Skills and knowledge need to be pooled to deal with unstructured and complex tasks, as in deciding how to reduce per unit costs during the coming year.
- Different ideas about the best means for dealing with a problem or task need to be resolved.
- Acceptance of the chosen solution is crucial to effective implementation.

Ask Students
How does this knowledge help you in your participation in student teams?

Because jobs at all levels increasingly involve task interdependence, the use of problem-solving teams, cross-functional teams, and self-managing teams is spreading rapidly.

Team Size. As size increases, changes occur in the team's decision-making process. The optimal team size seems to be from five to twelve members, depending on the team's tasks. Members of larger teams have difficulty in communicating directly with each other. In general, increasing team size causes the following effects.

Ask Students
How does this knowledge help you in your participation in student teams?

Ask Students
Think of a team that you have been in, such as a study team. What was its size and how did that size affect the team's effectiveness?

- Demands on leader time and attention are greater. The leader becomes more psychologically distant from the other team members. This problem is more serious in self-managing teams, where more than one person can take on leader roles.
- The team's tolerance of direction from the leader is greater, and the team's decision making becomes more centralized.
- The team atmosphere is less friendly, the actions are less personal, more cliques form within the team, and, in general, the members are less satisfied.
- The team's rules and procedures become more formalized.[50]

These findings suggest that team performance can be influenced by controlling team size. For innovative decision making, the ideal team size is probably between five and nine members.[51] If a team has more than nine members, cliques might form. If larger teams are required for some reason, subteams may be formed. The purpose of subteams is to encourage all team members to share ideas when analyzing task-related problems, information, and alternative solutions. The full team can then meet to discuss subteam assessments and recommendations. In some instances, different subteams work on the same set of problems and then share and discuss their conclusions with the entire team. The leader of a large team needs to be aware of the possibility that subteams, or cliques, may form on their own, each with its own leader and agenda. Although more resources are available to large teams, these resources can create a backlash that hurts overall team effectiveness if each unofficial subteam or clique lobbies strongly for its own position.

Very large groups usually follow highly formal procedures, such as *Robert's Rules of Order,* to maintain order and keep the group focused on the agenda. Large group meetings may be efficient when the primary purpose is to state, interpret, or reinforce new policies, procedures, or plans. Coupled with an adequate opportunity for questions and answers, a large group meeting may satisfactorily inform the membership. Voting is the method often used to reach agreement in large groups. Unfortunately, voting alone doesn't reveal the intensity of members' feelings, either positive or negative, or generate acceptable alternatives.

Team Leadership

Chapter 14 was devoted to a discussion of leadership. Hence our purpose here is to provide a few key ideas for effective team leadership. Team leaders shouldn't reject or promote ideas because of their own personal views. They must be receptive to member contributions and not judge them. Good team leaders summarize information, stimulate discussion, create awareness of problems, and detect when the team is ready to resolve differences and agree to a unified solution. In terms of the leader-participation model presented in Chapter 14, this behavior would represent the group decision style. You may recall that member participation is extremely high with this style. The group (team) style of decision making may seem strange to some people because it certainly isn't consistent with the popular conception of leadership. Support of disagreement, use of time, and introduction of change are three important aspects of the leadership role in teams.[52]

Ask Students
Is disagreement within a team good or bad? Explain.

Support of Disagreement. A skillful team leader can create an atmosphere for disagreement that stimulates innovative solutions while minimizing the risk of bad feelings. Disagreement can be managed if the leader is receptive to differences within the team, delays the reaching of decisions, and separates idea generation from idea evaluation. This last technique reduces the likelihood that an alternative solution will be identified with one individual rather than the team. The absence of disagreement on a team may be as destructive to its proper functioning as too much disagreement.

Ask Students
What are some of the things that leaders can do to encourage effective time management in teams? (Possibilities: having a set agenda and refocusing the team when the discussion digresses.)

Use of Time. To manage time effectively, a team leader must strike a proper balance between permissiveness and control. Rushing through a team session can prevent full discussion of the problem, lead to negative feelings, and poor solutions. However, unless the leader keeps the discussion moving, members will become bored and inattentive. Unfortunately, some leaders feel pushing for an early solution is necessary because of time constraints. Such a move ends discussion before the team has had a chance to work through a problem effectively.

Introduction of Change. When team members disagree, some have to change their opinions in order for the team to reach a consensus. If members offering the best alternatives are persuaded by other team members to abandon their arguments, the outcome suffers. The leader can protect individuals holding a minority view by discouraging other team members from expressing hostility toward them. The leader can also give individuals with a minority view the chance to influence the majority. Team leaders do so by keeping the minority view before the team, encouraging discussion of that view, and clarifying any misunderstanding.

Organizational Implications

Managers and some professionals (e.g., planners, market researchers, and quality control specialists) have a long history of team involvement within organizations. More recently, empowering nonmanagerial employees to undertake various managerial tasks—often in collaboration with managers—through teams has been stressed. This development is demonstrated by the system of teams at Texas Instruments Malaysia and the other Insight accounts in this chapter. The increasing use of teams is consistent with a growing shift from mechanistic to organic organizations. Recall that a mechanistic organization is one in which management breaks activities into separate, specialized tasks. Goals, authority, responsibility, and accountability are rigidly defined by level and position for both managers and subordinates. In contrast, in an organic organization, management fosters working together in teams and communicating openly. Employees are encouraged to form an association with anyone who might help solve the problem at hand. David Fearon, management consultant and professor, portrays the changing landscape for organizations in these words:

> *Effective teams are the leading edge of total quality accomplishments. Americans must learn, once again, how to be in teams, of many types, simultaneously and to give and take. It is time to rediscover the management power of teams and other groups. Management is knowledge of how and why to advance an organization in its environment. Few managers can think this out alone.*[53]

The growing importance of teams is reflected in the large amount of time managers and others spend in team meetings. These meetings usually are not the time traps they have a reputation for being. The good news about team meetings is how varied they are in purpose, style, length, format, and even technology. They range from quick huddles in someone's office to voice-mail get-togethers to multiday planning retreats. Many top managers report spending 50 percent or more of their time in team meetings. For first-line managers and professionals, time spent in such meetings may vary from 20 to 50 percent.[54] Most experts believe that the use of teams will continue to grow in organizations, especially among nonmanagerial employees.

4

Describe the core elements of organizational cultures and the basic types of cultures.

ORGANIZATIONAL CULTURES

An **organizational culture** is the unique pattern of shared assumptions, values, and norms that shape the organization's socialization activities, language, symbols, and practices.[55] It is like an *organizational personality* that is revealed through the employees as a whole. As with each individual's personality, an organizational culture provides predictable patterns and expectations that guide

- how to solve problems, meet goals, and deal with important customers, suppliers, and other stakeholders;
- how members are to relate to one another;
- how members are to perceive, think, and feel about the solutions that have been used in the past for dealing with various problems;
- how results are to be measured; and
- how rewards and punishments are to be determined.[56]

A strong organizational culture doesn't just happen. It is cultivated by management, learned and reinforced by employees, and passed on to new employees. Over time, it can change, though not easily. Where a well-developed, strong organizational culture exists, there is little to distinguish formal teams from informal groups in terms of their norms, activities, sentiments, and interactions. This uniformity doesn't mean that a culture simply can be written into a new-employee's handbook—although that *is* done by Hewlett-Packard, Southwest Airlines, and others—and learned by reading it or even that employees can fully explain the culture. The underlying shared assumptions and values may be unstated and organizational members may have trouble consciously verbalizing some of them.[57]

We focus on organizations with strong cultures, although not all organizations have a single, strong culture. Some organizations have several strong, distinct subcultures rather than a single culture. If the members of different subcultures don't trust and cooperate with one another, power struggles and gamesmanship may result. This situation has occurred with professional baseball players through their union and baseball owners through their association. Even in an effective organization with a strong culture, subcultures with some unique characteristics usually exist. Subcultures often express diversity in terms of management level (top management versus first-level management), management versus nonmanagement, functional specialty (manufacturing, research and development, accounting, engineering, marketing, human resources, etc.), gender, race, national origin, disability, and so on.

Ask Students
What are some of the subcultures on campus?

Most of the time subcultures coexist peacefully with one another and with the overall organizational culture.[58] For example, many universities and colleges have strong organizational cultures and distinct subcultures for undergraduate students, faculty, and administration. Figure 16.6 provides a general framework for examining organizational cultures and their linkages. We discuss these elements and linkages in the remainder of this chapter.

Macroculture

The broad outline of an organization's culture is shaped by its macroculture. For our purposes, the **macroculture** includes a combination of the assumptions and values of both the society and industry in which the organization (or one or its divisions) operates. Recall from Chapters 3 and 4 that we broadly differentiated societies and individ-

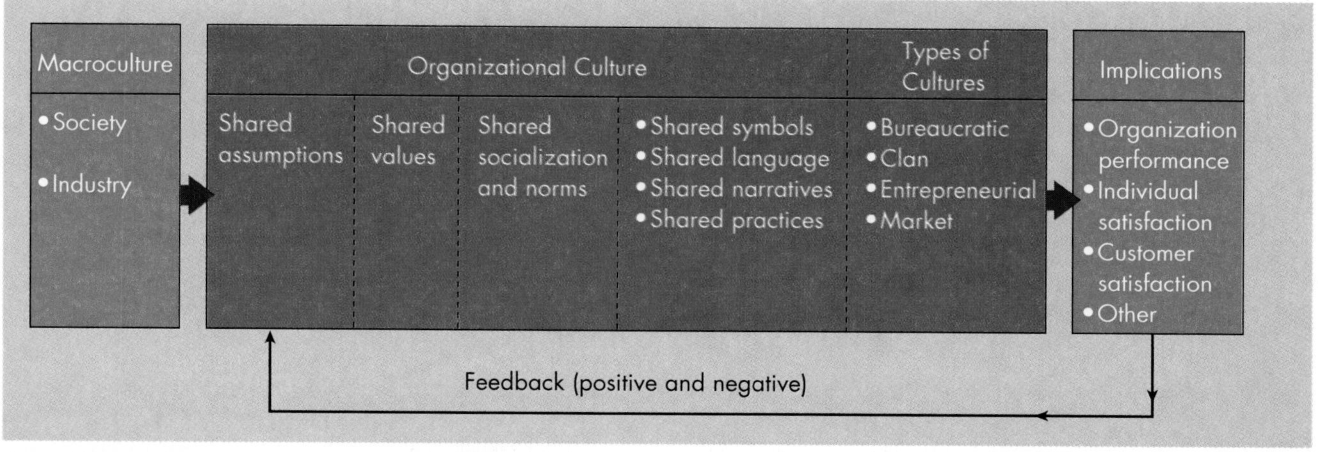

FIGURE 16.6

Framework for Understanding Organizational Cultures

uals in terms of values such as individualism versus collectivism and low versus high uncertainty avoidance.[59] We noted, for example, that the Canadian and U.S. societies rank relatively high on individualism and low on uncertainty avoidance. These value orientations support a competitive market-based economic system, individual merit, and individual incentive systems (or those based on efforts by small teams), selection based on individual merit, and the like.

Previous Industry Assumptions. An organization's culture may also be shaped by the presence of an *industry mindset* among competitors. This macroculture may shape how firms in the industry are expected to compete and deal with stakeholders such as governments, customers, and suppliers.[60] Until the last ten years or so, the Big Three auto firms—Chrysler, Ford, and General Motors—operated on the basis of some common industry assumptions. These assumptions included the following.

1. Production workers and the auto union were not to be trusted.
2. The key to increased productivity was the use of more robots and better contracts with the unions that required higher productivity.
3. Customers were more interested in new models with fancy features than reliable, low-maintenance autos.
4. Suppliers were to be squeezed to cut their prices and played off against one another by threatening to discontinue purchases.
5. Government proposals for new safety features should be strongly resisted because they drive up costs and customers do not care about safety.
6. Foreign auto firms compete unfairly, so government should restrict their imports.
7. Customers will pay the increasing price of gasoline to continue to drive their fuel-consuming models.[61]

Ask Students
What are some of the industry assumptions that high school administrators make?

Total Quality versus Traditional Assumptions. However, Japanese auto firms and auto customers in the United States and Canada generally did *not* hold these views. Thus U.S. auto firms had a macroculture that failed to fit the new realities created by foreign auto firms and changing customer expectations.[62] The enormous market share and financial losses by U.S. auto firms forced them to recognize the need for major changes. Over the past ten years, the Big Three auto firms have blended the features of a different macroculture—namely, total quality management—with their traditional assumptions and values.

TABLE 16.1

Core Assumptions and Values of Total Quality Management Versus Traditional Organizations

Dimensions	Total Quality Management Organizations	Continua of Assumptions and Values	Traditional Organizations
Priority organizational goals	Quality enhancement for long-term effectiveness and continuous improvement	|___|___|___|___|	Maximizing profits (i.e., shareholder wealth) and minimizing costs
Environment	Boundaries with environment blurred; suppliers, customers, and others part of organization's processes	|___|___|___|___|	Boundaries with environment clearly set; stakeholders viewed more as sources of threat and competition
Definition of quality	High value, meeting or exceeding customers' expectations	|___|___|___|___|	Conformance to standards a cost of doing business
Priority goals of individuals	Economic, social, and psychological: personal fulfillment and social acceptance	|___|___|___|___|	Economic: maximize income and minimize effort
Control	Active self-control; emphasis on self-management	|___|___|___|___|	Managers coordinate, direct, and monitor subordinates
Information	Open, timely, horizontal, and vertical flows	|___|___|___|___|	Restricted; follows vertical hierarchy
Role of employees	Empowered to make decisions, build relationships, and improve quality	|___|___|___|___|	Follow orders; reactive self-control; jobs limited to prescribed tasks

Sources: Adapted from Grant, R.M., Shani, R., and Krishnan, R. TQM's challenge to management theory and practice. *Sloan Management Review,* Winter 1994, 25–35; Spencer, B.A. Models of organization and total quality management: A comparison and critical evaluation. *Academy of Management Review,* 1994, 19, 446–471; Blackburn, R., and Benson, B. Total quality and human resources management: Lessons from Baldrige Award-winning companies. *Academy of Management Executive,* August 1993, 49–66.

This blending has been taking place in several industries. Table 16.1 summarizes the assumptions and values of total quality firms and those of traditional firms. We suspect that many firms exhibit various blends of these contrasting assumptions and values in their organizational cultures as a whole and in their subcultures. This situation is suggested by the continua in Table 16.1. Where the blend represents a relative balance, conflicts and uncertainties over priorities and how to deal with many problems are likely. That often is the case when organizations undertake major cultural changes, as at Chrysler, Ford, and General Motors.

The contrasting assumptions and values in Table 16.1 suggest that:

> *TQM is a revolutionary philosophy that requires radical and pervasive change within the firm. . . . TQM represents a challenge not only to conventional management practices but also to the assumptions and theories on which those practices are based.*[63]

Shared Assumptions

A specific organizational culture often reflects a blend of assumptions that are unique to the organization and assumptions from the macroculture.[64] In Chapter 6, we discussed two planning aids for diagnosing assumptions—dialectical inquiry and devil's advocacy. We also defined *assumptions* as the underlying thoughts and feelings of one or more individuals that are taken for granted and believed to be true. Assumptions for organizational culture relate to (1) the thoughts and beliefs that members hold about themselves and others (e.g., focus on self-interests versus common interests), (2) member relationships to others (e.g., compete versus cooperate), (3) the organization's relationship with the environment (e.g., dominate it, submit to it, cooperate with it), (4) time orientation (e.g., past, present, future), and so on.[65]

Laziness Assumption. Consider the potential implications if there were a common assumption in an organization that most human beings are lazy.[66] This assumption might create expectations of laziness that lead to perceptions of lazy behaviors. For instance, the assumption that success depends on sustained effort means that laziness is likely to be considered negatively. Then perceptions of laziness, along with negative thoughts and feelings about it, can easily lead to practices for controlling laziness, such as autocratic supervision and the use of rigid rules. Meanwhile, the laziness assumption reduces expectations of high-performing behaviors (because humans are lazy, why would they behave otherwise?) Thus perceptions of high-performing behaviors will be infrequent. This view suppresses the value that otherwise might be accorded autonomy and empowerment (because giving lazy people autonomy and empowerment almost certainly will lead to little or no effort being exerted).

Shared Values

Ask Students
What are some of this university's shared values?

Real-World Example
Some managers adopt missions and credos not out of any real commitment but because they seem fashionable (*Harvard Business Review,* March-April, 1995, 82). What happens to organizational culture when that occurs?

Ethics
Do shared values encourage ethical behavior or unethical behavior? How can you set values that will support ethical behavior?

Recall that a *value* is a basic belief about a condition that has considerable importance and meaning to individuals and is stable over time. A *value system* comprises multiple beliefs that are compatible and supportive of one another. For example, the societal values (macroculture) of private enterprise and individual rights are mutually supportive. There are a number of ways to develop the profile of shared values for an organization. The organization culture profile (OCP) provides one way.[67] The OCP provides a set of value statements for assessing both the extent to which certain values characterize an organization and an individual employee's preference for that set of values. A person-culture fit can be determined by relating the profile of organizational values to the profile of the employee's value preferences.

The OCP contains fifty-four statements that can express individual and organizational values. First, the employees sort the fifty-four value statements (each of which is on a separate card) into categories ranging from *most desirable* to *least desirable.* In doing so, they reveal their personal preferences for ideal values for their organization. Second, the employees sort the same fifty-four value statements from *most characteristic* to *least characteristic* of their organization. If these two ratings are closely related, shared values and a common organization culture probably exist.

The pattern of these value statements provide guidance for developing explicitly stated organizational principles and practices. For example, Johnson & Johnson is an organization with a strong culture. It has thirty-three major lines of business, with 168 operating companies in fifty-three countries. It sells baby oil, artificial cornea lenses, blood machines, fifty types of prescription drugs, surgery equipment, and hundreds of other products. Its core values and principles include the following.

- Let management and teams set goals for themselves. They will be tougher than you will.
- Put profits behind service and profits will come.
- Retain managers who make mistakes. They have learned their lesson.
- Use ethics to weed out bad employees and managers early; put trust in those who remain.
- Edicts from headquarters destroy morale.[68]

A variety of sources on Johnson & Johnson, including its stated principles and practices, suggest that, of those shown in Table 16.2, the following value statements are *most characteristic* of its value profile: flexibility, adaptability, being innovative, risk taking, autonomy, being team oriented, emphasizing a single culture throughout the organiza-

TABLE 16.2

Sample of Organizational Culture Value Statements

• Flexibility	• Emphasizing a single organizational culture	• Taking individual responsibility
• Stability	• Being people oriented	• Security of employment
• Predictability	• Respect for the individual's rights	• Low level of conflict
• Being innovative	• Tolerance	• Confronting conflict directly
• Risk taking	• Informality	• Enthusiasm for the job
• Being careful	• Being easygoing	• Working long hours
• Autonomy	• Being supportive	• An emphasis on quality
• Being rule oriented	• Being aggressive	• Being socially responsible
• Being analytical	• Taking initiative	• Being results oriented
• Paying attention to detail	• Being reflective	• Being highly organized
• Being team oriented	• Being demanding	
• Sharing information freely		

Source: Adapted from O'Reilly, C.A. III, Chatman, J.A., and Caldwell, D.F. People and organizational culture: A profile of comparison approach to assessing the person-organization fit. *Academy of Management Journal,* 1991, 34, 516.

Ethics
Maintaining an ethical culture needs to be emphasized strongly during organizational socialization.

tion, respect for the individual's rights, tolerance, taking initiative, confronting conflict directly, an emphasis on quality, being socially responsible, and being results oriented.[69]

Shared Socialization and Norms

Ask Students
How were you socialized into this college or university?

Organizational socialization is the systematic process by which an organization brings new members into its culture.[70] Individuals learn the ropes and are introduced to the norms of the organization. Strong organizational cultures generally have well-developed methods for selecting the right types of employees, and, once selected, for molding them. Molding, in terms of organizational norms, sentiments, activities, interactions, and practices, takes place in various ways.[71] The most powerful way is through consistent role modeling, teaching, coaching, and enforcement by co-workers and managers—starting at the top and spreading throughout the organization.

Disneyland parks emphasize predictability, paying attention to detail, being team oriented, emphasizing a single culture throughout the organization, enthusiasm on the job, and an emphasis on quality.

The socialization that takes place in an organization is determined by shared values, which are translated into more specific and observable organizationwide norms.[72] For example, Disneyland parks emphasize the following values (see Table 16.2): predictability, paying attention to detail, being team oriented, emphasizing a single culture throughout the organization, enthusiasm for the job, and an emphasis on quality. These values support specific norms (standards of behavior), rules, and practices related to who they serve (guests not customers), what they wear (costumes, not uniforms), who they are (cast members, not employees), and so on.

Fortune magazine noted the importance of socialization:

> *Many of the great American companies that thrive from one generation to the next . . . are organizations that have perfected their processes of socialization. Virtually none talk explicitly about socialization; they may not even be conscious of precisely what they are doing. Moreover, when one examines any particular aspect of their policy toward people—how they recruit or train or compensate—little stands out as unusual. But when the pieces are assembled, what emerges is an awesome internal consistency that powerfully shapes behavior.*[73]

The following Ethics Insight suggests how Johnson & Johnson's Credo has been consciously used and reviewed over time to ensure that its culture reflects ethical standards.

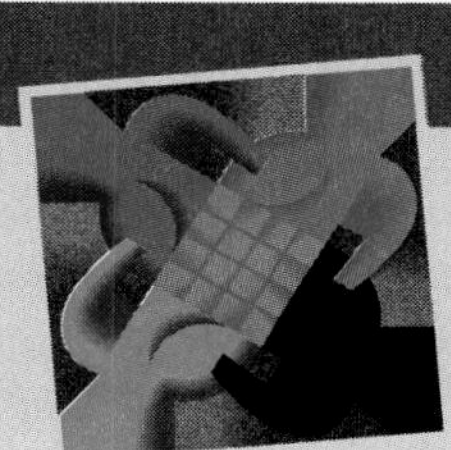

Ethics *Insight*

J&J's Credo Lives

What makes Johnson & Johnson's top executives so patient and trusting of their decentralized operations? Much of this trust can be traced to a deeply held companywide code of ethics. Those ethics are spelled out in the company's 308-word Credo, a copy of which is carved in stone at the company's New Brunswick, New Jersey, headquarters.

The Credo tells all employees who and what to care about—and in what order—such as: "We believe our first responsibility is to the doctors, nurses, and patients, to mothers and fathers." Its employees and the communities in which it operates come in the middle. Shareholders come last, even after suppliers and distributors. The Credo declares that shareholders will get a fair return if all other stakeholders have priority.

Because the Credo deemphasizes profits, says former CEO James Burke, managers are freer to operate long term. They aren't so worried about making mistakes and are under less pressure to cut corners.

The Credo almost faded away once. It got its start in 1935, when "General" Johnson spelled out the company's moral obligation to employees and local communities during the depression. It was lengthened and formalized eight years later. But Burke says that it had become stale by the late 1970s. He decided to challenge it and held a meeting with thirty-eight top managers, suggesting they should get rid of the Credo because it didn't mean anything. As he had hoped, many of the managers were indignant and leaped to its defense. "Violent arguments ensued that had the effect of reinvigorating the importance of the Credo," says Burke. Other managers were invited to challenge or modify it until virtually everyone had had a crack at it.

In 1982 some crank slipped cyanide into a few capsules of Tylenol and put them on a supermarket shelf in Chicago. Seven people died. It was then, says Burke, that the Credo became very real. "We had to put our money where our mouth was. We had committed to putting the public first, and everybody in the company was looking to see if we had lived up to our pretensions." They did, and spent $100 million pulling Tylenol from store shelves and replacing customers' supplies. It worked wonders for J&J's image—and helped saved Tylenol. As a result, says Burke, J&J employees will take the Credo seriously for at least a generation.[74]

Shared Symbols

A **symbol** is anything visible that can be used to represent an abstract shared value or special meaning.[75] Symbols are the simplest and most basic *observable* form of cultural expression. For example, Prudential Life Insurance uses the Rock of Gibraltar to represent continuity and dependability, which have great meaning to both employees and customers. Symbols may be expressed through logos, architecture, parking priorities (assigned versus unassigned spaces, in or out of the garage, and close versus far from building), uniforms, office (spaciousness, location, furniture, and carpeting), open versus closed door norms, common cafeteria or separate dining facility for higher management, plaques, lapel pins, type of art on walls, and types of awards (e.g., emphasizing awards for quality and customer service).

Ask Students
What are some visible shared symbols in this classroom?

Recall the Global Insight on TI Malaysia. To demonstrate mutual respect and embrace diversity, its cafeteria often is decorated with banners celebrating holidays such as the Chinese New Year or the Hindu Deepavali Festival. The cafeteria also has stalls that sell goods from the major ethnic cultures in Malaysia. The local bimonthly company magazine features articles and numerous pictures of employees and customers. This emphasis symbolizes the importance of both groups to the firm's success.[76]

Shared Language

From a cultural perspective, **language** is a shared system of vocal sounds, written signs, and/or gestures used to convey special meanings among members.[77] The elements of this system include shared jargon, slang, gestures, signals, signs, songs, humor, jokes, gossip, rumors, proverbs, metaphors, and slogans. In general, the greater the number and use of such language elements, the deeper is an organization's culture.[78]

Recall our discussion of Southwest Airlines through several Insights in Chapter 5. Herb Kelleher, the CEO, has championed the use of unique language to maintain and differentiate its culture. Consider these cultural statements: "Work should be fun . . . it can be play . . . enjoy it." "Work is important . . . don't spoil it with seriousness." "We give more for less, not less for less." "Fly the luv airline." "We dignify the CUSTOMER."

Ask Students
What are some of the words that express the shared symbols and language of the organizational culture of this college or university?

The word "customer" is always capitalized. Letters of commendation and appreciation to employees are known as "Love Reports." When interdepartmental problems occur, the employees must work them out at supervised sessions known as "Come to Jesus" meetings. "We draft great attitudes" is another slogan. "We are family" is a metaphor used to refer to all employees.

Shared Narratives

Narratives are the unique stories, sagas, legends, and myths in an organizational culture. A *saga* describes the unique accomplishments and beliefs of the organization and its leaders over time, usually in heroic and romantic terms.[79] A well-known saga is how Mary Kay founded a successful company while struggling to support herself and her children as a single parent.

Jim Burke, the recently retired CEO of Johnson & Johnson, tells the story of being a young executive in the mid-1950s and getting called to the office of the CEO, "General" Robert Wood Johnson. Burke states: "I thought I was going to get fired." He had led the development of a combination nose spray and drops for children. It flopped. Instead, Johnson stuck out his hand and said: "I want to congratulate you. Business is about taking risk. Keep doing it." Burke commented: "He (Johnson) felt the company was becoming risk-averse, and he knew I would tell everybody about what he had done."[80] As noted previously, two of the unique values at Johnson & Johnson are its tolerance for certain kinds of failure and support of risk taking.

Ask Students
What are some organizational legends with which you are familiar?

A *legend* is a well-known story about some significant person or event, based on historical fact but embellished with fictional details. Legends are passed on by organizational "storytellers," who help maintain cohesion and guidelines for employees to follow. These legends may even relate much of what it takes for the employees and organization to prosper. Sam Walton, who founded Wal-Mart, was a source of many stories and legends even before his death in 1992. One legend is that Sam Walton's favorite rule was "break all the rules." Although he made this statement many times, it was more symbolic than literal. His favorite rule was encompassed in the spirit of one guiding principle: The secret of successful retailing is to give your customers what they want.[81] He believed that, if a business isn't doing this, it should change its rules of operation.

Shared Practices

The most complex and *observable* cultural form is shared practices. These practices include taboos or rites and ceremonies. Taboos are behaviors that are forbidden in the organizational culture. A taboo at Johnson & Johnson is to put profits ahead of ethical responsibilities to doctors, nurses, and patients.

A **rite and ceremony** is the elaborate and formal activities designed to generate strong sentiments and carried out as a special event.[82] Commencement at a university or college is a *rite of passage*. The commencement program is the event, and the emotionally charged activities include the procession of faculty and honored guests, the procession of graduates, the invocation, the statement of welcome, the speech by a special guest, and the awarding of diplomas.

Ask Students
What are some examples of the rites and ceremonies of this college or university?

Discussion Question 5
What are the similarities between group characteristics and organizational cultures?

Teaching Tip
Ask students to identify rituals used by groups they belong to. (Example: a pledging or induction ceremony of a fraternity or sorority.)

A *rite of integration* involves the planned activities that create and reinforce the common goals, close ties, and positive sentiments among employees and with the organization. Employees at Wal-Mart are known as associates and partners, not workers or employees. Whenever an executive visits a Wal-Mart store, all the associates are assembled. After remarks, the executive leads them in a cheer: "Give me a W! Give me an A! Give me an L! Give me a Squiggly! (all do their versions of the twist.) Give me an M! Give me an A! Give me an R! Give me a T! What's that spell? Wal-Mart! What's that spell? Wal-Mart! Who's No. 1? THE CUSTOMER!"[83]

A *rite of enhancement* refers to planned activities that increase the personal status and social recognition of organization members. Awards programs of all types are examples. Mary Kay Cosmetics is well known for its dramatic annual awards ceremony in Dallas, which is the last event at its annual Mary Kay Seminars. The setting for the award presentations resemble the Oscar Award dinners of the motion picture industry. Most participants dress in formal evening clothes. To a large cheering audience, awards that include gold and diamond pins, fur stoles, and even the use of luxury automobiles are presented.[84]

Types of Organizational Cultures

Cultural elements and their relationships create a pattern that is distinct to an organization, just as a personality is unique to an individual. However, as with a classification of individuals that share some common characteristics, several general types of organizational cultures can be described. Of the many classification frameworks that have been proposed, one of the more useful ones is presented in Figure 16.7. The vertical axis reflects the relative formal control orientation, ranging from stable to flexible. The horizontal axis reflects the relative focus of attention, ranging from internal functioning to external functioning. The extreme corners of the four quadrants represent four pure types of organizational culture: bureaucratic, clan, entrepreneurial, and market.[85] Of course, a single organization may have various blends of these four types.[86]

Ask Students
What are some of the bureaucratic cultures you deal with?

Bureaucratic Culture. An organization in which employees value formalization, rules, standard operating procedures, and hierarchical coordination has a **bureaucratic culture.** Recall that the long-term concerns of a bureaucracy are predictability, efficiency, and stability. Its members highly value standardized goods and customer service. Managers see their roles as being good coordinators, organizers, and enforcers of writ-

FIGURE 16.7

Framework of Types of Cultures

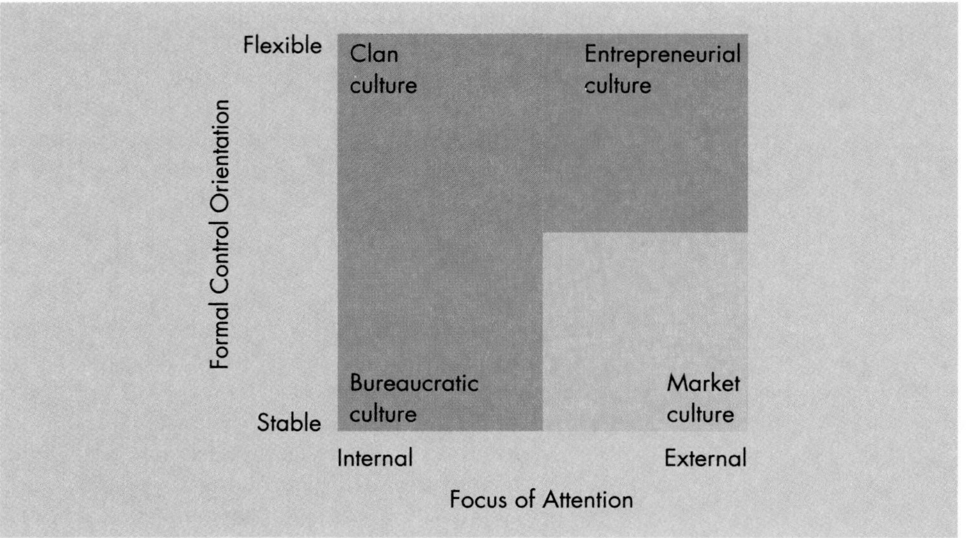

Sources: Adapted from Hooijberg, R., and Petrock, F. On cultural change: Using the competing values framework to help leaders execute a transformational strategy. *Human Resource Management,* 1993, 32, 29–50; Quinn, R.E. *Beyond Rational Management: Mastering the Paradoxes and Competing Demands of High Performance.* San Francisco: Jossey-Bass, 1988.

ten rules and standards. Tasks, responsibilities and authority for all employees are clearly defined. The many rules and processes are spelled out in thick manuals, and employees believe that their duty is to "go by the book" and follow legalistic procedures. Consider the following Insight.

Insight

Federal Government's Bureaucratic Culture

A recent task force on the U.S. federal bureaucracy released a report entitled the *National Performance Review.* This report recommended major changes in the way the federal bureaucracy draws up its budgets, organizes its departments and agencies, buys its equipment and supplies, and develops its procedures for hiring, promoting, and firing employees. The report provides numerous accounts of a bureaucratic culture being carried to extremes. According to the report, too often the results are ineffectiveness and inefficiency. Consider the following examples.

- How many government workers does it take to change a light bulb? Forty-three, according to a safety procedure proposed at the Rocky Flats nuclear-weapons plant in Colorado. The *Denver Post* disclosed the thirty-three-step process that a plant staff member wanted to adopt for replacing the light bulbs that warn workers of nuclear accidents. The proposed guidelines would require an estimated 1,087 worker hours per year, compared to 60 hours currently.
- The federal personnel manual, which spells out the rules for hiring and firing, totals 10,000 pages. There are 900 pages alone on how to fill out Standard Form 50 ("Notification of Personnel Action").
- The General Service Administration (GSA) is responsible for buying $10 billion of computer equipment annually. The GSA approval process for ordering a computer takes as long as three years. Over that time period, the equipment ordered sometimes becomes technologically obsolete and may no longer even be manufactured.[87]

Real-World Example
AT&T CEO Bob Allen said, "It's not easy to change a culture that was very control oriented and top down. We're trying to create an atmosphere of turning the organization chart upside down, putting the customers on top. The people closest to the customer should be making the key decisions" (*Fortune,* May 17, 1995, 57).

Clan Culture. Tradition, loyalty, personal commitment, extensive socialization, teamwork, self-management, and social influence are attributes of a **clan culture.** Its members recognize an obligation beyond the simple exchange of labor for a salary. They understand that contributions to the organization (e.g., hours worked per week) may exceed any contractual agreements. The individual's long-term commitment to the organization (loyalty) is exchanged for the organization's long-term commitment to the individual (security).

The clan culture achieves unity with a long and thorough socialization process. Long-time clan members serve as mentors and role models for newer members. These relationships ensure perpetuation of the organization's values and norms over successive generations of employees. The clan is aware of its unique history and often documents its origins and celebrates its traditions in various rites. Statements of its publicly held values are reinforced. Members have a shared image of the organization's style and manner of conduct.

Ask Students
Have you ever been a member of a clan culture? If so, briefly describe it.

In a clan culture, members share a sentiment of pride in membership. They have a strong sense of identification and recognize their interdependence. The up-through-the-ranks career pattern results in an extensive network of colleagues whose paths have crossed and who have shared similar experiences. Communication, coordination, and integration are facilitated by shared goals, perceptions, and behavioral tendencies. A clan culture generates feelings of personal ownership of a division, product, or ideas. In addition, peer pressure to adhere to important norms is strong. The richness of the culture creates an environment in which few areas are left totally free from normative pressures. Depending on the types of its norms, the culture may or may not generate risk-taking behavior or innovation. Success is assumed to depend substantially on sensitivity to customers and concern for people. Teamwork, participation, and consensus decision making are believed to lead to this success. The following Insight illustrates the clan culture and what can happen if it becomes too internally focused.

Insight

Tandem's Clan Culture

Tandem Computers, headquartered in Cupertino, California, resembles a clan culture. Its highly *flexible* formal controls and excessive *internal* focus may have contributed to its problems in the external marketplace, starting in about 1991. James Treybig, president and CEO, as well as founder, played a key role in creating the clan culture through five core assumptions and values by which Tandem would operate.

- All people are good.
- People, workers, management, and company are all the same thing.
- Every single person in a company must understand the essence of the business.
- Every employee must benefit from the company's success.
- You must create an environment where all of the above can happen.

Let's consider a few examples of how these assumptions and values work in practice. Several years ago Treybig was bumped up to first class on a United Airlines flight. He refused it! Treybig said: "I won't sit in front if my employees have to sit in the back." Tandem's 8,500 employees receive sabbaticals to "find" themselves, attend workshops to study Tandem values, and swim in the company pool. "We always felt that if you treat employees right, they will work hard and that loyalty will pay off," says Treybig.

During 1992 and 1993, Tandem had to lay off about 11 percent of its employees because of losses and slowed market growth. Consistent with its clan culture, these layoffs were made reluctantly, and departing employees received generous payouts. Other costs also were trimmed. The generous employee stock ownership plan was cut, and employee compensation was reduced by an average of 5 percent. Recently, new products have been successfully launched, and additional formal controls and procedures have been implemented. The clan culture at Tandem has been *softened,* not abandoned. Tandem appears to be more in tune with the intense pressures of its competitive environment.[88]

Ask Students
What would be needed to change this college or university into an entrepreneurial culture?

Entrepreneurial Culture. High levels of risk taking, dynamism, and creativity characterize an **entrepreneurial culture.** There is a commitment to experimentation, innovation, and being on the leading edge. This culture doesn't just quickly react to changes in the environment, it creates change. Effectiveness means providing new and unique products in order to grow rapidly. Individual initiative, flexibility, and freedom foster growth and are encouraged and well rewarded.

Entrepreneurial cultures usually are associated with small to middle-sized companies that are still run by a founder. An exception is the 3-M Corporation, which is headquartered in Minneapolis, Minnesota.

Insight

3M's Entrepreneurial Culture

The 3M Corporation has long been known for product innovation. It markets some 66,000 products, including Post-It message pads, Scotch videotapes, and household sandpaper. Until 1992, 3M consistently met its formal goal of deriving 25 percent of its revenues from products introduced within the past five years. With sales going relatively flat over a couple of years, 3M's chief executive officer, L. D. DeSimone, became alarmed. He discovered that too much energy was being spent on small products similar to those already on the market and that products were taking too long to progress from prototype to full production.

To reinforce the firm's entrepreneurial culture, DeSimone set a new goal: Accelerate innovation to the point where 3M generates 30 percent of its sales from products introduced within the past four years, a 30-and-4 goal, replacing the revered 25-and-5 goal. With the challenge of this new goal and greater concentration on products with large sales potential—like its recent innovative Scotch-Brite Never Rust soap pads—3M is approaching its growth targets in 1995.

Top management has long emphasized growth from the bottom— the project team—up. Under a concept called "grow and divide," successful project teams, consisting of an entrepreneur with an idea and a small team that buys into it, grow into departments. Some of them become large enough to spin off as separate divisions, such as Post-It-Notes. In turn, these divisions sponsor their own new projects. The usual approach for most firms is to form smaller units out of larger ones to facilitate formal and stable controls. In contrast, 3M encourages the small units created by innovation and entrepreneurship to grow into larger divisions and departments.

The values at 3M promote individual identity, innovation, and entrepreneurship. They are evident in sayings such as "Products belong to divisions, but technology belongs to the company." Through decades of cross-unit collaboration, employees have developed such mutual respect and cooperation that management hardly needs to intervene. The number of applications the company finds for even the simplest innovation often is amazing. For example, a nonwoven material was developed initially as a decorative ribbon. It generated scores of other products in nineteen divisions—from protective face masks to surgical tape to cleaning pads.[89]

Market Culture. The achievement of measurable and demanding goals, especially those that are financial and market-based (e.g., sales growth, profitability, and market share) characterize a **market culture.** Hard-driving competitiveness and a profits orientation prevail throughout the organization.

In a market culture, the relationship between individual and organization is contractual. That is the obligations of each party are agreed on in advance. In this sense, the formal control orientation is quite stable. The individual is responsible for some level of performance, and the organization promises a specified level of rewards in return. Increased levels of performance are exchanged for increased rewards, as outlined in an agreed schedule. Neither party recognizes the right of the other to demand more than was originally specified. The organization doesn't promise (or imply) security; the individual doesn't promise (or imply) loyalty. The contract, renewed annually if each party adequately performs its obligations, is utilitarian because each party uses the other to further its own goals. Rather than promoting a feeling of membership in a social system, the market culture values independence and individuality and encourages members to pursue their own financial goals and, by so doing, to help each other. For example, the salesperson who increases sales will make more money, and the firm will earn more profits through the salesperson's greater sales volume.

The market culture doesn't exert much informal, social pressure on an organization's members. They do not share a common set of expectations regarding management style or philosophy. Superiors' interactions with subordinates largely consist of negotiating performance-reward agreements and/or evaluating requests for resource allocations. Superiors aren't formally judged on their effectiveness as role models or mentors. The absence of a long-term commitment by both parties weakens the socialization process.

Ask Students
What would be needed to change this college or university into a market culture?

Social relations among co-workers are not officially emphasized, and few economic incentives are tied directly to cooperating with peers. Managers are expected to cooperate with managers in other departments only to the extent necessary to achieve their performance goals. As a result, they may not develop an extensive network of colleagues within the organization. The market culture often is tied to monthly, quarterly, and annual performance goals based on profits. The following Insight on PepsiCo reveals some of the attributes of a market culture.

Insight

PepsiCo's Market Culture

Wayne Calloway, CEO of PepsiCo, is described by his colleagues as "tough as nails." Calloway runs a boot camp for managers that makes Parris Island look like Coney Island. He sets back-breaking standards and raises them methodically each year. Those who can't cut it wash out. To the winners go the spoils— first-class air travel, fully loaded company cars, stock options, and bonuses. In good years, bonuses can hit 90 percent of salary for high-performing managers. Promotions come fast—every two to three years is standard.

The heart of PepsiCo's organizational culture is management evaluation, designed to weed out the weak and nurture the strong. The annual performance review requires a superior to sit down with each of his or her managers at least once a year and discuss performance. The focus is on what the manager actually did this year to contribute to the business, not whether she is a nice person or he wears the right clothes. Did she meet the sales target? Did he develop a successful new taco chip or soda commercial? Michael Jordan, the former hard-driving CEO of Frito-Lay, said: "Nothing is ever good enough." If the manager met the goals, fine. The superior then typically ups the standards for next year.

But pity the manager who isn't getting good bottom-line results. First the superior will try to find out why and try to help the manager fix it. But, after a year or two of missing the goals, the person's gone. Brenda Barnes, a chief operating officer in the Pepsi-Cola division of PepsiCo, sums up the culture this way: "We'll never be nor should we be a warm and cuddly environment."[90]

Organizational Implications

As suggested in Figure 16.6, organizational culture has the potential to enhance organizational performance, individual satisfaction, the sense of certainty (e.g., uncertainty reduction) about how problems are to be handled, and so on.[91] If the organizational culture gets out of step with the changing expectations of external stakeholders, it can hinder effectiveness, as illustrated in the Insight on Tandem Computers.[92]

Discussion Question 6
Should top management explicitly try to shape and change the culture of an organization? Why or why not?

The need to determine which attributes of an organization's culture should be preserved and which should be modified is constant.[93] In Chapter 21 we present the change process and describe approaches for making organizations more innovative and creative. Therefore we note here only a few of the things that managers and teams can do to maintain or change an organization's culture: set assumptions, state and reinforce desired values, and socialize through example.[94]

Do not underestimate the power of shared assumptions, norms, and socialization. Top management cannot delegate responsibility for creating and transmitting organizational culture. The strongest influences on culture formation often are top management's day-to-day assumptions and values, as perceived throughout the organization.

Managers and teams should be aware that they can influence the way employees think, feel, and act within the organization.[95] In the United States and Canada, with their macroculture value of individualism, socialization in firms such as Mary Kay Cosmetics, Johnson & Johnson, and Tandem Computers attempt to blend individuality with team and organizational processes. Organizations operating on the basis of TQM assumptions and values attempt to create a sense of unity without uniformity or blind conformity. Increasingly, organizations are encouraging entrepreneurship at lower organizational levels. They do so by creating strategic business units (SBUs), self-managing teams, cross-functional teams, product development teams, and the like. These units and teams may be empowered to undertake entrepreneurial initiatives.

A subtle bias of our presentation has been to emphasize the positive aspects of a strong organizational culture. However, we did note how a culture could become a misfit in dealing with its changing competitive environment. In addition, a strong organizational culture could have informal negative norms and practices such as "only white, Anglo-Saxon Protestants (WASPs) are promoted beyond the second-level of management." Moreover, strong cultures sometimes block recognition of the necessity for change, such as the need to actively recruit, develop, and promote women and minorities on their merits.[96]

CHAPTER SUMMARY

1 ***Describe the basic types of groups, their importance, and development stages.***

If designed and developed appropriately, teams may serve many important purposes, such as providing a forum for making decisions, sharing information, gaining acceptance and understanding of issues and decisions, building trust, and improving quality and efficiency. There are two basic types of groups in organizations:

formal and informal. An informal group is two or more individuals who meet more or less continually to engage in some activity or achieve some goal. Formal groups have specific goals and tasks that relate to broader organizational goals. During the early stages of group development, members usually are rather tentative and much sorting out occurs. In effective teams, bonds of trust and acceptance then develop. Members gain a clear sense of needed task and relationship behaviors. An effective team focuses on its goals, the tasks required to achieve those goals, and the processes that allow each member to participate fully and makes decisions by consensus whenever possible.

2 ***Explain the use of the model of group process to describe and diagnose informal and formal groups.***

The model of group process includes two basic parts: the internal system and the external system. The internal system includes the activities, interactions, sentiments, and norms that the group or team members develop over a period of time. These factors are interrelated and eventually determine the group's social structure and effects. The group or team process may include such effects as levels of quality, productivity, and member satisfaction. The external system affects the internal system. The variables in the external system that most often have some influence on shaping the internal system include the broader, societal and organizational cultures, type of technology, diversity of members, and the formal organization design.

3 ***Discuss the key issues—empowerment, types of teams, decision making, and leadership—in the establishment and use of teams.***

Empowerment is the process of delegating authority, responsibility, and discretion to teams to enable them to set goals, carry out tasks, be accountable for results. Increasingly, organizations are using many types of teams. The most common ones are functional teams, problem-solving teams, cross-functional teams, quality improvement teams, product development teams, and self-managing teams. The potential positive results of team decision making include greater knowledge, a diversity of approaches, increased acceptance, and better understanding than may be attainable from individual decision making. If teams have poor processes, the negative results may include blind conformity (possibly groupthink), domination by an individual, goal displacement, and wasted time. Teams usually are most appropriate when task interdependence exists among the members. For full participation by members, team size must be kept relatively small. Team leaders should be skilled in managing the process for dealing with disagreements, time, and change.

4 ***Describe the core elements of organizational cultures and the basic types of cultures.***

Organizational culture is the organizationwide personality—the way of thinking and doing things—of its members. Organizational culture is created and transmitted in many different ways, including shared assumptions, values, socialization, and norms. Ways of sustaining and reinforcing the organizational culture include shared symbols, language, narratives, and practices. Many organizations, even those with a strong organizationwide culture, have subcultures. Although all organizational cultures are unique in some way (just as each person is unique), some general types of cultures can be identified. The four pure types discussed are bureaucratic cultures, clan cultures, entrepreneurial cultures, and market cultures. These types are characterized by differences in formal control orientation—ranging from stable to flexible—and focus of attention—ranging from internal to external. Consistent with this framework, an organization could represent many blends of these pure types, either as a whole or through its subcultures. Strong cultures may work for or against organization performance, depending on their fit with demands of external stakeholders and the competitive environment.

QUESTIONS FOR DISCUSSION

1. What are the stages of group development? Which stage is most crucial?
2. Gail Stevens described her workplace as ". . . friendly, just great. All the people get along together, and we bowl and play softball after work." However, quality and production records show Gail's team to be one of least productive in the plant. Why might this be?
3. What are the primary differences between functional teams and cross-functional teams?
4. What are the main differences been problem-solving teams and self-managing teams?
5. What are the similarities between group characteristics and organizational cultures?
6. Should top management explicitly try to shape and change the culture of an organization? Why or why not?

FROM WHERE YOU SIT

1. List all the groups and teams of which you are currently a member and classify them by type.
2. Select one team to which you have belonged. Based on your personal experience, identify its desirable or undesirable effects on both task and relationship behaviors. Use the model of group process in Figure 16.2 to develop your response.
3. How well did your last superior help you meet the emotional problems often experienced when someone enters a new group? What steps did she or he take or fail to take to reduce those problems?
4. Based on the values presented in Table 16.2, identify the seven value statements that are most characteristic of the culture of an organization in which you have been involved. Do these values work for or against achieving the goals of the organization?
5. Based on the values presented in Table 16.2, identify the seven value statements that you think are most desirable for an ideal organization. Why did you choose them?
6. Use Table 16.1 to describe the profile of another organization with which you have been involved. Mark the continua of assumptions and values to reveal the extent to which it was a TQM or traditional organization.
7. Would you like to work in an organization that has a strong organizational culture? Why or why not?

SKILL-BUILDING EXERCISE

Assessing Team Development

INTRODUCTION: As a team begins its life and at several points during its growth and development, the leader and members might individually answer to the following questions and then spend some time sharing the responses. The answers to these questions indicate the perceptions that members have about the team and how it is developing. The answers also may reveal some difficulties that are blocking progress.

INSTRUCTIONS: Think of a team in which you have been or are now a member. Circle the number below each question that you perceive to be most descriptive of that team.

1. How clear are the goals?

2	4	6	8	10
No apparent goals	Goal confusion, uncertainty, or conflict	Average goal clarity	Goals mostly clear	Goals very clear

2. How much trust and openness are present in the team?

2	4	6	8	10
Distrust, a closed team	Little trust, defensiveness	Average trust and openness	Considerable trust and openness	Remarkable trust and openness

3. How sensitive and perceptive are team members?

2	4	6	8	10
No awareness or listening in the team	Most members self-absorbed	Average sensitivity and listening	Better than usual listening	Outstanding sensitivity to others

4. How much attention is paid to process? (The way the team is working?)

2	4	6	8	10
No attention to process	Little attention to process	Some concern with team process	A fair balance between content and process	Very concerned with process

5. How are team leadership needs met?

2	4	6	8	10
Not met, drifting	Leadership concentrated in one person	Some leadership sharing	Leadership functions distributed	Leadership needs met creatively and flexibly

6 How are team decisions made?

2	4	6	8	10
No decisions could be reached	Made by a few	Majority vote	Attempts at integrating minority vote	Full participation and mostly by consensus

7. How well are team resources used?

2	4	6	8	10
One or two contributed, but most silent	Several tried to contribute, but were discouraged	Average use of team resources	Team resources well used and encouraged	Team resources fully and effectively used

8. How much loyalty and sense of belonging to the team exist?

2	4	6	8	10
Members have no team loyalty or sense of belonging	Members not close, some friendly relations	About average sense of belonging	Some warm sense of belonging	Strong sense of belonging among members

9. How much discretion (empowerment) is provided to the team for determining the methods, procedures, and schedules used to accomplish its goals?

2	4	6	8	10
No discretion	Some discretion	Balance between team and higher management	Substantial discretion	Total discretion

10. How important is the work performed by the team in terms of serving customers' needs, either internal (other units) or external to the organization?

2	4	6	8	10
No importance	Some importance	Average importance	Significant importance	Great importance

INTERPRETATION: Add the points for all 10 questions to arrive at a team development score. Scores of 20 to 60 or so suggest that you perceive your team to be very ineffective to marginally effective. Scores of 70 to 80 suggest an average to good team, but one that is a little short of reaching its full potential. Scores of 90 to 100 suggest that you perceive this team to be remarkable and are very enthusiastic about its effectiveness.

CRITICAL THINKING CASE

Consolidated Life[97]

(This case is based on an actual situation. The names of the insurance company and individuals have been changed to protect their identities.)

Part I

It all started so positively. Three days after graduating with his degree in business administration, Mike Wilson started work in the policy issue department of a prestigious insurance company, Consolidated Life. The work of the department was mostly clerical and did not require a high degree of technical knowledge.

Rick Belkner was the division's vice-president, "the man in charge" at the time. Belkner was an actuary by training, a technical professional whose leadership style was laissez-faire. He was described in the division as "the mirror of whomever was the strongest personality around him." Also common knowledge was that Belkner made $90,000 a year and spent a lot of time doing crossword puzzles.

Mike Wilson was hired as a management trainee and promised a supervisory assignment within a year. However, a management reorganization placed him in charge of an eight-person unit only six weeks later. The reorganization was intended to streamline workflow, upgrade and combine clerical jobs, and make greater use of the computer system. Many of the clerical staff felt threatened.

Management realized that a flexible supervisory style was necessary to pull off the reorganization without considerable turnover. Thus they gave supervisors a free hand to run their units as they saw fit. Wilson used this freedom to implement team meetings and training classes in his unit. By promising raises, working long hours, participating in mundane tasks, and using a flexible management style, he increased productivity, reduced errors, and minimized lost time. The dramatic improvement of his unit earned Wilson the reputation of a "superstar," despite being viewed by upper management as unorthodox. The top managers tolerated his loose, people-oriented management style because of the excellent results.

A Chance for Advancement. After a year Wilson received an offer from a different division of Consolidated Life to manage a marketing office. The pay was excellent, and it offered an opportunity to turn around an office in disarray. The reorganization in his present division was almost complete, and most of his friends in management had moved on to other jobs. He decided to accept the offer. During the exit interview, he was assured of a position if he ever wanted to return.

The new job was satisfying for a short time, but Wilson soon realized that it didn't have the long-term potential he had been promised. After bringing in a new staff, computerizing the office, and auditing the books, he began looking for a position that would both challenge him and give him the autonomy he wanted.

Eventually, word got back to his former vice-president, Rick Belkner, that Wilson was looking for another job. Belkner offered Wilson a position at the same pay he was now receiving to supervise a fourteen-person unit in the division where he started. After considering other options, Wilson decided to return to his old division, believing that he would be able to progress steadily over the next several years.

Enter Jack Greely. Upon joining the policy issue department, Wilson become aware of several changes that had been made during the six months he had been away. The most important change was the hiring of a new divisional senior vice-president, Jack Greely, who had been given total authority to run the division. Greely's reputation was "tough but fair." It was necessary for people in the division to do things Greely's way and "get the work out." Belkner now reported to Greely.

Wilson found himself reporting to one of his former peers, Kathy Miller. She had been promoted to manager during the reorganization. Wilson had always "hit it off" with Miller and foresaw no problems in working with her.

After a week, Wilson realized the full extent of the changes. The loose casual atmosphere that had marked his first tour in the division was gone. Now management was stricter and task-oriented. Morale of the supervisory staff had declined alarmingly. As a result, the quality of work being done was poor. Jack Greely was the major topic of conversation in the division. People joked that MBO (management by objectives) now meant "management by oppression."

Wilson's Idea: A Supervisor's Forum. Wilson felt that a change in management style was necessary in order to improve a frustrating situation. He requested permission to form a supervisors' forum for all the managers at his level in the division. He explained to Belkner that the goal was to enhance the existing management-training program. The forum would include weekly meetings, guest speakers, and discussion of topics relevant to the division and the industry. Wilson thought that the forum would show Greely that he was serious about both his job and improving morale in the division. Belkner okayed the initial meeting of the forum.

At the first meeting, ten of Mike's peers in the company eagerly took the opportunity to "brainstorm" needed changes. The group drafted a memo to Belkner (with a copy to Greely). They outlined proposals for further training opportunities and exchanges of information among departments. The group members felt that the memo accurately and diplomatically stated their dissatisfaction with the current situation. Nonetheless, they pondered the likely results of their actions and what else they could have done.

Part II

Belkner called an emergency management meeting at Greely's request to address the "union" being formed by the supervisors. Four general managers, Belkner, and Greely attended the emergency meeting. One of them suggested that the forum be disbanded to "put them in their place." However, Belkner felt that if "guided" in the proper direction, the forum would die from lack of interest. Belkner's proposal was adopted, but everyone knew that Greely was strongly opposed to the forum and wanted its organizers dealt with. Wilson clearly was a marked man.

Wilson had always been a friendly and open supervisor. One of the main reasons for the effectiveness of his units was the attention Wilson paid to each individual and how they interacted with the group. He had a reputation for fairness, was seen as an excellent judge of personnel for new positions, and was noted for his ability to turn around employees who had been troublemakers. He motivated people through a dynamic, personable style and was known for his general lack of regard for the rules. Wilson treated rules as obstacles to management and usually used his own judgment in deciding what was important. His office had a sign reading, "Any fool can manage by the rules. It takes an uncommon man to manage without any." His approach flew in the face of company policy, but it had been overlooked in the past because of his results. Wilson's actions with the supervisors' forum resulted in his being regarded as a thorn in top management's side. He no longer was viewed as a superstar, and his oddball style only made things worse. Now, faced with rumors that he was on the way out, Wilson sat down to appraise the situation.

Part III

Wilson decided on the following course of action.

1. Keep the forum alive but moderate its tone so that it doesn't step on Greely's toes.
2. Don't panic. Simply outwork and outsmart the rest of the division by retraining and remotivating personnel.
3. Obtain praise from vendors and customers through excellent service and direct that praise to Greely.

Impressive Results. The results after eight months were impressive. Wilson's unit improved processing speed by 60 percent and lowered errors by 75 percent. His staff became the most highly trained in the division. He had copies of several letters sent to Greely by others that praised the unit's excellent service. In addition, the supervisors' forum had attained grudging credibility, although its scope of activity was restricted. Wilson had even begun submitting reports on time as a concession to higher management.

Wilson was confident that the results would speak for themselves. One month before his scheduled promotion and one month after receiving a merit raise in recognition of his exceptional work record, Miller called him into her office. She informed him that after long and careful consideration the decision had been made to deny him his promotion because of his lack of attention to detail. Wilson was stunned and said so. But before Wilson said anything else, he asked to see Belkner and Greely the next day.

The Showdown. Sitting face to face with Belkner and Greely, Wilson asked whether they agreed with Miller's appraisal. They both said they did. When asked if any other supervisor surpassed his ability and results, each stated that he was one of the best, if not the best they had. Then why, Wilson asked, would they deny him a promotion when others of less ability were approved. The answer came from Greely: "We just don't like you. We don't like your management style. You're an oddball. We can't run a division with ten supervisors all doing different things. We need people who conform to our style and methods so we can measure their results objectively. There's no room for subjective interpretation. It's our feeling that if you really put your mind to it, you can be an excellent manager. It's just that now you create trouble and rock the boat. We don't need that. It doesn't matter if you're the best now, sooner or later as you go up the ladder, you will be forced to pay more attention to administrative duties, and you won't handle them well. If we correct your bad habits now, we think you can go far."

Wilson was shocked. He turned to Belkner and demanded, "You mean it doesn't matter what my results are? All that matters is how I do things?" Belkner leaned back in his chair and said in a casual tone, "In so many words, yes."

Wilson left the office knowing that his career at Consolidated was over and immediately started looking for a new job.

Questions

1. Based on the model of group process (see Figure 16.2), how would you explain what happened with the supervisor's forum? (The supervisors' forum should be considered as the internal system.)
2. Did task type, team size, and leader role play a particularly important role in the supervisors' forum? Explain.
3. Does Consolidated Life appear to have a strong organizational culture? Explain your response by referring to the ways that organizational cultures are created and transmitted.
4. How would you characterize the values at Consolidated Life? Was there agreement or disagreement over one or more of these values? Explain. Use Tables 16.1 and 16.2 to guide your analysis.

VIDEO CASE

The People Behind the Products[98]

The evidence suggests that effective motivation of team members requires that they be given both the responsibility and the autonomy to make substantive decisions about team goals and tasks. The substantial reduction of traditional top-down forms of organizational control and the empowerment of teams are two important elements in creating *responsible autonomy* for teams. These and other such improvements in managerial styles and techniques are important steps in creating employee confidence, courage, and commitment.

Certain desirable values and shared norms will evolve to support responsible autonomy as an integral part of an organization's culture. Many decisions and actions will flow from the responsible autonomy value. For example, employees will develop skills in setting goals, performing new tasks, monitoring their own progress, and taking corrective actions, if necessary. Gaining the trust and commitment of top management to employees leads to organizational payoffs. Conversely, management's commitment fosters an increased employee commitment to the organization that goes beyond the stated mission and parameters of their jobs.

Let's consider the unique norms and values of different organizational cultures in three companies: Harbor Sweets, A.T. Cross Company, and Tom's of Maine.

Harbor Sweets

Harbor Sweets is a $3 million a year company, located in Salem, Massachusetts. It produces and markets a selection of high-quality, high-priced candies. The company founder and president, Benneville Strohecker, emphasizes having fun, trusts the ability and honesty of his employees, and encourages taking risks even if that means making mistakes. He jokingly says that his motto is: "If it's not fun, you are fired."

Strohecker considers the time clock in the red brick building where his company makes fifty tons of chocolates each year an odd testament to the trust between his employees and himself. He never wanted a time clock, and for years proudly touted the fact that there was no clock to punch. Instead, employees filled out their own timecards, and he paid them for whatever time they said they worked. He believed that doing so helped build that intangible foundation of trust that he considers to be as essential to his business as butter and brown sugar.

But about three years ago, his employees requested a time clock. "They said, 'It's a pain in the neck filling out these timecards. We know you trust us; let's be practical and just give us a clock,' " Strohecker recounts. In an age when psychological screenings for new employees are commonplace and workers are frequently subjected to drug testing, Strohecker's approach clearly is different.

Stohecker credits his employees with much of his success in bringing the company from a fledgling operation in the basement of his Marblehead, Massachusetts, home—when he sold his first box of candy to his mother for $2.95 in 1973—to a 19,000-square-foot waterfront space in Salem. "There would be no Harbor Sweets without trust," said Strohecker. "But I believe it's not just being nice. Relying on trust is good business."

Workers, for example, are encouraged to work in almost any position of their choosing. On a recent morning, Kathryn Carbone of Salem was wearing a red Harbor Sweets apron and operating a machine that wraps Marblehead Mints, but in the thirteen years she's worked with Strohecker, she's done nearly every job in production, from cooking to packing.

Strohecker doesn't view meeting the needs of his employees and meeting the requirements of running a healthy business as being mutually exclusive. Instead, he views them as being inexorably linked. And Strohecker said that, although the starting salary for employees is only $5 an hour, he always has a waiting list of prospective employees. He believes that money is not the only compensation employees seek; they also want a chance to be valued for their input.

A.T. Cross Company

The A.T. Cross Company is a major international manufacturer of fine writing instruments. The company also markets quality leather and gift products. Cross writing instruments are sold to the consumer gift market through fine stores worldwide and to the business gift market through a network of companies specializing in recognition and awards programs. Established in 1846, A.T. Cross Pens is America's oldest manufacturer of fine writing instruments and has become the leading manufacturer of high-quality pen and desk sets. When A.T. Cross was first established, the firm produced elegantly tooled gold and silver casings for wooden pencils. Today at its facility in Providence, Rhode Island, it is a major international manufacturer of fine writing instruments and the distributor of quality Fendi brand products.

The company attempts to prevent mistakes through its democratic work environment and total quality management (TQM) practices. For example, employees involved in assembling Cross's largely made-by-hand pens can reject any part that doesn't meet quality standards. Employees take a great deal of pride in their work because management trusts them to decide whether the pens meet the standards. Every employee is focused on continuous improvement and cost control. To bring new products to market faster while lowering costs, A.T. Cross has spent nearly two years reconfiguring its manufacturing facilities. In addition, the company has implemented an entirely new management information system that gives managers the ability to access and analyze the data necessary to make timely decisions.

Even with all the changes being made throughout the company, one thing remains the same: the strength of the Cross name. A.T. Cross products are trusted because consumers know them to be both reliable and beautifully made. The company is committed to total quality, customer satisfaction, and continuous improvement. Maintaining total quality will continue to be the focus at A.T. Cross as it expands its product line to meet the needs of consumers worldwide.

Tom's of Maine

Based in Kennebunk, Tom's of Maine markets personal care products, including natural toothpaste, deodorants, and shampoos. The firm markets "goodness," with a back-to-nature philosophy. This philosophy, which is the foundation of the company, is based on health and environmental concerns. The company goes further than most to instill in its employees the value that it will base decisions only on being a socially responsible citizen. For example, it pays regular wages to employees who spend part of their working time as volunteers in charitable efforts. Tom's sixty-five employees can spend as much as two hours a week or one day a month with pay working for causes of their choice. Tom's management believes that this program has the side benefit of enabling employees from different parts of the company to know and appreciate one another. One employee commented: "It's a morale booster, and better morale translates pretty directly into better productivity."

Tom Chappell, founder and president of Tom's of Maine, says this of his mission in the workplace:

> *To ensure that the Tom's of Maine mission continues to have life in the marketplace and in our community, we must be certain that it is lived here—in our offices, our factory, our warehouse. One employee summed it up very ably when he said, "Living the mission is a lot like living the Golden Rule, only the mission spells it out more." Like the Golden Rule, the mission helps us to be intentional about who we are, what we do, and how we do it. Certainly, living the mission has guided us through growth and change; and today, as we are poised for more new product launches, poised to build new relationships and strengthen existing ones, we feel energized and confident.*

The mission at Tom's of Maine is to acknowledge the value of each person's contribution to company goals and to foster teamwork in tasks. It comes to life in the New Products Development Team. The interdepartmental makeup of this team helps ensure that, as new products are developed, concerns associated with their manufacture and marketing can be aired and solved. Team members come away from monthly meetings with a keen appreciation of the perspectives of and the problems faced by various departments as all work toward a single goal.

There are many benefits to the team approach to developing new products at Tom's of Maine. Team members benefit from being exposed to various opinions, perspectives, and skills—and they carry that experience back to their departments. The team also helps ease the way toward product launches, as it keeps the whole company involved in the process virtually from the outset. One other benefit is the excitement generated by working on new ideas. Excitement is contagious, and it has spread beyond the team's membership. One team member put it eloquently when she said, "I have learned a lot more about Tom's of Maine. . . . I am more aware, I feel, of the products we package, the need to be as good as I can. . . ." It would be difficult to find a statement that more clearly illustrates an employee's understanding of the importance of her relationship with and contributions to her company and its customers.[98]

Questions

1. Compare and contrast the organizational cultures of Harbor Sweets, Cross Pens, and Tom's of Maine.
2. What are the missions of these three companies?
3. How are teams part of the environment of Harbor Sweets, Cross Pens, and Tom's on Maine?

Chapter *17*

Conflict and Stress Management

Learning *Objectives*

After studying this chapter, you should be able to:

1. State the different types and views of conflict in organizations.
2. Define and explain four types of role conflict and role ambiguity.
3. Explain the main interpersonal conflict-management styles and the conditions under which each may be used effectively.
4. Describe the process of negotiation for reducing or resolving conflict.
5. Discuss the causes and effects of job-related stress and actions that can be taken to manage stress.

Chapter *Outline*

Preview *Insight*

Conflict at Sunbeam-Oster

Paul Kazarian was hired as CEO of the Sunbeam-Oster Company in 1990. Headquartered in Providence, Rhode Island, the company makes appliances such as blenders, irons, and coffee makers. In 1993, at the age of 37, Kazarian was fired by the Board of Directors even though sales and profits were up. What happened?

"When we took over this company in 1990, it was a disaster," Kazarian says. "Everyone who analyzed it wrote it off as a disaster. When I came in, one of the first things I wanted to do was train the employees and managers, because there was, like, no real training. People did not even have the ability to analyze basic business decisions. I wanted to empower them, to get them to work their butts off and turn the company around. And I did. And people looked at me and said, 'Hey, like, you saved thousands of jobs.' "

Others don't share Kazarian's view of himself. He reportedly created an environment of intimidation and fear. Employees and managers, many of whom were required to work seven days a week and carry beepers, frequently complained that the stress of working for Kazarian began to disrupt their home lives. "Paul is an incredibly bright, intense guy, but he never left people alone. He never let people just do their jobs," says an employee. "He interfered way too much, and kept creating more and more work for people when we were already working beyond capacity. He would just throw more and more stuff at you, and he did not care about the impact on you or your family life." Kazarian counters: "You've got to shake things up, make a few waves. I was saving this company from bankruptcy. No pain, no gain."

Sunbeam's employees resent the implication that they needed a kick in the pants. "We've got some excellent people here, some of the hardest-working, brightest people you'll meet in business," says one employee. "Everybody here was committed to making this a great company."

Another source adds, "Kazarian's a great self-promoter. He loves telling people he was trying to change Sunbeam's culture. Actually what he wanted to do was turn the company into a cult of his personality. There is no grip on reality there. The only culture change he effected was to breed an atmosphere of mistrust, and to pit people against each other." Kazarian rejects this interpretation.

Over a number of months, the directors held secret meetings with disgruntled executives and even hired an outside consultant to investigate employee complaints. Three of the directors met with Kazarian and asked him to resign. When he refused, they fired him.[1]

1

State the different types and views of conflict in organizations.

Teaching Tip
Students, especially younger ones, often have negative attitudes toward conflict owing to lack of life and work experience. Such attitudes often lead to dysfunctional conflict management styles. Have the class create through free association a list of thoughts and feelings about conflict. Write the list on the board.

Ask Students
How do you define the term *conflict*? Is conflict good or bad? Explain your reasoning.

INTRODUCTION TO CONFLICT

We begin by presenting the basic types of conflict and three basic attitudes toward conflict. We then focus on individual conflict and role ambiguity in terms of role expectations, role episodes, and types of role conflict. Next, we examine five different interpersonal conflict-management styles that individuals use. Then we discuss the negotiation process and how it aids in conflict reduction or resolution. Finally, we consider one possible outcome of intense conflict—stress—and how to manage it.

Types of Conflict

Conflict is opposition arising from disagreements about goals, thoughts, or emotions within or among individuals, teams, departments, or organizations.[2] This definition recognizes three basic types of conflict.

- **Goal conflict** arises when results or preferred outcomes are incompatible.
- **Cognitive conflict** occurs when ideas or thoughts are perceived to be incompatible.
- **Affective conflict** involves negative feelings or emotions, such as anger.

Ethics
Is conflict ethical?

Ask Students
Give a personal example of this type of conflict.

Ask Students
Give a personal example of this type of conflict.

Ask Students
Give a personal example of this type of conflict.

Discussion Question 2
Why will there always be some conflict between two or more individuals, two or more departments, and two or more organizations?

Discussion Question 3
What are the differences between cognitive conflict and affective conflict?

Ask Students
How do you manage conflict in your own life?

Ethics
Are these types of conflict ever ethical?

All three types of conflict appeared to be operating with great intensity at Sunbeam-Oster during Paul Kazarian's reign as CEO. With regard to *goal conflict,* he gave the impression that he alone was committed to achieving Sunbeam-Oster's goals and that the other managers and employees weren't. He claimed that others had to be constantly pressured to strive for the organization's profit, growth, and efficiency goals. The people working for him sharply disagreed and felt that Kazarian's excessive pressures conflicted with their family-related goals.

In terms of *cognitive conflict,* consider a few examples: (1) Kazarian thought that many employees and managers lacked basic skills—they disagreed; (2) Kazarian thought that he saved the company—others thought that it was a joint effort; and (3) Kazarian thought that he had to be tough to change the organizational culture and save it from bankruptcy: others thought that he was trying to turn it into a cult of his personality.

In terms of *affective conflict,* others commented: (1) "Nobody liked this guy"; (2) "Paul's a great self-promoter"; and (3) "The only culture change he effected was to breed an atmosphere of mistrust, and to pit people against each other."

Conflict management consists of interventions designed to reduce excessive conflict or, in some instances, to increase insufficient conflict. Individuals and organizations use various approaches to manage conflict. The approach used is likely to be influenced by a person's fundamental attitude toward conflict: negative, positive, or balanced.

Negative Attitude

To some people the word conflict suggests negative situations: war, destruction, aggression, violence, and hostility. The traditional view of management (see Chapter 2) typically viewed conflict as being undesirable. Accordingly, conflict should be reduced or eliminated through careful selection of people, training, detailed job descriptions, elaborate rules, and incentive systems. These prescriptions still apply to conflict reduction and prevention under certain conditions.

Conflict in organizations can be especially destructive when management encourages interdependent individuals or groups to compete. In such situations, personal or team success is achieved at the expense of other individuals or teams.[3] Employees involved in frequent, intense competition and its resulting conflict may experience high levels of stress—as at Sunbeam-Oster—and may respond by withdrawing. Their discomfort may be expressed psychologically (apathy and indifference) or physically (tardiness, absenteeism, and high turnover). In more extreme cases, they may react with aggressive and hostile behavior, such as stealing from the organization or damaging its property.

Intense conflict often leads to biased perceptions and gross distortions of reality. When that happens, people may make decisions and take actions that increase conflict rather than reduce or resolve it. This tendency may have been part of Paul Kazarian's undoing at Sunbeam-Oster. In the heat of such situations, people often concentrate so hard on making their own points that they ignore the others' needs and points of view. Winning becomes more important than coming up with a mutually beneficial solution. Negative emotions can then interfere with efforts to resolve the issues at the root of the conflict.

Employees at all levels also may dislike conflict because they feel that it interferes with their productivity and efficiency. In other words, some managers and other employees believe that conflict disrupts organizational routines and therefore is undesirable.

Positive Attitude

Ask Students
Is this your attitude? Give a recent example to support your answer.

One of the roles of managers and team leaders is to ensure perpetual constructive conflict. Employees and teams with this positive attitude may view conflict situations as exciting, intriguing, and challenging. Conflict can result in better choices and improved performance if it stimulates a search for the reasons behind different viewpoints and for effective ways to resolve them. A positive attitude may thus lead to creativity, innovation, and change because conflict can reveal where corrective actions are needed. Those who hold a positive attitude about conflict, then, view it as a necessary condition for achieving individual and organizational goals.[4]

The dialectical inquiry and the devil's advocacy methods (Chapter 6) are based on a positive view of conflict. They represent interventions designed to stimulate conflict or allow it to "surface" in a controlled manner. The dialectical inquiry method is a process for examining issues systematically from two or more opposing points of view. The devil's advocacy method involves creating a conflict by selecting a person to critique a preferred plan or strategy.

Ask Students
Is this your attitude? Give a recent example to support your answer.

Balanced Attitude

A balanced attitude toward conflict is relative rather than absolute. It views organizational conflict as inevitable and at times desirable—that many conflicts can be prevented but that some need to be nurtured and managed instead. Through proper management, the negative outcomes of conflict can be reduced, and its positive effects can be increased.[5] One of the ways to achieve these results is to reduce role conflicts and ambiguity.

Ask Students
Is this your attitude? Give a recent example to support your answer.

2 Define and explain four types of role conflict and role ambiguity.

ROLE CONFLICT AND AMBIGUITY

Individuals often experience role conflict or role ambiguity. **Role conflict** occurs when a person experiences strong and *inconsistent* pressures or expectations.[6] A **role** is a set of related tasks and behaviors that an individual is expected to carry out. Roles abound within organizations (superior, subordinate, peer) and outside of organizations (husband or wife, parent or child). The role of student involves tasks and activities such as reading books, attending classes, writing papers, taking tests, and participating in student activities.

A **role set** is the collection of roles that relate directly to an individual. A role set for a student typically includes instructors, friends, family, significant other, members of team projects, manager (if working), and key people in organizations that the student belongs to.

For some individuals, the tensions and anxieties created by **role ambiguity** may be as serious as those created by role conflict. In terms of job-related experiences, role ambiguity involves (1) inadequate information about the person's expected performance goals, (2) unclear or confusing information about expected on-the-job behaviors, and/or (3) uncertainty about the consequences (e.g., pay raise, promotion, or dismissal) of certain on-the-job behaviors.[7] As we demonstrate later in the chapter, role ambiguity is a common source of intense stress for some individuals.

The issue of employee privacy revolves around role ambiguity, conflict, and stress for many managers and employees. Some of these issues are portrayed in the following Ethics Insight.

Ask Students
What role conflicts do you have? Describe their effects.

Discussion Question 4
Why does conflict occur within individuals?

Ask Students
Name five roles that you play.

Teaching Tip
Divide the class into two groups, one representing management and the other a new employee of an organization. Ask each group to generate a list of role expectations for the opposite group, as well as for itself. Ask the students to compare their role expectations.

Ethics *Insight*

Personal Privacy and Employers

In the 1920s, Henry Ford sent "sociology inspectors" to his workers' homes. Since 1986, Ted Turner, the principal owner and CEO of CNN and other TV programs, has refused to hire anyone who smokes—on or off the job. In Beaumont, Texas, the Mobil Oil Company has been monitoring the drinking habits of its employees for thirty years. An extension of Mobil's policy in 1989 to include marital, financial, and other personal problems resulted in the firing of a well-respected employee who had voluntarily sought marriage counseling.

There is a growing concern that technology, rising health care costs, and new employer initiatives designed to make the workplace safer and more productive are converging in an invasion of employees' privacy. Technology allows organizations to get information on their employees never previously available. Computerized databases and sophisticated medical testing can determine drug use, predisposition to genetic diseases, and even participation in dangerous sports.

Employers began saying, "We need well-adjusted employees, we need employees who don't have drinking problems, don't have unhealthy habits, who will be long-lived and productive," says Alan Westin, a Columbia University law professor who has written several books on privacy issues. As a result, the tension and conflict between what employers think they have a right to know and what employees think they have a right to keep private has become a major workplace issue.

"I thought we lived in a free society," says Carmella Mares, who lost her job at Longmont Foods, a Colorado turkey-processing plant. Mares refused to disclose, as part of a drug test, what prescribed medicines she took, what illnesses she had had in the past, and what she had told her doctors. "I did not realize your own employer could say, 'I need this, I need that.' I mean, what right do they have to my medical records?" Some employers claim a right to information that helps them control costs and promote safety.[8]

Ask Students
Name three role sets that you have.

Discussion Question 5
What is role ambiguity? Why is it important to an understanding of conflict and personal stress in organizations?

Ethics
Are CNN's and Mobil Oil's actions ethical? Why or why not?

Ask Students
Have you ever had privacy problems with an employer? If so, describe them.

Ask Students
What are some role expectations that others have of you? How do you know?

Ethics
Role pressure can motivate employees to surpass expectations, but role pressure also can create work-related stress. Is it ethical for an organization continually to exert pressure when only a *minority* of employees are involved in a win-win situation?

Ask Students
What type of power is associated with one role expectation that someone has of you?

Role Expectations

Role expectations are the views held by others about what an individual should or should not do. When role expectations are cloudy, an individual may experience role ambiguity. Moreover, the members of a role set are influenced by their own actions and by those of the other members. They may be rewarded or punished on the basis of someone else's behavior. For example, others may have to perform a task before they can perform their own.[9] This situation often occurs when students work on a team project.

Role pressure is created when *role senders* exert demands on a *focal person* to meet their expectations. An instructor who tells students that they must have an average of seventy or higher to pass the course is an example of a role sender creating role pressure. The sender exerts pressure through one or more types of power (reward, expertise, referent, coercive, or legitimate).[10] The instructor has been assigned legitimate power by the college and is exercising reward power in promising to pass the students (which is assumed to be a valued reward) if they achieve a 70 percent average.

So far, we have identified the role sender and the focal person as different people. Actually, one person can—and often does—play both roles. A person's *inner voice* provides do's and don'ts for each of the person's roles. These internal role expectations may exert just as great or even greater pressure on the individual than external expectations.[11]

For example, your ideal student role might conflict with your actual student role. Let's assume that your ideal student role is that of studying to be an artist. However, because of parental pressure, your actual student role involves studying to be an accountant. Hence the conditions that foster role conflict and stress are present. When too large a gap exists between these role expectations, the resulting conflict can lead to severe stress.

Role-Episode Model

A **role episode** involves attempts by one or more role senders to influence the behavior of a focal person and the responses of the focal person, which in turn, influence the role sender's *future* expectations of the focal person. Figure 17.1 provides a role-episode model. A manager's expectations communicated to an employee often become pressures. Under certain circumstances, the employee may exhibit strong negative emotional responses (yelling at others), physical responses (rising blood pressure), and cognitive responses (refusing to comply).

FIGURE 17.1

Role-Episode Model

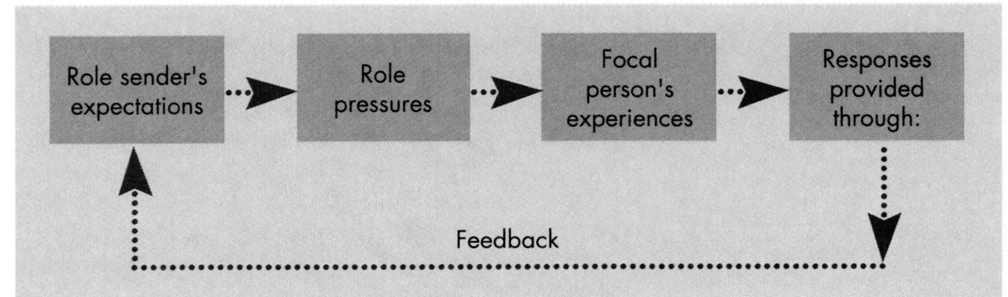

A person's *emotional response* is his or her feelings about role pressures—positively motivated, angry, frustrated, happy, or whatever. A person's *cognitive response* is his or her thoughts about those pressures. These feelings and thoughts influence the way an employee responds to a manager. The response provides feedback to the manager and influences the manager's future expectations of the employee. A manager may handle differently an employee who responds to pressure with hostility and an employee who responds with passive acceptance. If an employee responds to pressure by exhibiting signs of stress, the manager can react in several ways—ease up on the employee, reassign the employee, try to help the employee deal with the pressures, or even dismiss the employee under certain conditions.

Types of Role Conflict

As we stated previously, role conflict often occurs when a person experiences strong and inconsistent pressures or expectations. In other words, when the individual responds to one set of pressures, responding successfully to the other(s) becomes more difficult. The severity of the role conflict depends largely on the reward and coercive power exerted by the role sender and on both the focal person's personality and desire to cope with these pressures.[12] Two managers in an organization who pressure a single employee to complete different projects immediately may create severe role conflict for that person. Such conflicts often lead to stress for both the focal person and the role senders.

Let's now consider four basic types of role conflict: intrasender-role conflict, intersender-role conflict, interrole conflict, and person-role conflict.

Ask Students
Give an example of intrasender-role conflict.

Intrasender-Role Conflict. The receipt of mixed messages of do's and don'ts from a single role sender may create **intrasender-role conflict.** A manager might instruct an employee to complete a particular task today and then, a short time later, assign still another task to be completed the same day. If each task requires a full day to complete, intrasender conflict and stress result. Or an instructor might assign a paper to be completed and turned in during the same week in which that same instructor is giving a major exam.

Ask Students
Give an example of intersender-role conflict.

Intersender-Role Conflict. Pressures from one role sender that are incompatible with those from one or more other role senders may create **intersender-role conflict.** For example, managers and team members who must meet the expectations of multiple stakeholders with conflicting demands (e.g., shareholders, customers, peers, higher level managers, government agencies, and unions) often experience intersender role conflict and stress.[13] Intersender role conflict may be experienced by a conscientious employee who is part of a work team whose members have lower production norms than the output levels that management expects. Conflict occurs because the employee values friendly relations with fellow employees but also wants to be a high performer.

Interrole Conflict. When role pressures associated with membership in one group or organization conflict with those stemming from membership in others, the individual may experience **interrole conflict.** Pressure to work excessive overtime and on weekends may conflict with pressures from the person's spouse and children to devote more attention to the family. As indicated in the Preview Insight, most of the executives and managers at Sunbeam-Oster felt that the pressures from CEO Paul Kazarian were creating interrole conflicts for them. When this type of conflict becomes intense, individuals may experience severe stress and try to cope by withdrawing from one of the roles or eliminating the source of stress. At Sunbeam-Oster, the latter occurred when many of the executives and managers convinced the board of directors to fire Paul Kazarian.

Ask Students
Give an example of interrole conflict.

Interrole conflicts are common for both men and women who are parents and also want successful fast-track careers.[14] Interrole conflicts and stress can be especially severe for women who are attempting to blend their work, spousal, and parenting roles.[15] A recent study on U.S. working women shows that 300 hours of tasks have been added to their annual schedule since the late 1960s. Between their time at work and caring for the household, these women now have scheduled annual demands that are 140 hours above the national average for all U.S. adults.[16] We cover the need to rely on others and to learn how to manage these conflicts through constructive feedback in the section on stress management.

Person-Role Conflict. When differences arise between the pressures exerted by the focal person's role(s) and his or her needs, values, or abilities, **person-role conflict** occurs. Confronting stereotypes is an important source of person-role conflict. Stereotypes resist modification because they serve to (1) reduce internal conflicts and inner insecurities, (2) maintain basic values about an individual's role in society, and (3) provide a convenient way to maintain "inner" order and interpret others' behaviors.[17] Stereotypes serve these purposes by classifying individuals into groups according to simplistic criteria (gender, age, race, religion, national origin, occupation, or the like) and then assigning a common set of abilities, traits, and behaviors to everyone within that group.[18]

Another common source of person-role conflict occurs when employees must reconcile doing what they think is right and proper for current or prospective customers versus how their superior might pressure them to handle those customers. This problem is more common when managers or organizations adhere to traditional instead of total quality assumptions and values, such as striving to meet or exceed customers' expectations (refer back to Table 16.1). The following Quality Insight reveals the person-role conflict experienced by Herbert Schulte, a Prudential Insurance Company agent, when pressed by his manager to engage in questionable sales practices. These practices were at odds with (1) the assumptions and values of total quality management, and (2) the agent's personal values and activities, which created person-role conflict for him.

Ask Students
Give an example of person-role conflict.

Discussion Question 1
According to the Preview Insight, what types of role conflict did Paul Kazarian, former CEO at Sunbeam-Oster, experience?

Quality *Insight*

Herbert Schulte and Prudential

Herbert Schulte was a fifty-four-year-old agent at Prudential Insurance Company of America's tiny Lebanon, Illinois, office. He was facing dismissal for low sales in the summer of 1994 when a sales manager gave him a few tips.

The manager, the nineteen-year Prudential veteran says, printed out a list of Schulte's customers who were at least forty-five years old. He then handed Schulte sales material that repeatedly referred to a Prudential life insurance policy as nursing-home coverage. Instead of being pleased, Schulte took offense. The manager, he contends, was implicitly recommending that he "churn" the customers by pushing them to use the built-up cash value in an old policy to buy a new one—an arguably deceptively pitched new one. When he expressed those concerns, he says, the manager replied simply, "Trust me."

Schulte, who was dismissed in 1994, says that he was more concerned about his policyholders' trust in him: "I've built up a rapport with my clients. That's how it is in a small town. I'm not going to mislead them." At least one of his fears has been confirmed. Shown the sales material given to Schulte, a Prudential spokesperson termed it unauthorized and "a serious violation of company policy." Its distribution is under investigation, the spokesperson added, and so is Schulte's allegation that churning was encouraged. The sales manager declined to comment.

Many insurers have dispatched memos on acceptable sales practices, recalled promotional literature for inspection, ordered agents to take refresher compliance courses, revised training programs, beefed up audit procedures for field operations, randomly surveyed customers and contributed to an industry group running a nationwide consumer-education campaign.

Some insurers have gone even further: Prudential hired a law firm to review its sales practices. It also developed a process whereby a regional employee helps buyers complete applications by telephone. This system is designed partly to ensure that customers understand proposals for coverage made by the agents. Prudential has a special reason for eliminating such problems: Its Prudential Securities brokerage unit is expected to end up paying $1.2 billion in settlements and legal costs stemming from allegations that it sold limited partnerships improperly.[19]

There is no single cause of the role conflicts and ambiguities experienced by individuals. The personalities and the types of interpersonal relationships between a role sender and focal person enormously influence the intensity of conflicts and responses to them. Many different conflict-management styles are used by individuals in attempting to cope with conflict. Some of them actually may make a situation worse.

3

Explain the main interpersonal conflict-management styles and the conditions under which each may be used effectively.

Teaching Tip

Select a situation from the newspaper in which conflict management is required. Use it as an example in teaching this section.

CONFLICT-MANAGEMENT STYLES

Interpersonal conflict is broadly defined as (1) disagreements or incompatible interests over goals, policies, rules, and decisions and (2) incompatible behaviors that create anger, distrust, fear, rejection, or resentment. Everyone copes with interpersonal conflict through one or a combination of five interpersonal conflict-management styles: avoidance, smoothing, forcing, compromise, and collaboration.[20]

Figure 17.2 provides a useful model for understanding and contrasting these five conflict-management styles. The vertical axis indicates the degree to which a person focuses on her or his own view of the conflict. The horizontal axis indicates the degree to which the person focuses on the other's view of the conflict. The five interpersonal conflict-management styles represent the different combinations of attention that the person may give to self and others in a conflict situation.[21]

Avoidance Style

The **avoidance style** involves withdrawing from conflict situations or remaining neutral. The individual declines to confront the conflict. Employees who are unavailable for conferences, delay answering "problem" memos, or refuse to get involved in conflicts are using an avoidance style. Avoidance-prone individuals may act simply as a communication link, relaying messages between superiors, peers, or subordinates. When asked to take a position on controversial issues, these employees might say, "I haven't had time to study the problem fully," "I need more facts before making a judgment," or "Perhaps the best way is to proceed as you think best." When unresolved conflicts affect the achievement of goals, the avoidance style leads to negative results for the organization.[22]

FIGURE 17.2

Model of Interpersonal Conflict-Management Styles

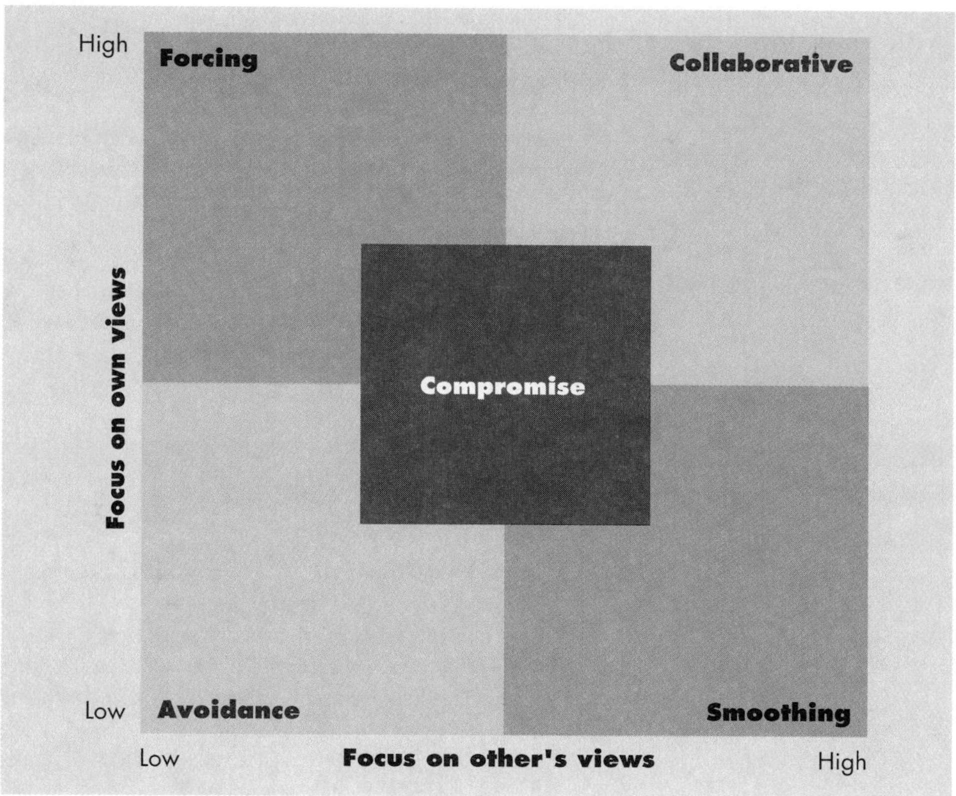

Source: Adapted from Nicotera, A.M. Beyond two dimensions: A grounded theory model of conflict-handling behavior. *Management Communication Quarterly*, 1993, 6, 282–306; Thomas, K.W. Conflict and negotiation processes in organizations. In M.D. Dunnette and L.M. Hough (eds.), *Handbook of Industrial and Organizational Psychology*, 2nd ed., vol. 3. Palo Alto, Calif.: Consulting Psychologists Press, 1992, 651–717.

Under certain circumstances, the avoidance style is desirable. For example, it is appropriate when

Ask Students
Have you used avoidance recently? Was it the appropriate conflict management style for the situation? Why or why not?

Ethics
Is avoidance ethical?

- the issue is minor or of only passing importance and thus not worth the person's time or energy to confront the conflict;
- there isn't enough information for the individual to deal with the conflict effectively at that time;
- the individual has so little power compared to the other person's that there is little chance of bringing about change; and
- others can resolve the conflict more effectively.

Smoothing Style

Discussion Question 6
When is the smoothing style likely to be more effective than the forcing style of conflict management?

The **smoothing style** represents minimizing or suppressing real or perceived differences while focusing on the other's views of the situation. The smoothing-prone person might reason, "If it makes others happy, I won't challenge their views" or "I don't want to hurt the feelings of others when discussing problems" or "We shouldn't risk our friendship, so let's not worry too much about the problem; things will work out." Individuals who use the smoothing style act as though the conflict will go away in time. They appeal for cooperation and try to reduce tensions and stress by offering reassurance and support for the other's views. This style shows concern about the emotional aspects of a conflict but does little to address the root causes of the conflict. The smoothing style simply encourages individuals to cover up or gloss over their feelings. Therefore it generally is ineffective when used as a dominant style.

Ask Students
Have you used smoothing recently? Was it the appropriate conflict management style for the situation? Why or why not?

Ask Students
Do you use a smoothing style whereby you minimize or suppress real or perceived differences? How do you respond to conflict?

However, the smoothing style may be effective when

- individuals are locked in a potentially explosive emotional conflict and smoothing is used to defuse the situation;
- keeping harmony and avoiding disruption are especially important in the short run; and
- the conflict is based primarily on the personalities of the individuals and cannot be easily resolved.[23]

The following Diversity Insight is based on a study of racial dynamics in close mentor-protégé, relationships. It addresses the following sensitive question: Are mentors and protégés more effective when they confront their differences openly or when they avoid and/or smooth them over?

Diversity *Insight*

Race in Developmental Relationships

The researcher interviewed junior and senior parties in twenty-two cross-racial developmental relationships. The sample contained men and women in both mentor and protégé roles. In some cases, the senior member of the pair was African-American; in most cases, the senior member was white.

Participants used one of two distinct strategies to manage cross-racial differences. The most common strategy, practiced in fourteen relationships, was called "denial and suppression." Here race either was not discussed at all or was discussed only in the most superficial way. In contrast, the strategy used by the other eight pairs was "direct engagement" of racial differences. Race was openly discussed and the cross-racial dynamics were viewed as a strength of the relationship. Pairs who chose to deal with racial dynamics openly were closer in age than pairs who preferred to deny or suppress their differences.

The key to success in managing racial dynamics in developmental relationships appears to be complementary. When both pair members had similar strategy preferences, regardless of whether it was direct engagement or denial and suppression, a mentor-protégé bond was likely to develop. Both career-oriented and psychological supportive activities were evident in pairs with complementary strategy preferences. In pairs with noncomplementary strategy preferences, there was no active mentor relationship other than sponsorship. Thus it was the complementary racial perspective rather than choice of a particular strategy that led to the full mentor-protégé bond. Relationships that were not complementary were more distant and less emotionally fulfilling.[24]

Forcing Style

Ask Students
Have you used forcing recently? Was it the appropriate conflict management style for the situation? Why or why not?

The **forcing style** involves the use of coercive and other forms of power to dominate another person or group and pressure others to accept one's own views of the situation. The forcing style produces outcomes that are satisfactory to only one of the parties. Forcing-prone managers may use phrases such as "If you don't like the way things are run, get out" and "If you can't learn to cooperate, I'm sure others can be hired who will." When someone disagrees with them, they often retaliate to ensure that their views prevail. Paul Kazarian used this style at the Sunbeam-Oster Company.

Forcing-prone individuals assume that conflicts involve win-lose situations.[25] One party can win only if the other party loses. When dealing with conflicts between subordinates or departments, forcing managers may threaten or actually use demotion, dismissal, negative performance evaluations, and other punishments in order to win. When conflicts occur between peers, an employee who exhibits the forcing style might try to get his or her way by appealing to a superior. This ploy attempts to use the superior to

Ask Students
Do you often use a forcing style to dominate another person and require the other person to agree with your position? In what management situation is this style effective?

Ethics
Is forcing ethical?

force one's own views on the opposing individuals. Especially for those subjected to it, the forcing style is likely to be associated with high levels of personal stress. This was clearly the experience of many managers and employees at Sunbeam-Oster when Paul Kazarian was CEO. Overreliance on forcing saps the motivation of others because their views are not considered. Relevant information and other possible alternatives usually are ignored.

Organizational situations in which the forcing style may be necessary include

- emergencies that require quick action;
- unpopular courses of action (e.g., cost cutting and the dismissal of employees for unsatisfactory performance) that must be taken in the name of long-term organizational effectiveness and survival; and
- taking action for self-protection and to stop others from taking advantage of the situation.[26]

Compromise Style

The **compromise style** involves the willingness of all parties to concede some of their own views and focus on some of the others' views to reach an agreement. The attitude of compromise-prone individuals might be expressed as "I let other people win something if they let me win something" or "I try to hit on a fair combination of gains and losses for both of us" or "I try to find a position between theirs and mine." Compromise is shown in the middle of Figure 17.2. It achieves a rough balance between differing views.

When it is used too early in conflict situations, the compromise style may create several problems. First, if too little effort is spent on diagnosing the issues, compromise is made on the stated rather than on the real issues. Second, accepting compromise on the initial positions presented may be easier than searching for alternatives that are more acceptable to all of the parties. Finally, compromise may be inappropriate to all or part of the situation. There may be a better way of resolving the conflict, such as through the collaborative style or mediation by a third party.[27]

Ask Students
Have you used compromising recently? Was it the appropriate conflict management style for the situation? Why or why not?

Ask Students
Do you use a compromise style whereby you tend to sacrifice some of your personal interests by making concessions to reach an agreement? Identify a situation in which you have actually used a compromise style.

Many people view the willingness to compromise by accepting other views as a positive form of cooperation.[28] The compromise is likely to be appropriate when

- agreement enables each party to be better off, or at least not worse off, than if no agreement is reached;
- achieving a total win-win agreement isn't possible because the parties can't agree to all of the views of the other parties; and
- conflicting views (including opposing goals and interests) block agreement.

Family businesses often are plagued by intense rivalries and conflicts among the family members who work in the firm.[29] As suggested in the following Small Business Insight, a willingness to compromise and collaborate is essential if the family business is to endure from generation to generation.

Small Business *Insight*

Family Succession at Choctaw Enterprise

Choctaw Enterprise is an industrial supply firm that was established by Gordon Gamble in Houston, Texas, in 1978. The transition from father to son and daughter happened gradually over a number of years, says Bret Gamble, the son. Bret took over as president of the firm in 1994. Bret's sister, Zoe Gamble-Jones, whom Bret considers his partner, serves as vice-president.

Bret was the company's first truck driver, and Zoe was the second. Over the years, they assumed more duties, met with key suppliers, and learned all aspects of the business. "It's not as rosy as it sounds. There were times when we had 'enlightened' discussions with each other, to put it mildly," Bret (age 37) says of talks with his father (age 71).

When the elder Gamble said he was going to retire, Bret and Zoe (age 35) went to the back of the warehouse and divvied up duties and responsibilities. There was no sibling fighting. "Zoe and I have been very close since we were kids. She put it good once: 'We can almost talk to each other in shorthand.' It's not a power thing," Bret says. "We got all that stuff out when we were kids."[30]

Collaborative Style

The **collaborative style** requires a willingness to identify the underlying causes of conflict, share information openly, and focus on both one's own and others' concerns by searching for mutually beneficial solutions. Collaboration-prone individuals might describe their approach by saying, "I try to deal with all concerns—theirs and mine" or "I try to get all viewpoints and issues out in the open" or "If we don't agree at first, we should spend some time thinking about why and then look for the best alternative that we can agree on." With the collaborative style, conflicts are recognized openly and evaluated by all concerned. Sharing, examining, and assessing the reasons for the conflict should lead to effective resolution of the conflict and acceptance of the solution by all parties.[31]

The guidelines for effective communication presented in Chapter 15 are essential for practicing the collaborative style. (See especially Tables 15.1 and 15.5.) All such guidelines are easy to state but difficult to use spontaneously and naturally. Effective collaboration requires more than opening up to others; it also demands opening up to oneself and gaining self-insight.[32]

Barriers to Use. If collaboration is so effective, you might ask, why isn't it used more frequently? The reason is that certain barriers to using the collaborative style may exist in a situation.

- Time limitations often constrain the direct sharing of feelings about issues involved in a conflict.
- Group norms may support the view that employees should not express negative feelings toward others.
- Traditional and out-of-date role expectations include the assumption that managers should command and firmly control subordinates. This top-down organizational norm sometimes makes use of the collaborative approach difficult for managers, even when it is their preferred style.

Ask Students
Have you used collaborating recently? Was it the appropriate conflict management style for the situation? Why or why not?

Ask Students
Do you use a collaborative style whereby you are willing to identify underlying causes of conflict, share information openly, and search for mutually beneficial solutions? Can a group actually adopt a collaborative style in which everyone is recognized openly and evaluated by everyone concerned? Why or why not?

The type of organizational culture (see Chapter 16) and the manager's leadership style (see Chapter 14) influence the use of collaboration. Supportive and participative managers use the collaborative style more than autocratic managers do. The collaborative style is more natural in open and supportive organizational cultures where there are trusting relationships than in those that are closed and autocratic.[33]

Conditions for Use. Collaboration often is regarded as the best overall style. However, as we have noted, each style may be useful in specific situations.[34] The collaborative style of conflict management is especially appropriate when

- the parties involved have one or more common goals and disagree mainly over the best *means* of achieving them;
- a consensus is needed to implement the best overall solution to the conflict;

- there is a need to make high-quality decisions on the basis of expert judgments and the best information available; and
- the parties need to work through negative feelings and distrust of each other that have interfered with their working relationships.[35]

4

Describe the process of negotiation for reducing or resolving conflict.

Teaching Tip
Select a situation from the newspaper in which negotiation is required. Use it as an example in teaching this section.

Teaching Tip
To discuss negotiation, ask students to identify situations in which they have actually been the negotiator and to identify which conflict management styles were used by the parties involved.

NEGOTIATION IN CONFLICT MANAGEMENT

Characteristics of Negotiation

Negotiation is a process by which individuals or groups with both common and conflicting goals or different preferences on how to achieve those goals present and discuss proposals for reaching an agreement.[36] Negotiation includes several elements.

Two or More Parties Are Involved. Negotiation isn't limited to the bargaining table in organizational disputes, as between management and unions. Everyone engages in negotiation. Children and parents negotiate over allowances, chores, and hours. Spouses negotiate over how money is to be spent, who is to perform what household duties, and so on.

The Parties Differ with Respect to One or More Issues. Without differences, there would be no need for negotiation. Most often, differences arise over one or more goals and/or the best way(s) to achieve the goal(s).

The Parties Share Some Commonalities. The parties have a common interest in reaching agreement, have some shared goals, and recognize that they are interdependent. In labor-management negotiations, both parties usually share the goal of reaching an agreement that will enable the continued survival, competitiveness, and success of the organization. The 1994–1995 major league baseball strike by the players association and their negotiations with team owners continued for months because of extreme distrust and the focus by each side on its own interests rather than the parties' mutual interests. There was little recognition that their economic survival and success was totally dependent on continued fan (customer) support. Supporters grew increasingly disenchanted and threatened to withdraw from the sport, which would result in fewer economic resources to negotiate over.

Negotiation Usually Is a Sequential Process. The parties present proposals and offer counterproposals to one another with the goal of reaching an agreement. The process involves exchanges of information, expression of key concerns or desires (which may not be revealed early in the process), and the continuous assessment of the other party's statements. Flexibility, some degree of trust, and a willingness to be responsive to the other party generally are necessary for true negotiation.

Negotiation Involves Arriving at a Shared Solution. The solution may involve an exchange of resources or mutually acceptable resolution of other issue(s)—such as how to schedule overtime work—that are in dispute. A common issue in labor-management negotiation involves the terms of exchanging union members' hours of work and productivity (a resource) for direct pay and other benefits (a resource).[37]

Teaching Tip
Have students pair up. One student is to state a negotiating situation. The other student is to use the diagnostic questions and interview the first. Have them switch when finished and repeat the exercise.

Diagnosis of the Situation

Initially, the issues that have created the need for negotiation should be diagnosed. Drawn-out and hostile negotiations may result if each party fails to diagnose the situation. An honest and thorough assessment of a series of questions by each party will help keep the negotiations on track—on the real issues and their underlying causes rather than on the personalities involved. At a minimum, the following questions should be asked and answered.

1. What do you want or need? Are you sure?
2. What do you think the other party wants or needs? Are you sure?
3. Do you and the other party differ over facts? Goals? Methods? Roles?
4. What could you lose if the conflict continues or escalates?
5. What goals do you and the other party share?
6. If you decide to collaborate during negotiation, what are the first steps you might take?[38]

Ask Students
What is the key to successful negotiation?

Relation to Conflict Styles

The traditional negotiating process involved each party's use of the forcing style and falling back on the compromise style only as a last resort. In fact, collaboration is a core ingredient in most successful negotiations. Consider the view of Leonard Greenhalgh, who writes on and teaches negotiation at Dartmouth's Tuck School of Business Administration.

> *North American managers have an old-fashioned notion of what competition is all about. When they think of competition, they think in adversary terms: You dump a supplier if you can find one with a cheaper product. You abandon the customer if you can find a more profitable one.*
>
> *But now we are dealing in a global market, where other managers are in collaborative business cultures. American managers do not have a really fine sense of what collaboration is all about. You cannot have an adversary, me-first mentality and get a complicated production program or an R&D joint venture to work. Managers must learn to evolve from a contractually oriented business culture where, if it is not in the contract, they do whatever they want. What is missing is good will, trust, and a genuine concern for the other person's welfare. Managers need to do business based on relationships.*[39]

Ask Students
Do you agree? Why or why not?

The use of various combinations of conflict-management styles in the negotiating process isn't unusual. This is especially true when the negotiations involve several important and complex issues, as in union-management negotiations and customer-supplier negotiations. The key to successful negotiation is the combination of styles and related assumptions that dominate the process.[40] If the collaborative and compromise styles dominate negotiations, the parties usually reach positive and effective solutions. Some use of the smoothing style also is likely in effective negotiations. Using the smoothing style as a gesture of "good will" by giving ground on some issues that are of considerable importance to the other party, but not critical to you, is relatively painless.[41]

In contrast, less effective negotiations often are dominated by the forcing and compromise styles. When neither party has the power to force its preferred solutions on the other, the compromise style may be used as a backup. Some use of the avoidance style also may come into play. The avoidance style may appear when the parties avoid addressing issues for which they feel no solution is possible at the present time. In effect, such issues are simply "tabled" for possible consideration during a future negotiation. These contrasting patterns of conflict-management styles and their different assumptions are found in a wide variety of negotiating relationships: between co-workers, managers and subordinates, customers and suppliers, departments, organizations, and even countries.[42]

Union-management relationships and negotiations may easily slip into the forcing pattern, with compromise being used only when the parties recognize that they don't have enough power to force for their own terms of settlement on the other. For example, during the major league baseball strike, the mind set of players and owners alike was to try to force their own terms on the other party. That prolonged the strike and indeed may ultimately make a mutually acceptable, negotiated settlement impossible. Increasingly, various formal and ongoing approaches for heading off bitter strikes, the

TABLE 17.1

Selected Mechanisms to Supplement Direct Negotiations

MECHANISM	BRIEF EXPLANATION
Voluntary arbitration	Parties agree to submit unresolved dispute(s) to a neutral third party (person or panel) for final and binding resolution.
Mediation	Parties meet with a neutral third party who listens to each side. Mediator fosters mutual understanding and collaboration and may provide advice and suggest new alternatives.
Ombudsman	An individual who helps employees cut through red tape, ensures that whistleblowers have an outlet for presenting their concerns (often confidentially), and provides information to aggrieved employees (often confidentially) on how to proceed.
Facilitator	A neutral third party who provides training and consultation to each party independently and jointly on effective ways of gathering data, identifying assumptions, defining problems, creating new alternatives, and negotiating. These efforts usually occur prior to actual negotiation.
Court system	One or both parties file a lawsuit, which states what the defendant did wrong and what the plaintiff wants as damages. This action assumes a win-lose relationship, seeks a court-imposed resolution, and is costly, time-consuming, and complex.

Source: Adapted from U.S. Department of Labor, *Fact Finding Report: Commission on the Future of Worker-Management Relations.* Washington, D.C.: U.S. Government Printing Office, 1994; Post, F.R., and Bennett, R.J. Use of the collaborative collective bargaining process in labor negotiations. *International Journal of Conflict Resolution,* 1994, 5, 34–61; McDowell, D.S. *Alternative Dispute Resolution Techniques: Options and Guidelines to Meet Your Company's Needs.* Washington, D.C.: Employment Policy Foundation, 1993.

forcing tendency, and hostilities both during the negotiation of new contracts and their implementation are being used.[43] As indicated in Table 17.1, a variety of supplemental dispute resolution mechanisms are available to help avoid, reduce, or resolve deadlocked negotiations. These mechanisms are aids to dispute resolution, not substitutes for negotiation.

The following Global Insight describes the supplemental dispute resolution mechanisms used by Telecom Australia (the major phone company in Australia) and the unions representing most of its nonmanagerial employees.

Global *Insight*

Telecom Australia Consultative Council

The Telecom Australia Consultative Council (TCC) was established under the terms of the *Telecommunications Act 1975.* It was intended to provide a regular forum for extensive consultation between management and union representatives on a wide range of matters.

The TCC has been relatively successful. Although the council is not a formal decision-making body, matters resolved in the TCC are expected to be translated into action. Subcommittees pursue issues raised at the council in greater depth, and the TCC usually endorses their recommendations. There appears to be meaningful union input at meetings of the TCC, and both parties seek to resolve differences between them in order to achieve positive outcomes. One major achievement of the TCC is agreement on the principles and procedures to be followed on the introduction of technological change.

The TCC hasn't been entirely without problems. Initially, management was reluctant to provide information on certain matters. One major union withdrew from the TCC for a period of time on the grounds that the council had no decision-making authority. Critics on both sides cite the slowness of the consultative process as an impediment to action. Others view it as a brake on hasty and ill-considered decisions. In general, both unions and management believe that the TCC is useful and productive. The effectiveness of consultative mechanisms depend on, among other things, the willingness of both sides to commit the necessary time and resources to the process.

The TCC meets regularly, and its meetings usually run for one or more days, in contrast to the single-afternoon meetings of many other Australian firms that have consultative councils. The TCC has a full-time secretary who prepares information for the representatives attending TCC and subcommittee meetings. The TCC has gained respect and influence in the decision-making system of Telecom Australia.[44]

Ethical Dilemmas

Ethical dilemmas are present in many negotiation and conflict situations. Recall that the resolution of ethical dilemmas is influenced by the stage of moral development of the individuals engaged in the conflict (refer back to Figure 7.2) and by the ethical approach they take (utilitarian, moral-rights, or justice; refer back to Table 7.2). One obvious ethical dilemma that arises in negotiations is the amount of information that should be shared with the other party.[45] Consider the following situation.

You are a real estate broker in the Lakes region. Times have been tough during the recession, but you now have a prospect for a lakefront home you have listed. The owner, who has relocated all the way across the country, has authorized you to negotiate the sale of the home within defined limits (including a minimally acceptable sales price). Your commission is based on a percentage of the sales price and increases as the sales price increases. If you close the sale, you could earn a commission of between $6,000 and about $10,000, depending on the sale price. The property has no boat dock, but you have overheard the prospective buyers (husband and wife) discussing where they would have a new dock built. The couple hasn't talked to you about the dock, but you know that having it is important to them. On this particular lake, you also know that getting the state licensing authority's approval to build a new dock is almost impossible. No new permits have been issued for two years.[46] You anticipate that the prospective buyers' knowledge of this problem would surely reduce the value of the property to them and might even result in their having no further interest in it. Would you discuss the dock problem with your prospective buyers?

Teaching Tip
Have students choose an organization, a team, or a manager. They are to find out what steps the subject is currently taking to reduce the intensity and number of stressors that affect their employees or to increase the employees' ability to cope with stress. Students may use library research or conduct personal interviews with representatives of organizations to do this exercise.

The real estate broker is faced with interrole and person-role conflict. Revealing the dock problem is the ethical action; not revealing it would be an economically motivated compromise of ethics. This incident also suggests the ethical problem of focusing exclusively on one's own interests, with no concern for the interests of others, when negotiating and making decisions.[47]

5

Discuss the causes and effects of job-related stress and actions that can be taken to manage stress.

JOB-RELATED STRESS

Individuals who experience extreme conflict, ambiguity, or the ineffective conflict-management styles of others may develop high levels of job-related stress. For example, the forcing style (especially when used repeatedly by a supervisor) is a possible source of job-related stress. Before expanding on the causes of stress, however, we need to define several terms.

Stress consists of the individual's responses—emotional, physical, and cognitive—to any situation that places excessive demands on that person. Stress often creates a **nonspecific** response, which means that certain emotional, physical, and cognitive responses occur automatically. That is, people do not consciously control them.[48] Heat (a physical stressor) produces sweating, cold (another physical stressor) produces shivering, and fear (an emotion) may produce a fight-or-flight response. Hans Selye, often regarded as the father of stress management, notes, however, that stress is not something to be avoided: "Complete freedom from stress is death."[49]

Ask Students
Have you experienced eustress within the last week? Describe the experience.

Ask Students
Have you experienced distress within the last week? Describe the experience.

Teaching Tip
Divide students into groups of 5–8 and ask them to brainstorm explanations for the effects of eustress and distress. Have them present their lists to the class to stimulate discussion of types of stress.

Teaching Tip
Get students to brainstorm work-related stresses. List them on the board or by using an overhead transparency.

What did Selye mean? Simply that not all conflict and ambiguity is negative, nor is all stress bad. There are two major types of stress: eustress and distress. **Eustress** is pleasant or constructive stress (e.g., the positive emotions a person experiences upon being congratulated for doing a good job, creating a novel solution, or negotiating a good agreement). Conversely, **distress** is unpleasant, detrimental, or disease-producing stress. Most of the literature dealing with stress focuses on distress, as we do in this chapter. Thus our use of the term *stress* refers primarily to *distress*. A **stressor** is any situation that places special demands on the individual. The individual may experience these demands consciously or unconsciously.[50]

Causes of Stress

There are many potential causes of stress in the workplace.[51] All of the types and causes of conflict and role ambiguity discussed earlier in this chapter are potential causes of stress. Table 17.2 identifies three common categories of job-related stressors: conditions that exist in the physical environment, role conflict, and role ambiguity.

Use Table 17.2 to assess your level of job-related stress in your present job or in one you had in the past. Scoring directions are included. In general, ratings of 8 or 10

TABLE 17.2

Stress Assessment Questionnaire

Listed below are various kinds of problems that may—or may not—arise in your job. Indicate to what extent you find each of them to be a problem or concern.

Factor	**Responses**				
This Factor Is ________ a Problem	*Never*	*Seldom*	*Sometimes*	*Usually*	*Always*
Physical Environment					
1. Feeling you are too hot or too cold	0	4	6	8	10
2. Thinking there is a good chance of being seriously injured on the job	0	4	6	8	10
3. Thinking there is a real possibility of getting some disease from this job	0	4	6	8	10
Role Conflict					
4. Feeling you must do things you personally feel to be unethical	0	4	6	8	10
5. Having a boss who keeps assigning different tasks and allowing too little time to complete them	0	4	6	8	10
6. Receiving too many incompatible pressures from too many people	0	4	6	8	10
7. Having to sacrifice too much of your personal and family life for this job	0	4	6	8	10
Role Ambiguity					
8. Not knowing what the people you work with expect you to accomplish	0	4	6	8	10
9. Being unclear about how you are to perform the tasks in your job	0	4	6	8	10
10. Not knowing how your manager evaluates your performance	0	4	6	8	10

- *Add the numbers you circled in each of the three categories and enter the totals in the blanks.*

  Physical environment (items 1–3) ________

  Role conflict (items 4–7) ________

  Role ambiguity (items (8–10) ________

- **Total** (add the three scores) ________

for a single factor or combination of factors in a category suggests potential problems that deserve your further attention. The overall score can range from 0 to 100. A total score of 74 or more suggests a more-than-desirable amount of stress in two or three categories. This level of stress could be a reason for low job satisfaction, a desire to quit the job, or high absenteeism.

Effects of Stress

Stress is associated with a variety of potentially negative effects.[52] These effects fall into one or more of the following categories.

- *Subjective effects:* Anxiety, aggression, apathy, boredom, depression, fatigue, frustration, guilt and shame, irritability and bad temper, moodiness, low self-esteem, threat and tension, nervousness, and loneliness.
- *Behavioral effects:* Accident proneness, illegal drug use, emotional outbursts, excessive eating or loss of appetite, excessive drinking and smoking, excitability, impulsive behavior, impaired speech, nervous laughter, restlessness, trembling, and excessive sleeping (or the inability to sleep).
- *Cognitive effects:* Inability to make decisions or concentrate, frequent forgetfulness, hypersensitivity to criticism, mental blocks, and denial.
- *Physiological effects:* Increased blood and urine catecholamines and corticosteroids, increased blood glucose levels, increased heart rate and blood pressure, dryness of the mouth, sweating, dilation of the pupils, difficulty in breathing, hot and cold spells, lump in the throat, numbness and tingling in parts of the limbs, hives, and indigestion.
- *Organizational effects:* Absenteeism, poor union-management relations, low productivity, high accident rates, high turnover rates, work of inferior quality, antagonism at work, and job dissatisfaction.[53]

Real-World Example
Harvard University President Neil L. Rudenstine, fifty-nine, went on "indefinite" medical leave owing to job stress. He was president from July 1991 to November 1994, when he took indefinite leave on the advice of his doctors. He said that he had "severe fatigue and exhaustion." He had spent two weeks resting in 1993 from fatigue. In his $227,000 per year job, he had to raise almost $1 million a day to achieve Harvard's five-year, $2.1 billion fund drive goal. Harvard has an operating budget of $1.3 billion a year. Roy Daniel, a director at McKinsey & Co. and member of Harvard's Governing Board, said that Rudenstine can't delegate or say "no." Apparently, Rudenstine micromanaged and got bogged down in details, especially by personally chairing the tenure committee, which took an entire day each week (*Wall Street Journal,* November 29, 1994, B1, B4; December 9, 1994, A1, A5; December 1, 1994, B1, B6; *U.S. News & World Report,* December 12, 1994, 82).

Ask Students
Have any of you ever said that you were burned out with school? If so, what made you feel that way?

Ethics
The effects of distress and burnout have received widespread attention in recent years from the general public, organizations, researchers, and news media. Ethically, should the organization or the employee be responsible for managing distress and burnout? Explain your reasoning.

A person under stress may show more than one adverse effect. However, an individual typically doesn't experience effects in all these categories, or all the specific effects within a single category, at the same time. Everyone experiences some negative effects of stress at times, but a severe problem is unlikely to arise unless stress is intense and frequent.

Individuals who experience a high level of stress over an extended period may suffer from burnout. **Burnout** is an unhealthy psychological process that is brought about by continuous and severe stress. It includes emotional exhaustion (lack of energy), depersonalization (detachment from others, treating people as objects, and cynical attitudes), and a sense of decreased personal accomplishments (evaluating oneself negatively, decline in sense of personal competence, and a self-perception of no progress or losing ground).[54] Some people experience burnout in response to intense job-related stressors.[55] Burnout and severe stress don't just happen. They involve a complex interplay of personal, job, group or team, and organization cultural characteristics.[56] Individuals who succumb to burnout seem to progress through the following stages:

1. Puzzlement, confusion, and the appearance of frustration.
2. Intense frustration and anger.
3. Apathy, withdrawal, and despair.[57]

The effects of stress and burnout have received widespread attention in recent years from the general public, business and health organizations, researchers, and the news media. Numerous suggestions have been advanced for managing stress and avoiding burnout. Methods of stress management can be both individual and organizational.

In October 1994, 11,500 employees of GM's Buick City complex walked off the job. Due to increasing demands for its cars and its attempt to downsize to improve productivity, workers had been forced to put in heavy overtime.

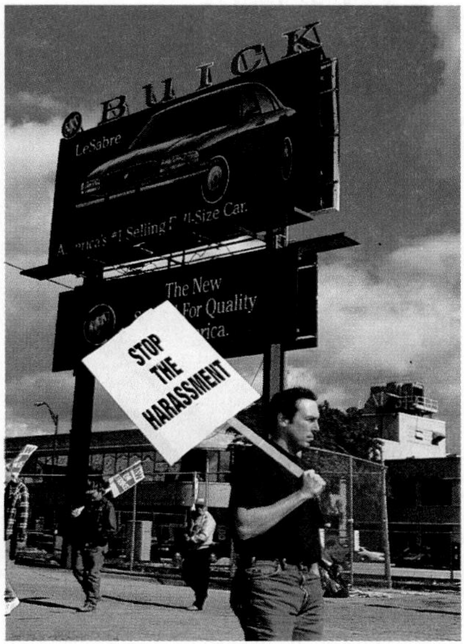

Individual Actions

Teaching Tip
As an introduction to coping with stress, have students brainstorm ways to cope with stress.

An awareness of the causes of stress and the responses (emotional, physical, and cognitive) to stressors are fundamental to positive individual actions for managing it. As suggested in Figure 17.3, there are many ways for eliminating or managing the negative effects of stress. The most direct individual actions that can be taken are the following.

1. ***Clarify your values.*** Not running on the fast track, but on your track, is what is important.
2. ***Improve your "self-talks."*** We all talk to ourselves, and many of our self-talks are needlessly negative: "I'm going to fail this test" or "There's no way I can get out of this mess." Discipline yourself not to overreact emotionally. Why be enraged when simple irritation will get the message across to yourself?
3. ***Learn how to relax.*** All you need is a quiet room. Get comfortable. Then close your eyes, breathe rhythmically (preferably from your abdomen), and blot out distractions for ten to fifteen minutes. Do this twice a day.
4. ***Exercise regularly.*** Try to exercise at least three times a week for twenty minutes at 75 percent of your maximum predicted heart rate. Be sure that your doctor approves, and start gradually.
5. ***Get the leisure you need.*** The best way to avoid burnout is to allow yourself proper leisure to renew your commitment to work and recharge your batteries. If you are a workaholic, consider that you owe it to yourself to take time off. Otherwise, you will jeopardize your chances of staying on top of a rough job over the long haul.
6. ***Adopt dietary goals.*** Maintain normal weight. Remember to eat a real breakfast.
7. ***Avoid "chemical haze."*** The use of nicotine, alcohol, and drugs in excessive amounts should be avoided.[58]

Teaching Tip
Try this now.

Ethics
People have many ways of dealing with work stress. Some employees try to cope by having a drink at lunch to "withdraw" from the stressors. Is it ethical for employees to have a couple of drinks during lunch (which is considered their own personal time), even though company rules and regulations stipulate "no drinking during working hours"? Why or why not?

In addition, two substantial *inner actions* are implied by several of the direct actions noted. You can manage stress better by resolving to *change what you can change* and *resolving not to live passively with what you can't change.*

Changes in Behaviors and Attitudes. Experiences associated with some stressors are more a result of personal attitudes and characteristics than the stressors in the situation. In other words, the same incident may be stressful for one person but not for another. Accordingly, individuals should be able to manage stress to some extent by mod-

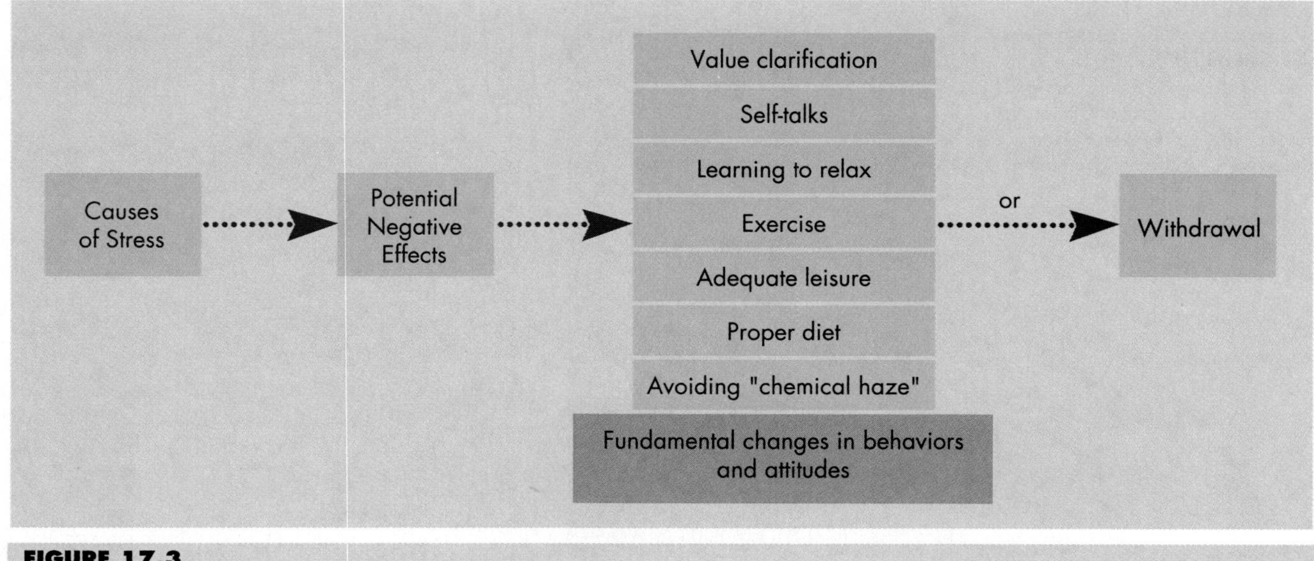

FIGURE 17.3

Individual Actions for Managing Stress

ifying their attitudes and behaviors. For example, they can learn to use the collaboration and compromise styles of conflict management and avoid the use of the forcing and avoidance styles. In this way they may be able to reduce the number of conflict incidents and resolve more effectively those that act as intense stressors. Individuals need to set reasonable goals, evaluate priorities carefully, allow more time for each task, improve time management, and simply reduce the total number of tasks. These actions may go a long way toward avoiding and reducing negative stress.

This advice is especially important for the individual who exhibits Type A behavior. The **Type A behavior pattern** refers to a "person who is aggressively involved in a chronic, incessant struggle to achieve more and more in less time, and if required to do so, against the opposing efforts of other things or other persons."[59] In contrast, the **Type B behavior pattern** refers to a person who is often contemplative, nonaggressive, realistic in goals pursued, and not hypercritical of self or others. Type A and Type B behavior patterns have been contrasted as follows:

> *The Type A individual is extremely competitive, constantly tending to challenge others—in sports, at work, and even in casual discussions. Type A people characteristically overreact and generally are hypercritical—both of themselves (to themselves) and of others (more openly). They might fume at something a Type B person would brush off as inconsequential.*
>
> *Type A's are said to have a great sense of urgency concerning time. They tend to thrive on deadlines and create them if none exist. Similarly, they establish difficult goals if none are set for them, and are quick to become impatient when goals and deadlines are not achieved. In contrast, Type B's are more contemplative. They take the time to ponder alternatives and usually feel there is plenty of time.*[60]

The type A and B patterns represent extreme profiles. Many individuals fall between these extremes.[61]

Ask Students
How many of you would identify yourselves as Type A individuals? What advantages and disadvantages do you associate with this behavior pattern?

Ask Students
How many of you would identify yourselves as Type B individuals? What advantages and disadvantages do you associate with this behavior pattern?

Ask Students
Could a business survive today if it employed only Type A or only Type B individuals? Explain.

Discussion Question 7
Is a Type A behavior pattern likely to be more effective in negotiations than a Type B behavior pattern? Explain your answer.

Withdrawal. The simplest way of coping with stress is to withdraw (flight) from the stressors. This may involve being absent, changing jobs, or even changing careers. Under certain circumstances, withdrawal may be an appropriate and healthy form of coping. Consider someone who works for a highly autocratic manager who constantly makes unrealistic demands and primarily uses the forcing style of conflict management.

One perfectly realistic coping strategy would be to transfer to another department or look for a job with another organization. However, withdrawal also can be an unhealthy way of attempting to avoid having to deal with reality.

Organizational Actions

Organizations, teams, and managers often are able to reduce the intensity and number of stressors on employees or increase their ability to cope with them.[62]

Real-World Example
Sixty percent of 1,000 companies surveyed offer flextime, and one-third offer job sharing. By the year 2000, 80 percent of companies may offer flextime (*Wall Street Journal,* March 22, 1994, A14).

Setting Goals. Participative goal setting should help reduce and resolve role conflicts and uncertainties. These factors often are major sources of stress and burnout. Clearly, delegating authority and encouraging employees to participate in decisions that affect their day-to-day work lives are likely to help control stress levels.

Real-World Example
In 1993, the cost of medical care in the United States exceeded 12 percent of total domestic expenditures. Of that total, employers paid about 52 percent; the federal government, about 34 percent; and Medicare and Medicaid, about 14 percent (*Business Week,* January 11, 1993).

Emotional Support. Emotional support is the empathy, caring, love, and trust displayed by others toward an individual. It appears to help individuals cope with stressors. Emotional and other forms of support in the workplace can be provided by superiors, cohesive teams, and subordinates. Organizational cultures that convey a sense of caring provide strong emotional support, helping employees cope successfully with performance expectations and pressures.[63] The use of collaborative, smoothing, and compromise conflict-management styles often creates a perception of caring, empathy, and trust. This perception builds mutual emotional support within the organization.

Real-World Example
Coors gets a return of $6.15 for each dollar it spends on worksite health promotion. Coors offers aerobics, strength training, cardiovascular monitoring, and an indoor running track to its employees (*Business Horizons.* November-December, 1994, 75).

Special Programs. Counseling and "wellness" programs, physical fitness facilities, leadership training, team decision making, organizational and job redesign, flextime, and career development activities represent some of the other actions that organizations can take to prevent and reduce severe stress experienced by employees.[64] **Flextime** allows employees, within certain limits, to vary their arrival and departure times to suit individual needs and desires. For example, flextime might enable a parent to be at home when the children arrive from school, thus eliminating stress about what they might be doing if left alone.

Wellness programs are designed to promote employees' physical and psychological health. Such programs are part of a growing preventive approach to health care whereby employees reduce their susceptibility to illness and ease the effects of stressors by changing the way they live. Wellness programs usually include courses in stress management, weight reduction, giving up smoking, exercise (aerobics), and the like.

The Menninger Clinic offers week-long seminars in which managers take a break from their routines and reflect on their work. One of the issues dealt with is the anxiety that comes from firing employees.

CHAPTER SUMMARY

1 ***State the different types and views of conflict in organizations.***

Goal conflict represents incompatibilities in desired results or preferred outcomes. Cognitive conflict represent differences in ideas or thoughts. Affective conflict refers to negative feelings or emotions between individuals. Conflict may be both positive (stimulating) and negative (destructive). It may stimulate a search for the reasons behind differences in approach and for innovative solutions to problems. Conflict may be destructive when interdependent employees or teams have to compete against each other. Most effective employees and managers have a balanced view of conflict. They attempt to manage positive conflict to make it work creatively and also try to eliminate negative conflict.

2 ***Define and explain four types of role conflict and role ambiguity.***

Intrasender role conflict often occurs when the role sender conveys mixed messages to the focal person. Intersender role conflict often occurs when pressures on the focal person from more than one role sender are incompatible. Interrole conflict often occurs when pressures associated with one role (demands on the person as an employee) conflict with those of another (demands on the person as a spouse or parent). Person-role conflict may occur when the focal person's roles are at variance with personal needs, attitudes, values, or abilities. Role ambiguity occurs when the person experiences uncertainties or confusion about expected performance, how to perform some of the job tasks, and the like. When severe, it can be a source of conflict and stress.

3 ***Explain the main interpersonal conflict-management styles and the conditions under which each may be used effectively.***

The avoidance style involves withdrawing from conflict. It is appropriate in various situations, as when others can resolve the conflict more effectively. The smoothing style minimizes differences and is appropriate for defusing intense emotions. The forcing style attempts to dominate the other party and assumes one party's gain is the other's loss. Its use may be necessary in special circumstances, as when an unpopular course of action must be taken and no other alternatives have been discovered. The compromise style involves both parties conceding some of their own views and preferences. It is appropriate when the parties are unable to agree in all respects and believe that they would be better off compromising than not reaching an agreement. The collaborative style involves seeking win-win solutions and is effective when consensus leads to the best overall solution.

4 ***Describe the process of negotiation for reducing or resolving conflicts.***

Two or more parties who differ over one or more issues are involved in the process of negotiation. However, the parties also share some common interests and need each other to achieve their own goals. The parties engage in a sequential process of presenting proposals and counterproposals, along with supporting information. They arrive at a voluntary sharing or exchange of resources, or resolution of other issues. Careful diagnosis of the issues initially is crucial to effective negotiation. Successful negotiations usually are dominated by use of the compromise and collaborative styles.

5 ***Discuss the causes and effects of job-related stress and actions that can be taken to manage stress.***

Three of the most common causes of job-related stress (distress type) are conditions that exist in the physical environment, role conflict, and role ambiguity. The effects of stress may be subjective, behavioral, cognitive, physiological, and/or organizational. Various individual and organizational actions can be taken to avoid or reduce stress. Individual actions include clarifying values, improving self-talks, learning how to relax, exercising regularly, taking enough time for leisure pursuits, following the proper diet, and avoiding "chemical haze." Of course, these actions often flow from fundamental choices, such as resolving to change behaviors and attitudes or even to withdraw from the situation. Organizational actions include participatory goal setting and decision making, promotion of an organizational culture that conveys a sense of caring and emotional support, and sponsorship of wellness programs.

QUESTIONS FOR DISCUSSION

1. According to the Preview Insight, what types of role conflict did Paul Kazarian, former CEO at Sunbeam-Oster, experience?
2. Why will there always be some conflict between two or more individuals, two or more departments, and two or more organizations?
3. What are the differences between cognitive conflict and affective conflict?
4. Why does conflict occur within individuals?
5. What is role ambiguity? Why is it important to an understanding of conflict and personal stress in organizations?
6. When is the smoothing style likely to be more effective than the forcing style of conflict management?
7. Is a Type A behavior pattern likely to be more effective in negotiations than a Type B behavior pattern? Explain your answer.

FROM WHERE YOU SIT

1. Drawing on your own experiences, give one example of each type of role conflict: intrasender, intersender, interrole, and person-role.
2. To what extent do you use each of the five interpersonal conflict-management styles?
3. Based on your response to Question 2, do your two most frequently used styles work well in dealing with conflict? Explain.
4. Think of a current or past relationship with someone who has much more power than you. How would you describe that person's relative use of the five interpersonal conflict-management styles? How would you evaluate that person's conflict-management effectiveness?
5. What are the major stressors in your life at the present time? Do any of these stressors create a sense of positive stress (eustress)? Do others create a sense of negative stress (distress)? Explain.
6. Do you see yourself as exhibiting more of a Type A or a Type B behavior pattern? What is your basis for this self-characterization? Would individuals who know you well agree with it? Why or why not?
7. What actions do you usually take to manage negative stress? Are the actions effective? Explain.

The Reluctant Clerk: A Supervisor's Challenge—Role Play Version[65]

Instructions: This case is well-suited to role playing as part of the class discussion. With each part of this progressive case, the roles of supervisor and employee can be assigned to students. The situation can be acted out by a pair of volunteers before the entire class or all students can pair up and role play the situation simultaneously. For simultaneous role playing, groups of three are suggested, with the third role being that of a nonparticipating observer who reports observations back to the small group and to the class as a whole. The role of Lynn Wilson, the supervisor, has been described in the case in such a way that this role can be played by either gender. When women play the role of Paul, simply change Paul to Paula, as nothing in the case description necessitates that Paul be male.

For the first round of the role play those playing the part of the *supervisor should read only Part I* of the case. Those playing *Paul should read both Parts I and II.* This beginning reflects what each would reasonably know in the actual situation. Those playing the observer roles *should not read either part* of the case in order to focus on process issues. Additional instructions for role playing this case, including those for Parts III and IV, will be provided by your instructor. Please do not read any of the parts of this case until instructed to do so.

Background

Shoshone Regional Medical Center (SRMC), the leading hospital for its county and the surrounding area, employs approximately 500 people. Several months ago operations were moved from a fifty-year-old building in the center of town to a new, modern two-story building. All of the employees were transferred to the new facility. However, because of the design of the new hospital and state-of-the-art equipment, including new computer systems in the business office, the jobs of some employees were eliminated. In accordance with hospital policy, these employees were reassigned to different responsibilities in the new facility.

Part I

Lynn Wilson, a supervisor in the business office at SRMC, is in charge of seventeen employees, including several patient account clerks. Lynn's job is to make sure that all applicable charges are received and entered into the computer by the clerks so that patients are accurately billed for all services and supplies used in their treatment.

The supervisor's job has, to say the least, been hectic since the move to the new facility, and everyone has been under pressure. Lynn's employees handled the pressure well, except for Paul, the new account clerk who used to work in the storeroom. Paul became a patient account clerk when his old storeroom clerk job was eliminated in the move to the new facility with its more automated storeroom accounting system. He was consulted about the change at the time and indicated he did not particularly like the new job, but he accepted the change anyway.

Paul's performance record in the storeroom had been excellent. However, Lynn has noticed a sharp drop in his performance over the last month or two in the new job. A number of billing errors have been attributed to him, and his relationships with other employees have gone from bad to worse. Paul is critical of everyone and everything and often falls behind schedule on billings. Other supervisors tell Lynn that Paul now refuses to search out and provide information that they need to complete their work or simply ignores their requests. This may be partly Lynn's fault because at one point Lynn issued an oral reprimand to Paul (the first formal step in SRMC's progressive discipline process) for falling behind. Lynn even suggested that he seek advice before handling the requests of other supervisors, but Paul does not seem to communicate at all anymore.

In any case, Paul's performance is substandard, and it is starting to affect other employees. It is a problem that Lynn feels can no longer be ignored. Something must be done.

Part II

Feeling the problem must be confronted, Lynn asks Paul to meet to discuss the situation. In the course of the discussion, Lynn learns that Paul had worked for SRMC for seven years. During most of that time, he was one of the storeroom clerks. His job involved checking incoming supplies, preparing supply orders, and arranging supplies for delivery to the various departments. Paul indicates that he enjoyed that work very much because of its variety and predictability. Consequently, he performed consistently well.

In the move to the new facility, Paul was given the new job as a patient account clerk at a slightly higher pay scale. Everyone has been under pressure since the move, and the new job has been hectic for Paul. It is more complicated than his old job. Paul sometimes encounters difficulty in checking to make sure that he has obtained all the necessary data to complete a patient's billing.

Other supervisors come to Paul with special requests for information from the records, which puts additional demands on his time. Although this doesn't ordinarily increase his workload that much, it does add to the confusion. He does not seem to know what to do first as he tries to please several different bosses. Paul is used to doing things in a neat, orderly, predictable way; hence the new job has become very frustrating. In fact, Paul is finding concentrating on his work difficult. As a result, he argues with co-workers a lot more and has been avoiding anyone who might have a special request. Paul is sure that the other supervisors are complaining to Lynn, and Lynn has already given him an oral reprimand for falling behind. Paul wishes that they would just give him back his old job where he was happy and productive.

PART III

As a result of this added information, Lynn decides that SRMC was at least partly responsible for Paul's behavior. Lynn talks to the other supervisors. They agree to seek needed information by coming through Lynn who could pass their requests along to Paul as part of his regular work schedule. Paul indicates that this should help reduce the pressure on him. He also says that additional training in the new job might help. Lynn agrees and schedules several training days for him over the next few weeks.

Despite the scheduling of special requests and the added training, Paul's performance continues to deteriorate. He still finds the pressure confusing and feels that he cannot please anyone anymore. He now says he hates his new job and this attitude seriously affects his performance. Paul is sullen, impatient, and complains constantly. On several occasions, Paul's carelessness has led to errors. Lynn decides to talk with Paul again and to deliver a last warning.

PART IV

Lynn has another discussion with Paul. They agree that Paul is really never going to be happy in the clerk's job. He prefers a job that is more routine and predictable and where he will not have to respond to so many special requests. Paul agrees to continue to do his best to meet Lynn's expectations in the clerk's job for some indefinite interim period. Lynn agrees to recommend Paul for a more suitable position when one opens up in the hospital.

CRITICAL THINKING CASE

The Reluctant Clerk: A Supervisor's Challenge—Discussion Version[65]

INSTRUCTIONS: Discussion questions are presented below for each part of the case presented in the preceding Skill-Building Exercise. Your instructor may elect to follow the role plays of this case with a class discussion and/or written assignments based on these questions. Or, your instructor may elect to proceed directly to these discussion questions. Please do not read the case, which appears in the Skill-Building Exercise section until you receive instructions from your instructor.

Discussion Questions for Part I

1. What is (are) the problem(s) faced by Lynn at this point?
2. What other issues may be involved in this situation?
3. What should Lynn attempt to accomplish, specifically?
4. How should Lynn proceed?

Discussion Questions for Part II

1. Based on this added information, what is (are) the problem(s) now?
2. What managerial issues are now involved in this situation?
3. How should Lynn proceed at this point?

Discussion Questions for Part III

1. What is the problem situation faced by Lynn now?

2. How should Lynn approach Paul this time?
3. Should Paul be terminated? Why or why not?

Discussion Questions for Part IV

1. How do you feel about the solution agreed to in Part IV?
2. What should Lynn do if no suitable position opens up in the near future?
3. If you had to terminate Paul, how would you do it?
4. What broader issues does this case indicate that may be problems for the hospital? Could this situation have been prevented? If so, how?

VIDEO CASE

Conflict: Is American Airlines' Management at Odds with Labor?[66]

As stated in an October 31, 1994 *Business Week* article, "In the high-stakes poker game known as the airline industry, American Airlines, Inc. holds a better hand than most." The Fort Worth-based carrier, currently enjoys a healthy cash flow, a strong brand name, a powerful route network, and a young jet fleet. The company had recorded $1.3 billion in losses over the preceding four years before posting record third-quarter 1994 profits of $205 million (before paying preferred dividends), and its first-half operating margin of 7 percent beat most major rivals. American is anticipating profits of $467 million for 1995, up 40 percent, on revenues of $16.8 billion.

Aviation Week and Space Technology calls American Airlines (AMR) Chairman Robert J. Crandall "the grand master of airline marketing." He made American one of the leading airlines of the 1980s. During that decade, Crandall was heavily involved in policy decisions to improve the traditionally adversarial relationship between labor and management. Crandall stated that the airline business had historically had a strong military bent and developed as a rather rigid, procedures-based, and confrontational workplace. In addition, the industry became heavily unionized. Early in the deregulation process, Crandall made the decision to make a sustained, long-term effort to change the confrontational, uncooperative, and nonparticipative environment into an environment based on trust and mutual respect. Were his efforts successful?

Between 1990 and 1993, employees took cuts in wages to help compensate for the company's losses. However, when American showed a net profit of $143 million for the first three quarters of 1993, employees no longer were willing to be the object of management's cost-cutting measures.

What management failed to convey was the fact that three consecutive quarters of profit couldn't offset three years of losses. The conflict between labor and management—and their failure to reach a mutually acceptable contract—resulted in a strike that began on November 18, 1993. The Association of Professional Flight Attendants, grounded two-thirds of American Airlines' flights during one of the industry's busiest seasons, Thanksgiving. Many people and the media asked, "What is the root of the problem?"

The initial problems of American Airlines have been traced to the market entry of several smaller airlines, such as Southwest, combined with a lagging travel market. The newer companies targeted specific geographic regions, had lower fixed costs, and were able to undercut American's fares. Initially, American attempted to counter the price differentials by promoting safety and better service. Flight attendants were required to attend training sessions at which they viewed films intended to improve the customer service they provided to passengers.

Despite these efforts, the average consumer was still swayed by lower prices. American responded by enforcing both salary cuts and caps. The company also began to consider seriously other cost-cutting measures, such as reducing staffing on some flights, assigning staff on an as-needed basis, and increasing health care prefunding for its flight attendants and pilots. As stated on its striker's signs, American had become "#1 in service, #1 in safety, but #6 in pay."

The proposed eleven-day strike was broken on November 22, 1993 by the intervention of President Clinton. Not since 1966 had a U.S. president been involved in an airline dispute. Both management and the Association of Professional Flight Attendants accepted binding federal arbitration, to be completed within sixty days. The results of this arbitration promised to have a great impact on the future of labor relations for several airlines faced with the same problem of cutting costs to remain competitive.

Ralph P. Craviso, former head of employee relations at American, stated that the arbitration set the tone for negotiations between management and all the unions in the airline industry. Arbitration may have provided an alternative to endless negotiations or the possibility of strikes. However, it also complicated labor negotiations, as in the 1960s when emergencies were declared unnecessarily in order to force arbitration.

Before the strike ended, American Airlines had lost almost $160 million, making 1993 its fourth consecutive year of losses. Flight attendants returned to the status quo to await the arbiter's decision.

The onus was on management to do what was required to avoid a future strike. Not only is a strike costly in economic terms, but political intervention also increases its costliness in strategic business terms. Thus airlines must be more innovative, not only in their dealings with unions but also in their strategic planning.

What does the future hold? Perhaps the toughest job is the one facing labor. The goal of long-term job protection through enhanced competitiveness will be more difficult for a group that now sees the possibility of easy, short-term victories.

Conflict continues as American currently wants $300 million in cost cuts from pilots. Allied Pilots Association President James G. Sovich says that the union will negotiate productivity gains but rejects the demand for $300 million in savings. Is management's demand legitimate? Crandall believes so and has threatened to shrink the airline even faster to concentrate investment in more lucrative nonairline units. One American board member warns that the pilots are misreading Crandall if they believe the threats to downsize are only a negotiating strategy. He insists that American will continue to downsize unless costs drop—the union will have to realize that's no bluff. The message to labor: Buy in—or get bashed.[66]

Questions

1. Describe the management-labor conflict at American Airlines. Was arbitration the best way to resolve this conflict? Why or why not?
2. How will that arbitration affect the role of American pilots in negotiations?
3. Using the contingency model of conflict, is the AMR strike situation a win-lose conflict, a mixed conflict, a collaborative situation, or a low-interdependency conflict?

"I Still Do My Job, Don't I?"

William Bonney had come to Yancey's Family Steakhouse of Nashville through a promotion. For the first time since he came to work for the parent company, United Foods, he would be responsible for an entire restaurant. As general manager, Bonney would be in charge of operations, which depended entirely on the performance of the employees and the management staff. He had a management staff of three: John Aston, the manager; Phillip Tate, the assistant manager, and Molly Houston, the intern trainee. In addition, forty-seven regular employees were on the work schedule when Bonney arrived.

The manager, John Aston, had been transferred in a few months before William's arrival. He also had come to Yancey's of Nashville with a promotion but not much money in his bank account. Thus he was pleased when he found an affordable garage apartment for rent and was able to move in quickly. His new landlords were the parents of three of the restaurant's teenaged employees, and the apartment was located over the garage of their house.

The landlords, Mr. and Mrs. Dan Murphy, their two daughters Theresa and Lisa, and their son Dennis, had been living in this area of Nashville for years. All three of the Murphy teenagers worked part time for Yancey's, which was located only a few miles from their home.

The Company

United Foods, a medium-sized restaurant corporation, owned and operated Yancey's Family Steakhouse chain. In addition to Yancey's, United Foods had two other fast-food restaurant chains that were franchised from the original companies. In all, United owned approximately 700 restaurants, all located in the southeastern United States.

The Yancey's division, which operated some 300 restaurants, was divided into several regions. Each region was the responsibility of a regional leader (RL), and comprised four to six districts, with a district leader (DL) responsible for each district. A district contained four to seven restaurants. Each restaurant was the responsibility of a general manager (GM), who directed operations through a management team (usually consisting of three managers in addition to the GM) and forty-five to fifty regular employees.

District leaders rose through the management ranks and were delegated formal authority by the regional leaders. The DLs were responsible for recruiting and selecting managers to fill any open management positions in their districts. Usually, DLs asked GMs who was ready for promotion because the GMs were in the best position to know. General managers and DLs often made joint disciplinary decisions concerning the lower level managers within the GMs' restaurants, but formal authority for final action rested with the DLs.

General managers exercised formal authority over all regular employees in their restaurants. The other three managers in each restaurant normally reported directly to the GM. They also were responsible for working with employees through a counseling procedure to resolve problems. Ultimately, however, only the GM had the authority to take formal disciplinary action.

The management staff under a GM formally was a hierarchy. For example, when the GM wasn't present, the Manager assumed responsibility for operations. Effective managers eventually were promoted to GMs, and effective assistant managers eventually were promoted to managers.

The Restaurant

Not quite four years old when William Bonney took over, Yancey's of Nashville didn't have the sales volume needed to break even. Although monthly sales always covered variable costs, the overhead assigned to the unit by the home office was almost never met. Many of the employees attributed the relatively low sales to the restaurant's location, which wasn't near the interstate highway where a mall and many of the other restaurants in the immediate area were located.

Bob Jackson, the DL for Bonney's restaurant, had a different theory, however. Jackson felt that the employees were the primary cause for the low sales. In his opinion, the restaurant was a local hangout for teenagers, which drove off the older customers that the restaurant needed as regular customers.

"They're all buddies," he told Bonney soon after Bonney became GM. "They all go to the same high school and hang out with each other, and when a bunch of them have to work, the rest come visit. The first thing I want you to do," Jackson told Bonney, "is to turn this restaurant into an establishment that the more mature customer will want to patronize. We need their repeat business to turn sales volume around, and these kids just run them off."

Source: This case was prepared by William Thomas Neese and Dan Cochran, Mississippi State University. Adapted and used by permission of the authors, 1995.

Rising food costs also were a concern, but what bothered the new GM the most was that the business was not as clean as it should have been. When Bonney supervised the nightly cleanup, he noticed employee reluctance to do a thorough job without being pushed. It aggravated him to have to interrupt his closing tasks to check and recheck their work, but eventually he could get them to do the job satisfactorily. He usually closed only two nights a week, which left five less-than-adequate cleanups. "Besides," he thought, "we shouldn't have to push so hard to get satisfactory work done around here."

Bonney was determined to get the management team to help him work out the restaurant's operational glitches. At the next weekly management meeting, he asked for their assistance in correcting a list of problems over the next few weeks. He asked them to address immediately the lack of cleanliness throughout the restaurant. He had previously spoken to John Aston and Phillip Tate about the need to improve the quality of the nightly cleanups, so he thought of this discussion as reinforcement. Intern trainees never closed, so Molly Houston was never responsible for nightly cleanups.

Feeling pretty good about the management meeting, Bonney left the restaurant in Aston's hands and went home for the night. The following morning, however, he was furious within minutes after coming in to open the unit. The restaurant wasn't as clean as it should have been and he found a case of four, one-gallon containers of very expensive blue cheese dressing that had been carelessly pushed under a shelf. Blue cheese dressing had to be refrigerated soon after arrival or it might be unsafe to consume. This case had been left out since the delivery at about the time the GM had left for home the night before. "There goes $30.00 down the drain!" he steamed. Thinking about the meeting of the day before, he just shook his head. It was then that the telephone rang.

The Telephone Call

"Why me?" Bonney asked himself, as he hung up the telephone. The call had been from Mrs. Murphy, the mother of the three Murphy teenagers who worked for Yancey's, and also John's landlady. Fuming and seemingly on the verge of tears, she demanded to know what Bonney was going to do "about this problem of ours!"

"Which one?" Bonney thought, but responded, "I don't even know what the problem is, much less what I can do about it!"

"Well I'll just tell you!" exclaimed Mrs. Murphy. "That man John Aston who works down there is corrupting my baby."

"Exactly what do you mean?" asked William.

"Your man—he's a manager at your restaurant—has been taking advantage of my child. She's still a schoolgirl, and he's a grown man!" was her answer. "We opened our home to that man, and I trusted him! That hurts the most," she mumbled in a tone of despair.

"Mrs. Murphy, I just don't see how. . ." Bonney was saying, when he was interrupted.

"How!? I'll tell you how!" Mrs. Murphy injected. "I caught the two of them in his room this morning!"

"Well I could. . ." attempted Bonney.

"Well you'd better," said Mrs. Murphy, "because none of my children are going to be allowed to come to work again as long as that man is working there! I'm going to an attorney!" she said, then banged down the receiver.

"I Still Do My Job, Don't I?"

That night after the crowd had thinned out, Bonney and his boss, Bob Jackson, sat in the office discussing the situation.

"Sir," Bonney began, "the more I think about it the more obvious it becomes. I've been scheduling all four of them to work the same shifts as much as possible. John wanted me to so they could all ride together. . . . I asked him about Theresa as soon as he came in this afternoon."

"Well, what did he say?" asked Jackson, in a somewhat disgusted tone of voice. "He knows he isn't supposed to become romantically involved with an employee. The guy wasn't born yesterday! Even if he hasn't paid attention to any of the horror stories he must have heard about this sort of thing, I told him about the policy when I transferred him into my district. Male managers just cannot be romancing female employees! He knows better!"

"He just said 'I still do my job, don't I?' " replied Bonney.

"What did you say then?" Jackson asked.

"Well, I told him that I didn't think he was doing his job," Bonney responded, and then continued: "I said that first, the nightly cleanups directly under his supervision simply were not acceptable and that they indicated a gross lack of management direction, especially for a manager occupying a position with his level of responsibility. 'After all,' I told him, 'you are second in command, and your records show that you've never had this problem before.' I told him I knew it was hard to get a good cleanup late at night from some of the employees but that it could be done if he tried hard enough. He seemed to agree. Then I told him I had found out about Phillip Tate."

"You mean the assistant manager?" asked Jackson, with concern in his voice. "What about him?"

"Phillip seems to think that if John can run around with the employees, he can too! I asked him at lunch today if he had known about John and Theresa, and he told me that everybody knew about them except their parents, me, and you—that is, at least until today. Then he told me that he had been out on a date with one of the waitresses, too!"

"Then what?" Jackson moaned.

"After I told him that John was a bad example and that dating an employee was against company policy, Phillip said he didn't see how it was any of Yancey's or my business what he and John did on their spare time! Do you know what John said when I told him about this little episode?"

"Tell me," said Jackson.

"He told me that Phillip was right, that it wasn't any of our business! What do you want to do about this mess?" asked Bonney.

"Right now," replied his boss, "I really don't know!"

Questions

1. Does a firm have the right to forbid fraternization between managers and employees? Why would a firm even want to have such a policy?
2. What motivational issues and group dynamics are involved? Give specific examples.
3. What sources of power are illustrated in this case?
4. What are your recommendations for resolving the conflicts?

Part *Six*

Controlling and Evaluating

Chapter 18

Controlling in Organizations

Learning *Objectives*

After studying this chapter, you should be able to:

1. Explain the foundations of control.
2. Discuss ways that organizations create effective controls.
3. Identify the six steps of the corrective control model.
4. Describe the primary types of organizational control.
5. Discuss ethical control issues confronting managers.

Chapter *Outline*

Preview *Insight*

Wright Express

Some of the union drivers for a large New Jersey service company thought that they had a good scam going for them. Using company credit cards, they would persuade gas station attendants to pad their charge slips and split the difference. Twenty bucks worth of gas into the tank, another ten bucks in the driver's wallet, and another ten for the gas station attendant. The company suspected that something was wrong, but couldn't prove it. The accounts payable department was flooded with suspicious credit card receipts but had no control system.

Top management contacted John Birk, president of Wright Express, a computer software company, to investigate the problem. After diagnosing the problem, Wright recommended that the company issue to all drivers a single credit card honored by more than 70,000 gas stations and truck stops in the United States. Wright collects the charges and sends the company a single monthly statement, highlighting drivers that apparently bought more gas at one stop than the tank could hold. Management began questioning drivers about these charges, and soon noticed, with its new control system, that its gasoline bills dropped by several hundred thousand dollars a month.

How does the new control system work? The pump attendant can't get the charge to clear unless the driver punches in a personal identification number and an odometer reading. The magnetic strip on the credit card triggers the electronic transfer of the following information: the vehicle number, the location of the filling station, type of fuel, amount, time, and date. This information is automatically recorded by Wright's computer system.

Wright processes more than 1.3 million such transactions on its computer system monthly. The client gets monthly bills and management reports on floppy disks or online. This system easily feeds data into accounting reports that show which drivers go the farthest each day and which trucks get the best mileage. It also prints out maintenance reviews based on odometer readings to alert fleet owners to needed oil changes and new tires.[1]

1

Explain the foundations of control.

Teaching Tip
See if this is so. Have students state what they think of when they think of control. Do their responses match the book's? Discuss the results with the class.

Ask Students
Why does the word *control* often have a negative connotation? Have you had a negative experience with being controlled? Describe it.

Ethics
Start a discussion and list on the board some of the ethical limits of organizational control.

Ask Students
Can control, in the absence of the other managerial functions, stand alone? Why or why not?

FOUNDATIONS OF CONTROL

Control refers to the mechanisms used to ensure that behaviors and performance conform to an organization's rules and procedures.[2] To most people the word *control* has a negative connotation—of restraining, forcing, delimiting, watching, or manipulating. Many shopping malls employ security guards during the peak season to keep a tight surveillance on shoppers' cars and on shoppers themselves when they are returning to their cars with goods. Most convenience stores (e.g., 7-Eleven and Magic-Mart, among others) have surveillance cameras that videotape customer movements throughout the store, but especially when they approach the cashier. Most employees and many shoppers resent such practices because of their deeply held values of freedom and individualism. Thus controls often are the focus of controversy and policy struggles within organizations.

However, controls are both useful and necessary for everyone in an organization. Effective control was one of the keys to increasing profits over the past decade for the New Jersey trucking company described in the Preview Insight. It also enabled the company to plan maintenance work more accurately. We can illustrate the need for controls by describing how control interacts with planning.

- Planning is the formal process of developing goals, strategies, tactics, and standards and allocating resources. Controls are measures that help ensure that decisions, actions, and results are consistent with those plans. Thus planning and controlling go hand in hand.
- Planning prescribes *desired* behaviors and results. Controls help maintain or redirect *actual* behaviors and results.

Discussion Question 1
How are planning and control linked?

- Managers and other employees cannot effectively plan without accurate and timely information. Controls provide some of this essential information.
- Managers and other employees need plans to indicate the purposes to be served by controls. Thus planning and control complement and support each other.

Preventive and Corrective Controls

Teaching Tip
College catalogs contain preventive controls.

Teaching Tip
Bring in the campus personnel handbook and use it as an example of a preventive control.

There are two general types of organizational controls: preventive and corrective.[3] **Preventive controls** are mechanisms intended to reduce errors and thereby minimize the need for corrective action. For example, convenience store robberies fell by 80 percent in Gainesville, Florida, after the city passed an ordinance to make such stores safer. The ordinance requires two clerks to be on duty from 8 P.M. to 4 A.M., well-lighted parking lots, a limit of $50 in the cash register, and an unobstructed view into the store. Similarly, air traffic controllers help prevent crashes by ensuring that airline pilots follow well-defined standards, rules, and procedures during takeoffs and landings.

Rules and regulations, standards, recruitment and selection procedures, and training and development programs function primarily as preventive controls. They all direct and limit the behaviors of employees and managers. The assumption is that, if employees comply with these requirements, the organization is likely to achieve its goals. Controls are needed to ensure that rules, regulations, and standards are being followed and are working.

Discussion Question 2
What types of control did Wright Express use in the Preview Insight?

Teaching Tip
An example of corrective control occurs when a student is placed on academic probation for having a low GPA.

Corrective controls are mechanisms intended to reduce or eliminate unwanted behaviors or results and thereby achieve conformity with the organization's regulations and standards. In the Preview Insight, when Wright Express notifies the trucking company that a driver's gasoline buying seems excessive, the company can call the driver in and discuss the situation. Similarly, an air traffic controller exercises corrective control by instructing a pilot to change altitude and direction to avoid another plane.

Sources of Control

The four primary sources of control in most organizations are stakeholders, the organization itself, groups, and individuals. They are shown in Table 18.1 along with examples of preventive and corrective controls for each.

Ask Students
Who are the stakeholders of your college or university?

Stakeholder control refers to pressures from outside sources on organizations to change their behaviors. Recall that stakeholders may be unions, government agencies, customers, shareholders, and others. General Motors will spend more than $1.3 billion between 1994 and 1997 to comply with California legislation that requires 10 percent of cars sold in the state to be emission-free by 1997. Automakers in Europe will spend $7

TABLE 18.1

Examples of Different Sources and Types of Control

	Type of Control	
Source of Control	**Preventive**	**Corrective**
Stakeholders	Maintaining quotas for hiring people in protected classes	Changing recruitment policies to attract qualified personnel
Organization	Using budgets to guide expenditures	Disciplining an employee for violating a "No Smoking" safety regulation in a hazardous area
Group	Advising a new employee about the group's norm in relation to expected level of output	Harassing and socially isolating a worker who doesn't conform to group norms
Individual	Deciding to skip lunch in order to complete a project on time	Revising a report you have written because you are dissatisfied with it

Ask Students
What are some of the organizational controls that your college or university exercises?

Ask Students
What are some of the group controls that student organizations use?

Ask Students
Name some of the self-controls you personally exercise.

Teaching Tip
Divide the class into small groups for brainstorming examples of stakeholder, organizational, group, and individual controls from students' work or school experiences.

billion in the near future to install pollution-reducing equipment in all new cars. Customers are demanding that companies provide environmentally safe products and often are willing to pay extra for these "green" products. British Telecom, which buys 250,000 products from some 25,000 regular suppliers, requires them to give assurances concerning product performance with regard to environmental safeguards; suppliers that don't comply are dropped.[4]

Organizational control refers to the formal rules and procedures for preventing or correcting deviations from plans and for achieving desired goals. Examples include rules, standards, budgets, and audits. **Group control** refers to the norms and values that group members share and maintain through rewards and punishments. Punishments, such as giving a group member the silent treatment, were described in Chapter 16.

Individual self-control consists of the guiding mechanisms that operate consciously and unconsciously within each person. Standards of professionalism are becoming an increasingly important underpinning for individual self-control. Becoming a professional involves acquiring detailed knowledge, specialized skills, and specific attitudes and ways of behaving. The entire process may take years of study and socialization. In doing their work, certified public accountants, lawyers, engineers, business school graduates, and physicians, among others, are expected to exercise individual self-control based on the guiding standards of their professions.

Patterns of Control

Stakeholder, organizational, group, and individual controls form patterns that differ widely from one organization to another. As we have pointed out previously, strong organizational cultures usually produce mutually supportive and reinforcing organizational, group, and individual controls. At Southwest Airlines, the culture focuses on treating the customer right. One senior vice-president oversees customer contact and personally answers more than 1,000 letters a month—and not with form letters. When five medical students complained that their regularly scheduled flight got them to class fifteen minutes late, Southwest moved the departure time forward by fifteen minutes to satisfy them. To maintain such a strong culture, Southwest hires employees who have a good sense of humor, who are broad-minded, and who are tolerant of individual differences. In keeping with its customer orientation, Southwest uses frequent flier customers to help select new flight attendants.[5]

In our discussions of motivation, leadership, and teams, we focused on managerial practices used to achieve compatibility and cooperation. Control patterns in organizations often are influenced by give and take among managers, teams, and individuals. The following Insight is an account of such give and take.

Insight

Control Patterns at AT&T Credit

AT&T Credit set up eleven teams consisting of ten to fifteen newly hired employees in a high-volume division serving small businesses. The three major lease-processing functions were combined in each team to eliminate calls being shunted from department to department. The company also divided its national staff of field agents into seven regions and assigned two or three teams to handle business from each region. That way the same teams worked with the same field agents, establishing personal relationships with them and their customers. Above all, team members took control of solving customers' problems.

The teams largely manage themselves. Members make most decisions on how to deal with customers, schedule their own time off, reassign work when people are absent, and interview new prospective employees. The only supervisors are seven regional managers who advise the team members rather than give orders. Team members control themselves and each other. Under this system, teams process up to 800 lease applications a day, compared to 400 under the old system. And instead of taking several days to give a final yes or no, the teams do it within twenty-four to forty-eight hours.[6]

Managers and teams cannot achieve effective control by relying only on formal organizational controls. They need to recognize that individual and group controls strongly influence employees' behavior and make use of that knowledge. In doing so, they can complement formal controls that directly affect employee behavior with informal mechanisms. The key to setting up such controls is to keep clearly in mind the purposes they are intended to serve.

2

Discuss ways that organizations create effective controls.

Ask Students
How do most organizations measure control effectiveness?

Ask Students
Who should be responsible for designing effective organizational controls and control systems? Why?

Teaching Tip
Select a problem facing your college or university that is out of control. Apply these three questions to it.

CREATING EFFECTIVE CONTROLS

One way to develop and measure the effectiveness of formal organizational controls is to compare their costs and benefits. Such a cost-benefit analysis addresses three basic questions.

1. For what desired behaviors and results should organizational controls be developed?
2. What are the costs and benefits of the organizational controls required to achieve the desired behaviors and results?
3. What are the costs and benefits of utilizing alternative organizational controls to obtain the desired behaviors and results?

The Prudential Insurance Company used these three questions to decide whether its general fitness program for white-collar workers was a success. The company provided smoke-free offices, an on-site fitness center with an instructor, and low-cholesterol food in the cafeteria and removed all candy and cigarette machines from the premises. A group of employees participated in a study of effects. Doctors measured each participant's level of cardiorespiratory fitness (aerobic capacity) with a treadmill exercise test prior to the experiment. After five years, Prudential reported that employees in the experiment had used 20 percent fewer sick days per year and that medical claims had declined by 46 percent. Annual disability and major medical costs were $120.60 per participant, compared to Prudential's average employee cost of $353.88. Prudential concluded that the program improved employees' fitness and saved the company money on medical costs.[7]

Cost-Benefit Model

Figure 18.1 shows a cost-benefit model for gauging the effectiveness of an organization's control system. The horizontal axis indicates the amount of organizational control, ranging from low to high. The vertical axis indicates the relationship between costs and benefits of control, ranging from zero to high. For simplicity, the cost-of-control curve is shown as a direct function of the amount of organizational control.

Managers have to consider trade-offs when choosing the amount of organizational control to use. With too little organizational control, costs exceed benefits and the controls are ineffective. As the amount of organizational control increases, effectiveness also increases—up to a point. Beyond a certain point, effectiveness declines with further increases in the amount of control. For example, an organization might benefit from reducing the average managerial span of control from twenty-one to sixteen employees. However, to further reduce it to eight employees would require doubling the number of managers. The costs of the increased control (managers' salaries) might far outweigh

FIGURE 18.1

Coast-Benefit Model of Organizational Control

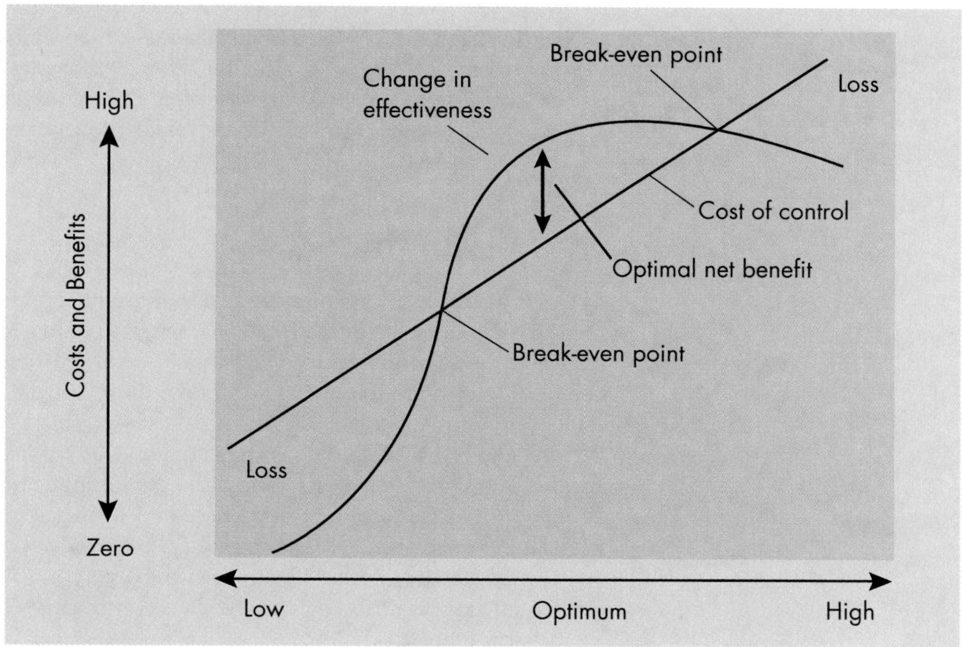

the expected benefits. Such a move might also make workers feel "micromanaged." That, in turn, could lead to increased dissatisfaction, absenteeism, and turnover.

Figure 18.1 shows two break-even points. They indicate where the amount of organizational control moves from a loss to a net benefit and then returns to a loss. Although the optimal amount of control is difficult to calculate, effective managers probably come closer to achieving it than do ineffective managers.

The following Small Business Insight illustrates how Francine Prokoski uses the cost-benefit model to sell the technology that she created. Her firm, Betac, uses facial thermogramming to recognize people. With just two other employees, she created a technology that could save organizations concerned about security (e.g., high-tech businesses, military bases, and prisons) millions of dollars in security guard costs.

Small Business *Insight*

Betac Technology

Francine Prokoski was doing work on pattern recognition of animals using biomedical data, scanning a few animals using normal procedures, such as CAT scans. She had the gut feeling that if she could combine her knowledge of biomedical research and her passion for photography, she might be able to create a business. Working with an infrared camera, a computer, and a few friends, she developed a technology whereby software reduces a person's facial image to several thousand thermograms.

From her biological training, she knew that the face provides its own invisible lighting: Because the blood comes from deep within the body, it is hotter than superficial tissue surrounding it and thus radiates heat (thermograms) that can be picked up at a distance. She learned that even plastic surgery doesn't change a thermogram unless it goes deep enough to reroute the flow of blood. The thermogram system is more accurate and faster than fingerprints.

Loral Vought Systems of Grand Prairie, Texas, uses it to identify employees at its plant to distinguish them from others who shouldn't be there. The system costs about $60,000 a year and saves Loral Vought thousands of dollars a year by reducing the number of round-the-clock security guards needed. Betac is attempting to sell its system to a federal agency for use in counterterrorism activities.[8]

Criteria for Effective Controls

Designing effective organizational controls and control systems isn't simple, because many issues must be considered.[9] However, control systems are more likely to be effective if they are linked to desired goals and are objective, complete, timely, and acceptable. These criteria refine and make more specific the ideas presented in the cost-benefit model.

As suggested by the assessment method in Table 18.2, a control may more or less satisfy each of these criteria. The table also implies that a particular control or control system should be designed and evaluated in terms of all five criteria. The total score from such an assessment can range from a low of 5 to a high of 25. The higher the total score, the greater is the likelihood that the control or control system is effective. Organizational controls that fail reasonably to satisfy the five criteria actually may do more harm than good.

Ethics
Ethics (utilitarianism, moral rights, and justice) should be emphasized at this stage.

Linkage to Desired Goals. Control or control systems should be linked to the desired goals of the organization. These goals often include improving customer service, protecting the organization's assets, and improving the quality of goods and/or services. The trucking company in the Preview Insight hired Wright Express to standardize its fuel billing process. This control process resulted in increasing the trucking company's overall profitability.

Teaching Tip
Actually, designing a complete control system that does not contradict itself is difficult, if not impossible. (Example: Reducing long distance phone and fax costs may be at odds with a goal to open up foreign markets.) Help students understand that control is a continuous series of trade-offs that constantly need reevaluation and redesign.

Objective. An objective control is impartial and cannot be manipulated by employees for personal gain. In the United States, the Financial Accounting Standards Board (FASB) and several government agencies devote a great deal of effort to developing principles and practices to ensure that financial statements objectively and accurately reflect reality as nearly as possible.

Complete. A complete control or control system encompasses all the desired behaviors and goals. A purchasing manager evaluated solely on the basis of cost per order may allow quality to slip. A computer salesperson evaluated only on the basis of sales volume may ignore after-sales service. Thus balancing quantitative (measurable) controls with more qualitative (subjective) controls is necessary.

TABLE 18.2

Methods for Assessing the Effectiveness of Organizational Controls

	Evaluation				
Criteria	**Definitely Not**	**Unlikely**	**Can't Tell**	**Probably**	**Definitely**
1. It is linked to desired goals.	1	2	3	4	5
2. It is objective.	1	2	3	4	5
3. It is complete.	1	2	3	4	5
4. It is timely.	1	2	3	4	5
5. It is acceptable.	1	2	3	4	5

Timely. A timely control or control system provides information when it is needed most. Timeliness may be measured in seconds for evaluating the safe movement of trains and planes or in terms of months for evaluating employee performance. Computer-based information systems have played a major role in increasing the timely flow of information. The computerized cash registers at Wal-Mart give store managers daily data on each department's sales, as well as profitability for the entire store.

Discussion Question 3
What are the characteristics of effective control systems?

Acceptable. An acceptable control is recognized as necessary and appropriate. If a control system is widely ignored, managers need to find out why. Perhaps the controls should be dropped or modified, should be backed up with rewards for compliance and punishments for noncompliance, or should be linked more closely to desired results.

Schlumberger is a six billion dollar a year multinational corporation that provides oil field services and high-tech measurement devices to customers throughout the world. The firm has more than 2,000 offices and field sites, scattered from Oklahoma to Japan and South America to Northern Europe. It has research centers in 100 countries. It is one of the most advanced organizations in the world in terms of control effectiveness, especially through the use of advanced information technologies. The following Global Insight focuses on the firm's use of advanced information technologies in its global information and control network.

Global *Insight*

Schlumberger's Information and Control Network

Schlumberger maintains communication links into remote parts of the world to market its technology-based measurement systems. Schlumberger's global activities present a challenge for geographically scattered employees to collaborate and stay informed about evolving projects and priorities. Management often attacks serious problems through task forces made up of employees from different locations. This approach brings people into direct contact with one another and promotes a strong flow of information throughout the company. But it also creates another problem—how to make working together possible without having employees spend all their time traveling to meetings in distant places.

Schlumberger's employees are fully aware of the Internet and regularly use the network. It helps keep employees connected to discussions and decisions that must be made. For a growing number of employees, a laptop computer with a modem is the first item packed for business trips and the last one put away in the hotel at night. The Internet is a valuable tool for bridging vast distances and promoting a common organizational control system. For example, use of the Internet features pictures and profiles of employees, tracks standards, and carries recommendations for restaurants and hotels and tips on getting from an airport to a company field site.

One reason for training and encouraging employees to use the Internet is so that they will use the same codes for essential information, instead of using personal codes to send information. With similar language (codes), employees can easily access data for a project that others may have worked on from around the world. Another reason for using the Internet is to communicate with customers. The data gathered from oil wells, seismic surveys, and the like are extremely time sensitive. Sending results to customers as quickly as possible is essential. In addition, Schlumberger has set up a special network that provides security for each customer using the Internet.

Even as interest in collaborating over the Internet continues to grow, Schlumberger is looking for better audio and video ways to overcome time and space. When the technology is improved, people will be able to collaborate in real time.[10]

3

Identify the six steps of the corrective control model.

Ask Students
Who should be responsible for setting standards within an organization? Why?

Teaching Tip
Ask students to visit a local business and interview a manager about the various preventive and corrective controls used there.

Teaching Tip
Have a student volunteer describe a problem at work and how the organization is approaching its solution. Use this example to explain the corrective control model.

Teaching Tip
Remind students that in previous chapters organizational culture was discussed as informal control.

CORRECTIVE CONTROL MODEL

The **corrective control model** is a process for detecting and eliminating or reducing deviations from an organization's established standards. This process relies heavily on information feedback and the needed reactions to it. As shown in Figure 18.2, the corrective control model has six interconnected steps: (1) define the subsystem (an individual, a department, or a process), (2) identify the key characteristics to be measured, (3) set standards, (4) collect information, (5) make comparisons, and (6) diagnose problems and make corrections.[11]

Define the Subsystem

A formal control subsystem might be created and maintained for an employee, a department, or an entire organization. The control mechanisms could focus on specific inputs, transformation processes, or outputs. Input controls often limit the amount by which raw materials used in the transformation process can vary from organization standards. For example, breweries use elaborate controls (including inspections and laboratory testing) to guarantee that the water and grains they use to make beer meet predetermined standards. Such controls ensure that the correct quantity and quality of inputs enter the production process.

Many formal controls are applied during production (the transformation process). For Coors, Miller, and other brewers, they include timing the cooking of the brew, monitoring temperature in the vats, sampling and laboratory testing of the brew at each stage of the process, and visual inspection of the beer prior to final packing.

Finally, output controls are used. For brewers, they range from specifying the levels of distributor inventories to monitoring consumer attitudes toward the beer and related services.

Identify Key Characteristics

The key types of information to be obtained about a person, team, department, or organization must be identified. Establishing a formal corrective control requires early determination of the characteristics that can be measured, the costs and benefits of obtaining information about each characteristic, and whether variations in each characteristic are likely to affect performance.

After identifying these characteristics, managers must choose the ones to be measured. The **principle of selectivity** (also known as Pareto's law) holds that a small number of characteristics always account for a large number of effects. For example, in brewing beer, three characteristics that greatly influence the final product's quality are

FIGURE 18.2

Corrective Control Model

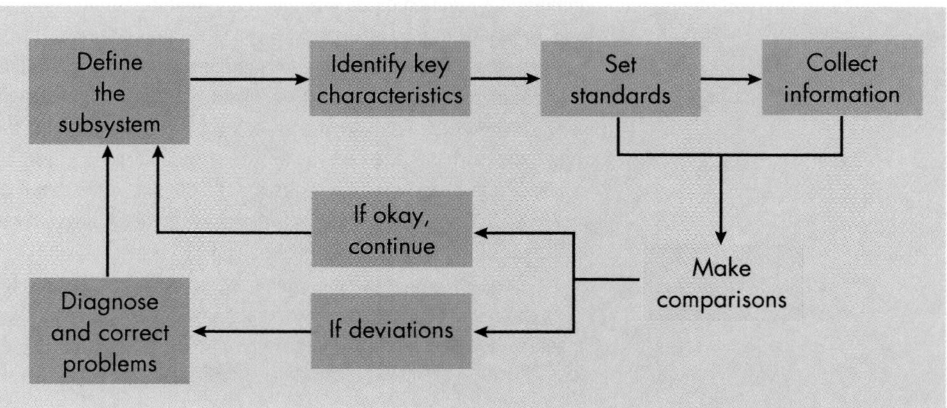

water quality, temperature, and length of brewing time. The control aspect of a management by objectives (MBO) system (discussed in Chapter 12) is based on the principle of selectivity. The direct control of objectives makes possible the control of a few vital characteristics that can account for major variations in results.

Set Standards

Standards are criteria for evaluating qualitative and quantitative characteristics and should be set for each characteristic measured. Because standards often are interrelated, a considerable amount of departmental coordination usually is required in setting them. Tuttle, Neidhart & Semyan, Inc., a global human resources consulting firm, has the goal of providing the highest quality services for its clients. According to John Semyan, a partner, its strict standards for screening job applicants include five years of work experience, excellent diagnostic abilities, ability to communicate effectively with diverse clients, ability to provide answers that clients will accept and implement, knowledge, and several essential attitudes (e.g., high ethical standards, empathy and trust, self-motivation, energy, and mobility).[12]

Increasingly, control systems are being based on performance standards (performance goals). There are many possible types of performance standards, of which the following are examples from five different functional areas.

Ask Students
Do these performance standards apply to your college or university and its various operations? Explain.

- *Inventory:* Monthly finished goods inventory should be maintained at the sales level forecast for the following two-month period.
- *Accounts receivable:* Monthly accounts receivable should be no more than the dollar value of the previous month's sales.
- *Sales productivity:* The dollar value of sales per salesperson should be $1,000 greater than the comparable month for the previous year and $12,000 greater annually.
- *Employee turnover:* The turnover of field sales personnel should be no more than 2 per 100 salespeople per month and no more than 20 per 100 salespeople annually.
- *Production waste:* Waste should amount to no more than $50 per month per full-time production worker, or no more than $600 per year per full-time production worker.

Collect Information

Information on each of the standards can be collected manually or automatically. Examples of the latter are the devices used at Disney World to count the number of people who use each ride or the turnstiles at libraries that count the number of people who enter.

If information is collected by the individual or group whose performance is to be controlled, its validity must be checked. Employees and managers have an incentive to distort or conceal information if negative results will be used to criticize or punish them. Moreover, when formal controls emphasize punishment, strong group controls (see Chapter 16 for a list) often emerge to distort the information that is reported to management. Such reporting often obscures responsibility for failure to achieve goals or meet standards.

Top managers may create special departments or rely on regular departments to collect information by monitoring or auditing certain activities. The human resources department at Dr Pepper/7-UP collects data from the U.S. Department of Labor and the company's competitors in order to determine whether starting salaries for various jobs are sufficient and affirmative action guidelines are being followed, among other items. Similarly, a controller's department will collect and analyze information to make sure that income and expenditures are being recorded in accordance with established accounting standards.

Teaching Tip

Ask the person in charge of scholarships at your college or university to come to class and describe how its scholarships compare with those of others.

Make Comparisons

Comparisons are needed to determine whether there is a difference between what *is* happening and what *should be* happening. In other words, information about actual results must be compared with performance standards. Making these comparisons allows managers and team members to concentrate on controlling deviations or exceptions. Overcontrolling becomes less likely and employees can use their time more effectively. If there is no apparent difference between what is and what should be happening, operations normally continue without any change.

Diagnose and Correct Problems

Diagnosis involves assessing the types, amounts, and causes of deviations from standards. Action is needed to eliminate those deviations and correct problems. However, the fact that a characteristic can be controlled doesn't necessarily mean that it should be controlled.[13] At times, the problem may be one of undercontrol because the timeliness of information and the linkage of corrective controls to desired results are inadequate. Computer-based management information systems often assist in overcoming inadequacies in corrective controls.

Mobil Oil Corporation used the six steps of the corrective control model to address a diversity problem. Mobil employs more than 65,000 people worldwide and, in 1988, moved its headquarters from Manhattan to Fairfax County, Virginia, for "compelling economic reasons." Besides saving an estimated $40 million annually, Mobil wanted to improve the quality of life for its employees. To do so, the company undertook the long-term diversity program described in the following Diversity Insight.

Diversity *Insight*

Mobil Oil Corporation

In 1990, Mobil's work force was 15 percent women, 5 percent African-American, 1 percent Hispanic, and the rest white men. These proportions were comparable to those of the other large oil companies (e.g., Exxon, Shell, and British Petroleum). However, the percentage of women and Hispanic employees was below that of companies not in the oil and gas industry. To achieve its goal of improving the quality of life for its employees, Mobil established targets for increasing the representation of professional women, African-Americans, and Hispanics by 10 percent, 30 percent, and 30 percent, respectively, in five years and launched four programs.

- *Outreach:* Mobil formed partnerships with outside organizations to enhance its public reputation and to encourage high school students to pursue technical studies in college.
- *Recruiting:* Mobil realized that hiring top-quality minority students meant getting them involved with the company while they were attending college. Fifty college sophomores are chosen to spend a week with Mobil during the school year and then are provided an internship for the following summer.
- *Training:* A "managing diversity" course was developed and offered to all employees to help them better understand the issues of diverse groups of people. An "efficacy program," designed for African-American and Hispanic professionals, provides career planning and self-development guidance.
- *Career development:* A career development program was designed to provide employees with "aggressive development experiences" in order to assess each individual's potential for advancement. Some development experiences require employees to live overseas, and/or work for months on oil platforms.

What has been accomplished by these programs? First, Mobil earmarks funds and lets employees donate time to organizations such as Adopt-A-School, the National Action Council for Minorities in Engineering, the American Indian Science & Engineering Society, and the National Urban League, to name a few. Second, Mobil involves more than 10,000 students in some type of recruiting program. Mobil recently hired nearly three times as many African-Americans and Hispanics and nearly twice as many women as their proportions are represented in the population as a whole. All were highly qualified. Third, more than 1,200 managers attended the "managing diversity" program and 450 professionals attended the "efficacy program" in two years.[14]

4

Describe the primary types of organizational control.

Teaching Tip

Ask students to interview a manager of a local business and write a short paper on its managerial controls. When students present their findings, have the class discuss how controls differ in different situations.

PRIMARY TYPES OF CONTROLS

Throughout the book, we have discussed various facets of control and have indicated how a firm's strategy helps focus (control) employees' behavior.[15] For example, Wal-Mart is a low-cost retailer compared to J.C. Penney. Therefore Wal-Mart's control systems focus on maintaining a low-cost strategy. In terms of human resources management, performance appraisal systems help managers assess the behaviors of employees and compare them with performance standards. Deviations are noted and corrective controls are used to reduce or eliminate problems.

In this section we explore five primary types of organizational control that are applicable to different situations and provide examples of specific methods utilized. These five types of organizational controls, shown in Figure 18.3, are bureaucratic and organic, market, financial, accounting, and automation.

Effective organizational control normally requires the use of a combination of methods from two or more of the five primary types of control. The methods available have the potential for complementing one another or working against one another. Thus management should select and assess control methods in relation to one another.

Bureaucratic versus Organic Controls

Bureaucratic controls are extensive rules and procedures, top-down authority, tightly written job descriptions, and other formal methods for preventing and correcting devi-

FIGURE 18.3

Primary Types of Organizational Controls

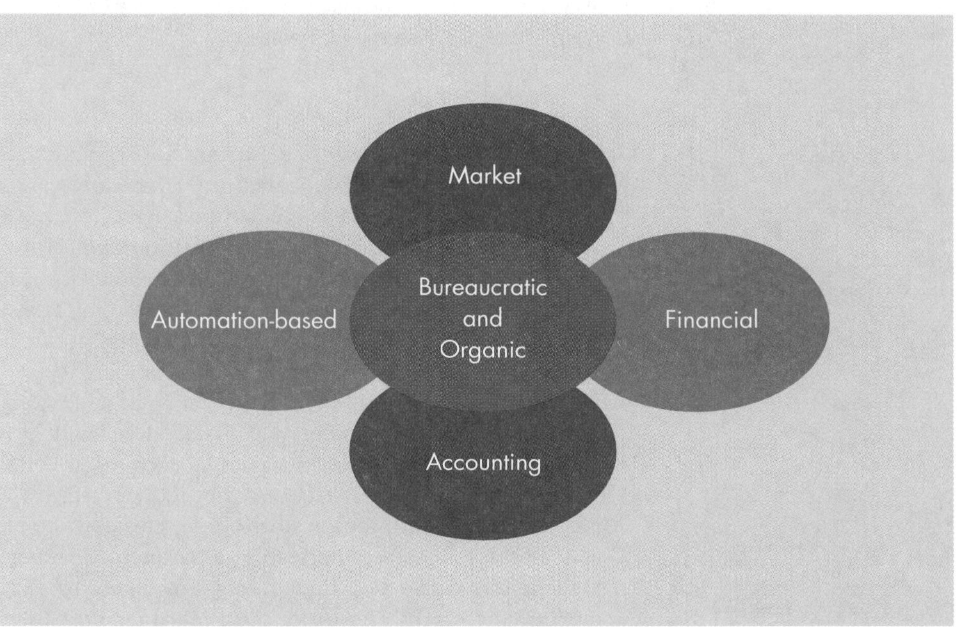

Ask Students
What types of bureaucratic and organic controls are simultaneously used at your college or university?

Teaching Tip
Divide students into groups for brainstorming the advantages and disadvantages of working for an organization that uses bureaucratic controls. Organic controls.

ations from desired behaviors and results. Bureaucratic controls are part of bureaucratic (mechanistic) management (see Chapters 2 and 11). In contrast, **organic controls** include flexible authority, relatively loose job descriptions, individual self-controls, and other informal methods for preventing and correcting deviations from desired behaviors and results. Organic controls reflect organic management (see Chapter 11).

Organic controls are consistent with a clan culture. Recall that a clan is simply a group united by common interests (goals) and characteristics. In clan cultures, such as Tandem, members share pride in membership and a strong sense of identification with management. In addition, peer pressure to adhere to certain norms is considerable. In addition, teams of self-managed employees control themselves with little direction from a supervisor. These self-managed teams use many organic controls, as illustrated in the following Quality Insight.

Quality *Insight*

Self-Managed Teams at A.O. Smith

In the early 1980s, life on the shop floor at A.O. Smith, a Milwaukee automobile parts manufacturer, was dull. Union stewards argued with management over work rules. Workers repeated the same task, either welding or riveting parts to truck frames, every twenty seconds. Absenteeism was running as high as 20 percent on some days. No one paid much attention to quality. Wages were based on piecework pay. Workers were encouraged to get the parts out the door, junk or not. Ford Motor Company was rejecting 20 percent of the door frames produced by Smith because they didn't fit. Something had to happen, or the company would go bankrupt.

Top management decided to involve employees in problem solving and formed several quality teams. The union strongly opposed these teams, but the company pressed ahead. As quality improved, the union's opposition lessened. Clearly, improving quality and cutting costs were the only ways the company was going to survive.

Now there are teams of five to seven workers who rotate from job to job. The members of the team select team leaders who assume managerial duties, such as scheduling production and overtime, ordering maintenance work, and monitoring quality control. All team members are involved in building a quality product. With team members taking over duties and controls from first-line supervisors, the company has been able to reduce their number. In 1980, the ratio of first-line supervisors to workers was 1 to 10; today it is 1 to 34. The company is training the remaining managers to put aside bureaucratic methods of control and adopt more organic methods.[16]

Ask Students
Would a change from bureaucratic management clan control be difficult? Why or why not?

Discussion Question 6
What controls do self-managed teams use to increase their effectiveness?

Table 18.3 contrasts bureaucratic and organic control methods. For example, the table indicates that detailed rules and procedures are used whenever possible as a bureaucratic control method. In contrast, detailed rules and procedures are used only when necessary as an organic control method. However, an organization or its units doesn't have to use totally bureaucratic or totally organic control methods. At Alcan Aluminum Corporation Metal Goods Division in Dallas, Texas, safety rules to protect life and property are uniform and highly detailed under both the bureaucratic and organic methods of control utilized within the company.

Rubbermaid, Merill Lynch, Procter & Gamble, and other large organizations consist of a number of departments which can differ widely in their emphasis on bureaucratic or organic controls. Mechanistic characteristics in certain departments and organic characteristics in others don't necessarily reduce a firm's overall effectiveness.[17] For example, at Rubbermaid, the production department operates within a relatively stable environment, whereas the marketing department operates within a changing environment. Managers of these two departments are likely to choose different ways to divide and manage the work. The production manager probably will choose a mechanistic struc-

TABLE 18.3

Characteristics of Bureaucratic and Organic Control Methods

BUREAUCRATIC CONTROL METHODS	ORGANIC CONTROL METHODS
Use of detailed rules and procedures whenever possible	Use of detailed rules and procedures only when necessary
Top-down authority, with emphasis on positional power	Flexible authority, with emphasis on expert power and networks of control
Activity-based job descriptions that prescribe day-to-day behaviors	Results-based job descriptions that emphasize goals to be achieved
Emphasis on extrinsic rewards (wages, pensions, status symbols) for controlling performance	Emphasis on both extrinsic and intrinsic rewards (meaningful work) for controlling performance
Distrust of team controls, based on an assumption that team goals conflict with organizational goals	Harnessing of group controls, based on an assumption that group goals and norms assist in achieving organizational goals
Organizational culture not recognized as a source of control	Organizational culture seen as a way of integrating organizational, group, and individual goals for greater overall control

ture, and the advertising manager probably will choose a more organic system. In fact, all organizations utilize some combination of bureaucratic and organic control methods in conjunction with their market, financial, accounting, and automation-based controls.

Teaching Tip
Students often say that they wish their university was market controlled. Tell them that market controlled schools often "sell degrees" in order to attract more business. These schools assign easy work or in some cases literally grant a degree to anyone who pays for it. Ask students whether they really would want a degree on their résumés from such a place.

Market Controls

Market controls involve the use of data to monitor sales, prices, costs, and profits, to guide decisions and evaluate results. The idea of market controls emerged from economics, and dollar amounts provide effective standards of comparison. To be effective, market controls generally require that

- the costs of the resources used in producing outputs be measured monetarily,
- the value of the goods and services produced be defined clearly and monetarily priced, and
- the prices of the goods and services produced be set competitively.

In one of its first attempts at variable pay for production workers, AlliedSignal cut the traditional annual raise from 3 to 2 percent at its spark plug plant in Fostoria, Ohio. However, if the employees meet rigorous productivity improvement goals, they stand to boost their salaries by as much as 6 percent. If they increase productivity by 6 percent, they get their old 3 percent raise; if they raise it 9 percent, they get a 6 percent raise.

Two of the control methods that can satisfy these requirements are profit-sharing plans and customer monitoring.

Profit-Sharing Plans. Recall that profit-sharing plans provide employees with supplemental income based on the profitability of an entire organization or a selected subunit.[18] The subunit may be a strategic business unit, a division, a store in a chain, or other organizational entity. Profit-sharing plans generally have four goals:

Ask Students
Does anyone here have profit sharing at work? How does it work? How does it compare to other forms of pay?

- to increase employee identification with the organization's profit goals, allowing greater reliance on individual self-control and group controls;
- to achieve a more flexible wage structure, reflecting the company's actual economic position and controlling labor costs;
- to attract and retain workers more easily, improving control of selection and lowering turnover costs; and
- to establish a more equitable reward system, helping to develop an organizational culture that recognizes achievement and performance.

Many factors influence whether the goals of a profit-sharing plan can be achieved. First, employees must believe that the plan is based on a reasonable, accurate, and equitable formula. The formula, in turn, must be based on valid, consistently, and honestly reported financial and operating information. Second, employees must believe that their efforts and achievements contribute to profitability. Third, employees must believe that the size of profit-based incentives will increase proportionally as profitability increases. These factors also are crucial in determining the effectiveness of gain-sharing plans. Recall that gain-sharing plans pass on the benefits of increased productivity, cost reductions, and improved quality through regular cash bonuses to employees.

Customer Monitoring. **Customer monitoring** consists of ongoing efforts to obtain feedback from customers concerning the quality of goods and services. Such monitoring is done in order to prevent problems or learn of their existence and solve them. Customer monitoring is being used increasingly in corrective control, in an attempt to assess or measure customers' perceptions.[19] Based on this assessment, management may take action to prevent the loss of further business because of customer dissatisfaction.

3M's medical and surgical products plant in Brookings, South Dakota, operates a program called Pulse to monitor customer satisfaction. All 750 employees meet face to face with doctors and nurses at three local hospitals. They go into the operating rooms to watch their products in action. As they observe, they note any improvements that could make their customers' jobs easier.

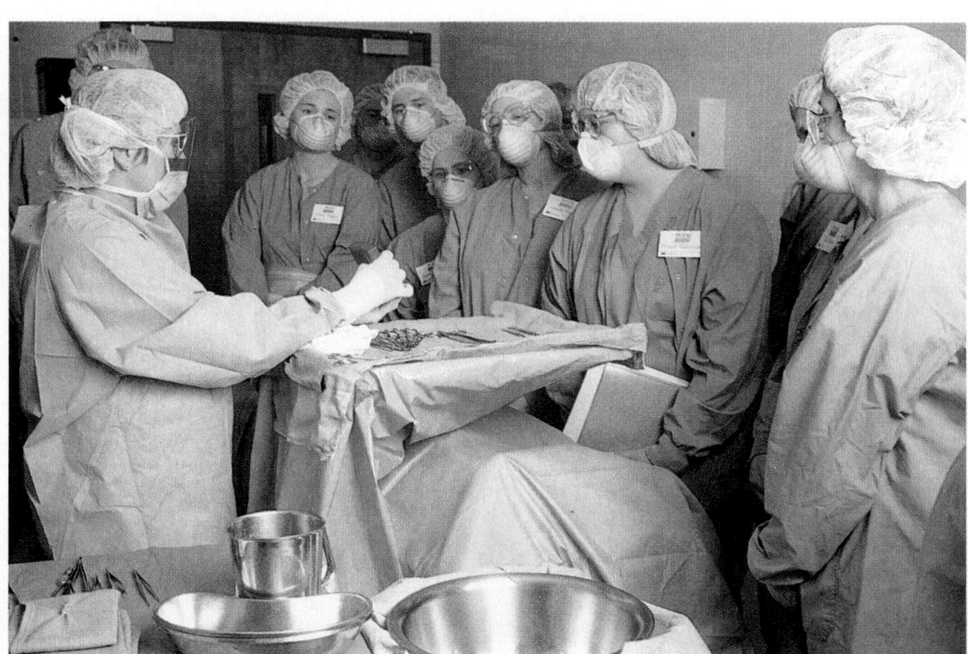

Teaching Tip
Bring a customer satisfaction card to class as a prop.

Teaching Tip
Focus groups, which students may have participated in, are an example of this approach.

Customer monitoring often is used by service providers. Hotels and restaurants may ask customers to judge the quality of their service by completing a "customer satisfaction card." After purchases of their products, many firms follow up with telephone interviews or mail questionnaires to obtain information from customers. Chemical Waste Management, Inc., the largest hauler of toxic wastes in the United States, uses a unique method of obtaining feedback from customers and the general public. The company's phone number is displayed prominently on each truck, and the local manager's name and home address are displayed at each storage facility. These displays are intended to improve the company's control in terms of its employees' compliance with laws and operating standards.

Financial Controls

Financial controls refer to the wide range of methods, techniques, and procedures intended to prevent or correct the misallocation of resources.[20] External auditors (certified public accounting firms, e.g., Arthur Andersen, Price Waterhouse, and Coopers & Lybrand) and/or internal auditing departments (e.g., accounting, controller, and treasurer) perform the monitoring aspect of financial controls. The primary responsibility of external auditors is to the shareholders. The auditors' role is to ensure shareholders that the firm's financial statements present its true financial position and are in conformity with generally accepted accounting principles.

Because there are so many methods, techniques, and procedures of financial control, we focus only on two of the essential ones: comparative financial analysis and budgeting.

Teaching Tip
Bring some corporate annual reports to class so that students can do comparative financial analysis.

Comparative Financial Analysis. The evaluation of a firm's financial condition for two or more time periods is called **comparative financial analysis.** When data are available from similar firms, they are used in making comparisons.[21] Industry trade associations often collect information from their members and publish it in summary form. Publicly owned firms publish income statements, balance sheets, and other financial statements. These sources often are used by managers and outsiders to assess changes in the firm's financial indicators and compare its financial health with that of other firms in the same industry. Companies that have multiple production facilities (e.g., GM, Ford, Exxon, and IBM), retail outlets (e.g., Kmart, Wal-Mart, Sears, J.C. Penney, and Foley's), restaurants (e.g., McDonald's, Wendy's, Red Lobster, and Bennigan's), hotels (e.g., Hilton, Holiday Inns, and Hyatt) compare the financial records of all units for control purposes.

The most common method of comparison is ratio analysis. **Ratio analysis** involves selecting two significant figures, expressing their relationship as a proportion or fraction, and comparing its value for two periods of time or with the same ratio of similar organizations. Of the many kinds of ratios, the types most commonly used by organizations are profitability, liquidity, activity, and leverage. They are summarized in Table 18.4.

TABLE 18.4

Examples of Financial Ratios

TYPE	EXAMPLE	CALCULATION	INTERPRETATION
Profitability	Return on investment (ROI)	$\frac{\text{Profit after taxes}}{\text{Total assets}}$	Productivity of assets
Liquidity	Current ratio	$\frac{\text{Current assets}}{\text{Current liabilities}}$	Short-term solvency
Activity	Inventory turnover	$\frac{\text{Sales}}{\text{Inventory}}$	Efficiency of inventory management
Leverage	Debt ratio	$\frac{\text{Total debt}}{\text{Total assets}}$	How a company finances itself

Return on investment (ROI) generally is considered to be the most important profitability ratio because it indicates how efficiently the organization is using its resources. A ratio value greater than 1.0 indicates that the organization is using its resources effectively. The *current ratio* indicates an organization's ability to pay bills on time. A current ratio should be well above 1:1 and if a firm has a ratio of 2:1, it should be financially sound. If an organization has a low current ratio, it might mean that it has unnecessary inventory, a lot of cash sitting idle, or heavy accounts receivable that are difficult to collect. *Inventory turnover* refers to the average number of times inventory is sold and restocked during the year. A high ratio means efficient operations—a relatively small amount of money is tied up in inventory—enabling the organization to use its resources elsewhere. *Debt ratio* is computed to assess an organization's ability to meet its long-term financial commitments. A value of 0.40 would indicate that this organization has $0.40 in liabilities for every $1.00 of assets. The higher this ratio, the poorer credit risk the organization is perceived to be by financial institutions. Generally, organizations with debt ratios above 1.0 are considered to be relying too much on debt to finance their operations.

Financial ratios have little value unless you know how to interpret them. For example, an ROI of 10 percent doesn't mean much unless you compare it to the ROIs of other organizations in the same industry. An organization with an ROI of 5 percent in an industry where the average ROI is 11 percent might be performing poorly. An inventory turnover rate of 5 at Pep Boys, Chief Auto Parts, and other auto-supply stores might be excellent but would be disastrous for Kroger, Grand Union, H.E.B., and other large supermarkets for which an inventory turnover of 15 is common. Organizations can improve their inventory turnover rate by offering "specials" to stimulate customer demand, lowering prices, or not carrying items that move slowly.

Budgeting. The process of categorizing proposed expenditures and linking them to goals is known as **budgeting.** Budgets usually express the dollar costs of various tasks or resources. For example, production budgets may be based on hours of labor per unit produced, machine downtime per thousand hours of running time, wage rates, and similar information. The main budget categories usually include labor, supplies and materials, and facilities (property, buildings, and equipment).[22]

Budgeting has three primary purposes: (1) to help in planning work effectively; (2) to assist in allocating resources; and (3) to assist in controlling and monitoring resource utilization during the budget period. When managers assign dollar costs to the resources needed, they sometimes realize that proposed tasks aren't worth the cost; they can then modify or abandon the proposals.

Budgeting for completely new tasks usually requires estimating costs. Budgeting for established tasks is easier because historical cost data are available. In either case, those who prepare budgets must exercise judgment, whether using historical data or forecasts of conditions and costs. Budgets often are developed for a year and then broken down by month. Managers thus are able to track their progress in meeting the budget as the year unfolds and to take corrective action as necessary.

The control aspect of budgeting may be either corrective or preventive. When budgeting is used as a corrective control, the emphasis is on identifying deviations from the budget. Deviations indicate the need to identify and correct their causes or to change the budget itself.

The power of a budget, especially when used as a preventive control, depends on whether it is viewed as an informal contract that has been agreed to. One study asked first-line managers about their companies' budgets. The question was: "Do you feel that budgets or standards are frequently a club held over the head of the manager to force better performance?" Twenty percent of the 204 respondents replied "yes" and 68 percent answered "no." Most employees who must live by budgets accept their use by top management as a control mechanism. However, some employees view budgets with fear and hostility. This reaction usually occurs when an organization enforces budget controls with threats and punishment.[23]

There is no single classification system for budgets. Specific individuals, sections, projects, teams, committees, departments, divisions, or SBUs may be given budgets within which they are expected to operate. The following are the most common types of budgets used in business.

- Sales budget—a forecast of expected revenues, generally stated by product line on a monthly basis and revised at least annually.
- Materials budget—expected purchases, generally stated by specific categories, which may vary from month to month because of seasonal variations and inventory levels.
- Labor budget—expected staffing, generally stated by number of individuals and dollars for each job category.
- Capital budget—targeted spending for major tangible assets (e.g., new or renovated headquarters building, new factory, or major equipment), often requires a time horizon beyond one year.
- Research and development budget—targeted spending for the refinement or development of products, materials, and processes.
- Cash budget—expected flow of monetary receipts and expenditures (cash flow), generally developed at least once a year for each month of the year.

The types of budgets and budget categories used are strongly influenced by organizational design and culture. An organization having a functional structure usually has a budget for each function (e.g., marketing, production, finance, and human resources). However, an organization having a product structure usually has a budget for each product line. For example, American Brands is structured by product—office, tobacco, distilled spirits, hardware & home improvements, specialty, and life insurance—and uses product-line budgeting. Management has found that this type of budgeting enables its control system to measure effectively the contributions of each product line.

Teaching Tip
Bring some organizational budgets to class so that students can compare them.

Accounting for Quality

Within the past decade, many organizations have needed to change their financial controls to reflect more accurately changes in their products. GE Medical Systems, Volkswagen Canada, Union Carbide, and others have had to change their accounting systems because of high overhead costs and because they began offering customers a diversity of products that required numerous variations in production runs and costly setups. Organizations also needed control systems that would enable them to measure accurately the cost of making quality products for the consumer. **Activity-based costing** is a system that focuses on activities as the fundamental cost centers.[24] It uses activity costs as building blocks for measuring the effectiveness of cost centers. Activities become the focal point for the organization. An activity is any event that is a cost driver, including energy consumed, miles driven, computer hours logged, quality inspections, shipments, and scrap/rework orders.

The number of these activities usually depends on the complexity of operations. The more complex the organization's operations, the more cost-driving activities it is likely to have. Equally important, managers have discovered that not all products have the same mix of these activities. If a product doesn't require the use of an activity, its cost would be zero for that activity. For example, at Motorola one product is low-volume but requires frequent machine setups, has many intricate parts requiring numerous purchase orders, and requires constant inspections to maintain quality. Another product is a high-volume item that requires few machine setups, few purchase orders, and few quality inspections. What happens if Motorola ignores the differences of these two products on its cost-driving activities and simply assigns a general overhead cost to the products on the basis of volume? The high-volume product will bear the lion's share of the overhead cost. This approach seriously distorts actual unit costs for each product.

Discussion Question 4
What are the basic elements of an activity-based costing system?

FIGURE 18.4

Activity-Based Costing Model

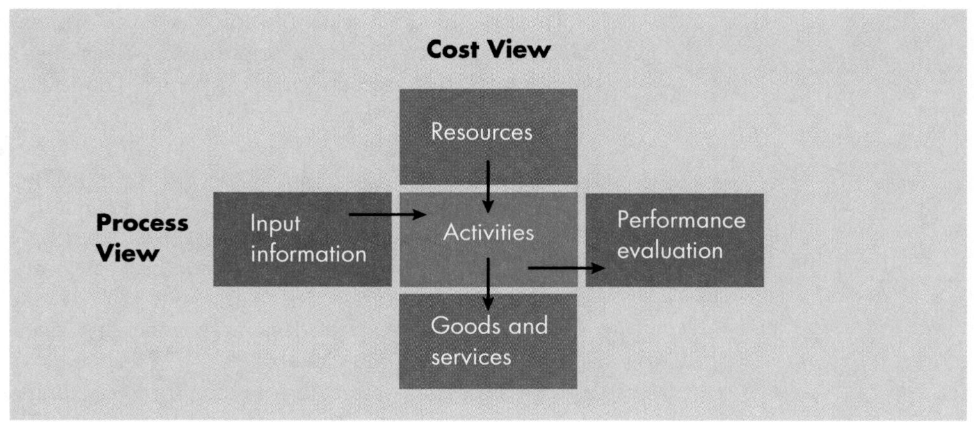

Figure 18.4 depicts a model of the flow of information in an activity-based accounting system. The information in this system is viewed from two perspectives: cost and process. The *cost view* reflects the flow of costs from resources to activities and from activities to products and services. At E-Systems, one of the activities is materials handling. The resources consumed in moving materials from one location to another at the plant is traced to each product based on the number of times an item has been moved. This cost view is the key concept underlying activity-based costing: *Resources are consumed by activities, and activities are consumed by products and services.*

The *process view* reflects the lateral flow from costs of input information to activities and from activities to performance evaluation. In the case of materials handling at E-Systems, information is gathered on the number of times an item is moved to determine the extent of activity during a period. This information provides the activity data needed to complete the costing of products. It also provides the data needed for performance evaluation.[25]

The following Quality Insight illustrates how Dana Corporation, an auto-parts maker headquartered in Toledo, Ohio, used activity-based costing to discover its true costs and then improve the quality of its parts.

Quality *Insight*

Activity-Based Costing at Dana

Dana Corporation installed an activity-based cost system at its Plymouth, Minnesota, factory to improve the quality of its parts. For six months in all areas of the plant, employees wrote down what they did each day to define their basic activities. For example, in the materials-control department, which buys components for the factory and fills customer orders, a customer representative spends about 30 percent of the time taking orders and 50 percent of the time processing them.

Based on these data, accountants took the expense data and applied activity-based costing to this department. The differences between the traditional way and the activity-based cost system are shown in the following table.

Traditional		*Activity-Based Costing*	
Salaries	$371,917	Process sales orders	$144,846
Fringe benefits	118,069	Source parts	136,320
Supplies	76,745	Expedite supplier orders	72,143

Fixed costs	23,614
Total	$590,345

Expedite internal processing	49,945
Resolve supplier quality	47,599
Reissue purchase orders	45,235
Expedite customer orders	27,747
Schedule intracompany sales	17,768
Request engineering changes	16,704
Resolve problems	16,648
Schedule parts	15,390
Total	$590,345

Dana was able to improve its quality by pinpointing activities that focused on quality. By working with suppliers more closely, it was able to save expediting costs and improve supplier quality. These activities saved Dana $99,742. As Dana develops standards for the cost of each activity, it will be able to determine quickly which activities are driving costs and which are directly related to customer satisfaction. The result will be higher profits.[26]

Benefits. Using an activity-based accounting control system yields at least three benefits.[27] First, costs are pinpointed by activity instead of being charged to overhead. Employees understand that their activities are translated into costs that define the performance level of their units and the organization as a whole. The system also gives them an incentive to think about how to reduce costs. Second, cost allocations are based on the portion of activities that can be directly traced to a product or job itself, as opposed to the volume of production. Third, costs associated with an activity for a particular product can now be traced. This result shows managers that the best way to control costs is to control the activities that generate them in the first place.

Limitations. The benefits of activity-based accounting control systems are offset somewhat by two limitations. First, managers must still make some arbitrary cost allocations based on volume. In many high-volume organizations, such as Siemens, obtaining accurate product costs is difficult because so many costs relate to buildings, land, and equipment. Second, high measurement costs are associated with multiple activity centers and cost drivers. For example, at a hospital, automatically recording the results each time a nurse takes someone's blood pressure would be expensive. Similarly, at banks, recording the length of time a teller and customer talk would be extremely difficult. Even if it were feasible, it might not be a good idea because most banks don't want tellers rushing customers and minimizing customer contact.

Automation-Based Controls

Automation refers to the use of devices and processes that are self-regulating and operate independently of people. Automation usually involves linking machines with other machines to perform tasks. **Machine controls** are methods that use instruments or devices to prevent and correct deviations from desired results. The use of machines in business has gone through several significant stages of development. Machines initially increased productivity by giving employees better physical control over certain tasks. Eventually the interaction of employee and machine created a mutual control system. A new threshold was reached with automation.

Machine control of other machines, as with computer-operated robots, takes over part of the managerial control function. That is, machines can now participate in the control process with managers. For example, computers in oil refineries collect data, monitor, and make automatic adjustments during refining processes. The impact of such automatic machine control on management has been reported in a number of studies. One researcher found that the introduction of an advanced automated system in one large factory reduced the number of middle management jobs by 34 percent.

There has been a steady shift toward machine controls in production operations. The shift began with machines being given control of some production tasks, such as using automatic sensors instead of visual inspection in steel production. With the advent of assembly lines and mass-production technology, machines supplemented rules and regulations as a means of directly controlling production workers. In continuous process or robotic operations, machines control machines.

Advanced machine control is widespread in the automobile industry. In its brake plant at Saginaw, Michigan, Chevrolet installed an automated system that controls four cranes, records inventory, directs five miles of conveyors, and diagnoses tool problems for the maintenance staff. Chrysler's computer-controlled system in its Syracuse, New York, plant expands or contracts a boring tool to adjust for temperature and tool wear. The system feeds the exact diameters of finished pistons to the machines tooling cylinder blocks so they can adjust their bits.

Real-World Example
James Wiggins of District Cablevision (Washington, D.C.) was fired after a background check—conducted after he had been given a raise—revealed that he was a cocaine user. Later, Equifax, a background checking firm, admitted that it investigated the wrong James Wiggins. Wiggins is suing both firms (*Los Angeles Times*, March 7, 1995, A1, A14).

ETHICS AND CONTROL

5

Discuss ethical control issues confronting managers.

Some methods of control, particularly those that are aimed directly at the behaviors of individuals, pose potential ethical dilemmas for managers and other employees.[28] To illustrate this problem, we present three controversial control methods: computer monitoring, drug testing, and undercover security agents.

Real-World Example
Greyhound fired bus cleaner Fred Huratado after a background check revealed that he had been arrested in 1979 for battery and in 1983 for unlawful use of a weapon and drinking in public. He was not convicted of two of the charges. The third charge was removed after he had successfully completed probation. The California Labor Code prohibits employers from asking about arrests that don't lead to felony convictions. Huratado is suing Greyhound and the background checker (*Los Angeles Times*, March 7, 1995, A1, A14).

Computer Monitoring

Computer monitoring refers to the use of special software to collect highly detailed quantitative information on employee performance. An estimated 10 million U.S. workers currently are being monitored electronically, often without their knowledge.[29] Employees who work at computer terminals in data processing service bureaus, insurance companies, airlines, telemarketing firms, and telephone companies are those most often monitored in this way. Information collected by computers may include the number of keystrokes, number of customers served, length of time required to serve each customer, minutes away from the computer terminal, number of corrections and changes made, and so on. At FedEx, if employees spend, on average, one second less on each phone call, the organization saves $500,000 a year.

Organizations such as FedEx, GE, among others, that monitor the work of their employees by computer indicate that doing so gives them an objective basis for giving employees precise feedback about their performance and for determining training needs.[30] The conversation between a customer and customer-service representative is that employee's work product. Thus the monitoring of both sides of the conversation may be the most accurate way to measure an employee's performance. However, customers should be asked whether they mind having their conversations monitored. At GE's Answer Center in Louisville, Kentucky, quality is stressed over quantity and counts for 70 percent of employee's performance evaluations. Handling problems related to warranties over the phone costs GE $4.00 per call, saving $16.00 a call by avoiding the need to send out a repair person. Monitoring also makes pinpointing problems easier in call centers, such as directory assistance centers, catalog order centers, and customer service departments of large organizations. These centers often have hundreds of employees who answer thousands of phone calls a day.

Real-World Example
African-Americans and low-income workers (those earning less than $15,000 per year) have the most concern about privacy violations (*Los Angeles Times*, August 19, 1994, D1-D2)

Ask Students
Does anyone in the class work under computer monitoring? If so, what is it like?

Ethics
Is computer monitoring ethical? Why or why not?

Computer monitoring is causing growing concern among unions, civil libertarians, and legislators because it invades employees' privacy to a greater degree than most other control methods used by organizations. The tensions associated with computer monitoring are demonstrated in the following Ethics Insight.

Ethics *Insight*

Computer Monitoring of Employees

Every morning for nearly two years, Meg Narducci came to work, logged onto her computer, logged on again to her terminal, plugged in her headphones, hit the ready button, and started to answer more than 200 calls in rapid succession, starting each one with "Hello, national customer service department. This is Meg."

Throughout the day, every second of her time was accounted for. Every conversation she had was subject to surveillance. Her manager knew everything she did. The computer she logged onto matched her name to every message she typed. The terminal next to her computer functioned like a high-tech stopwatch. It told her manager what time she punched in and out for the day, what time she took her scheduled lunch break, when she went to the bathroom, how long she stayed in the bathroom, how much time she was available to take calls, how many she took, and how long she spent on each one. For example, if she spent an extra minute in the bathroom that minute would be deducted from the six minutes she got the next hour.

Many employees who are monitored by computer complain of depression, anxiety, back pain, shoulder soreness, stiff and sore wrists, and fatigue. Most monitored employees complain that their managers have little idea about the job pressures because they have never been monitored.[31]

Real-World Example
In its franchised stores and at its Randolph, Massachusetts, corporate HQ, Dunkin' Donuts installed listening devices to pick up what employees and customers said. The donut shops have small stickers on the window that say "audio monitoring on the premises." The stickers say nothing about recording customers' private conversations. The company claimed that the bugs were for loss prevention purposes (*Houston Chronicle*, May 27, 1994, 2D; May 30, 1994, 6A).

Ethics
Is listening to customers' conversations ethical? Listening to employees' conversations?

Discussion Question 5
Do organizations have a right to monitor the work of their employees by computer? Explain your answer.

Real-World Example
Employees do want drug testing as a safety precaution but not other forms of testing (*Los Angeles Times*, August 19, 1994, D1-D2).

Drug Testing

President Reagan's 1987 Commission on Organized Crime recommended that all U.S. companies test employees for drug use. The commission was reacting to the increased use of illegal drugs in all segments of the society, the reluctance of employers to report known or suspected drug use by former employees for fear of lawsuits, and employer liability for negligent hiring. In addition, the Drug-Free Workplace Act of 1988 requires all federal government contractors and fund recipients to certify that they will maintain a drug-testing program. The requirements of the act do not include mandatory implementation of a drug-testing program. Instead, the primary focus is on employee awareness and drug rehabilitation.

Abuse of illegal drugs by employees cost U.S. organizations an estimated $100 billion per year.[32] Drug abuse leads to increased absenteeism, shoddy products, workplace accidents, and skyrocketing insurance claims. Health care costs and accident rates are more than 10 percent higher for abusers. According to a recent survey of 1,000 organizations, 48 percent of them test for drugs prior to employment, up from 21 percent just several years ago.[33] This survey found that the drug-testing programs of most of the nation's top 1,000 organizations cover both preemployment testing and testing of current employees.[34]

Preemployment Testing. Private sector employers may require any job applicant to submit to a drug-screening test, unless limited by state law. Most drug use is tested by examining body fluids, although hair analysis, video-based testing of eye-hand coordination, and pupillary reaction tests have been used. Employers can state a preference to hire only qualified candidates. As drug use may negatively affect job performance, these organizations can choose to hire only applicants who pass a drug-screening test. IBM, Kodak, Mellon Bank, and others use a plan that involves:

- *Notification.* Applicants are notified of the screening on the physical exam questionnaire to minimize claims of invasion of privacy.

- *No rescheduling of test.* Candidates are not allowed to postpone the test after appearing at the doctor's office and realizing that drug testing is part of the physical exam.
- *Test validity.* In the event of a positive test, the same sample is reanalyzed in order to ensure validity. Records of results usually are kept in the doctor's office for 180 days in case of a lawsuit.
- *Confidentiality.* Confidentiality is maintained by recording positive test results only in the patient's records at the doctor's office. Only the applicant is made aware of the test results. The doctor's office verbally notifies the applicant and a human resources specialist at the firm of the test results. The employing firm doesn't maintain records of the test results.

Testing Current Employees. The testing of current employees raises further issues. Employers who test employees usually follow one of three policies:

1. ***Random testing.*** All employees are tested at random. Those selected are tested on predetermined dates. Trucking companies report that drugs were found in nearly a third of all tractor-trailer drivers involved in accidents. Many trucking companies now perform random drug tests on their drivers.
2. ***Testing based on probable cause.*** An employee is tested only if the manager has reasonable cause to suspect drug abuse. Signs of probable abuse include possession of drug paraphernalia, suspicious behavior, and drastic mood or personality shifts.
3. ***Testing after an accident.*** All employees involved are tested after any accident or major incident on the job.

Some organizations have established elaborate policies and procedures to control drug and alcohol abuse among their current employees. For instance, General Dynamics spells out its program in a ten-page document. It requires managers to give employees, in writing, information on employee assistance programs, the effects of alcohol and drug abuse on co-workers and others, and how General Dynamics will conduct its tests. Capital Cities/ABC, a media conglomerate, also has an extensive program, including educational assistance, employee counseling, the use of various drug tests, drug-sniffing dogs, and undercover operations, if needed.

Undercover Security Agents

Employee theft is the unauthorized taking, control, or transfer of an organization's money and/or property by an employee. It costs employers more than $40 billion annually in the United States alone.[35] A rule of thumb says that any company loses 1 to 2 percent of its sales to employee theft. Employee theft includes pilferage (repeated stealing of small amounts), kickbacks, securities theft and fraud, embezzlement (taking assets entrusted to the employee's care), arson, burglary, vandalism (malicious destruction of assets), shoplifting, insurance fraud, check fraud, and credit card fraud. Although the news media have played up the role of outsiders in computer-related crime, most of it is committed by employees.

The primary reason for the growth of internal security staffs and security firms, such as Pinkerton, Brink's, Burns, and Guardsmark, is the need to bring the increasing rate of employee theft under control. These security firms provide companies with undercover security agents, often in response to suspicion that theft is taking place. Companies that sell their trash, such as Optigraphics, have used such agents posing as trash collectors because they suspect collusion between employees and trash collectors. Optigraphics manufacturers baseball cards and if a card doesn't meet the firm's standards, it is discarded in the trash. Some retail department stores use undercover agents to verify that salespeople are ringing up sales and not acting in collusion with "customers" in theft. A Pinkerton undercover agent who went to work as a production employee at a manufacturing company discovered that continual inventory shrinkage of 1 percent per year was due to widespread pilfering. Group norms had developed among employees in support of small amounts of stealing at that plant.

Undercover security seems to be tolerated and generally accepted—both legally and socially—as long as there is no hint of entrapment. **Entrapment** involves luring an individual into committing a compromising or illegal act.

CHAPTER SUMMARY

1 ***Explain the foundations of control.***

The foundations of organizational control are (1) the type of control, (2) the source of control, (3) the pattern of control, and (4) the purpose of control. Preventive controls, such as rules, standards, and training programs, are designed to reduce the number and severity of deviations that require corrective action. In contrast, corrective controls are designed to bring unwanted behaviors in line with established standards or goals. There are four sources of organizational control: stakeholders, the organization itself, groups, and individuals. Patterns of the different kinds of control vary from mutually reinforcing to independently operating to conflicting.

2 ***State how organizations create effective controls.***

The effectiveness of formal organizational controls is measured in terms of costs and benefits. The cost-benefit model highlights the trade-offs that occur with increases or decreases in control. At some point, increasing controls ceases to be effective. The effectiveness of specific controls is evaluated according to whether they achieve desired results and are objective, complete, timely, and acceptable.

3 ***Identify the six steps of the corrective control model.***

The corrective control model comprises six interconnected elements: (1) define the subsystem, (2) identify the characteristics to be measured, (3) set standards, (4) collect information, (5) make comparisons, and (6) diagnose and correct any problems.

4 ***Describe the primary types of organizational control.***

The primary types of organizational controls include (1) bureaucratic versus organic, (2) market, (3) financial, (4) accounting for quality, and (5) automation-based. Effective managerial control usually requires using several types and methods of control.

5 ***Discuss ethical control issues confronting managers.***

Ethical issues concerning control methods arise from the use of computer monitoring, drug testing, and undercover security agents.

QUESTIONS FOR DISCUSSION

1. How are planning and control linked?
2. What types of control did Wright Express use in the Preview Insight?
3. What are the characteristics of effective control systems?
4. What are the basic elements of an activity-based costing system?
5. Do organizations have a right to monitor the work of their employees by computer? Explain your answer.
6. What controls do self-managed teams use to increase their effectiveness?

FROM WHERE YOU SIT

1. If you were assigned to look for drug abuse on your campus or in an organization you belong to, what drugs would you look for? Why these drugs?
2. Talk with your local banker about the organizational controls used by that bank. Are they effective? If so, how does the banker know?
3. Recently, China and the United States have held talks on intellectual property rights. What controls can a government use to protect such rights?
4. What abuses of organizational control have you observed at work or school? When and how did these abuses occur?
5. Visit a local convenience store and note the controls used by store management. Are they effective in deterring theft (employee and/or customer)? Why or why not?
6. Apply the corrective control model to your studying behavior. What actions might you want to undertake to improve your grade-point average?

SKILL-BUILDING EXERCISE

Controlling Ethical Behavior

The following questionnaire lists behaviors that you and others might engage in on the job. For each item, circle the number that best indicates the frequency with which you would engage in that behavior. Then put an X over the number that you think best describes how others you know behave. Finally, put a check mark beside that behavior if you believe that management should design a system to control that behavior.[36]

Behavior	Most of the time	Often	About half the time	Seldom	Never
1. Blaming an innocent person or a computer for errors	5	4	3	2	1
2. Passing on information that was told in confidence	5	4	3	2	1
3. Falsifying quality reports	5	4	3	2	1
4. Claiming credit for someone else's work	5	4	3	2	1
5. Padding an expense account by more than 5 percent	5	4	3	2	1
6. Using company supplies for personal use	5	4	3	2	1
7. Accepting favors in exchange for preferred treatment	5	4	3	2	1
8. Giving favors in exchange for preferred treatment	5	4	3	2	1
9. Asking a person to violate company rules	5	4	3	2	1
10. Calling in sick to take a day off	5	4	3	2	1
11. Hiding errors					
12. Taking longer than necessary to do the job	5	4	3	2	1
13. Doing personal business on company time	5	4	3	2	1
14. Taking a longer lunch hour without approval	5	4	3	2	1
15. Seeing a violation and not reporting it	5	4	3	2	1
16. Overlooking boss's error to prove loyalty	5	4	3	2	1
17. Asking an aide to lie about one's whereabouts	5	4	3	2	1
18. Telling co-workers that one is going somewhere but actually going somewhere else	5	4	3	2	1

1. Do your co-workers seem to engage in these behaviors more often than you do?
2. Which behaviors occur most frequently?
3. What are the differences between the most and least frequently occurring behaviors?
4. What are the most important items that should be controlled? Why? What do these reveal about your own preferences for control?
5. How would management go about establishing programs for controlling them?

CRITICAL THINKING CASE

Sunflower, Inc.

Sunflower, Inc., is a large distribution company with more than 5,000 employees and annual sales of more than $550 million. The company distributes salty snack foods for Anheuser-Busch (Eagle snacks), Frito-Lay, Procter & Gamble (Pringles), Standard Brands (Planters Peanuts), and many local companies in twenty-two regions of the United States and Canada. Each region has its own warehouse, sales, marketing, finance, and distribution employees. Competition is intense between national distributors and large national brands, such as Frito-Lay, who often piggyback on local distributors for the distribution of their salty snacks.

In 1988, Sunflower began using a financial reporting system that compared sales, costs, and profits across the company's 22 regions. Top management was surprised to learn that profit ratios (e.g., profits per $1,000 of sales) varied widely among regions. By 1990, the differences were so great that management decided that additional controls were needed. It was concerned that highly profitable regions may sometimes use lower quality items, even seconds, to boost profit margins. This practice, if true, would hurt Sunflower's image as a quality distributor.

As these problems accumulated, Joe Steelman, president of Sunflower, decided to create a new position to monitor pricing and purchasing practices in all twenty-two regions. He hired Loretta Williams away from a competitor to head up this new department of pricing and purchasing. She was given great freedom in organizing her job and encouraged to establish whatever controls were necessary to get accurate and timely information from each region. Each regional manager was notified of her appointment by e-mail or fax and then sent a formal memo.

After three weeks on the job, Williams decided that two problems needed her attention. First, Sunflower needed to establish a better computer-based information system. She believed that a more sophisticated management information system could provide more effective information at headquarters for decision making and control. The regional managers were connected electronically to headquarters, but sales and warehouse employees weren't. However, only ten of the twenty-two regional managers regularly used e-mail, fax, or the Internet.

The second problem was that each regional manager made separate pricing and purchasing decisions. She wanted to standardize these decisions among the regions. Williams proposed that the financial person in each region notify her of any changes in regional prices of more than 3 percent. She also decided that all new contracts for local purchases of more than $5,000 be cleared through her office. She believed that the only way to standardize operations was for each region to notify the home office in advance of such changes in prices and purchases.

The regional managers had handled hundreds of items and were used to making their own decisions. Thus Steelman suggested that Williams personally visit each region to discuss these changes. Williams thought that such trips would be time-consuming, expensive, not really necessary, and cause her to postpone many of the things she needed to do at headquarters. She argued that the changes were needed now and convinced Steelman that the new procedures could be communicated electronically. The following day, she sent e-mail messages and faxes to all twenty-two regional managers. Seven of the twenty-two acknowledged receiving her communication and indicated that they would be happy to cooperate.

Three months later, Williams was surprised to discover that she hadn't received a single notice from any region requesting a price or purchase change. Executives from headquarters who visited the regions indicated that the managers and salespeople there were as busy as ever and doing business as normal. She randomly called one regional manager and discovered that he didn't know who she was and had never heard of the position she held. Besides, he said, "we have enough to worry about reaching profit goals without additional procedures from headquarters." Williams was surprised and became angry when she realized that the expected changes in procedures had had no impact on the regional managers. She wondered whether they were simply disobedient or whether she should have used some other control mechanism for obtaining compliance.[37]

Questions

1. What were some of the problems with Williams's approach?
2. What types of control did Sunflower use? What types did Williams use?
3. What advice would you give Williams about using control systems?

Chapter 19

Information Management Technologies

Learning *Objectives*

After studying this chapter, you should be able to:

1. State the far-reaching effects of information technologies on individuals and organizations.
2. Describe the role and value of information as a resource.
3. Explain the essential capabilities of information technologies that support and link the basic managerial functions.
4. Discuss the issues involved in information system design.
5. State the factors that facilitate effective implementation of information systems.
6. Identify several ethical concerns in the development and use of computer-based information technologies.

Chapter *Outline*

Preview *Insight*

The Blacksburg Electronic Village

The *Blacksburg electronic village project* is a plan to connect as many individuals and organizations (e.g., businesses, government agencies, schools, and Virginia Tech University) as possible in Blacksburg, Virginia to the Internet. The Internet links at least 35,000 computer-based networks and more than 30 million users worldwide as of 1995 and is expanding daily. The Blacksburg electronic village project is being coordinated by the town government, Virginia Tech University's computer systems department, and Bell Atlantic. The project so far has connected about 19,000 of Blacksburg's approximately 36,000 residents to the system. That makes Blacksburg the most networked community in the world. As of 1995, 35 to 50 people a week were signing up.

The Blacksburg electronic village project is an outgrowth of an online movement known as *freenets*—low-cost systems aimed at making both the Internet and municipal services accessible to everyone. In most cases, freenets rely on free connections through terminals in libraries, government offices, and other public places. A *World Wide Web* page on the Internet at the University of Saskatchewan listed 34 freenets in the United States and 14 more in other countries at the beginning of 1995. But none has launched as ambitious an undertaking as the electronic village. Note: The *World Wide Web* is a collection of files (called pages) stored in computers on the Internet that include text, graphics, sound, and video. The pages have links to other pages, which in turn have links to other pages.

The Blacksburg electronic village project has the following features.

- A series of discussion forums, where residents can talk about the things going on in their communities.
- High-speed connections to all student dorm rooms. Virginia Tech students can plug their computer modems directly into their phonejacks.
- Installation of high-speed network wiring in new construction. A nursing home being built in the area will be among the first to be so wired.
- The ability to apply for basic permits—leaf burning, animal licenses, public gatherings, and banners—online through the town government's Internet connection.
- Businesses communicating with customers, other businesses, and government agencies at little cost. Backstreets is perhaps the town's most popular locally owned pizza parlor. It made a name for itself when it began offering coupons on the Internet. Rusty Riley, a shift manager, urged the owner to post a menu and a coupon on the Internet (two strombolis and two drinks for $9.95). Customers can browse Chef James's specialties, print the coupons out and bring them in.

Marilyn Buyhoff, an officer at the National Bank of Blacksburg, said that other small banks have noticed her institution's home page and have gotten in touch with her. "We've talked about putting together a kind of information network of small banks, all of us on the Internet," said Buyoff. "We'd offer people who were moving from one town to another the ability to transfer accounts, order checks, and other services." Wade's Grocery sells flowers over the Internet and is experimenting with allowing complete shopping online. Customers would choose items from lists posted on the World Wide Web. The service also would let customers maintain standing grocery lists of items that they regularly purchase. Groceries could be purchased with a credit card or with *e-cash,* an electronic cash service.[1]

State the far-reaching effects of information technologies on individuals and organizations.

EFFECTS OF INFORMATION TECHNOLOGIES

Throughout the book, we have touched on the profound effects of new information technologies on organizations, their processes, and their managerial functions (decision making, planning, organizing, leading, and controlling). The Preview Insight provides a glimpse of how the people and organizations in one community are being linked in new and novel ways. The Blacksburg electronic village project is a portent of a digital world

Discussion Question 1
Develop a diagram of the communication network that represents the Blacksburg electronic village project, as described in the Preview Insight.

Ask Students
How many of you in this class are on the Internet?

Ask Students
How many of you have experienced virtual reality?

Ask Students
Do you agree or disagree with Negroponte? Explain.

Ask Students
How accurate were Leavitt and Whisler? Do you have any predictions for next the 20–25 years?

and cyberspace. The **digital world** is the linking of people (in business, in government, in the home, and on the road) via computers and computers with other computers. *Digital* refers to the method of data transmission, through on/off signals, by computers. The term **cyberspace** usually refers to real-time transmitting and sharing of text, voice, graphics, video, and the like over a variety of computer-based networks. However, cyberspace soon will become much more than communication connections between points A and B. Its broader attributes and capabilities will allow (1) people to come together from remote distances to dialogue in the same three-dimensional virtual electronic space, (2) computers to *talk* to other computers, and (3) individuals to interact with computer-based machines to create and shape three-dimensional virtual realities.[2]

Profound Predictions

Nicholas Negroponte, author of *Being Digital—Via Electronic Mail* suggests that networking through computers "will eventually be as ubiquitous as the phone, lights, and running water. But recognize that your connectivity may not be just your pecking at a keyboard. It may be your fridge ordering milk or your vacuum cleaner calling the police to report a 'breaking and entering.' The speed at which this will happen will knock the socks off of people."[3] For many organizations, computer-based networks have already become fundamental to their ability to produce and deliver goods and services—the organizations' nervous systems.

In 1958, in the *Harvard Business Review,* Harold J. Leavitt and Thomas L. Whisler forecast what organizations of the future would look like. Their predictions for the 1980s included the following:

- *The role and scope of middle managers will change.* Many middle management jobs will become more structured, have less status, and command less compensation. The number of middle managers will decline, creating flatter organizations. The middle management positions that remain will be more technical and specialized. New mid-level positions with titles such as analyst will be created.
- *Top management will focus more on innovating, planning, and creating.* The rate of obsolescence and change will quicken, and top management will continually have to address developments on the horizon.
- *Large organizations will recentralize.* New information technologies will give top managers more information. This advantage will extend top management's strategic control over crucial decisions. Some top managers choose to decentralize only because they are unable to keep up with the changing size and complexity of their organizations and external environments. Other top managers are using information technology in strategically planning, controlling, and leading their organizations.[4]

Observed Impacts

The information technology revolution continues to have a great impact on organizations. **Information technologies (ITs)** are electronic systems that help individuals and organizations assemble, store, transmit, process, and retrieve data and information. The new generation of managers and other employees naturally are more knowledgeable than their counterparts of a few decades ago about the uses and benefits of technological advances. Many organizations are using information technology as a strategic asset to maintain an edge in fiercely competitive world markets. Advances in telecommunications and networking allow people to exchange information more freely than ever. Computer-based systems are now available that can intelligently link, learn, and make recommendations to decision makers by applications of artificial intelligence, mainly through expert systems.[5]

Leavitt and Whisler's predictions were strongly criticized throughout the 1960s, 1970s, and early 1980s. But now they no longer seem farfetched. Organizations have in-

Discussion Question 2
Why are computer-based information technologies reducing the number of management levels in many organizations?

deed undergone radical changes in design and methods of operation because of new information technologies.[6] These advances, coupled with reengineering, make possible the reduction of the information *float* in organizations. In the past, decision making took a lot of time because information and proposals had to pass through numerous organizational layers before anything was decided or actually happened. Today's information technologies cut through several of those layers and even allow some to be eliminated.

Recall that the streamlining of decision and information flows, especially through the use of more horizontal networks, is a key feature of reengineering. The new information technologies are a vital component to most reengineering initiatives. Managers whose main function was to serve as assemblers and relayers of information are no longer needed. Organizations continue to reduce the number of first-line and middle managers because information technologies streamline many of the communication, coordination, and control functions that such managers traditionally performed. The managers who remain have been freed from most routine tasks and can take on more responsibility for tactical planning and decision making.

Ask Students
Do you have marketable knowledge worker skills? If so, what are they?

Organizations now need many more *knowledge workers* to help ensure the successful integration of information systems. Their skills allow them to deliver the appropriate technology and provide instructions for using it efficiently and effectively. The magnitude of the information revolution and the need for more knowledge workers is underscored by the following fact. In 1991, companies in the United States and Canada for the first time spent more money on computing and communications equipment than on industrial, mining, farm, and construction machines combined. In an automobile, the \$675 worth of steel is obvious, but the \$780 worth of microelectronics is less apparent.[7]

Changes in an organization's design and the composition of the work force often lead to decentralization of tactical decisions—but greater centralization of strategic decisions and controls, as predicted by Leavitt and Whisler in 1958. Decentralization results in the empowerment of lower level employees, managers, and teams, allowing them to engage in tactical planning, self- and mutual control, and day-to-day decision making. In some ways, organizations increasingly resemble professional firms (e.g., CPA firms, law firms, and group medical practices). The most successful of such firms attract, motivate, and retain skilled employees through a steady stream of challenging projects. In these organizations, few jobs consist solely of overseeing the work of others. Many employees take on managerial roles for short periods of time by serving as team leaders. Employees' jobs change all the time, depending on the project being worked on.[8]

The following Small Business Insight illustrates how new information technologies are affecting the options and life-styles of freelance professionals.

Small Business *Insight*

The Lone Eagles

Philip M. Burgess is president and CEO of the Center for the New West, a Denver-based think tank. The center studies the states west of the Mississippi, except Louisiana. Burgess studies and writes about the future of the American West from his eastern waterfront home near Annapolis, Maryland, at the mouth of Chesapeake Bay. Burgess's work and life-style began taking shape during one of the center's projects, a 1990 study of the future of the Great Plains states. "I kept meeting people who lived in small towns but were working for companies in New York, Los Angeles, Chicago," he says. "And it hit me—something new was happening in small-town America."

Out of those meetings emerged a full-fledged project at the center to study this phenomenon. Called the Lone Eagle Project, it ultimately changed his life. "When I started studying lone eagles, it hit me that I could do what I wanted to do. I didn't have to wait until I retired," says the 55-year-old Burgess. Lone eagles typically are freelance professionals—writers, analysts, brokers, accountants, and consultants, to name a few. Their products can be transmitted electronically in various ways, allowing them to pursue their profession wherever they live and travel.

Networked to clients through computers, faxes, voice-mail, and modems, lone eagles are able to obtain a sense of security and community now commonly believed impossible to find in some big cities. "Technology allows you to do things that five years ago you couldn't do," says Burgess. Whether as a result of corporate downsizing or more individuals desiring to escape urban life, the number of lone eagles—estimated at about nine million—is expected to continue to increase in the years ahead.

Burgess travels about half the time, as he did when he lived in Denver. He always takes his Mac Powerbook, which, he says, "contains his whole life." Burgess has a small but complete array of technologies to support him. His computer is a Macintosh 7100/66 Power PC with an AV/CD-ROM drive. An older Mac LC III serves as a backup. Burgess uses an Apple laser printer and a Hewlett-Packard color printer. He also has a Canon PC 11 copier and an H-P plain-paper copier with broadcast fax capability.[9]

2

Describe the role and value of information as a resource.

Teaching Tip
Have students pick an organization and research how it uses information as a resource for the three levels of management.

Teaching Tip
Invite a guest lecturer to speak to the class about how his or her organization uses information technology.

Teaching Tip
Ask an alum who is a CIO to come to class and tell what he or she does.

Real-World Example
Vinod Gupta grew up in a small village in India that had no electricity, roads, toilets, TVs, or cars. His firm, American Business Information, has annual sales of $75 million, derived largely from selling free information, and mailing lists to marketers (*Fortune,* February 6, 1995, 31).

Ask Students
Give an example of data and an example of information.

Ask Students
What is the impact of the difference between data and information for today's organizations?

ROLE OF INFORMATION

Organizations store and process vast amounts of data, which managers and other employee must turn into useful information. In turn, this information enables them to perform their jobs better. Although the terms *data* and *information* often are used interchangeably, we make a distinction between them in order to emphasize the unique role of information.

Effective organizations and managers control their information—they aren't controlled by it. At times, users' lack of knowledge places them at the mercy of an information systems department. To reduce this problem, some organizations, including J.C. Penney, have created the position of chief information officer. The **chief information officer (CIO)** usually is a top manager who provides leadership in assessing the organization's information processing needs and developing the information systems to meet those needs in collaboration with managers and key employees throughout the organization.[10]

Data and Information

Data are facts and figures. Every organization processes data about its operations to create current, accurate, and reliable information. Many decisions require data such as market statistics, operating costs, inventory levels, sales figures, and the like. However, raw data are much like raw materials—not very useful until they are processed. Processing data involves comparison, classification, analysis, and summarization to make them usable and valuable.

Information is the knowledge derived from data that people have transformed to make them meaningful and useful. In effect, data are subjected to a *value-added process* that yields meaningful information for decision making. Individuals use their **knowledge**—concepts, tools, and categories—to create, store, apply, and share information. Knowledge can be stored in a book, a person's mind, or a computer program as a set of instructions that gives meaning to streams of data.[11]

Value-Added Resource

In contrast to that of physical resources, the value of information can't be easily determined. The value added to data, especially through information technologies, is determined by those who use the resulting information to achieve desired goals. In organi-

A map display on a computer allows an employee of DU-WEST Foundation Repair in Pasadena, Texas, to locate any truck in the company's fleet.

Real-World Example
AT&T spends $4 billion per year on information technology. About 25,000 AT&T employees work in some aspect of information technology. CIO Ron Ponder says that AT&T "is a global leader in information management" (*Forbes*, April 10, 1995, 59).

Ask Students
How is information of value to managers today?

Discussion Question 3
Why is information increasingly viewed as a strategic asset and value-added resource?

Ask Students
How can a manager assess the value of information?

Teaching Tip
High-quality information for this course comes from the work of knowledgeable management researchers.

zations these goals may be wide ranging: (1) maintain or increase market share, (2) avoid catastrophic losses, (3) create greater flexibility and adaptability, and (4) improve the quality of goods and services.[12] Individuals at different organizational levels and in various functional, project, or product units or teams have different information needs. Certain information is essential to the specific types of decisions they must make to serve their customers, whether internal or external to the organization. For example, top managers typically are interested in information on overall organizational performance and new product ideas. Detailed information on daily production and quality at each manufacturing site isn't likely to be as useful to them as to self-managing teams in the plants. These teams need specific information about the availability of raw materials, changes in productivity, rates of defects, and similar operating characteristics. To sales managers, detailed information on various raw materials probably has little value. Sales personnel want to know the amounts and types of goods and services that can be promised for delivery at various times and at what prices.

To be considered a value-added resource, information must possess value over and above that of the raw data.[13] Figure 19.1 shows four common criteria used to assess the value of information: quality, relevance, quantity, and timeliness.

Quality. The quality of information refers to how accurately it portrays reality. The more accurate the information, the higher is its quality. The degree of quality required varies according to the needs of those who will use the information. Employees responsible for production inventory control need high-quality (precise) information about the amounts of raw materials available and resupply schedules required to meet customers' delivery expectations. Sales managers concerned with five-year sales forecasts might be able to use lower quality (less precise) information, such as general market trends and sales projections. Such long-term forecasting cannot be developed from detailed daily or weekly sales data.

Relevance. The relevance of information depends on the extent to which it directly assists decision making. Too often managers and other employees receive information

FIGURE 19.1

Criteria Used to Assess the Value of Information

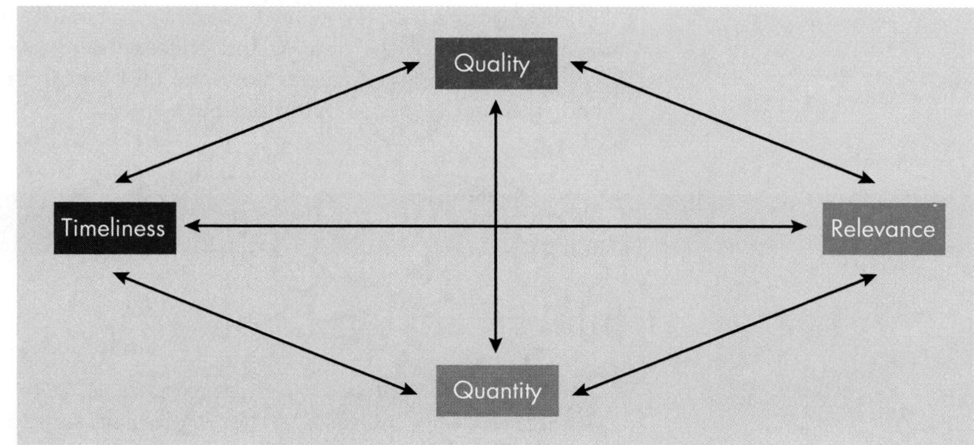

Teaching Tip
Relevance of the information from this course will help students in their careers as managers or non-managerial employees.

that is of little or no use. For example, a self-managing production team needs detailed information about production schedules, inventory levels, and promised delivery dates in order to make good decisions. Such information is relevant to providing quality goods when desired by customers. These team members don't need detailed information about the organization's global strategy. However, the relevance of information can differ for the same person or function at different times. For example, in January, summer sales estimates may not be relevant to Mattel managers trying to project next December's demand. But summer sales estimates may be very useful the following October when those same managers are trying to project next summer's demand before setting production goals.

Quantity. Quantity refers to the amount of information available when people need it. In the decision-making process, more information isn't always better. In fact, too much can lead to information overload, particularly if the extra information isn't relevant to the decisions being made. Therefore care must be taken in advance to determine the amount of information needed and wanted.[14] The provision of information—relevant or not—costs time and money, and information overload can cause stress and reduce effectiveness. For example, Charles Wang, Chairman of Computer Associates International—a software firm that sells an e-mail software package—no longer sends or receives e-mail. He also made the decision to shut down the company's e-mail system for five hours a day so that the employees would not be so distracted. He comments: "As a leader in a company, you have to go to an extreme to demonstrate a point. With subordinates copying their bosses on practically every memo they write [using e-mail], it has become a cover-your [self] tool."[15]

Teaching Tip
The quantity of information that students receive from this course is broad rather than specific, as it is a survey rather than an upper division elective course.

Timeliness. Timeliness means that managers and other employees must receive the information they need before it ceases to be useful for decision-making purposes. Top managers who make strategic plans may be interested in quarterly or monthly (or at most, weekly) production and sales information. In contrast, production managers and employees probably need daily—and sometimes even hourly or minute-by-minute information—concerning operations to ensure that they meet their production schedules. If they received such information only quarterly or even monthly, it wouldn't be timely and could hurt the quality and amount of outputs and slow promised deliveries to customers.

These four criteria—quality, relevance, quantity, and timeliness—are interrelated and are essential to the process and philosophy of total quality management. The following Quality Insight suggests how one firm initially blundered by discounting anticipated customer response based on these criteria.

Quality *Insight*

Intel's Pentium Error

Intel is the world's largest semiconductor company and the first such firm ever to sell more than $10 billion worth of products in a year. The company earned about $2.3 billion in 1994, even after charging off about $475 million to cover the estimated cost of replacing faulty Pentium chips. A top-of-the-line Pentium chip priced at about $1,000 in early 1994 cost about $600 at the end of the year. In February 1995, the cheapest Pentium chip cost only $275 when purchased by PC manufacturers.

In early November 1994, a trade publication reported that the Pentium chip makes errors in certain mathematical calculations. Intel, which had shipped at least 4 million of the chips at the time, claimed that the odds of a Pentium error were 1 in 9 billion division calculations—or once in 27,000 years of running a spreadsheet.

Intel's approach to its direct customers (e.g., IBM) and ultimate end users (e.g., home purchasers of IBM PCs containing Pentium chips) was to discount the significance of this flaw. Moreover, Intel knew about the problem in the summer of 1994 but didn't disclose it to customers until after it was reported in November 1994 by a trade publication—not through Intel.

IBM, one of Intel's largest customers, didn't learn of the Pentium flaw until it received a call November 22, 1994 from an Intel representative. The IBM executive was told that there would be a report on Cable News Network (CNN) on the chip problem. According to the IBM executive, the Intel representative added: "But don't worry about it." However, IBM temporarily suspended Pentium PC shipments on December 12, 1994, after its own researchers determined that the flaw would create inaccuracies in mathematical calculations up to 90 times more frequently than Intel claimed. IBM mounted a full-scale public campaign after its top management grew angry over what it contended was Intel's mishandling of the issue. "They were in denial," said the IBM executive, who was involved in the Intel negotiations. "We think Intel has handled this exceedingly poorly. First they hid the problem and then they tried to trivialize it."

Intel initially discounted the validity and relevance of tests on the Pentium chip conducted by IBM, *PC Week* magazine, and others. Soon after the strong negative publicity and outcry by customers, Intel assigned more than a thousand of its employees to answer customer questions. The firm quickly changed its production processes to accelerate shipments of an improved version of the Pentium chip. But Intel refused to announce that it would replace any customer's flawed Pentium chip with no questions asked.

Customers calling Intel's toll-free support lines faced a long series of questions about how they were using their machines. They were given detailed explanations about the flaw and how rarely it would occur, according to Intel's calculations. Intel also offered customers a lifetime guarantee to replace the chip if the problem ever cropped up in their own work.

Eventually, however, Intel had to relax its replacement policy. It no longer limited replacing chips to users involved in sophisticated calculations. Any customer who insisted on a replacement was given one, said Craig Barrett, Intel's chief operating officer. The reluctant change followed the more liberal return policies given to computer makers that buy Pentium chips.[16]

If Intel management had considered the criteria for valuable information (namely, quality, relevance, quantity and timeliness) from its customers' perspectives, it could have avoided the initial errors and later embarrassment. Ironically, fewer requests for replacements probably would have been made if the company had met the issue head on.

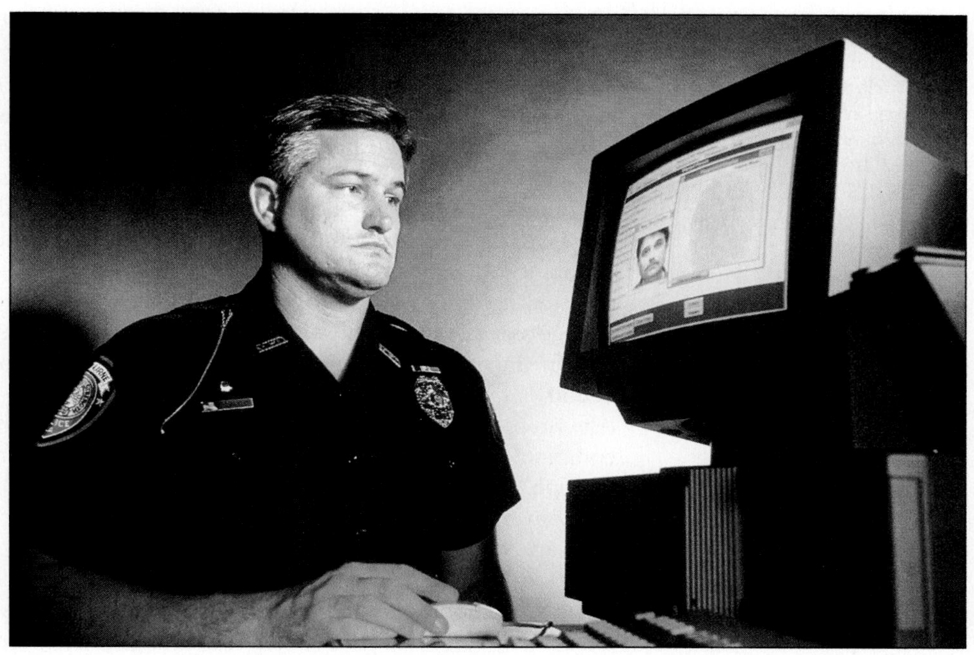

Harris' information-management system technology is making the FBI's database of 225,000 wanted felons instantly available to local, state, and federal law enforcement officers.

3

Explain the essential capabilities of information technologies that support and link the basic managerial functions.

Real-World Example
CEO Andy Grove said that he had mishandled the situation by trying to impose an engineering solution. He said, "To some people this seemed arrogant and uncaring: we apologize." Replacing all the chips requested could cost $1 billion, at $200 per replacement (*Los Angeles Times,* December 21, 1994, A1, A25).

Ask Students
What chip does your computer have? When did you buy it? How long after you bought it did the next generation come out?

CAPABILITIES OF INFORMATION TECHNOLOGIES

The capabilities and applications of computer-based (digital) information technologies are developing at a breath-taking pace. These technologies continue to become exponentially less expensive and exponentially more powerful. The most conservative forecasts claim that the cost-performance relationship for these technologies as a whole will improve by 15 to 25 percent annually into the foreseeable future.[17] Computer chip (microprocessor) manufacturers are on the leading edge of these cost-performance leaps. For example, the Intel 486 chip with 1.2 million transistors and an *initial* speed of 20 million instructions per second (MIPS) was introduced in 1989. The Intel Pentium chip with 3.1 million transistors and an initial speed of 100 MIPS for the top-end chip model was introduced only four years later in 1993. By early 1996, only 2.5 years later, Intel is expected to introduce its P6 chip with 5.5 million transistors and an initial speed of 250 MIPS. This new microprocessor will lead to rapid new developments and improvements in voice recognition, videoconferencing, multimedia, engineering workstations, and the like.[18]

In the remainder of this section, we focus on four interrelated categories of information technologies being used to support the basic managerial functions of planning, organizing, leading, and controlling. These categories are communication systems, decision support systems, expert systems, and executive support systems.[19] Information technologies that directly support operations and manufacturing processes are covered in Chapter 20.

Communication Systems

The ability to transmit and share all types of data and information has exploded with the introduction of inexpensive and improved communication systems. These systems enhance the ability of those in an organization to be in touch with everyone else in the organization—as well as important suppliers, customers, and other external stakeholders—from *anyplace* at *anytime*. **Communication systems** include teleconferencing,

Ask Students
How many of you have participated in a teleconference? How is it different from a face-to-face meeting?

Ask Students
How many of you have personal faxes? If you do have one, how often do you use it?

Teaching Tip
Tell the class what type of networks the university has.

Ask Students
How many of you use e-mail? How often?

facsimile machines, local and wide area networks, electronic mail, voice recognition systems, integrated systems, and the like.[20]

Teleconferencing allows people in one room (place) to participate in meetings with people in another room (place) by means of video transmission systems and television screens. *Facsimile (fax) machines* scan a sheet of paper electronically and convert the light and dark areas to electrical signals, which are transmitted over telephone lines. At the other end, a similar machine reverses the process and reproduces the original image. A *network* is the interconnection of computers, peripherals, and communication lines (signals) that allows users to transmit data and messages. A *local area network (LAN)* is a system of interconnected computers linked by cable that share data, software, and storage devices in a limited geographical area. A *wide area network (WAN)* often consists of linked multiple LANs in widely spaced geographic areas (all the way across a country or even between countries). The computers in a WAN may be linked through television or television cables, fiber optic cables, microwave signals, and/or satellite communications. *Electronic mail (e-mail)* allows users to transmit messages (text) through networked terminals or personal computers. *Voice recognition systems* involve the conversion of spoken words into electronic form for conversion by computer-based software systems into printed form.

Integrated systems are networks of information systems that were created to link the various functions, tasks, and decision-making processes in an organization and to permit direct information exchanges and dialog with customers, suppliers, and others outside the organization.[21] Integrated systems make horizontal communication and coordination within network organizations (see Chapter 11) easier and more effective, regardless of location. These integrated systems are fostering the development of global markets for goods and services giving small and large firms alike the opportunity to conduct business throughout the world. The following Global Insight describes Citicorp's integrated, worldwide communication systems.

Global *Insight*

Citicorp's Integrated Systems

Citicorp is a global financial services enterprise serving the financial needs of individuals, businesses, governments, and other financial institutions with offices in ninety countries. To meet the challenges of the marketplace, Citicorp has organized its activities and services around customer-oriented core businesses: the Individual Bank (serves consumers), Institutional Bank, Investment Bank, and Information Business, which work together to serve other customers. All are integrated through computer-based information technologies that permit communications to and from most anyplace around the world at anytime. The development and use of these technologies are keys to the provision of quality customer-driven services.

Citicorp touts its ability to serve high-income and mobile clientele globally. A Citigold account holder from Singapore can walk into a Frankfurt, Germany, branch, for instance, and cash a check of up to $5,000. One executive comments: "We thought we should make our 'globality' real to the customer." These accounts now make up about 45 percent of its Asian consumer deposits. In late 1992, Citicorp began capitalizing on this Asian experience by making Citigold available in the United States and Europe. Says an executive who worked with one of the bank's American competitors in Hong Kong for many years: "No one is in the same league in establishing a global consumer bank." In an organizational culture where ideas and people flow back and forth, that's the predictable result.

Customers who walk into one of Citicorp's branches, whether in New York City or Santiago, Chile, may see both more and different types of automatic teller machines (ATMs) than they are used to seeing.

Citicorp's ATMs can now handle more than 150 types of transactions, ranging from simple cash dispensing to mutual fund investing. Some U.S. customers can even use them to trade stocks. Citicorp's Hong Kong branches may be the world's most futuristic, offering customer accounts in ten different currencies. Hong Kong customers often call a Citicorp hotline from their mobile phones to check exchange rates and switch money among accounts.

The bank also is developing a sophisticated electronic system in Singapore that will allow a banker in any Asian branch to see all the information pertaining to a customer's account. Also on file will be notes on all conversations with the customer. Thus, if a Citicorp customer goes to a branch in Hong Kong, a representative there can pick up where one in Jakarta left off.

Help screens on their PCs provide employees with procedural guidance upon request. Moreover, software with structured, expert system capabilities now automatically assist employees as they move through complex transactions. For instance, a customer calling a service center with a dispute will be taken through a multipart information exchange that all Citicorp customer service representatives use. It is based on Citicorp's best customer service representatives' routines and ensures that all representatives can assist customers efficiently and comprehensively.[22]

Decision Support Systems

A **decision support system (DSS)** is a complex set of computer hardware and software that allows end users—usually managers and professionals—to analyze, manipulate, format, display, and output data in different ways. Such a system aids decision making because the user can pull together data from different sources, view them in ways that may differ from the original formats, and create information from them. The system allows data and information to be printed out or to be presented in the form of charts or graphs.[23]

Ask Students
How many of you use these types of software?

A DSS enables decision makers to represent features of the environment (e.g., customer purchasing practices) and business phenomena (e.g., changes in prices and inflation) and quickly evaluate many alternatives and assumptions within models. Actually, you may be familiar with DSS and not even know it. If you have used an electronic spreadsheet such as Lotus 1-2-3, Multiplan, Javelin, EXCEL, or QUATTRO, you have used one form of DSS software. These electronic spreadsheets will automatically recalculate a quantity when you change the value of one of the variables in a formula.

The capabilities of a DSS give the decision maker flexibility and the ability to explore and include:

- *Data collection and organization capabilities.* These capabilities allow the acquisition of needed data from internal and external sources. Current DSSs often have links to databases and LANs, enabling rapid creation of a database. A **database** is an organized collection of facts, figures, documents, and the like that have been stored for easy, efficient access and use. The computerized card catalog at a library is a database.
- *"What-is?" capabilities.* These capabilities provide the current status of developments from the DSS, external databases, or other internal databases.
- *"What-if?" capabilities.* These capabilities allow the decision maker to propose alternative actions (by means of a model) and test their likely consequences.
- *Goal-seeking capabilities.* These capabilities suggest actions to be taken to achieve a goal specified by the decision maker.
- *Presentation and report generation capabilities.* These capabilities allow the user to create various types of tables, graphs, text, pictures, art, audio, and video displays.[24]

The following Diversity Insight reveals the important role of DSS in tracking, assessing, planning, and controlling in human resources management. It emphasizes affirmative action compliance and decision support systems.

Diversity *Insight*

DSS and Compliance

Compliance with various laws, regulations, and policies is a major task in human resources. In the past, to obtain essential information to show compliance often meant a visit to the organization's law library, flipping through volumes of data, and more hours of processing data into usable information and reports. Many firms have developed software and database systems that provide easy access to data pertaining to all types of human resources decisions and actions. Among others, they relate to affirmative action requirements, work-force and promotion patterns, availability assessments of women and minorities in different job groups, injury illness patterns, benefits, training, and "what-if" scenarios. Firms that market human resources software and decision support capabilities include Oracle Corporation, Sybase, Inc., Gubta Corporation, Novell, Inc., Microsoft, ICONtrol, Inc., Optimum Management Insight Systems, Technical Difference, Inc., and Commerce Clearinghouse, Inc.

Let's briefly consider one such system—the HR Assistant—produced by Commerce Clearing House, Inc. (CCH). Users can compile information on about two dozen aspects of human resources management, from who should have access to personnel files to drug testing to family leave to workers' compensation to affirmative action. From a main menu, users first decide whether they want to find out about new developments, view summaries of federal or state laws, get quick answers to common questions (e.g., When may minors be employed as adults?), create a policy statement, or complete a compliance checklist for one of the laws. "What used to take hours is done in a matter of minutes," claims Lou Bahin, CCH's product manager for HR Assistant. Bahin goes on to explain, "We've tried to understand how HR people actually work. We've done market research and had a lot of contact with customers. We've tried for a product that matches up with tasks people do every day."

"For me, it's a very quick and efficient research tool," says Amy Johns, HR director at Precedent Financial Corporation in Indianapolis, Indiana. "People bring me an issue, such as pregnancy discrimination. I utilize HR Assistant, which gives the information to me. I hit Print, then give it to the person who asked for it."

The HR Assistant is interactive, asking questions and creating a draft document that users can review with legal staff if necessary. Amy Johns says that she uses the product successfully with no formal training. "I'm reasonably computer literate. I wouldn't call myself a guru by any means," she says. "The program prompts you. Everything is pretty much at your fingertips. It's definitely a time-saving alternative to sitting in a library, flipping through pages," Johns attests.[25]

Expert Systems

Recall that an *expert system (ES)* is a computer program based on the decision-making processes of human experts that stores, retrieves, and manipulates data, diagnoses problems, and makes limited decisions based on detailed information about a specific problem. These systems have problem-solving capabilities within a specific area of knowledge. Expert systems differ from decision support systems in that they actually recommend or make a decision. If requested, the system can explain its path of reasoning to the user. The expert system is an application of artificial intelligence (AI), the ability of computers to simulate some thought processes of human beings.[26]

Expert systems vary in complexity, both in terms of knowledge and technology. An example of the simplest type of system is a personal budgeting system running on a PC. The thrust of low-level expert systems is to improve personal decision making and thereby increase productivity. In contrast, strategic impact expert systems involve high levels of knowledge and technological complexity. Lincoln National's Life Underwriting System is an example. The process of underwriting an individual's life insurance application requires complex medical, financial, and insurance knowledge. Lincoln National also requires that an applicant's hobbies (e.g., mountain climbing) and vocation (e.g.,

Discussion Question 4
What are the similarities and differences between communication systems and expert systems?

possibly requiring frequent travel to politically unstable countries) be factored into policy evaluation and pricing. In many of these areas, the information that an underwriter receives needs to be clarified and interpreted. Lincoln National's four best senior underwriters spent much of their time for several years as consulting experts helping develop this expert system.[27] (See Chapter 9 for more on expert systems.)

Executive Support Systems

An **executive support system (ESS)** is an organized network of electronic messaging systems, multimedia presentation systems, management information systems, and/or group decision support systems. Some people are beginning to call such a system an *enterprise support system (ESS)* because these systems are being made available to lower level managers and professionals, not just executives. The information technologies that comprise an ESS can integrate managers and other professionals—not just top executives—into an organization's information and decision-making flows. Users of electronic messaging systems may send messages over the phone that can be stored, annotated with comments, and distributed to many different people. Multimedia presentation systems increasingly utilize computer graphics, voice, motion, and other features to enhance presentations to groups. This book's illustrations exemplify the types of graphics that a fairly sophisticated executive presentation system can produce. **Management information systems** provide up-to-date financial, market, human resources, or other information about the status of an organization, its major departments or divisions, and its environment.

Finally, a **group decision support system (GDSS)** is a set of software, hardware, and language components that support a team of people engaged in a decision-making meeting.[28] A GDSS aims to improve the process of team decision making by removing common communication barriers, providing techniques for guiding the decision process, and systematically directing the pattern, timing, or content of the discussion. Facilitators play a crucial role in the use of GDSS. They allow the participants to concentrate on the issues at hand rather than struggling to use the technology themselves.

Most executives and many managers aren't proficient on a computer and lack keyboard skills, which must be taken into account in designing and implementing ESSs. A requirement that executives be fully computer proficient to use executive support systems, such as GDSS, is likely to minimize their use. Slowness in manipulating data and the resulting frustration may even lead to disinterest and lack of support. Several estimates indicate that, in 1995, only 25 percent of senior executives worldwide were fully using executive support systems.[29] Even computer-literate users need time to become familiar with the GDSS. A typical GDSS room might include a series of terminals or workstations linked by some form of computer-based network, a large main screen visible to everyone and controlled by the facilitator, a photocopying whiteboard on which to record the options as they emerge, and a three-color video projector or large monitor.[30]

Discussion Question 5
Why are the information needs of top managers different from those of first-line managers?

Seven executives from one of Marriott's large Washington-area hotels participated in their first electronic meeting using VisionsQuest, a type of GDSS software. Their challenge was to find new ways of improving guest satisfaction. They generated 139 ideas in only twenty-five minutes. Then they rated each idea twice on a scale of 1 to 5, first according to its likely effect on guests and second according to its probable cost. The Marriott executive team emerged with a consensus on the specific forms of additional training needed by hotel employees.[31]

4

Discuss the issues involved in information system design.

INFORMATION SYSTEM DESIGN

Four major interrelated issues affect information system design: (1) determine information needs, (2) identify system constraints, (3) set goals, and (4) work through the developmental stages.

Determine Information Needs

Teaching Tip
Ask students to brainstorm reasons that some information systems fail to be effective. List them on the board or an overhead transparency.

Ask Students
What have been your experiences with student registration? Does the process work effectively? Why or why not?

The most important decision concerning the development of any form of information system may well be determining what information actually is needed. Far too often organizations develop information systems without an adequate understanding of their true needs or the costs involved. An organization wouldn't construct a new manufacturing plant unless it was essential. Information system development should be approached in the same way. Many organizations have a strategic plan, either by design or by default. Managers should ensure that any proposed information system will fit the organization's overall mission and strategy. In other words, the information system should make sense in terms of organizational plans, financial and technical resources, customers, competitors, and desired return or investment. Questions that need to be asked include: Is the organization planning to change or add to its customer base or its goods and services? What are the current financial constraints? Do competitors use such technology? What type, quality, relevance, quantity, and timeliness of data and information do employees currently use?

Figure 19.2 illustrates the transformation of raw data into information and then into decisions. Note that knowledge of the environment progresses from disorganized data to refined and sharply focused information.

Information needs often vary by organizational level, department, and individual employee and according to the type of decision to be made. Decision-making activities occur at three levels: strategic, tactical, and operational. The characteristics of information most used by employees and managers at these levels are summarized in Table 19.1: focus, scope, aggregation level, time horizon, currency, frequency of use, and type. Note that strategic decisions often require information from external sources, such as customers, suppliers, and competitors. The information must be broad in scope, composite (highly aggregated), future-oriented, and both qualitative and quantitative. In contrast, information needs for operational decisions are substantially different. Operational decisions basically require internal information (e.g., inventory levels) that is well defined, detailed, reported daily or weekly, precise, and quantitative. Tactical decisions, which are of most concern to middle managers and professionals, represent the middle ground between strategic and operational decisions.[32]

Identify System Constraints

After the organization's information needs have been identified, prospective users and system developers must consider the constraints on the existing system. Constraints are the limitations on the discretion available to decision makers and may be internally or externally imposed. External constraints vary from organization to organization and may include government regulations, supplier requirements, technological progress, and cus-

FIGURE 19.2

Evolution in Information Needs

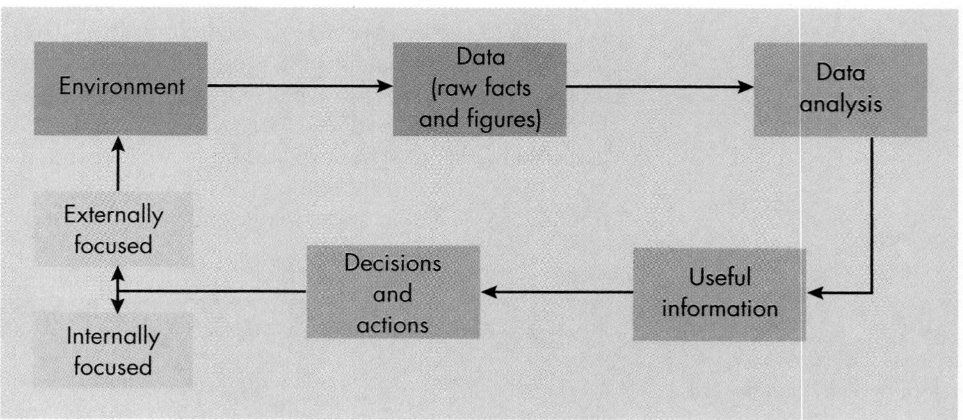

TABLE 19.1

Information Requirements by Decision Level

Information Characteristic	Requirement: At Operational Level	At Tactical Level	At Strategic Level
Focus	Internal to external		External to internal
Scope	Narrow, well defined		Broad
Aggregation level	Detailed		Composite
Time horizon	Historical		Future-oriented
Currency	Recent		Long term
Frequency of use	Continuous		Periodic
Type	Quantitative		Qualitative and quantitative

Sources: Developed from Gorry, G.A., and Scott Morton, M.S. A framework for management information systems. *Sloan Management Review.* Fall 1971, 59–62; Markus, M.L., and Keil, M. If we build it, they will come: Designing information systems that people want to use. *Sloan Management Review.* Summer 1994, 11–26.

tomer demands. For example, government regulations require automobile manufacturers to produce cars with safety features such as seatbelts, exhaust systems that emit limited amounts of certain chemicals, and engines that meet fuel efficiency standards.

Teaching Tip
Have students brainstorm about system constraints they would expect to encounter in a specific organization.

Internal constraints are created by the organization itself. They also vary among organizations and even among departments within an organization. Probably the most common internal constraint on the development of an information system is cost. Everyone usually wants the best system possible. Unfortunately, the best available information technology may be very costly. That is true even though the price-performance relationships for information technologies continue to improve dramatically year-by-year. Another internal constraint is lack of support from employees and top management. Without top management's support, or with only its limited support, an information system is unlikely to be successful.[33]

Set Goals

Ask Students
Why is setting goals for an information system early in the design process essential?

After the organization's information needs have been established and system constraints identified, the general and operational goals for the information system should be set. They should focus on the purposes the information will serve, who will use it, and how it will be used. One goal for Rockwell International's executive information system was that it had to be useful as an investigative tool, that is, for answering "what-if" questions such as: What would happen if the company relied on more overtime to meet an increase in demand rather than adding more employees?[34] Goals also should be established for the number and type of operating personnel and the system's cost. Setting goals provides the direction for developing and implementing the information system.

Working Through the Developmental Stages

An information system may be created in various ways. However, the basic underlying developmental process generally is the same.[35] Figure 19.3 shows the four stages in the development of information systems. The dashed arrows indicate feedback loops, illustrating that the process is never cut and dried.

FIGURE 19.3

Stages in Information Systems Development

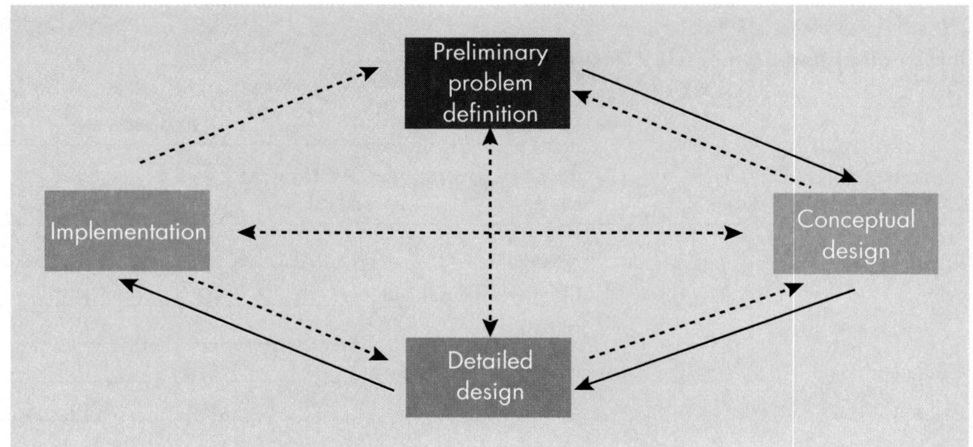

Preliminary Problem Definition. A team of information users, with technical support personnel, may be given the tasks of determining information needs, rough cost estimates, constraints, and goals.

Conceptual Design. The conceptual design stage should be primarily user led, although system development experts can act as resources. During this stage, information generated in the preliminary problem definition stage is used to develop alternative designs. They are evaluated in terms of how well they satisfy organizational needs and goals. More accurate cost estimates are obtained at this stage. This evaluation usually leads to a preliminary selection of specific system characteristics for further review. However, it also may lead back to the problem definition stage.

Detailed Design. During the detailed design stage, performance specifications are established. The team selects or develops hardware and software components. Information system experts are heavily involved, mapping information flows, preparing specialized programs, and defining databases. They also create a prototype of the information system and evaluate, test, refine, and reevaluate it until the stated requirements are satisfied.[36] Users are still involved, but their role is primarily advisory. If problems arise, returning to the conceptual design stage or even to a reanalysis of the problem definition may be necessary.

Implementation. During the final stage, modules of the information system are connected and users begin testing the system. As operational problems are identified and corrected, one module after another is added. Eventually, the entire system is assembled and tested for all conceivable types of errors. Corrections continue to be made until the information system's performance satisfies all the performance criteria. At that point, the information system is ready to be phased into the organization for full-time use. In some situations, the design process may even have to begin again after implementation. For example, a Pennsylvania bank decided to automate its branches with a new automatic teller computer system. Six months after installation, the system response time was four times longer than expected, customers waited in long lines, and daily processing differences were out of control. A large write-off and a new design were required. How could such a fiasco occur? The primary reason was too little user involvement from the beginning.[37]

In contrast, the Merrill Lynch brokerage and financial services firm has been on the cutting edge in developing and improving its information systems. The firm has more than 13,000 retail brokers and salespeople (now called financial consultants) and a total of 42,000 employees worldwide. The firm's budget for information technologies is about $1 billion per year. The following Insight describes Mike Sullivan's experience with a few of this technology's applications.

Insight

Merrill Lynch's Prism

Mike Sullivan is a vice-president with Merrill Lynch's private client group's New York sales office. The PC on Sullivan's desk runs the firm's new version of Prism. It allows him to (1) view customer portfolios and executive trades; (2) browse breaking Dow Jones, Reuters, and Knight-Ridder news stories and market data delivered via satellite; and (3) even watch television and videos broadcast internally through a new Merrill Lynch service.

Typing a command, Sullivan calls up the portfolio of one of his customers—the head of fixed-income trading at a major Manhattan bank—and goes through a list of dozens of stock and bond holdings. If Merrill Lynch had kept the traditional method of printing customer statements on a monthly basis, it would be a twelve-page list, broken into seven separate accounts. The dollar value of the portfolio would be somewhat outdated by the time it was printed. Now, however, Sullivan can get an instant profit-and-loss statement—of both realized and unrealized earnings—with just three keystrokes. He can view summary data and key ratios. And he knows he's looking at the current valuation of the client's massive portfolio: no need to wait until the first of the month for an update. "We used to have to do this manually," says Sullivan, who adds that the ability to calculate a profit-and-loss statement with current market data was installed in February 1994.

A recent addition to Prism is customer asset allocation charts. An essential aspect of any customer's financial plan is an optimal mix of investment types (e.g., corporate bonds, government securities, and low- and high-risk stocks) that match the customer's risk and return goals. Previously, lengthy manual calculations were required to determine whether the current asset allocation for the portfolio reflected the customer's goals. No longer. Sullivan says, "The fact that it's done for me automatically is superb. I save two hours a day because of this feature alone."[38]

5

State the factors that facilitate effective implementation of information systems.

EFFECTIVE INFORMATION SYSTEM IMPLEMENTATION

Each information system has unique characteristics. However, the seven factors shown in Figure 19.4 commonly influence the effective implementation of information systems and thus are called implementation building blocks. They emerge during the initial stages of system development, continue through implementation, and then become important to everyday operations.[39]

Ethics

Sociologists and psychologists say that the spread of communication devices such as fax machines, beepers, and cellular telephones may diminish face-to-face human contact, disrupt etiquette and social customs, and spark new fears in the workplace. Is it ethical for organizations to encourage this spread of technology?

User Involvement

As noted previously, information system users must be heavily involved in the design process. Their input normally gives system designers a fairly accurate picture of current work flows, costs, and time requirements for various functions. This input usually helps in the identification of current operational inefficiencies that the new system should correct. Users typically know how information affects decision making, but designers often do not. For example, employees in an accounting department understand the flow of financial information and how financial reports are prepared and distributed. By working with the accounting staff, systems experts can tailor the system to these users' needs.

FIGURE 19.4

Building Blocks for Effective Implementation of Information Systems

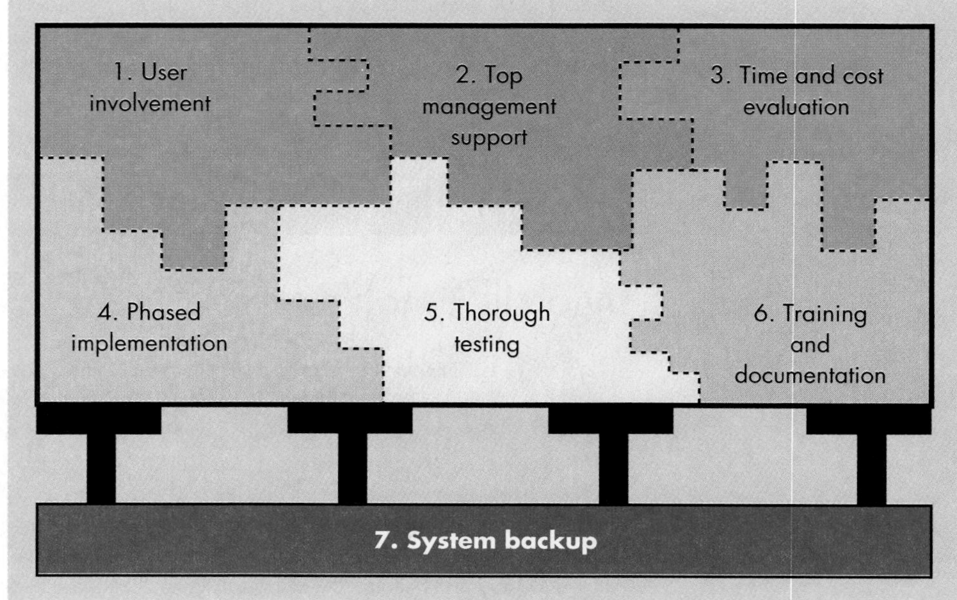

Teaching Tip
Ask the CIO for the university to come to class and explain implementation of an information system at the university. Ask him or her to describe each stage of the process.

Teaching Tip
Have students brainstorm about the key issues involved in implementation of new information technologies in an organization.

Ask Students
"How many of you have ever experienced computer anxiety? What was its basis? In general, does this type of anxiety seem as prevalent as ten years ago? Why or why not?"

Teaching Tip
Have students interview a top manager of an organization that has installed new information technology about how the organization overcame employees' resistance.

User participation during the implementation stage is crucial because those who are to apply it can often spot problems or deficiencies before the new system becomes fully operational. Taking part in implementation also helps users understand the reasons for the new system and prepares them for the necessary changes in the way that tasks are performed.

Top Management Support

Another key factor in the effective implementation of information systems is strong, visible support from top management. Like any major organizational undertaking, information technology applications must involve top managers in order to succeed. Without their support, information technology is less likely to be integrated into the organization. Thus strategic information systems planning involving top management is essential to foster a positive attitude toward system development from the beginning.

Evaluation of Time and Cost

A third important factor involved in effective implementation of information systems is a thorough evaluation of time and cost requirements. New information systems often require more time to develop and cost more than anticipated. During the initial development stages, predicting these requirements accurately is difficult. However, management initially should have some idea of the cost of not improving the organization's information system.

To keep the developmental process on schedule and within budget, systems designers must project time and costs in detail. The projected schedule should include project milestones and perhaps even a PERT network (see Chapter 6), as is common for many construction projects. Justification of the design, installation, and projected maintenance costs helps prevent cost overruns and guides decision making.

Phased Implementation

Any significant new technology normally should be introduced in phases. A new information system should not be turned on one day and the old system abandoned at the same time. Too many things can and will go wrong: The new system does not work as

Discussion Question 6
Why should new or major changes in information systems normally be implementaed in phases?

Teaching Tip
Select various students to role-play as outside consultants, employees, and top management in a company that is considering implementing a new information system. Have some "employees" and "managers" express resistance to the system and have others support the system.

expected, it generates bad information, no one knows how to use it, and so on. By implementing the system in phases, problems owing to design glitches and unforeseen events can be managed. Software problems can be resolved before employees become too dependent on the system. Technical support staff can train users to work with the new system before their jobs depend on it. Gradual implementation also gives employees time to adjust, thus minimizing resistance to change.

As recently as 1985, students at Texas A&M University (and many other universities) had to pick up computer cards for each class during registration. Because they had to go to so many different locations around campus and wait in lines, the registration process often took at least a full day. Then a new registration system was slowly phased in. At first data entry personnel entered only late registrations on terminals linked to the main computer. By 1987 the entire registration process was handled by the information system. Students now register through the telephone by contacting the main computer directly. They enter class section and fee information from a push-button telephone and respond to a computer-triggered voice. The problems and confusion that an immediate and direct transition from computer cards to telephone registration were avoided.

Thorough Testing

Another factor that affects the effective implementation of information systems is thorough testing of both hardware and software. Testing should be performed on individual modules, on sets of modules as the system is assembled, and then on the entire system before it becomes fully operational. The testing process should anticipate probable errors and those that aren't likely to occur. The effects of incorrect commands, improper data, poor environmental conditions, and other possible problems all should be checked. The biggest problems with new technologies arise from events that system designers claim are not expected to occur or could not occur—but do. Users should be intensively involved in this testing and debugging process.

Training and Documentation

The introduction of new technologies requires training of users and adequate documentation of operational procedures. An information system is of little value if no one knows how to use it properly. At times, those in charge of the information system have gained power because many others in the organization are overly dependent on them. As a result, a power struggle may develop between managers and other employees who formerly controlled the flow of information and the system development staff. Organizations can avoid this sort of interdepartmental conflict by fostering cooperation. Users don't have to know how to program computers, but they should understand the capabilities and limitations of their information system. And systems development personnel must understand the capabilities and information needs of the users.

System Backup

The last factor, but not the least important by any means, that influences the effective implementation of information systems is the presence of an alternative information system for accomplishing the same task in case of system failure. Computer systems are notorious for developing problems, especially software problems, at the wrong time. If users are too dependent on a single information system, they may believe that the quicker the fix, the better. However, quick system fixes may overlook real problems that lead to other problems. A backup procedure—or even access to a backup computer system—will give analysts time to track down such problems, carefully evaluate them, and properly correct them. This approach does not ensure a problem-free future, but it does encourage solutions that are less likely to create additional problems.

Perhaps the most extreme example of system backup is the computer-based *voting* system developed for NASA's space shuttle program. Four identical computers run IBM software. A fifth computer runs software designed by Rockwell International. If the first four computers disagree, they decide what to do by majority vote. In the event of an even split, the Rockwell system steps in to break the tie. Should some subtle software bug common to all the IBM machines cause them to stop in their tracks at once, the Rockwell backup stands ready to take over crucial functions. The use of independently designed systems is known as *dissimilar redundancy*. "We've never had to use that backup computer in flight," stated Ted W. Keller, IBM's manager for the shuttle's on-board software. He claims that statistical models predict less than 3.6 bugs per million lines for the software. Thus the normal 500,000-line program should have at most 2 bugs, but nobody knows for sure.[40]

The following Insight on DuPont Canada reveals the process and results of effective development and implementation of its executive support system (ESS).

Insight

DuPont Canada's ESS

Top executives at DuPont Canada, Inc., believe that its ESS has led to better management, both by changing the way managers work and by changing the way they view the company. DuPont began installing its system in 1989. It rolled the system out gradually, making it available first to 125 managers and other professionals. It also formed a decision support team, including senior executives, to help determine the system's final shape. Executive involvement was important. Not only did it help ensure that the system was useful and relevant, but it also created peer pressure within the executive ranks to use the ESS.

DuPont Canada's ESS provides links with the company's electronic-mail (e-mail) software. This linkage enables executives to send each other charts, graphs, and other material when they come across something of interest. The ESS is connected to the Dow Jones news wire, so executives can monitor market developments and news about competitors. Senior executives can also run "what-if" scenarios over the breadth of the company, to see the ripple effect of a decision in one business segment on all the others, and on the consolidated results.

The company's ESS also is linked with its parent company's global financial database. Executives can examine information from DuPont operations all over the world and benchmark its Canadian operations with DuPont operations elsewhere. A Canadian manufacturing executive, noticing a drop in variable costs at a U.S. plant, can phone and ask why that is occurring. A sales executive with DuPont's plastics business, noticing a sudden increase in sales in Japan, can do the same. They might just hear about a new way to arrange a factory floor or an innovative sales technique.

Before DuPont Canada's ESS came into the plastics segment, says Dennis Layfield, then the segment's controller, executives were making marketing decisions based on cash flow and profit statements. These statements weren't segmented by market, and the executives were making some serious mistakes. "We had some products we thought were profitable in certain markets that weren't, and others we thought weren't profitable that were," say Layfield. "It was a revelation." DuPont Canada wound up dropping some products and emphasizing others. Executives could better tell where their products fit, where they delivered the greatest value for the customer (and where, by extension, to raise prices) and where additional opportunities lay. "It created an outward focus," says Layfield, "and put us closer to the customer."[41]

One closing word of caution about implementation: Even if all seven of the interrelated building blocks for information system implementation are addressed (see Figure 19.4), there is no guarantee that it will be effective. However, the risks and uncertainties will be reduced and better understood if those seven factors are considered thoroughly. Also, the recognition of the potential sources of uncertainties will motivate decision makers to invest in system backup. Like many major organizational changes, the development and implementation of information technologies may meet with resistance. In Chapter 21 we present some ways for dealing with such resistance.

6

Identify several ethical concerns in the development and use of computer-based information technologies.

ETHICS AND INFORMATION TECHNOLOGIES

As the capabilities and pervasiveness of computer-based information technologies increase, concern with their ethical—and unethical or criminal—uses is deepening in the United States, Canada, and other countries characterized as information societies.

Computer Ethics

Some ethicists are even specializing in a subfield known as **computer ethics,** or the analysis of the nature and social impact of computer technology and the corresponding formulation and justification of policies for its ethical use.[42]

Why are an increasing number of individuals and organizations concerned with computer ethics? The reason is that ethical issues surrounding computers arise from their unique technological characteristics.

- They make mistakes that no human being would make.
- They communicate over great distances at high speed and low cost.
- They have huge capacities to store, copy, erase, retrieve, transmit, and manipulate information quickly and economically.
- They have the effect of radically distancing (depersonalizing) originators, users, and subjects of programs and data from each other.
- They may collect and store data for one purpose that can easily be used for another and be kept for long periods of time.

Discussion Question 7
Why is computer ethics of great interest to many individuals?

The Computer Ethics Institute, a professional association headquartered in Washington, D.C., was formed because of the growing interest in this area. It has issued a "ten commandments" of computer ethics, which are listed in Table 19.2. The commandments provide an ethical code of conduct for guidance in situations that may not be covered by law.

Ethics
Is sending anonymous computer messages ethical?

If employees, the media, and general population reflected on and accepted these commandments, many would come to hold much different attitudes toward computer crime, as discussed in the following Ethics Insight.

TABLE 19.2

Ten Commandments of Computer Ethics

1. Thou shall not use a computer to harm other people.
2. Thou shall not interfere with other people's computer work.
3. Thou shall not snoop around in other people's computer files.
4. Thou shall not use a computer to steal.
5. Thou shall not use a computer to bear false witness.
6. Thou shall not copy or use proprietary software for which you have not paid.
7. Thou shall not use other people's computer resources without authorization or proper compensation.
8. Thou shall not use other people's intellectual output.
9. Thou shall think about the social consequences of the program you are writing or the system you are designing.
10. Thou shall always use a computer in ways that demonstrate consideration and respect for your fellow humans.

Source: Computer Ethics Institute, Washington, D.C.

Ethics *Insight*

Attitudes Toward Computer Crime

Keven D. Mitnick, thirty-one years old, was accused of breaking into dozens of corporate computers, pilfering thousands of credit card records, and stealing a fortune in software. To his fans on the Internet, Mitnick is a "legend," a "technology-wielding genius," and a "hero." Soon after his arrest in February 1995 by federal agents in Raleigh, North Carolina—after eluding authorities for more than two years—Internet bulletin boards lit up with supportive slogans: "Long live Mitnick," "Free Mitnick," and "Mitnick for President." "Mitnick will go down in infamy as the one who truly showed the system," one admirer wrote in a post on the Internet's alt.2600: news group. "He should be freed. . . . He will be freed."

"I don't see them as romantic figures. They're criminals—they're spoiled kids who are doing whatever they want to do," says Donald Hutchison, a vice-president at Netcom Online Communications, Inc., an Internet service. Netcom had 20,000 credit card numbers stolen during Mitnick's alleged crime spree. But Hutchinson says, "People don't turn in heroes."

Whether hacker or disgruntled employee, the computer thief is not a romantic figure, and there is no glamour about computer theft. It is a betrayal of trust, like any other form of embezzlement. Unfortunately, the public's attitude isn't significantly different from its attitude toward old-fashioned bank robbery. The computer-age robber is admired not for swashbuckling, guns-blazing bravado but for cleverness and intelligence. After all, no one gets killed. The villain is still the big impersonal bank or, more likely, the bank's computer. But the money stolen from the bank (or any organization) doesn't belong to the bank or its computer; it belongs to the bank's depositors, most of whom are individuals and some of whom are smaller client banks.

The public's attitude toward hackers and their crimes is a bit different, springing mainly from the media's attitude toward them. Unlike the disgruntled bank employee, hackers have a romantic view of themselves. The names they give themselves clearly indicate that view: the Legion of Doom, the Dream Team, Video Vindicator, and Chaos. They think of themselves as secret agents, outlaws, or heroes of an underground counterculture.

Television and the print media buy into this fantasy. Hackers appear on news and talk shows, where they demonstrate their talents to seemingly admiring hosts. They are interviewed in news magazines and boast of the databanks they have ripped off. One hacker provided the cover story in one issue of *People* magazine, and the article about him was flattering, even fawning.[43]

Privacy Issues

Ethics
Are hackers heroes or criminals?

A wide range of privacy issues are central to computer ethics, as suggested in previous chapters. The types of information available about most individuals in the United States to just about any business (or individual in that business) or government agency is astounding. Most of this information originates with the individual through the process of borrowing money, participating in a government program, or purchasing goods. Consumers and borrowers routinely give information voluntarily to retailers and creditors so that they can purchase goods on credit. At least once a month, millions of banks, retailers, credit card companies, and mail-order houses send computer tapes or other electronic files detailing their customers' purchases and payment activities to credit bureaus.[44]

The three large credit rating companies—TRW, Trans Union, and Equifax—maintain credit information on more than 160 million people in the United States. This information is accessible in a matter of seconds to merchants, clerks, and, in essence, just about anyone. A group of newspaper journalists, who acquired and published the credit rating of a U.S. vice-president, demonstrated this situation. In addition to credit ratings, a large amount of information on nearly everyone in the United States—ranging from medical histories and insurance information to buying habits—is stored in computer-readable form and widely disseminated among credit bureaus, resellers of data purchased from bureaus, and many businesses.[45]

According to recent studies, information that used to be inaccessible or very difficult to obtain is now instantly available for use by almost anyone. The advances in information technologies permit the sharing of all sorts of personal data. The legal system, organizational and managerial policies and practices, self-regulation through professional and trade associations, and consumer groups have not caught up with technological developments.[46]

Ethics
Is it ethical for a company like Kraft to be able to obtain information on its customers?

Kraft General Foods has computer-based information on thirty million customers, including their ages, how often they shop, and much more. The marketing and research staff can figure out (1) whether the company's customers fill the grocery cart in one trip or grab a few items several times a week, (2) whether they spend afternoons clipping coupons and how many children they have, (3) whether they eat out or entertain friends at home, and (4) whether they earn their living behind a desk or on a factory floor. The information on Kraft's customers comes from returned coupons, other promotions, surveys, and scanners used at most supermarket checkout counters. Every time a clerk whisks a purchase over the scanner it electronically records what was bought, who made it, the size, and the price. Those data are then merged with information derived from returned coupons and surveys into what shoppers watch on television, the type of neighborhood they live in, and their shopping patterns.[47]

CHAPTER SUMMARY

1 ***State the far-reaching effects of information technologies on individuals and organizations.***

Information technologies continue to have profound effects on the design of organizations, the roles of managers, and the ways employees perform their jobs. The numbers of organizational levels and middle managers are being reduced, top managers are gaining more strategic control over critical decisions, information technologies often are used as a strategic asset necessary to compete in the marketplace, more knowledge workers are needed by organizations, knowledge workers are taking on temporary managerial roles as team leaders of special projects, information float (e.g., delay) among positions and organizational levels is being sharply cut, and real-time information networks are enabling an increasing number of knowledge workers to perform their tasks any place at any time.

2 ***Describe the role and value of information as a resource.***

Some organizations have created the role of chief information officer to provide leadership in developing information systems as a strategic asset for use by employees. Information is a value-added resource derived from data that have been transformed to make them useful. Knowledge is used by individuals to create, store, share, and apply information. Four interrelated criteria may be used to assess the value of information: quality, relevance, quantity, and timeliness.

3 ***Explain the essential capabilities of information technologies that support and link the basic managerial functions.***

Information technologies continue to become exponentially less expensive and exponentially more powerful. By means of real-time communication networks and other computer-based capabilities, the basic managerial functions of planning, organizing, leading, and controlling are dramatically changing, rapidly improving, and quickly becoming more closely linked. Four categories of interrelated information technologies are the primary sources of these capabilities: communication systems (e.g., teleconferencing, facsimile machines, local and wide area networks, electronic mail, voice recognition systems integrated systems, and the like), decision support systems (DSS), expert systems (ES), and executive support systems (ESS).

4 ***Discuss the issues involved in information system design.***
The creation of an information system should begin with a careful determination of information needs. This assessment should be linked to the organization's market-related goals, strategies, and plans. System constraints, which are the internal and external limitations on decision-making discretion, must be identified and assessed. The general and operational goals for the information system should then be developed. The last task is to specify the content of the developmental stages for the system. These stages include preliminary problem definition (which normally reflects the information needs, system constraints, and system goals), conceptual design, detailed design, and implementation.

5 ***State the factors that facilitate the effective implementation of information systems.***
Seven interrelated building blocks contribute to effective information system implementation: (1) user involvement, (2) top management support, (3) evaluation of time and cost, (4) phased implementation, (5) thorough testing, (6) training and documentation, and (7) system backup.

6 ***Identify several ethical concerns in the development and use of computer-based information technologies.***
Concerns about the unethical and criminal uses of computer-based information technologies are deepening in the United States, Canada, and other information societies. Ethical issues arise from the unique technological characteristics of computers. The ten commandments of computer ethics suggest that radically different attitudes and actions are needed by many individuals and the media toward computer crime and the unethical use of computer-based technologies. A wide range of privacy issues also are central to computer ethics. The private and government sectors have yet to put significant controls on the current wide-open access and use of all types of data and information about individuals.

QUESTIONS FOR DISCUSSION

1. Develop a diagram of the communication network that represents the Blacksburg electronic village project, as described in the Preview Insight.
2. Why are computer-based information technologies reducing the number of management levels in many organizations?
3. Why is information increasingly viewed as a strategic asset and value-added resource?
4. What are the similarities and differences between communication systems and expert systems?
5. Why are the information needs of top managers different from those of first-line managers?
6. Why should new or major changes in information systems normally be implemented in phases?
7. Why is computer ethics of great interest to many individuals?

FROM WHERE YOU SIT

1. How does your community and college compare with what's being done in the Blacksburg electronic village project discussed in the Preview Insight?
2. Review the Small Business Insight on the lone eagles. If you took a lone-eagle type of job after graduation, what aspects of career progression do you need to consider?
3. Evaluate the degree of effectiveness of your college's student registration system in terms of quality, relevance, quantity, and timeliness.

4. Identify three ways that your life has been affected by one or more of the types of information technologies described in this chapter.
5. Identify a decision—either personal or organizational—that you (or your superior or a friend) have recently made (or are making). What information technologies were used or might have been used to make this decision?
6. Develop a scenario of how students might use the capabilities of executive support systems to obtain a college degree.
7. Has your right to privacy and sense of individualism ever been violated by a computer-based information technology? Explain.

SKILL-BUILDING EXERCISE

Computer Ethics Survey[48]

INSTRUCTIONS: Twenty statements appear in this survey. You should evaluate each statement in terms of the following five point scale:

1	2	3	4	5
TRUE	SOMEWHAT TRUE	NEITHER TRUE NOR FALSE	SOMEWHAT FALSE	FALSE

If you think a statement is true, record a "1" next to it. If you think a statement is *neither true or false,* place a "3" next to it, and so on. Do not skip any statements.

_______ 1. The courts have provided clear guidance on who should have access to electronic mail at work.

_______ 2. Employees are usually informed by employers if their voice mail is going to be monitored.

_______ 3. Medical records are not available to employers.

_______ 4. Most organizations have clear written policies and procedures regarding the use of electronic mail.

_______ 5. The confidentiality of faxes is generally well maintained.

_______ 6. Nothing inherent in computer technology raises unique ethical questions.

_______ 7. Public perceptions of computers and computer professionals generally has been good.

_______ 8. Computer professionals have a level of influence that is matched by equivalent levels of organizational controls and professional association guidance.

_______ 9. The best way to deter unethical behavior in the use of computers is through legal deterrents and remedies.

_______ 10. The best way to deter unethical behavior in the use of computers is through professional codes of conduct.

_______ 11. The majority of computer science graduates have had at least one course in computer ethics by the time they graduate.

_______ 12. There are many controls over what information is kept on private citizens, who keeps it, and who can access it.

_______ 13. The majority of businesses in the United States have well-documented policies regarding what employee information is kept in personnel databases and who has access to it.

_______ 14. Computerized medical records pose no greater danger to privacy and potential for misuse than do paper records.

_______ 15. Electronic bulletin boards are fairly well "policed" and do not contain potentially harmful information.

_______ 16. The majority of computer crimes are reported, and the perpetrators are successfully prosecuted.

_______ 17. Computer abuse, such as gaining unauthorized access to a system or placing a virus or other potentially damaging program into a computer, is a minor problem.

_______ 18. Software theft, including unauthorized copying of software, is clearly a problem, but monetary losses are not yet significant.

———19. Although the failures of computer systems have been reported in the media, none have resulted in serious injury or significant property loss.

———20. Because computer ethics is a relatively new application of older ethical concepts to new technology, there is little understanding about what can and should be done.

Scoring: Sum the point values for statements 1-20. The total points may range from 100 to 20. Most experts on computer ethics would consider a perfect score as 100; that is, all statements are considered to be *false.*

CRITICAL THINKING CASE

Frito-Lay—In the Know[49]

Paul Davis noticed the beginnings of a disturbing trend in the weekly sales data for the Dallas division of Frito-Lay, Inc., which he headed. Sales of the company's Lay's and Ruffles potato chips brands were headed down—by all comparisons. The declining sales numbers showed up in red on his computer screen. With a few keystrokes, Davis quickly called up information that showed him the cause—a competitor was making inroads. Not only that, the competitor was doing the damage by deeply discounting its products and getting key display space in stores of a leading grocery chain. Because salty snacks such as potato chips often are bought on impulse, the location and amount of supermarket display space are critical.

Davis and his regional managers were able to react immediately. They pulled comparative data—from the retailer's own sales—that convinced the retailer that the deep discounts were hurting the store's bottom line, that reallocating space in Frito-Lay's favor would be more profitable for the supermarket. The system that allowed Davis to assemble quickly a detailed presentation based on the chain's own scanner data is, in his words, "powerful." Frito-Lay's managers and planners can pinpoint sales, turnover, and space allocations for its own products and those of its competition. They can compare a retailer's return on inventory for Frito-Lay products, competitors' products, and other food categories. "We have a one-week report on new promotions," said Allen Dickason, director of systems development. "We can respond to competition's response to us."

Frito-Lay—with roughly half the $10 billion U.S. market for chips—took an early lead in using scanner data, although its competitors weren't far behind. "Every one of [its] large competitors is working on something like this," said Lynda Applegate, a Harvard Business School professor who researches strategic use of information technology. She states: "What's different about Frito-Lay is that they are going not only faster but further than most. They are building an information infrastructure that enables them to package information and deliver it to all levels of the organization."

Frito-Lay credits its system, an initial $40 million investment, with savings of $39 million a year on returned products. More important, Frito-Lay's executives consider the system crucial to the company's strategy of decentralization. Frito-Lay faces intense competition and a sophisticated, fragmented market. The firm had to learn to move quickly and in several directions at once.

"This is really a bag-by-bag kind of business. It's 10,000 people doing thousands of things a day," said Charles Feld, vice-president of management services and the architect of Frito-Lay's system. Bobby R. Wright is one of the 10,000. Every working day he drives a delivery truck to customers on a specified route. For more than two years, he's had something different on his truck. Right above the cartons of bean dip, salsa, and Grandma's Cookies is a mount for a handheld computer. These devices kicked off Frito-Lay's internal information revolution. Wright's route takes him to a number of small accounts: convenience stores, service stations, and sandwich shops. At each stop, he casts an experienced eye over the display shelves. He doesn't need to count. He knows how many bags of Doritos or Ruffles will fill the empty space, and he keys the number into the handheld computer. When Wright finishes the call, the computer prints out an itemized sales ticket, automatically factoring in any promotional allowances for the retailer and cutting the potential for error. At the end of the day, instead of tallying his accounts, Wright simply downloads the computer at the district warehouse to send the information into a central database. At the same time, new information can be uploaded into the computer. Every week, Wright's district manager can hold a "one-on-one" with him, spotting problem areas or sales potential.

Two management layers above the district managers, Paul Davis scrutinizes a large amount of information every week, packaged to fit his needs. Included in his executive information package is another huge block of data—supermarket scanner transactions purchased from Information Resources, Inc. The division manager can use these data to find out who's hurting Frito-Lay the most and how, and then allocate dollars to move against the competitive threats or seize new opportunities.

"Strategic advantages never last. You are always only six months to a year ahead of everyone else," explains Feld. By 1994, Feld and Dickason had manufacturing, logistical, and marketing data integrated into the system. All managers are now online with executive information software. "We know people are using handheld computers out there," Dickson said. "But we don't believe they've built the systems behind [them] to sum up that information, capture it accurately, and make it work on a day-to-day basis." These information technologies and the creation of many self-managing teams have also enabled Frito-Lay to reduce significantly the number of managers.

1. What types of information technologies are being used at Frito-Lay?
2. What was the likely effect of implementing the new system at each organizational level mentioned? Explain.
3. Why is Frito-Lay's new system considered to be a strategic competitive weapon?

VIDEO CASE

Technology: The Interactive Future of Television

David Lockton, CEO of Interactive Network (IN), says that his company will soon change the way in which TV is used with the creation of two-way television entertainment. Viewers will be able to "play along" with TV game shows and sporting events by using a hand-held wireless control unit that receives a data stream by means of FM radio signals. This service requires the purchase of a control unit and payment of a monthly basic service fee of about $15.00. And it is just the first step for interactive television. Bruce Judson, general manager of multimedia products and services at Time, Inc., believes that interactive television will change the face of advertising and marketing and in turn create completely new viewing, shopping, and buying habits.

Interactive media is a not a new concept and is not exclusive to Interactive Network. *Modern Media* views it as a "continuum that ranges from the most simple interactive media such as 800-number telephone promotions, interactive fax programs, interactive kiosks, scanning technologies and on-line services (i.e., Prodigy, CompuServe), to more complex vehicles such as interactive compact disks and video games." Other companies also are entering the interactive arena. E-ON, formerly TVAnswer, was incorporated in 1986 and offers two-way television service that allows the viewer to shop, order food, perform banking transactions, interact with educational programs, news and entertainment, and even vote in polls. NTN Communications, Inc., established in 1983, produces, programs, and broadcasts interactive TV games and shows twenty-four hours a day.

According to a survey by the Rand Corporation, more than 40 percent of U.S. households will pay for interactive entertainment and information services by the end of the decade. The industries that are betting heavily on an interactive future include telecommunications, media, consumer electronics, computers, and advertising. Investors also have been swayed by leaders in the industry, such as Lockton, and Paul Kagan, one of the founding investors of IN. Kagan provided much of the funding needed to spurn cable companies in the 1970s and 1980s and through IN's success gained a reputation as a "visionary" in the field. Companies testing interactive television include J.C. Penney, which conducted a 150-household test in Denton, Texas, in which they offered selected catalog merchandise, including clothing, home furnishings, and fitness equipment. Chrysler Corporation also has experimented with interactive television with postcommercial surveys and the delivery of electronic coupons to viewers.

Despite the anticipated success of interactive media, some in the industry believe that the forecasts are too optimistic. These people ask: "Will 40 percent of U.S. households pay for interactive television when only 60 percent currently subscribe to cable?" and "Will consumers pay for the extra devices needed for two-way communication?" Another problem to be considered is similar to the one currently facing online computer information services. The companies that pioneered this technology have become its victim as technological advances move faster than they can be marketed. Solutions to these problems remain to be obtained as the industry nudges consumers toward an increasingly interactive world.[50]

Questions

1. How can new technologies such as interactive media contribute to today's business organizations?
2. In the future, more and more uses for interactive technology are likely to be found. What are some of the possibilities for this technology beyond telecommunications, media, consumer electronics, computers, and advertising?
3. What types of resistance to information technologies may workers exhibit? How can employees best be introduced to, oriented to, and encouraged to be participative in these new information technologies?

Chapter 20

Operations Management

Learning *Objectives*

After studying this chapter, you should be able to:

1 Answer four basic questions about operations management.

2 Explain traditional positioning strategies and an emerging alternative to them.

3 Provide examples of choices in office, service, and manufacturing technologies.

4 Describe the differences between traditional quality control and total quality management and control.

5 Explain the main concepts and practices of inventory management and control.

Chapter *Outline*

Preview *Insight*

Xerox—World Class Manufacturer

Xerox Corporation, which makes more than 250 types of document processing equipment, carried away the coveted Malcolm Baldrige National Quality Award in 1989. That same year Xerox Canada, Inc., won Canada's first National Quality Award. The quest for total quality continues to be a top priority at Xerox, according to David T. Kerns, its former CEO and chairman.

About a decade ago Xerox introduced its Leadership Through Quality process—a management system that depends heavily on employee involvement in teams and focuses the entire company on achieving total quality. For example, individual assemblers have the authority to stop production when they spot problems. Operators working as a team fix the problems on the spot. The role of first-line management was changed from that of traditional, directive supervisor to that of coach and expediter. Defining customer satisfaction as the top priority changed the company's organizational culture. Quality now means meeting and exceeding the requirements of Xerox customers.

The first step in implementing the new process was to train teams of managers who had to plan, coordinate, and solve problems together. Usually conducted off-site and lasting about three-and-a-half days, the training was similar to that Xerox had already been giving manufacturing supervisors. Management emphasized identifying quality shortfalls and problems, determining root causes, and developing and implementing solutions. Teams at all levels are taught interpersonal skills, a six-step problem-solving process, and a nine-step quality improvement process. To ensure the commitment of managers at every level, the Leadership Through Quality program began with top management. It then spread throughout the organization (led by senior staff), gradually reaching all employees worldwide.

At the same time, Xerox intensified and formalized the analysis of its position in the marketplace. In addition to conversations with customers and periodic surveys of the marketplace, the company now uses benchmarking. It measures Xerox's goods, services, and practices against those of its toughest competitors and other firms who are among the best at doing certain things. For example, Xerox benchmarked L.L. Bean for distribution procedures, Deere Company for central computer operations, and Procter & Gamble for marketing. Benchmarking is the responsibility of each of Xerox's approximately 200 departments and units.

Xerox also is a leader in one of the newest manufacturing trends, called design for disassembly (DFD). The goal of DFD is to close the production loop by conceiving, developing, and building a product with a long-term view of how its components can be refurbished and reused—or disposed of safely—at the end of the product's life. Xerox implemented DFD in 1992, and it now is an integral part of what is called green manufacturing. The word *green* is a reference to the company's concern with environmental effects. Moreover, green manufacturing, from transforming raw materials into products to remanufacturing and recycling of parts, is paying off financially for Xerox at the rate of about $500 million a year.

At first Xerox disassembled used up products without having designed them with that final stage in mind. The cartridge assembly for copier toner, for instance, was welded together ultrasonically and had to be torn apart by hand. Xerox replaced this assembly with a design that anticipates recycling. Potentially reusable parts were put in easily accessible places and snaps replaced screws. Common parts, such as plastic panels, now are standardized for use in different products. Engineers were taught the elements of disassembly. A 35-person team called the asset recycle management organization helped them master the new discipline. Because of its total quality and other initiatives, Xerox now is widely viewed as a world-class manufacturer.[1]

1

Answer four basic questions about operations management.

INTRODUCTION TO OPERATIONS MANAGEMENT

Xerox Corporation had lost its dominance of the copier industry that it had created by becoming complacent about operations management. Then the company renewed itself, literally from top to bottom, to become a world-class manufacturer. Every organization—private or public, manufacturing or service—engages in operations manage-

Discussion Question 1
Based on the discussion of Xerox in the Preview Insight, why did the firm adopt a total quality management philosophy and system?

ment. **Operations management (OM)** is the systematic direction, control, and evaluation of the entire range of processes that transform inputs into finished goods or services.[2] Originally, OM was known as *production management,* but this term often was associated only with manufacturing operations. The efficiency and effectiveness of OM play a central role in determining whether an organization achieves its overall goals.

In this chapter we describe the nature of operations management and its importance to quality and productivity in the manufacturing and service sectors of the economy. We identify nine key decisional areas of operations management and then discuss four of them in some detail: positioning strategy, technology choices, quality management and control, and inventory management and control. In this introductory section, we answer four basic questions about OM.

How Does OM Relate to a Systems View of Organizations?

We consider operations management (OM) from a systems view of organizations that involves four primary components: environmental factors, inputs, transformations, and outputs. Figure 20.1 depicts these components and illustrates their interactions.

Environmental factors, which we have discussed in several previous chapters, influence operations management in numerous ways. Recall that such factors can be grouped into cultural, political, and market influences, examples of which are group norms (cultural), health and safety legislation and standards (political), and price competition (market).

Inputs include human resources (managers and workers), capital (equipment, facilities, and money), materials, land, energy, and information. Examples are assembly-line workers and dentists (human resources), a factory and zero-coupon bonds (capital), seed corn (materials), a farm (land), electric power (energy), and market analyses (information).

Transformations are the operations that convert inputs into outputs. Examples are turning bauxite (a raw material, or mineral) into aluminum ingots in an electric furnace, saltwater into freshwater through desalinization, and cavities into fillings through various dental skills (use of a drill) and materials (metal or porcelain). The five numbered circles in the transformations box in Figure 20.1 indicate that production of a good or

FIGURE 20.1

Systems View of Operations Management

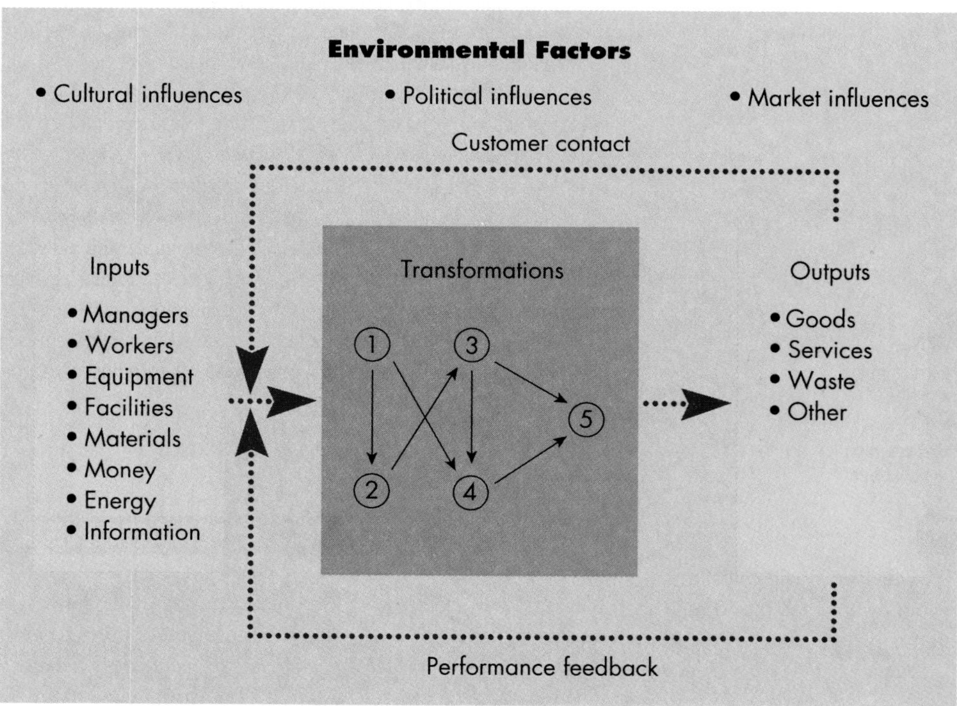

service often requires several operations. An operation can be manufacturing a part or assembling parts manufactured elsewhere, combining fresh vegetables into a salad at a salad bar, or entering a code number and transaction information into an automated teller machine.[3]

Outputs are the goods, services, and waste products created through transformations. Examples are copiers from Xerox factories, government Social Security checks, and garbage, air pollution, and water pollution.[4]

Customer contact often occurs in operations management. Customers actively participate in the transformation process in self-service operations, as when they fill their cars' gas tanks at service stations or their soft drink cups at dispensers and take them to their tables. Customers also provide essential feedback by expressing satisfaction or dissatisfaction with purchased goods and services. *Performance feedback* (e.g., records of the frequency of equipment breakdowns), much of which is provided by customers, closes the system loop. This information helps organizations decide whether to make changes in the goods or services provided, the transformation processes used, and/or the inputs utilized.

What Are the Differences Between Goods and Services Producers?

The application of operations management concepts must recognize differences in the production of goods and the provision of services. Table 20.1 summarizes five such differences. These distinctions often are a matter of degree, as suggested by the continuum of characteristics. For example, McDonald's may be considered a service provider, yet it produces meals (tangible, nondurable products). Goods producers, such as Xerox and Ford, also provide services in the form of credit and technical advice to their customers.

The ability of goods producers to hold items in inventory gives them flexibility in scheduling flows in the transformation process. They can partially offset peaks and valleys in demand by drawing down or adding to inventories. Service providers are more at the mercy of day-to-day and even hour-by-hour fluctuations in customer demand. For example, First National Bank of Chicago has had to shift personnel to eliminate backups in telephone-initiated funds transfer during peak periods each day.

Discussion Question 2
Why is operations management important in the service sector?

Customers themselves often are inputs to the transformation process for service providers (e.g., doctors or hairdressers). In contrast, most customers for manufactured goods have little or no direct contact with the transformation process. Customer contact is left to the marketing department, distributors, and retailers.

Service providers often must respond quickly—within minutes or hours—to customer demand. Examples are checkout lines at supermarkets, service at fast-food restaurants, and auto repairs. Thus the matching of short-term productive capacity (especially the number of employees) to customer demand can be much more difficult for service providers than for manufacturers. Customers for many tangible, durable goods (e.g., cars, furniture, computers, and buildings) know that they may have to wait days, weeks, or even months for those products.

Goods producers generally are capital intensive (i.e., require relatively more investment in building and equipment for their operations). Services producers generally

TABLE 20.1

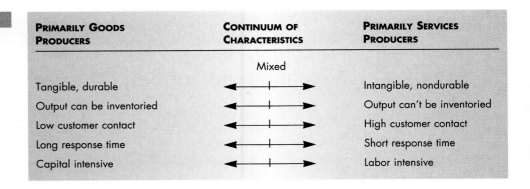

Typical Characteristics of Goods and Services Producers

Primarily Goods Producers	Continuum of Characteristics	Primarily Services Producers
	Mixed	
Tangible, durable	◄——+——►	Intangible, nondurable
Output can be inventoried	◄——+——►	Output can't be inventoried
Low customer contact	◄——+——►	High customer contact
Long response time	◄——+——►	Short response time
Capital intensive	◄——+——►	Labor intensive

are labor intensive (i.e., require relatively more employees for their operations). The need for larger plants and more and better equipment runs up the cost of many manufacturing operations. For example, Chrysler's Windsor, Ontario, assembly plant has 2.5 million square feet, but a NationsBank branch in Corpus Christi, Texas, might have less than 10,000 square feet.

Why Is OM Important to Productivity?

Teaching Tip
Have students brainstorm the reasons that productivity improvement is important to their countries. List responses on the board or an overhead transparency.

Productivity improvement is important from a national and even a global perspective.[5] The impacts of computer-based information technologies are beginning to show up in government productivity statistics. Manufacturing productivity increased by at least 3 percent annually and service industry productivity rose by about 2 percent annually in the first half of the 1990s. Critics claim that government statistics understate productivity gains, especially in services. For example, telephone service has greatly improved and its price has dropped. But the productivity increase is understated because the price decrease usually doesn't fully reflect product improvements. Quality increases—such as variety, reliability, service, and timeliness—often are unrecognized or underrecognized because they are hard to quantify.[6]

The continuous increase in productivity is a key to restoring and maintaining the competitive positions of U.S. and Canadian firms internationally in the manufacture of automobiles, electronic equipment, bicycles, motorcycles, cameras, small appliances, and steel. International differences in rates of productivity growth influence exports, standards of living, and choice of jobs.[7]

Operations management can greatly improve productivity, a primary concern of both goods and services producers. In particular, three applications of operations management principles have resulted in improved productivity.[8] First, the investment of capital in new technology and carefully managing its introduction are essential to long-term productivity growth in both sectors. Second, the reduction of waste, rejects, and returns through improved quality control pays off immediately in both sectors. Third, the reduction in work-in-progress materials in the manufacturing sector reduces the amount of money tied up in inventories and physical space requirements.

No standard measures of productivity apply to all organizations. The most commonly used general measure is **total-factor productivity,** which is the ratio of total outputs (amount of goods and services produced) to total inputs (quantities of labor, capital, and materials used).[9] This indicator of economic efficiency is normally expressed in monetary terms. In contrast, **partial productivity** is the ratio of total outputs to a single input. Examples of partial productivity ratios are (1) units produced per day divided by labor hours of production employees per day, and (2) store sales per month divided by labor hours of sales personnel per month.[10]

These and other measures are meaningful only if the outputs produced are sold. The assessment and improvement of productivity in service operations, such as retailing, is especially challenging. The following Global Insight describes one of the more dramatic examples of productivity improvement in a retailing organization through the application of new information technologies.

Global *Insight*

Technologies at Seiyu Supermarkets

In Japan, Seiyu Supermarkets set out to develop a model store that would significantly increase retail productivity. Containing about 5,000 square feet each, its new stores feature many technological innovations. Management worked directly with manufacturers to design the new equipment. The results have revolutionized the company's operations.

Technological innovations used in the stores include (1) a computer-driven robotic system for loading and unloading delivery trucks, (2) a programmable robot that places merchandise in appropriate aisles, (3) an automatic cold-cut dispenser (type of meat, slicing thickness, and cost or number of slices desired are programmed by the customer), (4) online liquid crystal diode (LCD) displays of merchandise prices, and (5) automatic audio descriptions of products and recipes in which they can be used (activated when the merchandise is picked up by shoppers).

Data provided by management show significant gains in productivity, with the ultimate potential of reducing the number of employees by 20 percent. The time required for materials handling and other routine management tasks has been cut by nearly one-third. The time gained is now spent on planning and decision making—almost three times as much as can be devoted to such functions as Seiyu's conventional stores.

The technologies developed also serve as a profit center. Seiyu is making them available to others through licensing agreements. In addition, the level of customer service has significantly increased.[11]

What Types of Decisions Are Made in OM?

Operations management involves at least sixteen categories of decisions. An effective OM system will link all sixteen, some of which you will recognize as strategic. Nine of the categories are:

1. ***Product plans.*** What products (goods or services) should be offered?
2. ***Competitive priorities.*** Should low price, high quality, fast delivery time, or product choice be emphasized?
3. ***Positioning strategy.*** Should resources be organized around products or processes?
4. ***Location.*** Should facilities be expanded on-site, at a new site abroad, or in a relocated existing facility?
5. ***Technological choices.*** What transformation operations should be automated to improve productivity?
6. ***Quality management and control.*** How can the quality levels necessary to maintain or better the organization's competitive position be achieved?
7. ***Inventory management and control.*** What are the best methods of determining and maintaining the proper inventory levels?
8. ***Materials management.*** How should suppliers be selected and evaluated?
9. ***Master production scheduling.*** Should the organization make to inventory or make to order.[12]

Space limitations prevent us from discussing all nine of these types of decisions. Thus we concentrate on four of the most significant ones: positioning strategy, technological choices, quality management and control, and inventory management and control.

POSITIONING STRATEGY

2

Explain traditional positioning strategies and an emerging alternative to them.

Positioning strategy is the approach selected for managing resource flows in the transformation process. Figure 20.2 provides a framework for comparing traditional positioning strategies. The vertical axis indicates that resource flows can range from sporadic (unstable and unpredictable) to continuous (stable and predictable). The horizontal axis indicates that product type and volume can range from low-volume custom products to high-volume standard products. The three boxes indicate the likely range of three traditional positioning strategies: process focus, intermediate, and product focus.[13]

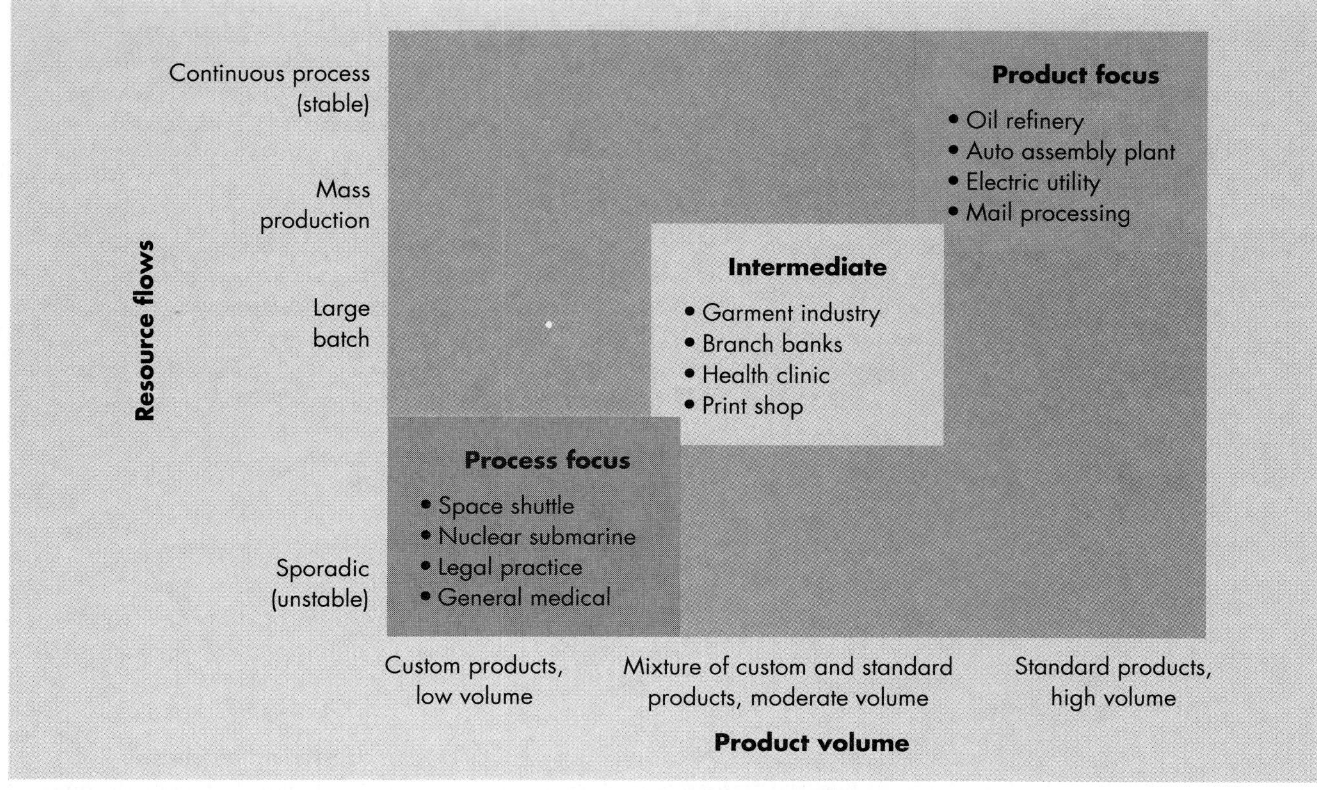

FIGURE 20.2

Traditional Positioning Strategies

Sources: Adapted from Brown, H.K., Clark, K.B., Holloway, C.A., and Wheelwright, S.C. *The Perpetual Enterprise Machine: Seven Keys to Corporate Renewal Through Successful Product and Process Development.* New York: Oxford University Press, 1994; Upton, D.M. The management of manufacturing flexibility. *California Management Review,* Winter 1994, 72–89.

Traditional Positioning Strategies

Teaching Tip
Drilling for oil is an unpredictable process.

A **process-focus strategy** organizes the physical layout of equipment and the work force around each operation in the transformation process. This strategy meets the requirements of custom-made products and low-volume production. This is because a variety of products share each resource and transformation routines for different products vary. Thus, scheduling is crucial. The resource flow pattern is unstable, changing from one order to the next. Similar equipment and operations (e.g., painting stations, drill presses, and welding stations) usually are grouped in separate areas of the facility. For example, one department may perform welding operations for all products passing through the transformation process. Similarly, in a general medical practice, each patient is unique and treatment (product) is based on an individualized diagnosis of symptoms (unstable flow pattern).

Flexibility is at the heart of the process focus. The following are three types of flexibility for manufacturing operations.

- *Product flexibility* is (1) the speed with which new products are created, designed, manufactured, and introduced; (2) the ability to design a product to a particular customer's specifications; and (3) the ability to modify existing products for special needs.
- *Volume flexibility* is (1) the ability to respond to sudden changes in market demand for a particular product; and (2) the speed with which new manufacturing processes can go from small volumes to full-scale production.

Teaching Tip
Movies are an example of one-of-a-kind products.

- *Process flexibility* is (1) the ability to manufacture a variety of products, over a short period of time, without modifying existing facilities; (2) the ability to adjust smoothly to changes in product mix over the long term; and (3) the ability to accommodate variations in raw materials and raw materials substitutions.[14]

A **product-focus strategy** organizes the physical layout of equipment and the work force around a few outputs. As indicated in Figure 20.2, this strategy is designed to fit high-volume, highly automated production of a few standard products with a continuous process or mass-production flow of resources. The transformation process is linear, with various operations arranged in a fixed sequence. This organization is typical of cafeterias, oil refineries, and assembly lines. In a traditional automobile assembly plant, welding machines are stationed along several different assembly lines to perform the same operation on different products. A service example is the automated teller machine (ATM), which provides a limited set of standard financial services (products) continuously by using a well-defined (stable) process.

Discussion Question 3
Do the three traditional positioning strategies apply to both large and small organizations? Why or why not?

An **intermediate strategy** organizes the physical layout of equipment and the work force so that they reflect some features of both the process focus and product focus. Some batching can be done by merging and handling several similar orders at the same time. Some standard products or standard component parts might be made in advance and put in inventory. Kinko's and other print shops adjacent to universities and colleges use an intermediate strategy. They often run off batches of course supplements in advance for later purchase by students, but they also provide immediate customer service in response to a variety of customer orders.

Agile Manufacturing Strategy

Real-World Example
Over the past ten years a much wider choice of cars has become available. This variety is due in part to flexible manufacturing techniques.

An **agile manufacturing strategy** is a system that allows the mass customization of goods by means of advanced fabrication, information, and delivery technologies that are utilized by skilled and empowered individuals and teams.[15] This strategy represents a *paradigm shift* (i.e., a fundamental change in thinking) from the three traditional positioning strategies. Agile manufacturing integrates key features of the process focus (especially customization and flexibility) with the product focus (especially continuous processes and low costs).[16] In the past, these features were, for the most part, considered inconsistent and mutually exclusive, as suggested in Figure 20.2.

Agile manufacturing gives OM the capability to switch from rapid product development to low-cost production quickly and with minimal resources. It rejects (or at least minimizes) the view that the choices have to be among the conflicting priorities of low cost, high quality, and flexibility.[17] With an agile manufacturing strategy, *flexibility* takes on special meaning: the ability to change or react with little or no adverse consequences in terms of the amount of time required and effort expended, the cost of resources, or the quality and quantity of performance.

Some experts forecast that many goods (e.g., autos, computers, and clothes) will be manufactured to each customer's specifications (taste and budget) within the next five to ten years. Companies moving toward agile manufacturing are being forced to cut cycle times—the period between receiving an order and delivering the goods. For that reason some of the production work that left the United States and Canada in the 1980s is beginning to return. In addition, one of the goals of agile manufacturing is to create real-time links between the manufacturer and its customers and suppliers. Advanced information technologies allow networked manufacturers to send their orders electronically into their suppliers' computers. These computers, in turn, relay the suppliers' needs to their own suppliers. Ultimately, the computer-based real-time communications web will extend to individual machines on the shop floor. Robert Nagel, deputy director of Lehigh University's Iacocca Institute (the think tank where the concept of agile manufacturing was born in 1992), states: "If ever the term *paradigm shift* was appropriate, this is it."[18] The following Global Insight indicates how one firm is evolving into an agile manufacturer.

Global *Insight*

John Crane Goes Agile

The U.K. firm, John Crane, Ltd., is a multinational manufacturer of mechanical seals used with assemblies of machined metal components. They provide a barrier between different fluids on each side of rotating shafts, such as around the drive shaft of an oil pump.

During the 1980s, seals were becoming more complex and often were used in capital-intensive plants, which relied heavily on the seals in their systems. If a seal failed, a plant had to shut down. Crane identified a need for quick response to customer demand for both standardized and specialized seals. In addition, the company felt strong pressure to reduce finished goods inventory of the more standardized seals. Crane identified the need for flexibility in the ability to (1) shift between products to meet a customer's requirements (the general time frame was day-to-day and less than a day); (2) switch between products quickly to make smaller runs economical (thus reducing inventories); and (3) provide quick response to customer requests.

Crane achieved mobility in its manufacturing system by using computer integrated manufacturing (CAM) techniques and advanced programmable machine tools. The company developed a system for computer-aided design (CAD) representations of components that could be used quickly and automatically to generate computerized instructions for machines on the shop floor. This advance made the time-consuming step of manually reprogramming machines unnecessary and greatly eased the process of switching from one component to another. Its new-found mobility enabled Crane to achieve low costs and remain competitive in an increasingly tight market.

Although management readily identified the need for quick response and mobility, Crane also had to deal with growing external pressure to customize seals to meet a particular requirement in an order (customers were demanding that Crane be more *flexible*). To provide customization of seals, Crane's manufacturing system needed the ability to adapt to a large range of product characteristics. For example, many different sizes and shapes of holes and slots were required. To meet such requirements, Crane installed general-purpose machine tools with large, well-stocked tool cribs and relied on the ability of trained operators to work on a variety of machines. Crane's evolving agile manufacturing strategy and new capabilities have made it a world-class competitor in its field.[19]

Link to Reengineering

The creation of an agile manufacturing (or service) process usually calls for organizational reengineering. As discussed further in Chapter 21, *reengineering* is the fundamental redesign of an organization's processes (e.g., product development, logistics, distribution, customer service, and manufacturing) to lower costs, improve quality, and increase speed.[20] Reengineering focuses on selected activities that can be improved to yield benefits quickly.

The purpose of reengineering is to do things right the first time: improving quality, eliminating repeated work, spending less time on bureaucratic rules and procedures by cutting them, tearing down barriers between departments, empowering employees and teams, substituting information technologies for paper handling, and organizing processes to serve internal customers (which a human resources department or payroll department often does) or external stakeholders (especially customers).[21] Some reengineering efforts have achieved dramatic results; others have had disappointing outcomes or have failed entirely. The essential ingredient lacking in the disappointing cases and failures often was inadequate management in terms of (1) poor goal development, (2) not creating a motivating environment, (3) inadequate empowerment at lower levels, (4) lack of meaningful measures of performance, and (5) failure to communicate with employees throughout the reengineering effort.[22] The following Quality Insight about Texas Commerce suggests that its management did not make these errors and demonstrates the relevance of reengineering to a service organization.

Discussion Question 4
Why is reengineering often a component of implementing an agile manufacturing strategy?

Quality *Insight*

Texas Commerce Reengineers

Texas Commerce is a unit of the Chemical Bank of New York. In 1993, Texas Commerce had a problem with its return on assets, a standard measure of bank profitability. Other large regional banks were getting returns about a third higher than it was.

One obvious approach was to cut expenses. But after sitting down and listening to more than 4,000 employees in organized focus groups, bank leaders selected a better approach. Don't concentrate on cutting expenses, the employees had said. Instead, look at breaking down bureaucratic barriers in the bank itself—barriers that not only add expenses, but also result in poor service to customers.

So the bank got 1,850 of its 4,000 employees involved in process improvement action teams—groups working to find better ways of doing business. Management also sought suggestions from everyone working in the bank about streamlining procedures in their areas. The program, which started early in 1994 and was completed in February 1995, produced 1,005 recommendations—95 percent of which were adopted. The bank cut expenses and improved customer services.

Some of the changes require new equipment. Texas Commerce will have a one-time expense of $42 million in new systems and technology but should save $53 million a year after paying for the new equipment and transition costs. Some of the changes will have to wait on that new equipment. For example, by the middle of 1995, when a customer cashes a check at Texas Commerce, the tellers no longer will manually type in account information. Instead they will use electronic devices to retrieve instantly information that is already printed on the check. Other improvements were as simple as deciding that the bank didn't need to keep the same records on both paper and microfiche—eventually it had just dumped the paper. Even simpler, the commercial loan process that had required entering the same information in seven different places was simplified so that the information is entered only once.

When a firm learns to do more with less, fewer people are needed. At Texas Commerce, about 1,100 fewer employees will be needed by the end of 1996. The bank has a normal turnover of about 700 people a year, which should ease the pain of layoffs. The bank also has offered an early retirement program and a job deployment scheme for those willing to learn new skills. Ultimately, no more than 200 people will be laid off, bank officials estimate.[23]

3

Provide examples of choices in office, service, and manufacturing technologies.

TECHNOLOGICAL CHOICES

The explosion in the number and types of technologies available for improving productivity and quality continues unabated. These new technologies usually involve computer-based capabilities. Let's consider some of these developments in office, service, and manufacturing technologies.

Office Technologies

Teaching Tip
Have students identify office technologies they have used and rate their efficiency. List their responses on the board or an overhead transparency.

Ask Students
How many of you have PCs, laptop PCs, or notebook PCs?

Computer-based information technologies continue to revolutionize the office environment, with personal computers (PCs) being the dominant force. Today's most powerful PCs have more capabilities (because of software developments) than a 1970s mainframe that cost several million dollars. Managers and professionals in virtually all leading organizations use PCs to communicate with each other, subordinates, customers and suppliers, and large computers. The following are some additional uses of PCs and other computer-based office technologies.

- PCs are now the workstation of choice in many organizations for accessing databases. They also are capable of inputting to fax machines or acting as telex/TWX terminals.

- Pioneering users are now applying video imaging to their use of optical disks, graphics workstations, and new control software to merge video images with text and data.
- An increasing number of organizations utilize voice communication systems as part of their office automation. In certain applications—in credit and collections, for instance—telephone signals interface with computer files.
- Organizations are using information technologies to exchange data and documents—everything from memos and price lists to orders and inventory status—electronically. These systems cut internal costs and create real-time networks for communication anytime and anyplace.[24]

Ask Students
How many of you own cellular phones?

Ask Students
How many of you have call forwarding?

Personal communication services (PCS) represent an emerging set of capabilities based on wireless equipment that will enable users to stay in touch with almost anyone, anytime, anywhere.[25] At present, PCS extends the capabilities of cellular phones, which allowed development of mobile offices. Cellular phone technology allows oral or electronic air borne transmissions to be "handed off" automatically over special frequencies from one geographic area (cell) to another. The first cellular communication system was started in Chicago in 1983. At that time, AT&T predicted that 1 million people would utilize such services by the year 2000. By 1994, there were more than 17 million cellular subscribers in the United States and Canada, with as many as 14,000 new users signing up every working day.[26] With PCS, a single phone number can seamlessly follow a user, and some cellular phone providers are already moving toward this capability. Personal communication services are expected to include wireless e-mail messages, faxes, access to information services, and even video images.[27] They operate at higher frequencies, with towers twice as close together as those for cellular phones. Thus the equipment doesn't require as much battery power and thus can be smaller and lighter.

The following Small Business Insight reveals how one law firm, Harris and Graves, reengineered and adopted advanced office technologies to change its processes radically.

Small Business *Insight*

Harris and Graves: Law Firm Without Secretaries

The Harris and Graves law firm is located in Columbia, South Carolina, the home of the University of South Carolina. The firm has sixty attorneys, paralegals, and administrators. It used to have four support employees for every attorney. Now there are just three for each attorney. All employees have 66-megahertz Pentium machines with many features.

In 1994, the firm installed CaseWarder, an integrated case management system based on Windows products and imaging technology. Managing partner Shipp Harris didn't select this technology without making some rather dramatic organizational changes. He eliminated all secretarial positions. Clerical duties formerly performed by the secretarial staff have either vanished (because of automation) or have been taken on by teams of attorneys and paralegals. "We'd already noticed that the sorts of things secretaries did for attorneys were disappearing," says Harris. "Imaging technology did the rest."

Harris had been eyeing imaging for years but was dismayed by the high price tag. Then, new desktop imaging technology became available, priced at just $295 or less per workstation. Five years earlier, says Harris, this type of capability would have cost $10,000 per workstation—and limited Harris and

Graves to a cumbersome proprietary system. Using off-the-shelf products the firm pulled together CaseWarder, a suite of applications that automates legal case management.

Previously, Harris and Graves had a traditional mailroom where paper documents were sorted into cubbyholes, then distributed to secretaries. The secretaries would then re-sort the mail and send it on to the attorneys and paralegals. If action was needed, instructions were either scribbled on a legal pad or spoken into a tape recorder, eventually finding their way onto paper. Now the firm scans all incoming mail into CaseWarder as soon as it arrives. The software indexes each document and places it in an electronic file folder dictated by case number. The program automatically embeds a copy of each document in an e-mail message that it sends to the appropriate attorney or paralegal. That person immediately sees the "mail" icon flashing on his or her screen. Clicking on the icon displays the actual image of the just-arrived document. The image can then be printed, faxed, or sent via e-mail to any other Harris and Graves employee. Automatic links to the electronic case file let employees pull up related documents, as well as type or add spoken instructions "on top" of the image before routing it to another employee.

The productivity benefits of this new way of working have already proved tremendous, says Harris. For example, in litigation an opposing attorney commonly requests copies of medical reports or depositions of expert witnesses for inspection. In the past, when such a request came in, a Harris and Graves employee physically had to locate the file, copy it, and either fax or mail it to the opposing counsel. Now an employee can handle it in a twenty second telephone call.[28]

Service Technologies

Airlines' computerized reservation systems, banks' ATMs, and credit card companies' billing and customer service systems are only three of the many consumer-oriented service technologies.[29] Other computer-based service technologies used by organizations are bar coding, integrated computer order systems, open networks, and voice recognition systems.[30]

A **bar code** is a series of black bars of varying widths alternating with spaces that represent information and can be read by an optical scanner into a computer. Information contained in a bar code may include product name, lot number, manufacturing location, shelf location, and price. Bar coding has greatly increased productivity in supermarkets during the past decade. It speeds up the checkout process, reduces checkout errors, and makes inventory control more effective. Many new applications of bar coding are being developed, including some for goods producers. For example, some goods, such as appliances, are being tracked in inventories through the use of bar codes.

Real-World Example
Amity Leather Products uses bar-codes to pack customers' orders, which may contain hundreds of different items per order (*Material Handling Engineering*, January 1994, 44).

Integrated order systems involve connecting suppliers' computers to customers' computers so that orders may be placed at any time. Such systems eliminate telephoned orders, mailed hard-copy order forms, and hard-copy invoices. American Hospital Supply has placed terminals in the purchasing offices of many hospitals, allowing purchasing agents to order supplies easily and efficiently. The hospitals can keep smaller inventories of many supplies, thus reducing their inventory costs. American Hospital Supply also benefits by making it less convenient for these customers to switch to other suppliers.

An **open network** is a computer-based information system that enables parts of highly dispersed service operations (including customers) to interact readily. Such a system is best thought of as a spider web because of the intricate and structured quality of its interconnections. Such information networks are being used increasingly by multinational banks, financial and professional service companies, engineering and construction enterprises, research and health care firms, and accounting and advertising organizations.[31]

Voice recognition systems are methods of analyzing and classifying speech or vocal tract patterns and converting them into digital codes for entry in a computer system. The U.S. Postal Service uses voice recognition systems in thirty large postal centers to sort bundles that cannot be processed by its automatic equipment. A clerk reads the ZIP codes off the labels, and the system directs the packages to the proper chutes. Postal Service management believes that buying a computer to do the job is cheaper than having people memorize ZIP code locales. Some of the authorizations at American Express are now being given by computers that ask for account numbers and purchase prices and then check cardholders' accounts automatically. Voice recognition systems also are being used in manufacturing applications.[32]

The following Diversity Insight highlights how voice recognition systems and other computer-based information technologies enable disabled people to provide services to others. Dramatic new developments in these technologies are anticipated during the next five years.

Diversity *Insight*

Enabling the Disabled

IBM launched VoiceType in the fall of 1993. It is capable of recognizing 32,000 spoken words at approximately 70-100 words a minute, with about 97 percent accuracy. A two-hour enrollment session familiarizes the computer with a user's voice. Upon completion, the system is ready for use. DragonDictate for Windows and Kurzweil Voice for Windows are other popular dictation systems. Both have vast vocabularies that can be updated; their enrollment sessions last less than thirty minutes. These systems allow dictation directly into word processor.

Phil Terry, a technical trainer at Moody's Investors Service has limited hand use owing to a repetitive strain injury. He uses the Kurzweil system as his primary mode of input. "It's not as fast as typing," he admits, "but I can do just about everything by voice." He sends mail, roams the Internet, and does most of his daily work by voice.

Also gaining popularity are voice navigators, which control and command the computer, replacing basic keyboard and mouse functions. They are easier to use than dictation systems.

Don Dalton, who is paralyzed from the chest down and confined to a wheelchair, started Micro Overflow Corporation in his garage. He relied heavily on a microcomputer, initially operating the keyboard with a stick held in his mouth. Now he uses a microphone in a headset connected to a microcomputer and can activate all the computer's functions by voice, type 100 words per minute, and manage the company's finances and scheduling. Micro Overflow is a distributorship that adapts computer technology for the disabled. Dalton is helping other disabled entrepreneurs profit from computer technology just as he did.

Dr. Alan Brightman, manager of Apple Computer's Worldwide Disability Solutions Group suggests that people with disabilities do not need a personal computer as much as they need a *personalized* computer—one modified by enhancements suited to their particular disabilities. To make such enhancements widely available, Apple opened Aisle 17 in the Spring of 1994. Aisle 17 is a mail order disability solutions store that provides a "one-stop shop" for Macintosh computers and assistive technology packages.[33]

Manufacturing Technologies

As suggested in the discussion of traditional positioning strategies, agile manufacturing, and reengineering, a wide variety of manufacturing technologies are available. In this section, we describe two more new-generation technologies: robots and computer-aided manufacturing.[34]

Robots are reprogrammable, multifunctional machines. A robot's frame often is a substitute for the human arm, and its microprocessor (computer) takes the place of the

Discussion Question 5
What types of problems should management anticipate because of the increasing use of robots?

Ethics
Is it ethical for companies to sacrifice employees' job security by increasing the utilization of robots?

human brain by providing instructions for routine and standardized tasks. Robots have been programmed to perform numerous tasks in materials handling, welding, spray painting and other finishing operations, assembling, inspection and testing, materials removal, and water-jet cutting. Robots perform repetitive tasks without tiring or complaining about poor working conditions.

A robot can be programmed to move in various ways, depending on the task it is to perform. Tactile (feel) and optical (sight) sensing and hand-to-hand coordination systems represent major aspects of robot development.[35] In the Matsushita Electric factory that makes Panasonic VCRs, a robot winds wire thinner than a human hair through a pinhole in the video head sixteen times and then solders it. The 530 robots in the factory wind wire twenty-four hours a day. They do this job five times faster and much more reliably than the 3,000 Japanese homemakers who used microscopes to do the work on a subcontract basis in their homes. The robots can even inspect their own work.[36]

In the service sector, robots have been used for years in nuclear power plants to avoid employee exposure to radiation, and in the ocean to replace divers who require cumbersome and costly life-support systems. Anticipated and evolving applications of robots include assisting with the care of the handicapped and elderly, picking oranges, cleaning office buildings and hotel rooms, guarding buildings, and even helping surgeons. In fact, some brain surgeons already are using a type of robot that drills into the skull with great precision.[37]

Computer-aided manufacturing (CAM) encompasses a wide variety of computer-based technologies used to produce goods.[38] The complete CAM process begins with **computer-aided design (CAD),** which uses special software to instruct a computer to draw specified configurations, including dimensions and details, on a display screen. This method reduces the time spent in the design process and simplifies the exploration of alternative designs. The database resulting from CAD is used to help generate the instructions needed to guide the CAM process, including sequentially routing components to various machines, operating instructions for each machine, and providing for testing components against specifications. It also reports the unit cost of each operation, combines design information with materials specifications, and estimates waste and scrap rates that may affect purchasing requirements.

Teaching Tip
Take the students to the engineering school and have an instructor show them how CAD works and fits into CAM.

In the future, CAM will have an even greater impact on many activities in the manufacturing sector. They include process planning, production scheduling and control, machining instructions, matching performance, parts testing, assembly operations, shipping, cost accounting, personnel assignments, finished goods inventories, work-in-progress inventories, and procurement. The technology has become an important part of the competitive strategy of Xerox, Westinghouse, Texas Instruments, and Hewlett-Packard, among others.

Computer-aided manufacturing is compatible with the product variety and flexibility associated with a process-focus strategy and the low per unit costs associated with a product-focus strategy (see Figure 20.2). Its most direct effects are reduction of the cost versus variety trade-off for goods producers and removal of rigid plant setups as a barrier to rapid product innovation. The demand for CAM has grown rapidly because flexibility is needed to meet ever-changing competition and customer demand. Thus CAM is an important aspect of implementation of the agile manufacturing strategy. Moreover, shorter product life cycles mean that manufacturing plants long outlive the goods they originally were designed to produce. The lives of many products now are so short that 50 percent of their sales often occur in less than three years after they are introduced. In addition, technological advances have accelerated to the point that new goods, materials, and processes are being introduced almost daily.[39]

Real-World Example
Cimplex Corporation of San Jose, California, sells software that costs $52,000 per copy to customers such as Rockwell and Ingersoll Milling. The software translates an engineer's 3-D drawing into a program that runs machines to cut parts (*Fortune*, February 14, 1994, 160).

To take full advantage of CAM and other new manufacturing technologies, some operations actually are becoming more efficient with less use of robots. Consider the changes made by Toyota, as described in the following Insight.

Insight

Toyota Fosters Agility

Toyota Motor Corporation, the world's most efficient manufacturer of automobiles, modified its vision of factories dominated by robots. In 1994, it reduced its heavy emphasis on automation in favor of the flexibility of human employees.

In an old plant south of Tokyo, Toyota has broken the assembly line into five subsections to produce a new four-wheel drive vehicle, called the RAV4. The new assembly line, with buffer zones between the sections, allows workers to control the pace of production better. The payoffs, along with less stress—say company executives—are lower costs and higher productivity.

This change reversed Toyota's earlier expectations and policies. In the early 1990s, in an attempt to cope with a rising yen and a threatened shortage of workers in Japan, Toyota bet big on robots—investing $10 billion in outfitting car plants at Tahara in central Japan with the latest in automation. It also stressed automation for its worldwide operations, including a parts distribution center in Chicago. But it didn't achieve the savings it expected, either in Tahara or Chicago.

Toyota intends to apply its new production techniques to other plants, including its complex at Georgetown, Kentucky, which is now being run by Mikio Kitano. He is the manager who oversaw the RAV4 experiment in Tokyo and was promoted for its success. Kitano says, "Workers can earn high wages because they are capable of improving the job they are doing; machines have not progressed to that point." He adds that a sectioned, buffered assembly line is "not necessarily" slower because the buffers help employees do their jobs better.

Toyota has long had a system in which employees had to be capable of multiple tasks and taking responsibility for improving production. Toyota practically eliminated supervisors and inspectors and cut out repair centers to fix defects at the end of the assembly line. Thus the company instituted basic elements of total quality management several decades before it began to catch on in Canada and the United States.[40]

4

Describe the differences between traditional quality control and total quality management and control.

QUALITY MANAGEMENT AND CONTROL

The Preview Insight emphasized the importance of quality management and control at Xerox. In this section, we discuss the importance of quality management to competitive strategy, the key dimensions of quality, and the meaning and process of total quality control.

Teaching Tip
Ask students to interview the manager of a local company about the company's quality management program (internal and suppliers).

Ask Students
What is quality?

Ask Students
Who defines quality for an organization?

Ask Students
Give examples of value. List them on the board or on an overhead transparency.

Quality and Competitive Strategy

Increasingly, quality management and control is being viewed as a strategic component of effective competition.[41] *Fortune* magazine's annual ranking of America's most admired corporations has always included "quality of products or services" as one of eight key aspects of reputation. For 1994, three of the most-admired corporations that ranked high on quality were Rubbermaid (rubber and plastic products), Motorola (electronics and electrical, equipment), and Procter & Gamble (soaps and cosmetics).[42] Many managers, professionals, and other employees recognize the organizational benefits of offering superior quality (as perceived by customers). These benefits include strong customer loyalty (more repeat purchases), low vulnerability to price wars, ability to command a higher relative price without losing customers, low marketing costs, and low warranty costs.

From a competitive perspective, **value** is the relationship between quality and price. Figure 20.3 presents a competitiveness value map on which an organization can determine its price versus quality position relative to competitors.[43] Recall that Xerox diag-

FIGURE 20.3

Competitiveness Value Map

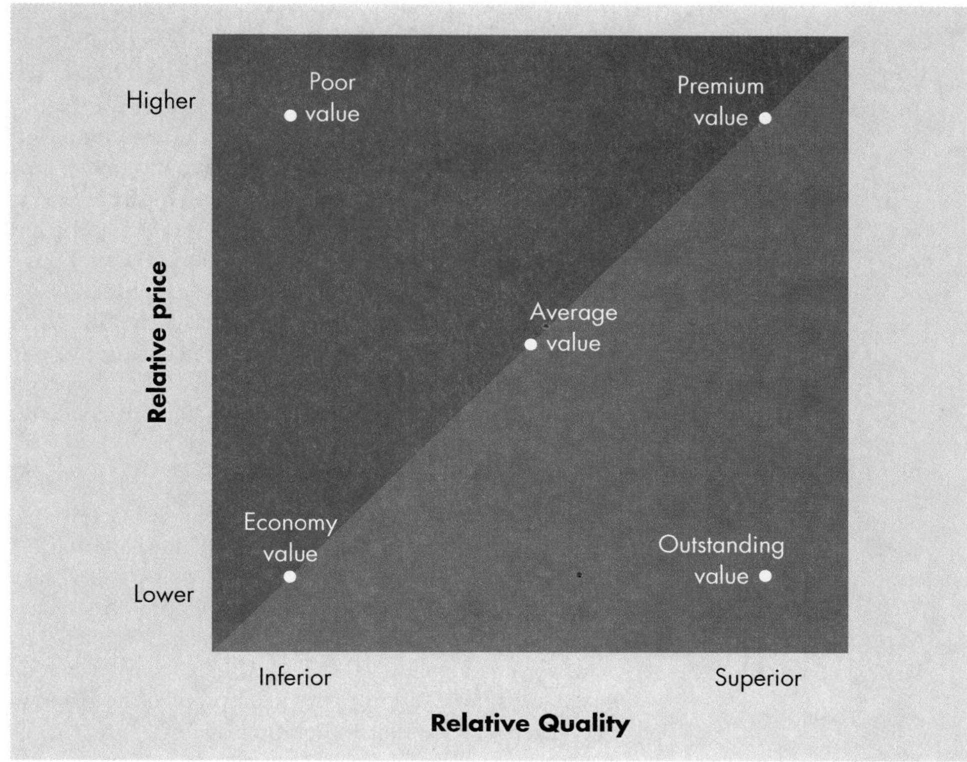

Source: Adapted from Gale, B.T., and Buzzell, R.D. Market perceived quality: Key strategic concept. *Planning Review,* March-April, 1989, 10.

nosed its products' competitiveness values through benchmarking, the process of measuring an organization's goods, services, or practices against those of its toughest competitors or other firms that perform a specific task in an outstanding manner.

As Figure 20.3 suggests, customers who perceive superior quality at a lower relative price receive outstanding value. Organizations that provide such value are likely to grow and prosper. In contrast, the provision of inferior quality at a higher relative price results in poor value for the customer. This situation is likely to invite new competitors. If organizations continue to offer poor value, they will wither and die. Figure 20.3 also indicates a premium value, or high price and superior quality. Competitive pressures continue to challenge organizations to provide greater relative quality at the same or lower price as competitors.[44]

Ask Students

What country was your car designed in? Manufactured in? Did you base your choice of car on the country it was designed and/or manufactured in?

In the mid-1980s, North American automobile firms undertook a massive transformation to become competitive with foreign automakers that had been offering superior quality at a comparable price. A similar incentive operated at Xerox, according to David T. Kearns (Xerox's former CEO):

> *Initially, we dismissed the Japanese by telling ourselves that they were catering to low-volume users, a market segment of only marginal interest to us. We had always been successful, and we assumed that we would continue to be successful. Then we discovered that they were cutting into our market share by selling better, more reliable copiers at prices approximating our cost for producing comparable products. We learned firsthand how far we had fallen behind when we began producing and marketing a copier in the United States that had been designed by our own Japanese affiliate, Fuji Xerox. To our amazement, the reject rate for the Fuji Xerox parts proved to be a fraction of the rate for American parts.*[45]

Heightened global competition has been a major force behind management's sharpened interest in quality management and control. North American manufacturers and service providers used to focus solely on the costs of maintaining or increasing quality. Now, product quality and costs increasingly are being viewed as inversely related—at least up to a point. That is, the costs of improving quality are often less than the resulting savings in reworking, scrap, warranty expenses, and product liability.[46]

Total costs for quality management and control typically include expenditures for prevention (quality planning, worker training, and supplier education), appraisal (product inspection and testing), internal failures (reworking and scrap), and external failures (warranty and product liability). These categories of costs suggest that improving quality can lead to increased productivity. This attitude is widely held among Japanese manufacturers and explains much of their dedication to improving product quality and ultimately attaining the goal of zero defects. And it is an outlook that is increasingly shared by managers and employees of North American manufacturers and service providers.[47]

Meaning of Quality

There are two underlying views of quality: internal and external. The internal view is that quality means meeting the organization's established specifications and standards. This view is rather limited because it ignores customers and actions by competitors. As suggested previously, the external view is that quality means achieving or exceeding the results that customers value and expect.[48] Organizations such as Motorola, Rubbermaid, Ford, and Xerox, among others, emphasize the external view of quality and consider it to be the starting point in defining quality.

TABLE 20.2

The Meaning of Quality

Quality Dimension	Examples		
	Definition	**Stereo Amplifier**	**Checking Account at Bank**
Performance	Primary good or service characteristics	Signal-to-noise ratio, power	Time to process customer requests
Features	Added touches, secondary characteristics	Remote control	Automatic bill paying
Conformance	Fulfillment of specifications, documentation, or industry standards	Workmanship	Accuracy
Reliability	Consistency of performance over time	Mean time to failure	Consistency of time to process requests
Durability	Useful life	Useful life (with repair)	Keeping pace with industry standards
Serviceability	Resolution of problems and complaints	Ease of repair	Resolution of errors
Responsiveness	Person-to-person contact, including timeliness, courtesy, and professionalism	Courtesy of dealer	Courtesy of teller
Aesthetics	Sensory effects, such as sound, feel, and look	Oak-finished cabinet	Appearance of bank lobby
Reputation	Past performance and other	*Consumer Reports* ranking	Advice of friends, years in business

Sources: Adapted from Garvin, D.A. *Managing Quality: The Strategic and Competitive Edge*. New York: Free Press, 1988; Reeves, C.A., and Bednar, D.A. Defining quality: Alternatives and implications. *Academy of Management Review*, 1994, 19, 419–445; Berry, L.L. *On Great Service: A Framework for Action*. New York: Free Press, 1995.

The quality of goods and services can't be effectively represented as a single dimension. Nine of the most common dimensions of quality are performance, features, conformance, reliability, durability, serviceability, responsiveness, aesthetics, and reputation.[49] Table 20.2 provides a brief definition of these dimensions, along with examples of how they are reflected in goods (for a stereo amplifier) and services (for a checking account). These dimensions indicate that customers' expectations and perceptions, as well as competitors' products and services, must be monitored and assessed continuously to ensure effective quality management and control. As we have mentioned, the past failures of U.S. automakers to assess adequately customer perceptions and foreign competition resulted in staggering declines in sales and market share.

Teaching Tip
Have students talk to their neighbors and apply these dimensions to a product they bought recently.

Table 20.2 doesn't represent a comprehensive definition of quality. For example, we could develop indicators of service quality for a specific task or process, such as ordering and delivering goods. The following four dimensions illustrate this idea.

- *Accuracy:* whether the correct products were delivered in the ordered quantities.
- *Speed:* the elapsed time between placing the order and delivery of the product to the customer and how well that matches the customer's expectations.
- *Information accessibility:* the degree to which information is available about a shipment when the customer requests it.
- *Ease of ordering:* the degree to which customer expectations are met with respect of order preparation assistance, ability to receive orders electronically, or providing customers immediate notification of items that are out of stock.[50]

Total Versus Traditional Quality

Total quality management (TQM) is an organizational philosophy and strategy that make quality a responsibility of *all* employees. Organizations pursue TQM through various preventive and corrective control methods that are intended to ensure customer satisfaction.[51] As discussed previously, TQM involves building in quality from product planning to design to design evaluation to preproduction to purchasing to production to sales and service. The TQM strategy gives quality rather than short-term profits top priority. The only constraints are economic feasibility and competitiveness.

In contrast to total quality management, **traditional quality control** relies mainly on product inspection during or at the end of the transformation process. A particular department, such as a quality control department or a relatively small group of inspectors and lab technicians, often is given the responsibility for ensuring quality. The focus is on corrective controls, that is, fixing mistakes after the fact rather than making the product right the first time.[52] Table 20.3 shows the principal differences between traditional quality control and total quality management. Let's now consider some of the specific things that managers and other employees can do to implement total quality.

TABLE 20.3

Traditional Versus Total Quality

TRADITIONAL QUALITY CONTROL	TOTAL QUALITY MANAGEMENT
Screen for quality.	Plan for quality.
Quality is the responsibility of the quality control department.	Quality is everybody's responsibility.
Some mistakes are inevitable.	Strive for zero defects.
Quality means inspection.	Quality means conformance to requirements that meet or exceed customers' expectations.
Scrap and reworking are the major costs of poor quality.	Scrap and reworking are only a small part of the costs of nonconformance.
Quality is a tactical issue.	Quality is a strategic issue.

Deming's Recommendations

W. Edwards Deming, ninety-three years old at the time of his death in 1993, taught the Japanese about quality control. He designed a four-day seminar for Japanese executives in 1950 and subsequently became almost a "guru" to Japanese industry. To honor his contributions, Japanese industry created the Deming Prize in 1951. Highly esteemed in Japan, this annual prize recognizes organizations that have met the qualifications for applying companywide quality control (CWQC). Ten major categories of criteria (e.g., policies and objectives, analysis, and quality assurance) are used to judge applicants for the prize, and each category is divided into subcategories. Although all who apply can be recognized, only a small number of awards are made each year because the standards are very high. The Deming Prize is awarded to several classes of applicants, including individuals, factories, and divisions or small companies.[53]

Until 1980, Deming's work received relatively little notice from top management in North American industry. Then NBC television broadcast a documentary contrasting Japanese and American product quality. Prominently featured on the program as the world's major authority on quality control, Deming soon was in great demand and he signed a long-term consulting contract with Ford. Deming asserted, "We in America will have to be more protectionist or more competitive. The choice is very simple. If we are to become more competitive, then we have to begin with quality."[54]

Deming believed that poor quality is 85 percent a management problem and 15 percent a worker problem. His recommendations for total quality are deceptively simple. Here, we expand on a few of Deming's key ideas that we introduced in Chapter 1.

- Adopt the new philosophy of quality.
- Accept the doctrine that poor quality is flatly unacceptable. Defective materials, workmanship, products, and service will *not* be tolerated. Improve constantly and forever the system of production and service, to improve quality and productivity and thus decrease costs.
- Gather statistical evidence of quality problems before (e.g., from suppliers) and on a real-time basis as they occur during the process, not at the end of the process. The earlier an error is caught, the less is the cost to correct it. Cease dependency on inspection to achieve quality. Eliminate the need for inspection on a mass basis by building quality into the product in the first place.
- Rely on suppliers that have historically provided quality, not on sampling inspections to determine the quality of each delivery. Instead of many suppliers, select and stay with a few sources that furnish consistent quality. Establish long-term relationships with suppliers and stop the practice of awarding contracts to suppliers merely on the basis of price.
- Emphasize training and education of employees to use statistical methods in their jobs and to develop other skills. Do not use slogans to improve quality.
- Employees should feel free to report any conditions that detract from quality. Drive out fear so that everyone may work effectively. Remove barriers to pride of workmanship.
- Managers should introduce statistical methods to help people do their work better, not continue to enforce rigid production standards. Statistical techniques detect *sources* of poor quality. Teams of designers, managers, and employees can then eliminate those sources. This result can be achieved by breaking down barriers between departments.[55]

Baldrige Framework and Award

Teaching Tip
Bring a Baldrige application to class and go through it with the students.

The Malcolm Baldrige National Quality Award annually recognizes U.S. companies that excel in quality achievement and management. The award, a gold-plated medal encased in a crystal column, was created by the U.S. Congress in 1987. Six prizes are possible every year (but aren't automatically awarded): two to manufacturing companies, two to service companies, and two to small businesses with fewer than 500 employees. Three of the manufacturers who have won the award are Motorola (1988), Xerox Business Products Division (1989), and Eastman Chemical Company (1993). Federal Express Corporation (1990) and the Ritz-Carlton Hotel Company, Atlanta (1992), are two of the firms that have received the award in the service category. Two of the firms in the small businesses category that have received the award are the Wallace Company of Houston (1990), a distributor to firms in the energy industry, and Ames Rubber Company (1993).

Companies participating in the award process submit applications and complete an examination. This examination is reviewed by a team of U.S. quality experts, who also visit the companies that pass the initial screening. The 1995 application guidelines and related information fill a fifty-page booklet. A summary of the seven examination categories for 1995, along with their maximum point values (totaling 1,000 points), follows.

Teaching Tip
Apply these criteria to your college or university.

1. ***Leadership*** (90 points): Senior executives' personal leadership and involvement in creating and sustaining a customer's focus, clear values and expectations, and a leadership system that promotes performance excellence.
2. ***Information and Analysis*** (75 points): The management and effectiveness of the use of data and information to support customer-driven performance excellence and marketplace success.
3. ***Strategic Planning*** (55 points): The effectiveness of the company in setting strategic directions and how it determines key plan requirements. Also examined is how the plan requirements are translated into an effective performance management system.
4. ***Human Resources Development and Management*** (140 points): Examines how the work force is developed and utilized to its full potential, in accordance with the company's performance goals. Also, examined are the company's efforts to build and maintain an environment conducive to performance excellence, full participation, and personal and organizational growth.
5. ***Process Management*** (140 points): The effectiveness of key aspects of process management, including customer-focused design, product and service delivery processes, support services, and supply management involving all work units, including research and development.
6. ***Business Results*** (250 points): The company's performance and improvement in key business areas—product and service quality, productivity and operational effectiveness, supply quality, and financial performance linked to these areas. Also examined are performance levels relative to competitors.
7. ***Customer Focus and Satisfaction*** (250 points): The company's systems for customer learning and for building and maintaining customer relationships. Also examined are levels and trends in key measures of business success—customer satisfaction and retention, market share, and satisfaction relative to competitors.[56]

Ethics
Note that ethics is not part of these criteria. How does ethics relate to quality? Should ethics be built into quality criteria? How can it be?

Together the seven examination categories cover all the main components of an integrated, prevention-based quality system built around continuous quality improvement. Most of Deming's prescriptions are represented in these categories.

The following Quality Insight highlights Motorola's progress to the Baldrige Award in 1988 and its continuous quality improvement process since. Motorola is a global firm headquartered in Schaumburg, Illinois, thirty miles west of Chicago. It manufactures pagers, cellular telephone systems, computers, semiconductors, modems, automotive electronics, military and space electronics, and similar products. It is one of the few North American firms that didn't hesitate to accept, refine, and use the best Japanese manufacturing methods.[57]

Quality *Insight*

Motorola's March to Total Quality

In 1981, Motorola set itself a goal of reducing defects by 90 percent by 1986. Robert Galvin, the former chairman, provided the leadership for implementing a series of quality improvement concepts and techniques, including statistical measures, training, employee involvement, emphasis on customer satisfaction, and the like. The company achieved that goal, and product quality became good enough for Motorola to export its pocket pagers to Japan. In 1987 the company set a new goal: another 90 percent improvement by 1989. Since then, Motorola has continued to set and achieve new, demanding quality goals.

For example, the corporate goal was to achieve a quality level by 1992 that is equivalent to what the statisticians and industrial engineers call "six sigma," which means six standard deviations from a statistical performance average. Six sigma translates into only 3.4 defects per million opportunities, or a production process that is 99.99966 percent defect-free. Five sigma is 233 defects per million, and four sigma is 6,210. As a group airlines achieve 6.5 sigma in safety—counting fatalities as defects—but only 3.5 to 4 sigma in baggage handling. Doctors and pharmacists achieve an accuracy of just under 5 sigma in writing and filling prescriptions. As a whole, Motorola is now operating beyond five sigma. At some Motorola factories, quality is so high that they have stopped counting defects per million and have started counting defects per billion. Overall, the company strives to reduce its error rate tenfold every two years.

In applying the six sigma guideline to support services and white-collar operations, every administrative department must go through the following six steps.

1. Define the major functions or services performed.
2. Determine the internal customers and suppliers of these services.
3. Identify the customer's requirements, as well as quantitative measures to assess customer satisfaction with respect to those requirements.
4. Identify the requirements and measurement criteria that the supplier to the process must meet.
5. Flow-chart or map the process at the macro, or interdepartmental, level and at the micro, or intradepartmental, level.
6. Continuously improve the process with respect to effectiveness, quality, cycle time, and cost.

Because speed is an element of quality, Motorola also strives to do things faster. The company cut the time it takes to fill an order for portable radios from fifty-five days to fifteen days and then to an average of seven days. The goal is to increase the speed of its processes—cycle time—tenfold every five years. Not even the corporate legal department is exempt. Motorola's patent lawyers used to take eighteen to thirty-six months to write and file a patent claim. That time has been cut in many cases to two months, and the six sigma goal is *one day* for getting the information about an invention from the engineers and filing the claim.[58]

Quality Control Process

The quality control process generally focuses on measuring inputs (including customer expectations and requirements), transformation operations, and outputs. The results of these measurements enable managers and other employees to make decisions about product or service quality at each stage of the transformation process.

Teaching Tip
Invite a local manager to speak to the class about what his or her company is doing to ensure quality control by *all* employees.

Inputs. Quality control generally begins with inputs, especially the raw materials and parts used in the transformation process. Automobile assembly plants, such as Chrysler's Windsor, Ontario T-van (minivan) plant, couldn't function if suppliers' materials and parts failed to meet or exceed predetermined standards. Fierce global competition has caused all North American automakers to toughen and more vigorously enforce the quality standards for inputs.

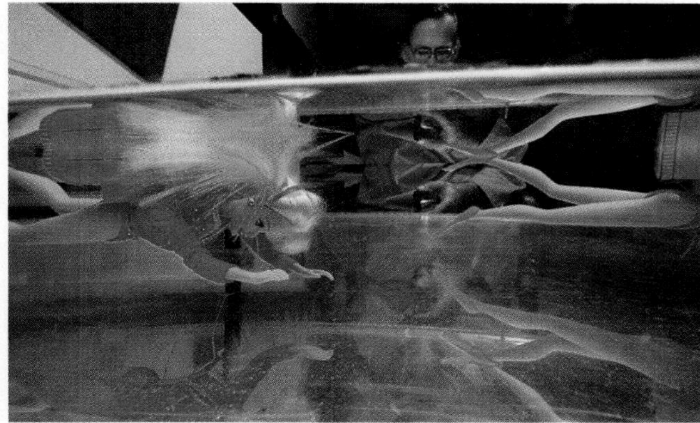

Mattel puts Barbie through rigorous testing to insure quality. At the left, two steel jaws clamp Barbie's foot to make sure her "skin" won't crack, cut, or choke future owners. At the right, Barbie must swim and kick for 15 straight hours to assure Mattel that she'll last for one year. The technician makes sure her batteries stay dry.

Transformation Operations. Quality control inspections, often by production teams, are made during and between successive transformation stages. Work-in-progress inspection can result in the reworking or rejecting of an item before the next operation is performed on it.

The systematic and widespread use of statistical process control is one of Deming's key recommendations. **Statistical process control** is the use of statistical methods and procedures to determine whether production operations are being done correctly, to detect any deviations, and to find and eliminate their causes. Statistical process control methods have been available for decades but only recently have been widely used. They serve primarily as preventive controls.[59] Ford makes extensive use of statistical process control and, since 1984, has offered three-day courses on this method to its suppliers. The suppliers, such as Velcro (a manufacturer of fasteners), are required to demonstrate that they have a commitment to quality improvement.[60] Obviously, improvements in suppliers' outputs improve the quality of Ford's inputs.

Outputs. The most traditional and familiar form of quality control is the assessment made after completion of a product or provision of a service. With goods, quality control tests may be made before the items are shipped to customers. The amount returned by customers because of shoddy workmanship or other problems is one indicator of the effectiveness of the quality control process. Service providers, such as barbers and hairdressers, usually involve their customers in checking the quality of outputs by asking if everything is okay. However, the satisfactory provision of a service often is more difficult to assess than the satisfactory quality of goods.

Determining the amount or degree of the nine dimensions of quality shown in Table 20.2 is fundamental to quality control. The more accurate the measurement, the easier comparing actual to desired results becomes. Quality dimensions generally are measured by variable or by attribute. **Measuring by variable** assesses product characteristics for which there are quantifiable standards (length, diameter, height, weight, or temperature). **Measuring by attribute** assesses product characteristics as acceptable or unacceptable. Measuring by attribute usually is easier than measuring by variable. For example, testing TVs by turning them on as a final check results in a simple yes or no answer regarding acceptable quality. However, the setting and achievement of quality standards usually isn't that simple. In the production of a new kind of bus—called the flexible bus—several years ago, the trade-off between the strength needed in the bus frame and the light weight needed to improve fuel efficiency was misjudged. Several cities that purchased this "new generation" of bus experienced numerous problems, including cracked frames.

The assessment of product quality doesn't reveal what the quality level should be. Desired levels of quality are strongly influenced by an organization's strategy and culture (as at Maytag) and by its competition (as at Ford, GM, Chrysler, Honda, and Toyota).

Response to Quality Problems

The provision of quality services and goods—constantly and from the beginning—is an ideal that isn't always attained. Therefore how managers and employees respond to quality problems is crucial. The following are three specific prescriptions for recovering from quality problems.

Teaching Tip
Have the students locate the names and addresses or (800) phone numbers of the manufacturers of five products they bought recently. Ask them to call or write to these manufacturers and comment on their satisfaction with those products. Have them write up and turn in any responses they receive.

Teaching Tip
Have students write a letter of complaint about an unsatisfactory product or service. Have them keep a record of how long the response took, what the organization did initially, how long resolution of the matter took, and whether they were satisfied with the outcome.

- *Encourage customers to complain and make it easy for them to do so.* Comment cards in service delivery facilities and toll-free telephone numbers are two of the more common approaches used. Fred Brown is a key partner in Ford, Mazda, and BMW dealerships in Texas. The sales associates don't just follow up with customers to determine whether there are any problems two weeks or so after the purchase of a car. They follow up by phone six months and again a year after the purchase to determine whether the customer has had any problems with the car or the service being received. Fred Brown often follows up with a personal call when customers express concerns. His dealerships have won many awards for quality service from car manufacturers.
- *Make timely, personal communication with customers a key part of the strategy.* Organizations frequently make two fatal mistakes in problem resolution: They take too long to respond to customers, and they respond impersonally. Timely, personal communication with unhappy customers offers the best chance to regain the customer's favor. North Carolina's Wachovia Bank & Trust has a *sundown rule:* "Employees must establish contact with a complaining customer before sunset on the day a complaint is received." Motorola expects employees to demonstrate empathy for customers' problems through such statements as, "I can identify with you on what has happened." Motorola wants the customers to feel heard, affirmed, and cared about.
- *Encourage employees to respond effectively to customer problems and give them the means to do so.* Organizations must market the idea of problem resolution to employees. Among other things, this approach involves setting and reinforcing problem-resolution standards and giving employees the freedom to solve customer problems. Employees are less likely to try to solve customer problems if doing so creates for them a small mountain of red tape. When American Express cardholders telephone the 800 number on their monthly statements, they talk to a highly trained customer service representative. This person has the authority to solve 85 percent of the problems on the spot and the ability to do so by means of the company's advanced information technology capabilities. At the Ritz-Carlton hotel chain, employees are authorized to spend up to $2,000 to handle a customer problem on the spot.[61]

5

Explain the main concepts and practices of inventory management and control.

INVENTORY MANAGEMENT AND CONTROL

Ask Students
How many of you have taken an inventory? If you have, describe what it involved.

Inventory management and control is one of the most important aspects of operations management. **Inventory** is the amount and type of raw materials, parts, supplies, and unshipped finished goods an organization has on hand at any one time. **Inventory control** is concerned primarily with setting and maintaining minimum, optimum, and maximum levels of inventory. In part, such control is achieved by obtaining feedback about changes in inventory levels that signal the need for action to avoid going above or below the predetermined levels. The amount of inventory may have an enormous effect on a firm's capital requirements and the productivity of its capital. If a firm can cut its average inventory value from $10 million to $8 million, with everything else being equal, it can operate with $2 million less in capital or borrowed funds on which it would have to pay interest. This reduction in the amount of money tied up in inventory has the effect of increasing the productivity of the $8 million in inventory by 20 percent. Inventory management and control is of interest to goods producers and service producers alike. For example, supermarkets are constantly analyzing the quantity of each good they should stock, where it should be located, and how much shelf space should be allocated to it.

Goals of Maintaining Inventories

Five important goals of maintaining inventories are (1) to achieve some independence in transformation operations, (2) to allow flexibility in the production schedule, (3) to safeguard against problems caused by variations in delivery of input materials, (4) to meet variations in product demand, and (5) to take advantage of economic order quantities.

Input materials and partially completed goods sometimes are stocked at each workstation to provide some independence of operation. Thus, an equipment breakdown at one station won't delay work at any of the workstations farther on.

Inventories allow flexibility in the production schedule because a stockpile of finished goods lessens the pressure to produce a certain amount by a particular date and provides for shorter lead times. **Lead time** is the elapsed time between placing an order and receiving the finished goods. In general, larger finished goods inventories result in shorter customer lead times. For example, some auto dealers use the availability of a large number of cars as part of their marketing strategy. They advertise that customers can get the car of their choice today.

Inventories provide a safeguard against problems caused by variations in the delivery of input materials. An operations manager can't always count on raw materials arriving on a specific date. Possible reasons for delays include labor strikes, transportation holdups, bad weather, and late shipments by suppliers. Without a backup inventory of input materials, even slight delays can shut down an entire operation.

Inventories help meet variations in market demand for the firm's outputs. A company can seldom produce or provide the number of items needed to match market demand exactly. Therefore a common practice is to maintain a safety, or buffer, inventory to meet unanticipated market demand. For example, hospitals must maintain certain quantities of surgical supplies, blood, and medicines to be ready for possible disasters

Hospitals must maintain certain quanities of surgical supplies, blood, and medicines to be ready for possible emergencies. At Baxter's new ValueLink® warehouse in San Francisco, an employee prepares products for "just-in-time" delivery to California Healthcare System hospitals.

requiring the treatment of many patients. However, the agile manufacturing strategy is dramatically reducing the amount of inventory required to meet variations in demand. Inventories also are needed to meet seasonal changes in demand for items such as swimsuits. Retailers constantly try to forecast shifts in customer demand in setting inventory levels.

Inventories enable management to take advantage of economic order quantities. Purchasing materials and carrying those materials in inventory costs money. These costs—along with any offsetting supplier discounts for quantity ordering—are important in determining the most economical size of an order.

Ask Students
What is the most important purpose of maintaining inventory?

Inventories also are used to achieve other goals, such as stabilizing employment, hedging against inflation, reducing the risk of possible future shortages, and eliminating the need for possible future overtime.[62]

Inventory Costs and Trade-Offs

Inventory costs are the expenses associated with maintaining inventory, including ordering costs, carrying costs, shortage costs, and setup costs. All must be considered in making decisions about inventory levels.

- *Ordering costs* are the expenses associated with placing the order and/or preparing the purchase order. They generally aren't very large.
- *Carrying costs* are the expenses of holding goods in inventory. They include losses owing to obsolescence, insurance premiums, rent on storage facilities, depreciation, taxes, breakage, pilferage, and capital invested in inventory.
- *Shortage costs* are the losses that occur when there is no stock in inventory to fill a customer's order. The customer must either wait until the inventory is restored or cancel the order. Determining the costs resulting from a customer's decision to cancel an order or to place future orders elsewhere is difficult.
- *Setup costs* are the expenses of changing over to make a different product. They include the time required to get new input materials, make equipment changes, make changes in the sequence of transformation processes, and clear out inventories of other items. They also include the costs of additional administrative time, employee training, idle time, and overtime.

Evaluating specific inventory goals and costs is part of the control process for determining desirable inventory levels and the ideal size of orders to replenish inventories. "How much do I order?" is a practical question whose answer depends on cost trade-offs that every inventory manager must evaluate. Figure 20.4 identifies the typical cost trade-offs involved in determining appropriate order quantities. It shows that, as the quantity ordered increases, the cost of orders declines. The total cost also declines (but not as fast because carrying costs are accumulating), reaches a low point, and then begins to rise. Why? As order quantity and average inventory level increase, the carrying cost of the inventory also increases as more money and space are tied in inventory. The optimum order quantity yields the lowest total inventory costs. This quantity, labeled Q1, is called the **economic order quantity.** Calculations based on inventory records, ordering practices, and costs yield the actual values of economic order quantities.[63]

Systems for Inventory Planning and Control

Two developments that have significantly affected inventory management and control are materials resource planning and the just-in-time system. Materials resource planning appears to have the greatest application with process-focus and intermediate positioning strategies (see Figure 20.2). In contrast, the just-in-time system provides tighter inventory control with a product-focus strategy.

Materials Resource Planning II (MRP II). A widely used computerized information system for managing dependent demand inventories and scheduling stock replen-

FIGURE 20.4

Cost Trade-Offs in Determining Inventory Levels

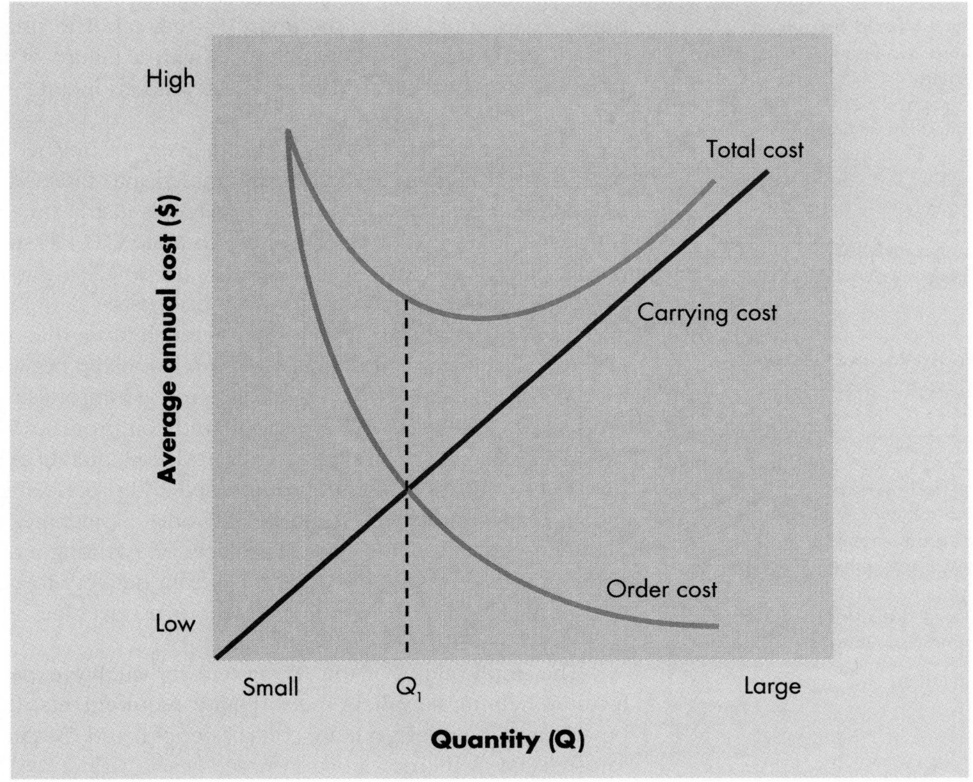

ishment orders is the **materials resource planning II (MRP II)** system. It is programmed to initiate production of various components, release orders, and offset inventory reductions. The dependent demands for components, subassemblies, and raw materials (inputs to the transformation process) are calculated from the demand schedules of those who will use the outputs (customers) or from forecasts. Replenishment orders are time-phased relative to the date the stock is needed. For example, if a firm needs to replenish the stock of an item in week 6 to avoid a stockout and the lead time is four weeks, the purchase order will be issued in week 2. Ideally, items arrive just before they are needed, and finished goods are produced just before they are to be shipped. Based on the assumption of uneven demand, MRP II attempts to minimize inventory investment while achieving zero stockouts, maximize operating efficiency, and improve customer service.[64]

Materials resource planning II helps meet three basic information requirements of operations management: (1) What is needed? (2) How much is needed? (3) When is it needed? The following components provide this information.

Real-World Example

Hooper Specialty Company is the largest industrial hardware distributor in northwest New Mexico. Founder Joe Hooper built the business from a small storefront. He was proud when he purchased NCR's Warehouse Manager computer system. Four months prior to Hooper's buying the software, NCR stopped selling the package because engineers could not work out the bugs. The computer system altered data and created havoc with the accounting and ordering systems (*Wall Street Journal*, August 8, 1994, A1).

- A *master production schedule* shows which goods are to be produced, when, and in what quantities.
- A *bill of materials* describes the inputs—raw materials, parts, or subassemblies—for each finished good or component to be produced.
- An *inventory-status file* shows inventory on hand and on order for each stock item by time period (day, week, or month), including information on lead time, order size, and supplier.

Materials resource planning II also calculates gross and net financial requirements for inputs and outputs by time period. To be successful this system requires precise information, as well as extensive coordination and cooperation among individuals and departments. The intent is to get all departments to work to the same schedules and priorities. For example, the failure of sales personnel to report sales precisely and on a

Real-World Example
Merry Go Round Enterprises distributes 44 million separate pieces of apparel per year to 1,500 retail outlets in 44 states. Most items are shipped 2-3 days after receipt of an order. The firm uses a computer- based system to manage its inventory (*Modern Materials Handling*, November 1993, 48).

Real-World Example
Chrysler's Toledo plant, like most plants in the company, consists of two locations, which in this case are four miles apart. Its JIT system needed an automated storage and retrieval system (AS/R) to keep automobile bodies moving at a pace which would neither slow production or create a stockpile of parts (*Modern Materials Handling*, December 1993, 38).

Discussion Question 6
Why is the JIT system not useful for all types of transformation operations?

timely basis could throw the entire system off. The primary problems with the use of MRP II usually have been associated with a failure of individuals in different departments or organizations to communicate and cooperate.[65]

Just-in-Time (JIT) System. The delivery of finished goods just in time to be sold, subassemblies just in time to be assembled into finished goods, parts just in time to go into subassemblies, and purchased materials just in time to be transformed into parts is called, as you may surmise, the **just-in-time (JIT) system.** At each stage of the transformation process, a JIT system delivers the smallest possible quantities at the latest possible time in order to minimize inventory costs.

Like MRP II, the JIT system affects much more than just the purchasing department. It requires fundamental changes in the relationship between a manufacturer and its suppliers. The traditional use of forcing and compromise as conflict-management styles must shift to the use of collaboration and compromise. The JIT system has major implications for quantities purchased and produced, quality expectations, and suppliers used. The implications for quantities purchased and produced include (1) a steady output rate by the manufacturer, (2) frequent deliveries (sometimes twice or more a day) in small quantities by suppliers to the manufacturer, (3) long-term contracts and blanket orders with suppliers, (4) variable quantities from delivery to delivery but a fixed quantity for the overall contract term, and (4) little or no overage or underage acceptable in deliveries.

The implications of the JIT system for quality expectations include (1) the manufacturer helping suppliers meet quality requirements, (2) close relationships between buyer's and suppliers' quality control people, and (3) the manufacturer urging suppliers to use TQM in their production processes.[66]

The implications of the JIT system for suppliers include (1) few suppliers, who often are located near the manufacturing plant, (2) repeat business with the same suppliers and competitive bidding mostly limited to new parts, (3) suppliers encouraged to extend the JIT system to their suppliers, and (4) supplier control of shipping by using company-owned trucks or contract trucks, contract warehousing, and trailers for freight consolidation storage where possible, instead of common carriers.[67]

As these implications suggest, JIT is a very demanding system for employees and managers. It requires high levels of communication, coordination, and cooperation. With the JIT system, buffer inventories, idle time, and other forms of slack are drastically reduced. Everyone must be constantly on their toes for JIT to work. Even coffee breaks must be carefully coordinated within and between work teams.

The following Quality Insight relates how Caterpillar reengineered its processes, including its inventory management and control system.

Quality *Insight*

Caterpillar Reengineers for Quality and Inventory Management

Caterpillar is typical of the old-line manufacturers that reengineered key processes in response to reverses in the marketplace. Beginning in the mid-1980s, Caterpillars launched a $2 billion program to modernize its seventeen factories. The goal was to increase product quality and plant flexibility while slashing inventories and production-cycle time. The company recouped its investment by 1993, and since then the return on its investment has been running at a 20 percent annual rate. What happened is illustrated by the changes that were made at one of its plants.

Caterpillar's plant in Aurora, Illinois, makes earth-moving vehicles. With the help of experts from Electronic Data Systems (EDS), Caterpillar redesigned the production process there, spending $250 million on new systems and equipment. Jim Bishop, an EDS regional manager who worked with Caterpillar stated: "Computer technology is a minor part of it—an enabler, not a creator. The real secret was the reengineering of the assembly process."

Prior to reengineering, the Aurora plant built several different vehicle models on just two assembly lines. This approach resulted in frequent, time-consuming setup changes. The redesigned factory runs eight shorter, more specialized lines. Employees now work together in teams called *cells.* The biggest savings came from integrated materials-handling systems that cut inventories of tens of thousands of components by nearly 40 percent. Components now are delivered when needed as vehicles, automatically guided by cranes and a monorail system, move down each of the assembly lines.

Networked computer terminals on the factory floor require workers to alert the system at key stages of the assembly process. Their input—often a single keystroke in response to the computer's query—triggers automatic replenishment of components. Similarly, the computer monitors parts consumption and automatically transmits reorders to suppliers. It also sends information on inventory levels and finished products, along with other crucial data, to the financial tracking system at Caterpillar headquarters in Peoria, Illinois.

Bruce Schuver, operations manager of the Aurora plant, says that increased customer satisfaction, not just cost savings, is the ultimate reason for the modernization program. The company can now produce wheel-loaders—which weigh as much as 173 tons and scoop, carry, and dump materials such as sand or gravel—in five days rather than the sixteen days required before. Customers benefit from faster delivery, lower prices, and a defect rate that is half what it used to be.[68]

CHAPTER SUMMARY

1 ***Answer four basic questions about operations management.***

Operations management (OM) takes a systems view that begins with four basic components: environmental factors, inputs, transformations, and outputs. The typical differences between goods and services producers are in the degree to which (1) outputs are tangible and durable, (2) outputs can be inventoried, (3) direct customer contact is involved, (4) response time is long or short, and (5) the operations are capital intensive or labor intensive. Improvements in an OM system often are key to productivity improvements which, in turn, affect the organization's efficiency and competitiveness, as well as a nation's standard of living. We identified nine of the principal categories of decisions in OM and discussed four of them: positioning strategy, technological choices, quality management and control, and inventory management and control.

2 ***Explain traditional positioning strategies and an emerging alternative to them.***

The three traditional positioning strategies are the process-focus strategy, product-focus strategy, and intermediate strategy. The agile manufacturing strategy represents a paradigm shift away from these traditional strategies by providing a system and set of capabilities that allow mass customization of goods. Reengineering is one of the methods used to assist in the implementation of an agile manufacturing strategy.

3 ***Provide examples of choices in office, service, and manufacturing technologies.***

Technological choices for improving quality and productivity in OM systems, most of them computer-based, are increasing rapidly. Innovative office technologies revolve around the personal computer and the revolution in software. Four increasingly used service technologies are bar coding, computerized order systems, open networks, and voice recognition systems. In manufacturing, two important technologies are robots and computer-aided manufacturing. Recent developments in computer-aid design and computer-aided manufacturing have made agile manufacturing strategies feasible.

4 ***Describe the differences between traditional quality control and total quality management and control.***

Total quality management and control is a strategic method of competing effectively and efficiently. Nine basic dimensions of quality are (1) performance, (2) features, (3) conformance, (4) reliability, (5) durability, (6) serviceability, (7) responsiveness, (8) aesthetics, and (9) reputation. Total quality management involves building in quality from product planning through sales and services. In contrast, traditional quality control refers to the inspections that take place during or at the end of the production process. The quality control process focuses on measuring inputs (including customer expectations and requirements), transformation operations, and outputs to determine whether goods or services are of acceptable quality. Deming's prescriptions and the Baldrige framework provide examples of the philosophy and strategy, processes, and methods that comprise total quality management and control.

5 ***Explain the main concepts and practices of inventory management and control.***

Five goals for maintaining inventories are (1) to achieve increased flexibility and reduced dependence between transformation operations, (2) to allow flexibility in the production schedule, (3) to safeguard against unexpected delivery problems, (4) to meet variations in demand, and (5) to take advantage of economic order quantities. Decisions about how much inventory to keep on hand usually involve evaluation of four types of costs: ordering, carrying, shortage, and setup. The optimum inventory level (and economic order quantity) is determined by weighing certain cost trade-offs. Materials resource planning II (MRP II) is a computerized system for managing inventories and scheduling orders. The just-in-time (JIT) system aims to deliver the smallest possible quantities at the latest possible date at all stages of the transformation process in order to minimize inventory costs.

QUESTIONS FOR DISCUSSION

1. Based on the discussion of Xerox in the Preview Insight, why did the firm adopt a total quality management philosophy and system?
2. Why is operations management important in the service sector?
3. Do the three traditional positioning strategies apply to both large and small organizations? Why or why not?
4. Why is reengineering often a component of implementing an agile manufacturing strategy?
5. What types of problems should management anticipate because of the increasing use of robots?
6. Why is the JIT system not useful for all types of transformation operations?

FROM WHERE YOU SIT

1. Give an example of each of the following for both a services provider and a goods producer: (a) inputs, (b) transformation process, (c) outputs, and (d) feedback.
2. Choose a good or service that you consume. Assume that you are a manager of the organization that provides this good or service. What measures might you use to track changes in its productivity?

3. Describe and evaluate an organization (public or for-profit) with which you have had one or more transactions during the past three months in terms of five of the nine dimensions of quality shown in Table 20.2.
4. Some people claim that North American industries are losing their competitive edge because the quality of foreign-made goods is superior and their prices are competitive. Do you agree? Why or why not? Cite a specific personal experience.
5. Recall an instance in which you had problem with product quality. How would you assess the organization's responses to this problem?

SKILL-BUILDING EXERCISE

Quality Assessment of the Computing Service at Your College[69]

This survey is intended to obtain your views on the quality of the computing service at your college. Please indicate your response to each statement by using the following scale.

5	4	3	2	1
STRONGLY AGREE	**AGREE**	**NEITHER AGREE NOR DISAGREE**	**DISAGREE**	**STRONGLY DISAGREE**

If you *strongly agree* with a statement, you should place a 5 on the blank line next to it. If you *strongly disagree,* you should place a 1 on the blank line next to the statement, and so on.

_______ 1. The college's computing service has up-to-date equipment.

_______ 2. The college computing service's physical facilities are visually appealing.

_______ 3. The college computing service's employees are neat in appearance.

_______ 4. Materials associated with the college's computing service (e.g., documentation, equipment, screen displays, etc.) are visually appealing.

_______ 5. When the college's computing service promises to do something by a certain time, it does so.

_______ 6. The college's computing service performs services right the first time.

_______ 7. The college's computing service provides its services at the time it has promised to do so.

_______ 8. The college's computing service maintains fully functional equipment and software.

_______ 9. Employees in the college's computing service tell me exactly when services will be performed.

_______ 10. Employees in the college's computing service give me prompt service.

_______ 11. Employees in the college's computing service are always willing to help me.

_______ 12. Employees in the college's computing service are never too busy to respond to my requests.

_______ 13. The behavior of employees in the college's computing service instills confidence in me.

_______ 14. I feel safe in my transactions with the college's computing service.

_______ 15. Employees in our college's computing service are consistently courteous with me.

_______ 16. Employees in my college's computing service have the knowledge to answer my questions.

_______ 17. The college's computing service gives me individual attention.

_______ 18. The college's computing service has operating hours convenient to me.

_______ 19. The college's computing service has employees who give me personal attention.

——— 20. Employees in the college's computing service understand my specific needs.

Scoring: Please record the point values you gave each numbered statement in the appropriate column.

	Column I Tangibles	Column II Reliability	Column III Responsiveness	Column IV Assurance	Column V Empathy
	1 ———	5 ———	9 ———	13 ———	17 ———
	2 ———	6 ———	10 ———	14 ———	18 ———
	3 ———	7 ———	11 ———	15 ———	19 ———
	4 ———	8 ———	12 ———	16 ———	20 ———
Column Totals	———	———	———	———	———

Scoring and Interpretation

Add the scores from the totals in each column. Total overall scores can vary from 100 (which means that you perceive the quality of services offered by your college's computing operation as outstanding) to 20 (which indicates that you perceive the services of this operation as terrible). Most individuals' perceptions are likely to fall somewhere between these extremes. How might such data and information be used by any service unit, including your college's computing service. Does your college's computing service have any *customer*-driven initiatives to obtain such data and information.

Each of the scoring columns provide a subscore, which can vary from 20 to 4, on a dimension of service quality. These dimensions are defined as follows.

- *Tangibles:* the degree to which the appearance of physical facilities, equipment, personnel, and communications materials match or exceed the customer's expectations.
- *Reliability:* the degree to which the promised services are performed dependably and accurately.
- *Responsiveness:* the degree of willingness to help customers and provide prompt service.
- *Assurance:* the degree of knowledge of employees and their ability to convey trust and confidence.
- *Empathy:* the degree of caring, individualized attention provided to customers.

CRITICAL THINKING CASE

Longhorn Products[70]

David Ream achieved his lifelong dream of starting his own company in 1974. Longhorn Products is a machine shop located in San Antonio, Texas. After two difficult years, the firm grew steadily and annual sales now exceed $500,000.

Longhorn Products produces a variety of small metal parts that it sells to other manufacturers in the Southwest. About 50 percent of customer orders are for one-of-a-kind parts. The average order is for 35 pieces, and order quantities range from 1 to 500 pieces. Delivery lead times (which Ream calls "cycle times") vary from one to four months, depending on work content, materials requirements, and capacity bottlenecks. Ream's competitive priorities are to produce a wide range of customized jobs, handle peaks and valleys in demand, and consistently meet due dates promised to customers.

One of Ream's main tasks is to decide how a job will be performed, including the manufacturing operations and materials needed. He uses two sources of information: a blueprint of the detailed design provided by the customer and a routing sheet listing each operation to be performed, time standards, and materials costs.

Longhorn primarily uses general-purpose machines that provide production flexibility. Most workers are trained to operate several different machines, giving them job variety and necessitating frequent interaction among the workers, shop manager, and Ream.

Ream and the shop managers constantly look for new ways to reduce setup times (the time to change a machine over from one job to the next), improve tooling, perform an operation on a more efficient machine, make (rather than buy) a component, change routing sequences, or even redesign a product.

Longhorn operates one full shift of twenty-six workers supplemented by a second shift of only six workers. Machine capacity is the main limitation. Work overloads are handled with overtime and increased use of machines and employees on the second shift. Equipment capacity is not well balanced. Weekly usage per machine varies from three to eighty hours, with an average of four and a half. Because of variations in product mix, Ream describes the workload at most machines as "feast-or-famine." However, there is enough machine flexibility to reroute jobs to other machines temporarily.

Space is cramped, and Ream is looking at relocation options. The current layout groups workers and equipment functionally: an area for drill presses, one for welding stations, another for brake presses, and so on. A fair amount of shop space is needed to store in-process jobs. Materials handling paths are complex, with considerable criss-crossing from one area of the plant to another. Materials are moved by the machine operators themselves.

In order to buffer operations and reduce bottlenecks, Ream quotes reasonably long delivery lead times—averaging two months—to customers. With a typical job actually taking only 100 work hours for all setup and processing activities, work-in-progress inventory is large.

Longhorn has little influence over its suppliers because of its low volumes. Vendor relationships are informal, and there are no long-term purchasing agreements. Few purchased items are stocked in inventory, which minimizes inventory but lengthens production time. Ream currently is considering stocking some high-usage raw materials and manufactured subassemblies to cut delays. Because of their customized nature, finished goods are rarely stocked. Usually, as soon as an order is finished, it is shipped directly to the customer.

Production planning isn't formalized or projected very far into the future. Using lead-time estimates and orders already booked, Ream forecasts total monthly output for three months ahead. His projections influence how aggressively he bids on new jobs.

Ream uses a manual system to release and follow up on orders. When all necessary materials and tooling are available, he releases the order to the shop. The routing sheet, a record card, and the blueprint are placed in a folder and sent to the shop managers, signaling that work can begin.

Scheduling of work is complex. It demands much of the shop manager's time. He schedules work assignments only a day or two in advance. Longer schedules are of little value because of unexpected bottlenecks, rush orders, and rework problems. Longhorn workers are responsible for the quality of their work. Only spot checks of outgoing shipments are made. Scrap and rework sometimes are a problem.

Questions

1. Which of the nine types of operations management decisions are illustrated in this case?
2. What positioning strategy is used at Longhorn Products? Is it appropriate? Why?
3. Should Ream establish a just-in-time (JIT) system? Why or why not?
4. Should Ream establish a materials resource planning II system? Why or why not?
5. Does Longhorn Products practice traditional quality control or total quality management? Should any changes be made in this area?

The PTL Ministry: An Audit Plum? (B)

Bill Spears, audit engagement partner, initiated the Laventhol and Horwath (H&L) paperwork on May 14, 1985, requesting the national office in Philadelphia to grant client acceptance. In his discussions with PTL, Spears had negotiated an audit fee based on time spent on the engagement rather than a fixed-fee arrangement. The paperwork (Form SEC-6) was forwarded to two members of the client acceptance committee with a copy to the regional audit director in accordance with prescribed policy.

In the request form, Spears revealed to the acceptance committee members and the national office that Jim Bakker and PTL had been the target of unfavorable media attention and that there was an ongoing IRS audit. However, he did not mention the 1979-1982 FCC investigation. The Philadelphia L&H office did not ask about the status of the IRS investigation. An examination of the client acceptance paperwork reveals that one of the client acceptance committee members signed off on May 18, 1985 but that the second committee member didn't sign until November 4. The paperwork indicating formal acceptance of PTL as an audit client was not finalized until November 5, 1985—six days after the L&H audit was completed.

Behind the Scenes

Unknown to Bill Spears, as the IRS investigation intensified in 1984 and early 1985, strategy sessions between PTL officials, its outside legal counsel, and Deloitte Haskins & Sells (DH&S) had increased. Following one such conference, in a January 1984 memorandum, John Yorke, PTL's outside legal counsel with the firm of Wardlow, Knox and Knox in Charlotte, expressed concern that the IRS inquiry could actually lead to the revocation of PTL's tax-exempt status due to private inurement. Yorke addressed the memo to his superior, and its contents described a recent office conference held between the legal counsel and DH&S officials. The memo addressed suspect expenditures, including $2,100 for moving Tammy Bakker's parents to Charlotte. (Bill Spears didn't have access to a copy of this memo as of May 1985.) The memo goes on:

> *The parsonage account is particularly interesting. The offering from the church services goes into the parsonage account so that they can say on the air that Jim and Tammy's salary is paid by the Church members who attend services out there. Out of this account comes their salaries, note payments on the house and other things, expenses for the house, withholdings, telephone, power, Tega Cay Homeowners fee, etc. (It is really a secondary payroll account, for all practical purposes.) Jim and Tammy also get $1000 each per month that they do not have to account for and which is designated as living expenses. This was included on their last return as income to them. The miscellaneous expenses for the parsonage included a payment to the maid of $600 for food, payment for The Charlotte Observer; property additions, a vibrator massage apparatus, and lots of nik naks [sic] for the parsonage. Everything in the parsonage is paid for by the Church. Evan Webster [the DH&S audit manager for the prior year] commented that if Jim and Tammy ever leave the Ministry they would have to walk out with nothing but the clothes on their back. I am not sure why he thinks they could walk out with the clothes, since they are paid for with church funds too!*
>
> *Concerns about cash advances to Jim and Tammy Bakker for travel were also expressed. The questions centered around a lack of supporting receipts following cash advances as well as expenses incurred from the trips that were charged on PTL's American Express account. In one instance, over $23,000 was charged for wardrobe items for the Bakkers. On another occasion, the ministry could not account for a charge of $22,000 made by the Bakkers. Yorke expressed concerns that the expenditures appeared to be personal but were never recognized as income by the Bakkers. In each instance, the amounts were simply charged to various ministry expense accounts. The issue of nepotism is also addressed in the memo. The fact that seven Bakker relatives were on the PTL payroll was a matter for concern. The relatives included various siblings as well as parents of the couple. Each of the individuals held salaried positions with the ministry and often received perquisites. Both of Jim Bakker's parents were allocated PTL owned cars and resided in a ministry-owned house. Yorke later said he had reservations in 1984 regarding PTL's management of the executive payroll account. When asked to explain his firm's involvement with the account, Yorke said*

Source: This case was prepared by A. James McKee, Jr., and Roger B. Daniels, College of Charleston, and published in the *Case Research Journal,* 1993. Adapted and used with permission of the authors, 1995.

PTL wanted Deloitte Haskins & Sells to handle the paying of their top executives so that information wouldn't be in the finance division, so that one person wouldn't know what another person was making. And Deloitte, Haskins & Sells—I believe, discovered [that] an auditor couldn't audit an account if they were a signatory on the account. So they needed somebody else to actually put a stamp in the signature line and they called and asked if we would put the stamp in the signature line.

Yorke explained that the law firm agreed to perform this function until a major problem arose.

My secretary, Ann Fox, was the one who put the stamps on the checks, and she would receive a package from Deloitte and she would stamp them, the checks, put them back in the package and call whoever was going to pick them up. And she brought the checks to me one time and said . . . they are coming more frequently than we thought, and she said I think you need to look at the size of the checks that are coming. I went to Eddie [Knox] and we got with Charlie Knox, the other senior partner in the firm, and decided that PTL might consider our stamping those checks to be acquiescing in the amount that [was] being paid and we decided we didn't want to do that.

When asked why they had a problem with the amounts being paid through the PTL payroll, Yorke said, "It was contrary to the advice that we had been giving them about payroll and salaries." Furthermore, DH&S officials were concerned about the increasing audit risk of the PTL client. The rapid building that was taking place at PTL's Heritage USA and the uncertainty of cash flow for the project's completion raised the question of whether the minister was a going concern. Reference was made in DH&S memoranda to the fact that a "subject to" qualification relating to the going-concern question was a strong possibility for 1985. [In May 1985, a "subject to" qualification could be used in the audit opinion. In 1988, the Auditing Standards Board issued nine new Statements on Auditing Standards (SAS), including No. 58, which abandoned the "subject to" qualification.]

The internal memorandum concluded by stating that "with ever-increasing outstanding debt, the possible challenge to its nonexempt status by the IRS . . . together with the fact that this is a 'one-mall show,' the exposure is at an all-time high." The concerns of DH&S were becoming evident to PTL officials by the end of the 1984 audit. Thus the ministry began the search for new auditors.

The Demise of L&H

L&H accepted PTL as an audit client, which later would prove to be the "kiss of death" for the firm. L&H filed for bankruptcy in the midst of a civil class action suit brought against the firm by PTL contributors. The suit centered on the defrauding of the PTL "lifetime partners," who had invested approximately $158 million in the various lodging programs at PTL. The partners claimed that Jim Bakker and PTL had defrauded them by overselling the Lifetime Partnerships. More than 158,000 Lifetime Partnerships had been sold against a lodging capacity of 55,000. As disclosed in Note 7 of the 1984 financial statements, PTL had projected that the Towers Hotel project would result in excess revenues over construction costs of $15 million. However, the Towers contract wasn't signed by PTL officials until November 1986, after L&H had completed its second audit. Furthermore, Bakker's penchant for changes in design resulted in nearly a $13 million cost overrun for the Towers project by the time the contract was finally signed. Thus the excess of revenues over construction costs was ultimately significantly less than the original estimate of $15 million. Meanwhile, Bakker continued to sell Lifetime Partnerships in the project (beyond his promised cap of 30,000), even when it became a physical impossibility to honor lodging privileges. At the L&H trial one of the defense attorneys was asked whether the PTL account was the proverbial "straw" for the firm. His response was, "More like the girder dropped from the fifteenth floor!" In a settlement finalized in January 1993, third parties victimized by PTL ranked among the major L&H creditors who were awarded a total of $48 million in the judgment against the former L&H partners. At the time of the judgment (rendered by Cornelius Blackshear of the U.S. Bankruptcy Court, Southern District of New York), there were 609 practicing and retired L&H partners, 427 of whom agreed to personal assessment in return for permanent indemnification against any further legal action regarding the matter.

The Historical Significance of the PTL Audits

The PTL audits resulted in the setting of two U.S. records. First, Reverend Jim Bakker was convicted of perpetrating the largest consumer wire and mail fraud in U.S. history. Second, Laventhol & Horwath became the largest U.S. professional firm ever to go bankrupt. The PTL debacle should rank among the numerous landmark lawsuits—including McKesson & Robbins and Continental Vending—that have had a significant impact on shaping the rules that govern audit practice.

The American Institute of Certified Public Accountants (AICPA) originally issued Statement on Quality Control Standards No. 1 (SQCS-l) in July 1980, requiring accounting firms to establish procedures to determine whether a client should be accepted. Recently the AICPA has again cautioned its membership on these matters. Some firms are now hiring investigative agencies to do background checks on the prospective clients' principals in order to assess the integrity of management. Indeed, audit risk begins with client acceptance.

Questions

1. What control and quality of information problems does this case present?
2. What features of a control system could be used to avoid these problems in the future?
3. What ethical guidelines were violated by all the parties involved?

Part *Seven*

Change and Innovation

Chapter 21

Organizational Changes and Innovations

Learning *Objectives*

After studying this chapter, you should be able to:

1. Describe the features of the learning organization that enable it to anticipate and effectively deal with change.
2. Explain the process of planned organizational change.
3. Describe the sociotechnical system and information technologies as methods in the technology approach to change.
4. Explain how restructuring and reengineering can be used to change the design of an organization.
5. Discuss job simplification and job enrichment as ways to change the tasks that employees perform.
6. Describe how survey feedback and team-building change processes can affect employees' attitudes and behaviors.

Chapter *Outline*

Preview *Insight*

Compaq Computer

When Eckhard Pfeiffer took over as CEO of Compaq Computer in August 1992 from founder Rod Canion, his first task was to develop new goals and strategies for the company. Compaq traditionally had sold computers to corporations through distributors. However, as per unit manufacturing costs climbed and sales began to lag Compaq's management realized that changes were in order. Other computer companies (e.g., Dell, Apple Computer, IBM and Toshiba) had developed PCs to compete directly with Compaq's line. Compaq posted its first-ever quarterly loss in 1992 and was forced to lay off more than 1,700 employees.

Pfeiffer and his management team developed a new goal: to be number one in PC and workstation market share by 1995. To achieve this goal, Compaq had to change the way it did business. It had to sell its computers in every market segment, not just to corporations. Compaq's new plan to reach these goals included four interrelated strategies.

1. Design and make competitively priced computers for each specific market segment and advertise them aggressively. Television ads for Compaq's new Presario line of home computers started in late 1994. Design changes had to be made to install user friendly features, such as factory installed software, a built-in telephone answering machine and a CD-ROM drive to play music.
2. Change distribution methods. To make its computers accessible to the home market, Compaq had to sign up retailers such as Wal-Mart to carry its line.
3. Cut manufacturing and inventory costs. Subassembly is now performed by contract workers in Texas and Scotland to cut labor costs. To slash inventory costs, computers are no longer stockpiled, like cars, but are built to order.
4. Establish strong alliances with other computer-related companies. An alliance was formed with Microsoft to fine-tune Windows software for Compaq's Contura Aero, a tiny notebook computer. For the 1994 holiday season, Compaq and Microsoft offered a free voucher for a ticket on Delta Airlines to customers who purchased two Microsoft home products and either a Presario desktop computer or a Contura subnotebook computer.

So far, Compaq's new strategies and goals seem to fit marketplace needs. Competitors have been stunned by Compaq's revived ability to sell computers and bring new products to the market. Because of these changes, its share of the PC market has climbed from 4 percent to more than 10 percent. Sales in Asia, Latin America, and Europe doubled from 1993 to 1995. Its sales have topped $10 billion, and Compaq reached its goal of selling more PCs than IBM by 1995.[1]

LEARNING ORGANIZATIONS

1

Describe the features of the learning organization that enable it to anticipate and effectively deal with change.

Discussion Question 2
What global changes are affecting organizations.

You may wonder how companies such as Compaq, Merck, and Hewlett-Packard, among others, always seem to have new products on the market. Behind each of these successful companies is a well-designed strategy for planned change. For example, Compaq assigns a design-team leader to each promising new product. The team leader is responsible for shepherding the product through the entire process—from basic research to the marketplace. The team leader must also persuade other employees to join his or her team. This approach builds unity and helps employees feel that they have something invested in a project.[2]

You may also wonder why some companies that were successful at one time no longer are successful.[3] The answer is simple: They become static. Organizations can continue to be successful only if they change and adapt. Handy Dan Home Improvement Center, Greyhound, Pan Am, Herman's Sporting Goods, and many savings & loan associations have failed. These once highly profitable companies were unable to maintain their past successes because they didn't adapt fast enough to the market.

In the 1960s, Greyhound's market share of the interstate travel industry was 30 percent. By 1995, its share had slipped to less than 6 percent. Increased automobile ownership and discount airlines, such as Southwest and Continental, have taken passengers away from Greyhound. But these weren't Greyhound's only problems. After a series of unprofitable years, Greyhound replaced its top managers in 1991. The new managers are described by employees as numbers-oriented, intimidating, and aloof. Through relentless cost cutting (employees, routes, and buses) customer service has suffered. Unionized drivers struck Greyhound for higher pay and to improve working conditions, leaving passengers stranded at bus depots throughout the United States. Greyhound's new Trips project, a complex reservation system designed to integrate bus scheduling and passenger demand, was driven more by promises than by reality. An American Airlines flight from New York City to Seattle might make one stop, but a Greyhound bus might make ten or more stops between the two cities. At each stop, some passengers get off and other passengers fill their seats. Thus the demands on Greyhound's reservation system are far more complex than on those of the airlines. Moreover, to run effectively, the system would have to be simple enough to be used in terminals where clerk turnover is more than 100 percent a year and few employees have more than a high-school education. Finally, as most of Greyhound's passengers have low incomes, payment in advance by credit card to reserve a seat is infrequent.[4]

In Chapters 3–5, we discussed how shifts in consumer preferences, technological breakthroughs, heightened competition, and demands from diverse interest groups combine to create powerful forces that require organizational change. Most people—whether students, employees, managers, or consultants—are involved with organizations that need to change. To be effective, employees or managers must learn how to deal creatively with day-to-day conditions that require adaptation and cause tension and frustration.

Discussion Question 3
Respond to the following statement: "A system that performs a certain function or operates in a certain way will continue to operate in that way regardless of need or changed conditions."

The major purpose of this chapter is to help you understand how organizations can survive, operate effectively, and innovate in a changing world. A new way of thinking about how organizations may change has emerged during the past few years. This new way of thinking has given rise to the learning organization.

Teaching Tip
Have students write a one-page paper identifying several changes in consumer preferences and technology that have occurred during their lifetimes.

A **learning organization** involves all employees in identifying and solving problems, thus enabling the organization continuously to experiment, improve, and increase its capacity to deliver new goods or services to its customers.[5] The learning organization encourages the development of critical thinking, communication, interpersonal, and technical skills by everyone in an organization. The capacity to create, anticipate, and respond to changing customer demographics and demand are its hallmarks. The learning organization adds value for the customer by responding quickly to new needs by developing ways to satisfy them. The learning organization finds ways to create sustainable competitive advantages in its industry.

Ethics
Does the learning organization demand a higher standard of ethics (by requiring all employees to identify and solve problems) than the bureaucratic organization (which requires employees to do only what is in their narrowly defined job descriptions)?

Figure 21.1 presents the basic characteristics of a learning organization. Employees working in learning organizations tell one another the truth. Information on performance, quality, consumer satisfaction, and competition is circulated widely. Rewards are distributed equitably among all employees. An extraordinarily high degree of trust develops between managers and employees based on a common set of customer-oriented values. All employees are actively involved in solving customer-related problems. Thus employees don't simply have to learn more about accounting or marketing. Rather they also must learn to expand their knowledge and ability to do things differently. These skills are not acquired from textbooks or past experience but from continuously experimenting with new ideas and methods to satisfy customers. Employees are respected, trusted, and given opportunities to grow in their jobs. Learning organizations invest heavily in training by providing opportunities for everyone. Top managers believe that employees are motivated by curiosity and should experience the joy of learning.

Ask Students
Does this sound like an organization that you belong to or have belonged to in the past?

Discussion Question 4
Describe the basic features of a learning organization. How are they different from those of a bureaucratic organization?

At Southwest Airlines, clerks suggested doing away with tickets. Herb Kelleher, Southwest's CEO, believed that this was an interesting idea and permitted clerks to ex-

FIGURE 21.1

Characteristics of a Learning Organization

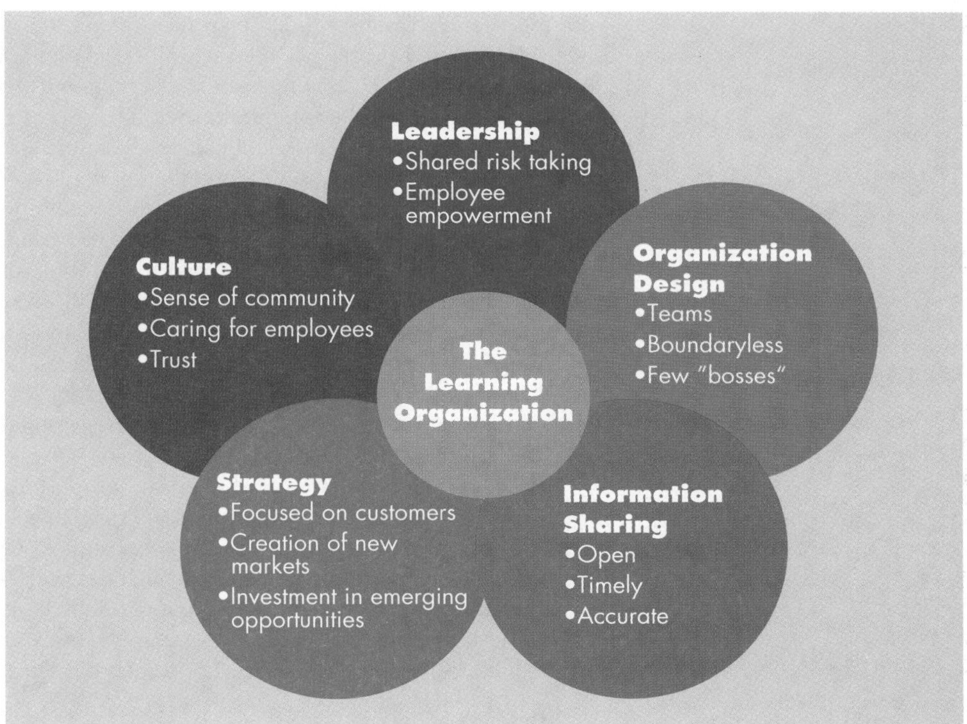

Teaching Tip
Divide the class into small groups. Have them come up with innovative suggestions for registering for classes, as the employees at Southwest Airlines did for eliminating tickets.

periment with it on selected routes. Customers calling for a reservation receive a PIN number. When arriving at the gate, the gate attendant asks the passenger for that PIN number and issues a plastic reusable boarding pass, color coded for seat selection (first come, first served). For passengers needing a receipt, it is mailed to them that day. Southwest estimates that, if this procedure is adopted systemwide, it will save $1.25 per ticket.[6]

In addition to increased employee responsibility, other behaviors need to occur and be positively reinforced. The building blocks of a learning organization include leadership, culture, strategy, design, and information sharing.

Leadership

Teaching Tip
Have students break into groups of 3. The first student is to tell about a group or organization that she or he belonged to but resisted buying into its goals. The second student is to interview the first to find out why. The third student is to listen and ask further questions. Have the students rotate until each one has done each task.

In a bureaucratic organization, top management is responsible for making decisions, directing operations, and achieving organizational goals. Employees are treated simply as one of the factors of production, along with capital and equipment. Workers often are assigned to routine tasks that allow little experimentation. In a learning organization, managers and other employees share leadership. They have the freedom to identify and experiment with new methods and approaches to help the organization reach its goals. Shared leadership provides a way to integrate departments and systems and allow employees to buy into the organization's goals. Max Depree, CEO of the Herman Miller Company, believes that leaders in learning organizations should liberate employees by removing roadblocks that prevent them from doing their jobs to the best of their abilities and supporting employees who experiment with new approaches to satisfy customers.[7]

Culture

What does the culture of a learning organization look like? To become a learning organization, an organization should remove boundaries between departments so that all work together. Problems in one department aren't "thrown over the wall" to become another department's problems. Removing boundaries enables the free flow of people, ideas, and information. Creating a sense of community, compassion, and caring for other employees is essential. People like to belong to something, and the learning organization becomes a place where relationships are nurtured and developed.

At Thermos Company, CEO Monte Peterson used employees from marketing, manufacturing, distribution, finance, and sales to create a new electric grill.[8] As members of this multidepartmental team, employees learned to appreciate and value others' perspectives. After the team had developed a prototype electric grill, Thermos sampled a group of customers. It asked them to use the grill—free—for a month. Team members then interviewed them to learn what they liked and what needed improvement. After using many of their suggestions, Thermos introduced its grill. In less than one year, the new electric grill has captured a 20 percent share of the electric grill market. What Thermos employees learned is that learning from others how to improve a process requires no apology.

Teaching Tip
List on the board the characteristics of the organizational culture of a learning organization. Pick an organization familiar to the students (e.g., the U.S. Postal Service, the Department of Motor Vehicles, or their university). Have students match what they know about this organization with the characteristics listed.

The organization's culture also needs to support learning from competitors, suppliers, and others through the formation of strategic alliances. Successful alliances are built on trust and mutual respect.[9] They are so central to Corning that it describes itself as a "network of organizations." Corning's alliances with Vitro of Mexico and Siemens of Germany have been successful because it carefully considers the needs of each partner and has the leadership ability to cultivate and nurture these relationships over the long term. A culture that emphasizes trust and mutual respect is a cornerstone of success.

Strategy

The strategy of a learning organization emerges from the bottom up as well as from the top down. Being in touch with customers, suppliers, and new technologies allows employees to identify their needs, which strongly influence an organization's strategy.[10] Employees are urged to ask customers want they want and look for what the customer may desire in the future. For example, Nucor Steel developed a strategy of low-cost production that reflects the vision that CEO Ken Iverson and his employees share. Iverson learned from his employees about a new technology for making steel. After carefully studying it, Nucor management then took a chance and built a $270 million plant for a thin-slab minimill. Its employees helped Nucor acquire the new technology and generated new products that used the process. Nucor now makes a ton of sheet steel in forty-five minutes (of labor), versus three hours (of labor) for other big steelmakers.[11]

Nucor Steel can forge a ton of steel three to four times as fast as the typical mill; that has made the North Carolina-based company the world's most productive producer.

Organization Design

Teaching Tip
Many students typically have unrealistic expectations of getting a degree and finding a fast-track job. Discuss the likelihood that flattening hierarchies and increasing the time between promotions translates into less vertical advancement and fewer pay raises. Have students explain how they may have to adjust their high expectations and life and career plans to meet the new realities.

Some management consultants predict that the typical organization in the near future will have half the management levels it has today. As companies flatten their structures to become more competitive, they reduce the number of rungs on the managerial ladder. That also will lengthen the time between promotions—tomorrow's managers will hold each position longer. They will have to move laterally within the organization to learn new skills and continue to be personally challenged. Personal growth will be essential because managers in the future will need to be generalists who are knowledgeable in several areas, as opposed to specialists who understand only finance, production, or marketing.

Teams are the key building blocks in learning organizations. People work together in cross-functional teams to create a product, deal with customers, suggest improvements, and make changes. In learning organizations, "bosses" are practically eliminated as team members take responsibility for training, safety, scheduling vacations, and purchases. The following Quality Insight illustrates how General Electric uses teams to improve its quality.

Quality *Insight*

Absence of Management

In its Bayamon, Puerto Rico, plant, General Electric employs 172 hourly workers and just 15 salaried "advisers," in addition to its plant manager. Advisors have technical knowledge that may be helpful to employees when they are trying to solve specific problems. The plant has only three levels of management.

Every hourly worker is on a team with ten or more other workers. These teams meet weekly to discuss problems. Each team "owns" part of the manufacturing process (e.g., assembly, shipping, or receiving). Team members come from all the plant's departments so that their concerns can be expressed. An adviser speaks up only when asked to by a team member. Every six months workers rotate through the plant's four major areas.

The rewards for learning a new task are threefold: skill, knowledge, and business performance. The first time on a new job, the employee gets a $0.25 per hour raise. Upon learning the job, say, statistical quality control, and declaring themselves "masters," they get a $0.50 per hour raise. Employees also can earn additional pay by passing courses on English and business practices, among others. If the entire plant reaches its quality goals, all workers can earn an additional $225 bonus. Promotions, demotions, and firings are based on proficiency, not on seniority. In just one year, this plant has become 20 percent more productive than its sister plant, and its quality is 50 percent higher.[12]

Teaching Tip
Many students typically experience culture shock when they begin their first jobs. They are accustomed to "bosses" (teachers, parents) telling them exactly what to do and how to do it, and getting clear feedback (grades, grounding). As work teams replace bosses, personal responsibility and initiative must increase. Engage students in a discussion of how they will move from their present states of dependency to becoming a member of a semiautonomous work team.

Information Sharing

The learning organization is a sea of information.[13] To solve customer problems, employees need to be aware of what's going on. Data on profits and losses, market share, and competitors strategy are freely exchanged by employees. Employees believe that too much information sharing is better than too little, and they can pick and choose the information they need to perform their tasks. E-mail, video conferencing, and the Internet allow employees in distant locations to communicate freely with one another.

At Four-Gen Technologies Software, employee computers have an electronic mailbox. Employees can contribute advice to other employees, no matter where they work. As a result, good ideas are shared widely. At Springfield Remanufacturing, managers make available all production and financial figures, and employees are encouraged to ask tough questions about them. Employees also have access to daily printouts that provide detailed cost information on all products. The days of managers hoarding information are long gone in learning organizations.[14]

2

Explain the process of planned organizational change.

Teaching Tip

Learning organizations empower their workers by pushing information down to the lowest level. That is, the least senior worker may have access to almost all the organization's information. By having such access to information, employees are expected to "learn the business" and actually help run it. Have students discuss how they can transform themselves from students (limited tasks and information) to employees of learning organizations (varied tasks with much information).

Ethics

When a bureaucracy is changed into a learning organization, an ethical change is required: from hoarding information to gain personal power to sharing information for the good of the organization.

PROCESS OF PLANNED CHANGE

Organizational change has two interrelated goals: (1) fitting the organization to its environment and (2) changing employee behavior.[15] The process of planned organizational change comprises the nine steps shown in Figure 21.2. Although change programs don't always proceed in the order shown, these steps constitute their basic components regardless of the sequence followed.

Assess the Environment

An organization's external environment constantly changes. Both the degree and rate of that change are important. The environmental factors most responsible for change are customers, competition, technology, politics, culture, and the work force. One of management's primary functions is to monitor these elements and the changes they bring so that the organization can operate effectively.

The degree and rate of change determines whether an organization's external environment is relatively stable or unstable. Relatively stable environments exist in the brewing, auto, insurance, and ice cream industries. In each, the products, customers, suppliers, methods of distribution, and prices are similar. Companies try to differentiate their products and advertise extensively to create demand. Ford and Chrysler generally compete for the same car buyers, charge similar prices, negotiate with the same international labor union, and face similar distribution problems. Insurance premiums charged by large insurance companies (e.g., State Farm, Allstate, Prudential, Travelers, and Hartford) are similar. They differentiate their products by the services they provide to policyholders.

As we've stressed before, most industries have undergone—and are still undergoing—tremendous technological change. In some industries the technology of only five

FIGURE 21.2

Planned Organizational Change

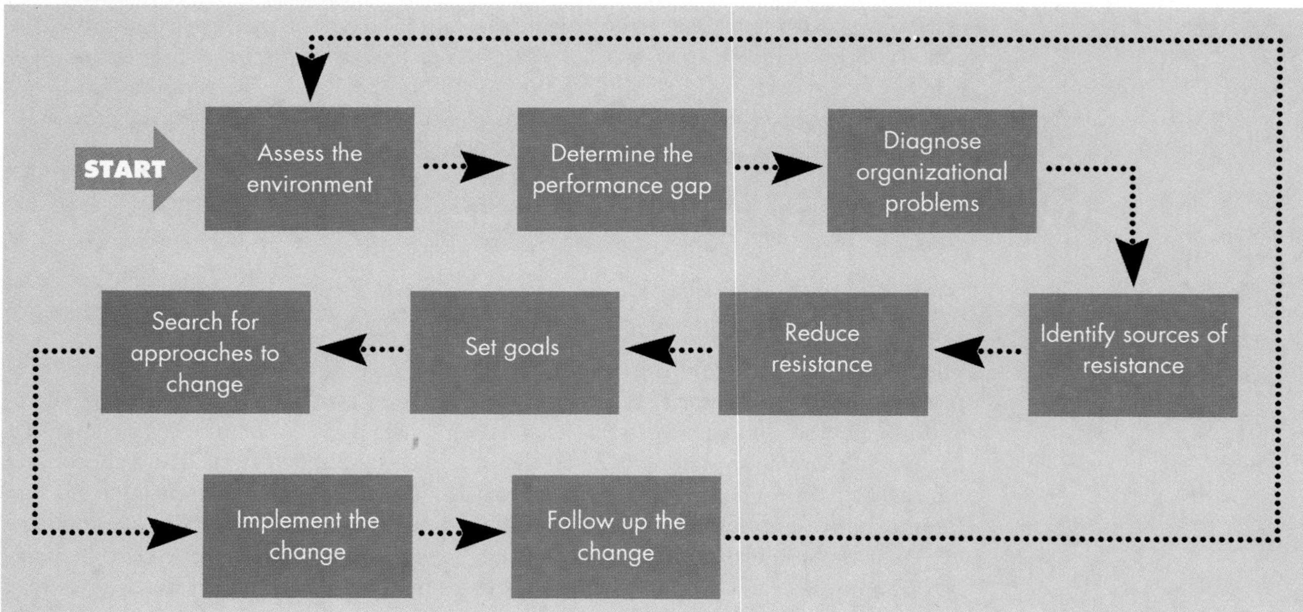

Ask Students
An executive for a transportation company said, "Management must guide the forces of change." What did he mean?

Ask Students
Why is change considered to be an integral part of life?

Teaching Tip
Younger students typically seek the security they have known with their families. Many students believe that they will find it by going to work for an organization with a stable environment. Find a recent news story that described an organization in a supposedly stable environment that surprised most people by failing.

years ago is now outdated. For example, many of the same challenges facing Compaq Computer, highlighted in the Preview Insight, face other organizations in industries where technological change is an everyday occurrence.

Determine the Performance Gap

The next step in the change process is to determine the performance gap. The **performance gap** is the difference between what the organization aspires to do to take advantage of its opportunities and what it actually does.

A performance gap may be created by competitors, government regulation, or new technological breakthroughs. Moreover, a gap may persist for some time before it is recognized. (In fact, it may never be recognized.) Recognition of a performance gap—regardless of its cause—doesn't automatically mean that it should be narrowed or filled. It must have significant consequences for the organization to warrant such action. However, small businesses often seize on performance gaps of larger organizations and move rapidly to fill them. The following Small Business Insight shows how David Potter, founder of Source, Inc., has built a business on trading new and used telephones. One performance gap that his organization fills is to provide low-cost phones to customers who couldn't afford new ones. The other gap being filled is to buy used phones from organizations that have upgraded their equipment and couldn't resell the used phones to the original manufacturers.

Small Business *Insight*

Source, Inc.

David Potter surveys his 19,000-square-foot trading floor, watching his 50 employees working deals on the phone and punching data into desktop terminals. These employees buy and sell new and used phones. Another 175 employees pull apart, clean, fix, and reassemble an assortment of phones, switches, and parts. By the end of the process, most of the used equipment is transformed into new-looking equipment to be boxed and warranted. Some of it, however, will be buried in a local landfill.

Source, Inc., buys phones that other people have discarded. Customers include organizations that ordered too many phones and don't know what to do with the extras and organizations that are upgrading their systems and have no customers for their old phones. Top managers at Arcata Corporation, which was in the printing business, thought that selling phones might be lucrative. Unfortunately, the firm lost the contract to print the West Coast Yellow Pages and decided that it didn't want to be in the phone business after all. Potter was able to buy all of Arcata's phones for ten cents on the dollar.

As a broker of phones, Potter is constantly looking for deals. Once he was able to buy 2,000 new telephones for $1,800 while eating breakfast with a manager of an ad agency at a Beverly Hills deli. The phones had been bartered for advertising time when the manufacturer couldn't sell them. As more organizations decide to sell and lease back their phone systems to free up cash, Source, Inc., also acts as a third party to establish the value of such deals.

Who buys used phones? An organization in Russia wanted 50,000 phones but could afford to pay only $5 for each one. Potter worked a deal. Potter also bought a $2 million switch for less than $100,000 and sold its parts to the University of Chicago for more than double that amount.[16]

Diagnose Organizational Problems

Teaching Tip
Have students interview an older adult about some of the changes that have occurred in the U.S. work force during that person's lifetime.

The aim of the diagnostic step of the change process is to identify the nature and extent of problems before taking action. The idea that diagnosis should precede action may seem obvious, but its importance is often underestimated.[17] All too often the change process is started prematurely—early in the diagnostic step—depending on who does the diagnosis and the methods chosen for analyzing the problem. Harassed and

Ask Students
What three performance gaps are you currently dealing with?

Teaching Tip
Have some students interview a sole proprietor, some interview a partner in a small firm, and some interview a corporate manager about challenges facing their organizations. Discuss their findings in class.

Ask Students
What three personal performance gaps aren't worth dealing with? Explain why.

Teaching Tip
Select a current issue to which these diagnostic questions can be applied. Have the students divide into groups of 5-8 and use the questions to diagnose the issue.

results-oriented managers often impatiently push for solutions before the problem itself is clear.

Most organizational problems have multiple causes; seldom is there a simple and obvious one. As part of the diagnostic step, a manager might begin by asking the following questions,

1. What specific problems have to be corrected?
2. What are the causes of these problems?
3. What must be changed to solve these problems?
4. What forces are likely to work for and against these changes?
5. What are the goals of these changes, and how will they be measured?

A variety of data-gathering techniques (e.g., attitude surveys, conferences, informal interviews, and team meetings) have been used successfully to diagnose problems. The purpose of these techniques is to gather and analyze unbiased data.

Interpersonal problems usually require the use of attitude surveys, perhaps handled by outside consultants who conduct the interviews and analyze the data. Attitude surveys usually tap the feelings of employees effectively and can provide insight into many potential problems. This technique enables management to evaluate employee attitudes about their pay, tasks, and working conditions. Survey responses should be recorded anonymously so that employees will feel free to express themselves without fear of reprisal. Managers and/or consultants should carefully formulate questions covering a wide variety of work-related factors before conducting a survey.

Identify Sources of Resistance

Teaching Tip
Divide the class into groups to brainstorm about why some people and organizations resist change. Have each group present its results.

Few organizational changes are complete failures. However, few go as smoothly as management would like because change efforts often run into various forms of resistance. Experienced managers are all too aware of them. Some managers don't even initiate needed changes because they feel incapable of successfully carrying them out. Such managers need to think through why people resist change and what can be done to overcome such resistance. In general, people—and sometimes even entire organizations—tend to resist change for six reasons: fear, vested interests, misunderstanding or lack of trust, differences in assessment of the situation, limited resources, and interorganizational agreements.[18]

Fear. Some people resist change because they fear they'll be unable to develop the new skills and behaviors required of them. A major obstacle to organizational change often is managers' inability to change their own attitudes and behaviors as rapidly as their organizations require. Even when managers understand that they need to change, doing so often is difficult.

Ask Students
What should management do when employees resist change because of fear of losing their jobs?

Vested Interests. People who have a vested interest in maintaining things as they are often resist change.[19] The downsizing, cost cutting, and restructuring begun by many organizations in the 1980s to improve performance will continue throughout the 1990s. At times, downsizing has hurt product quality, alienated customers, and actually cut productivity. As we discuss later in this chapter, employees who are anxious about where the ax will fall next may spend too much of their time trying to make sure that it does not fall on them. Wary of losing their jobs, these employees become reluctant to take risks or innovate.

Ask Students
Have you ever been in a situation where individuals resisted a change in spite of the fact that the change was in their best interests? Why did that happen?

Misunderstandings. People resist change when they don't understand its implications. Unless it is quickly addressed, any misunderstanding or lack of trust builds resistance. This type of resistance often takes others by surprise because many managers assume that employees resist change only when it isn't in their best interests. The "not invented here" mentality often is a source of resistance. Employees ask, "What happens to me now? Is there a job for me? Is it the one I want? How do I prove my value in the new environment?" Top managers must be visible during the change to spell out clearly the new direction for the organization and what it will mean for others. Getting employees to discuss their problems openly is crucial to overcoming resistance to change.

Ask Students
Has an instructor ever made a change believing that everyone in the class would respond to it in the same way? Explain what happened.

Differing Assessments. Employees also may resist change if they assess the situation differently than do their managers or team members. Some people initiate change believing that anyone with the same information would make the same decision. This assumption isn't always correct.

Limited Resources. Although some organizations emphasize stability, others would prefer to change if they had the resources needed to do so. General Electric's alliance with Samsung saved GE millions of dollars that it would have had to invest in new plant and equipment to compete effectively in microwave manufacturing. In 1983, GE produced microwave ovens for $218 each, compared to Samsung's $155. The number of ovens produced per day per person showed an even more glaring difference: GE got four units per person per day, and Samsung got nine. So, instead of sinking millions of dollars into the microwave business, GE invested its money in plastics, medical equipment, and lighting products for which it had global competitive advantages.[20]

Teaching Tip
Have students break into small groups. One student is to tell of a situation in which he or she resisted change. The situation may be at home, work, a sports team, or school. The others are to take turns asking about the reasons for resisting.

Interorganizational Agreements. Labor contracts are the most common examples of interorganizational agreements that limit options for change. Actions once considered major rights of management (e.g., to hire and fire, assign personnel to jobs, and promote) have become subjects of negotiation. Advocates of change also may find their plans delayed because of agreements with competitors, suppliers, public officials, or contractors. Although agreements sometimes are ignored or violated, the legal costs of settlement can be expensive.

The following Global Insight describes some of the resistance that Sir Colin Marshall faced when he instituted changes at British Airways.

Global *Insight*

British Airways

When Sir Colin Marshall, CEO of British Airways (BA), declared that British Airways would become the "world's favourite airline," few employees thought that was possible. Many employees saw little reason to change because they felt secure in their jobs at this government-subsidized airline. Before its turnaround in the 1980s, the airline reported frequent maintenance delays, served poor food, and had been dubbed by customers as BA for "Bloody Awful." Sir Colin needed to impress upon BA's employees that they needed to change their behaviors—and that included everybody. Being best in customers' eyes meant everything from making sure that the concourse lights were always on to making sure that meals on short flights were easy to deliver and unwrap. It also meant that employees had to change their attitude toward customers from that of moving "packages" to a concern for the passenger as a human being.

Customer-service training was provided to all employees. Flight crew members had to attend language training to help them become proficient in French, Italian, German, or Spanish. The trainers themselves were crew members who flew for half the year and taught for the other half. Thus they knew and understood customer-service problems, the questions most likely to be asked, and the vocabulary most often used. The courses last about two and a half months, alternating full-time classroom work with flying duties. The development program included a week living abroad with a non-English speaking family. This program has helped British Airways attain its goal of being one of the best airlines in the world.[21]

Reduce Resistance

Not all resistance to change is bad. Employees can operate as a check-and-balance mechanism to ensure that management properly plans and implements change.

TABLE 21.1

Methods of Overcoming Resistance to Change

METHOD	SITUATIONS	ADVANTAGES	DRAWBACKS
Education	When there is a lack of information or inaccurate information and analysis	Once persuaded, people will often help with the implementation of the . change.	Can be very time-consuming if many people are involved
Participation	When the initiators do not have all the information they need to design, and others have considerable power to resist	People who participate will be committed to implementing change, and any relevant information they have will be integrated into the change plan.	Can be very time-consuming if participators design an inappropriate change
Negotiation	When someone or some group will clearly lose out in a change, and that person or group has considerable power to resist	Sometimes it is a relatively easy way to avoid resistance.	Can be expensive in many cases if it alerts others to negotiate for compliance
Manipulation	When other tactics will not work or are too expensive	It can be a relatively quick and inexpensive solution to resistance problems.	Can lead to future problems if people feel manipulated

Source: Adapted from Kotter, J.P., and Schlesinger, L.A. Choosing strategies for change. *Harvard Business Review,* March-April 1979, 111.

Ask Students
How do you deal with individuals who resist change at school? In a social setting?

Ask Students
Have you ever been in a situation where your resistance to change resulted in a good outcome? Explain.

Ask Students
Can resistance to change ever be overcome completely? Why or why not?

Teaching Tip
Have students brainstorm to identify factors that can overcome resistance to change.

Justifiable resistance that causes management to think through its proposed changes more carefully may result in better decisions. Although resistance to change will never disappear completely, managers can learn to overcome it. Table 21.1 describes four commonly used methods for doing so: education, participation, negotiation, and manipulation.

Education. One method for overcoming resistance to change is through education and communication. This method is ideal when resistance is based on inadequate or inaccurate information and analysis, and the resisters are the ones who must carry out the change. British Airways used this method to implement its needed changes.

Participation. Organizations often meet with less resistance to change when they allow participation and involvement. In other words, when potential resisters are involved in the design and implementation of proposed changes, they are less inclined to oppose the changes. Figure 21.3 suggests an inverse relationship between participation and resistance: the greater the participation, the less the resistance.

Many individuals have strong feelings about participation. Some employees feel that they should be allowed to participate in various aspects of change efforts; others feel that participation usually is a mistake. Participation seems to work best when those proposing change need information from others to design and implement the change. Research shows that participation usually leads to commitment.[22] Nevertheless, participation can have its drawbacks, as we described earlier (Chapters 14 and 16). If participation isn't carefully managed, it can lead to poor solutions. It also can be very time-consuming. When change must be made quickly and will probably be resisted in any event, involving others simply may not be worth the effort.

Negotiation. Another way to deal with resistance to change is to negotiate and offer incentives or rewards to potential or active resisters. This method of dealing with resistance is especially appropriate when someone clearly is going to lose as a result of the change. For example, at Oryx, an oil and gas producer, the company eliminated rules, procedures, reviews, and reports that had little to do with exploration for hydrocarbons. As the price of oil continued to drop, the company had to cut 1,500 managerial jobs. The company negotiated wage and benefit concessions with those who remained. They were committed to the changes and began to look for ways to further increase Oryx's efficiency.[23]

FIGURE 21.3

Effect of Participation on Resistance to Change

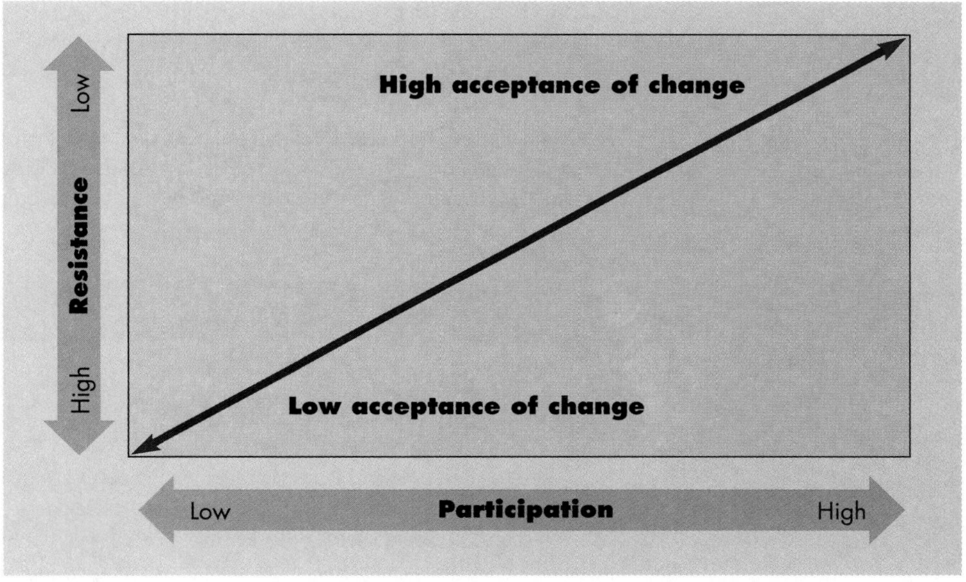

Manipulation. In some situations, management attempts to manipulate others in an attempt to change their attitudes or behavior. This method normally involves selective use of information and may involve cooptation. *Cooptation* is a political maneuver that brings people into the decision-making process to obtain their endorsement of change or, at least, get them not to resist it. Coopting a group involves giving one of its leaders a role in the change process. This method isn't a form of participation because those who are proposing the change don't really want advice from those coopted.

Teaching Tip
In the newspaper find a case of resistance to change that President Clinton currently is dealing with. How might he reduce that resistance with the methods discussed?

However, people who feel that they have been tricked into not resisting, are not being treated fairly, or are being lied to, may respond negatively to a change.[24] Many managers have found that, by manipulating subordinates, they have ultimately created more resistance to the change than if they had chosen another tactic. Managers face a whole new set of problems if those who were manipulated use their ability and influence to propose changes that aren't in the best interests of the organization.

Selecting a Method. Five issues need to be diagnosed in selecting a method to overcome resistance to change.[25]

1. ***Amount and types of resistance anticipated.*** All other things being equal, the greater the anticipated resistance, the more difficult overcoming it will be. Education and participation probably are the most appropriate methods of combating strong resistance.
2. ***Power of resisters.*** The greater the power of the resisters, the more the proponents of change must involve the resisters. Conversely, the stronger the proponent's position, the greater is the opportunity for negotiation.
3. ***Location of needed information and commitment.*** The greater the need for information and commitment from others to help design and implement change, the more the advocates of change should use education and participation. Gaining vital information and commitment from others requires time and their involvement.
4. ***Stakes involved.*** The greater the short-run potential for damage to the organization's performance and survival if the situation isn't changed, the greater is the need for managers to negotiate and/or use manipulation to overcome resistance.
5. ***Short-term and long-term effects.*** Accurate assessment of the first four factors still leaves the manager with the choice between short-term and long-term effects. Forcing change on people can have many negative effects, both in the short term and the long term. Education and negotiation often can overcome initial resistance

and can lead to long-term benefits. Participation can lessen both short-term and long-term resistance. Cooptation method may be quickest in the short run but can lead to long-term resistance.[26]

Teaching Tip
Select a key issue that President Clinton currently is working on and a method to overcome any resistance to that change.

The San Diego Zoo used a combination of these methods to change elephant trainers' behaviors, as described in the following Insight. Zookeepers quickly learned that the elephants changed their behaviors more easily and quickly than their trainers did.

Insight

Training Elephants

In 1991, tragedy struck at the San Diego Zoo. While working with an elephant, one of the keepers was killed instantly when an elephant accidentally stepped on her. That fatality, combined with high staff turnover, intense pressure from the California Occupational Safety and Health Administration to handle elephants differently, and an organizational design that no longer met the needs of the zoo, galvanized the zoo's managers to take action.

The managers met with all the employees and announced the decision to hire an employee with a strong background in behavioral modification and experience in working with exotic animals to train employees in new methods. Old-time zoo employees doubted that changes would occur in elephants' behaviors. Wild elephants for centuries have been controlled by a dominant cow, who was usually the oldest and most experienced member of the herd. When this cow moved, other members of the herd moved. Challenges to her authority were rare, and, when they occurred, the matriarch retaliated swiftly. To control the herd, trainers taught elephants to be subordinate to them, just as they would be to the matriarch cow. Physical discipline was used by trainers to keep the herd and cow in line. Keepers who trained elephants were self-assured and believed that they could control their own fates.

The new training required that the keepers no longer go into an elephant's pen. A protective barrier was erected, preventing the keepers from using physical control. The use of positive reinforcers—apples or carrots—to control the elephant's behavior was introduced. An elephant that didn't obey didn't receive a positive reinforcer. Within days the elephants learned the connection between doing what the keepers wanted them to do and obtaining a positive reinforcement.

The old-time keepers who resisted the new system did so because it required them to behave differently. They had to attend classes on behavioral modification, take examinations, and pass (85 percent or higher) an internally administered test before they could continue to work with the elephants. Keepers who didn't try the new system or couldn't pass the test were dismissed. Keepers who passed the test and practiced new behaviors were rewarded with challenging jobs and higher salaries.[27]

Set Goals

Ask Students
Why should objectives be set before a change effort is begun?

Ask Students
Set a change goal for one of your extracurricular activities.

For change to be effective, goals should be set before the change effort is started. If possible, the goals should be (1) based on realistic organizational and employee needs, (2) stated in clear and measurable terms, (3) consistent with the organization's policies, and (4) attainable. For example, the new system at the San Diego Zoo was designed to measure the behaviors needed to train exotic animals without the use of punishment. How an elephant performed without the use of physical punishment was one indicator of a keeper's effectiveness, as was the aggressiveness of the elephant. Specific measurable behaviors indicating aggressiveness were established.

Search for Approaches to Change

The next step in planned organizational change is to look for practical approaches to achieve it. Successful change can be brought about only through modification of certain

FIGURE 21.4

Approaches to Organizational Change

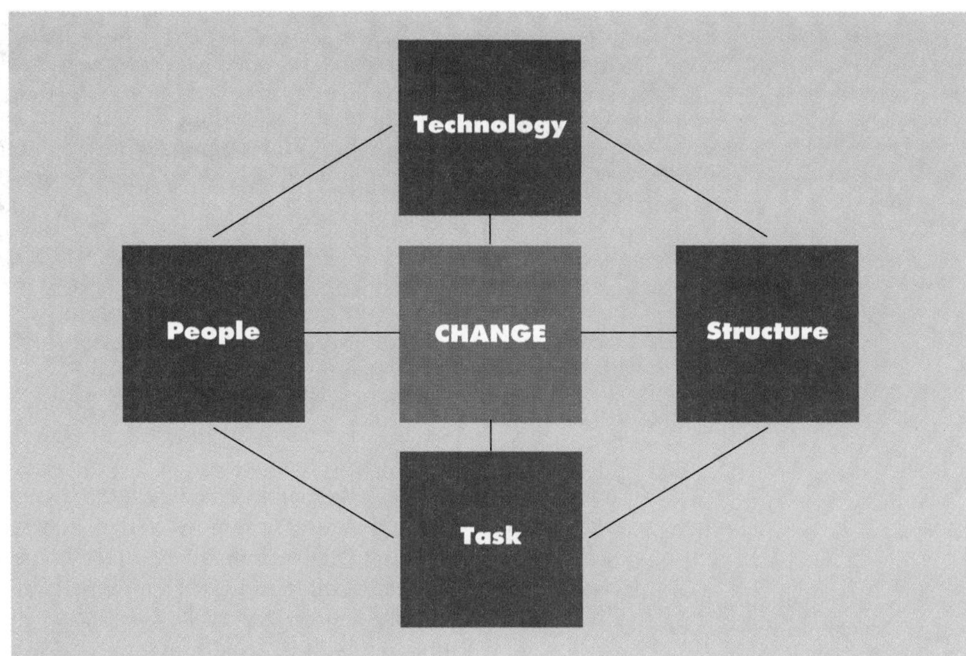

Source: From Leavitt, H. Applied organizational change in industry: Structural, technological and humanistic Approaches. In J.G. March (ed.), *Handbook of Organizations*. Chicago: Rand McNally, 1965. Used with permission.

factors. The four interrelated approaches presented here—technology, design, task, and people—are identified by the factors they seek to change. These approaches are depicted in Figure 21.4.

The technology approach focuses on change in workflows, production methods, materials, and information systems. Greyhound's Trip program is an example of this approach. It was intended to provide an integrated management information system to monitor the millions of miles its buses travel.

The design approach emphasizes internal structural changes: realigning departments, changing who makes decisions, and merging or reorganizing departments that sell the company's products. The Preview Insight on Compaq Computer highlighted this approach.

The task approach concentrates on changing specific employee job responsibilities and tasks. This approach could increase or decrease the quality of the work experience for employees and their job performance, as illustrated in the San Diego Zoo Insight.

Ask Students
Do you believe that effective implementation of change requires rewards? Why or why not?

The people approach usually is aimed at improving individual skills and organizational effectiveness through training and development programs. For managers, the people approach would focus on improving the skills needed to perform one or more of the ten managerial roles presented in Chapter 1 or to train employees in customer service, as highlighted in the British Airways Global Insight.

Implement the Change

The next step in the change process is to implement and reinforce the change over a period of time. The ability to sustain change depends primarily on how well the organization reinforces newly learned behaviors during and after the change effort. In other words, employees should be properly rewarded for learning new behaviors. A combination of money, pats on the back, and new job opportunities reinforces new behaviors. If employees view the rewards as fair, they are likely to continue to develop and maintain those behaviors. Effective implementation of change also is enhanced when the people being asked to change their behaviors have been allowed to participate in designing the change program.

Ask Students
How would you use each of the four change approaches to change the makeup or direction of one of your extracurricular organizations?

Follow Up the Change

In the follow-up step managers need to determine whether the change process has been successful. This determination is based on measurement of the trends in levels of satisfaction, productivity, new-product development, market share, or other factors since the change process began; the size of the improvement or decline; and the duration of the improvement or decline. Before implementing the change program, management should have set goals and benchmarks to use in measuring the program's success. The effectiveness of a change program shouldn't be determined by measuring only attitudes or performance. An index containing both attitudinal and performance benchmarks and accomplishments should be used. For example, if a people approach to change was used, the levels of employee attitudes, knowledge, skills, and job satisfaction would be measured against predetermined goals for these characteristics.

Ideally, the effectiveness of change should be checked continuously. However, because this type of assessment usually is too costly and time-consuming, most managers make assessments at predetermined intervals. One set of measurements should be made immediately after a change is implemented.[28] To avoid an inaccurate assessment based only on temporary changes in attitudes and behaviors, another set of measurements should be made later, after the immediate effect of the change has worn off. This second set of measurements often indicates attitudinal and behavioral changes that the first one didn't reveal. One reason is that, at the time of the first set of measurements, the organization hadn't yet had the opportunity to reinforce newly developed employee attitudes and behaviors.

Teaching Tip
Use the recent ban on smoking in many restaurants to discuss with students how the effectiveness of the change can be determined.

Describe the sociotechnical system and information technologies as methods in the technology approach to change.

TECHNOLOGY APPROACH

At the turn of the century, Frederick Taylor changed the workplace with his ideas of scientific management. Recall that his basic aim was to increase organizational efficiency by the application of scientific principles. In 1908, Henry Ford launched the mass production of cars. In an age of mass consumption, assembly lines were ideal for making identical goods in volume. No longer were skilled craftsmen needed to piece together one-of-a-kind vehicles from nonstandard parts. Employees became replaceable parts.

In many of today's markets, customers and competition are pushing companies to add niche items and shorten production schedules.[29] For example, the NEC Corporation now offers nineteen models of cellular and cordless phones, up from three just ten years ago, and phone-product life cycles have shrunk to one year or less from two or three. Hence many organizations—forced to turn out goods in smaller lots and changes lines quickly—can't mass produce the quantities needed to make traditional assembly lines profitable. "We can't cope just by improving mass-production-based manufacturing," says Toru Mikami, a vice-president at NEC.

If traditional mass-production assembly lines are posing problems for organizations, what is the next technology? Sony, USAA, Stanley Works, and Toyota are among those that have dismantled their assembly lines in favor of sociotechnical systems.

Teaching Tip
Most universities are designedby product (e.g., liberal arts, business, engineering, and law). Brainstorm with students about how to apply a sociotechnical systems approach in redesigning your university's structure. Throw out a few suggestions: permanent study cubicles and lockers for students, more telephones and copiers, a day care center, and the like.

Sociotechnical Systems

Sociotechnical systems involve the consideration of the needs of both employee and organization in devising ways to satisfy customer demand.[30] That is, employees must be able to satisfy their needs at the same time that the organization must be able to produce the goods and/or services desired by its customers. An essential aspect of the sociotechnical approach to change is to give teams of employees the responsibility for a product or service and allow them to make decisions about task assignments and work methods. Team members then are expected to learn how to do all the jobs within the control of their team and frequently are paid on the basis of their knowledge and skills, rather than on seniority.

The following Global Insight highlights how Sony has redesigned its technology for manufacturing cameras using sociotechnical concepts. Note how the new system jointly satisfies the needs of employees and Sony's customers.

Global *Insight*

The Death of the Assembly Line at Sony

In Kohda, Japan, the Sony assembly line that made cameras has been dismantled. Tables have been set up to form a snail-shaped cell for four people. Walking through this cell permits workers to assembly an entire camera themselves, doing everything from soldering to testing. Output from the line is running 10 percent more than former assembly line's. Sony believes that this productivity gain is the result of freeing efficient assemblers to work at their own speed instead of limiting them to the conveyor belt's speed. People, not conveyors, pace the work. And if something goes wrong, only a small section of the entire plant is affected.

Sharper workers are now needed. On Sony's old assembly line, workers did only one or two tasks; now they do a dozen or more. Sony puts trainees through an apprenticeship, often lasting up to 100 hours, during which they practice at tables on the factory floor until they learn their basic duties. Sony now spends 5 percent of its revenues on employee training. The company has been able to free up technical employees to help increase the plant's efficiency. It has assigned 156 technicians to an in-house development department to design low-end camcorders and other products. Because these employees also know how to make the products, they can squeeze costs better than the off-site engineers who once did that work.

Sony's change has not been without some pain. In Japan, the emphasis on maximizing individual output may create social tensions in a teamwork-oriented culture. Rather than fire slow people, management tries to retrain or reassign them. Sony faces another choice: fewer jobs or no jobs. When it changed over to this new technology, Sony found that 500 of its 3,000 employees were unnecessary. In keeping with the tradition of "life-time employment," Sony is relying on employees quitting and is not replacing female workers who quit to have children to reduce the size of its work force.

Despite these problems, the cell assembly system is a success. Cameras are assembled in fifteen minutes compared to seventy minutes on the old assembly line. Sony now makes cameras only as customers order them instead of basing production on sales estimates. The cells are 100 times cheaper to set up than assembly lines and can be set up in two to three weeks compared to two or three months for assembly lines. The cells also use less space, enabling Sony to slash its space costs.[31]

Information Technologies

Coping with competition often requires information flexibility. **Information technology (IT)** comprises complex networks of computers, telecommunications systems, and remote-controlled devices. As discussed previously, information technology is having a profound impact on organizational operations, power relationships, and change methods.[32]

An organization now can have an electronic link to its suppliers and customers. It can link its manufacturing and inventory functions so that, as soon as the system runs low on a part, a central computer automatically executes an electronic purchase order signaling the supplier to ship new parts. Consider, for example, how Motorola makes and sells its Bravo pocket pagers. A salesperson in Foster City, California, types an order into a Macintosh laptop computer, specifies the unique code that will cause each pager to beep, and asks for delivery in two weeks. The order moves over phone lines to a mainframe computer in Motorola's factory in Boynton, Florida. The computer automatically schedules the pagers for production, orders the proper components, and informs the shipping employees to Express Mail them to Pacific Telesis Group in California.[33]

Computer-integrated manufacturing uses technology to link sales, production, and shipping functions. This technology breaks down barriers between departments, improves quality control, and reduces inventory costs by creating just-in-time manufacturing processes. The employees involved can use their computers to "talk" to each other and watch the manufacturing process unfold as the product moves through the system.[34]

4

Explain how restructuring and reengineering can be used to change the design of an organization.

DESIGN APPROACH

Managers are being bombarded by ideas on how to redesign their organizations to improve customer satisfaction. Some of the recommendations include delayering, downsizing, reengineering, restructuring, and rightsizing.[35] Whatever method is chosen, its intent usually is to clarify what gives the organization its leadership position with its customers. That is, capitalizing on the organization's capabilities that distinguish it from its competitors. Businesses, products, or services that don't contribute to this goal are candidates for elimination or sale.

Table 21.2 highlights some of the major differences between two approaches to changing an organization's design—restructuring and reengineering—which we focus on first. We then summarize restructuring tactics (see Chapter 11 for a full discussion of organization design).

Discussion Question 5
Evaluate the following statement: "We trained hard, but it seemed that every time we were beginning to form into teams, we would be reorganized. We tend to meet any new situation by reorganizing, and what a wonderful method it can be for creating the illusion of progress while producing confusion, inefficiency, demoralization." (Petronius, 210 B.C.)

Restructuring

Restructuring typically means reconfiguring—changing levels of authority, responsibility, control—the organization.[36] That is, entire businesses or divisions might be combined or spun off. For example, in 1994, Sears, Roebuck & Company restructured. It sold off interests in insurance (Allstate Insurance Company), real estate (Coldwell Banker), and finance (Dean Witter Reynolds) to focus on its core competency of merchandising. Sears, Digital Equipment, and ABB Asea Brown Boveri, among others, have restructured to survive by taking drastic measures to reduce overhead. Clearly, stifling bureaucracies and inefficiencies cannot weather competition in the years ahead. Restructuring decisions almost always are made by top management because of the impact such decisions have on employees' lives and the profitability of the organization.

Ethics
Do you agree with Barnevik's ethical reasoning? Is gradual or sudden restructuring more ethical? Argue the worker's side first. Then argue management's viewpoint.

When Percy Barnevik, CEO of Zurich-based ABB Asea Brown Boveri, took over in 1987, top management developed a goal to create the world's largest electrical engineering company. He wanted to create a company with no national boundaries. To

Teaching Tip
Find out what these and equivalent ratios are at your university.

TABLE 21.2

Two Approaches to Changing the Design of an Organization

CHARACTERISTICS	RESTRUCTURING	REENGINEERING
Target	Organizational structure—levels, span of control	Business processes and work systems
Rationale	Survival, repositioning, reduced costs	Simpler and faster processes
Performance criteria	Efficiency satisfaction	Efficiency and customer
Method	Benchmark and compute ratios	Flow-charting work processes
Advantages	Reduced costs	Reduced costs
Disadvantages	Organizational personal and stress	Time, cost, and personal stress

Source: Adapted from Keidel, R. Rethinking organizational design. *Academy of Management Executive,* 1994, 8(4), 14.

Ask Students
Have you personally been laid off, or do you know anyone who has been? In what ways, if any, did your (their) motivation decline?

Real-World Example
According to James Champy, coauthor of the best-selling book *Reengineering the Corporation,* "We're going to see five to ten years of very difficult dislocation for a large number of people. I'd like to say we have the growth engine of business moving to a point where we'll quickly absorb those people into high-value-added jobs. I don't believe that." Do you agree with Champy's view? If he's right, how will you adapt?

Real-World Example
According to the authors of the best-selling book *Reengineering the Corporation,* Michael Hammer and James Champy, middle managers' jobs that concentrated on managing information have been reengineered to eliminate the function or give it to nonmanagerial workers (*Wall Street Journal,* February 21, 1995, B1).

Real-World Example
According to Michael Hammer, coauthor of the best-selling book *Reengineering the Corporation,* "I think there are a lot of people who will never find a job again. The market is over for bureaucrats. If you can't design or sell products, I'd get real nervous." Do you agree with Hammer's view? If he is right, how will you adapt?

Real-World Example
Attempts to balance work and life, through programs such as flextime and telecommuting, are being hampered by reengineering efforts. Employees are fearful and want to hang on to what they already have, especially their jobs. They don't want to ask for anything more (*Wall Street Journal,* March 1, 1995, B1).

reach this goal, he reorganized by (1) slashing staff at headquarters from 4,000 to 200 people, (2) creating 5,000 profit centers, (3) cutting three layers of management, and (4) carving ABB's global businesses into a triad—America, Asia, and Europe—to gain more control over operations. To survive the 1993-1994 worldwide drop in demand for electrical products, the firm closed fifteen plants around the world and laid off more than 4,000 employees, despite labor protests in Germany. Barnevik reasoned that making a series of small changes over time would be more demoralizing than restructuring in one fell swoop.[37]

What needs to be restructured is often assessed through the computation of ratios. Ratios used to make restructuring decisions include total employees to sales, corporate staff to operating employees, and managerial span of control (the number of people reporting to a manager). An organization typically benchmarks competitors to determine how its ratios compare with those of competitors. For example, DEC's CEO Robert Palmer justified the restructuring of that organization by comparing DEC's revenue per employee with those of IBM and Hewlett-Packard. Finding that DEC's competitors were producing more with fewer people, he ordered massive layoffs until DEC's ratios were in line with IBM's and Hewlett-Packard's.

The potential disadvantages to restructuring are shown in Table 21.2; restructuring is not guaranteed to work. Several researchers found that 75 percent of restructured firms ended up in worse financial shape than they were before.[38] Obviously, no one knows whether they would have even survived without the radical changes undertaken. Moreover, restructuring often is a painful emotional experience for both those who were let go and those who survive. The survivors often feel guilty that, somehow, they have been spared and are anxious that they might be next. Survivors often have trouble maintaining a commitment to an organization when they just might be "doing time" until the next layoff is announced.[39]

Reengineering

Whereas restructuring is concerned with eliminating organizational units, **reengineering** has to do with changing the way work is carried out.[40] Recall that reengineering is the redesign of an organization's processes (e.g., logistics, distribution, and manufacturing) to cut costs, improve quality, increase speed, and enhance competitiveness. Processes that are crucial to customer satisfaction are candidates for reengineering. Thus the starting point is to assess current processes from the customer's point of view.

Successful reengineering requires employees to examine the *breadth* of activities to be redesigned and the *depth* of these changes. In terms of breadth, although reengineering a single activity or function may be important to an organization, including more activities is more likely to extend its benefits throughout the organization. Often, a reengineered process is interrelated with other key activities. Recall that many organizations are structured by function and that employees' ideas about change typically are based on its effect on their department. However, reengineering requires employees to think across functions. To oversimplify, reengineering decreases the amount of "hand-offs" between departments by increasing the amount of resources that are brought together simultaneously to meet customers' needs, such as faster delivery time, more accurate billing, and fewer defective products that must be returned.

The depth of the reengineering effort is measured by the number of roles, responsibilities, rewards, incentives, and information technologies to be changed. Successful reengineering requires in-depth changes. If reengineering efforts are sufficiently deep, the old support systems will become obsolete. Starting from scratch, in effect, the organization can redesign itself and new support systems will emerge.

The following Global Insight illustrates how Banca di America e di Italia (BAI) used reengineering to improve customer service. One of the most important aspects of this reengineering effort was the investment by top managers of resources and time to support the reengineering change continuously over two years. BAI's top managers understood the necessity of setting challenging and specific goals and were dedicated to doing whatever it took to implement the reengineering program. They tried to ensure that all personnel had the time to work on the project. Daily "crises" had to be solved by others not directly involved in the reengineering program.

Global *Insight*

Reenginering at Banca di America e di Italia

Top management of Banca di America e di Italia (BAI) set out to improve customer-service levels, as well as front-office efficiency and effectiveness, in its banks. It needed to reduce the number of people per branch and open new branches to remain competitive. With 85 percent of BAI's revenues coming from retail banking, the primary need was to reengineer key customer-service processes.

Two teams of BAI employees diagnosed customer transactions and categorized them as payments, deposits, withdrawals, money orders, and the like. Each team carefully documented the flow of specific processes for each transaction (e.g., depositing a check drawn on another bank into a customer's account). The team discovered that completing a simple deposit transaction required sixty-four activities and nine forms. After the reengineering program, the same transaction required only twenty-five activities and two forms.

The team then began to consider the key organizational activities that would determine whether the program succeeded. What types of back-office and front-office changes would be needed? What new skills or positions were required? What types of new physical layout would complement the new organizational design?

After wrestling with these questions and suggesting answers to top management, the teams reengineered the customer-service processes for check depositing. The customer now fills out a deposit slip, indicating the total number and amount of the checks being depositing and the amount to be withdrawn. The teller types in the account number, total amount of the deposit, and then feeds the checks through a scanner. While the customer is waiting two or three seconds for the checks to be recorded, the teller calls up the customer's profile on the CRT screen and sees that the customer looks like an excellent candidate for a CD. As a receipt containing detailed information about the checks deposited prints out, the teller asks the customer whether he or she is interested in a CD. Meanwhile, on another screen, the teller provides the customer with detailed information on CDs. After the discussion, the teller hands the customer the deposit slip and some promotional material on CDs. The entire transaction takes less than thirty seconds. If the customer purchases a CD, the teller also handles that transaction. The teller will handle the checks only once more: when counting the total number at the end of the day and reconciling that total to the one on her computer. This new approach requires tellers to learn marketing and information processing skills.

What were the results? First, BAI has been able to open fifty new branches without adding personnel. Second, the average number of employees per branch has dropped from nine to three or four. Third, daily teller closing time has dropped from more than two hours to ten minutes. Finally, BAI's revenues have increased by 24 percent and the number of customers buying CDs has increased by 306 percent during the past four years.[41]

Discussion Question 7
What are the primary differences between restructuring and reengineering?

Reengineering often is expensive, time-consuming, and seems best suited to organizations that face major shifts in the nature of competition. It requires employees to change their behaviors and managers to communicate openly with employees. Managers must give employees sound reasons and explanations for the new design. Feedback is essential to show employees that their concerns are being heard because employees may feel that their jobs are under attack. Ultimately, reengineering projects succeed and can produce long-lasting results only if managers and other employees invest their time and energy in bringing about the change.[42]

5

Discuss job simplification and job enrichment as ways to change the tasks that employees perform.

TASK APPROACH

Whenever a job is changed—whether because of new technology, internal reorganization, or reengineering—tasks also change. Two dramatically different methods of changing a task are job simplification and job enrichment.

Job Simplification

The oldest task approach to change is job simplification. Recall that the scientific management techniques developed by Frederick Taylor define jobs and design tasks on the basis of engineering concepts, such as time-and-motion studies. The job specification states the tasks to be performed, the work methods to be used, and the work flow between individuals, if any, that is to occur. **Job simplification** involves the scientific analysis of tasks performed by employees in order to discover procedures that produce the maximum output for the minimum input. This type of analysis generally results in tasks with high levels of specialization and specification. Employee turnover is high and commitment to the organization is low.[43]

Many fast-food restaurants, such as McDonald's, Burger King, and Hardee's, use such designs because (1) employees can learn tasks rapidly, (2) short work cycles allow task performance with little or no mental effort, and (3) low-skilled and low-paid employees can be hired and trained easily. However, most current competitive challenges require a committed and involved work force that is able to make decisions and to experiment with new ways to do things. Because many people seek jobs that allow greater discretion and offer more of a challenge, designing jobs with employee needs in mind requires a different approach.

Ask Students

Did you ever have a job that was simplified after you started work? Did it have the characteristics described here? Explain.

Job Enrichment

Recall that changing job specifications to broaden and add challenge to the tasks required in order to increase productivity is called **job enrichment.**[44] Let's briefly review its main characteristics.

Job enrichment has four unique aspects. First, it changes the basic relationships between employees and their work. Job enrichment is based on the assumption that

Many fast-food restaurants use job simplification methods to increase the productivity of their employees.

Ask Students
How does job enrichment actually change a job?

Teaching Tip
Compare in two columns on the board the job of a typical undergraduate who reads the textbook and takes scantron tests and that of a doctoral student who must write a dissertation and defend it before a faculty committee. Which one has the simplified job? The enriched job? Ask students which of these jobs they would prefer and why.

work itself may be a powerful motivator, increasing satisfaction and productivity. If a job is satisfying only lower order needs (physiological or security), job enrichment lets employees move toward satisfying higher order needs (esteem or self-actualization).

Second, job enrichment directly changes employees' behaviors in ways that gradually lead to more positive attitudes about work and the organization and a better self-image. Because enriched jobs usually increase feelings of autonomy and personal freedom, employees are likely to develop attitudes that support the new job-related behaviors.

Third, job enrichment offers numerous opportunities for initiating other organizational changes. Technical problems are likely to develop when jobs are changed, which offers management an opportunity to refine the technology used. Interpersonal problems almost inevitably arise between managers and subordinates and sometimes among co-workers who have to relate to one another in different ways. These situations offer opportunities for developing new skills and teamwork.

Finally, job enrichment can humanize an organization. Individuals can experience the psychological lift that comes from developing competence in their work and doing a job well. Individuals are encouraged to grow and push themselves.

6

Describe how survey feedback and team-building change processes can affect employees' attitudes and behaviors.

PEOPLE APPROACH

Technology, design, and task approaches try to improve organizational performance by changing the way work is done. They are based on the belief that employees will be most productive in an interesting and challenging work situation. People approaches, on the other hand, attempt to change the behavior of employees indirectly by focusing on changing their skills, attitudes, perceptions, and expectations. New attitudes, skills, and expectations may, of course, encourage employees to seek changes in the organization's design, technology, or tasks.

Methods of changing job-related behaviors and attitudes can be directed at individuals, groups, or the entire organization. Many of these methods are commonly grouped under a broad label—organization development methods. **Organization development (OD)** is a planned, long-range behavioral science strategy for understanding, changing, and developing an organization's work force in order to improve its effectiveness.[45] Although OD methods frequently include design, technological, and task changes, their primary focus is on changing people. Typical OD methods include survey feedback, team building, conflict resolution, and improvement of interpersonal relations. Managers and team leaders can use these methods and others to resolve problems and conflicts within or between work groups.

Organization development emphasizes three major sets of values that make it a unique approach to organizational change:

- *People values.* People have a natural desire to grow and develop. Organization development aims to overcome obstacles to individual growth and enable employees to give more to the organization. It stresses treating people with dignity and respect, behaving genuinely rather than playing games, and communicating openly.
- *Group values.* Acceptance, collaboration, and involvement in a group lead to expressions of feelings and perceptions. Hiding feelings or not being accepted by the group diminishes the individual's willingness to work constructively toward solutions to problems. Openness can be risky, but it can usually help people effectively plan solutions to problems and carry them out.
- *Organization values.* The way groups are linked strongly influences their effectiveness. Organization development recognizes the importance of starting change at the top and gradually introducing it throughout the rest of the organization. As one manager put it, "Successful change is like a waterfall. It cascades from the top to

Ethics
Some people argue that simplified jobs are unethical because they are dehumanizing and that enriched jobs are superior. Others argue that simplified jobs are ethical for recent immigrants, uneducated workers, and mentally challenged people who cannot handle enriched jobs.

Teaching Tip
Invite an organization development (OD) consultant to class to explain what she or he does.

Ask Students
What is the difference between organization development and management development? (Answer: OD focuses on the *entire* organization.)

the bottom." The links between the top and the bottom are accomplished through groups.

Of the many OD methods used, we examine only two of the most common ones: survey feedback and team building.

Survey Feedback

Survey feedback is an OD method that allows managers and employees to provide feedback about the organization and receive feedback about their own behaviors.[46] This information becomes the basis for group discussion and the stimulus for change. Accurate feedback from others about behaviors and job performance is one of the primary characteristics and values on which OD is based.

Ethics
Managers frequently argue with consultants that, as they paid for the survey, they should know who said what, even if anonymity was agreed to beforehand. Some managers even ask to see the results of personality tests. Are management's attempts ethical? Why or why not?

Feedback is obtained by means of a questionnaire, which is developed and distributed to all employees, who complete it and turn it in anonymously. The questionnaire shown in Figure 21.5 was designed to measure the corporate culture of the Fort Worth, Texas, Museum of Science and History. The data obtained from such a questionnaire are summarized, usually by a consultant or someone from the organization's human resources department. The summarized data are then used in group problem-solving activities. Group meetings are chaired by a manager or team leader. The group leader's job is to help group members interpret the data, make plans for constructive

FIGURE 21.5

Corporate Culture Survey, Fort Worth Museum of Science and History

Instructions: We would like you to describe the environment in which you work. By environment, we mean the fundamental internal character of the museum that sets the pattern for how things get done. It is the core values and rules of the game that have evolved over the years. These values and rules have been shaped daily by both he content and style of top management. Make your descriptions as objectively and factually as possible. THERE ARE NO RIGHT OR WRONG ANSWERS. Please read each statement and assign it a number using the following scale. Your first reaction is probably the best response. DO NOT SIGN YOUR NAME.

9	Most characteristic	4	Somewhat uncharacteristic
8	Quite characteristic	3	Fairly uncharacteristic
7	Fairly characteristic	2	Quite uncharacteristic
6	Somewhat characteristic	1	Most uncharacteristic
5	Neutral		

Statements:

_____ High performance expectations
_____ Emphasis on quality
_____ Being competitive
_____ Being highly organized
_____ Being decisive
_____ Fitting in
_____ Being careful
_____ Paying attention to detail
_____ Having a clear, guiding philosophy

Source: Slocum, John W., Jr. Cox School of Business, Southern Methodist University, Dallas, 1995.

FIGURE 21.6

Team-Building Program

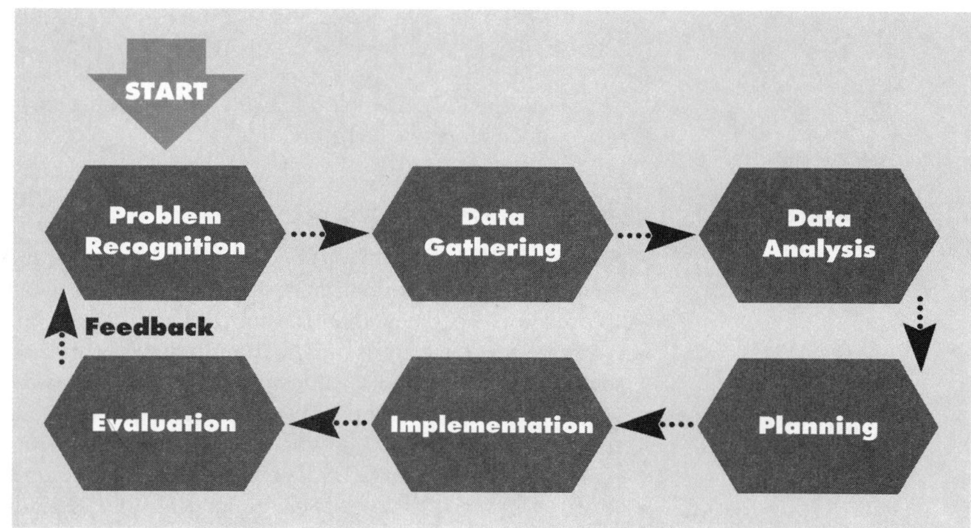

Source: Dyer, W.G. Team Building: *Issues and Alternatives,* 2nd ed. Reading, Mass.: Addison-Wesley, 1987, 53.

change, and prepare the results for distribution to others in the organization. If the group leader and members decide that additional data are needed, another questionnaire could be developed.

Survey feedback is a highly successful OD method. It has been used by a variety of organizations, including the U.S. Navy, schools, hospitals, museums, and businesses. Survey feedback works best as a bridge between the diagnosis of organizational problems and the implementation of a people approach to change. There is little evidence to suggest that survey feedback alone will result in changes in individual behavior or organizational effectiveness. However, it does enable managers to collect data from a large number of employees and to feed that information back to them for purposes of solving organizational problems.

Teaching Tip
Student's evaluations of teachers are an example of survey feedback. Use one of these forms as a visual aid.

Teaching Tip
Divide students into groups for brainstorming the advantages and disadvantages of team building. Have the groups share their results with the class.

Discussion Question 6
What are the main differences among the four approaches to achieving change?

Discussion Question 1
Why do you resist change?

Team Building

Team building is an OD method that helps teams operate more effectively by testing and improving their structure, processes (leadership, communication, and conflict resolution), and member satisfaction.[47] Team building normally begins at the top of an organization and extends downward. Ideally, it focuses on solving problems within a group or department. Team-building sessions may last from half a day to several days. Ordinarily, a team-building program will follow a pattern similar to that shown in Figure 21.6. The program begins when someone recognizes a problem. Data are then gathered and analyzed to diagnose the problem and its cause(s). Following the diagnosis, the team begins to plan and identify ways to solve the problem. The solution is then implemented and the results are openly evaluated by the team.

An important aspect of team building is recognizing, valuing, and managing diversity in an organization. For several years the City of San Diego had been losing high-performing employees and had been besieged by residents complaining about poor city services. The city's management team felt that cultural differences and lack of appreciation for diversity might be one of the major causes of these problems. After looking into methods to research the problems and achieve a change in direction, the city chose a team-building approach. The following Diversity Insight illustrates how this approach helped the city reach its goal.

Diversity *Insight*

San Diego's Diversity Program

The team selected by the City of San Diego comprised consultants, city employees, and residents. In doing its work, the team followed the steps shown in Figure 21.6. It established liaison with all key city functions (e.g., personnel and employment opportunity) and concerned citizens to communicate the team's task and identify goals. The team made a concerted effort to involve everyone with a vested interest in the program. To identify issues and challenges, the team conducted seventy-four interviews with a random selection of employees who reflected the varied composition of the city's work force. The interviewees identified career development, communication, and promotion as priority areas for improvement.

The team then developed goals, a diversity program, and plans to implement it. Short-term strategies included creating multicultural and bigender selection and promotion interview panels to make the selection process more representative. The personnel department agreed to make test and interview results available. The team also made available diversity training for all existing city employees. Task forces were formed to remove language barriers and improve the promotion process. The team also made 225 presentations during the next two years to interested groups of citizens and city employees. The city manager now holds monthly meeting with other managers regarding the goals and expectations for diversity management and has established a time each Friday to talk with employees who have completed diversity courses.

What have been the results? City employees now rate their understanding of diversity as "excellent" as opposed to "average" before the program started. Discrimination complaints have dropped, saving the city more than $300,000 in legal fees. City employees have a greater sense of equity and fairness in hiring and promotion opportunities. The city's logo has been redesigned to reflect multicolored ribbons being woven into a fabric by figures representing individuals from various cultures. A symbol of teamwork, the logo promotes esprit de corps among city employees. Finally, trained city employees are spending considerable time helping other employees implement their own diversity activities.[48]

Team building is a successful approach for several reasons. First, it focuses mainly on the feelings and attitudes of group members, which can be stumbling blocks to change unless they are adequately addressed. Second, off-site team meetings—a commonly used method—allow people to focus on interpersonal issues and not be concerned about being interrupted or preoccupied with tasks they otherwise would be doing. Finally, team building can improve group performance, particularly for tasks that are complex, unstructured, and require a group decision.

CHAPTER SUMMARY

1 ***Describe the features of the learning organization that enable it to anticipate and effectively deal with change.***

Organizations are redesigning themselves to become learning organizations capable of quickly adapting their practices to satisfy the needs of their customers. The basic features of such organizations are culture, leadership, strategy, organization design, and information sharing.

2 ***Explain the process of planned organizational change.***

Planned organizational change consists of (1) assessing changes in the environment; (2) determining whether a performance gap exists and, if so, its nature and magnitude; (3) diagnosing organizational problems; (4) identifying sources of resistance to change, both individual and organizational; (5) selecting methods for reducing resistance; (6) setting clear, realistic, and attainable goals for change; (7) searching for a change strategy that will accomplish the stated goals; (8) implementing the change; and (9) following up to determine whether the change has been successful.

3 ***Describe the sociotechnical system and information technologies as methods in the technology approach to change.***
Changing technology means altering the methods that organizations use to produce goods and services. The sociotechnical system balances the needs of employees with those of the firm. The use of e-mail, video conferencing, and other methods to process information changes the technology available to employees to perform their jobs.

4 ***Explain how restructuring and reengineering can be used to change the design of an organization.***
Restructuring involves changing the levels of authority, control, and responsibility. Entire divisions may be spun off in an attempt to reduce costs. Reengineering is concerned with changing the way work is carried out, that is, changing the organization's processes to improve costs, quality, and speed.

5 ***Discuss job simplification and job enrichment as ways to change the tasks that employees perform.***
Changing tasks requires changing the basic relationships between employees and their work. Job simplification and job enrichment are two methods that can be used to achieve such a change. Job simplification uses scientific management principles to redesign the task. Job enrichment permits employees to satisfy their needs by permitting them to do various tasks. Creating self-managed work teams is one result of job enrichment.

6 ***Describe how survey feedback and team-building change processes can affect employees' attitudes and behaviors.***
Survey feedback permits managers and other employees to provide information about their own behaviors. Such information is then used to provide a stimulus for change. Team building is a method designed to help groups operate more effectively by improving the processes—leadership, communication, and conflict resolution—by which they make decisions and take actions.

QUESTIONS FOR DISCUSSION

1. What approaches to change did management at Compaq Computer use to turn that company around?
2. What global changes are affecting the design of organizations?
3. Respond to the following statement: "A system that performs a certain function or operates in a certain way will continue to operate in that way regardless of need or changed conditions."
4. Describe the basic features of a learning organization. How are they different from those of a bureaucratic organization?
5. Evaluate the following statement: "We trained hard, but it seemed that every time we were beginning to form into teams, we would be reorganized. We tend to meet any new situation by reorganizing, and what a wonderful method it can be for creating the illusion of progress while producing confusion, inefficiency, and demoralization." (Petronius, 210 B.C.)
6. What are the main differences among the four approaches to achieving change?
7. What are the primary differences between restructuring and reengineering?

FROM WHERE YOU SIT

1. Why do you resist change?
2. Based on your knowledge of the ways that people and organizations resist change, evaluate the following remark that Charlie Brown made to Snoopy: "Once a dog, always a dog."
3. Reengineer the way you study for this class. What changes did it involve?
4. Design a team-building process to improve the effectiveness of a team you belong to. Be sure to address the motivation for the change and political concerns.
5. Values play an important role in organizational development practices. What are some of your key values that could be used to humanize an organization?

How Innovative Are You?

Instructions: To find out how innovative you are, respond to eighteen statements using the following scale. There is no right or wrong answer. Rather, the intent is to help you explore your attitudes.

SA = Strongly Agree
A = Agree
? = Undecided
D = Disagree
SD = Strongly Disagree

Questions

1.	I try new ideas and new approaches to problems.	SA	A	?	D	SD
2.	I take things or situations apart to find out how they work.	SA	A	?	D	SD
3.	I can be counted on by my friends to find a new use for existing methods or existing equipment.	SA	A	?	D	SD
4.	Among my friends, I'm usually the first person to try out a new idea or method.	SA	A	?	D	SD
5.	I demonstrate originality.	SA	A	?	D	SD
6.	I like to work on a problem that has caused others great difficulty.	SA	A	?	D	SD
7.	I plan on developing contacts with experts in my field located in different companies or departments.	SA	A	?	D	SD
8.	I plan on budgeting time and money for the pursuit of novel ideas.	SA	A	?	D	SD
9.	I make comments at meetings on new ways of doing things.	SA	A	?	D	SD
10.	If my friends were asked, they would say I'm a wit.	SA	A	?	D	SD
11.	I seldom stick to the rules or follow protocol.	SA	A	?	D	SD
12.	I discourage formal meetings to discuss ideas.	SA	A	?	D	SD
13.	I usually support a friend's suggestion on new ways to do things.	SA	A	?	D	SD
14.	I probably will not turn down ambiguous job assignments.	SA	A	?	D	SD
15.	People who depart from the accepted organizational routine should not be punished.	SA	A	?	D	SD
16.	I hope to be known for the quantity of my work rather than the quality of my work when starting a new project.	SA	A	?	D	SD
17.	I must be able to find enough variety of experience on my job or I will leave it.	SA	A	?	D	SD
18.	I am going to leave a job that doesn't challenge me.	SA	A	?	D	SD

Scoring

Give yourself the following points for each circled response.

SA = 5 points
A = 4 points
? = 3 points
D = 2 points
SD = 1 point

Interpretation

Total your scores for all responses. The higher the score, the more willing you are to be innovative and to welcome change. A score of 72 or greater is high; a score of 45 or less is low. People who aren't innovators have a tendency to maintain the status quo. Innovative people like to create planned changes in their organizations to increase performance.[49]

CRITICAL THINKING CASE

Harley Hogs Ride Again

Employees of Milwaukee-based Harley-Davidson Motorcycle Company have seen it all. During the 1960s, Harley had 100 percent of the motorcycle market. The bikes rumbled through streets and became a symbol of street gangs and blue-collar workers. But buyers of "hogs" complained of leaky gaskets, unstable bikes, and vibrating engines. Half the bikes that came off the assembly line had to be reworked. Dealers complained that they couldn't get parts and that the workmanship on the bikes was poor. Union-management relations were terrible, and absenteeism and grievances were high.

In the mid-1970s, the Japanese introduced their version of the motorcycle. Their ads changed the motorcycle "gang" image with sayings such as, "You meet the nicest people on a Honda." The Japanese targeted the small-bike market and grabbed a large share of it with bikes that were low in cost and high in quality. Honda and other Japanese motorcycle companies talked to dealers and vastly improved relations with them. By 1980, Harley's market share was 23 percent, and the organization was on the brink of closing its doors.

When CEO Vaughn Beals took over in 1980, he and his top management team visited the Honda plant in Japan. They learned that the Japanese were more efficient and had employees who were highly motivated. Working with Arthur Andersen Consulting, Harley-Davidson management almost overnight changed the way the organization worked.

Beals initiated an open-door policy. That gave employees the chance to air grievances and provided Beals with feedback on a host of problems that never before had reached top management. To achieve a more highly motivated work force, his goal was to develop a more participative and less adversarial relationship with the union. The union label now was printed on the bike and management volunteered to share financial information with the union's leadership. In addition, team-building sessions were held to teach first-line managers how to treat employees more humanely.

A peer review system was created by employees to evaluate each others' performance instead of relying solely on first-line supervisors' evaluations. To create a strong team culture, layers of management were eliminated, thereby giving employees authority to make decisions that once had been reserved for management. Employees in each work area determined the best way to set up their own work, what job descriptions should be, and what assembly line rates were optimal for achieving the highest quality. This approach also was extended to sales and other managerial employees. Quality circles were implemented and became a source of bottom-up ideas for improving quality. These circles also became a vehicle for breaking down communication and status barriers between managers and workers.

To attack the quality problems, managers and employees designed a just-in-time (JIT) inventory system and statistical process control techniques. The JIT inventory system scheduled raw materials to arrive only as needed, which produced huge inventory savings. Harley gradually invested money in new technology, such as robots and computer-aided manufacturing techniques, to help employees improve quality. The statistical process controls enabled employees to monitor quality and make corrections immediately rather than waiting for them to show up in a dealer's showroom. Dealer satisfaction improved dramatically as customer complaints about quality dropped. Dealers were stocking fewer parts because of higher quality and, when they needed a part, it was shipped immediately. These improvements allowed Harley to slash the cost while greatly improving the quality of the bike. In 1993, Harley reached Six Sigma (i.e., error rate expressed in parts per million) in quality for the first time.

To deal with the Japanese invasion, Beals sought and received help from the U.S. government. The Reagan administration found that the Japanese were dumping (selling for below cost) excess bikes on the U.S. market and responded with a five-year tariff on heavyweight bikes. This action gave Harley some additional time to make needed changes.

Beals also repaired strained relationships with customers by visiting motorcycle rallies and meetings on his Harley. Arriving at these rallies with his own black leather jacket and jeans boosted customer relations. In 1992, he biked through Germany, France, and England. He learned that German owners often ride their bikes at more than 100 miles per hour. That led Harley to look at other ways of creating a smoother ride and to emphasize the sale of options that offered more rider protection.

Sales managers also took new Hogs to these rallies and let potential customers drive them. In addition, the company formed the Harley Owners Group (H.O.G.), which now has more than 185,000 members, and sponsored rides and activities for customers. It is a roaring marketing success, and its fame isn't limited to the United States. In 1992, Harley sponsored its first rally in Southeastern France, where people tend to keep late hours. Harley supplied beer and rock-and-roll music until midnight, then turned off the lights. The bikers called headquarters and persuaded them to keep the band playing and bar open until 4:00 A.M.

Beals retired and Richard Teerlink took over in 1988. Teerlink maintained the same practices that Beals had started. His values are: (1) tell the truth, (2) keep your promises, (3) be fair, (4) respect the individual, and (5) encourage intellectual curiosity. He believes that empowered employees make the best decisions. By giving them the authority and resources to make decisions, they learn that they can make a difference. Teams are now in charge of producing products and have come up with new engines, transmissions, and frames.

In 1992, for the first time in the company's ninety-year history, marketing staff from around the world gathered in Milwaukee to share ideas and information. From these discussions, the company decided to eliminate the positions of senior vice-president of marketing and of operations. Those jobs were eliminated because they didn't add value to the products. Today, Harley has an 85 percent share of the big-bike market and views itself as being customer focused. One of its hottest selling motorcycles didn't originate in the company but was designed by a customer. Harley's close-to-the-customer marketing philosophy creates the opportunity for company employees to receive direct input from both dealers and customers. Harley now treats each customer like family. Even though the demand for Harley's bikes exceeds supply, Harley pledges not to abuse its customers by charging excessive prices or cutting back on quality to speed up production.[50]

Questions

1. Is Harley-Davidson a learning organization? If so, what features can you pinpoint that support your answer?
2. What concepts from this chapter explain the successful turnaround of Harley-Davidson?

Chapter 22

Entrepreneurship and Small Business

Chapter *Outline*

Learning *Objectives*

After studying this chapter, you should be able to:

1. Explain who entrepreneurs are and how they develop.
2. Recognize the personal attributes and behaviors associated with successful entrepreneurs.
3. Describe the planning issues associated with becoming an entrepreneur.
4. Recognize the characteristics of organizations that encourage intrapreneurship.

Preview *Insight*

Super Bakery, Inc.

Super Bakery is a company owned by former Pittsburgh Steeler football star Franco Harris. It was formed in 1983 as a baker of donuts and baked goods for the institutional food market. The industry has sales of more than $120 billion per year and is growing at the rate of 1 to 2 percent a year. Super Bakery sales are slightly more than $6 million, a minuscule share of the industry total. The bakery makes more than four million donuts a month and sells its products in five cities and four states.

Super Bakery has a flat management structure, employees and managers work side by side, and there are few rules and regulations. Managers also frequently ask employees for suggestions on day-to-day operational issues. To ensure that they have a broad knowledge of all bakery operations, employees are trained to perform different functions (mixing dough, baking, delivery, and the like). This cross-training permits employees to fill in for each other when needed, expands their responsibilities, and makes full use of their capabilities. It also has made the bakery a more satisfying and motivating place to work.

Super Bakery collects a great deal of information that it uses to improve service. A database is maintained on each competitor, including credit policies, nutritional ingredients, and lead time(the length of time required to fill an order). Employees are trained to know the location of each facility, the people who work for each customer, their routines, jobs, and key decision makers. Employees normally visit a customer at least once a year to stay abreast of customers' needs. The company maintains strong ties to local schools and distributors because bids on public contracts are a matter of public record.

Distributors are important to Super Bakery because they deliver a variety of noncompeting goods to small school districts. Super Bakery works with other food manufacturers to provide complete meals to schools. It also makes school districts aware of various state and federal programs and resources that might be available to them. By staying in close touch with current and pending legislation, Super Bakery often is able to introduce new products and services that help customers comply with changes in government rules, beating its competitors in the process. Super Bakery baked a "Super Donut," one low in fat, protein-enriched, and vitamin-fortified. This new donut was among the first products approved by the U.S. Department of Agriculture for high school breakfasts. The company also has pioneered the use of government commodities—flour, butter, sugar—in its products to reduce the cost to schools. It worked innovatively with suppliers and schools to provide children attending the Chicago Zoo with box lunches at a reasonable price. Super Bakery also sells donuts to a distributor who combines a donut, piece of fruit, sandwich, container of milk, straw, and napkin to create a packaged lunch.[1]

1

Explain who entrepreneurs are and how they develop.

ENTREPRENEURS: BORN OR MADE?

Why have a chapter on entrepreneurship in a textbook about management? Some people believe that entrepreneurs are born, not made, or are influenced by circumstances. Others believe that entrepreneurs may be good at creating a business but that they can't manage one. Franco Harris and his team at Super Bakery illustrate that some entrepreneurs can be good at creating *and* running a business.

Teaching Tip
Have students prepare a one-minute definition of the term *entrepreneur*. Compare the definitions.

Entrepreneur is the label usually given to someone who creates new business activity in the economy. Managers in large corporations also engage in entrepreneurial activity when they develop new product lines or establish new companies to enter markets they had not penetrated before. In fact, one of the roles of a manager is to be entrepreneurial. In the broadest sense, then, an entrepreneur manages resources in order to create something new or innovative—generally a business or a product.

Individuals often become entrepreneurs when they discover that they can't accomplish their career goals in a large organization. For example, Ron Canion's idea for a compact computer wasn't supported by Canion's employer, Texas Instruments. Canion and a group of Texas Instruments employees quit and formed Compaq Computer Com-

Seeing few women executives in corporate America and worried that motherhood would prevent her advancement, Gigi Goldman left her marketing job to found Gianna International, which sells picture frames to department stores.

pany. Canion's entrepreneurial talents ensured success for almost a decade. Then competition caught up, prices dropped, and Compaq faced a serious decline in sales. As a result, the Compaq board of directors replaced Canion.

The term **incubator organization** is used for organizations that support entrepreneurs.[2] In recent years, incubator organizations have sprung up in all parts of the world. These organizations rent space to new businesses or to people wanting to start businesses. They often are located in recycled buildings, such as warehouses or schools. In addition to making space available, they serve fledging businesses by offering administrative services and providing management advice. An incubator tenant can be fully operational the day after moving in, without buying phones, renting a copier, or hiring office employees. Studies show that people tend to start businesses in the same general geographic area as their incubator organizations and to use the skills and knowledge they gained from those organizations.

Ask Students
How many of you have worked in a small business? What size business was it? What was its main product?

Another reason for dealing with the topic of entrepreneurship in a management text is sheer numbers.[3] You may well be involved in an entrepreneurial venture when you graduate because that is where the new jobs are. During the 1980s, new ventures were started in record numbers. More recently, almost one million new companies have been formed in the United States—compared to 200,000 in 1965 and only 90,000 in 1950. More than 300,000 entrepreneurs started their own businesses for the first time. Forecasters predict a large number of organizational births well into the future. In particular, an explosion in venture creation by women, immigrants, and members of minority groups is anticipated. The proportion of new ventures involving female entrepreneurs rose from 24 percent in 1975 to 33 percent in 1994.[4] Entrepreneurship also has created several million new businesses in nations throughout the world, including China, Hungary, and Poland. Does this explosion reflect a boom in "born entrepreneurs" a generation ago? No. More people simply have come to view business ownership as a realistic career option and have begun learning how to achieve it.

Teaching Tip
People who buy franchises are not technically entrepreneurs.

For their enterprises to survive, however, entrepreneurs typically have to manage their limited resources differently than managers of large organizations do. In this chapter we describe what seem to be emerging as the management styles and characteristics of successful and unsuccessful entrepreneurs.

Teaching Tip
Have students interview the manager of a local franchise and discuss the advantages and disadvantages of becoming a franchisee.

The term *entrepreneur* often is used incorrectly to mean *small-business owner.* People become small-business owners by purchasing companies, inheriting them, buying franchises, and other means. They also are usually content to keep the business small. In contrast entrepreneurship involves the creation of something new or innovative that grows large, usually rapidly. In this sense, the purchase or inheritance of an ongoing business isn't entrepreneurial unless innovative decisions cause it to move rapidly in new directions.

Early Experiences

Let's consider the stereotypical entrepreneur: the owner of a small, independent business who created it.[5] The U.S. Small Business Administration (SBA) draws the line at 500 employees to distinguish small from large firms. According to *Inc.*, a magazine that publishes articles and conducts research on entrepreneurs, the top 100 entrepreneurial firms in the United States have the following characteristics: 98 percent are run by men, their annual sales exceed $62 million, and they have an average of 441 employees.[6]

Over 95 percent of the approximately 22 million businesses in Canada and the United States are small. Thus millions of people are in business for themselves, each possessing a unique set of personal characteristics and experiences. Researchers have studied samples of business owners for years to determine whether any characteristics or experiences consistently set these owners apart from the rest of the population.

The family environment has been shown to affect the development of an entrepreneur. For example, first-born female children tend to be more entrepreneurial than females born as later children, perhaps because the first child receives special attention and thereby develops more self-confidence. There also is strong evidence that entrepreneurs tend to have had self-employed parents. The independent nature and flexibility shown by the self-employed mother or father is learned at an early age. Such parents are supportive and encourage independence, achievement, and responsibility.[7]

Teaching Tip
Have students interview a local small-business owner or entrepreneur. Then have the students prepare an oral or written report, describing the advantages and disadvantages the interviewee mentions and the individual's personal attributes.

Teaching Tip
Invite a graduate of the school who also is a successful entrepreneur to class to tell his or her story and encourage students to explore entrepreneurship opportunities.

Teaching Tip
Have students write down the steps they would follow to ensure that their small businesses would not be among the 50 to 55 percent that fail in the first year of operation. Discuss this crucial time in the life of a small business.

Ethics
Haägen-Dazs distributes its products nationwide, whereas Ben & Jerry's Homemade Ice Cream is distributed only in thirty-five states. Haägen-Dazs would like to require that distributors and retailers that handle its product handle no other ice cream. What are the legal and ethical aspects of this situation?

Today's entrepreneurs are, on average, younger and better educated than in the past. Some earlier business founders substituted on-the-job experience for college education. Today, many entrepreneurs develop their business ideas—and even start their companies—while still in college.[8]

- Phil Knight, a long-distance runner at the University of Oregon, and his coach, Bill Bowerman, discussed the poor quality of U.S.-made running shoes. Two years after receiving his graduate degree, Knight entered into partnership with Bowerman to establish NIKE, Inc.
- Linda Richardson actually started her first business in high school—selling makeup. During college, she formed companies to make and sell handbags and distribute antique jewelry. After graduation, she attempted more traditional careers in education and banking, but eventually her entrepreneurial spirit reasserted itself, and she opened a bank sales training company.
- As a marketing class project at Harvard, Daniel Fylstra invested $500 to create Personal Software. The company introduced VisiCalc, the first personal computer planning and budgeting software package to be a major commercial success.
- Jody Gessow, owner of three Atlanta-based businesses, was featured in *People* magazine as the youngest travel broker in the nation. At the time, he was a student at Emory University and had a partner studying at the University of Virginia.

What Successful and Unsuccessful Entrepreneurs Do

The image of a successful entrepreneur brings to mind words such as *create, innovate, risk,* and *grow*. The successful entrepreneur values independence and creativity, has the ability to find market opportunities that others may have overlooked, can't stand the "red tape" that often strangles large organizations, and has a vision that can be sold to potential employees and investors.

Entrepreneurs position themselves well in markets that are shifting or are untapped. Ben Cohen and Jerry Greenfield started Ben & Jerry's Ice Cream in 1963 after enrolling in a $5 dollar correspondence course on ice cream making from Penn State. They started making super premium ice cream with chunks of fruit, which appealed to customers

Teaching Tip
Ask students to brainstorm and prepare lists of what successful and unsuccessful entrepreneurs do. Display these lists either by using an overhead transparency or on the board, and compare them.

Ask Students
Do the personal attributes that characterize successful entrepreneurs develop, or are they innate? That is, are entrepreneurs *made* or *born*?

Discussion Question 1
What's required for successfully starting an entrepreneurial business? Why do so many entrepreneurs fail?

Ask Students
Are similar or different personal attributes required in managing a large business and managing a small business? Explain your opinion.

who didn't like regular ice cream. At that time, the big ice cream manufacturers (e.g., Kraft, Pillsbury, Sealtest, and Borden's) weren't in the super premium market.[9]

Not all new ventures, however, are success stories. Thousands fail each year. According to Dun & Bradstreet and other credit-reporting agencies, the majority of failures can be traced to poor management. Also, many of those who fail don't have the stomach for hard work. There is no substitute in a firm just starting up for hard work, which must often include sixty-plus-hour weeks. One investor remodeled a vacant service station, filled it with cases of beer, hired a few part-time college students at minimum wage to collect the customers' money, and sat back to wait for the profits to roll in. They never did. The owner's absence and failure to exert leadership led to low sales, theft, and general physical deterioration of the business.

However, hard work alone isn't enough, either. The entrepreneur must "work smart" and use time effectively. Some of the owner-managers who put in the most hours lose their businesses because their efforts are misdirected. They also aren't able to put the right management team together. A typical example is the inventor who spent all his time trying to sell a new product rather than hiring someone with marketing expertise to stimulate sales. Doing so would have freed the inventor to spend time in the workshop doing what he did best.

Unsuccessful entrepreneurs also fail to plan and don't prepare for expansion.[10] They don't recognize that their role must change as their organization changes. As a company grows from a one-person enterprise to a team effort to an organization requiring more than one level of management, the entrepreneur must be flexible enough to change managerial roles. The owner starts out as a creator, becomes an operator and manager, and gradually evolves into a leader. But each role requires different patterns of behavior.

Poor and reckless money management can cripple an organization from the start. Too much capital may have been put into fixed assets (land, buildings, or equipment). Record keeping may be sloppy and haphazard. The owner may be taking out too much money in salary, perks, and expenses. Cash flow problems may be caused by poor credit-granting practices or by faulty inventory management. All these factors may spell doom for a business just as it is on the verge of success.[11] Many of these causes of failure are highlighted in the following Small Business Insight.

Small Business *Insight*

Tortilla Flap

Doug Foreman dreamed up a recipe for a low-fat version of tortilla chips in an attempt to eliminate fried foods from his personal diet. He started selling his chips, and they became so popular that he found himself baking chips day and night. Then he met Drew Westbrook, a crackerjack salesperson for a local Austin, Texas, radio station. Westbrook was interested in Foreman's business but wanted equity in the firm in exchange for $6,500. Foreman agreed and Westbrook became the owner of 49 percent of the business.

The demand for the new low-fat chips rose dramatically and forced the partners to move into new headquarters and buy new tortilla-baking equipment. As interest in low-fat foods grew, sales continued to grow. However, Westbrook had written some unprofitable orders and made some sales promises to customers that he later broke. Many of his deals were written on cocktail napkins, and he failed to inform manufacturing when and how to fill these orders. Often he couldn't be found to straighten out the orders.

Foreman kept busy filling orders and doing his partner's job. Sales were approaching $370,000 a month and additional money was needed to build another chip factory. He approached two other entrepreneurs, who had started Barq's Rootbeer, Inc., about lending him capital. They agreed to lend Foreman cash but wanted a voice in decisions involving compensation, hiring and firing key managers, licensing agreements, and purchases of major assets.

With this infusion of cash, sales grew even more rapidly. Now it was a $10 million dollar company with a network of distributors and regional sales representatives. However, because of Westbrook's lack of attention, customer service was terrible. Foreman finally asked Westbrook to take a six-week leave of absence because he could no longer cover for his shortcomings. Westbrook immediately hired an experienced sales manager and shortly after that, customer service and lack of product complaints stopped.

When Westbrook returned, Foreman asked him to go to lunch. During lunch, Foreman bought his partner out for $1.28 million. According to Foreman, Westbrook got a great return on his original $6,500 and two years of work.[12]

2

Recognize the personal attributes and behaviors associated with successful entrepreneurs.

CHARACTERISTICS OF ENTREPRENEURS

The many studies of entrepreneurs that have been conducted over the years indicate that those who succeed have several characteristics in common. These attributes and behaviors are listed in Table 22.1.[13]

Key Personal Attributes

Although possible, changing personal attributes isn't easy. These characteristics tend to be deeply ingrained and are formed over a lifetime. Some personal attributes that are clearly related to entrepreneurial success may well be worth the effort to develop. In addition, personal attributes appear to develop from behavioral changes. Thus engaging in entrepreneurial behavior may itself lead to the development of desired motivations and ways of thinking.

Teaching Tip

Just because someone is highly independent and dislikes bureaucratic organizations (e.g., universities) doesn't mean that she or he will be unsuccessful. Becoming an entrepreneur may be an option worth exploring.

Need for Achievement. Heading the list in Table 22.1 is the *need for achievement*—a person's desire either for excellence or to succeed in competitive situations. High achievers take responsibility for attaining their goals, set moderately difficult goals, and want immediate feedback on how well they have performed.

David McClelland and others have conducted extensive research into three human needs: for power, affiliation, and achievement. Their findings indicate that only perhaps 5 percent of the U.S. population is characterized by a predominant need to achieve.[14] Yet this need is consistently strong in successful entrepreneurs.

Ethics

How can the excessive need for achievement lead to ethical problems?

TABLE 22.1

Characteristics of Successful Entrepreneurs

Personal Attributes	Behaviors
Need for achievement	Technically competent
Desire for independence	Good grasp of business finance
Not motivated to work in large organizations	Willing to delegate
Ambition	Hard-working; task-oriented
Self-confidence	Effective leader
Future-oriented	Self-starter
High reward expectations	Decisive and methodical
Tolerance for ambiguity	Reliable
Self-sacrificing	

Sources: Adapted from Vaught, B.C., and Hoy, F. Have you got what it takes to run your own business? *Business,* July-August 1981, 4; Sexton, D.L., and Bowman-Upton, N. Female and male entrepreneurs: Psychological characteristics and their role in gender-related discrimination. *Journal of Business Venturing,* 1990, 5, 29–36; Main, J. A golden age for entrepreneurs. *Fortune,* February 12, 1990, 120–125.

Entrepreneurs strive to achieve goals and measure success in terms of what those efforts have accomplished. Entrepreneurs learn to set challenging but achievable goals for themselves and for their businesses and, when they achieve them, to set new goals. Goals that are too high *and* those that are too low don't work. Goals that are too high to achieve breed frustration, and goals that are too low breed complacency.

Teaching Tip
Before you cover this list, ask the students to consider each attribute in relation to themselves. After you have discussed the list, ask the students who believe that they are entrepreneurial material to raise their hands.

Desire for Independence. Entrepreneurs often seek independence from others. As a result, they generally aren't motivated to perform well in large, bureaucratic organizations. They have internal drive, are confident of their own abilities, and possess a great deal of self-respect. They may be ambitious without being concerned about social image.

Self-Confidence. A successful track record of accomplishment does much to improve an entrepreneur's self-confidence and self-esteem. It enables the person to be optimistic in representing the firm to employees and customers alike. Expecting, obtaining, and rewarding high performance from employees is personally reinforcing, and it also provides a role model for others. Most people want an optimistic and enthusiastic leader—someone they can look up to. Because of the risks involved in running an entrepreneurial organization, having an "upbeat" attitude is essential.

Ethics
How can excessive self-confidence lead to ethical problems?

Future Oriented. Successful entrepreneurs are future- and money-oriented. They have high expectations of reward and use rewards (e.g., salary and status) as indicators of their achievements. They are optimistic but still have a reasonably objective outlook on the world in which they work. They are tolerant of the uncertainties they face daily.

Discussion Question 2
Which attitudes and behaviors listed in Table 22.1 are more useful in managing an entrepreneurial company than in being an entrepreneur?

Self-Sacrificing. Finally, successful entrepreneurs have to be self-sacrificing. They recognize that nothing worth having is free. That means giving up the two-week vacation, the every Saturday golf game, or the occasional trip to the mountains. Success has a high price tag, and they are willing to pay it.

The following Diversity Insight illustrates how these key behaviors influenced one entrepreneur. She started her business with employees who had been on Chicago's welfare rolls for years. With the financial backing of the First National Bank of Chicago, Deborah Payne successfully launched her own dressmaking company.

Diversity *Insight*

Redefining What's Possible

Deborah Payne is a dressmaker and designer who had been sewing for her friends since she was fourteen. She spent many years just trying to earn a paycheck and wanted to break free from the long hours, low wages, and other things that defined her employment. As a single mother, she was afraid to go out on her own until a friend told her about the Chicago-based Women's Self-Employment Project (WSEP). WSEP is a nonprofit entrepreneurial service program targeting low- and moderate-income women in the city. Many of the people who come to WSEP have poor or no credit histories and are on welfare. They lack the collateral that banks normally require to start a business.

WSEP arranged a loan that enabled Payne to buy a sewing machine. WSEP also holds free monthly meetings because its clients often need technical support and advice, not just money. Handling disagreements with children or employees are topics usually discussed at these meetings. Through connections at WSEP, Payne landed an interview with the publishers of the Spiegel catalog. That led to the catalog's carrying some of her designs, which are targeted at the African-American community. The demand for her clothes has been so strong that she has hired four people to sew for her. She now spends her days designing and working with buyers from large department stores. She delegates the authority and responsibility for sewing to her employees.[15]

For some people entrepreneurship itself becomes a career. Rather than managing a business solely for income or growth, these individuals use their companies as springboards to start or acquire other ventures and then repeat the process, which is known as the **corridor principle.**[16] That is, opening a business is analogous to entering a passageway. As these individuals walk along it, they see new corridors that they may explore. Had they not entered the first one, they would never have learned of the others. The entrepreneur thus encounters many business opportunities that otherwise would have remained hidden.

Key Behaviors

Patterns of behavior become habits, and such habits are certainly easier to change than personal attributes. But taking on some of the behaviors associated with successful entrepreneurship can still cause discomfort if the individual isn't prepared. For example, before launching an entrepreneurial effort, a person must have the necessary technical skills and be confident about handling interpersonal relations and decision making.

Teaching Tip
Caution students that entrepreneurs need to exhibit all these behaviors.

Technical Skills. As shown in Table 22.1, entrepreneurs often demonstrate high levels of technical competence.[17] They typically bring some related experience to their business ventures. For example, owners of successful automobile dealerships usually have acquired a significant amount of technical knowledge about selling and servicing automobiles before opening their dealership. Some people believe that successful entrepreneurs are lucky. In reality, successful entrepreneurs have developed the skills, experience, and resources they need to take advantage of opportunities.

Financial Savvy. Entrepreneurs must have accurate, meaningful, and timely information if they hope to make sound financial decisions. Although few owners of small businesses can expect to be experts in accounting, they need to know about key financial indicators. These include an income statement that shows a profit or loss, a balance sheet, which provides a snapshot of the firm's financial position, and a cash flow statement. Without understanding these basic statements, the owner cannot have a grasp on the firm's financial picture.

Ask Students
Have you ever worked for an entrepreneur who expected you to have as much commitment to the business and drive as your employer did? If so, describe the experience.

Interpersonal Skills. To take advantage of opportunities, entrepreneurs also must be good managers. Those who are successful have acquired the skills necessary to manage the human and the financial resources of their firms. Like Deborah Payne, they must be willing to delegate to their subordinates the authority and responsibility needed to get the job done. At the same time, they must be willing to be accountable for their decisions and actions. Soliciting constructive feedback is part of accountability.

Real-World Example
Wanda Gibbs, an entrepreneur who started a grocery delivery business in Southfield, Michigan, collapsed in December 1992 in a customer's living room. Burnout, like that experienced by Gibbs, is a serious problem among owners of small businesses. Physicians and therapists say that emotional and physical burnout is common from overwork and not enough rest (*Los Angeles Times,* January 10, 1995, D3).

Successful entrepreneurs are extremely hard working and task-oriented, yet they have learned how to temper this drive and dedication with the interpersonal skills of effective leaders. They are self-starters who usually support their subordinates and programs enthusiastically. Not insignificant to these behaviors are highly developed communication skills.[18]

Many day-to-day problems that entrepreneurs encounter are behavioral. Employees and customers interpret situations from their own unique perspectives. In some cases, a problem may exist *only* in the mind of an employee or customer, but to that employee or customer, the problem is very real. For instance, the owner of a small parts-manufacturing firm witnessed the constant recurrence of a scheduling problem between the production control manager and the manufacturing superintendent. Several meetings and procedural changes later, the "problem" still existed. Only in-depth interviews with the two men conducted by an outside consultant exposed the real, human problem: The older superintendent resented the younger production control manager telling him what to manufacture and when. The moral: Entrepreneurs won't make the right decisions if they can't diagnose the problem accurately.

Decision-Making Skills. Successful entrepreneurs are good at making crucial decisions affecting their operations. They are decisive and methodical—as opposed to impulsive—in reaching their decisions. They think with their heads more than with their hearts. Decisions are right, in their minds, if they lead to accomplishment of the goal.

Teaching Tip
Business students may judge entrepreneurs who aren't so inclined or don't have time to use quantitative decision models as not being sound businesspeople. Students need to understand that the diversity among people and viewpoints makes others *different* from them, not better or worse.

Most entrepreneurs don't have the time or the inclination to develop quantitative decision models for solving specific operational problems. They learn, often by trial and error, how to build quality into their operations. They find that few quality problems can be solved perfectly and that not many problems can be solved once and for all time.

The following Quality Insight illustrates how Margot Fraser of Birkenstock Footprint Sandals got into the sandal business and has operated it. We have highlighted the key behaviors she demonstrates in running the company.

Quality *Insight*

Feet: Don't Fail Me Now

Margot Fraser discovered Birkenstock sandals while visiting Germany more than twenty years ago. She brought a pair, and they felt so comfortable that she arranged a meeting with the president of the sandal company, Karl Birkenstock. Birkenstock had taken over his family's 192-year-old business and was making sandals that were orthopedically correct for his friends and customers in the German village where he lived.

Fraser impressed Birkenstock with her drive and business sense (technical skills), and he agreed to let her have exclusive rights to distribute his sandals in the United States. Fraser and a friend started selling the sandals in health-food and hole-in-the wall stores and offered 5 percent discounts to retailers who paid their bills within ten days.

After slow sales growth for nearly twenty years, the leather-strapped, molded-cork-base shoes became the casual shoe of choice after several women's magazines featured them. Fraser became the spokesperson for the sandals in the United States (interpersonal skill). Companies such as The Gap and Timberland promoted the shoe, and sales climbed from $9 million to $50 million a year. By 1989, Fraser's company had grown to 145 employees, and she was buying almost all of the sandals produced by Birkenstock's German factory.

When the Berlin Wall fell in 1989, the German government offered financial incentives for companies to move into what was once East Germany. Birkenstock moved. But former garment workers had to be trained to read leather hides for imperfections, and Birkenstock had to wait weeks or even months to get machine parts. While Birkenstock was patching up inconsistent supply lines, knockoff sandals started to appear on the gray market. Knockoff companies were able to copy the sandal and offer them to customers at a quarter of the price. More than 10,000 pairs of shoes at a time were showing up at European flea markets and in U.S. discount chains. At the same time, other manufacturers, such as NIKE and Deckers, started manufacturing their own sandals, which were similar in price and style.

To counter such attacks, Fraser and Birkenstock hired models to wear their shoes at fashion shows. Fraser renewed her efforts to sell sandals to independent shoe stores by starting an extensive advertising campaign (decision making). Fraser pledged extraordinary service to these stores, which included shipping single pairs to retailers overnight to satisfy them (quality). Fraser also ran advertisements in local newspapers and dropped in store names and addresses for a small fee.

In December 1993, the head of sales and marketing left to join a competitor and took a key salesperson with her. Fraser says that it was a "personality issue" and faced hiring an essential member of her team.[19]

3

Describe the planning issues associated with becoming an entrepreneur.

BECOMING AN ENTREPRENEUR

Research has shown that, before going into business, entrepreneurs who are successful typically plan more carefully than those who fail. One tool that helps them do so is the business plan.[20] A **business plan** is a step-by-step outline of how an enterprise expects to turn ideas into reality. A business plan also provides prospective investors with information about the new business. Table 22.2 shows the major components of a business plan.

Entrepreneurs must answer the following types of questions in their business plans.

Teaching Tip
Have students select businesses they would be interested in owning, draw up quick one-page business plans, and share their plans with the class.

1. What kind of business should I own?
2. Should I start or buy a business?
3. What and where is the market for my product or service?
4. How much will it cost to own the business, and where will I get the money?
5. What skills will I need to manage a changing or a family enterprise successfully?

Kinds of Businesses

People become business owners for various reasons. Some want to make a hobby or craft pay off, and others enter businesses owned by family members. Still others choose an industry on the basis of their assessment of the growth and profit potential in that industry. One way to think about business opportunities is to classify them as lifestyle, smaller profitable, and high-growth ventures.

Teaching Tip
Have students identify the types of business they would engage in if they had an opportunity to do so. Classify those identified as lifestyle ventures, small profitable ventures, or high-growth ventures.

1. ***Lifestyle ventures.*** Independence, autonomy, and control are the overriding goals.
2. ***Smaller profitable ventures.*** Cash flow and profits are important goals, as long as they don't jeopardize the owner's ability to control the firm.
3. ***High-growth ventures.*** Significant levels of sales and profits are sought, with outside investment and eventual buyout expected.

As we have noted, new ventures frequently spring from an incubator organization, where entrepreneurs may develop skills and knowledge to use in starting their own

TABLE 22.2

Components of a Business Plan

Business concept	Description of the product Market identification, target customers, and descriptive and economic data on demand Competition defined and market analysis completed Marketing strategy clearly articulated Location information on business, facilities, outlets, and service Management, leading entrepreneur profile, key employees
Financial support	Financial needs and planned sources of capital, debt, and personal equity positions Supporting documentation of financial plans: • Projected income statement (profit-and-loss operating statement) • Projected cash flow statement • Projected balance sheet • Break-even analysis of sales quantity
Incidental information	Customer surveys, market information, forecasts of demand and sales Personal data sheets on owners, lead entrepreneurs, key skilled managers Support information on materials purchasing, vendors, quotes, and prices Facility plans, layouts, manufacturing requirements, equipment needs Credit reports, bids, contracts, and other appendices helpful to investors

Sources: Adapted from Longenecker, J.G., Moore, C.W., and Petty, J.W. *Small Business Management: An Entrepreneurial Emphasis.* Cincinnati: South-Western, 1994.

businesses. When deciding what type of business to own, people should begin by examining the abilities, interests, and contacts they can bring to their future company. Prospective entrepreneurs should examine various alternatives carefully in terms of expected revenue, the initial investment required, and the intensity of competition. This analysis often turns up existing businesses that may be purchased. Business magazines, such as *Inc.*, *Entrepreneur*, and *Venturing*, can be a good source of new-venture ideas.

Starting or Buying a Business

Prospective entrepreneurs who have the option to "start or buy" begin by weighing the advantages and disadvantages of each strategy. Sometimes, of course, the decision is made *for* them because they don't have the financial resources necessary to purchase an existing company.

In deciding whether to *start* a business, the prospective entrepreneur should consider the following questions, among others.

Teaching Tip
Invite two alums to class—one who purchased a business and the other who started a business. Ask them to share, compare, and contrast their initial decisions and subsequent experiences.

- Is there a way that I can begin the enterprise in stages or with a limited investment?
- Can I run the company at first as a home-based business?
- Can I continue working for someone else and put in time on my own business after hours?
- To what extent can I draw on relatives to help me, perhaps simply by answering the phone while I work at my regular job?

In answering these questions, German banker Bertolt Brecht discovered that the bank he had founded on environmental issues couldn't survive unless he changed the bank's policies. The following Ethics Insight highlights the ethical issues that he considered important.

Ethics *Insight*

Hippy Bank

Bertolt Brecht founded one of Europe's few "alternative banks" in the mid-to-late 1980s when Germany was experiencing a social revolution—collapse of the Berlin Wall, influx of immigrants, and rise of far-right political groups. He knew when he founded the bank that maintaining its ethical principles and surviving would be a struggle. His alternative bank mixes ecological awareness with social responsibility. All loan requests are measured against the bank's social and environmental criteria. It won't lend money to companies and projects deemed to be damaging on either account. A special investment fund division channels money to companies involved in Third World development, alternative energy sources, and women's issues, among others. Depositors choose which fund, and therefore which activities, they want to support.

Although this policy seems to work for existing customers, the bank is having difficulty attracting new ones. With concerns for the environment now a major issue in Germany, other mainstream German banks, which offer higher returns, are offering their customers "ethical financing."

Another problem facing the bank is that 80 percent of its customers live outside Frankfurt and Freiburg, its two major centers. Thus customers' transactions are delayed because electronic banking is still relatively rare in Germany. With few branches, it can't offer the same level of customer service as other German banks.

These problems may leave the bank on high moral ground, but they are unlikely to boost its profits. Similarly, environmental issues aren't restricted by national boundaries. As the bank starts to internationalize, that will pose additional ethical problems. That is, an organization may be able to practice social and environmental responsibility in one country, but not in another.[21]

Real-World Example
There is an ethical controversy over franchising. Some franchisors make more money selling supplies and management services to franchisees than they do from selling to the public. Franchisors say that they must sell their own supplies and services to the franchisees to ensure the consistent delivery of quality and service and to protect their names. Franchisees say that they are being overcharged for supplies and services and that franchisors are restraining trade and hold a monopoly (*Los Angeles Times,* Feb. 20, 1994, D3). What do you think?

Teaching Tip
Students often mistakenly believe that, after graduating from college, they can easily find employment with some big company who will hire, train, and pay them well. (This expectation frequently is a wish to be taken care of.) Suggest to them that, if they can't find employment, buying into a franchise or existing firm, especially if they have partners, may be easier than they think.

Teaching Tip
A good question to ask when buying an existing business: Why do you, as the owner of a successful business, want to sell it?

Discussion Question 4
Why would an entrepreneur prefer to launch an entirely new venture rather than buy an existing firm?

Teaching Tip
Have your students learn about small business by following a SCORE consulting team on a case.

Discussion Question 3
A recent survey published by *Inc.*, a magazine widely read by entrepreneurs, revealed the following data. Many of the 600 fastest-growing entrepreneurial firms didn't exist a decade earlier. Over 40 percent of these firms are in computer-related fields. Why has the computer industry—unlike, say, those producing energy- related or consumer goods—been such a hotbed of entrepreneurial activity?

A middle ground between starting your own business and buying an existing independent business is to run a franchise. A **franchise** is a business run by a person to whom a *franchisor* grants the right to market a good or service. The *franchisee* pays a franchise fee and a percentage of the sales.[22] The franchisee often receives financial help, training, guaranteed supplies, a protected market, and technical assistance in site selection, accounting, and operations management. Sometimes a franchise is referred to as **turnkey operation** because it is ready to open when purchased or leased, virtually by the entrepreneur turning a key in the lock. More than 558,000 franchise outlets were being operated in 1994.[23] McDonald's, Domino's Pizza, Jiffy Lube, AAMCO Transmissions, and Jenny Craig Diet Centers all use franchises to market their products. Whoever enters a franchise agreement obtains a brand name that enjoys recognition among potential customers. However, franchisees are their own bosses only to a degree. They can't run their businesses exactly as they please. They usually have to conform to standards set by the franchisor, and sometimes they must buy the franchisor's goods and services. But many people want to operate a franchise in the first place for these very reasons.

Buying a nonfranchise existing firm is more complex and may involve more risk. The seller may not reveal some hidden problems—and may not even be aware of others. Also, many a new owner has thought that she or he was buying goodwill, only to have the previous owner open a competing firm and lure away the established clientele. The prospective buyer is wise to specify, in the purchase agreement, restrictions limiting the previous owner's ability or right to compete with the new owner. Such restrictions may limit the types of businesses that the previous owner can operate in a certain region or for a stipulated period of time.

Learning about businesses available for purchase and negotiating the purchase agreement often require the assistance of experts. Bankers, accountants, attorneys, and other professionals may be aware of an opportunity to buy a business before it is publicly announced. A business broker may help find a firm and act as intermediary for the sale. Usually, an attorney prepares or reviews the sale documents.

The Market

The forecasting techniques described in Chapter 6 often are overlooked in planning for business ownership. Entrepreneurs frequently are so excited about their business ideas that they assume others will feel the same way. Their market research may consist of asking the opinion of a few friends or relatives about the salability of a product.

Help in targeting and analyzing markets is available to the prospective entrepreneur from numerous sources. The federal government compiles an enormous amount of data on products, industries, consumers, and other market-related categories. The business development programs supported by the U.S. Small Business Administration, such as the Service Corps of Retired Executives (SCORE) and Small Business Development Centers (SBDC), can help entrepreneurs sort through the data.

How should a business plan identify the target market? Typical questions derived from a business plan (see Table 22.2) are listed in Table 22.3. These questions focus on the attractiveness of the market and on the firm's ability to capture some share of that market.

Sources and Uses of Funds

Just as entrepreneurs are likely to overestimate their income, they also tend to underestimate their costs. The new-venture plan should identify anticipated costs of opening the business (e.g., deposits, fixtures, and incorporation fees). It should also project, month by month, the expenses that reasonably can be expected for the first one to three years. These include the cost of goods or services sold and the expenses of operating the firm.

TABLE 22.3

Market Issues Facing the Entrepreneur

1. Who exactly is your market? Describe the characteristics (age, sex, profession, income, and so on) of your various market segments.
2. What is the present size of the market?
3. What percentage of the market will you have?
4. What is the market's growth potential?
5. How will you attract, expand, and keep this market?
6. How are you going to price your service, product, or merchandise to make a fair profit and, at the same time, be competitive?
7. What special advantages do you offer that may justify a higher price?
8. Will you offer credit to your customers? If so, is this really necessary? Can you afford to extend credit? Can you afford bad debts?

Source: *How to Start and Manage a Business* (workbook). Athens: University of Georgia, North Georgia Regional Small Business Development Center, 1990.

The entrepreneur must plan for obtaining funds to handle expenses, such as those associated with the start-up phase, that can't be covered initially by revenues. Sources are most likely to be the entrepreneur and other members of the venture team and family and friends. Beyond these sources, a sound business plan is essential in demonstrating to potential lenders and investors the viability of the proposed enterprise.

Real-World Example
As domestic markets become saturated with small franchises, franchisors are seeking overseas markets. Kidsports International, a Sinking Springs, Pennsylvania, family fun and fitness facility, is seeking outlets in Argentina (*Entrepreneur*, January 1995).

The following Global Insight illustrates how Wendy Wigtil, president of Barnyard Babies, started exporting her toys. For small organizations such as Wigtil's, opportunities to profit from exporting have been influenced by passage of the North American Free Trade Agreement (NAFTA), declining interest rates, declining value of the dollar, opening of new markets (e.g., Vietnam and the Czech Republic), and stepped-up government initiatives to improve access to export services.

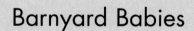

Global *Insight*

Barnyard Babies

Wendy Wigtil is president of Barnyard Babies, which produces cloth designs for children to color and is headquartered in Annapolis, Maryland. Her toy company has six full-time employees and from ten to thirty part-time workers, depending on demand. Wigtil plans to sell toys in Japan, France, Canada, and Brazil.

Why export? Wigtil was forced to sell overseas because of the decline in the U.S. market for her goods and the rise in domestic competition. The provisions in the General Agreement on Tariffs and Trade (GATT) regarding patents and copyrights will give her some protection for her original toy designs. More and more untapped markets are opening up, and consumers in them may have the money to spend on products such as hers. Her success depends on being able to get the more sophisticated buyers, who prefer U.S.-made products, to buy her toys. She knows that foreign buyers have high expectations for quality and performance, and she must meet or exceed them.

She has positioned her company to be a successful exporter by (1) establishing a small, but financially viable market in the United States, (2) being able to adapt her product and offer it at a competitive price in various countries, (3) realizing that success won't come instantly and setting up a financial plan to help the firm, and (4) committing her firm to quality. Her plan called for her to use foreign distributors to find lucrative markets for Barnyard Babies' products instead of doing her own market research. Wigtil pays a commission, but having distributors allows her to concentrate on designing new toys instead of flying all over the world trying to sell her toys to individual stores.[24]

TABLE 22.4

Business Dimensions of Entrepreneurial and Formal Organizations

Business Dimension	Entrepreneurial Organization	Formal Organization
Strategic orientation	Seeks opportunity	Controls resources
Commitment to opportunity	Revolutionary and of short duration	Evolutionary and of long duration
Commitment to resources—capital, people, equipment	Lack of stable resource needs and bases	Systematic planning systems
Control of resources	Lack of commitment to permanent ventures	Power, status, and financial rewards for maintaining the status quo
Management structure	Flat, with many informal networks	Clearly defined authority and responsibility
Compensation policy	Unlimited; based on team's accomplishments	Short-term driven; limited by investors

Sources: Adapted from Stevenson, H.H., Roberts, M.J., and Grousbeck, H.I. *New Business Ventures and the Entrepreneur,* 3rd ed. Boston: Irwin, 1989, 18–19; Stevenson, H.H., and Jarillo, J.C. A paradigm of entrepreneurship: Entrepreneurial management. *Strategic Management Journal,* 1990 Summer Special Issue, 11, 17–27.

Discussion Question 5
What changes in a firm's marketing plan, if any, may be required when the firm begins selling in foreign markets?

Wendy Wigtil could have done many things differently, including starting with a different initial product—one with which she could have made more money more rapidly. She also discovered that many aspects of her plan had to be changed in response to unforeseen events, such as the breakup of the former Soviet Union. Nevertheless, she found that her plan was extremely valuable in helping her organize her thoughts and plot a course of action. It also helped her raise the money she needed from outside investors and lenders. Many of these outsiders, encouraged by her well-developed business plan, contributed both funds and critical managerial skills to the venture in its formative years.

Growth Pressures on Entrepreneurs

Teaching Tip
Students typically do not understand growth models beyond the concept. Impress upon them that the inability to manage growth is a leading reason that small businesses fail.

Entrepreneurs such as Franco Harris (Super Bakery, Inc.), Wendy Wigtil (Barnyard Babies), and Deborah Payne (Redefining What's Possible) often find that as their businesses grow, they feel more and more pressure to use formal methods to lead their organizations. Entrepreneurial and formal organizations differ in terms of six business dimensions: strategic orientation, commitment to opportunity, commitment to resources, control of resources, management structure, and compensation policy. These differences are compared in Table 22.4. To illustrate them, let's consider the experience of Gail Ray, founder of Personal Computer Rentals, as described in the following Insight, and then analyze her company's behavior in terms of Stevenson's dimensions.

Insight

Personal Computer Rentals

It is hard to imagine a more entrepreneurial endeavor than Personal Computer Rentals (PCR) when Gail Ray founded it in 1983. She was the stereotypic "one-woman band." She met with customers, negotiated with suppliers, picked up equipment, delivered and installed it, answered the phone, and handled correspondence. She did anything and everything to get her company off the ground.

Ray hit on the idea for PC rentals while working in sales for IBM. She frequently received calls from people who wanted to lease equipment. In emergency situations, they were willing to pay almost anything. Because IBM chose not to get into the business of leasing personal computers, Ray saw an opportunity. Her instincts proved correct, and she was swamped immediately with orders as she tried to run her business from the file room of her accountant's office.

Ray was encouraged by her initial backer, Edward Miranda, a stockbroker, to expand through franchising. But before it could become a national company, PCR had to get its own house in order. Gail hired Bruce Minker to manage rentals in 1984. He found what he later described as a "seat-of-the-pants operation." Everything from equipment purchases to marketing to collections was handled on an ad hoc basis. Minker and Ray overcame the disorganization by putting in long hours and scrutinizing every detail. PCR sold its first franchise in 1985.

Immediately obvious was the fact that growth required more financing. Banks weren't interested in making loans to unproven ventures in industries that have high failure rates. With Miranda's help, Ray was able to get more equity investors. In 1987, she sold the company to a group of venture capitalists who made PCR their only investment, renaming the company PCR International. These investors wanted PCR International to become the Hertz of the computer rental market. They intended to achieve this goal by aggressively franchising Ray's concept.

One of its most successful franchise operators is Orin Knopp, who has more than seventy offices nationwide and offers an 800-number for clients. As a franchisee, Knopp pays a fee to PCR International and seeks their advice when needed.[25]

Looking at the dimensions listed in Table 22.4 reveals how well a venture such as PCR in its early stages fits the pattern of an entrepreneurial organization. Gail Ray sought an opportunity that larger corporations ignored or were not in a position to seize. Actually, her first idea was to start a chain of personal computer service centers. She abandoned that plan when she learned that Xerox intended to do the same thing. She expected competition in the rental business from computer retail chains. Her timing turned out to be an advantage, though, because the retail market hit a saturation point in the early 1980s, and the big retailers had to concern themselves with controlling their existing resources and couldn't expand into rentals. That gave her a window of opportunity to launch her firm.

Ray's management of PCR showed a focus on market potential. She refused to be restricted by limited resources. She was even willing to sacrifice ownership of the company to obtain the resources necessary to finance its growth. Ray recognized that she was giving up the security offered by IBM for the risks associated with business ownership. She also recognized that the rewards could be virtually limitless. She and her investors foresee a time when they will sell off the enterprise for an enormous return.

Ask Students
How do small businesses (e.g., family-owned businesses) contribute to economic growth, productivity, and change in the United States?

Real-World Example
According to *Inc.* magazine (January 1995, 46–48), family-owned businesses are more likely to succeed in certain industries than in others. Plumbing shops seem to offer the best chance for success and stationery stores the worst. Market niches exist for mom-and-pop hardware stores.

Teaching Tip
Understandably, many students shun family businesses in an effort to separate from their families psychologically and financially and make it on their own. However, in today's economy, students fortunate enough to have a family business to fall back on should consider getting a start in it. Later, they might be able to start a spin-off business of their own or land a job somewhere else by citing their experience.

Managing a Family Business

Family-owned businesses are an integral part of the U.S. economy, responsible for nearly half of the nation's gross domestic product (GDP). Chances are that, when most families enter a business, friends and others say, "Isn't it great that you all can work together?" But for a family business to succeed, a family should take the following steps.

1. Decide who is responsible for what. Jobs in companies just starting up should not be too narrowly defined. Families should recognize each other's areas of expertise to determine who is best able to make each decision.
2. Draw up a legal agreement on disposing of the business. Investors and other outsiders have an interest in family members being in accord on this outcome.
3. Agree on whether and when to sell the business.
4. Decide whether the business will employ other family members and, if so, what hiring criteria will be used.
5. Settle fights as they come up. If a co-worker/family member does something on the job that makes another angry, correcting the problem requires that it be brought into the open.

Teaching Tip
Many students' families operate family-owned businesses. A panel discussion among such class members reflecting the experiences of the small businesses represented is a worthwhile activity that students thoroughly enjoy. Ask class members to generate questions such as, "What made your family decide to go into this type of business?"

Ask Students
What potential problems are associated with working for a mom-and-pop business?

Real-World Example
Substance abuse is a particularly difficult problem to deal with in family-owned business because of family ties. *Entrepreneur* magazine (January 1995, 75) suggests using trained professionals and consultants, if family members and/or an outside board of directors are unable to confront the problem and encourage the person to get help.

6. Establish a board of advisers. Sometimes outsiders are needed to mediate a conflict or at least to provide a fresh perspective.[26]

The issues that most family businesses have to address at some time in their existence may be classified as *survival* and *operational*. Survival issues may arise only once in the lifetime of the owners and the enterprise, but the way they are resolved may determine whether the firm will continue to exist. More than two-thirds of family-business owners want family ownership to continue into the next generation, but few have tackled the issues that need to be addressed to make this happen. Such issues include

1. ensuring equitable estate treatment,
2. preparing for ownership transfer,
3. minimizing estate taxes,
4. ensuring the financial security of the senior generation, and
5. selecting and developing a successor.

Operational issues aren't so crucial, but they may occur daily. Left unattended, they may become survival issues. They include

1. suppressing or avoiding conflict among family members,
2. retaining nonfamily members,
3. handling unproductive family members, and
4. participating in executive decisions.

If you are employed in a family firm, these issues affect you whether or not you are a family member. They influence the company's survival prospects, career advancement opportunities, employee motivation and morale, the company's competitive position, and work-life quality. Because of the high percentage of U.S. businesses that are family-owned and -managed, these issues shouldn't be taken lightly. If they aren't resolved, the family itself may not survive, as illustrated in the following Small Business Insight.

Small Business *Insight*

Death of a Marriage

Six months after Mary and Phil Baechler, of Yakima, Washington, had their first child, Travis, Phil invented a jogger's stroller. When Phil and Mary took turns jogging, with Travis in the stroller, people would ask where they could purchase one. Mary's father finally convinced them to start a business. So with $8,000, they founded Racing Strollers in 1984.

Mary was talked into running the office from the couple's kitchen table. Phil and Jim, a close friend of the family, rented a little garage and built strollers every weekend. They often worked until the wee hours of the morning trying to fill orders.

After the Baechlers placed a small ad in *Runner's World,* customers started calling at all times of the day and night, assuming that operators were standing by to take orders. Mary couldn't stand putting a customer on the answering machine and spent countless hours taking orders. Phil just let customers put their orders on the answering machine. Mary had the ambition to make it big, always going that extra mile for a customer. Phil wasn't as driven and didn't go that extra mile. Phil enjoyed being an artist and designer. All he wanted was financial security. Mary wanted Phil to become a manager and take as much interest in their employees and customers as she did. She viewed the business as a religion and got hooked on making money. Phil wanted a life away from work once they got home. He didn't want to hear about problems at Racing Stollers. He'd been there all day and was bored with the employees' and customers' problems. Mary took all problems home and wanted to discuss them.

After several years of nearly going broke, the business became profitable in 1988. In 1994, the ten-year-old company had sales in excess of $5 million dollars. The Baechlers' family income rose, enabling them to move into a larger house. Both were working long, hard hours and joked that they each needed a spouse.

Employees at the business needed Mary to advise them because business was doubling at least once a year. The strain, urgency to move the business forward, and the neglect of the family had put too much strain on their marriage. Mary finally chose business over marriage, and the couple started divorce proceedings.[27]

4

Recognize the characteristics of organizations that encourage intrapreneurship.

CORPORATE INTRAPRENEURSHIP

Many large organizations now recognize that entrepreneurial behavior can produce growth and profits. Corporate entrepreneurship, once considered a contradiction in terms, is becoming more and more widespread.

Consider for a moment *why* an organization exists. It has some mission—some goals to be accomplished—that requires the efforts of more than one person. At the very least, a business has the goal of satisfying customers so that it can be profitable over the long run.

Ethics
Ask students to suppose that they are working for a family-owned business. The family is involved in a dispute, and the students are asked to take sides. Have them identify the ethical issues that arise specifically because the business is family-owned. Does family ownership make resolution of some problems *easier*? If so, what types of problems and why?

Fundamental to organizing is dividing up the work. Managers may think that they have organized successfully when they have brought different interests together, minimized conflict, increased stability, and reduced uncertainty. Imagine the effects of those organizing efforts on entrepreneurial tendencies. Is the climate conducive to change? Will disruption be tolerated? Is redirection possible?

Large organizations usually are formally structured for efficiency. Their managers run operations in such a way that the same activities will continue indefinitely into the future. Obviously, this approach often is at odds with innovation and change. What then can be done to encourage entrepreneurship when a company needs to be revitalized? The answer lies in changing—perhaps even inciting a revolution in—an organization's practices. Recall, however, that over time organizations develop cultures infused with traditions, norms, rituals, and values. Employees come to take the working environment for granted, and individual efforts to foster change may be met with resistance.

Gifford Pinchot III coined the term **intrapreneur** to describe someone in an organization who turns ideas into profitable realities.[28] Jacques Robinson and Howard R. Stevenson, Jr., who teamed up to rejuvenate General Electric's video products division, are intrapreneurs. Robinson provided the risk-taking environment in which Stevenson was able to design circuitry that brought the quality of standard television sets up to the level of computer monitors. This advance made using ordinary sets with home computers, video games, and video cameras more practical than it had been.

Teaching Tip
Many professors operate like intreprenuers in starting up their own research centers within universities. Cite some examples for students.

Discussion Question 6
Why have companies such as 3M and Kodak, among others, been successful in spawning so many intrapreneurs?

The introduction of the IBM personal computer represents another intrapreneurial activity. IBM gave the assignment of developing the PC to Philip Estridge. Estridge and his group proceeded to violate many time-honored IBM traditions. They used outside suppliers to speed up development and hold down costs, rather than depending solely on other IBM divisions. And they marketed PCs directly through retailers, rather than relying on IBM's sales organization. Estridge was able to accomplish his vision because initially he had the support of top management. Owing to differences that eventually arose between Estridge and corporate management, he left IBM in 1994.

Characteristics of Intrapreneurs

A person must possess certain attributes to be a successful intrapreneur within an organization. They include vision, ability to build and lead teams, and persistence.

Vision. The person who is going to establish a new intrapreneurial venture must have a dream. To establish the new venture, the individual will have to sell that dream to others. Arthur Fry did so at 3M with his Post-it Notes pads.

Ability to Build and Lead Teams. By challenging the beliefs and assumptions of the organization, the intrapreneur has an opportunity to create something new. This person must encourage teamwork and must be a diplomat, skilled in crossing departmental lines, structures, and reporting systems. Intrapreneurial activities can cause some disruption, particularly in large organizations where each manager's "turf" has been staked out carefully over the years. One of the keys to success in team building is to avoid win-lose conflicts.

Ask Students
Do you have these characteristics? Would you like to be an intrapreneur?

Discussion Question 7
What are the social implications of the growing trend for women to become successful entrepreneurs?

Persistence. Frustrations occur throughout the establishment of any new intrapreneurial venture. Thus the intrapreneur needs a strong support group. Even then, only through persistence will the intrapreneur overcome obstacles and achieve success.

Fostering Intrapreneurial Activity

Top management can foster an intrapreneurial culture by eliminating obstacles and providing incentives for intrapreneurship.[29] Organizations that redirect themselves through innovation have the following characteristics:

- *Commitment from senior management.* Don't expect changes to occur unless top management is committed to supporting them. This support must include a willingness to tolerate failure. Top managers must regularly communicate their commitment to intrapreneurial activities—and back their words with actions.
- *Flexible organization design.* Intrapreneurial organizations are designed for fast action. Management gives information and the authority to make decisions to those best positioned to react to changing market conditions. These people often are first-line managers. Intrapreneurial organizations frequently have profit centers and may have internal new-venture teams or task forces, such as 3M does, that act as incubators.

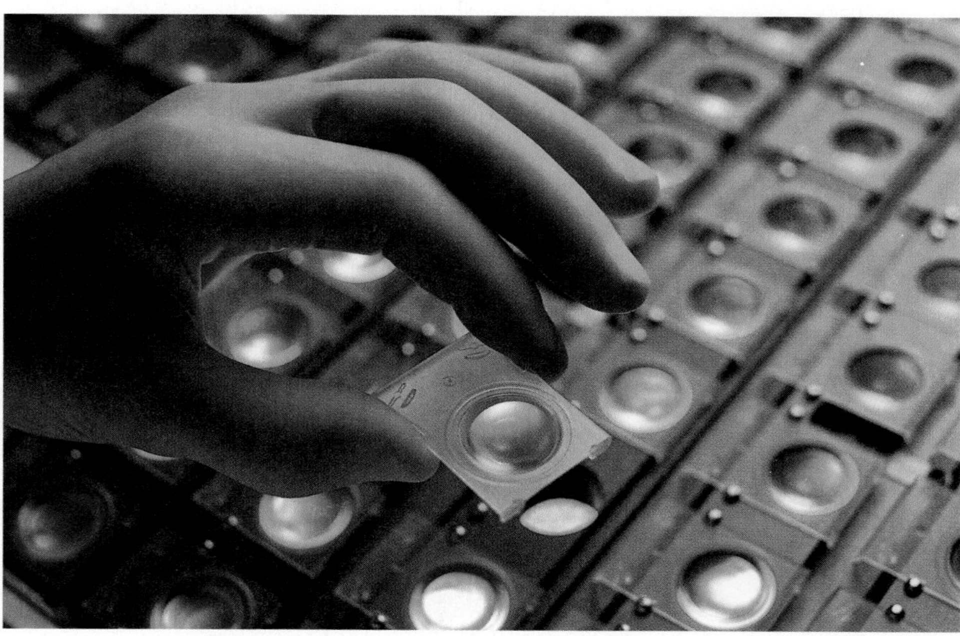

A new factory in Jacksonville, Florida, produces contact lenses cheap enough to be replaced every day, and helps make Johnson & Johnson's Vistakon company the world's largest manufacturer of contacts.

- *Autonomy of the venture team.* Closely aligned with flexibility is maintaining a hands-off policy in day-to-day management of the team charged with implementing an innovation. Successful intrapreneurs, such as Arthur Fry at 3M, usually are volunteers who are allowed considerable leeway in their actions.
- *Competent and talented people who exhibit entrepreneurial behaviors and attitudes.* A willingness to volunteer isn't sufficient reason to assign someone to a venture team—that person also must be competent in that or a related area. Competent volunteers usually have experience in, or have received training for, new-venture creation. Some companies conduct formal training programs; others establish mentor or coaching relationships. Even so, most intrapreneurs have experienced at least one failure before achieving successes that more than offset early losses.
- *Incentives and rewards for risk taking.* Intrapreneurs may not be willing to risk their careers and undergo the frustration of forcing change only for the satisfaction of giving life to their ventures. The developers of successful ventures should be generously compensated. Intrapreneurship should not be a dead-end activity; rather, it should be linked to an identifiable career path of advancement. This recognition is especially important because it helps ensure that the intrapreneur's next new venture won't be a spinoff from the company!
- *An appropriately designed control system.* Nothing is more stifling to an intrapreneurial activity than bureaucratic controls. Nevertheless, despite the potential contradiction between strong controls and the intrapreneurial spirit, senior management cannot give up its accountability for new-venture projects. Controlling internal innovations means collecting and analyzing data that enable management to predict, to a reasonable degree, where the new-venture team is headed. It also involves ensuring that the team understands the difference between intrapreneurial behavior and irresponsible risk taking. Obstacles that inhibit intrapreneurial management generally are structural and deeply ingrained within the firm. Unfortunately, those obstacles are considered practice under some styles of management.

Ask Students
What are some of the reasons that organizations would not want intrapreneurs to succeed? (Examples: fear of losing control, intolerance of nonconformity, and jealousy.)

Integrating Intrapreneurship into an Organization

Top management must meet at least four challenges to stimulate intrapreneurial activity in an organization. First, it must allow intrapreneurial activities to flourish as a part of the organization's normal day-to-day operations. These islands of intrapreneurial activity have been called **skunkworks,** which often violate formal review and reporting policies.[30] Top management must create subcultures wherein these violations are tolerated, if not rewarded. The new-venture team members can then focus their attention on nonroutine and innovative tasks.

Second, intrapreneurship should generate ideas that result in products that the organization can market. The challenge every new-venture team faces is to shape ideas into commercially successful ventures. Organizations' intrapreneurial teams (e.g., Hallmark's technology and innovation center and Kodak's office of innovation) are made up of competent people who are committed to transforming their ideas into profitable ventures for the firm.[31]

Third, rewards need to be tied to performance of intrapreneurial units. By reaping the benefits of their efforts directly, team members are likely to work harder and compete more effectively. Compensation usually is in the form of salary. However, incentives should be established to reward cooperation with other parts of the organization, as well as to reward those units that cooperate with and support the intrapreneurial project.

Fourth, in order for intrapreneurial activities to occur, top management must provide appropriate leadership. People generally are recruited to intrapreneurial activities by charismatic leaders. Shared norms and values are crucial; they create a spirit that fosters innovative activity within the organization.

CHAPTER SUMMARY

1 ***Explain who entrepreneurs are and how they develop.***
An entrepreneur is someone who creates new business activity in the economy. Entrepreneurship may create an independent venture or it may occur in large organizations. However, shepherding a new venture to success requires different skills than those regularly used by managers in large, complex organizations.

2 ***Recognize the personal attributes and behaviors associated with successful entrepreneurs.***
Among the attributes that characterize successful entrepreneurs are the need for achievement, a desire for independence, self-confidence, future orientation, and a capacity for self-sacrifice. Key behaviors include technical competence, strong interpersonal skills, and decision-making ability.

3 ***Describe the planning issues associated with becoming an entrepreneur.***
Entrepreneurs can improve their chances for success by creating a business plan and following it. A prospective entrepreneur must consider issues such as (1) the kind of business to own, (2) whether to start a business or buy one, (3) whether there is an adequate market for the product, (4) where start-up funds will come from and how they will be used, and (5) the skills needed to run the organization successfully.

Operating a family business leads to some unique opportunities and some special problems. The issues that family members must decide include who is responsible for what jobs and whom to hire. They also should agree on legal matters and establish a board of advisers.

4 ***Recognize the characteristics of organizations that encourage intrapreneurship.***
Intrapreneurship involves turning ideas into marketable products in an organization. As such, it is more closely associated with a process than with a personality. Companies that successfully market new ventures are characterized by commitment from senior management, flexible organizational structures, autonomous venture teams, competent and talented intrapreneurs, incentives and rewards for risk taking, and appropriate control systems.

QUESTIONS FOR DISCUSSION

1. What does it take to be successful in starting an entrepreneurial business? Why do so many entrepreneurs fail?
2. Which attitudes and behaviors listed in Table 22.1 are more useful in managing an entrepreneurial company than in being an entrepreneur?
3. A recent survey published by *Inc.*, a magazine widely read by entrepreneurs, revealed the following data: Many of the 600 fastest-growing entrepreneurial firms didn't exist a decade earlier. Over 40 percent of these firms are in computer-related fields. Why has the computer industry—unlike, say, those producing energy-related or consumer goods—been such a hotbed of entrepreneurial activity?
4. Why would an entrepreneur prefer to launch an entirely new venture than buy an existing firm?
5. What changes in a firm's marketing plan, if any, may be required when selling to foreign markets?
6. Why have companies such as 3M and Kodak, among others, been successful in spawning so many intrapreneurs?
7. What are the social implications of the growing trend for women to become successful entrepreneurs?

FROM WHERE YOU SIT

1. Based on your personal experience as an employee, customer, or observer of a small business, how would you rate the ethical behaviors of the owner? What criteria did you use in rating those behaviors?
2. Would you like to run a franchise? Explain the reasons for your answer.
3. Visit a small business and evaluate its customer service. What organization design does it use to provide the level of customer service you observed?
4. Suppose that you are trying to recruit a well-qualified friend from your school to start a new business with you. What arguments would you use to persuade the student to join your venture?
5. Give an example of leadership behavior by a small business owner. How has that behavior helped the owner?

Do You Have What It Takes to Be an Entrepreneur?

Wondering whether you have what it takes to succeed as an entrepreneur? No one can predict your success. But studies of successful entrepreneurs have revealed some characteristics that many have in common, including family background, motivation, and personality traits. Northwestern Mutual Life Insurance Company in Milwaukee has prepared this quiz to help give you an idea whether you'll have a head start or a handicap if you go into business for yourself. Add or subtract from your score as you respond to each item.

1. Significantly high numbers of entrepreneurs are children of first-generation U.S. citizens. If your parents were immigrants, score plus 1. If not, score minus 1.
2. Successful entrepreneurs were not, as a rule, top achievers in school. If you were a top student, subtract 4. If not, add 4.
3. Entrepreneurs were not especially enthusiastic about participating in group activities in school. If you enjoyed group activities—clubs, team sports, group dates—subtract 1. If not, add 1.
4. Studies of entrepreneurs show that, as youngsters, they often preferred to be alone. Did you prefer to be alone as a youngster? If yes, add 1. If no, subtract 1.
5. Those who started an enterprise during childhood—lemonade stands, family newspapers, greeting card sales—or ran for elected office at school can add 2 because enterprise usually appeared at an early age. Those who didn't initiate enterprises, subtract 2.
6. Stubbornness as a child seems to translate into determination to do things one's own way—certainly a hallmark of proven entrepreneurs. So, if you were a stubborn child, add 1. If not, subtract 1.
7. Caution may involve an unwillingness to take risks, a handicap for those embarking on previously uncharted territory. Were you cautious as a youngster? If yes, subtract 4. If no, add 4.
8. If you were daring, add 4.
9. Entrepreneurs often speak of pursuing different paths—despite the opinions of others. If the opinions of others matter to you, then subtract 1. If not, add 1.
10. Being bored with a daily routine is often a precipitating factor in an entrepreneur's decision to start an enterprise. If an important motivation for starting your own enterprise would be changing your daily routine, add 2. If not, subtract 2.
11. If you really enjoy work, are you willing to work long nights? If yes, add 2. If no, subtract 6.
12. If you would be willing to work "as long as it takes" with little or no sleep to finish a job, add 4.
13. Entrepreneurs generally enjoy their activity so much they move from one project to another—non-stop. When you complete a project successfully, do you immediately start another? If yes, add 2. If no, subtract 2.
14. Successful entrepreneurs are willing to use their savings to start a project. If you would be willing to spend your savings to start a business, add 2. If not, subtract 2.
15. If you would be willing to borrow from others, too, add 2. If not, subtract 2.
16. If your business failed, would you immediately work to start another? If yes, add 4. If no, subtract 4.
17. If you would immediately start looking for a good paying job, subtract 1.

18. Do you believe entrepreneurship is "risky"? If yes, subtract 2. If no, add 2.

19. Many entrepreneurs put long-term and short-term goals in writing. If you do, add 1. If you don't, subtract 1.

20. Handling cash flow can be critical to entrepreneurial success. If you believe you have more knowledge and experience with cash flow than most people, then add 2. If not, subtract 2.

21. Entrepreneurial personalities seem to be easily bored. If you are easily bored, add 2. If not, subtract 2.

22. Optimism can fuel the drive to press for success. If you're an optimist, add 2. Pessimists subtract 2.

YOUR ENTREPRENEURIAL QUOTIENT

A score of 35 or more: You have everything going for you. If you decide to become an entrepreneur, you ought to achieve spectacular success (barring acts of God or other variables beyond your control).

A score of 15 to 34: Your background, skills, and talents give you excellent chances for success in starting your own business. You should go far.

A score of zero to 14: You have a head start on the ability and/or experience in running a business and ought to be successful in opening an enterprise of your own if you apply yourself and learn the necessary skills to make it happen.

A score of Minus 15 to Minus 1: You might be able to make a go of it if you ventured on your own, but you would have to work extra hard to compensate for a lack of built-in advantages and skills that give others a "leg up" in beginning their own businesses.

A score of Minus 43 to Minus 16: Your talents probably lie elsewhere. You ought to consider whether building your own business is what you really want to do because you may find yourself swimming against the tide if you make the attempt. Another work arrangement—such as working for someone else, or developing a career in a profession or an area of technical expertise—may be far more congenial to you and, therefore, allow you to enjoy a lifestyle appropriate to your abilities and interests.[32]

CRITICAL THINKING CASE

Pipe Dreams

Ron Inscoe's yellow van trundles along the leafy streets of suburban Bethesda, Maryland, and pulls up at Cornelia Hyatt's house at 5:00 o'clock on a Friday afternoon in late April. Inscoe, Hyatt's heating and cooling mechanic, is here for the springtime inspection. Half an hour later he packs up his tools and pronounces Hyatt's air-conditioning system fit for action.

Inscoe is a heating, ventilation, and air-conditioning technician—an HVAC guy, in trade lingo. But he's also an "area technical director" (ATD) for his employer, Warner Corporation. Instead of making service calls all over Maryland's huge Montgomery County, seldom seeing the same customer twice, he now focuses strictly on Bethesda zip codes 20814 and 20817. The ATD program is the brainchild of company president Tom Warner, who credits it with revitalizing his 260-person business. He has about eighty such directors now, with many more to come. They are plumbers, electricians, and HVAC technicians—the company's operational triad. Each has his or her own zip code or two, covering roughly 10,000 households. The directors are responsible for making a profit, billing customers, and other managerial tasks.

In essence, Warner has given each of them a business to manage—within Warner Corporation. The idea is to field a corps of technically superb, friendly, and ambitious mechanics who operate like small-town tradesmen, despite the big-city reality. By turning his technicians into business people who make decisions and think responsibly about profits and losses, Warner has engendered in them a new sense of pride and ownership. "In the Washington area," he says, "there's a social stigma to working with your hands. This program is a real ego booster.

Running their own businesses, these guys really feel good about themselves."

The upside is more than improvement in self-esteem. Before Ron Inscoe, a 34-year-old with a high school education, joined the Warner team, the most he'd earned in a year was $60,000. But last year, as he began to develop his area, he made $103,000. This year he's on track for $126,000. And when Inscoe does well, so does Tom Warner.

A central feature of Warner's ATD program is a generous incentive system that ensures that Inscoe and others like him will go the extra mile to please customers. "If someone needs an appointment at 6:00 A.M. before work, no problem," he says. "I even give out my pager number to my customers. One of them, a surgeon, paged me at 11:00 o'clock one night. His basement was flooded—there was a bad valve on his boiler. I hopped into my truck and drove over."

Founded in the 1940s, Warner Corporation is the largest plumbing contractor in the Washington area. For decades this family-owned business thrived as Washington's premier contractor for big plumbing projects—office high-rises and apartment buildings. In late 1989, however, just as Tom Warner gained control of 100 percent of the company's equity, Washington's red-hot commercial real estate industry began to flicker, a victim of overbuilding and tax-law changes. Facing cash-flow crises, many property managers hired handymen to handle plumbing work in-house.

Warner saw that his only option was to engineer a massive shift to the previously shunned residential sector. It wouldn't be easy. The area's yellow pages listed hundreds of plumbing and HVAC companies, mostly mom-and-pop operations. Though Warner Corporation is huge, few homeowners had considered its services. Its commercial image was so strong.

But Warner knew that the switch could prove lucrative. Commercial property managers demand discounted labor rates and many of them supply their own parts, canceling the contractor's opportunity to apply margin-fattening markups. And commercial accounts receivable often run to 90 or 120 days. Residential work is more profitable. There is no discount on labor, contractors sell parts at a considerable markup, and customers usually pay immediately. But individual jobs are small. So, to keep revenues up, there's an ongoing need for promotion and advertising.

To introduce the ATD campaign, Warner mailed out flyers on each new director to every address in each director's zip codes— well over 100,000 pieces in all. Each flyer featured a color photo of the zip code's ATD and described the person's experience. It contained a general number to call, day or night (1-800-4-HOT-WATER), along with the number of the director's own line.

The quickest way to build a clientele is to sell a $100 Homeguard service contract. It requires the mechanic to be in the house at least twice a year for routine inspections. So the flyer included a 10 percent off coupon for Warner's service contract.

Andy Kondas, an HVAC mechanic in the Fairfax, Virginia, branch, was among the first ATD volunteers. A self-described workaholic, Kondas likes the compactness of his new territory. But the program's best feature, he says, is that he has his own customers: "Why should there be five different people in a customer's home on five different occasions? Nobody knows what's been done, and the customers never get to know you."

Mary Jane Sherman, one of Kondas's customers, likes the arrangement, too. Warner's superplumber spots on TV enticed her to call, and now she's a convert. "It's like having a family doctor," she says. "He knows my house and all the quirks of its system."

"Two or three years ago," Warner says, "I had to think of everything, and people just waited for me. Now our people come up with their own ideas, and I'm cheering more than leading."

He's got plenty to cheer about. The company recently had revenues of $15.6 million, with after-tax earnings of $544,000—a margin of roughly 3.5 percent. In the near future, Warner expects revenues to jump to $20 million and have a margin of about 8.3 percent.[33]

Questions

1. What personal attributes and key behaviors is Warner looking for when he hires people?
2. What are some growth pressures on Warner's business?
3. If you were Inscoe, why would you work for Warner?

VIDEO CASE

Entrepreneurial Spirit: How Sweet It Is

Entrepreneurs and small-business owners have always been the backbone of any private enterprise system, providing the competitive zeal needed to keep the system running. Entrepreneurs are complex individuals, and researchers have attempted to analyze their personalities, skills, and attitudes and the conditions that foster their development. Research shows that entrepreneurs need self-confidence, drive, optimism, and courage to engage in a new business. Entrepreneurs often base a decision to launch a new venture on a vision, and they are willing to risk security for financial gain. Entrepreneurs also may be victims of corporate cutbacks. In 1987, approximately 3 percent of those who lost corporate jobs turned to entrepreneurship. In 1994, that proportion tripled.

Rob Smith, Jr., previously a manager at Electric Boats, a division of General Dynamics in Connecticut, found himself a victim of defense budget cutbacks after being employed with that company for nine years. After being laid off and subsequently working as a waiter, Smith decided to pursue his entrepreneurial vision to open a small gourmet ice cream shop.

He turned to the Connecticut Small Business Development Center to help him create a business plan. Only one bank was willing to make a small business loan, which was contingent on a financial guarantee from the Small Business Administration (SBA). The SBA declined to give the guarantee because of a lack of assets. After receiving a signature loan from his parents, Smith opened *How Sweet It Is* in Mystic, Connecticut, in 1992. The business was a family affair with his wife designing the shop's decor, his father assisting with the counter, his mother keeping the books, and his sister making the baked goods.

Upon opening, Smith faced a multitude of challenges: products not showing up on time, people not returning his calls, and multiple power failures. However, his tenacity prompted a move of the shop to the heart of Main Street because he knew that location was crucial for success. Business soon doubled. Another key to his sweet success is the extraordinary care that he puts into making ice cream to differentiate his product from that of his competition.

When asked what advice he would give others thinking about pursuing an entrepreneurial vision, he states, "You have to be willing to give up everything." Smith's work ethic isn't a 9-to-5 job—he puts in fifteen-hour days, seven days a week, giving up large chunks of family time. One of Smith's greatest assets is his interpersonal skills, which he exhibits throughout the day as he visits with customers and listens to their suggestions. Along with other entrepreneurs, Smith enjoys controlling his own destiny and building his own sense of job security.

In actuality, though, being an entrepreneur means living without a safety net, making it both thrilling and dangerous. Misjudgments can be deadly, and bureaucratic trampling or a lawsuit can break a small company. Yet, the entrepreneurial spirit continues to thrive. Recent successful ventures include Lone Star Steakhouse and Saloons, Gateway Computers, and Bombay retail furniture stores—all now relatively large operations. However, small businesses do not have to evolve into such highly visible companies with large market shares to be successful, as illustrated by the emergence of How Sweet It Is. As John F. Welch, Jr., chairman of General Electric, has said: "Size is no longer the trump card it once was in today's brutally competitive world marketplace—a marketplace that . . . demands value and performance."[34]

Questions

1. Do you agree with John Welch's statement that "size is no longer the trump card it once was in today's brutally competitive world marketplace—a marketplace that . . . demands value and performance"?
2. In a 1993 article in the *Journal of Business Venturing,* entitled "Personal Value Systems of Men and Women Entrepreneurs Versus Managers," Ellen A. Fagenson states that entrepreneurs tend to value "self-respect, freedom, a sense of accomplishment, and an exciting lifestyle." She goes on to say that, in contrast, managers tend to value "true friendship, wisdom, salvation, and pleasure." Based on Rob Smith's story, would you characterize him as a typical entrepreneur? Why or why not?
3. What are some of the long-term challenges that Rob Smith is likely to face as an entrepreneur?
4. How does entrepreneurship differ from management?

Western Distribution Center, Inc.

"This is a can-do company, a company that people are proud to work for," Mike Henley told himself. "Then why is it that we can't solve our safety problem? I love this company too. I am fully committed to it and to my people! But right now I certainly could use some inspiration. . . ."

Henley was the middle-level manager responsible for daily operations in the regional distribution center of a major mail- order catalog company. The center was located in a small and cohesive community in which traditional values such as close-knit families and patriotism were highly regarded. Mike had been working for the company for twelve years, and many of his employees had been with the company even longer. The company was run like a large and friendly family in which the norm was to work with diligence and enthusiasm. Employees were seldom fired.

Depending on the time of year, Mike supervised between 60 and 100 hourly and salaried associates (nonunion). Their duties were to receive, store, and ship merchandise advertised in the quarterly catalog. More specifically, the associates packed orders, hand carried merchandise, ran a forklift operation, counted stock, stacked and opened cartons, and handled related paperwork. The company was known locally as a good—even inspiring—place to work, and turnover was low.

In recent months Mike Henley had become deeply concerned about an increase in the frequency of accidents at the center. Injuries were up from the same period last year, and the fall and holiday shipping seasons—traditionally the busiest months of the year—were still to come. At the same time, cost reductions had become a special concern in the highly competitive mail-order business, and upper management had been urging middle-level supervisors to examine expenditures closely. In recent years, the average cost per injury at Western, including first aid, medical care, and time lost from work, had been high.

Henley was determined to reverse the accident trend. He decided to challenge himself and his associates. Even though the busiest seasons were yet to come, involving more associates and more orders, he wanted some improvement by the end of the year, and next year he wanted significant improvement in the safety record.

Henley consulted the corporate organizational development (OD) staff in Chicago, who suggested that he might want to use behavior modification and feedback techniques to get associates to work more safely. The OD staff suggested that, even though the company already had a highly positive culture, setting specific goals and carefully managing rewards could still have strong payoffs. Henley was a willing listener; he felt as though he had tried everything else without success.

However, the OD staff tried to temper his eagerness to get started right away. In fact, they cautioned him about several things. For instance, to use these techniques effectively he would have to know exactly what the problem was. Also, he would have to make a commitment to involving and training the associates. Furthermore, if he wanted the program to succeed for more than just a few months, he would have to understand how behavior is maintained for the long term. The OD staff noted that the corporate culture probably would support the change, but that he must be careful not to challenge that culture by his efforts. After several detailed discussions with the OD staff, Henley decided to take a course on behavior modification techniques and to design a program to reduce the warehouse accident rate.

As he learned more about the theory of behavior modification, Henley decided to research systematically the causes of the accident rate. He wanted to know exactly what the problem was. Initially, he formed a representative team of workers and managers to study facility safety. Its job was to get answers to the following questions.

- Have conditions in the facility been unsafe?
- Have the workers lacked training in safety procedures?
- Does some human fallibility contribute to the accidents?

To answer these questions, the team first tested workers on their knowledge of safety procedures: Each associate was interviewed by his or her immediate manager about safety procedures pertinent to their job. Next, through additional interviews and examination of records, the team made a detailed analysis of the causes of previous accidents.

The results of this investigation indicated that workers' actual knowledge of safety procedures was extremely high. Accidents occurred most frequently when people "forgot" about safety—for example, when they were distracted from their task or were in a hurry. The team con-

Source: This case was prepared by Rae Andre, Northeastern University, under a grant from the Minerva Education Institute. Adapted and used with permission of the author, 1995.

cluded that 97 percent of all accidents had been caused by mistakes, not by inadequate training or unsafe conditions.

Henley accepted the team's analysis that people's behavior on the job should be targeted for change. He believed that improving people's attention would translate into safer behaviors. He decided that his next step should be to design a program to motivate people to behave safely.

Questions

1. Why did the OD staff caution Mike Henley? Discuss the issues that the staff raised in light of what you know about application of behavior modification principles in the workplace.
2. What additional problems should Henley anticipate, if any?
3. How would you design the program? Consider each step, from diagnosis of the problem through implementation and follow up.
4. Why should Henley use behavior modification instead of other approaches (e.g., a change in leadership style, team building, or employee training) to address this issue?

References

Chapter 1

1. Adapted from Laabs, J.J. Hewlett-Packard's core values drive HR strategy. *Personnel Journal,* 1993, 72(12), 38–46; Deutschman, A. How H-P continues to grow and grow. *Fortune* May 2, 1994, 90–96; Hage, D. and Grant, L. How to make America work. *U.S. News & World Report,* December 6, 1993, 48–53.

2. Lei, D., and Slocum, J.W., Jr. Global strategic alliances: Payoffs and pitfalls. *Organizational Dynamics,* Winter 1991, 44–62.

3. Sherman, S.S. Smart ways to handle the press. *Fortune,* June 19, 1989, 69–75.

4. Goren, B. Personal interview, September 1994, Dallas.

5. McDonald's net rose 16% in period, topped $1 billion for year. *Wall Street Journal,* January 28, 1994, C13; Casper, C. Hot heros. *Restaurant Business,* January 20, 1994, 109–114.

6. Adapted from BE automobile dealer of the year. *Black Enterprise,* June 1993, 123–129.

7. Vogel, T., and Hawkins, C. Can UPS deliver goods in the new world? *Business Week,* June 4, 1990, 80–82.

8. Katz, D. *Just Do It: The NIKE Spirit in the Corporate World.* Toronto: Random House, 1994.

9. Adapted from McGill, M.E., and Slocum, J.W., Jr. *The Smarter Organization.* New York: John Wiley & Sons, 1994.

10. Mintzberg, H. *The Nature of Managerial Work.* New York: Harper & Row, 1973.

11. Maxon, T. Fare-market competition. *Dallas Morning News,* August 21, 1994, H1.

12. Fox, B. Staying on top with Wal-Mart. *Chain Store Age Executive,* April 1994, 47–49; Saporito, B. And the winner is still. . . Wal-Mart. *Fortune,* May 2, 1994, 62–68.

13. Adapted from Eyerdam, R. Wayne's world topsy-turvy. *South Florida Business Journal,* January 14, 1994, 1–3; Fabrikant, G. Blockbuster's chief viewed as wary on Viacom deal. *New York Times,* March 25, 1994, C6; Boroughs, D. Pressing fast-forward; Wayne Huizenga quickly pushes Blockbuster beyond video rentals. *U.S. News & World Report,* May 16, 1994, 53–56.

14. Kraut, A.I., Pegrego, P.R., McKenna, D.D., and Dunnette, M.D. The role of the manager: What's really important in different management jobs. *Academy of Management Executive,* 1989, 3, 286–293.

15. John Burson does it all. *Ft. Lauderdale Sun-Sentinel,* January 24, 1994.

16. Trevino, L.K. Moral reasoning and business ethics: Implications for research, education and management. *Journal of Business Ethics,* 1992, 11, 445–459; Trevino, L.K. *Business Ethics.* New York: John Wiley & Sons, 1995.

17. Adapted from Fuschsberg, G. Sears reinstates sales incentives in some centers. *Wall Street Journal,* March 7, 1994, B1, B6; Paine, L.S. Managing for organizational integrity. *Harvard Business Review,* March-April 1994, 106–117.

18. Johnson, W.B. Global work force 2000: The new world labor market. *Harvard Business Review,* March–April 1991, 115–127; Cox, T., Jr. *Cultural Diversity in Organizations.* San Francisco: Berett-Koehler, 1994.

19. Powell, G.N. and Butterfield, D.A. Investigating the "glass ceiling" phenomenon: An empirical study of actual promotions to top management. *Academy of Management Journal,* 1994, 37, 68–87.

20. Adapted from Roddick, A. *Body and Soul.* New York: Crown Trade Paperbacks, 1991; Bartlett, C.A. *The Body* Shop International. Boston: Harvard Business School, Case #9-392-032, rev. ed., April, 1994.

21. Reich, R. *The Work of Nations.* New York: Vintage Press, 1991.

22. Castro, J. Get set: Here they come. *Time Special Issue: Women, the Road Ahead.* Fall 1990, 50–52.

23. Mitroff, I.I., Mason, R.O., and Pearson, C.M. *Framebreak.* San Francisco: Jossey-Bass, 1994; Marks, M.L. *From Turmoil to Triumph.* New York: Lexington Books, 1994.

24. Hoskisson, R.E., and Hitt, M.A. *Downscoping.* New York: Oxford University Press, 1994.

25. Turnage, J.J. The challenge of the new workplace technology in psychology. *American Psychologist,* 1990, 45, 171–178; Hakim, C. *We Are All Self-Employed.* San Francisco: Berrett-Koehler, 1994.

26. Parker, G.M. *Cross-Functional Teams.* San Francisco: Jossey-Bass, 1994; Manz, C.C., and Sims, H.P., Jr. *Business Without Bosses.* New York: John Wiley & Sons, 1994.

27. Cox, T. The multicultural organization. *Academy of Management Executive,* 1991, 5, 34–47; Fernandez, J.P., and Barr, M. *The Diversity Advantage.* New York: Lexington Books, 1994.

28. Noer, D.M. *Healing the Wounds.* San Francisco: Jossey-Bass, 1993.

29. Root, F.R. *Entry Strategies for International Markets.* New York: Lexington Books, 1994; Pucik, V., Tichy, N.M., and Barnett, C.K. *Globalizing Management.* New York: John Wiley & Sons, 1994.

30. Gavin. D. How the Baldrige award really works. *Harvard Business Review,* November–December 1991, 80–95; Snyder, N.H., Dowd, J.J., Jr., and Houghton, D.M. *Vision, Values & Courage.* New York: Free Press, 1994.

31. Loudermilk, S. Motorola continues to go mobile. *PC Week,* April 12, 1993, 54–55; Carson, P. Motorola to expand pager manufacturing. *South Florida Business Journal,* April 23, 1993, 1A–3A; Pope, K. Motorola plans a new pager for next year. *Wall Street Journal,* April 8, 1994, B2.

32. Katz, R.L. Skills of an effective administrator. *Harvard Business Review,* January–February 1974, 90–101.

33. Wriston, W.B. The state of American management. *Harvard Business Review,* January–February 1990, 78–83.

34. Bloom, B.S. *Taxonomy of Educational Objectives.* New York: David McKay, 1958.

35. Abegglen, J.C. *Sea Change.* New York: Free Press, 1994.

36. Walton, M. *The Deming Management Method.* New York: Dodd, Mead, 1986.

37. Adapted with permission from *The 1994 Annual: Developing Human Resources.* San Diego: Pfieffer, 1994, The Diversity Quiz.

38. Adapted from Tichy, N.M. Revolutionize your company. *Fortune,* December 13, 1993, 114–117; Tichy, N.M., and Sherman, S. Walking the talk at GE. *Training & Development,* June 1993, 26–36.

39. Adapted from Interview with Lou Gerstner, *Fortune,* May 31, 1993; Big blue language, *Fortune,* October 18, 1993; An exclusive account of Lou Gerstner's first six months, *Business Week,* October 4, 1993; Gerstner vows better service, lower prices, *Computerworld,* January 17, 1994; Lou Gerstner unveils his battle plan, *Business Week,* April 4, 1994; August 1994; Gerstner to staff: Don't relax, *Computerworld,* August 15, 1994; Sherman, S. Is he too cautious to save IBM? *Fortune,* October 3, 1994; Sager, I., and Cortese, A. IBM: Why the good news is not good enough. *Business Week,* January 23, 1995.

Chapter 2

1. Stewart, T.A. Managing in a wired company. *Fortune,* July 11, 1994, 44–60.

2. Weber, M. *The Theory of Social and Economic Organization,* trans. by M.A. Henderson and T. Parsons. New York: Free Press, 1947. Also see Wren, D.A. Management history: Issues and ideas for teaching and research. *Journal of Management,* 1987, 13, 239–250.

3. Howard, R. The CEO as organizational architect: An interview with Xerox's Paul Allaire. *Harvard Business Review,* September-October 1992, 106–123.

4. Hummel, R.P. *The Bureaucratic Experience.* New York: St. Martins, 1987.

5. Adapted from Salwen, K.G., and Thomas, P. Beltway bog—How Washington frustrates change. *Wall Street Journal,* December 16, 1993, 1A.

6. Labich, K. Big changes at big brown. *Fortune,* January 18, 1988, 56–64; Sonnenfeld, J.A. A year of living differently. *Harvard Business School Bulletin,* June 1987, 47–50; Karlgaard, R. An interview with Frank Erbrick, Vice-President of Information Services. *Forbes,* October 25, 1993, 69–74.

7. Taylor, F.W. *Scientific Management.* New York: Harper & Row, 1947, 66–71.

8. Koontz, H. The management theory jungle revisited. *Academy of Management Review,* 1980, 5, 175–188.

9. Krajewski, L.J., and Ritzman, L.P. *Operations Management: Strategy and Analysis,* 3rd ed. Reading, Mass.: Addison-Wesley, 1990.

10. Apte, U.M., and Reynolds, C.C. Quality management at Kentucky Fried Chicken. *Interfaces,* 1995 (in press).

11. Fayol, H. *General and Industrial Management.* London: Pitman and Sons, 1949.

12. Follett, M.P. Dynamic administration. In Metcalf, H., and Urwick, L.F. (eds.), *Dynamic Administration: The Collected Papers of Mary Parker Follett.* New York: Harper & Row, 1942.

13. Adapted from Reed, J., and Cunningham, R. *Team Member General Information Guidebook.* Austin, Tex.: Whole Foods Market, 1993.

14. Barnard, C. *The Functions of the Executive.* Cambridge, Mass.: Harvard University Press, 1938.

15. Mayo, E. *The Social Problems of an Industrial Civilization.* Boston: Harvard Business School, 1945.

16. Greenwood, R., Bolton, A., and Greenwood, R. Hawthorne: A half century later: Relay participants remember. *Journal of Management,* 1983, 9, 217–231; Sonnenfeld, J.A. Shedding light on the Hawthorne studies. *Journal of Occupational Behavior,* 1985, 6, 111–130.

17. Adapted from Labbs, J.L. Family issues are a priority at Stride Rite. *Personnel Journal,* July 1993, 48–56.

18. Wagner, J.A. III. Participation's effect on performance and satisfaction: A reconsideration of the research. *Academy of Management Review,* 1994, 312–330; Kahn, W.A., and Kram, K.E. Authority at work: Internal models and their organizational consequences. *Academy of Management Review,* 1994, 17–50.

19. Markland, R.E., Vickery, S.K., and Davis, R.A. *Operations Management.* St. Paul, Minn.: West, 1995.

20. Reed, S., and Maier, A, Cleared for take-off. *People,* May 2, 1994, 67–72.

21. Adapted from Labbs, J.L. How Gillette grooms global talent. *Personnel Journal,* August 1993, 65–75.

22. Tosi, H. *The Environment/Organization Person Contingency Model: A Neso Approach to the Study of Organizations.* Greenwich, Conn.: JAI Press, 1992.

23. Dean, J.W., Jr., and Evans, J.R. *Quality Management.* St. Paul, Minn.: West, 1994; DeSantis, G., and Poole, M.S. Capturing the complexity of advanced technology use: Adaptive structuration theory. *Organization Science,* 1994, 5, 121–147.

24. Woodward, J. *Industrial Organization: Theory and Practice.* London: Oxford University Press, 1980.

25. For an excellent review of the contingency variables that influence an organization's design, see Huber, G.P., and Glick, W.H. *Organizational Change and Redesign.* New York: Oxford University Press, 1993.

26. Adapted from Marcic, D. Bribery in international business. In *Management International: Cases, Exercises and Readings,* D. Marcic and S.M. Puffer (eds.). St. Paul, Minn.: West, 1994, 93–95.

27. Walton, M. *The Deming Method.* New York: Dodd Mead, 1986; Byrne, J.A. Remembering Deming, the godfather of quality. *Business Week,* January 10, 1994, 45; Dean, J.W., Jr., and Bowen, D.E. Management theory and total quality: Improving research and practice through theory development. *Academy of Management Review,* 1994, 19, 392–418; Spencer, B.A. Models of organization and total quality management: A comparison and critical evaluation. *Academy of Management Review,* 1994, 19, 446–471.

28. Used by permission of Professor R. Keller, College of Business, University of Houston, Houston, Texas, 1995.

29. Adapted from Andre, R. Northern industries. In *Management International: Cases, Exercises and Readings.* D. Marcic and S.M. Puffer (eds.). St.Paul, Minn.: West, 1994, 191–192.

Chapter 3

1. Adapted from Everglades sugar firm signs cleanup accord. *ENR,* January 24, 1994, 14; Everglades clean-up announced. *Sun Sentinel,* July 14, 1993; 1A; U.S. Sugar Corporation. *New Horizon,* July–August, 1993.

2. Smith, G. Mexico. *Business Week,* August 22, 1994, 41–47; Smith, G. NAFTA: A green light for red tape. *Business Week,* July 25, 1994, 48.

3. Dechant, K., and Altman, B. Environmental leadership: From compliance to competitive advantage. *Academy of Management Executive,* 1994, 8(3), 7–27.

4. Cairncross, F. *Costing the Earth: The Challenge for Governments, The Opportunities for Business.* Boston: Harvard Business School Press, 1992, 317–318.

5. Sharpe, R. Unequal opportunity. *Wall Street Journal,* September 14, 1993, 1Aff; Allen, F.E. Work and family (a special report). *Wall Street Journal,* June 21, 1993, 7A; Waterman, R.H., Jr., Waterman, J.A., and Collard, B.A. Toward a career-resilient workforce. *Harvard Business Review,* July–August 1994, 87–95; Pulley, B., and Bailey, J. Management: Pool of qualified blacks expands, but very few sit on corporate boards. *Wall Street Journal,* June 28, 1994, 1B.

6. Blum, T.C., Fields, D.L., and Goodman, J.S. Organizational-level determinants of women in management. *Academy of Management Journal,* 1994, 37, 241–268; Tharenou, P., Latimer, S., and Conroy, D. How do you make it to the top? An examination of the influences on women's and men's managerial advancement. *Academy of Management Journal,* 1994, 37, 899–931.

7. Leonard, J.S. The changing face of employees and employment regulation. *California Management Review,* Winter 1989, 29–38.

8. Richman, L.S. How to get ahead in America. *Fortune,* May 16, 1994, 46–51; Mainiero, L.A. The political seasoning of powerful women executives. *Organizational Dynamics,* Spring 1994, 5–22.

9. Minorities scarce at the top: Women hold 20% of senior spots at large employers. *Triangle Business Journal,* August 30, 1993, 1ff.

10. Schmid, R.E. Latinization of America. *Bryan-College Station Eagle,* March 23, 1990, 7B; Nuiry, O.E. Spin doctors. *Hispanic,* July 1994, 20–26.

11. Adapted from Border crossing. *Business Week,* November 1993, 40–42; deFrost, M. Thinking of a plant in Mexico? *Academy of Management Executive,* 1994, 8, 33–40.

12. Hofstede, G. *Culture's Consequences: International Differences in Work-Related Values.* London: Sage, 1980, 25–28

13. Erez, M., and Earley, P.C. *Culture, Self-Identity and Work.* New York: Oxford University Press, 1993.

14. Aguilar, F.J. *Managing Corporate Ethics.* New York: Oxford University Press, 1994.

15. Martin, J. *Cultures in Organizations.* New York: Oxford University Press, 1993.

16. Hofstede, G. The cultural relativity of the quality of life concept. *Academy of Management Review,* 1984, 9, 389–398. Also see Cartwright, S., and Cooper, C.L. The role of culture compatibility in successful organizational marriage. *Academy of Management Executive,* 1993, 7(2), 57–70.

17. Hofstede, G. National cultures in four dimensions: A research-based theory of cultural dimensions among nations. *International Studies of Management and Organization,* 1983, 13, 46–74; Slocum, J.W., Jr., and Lei, D. Designing global strategic alliances: Integrating cultural and economic factors. In G. Huber and Wm. Glick (eds.), *Organizational Change and Redesign.* New York: Oxford University Press, 1993, 295–322.

18. Adler, N.J. Women in management worldwide. *International Studies of Management and Organizations,* Fall–Winter, 1986–1987, 3–32.

19. D'Aveni, R.A. *Hypercompetition: Managing the Dynamics of Strategic Maneuvering.* New York: Free Press, 1994.

20. Duncan, R.B. What is the right organization structure: A decision tree analysis provides the answer. *Organizational Dynamics,* Winter 1979, 63–69; Bluedorn, A.C., Johnson, R.A., Cartwright, D.K., and Barringer, B.R. The interface and convergence of strategic management and organizational environment domains. *Journal of Management,* 1994, 20, 201–263.

21. Drucker, P.F. *Managing in Turbulent Times.* New York: Harper & Row, 1980, 3, 153–154. Also see, Hamel, G. and Prahalad, C.K. *Competing for the Future.* Boston: Harvard Business School Press, 1994.

22. Adapted from Carter, N.N. Small firms adaptation: Responses of physicians' organizations to regulatory and competitive un-

certainty. *Academy of Management Journal,* 1990, 33, 106–128.

23. Maister, D.H. *Managing the Professional Service Firm.* New York: Free Press, 1993.

24. Porter, M.E. *Competitive Strategy: Techniques for Analyzing Industries and Competitors.* New York: Free Press, 1980.

25. Henderson, B.D. The anatomy of competition. *Journal of Marketing,* Spring 1983, 7–11.

26. Adapted from Wentz, L. Playing from the same rules: Harmonization of children's ads sought via self-regulation. *Advertising Age International Special Report,* December 1991, S-2.

27. Miller, D., and Chen, M. Sources and consequences of competitive inertia: A study of the U.S. airline industry. *Administrative Science Quarterly,* 1994, 39, 1–23.

28. Labich, K. Should airlines be reregulated. *Fortune,* June 19, 1990, 82–90.

29. Adapted from Magnet, M. Let's go for growth. *Fortune,* March 7, 1994, 60–72.

30. Yang, D.J., and O'neal, M. How Boeing does it. *Busness Week,* July 9, 1990, 46–50.

31. Oster, S.M. *Modern Competitive Analysis.* New York: Oxford University Press, 1994.

32. The flying monopolists: Boeing and Airbus should be forbidden to team up to build a super-jumbo. *The Economist,* June 19, 1993, 20–21; Wilhelm, S. Boeing nosedive won't end soon. *Puget Sound Business Journal,* January 29, 1993, 1–3; Tully, S. Can Boeing reinvent itself? *Fortune,* March 8, 1993, 66–68, 72–73.

33. Lei, D., and Slocum, J.W., Jr. Global strategy, competence building and strategic alliances. *California Management Review,* Fall 1992, 81–97.

34. Henderson, R.M. Technological change and the management of architectural knowledge. In Kochan T.A., and Useem, M. (eds.), *Transforming Organizations.* New York: Oxford University Press, 1992, 118–132.

35. Quinn, J.B., and Maily, M.N. Information technology: Increasing productivity in services. *Academy of Management Executive,* 1994, 8(3), 28–51.

36. Harbison, E.H., Jr. Society and technology. *World Link,* January–February 1990, 28–30.

37. Zammuto, R.F., and O'Connor, E.J. Gaining advanced manufacturing technologies benefits: The roles of organization design and culture. *Academy of Management Review,* 1992, 17, 701–728.

38. Adapted from Bylinsky, G. A U.S. comeback in electronics. *Fortune,* April 20, 1992, 77–84; Tetzeli, R. Cargo that phones home. *Fortune,* November 15, 1993, 143–144; Deutschman, A. The next big infotech battle. *Fortune,* November 29, 1993, 38–46; Levine, J.B., Shares, G.E., Flynn, J., Dwyer, P., and Rossant, J. The continent's wakeup call. *Business Week,* December 20, 1993, 96–99.

39. Bazerman, M.H., and Neale, M.A. *Negotiating Rationally.* New York: Free Press, 1992.

40. Dalton, D.R., Metzger, M.B., and Hill, J.W. The new corporate sentencing commission guidelines: A wake-up call for corporate America. *Academy of Management Executive,* 1994 8(1), 7–17.

41. Levitan, S., and Cooper, M. *Business Lobbies: The Public Good and the Bottom Line.* Baltimore: Johns Hopkins Press, 1984.

42. Mitchell, L.A. Small manufacturer, big role. *Arizona Business Gazette,* June 23, 1994, 1.

43. Clark, L.H., Jr. Speaking of business: How the biggest lobby grew. *Wall Street Journal,* January 27, 1994, 14A.

44. Brinkerhoff, R.O., and Gill, S.J. *International Multilateral Negotiation.* San Francisco: Jossey-Bass, 1994.

45. Rugman, A.M., and Hodgetts, R. *International Business: A Strategic Approach.* New York: McGraw-Hill, 1995.

46. Merchant, H. The expected performance of international joint ventures: An event study approach. Paper presented at *Second World Conference on Management,* International Federation of Scholarly Associations of Management, Dallas, August, 1994.

47. Stearns, L.B. Board composition and corporate financing: The impact of financial institution representation on borrowing. *Academy of Management Journal,* 1993, 36, 603–618.

48. Graves, S.B., and Waddock, S.A. Institutional owners and corporate social performance. *Academy of Management Journal,* 1994, 37, 1034–1046.

49. Welch, J. Speed and simplicity. *Harvard Business Review,* September–October 1989, 112–116.

50. Adapted from Budner, S. Intolerance for ambiguity. *Journal of Personality,* 1962, 30, 29–59.

51. Adapted from U.S. car image improves. *Detroit Free Press,* February 17, 1994; The electric tropica. *Car and Driver,* March, 1994; Saturn doesn't foresee being in neon's mirror. *Automotive News,* February 7, 1994; Suris, O. Supercar draws federal funds to big three. *Wall Street Journal,* February 17, 1994. 1B.

52. Adapted from *Glaxco Annual Report,* 1993; Training key to success in sales, *Toronto Star,* November 11, 1993; Drug firms join forces, *News and Observer,* July 29, 1993; Faces behind the figures, *Forbes,* August 2, 1993; Glaxo to join with Warner to push OTC drugs, *Marketing,* December 16, 1993; Having an ulcer is getting a lot cheaper, *Business Week,* May 9, 1994.

Chapter 4

1. Adapted from Smith, G. Mexico's no frills mogul. *Business Week,* March 7, 1994, 62–64; Perry, N.J. What's powering Mexico's success. *Fortune,* February 10, 1992, 109–115; Smith, G., Baker, S., and Glasgall, W. Mexico: Will economic reform survive the turmoil? *Business Week,* April 11, 1994, 24–27; Malklin, E. Will rivals unplug Telmex? Don't bet on it. *Business Week,* September 19, 1994, 102.

2. Kinnock, N. Beyond free trade to fair trade. *California Management Review,* Summer 1994, 12–135.

3. Stewart, T.A. Welcome to the revolution. *Fortune,* December 13, 1993, 66–77.

4. Ibid.

5. Sesit, M.R. Flocking to the frontier. *Wall Street Journal,* September 24, 1993, R4; Institute for the Future. *Global Opportunities: Searching for Markets and Working Across Borders.* Corporate Associates Program, Vol. 4., No. 1. Menlo Park, Calif.: Institute for the Future, 1993.

6. O'Hara-Devereaux, M., and Johansen, R. *Global Work: Bridging Distance, Culture, and Time.* San Francisco: Jossey-Bass, 1994, 4–30.

7. Cavaleri, S., and Obloj, K. *Management Systems: A Global Perspective.* Belmont, Calif.: Wadsworth, 1993, 31–38.

8. Adapted from Barrier, M., and Zuckerman, A. Quality standards the world agrees on. *Nation's Business,* May 1994, 71–73; Zuckerman, A. ISO 9000: A program in transition. *Trade & Culture,* September–October 1994, 24–28; Omachanu, V.K., and Ross, J.E. *Principles of Total Quality.* Delray Beach, Fla.: St. Lucie Press, 1994, 271–288.

9. Woodcock, C.P., Beamish, P.W., and Makino, S. Ownership-based entry mode strategies and international performance. *Journal of International Business Studies,* 1994, 25, 253–273.

10. Sullivan, D. Measuring the degree of internationalization of a firm. *Journal of International Business Studies,* 1994, 25, 325–342.

11. Adapted from Farnham, A. Global or just globaloney? *Fortune,* June 27, 1994, 97–100.

12. Daniel, J.D., and Radebaugh, L.H. *International Business: Environments and Operations,* 6th ed., rev. Reading, Mass.: Addison-Wesley, 1994.

13. Adapted from Roha, R.R. Making it big overseas. *Kiplinger's Personal Finance Magazine, November 1992, 95–97.*

14. Dunning, J.H. *Multinational Enterprises and the Global Economy.* Reading, Mass.: Addison-Welsey, 1994.

15. Out from the salt mines. *Forbes,* January 3, 1994, 115; *1993 Morton International Annual Report,* 1994.

16. Beamish, P.W., Killing, J.P., and LeCraw, D.J. *International Management: Text and Cases,* 2nd ed. Burr Ridge, Ill: Irwin, 1994.

17. Rosenzweig, P.M. The new American challenge: Foreign multinationals in the United States. *California Management Review,* Spring 1994, 107–123.

18. Mallory, M. Behemoth on a tear. *Business Week,* October 3, 1994, 54–55; Pearce, J.A. II, and Robinson, R.B., Jr. *Formulation Implementation and Control of Competitive Strategy.* Burr Ridge, Ill.: Irwin, 1994, 135–139, 328–336, 375–379.

19. Ghoshal, S., and Nohria, N. Horses for courses: Organizational forms for multinational corporations. *Sloan Management Review,* Winter 1993, 23–35.

20. Cox, H., Clegg, J., and Letto-Gillies, G. (Eds.) *The Growth of Global Business.* New York: Routledge, 1994.

21. Harbrecht, D. Exports: This show has legs. Business Week, September 19, 1994, 48–49.

22. *Form 10-K for Harley-Davidson, Inc.* Milwaukee, 1994.

23. Zurawicki, L. *International Countertrade.* New York: Pergamon, 1994.

24. Agmon, T., and Drobnick, R. *Small Firms in Global Competition.* New York: Oxford University Press, 1994.

25. Rebello, K., Sager, I., and Brandt, R. Spindler's Apple. *Business Week,* October 3, 1994, 88–96; Carlton, J. Apple will be more aggressive about licensing Power Mac line. *Wall Street Journal,* September 19, 1994, E6.

26. Hisrich, R.D., and Peters, M.P.

Entrepreneurship: Starting, Developing, and Managing a New Enterprise. Burr Ridge, Ill.: Irwin, 1995, 510–530.

27. Doolin, W. Taking your business on the road abroad. *Wall Street Journal,* July 25, 1994, A16.

28. Lanier, S. Joint ventures are not just for giants. *Trade & Culture,* September–October 1994, 37–38.

29. Kanter, R.M. Collaborating advantage: Successful partnerships manage the relationship, not just the deal. *Harvard Business Review,* July–August 1994, 96–108; Grossman, L.M. Royal crown seeks to boost Mexican sales. *Wall Street Journal,* September 20, 1994, A10; Walters, B.A., Peters, S., and Dess, G.G. Strategic alliances and joint ventures: Making them work. *Business Horizons,* July–August 1994, 5–10.

30. Pucek, V., Tichy, N.M., and Barnett, C.K. *Globalizing Management: Creating and Leading the Competitive Organization.* New York: John Wiley & Sons, 1993.

31. Pearce, J.A. II, and Robinson, R.B., Jr. *Formulation, Implementation, and Control of Competitive Strategy.* Burr Ridge, Ill.: Irwin, 1994, 328–336.

32. Weber, J. Campbell: Now it's M-M-global. *Business Week.* March 15, 1993, 52–54.

33. Caminiti, S. A star is born. *Fortune.* Autumn/Winter 1993, 44–47.

34. Yip, G. *Total Global Strategy.* Englewood Cliffs, N.J.: Prentice-Hall, 1995.

35. The world according to Andy Grove. *Business Week/The Information Revolution,* Special Issue 1994, 76–78.

36. Arnst, C, and Edmondson, G. The global free-for-all. *Business Week,* September 26, 1994, 118–126.

37. Adapted from Meeks, F. Watch out Motorola. *Forbes,* September 12, 1994, 192–198; Kennedy, C. How Nokia is going high tech. *Long Range Planning,* April 1992, 16–25; Zipper, S., and Lineback, J.R. Tandy sets cellular sale to Nokia. *Electronic News,* July 12, 1993, 11.

38. Alkhafaji, A.F. *Competitive Global Management: Principles and Strategies.* Delray Beach, Fla.: St. Lucie Press, 1995.

39. Coplin, W.D., and O'Leary, M.K. *The Handbook of Country and Political Risk Analysis.* East Syracuse, N.Y.: Political Risk Services, 1994, 3–9.

40. Ibid.

41. Holt, D.H., Ralston, D.A., and Terpstra, R.H. Constraints on capitalism in Russia: The managerial psyche, social infrastructure, and ideology. *California Management Review,* Spring 1994, 124–141.

42. The cost of export controls. *Fortune,* October 3, 1994, 29.

43. Mintz, B. When national security, economies conflict. *Houston Chronicle,* August 29, 1993, 1E, 7E.

44. Adapted from Rayfield, G. General Motors political risks ratings: Assessment of a track record. In Rodgers, J. (Ed.). *Global Risk Assessment: Issues, Concepts, and Applications,* Riverside, Calif.: Global Risk Assessment, 1988, 172–186.

45. Ignatius, A. GM dealer hits rough road in Russia. *Wall Street Journal,* July 28, 1994, A15.

46. Berman, P., and Khalaf, R. The Fanjuls of Palm Beach: The family with a sweet tooth. *Forbes,* May 14, 1990, 56–69.

47. *Investment Mission Program for U.S. Business Executives.* Washington, D.C.: Overseas Private Investment Corporation, 1987.

48. Stocking, G.W., and Watkins, M.W. *Cartels or Competition?* New York: Twentieth Century Fund, 1984, 3.

49. Agmon, T., and Drobnick, R. *Small Firms in Global Competition.* New York: Oxford University Press, 1994.

50. Pennar, K. The destructive costs of greasing palms. *Business Week,* December 6, 1993, 133–138.

51. Jacoby, N.H., Nehemkis, P., and Ells, R. *Bribery and Extortion in World Business.* New York: Macmillan, 1977, 90.

52. Interviews. The Russian investment dilemma. *Harvard Business Review,* May–June 1994, 35–44.

53. Boddewyn, J.J., and Brewer, T.L International-business political behavior: New theoretical directions. *Academy of Management Review,* 1994, 19, 119–143.

54. Greanias, G.C., and Windsor, D. *The Foreign Corrupt Practices Act: Anatomy of a Statute,* Lexington, Mass.: Lexington Books, 1982.

55. Example provided by P.A. Golden, Florida International University, 1994.

56. Dryden, S. *The Trade Warriors: USTR and the American Crusade for Free Trade.* New York: Oxford University Press, 1995.

57. Harbrecht, D. GATT: It's yesterday's agreement. *Business Week,* December 27, 1993, 36.

58. Schlegel, P.K., and Cowan, M.E. The General Agreement on Tariffs and Trade. Technical Note. Charlottesville, Va.: Darden Graduate Business School Foundation, 1988.

59. Adapted from Antosh, N. U.S. beekeepers seek relief from Chinese honey imports. *Houston Chronicle,* October 5, 1994, 1B, 6B.; Flynn, A.A. New U.S. recipe for China relations: More honey, less vinegar. *China Business Review,* November/December 1993, 4–5.

60. Davis, B., and Hamilton, D.P. U.S. trade pact with Japanese is a trade-off. *Wall Street Journal,* October 3, 1994, A2, A8.

61. This section is based substantially on Gruben, W.C., and Welch, J.H. Is NAFTA economic integration. *Economic Review,* Second quarter 1994, 35–51.

62. Bierman, L., Fraser, D.R., and Kolari, J.W. NAFTA: A market analysis. *Vanderbilt Journal of Transnational Law* (in press).

63. Rudman, A.M. A Canadian perspective on NAFTA. *International Executive,* January/February 1994, 33–54.

64. Gumbel, P. Customs of the countries. *Wall Street Journal,* September 30. 1994, R10.

65. Story, J. *The New Europe: Politics, Government and Economy Since 1945.* Cambridge, Mass.: Blackwell, 1993.

66. Roth, T. Gordion knot. *Wall Street Journal,* September 30, 1994, R4.

67. Rapoport, C. The new U.S. push into Europe. *Fortune,* January 10, 1994, 73–74.

68. Dykes, H. Watch on the EC: Investment opportunities. *Business Strategy,* March/April 1993, 22–25; Calingaert, M. Government-business relations in the European Community. *California Management Review,* Winter 1993, 118–133.

69. Maruca, R.F. The right way to go global: An interview with Whirlpool CEO David Whitwam. *Harvard Business Review,* March–April 1994, 134–145.

70. Gannon, M.J., and Associates. *Understanding Global Cultures: Metaphorical Journeys Through 17 Countries.* Thousand Oaks, Calif.: Sage, 1994.

71. Meyer, C. *Fast Cycle Time: How to Align Purpose Strategy and Structure for Speed.* New York: Free Press, 1993.

72. Goldman, D.P. The Mexican revolution: Phase II. *Forbes,* October 25, 1993, 132–135.

73. Tung, R.L. Strategic management thought in East Asia. *Organizational Dynamics,* Spring 1994, 55–65.

74. Adapted from deForest, M.E. Thinking of a plant in Mexico? *Academy of Management Executive,* February 1994, 33–40.

75. Adapted from Mitchell, R., and O'Neal, M. Managing by values: Is Levi Strauss approach visionary—or flaky! *Business Week,* August 1, 1994, 46–52; Zachary, G.P. Levi tries to make sure contract plants in Asia treat workers well. *Wall Street Journal,* July 28, 1994, A1, A5; Doing the right things. *Business Ethics,* July/August 1993, 9.

76. Morris, M.H., Davis, D.L., and Allen, J.W. Fostering entrepreneurship: Cross-cultural comparisons of the importance of individualism versus collectivism. *Journal of International Business Studies,* 1994, 25, 65–89.

77. Hodgson, J. *The Wondrous World of Japan.* Washington, D.C.: American Enterprise Institute, 1978, 3.

78. Beecher, S., and Zhuang Yang, J. The transfer of Japanese-style management to American subsidiaries: Contingencies, constraints and competencies. *Journal of International Business Studies,* 1994, 25, 467–491.

79. Elger, T., and Smith, C. (Eds.) *Global Japanization.* New York: Rutledge, 1994.

80. Williams, M. Toyota creates work contracts challenging lifetime-job system. *Wall Street Journal,* January 24, 1994, A10.

81. Schlender, R.R. Japan: Is it changing for good? *Fortune,* June 13, 1994, 123–134.

82. Cody, J. To forge ahead, Career women are venturing out of Japan. *Wall Street Journal,* August 29, 1994, B1.

83. Characteristics used in this instrument were developed from Kras, E.S. *Management in Two Cultures.* Yarmouth, Me.: Intercultural Press, 1988; Casse, P., and Deol, S. *Managing Intercultural Negotiations.* Washington, D.C.: Setnar International, 1985.

84. This case was presented originally by Professors Ellen Cook, Phillip Hunsaker, and Mohammed Ali Alireza, all of the University of San Diego, as a basis for class discussion rather than to illustrate either effective or ineffective handling of an administrative situation. Copyright 1984 by Ellen Cook, Phillip Hunsaker, and Mohammed Ali Alireza. Adapted with permission.

85. Business in China: A wild card, *Fortune,* November 1, 1993; Chine: Struggle for control, The *Economist,* December 25, 1993; Nirvana by numbers, *Fortune,* December 27, 1993; To get in on growth in Asia, try U.S. companies already there, *Business Week,* January 31, 1994; China: Birth of a new economy, *The Economist,* April 16, 1994; Multinationals in Asia: Slow car to China, *Business Marketing,* May 1994; U.S. marketers work to secure MFN for China, *China Business Review,* September/October 1994; Tucker, M.F., and Chen, S. China: Building business relation-

ships in Asia. *Trade & Culture,* January-February 1995

Chapter 5

1. Adapted from Banks, H. A sixties industry in a nineties economy. *Forbes,* May 9, 1994, 107–112; Labich, K. Is Herb Kelleher America's best CEO? *Fortune,* May 2, 1994, 45–52; Quick, J.C. Crafting an organizational culture: Herb's hand at Southwest Airlines. *Organizational Dynamics,* Autumn 1992, 45–55.

2. Lorange, P. *Strategic Planning and Control.* Cambridge, Mass.: Blackwell, 1993.

3. Redding, J.C., and Catalanello, R.F. *Strategic Readiness: The Making of the Learning Organization.* San Francisco: Jossey-Bass, 1994; AT&T study warns: If you fail to plan, plan to fail. *Managing Office Technology,* February 1994, 28–29.

4. Bhide, A. How entrepreneurs craft strategies that work. *Harvard Business Review,* March–April 1994, 150–161.

5. O'Brian, B. Southwest Airlines fares well, despite getting the boot. *Wall Street Journal,* August 3, 1994, B4.

6. Does G.E. really plan better? *MBA,* 1975, 9; 42–45.

7. Nutt, P.C., and Backoff, R.W. Strategic issues as tensions. *Journal of Management Inquiry,* 1993, 2, 28–42.

8. Hart, S., and Banbury, C. How strategy-making processes can make a difference. *Strategic Management Journal,* 1994, 15, 251–269.

9. Ansoff, H.I., and Sullivan, P.A. Optimizing profitability in turbulent environments: A formula for strategic success. *Long Range Planning,* October 1993, 11–23.

10. Mintzberg, H. *The Rise and Fall of Strategic Planning.* New York: Free Press, 1994.

11. Adapted from Austin, B. Book Review of *The Rise and Fall of Strategic Planning. Academy of Management Executive,* August 1994, 109–111.

12. Thompson, A.A., Jr., and Strickland, A.J. III. *Strategic Management: Concepts and Cases,* 7th ed. Burr Ridge, Ill.: Irwin, 1995.

13. Bloom, M.J., and Menefee, M.K. Scenario planning and contingency planning. *Public Productivity and Management Review,* 1994, 17, 223–231.

14. Egan, G. *Adding Value: A Systematic Guide to Business-Driven Management and Leadership.* San Francisco: Jossey-Bass, 1993.

15. *Southwest Airlines 1993 Annual Report.* Dallas: Southwest Airlines, 1994.

16. *AT&T 1993 Annual Report.* New York: AT&T, 1994.

17. *Cupertino National Bancorp 1993 Annual Report.* Cupertino, Calif.: Cupertino National Bancorp, 1994.

18. *Reader's Digest Association Inc. 1993 Annual Report.* Pleasantville, N.Y.: Reader's Digest Association, Inc., 1994.

19. Quigley, J.V. Vision: How leaders develop it, share, and sustain it. *Business Horizons,* September–October 1994, 37–41.

20. Teitelbaum, R.S. Where service flies right. *Fortune,* August 24, 1992, 115–116.

21. *AT&T 1993 Annual Report.* New York: AT&T, 1994.

22. *General Motors 1993 Annual Report.* Detroit: General Motors Corporation, 1994.

23. Labich, K. Is Herb Kelleher America's best CEO? *Fortune,* May 2, 1994, 43–52.

24. *Reader's Digest Association Inc. 1993 Annual Report,* Pleasantville, N.Y.: Reader's Digest Association, Inc., 1994.

25. Shivastava, P. *Strategic Management: Concepts and Cases.* Cincinnati: South-Western, 1994.

26. Shank, J.K., and Govindarajan, V. *Strategic Cost Management: The New Tool for Competitive Advantage.* New York: Free Press, 1993.

27. Sherman, S. Is he too cautious to save IBM? *Fortune,* October 3, 1994, 78–90.

28. O'Brian, B. Southwest Air says it will add longer flights. *Wall Street Journal,* July 5, 1994, A3, A6.

29. Adapted from Caggiano, C. The profit-promoting daily scorecard. *INC,* May 1994, 101–103.

30. Lubatkin, M., and Chatterje, S. Extending modern portfolio theory into the domain of corporate diversification: Does it apply? *Academy of Management Journal,* 1994, 37, 109–136.

31. *General Motors 1993 Annual Report.* Detroit: General Motors Corporation, 1994.

32. Hoskisson, R.E., and Hitt, M.A. *Downscoping: How to tame the diversified firm.* New York: Oxford University Press, 1994.

33. Buckeley, W.M. Conglomerates make a surprising comeback—With a '90s twist. *Wall Street Journal,* March 1, 1994, A1, A6.

34. Adapted from Kraar, L. Korea goes for quality. *Fortune,* April 18, 1994, 153–158; Nakarmi, L., and Neff, R. Samsung's radical shakeup: Chairman Lee Kun-hee is formenting a management revolution. *Business Week,* February 28, 1994, 74–76; Nakarmi, L. Samsung: Korea's great hope for high tech. *Business Week,* February 3, 1992, 44–45; Ristelhueber, R. Samsung's next step. *Electronic Business Buyer,* February 1994, 46–50+.

35. Goold, M., and Luchs, K. Why diversify? Four decades of management thinking. *Academy of Management Executive,* August 1993, 7–26; Pennings, J.M., Barkema, H., and Douma, S. Organizational learning and diversification. *Academy of Management Journal,* 1994, 37, 608–640.

36. *Dick Clark Productions, Inc., 1993 Annual Report.* Los Angeles, Calif.: Dick Clark Productions, Inc., 1994.

37. Ibid.

38. O'Reilly, B. Why Merck married the enemy. *Fortune.* September 20, 1993, 60–64.

39. Borrus, A. Mergers today, trouble tomorrow? *Business Week,* September 12, 1994, 30–33.

40. *Chrysler Corporation 1993 Annual Report.* Highland Park, Mich.: Chrysler Corporation, 1994.

41. Kirkpatrick, A. Could AT&T rule the world? *Fortune,* May 17, 1993, 55–66.

42. Gubernick, L. Carry on, Mr. Sheinberg. *Forbes,* July 18, 1994, 72–73.

43. Zellner, W. Dogfight over California. *Business Week,* August 15, 1994, 32.

44. Adapted from Banks, H. A sixties industry in a nineties economy. *Forbes,* May 9, 1994, 107–112; O'Brian, B. Southwest Air says it will add longer flights. *Wall Street Journal,* July 5, 1994, A3, A6; Baird, J. Southwest flying its own route to success. *Houston Chronicle,* October 25, 1992, 1E, 4E.

45. Lado, A.A., and Wilson, M.C. Human resource systems and sustained competitive advantage: A competency based perspective. *Academy of Management Review,* 1994, 19, 699–727; Schuler, R.S., Dowling, P.J., and De Cieri, H. An integrative framework of strategic international human resource management. *International Journal of Human Resource Management,* 1993, 4, 717–764.

46. Adapted from Quick, J.C. Crafting an organizational culture: Herb's hand at Southwest Airlines. *Organizational Dynamics,* Autumn 1992, 34–44; Labich, K. Is Herb Kelleher America's best CEO? *Fortune,* May 2, 1994, 44–52; Barrett, C. Service turbulent decade, HR excels. *Personnel Journal,* January 1994, 54–55.

47. Rajagopalan, N., Rasheed, A.M.A., and Datta, D.K. Strategic decision processes: Critical review and future directions. *Journal of Management,* 1993, 19, 349–384.

48. Adapted from Plevel, M.J., Lane, F., Nellis, S., and Schuler, R.S. AT&T Global Business Communications Systems: Linking HR with business strategy. *Organizational Dynamics,* Winter 1994, 59–71; Anfuso, D. Through AT&T's begin at home: Southwest Airlines' employee service program. *Sales Marketing Management,* March 1994, 27–28; Bovier, C. Teamwork: The heart of an airline. *Training,* June 1993, 53–55+.

49. Benveniste, G. *Mastering the Politics of Planning.* San Francisco: Jossey-Bass, 1989.

50. Porter, M.E. *Competitive Strategy: Techniques for Analyzing Industries and Competitors.* New York: Free Press, 1980; Porter, *M.E. Competitive Advantage: Creating and Sustaining Superior Performance.* New York: Free Press, 1985. See also Porac, J.F., and Thomas, H. Taxonomic mental models in competitor definition. *Academy of Management Review,* 1990, 15, 224–240.

51. Fenster, J.M. Detroit opens the door for Japan. *Audacity,* Winter 1993, 28–37.

52. Hamel, G. and Prahalad, C.K. *Competing for the Future: Breakthrough Strategies for Seizing Control of Your Industry and Creating the Strategies of Tomorrow.* Boston: Harvard Business School Press, 1994.

53. Keller, M. Collision: *GM, Toyota, Volkswagen and the Race to Own the 21st Century.* New York: Doubleday, 1993.

54. Porter, M.E. *Competitive Strategy,* 24–27.

55. Ibid., 27–28.

56. *Compaq Computer Corporation 1993 Annual Report.* Houston: Compaq Computer Corporation 1994.

57. Treece, J.B. ALCOA want to take its show on the road. *Business Week,* August 1, 1994, 58–59.

58. Adapted from Cole, J., and Carey, S. Airlines are keeping aging planes aloft, testing repair rules. *Wall Street Journal,* November 3, 1994, A1, A15; Banks, H. Outfaxed. *Forbes,* May 10, 1993, 40–41; Chandler, S. Nothing but blue sky at Northwest. *Business Week,* October 17, 1994, 190–192; Kleit, A.N. Competition without apology: Market power and entry into the deregulated airline industry. *Regulation,* Summer 1991, 68–75.

59. Zellner, W. Dogfight over California. *Business Week,* August 15, 1994, 32; Zellner, W. This is captain Ferguson, please hang onto your hats. *Business Week,* May 24, 1994, 54–56.

60. Amit, R., and Schoemaker, P.J.H. Strategic assets and organizational rent. *Strategic Management Journal,* 1993, 14, 33–46; McGill, M.E., and Slocum, J.W., Jr. *The Smarter Organization: How to Build a Business That Learns and Adapts to Marketplace Needs.* New York: John Wiley & Sons, 1994.

61. Quinn, J.B., and Helmer, F.G. Strategic outsourcing. *Sloan Management Review,* Summer 1994, 43–55.

62. Taylor, A. III Here come Japan's carmakers—Again. *Fortune,* December 13, 1993, 131–134; Lowry Miller, K. A car is born. *Business Week,* December 13, 1993, 64–73.

63. Taylor III, A. GM's $11 Billion turnaround. *Fortune,* October 17, 1994, 53–74; McWhirter W., and Szczesny, J.R. What went wrong? *Time,* November 9, 1992, 43–51.

64. Hill, C.W.L., and Jones, G.R. *Strategic Management: An Integrated Approach.* Boston: Houghton Mifflin, 1995.

65. Hitt, M.A., Hoskisson, R.E., and Ireland, R.D. *Strategic Management: Theory and Cases.* St. Paul, Minn.: West, 1995.

66. Adapted from Rice, F. How to make diversity pay. *Fortune,* August 8, 1994, 78–86; Anfuso, D. Through AT&T's turbulent decade, HR excels. *Personnel Journal,* January 1994, 54–55.

67. Ohmae, K. *Triad Power: The Coming Shape of Global Competition.* New York: Free Press, 1985.

68. Oster, S.M. *Modern Competitive Analysis,* 2nd ed. New York, Oxford University Press, 1994, 252–288; Anderson, C.R., and Zeithaml, C.P. Stage of the product life cycle, business strategy and business performance. *Academy of Management Journal,* 1984, 27, 5–24.

69. Hayden, C. *The Handbook of Strategic Expertise.* New York: Free Press, 1986, 265–271.

70. Porter, *Competitive Strategy,* 34–46.

71. Miller, A., and Dess, G.G. Assessing Porter's (1980) Model in terms of its generalizability, accuracy, and simplicity. *Journal of Management Studies,* 1993, 30, 553–585.

72. Johnson, H.H. Marzilli's Fine Italian Foods: An introduction to strategic thinking. Adapted from *The 1989 Annual: Developing Human Resources* (pp. 58–59), by J.W. Pfeiffer (Ed.). Copyright © 1989 by Pfeiffer & Company, San Diego, Ca. Used with permission.

73. Adapted from *Carnival Cruise Lines 10-0 Report, 1993;* Dean Witter Reynolds Company Report, August 18, 1993; Islands, Cruise Lines Debate Marine Environment at CTO Talks. *Travel Weekly,* May 17, 1993; Some Cruise Lines May Collapse Before Year 2000, Consultant Warns. *Journal of Commerce and Business,* March 9, 1993; With Shorter Trips, Carnival Attracts First Time Passengers. *Travel Weekly,* September 6, 1993; Marcial, G.C. Carnival's cruise isn't over. *Business Week,* January 24, 1994, 86; Underwood, E. Carnival caught a wave, positioned cruising as fun. *Brandweek,* October 11, 1993, 22–24.

74. Allied-Signal *Form 10-K,* 1993; A master class in radical change, *Fortune,* December 13, 1993; Allied-Signal's no-excuse boss tried, *New York Times,* November 1, 1992; Allied-Signal's turnaround blitz, *Fortune,* November 30, 1992; Reaching for a broader market, *Air Transport World,* March 1993; Corporate focus: Allied-Signal's chairman outlines strategy for growth: He tries new management and manufacturing approaches to boost efficiency, *Wall Street Journal,* August 17, 1993; Turnaround earns Allied new credibility, *Aviation Week & Space Technology,* August 15, 1994.

Chapter 6

1. Adapted from Lubove, S. It ain't broke, but fix it anyway. *Forbes,* August 1, 1994, 56–60; Knight, C.F. Emerson Electric: Consistent profits, consistently. *Harvard Business Review,* January–February 1992, 57–70.

2. Webster, J.L., Reif, W.E., and Bracker, J.S. The manager's guide to strategic planning tools and techniques. *Planning Review,* November/December 1989, 4–12, 47, 48.

3. Boulding, E., and Boulding, K.E. *The Future: Images and Prophecies.* Thousand Oaks, Calif. Sage, 1994.

4. Makridakis, S.G. *Forecasting, Planning, and Strategy for the 21st Century.* New York: Free Press, 1990.

5. Sherman, S. Is he too cautious to save IBM. *Fortune,* October 3, 1994, 78–90.

6. Bloom, M.J., and Menefee, M.K. Scenario planning and contingency planning. *Public Productivity & Management Review,* 1994, 18, 223–230.

7. Foster, J.F. Scenario planning for small businesses. *Long Range Planning,* 1993, 26, 123–129.

8. Henkoff, R. How to plan for 1995. *Fortune,* December 31, 1990, 70–78.

9. Jain, C.L. Delphi—Forecast with experts' opinions. *Journal of Business Forecasting,* Winter 1985–1986, 22–23.

10. Opren, C. The relative accuracy of individual, group, and Delphi process strategic forecasts. In W.D. Guth (ed.), *Handbook of Business Strategy; 1986/1987 Yearbook,* Boston: Warren, Gorham & Lamant, 1986, 19–1–19–9; Kastein, M.R. Delphi, the issues of reliability: A qualitative Delphi study in primary health care in the Netherlands. *Technological Forecasting & Social Change,* 1993, 44, 315–323.

11. Kudon, D.A., and Frankel, M.R. Going to the oracle of strategic planning: The Delphi process. In H.E. Glass (ed.) *Handbook of Business Strategy 1988/1989 Yearbook.* Boston: Warren, Gorham & Lamont, 1988, 1–1–1–10.

12. Hayden, C.L. *The Handbook of Strategic Expertise.* New York: Free Press, 1986, 98–99; de Haan, J., and Peters, R. The future implementation of advanced manufacturing techniques: Experiences from a Dutch Delphi study. *International Journal of Technology Management,* 1993, 8, 282–293.

13. Tumay, K., and Harrell, C. *Simulation of Manufacturing and Service Systems.* Norcross, Ga.: Industrial Engineering & Management Press, 1994.

14. Wild, W.G., Jr., and Port, O. The video "game" is saving manufacturers millions. *Business Week,* August 17, 1987, 82–84; Reiman, M.I., and Weiss, A. Sensitivity analysis for simulations via likelihood ratios. *Operations Research,* 1989, 37, 830–844.

15. McCluskey, J. A primer on virtual reality. *T.H.E. Journal,* December 1992, 56–59; Sheridan, T.B., and Zeltzer, D. Virtual reality check. *Technology Review,* October 1993, 20–28.

16. Senge, P.M. *The Fifth Discipline: The Art and Practice of the Learning Organization.* New York: Doubleday, 1990, 257–259.

17. Adapted from Hamilton, J.O. Virtual reality: How a computer-generated world could change the real world. *Business Week,* October 5, 1992, 97–105; Mitchell, R. Fantastic journeys in virtual labs. *Business Week,* September 19, 1994, 76–88; Winter, D. These games aren't for kids: Virtual reality automobile applications include designing new manufacturing operations and simulating plant layouts and processes. *Ward's Auto World,* December 1993, 86–88.

18. Lane, H.W., and DiStefans, J.J. *International Management Behavior,* 2nd ed. Boston: PWS-Kent, 1992, 20–22.

19. Senge, P.M., Roberts, C., Ross, R.B., Smith, B.J., and Kleiner, A. *The Fifth Discipline Fieldbook: Strategies and Tools for Building a Learning Organization.* New York: Doubleday, 1994, 378–380.

20. Adapted from Hofstede, C. Cultural constraints in management theories. *Academy of Management Executive,* February 1993, 81–94; Kraar, L. The overseas Chinese: Lessons from the world's most dynamic capitalists. *Fortune,* October 31, 1994, 91–114.

21. Mason, R.O. A dialectical approach to strategic planning. *Management Science,* 1969, 15, B402–B414.

22. Mitroff, I.I. *Break-Away Thinking.* New York: John Wiley & Sons, 1988.

23. Chanin, M.N., and Shapiro, H.J. Dialectical inquiry in strategic planning: Extending the boundaries. *Academy of Management Review,* 1985, 10, 663–675.

24. Schwenk, C. A meta-analysis on the comparative effectiveness of devil's advocacy and dialectical inquiry. *Strategic Management Journal,* 1989, 10, 303–306; Nutt, P.C. *Making Tough Decisions: Tactics for Improving Managerial Decision Making,* San Francisco: Jossey-Bass, 1989.

25. Cosier, R.A., and Schwenk, C.R. Agreement and think alike: Ingredients for poor decisions. *Academy of Management Executive,* February 1990, 69–74.

26. Schwenk, C.R. Devil's advocacy and the board: A modest proposal. *Business Horizons,* July–August 1989, 22–27.

27. The discussion in this section draws from a variety of sources, including: Holoviak, S.J. *Golden Rule Management: Give Respect, Get Results.* Reading, Mass.: Addison-Wesley, 1993; Mink, O.G., Mink, B.P., Downes, E.A., and Owen, K.Q. *Open Organizations: A Model for Effectiveness, Renewal, and Intelligent Change.* San Francisco: Jossey-Bass, 1994; Redding, J.C., and Catalanello, R.F. *Strategic Readiness: The Making of the Learning Organization.* San Francisco: Jossey-Bass, 1994.

28. Mali, P. *MBO Updated.* New York: John Wiley & Sons, 1986.

29. Adapted from Rice, R. How to make diversity pay. Fortune, August 8, 1994, 78–86; *1993 Hoeschst Celanese Annual Report,* 1994.

30. Locke, E.A., and Latham, G.P. *A Theory of Goal Setting and Task Performance,* Englewood Cliffs, N.J.: Prentice-Hall, 1990.

31. Morrisey, G.L., Below, P.J., and Acomb, B.L. *The Executive Guide to Operational Planning.* San Francisco: Jossey-Bass, 1988.

32. Fry, L.W., and Hellriegel, D. The role

and expectancy participation model: An empirical assessment and extension. *Journal of Occupational Behavior,* 1987, 8, 295–309.

33. Slocum, J.W., Jr., McGill, M., and Lei, D.T. The new learning strategy: Anytime, anything, anywhere. *Organizational Dynamics,* Autumn 1994, 33–47.

34. Carson, P., and Carson, K.D. Deming versus traditional management theorists on goal setting: Can both be right? *Business Horizons,* September–October 1993, 79–84.

35. Hirschhorn, L. *Managing in the New Team Environment: Skills, Tools, and Methods.* Reading, Mass.: Addison-Wesley, 1991.

36. Reeves, C.A., and Bednar, D.A. Defining quality: Alternatives and implications. *Academy of Management Review,* 1994, 19, 419–445.

37. Dean, J.W., Jr., and Bowen, D.E. Management theory and total quality: Improving research and practice through theory development. *Academy of Management Review,* 1994, 19, 392–418.

38. Omachonu, V.K., and Ross, J.E. *Principles of Total Quality.* Delray Beach, Fla.: St. Lucie Press, 1994, 137–154.

39. Adapted from Shetty, Y.K. Aiming high: Competitive benchmarking for superior performance. *Long Range Planning,* 1993, 26, 39–44.

40. Fitz-Enz, J. *Benchmarking Staff Performance: How Staff Departments Can Enhance Their Value to Customers.* San Francisco: Jossey-Bass, 1993.

41. George, S., and Weinerskirch, A. *Total Quality Management: Strategies and Techniques Proven at Today's Most Successful Companies.* New York: John Wiley & Sons, 1994.

42. Taylor, A. III. Will success spoil Chrysler? *Fortune,* January 10, 1994, 88–92.

43. Altier, W.J. Process expertise—A critical managing function. *Business Horizons,* January–February 1993, 10–15.

44. Adapted from Main, J. How to steal the best ideas around. *Fortune,* October 19, 1992, 102–106; Port, O. and Smith, G. Beg, borrow—and benchmark. *Business Week,* November 30, 1992, 74–75; White, M.L. Doing the right things right the first time: Mellon total quality improvement process. *Trusts & Estates,* September 1993, 30–33.

45. Walton, M. *Deming Management at Work.* New York: G.P. Putnam's Sons, 1990, 20–24.

46. Deming, W.E. *The New Economics for Industry, Government Education.* Cambridge, Mass.: Center for Advanced Engineering Study, Massachusetts Institute of Technology, 1993.

47. Adapted and modified from Langley, G., Nolan, K., Nolan, T. The foundation of improvement. Presented at the Sixth Annual International Deming's User's Group Conference. Cincinnati: August 1992; Dean, J.W., Jr., and Evanse, J.R. *Total Quality: Management, Organization, and Strategy.* St. Paul, Minn.: West, 1994, 81–82.

48. Knutson, J. and Bitz, I. *Project Management: How to Plan and Manage Successful Projects.* New York: AMACOM, 1991; Frame, J.D. *The New Project Management.* San Francisco: Jossey-Bass, 1994.

49. Code of ethics for the project management profession. *PM Network,* February 1991, 32.

50. Dinsmore, P.C. (ed.) *The AMA Handbook of Project Management.* New York: AMACOM, 1993; Badiru, A.B. *Project Management Tools for Engineering and Management Professionals.* Norcross, Ga.: Institute of Industrial Engineers, 1991.

51. Randolph, W.D., and Posner, B.Z. What every manager needs to know about project management. *Sloan Management Review,* Summer 1988, 65–73.

52. Slutsker, G. Good-bye cable TV, hello fiber optics. *Forbes,* September 19, 1988, 174–179.

53. Reagon, G. Total Quality Management (TQM) inventory. Adapted from *The 1992 Annual: Developing Human Resources* (pp. 157–161) by J.W. Pfeiffer (Ed.). Copyright © 1992 by Pfeiffer & Company, San Diego, Ca. Used with permission.

54. Adapted from Stoffman, D. Locking up profits. *Canadian Business,* February 1987, 102–109. Case within this article was prepared by Stephen Tax under the direction of Walter Good, professor of management studies at the University of Manitoba, Winnipeg, Canada. Used with permission.

55. The car industry: On another planet, *The Economist,* October 17, 1992; No-haggle pricing going full throttle, *Advertising Age,* March 22, 1993; Loyalty and the renaissance of marketing, *Marketing Management,* 1994, 2(4); The death and rebirth of the salesman, *Fortune,* July 25, 1994; Saturn "homecoming": Publicity stunt, or triumph of relationship marketing? *Brandweek,* August 8, 1994; The Saturn story: Building a brand, *California Management Review,* Winter 1994.

Chapter 7

1. Adapted from Sharp Paine, L. Managing for organizational integrity. *Harvard Business Review,* March–April 1994, 106–117; Martin Marietta team urges tighter controls in space age group. *Aviation Week Space Technology,* January 10, 1994, 26–27; Barnhart, P. The ethics game. *Training,* June 1993, 65–67.

2. Sharp Paine, L., 113–114.

3. Weiss, J.W. *Business Ethics: A Managerial, Stakeholder Approach.* Belmont, Calif.: Wadsworth, 1994.

4. Berry, L.L. Playing fair in retailing. *Arthur Anderson Retailing Issues Letter,* March 1993, 1–5.

5. Stark, A. What's the matter with business ethics. *Harvard Business Review,* May–June 1993, 38–40, 43–46, 48.

6. Harris, C.E., Jr. *Applying Moral Theories.* Belmont, Calif.: Wadsworth, 1990, 7–11.

7. Sims, R.R. *Ethics and Organizational Decision Making.* Westport, Conn.: Quorum Books, 1994.

8. Harris poll: Is an antibusiness backlash building? *Business Week,* July 20, 1987, 71; Gudridge, K., and Byrne, J.A. A kinder, gentler generation of executives? *Business Week,* April 23, 1990, 86–87.

9. Posner, B.Z., and Schmidt, W.H. Ethics in American companies: A managerial perspective. *Journal of Business Ethics,* 1987, 6, 383–391.

10. Bhide, A., and Stevenson, H.H. Why be honest if honesty doesn't pay? *Harvard Business Review,* September–October 1990, 126.

11. Aquilar, F.J. *Managing Corporate Ethics.* New York: Oxford University Press, 1994.

12. Vietell, S.J., Nwachukwu, S.L., and Barnes, J.H. The effects of culture on ethical decision-making: An application of Hofstede's Typology. *Journal of Business Ethics,* 1993, 12, 753–760.

13. Adapted from Kohls, J., and Buller, P. Resolving cross-cultural ethical conflict: Exploring alternative strategies. *Journal of Business Ethics,* 1994, 13, 31–38; Beauchamp, T. *Case Studies in Business, Society, and Ethics.* Englewood Cliffs, N.J.: Prentice-Hall, 1989.

14. Jennings, M.M. *Business: Its Legal, Ethical, and Global Environment.* Belmont, Calif.: Wadsworth, 1994.

15. Twomey, D. P. *Labor and Employment Law: Text and Cases,* 9th ed. Cincinnati: South-Western, 1994.

16. Adapted from Burck, C. The real world of the entrepreneur. *Fortune,* April 5, 1993, 62–80.

17. *Corporate Ethics: A Prime Business Asset.* New York: Business Roundtable, 1988.

18. Trevino, L.K., and Nelson, K. *Business Ethics.* New York: John Wiley & Sons, 1995.

19. Cullen, J.B., Victor, B., and Stephens, C. An ethical weather report: Assessing the organization's ethical climate. *Organizational Dynamics,* Autumn 1989, 50–62; Victor, B., and Cullen, J.B. The organizational bases of ethical work climates. *Administrative Science Quarterly,* 1988, 33, 101–125.

20. Adapted from Shepard, A.C. Should journalists go on record with ethics? *Ethics: Easier Said Than Done.* Issue 25, 1994, 53–56.

21. Kohlberg, L. Stage and sequence: The cognitive-developmental approach to socialization. In D.A. Goslin (ed.), *Handbook of Socialization Theory and Research.* Chicago: Rand McNally, 1969, 347–380.

22. Kohlberg, L. The cognitive-developmental approach to moral education. In P. Scharf (ed.), *Readings in Moral Education.* Minneapolis: Winston Prisa, 1978, 36–51; Boxter, G.D. and Rarick, C.A. Education and moral development of managers: Kohlberg's stages of moral development and integrative education. *Journal of Business Ethics,* 1987, 6, 243–248.

23. Barnett, T., Bass, K., and Brown, G. Ethical ideology and ethical judgment regarding ethical issues in business. *Journal of Professional Ethics,* 1994, 13, 469–480.

24. Ford, R.C., and Richardson, W.D. Ethical decision making: A review of the empirical literature. *Journal of Business Ethics,* 1994, 13, 205–221.

25. Cavanagh, G.F., Moberg, D.J., and Velasquez, M. The ethics of organizational behavior. *Academy of Management Review,* 1981, 5, 363–374; Brady, F.N. *Ethical Managing: Rules and Results:* New York: Macmillan, 1990.

26. Mill, J.S. *Utilitarianism.* Indianapolis: Bobbs-Merrill, 1957 (originally published 1863).

27. Wilson, J.Q. Adam Smith on business ethics. *California Management Review,* Fall 1989, 59–72.

28. Aram, J.D. *Presumed Superior: Individualism and American Business.* Englewood Cliffs, N.J.: Prentice-Hall, 1993.

29. Adapted from Yu, D. Multicultural marts: Big retailers increasingly target ethnic customers. *Houston Chronicle,* August

29, 1993, 4E; Chakravarty, S.N. The best-laid plans: Kmart's turnaround plan. *Fortune,* January 3, 1994, 44–45; Watching over Kmart's special concepts. *Discount Merchandiser,* February 1993, 38–67.

30. Velasquez, M., Moberg, D.V., and Cavanagh, G.F. Organizational statesmanship and dirty politics: Ethical guidelines for the organizational politician. *Organizational Dynamics,* Autumn 1983, 65–80.

31. Cavanagh, G.F. *American Business Values,* 2nd ed. Englewood Cliffs, N.J.: Prentice-Hall, 1984.

32. Murphy, K.R. *Honesty in the Workplace.* Belmont, Calif.: Wadsworth, 1993.

33. Boisseau, C. Flying a route to controversy. *Houston Chronicle,* July 3, 1994, 1F, 5F.

34. Kidwell, R.E., Jr., and Bennett, N. Employee reactions to electronic control systems. *Group & Organization Management,* 1994, 19, 203–218; Jossi, F. Eavesdroppers in cyberspace. *Business Ethics,* May/June 1994, 22–25; Comer, D.R. Crossroads: A case against workplace drug testing. *Organization Science,* 1994, 5, 259–267.

35. Adapted from Chura, H. Don't talk and chew anymore. *Houston Chronicle,* May 27, 1994, 2D; Doughnut shop got a hole lot of juicy gossip. *Houston Chronicle,* May 30, 1994, 6A.

36. Ewing, D.W. Your right to fire. *Harvard Business Review,* March–April 1983, 32–34ff.

37. Sitkin, S.B., and Bies, R.J. (eds.). *The Legalistic Organization.* Thousand Oaks, Calif.: Sage, 1994.

38. Near, J.P., Moorehead Dwarkin, T., and Miceli, M. P. Explaining the whistle-blowing process: Suggestions from power theory and justice theory. *Organization Science,* 1993, 4, 393–411.

39. Driscoll, L. A better way to handle whistle-blowers: Let them speak. *Business Week,* July 27, 1992, 36.

40. Brooks, L.L. Whistleblowers: Learn to love them. *Canadian Business Review,* Summer 1993, 19–21.

41. Driscoll, L., 36.

42. Friedman, D.D. The world according to Coase. *Law School Record,* Spring 1992, 4–9.

43. Locke, J. *Concerning Civil Government,* London,: J.M. Dent, 1924, 180.

44. Rawls, J. *A Theory of Justice,* Cambridge, Mass.: Harvard University Press, 1971; Greenberg, J. A taxonomy of organizational justice theories. *Academy of Management Review,* 1987, 12, 9–22.

45. Fisher, C.D., Schoenfeldt, L.F., and Shaw, J.B. *Human Resource Management,* Boston: Houghton Mifflin, 1994.

46. Rawls, J., 111–112; Donaldson, T., and Dunfee, T.W. Toward a unified conception of business ethics: Integrative social contracts theory. *Academy of Management Review,* 1994, 19, 252–284.

47. Folger, R., and Konovsky, M.A. , Effects of procedural and distributive justice on reactions to pay raise decisions. *Academy of Management Journal,* 1989, 32, 115–130; Niehoff, B.P., and Moorman, R.H. Justice as a mediator of the relationship between methods of monitoring and organizational citizenship behavior. *Academy of Management Journal,* 1993, 36, 527–556.

48. Adapted from Fierman, J. The perilous new world of fair pay. *Fortune,* June 13, 1994, 57–64; McCausland, R. Marshall ends commissions: Rivals wary. *Electronic News,* September 7, 1992, 1–3.

49. Ewing, D.W. Your right to fire. *Harvard Business Review,* March–April 1983, 32–34ff.

50. Barton, L. *Ethics: The Enemy in the Workplace.* Cincinnati: South-Western, 1995.

51. Litzinger, W.D., and Schaefer, T.E. Business ethics bogeyman: The perpetual paradox. *Business Horizons,* March–April 1987, 21.

52. Friedman, M. A Friedman doctrine: The social responsibility of business is to increase its profits. *New York Times Magazine,* September 13, 1970, 32ff.

53. Friedman, M., 126.

54. Carson, T. Friedman's theory of corporate social responsibility. *Business & Professional Ethics Journal,* 1993, 12, 3–32.

55. Coye, R., and Belohlav, J. Disciplining: A questions of ethics? *Employee Rights and Responsibilities Journal,* 1989, 2, 155–162.

56. Buchholz, R. *Business Environment and Public Policy,* 5th. ed. Englewood Cliffs, N.J.: Prentice-Hall, 1995.

57. Drucker, P.F. The new meaning of corporate social responsibility. *California Management Review,* Winter 1984, 62.

58. Carroll, A.B. *Business and Society: Ethics and Stakeholder Management,* Cincinnati: South-Western, 1993.

59. Kraft, K.L., and Hage, J. Strategy, social responsibility and implementation. *Journal of Business Ethics,* 1990, 9, 11–19; McGuire, J.B., Sundgren, A., and Schneeweis, T. Corporate social responsibility and firm financial performance. *Academy of Management Journal,* 1988, 31, 854–872.

60. Adapted from Rice, F. Who scores best on the environment. *Fortune,* July 26, 1993, 114–122; *AT&T Environment and Safety Report.* Basking Ridge, N.J.: AT&T, Department AR, 1994.

61. Epstein, E.M. Business ethics, corporate good citizenship and the corporate social policy process: A view from the United States. *Journal of Business Ethics,* 1989, 8, 583–595.

62. Gibson, R. McDonald's will put nutritional data for menu on wall posters, tray liners. *Wall Street Journal,* June 11, 1990, B4.

63. Sethi, S.P. A conceptual framework for environmental analysis of social issues and evaluation of business response patterns. *Academy of Management Review,* 1979, 8, 63–74; Mahoney, J.T., Huff, A.S., Huff, J.O. Toward a new social contract theory in organization science. *Journal of Management Inquiry,* 1994, 3, 153–168.

64. Greengard, S. Face values. *US Air Magazine,* November 1990, 89–97; Franssen, M. Beyond profits: The Body Shop does. *Business Quarterly,* Autumn 1993, 14–20; Roddick, G. Letter to Business Ethics subscribers. September 22, 1994, 1–10; Entine, J. Shattered image. *Business Ethics,* September/October 1994, 23–28.

65. Weiss, J.W. *Business Ethics: A Managerial Stakeholder Approach.* Belmont, Calif.: Wadsworth, 1994.

66. Walley, N., and Whitehead, B. It's not easy being green. *Harvard Business Review,* May–June 1994, 46–52.

67. Bowen, E. Looking to its roots. *Time,* May 27, 1987, 26.

68. Scenario 1: Harris, James R. *The Harris Survey,* Auburn University; Scenario 2: Posner, B.Z., and Schmidt, W.H. Ethics in American companies: A managerial perspective. *Journal of Business Ethics,* 1987, 6, 383–391; Scenario 3: Fritzsche, D.J., and Becker, H. Linking management behavior to ethical philosophy: An empirical investigation. *Academy of Management Journal,* 1984, 27, 1, 172–173.

69. Adapted from Josephson, M. *Ethical Obligations and Opportunities in Business: Ethical Decision Making in the Trenches.* Marina del Rey, Calif.: Josephson Institute of Ethics, 1990, 39. Address: 4640 Admiralty Way, Suite 1001, Marina del Ray, CA 90292.

70. Adapted from *The Body Shop Annual Report,* 1992; *Ward's Business Directory of U.S. Private and public Companies,* 1992; Shoppers buy up a bounty of natural beauty products, *Wall Street Journal,* June 8, 1994; Body shop has a few aches and pains, *Wall Street Journal,* August 6, 1993; Storm in a bubble bath, *The Economist,* September 3, 1994; Not free trade but fair trade, *Across the Board,* June 1994; The seven (almost) deadly sins of high-minded entrepreneurs, *INC.,* July 1994.

Chapter 8

1. Adapted from Sacasas, R., and Cava, A. Law ethics and management: Toward an effective audit. *Business Forum.* February 1990, 18–21.

2. This case is based on the facts and legal arguments presented in *Crinkley v. Holiday Inn,* 844 F.2d 156 (4th Cir. 1988).

3. MacCrimman, K.R., and Taylor, R.N. Decision making and problem solving. In M.D. Dunnette (ed.), *Handbook of Industrial and Organizational Psychology.* Chicago: Rand McNally, 1976, 1397–1453; Cowan, D.A. Developing a classification structure of organizational problems: An empirical investigation. *Academy of Management Journal,* 1990, 33, 366–390.

4. March, J.G. *A Primer on Decision Making: How Decisions Happen.* New York: Free Press, 1994.

5. Harrison, F.E. *The Managerial Decision-Making Process,* 4th ed. Boston: Houghton Mifflin, 1994.

6. Bell, D. *Risk Management.* New York: Cambridge University Press, 1988.

7. Miller, K. Insurance claims data don't show advantage of some auto devices. *Wall Street Journal,* March 13, 1994, A1, A6.

8. Garcia, M. Fear of crime drives Florida's motorists to break laws. *Houston Chronicle,* October 2, 1993, 8A.

9. Boynoton, A.C., Gales, L.M., and Blackburn, R.S. Managerial search activity: The impact of perceived role uncertainty and role threat. *Journal of Management,* 1993, 19, 725–747.

10. Bazerman, M.H. *Judgment in Managerial Decision Making,* 3rd ed. New York: John Wiley and Sons, 1994.

11. Boulding, K.E. Irreducible uncertainties. *Society,* November–December 1982, 17.

12. McCall, M.W., Jr., and Kaplan, R.E. *Whatever It Takes: The Realities of Managerial Decision Making,* 2nd ed. Englewood Cliffs, N.J.: Prentice-Hall, 1990.

13. Adapted from Maruca, R.F. The right way to go global: An interview with Whirlpool CEO David Whitwam. *Harvard*

Business Review, March–April 1994, 134–145;

14. Fagenson, E.A. *Women in Management.* Thousand Oaks, Calif.: Sage, 1993.

15. Lewyn, M., and Jones Yang, D. Boeing: For want of a pin. *Business Week,* July 5, 1993, 96–97.

16. Nutt, P.C. The formulation processes and tactics used in organizational decision making. *Organization Science,* 1993, 4, 226–251.

17. Dean, J.W., and Bowen, D.E. Management theory and total quality: Improving research and practice through theory development. *Academy of Management Review,* 1994, 19, 392–418.

18. Port, O. Back to basics. *Business Week,* 1989, 16.

19. Dean, J.W., Jr., and Evans, J.R. *Total Quality: Management, Organization, and Strategy.* St. Paul, Minn.: West, 1994.

20. Welsh, T. Best and worst corporate reputations. *Fortune,* February 7, 1994, 58–60.

21. Adapted from Farnham, A. America's most admired company. *Fortune,* February 7, 1994, 50–54; Schiller, Z. At Rubbermaid, little things mean a lot. *Business Week,* November 11, 1991, 126.

22. Mitroff, I.I., Mason, R.O., Pearson, C.M. *Framebreak: The Radical of American Business.* San Francisco: Jossey-Bass, 1994.

23. Senge, P.M. The leader's new work: Building learning organizations. *Sloan Management Review,* Fall 1990, 20.

24. Nolan, R.L. *Creative Destruction: A Six-Stage Process for Transforming the Organization.* Boston: Harvard Business School Press, 1995.

25. Maruca, R.F., 135–145.

26. Ibid., 137.

27. Richards, M.D. *Setting Strategic Goals and Objectives.* St. Paul, Minn.: West, 1986.

28. Wallace, D. It's all about goals. *Success,* September 1991, 39–43.

29. Locke, E.A., and Latham, G.P. *A Theory of Goal Setting and Task Performance.* Englewood Cliffs, N.J.: Prentice-Hall, 1990.

30. Adapted from Wallace, D., 39–43.

31. Stewart, R. *Choices for the Manager.* Englewood Cliffs, N.J.: Prentice-Hall, 1982.

32. Mitroff, I.I. Crisis management and environmentalism: A natural fit. *California Management Review,* Winter 1994, 101–113.

33. Worthy, J.C. *William C. Norris: Portrait of a Maverick.* Cambridge, Mass.: Ballinger, 1987; Norris, W.C. *New Frontiers for Business Leadership.* Minneapolis: Dorm Books, 1983.

34. Imparato, N., and Harari, O. *Jumping the Curve: Innovation and Strategic Choice in an Age of Transition.* San Francisco: Jossey-Bass, 1995.

35. Schultz, R. *Unconventional Wisdom.* New York: HarperCollins, 1994.

36. Kiesler, S., and Sproull, L. Managerial response to changing environments: Perspectives on problem sensing from social cognition. *Administrative Science Quarterly,* 1982, 27, 548–570; Bowen, M.G. The escalation phenomenon reconsidered: Decision dilemmas or decision errors? *Academy of Management Review,* 1987, 12, 52–66.

37. Ray, M. and Myers, R. *Creativity in Business.* Garden City, N.Y.: Doubleday, 1986, 94–96.

38. Handy, C. *The Age of Paradox.* Boston: Harvard Business School Press, 1994.

39. Fandt, P.M. *Management Skills: Practice and Experience.* St. Paul, Minn.: West, 1994.

40. Czander, W.M. *The Psychodynamics of Work and Organizations.* New York: Guilford, 1993.

41. Payne, J.W., Bettman, J.R., and Johnson, E.J. *The Adaptive Decision Maker.* New York: Cambridge University Press, 1993.

42. Simon, H.A. *Reason in Human Affairs.* Stanford, Calif.: Stanford University Press, 1983; Simon, J.A. Making management decisions: The role of intuition and emotion. *Academy of Management Executive,* 1987, 1, 57–64; Martin, J.E., Kleindorfer, G.B., and Brashers, W.R., Jr. The theory of bounded rationality and the problem of legitimation. *Journal for the Theory of Social Behavior,* 1987, 17, 63–82.

43. Silver, W.S. The status quo tendency in decision making. *Organizational Dynamics,* Spring 1990, 34–36.

44. Roach, J.M. Simon says: Decision making is a "satisficing" experience. *Management Review,* January 1979, 8–9.

45. Saunders, C., and Jones, J.W. Temporal sequences in information acquisition for decision making: A focus on source and medium. *Academy of Management Review,* 1990, 15, 29–46.

46. Adapted from Custred, J. Women teed off at private clubs. *Houston Chronicle,* July 24, 1994, 1B, 6B.

47. Developed from Hogarth, R.M., and Makridakis, S. Forecasting and planning: An evaluation. *Management Science,* 1981, 27, 117–120; Schoemaker, P.J.H., and Russo, J.E. A pyramid of decision approaches. *California Management Review,* Fall 1993, 9–31.

48. Dawes, C. Risky business. *Columns,* March 1993, 20–25.

49. Fimbel, N. Communicating realistically: Taking account of politics in internal business communications. *Journal of Business Communication,* 1994, 31, 7–26.

50. Voyer, J.J. Coercive organizational politics and organizational outcomes: An interpretive study. *Organization Science,* 1994, 5, 72–85.

51. Braaten, D.O., Cody, M.J., and DeTienne, K.B. Account episodes in organizations: Remedial work and impression management. *Management Communication Quarterly,* 1993, 6, 219–250.

52. Pfeffer, J. *Power in Organizations.* Boston: Pitman, 1981; Mesch, D.J. A union/management cooperative program gone wrong: Some unintended consequences of a fact-finding program. *Journal of Applied Behavioral Science,* 1994, 30, 43–62.

53. Greiner, L.E., and Schein, V.E. *Power and Organizational Development.* Reading, Mass.: Addison-Wesley, 1988; Rosenblatt, Z., Rogers, K.S., and Nord, W.R. Toward a political framework for flexible management of decline. *Organization Science,* 1993, 4, 76–91.

54. Yates, D., Jr. *The Politics of Management.* San Francisco: Jossey-Bass, 1985; Finet, D. Effects of boundary spanning communication on the sociopolitical delegitimation of an organization. *Management Communication Quarterly,* 1993, 7, 36–66.

55. Selznik, P. *TVA and the Grass Roots.* Berkeley: University of California Press, 1949.

56. Adapted from Saxe, L. Lying: Thoughts of an applied social psychologist. *American Psychologist,* 1991, 46, 409–415; Taylor, S.E. *Positive Illusions: Creative Self-Deception and the Healthy Mind.* New York: Basic Books, 1990.

57. Coping with ambiguity. Adapted from *The 1982 Annual for Facilitators, Trainers, and Consultants* (pp. 110–116) by J.W. Pfeiffer & L.D. Goodstein (Eds.). Copyright © 1982 by Pfeiffer & Company, San Diego, Ca. Used with permission.

58. Wallace, D. A risk of disclosure. *Business Ethics,* November–December 1993, 33. This article reprinted with permission from: *Business Ethics Magazine,* 52 S. 10th St., Suite 110, Minneapolis, MN 55403-2001. (612-962-4702 in Minnesota.)

59. General opens marketing doors, *Rubber and Plastics News,* August 15, 1994; General debuts tires, *Tire Business,* January 24, 1994; Re-inventing the tire, *Fleet Equipment,* March 1993.

Chapter 9

1. Adapted from Perelman, L.J. How hypermation leaps the learning curve. *Forbes ASAP,* October 25, 1993, 77–90.

2. Schoemaker, P.J.H., and Russo, J.E. A pyramid of decision approaches. *California Management Review,* Fall 1993, 9–31.

3. Bazerman, M.H. *Judgment in Managerial Decision Making,* 3rd. ed. New York: John Wiley & Sons, 1994.

4. Harrison, F.E. *The Managerial Decision-Making Process,* 4th ed. Boston: Houghton Mifflin, 1995.

5. Turban, E. *Expert Systems and Applied Artificial Intelligence.* New York: Macmillan, 1993.

6. Goodsell, C.T. *The Case for Bureaucracy: A Public Administration Polemic,* 3rd. ed., Chatham, N.J.: Chatham House, 1994.

7. Harris, R. (ed.), *Partners in Learning: Guidelines for Working with Students with Disabilities at Texas A&M University,* College Station, Texas A&M University, 1994.

8. Ibid., 1–2.

9. Adapted from Josephson, M. *Ethical Obligations and Opportunities in Business: Ethical Decision Making in the Trenches.* Marina del Rey, Calif.: Joseph & Edna Josephson Institute, 1990, 12–14; Weiss, J.W. *Business Ethics: A Managerial, Stakeholder Approach.* Belmont, Calif.: Wadsworth, 58–81.

10. Illovsky, M.E. Counseling, artificial intelligence and expert systems. *Simulation & Gaming,* 1994, 25, 88–98.

11. Treleaven, P., and Goonatilake, S. *Intelligent Systems for Finance and Business.* New York: John Wiley & Sons, 1994.

12. Turban, E. *Decision Support and Expert Systems.* 3rd ed. New York: Macmillan, 1993.

13. Adapted from France, M. Smart contracts. *Forbes ASAP,* August 28, 1994, 117–118; Bylinsky, G. Computers that think. *Fortune,* September 6, 1993, 96–102; Treece, J.B. Breaking the chains of command. *Business Week/The Information Revolution,* 1994, 112–114; Byrne, J.A. The pain of downsizing: Nynex. *Business Week,* May 9, 1994, 60–63ff.

14. Bylinsky, G. Computers that think. *Fortune,* September 6, 1993, 102.

15. Arinze, B. *Microcomputers for Managers.* Belmont, Calif.: Wadsworth, 1994, 250–259.

16. Powers, T.L. Break-even analysis with semi-fixed costs. *Industrial Marketing Management,* 1987, 16, 35–41; Haines, L. The small-sales syndrome: Those marginal orders could be eating you alive. *Success,* October 1990, 12.

17. Watson, S.R., and Buede, D.M. Decision Synthesis: The *Principles and Practice of Decision Analysis.* New York: Cambridge University Press, 1987.

18. Omachonu, V.K., and Ross, J.E. *Principles of Total Quality.* Delray Beach, Fla.: St. Lucie Press, 1994, 240–243.

19. Adapted from Howard, N.L. (ed.) *Total Quality Management: Facilitator and Team Leader Training.* Corvallis: Oregon State University, Department of Human Resources, 1991, 47–50; Murphy, P., Brelin, H., Jennings, L.P., and Davenport, K. *Focused Quality: Managing for Results.* Delray Beach, Fla.: St. Lucie Press, 1994.

20. Paul, R.W. The logic of creative and critical thinking. *American Behavioral Scientist,* 1993, 37, 21–39.

21. This section draws on Boone, L.W., and Hollingsworth, A.T. Creative thinking in business organizations. *Review of Business,* Fall 1990, 3–12; Morgan, G. *Imaginization: The Art of Creative Management.* Newbury Park, Calif.: Sage, 1993; Harre, R., and Gillett, G. *The Discursive Mind.* Newbury Park, Calif.: Sage, 1994.

22. Basadur, M., and Robenson, S. The new creative thinking skills needed for total quality management to become fact, not just philosophy. *American Behavioral Scientist,* 1993, 37, 121–138.

23. Miller, W.C. *The Creative Edge: Fostering Innovation Where You Work.* Reading, Mass.: Addison-Wesley, 1987, 90–91.

24. Ibid., 7.

25. Adapted from Norton, R. Strategies for the new export boom. *Fortune,* August 22, 1994, 124–130; Double-barreled bigots: UNIX weds Acucobol Inc.'s COBOL development tool. *Datamation,* October 15, 1992, 80; Coker, P. Let customers know you love them. *Nation's Business,* August 1992, 9.

26. Purser, R.E., and Montuori, A. (eds.). *Social Creativity in Organizations.* Creskill, N.J.: Hampton Press, 1995; Ford, C.M., and Gioia, D. (eds.). *Creativity in Organizations.* Newbury Park, Calif.: Sage, 1995.

27. Adapted from Thornton, E. Japan's struggle to be creative. *Fortune,* April 9, 1993, 129–134; Schlender, B.R. Japan: Is it changing for good? *Fortune,* June 13, 1994; Williams, M., and Kanabayashi, M. Some maverick firms are changing its business climate. *Wall Street Journal,* April 29, 1994, A1, A5.

28. Osborn, A.F. *Applied Imagination,* 3rd rev. ed. New York: Scribner's, 1963; Evans, J.R. *Creative Thinking in the Decision and Management Sciences.* Cincinnati, South-Western, 1991.

29. Morgan, T.F., and Ammentorp, W.M. Practical creativity in the corporate world: Capturing expert judgment in the corporate world. *American Behavioral Scientist,* 1993, 37, 102–111.

30. Van Gundy, A.B., Jr. *Techniques for Structured Problem Solving.* New York: Van Nostrand Reinhold, 1981, 92–101.

31. Osborn, 124; Alvino, J. Future problem solving in the year 2000—Challenges and opportunities for business. *Business Horizons,* November–December 1993, 16–22.

32. Osborn, 229–290.

33. Ibid., 155–158.

34. Treffinger, D.J., and Isaksen, S. *Creative Problem Solving: An Introduction.* Sarasota, Fla.: Center for Creative Learning, 1992.

35. Osborn, 156.

36. Adapted from "Building the creative organization" by Lisa K. Gundry, Ph.D., from ORGANIZATIONAL DYNAMICS, pp. 22–37. Reprinted, by permission of the publisher, from ORGANIZATIONAL DYNAMICS (Spring 1994) © 1994. American Management Association, New York. All rights reserved.

37. Gallupe, R.B., Bastianutti, L.M., and Cooper, W.H. Unlocking brainstorms. *Journal of Applied Psychology,* 1991, 76, 137–142.

38. Valacich, J.S., Dennis, A.R., and Connolly, T. Idea for generation in computer-based groups: New ending to an old story. *Organizational Behavior and Human Decision Processes,* 1994, 448–467.

39. Gallupe, R.B., Cooper, W.H., Grise, M.L., and Bastianutti, L.M. Blocking electronic brainstorms. *Journal of Applied Psychology,* 1994, 79–77, 86.

40. Ishikawa, K. *What Is Total Quality Control? The Japanese Way.* Englewood Cliffs, N.J.: Prentice-Hall, 1995.

41. Based on Howard, 86–90; Schmidt, W.H., and Finnigan, J.P. *The Race without a Finish Line: America's Quest for Total Quality.* San Francisco: Jossey-Bass, 1992, 212–213.

42. DeCosmos, Richard D., Parker, Jerome S., and Heverly, Mary Ann. "Total Quality Management Goes to Community College," exerpt from pp. 16–20. In L.A. Sherr and D.J. Teeter (Eds.), *Total Quality Management in Higher Education,* no. 71. Copyright 1991 Jossey-Bass Inc., Publishers.

43. Ross, J.E. *Total Quality Management: Text, Cases and Readings,* 2nd ed. Delray Beach, Fla.: St. Lucie Press, 1994.

44. Developed from Curran, J.J. Why investors make the wrong choices. *Fortune/1987 Investor's Guide.* 1987, 63ff; Curran, J.J. Why investors misjudge the odds. *Fortune/1989 Investor's Guide,* 1989, 85–97; Tversky, A., and Kahneman, D. Rational choice and the framing of decisions. *Choice: The Contrast between Economics and Psychology.* Chicago: University of Chicago Press, 1987, 67–94.

45. Ibid.

46. Martin, L.P. Inventory of barriers to creative thought and innovative action. Adapted from *The 1990 Annual: Developing Human Resources* by J.W. Pfeiffer (Ed.). Copyright © 1990 by Pfeiffer & Company, San Diego, Ca. Used with permission.

47. Adapted from case prepared by Nabil Hassan, Paula Saunders, and Herbert Brown, all of Wright State University, and Jeffrey R. Liles of *Lexington Herald Leader,* and is intended to be used as a basis for class discussion rather than to illustrate either effective or ineffective handling of the situation. The names of the firms, individuals, locations, and financial information have been disguised to preserve the firm's desire for anonymity. Presented to and accepted by the Society for Case Research. All rights reserved to the authors and the SCR. Copyright © 1992 by Nabil Hassan, Paula Saunders, Herbert Brown, and Jeffrey R. Liles. Used with permission. Case appears in Meadows, R.E. (ed.), *Annual Advances in Business Cases, 1992.* Nacogdoches, Texas: Society for Case Research, 1993, 440–443.

Chapter 10

1. Adapted Henkoff, R. Service is everybody's business. *Fortune,* June 27, 1994, 48–60; Schlesinger, L.A., and Heskett, J.L. The service driven service company. *Harvard Business Review,* September–October 1991, 71–81.

2. Daft, R.L. *Organization Theory and Design,* 5th ed. St. Paul, Minn.: West, 1995.

3. Rummler, G.A., and Brache, A.P. *Improving Performance: How to Manage the White Space on the Organization Chart.* San Francisco: Jossey-Bass, 1990.

4. McGill, M.E., and Slocum, J.W., Jr. *The Smarter Organization: How to Build a Business That Learns to Adapt to Marketplace Needs.* New York: John Wiley & Sons, 1994, 93–96.

5. Adapted from Napier, N. Change is big even for a little guy. *Arthur Andersen: Retailing Issues Letter,* May 1994.

6. Huber, G.P., and Glick, W.H. *Organization Change and Redesign.* New York: Oxford University Press, 1993.

7. Adapted from *1993 Annual Report, Broadcasting Partners, Inc.,* and personal conversation with D. Bitterman, November 1994.

8. Adapted from *1993 Annual Report, Harrisons & Crosfield,* 1993, and personal conversation with I. Caballero, June 1994.

9. Kochan, T.A. and Useem, M. *Transforming Organizations.* New York: Oxford University Press, 1992.

10. Adapted from *1993 Annual Report, Fluor Corporation.*

11. Tosi, H. *The Environment/Organization/Person Contingency Model: A Meso Approach to the Study of Organizations.* Greenwich, Conn.: JAI Press, 1992, 63–64.

12. D'Aveni, R.A. *Hyper-Competition: The Dynamics of Strategic Maneuvering.* New York: Free Press, 1994.

13. *1992 Annual Report, Rhone-Poulenc Rorer.* Collegeville, Pa: Rhone-Poulenc Rorer, Investor Relations, 1993.

14. *1994 Annual Report, Comair Holdings, Inc.* Cincinnati: Comair Holdings, Inc., 1994.

15. Kiam, V.H. Growth strategies at Remington. *The Journal of Business Strategy,* January–February 1989, 22–26.

16. Clawson, J.G., and Pitts, T. *Organizational Structure.* Charlottesville: University of Virginia, Darden Graduate School of Business, 1988.

17. Allen, L.A. *The Professional Manager's Guide.* Palo Alto, Calif.: Louis A. Allen, 1981.

18. Barnard, C. *The Functions of an Executive.* Cambridge, Mass.: President and Fellows of Harvard University, 1938.

19. Morrison, E.W., and Herlihy, J.M. Becoming the best place to work: Managing diversity at American Express Travel Related Services. In *Diversity in the Workplace* S.E. Jackson and Associates (eds.). New York: Guilford Press, 1992, 203–226.

20. Eichenwald, K. Prudential execs ignored churning by Dallas brokers. *Dallas Morning News,* May 24, 1993, D1–D2; Zimmerman, M. Prudential, investors in a tactical tug of war. *Dallas Morning News,* March 20, 1994, H1–H2.

21. Leana, C.R. Predictors and consequences of delegation. *Academy of Management Journal,* 1986, 29, 754–774; Nelson, R.B. *Empowering Employees Through Delegation.* Burr Ridge, Ill.: Irwin Professional Publishing, 1994, 17–38.

22. Hrebiniak, L.G. *The We-Force in Management.* New York: Lexington, 1994.

23. Capers, R.S. NASA post-Hubble: Too little, too late? *The Academy of Management Executive,* May 1994, 68–72.

24. Kahn, W.A., and Kram, K.E. Authority at work: Internal models and their organizational consequences. *Academy of Management Review,* 1994, 19, 17–50.

25. Tichy, N., and Charan, R. Speed, simplicity, self-confidence: An interview with Jack Welch. *Harvard Business Review,* September–October 1989, 112–121.

26. Trice, H.M., and Beyer, J.M. *The Cultures of Work Organizations.* Englewood Cliffs, N.J.: Prentice-Hall, 1993.

27. Sellers, P. Pepsi opens a second front. *Fortune,* August 8, 1994, 71–76.

28. Interview with R. Hinton, president of Burgundy Group, July 1994.

29. Daft, R.L., 146–147.

30. Reprinted by permission from pp. 158–160 of *The Dynamics of Organization Theory: Gaining a Macro Perspective* by John F. Veiga and John W. Yanouas; Copyright © 1979 by West Publishing Company. All rights reserved.

31. Adapted from *Kimberly-Clark 1994 Annual Report;* McCarthy, M.J. Airline squeeze play: More seats, less leg room. *Wall Street Journal,* April 18, 1994, B1.

32. Adapted from CEO Interview: Edward Brennan of Sears, Roebuck, & Co., *Institutional Investor,* April 1994; England, R.S. Penney-wise. FW, April 26, 1994; Loomis, C.J. "Dinosaurs?" *Fortune,* May 3, 1993; Corporate Growth Report, October 5, 1992; Chandler, S. Sears' turnaround is for real—for now. *Business Week,* August 15, 1994; Feltes, P., Kopp, D., and Shufeldt, L. Fall of Sears' great retail empire. *Business Case Journal,* Fall 1993.

Chapter 11

1. Adapted from Jacob, R. The search for the organization of tomorrow. *Fortune,* May 18, 1992, 93–96; McGill, M.E., and Slocum, J.W., Jr. *The Smarter Organization.* New York: John Wiley & Sons, 1994, 87–120; Richman, L.S. The new work force builds itself. *Fortune,* June 27, 1994, 68–76.

2. Chandler, A.D. *Strategy and Structure.* Cambridge, Mass.: MIT Press, 1962.

3. Huber, G.P., and Glick, W.H. *Organizational Change and Redesign.* New York: Oxford University Press, 1993, 10–11; Ketchen, D.J., Jr., Thomas, J.B., and Snow, C.C. Organizational configurations and performance: A comparison of theoretical approaches. *Academy of Management Journal,* 1993, 36, 1278–1313.

4. Hellriegel, D., Slocum, J.W., Jr., and Woodman, R.W. *Organizational Behavior,* 7th ed. St. Paul, Minn.: West, 1995, 108.

5. Schilit, W.K. *Rising Stars and Fast Fades.* New York: Lexington Books, 1994.

6. Adapted from Paperiernik, R.L. Mac attack. *Financial World,* April 12, 1994, 28–31; Whalen, J. McDonald's mulls hearth takeout units. *Advertising Age,* March 14, 1994, 43–44; Love, J.F. *Behind the Golden Arches.* New York: Bantum Books, 1986; Serwer, A.E. McDonald's conquers the world. *Fortune,* October 17, 1994, 103–105ff.

7. Hamel, G., and Prahalad, C.K. *Competing for the Future.* Boston: Harvard Business School Press, 1994.

8. Carvell, T. The new worker elite. *Fortune,* August 22, 1994, 56–66. Also see Jelinek, M., and Schoonhaven, C.B. *The Innovation Marathon.* San Francisco: Jossey-Bass, 1993.

9. Adapted from Diesenhouse, S. A textile manufacturer wins by breaking all the rules. *New York Times,* July 24, 1994, 5F.

10. Burns, T., and Stalker, G.M. *The Management of Innovation.* London: Tavistock, 1961.

11. Katz, D. *Just Do It.* New York: Random House, 1994; Yang, D.J., O'Neal, M., and Hoots, C. Can Nike do it? *Business Week,* April 18, 1994, 86–90.

12. Lawrence, P.R., and Lorsch, J.W. *Organization and Environment.* Homewood, Ill.: Irwin, 1967. Also see Keck, S.L., and Tushman, M.L. Environmental and organizational context and executive team structure. *Academy of Management Journal,* 1993, 36, 1314–1344.

13. Adapted from Cosco, J. Black & Deckering Black & Decker. *Journal of Business Strategy,* January–February 1994, 59–62; Travers, P.J. Home appliance industry. *Value Line,* March 18, 1994, 128–136; Caminiti, S. A star is born. *Fortune,* Autumn/Winter 1993, 45–47.

14. Thompson, J.D. *Organizations in Action.* New York: McGraw-Hill, 1967, 51–67; Keller, R.T. Technology-information processing fit and the performance of R & D project groups: A test of contingency theory. *Academy of Management Journal,* 1994, 37, 167–179.

15. Miles, R.E., and Snow, Charles C. *Fit, Failure, and the Hall of Fame.* New York Free Press, 1994.

16. Henkoff, R. Service is everybody's business. *Fortune,* June 27, 1994, 48ff; Henkoff, R. Finding training and keeping the best service workers. *Fortune,* October 3, 1994, 110ff.

17. Quinn, J.B. *Intelligent Enterprise: A Knowledge and Service Based Paradigm for Industry.* New York: Free Press, 1992; Quinn, J.B., and Baily, M.N. Information technology: Increasing productivity in services. *Academy of Management Executive,* 1994, 8(3), 28–51; Kaplan, D.I. *Service Success.* New York: John Wiley & Sons, 1994.

18. Adapted from *PETsMART Annual Report,* 1994; and *PETsMART Prospectus,* July 22, 1993.

19. Watkins, K.E., and Marsick, V.J. *Sculpting the Learning Organization.* San Francisco: Jossey-Bass, 1994.

20. Galbraith, J.R. *Organization Design.* Reading, Mass.: Addison-Wesley, 1977; D'Aveni, R.A., and Ravenscraft, D.J. Economies of integration versus bureaucracy costs: Does vertical integration improve performance? *Academy of Management Journal,* 1994, 37, 1167–1206.

21. Adapted from Neuborne, E. Firm takes season rush in stride. *USA Today,* December 17, 1993, 1–2.

22. Adapted from McAra, A., and Vorstenbos, P. *Expertise in Electronics.* Eindhoven, Netherlands: Philips, 1994.

23. For reviews of the advantages and disadvantages of matrix designs, see Davis, S.M., and Lawrence, P.R. *Matrix.* Reading, Mass.: Addison Wesley, 1977; Hammerly, H. Matching global strategies with national responses. *Journal of Business Strategy,* March/April 1992, 8–12; Dinsmore, P.C. *The AMA Handbook of Project Management.* New York: American Management Association, 1993, 90–93, 111; Hrebiniak, L.G. The *We-Force in Management.* New York: Lexington, 1994.

24. Bowen, H.K., Clark, K.B., Holloway, C.A., Barton, D.L., and Wheelwright, S.C. Regaining the lead in manufacturing. *Harvard Business Review,* September–October 1994, 108–144.

25. Devereaux, M.O., and Johansen, *Globalwork.* San Francisco: Jossey-Bass, 1994; McGill, M.E., and Slocum, J.W., Jr. *The Smarter Organization: How to Build a Business That Adapts to Marketplace Needs.* New York: John Wiley & Sons, 1994, 100–108.

26. *Nike, Inc., Annual Report,* 1994; Katz, D. *Just Do It.* New York: Random House, 1994.

27. For excellent sources that review these points see D'Aveni, R.A. *Hyper-Competition: Managing the Dynamics of Strategic Maneuvering.* New York: Free Press, 1994; Mitroff, I.I., Mason, R.O., and Pearson, C.M. *Framebreak: The Radical Design of American Business.* San Francisco: Jossey-Bass, 1994.

28. Uzzi, B.S. Organizational networks, structural embeddedness and firm survival. Paper presented at Academy of Management Meetings, Dallas, August 16, 1994; Lechner, A. Understanding the natural nature of the networked organization. Paper presented at Academy of Management Meetings, Dallas, August 16, 1994.

29. Sashkin, M., and Morris, W.C. *Organizational Behavior.* Reston, Va.: Reston Publishing, 1984, 360–361.

30. Adapted from Pine, B.J. II, Victor, B., Boynton, A.C. Making mass customization work. *Harvard Business Review, September–October 1993, 108–121; Pietrocini, T. W. The future belongs to the leaders.* Frozen Food Digest, April–May 1993, 6–7.

31. Adapted from Anfuso, D. L.L. Bean's TQM efforts put people before processes. *Personnel Journal,* July 1994; Ettorre, B. Phenomenal promises that mean business. *Management Review,* March 1994; L.L Bean quality starts with people, *Personnel Journal,* January 1994; Bean lights the home fires, *Catalog Age,* September 1994; Poirier, M. Management alternatives. *Catalog Age,* February 1993; Caudron, S. Change keeps TQM programs thriving. *Personnel Journal,* October 1993; 10 years in review, *Catalog Age,* March 1993.

Chapter 12

1. Adapted from Blackburn, R.J., and Rosen, B. Total quality and human resources management: Lessons learned from Baldrige Award-Winning Companies. *Academy of Management Executive,* 1993, 7(3), 49–66; Chaudron, S. Change keeps

TQM programs thriving. *Personnel Journal,* October 1993, 104–109.

2. Fisher, C.D., Schoenfeldt, L.D., and Shaw, J.B. *Human Resource Management,* 2nd ed. Boston: Houghton Mifflin, 1993, 5; French, W.L. *Human Resources Management,* 3rd ed. Boston: Houghton Mifflin, 1994, 4–5.

3. For an excellent discussion of strategic human resource management, see Greer, C.R. *Strategy and Human Resources.* Englewood Cliffs, N.J.: Prentice-Hall, 1995.

4. Arthur, J.B. Effects of human resource systems on manufacturing performance and turnover. *Academy of Management Journal,* 1994, 37, 670–687.

5. Bowen, D.B., and Lawler, E.E. III. Total quality-oriented human resources management. *Organizational Dynamics,* Spring 1992, 29–41.

6. U. S. Bureau of the Census, *Statistical Abstract of the United States: 1993,* 113th ed. Washington, D. C., 1993, 859, Table 1404.

7. Bjarvall, K. Boy aims to end forced child labor. *South Bend Tribune,* November 8, 1994, A6; Quindlen, A. Child labor is slavery, unworthy of GATT. *South Bend Tribune,* November 27, 1994, A23.

8. Baker, S., Smith, G., and Weiner, E. The Mexican worker. *Business Week,* April 19, 1993, 84–87ff.

9. For a discussion of the nature of work in the future see Kiechel, W. III, How we will work in the year 2000. *Fortune,* May 17, 1993, 38–52; Church, G.J. Jobs in an age of insecurity. *Time,* November 22, 1993, 32–39.

10. Adapted from Caudron, S. Successful companies realize that diversity is a long-term process, not a program. *Personnel Journal,* April 1993, 54–55. Also see Wright, P., Ferris, S.P., Hiller, J.S., and Kroll, M. Competitiveness through management of diversity: Effects on stock price evaluation. *Academy of Management Journal,* 1995, 38, 272–287.

11. For an excellent discussion of these laws, see Fisher, C.D., Schoenfeldt, L.D., and Shaw, J.B., 178–219, 551–554, and 674–681.

12. Adapted from Barrett, A. How can Jenny Craig keep on gaining? *Business Week,* April 12, 1993, 52–53; Carton, B., Muscled out? At Jenny Craig, men are ones who claim sex discrimination. *Wall Street Journal,* November 29, 1994, A1, A7.

13. Schneider, B., and Schmitt, N. *Staffing Organizations,* 2nd ed. Glenview, Ill.: Scott, Foresman, 1986; Rynes, S.L., and Barber, A.E. Applicant attraction strategies: An organizational perspective. *Academy of Management Review,* 1990, *15*: 286–310.

14. Calloway, W. Building a culture of growth. *Fortune,* March 7, 1994, 70–72.

15. Feuer, M.J., Niehaus, J.R., and Sheridan, J.E. Human resource forecasting: A survey of practice and potential. *Human Resource Planning,* 1988, 7(2), 85–97.

16. French, W.L., 464.

17. Hughes, M. In need of a job? Meijer has hundreds to fill. *South Bend Tribune,* December 28, 1994, A1, A2.

18. McDaniel, M.A., Whetzel, D.L., Schmidt, F.L., and Maurer, S.D. The validity of employment interviews: A comprehensive review and meta-analysis. *Journal of Applied Psychology,* 1994, 79, 599–616.

19. Powell, G.N. Applicant reactions to the initial employment interview: Exploring theoretical and methodological issues. *Personnel Psychology,* 1991, 44, 67–83; Dougherty, T.W., Turban, D.B., and Callender, J.C. Confirming first impressions in the employment interview: A field study of interviewer behavior. *Journal of Applied Psychology,* 1994, 79, 659–665.

20. Liden, R.C., Martin, C.R., and Parsons, C.K. Interviewer and applicant behaviors in employment interviews. *Academy of Management Journal,* 1993, 36, 372–386.

21. Kelley, P.L., Jacobs, R.R., and Farr, J.L. Effects of multiple administrations of the MMPI for employee screening. *Personnel Psychology,* 1994, 47, 575–591.

22. Battagliola, M. The results are in: Drug testing saves money. *Business & Health,* August 1993, 22–26.

23. Tepper, B.J. Investigation of general and program-specific attitudes toward corporate drug-testing policies. *Journal of Applied Psychology,* 1994, 79: 392–401.

24. Brookler, R. Industry standards in workplace drug testing. *Personnel Journal,* April 1992, 128–132; Oliver, B. Fight drugs with knowledge. *Training & Development,* May 1994, 105–108.

25. Greengard, S. Theft control starts with HR strategies. *Personnel Journal,* April 1993, 80–91; Bernardin, H.J., and Cooke, D.K. Validity of an honesty test in predicting theft among convenience store employees. *Academy of Management Journal,* 1993, 36, 1097–1108.

26. Ones, D., Viswesvaran, S.C., and Schmidt, F.L. Comprehensive meta-analysis of integrity test validities: Findings and implications for personnel selection and theories of job performance. *Journal of Applied Psychology Monograph,* 1993 78: 679–703.

27. Kerlinger, F.N. *Foundations of Behavioral Science Research.* New York: Holt, Rinehart and Winston, 1986.

28. Kleinmann, M. Are rating dimensions in assessment centers transparent for participants? Consequences for criterion and construct validity. *Journal of Applied Psychology,* 1993, 78, 988–993.

29. Tziner, A., Ronen, S., and Hacohen, D. A four-year study of an assessment center in a financial corporation. *Journal of Organizational Behavior,* 1993, 14(3), 225–237.

30. Adapted from Henkoff, R. Finding, training, and keeping the best service workers. *Fortune,* October 3, 1994, 110–122.

31. Lawler, E.E. III. *Strategic Pay: Aligning Organizational Strategies and Pay Systems.* San Francisco: Jossey-Bass, 1990; Greene, R.J. Person-focused pay: Should it replace job-based pay? *Compensation & Benefits Management,* Autumn 1993, 9(4), 46–55.

32. Greenberg, J. Stealing in the name of justice: Informational and interpersonal moderators of theft reactions to underpayment inequity. *Organizational Behavior and Human Decision Processes,* 1993, 54, 81–103; Schaubroek, J., May, B., and Brown, F.W. Procedural justice explanations and employee reactions to economic hardship: A field experiment. *Journal of Applied Psychology,* 1994, 79, 455–460.

33. Adapted from Motivation the old-fashioned way. *INC.,* November 1994, 134.

34. Kelley, B. The power of incentive. *Incentive,* May 1992, 6–9.

35. Fisher, C.D., Schoenfeldt, L.F., and Shaw, J.B., 573–577.

36. Ibid.

37. Cherrington, D.J. *The Management of Human Resources,* 4th ed. Englewood, Cliffs, N.J.: Prentice-Hall, 1995, 452–453.

38. Guthrie, J.P. and Cunnigham, E.P. Pay for performance for hourly workers: The Quaker Oats alternative. *Compensation & Benefits Review,* March-April 1992, 18–23.

39. Wilkinson, J.G. Duke Power integrates employee rewards with its business vision of excellence. *National Productivity Review,* Summer 1993, 325–335.

40. Koshuta, M., and McCuddy, M.K. Improving productivity in the health care industry: An argument and supporting evidence from one hospital. *Health Care Supervisor,* 1989, *8(1):* 15–30.

41. Hanlon, S.C., Meyer, D.G. and Taylor, R.R. Consequences of gainsharing: A field experiment revisited. *Group & Organization Management,* 1994, 19(1), 87–111.

42. Masternak, R.L. Gainsharing: Overcoming common myths and problems to achieve dramatic results. *Employment Relations Today,* Winter 1993–1994, 425–436.

43. Kumbhakar, S.C., and Dunbar, A.E. The elusive ESOP-productivity link: Evidence form U. S. firm-level data. *Journal of Public Economics,* 1993, 52(2), 273–283.

44. Wolfe, R.A., and Parker, D.F. Employee health management: Challenges and opportunities. *Academy of Management Executive,* May 1994, 8(2), 22–31.

45. McCaffery, R.M. *Employee Benefit Programs: A Total Compensation Perspective,* 2nd ed. Boston: PWS-Kent, 1992, 130–131.

46. Twer, D. Linking pay to business objectives. *Journal of Business Strategy,* July-August 1994, 15, 15–18; Saunier, A.M., and Hawk, E.J. Realizing the potential of teams through team-based rewards. *Compensation and Benefits Review,* July-August 1994, 26(4), 24–33; Lucero, M.A., and Allen, R.E. Employee benefits: A growing source of psychological contract violations. *Human Resource Management,* Fall 1994, 33, 425–446.

47. For an excellent discussion of how performance standards can affect employees' satisfaction and motivation see Bobko, P., and Calella, A. Employee reactions to performance standards: A review and research propositions. *Personnel Psychology,* Spring 1994, 47, 1–29; Becker, T.E., and Martin, S.L. Trying to look bad at work: Methods and motives for managing poor impressions in organizations. *Academy of Management Journal,* 1995, 38, 174–199.

48. Locke, E.A., and Latham, G.P. *A Theory of Goal Setting and Task Performance.* Englewood Cliffs, N.J.: Prentice-Hall, 1990, 252–267.

49. Milliman, J.F., Zawacki, R.A., Norman, C., Powell, L., and Kirksey, J. Companies evaluate employees from all perspectives, *Personnel Journal,* November 1994, 99–103.

50. Harris, M.H. Rater motivation in the performance appraisal context: A theoretical framework. *Journal of Management,* 1994, 20(4), 737–756; Lance, C.E. Test of a latent structure of performance ratings derived from Wherry's (1952) theory of rating. *Journal of Management,* 1994, 20(4), 757–771; Wayne, S.J., and Liden, R.C. Effects of impression management on performance ratings: A longitudinal study. *Academy of Management Journal,* 1995, 38, 232–260.

51. Longnecker, C.O., Sims, H.P., Jr., and

Goia, D.A. Behind the mask: The politics of employee appraisal. *Academy of Management Executive,* 1987, 1, 183–193.

52. Goia, D.A., and Longnecker, C.O. Delving into the dark side: The politics of executive appraisal. *Organizational Dynamics,* Winter 1994, 47–57.

53. Adapted from Scholtes, P.R. Total quality or performance appraisal: Choose one. *National Productivity Review,* Summer 1993, 349–363; Bowman, J.S. At last, an alternative to performance appraisal: Total quality management. *Public Administration Review,* March/April 1994, 54(2), 129–136.

54. Adapted from Schuler, R.S., and Harris, D.L. Deming quality improvement: Implications for human resource management as illustrated in a small company. *Human Resource Planning,* 1991, 14(3), 191–207; Nelton, S. How a Pennsylvania company makes the sweet sounds of innovation. *Nation's Business,* December 1991, 16.

55. Ready, D.A., Vicere, A.A., and White, A.F. Towards a systems approach to executive development. *Journal of Management Development,* July 1994, 13(5): 64–71; Bartel, A.P. Productivity gains from the implementation of employee training programs. *Industrial Relations,* October 1994, *33(4)*: 411–425.

56. Cooper, H. The new educators: Carpet firm sets up an in-house school to stay competitive. *Wall Street Journal,* October 5, 1992, A1, A5.

57. Lombardo, M., McCall, M., and DeVries, D. *Looking Glass, Inc.* Greensboro, N.C.: Center for Creative Leadership, 1991.

58. Dowling, P.J., Schuler, R.S., and Welch, D.E. *International Dimensions of Human Resource Management,* 2nd ed. Belmont, Calif.: Wadsworth, 1994, 129–134.

59. Adapted from Solomon, C.M. Staff selection impacts global success. *Personnel Journal,* January 1994, 88–101; Solomon, C.M. Global operations demand that HR rethink diversity. *Personnel Journal,* July 1994, 40–50.

60. Adapted from Pfeiffer, J.W. What's legal? Investigating employment interview questions. *The 1989 Annual: Developing Human Resources.* San Diego: University Associates, 1989, 23–37. Used by permission, 1995.

61. Adapted from Vosmik, P. In pursuit of quality human resources at AT&T universal card services. *Employment Relations Today,* Spring 1993, 29–35; Anfuso, D. Through AT&T's turbulent decade, HR excels. *Personnel Journal,* January 1994, 54–55; Pevel, M.J., Nellis, S., Lane, F., and Schuler, R.S. AT&T global business communications systems: Linking HR with business strategy. *Organizational Dynamics,* Winter 1994, 22(3), 59–72.

62. Adapted from O'Reilly, B. 360 feedback can change your life. *Fortune,* October 17, 1994; Lublin, J. It's shape-up time for performance reviews. *Wall Street Journal,* October 3, 1994; Hirsch, M.S. 360 degrees of evaluation. *Working Woman,* August 1994; Positive peer pressure boosts productivity, morale. *Supervisory Management,* March 1993; Grote, D., and Wimberly, J. Peer review. *Training,* March 1993; Ramsay, M., and Lehto, H. The power of peer review. *Training & Development,* July 1994; Kinni, T. Judge and be judged. *Industry Week,* August 2, 1993; Machan, D. Operation deadwood. *Forbes,* March 24, 1993; The team building tool kit, *Compensation & Benefits Review,* March-April 1994.

Chapter 13

1. Adapted from McGeady, M.R. Disconnected kids: An American tragedy. *America,* June 15, 1991, 639–645; Doyle, K. Lean and Mean. *Incentive,* January 1993, 28–3.

2. For reviews of the literature, see Landy, F.J., and Becker, W.S. Motivation theory reconsidered. In L.L. Cummings and B.M. Staw (eds.). *Research in Organizations,* vol. 9, Greenwich, Conn.: JAI, 1987, 1–38.

3. Wilkinson, J.G. Duke Power integrates employee rewards with its business vision of excellence. *National Productivity Review,* Summer 1993, 325–335.

4. Adapted from Woodruff, M.J. Understanding and supervising the twenty-somethings. *Supervision,* April 1992, 10–12; Ratan, S. Generational tension in the office: Why busters hate boomers. *Fortune,* October 4, 1993, 57–70.

5. Maslow, A.H. *Motivation and Personality,* 2nd ed. New York: Harper & Row, 1970.

6. Caudron, S. Motivating creative employees calls for new strategies. *Personnel Journal,* May 1994, 103–106.

7. Betz, E.L. Two tests of Maslow's theory of need fulfillment. *Journal of Vocational Behavior,* 1984, 24: 204–220; Hugman, R., and Hadley, R. Involvement, motivation, and reorganization in a social services department. *Human Relations,* 1993, 46: 1338–1349.

8. Spera, S.P., Buhrfeind, E.D., and Pennebaker, J.W. Expressive writing and coping with job loss. *Academy of Management Journal,* 1994, 37, 722–733.

9. Welsh, D.H.B., Luthans, F., and Sommer, S.M. Managing Russian factory workers: The impact of U.S.-based behavioral and participative techniques. *Academy of Management Journal,* 1993, 36: 58–79.

10. Alderfer, C.P. *Existence, Relatedness and Growth: Human Needs in Organizational Settings,* New York: Free Press, 1972.

11. Alderfer, C.P. An empirical test of a new theory of human needs. *Organizational Behavior and Human Performance,* 1969, 5: 142–175; Alderfer, C.P. *Existence, Relatedness and Growth;* Wanous, J.P., and Zwany, A.A. A Cross-sectional test of need hierarchy theory. *Organizational Behavior and Human Performance,* 1977, 18: 78–97.

12. Adapted from Horwitz, T. Jobless male managers proliferate in suburbs, causing subtle malaise. *Wall Street Journal,* September 20, 1993, A1, A5; DeMott, J.S. Out on a limb and on their own. *Nation's Business,* March 1994, 33–34.

13. McClelland, D.C. *Motivational Trends in Society,* Morristown, N.J.: General Learning Press, 1971.

14. McClelland, D.C. The two faces of power. *Journal of International Affairs,* 1970, 24: 29–47.

15. Herzberg, F., Mausner, B., and Snyderman, B. *The Motivation to Work,* New York: John Wiley & Sons, 1959.

16. Adapted from Miller, K.L. Stress and uncertainty: The price of restructuring. *Business Week,* March 29, 1993; Ono, Y. Unneeded workers in Japan are bored, and very well paid. *Wall Street Journal,* April 20, 1993, A1, A8; Rogers, R.E. Managing for quality: Current differences between Japanese and American approaches. *National Productivity Review,* Autumn 1993, 503–517.

17. Brockner, J., Wiesenfeld, B.M., Reed, T., Grover, S., and Martin, C. Interactive effect of job content and context on the reactions of layoff survivors. *Journal of Personality and Social Psychology,* 1993, 64: 187–197.

18. Campion, M.A., and McClelland, C.L. Follow-up and extension of the interdisciplinary costs and benefits of enlarged jobs. *Journal of Applied Psychology,* 1993, 78: 339–351; Denton, D.K. !*#*@#! I hate this job. *Business Horizons,* January-February 1994, 46–52; Denton, D.K. The power of flexibility. *Business Horizons,* July-August 1994, 43–46.

19. Hackman, J.R., and Oldham, G.R. *Work Redesign,* Reading, Mass.: Addison-Wesley, 1980.

20. Fried, Y., and Ferris, G.R. The validity of the Job Characteristics Model: A review and meta-Analysis. *Personnel Psychology,* 1987, 40: 287–322; Cunningham, J.B., and Eberle, T. A guide to job enrichment and design. *Personnel,* February 1990, 56–61; Spector, P.E., and Jex, S.M. Relations of job characteristics from multiple data sources with employee affect, absence, turnover intentions, and health. *Journal of Applied Psychology,* 1991, 76: 46–53.

21. Goldman, R.B. *A Work Experiment: Six Americans in a Swedish Plant.* New York: Ford Foundation, 1976.

22. Templin, N. Team spirit: A decisive response to crisis brought Ford enhanced productivity. *Wall Street Journal,* December 15, 1992, A1, A13.

23. Adapted from Selz, M. Enterprise: Testing self-managed teams, entrepreneur hopes to lose job. *Wall Street Journal,* January 11, 1994, B1.

24. Vroom, V.H. *Work and Motivation,* New York: John Wiley & Sons, 1964.

25. Stayer, R.C. How I learned to let my workers lead. *Harvard Business Review,* November-December 1990, 66ff.

26. Porter, L.W., and Lawler, E.E. III. *Managerial Attitudes and Performance,* Homewood, Ill.: Irwin, 1968.

27. Adapted from Eisman, R. The Ritz-Carlton. *Incentive,* January 1993, 24–27; Galagan, P.A. Putting on the Ritz. *Training & Development,* December 1993, 40–45.

28. Nadler, D.A., Hackman, J.R., and Lawler, E.E. III. *Managing Organizational Behavior,* Boston: Little, Brown, 1979, 32.

29. Hall, J. Americans know how to be productive if managers will let them. *Organizational Dynamics,* Winter 1994, 22: 33–46.

30. Blau, G. Operationalizing direction and level of effort and testing their relationships to individual job performance. *Organizational Behavior and Human Decision Processes,* 1993, 55: 152–170; Tubbs, M.E., Boehne, D.M., and Dahl, J.B. Expectancy, valence, and motivational force functions in goal-setting research: An empirical test. *Journal of Applied Psychology,* 1993, 78: 361–373; Farrell, J.N., Lord, R.G., Alexander, R.A., and Gradwohl, W.C. The measurement of performance valence: An examination of construct-related evidence. *Organizational Behavior and Human Decision Processes,* 1994, 60: 157–178.

31. Peery, N.J. Here come richer, riskier pay plans. *Fortune,* December 19, 1988, 51.

32. Adams, J.S. Toward an understanding of equity. *Journal of Abnormal and Social Psychology,* 1963, 67: 422–436.

33. Quinn, J. Avon's new face. *Incentive,* June 1994, 26–30.

34. Adapted from Sonnenberg, F.K., and Goldberg, B. Business integrity: An oxymoron? *Industry Week,* April 6, 1992, 53–56; Sonnenberg, F.K., and Goldberg, B. New bottom lines? *Executive Excellence,* December 1992, 3–4.

35. Schaubroek, J., May, D.R., and Brown, F.W. Procedural justice explanations and employee reactions to economic hardship: A field experiment. *Journal of Applied Psychology,* 1994, 79: 455–161; Konovsky, M.A., and Pugh S.D. Citizenship behavior and social exchange. *Academy of Management Journal,* 1994, 37, 656–669.

36. Kidwell, R.E., Jr., and Bennett, N. Employee propensity to withhold effort: A conceptual model to intersect three avenues of research. *Academy of Management Review,* 1993, 18: 429–456.

37. Greenberg, J. Employee theft as a reaction to underpayment inequity: The hidden costs of pay cuts. *Journal of Applied Psychology,* 1990, 75: 561–568; Greenberg, J. Stealing in the name of justice: Informational and interpersonal moderators of theft reactions to underpayment inequity. *Organizational Behavior and Human Decision Processes,* 1993, 54: 81–103.

38. Skinner, B.F. *Contingencies of Reinforcement,* New York: Appleton-Century-Crofts, 1969; Skinner, B.F. *Beyond Freedom and Dignity,* New York: Bantam, 1971; Skinner, B.F. *About Behaviorism,* New York: Knopf, 1974.

39. Latham, G.P., and Huber, V.L. Schedules of reinforcement: Lessons from the past and issues for the future. *Journal of Organizational Behavior Management,* 1992, 12: 125–149.

40. Stuart, P. Employees buy awards with rideshare points. *Personnel Journal,* January 1993, 65–69.

41. Luthans, F., and Kreitner, R. *Organizational Behavior Modification and Beyond: An Operant and Social Learning Perspective,* Glenview, Ill.: Scott, Foresman, 1985.

42. Adapted from Steinmetz, G. Former agents draw a picture of Met Life's sales practices. *Wall Street Journal,* October 8, 1993, B1, B5; Steinmetz, G. Met Life got caught; Others sent same letter. *Wall Street Journal,* January 6, 1994, B1, B6.

43. Ball, G.A., Trevino, L.K., and Sims, H.P., Jr. Just and unjust punishment: Influences on subordinate performance and citizenship. *Academy of Management Journal,* 1994, 37: 299–322.

44. Kazdin, A.E. *Behavior Modification in Applied Settings,* 3rd ed. Homewood, Ill.: Dorsey Press, 1984, 143.

45. Miller, L.M. *Behavior Management; The New Science of Managing People at Work.* New York: John Wiley & Sons, 1978, 126–151; Kazdin, A.E., 93–98.

46. Kazdin, A.E., 142–146.

47. Kreitner, R., and Luthans, F. A social learning approach to behavioral management: Radical behaviorists mellowing out. *Organizational Dynamics,* Autumn 1984, 47–65.

48. Adapted from Deutschman, A. Bill Gates' next challenge. *Fortune,* December 28, 1992, 30–41; McKenna, J.F. America's most admired CEOs. *Industry Week,* December 6, 1993, 22–32; Boyd, M. Corporate cult or corporate culture? *Incentive,* January 1994, 18–23; Deutschman, A. The managing wisdom of high-tech superstars. *Fortune,* October 17, 1994, 197–206.

49. Adapted from Gerstner, J. Good communication. *Communication World,* March 1994; Henkoff, R. Getting beyond downsizing. *Fortune,* January 10, 1994; Marshall, R., and Yorks, L. Planning for a restructured revitalized organization. *Sloan Management Review,* Summer 1994; Hulsizer, G. Successful transitions. *Executive Excellence,* April 1994; Navran, F. Surviving a downsizing. *Executive Excellence,* July 1994; Hodge, J. Healing the wounds of downsizing. *HRM Magazine,* August 1994; Byrne, J.A. There is an upside to downsizing. *Business Week,* May 9, 1994; Managers remain cynical about the real reason for delayering, *Personnel Management,* September 1994; The anorexic corporation, *The Economist,* September 3, 1994; Romano, C. Pressed to service. *Management Review,* June 1994.

Chapter 14

1. Adapted from Semler, R. Managing without managers. *Harvard Business Review,* September-October 1989, 76–84; Fierman, J. Winning ideas from maverick managers. *Fortune,* February 6, 1995, 70, 74, 78.

2. Rehfeld, J.E. *Alchemy of a Leader.* New York: John Wiley & Sons, 1994; Greenwood, R.G. Leadership theory: A historical look at its evolution. *Journal of Leadership Studies,* November 1993, 3–20.

3. Phillips, A.S., and Bedeian, A.G. Leader-follower exchange quality: The role of personal and interpersonal attributes. *Academy of Management Journal,* 1994, 37, 990–1001; Kotter, J.P. *The Leadership Factor.* New York: Free Press, 1988.

4. Personal communication with Kerr, S., vice-president, corporate management development, General Electric Company, February 1995.

5. Adapted from Sellers, P. Don't call me a slacker. *Fortune,* December 12, 1994, 181–196.

6. Hinkin, T.R., and Schriesheim, C.A. Relationship between subordinate perceptions of supervisory influence and attributed power bases. *Human Relations,* 1990, 43, 221–238; Hinkin, T.R., and Schriesheim, C.A. An examination of subordinate-perceived relationships between leader reward and punishment behavior and leader bases of power. *Human Relations,* 1994, 47, 779–801.

7. French, J.R.P., and Raven, B.H. The bases of social power. In D. Cartwright and A. Zander (eds.), *Group Dynamics: Research and Theory,* 2nd. ed. New York: Harper & Row, 1960, 607–623.

8. Kets de Vries, M.F.R. The leadership mystique. *Academy of Management Executive,* 1994, 8(3), 73–89; Kinder, A., and Robertson, I.T. Do you have the personality to be a leader? The importance of personality dimensions for successful managers and leaders. *Leadership & Organization Development Journal,* 1994, 15(1), 3–13.

9. Gastil, J. A definition and illustration of democratic leadership. *Human Relations,* 1994, 47, 953–976; Pfeffer, J. *Managing with Power.* Boston: Harvard Business School Press, 1994.

10. Adapted from Treacy, M., and Wiersema, F. How market leaders keep their edge. *Fortune,* February 6, 1995, 88–98.

11. Bass, B.M. *Bass and Stodgill's Handbook of Leadership.* New York: Free Press, 1990.

12. Badaracco, J.L., Jr. *Leadership and the Quest for Integrity.* Boston: Harvard Business School Press, 1994.

13. McGregor, D. *The Human Side of the Enterprise.* New York: McGraw-Hill, 1960, 33–58.

14. Adapted from Dumaine, B. America's toughest bosses. *Fortune,* October 18, 1993, 39–50.

15. Stogdill, R.M. *Handbook of Leadership: A Survey of the Literature.* New York: Free Press, 1974.

16. Schriesheim, C.A., and Bird, B.J. Contributions of the Ohio State studies to the field of leadership. *Journal of Management,* 1979, 5, 135–145; Rotemberg, J.J., and Saloner, G. Leadership style and incentives. *Management Science,* 1993, 39, 1299–1319.

17. Likert, R. From production-and-employee centeredness to systems 1–4. *Journal of Management,* 1979, 5, 147–156.

18. Blake, R.R., and Mouton, J.S. *The Managerial Grid.* Houston: Gulf, 1985; Lewis, C.T., and Jobs, S.M. Conflict management: The essence of leadership. *Journal of Leadership Studies,* November 1993, 47–60.

19. Yukl, G.A. *Leadership in Organizations,* 2nd ed. Englewood Cliffs, N.J.: Prentice-Hall, 1989.

20. Fiedler, F.E. *A Theory of Leadership.* New York: McGraw-Hill, 1967.

21. Adapted from Fierman, J., 78–79; Menagh, M. Calling all road warriors. *CIO,* June 1, 1993, 76–77; Glines, S. ANI keeps C.R. England truckin' to profits. *Communication News,* July 1993, 12–13.

22. Schriesheim, C.A., Tepper, B.J., and Tetrault, L.A. Least preferred co-worker score, situational control, and leadership effectiveness: A meta-analysis of contingency model performance predictions. *Journal of Applied Psychology,* 1994, 79, 561–574.

23. Potter, E.H. III, and Fiedler, F.E. Selecting leaders: Making the most of previous experience. *Journal of Leadership Studies,* November 1993, 61–70.

24. Hersey, P., and Blanchard, K.H. *Management of Organizational Behavior: Utilizing Human Resources,* 6th ed. Englewood Cliffs, N.J.: Prentice-Hall, 1993.

25. Adapted from Hirsch, J.S. Hired to rev up AAA, an outsider discovers changing it is tough. *Wall Street Journal,* August 30, 1994, 1A & 4A; AAA names new president for U.S., Canada clubs. *Wall Street Journal,* November 2, 1994, 10B.

26. Blanchard, K.H., Zigarmi, D., and Nelson, R.B. Situational leadership after 25 years: A retrospective. *Journal of Leadership Studies,* November 1993, 21–36.

27. Norris, W.E., and Vecchio, R.P. Situational leadership theory: A replication. *Group & Organization Management,* 1992, 17, 331–343.

28. House, R.J., and Mitchell, T.R. Path-goal theories of leadership. *Journal of Contemporary Business,* 1974, 3, 81–97.

29. Adapted from Finegan, J. Unconventional wisdom. *INC.,* December 1994, 44–59.

30. Wofford, J.C., and Liska, L.Z. Path-goal theories of leadership: A meta-analysis. *Journal of Management,* 1993, 857–876.

31. Vroom, V.H., and Jago, A.G. *The New Leadership*. Englewood Cliffs, N.J.: Prentice-Hall, 1988.

32. Field, R.H.G., and House, R.J. A test of the Vroom-Yetton model using manager and subordinate reports. *Journal of Applied Psychology,* 1990, 75, 362–366; Pasewark, W.E., and Strawser, J.R. Subordinate participation in auditing budgeting decisions: A comparison of decisions influenced by organizational factors to decisions conforming with the Vroom-Jago model. *Decision Sciences,* 1994, 25, 281–300.

33. Shamir, B., House, R.J., and Arthur, M.B. The motivational effects of charismatic leadership: A self-based theory. *Organization Science,* 1993, 4, 577–594; Snyder, N.H., and Graves, M. Leadership and vision. *Business Horizons,* January-February 1994, 1–7; Scandura, T.A., and Schriesheim, C.A. Leader-member exchange and supervisor career mentoring as complementary constructs in leadership research. *Academy of Management Journal,* 1994, 37, 1588–1602.

34. Howell, J.M., and Avolio, B.J. Transformational leadership, transactional leadership, locus of control, and support for innovations: Key predictors of consolidated-business-unit performance. *Journal of American Psychology,* 1993, 78, 545–568; Avolio, B.J. The "natural": Some antecedents to transformational leadership. *International Journal of Public Administration,* 1994, 17, 1559–1581.

35. House, R.J., Spangler, W.D., and Woycke, J. Personality and charisma in the US presidency: A psychological theory of leader effectiveness. *Administrative Science Quarterly,* 1991, 36, 364–395; Kets de Vries, M.F.R. The leadership mystique. *Academy of Management Executive,* 1994, 8(3), 73–93.

36. Adapted from Rossant, J. The man who's driving Fiat like a Ferrari. *Business Week,* January 23, 1995, 82–83; Kurylko, D.T. Fiat breathes new life into Poland. *Automotive News,* March 28, 1994, 18–19; Kurylko, D.T. Plant pays extra attention to the small details. *Automotive News,* May 30, 1994, 26–27.

37. Howell, J.M., and Avolio, B.J. The ethics of charismatic leadership: Submission or liberation? *Academy of Management Executive,* 1992, 6(2), 43–55. Also see Bass, B.M., and Avolio, B.J. The implications of transactional and transformational leadership for individual, team, and organizational development. In W.A. Pasmore and R.W. Woodman (eds.), *Research in Organizational Change and Development,* Vol. 4. Greenwich, Conn.: JAI Press, 1990, 231–272.

38. Adapted from Henriques, D. A celebrity boss faces exile from 2d corporate kingdom. *New York Times,* February 10, 1995, 1C—4C; Storied executive Agee ousted from Morrison Knudsen, *Dallas Morning News,* February 11, 1995, 1–2F; Dorfman, J. Call to duty: Why Morrison board fired Agee. *Wall Street Journal,* February 14, 1995, 1–2B.

39. Schriesheim, C.A. *Leadership Instrument*. Coral Gables, Fla.: University of Miami, 1995. Used by permission.

40. Adapted from Burck, C. Succeeding with tough love. *Fortune,* November 29, 1993, 188; McCune, J.C. The best revenge: Your own business. *Success,* May 1991, 19–20.

41. Adapted from Hunter, D. Dow's Popoff sounds an upbeat note. *Chemical Week,* November 2, 1994; Stewart, T.A. Your company's most valuable asset: Intellectual capital. *Fortune,* October 3, 1994; Lederer, J. CEO compensation. *Chief Executive,* September 1994; Popoff on challenges for Dow and for the industry, *Chemical Week,* May 18, 1994; Full-cost accounting for the environment, *Chemical Week,* March 9, 1994; Dow Chemical: Leading a quiet revolution, *Chemical Week,* September 29, 1993; Industry leaders, setting the agenda in the '90's, *Chemical Week,* August 4, 1993; Staying off the scrap heap and preparing for the next century, *Chemical Week,* May 12, 1993; CEO's on the long march to quality, *Chemical Week,* September 30, 1992.

Chapter 15

1. Adapted from Treece, J.B. Breaking chains of command. *Business Week/The Information Revolution,* November 16, 1994, 112–114.

2. Davis, S.M., and Botkin, J.W. *The Monster Under the Bed: How Business Is Mastering the Opportunity of Knowledge for Profit*. New York: Simon & Schuster, 1994.

3. Eisenbereg, E.M., and Goodall, H.L., Jr. *Organizational Communication: Balancing Creativity and Constraint*. New York: St. Martin's Press, 1993.

4. Adapted from Mitroff, I.I., Mason, R.O., and Pearson, C.M. *Frame Break: The Radical Redesign of American Business*. San Francisco: Jossey-Bass, 1994.

5. Rasberry, R.W., and Lindsay, L.L. *Effective Managerial Communications*. Boston: Wadsworth, 1994; Argyris, C. Good communication that blocks learning. *Harvard Business* Review, July-August 1994, 77–86.

6. Miller, R. Business Day. *Dallas Morning News,* November 16, 1994, 3D.

7. Ornstein, S. The hidden influences of office design. *Academy of Management Executive,* 1989, 3, 144–147; Narisetti, R. Executives suites' walls come tumbling down. *Wall Street Journal,* June 29, 1994, 1B.

8. Morrow, P.C. Physical attractiveness and selection in decision making. *Journal of Management,* 1990, 16, 45–60; Liden, R.C., Martin, C.L., and Parsons, C.K. Interviewer and applicant behaviors in employment interviews. *Academy of Management Journal,* 1993, 36, 372–386.

9. Adapted from Winsor, A. *The Complete Guide to Doing Business in Mexico*. New York: American Management Association, 1994; Hecht, L., and Morci, P. Managing risks in Mexico. *Harvard Business Review,* July-August 1993, 32–41.

10. Daft, R.L. *Organization Theory,* 5th ed. St. Paul, Minn.: 1995; Daft, R.L., Bettenhausen, K.R., and Tyler, B.B. Implications of top managers' communication choices for strategic decisions. In G.P. Huber and Wm. H. Glick (eds.), *Organizational Change and Redesign*. New York: Oxford University Press, 1993, 112–146.

11. Main, J. How to steal the best ideas around. *Fortune,* October 19, 1992, 102–106.

12. Krackhardt, D. and Hanson, J.R. Informal networks: The company behind the chart. *Harvard Business Review,* July-August 1993, 104–113.

13. Adapted from Hall, C. Computers make at-home agency a virtual reality. *Dallas Morning News,* November 6, 1994, 1H-2H; Kunde, D. "Hoteling" helping companies trim office costs. *Dallas Morning News,* November 16, 1994, 1D-3D.

14. Hoskisson, R.E., and Hitt, M.A. *Downscoping*. New York: Oxford University Press, 1994; Cameron, K.S., Freeman, S.J., and Mishra, A.K. Downsizing and redesigning organizations. In G.P. Huber and Wm. H. Glick (eds.), *Organizational Change and Redesign*. New York: Oxford University Press, 1993, 19–65.

15. Rasberry, R.W., and Lemoine, L.F. *Effective Managerial Communications*. Boston: Kent, 1986, 168–170.

16. Sutcliffe, K.M. What executives notice: Accurate perceptions in top management teams. *Academy of Management Journal,* 1994, 37.

17. Kunde, D. Engendering a change. *Dallas Morning News,* January 13, 1991, 1H-3H.

18. Adapted from DeLuca, J.M., and McDowell, R.N. Managing diversity: A strategic "grass-roots" approach. In S. E. Jackson and Associates. *Diversity in the Workplace*. New York: Guilford Press, 1992, 227–247.

19. Griffith, T.L., and Northcraft, G.B. Distinguishing between the forest and trees: Media, features, and methodology in electronic communications research. *Organization Science,* 1994, 5, 272–285.

20. Tetzeli, R. The Internet and your business. *Fortune,* March 7, 1994, 86–88.

21. Adapted from *Intel Corporation, 1994 Annual Report*. Santa Clara, Calif.: Intel Corporation, 1994; Fisher, L.M. Sharing sights and sounds with your PC correspondents. *New York Times,* May 15, 1994. 12F; Manning, J. Ambitious executive uses customer-driven strategy at Intel Corp. *Business Journal-Portland,* May 13, 1991, 10–11.

22. Tetzeli, R., 92.

23. Adapted from Sager, I. The great equalizer. *Business Week/The Information Revolution,* November 16, 1994, 100–107; Spindler, A.M. Underwear on the Internet. *New York Times,* February 22, 1994, 19A; Baig, E. Ready, set, go on-line. *Business Week/The Information Revolution,* November 16, 1994, 124–130; Carroll, P.B. Onto the highway: Foreign competition spurs Mexico to move into high-tech world, and more data are becoming available on nation's businesses. *Wall Street Journal,* July 5, 1994, 1A; Jarvenpaa, S., and Ives, B. Digital Equipment Corporation: The Internet Company. Unpublished case. Dallas: Southern Methodist University, Cox School of Business, 1995.

24. Stack, B. Survival tactics: When the facility must close down. *Management Review,* May 1990, 54–57.

25. Personal communications with Dan Pryor, November 23, 1994.

26. Rodgers, E.M. *A History of Communication Study*. New York: Free Press, 1994.

27. Adapted from Ricks, D., and Mahajan, V.J. Blunders in international marketing:

Fact or fiction. *Long Range Planning,* 1984, 17(1), 78–82; Yan, R. To reach China's consumers, adapt to guo qing. *Harvard Business Review,* September-October 1994, 66–75; Waldmann, S. Making presentations to German audiences. *Trade and Culture,* September-October 1994, 66–67.

28. These are abridged from *Ten Commandments for Good Communications.* New York: American Management Association, 1955; Argyris, C. Good communication that blocks learning. *Harvard Business Review,* July-August 1994, 77–86.

29. Adapted from Aguilar, F.J. *Managing Corporate Ethics.* New York: Oxford University Press, 1994, 72–79.

30. Burton, G.E. *Exercises in Management.* (Boston: Houghton-Mifflin 1990) 199–202. Used by permission.

31. Adapted from Kalellcar, A.S. Investigation of large-magnitude incidents: Bhopal as a case study. Presented at the Institute of Chemical Engineers Conference on Preventing Major Chemical Accidents, London, May 1988; Browning, J.B. Union Carbide: Disaster at Bhopal. In J.A. Cottschalk (ed.), *Crisis Response: Inside Stories on Managing Under Siege.* Detroit: Visible Ink Press, 1993; Sharplin, A. Union Carbide of India, Ltd.: The Bhopal tragedy. *Case Research Journal,* 1985.

Chapter 16

1. Adapted from Yeatts, D.E., Hipskind, M., and Barnes, D. Lessons learned from self-managed work teams. *Business Horizons,* July-August 1994, 11–18; De Llosa, P. What business am I in? *Fortune,* November 4, 1994; 54; Whetsell, T. Jostens: Wrung dry. *Financial World,* September 27, 1994, 18; Schifrin, M. Look before you leap. *Forbes,* July 18, 1994, 80–81.

2. Katzenbach, J.R., and Smith, D.K. *The Wisdom of Teams: Creating the High Performance Organization.* Boston: Harvard Business School Press, 1993.

3. Lawler, E.J., and Markovsky, B. (eds.). *Social Psychology of Groups: A Reader.* Greenwich, Conn.: JAI Press, 1995.

4. Galbraith, J.R. *Competing with Flexible Lateral Organizations.* Reading, Mass.: Addison–Wesley, 1994.

5. Trist, E., and Murray, H. (eds.). *The Social Engagement of Social Science. Volume II: The Socio-Technical Perspective.* Philadelphia: University of Pennsylvania Press, 1993.

6. Whyte, W.F., and Whyte, K.K. W. *Making Mondragon.* Ithaca, N.Y.: ILR Press, 1988.

7. Frankling, S. Survey finds workers grumbling louder, saying bosses don't listen. *Houston Chronicle,* December 29, 1994, 1D, 3D; *Report of Commission for the Future of Labor-Management Relations.* Washington, D.C.: U.S. Department of Labor, 1995.

8. Montebello, A.R. *Work Teams That Work: Skills for Managing Across the Organization.* Minneapolis: Best Sellers, 1994, 33–39; Worchel, S. You can go home again: Returning group research to the group context with an eye on developmental issues. *Small Group Research,* 1994, 25, 205–223; Gersick, C.J.G. Marking time: Predictable transitions in task groups. *Academy of Management Journal,* 1989, 32, 274–309.

9. Montebello, A.R., 40–47; Worchel, S., Wood, W., and Simpson, J.A. (eds.). *Group Process and Productivity.* Newbury Park, Calif.: Sage, 1992; Klimoski, R., and Mohammed, S. Team mental model: Construct or metaphor. *Journal of Management,* 1994, 20, 403–437.

10. Stevens, M.J., and Campion, M.A. The knowledge, skill, and ability requirements for teamwork: Implications for human resource management. *Journal of Management,* 1994, 20, 503–530; O'Leary, A.M., Martocchio, J.J., and Frink, D.D. A review of the influence of group goals on group performance. *Academy of Management Journal,* 1994, 37, 1285–1301.

11. Adapted from Sixel, L.M. Bag manufacturing growing up fast. *Houston Chronicle,* October 16, 1994, 1E, 4E.

12. Adapted from Homans, G.C. *The Human Group.* New York: Harcourt, Brace, 1950; Homans, G.C. *Social Behavior: Its Elementary Forms.* New York: Harcourt, Brace, 1961.

13. Burkhardt, M.E. Social interaction effects following a technological change: A longitudinal investigation. *Academy of Management Journal,* 1994, 37, 869–898.

14. Cooke, R.A., and Szumal, J.L. The impact of group interaction styles on problem-solving effectiveness. *Journal of Applied Behavioral Science,* 1994, 30, 415–437.

15. Mueller, C.W., Boyer, E.M., Price, J.L., and Iverson, R.D. Employee attachment and noncoercive conditions of work. *Work and Occupations,* 1994, 21, 179–212.

16. Rabbie, J.M. Determinants of ingroup cohesion and outgroup hostility. *International Journal of Group Tensions,* 1993, 23, 309–328.

17. Hackman, J.R. Group influences on individuals in organization. In M.D. Dunnette and L.M. Hough (eds.), *Handbook of Industrial and Organizational Psychology,* 2nd ed., vol. 3. Palo Alto, Calif.: Consulting Psychologists Press, 1992, 199–267.

18. Zander, A. *Making Groups Effective,* 2nd ed. San Francisco: Jossey-Bass, 1994.

19. Early, P.C. Self or group? Cultural effects of training on self-efficacy and performance. *Administrative Science Quarterly,* 1994, 39, 89–117.

20. Kidwell, R.E., Jr., and Bennett, N. Employee propensity to withhold effort: A conceptual model to intersect three avenues of research. *Academy of Management Review,* 1993, 18, 429–456.

21. Feldman, D.C. The development and enforcement of group norms. *Academy of Management Review,* 1984, 9, 47–53.

22. Krackhardt, D., and Hanson, J.R. Informal networks: The company behind the chart. *Harvard Business Review,* July-August 1993, 104–111; Frey, L.R. (ed.. *Group Communication in Context: Studies in Natural Groups.* Hillsdale, N.J.: Lawrence Erlbaum Associates, 1994.

23. Triandis, H.C., Kurowski, L.L., and Gelfand, M.J. Workplace diversity. In H.C. Triandis, M.D. Dunnette, and L.M. Hough (eds.), *Handbook of Industrial and Organizational Psychology,* 2nd. ed., vol. 4. Palo Alto, Calif.: Consulting Psychologists Press, 1994, 769–827.

24. Adapted from Konrad, W. Welcome to the woman–friendly company. *Business Week,* August 6, 1990, 48–55; Segal, A.T., and Zellner, W. Corporate women: Progress? Sure. But the playing field is still far from level. *Business Week,* June 8, 1992, 74–83; Powell, G.N. *Women & Men in Management,* 2nd ed. Newbury Park, Calif.: Sage, 1993; Jacobs, J.A. (ed.) *Gender Inequality at Work.* Thousand Oaks, Calif.: Sage, 1994.

25. Sagie, A. Participative decision making and performance. A moderator analysis. *Journal of Applied Behavioral Science,* 1994, 30, 227–246; Kahn, W.A., and Kram, K.E. Authority at work: Internal models and their organizational consequences. *Academy of Management Review,* 1994, 19, 17–50.

26. Maznevski, M.L. Understanding our differences: Performance in decision–making groups with diverse members. *Human Relations,* 1994, 47, 531–552; Watson, W.E., Kumar, K., and Michaelson, L.K. Cultural diversity's impact on interaction process and performance: Comparing homogeneous and diverse task groups. *Academy of Management Journal,* 1993, 36, 590–602.

27. Gentile, M.C. (ed.). *Differences That Work: Organizational Excellence Through Diversity.* Boston: Harvard Business School Press, 1994.

28. Campion, M.A., Medsker, G.J., and Higgs, A.C. Relations between work group characteristics and effectiveness: Implications for designing work groups. *Personnel Psychology,* 1993, 46, 823–850.

29. Adapted from Caudron, S. Teamwork takes work. *Personnel Journal,* February 1994, 41–49; Shelby Die Casting may move out of Mississippi to Alabama, where it can get literate workers. *New York Times,* March 3, 1994, B8.

30. Katzenbach, J.R., and Smith, D.K. The discipline of teams. *Harvard Business Review,* March-April 1993, 111–120.

31. Wetlaufer, S. The team that wasn't. *Harvard Business Review.* November-December 1994, 22–38; Reagan-Cirincione, P. Improving the accuracy of group judgment: A process intervention combining group facilitation, social judgment analysis, and information technology. *Organizational Behavior and Human Decision Processes,* 1994, 58, 246–270.

32. Nohavandi, A., and Aranda, E. Restructuring teams for the re-engineered organization. *Academy of Management Executive,* November 1994, 58–68.

33. Adapted from Dumaine, G. The trouble with teams. *Fortune,* September 5, 1994, 86–92; Kearney, R.C., and Hays, S.W. Labor-management relations and participative decision-making: Toward a new paradigm. *Public Administration Review,* January/February 1994, 44–51; Allina has been formed by a merger between Health Span Health Systems and Medica. *Milwaukee Journal,* July 28, 1994, D1.

34. Parker, G.M. *Cross-Functional Teams: Working with Allies, Enemies, and Other Strangers.* San Francisco: Jossey-Bass, 1994.

35. Isabella, L.A., and Waddock, S.A. Top management team certainty: Environmental assessments, teamwork, and performance implications. *Journal of Management,* 1994, 20, 835–858.

36. Lawler, E.E. III. Total quality management and employee involvement: Are they compatible? *Academy of Management Executive,* February 1994, 68–76.

37. Mears, P. *Team Building: A Structured Learning Approach.* Delray Beach, Fla.: St. Lucie Press, 1994.

38. Wellins, R.S., Byham, W.C., and Dixon, G.R. Inside Teams: *How 20 World-Class Organizations Are Winning Through Teamwork.* San Francisco: Jossey-Bass, 1994; Van Aken, E.M., Monetta, D.J., and Sink, D.S. Affinity groups: The missing link is employee involvement. *Organizational Dynamics,* Spring 1994, 38–54.

39. Parker, G.M.; Clark, K.B., and Wheelwright, S.C. *The Product Development Challenge: Competing Through Speed, Quality, and Creativity.* Boston: Harvard Business School Press, 1995.

40. Schneider, B., and Bowen, D.E. *Winning the Service Game.* Boston: Harvard Business School Press, 1995.

41. Dumaine, B., 86–92; Wellins, R.S., Byham, W.C., and Dixon, G.R. *Inside Teams: How 20 World-Class Organizations Are Winning Through Teamwork,* San Francisco: Jossey-Bass, 1994.

42. Mohrman, S.A., Cohen, S.G., and Mohrman, A.M., Jr. *Designing Team-Based Organizations.* Jossey-Bass, 1995; Cohen, S.G. and Ledford, G.E., Jr. The effectiveness of self-managing teams. *Human Relations,* 1994, 47, 13–43.

43. Adapted from Cheney, A.B., Sims, H.P., Jr., and Manz, C.C. Teams and TQM. *Business Horizons,* September-October 1994, 16–25; Manz, C.C., and Sims, H.P., Jr. *Business Without Bosses: How Self-Managing Teams Are Building High Performance Companies.* New York: John Wiley & Sons, 1993; Nielson, L.C. The only unique resource. Across the Board, July/August 1994, 56–57; Junkins, J.R. Confessions of a Baldrige winner. *Management Review,* July 1994, 58.

44. Maier, N.R.T. Assets and liabilities in group problem-solving: The need for an integrative function. Psychology Review, 1967, 74, 239–249; Pacanowsky, M. Team tools for wicked problems. *Organizational Dynamics,* Winter 1995, 36– 51.

45. Dennis, A.R., and Valacich, J.S. Group sub-group, and nominal group idea generation: New rules for a new media? *Journal of Management,* 1994, 20, 723–736.

46. Glaser, S.R. Teamwork and communication: A 3-year case study of change. *Management Communication Quarterly,* 1994, 7, 282– 296.

47. Bazerman, M.H. *Judgment in Managerial Decision Making,* 3rd ed. New York: John Wiley & Sons, 1994.

48. Mullen, B., Anthony, T., Salas, E., and Driskell, J.E. Group cohesiveness and quality of decision making: An integration of tests of the groupthink hypothesis. *Small Group Research,* 1994, 25, 189–204; Miranda, S.M. Avoidance of groupthink: Meeting management using group support systems. *Small Group Research,* 1994, 25, 105–136.

49. Wagner, J.A. III. Participation's effects on performance and satisfaction: A reconsideration of research evidence. *Academy of Management Review,* 1994, 19, 312–330.

50. Hare, A. P. Group size. *American Behavioral Scientist,* 1981, 24, 695–708; Albanese, R., and Van Fleet, D.D. Rational behavior in groups: The free-riding tendency. *Academy of Management Review,* 1985, 10, 244–255.

51. Sundstrom, E., DeMeuse, K.P., and Futrell, D. Work teams: Applications and effectiveness. *American Psychologist,* 1990, 45. 120–133; Smith, K.G., Smith, K.A., Olian, J.D., Sims, H.P., Jr., O'Bannon, D.P., and Scully, J.A. Top management team demography and process: The role of social integration and communication. *Administrative Science Quarterly,* 1994, 39, 412–438.

52. Zenger, J.H., Musselwhite, E., Hurson, K., and Perrin, C. *Leading Teams: Mastering the New Role.* Homewood, Ill.: Business One Irwin, 1993; Belasco, J.A., and Stayer, R.C. Why empowerment doesn't empower: The bankruptcy of current paradigms. *Business Horizons,* March-April 1994, 29–41; Caminiti, S. What team leaders need to know. *Fortune,* February 20, 1995, 93–100.

53. Fearon, D. Correspondence with the authors. January 11, 1991.

54. Hirschhorn, L. *Managing in the New Team Environment: Skills, Tools, and Methods,* Reading, Mass.: Addison-Wesley, 1991; Steckler, N. and Fondas, N. Building team leader effectiveness: A diagnostic tool. *Organizational Dynamics,* Winter 1995, 20–35.

55. Adapted from Trice, H.M., and Beyer, J.M. *The Culture of Work Organizations,* Englewood Cliffs, N.J.: Prentice-Hall, 1–32.

56. Schein, E.H. What is culture? In P.J. Frost, L.F. Moore, M.R. Louis, C.C. Lundberg, and J. Martin (eds.), *Reframing Organizational Culture.* Newbury Park, Calif.: Sage, 1991, 243–253.

57. Schultz, M. *On Studying Organizational Cultures.* New York: deGruyter, 1994.

58. Trice, H.M., and Beyer, J.M., *The Culture of Work Organizations,* 175–253.

59. Black, B. Culture and effort: British and Irish work–related values and attitudes. *International Journal of Human Resource Management,* 1994, 5, 875–892; Storey, J., and Bacon, N. Individualism and collectivism: Into the 1990s. *International Journal of Human Resource Management,* 1993, 4, 665–684.

60. Abrahamson, E., and Fombrun, C.J. Macrocultures: Determinants and consequences. *Academy of Management Review,* 1994, 19, 728–755; Phillips, M.E. Industry mindsets: Exploring the cultures of two macro–organizational settings. *Organization Science,* 1994, 5, 384–402.

61. Mitroff, I. *Break-Away Thinking.* New York: John Wiley & Sons, 1988; Senge, P.M. *The Fifth Discipline: The Art and Practice of the Learning Organization.* New York: Doubleday, 1990, 174–204.

62. Keller, M. *Collision: GM, Toyota, Volkswagen and the Race to Own the 21st Century.* New York: Doubleday, 1993.

63. Grant, R.M., Shani, R., and Krishnan, R. TQM's challenge to management theory and practice. *Sloan Management Review,* Winter 1994, 34.

64. Chatman, J.A., and Jehn, K.A. Assessing the relationship between industry characteristics and organizational culture: How different can you be? *Academy of Management Journal,* 1994, 37, 522–553.

65. Schein, E.H. *Organizational Culture and Leadership.* San Francisco: Jossey-Bass, 1985.

66. Developed from Hatch, M.J. The dynamics of organizational culture. *Academy of Management Review,* 1993, 18, 657–693.

67. Adapted from O'Reilly, C.A. III, Chatman, J., Caldwell, D.F. People and organizational culture: A profile comparison approach to assessing person-organization fit. *Academy of Management Journal,* 1991, 34, 487–516; Sheridan, J.E. Organizational culture and employee retention. *Academy of Management Journal,* 1992, 35, 1036–1056.

68. Adapted from O'Reilly, B. J&J is on a roll. *Fortune,* December 26, 1994, 178–192; Weber, J. A big company that works. *Business Week,* May 4, 1992, 124–132.

69. Adapted from O'Reilly, B., 178–192; Farnham, A. State your values, hold the hot air. *Fortune,* April 19, 1993, 117–124.

70. Allen, N.J., and Meyer, J.P. Organizational socialization tactics: A longitudinal analysis of links to newcomers' commitment and role orientation. *Academy of Management Journal,* 1990, 33, 847–858.

71. Schneider, B., Gunnarson, S.K., and Niles-Jolly, K. Creating the climate and culture of success. *Organizational Dynamics,* Summer 1994, 17–29.

72. Dutton, J.E., Dukerich, J.M., and Harquail, C.V. Organizational images and member identification. *Administrative Science Quarterly,* 1994, 39, 239–263; Rafaeli, A., and Pratt, M.G. Tailored meanings: On the meaning and impact of organizational dress. *Academy of Managment Review,* 1993, 18, 32–55.

73. Pascale, R. Fitting new employees into the company culture. *Fortune,* May 28, 1984, 28.

74. Adapted from O'Reilly, B., 178–192; Farnham, A. State your values, hold the hot air. *Fortune,* April 19, 1993, 117–124; Hurstak, J.M., and Pearson, A. *Johnson & Johnson: Hospital Services.* Case 9-392-050. Boston: Harvard Business School, 1992.

75. Hatch, M.J. The dynamics of organizational culture. *Academy of Management Review,* 1993, 18, 657–693.

76. Cheney, A.B., Sims, H.P., Jr., and Manz, C.C. Teams and TQM. *Business Horizons,* September-October 1994, 16–25.

77. Trice, H.M., and Beyer, J.M., *The Culture of Work Organizations,* 78–79.

78. Difonzo, N., Bardia, P., and Rosnow, R.L. Reining in rumors. *Organizational Dynamics,* Summer, 1994, 47–62; Noon, M., and Delridge, R. News from behind my hand: Gossip in organizations. *Organization Studies,* 1993, 14, 23–36.

79. Trice, H.M., and Beyer, J.M., *The Culture of Work Organizations,* 79.

80. O'Reilly, B., 178–192.

81. Walton, S., with Huey, J. *Sam Walton: Made in America.* New York: Doubleday, 1992.

82. Trice, H.M., and Beyer, J.M. Cultural leadership in organizations. *Organization Science,* 1991, 2, 149–169.

83. Saparito, B. And the winner is still...Wal–Mart. *Fortune,* May 2, 1994, 62–70.

84. Trice, H.M., and Beyer, J.M., 149–169.

85. Hooijberg, R., and Petrock, F. On cultural change: Using the competing values framework to help leaders execute a transformational strategy. *Human Resource Management,* 1993, 32, 29–50.

86. Cartwright, S., and Cooper, C.L. The role of culture compatibility in successful organizational marriage. *Academy of Management Executive,* May 1993, 57–70; Kotter, J.P., and Heskett, J.L. *Corporate Culture and Performance.* New York: Free Press, 1992; Kerr, J., and Slocum, J.W., Jr. Managing corporate culture through reward systems. Academy of *Management Executive,* 1987, 1, 98–108; Ouchi, W. *Theory Z,* Reading, Mass.: Addison-Wesley, 1981; Denison, D.R. *Corporate Culture and*

Organizational Effectiveness. New York: John Wiley & Sons, 1990.

87. Adapted from *National Performance Review*. Washington, D.C.: U.S. Government Printing Office, 1993; Church, G.C. Gorezilla zaps the system. *Time*, September 13, 1993, 25–29.

88. Adapted from Machan, D. A too proud papa. *Forbes,* September 27, 1993, 46–48; *1994 Annual Report: Tandem Computers, Inc.,* Cupertino, Calif.: Tandem Computers, Inc., 1995; Waurzyniak, P. Tandem changes its business model. *Electronic Business Buyer,* May 1994, 76–78; Zipser, A. Do-gooder does well. *Barrons,* July 26, 1993, 28–29; Orlin, J.M. Selling in teams: Consultative selling teams training at Tandem and Data General. *Training and Development,* December 1993, 26–32.

89. Adapted from Loeb, M. Ten Commandments for managing creative people. *Fortune,* January 16, 1995, 135–136; Tully, S. Why to go for stretch targets. *Fortune,* November 14, 1994, 145–155; Ghoshal, S., and Bartlett, C.A. Changing the role of top management: Beyond structure to processes. *Harvard Business Review,* January-February 1995, 86–96; Collins, J.C., and Porras, J.I. Built to Last: *Successful Habits of Visionary Companies*. New York: Harper Business, 1995.

90. Adapted from Dumaine, B. Those high flying PepsiCo managers. *Fortune,* April 10, 1989; Zinn, L., Berry, J., and Burns, G. Will the Pepsi brass be drinking hemlock? *Business Week,* July 25, 1994, 31; Lubove, S. We have a big pond to play in. *Forbes,* September 12, 1993, 216–224; Wolfe, J. PepsiCo and the fast food industry. In M.A. Hitt, R.D. Ireland, and R.E. Hoskisson (eds.), *Strategic Management: Competitiveness and Globalization*. St. Paul, Minn.: West, 1995, 856–879.

91. Morgan, M.J. How corporate culture drives strategy. *Long Range Planning,* 1993, 26(2), 110–118.

92. McAuley, J. Exploring issues in culture and competence. *Human Relations,* 1994, 47, 417–430; Byron, W.J. Coming to terms with the new corporate contract. *Business Horizons,* January-February 1995, 8–15.

93. Clement, R.W. Culture leadership and power: The keys to organizational change. *Business Horizons,* January-February 1994, 33–39.

94. Lawler, E.E. III, and Galbraith, J.R. Avoiding the corporate dinosaur syndrome. *Organizational Dynamics,* Autumn 1994, 5–17.

95. Bennett, R.H. III, Fadil, P.A., and Greenwood, R.T. Cultural alignment in response to strategic organizational change: New considerations for changing framework. *Journal of Management Studies,* 1994, 6, 474–490.

96. Pfeffer, J. *Competitive Advantage through People: Unleashing the Power of the Work Force*. Boston: Harvard Business School Press, 1995.

97. Adapted from Weiss, J., Wahlstrom, M., and Marshall, E. The Consolidated Life: Caught between corporate cultures, *Journal of Management Case Studies,* 1986, 2, 238–243. Elsevier Science Publishing Co., Inc., 52 Vanderbilt Ave., New York, NY 10017. Used with permission.

98. Adapted from Schuman, M. Thin is out, fat is in. *Forbes,* May 9, 1994; A.T. Cross Company, *Incentive,* October 1993; Quinn, J. Tom's of Maine. *Incentive,* December 1993; Success, *Working Woman,* November 1993; Paying employees to work elsewhere, *INC.,* February 1993; Chappell, Tom. *The Soul of a Business*. New York: Bantam, 1993; Benson, Tracy. In trust we manage. *Industry Week,* March 4, 1991; Mangelsdorf, Martha. Managing the new work force. *INC.,* January 1990.

CHAPTER 17

1. Adapted from Brewer, G. The demotivator? *Incentive,* April 1993, 26–30; Sunbeam-Oster unexpectedly dismisses chairman Paul B. Kazarian. *New York Times,* January 1, 1993, C1; Sunbeam-Oster will pay $173 million to Paul Kazarian and two partners to settle litigation over his ouster. *New York Times,* July 23, 1993, C15; DeGeorge, G. Why Sunbeam is shining brighter. *Business Week,* August 29, 1994, 74–75.

2. Rahim, M.A. *Managing Conflict in Organizations,* 2nd ed. Westport, Conn.: Praeger, 1992.

3. Boettger, R.D., and Greer, C.R. On the wisdom of rewarding A while hoping for B. *Organization Science,* 1994, 5, 569–582; DiBella, A.J. The role of assumptions in implementing practices across cultural boundaries. *Journal of Applied Behavioral Science,* 1993, 29, 311–327.

4. Tjosvold, D. *The Conflict-Positive Organization: Stimulate Diversity and Create Unity*. Reading, Mass.: Addison-Wesley, 1991.

5. Hrebiniak, L.G. *The We-Force Management: How to Build and Sustain Cooperation*. New York: Lexington, 1994.

6. Kahn, R., Wolfe, D., Quinn, R., and Snoek, J. *Organizational Stress: Studies in Role Conflict and Ambiguity*. New York: John Wiley & Sons, 1964.

7. Teboul, J.B. Facing and coping with uncertainty during organizational encounter. *Management Communication Quarterly,* 1994, 8, 190–224; Van Sell, M., Brief, A.P., and Schuler, R.S. Role conflict and role ambiguity: Integration of the literature and directions for future research, *Human Relations,* 1981, 34, 43–71.

8. Adapted from Mendoza, M. Privacy and the job. PBS looks at an issue that's taking on heat. *Dallas Morning News,* August 23, 1994, 1C, 2C; Schultz, E.E. Employee beware: The boss may be listening. *Wall Street Journal,* July 29, 1994, C1, C16; Yates, R.E. Workers fear counseling backlash. *Orlando Sentinel,* June 19, 1994, E1, E7; Geyelin, M. Cellular phones may betray client confidences. *Wall Street Journal,* September 1, 1994, B1, B7.

9. Kahn, W.A., and Kram, K.E. Authority at work: Internal models and their organizational consequences. *Academy of Management Review,* 19, 1994, 17–50.

10. Wiersma, U.J. A taxonomy of behavioral strategies for coping with work-home conflict. *Human Relations,* 1994, 47, 211–221.

11. Wharton, A.S., and Erickson, R.J. Managing emotions on the job and at home: Understanding the consequences of multiple emotional roles. *Academy of Management Review,* 1993, 18, 457– 486.

12. Quenk, N.L. *Besides Ourselves: Our Hidden Personalities in Everyday Life*. Palo Alto, Calif.: Consulting Psychologists Press, 1993.

13. Ibarra, H. Personal networks of women and minorities in management: A conceptual framework. *Academy of Management Review,* 1993, 18, 56–87.

14. Powell, G.N. *Women & Men in Management*. 2nd ed., Newbury Park, Calif.: Sage, 1993.

15. Fagenson, E.A. (ed.). *Women in Management: Trends, Issues and Challenges in Managing Diversity*. Newbury Park, Calif.: Sage, 1993.

16. Condor, B. All work, no play not healthy. *Houston Chronicle,* February 6, 1995, 2D; Pittman, J.F. Work-family fit as a mediator of work factors on marital tension: Evidence from the interface of greedy institutions. *Human Relations,* 1994, 47, 183–207.

17. Falkenberg, L. Improving the accuracy of stereotypes within the workplace, *Journal of Management,* 1990, 16, 107–118.

18. Triandis, H.C., Kurowski, L.L., and Gelfand, M.J. Workplace diversity. In H.C. Triandis, M.D. Dunnette, and L.M. Hough (eds.), *Handbook of Industrial and Organizational Psychology*. Palo Alto, Calif.: Consulting Psychologists Press, 1994, 769–827.

19. Adapted from Scism, L. Life insurers struggle with "churning." *Houston Chronicle,* January 8, 1995, 1E, 8E; Fierman, J. The death and rebirth of the salesman. *Fortune,* July 25, 1994, 80–91; Clark, R.W., and Darnel Lattal, A. The ethics of sales: Finding the right balance. *Business Horizons,* July-August 1993, 66–69; Crosson, C. Class suit alleges churning by Pru. *National Underwriter,* April 4, 1994, 1, 3; Pare, T.P. Scandal isn't all that ails the Pru. *Fortune,* March 21, 1994, 52–56.

20. Blake, R.R., and Mouton, J.S. *Solving Costly Organizational Conflicts,* San Francisco: Jossey-Bass, 1984; Korabik, K., Baril, G.L., and Watson, C. Managers' conflict management style and leadership effectiveness: The moderating effects of gender. *Sex Roles,* 1993, 29, 405–420; Tjosvold, D. *Learning to Manage Conflict: Getting People to Work Together Productively*. New York: Lexington, 1993.

21. Thomas, K.W. Conflict and negotiation processes in organizations. In M.D. Dunnette, and L.M. Hough (eds.), *Handbook of Industrial and Organizational Psychology,* 2nd ed., vol. 3. Palo Alto, Calif.: Consulting Psychologists Press, 1992, 651–717; Nicotera, A.M. Beyond two dimensions: A grounded theory model of conflict-handling behavior. *Management Communication Quarterly,* 1993, 6, 282–306.

22. Gwartney-Gibbs, P.A., and Lach, D.J. Gender differences in clerical workers' disputes over tasks, interpersonal treatment, and emotion. *Human Relations,* 1994, 47, 611–639.

23. Roy, B. From community mayhem to effective mediation: The usefulness of research. *NIDR Forum,* Summer 1994, 4–11; Yukl, G., and Falbe, C.M. Influence tactic and objectives in upward, downward, and lateral influence attempts. *Journal of Applied Psychology,* 1990, 75, 132–140.

24. Adapted from Kaplan, E. Confronting the issue of race in developmental relationships: Does open discussion enhance or suppress the mentor-protégé, bond? *Academy of Management Executive,* May 1994, 78–80; Thomas, D. Racial dynamics in cross-race developmental relationships. *Administrative Science Quarterly,* 1993, 38, 169–194.

25. Ball, G.A., Trevino, L.K., and Sims,

H.P., Jr. Just and unjust punishment: Influences on subordinate performance and citizenship. *Academy of Management Journal,* 1994, 37, 299–322; Moore, J.E. Predators and prey: A new ecology of competition. *Harvard Business Review,* May-June 1993, 75–86.

26. Connelly, J. Have we become mad dogs in the office? *Fortune,* November 28, 1994, 197–199; Jamieson, K.H. *Beyond the Double Bind.* New York: Oxford University Press, 1995.

27. Bazerman, M.H., and Neale, M.A. *Negotiating Rationally.* New York: Free Press, 1993; Lewicki, R.J., Sheppard, B.H., and Bies, R. (eds.). *Research on Negotiations in Organizations.* Vol. 4. Greenwich, Conn.: JAI Press, 1994.

28. Thacker, R.A., Stein, M., and Bresler, S.J. Mediation keeps complaints out of court. *HR Magazine,* May 1994, 72–75; Carver, T.B., and Vondra, A.A. Alternative dispute resolution: Why it doesn't work and why it does. *Harvard Business Review,* May-June 1994, 120–130.

29. Kets de Vries, M.F.R. The dynamics of family controlled firms: The good and the bad news. *Organizational Dynamics,* Winter 1993, 59–71; Berman, P., and Alger, A. Reclaiming the patrimony. *Forbes,* March 14, 1994, 50–54.

30. Adapted from Boisseau, C. Making succession succeed: Transition often difficult for family-owned business. *Houston Chronicle,* July 12, 1994, 1B, 3B.

31. Weeks, D. *The Eight Essential Steps to Conflict Resolution.* Los Angeles: Jeremy P. Tarcher, 1992.

32. Hayes, J. *Interpersonal Skills: Goal Directed Behavior at Work.* New York: Routledge, 1994.

33. McAllister, D.J. Affect- and cognition-based trust as foundations for interpersonal cooperation in organizations. *Academy of Management Journal,* 1995, 38, 24–59.

34. Blair, J.D., Savage, G.T., and Whitehead, C.J. A strategic approach for negotiating with hospital stakeholders, *Health Care Management Review,* 1989, 14, 13–23; Prein, H. A contingency approach for conflict intervention, *Group and Organization Studies,* 1984, 9, 81–102.

35. Argyris, C. Good communication that blocks learning. *Harvard Business Review,* July-August 1994, 77–85.

36. Walton, R.E., Cutcher-Gershenfeld, J.E., and McKersie, R.B. *Strategic Negotiations: A Theory of Change in Labor-Management Negotiations.* Boston: Harvard Business School Press, 1994.

37. Kochan, T.A., and Osterman, P. *The Mutual Gains Enterprise: Forging a Partnership Among Labor, Management, and Government.* Boston: Harvard Business School Press, 1994; Ware, J.P. *Bargaining Strategies: Collaborative Versus Competitive Strategies.* Teaching note. Boston: Harvard Business School, 1980.

38. Fisher, R., Kopelman, E., and Schneider, A.K. *Beyond Machiavelli: Tools for Coping with Conflict.* Boston: Harvard University Press, 1994; Mnookin, R.H. Why negotiations fail: An exploration of barriers to the resolution of conflict. *NIDR Forum,* Summer 1993, 21–32.

39. Greenhalgh, L. I would abandon business contracts. *Fortune,* March 26, 1990, 49.

40. Post, F.R., and Bennett, R.J. Use of collaborative collective bargaining process in labor negotiations. *International Journal of Conflict Management,* 1994, 5, 34–61; Pinkley, R.L., and Northcraft, G.R. Conflict frames of reference: Implications for dispute processes and outcomes. *Academy of Management Journal,* 1994, 37, 193–205.

41. Ramundo, B.A. *The Bargaining Manager: Enhancing Organizational Results Through Effective Negotiations.* Westport, Conn.: Quarum, 1994; Susskind, L.E., and Landry, E.M. Implementing a mutual gains approach to collective bargaining. *Negotiation Journal,* January 1991, 5–10.

42. Griffin, T.J., and Daggatt, W.R. *The Global Negotiator: Building Strong Business Relationships Anywhere in the World.* New York: Harper Business, 1990; Klein, G., and Rothman, J. The role of pre-negotiation in addressing "intransigen" conflicts. *International Journal of Group Tensions,* 1993, 23, 225–243.

43. Wever, K.S. *Negotiating Competitiveness: Employment Relations and Organizational Innovation in Germany and the United States.* Boston: Harvard Business School Press, 1995; Feuille, P., and Chachere, D.R. Looking fair or being fair: Remedial voice procedures in nonunion workplaces. *Journal of Management,* 1995, 21, 27–42.

44. Adapted from Lansbury, R.D., and Marchington, M. Joint consultation and industrial relations: Experience from Australia and overseas. *Asia Pacific Journal of Human Resources,* 1993, 31, 62–82; Alexander, M.J., and Green, R. Workplace productivity and joint consultation. *Australian Bulletin of Labour,* 1992, 18, 95–118; Lansbury, R.D., and Macdonald, D. *Workplace Industrial Relations: Australian Cases.* Melbourne, Australia: Oxford University Press, 1992.

45. Weiss, S.E. Negotiating with "Romans"—Part 1. *Sloan Management Review,* Winter 1994, 51–61; Weiss, S.E. Negotiating with "Romans"—Part 2. *Sloan Management Review,* Spring 1994, 85–99.

46. Adapted form Barnett, J.H., and Karson, M.J. Personal values and business decisions: An explanatory investigation, *Journal of Business Ethics,* 1987, 6, 371–382.

47. Frederick, W.C. Values, *Nature, and Culture in the American Corporation.* New York: Oxford University Press, 1995.

48. Seyle, H. The stress concept today. In I.L. Kutash, L.B. Schlesinger, and Associates (eds.), *Handbook on Stress Anxiety,* San Francisco: Jossey-Bass, 1980, 127–143.

49. Seyle, H., 128; Seeman, J. Toward a model of positive health, *American Psychologist,* 1989, 44, 1099–1109.

50. Quick, J.C., and Quick, J.D. *Organizational Stress and Preventive Management,* New York: McGraw-Hill, 1984, 1–14.

51. Ross, R.R., and Altmaier, E.M. *Intervention for Occupational Stress.* Thousand Oaks, Calif.: Sage, 1994.

52. Williams, K.J., and Alliger, G.M. Role stressors, mood spillover, and perceptions of work-family conflict in employed parents. *Academy of Management Journal,* 1994, 37, 837–868; Fox, M.J., Dwyer, D.J., and Ganster, D.C. Effects of stressful job demands and control on physiological and attitudinal outcomes in a hospital setting. *Academy of Management Journal,* 1993, 36, 289–318.

53. Adapted from Cox, T. Stress, Baltimore: University Park Press, 1978; Quick, J.C., Nelson, D.L., and Quick, J.D. *Stress and Challenge at the Top: The Paradox of the Successful Executive,* New York: John Wiley & Sons, 1990.

54. Cordes, C.L., and Dougherty, T.W. A review and integration of research on job burnout. *Academy of Management Review,* 1993, 18, 621–656.

55. Leiter, M.P., Clark, D., and Durup, J. Distinct models of burnout and commitment among men and women in the military. *Journal of Applied Behavioral Science,* 1994, 30, 63–82.

56. Ray, E.B., and Miller, K.I. Social support, home/work stress, and burnout: Who can help? *Journal of Applied Behavioral Science,* 30, 1994, 357–373.

57. Golembiewski, R.T., and Munzenrider, R. *Phases of Burnout: Developments in Concepts and Applications.* New York: Praeger, 1988.

58. Adapted from O'Reilly, D. New truths about staying healthy, *Fortune,* September 25, 1989, 58–66; Newton, T., Handy, J., and Fineman, S. *Managing Stress: Subjectivity and Power in the Workplace.* Thousand Oaks, Calif.: Sage, 1995; Wharton, A.S., and Erickson, R.J., 457–486.

59. Friedman, M., and Roseman, R. *Type A Behavior and Your Heart.* New York: Knopf, 1974, 84.

60. McLean, A.A. *Work Stress,* Reading, Mass.: Addison-Wesley, 1979, 69.

61. Schhaubroeck, J., Ganster, D.C., and Kemmerer, B.E. Job complexity "Type A" behavior and cardiovascular disorder: A prospective study. *Academy of Management Journal,* 1994, 37, 426–439.

62. Beehr, T.A. *Psychological Stress in the Workplace.* New York: Routledge, 1995; Hellriegel, D., Slocum, J.W., Jr., and Woodman, R.W. *Organizational Behavior,* 7th ed., St. Paul, Minn.: West, 1995.

63. French, W., and Zawacki, R. (eds.). *Organization Development and Transformation,* 4th ed. Burr Ridge, Ill.: Irwin, 1994.

64. Schuler, R.S. *Human Resource Management,* 5th ed. St. Paul, Minn.: West, 1995.

65. Adapted from Stratton, W.E. The reluctant clerk: A supervisor's challenge. In R.E. Meadows (ed.). *Annual Advances in Business Cases* 1993. Nacogdoches, Tex.: Society for Case Research, 1994, 389–391. This case was prepared by William E. Stratton of Idaho State University and is intended to be used as a basis for class discussion rather than to illustrate either effective or ineffective handling of the situation. The names of the organization, individuals, and location have been disguised to preserve the organization's desire for anonymity. Presented to and accepted by the refereed Society for Case Research. All rights reserved to the author and the SCR. Copyright © 1993 by William E. Stratton. Used with permission.

66. Adapted from American Airlines may be too healthy, *Business Week,* October 31, 1994; Donoghue, J.A. Turning point. *Air Transport World,* January 1994; News briefs, *Air Transport World,* January 1994; Halcrow, A. At odds with the future. *Personnel Journal,* January 1994; AMR posts 1993 loss, *Aviation Week & Space Technology,* January 24, 1994; Say it ain't so, Bob. *Air Transport World,* January 1994; Did Clinton scramble American's profit picture? *Business Week,* December 6, 1993; Cardona, M.M. Airline strike over, but problems linger. *Pensions and Investments,* November 29, 1993; McKenna, J. T. Clinton strike action may open new era. *Aviation Week and Space Technology,* November 29, 1993; Drastic steps in such troubled times,

Aviation Week and Space Technology, November 22, 1993.

Chapter 18

1. Adapted from Churbuck, D.C. Don't leave headquarters without it. *Forbes,* December 20, 1993, 242–243.

2. Simons, R. Control in an age of empowerment. *Harvard Business Review,* March-April, 1995, 80–88.

3. Simons, R. *Levers of Control: How Managers Use Innovative Control Systems to Drive Strategic Renewal.* Boston: Harvard University Press, 1995.

4. Corbett, C.J., and Van Wassenhove, L.N. The green fee: Internalizing and operationalizing environmental issues. *California Management Review,* 1993, 36(1), 116–135; Clarkson, M.B.E. A stakeholder framework for analyzing and evaluating corporate social performance. *Academy of Management Review,* 1995, 20, 92–117.

5. Quick, J.C. Crafting an organizational culture: Herb's hand at Southwest Airlines. *Organizational Dynamics,* Autumn 1992, 45–56.

6. Adapted from Dean, J.W., and Evans, J.R. *Total Quality: Management, Organization, and Strategy.* St. Paul, Minn.: West, 1994, 205; Meyer, C. How the right measures help teams excel. *Harvard Business Review,* May-June 1994, 95–103.

7. Bowne, D.W., Russell, M.L., Morgan, S.A., Optenberg, S., and Clarke, A. Reduced disability and health care costs in an industrial fitness program. *Journal of Occupational Medicine,* 1984, 26, 809–816; Eurfurt, J.C., Foote, A., and Heirich, M.A. The cost effectiveness of worksite wellness programs for hypertension control, weight loss, smoking cessation, and exercise. *Personnel Psychology,* 1992, 45(1), 5–29.

8. Adapted from Ross, P.E. I can read your face. *Forbes,* December 1994, 304–305.

9. Yan, A., and Gray, B. Bargaining power, management control, and performance in the United States-China joint ventures: A comparative study. *Academy of Management Journal,* 1994, 37, 1478–1517; Arthur, J.B. Effects of human resource systems on manufacturing performance and turnover. *Academy of Management Journal,* 1994, 37, 670–687.

10. Adapted from Cronin, M.J. *Doing Business on the Internet: How the Electronic Highway Is Transforming American Companies.* New York: Van Nostrand Reinhold, 1994.

11. Lowe, T., and Machin, J.L. *New Perspectives on Management Control.* New York: Macmillan, 1987.

12. Personal interview with John Semyan, Dallas, Texas, March 5, 1995.

13. Sitkin, S.B., Sutcliffe, K.M., and Schroeder, R.G. Distinguishing control from learning in total quality management: A contingency perspective. *Academy of Management Review,* 1994, 19, 537–564.

14. Adapted from Winterle, M.J. Toward diversity, with carrots and sticks. *Across the Board,* January-February 1993, 50–51; Hogan, E. Mobil Oil Corporation. In C.P. Harvey and M.J. Allard (eds.), *Understanding Diversity.* New York: HarperCollins, 1995, 212–222.

15. Hamel, G., and Prahalad, C.K. *Competing for the Future.* Boston: Harvard Business School Press, 1994; Pitts, R., and Lei, D. *The Challenge of Strategic Management.* St. Paul, Minn.: West, 1996.

16. Adapted from Hoerr, J. The cultural revolution at A.O. Smith. *Business Week,* May 29, 1989, 66–68.

17. Gupta, P.P., Dirsmith, M.W., and Fogarty, T.J. Coordination and control in a government agency: Contingency and institutional perspectives on GAO audits. *Administrative Science Quarterly,* 1994, 39, 264–284; Miles, R.E., and Snow, C.C. *Fit, Failure and the Hall of Fame.* New York: Free Press, 1994.

18. Schuler, R.S. *Managing Human Resources,* 5th ed. St. Paul, Minn.: West, 1995, 424–459.

19. Ghorpade, J., and Chen, M.M. Creating quality-driven performance appraisal systems. *Academy of Management Executive,* 1995, 9(1), 32–41.

20. Kaplan, R.S., and Norton, D.P. The balanced scorecard—Measures that drive performance. *Harvard Business Review,* January-February 1992, 71–79.

21. Simons, R. *Levers of Control: How Managers Use Innovative Control Systems to Drive Strategic Renewal.* Boston: Harvard Business School Press, 1995.

22. Horngren, C.T., and Foster, G. *Cost Accounting: A Managerial Emphasis.* Englewood Cliffs, N.J.: Prentice-Hall, 1994.

23. Sord, B., and Welsh, G. *Managerial Planning and Control.* Austin: University of Texas Press, 1964, 93–99. For additional work on related topics, see Boettger, R.D., and Greer, C.R. On the wisdom of rewarding A while hoping for B. *Organization Science,* 1994, 5, 569–582.

24. Garrison, R.H., and Noreen, E.W. *Managerial Accounting: Concepts for Planning, Control and Decision Making,* 7th ed. Burr Ridge, Ill.: Irwin, 1994, 187–213.

25. Beischel, M.E. Improving production with process value analysis. *Journal of Accountancy,* September 1990, 55–63.

26. Adapted from Pare, T.P. A new tool for managing costs. *Fortune,* June 14, 1993, 124–129.

27. Southerst, J. Suddenly, it all makes sense. *Canadian Business,* March 1994, 39–42; Worthy, F.S. Japan's smart secret weapon. *Fortune,* August 12, 1991, 72–75.

28. Donaldson, T., and Diunfee, T.W. Toward a unified conception of business ethics: Integrative social contracts theory. *Academy of Management Review,* 1994, 19, 252–284; Daboub, A.J., Rasheed, A.M.A., Priem, R.L., and Gray, D.A. Top management team characteristics and corporate illegal activity. *Academy of Management Review,* 1995, 20, 138–170.

29. Picard, M. Working under an electronic thumb. *Training,* February 1994, 47–51.

30. Sheeline, W.E. How companies spy on employees. *Fortune,* November 4, 1991, 131–136; Griffith, T.L. Teaching big brother to be a team player: Computer monitoring and quality. *Academy of Management Executive,* 1993, 7, 73–80.

31. Adapted from Picard, M. Working under an electronic thumb. *Training,* February 1994, 47–51.

32. Bennett, N., Blum, T.C., and Roman, P.M. Presence of drug screening and employee assistance programs. *Journal of Organizational Behavior,* 1994, 15, 549–562.

33. Barnum, D.T., and Gleason, J.M. The credibility of drug tests. *Industrial and Labor Relations Review,* 1994, 47, 610–621; Tepper, B.J. Investigation of general and program-specific attitudes toward corporate drug-testing policies. *Journal of Applied Psychology,* 1994, 79, 392–402.

34. Solomon, R.M., and Usprich, S.J. Employment drug testing. *Business Quarterly,* Winter 1993, 73–79; Crow, S.M., Fok, L.Y., and Hartman, S.J. Drug testing in labor arbitration: Does it impact the decision-making process? *Journal of Managerial Issues,* 1994, 6, 297–311.

35. Bass, D.D. Combating crime. *Nation's Business,* March 1994, 16–24; Survey puts 1994's shrink at 1.79% of retail volume. *Supermarket News,* January 9, 1995, 13–14.

36. Adapted from Jaunch, L.R., Coltrin, S.A., Bedeian, A.G., and Glueck, W.F. *The Management Experience: Cases, Exercises and Readings,* 4th ed. Chicago: Dryden, 1986, 254–255.

37. Adapted from Daft, R.L. *Organization Theory & Design,* 5th ed. St. Paul, Minn.: West, 1995, 326–328.

Chapter 19

1. Adapted from Silverman, D. On-line experiment's goal is to link entire town. *Houston Chronicle,* February 5, 1995, 22A; Seaman, B. The future is already here. *Time Special Issue,* Spring 1995, 30–33; Hays, L. Working it out: Computer networks are profoundly changing the workplace. *Wall Street Journal,* November 14, 1994, R22; Karlgaard, R., and Malone, M. City versus country: Tom Peters and George Gilder debate the impact of technology on location. *Forbes ASAP,* February 22, 1995, 56–61; Baig, E. WEB—Weary? Let your browser do the walking. *Business Week,* March 27, 1995, 192–193.

2. Elmer-DeWitt, P. Welcome to cyberspace: What is it? Where is it? And how do we get there? *Time,* Spring 1995, 4–11; O'Hara-Devereaux and Johansen, R. *Globalwork: Bridging Distance, Culture, and Time.* San Francisco: Jossey-Bass, 1994.

3. Silverman, D., 22A.

4. Leavitt, H. J., and Whisler, T.L. Management in the 1980's. *Harvard Business Review,* November-December 1958, 41–48; Friedman, A.L. The information technology field: Using fields and paradigms for analyzing technological change. *Human Relations,* 1994, 47, 367–392.

5. Zahedi, F. *Intelligent Systems for Business: Expert Systems with Neural Networks.* Belmont, Calif.: Wadsworth, 1993.

6. McKenny, J.L., with Mason, R.O. and Copeland, D.G. *Waves of Change: Business Evolution through Information Technology.* Boston: Harvard Business School Press, 1995.

7. Stewart, T.A. The information age in charts. *Fortune,* April 4, 1994, 75–78.

8. Schlender, B. Planning a career in a world without managers. *Fortune,* March 20, 1995, 72–80; Thach, L., and Woodman, R.W. Organizational change and information technology: Managing on the edge of cyberspace. *Organizational Dynamics,* Summer 1994, 30–46.

9. Adapted from D'Amico, M. New man and the sea. *Forbes ASAP,* August 29, 1994,

31; LaPlante, A. Imaging your sea of data. *Forbes ASAP,* August 29, 1994, 21–23; Feinberg, A. Wired promoter. *Forbes ASAP,* February 27, 1995, 26–28; Kupfer, A. Alone together: Will being wired set us free? *Fortune,* March 20, 1995, 94–104.

10. Earl, M.J., and Feeny, D.F. Is your CIO adding value? *Sloan Management Review,* Spring 1994, 11–20; Kessler, A. Fire your MIS director. *Forbes ASAP,* February 27, 1995, 23.

11. Laudon, K.C., and Laudon, J.P. *Information Systems: A Problem-Solving Approach,* 3rd ed. Orlando: Dryden, 1995.

12. Quinn, J.B., and Baily, M.N. Information technology: Increasing productivity in services. *Academy of Management Executive,* August 1994, 28–51.

13. Zahedi, F. *Quality Information Systems.* Danvers, Mass.: Boyd and Fraser, 1995.

14. Rheingold, H. *The Virtual Community: Homesteading on the Electronic Frontier.* Reading, Mass.: Addison-Wesley, 1993.

15. Zachary, G.P. It's a mail thing: Electronic messaging gets a rating—Ex. *Wall Street Journal,* June 22, 1994, A1, A10.

16. Adapted from Clark D. Intel seeks to mollify Pentium owners but balks at unquestioned replacement. *Wall Street Journal,* December 14, 1994, A3; Mossberg, W.S. Intel isn't serving millions who bought its Pentium campaign. *Wall Street Journal,* December 15, 1994, B1; Sager, I., and Hof, R.D. Bare knuckles at big blue. *Business Week,* December 26, 1994, 60–63; Hof, R.D. Intel: Far beyond the Pentium. *Business Week,* February 20, 1995, 88–90.

17. Hedterick, R.C. Paradigms and paradoxes: Preparing for the information revolution. *Higher Education Product Companion,* 1994, 3(1), 8–13; McLeod, R., Jr. *Management Information Systems,* 6th ed. Englewood Cliffs, N.J.: Prentice-Hall, 1995.

18. Hof, R.D. Intel: Far beyond the Pentium. *Business Week,* February 20, 1995, 88–90; Port, O. Wonder chips: How they'll make computing power ultrafast and ultracheap. *Business Week,* July 4, 1994, 86–92.

19. O'Brien, J.A. *Introduction to Information Systems,* 7th ed. Burr Ridge, Ill.: Irwin, 1994.

20. Eilipczak, B. The ripple effect of computer networking. *Training,* March 1994, 40–47; Verity, J.W., and Hof, R.D. The Internet: How it will change the way you do business. *Business Week,* November 14, 1994, 80–88; Tetzeli, R. The Internet and your business. *Fortune,* March 7, 1994, 86–90.

21. Arinze, B. *Microcomputers for Managers,* Belmont, Calif.: Wadsworth, 1994; Herman, J. Network management inches forward. *Business Communications Review,* May 1994, 45–50.

22. Adapted from Holland, K., Dwyer, P., and Edmondson, G. Technobanking takes off. *Business Week/21st Century Capitalism,* 1995, 52–53; Jacob, R. Capturing the global consumer. *Fortune,* December 13, 1993, 166–170; Nemeroff, D. Quality in consumer financial services. In J.W. Spechler (ed.), *When America Does It Right: Case Studies in Service Quality.* Norcross, Ga.: Institute of Industrial Engineers, 1991, 72–83; Milligan, J.W. Citicorp changes its retail prescription. *US Banker,* July 1994, 32–36.

23. Lofti, V., and Pegels, C.C. *Decision Support Systems for Production and Operations Management,* 3rd ed. Burr Ridge, Ill.: Irwin, 1995.

24. Arinze, B. *Microcomputers for Managers,* Belmont, Calif.: Wadsworth, 1994, 240–247; Hofstetter, F.T. *Multimedia Presentation Technology.* Belmont, Calif.: Wadsworth, 1994.

25. Adapted from Meade, J. Check your compliance with up-to-date HR Assistant. *HR Magazine,* March 1995, 127–130; Greengard, S. The next generation. *Personnel Journal,* March 1994, 40–46; Davis, B. *JO Base* eases status checks on affirmative action. *HR Magazine,* January 1995, 144–145.

26. Zahedi, F. *Intelligent Systems for Business: Expert Systems with Neural Networks.* Belmont, Calif.: Wadsworth, 1993.

27. Meyer, M.H., and Curley, K.F. Putting expert systems to work, *Sloan Management Review,* Winter 1991, 21–31; Ashton, A.H. and Davis, M.N. White-collar robotics: Levering managerial decision making. *California Management Review,* Fall 1994, 83–109.

28. Jessup, L., and Valacich, J.S. *Group Support Systems: New Perspectives.* New York: Macmillan, 1993.

29. Frolick, M.N. Management support systems and their evolution from executive information systems. *Information Strategy: The Executive Journal,* Spring 1994, 31–38.

30. Beekman, G. *Computer Currents—Navigating Tomorrow's Technology.* Reading, Mass.: Addison-Wesley, 1994.

31. Kirkpatrick, D. Here comes the payoff from PCs. *Fortune,* March 23, 1993, 24–25.

32. Teng, J.T.C., Grover, V., and Fiedler, K.D. Re-designing business processes using information technology. *Long Range Planning,* 1994, 27(1), 95–106; Drucker, P.F. The information executives truly need. *Harvard Business Review,* January-February 1995, 54–62.

33. McLeod, R., Jr., Jones, J.W., and Saunders, C. The difficulty in solving strategic problems: The experiences of three CIOs. *Business Horizons,* January-February 1995, 28–38.

34. Armstrong, D.A. How Rockwell launched its EIS, *Datamation,* March 1, 1990, 69–71; Plante, A. Data liberation. *Forbes ASAP,* February 28, 1994, 59–67.

35. Osterle, H., Brenner, W., and Hilbers, K. *Total Information Systems Management: A European Approach,* New York: John Wiley & Sons, 1994.

36. Hoffman, J.D., and Rockart, J.F. Application templates: Faster, better, and cheaper systems. *Sloan Management Review,* Fall 1994, 49–60.

37. Heckman, R.L. Managing the risks of investing in information technology. *Bankers Magazine,* November-December 1989, 18–20.

38. Adapted from LaPlante, A. Merrill's wired stampede. *Forbes ASAP,* June 6, 1994, 76–80; Benjamin, R., and Wigand, R. Electronic markets and virtual chains on the information superhighway. *Sloan Management Review,* Winter 1995, 62–72; Labe, R.P., Jr. Database marketing increases prospecting effectiveness at Merrill Lynch. *Interfaces,* September/October 1994, 1–12.

39. Pollalis, Y.A., and Hanson Frieze, I. A new look at critical success factors in IT. *Information Strategy: The Executives Journal,* Fall 1993, 24–34.

40. Ross, P.E. The day the software crashed. *Forbes,* April 25, 1994, 142–156; Cringely, R.X. When disaster strikes IS. *Forbes ASAP,* August 29, 1994, 60–64.

41. Adapted from Stevenson, M. He sees all, he knows all. *Canadian Business,* Spring 1994, 30–35; Vandenbosch, B. *Executive Support System Impact Viewed from a Learning Perspective.* Ph.D. dissertation. London, Ontario: University of Western Ontario, 1993; DuPont has most advanced use of IT in chemical industry along with Dow. *Chemical Week,* July 7, 1994, 20–23.

42. Moor, J.H. Computing and the ring of invisibility: A philosopher explains why we shouldn't trust computers. *Ethics: Easier Said Than Done,* 1991, Issue 15, 40–41; Mantovani, G. Is computer-mediated communication intrinsically apt to enhance democracy in organizations? *Human Relations,* 1994, 47, 45–62.

43. Adapted from Sandberg, J. Immorality play: Acclaiming hackers as heroes. *Wall Street Journal,* February 27, 1995, B1, B6; Radlow, J. *Computers and the Information Society,* 2nd ed. Danvers, Mass.: Boyd & Fraser, 1995, 349–352; Godwin, M. Cops on the I-Way. *Time Special Issue,* Spring 1995, 62–64.

44. Laudon, K.C., and Laudon, J.P., 90–95.

45. Arinze, B., 440–446.

46. Branscomb, A.W. *Who Owns Information?: From Privacy to Public Access.* New York: Basic Books, 1994; Smith, H.J. *Managing Privacy: Information Technology and Corporate America.* Chapel Hill: University of North Carolina Press, 1994.

47. Berry, J.A. A potent new tool for selling: Database marketing. *Business Week,* September 5, 1994, 56–62; Power, C. How to get closer to your customers. *Business Week/Enterprise,* 1993, 42–46; Caminiti, S. What the scanner knows about you. *Fortune,* December 3, 1990, 51–52.

48. Adapted from Kelsey, D. Computer ethics: An overview of the issues. *Ethics: Easier Said Than Done,* 1991, Issue 15, 30–33. Jossi, F. Eavesdroppers in cyberspace. *Business Ethics,* May/June 1994, 22–25; Cortese, A. Warding off the cyberspace invaders. *Business Week,* March 13, 1995, 92–93; Forester, T. and Morrison, P. *Computer Ethics.* Cambridge, Mass.: MIT Press, 1990.

49. Adapted from Boynton, A.C. Achieving dynamic stability through information technology. *California Management Review,* Winter 1993, 58–77; Kunde, D. In the chips: Frito-Lay data system feed ideas for boosting sales to employees. *Dallas Morning News,* July 29, 1990, H1–H2; Main, J. Computers of the world, unite! *Fortune,* September 24, 1990, 115–122; Johnson, R. In the chips, *Wall Street Journal Reports,* March 22, 1991, BH1–B2.

50. Adapted from Miller, C. Advertisers face an interactive future. *New York Times,* July 4, 1994; Clark, T. Marketing chic. *Business Marketing,* February 1994; Abe, B. ICTV squares off against giants. *Advertising Age,* December 13, 1993; Lang, C. The pied piper of convergence. *Advertising Age,* December 6, 1993; A user's guide to today's technology, *Direct Marketing,* September 1993.

Chapter 20

1. Adapted from Bylinsky, G. Manufacturing for reuse. *Fortune,* February 6, 1995, 102–112; Kearns, D.T. Leadership through quality. *Academy of Management Executive,* May 1990, 86–89; Juran, J.M.

Made in U.S.A.: A renaissance in quality. *Harvard Business Review,* July–August 1993, 42–50; Cooney, J.F. Xerox: A leadership approach to total customer satisfaction. In J.W. Speckler (ed.), *Managing Quality in America's Most Admired Companies.* San Francisco: Berrett-Kohler, 1993, 135–140.

2. Krajewski, L.L., and Ritzman, L.R. *Operations Management: Strategy and Analysis,* 3rd ed. Reading, Mass.: Addison-Wesley, 1993.

3. Fogerty, D.W., Blackstone, J.H., and Hoffman, T.R. *Production and Inventory Management,* Cincinnati: South-Western, 1990; Adams, E.E. Jr. Towards a typology of production and operations management systems. *Academy of Management Review,* 1983, 8, 353–375.

4. Krajewski, L.L., and Ritzman, L.R., 2–5.

5. Committee for Economic Development, *Productivity Policy: Key to the Nation's Economic Future,* New York: Committee for Economic Development, 1983, 23.

6. Magnet, M. The productivity payoff arrives. *Fortune,* June 27, 1994, 79–84; Cooper, J.C. The new golden age of productivity. *Business Week,* September 26, 1994, 62; Richman, L.S. Why the economic data mislead us. *Fortune,* March 8, 1993, 108–114.

7. Edmondson, H.E., and Wheelwright, S.C. Outstanding manufacturing in the coming decade, *California Management Review,* Summer 1989, 70–90; Port, O. The productivity paradox, *Business Week,* June 6, 1988, 100–113.

8. Harmon, R.L., and Peterson, L.D. *Reinventing the Factory: Productivity Breakthroughs in Manufacturing Today,* New York: Free Press, 1990.

9. Ciscel, D.H., and Lewis, L.S. The meaning of productivity, *Mid-South Business Journal,* April 1987, 17–20.

10. Riggs, J.L., and Felix, G.H. *Productivity by Objectives,* Englewood Cliffs, N.J.: Prentice-Hall, 1983; Bouchkaert, G. Measurement and meaningful management. *Public Productivity & Management Review,* 1993, 17, 31–43.

11. Adapted from Samiee, S. Productivity planning and strategy in retailing, *California Management Review,* Winter 1990, 54–76; Seiyu relies on Rainbow Project to use information that will help simplify wholesale retail activities. *Office Equipment,* April 1994; 31–32.

12. Krajewski, L.J., and Ritzman, L.P., 10–15.

13. Ibid, 15–20.

14. Garvin, D.A. Manufacturing strategic planning. *California Management Review,* Summer 1993, 85–106; Schroeder, R.G., and Pesch, M.J. Focusing the factory: Eight lessons. *Business Horizons,* September-October 1994, 76–81.

15. Nagel, R.N. *Agile Manufacturing: The 21st Century Vision.* Paper. Bethlehem, Pa.: Iacocca Institute, Lehigh University, 1993.

16. Womack, J.P., and Jones, D.T. From lean production to the lean enterprise. *Harvard Business Review,* April 1994, 93–103; Cusumano, M.A. The limits of lean. *Sloan Management Review,* Summer 1994, 27–32.

17. Hayes, R.H., and Pisano, G.P. Beyond world-class: The new manufacturing strategy. *Harvard Business Review,* January-February 1994, 77–86.

18. Port, O. The Agile factory: Custom-made, direct from the plant. *Business Week/21st Century Capitalism,* 1995, 158–160; Pine, B.J. II. *Mass Customization: The New Frontier in Business Competition.* Boston: Harvard Business School Press, 1993.

19. Adapted from Upton, D.M. The management of manufacturing flexibility. *California Management Review,* Winter 1994, 72–89; Kinni, T.B. John Crane Belfab. *Industry Week,* October 18, 1993, 37–39.

20. Dixon, J.R., Arnold, P., Heineke, J., Kim, J.S., and Mulligan, P. Business process reengineering: Improving in new strategic directions. *California Management Review,* Summer 1994, 93–108; Teng, J.T.C., Grover, V., Fiedler, K.D. Business processes reengineering: Charting a strategic path for the information age. *California Management Review,* Spring 1994, 9–31.

21. Schonberger, R.J. Human resource management: Lessons from a decade of TQM and reengineering. *California Management Review,* Summer 1994, 109–123; Talwar, R. Business re-engineering—a strategy driven approach. *Long Range Planning,* December 1993, 22–40; Harbour, J.I. *The Process Reengineering Workbook.* Norcross, Ga.: Industrial Engineering Management Press, 1994.

22. Champy, J. *Reengineering Management: The Mandate for New Leadership.* New York: Harper Business, 1994.

23. Adapted from Barlow, J. Last frontier of productivity. *Houston Chronicle,* February 19, 1995, 1E; Texas Commerce benefiting from use of viewstar imaging & workflow system. *Computer World,* June 6, 1993, 8–9.

24. Radlow, J. *Computers and the Information Society.* Danvers, Mass.: Boyd & Fraser, 1995; Buskin, J. Warning: Technology ahead. *Wall Street Journal,* March 20, 1995, R24.

25. Naik, G. No big deal?—PCS is coming. *Wall Street Journal,* March 20, 1995, R16.

26. Dunkin, A. Hardware: Smart, useful. *Business Week,* May 30, 1994, 141–142.

27. Cauley, L. The urge to merge: The cellular industry, facing competition from PCS, is in the midst of a major shake–up. *Wall Street Journal,* March 20, 1995, R16.

28. Adapted from LaPlante, A. Imaging your sea of data. *Forbes ASAP,* August 29, 1994, 36–41; Symands, W.C. Getting rid of paper is just the beginning. *Business Week,* December 21, 1992, 88–89; McCarroll, T. Ending the paper chase. *Time,* June 14, 1993, 60–65.

29. Quinn, J.B., Doorley, T.L., and Paquette, P.C. Beyond products: Services–based strategies. *Harvard Business Review,* March-April 1990, 58–60.

30. Salvendy, G. (ed.). *Handbook of Industrial Engineering.* Norcross, Ga.: Industrial Engineering & Management Press, 1994.

31. O'brien, J.A. *Introduction to Information Systems.* Burr Ridge, Ill.: Irwin, 1994, 59–66.

32. Elmer-Dewitt, P. The machines are listening. *Time,* August 12, 1992, 45; Schwind, G.F. Voice recognition deserves a second listen. *Material Handling Engineering,* February 1994, 63–67.

33. Adapted from Beck, R. Computers can now be controlled by verbal commands. *Houston Chronicle,* March 20, 1995, 3B; A disability friendly workplace, *Business Week,* May 30, 1994, part 4, special advertising section (unpaginated); Hoffman, T. Knocking down barriers. *Computerworld,* August 30, 1993, 5–7.

34. Chase, R.B., and Aguilano, N.J. *Production and Operations Management: Manufacturing and Services.* Burr Ridge, Ill.: Irwin, 1995.

35. Bowonder, B., and Miyake T. Creating and sustaining competitiveness: An analysis of the Japanese robotics industry. *International Journal of Technology Management,* 1994, 9(5–7), 575–611.

36. Sprout, A.L. Talking to robots made easy. *Fortune,* October 31, 1994, 240; Baker, S. A surgeon whose hands never shake. *Business Week,* October 4, 1993, 111–114.

37. Leonard–Barton, D., Bowe, H.K., Clarke, K.B., Holloway, C.A., and Wheelwright, S.C. How to integrate work and deepen expertise. *Harvard Business Review,* September-October 1994, 121–130.

38. Hill, T. *Manufacturing Strategy: Text and Cases.* Burr Ridge, Ill.: Irwin, 1994.

39. Duimering, P.R., Safayeni, F., and Purdy, L. Integrated manufacturing: Redesign the organization before implementing flexible technology. *Sloan Management Review,* Summer 1993, 47– 56.

40. Adapted from Flanigan, J. Toyota putting robots aside. *Houston Chronicle,* March 25, 1995, 1D; Keller, M. *Collision: GM, Toyota, Volkswagen and the Race to Own the 21st Century.* New York: Doubleday, 1994.

41. Mears, P., and Voehl, F. *The Executive Guide to Implementing Quality Systems.* Delray Beach, Fla.: St. Lucie Press, 1995.

42. Jacob, R. Corporate reputations. *Fortune,* March 6, 1995, 54–64.

43. Gale, B.T., and Buzzell, R.D. Market perceived quality: Key strategic concept. *Planning Review,* March-April 1989, 6–12.

44. Evans, J.R., and Lindsay, W.M. *The Management and Control of Quality,* 2nd ed. St. Paul, Minn.: West, 1993; Grant, R.M., Shani, R., and Krishnan, R. TQM's challenge to management theory and practice. *Sloan Management Review,* Winter 1994, 25– 35.

45. Kearns, D., 86.

46. Chase, R.B., and Stewart, D.M. Make your service fail safe. *Sloan Management Review,* Spring 1994, 35–44; Griffin, A., Gleason, G., Preiss, R., and Shevenaugh, D. Best practice for customer satisfaction in manufacturing firms. *Sloan Management Review,* Winter 1995, 87–98.

47. Schmidt, W.H., and Finnigan, J.P. *The Race Without a Finish Line: America's Quest for Total Quality,* San Francisco: Jossey-Bass, 1992.

48. Berry, L.L., Parasuraman, A., and Zeithaml, V.A. Improving service quality in America: Lessons learned. *Academy of Management Executive,* May 1994, 32–52.

49. Garvin, D.A. Manufacturing strategic planning. *California Management Review,* Summer 1993, 85–106; Milakovich, M.E. *Improving Service Quality: Achieving High Performance in the Public and Private Sectors.* Delray Beach, Fla.: St. Lucie Press, 1995.

50. Garvin, D.A., 94–97; Gehani, R.R. Quality value-chain: A meta-synthesis of frontiers of quality movement. *Academy of Management Executive,* May 1993, 29–42.

51. Omachonu, V.K., and Ross, J.E. *Principles of Total Quality Management.* Delray Beach, Fla.: St. Lucie Press, 1994.

52. Juran, J.M. *Managerial Breakthrough: The Classic Book on Improving Performance,* rev. ed. New York: McGraw-Hill, 1995.

53. Bush, D., and Dooley, K. The Deming

Prize and Baldrige Award: How they compare. *Quality Progress,* January 1989, 28–30.

54. Halberstam, D. Yes we can. *Parade Magazine,* July 8, 1984, 5.

55. Deming, W.E. *Out of the Crises.* Cambridge, Mass.: MIT Center for Advanced Engineering Study, 1986; Delavigne, K.T., and Robertson, J.D. *Deming's Profound Changes: When Will the Sleeping Giant Awaken.* Englewood Cliffs, N.J.: PTR Prentice-Hall, 1994; Phillips Carson, P., and Carson, K.D. Deming versus traditional management theorists on goal setting: Can both be right? *Business Horizons,* September-October 1993, 79–84.

56. National Institute of Standards and Technology, *Malcolm Baldrige National Quality Award: 1995 Award Criteria.* Gaithersberg, Md.: U.S. Department of Commerce, 1995.

57. *Motorola 1994 Annual Report.* Schaumburg, Ill.: Motorola, Inc., 1995.

58. Adapted from Slutsker, G. The company that likes to obsolete itself. *Forbes,* September 13, 1993, 139–144; Henkoff, R. Motorola's plantation factory. *Fortune,* April 18, 1994, 26–30; Main, J. How to win the Baldrige Award, *Fortune,* April 23, 1990, 101–116; Bhote, K.R. Motorola's long march to the Malcolm Baldrige National Quality Award. *National Productivity Review,* 1989, 8, 365–3475; Wiggenhorn, W. Motorola U: When training becomes an education. *Harvard Business Review,* July-August 1990, 71–83; Belohlav, J.A. Quality, strategy, and competitiveness. *California Management Review,* Spring 1993, 55–67.

59. Pitt, H. *SPS for the Rest of Us: A Personal Path to Statistical Process Control.* Reading, Mass.: Addison-Wesley, 1994; Roberts, H.V. *Statistics and Total Quality Management.* New York: Blackwell, 1995.

60. Krantz, K.T. How velcro got hooked on quality. *Harvard Business Review,* September-October 1989, 34–38.

61. Adapted from Berry, L.L., Zeithaml, V.A., and Parasuraman, A. Five imperatives for improving service quality. *Sloan Management Review,* Summer 1990, 29–38; Berry, L.L. *On Great Service: A Framework for Action.* New York: Free Press, 1995; Hodgetts, R.M. Quality lessons from America's Baldrige winners. *Business Horizons,* July-August 1994, 74–79.

62. Fisher, M.L., Hammond, J.H., Obermeyer, W.R., and Raman, A. Making supply meet demand in an uncertain world. *Harvard Business Review,* May-June 1994, 83–93; Tully, S. Purchasing's new muscle. *Fortune,* February 20, 1995, 75–83.

63. Waters, D.C. *Inventory Control and Management.* New York: John Wiley & Sons, 1992.

64. Zenz, G. *Purchasing and the Management of Materials.* New York: John Wiley & Sons, 1994.

65. Fernandez, R.R. *Total Quality in Purchasing and Supplier Management.* Delray Beach, FL: St. Lucie Press, 1994.

66. Mooney, M., and Hessel, M. *Quality Dimensions of Operations Management.* Cambridge, Mass.: Blackwell, 1995; Ansari, A. and Modarress, B. *Just-In-Time Purchasing.* New York: Free Press, 1990.

67. Klein, J.A. The human costs of manufacturing reform. *Harvard Business Review,* March-April 1989, 60–61.

68. Adapted from Sherman, S. How to bolster the bottom line: Information technology special report. *Fortune,* Autumn 1993, 15–28; Rose, R.L. UAW's long strike fails to crimp output at Caterpillar's plants. *Wall Street Journal,* October 14, 1994, A1, A12; Bartholomew, D. Caterpillar digs in. *Information Week,* June 7, 1993, 1–3.

69. Adapted from Kettinger, W.J., and Lee, C.C. Perceived service quality and user satisfaction with the information services function. *Decision Sciences,* 1994, 25, 737–766; Parasuraman, A., Zeithmal, V.A., and Berry, L.L. Reassessment of expectations as a comparison in measuring service quality: Implications for further research. *Journal of Marketing,* 1994, 58, 111–124; Conrath, D.W., and Mignen, O.P. What is being done to measure user satisfaction with EDP/MIS. *Information and Management,* 1990, 19(1), 7–19; Rands, I. Information technology as a service operation. *Journal of Information Technology,* 1992, 7, 189–201.

70. Lee L. Krajewski and Larry P. Ritzman, OPERATIONS MANAGMENT: STRATEGY AND ANALYSIS (excerpted and adapted from pp. 54–58), © 1987 by Addison-Wesley Publishing Company, Inc. Reprinted by permission of the publisher.

Chapter 21

1. Adapted from Goldstein, A. Shopping frenzy boosts Compaq to the top of the computer world. *Dallas Morning News,* December 29, 1994, 1–2B; McCartney, S. Financial performance, company reports: Compaq Computer. *Wall Street Journal,* October 20, 1994, 3A; McCartney, S. Compaq to unveil two powerful servers as AST also will launch new line. *Wall Street Journal,* September 12, 1994, 11E; Technology & health: Compaq to unveil its latest PC models as home appliances. *Wall Street Journal,* September 14, 1994, 7B; Burrows, P. The computer is in the mail (really). *Business Week,* January 23, 1995, 76–77.

2. *Annual Report,* Merck.

3. D'Aveni, R.A. *Hyper-Competition.* New York: Free Press, 1994; McKinley, Wm. Organizational decline and adaptation: Theoretical controversies. *Organization Science,* 1993, 4, 1–9.

4. Tomsho, R. Real dog: How Greyhound lines re-engineered itself right into a deep hole. *Wall Street Journal,* October 20, 1994, 1A.

5. Senge, P. *The Fifth Discipline: The Art and Practice of the Learning Organization.* New York: Doubleday, 1990; Huber, G. Organizational learning: The contributing processes and literature. *Organization Science,* 1991, 2, 88–115.

6. Maxon, T. Southwest to go "ticketless" on all routes January 31. *Dallas Morning News,* January 11, 1995, 1D.

7. McGill, M.E., and Slocum, J.W., Jr. *The Smarter Organization: How to Build an Organization That Learns to Adapt to Marketplace Needs.* New York: John Wiley & Sons, 1994; DePree, M. *Leadership is an Art.* New York: Doubleday, 1992.

8. McGill, M.E., Slocum, J.W., Jr., and Lei, D. Management practices in learning organizations. *Organizational Dynamics,* Summer 1992, 5–17; Nevis, E., DiBella, A.J., and Gould, J.M. Understanding organizations as learning systems. Sloan *Management Review,* Winter 1995, 87–98.

9. Lei, D., and Slocum, J.W., Jr. Global strategy, competence-building and strategic alliances. *California Management Review,* Fall 1992, 81–97; Hill, R.C., and Hellriegel, D. Critical contingencies in joint venture management: Some lessons from managers. *Organization Science,* 1994, 5, 594–607.

10. Slocum, J.W., Jr., McGill, M.E., and Lei, D. The new strategy: Anything, anytime, anywhere. *Organizational Dynamics,* Autumn 1994, 33–47.

11. Welles, E.O. Bootstrapping for billions. *INC.,* September 1994, 78–86.

12. Adapted from Jacob, R. Absence of management. *American Way,* February 15, 1993, 38–42; Tully, S. The modular corporation. *Fortune,* February 8, 1993, 106–116; Kiechel, W. III. The organization that learns. *Fortune,* May 18, 1992, 93–98.

13. Kiernan, M. The new strategic architecture: Learning to compete in the twenty-first century. *Academy of Management Executive,* February 1993, 7–21.

14. Stack, J. The great game of business. *INC.,* June 1992, 53–66.

15. Kanter, R.M., Stein, B.A., and Jick, T.D. *The Challenge of Organizational Change.* New York: Free Press, 1992.

16. Adapted from Hall, C. Broker finds calling in discarded phones. *Dallas Morning News,* August 28, 1994, 1–3H; Hall, C. Still going. *Dallas Morning News,* January 1, 1995, 1–2H.

17. Huber, G.P., and Glick, Wm.H. *Organizational Change and Redesign.* New York: Oxford University Press, 1993.

18. Skoldberg, K. Tales of change. *Organization Science,* 1994, 5, 219–238.

19. Pennings, J.M., Barkema, H., and Douma, S. Organizational learning and diversification. *Academy of Management Journal,* 1994, 37, 608–641.

20. McFarlan, F.W., and Nolan, R.L. How to manage an IT outsourcing alliance. *Sloan Management Review,* Winter, 1995, 9–24.

21. Adapted from Lovelock, C.H. What language shall we put it in? *Marketing Management,* Winter 1994, 41; Valente, J. British Airways sees strong gains, challenges ahead. *Wall Street Journal,* November 8, 1994, 4B; Dwyer, P. British Air: Not cricket. *Business Week,* January 25, 1993, 50–51

22. Mathieu, J.E., and Zajkac, D.M. A review and meta-analysis of the antecedents, correlates, and consequences of organizational commitment. *Psychological Bulletin,* 1990, 108, 171–194; Brett, J.F., Cron, Wm.L., and Slocum, J.W., Jr. Economic dependency on work: A moderator of the relationship between organizational commitment and performance. *Academy of Management Journal,* 1995, 38, 261–271.

23. Jones, G. Oryx plan drives stock down 15%. *Dallas Morning News,* January 21, 1995, 1F; James, G. Oryx rolls out cost-cutting plans. *Dallas Morning News,* January 20, 1995, 1D.

24. Cummings, T.G., and Worley, C.G. *Organizational Change and Development,* 5th ed. St. Paul, Minn.: West, 1993, 147–148.

25. Hellriegel, D., Slocum, J.W., Jr., and Woodman, R.W. *Organizational Behavior,* 7th ed. St. Paul, Minn.: West, 1995, 647–675.

26. Amburgey, T.L., and Dacin, T. As the left foot follows the right? The dynamics of strategic and structural change. *Academy of Management Journal,* 1994, 37, 1427–1452; Romanelli, E., and Tushman, M.L. Organizational transformation as a punctuated equilibrium: An empirical test. *Academy of Management Journal,* 1994, 37, 1141–1166.

27. Adapted from Priest, G. Zoo story. *INC.,* October 1994, 27–28.

28. Goldstein, I.L. Training in work organizations. In M.D. Dunnette and L.M. Hough (eds.), *Handbook of Industrial and Organizational Psychology,* 2nd ed., vol. 2. Palo, Alto, Calif.: Consulting Psychologists Press, 1991, 507–620.

29. Pfeffer, J. *Competitive Advantage Through People.* Boston: Harvard Business School Press, 1994.

30. Cummings and Worley, 353.

31. Adapted from Williams, M. Back to the past. *Wall Street Journal,* October 24, 1994, 1A; Michaels, J.W. Why Sony is ahead. *Forbes,* December 20, 1993, 10–11.

32. McKenney, J.L. *Waves of Change: Business Evolution Through Information Technology.* Boston: Harvard Business School Press, 1995.

33. Yoder, S.K. Putting it all together. *Wall Street Journal Reports: Workplace of the Future,* June 4, 1990, 24.

34. Thach, L., and Woodman, R.W. Organizational change and information technology: Managing on the edge of cyberspace. *Organizational Dynamics,* Summer 1994, 30–46.

35. Keidel, R.W. Rethinking organization design. *Academy of Management Executive,* 1994, 8(4), 12–29; Miles, R.E., and Snow, C.C. The new network firm: A spherical structure built on a human investment philosophy. *Organizational Dynamics,* Spring 1995, 5–18.

36. DeWitt, R.L. The structural consequences of downsizing. *Organization Science,* 1993, 4, 30–40.

37. Schares, G.E. Percey Barnevik's global crusade. *Business Week/Enterprise 1993,* 204–211.

38. Cameron, K.S., Freeman, S.J., and Mishra, A.K. Downsizing and redesigning organizations. In G.P. Huber and Wm.H. Glick (eds.), *Organizational Change and Redesign.* New York: Oxford University Press, 1993, 19–65.

39. Freeman, S.J., and Cameron, K.S. Organizational downsizing: A convergence and reorientation. *Organization Science,* 1993, 4, 10–29.

40. Hammer, M., and Champy, J. *Reengineering the Corporation.* New York: HarperCollins, 1993.

41. Adapted from Hall, G., Rosenthal, J., and Wade, J. How to make reengineering really work. *Harvard Business Review,* November-December 1993, 124–126.

42. Nahavandi, A., and Aranda, E. Restructuring teams for the reengineered organization. *Academy of Management Executive, 1994,* 87(4), 58–68; Lancaster, H. Managing your career. *Wall Street Journal,* January 17, 1995, 1B.

43. Yeatts, D.E., Hipskind, M., and Barnes, D. Lessons learned from self-managed teams. *Business Horizons,* July-August 1994, 11–19; Manz, C.C., and Sims, H.P., Jr. *Businesses Without Bosses.* New York: John Wiley & Sons, 1994.

44. Roberts, H.V., and Sergesketter, B.F. *Quality Is Personal: A Foundation for Total Management.* New York: Free Press, 1994.

45. Cummings and Worley, 1–6.

46. Dunham, R., and Smith, F.J. *Organizational Surveys.* Glenview, Ill.: Scott Foresman, 1979.

47. Dyer, Wm.G. *Team Building: Issues and Alternatives.* Reading, Mass.: Addison-Wesley, 1987.

48. Adapted from Dobbs, M.F. San Diego's diversity commitment. *The Public Manager,* Spring 1994, *59–62.*

49. Adapted from Ettlie, J.E., and O'Keefe, R.D. Innovative attitudes, values, and intentions in organizations. *Journal of Management Studies,* 1982, 19, 176. Used by permission of the authors, 1995.

50. Adapted from Teresko, J. Mass customization or mass confusion? *Industry Week,* June 20, 1994, 45–48; Moskal, B.S. Born to be real. *Industry Week,* August 2, 1993, 14–19; Slutsker, G. Hog wild. *Forbes,* May 24, 1993, 45–46; Kelly, K., and Lowry Miller, K. The rumble heard round the world: Harleys. *Business Week,* May 24, 1993, 58–60.

Chapter 22

1. Adapted from Darling, B.L., and Davis, T.R.V. Super Bakery, Inc. *Planning Review,* January-February 1994

2. Cooper, A.C. The role of incubator organizations in founding of growth-oriented firms. *Journal of Business Venturing,* 1985, 1, 75–86; Steffens, R. What the incubators have hatched: An assessment of a much-used economic tool. *Planning,* 1992, 58(5), 28–31.

3. Longenecker, J.G., Moore, C.W., and Petty, J.W. *Small Business Management: An Entrepreneurial Emphasis.* Cincinnati: South-Western, 1994.

4. Shane, S. Why do rates of entrepreneurship vary over time? In D.P. Moore (ed.). *Academy of Management Best Paper Proceedings,* 1994. Madison, Wis.: Omni Press, 1994, 90–93; Fischer, E.M., Reuber, R.A., and Dyke, L.S. A theoretical overview and extension on sex, gender, and entrepreneurship. *Journal of Business Venturing,* 1993, 8, 151–159.

5. Fenn, D. Are your kids good enough to run your business? *INC.,* August 1994, 36–38.

6. Ehrenfeld, T. Growing up in public., *INC.,* May 1994, 108.

7. Virarelli, M. The birth of new enterprises. *Small Business Economics,* 1991, 3(3), 215–233; Bhave, M.P. A process model of entrepreneurial venture creation. *Journal of Business Venturing,* 1994, 9, 223–243.

8. Bull, I., and Willard, G.E. Toward a theory of entrepreneurship. *Journal of Business Venturing,* 1993, 8, 183– 196.

9. Bulkeley, W.M. Ben and Jerry's is looking for Ben's successor. *Wall Street Journal,* June 14, 1994, B1; Theroux, J. *Ben & Jerry's Homemade Ice Cream Inc.: Keeping the Mission(s) Alive.* Boston: Harvard Business School Press, 1991.

10. Broome, J.T., Jr. How to write a business plan. *Nation's Business,* February 1993, 29–30; Osborne, R.L. Second phase entrepreneurship: Breaking through the growth wall. *Business Horizons,* January-February 1994, 80–87.

11. Cooper, A.C. Challenges in predicting new firm performance. *Journal of Business Venturing,* 1993, 8, 241–154.

12. Adapted from Prior, T.L. Torilla flap., *INC.,* June 1994, 46– 50.

13. McGrath, R.G., MacMillan, I.C., Scheinberg, S. Elitists, risk-takers, and rugged individualists? An exploratory analysis of cultural differences between entrepreneurs and non-entrepreneurs. *Journal of Business Venturing,* 1992, 7(2), 115– 135.

14. McClelland, D.C. Characteristics of successful entrepreneurs. *Journal of Creative Behavior,* 1987, 21, 219–233; Robinson, P.B., and Sexton, E.A. The effect of education and experience on self-employment success. *Journal of Business Venturing,* 1994, 9, 141–156.

15. Adapted from Welles, E.O. It's not the same America. *INC.,* May 1994, 82–98.

16. Ronstadt, R.C. *Entrepreneurship.* Dover, Mass.: Lord, 1984.

17. Woo, C.Y., Cooper, C.A., and Dunkelberg, W.C. The development and interpretation of entrepreneurial typologies. *Journal of Business Venturing,* 1991, 6(2), 93–114; Birley, S. and Westhead, P. A taxonomy of business start-up reasons and their impact on firm growth and size. *Journal of Business Venturing,* 1994, 9, 7–32.

18. Hisrich, R.D. Entrepreneurship/Intrapreneurship. *American Psychologist, 1990,* 45, 209–222.

19. Adapted from Brokaw, L. Feet, don't fail me now. *INC.,* May 1994, 70–81.

20. Longenecker, J.G., Moore, C.W., and Petty, J.W., 161–296.

21. Adapted from Studermann, F. Green bank puts principles to test. *International Management,* October 1993, 32–33.

22. Sexton, D.L., and Bowman, N.B. *Entrepreneurship.* New York: Macmillan, 1991.

23. Johnson, G., and Christian, S. A litany of complaints in the booming franchise industry. *Los Angeles Times,* February 20, 1994, D3.

24. Adapted from Maynard, R. A good time to export. *Nation's Business,* May 1994, 22–29, 32.

25. Adapted from McDermott, K. Going it alone. *D & B Reports,* March/April 1989, 31–35, and Garrett, E.M. The empire builders. *INC.,* September 1993, 115–119.

26. Family business: Why some succeed while others fail. *Rothman Ink,* Spring/Summer 1994, 3, 6.

27. Adapted from Baechler, M. The death of a marriage. *INC.,* April 1994, 74–78.

28. Pinchott, G. III. *Intrapreneurship.* New York: Harper & Row, 1985.

29. Hornsby, J.S., Naffziger, D.W., Kuratko, D.F., and Montagno, R.V. An interactive model of corporate entrepreneurship. *Entrepreneurship: Theory and Practice,* Winter 1993, 29–38.

30. Peters, T.L., and Waterman, R.H., Jr. *In Search of Excellence.* New York: Harper & Row, 1982.

31. McGill, M.E., and Slocum, J.W., Jr. *The Smarter Organization: How to Adapt to Meet Marketplace Needs.* New York: John Wiley & Sons, 1994.

32. Tally your chances on making it on your own. *USA Today,* May 11, 1987, 10E

33. Adapted from Finegan, J. Pipe dreams. *INC.,* August 1994, 64–72.

34. Adapted from Byrne, J.A. Enterprise: How entrepreneurs are reshaping the economy—and what big companies can learn. *Business Week/Enterprise 1993,* Special Issue, 11–18; Hartley-Leonard, D. The entrepreneurial spirit. Special advertising section. *INC.,* December 1993, 15. Burck, C. The real world of the entrepreneur. *Fortune,* April 5, 1993.

Glossary

A

360-degree appraisal system A performance review system that gathers feedback from an employee's colleagues inside the organization and from people outside the organization with whom the employee does business. (p. 388)

ability An individual's mastery of the skills required to do a job. (p. 427)

acceptance theory of authority The theory that holds that employees will choose to follow management's orders if they understand what is required, believe the orders to be consistent with organizational goals, and see positive benefits to themselves in carrying out the orders. (p. 53)

accountability The expectation that each employee will accept credit or blame for results achieved in performing assigned tasks. (p. 318)

achievement motive The desire to succeed relative to some standard of excellence or in competitive situations. (p. 418)

achievement-oriented leadership Setting challenging goals and expecting followers to perform at their highest level. (p. 463)

act utilitarianism An emphasis on the consequences of providing the greatest good for the greatest number. (p. 219)

activity-based costing A system that focuses on activities as the fundamental cost centers. (p. 601)

adaptive decisions Choices made in response to a combination of moderately unusual and only partially known problems and alternative solutions. (p. 245)

administrative management A traditional management system that focuses on the manager and basic managerial functions. (p. 48)

affective conflict Negative feelings or emotions, such as anger, directed at another. (p. 552)

affiliation motive The desire to develop and maintain close, mutually satisfying interpersonal relationships with others. (p. 418)

affiliation needs The desires for friendship, love, and belonging (the third level of Maslow's hierarchy). (p. 414)

affirmative action programs Efforts intended to ensure that a firm's hiring practices and procedures guarantee equal employment opportunity, as specified by law. (p. 376)

affirmative social responsibility The belief that managers and other employees are obligated to avoid problems by anticipating changes in their environment, blending the organization's goals with those of stakeholders and the public, and promoting their mutual interests. (p. 229)

agile manufacturing strategy A system and set of capabilities that enable the mass customization of goods through advanced fabrication, information, and delivery technologies that are implemented by skilled and empowered individuals and teams. (p. 647)

alliance The uniting of two or more organizations, groups, or individuals to achieve common goals with respect to a particular issue. (p. 98)

alliance strategy The pooling of companies' physical and human resources to achieve common goals. (p. 116)

artificial intelligence The ability of a properly programmed computer system to perform functions normally associated with human intelligence. (p. 270)

assessment center Simulation of job situations in order to assess potential employees' performance. (p. 380)

assumptions The underlying thoughts and feelings of one or more individuals that are taken for granted and believed to be true. (p. 177)

authority The right to decide and act. (p. 302)

automation The use of devices and processes that are self-regulating and operate independently of people. (p. 603)

availability bias A person who easily recalls specific instances of an event may overestimate how frequently the event occurs. (p. 257)

avoidance style Withdrawing from conflict situations or remaining neutral. (p. 558)

B

backward integration When a company enters the businesses of its suppliers, usually to ensure component quality, on-time delivery, or stable prices. (p. 93, 149)

bar code A series of black bars of various widths alternating with spaces that represent information and can be read by an optical scanner into a computer. (p. 651)

behavioral models Leadership models that focus on differences in the actions of effective and ineffective leaders. (p. 451)

behavioral viewpoint One of the five principal viewpoints of management, which focuses on helping managers deal effectively with the human side aspects of organizations. (p. 51)

behaviorally anchored rating scale (BARS) A type of performance appraisal that describes specific job behaviors along a continuum of intensity. (p. 391)

benchmarking The continuous process of comparing an organization's functions, products, or processes with those of best-in-class organizations. (p. 185)

bonuses Lump-sum payments given for achieving a particular performance goal. (p. 384)

bounded rationality model An individual's tendencies (1) to select less than the best goal or alternative solution (i.e., to satisfice), (2) to engage in a limited search for alternative solutions, and (3) to have inadequate information and control over external and internal environmental forces influencing the outcomes of decisions. (p. 255)

brainstorming An unrestrained flow of ideas in a group with all critical judgments suspended. (p. 283)

break-even analysis Examination of the various relationships among sales (revenues) and costs in order to determine the point where total sales equal total costs. (p. 272)

bribe An improper payment made to induce the recipient to do something for the payer. (p. 122)

budgeting The process of categorizing proposed expenditures and linking them to goals. (p. 600)

bureaucratic controls Extensive rules and procedures, top-down authority, tightly written job descriptions, and other formal methods for preventing and correcting deviations from desired behaviors and results. (p. 595)

bureaucratic culture An organization in which employees value formalization, rules, standard operating procedures, and hierarchical coordination. (p. 537)

bureaucratic management A traditional management system that relies on rules, set hierarchy, a clear division of labor, and firm procedures and that focuses on the overall organizational structure. (p. 40)

burnout An unhealthy psychological process that is brought about by severe and continuous stress. (p. 568)

business plan A step-by-step outline of how an enterprise expects to turn ideas into reality. (p. 716)

business-level strategy A guide for the operations of a single business and answers questions such as "How do we compete?" (p. 150)

C

capital requirements The dollars needed to finance equipment, supplies, R&D, and the like. (p. 92)

cartel An alliance of producers engaged in the same type of business, formed to limit competition. (p. 122)

cause and effect diagram A chart that helps team members display, categorize, and evaluate all the possible causes of an effect, which is generally expressed as a problem. (p. 286)

central tendency A rating error that occurs when all employees are given an average rating, even when their performance varies. (p. 389)

centralization of authority The concentration of authority at the top of an organization or department. (p. 321)

certainty The condition under which individuals are fully informed about a problem, alternative solutions are obvious, and the possible results of each solution are clear. (p. 240)

changing environment A setting that is unpredictable because of frequent shifts in products, technology, competitive forces, markets, or political forces. (p. 337)

channel The path a message follows from sender to receiver. (p. 489)

chief information officer (CIO) A top manager who provides leadership in assessing the organization's information processing needs and developing the information systems to meet those needs in collaboration with managers and key employees throughout the organization. (p. 615)

clan culture The attributes of tradition, loyalty, personal commitment, extensive socialization, teamwork, self-management, and social influence. (p. 539)

closed system A system that doesn't interact with its environment. (p. 56)

clout Someone's pull or political influence within an organization. (p. 449)

co-optation Involves bringing new stakeholder representatives into the strategic decision-making process as a means of averting threats to an organization's stability or existence. (p. 258)

coercive power The ability of a leader to obtain compliance through fear of punishment. (p. 448)

cognitive ability test A written test that measures general intelligence, verbal ability, numerical ability, reasoning ability, and so on. (p. 379)

cognitive conflict Ideas or thoughts perceived to be incompatible. (p. 552)

cohesiveness The strength of members' desires to remain in the group or team and their commitment to it. (p. 517)

collaborative style A willingness to identify the underlying causes of conflict, share information openly, and focus on both one's own and others' concerns by searching for mutually beneficial solutions. (p. 562)

collectivism Hofstede's value dimension that measures the tendency of group members to focus on the common welfare and feel loyalty toward one another (the opposite of individualism). (p. 85)

commission agent A person or firm who represents businesses in foreign transactions in return for a negotiated percentage of each transaction's value (a commission). (p. 109)

commissions Compensation paid as percentages of salespeople's total sales. (p. 384)

communication The transfer of information and understanding from one person to another through meaningful symbols. (p. 482)

communication skills The abilities to send and receive information, thoughts, feelings, and attitudes. (p. 26)

communication systems Teleconferencing, facsimile machines, local and wide area networks, electronic mail, voice recognition systems, integrated systems, and the like. (p. 619)

comparative financial analysis The evaluation of a firm's financial condition for two or more time periods. (p. 599)

compromise style A willingness of all parties to concede some of their own views and focus on some of the others' views to reach an agreement. (p. 561)

computer ethics The analysis of the nature and social impact of computer technology and the corresponding formulation and justification of policies for its ethical use. (p. 631)

computer monitoring The use of special software to collect highly detailed quantitative information on employee performance. (p. 604)

computer-aided design (CAD) The use of special software to instruct a computer to draw specified configurations on a display screen. (p. 653)

computer-aided manufacturing (CAM) A wide variety of computer-based technologies used to produce goods. (p. 653)

concentric diversification Acquisition of or starting a business related to a firm's existing business in terms of technology, markets, or products. (p. 149)

conceptual skills The ability to view a problem, an issue, or the organization as a whole and its interrelated parts. (p. 26)

concrete information bias Vivid, direct experience usually dominates abstract information. (p. 257)

conditional value (CV) An outcome based on a particular state of nature and a specific strategy in a payoff matrix. (p. 274)

conflict Opposition arising from disagreements about goals, thoughts, or emotions within or among individuals, teams, departments, or organizations. (p. 552)

conflict management Interventions designed to reduce excessive conflict or, in some instances, to increase insufficient conflict. (p. 553)

conglomerate diversification The addition of unrelated goods or services to a firm's line of businesses. (p. 150)

consideration leadership style Exhibiting concern for employees' well-being, status, and comfort. (p. 453)

content approach Models of motivation that address the question: What motivates behavior? The answers are based on the assumption that employees are motivated by the desire to fulfill inner needs. (p. 412)

contingency models Leadership models based on the idea that the situation determines the best style to use. (p. 456)

contingency planning Preparation for unexpected and rapid changes (positive and negative) in the environment that will have a large impact on the organization and that will require a quick response. (p. 142)

contingency viewpoint One of the five principal viewpoints of management; contends that different situations require different practices and advocates the use of the traditional, behavioral, and systems viewpoints separately or in combination to deal with various problems. (p. 59)

continuous improvement Streams of adaptive decisions made over time in an organization that result in a large number of small, incremental improvements year after year. (p. 245)

continuous punishment schedule A special type of fixed ratio schedule in which the ratio of punishment to number of target responses is 1:1. (p. 436)

continuous reinforcement schedule A special type of fixed ratio schedule in which the ratio of reinforcement to number of responses is 1:1. (p. 436)

contrast error Basing a candidate's rating on a comparison with the preceding interviewee. (p. 379)

control Mechanisms used to ensure that behaviors and performance conform to an organization's rules and procedures. (p. 585)

controlling The process by which a person, group, or organization consciously monitors performance and takes corrective action. (p. 9)

coordination The formal and informal procedures that integrate the activities performed by separate individuals, teams, and departments in an organization. (p. 302)

core competencies The complementary strengths that make a company distinctive and presumably more competitive by providing unique value to customers. (p. 156)

corporate culture The norms, values, and practices that characterize a particular organization. (p. 322)

corporate-level strategy A guide for the overall direction of a firm having more than one line of business. (p. 148)

corrective control model A process for detecting and eliminating or reducing deviations from an organization's established standards. (p. 592)

corrective controls Mechanisms intended to reduce or eliminate unwanted behaviors and thereby achieve conformity with the organization's regulations and standards. (p. 586)

corridor principle Using one business to start or acquire others and then repeating the process. (p. 714)

cost leadership strategy An emphasis on competing in the industry by providing a product at a price as low as or lower than competitors. (p. 162)

counter trade An arrangement in which the export sale of goods and services by a producer is linked to an import purchase of other goods and services. (p. 115)

creativity The ability to visualize, foresee, generate, and implement new ideas. (p. 279)

critical path The path with the longest elapsed time, which determines the length of the entire project. (p. 190)

critical thinking The careful consideration of the implications of all known elements of a problem. (p. 27)

cross-cultural training Training that prepares expatriates for global job assignments; this training includes cultural awareness, language instruction, and practical assistance. (p. 396)

cross-functional team Five to thirty employees from various functions and sometimes two organizational levels who collectively have specific goal-oriented tasks. (p. 523)

culture The shared characteristics (e.g., language, religion, and heritage) and values that distinguish one group of people from another. (p. 83)

customer departmentalization Organizing around the type of customer served. (p. 311)

customer monitoring Ongoing efforts to obtain feedback from customers concerning the quality of goods and services. (p. 598)

cyberspace The real-time transmission and sharing of text, voice, graphics, video, and the like over a variety of computer-based networks. (p. 613)

data Facts and figures. (p. 615)

database An organized collection of facts, figures, documents, and the like that have been stored for easy, efficient access and use. (p. 621)

decentralization of authority A high degree of delegated authority throughout an organization or department. (p. 321)

decision making The process of defining problems, gathering information, generating alternatives, and choosing a course of action. (p. 239)

decision support system (DSS) A complex set of computer hardware and software that allows end users to analyze, manipulate, format, display, and output data in different ways. (p. 621)

decoding Translating encoded messages into a form that has meaning to the receiver. (p. 484)

defined benefit retirement plan A pension plan funded by the employer that relies on some type of formula for specifying participant benefits. (p. 386)

defined contribution retirement plan A pension plan in which each participant has a retirement account funded by contributions from the employer, the employee, or both. (p. 386)

delegating style Recognition that others are ready to accomplish a particular task and are both competent and motivated to take full responsibility for it. (p. 461)

delegation of authority The process by which managers assign the right to act and make decisions in certain areas to subordinates. (p. 319)

Delphi technique A forecasting aid based on a consensus of a panel of experts. (p. 173)

Deming Cycle Four stages—plan, do, check, and act—that should be repeated over time to ensure continuous improvements in a function, product, or process. (p. 188)

demographics The characteristics of work group, organization, specific market, or national populations. (p. 82)

departmentalization Subdividing work and assigning it to specialized groups within an organization. (p. 304)

development programs Improving an employee's conceptual and human skills in preparation for future jobs. (p. 394)

devil's advocacy method The selection of one person in a decision-making group (the devil's advocate) to critique a preferred plan or strategy. (p. 180)

dialectical inquiry method A process for systematically examining issues from two or more opposing points of view. (p. 178)

differentiation The measure of the differences among departments with respect to structure, tasks, and goals. (p. 341)

differentiation strategy An emphasis on competing with all other firms in the industry by offering a product that customers perceive to be unique. (p. 162)

digital world The linking of people (in business, government, and the home and on the road) via computers and computers with other computers. (p. 613)

direct compensation An employee's base wage or salary and any incentive pay received. (p. 382)

directive behavior Reliance on one-way communication, spelling out duties, and telling followers what to do and when and how to do it. (p. 459)

directive leadership Letting followers know what's expected of them and telling them how to perform their tasks. (p. 463)

disseminator role The informational role that managers play when they share knowledge or data with subordinates and other members of the organization. (p. 12)

distress Unpleasant, detrimental, or disease-producing stress. (p. 567)

distributive justice principle A moral requirement that individuals not be treated differently because of arbitrarily defined characteristics. (p. 223)

disturbance handler role The decisional role played by managers when they deal with problems and changes beyond their immediate control, such as a strike or a supplier's bankruptcy. (p. 13)

diversification The variety of goods and/or services an organization produces and the number of different markets it serves. (p. 145)

domestic instability The amount of subversion, revolution, assassinations, guerrilla warfare, and government crisis in a country. (p. 119)

dominant-business firm An organization that serves various segments of a particular market. (p. 146)

downsizing The process of letting employees go in an attempt to cut costs by reducing payroll. (p. 21)

downsizing strategy Reliance on fewer resources—primarily human—to accomplish the organization's goals. (p. 144)

downward channel A communication path that managers use to send messages to employees or customers. (p. 489)

dual-career couple Any couple in which both husband and wife are employed. (p. 20)

E

economic climate The extent of government controls of markets and financial investments, as well as government support services and capabilities. (p. 120)

economic order quantity The optimum amount to order to achieve the lowest total inventory costs. (p. 664)

economies of scale The decreases in per unit costs as the volume of goods and/or services produced increases. (p. 92)

electronic brainstorming Use of technology to input and automatically disseminate ideas in real time over a computer network to all team members, each of whom may be stimulated to generate other ideas. (p. 285)

electronic mail (e-mail) Use of computer text-editing to send and receive written information. (p. 494)

emotion A subjective reaction or feeling. (p. 500)

employee effort The amount of physical and/or mental energy exerted to perform a task. (p. 427)

employee stock ownership plans (ESOPs) Incentive plans whereby the company funds the purchase of its stock to be held in individual employee investment accounts. (p. 385)

employee-centered leadership style Encouraging employees to participate in making decisions and making sure that they are satisfied with their work. (p. 453)

employment-at-will A traditional common-law concept holding that employers are free to discharge employees for any reason at any time, and that employees are free to quit their jobs for any reason at any time. (p. 213)

empowerment The delegation of authority, responsibility, and discretion to an individual or a team. (pp. 446, 521)

encoding Translating thoughts or feelings into a medium—written, visual, or spoken—that conveys the meaning intended. (p. 483)

entrapment Luring an individual into committing a compromising or illegal act. (p. 607)

entrepreneur Someone who creates a new business activity in the economy. (p. 708)

entrepreneur role The decisional role played by managers when they design and implement a new project, enterprise, or business. (p. 12)

entrepreneurial culture Exhibits high levels of risk taking, dynamism, and creativity. (p. 540)

environmental forces External events and the influences, direct and indirect, that can affect the decisions and actions of an organization. (p. 77)

environmental uncertainty The ambiguity or unpredictability of certain factors in an organization's external environment (e.g., government regulation). (p. 88)

equity model A process approach to motivation that is concerned with individuals' beliefs about how fairly they're treated compared with their peers. (p. 429)

ERG model Alderfer's content approach to motivation, which specifies a hierarchy of three need categories: existence, relatedness, and growth. (p. 416)

esteem needs The desires for self-respect, a sense of personal achievement, and recognition from others (the fourth level of Maslow's hierarchy). (p. 414)

ethics A set of moral principles, values, and conduct that decision makers apply to issues that are not specifically addressed by law. (p. 17) A set of rules and values that define right and wrong conduct. (p. 210)

eustress Pleasant or constructive stress. (p. 567)

executive support systems (ESS) An organized network of electronic messaging systems, multimedia presentation systems, management information systems, and group decision support systems. (p. 623)

exempt employees Employees who are not covered by the minimum wage and overtime provisions of the Fair Labor Standards Act. (p. 370)

existence needs The desires for material and physical well-being (the lowest level in Alderfer's hierarchy). (p. 416)

expatriate employees Employees working in a nation other than their home country. (p. 395)

expectancy The belief that effort will lead to first-order outcomes. (p. 424)

expectancy model A process approach to motivation based on the assumption that people choose among alternative behaviors because they anticipate that a particular behavior will lead to one or more desired outcomes and that other behaviors will lead to undesirable outcomes. (p. 424)

expected value (EV) The weighted-average outcome for each strategy in a payoff matrix. (p. 274)

expert power Influence based on a leader's specialized knowledge. (p. 448)

expert system A computer program based on the decision-making processes of human experts that stores, retrieves, and manipulates data, diagnoses problems, and makes limited decisions based on detailed information about a specific problem. (p. 270)

export department A unit that represents foreign customers to the firm's other departments and to top management and provides various export-related services. (p. 110)

export manager Someone who actively searches out foreign markets for a firm's goods and services. (p. 110)

exporting strategy Maintaining facilities in a home country and transferring goods and services abroad, for sale in foreign markets. (p. 114)

external system Outside conditions and influences that exist before and after the group is formed. (p. 519)

extinction The absence of any reinforcement, either positive or negative, following the occurrence of a target behavior. (p. 435)

extortion A payment made to ensure that the recipient does not harm the payer in some way. (p. 123)

extrapolation The projection of some tendency from the past or present into the future. (p. 172)

extrinsic rewards Outcomes supplied by the organization, such as pleasant working conditions, a fair salary, status, job security, and fringe benefits. (p. 428)

fairness principle A moral requirement that employees support the rules of the organization when certain conditions are met. (p. 223)

feedback Information about a system's status and performance. (p. 56) The receiver's response to the sender's message. (p. 492)

femininity Hofstede's value dimension that measures the tendency to be nurturing and people-oriented (the opposite of masculinity). (p. 86)

Fiedler's contingency model A model that suggests that successful leadership depends on matching a leader's style to a situation's demands. (p. 456)

figurehead role The interpersonal role played by managers when they represent the organization at ceremonial and symbolic functions. (p. 11)

financial control A wide range of methods, techniques, and procedures intended to prevent the misallocation of financial resources. (p. 599)

firewalls Workstations with special software that screen incoming messages to ensure that an outsider is authorized to access a certain computer in the company and doesn't leave confidential information on the Internet. (p. 496)

first-line managers Managers directly responsible for the production of goods or services. (p. 6)

first-order outcome Any work-related behavior that is the direct result of the effort an employee expends on a job. (p. 424)

fixed interval punishment schedule A schedule that provides punishment at fixed time intervals. (p. 436)

fixed interval reinforcement schedule Providing reinforcement at fixed intervals of time. (p. 436)

fixed ratio punishment schedule Providing punishment after a fixed number of target behaviors have occurred. (p. 436)

fixed ratio reinforcement schedule Providing reinforcement after a fixed number of target behaviors have occurred. (p. 436)

flextime Allowing employees, within certain limits, to vary their arrival and departure times to suit individual needs and desires. (p. 571)

focus strategy An emphasis on competing in a specific industry niche by directing efforts to the unique needs of certain customers or a narrowly defined geographic market. (p. 163)

forcing style Use of coercive and other forms of power to dominate another person or group and put pressure on others to accept one's own views of the situation. (p. 560)

forecasting Predicting, projecting, or estimating future events or conditions in an organization's environment. (p. 172)

foreign conflict The degree of hostility that one nation shows toward others. (p. 119)

formal group People who jointly have and work toward goals that relate directly to the achievement of organizational goals. (p. 512)

forward integration When a company enters the businesses of its customers, moving it closer to the ultimate consumer. (p. 149)

framing A process whereby leaders define the purpose of their movement in highly meaningful terms for their followers. (p. 471)

franchise A business run by an individual to whom a franchisor grants the right to market a certain good or service. (p. 718)

franchising strategy A parent organization (franchiser) grants other companies or individuals (franchisees) the rights to use its trademarked name and to produce and sell its goods or services. (p. 115)

free riding Not contributing fully to group performance because she or he can share in group rewards despite making less effort than others. (p. 518)

frustration-regression hypothesis The idea that frustration in fulfilling a higher level need will result in the reemergence of the next lower level need as a motivator of behavior. (p. 416)

functional departmentalization The grouping of employees according to their areas of expertise and the resources they draw on to perform a common set of tasks. (p. 305)

functional foremanship System developed by Taylor to link each foreman's area of specialization to that foreman's scope of authority. (p. 46)

functional managers Managers who supervise employees having specialized skills in a single area of operation, such as accounting, personnel, payroll, finance, marketing, or production. (p. 7)

functional team A manager and subordinates who consider common issues and solve problems common to their area of responsibility and expertise for which they are interdependent. (p. 523)

functional-level strategy A guide for managing a firm's functional areas, such as manufacturing, marketing, human resources, and finance. (p. 151)

G

gainsharing reward system Team sharing in the gains (or cost savings) realized by measurable improvements in productivity. (p. 385)

gambler's fallacy bias Seeing an unexpected number of similar chance events can lead to the conviction that an event not seen will occur. (p. 257)

Gantt chart A visual plan and progress report that identifies work stages, completion deadlines, and project accomplishments. (p. 47)

general environment External factors, such as inflation and demographics, that usually affect indirectly all or most organizations (also called the macroenvironment). (p. 78)

general goals Broad direction for decision making in qualitative terms. (p. 249)

general managers Managers responsible for the overall operations of a complex unit such as a company or a division (p. 7)

generic strategies model A framework of three basic business-level strategies that can be applied to a variety of organizations in diverse industries. (p. 161)

global strategy Operating with worldwide consistency, standardization, and low relative cost. (p. 117)

goal conflict Incompatible results or preferred outcomes. (p. 552)

goals What a firm is committed to and where it is going. (p. 143) Results to be attained. (p. 248)

Golden Rule "Do unto others as you would have them do unto you." (p. 270)

grapevine An organization's informal communication system. (p. 491)

graphic rating method A type of performance appraisal that evaluates employees on a series of performance dimensions, usually along a five- or seven-point scale. (p. 391)

grease payments Small payments—almost gratuities—used to get lower level government employees to speed up required paperwork. (p. 123)

group Two or more individuals who come into personal and meaningful contact on a continuing basis. (p. 512)

group control The norms and values that group members share and maintain through rewards and punishments. (p. 587)

group decision support system (GDSS) A set of software, hardware, and language components that support a team of people engaged in a decision-making meeting. (p. 623)

group social structure Formation of a relatively consistent pattern of activities, interactions, sentiments, and norms. (p. 518)

groupthink An agreement-at-any-cost mentality that results in an ineffective team decision-making process and possibly poor solutions. (p. 527)

growth needs The desires to be creative, to make useful and productive contributions, and to have opportunities for personal development (the top level in Alderfer's hierarchy). (p. 416)

growth-need strength The extent to which a person desires a job that provides personal challenges, sense of accomplishment, and learning (personal growth). (p. 422)

H

halo effect A rating error that occurs when the rater's knowledge of a job candidate or employee's performance on one dimension colors the rating on all others. (p. 389)

Hawthorne effect The fact that, when workers receive special attention, their productivity is likely to improve whether or not working conditions actually change. (p. 53)

Hersey and Blanchard's situational leadership model A model that suggests that the levels of directive and supportive leader behaviors should be based on the readiness level of followers. (p. 459)

hierarchy of goals The formal linking of goals between organizational levels so that meeting the goals of the lowest level units helps achieve goals at the next higher level, and so on, until the goals of the organization as a whole are achieved. (p. 250)

hierarchy of needs model Maslow's content approach to motivation that suggests that people have a complex set of needs arranged on five levels, which they attempt to meet in sequence, from the bottom (most basic) up. (p. 412)

honesty test A specialized paper-and-pencil measure that attempts to gauge a person's tendency to behave dishonestly. (p. 380)

horizontal channel A communication path that managers and other employees use when communicating across departmental lines. (p. 491)

horizontal integration When a company acquires a competitor to consolidate and extend its market share. (p. 149)

House's path-goal model A model that indicates that effective leaders specify the task and clear roadblocks to task achievement, thereby increasing subordinates' satisfaction and job performance. (p. 462)

human resources management The philosophies, policies, programs, practices, and decisions that affect the people who work for an organization. (p. 366)

human resources planning Forecasting the organization's human resource needs and developing the steps to be taken to meet them. (p. 374)

hygiene factors Characteristics of the work environment outside the job (working conditions, company policies, supervision, co-workers, salary, formal status, and job security that, when positive, maintain a reasonable level of job motivation but don't necessarily increase it. (p. 419)

I

impression management A leader's attempt to control the impressions that others form about the leader through practicing behaviors that make the leader more attractive and appealing to others. (p. 471)

incentive pay Pay that links at least a portion of pay to job performance to encourage superior performance. (p. 384)

incubator organization An organization that supports entrepreneurs. (p. 709)

indirect compensation Benefits that are required by law and those that are provided voluntarily by the employer. (p. 382)

individual differences Personal needs, values, attitudes, interests, and abilities that people bring to their jobs. (p. 410)

individual self-control The guiding mechanisms that operate consciously and unconsciously within each person. (p. 587)

individualism Hofstede's value dimension that measures the extent to which a culture expects people to take care of themselves and/or individuals believe they are masters of their own destiny (the opposite of collectivism). (p. 85)

informal group A small number of people who jointly participate in activities frequently, otherwise interact, and share sentiments for the purpose of meeting their mutual needs. (p. 512)

information The knowledge derived from data that people have transformed to make them meaningful and useful. (p. 615)

information richness The information carrying capacity of a channel of communication. (p. 489)

information technologies (ITs) Complex networks of computers, telecommunications systems, and remote-controlled devices that help individuals and organizations assemble, store, transmit, process, and retrieve data and information. (pp. 613, 693)

initiating-structure leadership style Actively planning, organizing, controlling, and coordinating subordinates' activities. (p. 453)

innovative decisions Choices based on the discovery, identification, and diagnosis of unusual and ambiguous problems and the development of unique or creative alternative solutions. (p. 246)

inputs The physical, human, material, financial, and information resources that enter the transformation process. (p. 55) What an employee gives to a job, such as time, effort, education, in order to obtain a desired outcome. (p. 430)

instrumentality The perceived relationship between first-order outcomes and the attainment of second-order outcomes. (p. 425)

integrated order systems Connecting suppliers' computers to customers' computers so that orders may be placed at any time. (p. 651)

integration The measure of coordination among various departments with respect to structure, tasks, and goals. (p. 341)

intermediate strategy Organizing the physical layout of equipment and the work force so that they reflect some features of both the process focus and product focus. (p. 647)

internal system The activities (tasks), interactions, sentiments, norms, and social structure that group members develop over time. (p. 516)

international corporation An organization that has significant business interests that cut across national boundaries, often focuses on importing and exporting goods or services, and operates production and marketing units in other countries. (p. 111)

Internet A loosely configured, rapidly growing web of 25,000 corporate, educational, and research computer networks around the world. (p. 495)

interpersonal conflict The disagreements or incompatible interests over goals, policies, rules, and decisions and incompatible behaviors that create anger, distrust, fear, rejection, or resentment. (p. 558)

interpersonal skills The ability to lead, motivate, manage conflict, and work with others. (p. 26)

interrole conflict A result of role pressures associated with membership in one group or organization that conflict with those stemming from membership in others. (p. 557)

intersender role conflict A result of receiving pressures from one role sender that are incompatible with those from one or more other role senders. (p. 556)

intrapreneur Someone in an existing organization who turns new ideas into profitable realities. (p. 723)

intrasender role conflict A result of receiving mixed messages of do's and don'ts from a single role sender. (p. 556)

intrinsic rewards Rewards that are personally satisfying outcomes, such as achievement, self-recognition, or personal growth. (p. 428)

intuition The ability to scan a situation, anticipate changes, take risks, and build trust. (p. 447)

inventory The amount and type of raw materials, parts, supplies, and unshipped finished goods an organization has on hand at any one time. (p. 662)

inventory control Setting and maintaining minimum, optimum, and maximum levels of inventory. (p. 662)

inventory costs The expenses associated with maintaining inventory. (p. 664)

J

job analysis A breakdown of the tasks and responsibilities for a specific job and the personal characteristics, skills, and experience necessary for their successful performance. (p. 374)

job characteristics The aspects of a position that determine its limitations and challenges. (p. 410)

job description A detailed outline of a position's essential tasks and responsibilities. (p. 374)

job enrichment Changing job specifications to broaden and add challenge to the tasks required in order to increase productivity. (p. 697)

job evaluation A procedure for determining the monetary worth of the important characteristics of a job. (p. 382)

job simplification Scientific analysis of tasks performed by employees in order to discover procedures that produce the maximum output for the minimum input. (p. 697)

job specification A list of the personal characteristics, skills, and experience a worker needs to carry out a job's tasks and assume its responsibilities. (p. 374)

job-based pay Compensation that is linked to the specific tasks a person performs. (p. 382)

job-enrichment models An extension of the two-factor model that emphasizes changing specific job characteristics in order to address employees' higher level needs. (p. 421)

joint ventures Partnerships between two or more firms to create another business to produce a product or service. (p. 23)

just-in-time (JIT) system The delivery of finished goods just in time to be sold, subassemblies just in time to be assembled into finished goods, parts just in time to go into subassemblies, and purchased materials just in time to be transformed into parts. (p. 666)

justice model Judging decisions and behavior by their consistency with an equitable, fair, and impartial distribution of benefits (rewards) and costs among individuals and groups. (p. 218)

K

knowledge Concepts, tools, and categories of information. (p. 615)

L

language A shared system of vocal sounds, written signs, or gestures used to convey special meanings among members. (p. 536)

lateral relations An information processing strategy by which decision making is placed in the hands of those who have access to the information needed to make the decision. (p. 349)

law of small numbers bias A few incidents or cases may be viewed as representative of a larger population (a few cases "prove the rule"), even when they aren't. (p. 257)

laws Society's values and standards that are enforceable in the courts. (p. 213)

lead time The elapsed time between placing an order and receiving the finished goods. (p. 663)

leader-member relations The extent to which the leader is accepted by followers. (p. 457)

leader-participation model A set of rules to determine the amount and form of participative decision making that should be encouraged in different situations. (p. 465)

leader position power The extent to which a leader has legitimate, coercive, and reward power. (p. 457)

leader role The interpersonal role that managers play when they direct and coordinate the activities of subordinates to accomplish organizational objectives. (p. 11)

leadership Influencing others to act toward the attainment of a goal. (p. 445)

leading The managerial function of communicating with and motivating others to perform the tasks necessary to achieve the organization's objectives. (p. 9)

learned needs model McClelland's content approach to motivation, which specifies that people acquire three needs or motives—achievement, affiliation, and power—through interaction with their social environments. (p. 418)

learning organizations Involvement of all employees in identifying and solving problems, thus enabling the organization continuously to experiment, improve, and increase its capacity to deliver new goods or services to customers. (p. 680)

least preferred co-worker (LPC) The employee with whom the manager can work least well. (p. 456)

legitimate power Influence based on the leader's formal position in the organization's hierarchy. (p. 447)

leniency A common, often intentional, rating error that occurs when an individual rates all employees in a group higher than they deserve. (p. 389)

leveraged buyout The acquisition of a company, financed through borrowing by a group of investors. (p. 23)

liaison role The interpersonal role played by managers when they deal with people outside the organization. (p. 12)

licensing strategy A firm (the licensor) in one country gives other domestic or foreign firms (licensees) the right to use a patent, trademark, technology, production process, or product in return for the payment of a royalty or fee. (p. 115)

line authority The right to direct and control immediate subordinates who perform activities essential to achieving organizational objectives. (p. 323)

listening Paying attention to a message, not merely hearing it. (p. 484)

lobbying An attempt to influence government decisions by providing officials with information on the anticipated effects of legislation or regulatory rulings. (p. 97)

M

machine controls Methods that use instruments to prevent and correct deviations from desired results. (p. 603)

macroculture A combination of the assumptions and values of both the society and industry in which the organization (or one of its divisions) operates. (p. 530)

Malcolm Baldrige Award The award created by the Malcolm Baldrige National Quality Improvement Act of 1987 to create standards for measuring total quality in both small and large service and manufacturing companies. (p. 23)

management Planning, organizing, leading, and controlling the people working in an organization and the ongoing set of tasks and activities they perform. (p. 5)

management by objectives An approach that emphasizes the development of objectives (goals) for organizational units and individual employees and the review of performance against those objectives. (p. 181)

management information systems Provision of up-to-date financial, market, human resources, or other information about the status of an organization, its major departments or divisions, and its environment. (p. 623)

manager A person who allocates human and material resources and directs the operations of a department or an entire organization. (p. 5)

managerial grid model A model that identifies five leadership styles, each combining different proportions of concern for production and concern for people. (p. 454)

market controls The use of data to monitor sales, prices, costs, and profits, to guide decisions, and to evaluate results. (p. 597)

market culture Values achievement of measurable and demanding goals, especially those that are financial and market-based. (p. 541)

market development strategy Involves seeking new markets for current products. (p. 158)

market penetration strategy Involves seeking growth in current markets with current products. (p. 158)

masculinity Hofstede's value dimension that measures the degree to which the acquisition of money and things is valued and a high quality of life for others is not (the opposite of femininity). (p. 86)

materials resource planning II (MRP II) A computerized information system for managing dependent demand inventories and scheduling stock replenishment orders. (p. 665)

matrix organization A design that combines the advantages of the functional and product structures to increase the ability of managers and other employees to process information. (p. 350)

measurable behavior Work-related action that can be observed and expressed in quantitative terms. (p. 432)

measuring by attribute Assessment of product characteristics as acceptable or unacceptable. (p. 661)

measuring by variable Assessment of product characteristics for which there are quantifiable standards. (p. 661)

mechanistic structure An organization design in which activities are broken down into specialized tasks and decision making is centralized at the top. (p. 339)

merit pay A permanent increase in base pay linked to an individual's performance during the preceding year. (p. 385)

message The verbal (spoken and written) symbols and nonverbal cues that represent the information the sender wants to convey to the receiver. (p. 485)

middle managers Managers who receive broad, overall strategies and policies from top managers and translate them into specific objectives and plans for first-line managers to implement. (p. 7)

mission An organization's purpose or reason for existing. (p. 142)

modular corporation A company whose operating functions are performed by other companies. (p. 10)

monitor role The informational role played by managers when they seek, receive, and screen information that may affect the organization. (p. 12)

moral principles General rules of acceptable behavior that are intended to be impartial. (p. 211)

moral rights model Judging decisions and behavior by their consistency with fundamental personal and group liberties and privileges. (p. 218)

motivation Any influence that brings out, directs, or maintains people's goal-directed behavior. (p. 409)

motivator factors Job characteristics (challenge of the work, responsibility, recognition, achievement, and advancement and growth) that, when present, should create high levels of motivation. (p. 419)

multicultural organization An organization with a work force representative of the population at large. (p. 7)

multidomestic strategy Adjusting a firm's products, services, and practices to individual countries or regions. (p. 117)

multinational corporation An organization that takes a worldwide approach to markets (customers), services, and products and that has a global philosophy of doing business. (p. 112)

multiple scenarios Written descriptions of several alternative futures. (p. 172)

narratives The unique stories, sagas, legends, and myths in an organizational culture. (p. 536)

natural duty principle A moral requirement that decisions and behaviors be based on a variety of universal obligations. (p. 224)

need A strong feeling of deficiency in some aspect of a person's life that creates an uncomfortable tension. (p. 412)

negative reinforcement Engaging in behavior to avoid impending unpleasant consequences or to escape from existing unpleasant consequences. (p. 435)

negotiation A process by which two or more individuals or groups with both common and conflicting goals or different preferences on how to achieve those goals present and discuss proposals for reaching an agreement. (pp. 97, 563)

negotiator role The decisional role played by managers when they meet with individuals or groups to discuss differences and reach some agreement. (p. 13)

network organization An organization that subcontracts some or all of its operating functions to other organizations to perform and coordinates their activities through managers and other employees at its headquarters. (p. 354)

nonexempt employees Employees who are covered by the minimum wage and overtime provisions of the Fair Labor Standards Act. (p. 370)

nonroutine service technology Methods used by organizations operating in a complex and changing environment and serving customers or clients who are unaware of their needs or imprecise about their problems. (p. 345)

nonspecific response Emotional, physical, and cognitive responses that occur automatically. (p. 566)

nonverbal messages The use of facial expressions, movements, body language to convey meaning. (p. 485)

normative decision making Any prescribed step-by-step process that individuals may use to help them make choices. (p. 268)

norms The informal rules of behavior that are widely shared and enforced by the members of a group. (p. 514)

O

objective probability The likelihood that a specific outcome will occur, based on hard facts and numbers. (p. 241)

open network A computer-based information system that enables parts of highly dispersed service operations to interact readily. (p. 651)

open system A system that interacts with its external environment. (p. 56)

operational goals What is to be achieved in quantitative terms, for whom, and within what time period. (p. 249)

operations management (OM) The systematic direction, control, and evaluation of the entire range of processes that transform inputs into finished goods or services. (p. 642)

organic control Flexible authority, loose job descriptions, individual self-controls, and other informal methods of preventing and correcting deviations from desired behaviors and results. (p. 596)

organic structure An organization design that stresses teamwork, open communication, and decentralized decision making. (p. 340)

organization Any structured group of people brought together to achieve certain goals that the individuals could not reach alone. (p. 5)

organization chart A diagram showing the reporting relationships of functions, departments, and individual positions within an organization. (p. 302)

organization design The process of determining the structure and authority relationships for an entire organization. (p. 332)

organization development (OD) A planned long-range behavioral science strategy for understanding, changing, and developing an organization's work force in order to improve its effectiveness. (p. 698)

organizational control Formal rules and procedures for preventing and correcting deviations from plans and for pursuing goals. (p. 587)

organizational culture The unique pattern of shared assumptions, values, and norms that shape the organization's socialization activities, language, symbols, and practices. (p. 530)

organizational practices The rules, human resources policies, managerial practices, and reward systems of an organization. (p. 411)

organizational socialization The systematic process by which an organization brings new members into its culture. (p. 534)

organizational structure A formal system of working relationships that both separates and integrates tasks, (clarifies who should do what and how efforts should be meshed). (p. 301)

organizing The managerial function of creating a structure of relationships that will enable employees to carry out management's plans and meet its objectives. (p. 9)

orientation A formal or informal program that introduces new employees to their job responsibilities, their co-workers, and the organization's policies. (p. 380)

Osborn's creativity model A three-phase decision-making process that involves finding facts, ideas, and solutions. (p. 282)

outcomes Rewards obtained from work, such as promotions, challenging assignments, pay, and friendly co-workers. (p. 430)

outputs The results of a transformation process. (p. 55)

outsourcing Letting other organizations perform a service and/or manufacture parts or a product. (p. 10)

P

Pareto analysis An aid for focusing on the sources and relative priorities of the causes of problems. (p. 276)

Pareto diagram A chart used to determine the relative priorities of issues or problems. (p. 277)

Pareto principle Recognition that a small number of causes (usually 20 percent) accounts for most of the problems (usually 80 percent) in any situation. (p. 276)

partial productivity The ratio of total outputs to a single input. (p. 644)

participating style Sharing decision making when directive behavior no longer is required. (p. 461)

participative leadership Consulting with followers and asking for their suggestions. (p. 463)

payoff matrix A table of figures or symbols used to identify the possible states of nature, probabilities, and outcomes (payoffs) associated with alternative strategies. (p. 273)

perceived effort-reward probability A person's perception of the linkage between expending effort and obtaining certain rewards. (p. 427)

perceived equitable rewards The amount of compensation and perks that employees believe they should receive relative to what other employees receive. (p. 428)

perception The meaning ascribed to a message by a sender or receiver. (p. 493)

performance The level of the individual's work achievement that comes only after effort has been exerted. (p. 427)

performance appraisal The process of systematically evaluating each employee's job-related strengths, developmental needs, and progress toward meeting goals and determining ways to improve the employee's job performance. (p. 387)

performance gap The difference between what the organization aspires to do to take advantage of its opportunities and what it actually does. (p. 685)

performance test A test that requires job candidates to perform simulated job tasks. (p. 379)

perquisites Also known as perks, these are the extra benefits provided for managers and executives. (p. 387)

person–role conflict A result of differences that arise between the pressures exerted by the focal person's role(s) and his or her own needs, values, or abilities. (p. 557)

personal communication services (PCS) An emerging set of capabilities based on wireless equipment that will enable users to stay in touch with almost anyone, anytime, anywhere. (p. 650)

personality The unique blend of characteristics that define an individual. (p. 379)

PERT network A diagram showing the sequence and relationships of the activities and events needed to complete a project. (p. 190)

physiological needs The most basic desires for food, clothing, shelter (the first level in Maslow's hierarchy). (p. 412)

piece-rate incentives Adjustment of the fixed amount of money paid for each unit of output produced when the number of units exceeds a standard output rate. (p. 384)

place departmentalization The grouping of all functions for a geographic area at one location under one manager. (p. 307)

planning The formal process of (1) choosing an organizational mission and overall goals for both the short run and long run, (2) devising divisional, departmental, and even individual goals based on organizational goals, (3) choosing strategies and tactics to achieve those goals, and (4) allocating resources (people, money, equipment, and facilities) to achieve the various goals, strategies, and tactics. (pp. 8, 140)

political climate The likelihood that a government will swing to the far left or far right politically. (p. 120)

political model A description of decision-making process in terms of the particular interests and goals of powerful external and internal stakeholders. (p. 258)

political risk The probability that political decisions or events in a country will negatively affect the long-term profitability of an investment. (p. 119)

pooled interdependence The type of technological interdependence that involves little sharing of information or resources among individuals and departments. (p. 343)

Porter–Lawler expectancy model A process approach to motivation that suggests that job satisfaction is the result rather than the cause of performance. (p. 426)

positioning strategy The approach selected for managing resource flows in the transformation process. (p. 645)

positive reinforcement Creating a pleasant consequence by using rewards to increase the likelihood that a behavior will be repeated. (p. 434)

power The ability to influence or control individual, departmental, team, or organizational decisions and goals. (pp. 258, 447)

power distance Hofstede's value dimension that measures the degree to which influence and control are unequally distributed among individuals within a particular culture. (p. 84)

power motive The desire to influence and control others and the social environment. (p. 418)

preventive controls Mechanisms intended to reduce errors and thereby minimize the need for corrective action. (p. 586)

principle of selectivity A small number of characteristics always account for a large number of effects (also known as Pareto's principle). (p. 592)

probability The percentage of times that a specific outcome would occur if an individual were to make a particular decision a large number of times. (p. 241)

problem-solving team Five to twenty hourly and salaried employees from different areas of a department who consider how something can be done better. (p. 523)

process approach Models of motivation that emphasize how and why people choose certain behaviors in order to meet their personal goals. (p. 412)

process-focus strategy Organizing the physical layout of equipment and the work force around each operation in the transformation process. (p. 646)

product departmentalization The division of an organization into self-contained units, each capable of designing and producing its own goods and/or services. (p. 309)

product development strategy Involves developing new or improved goods or services for current markets. (p. 158)

product development team A temporary group that exists for the period of time required to bring a product to market, which could vary from a couple of months to several years. (p. 524)

product differentiation Uniqueness in quality, price, design, brand image, or customer service that gives a product an edge over the competition. (p. 92)

product life cycle model The market phases that many products go through during their lifetimes. (p. 160)

product-focus strategy Organizing the physical layout of equipment and the work force around a few outputs. (p. 647)

production-centered leadership style Setting standards, organizing and paying close attention to employees' work, keeping production schedules, and stressing results. (p. 453)

profit center An organizational unit that is accountable for both the revenues generated by its activities and the costs of those activities. (p. 117)

profit sharing Employee sharing in the actual profits a business earns. (p. 385)

program evaluation and review technique (PERT) A method of scheduling the sequence of activities and events required to complete a project, estimating their costs, and controlling their progress. (p. 190)

project A one-time activity with a well-defined set of desired results. (p. 189)

project management The principles, methods, and techniques used to establish and implement a project and achieve its goals. (p. 189)

protected groups Categories of existing and prospective employees covered by EEO laws. (p. 370)

protectionism The use of various mechanisms to help a home-based industry or firms avoid (or reduce) potential (or actual) competitive or political threats from abroad. (p. 122)

proxemics The study of ways people use physical space to convey a message about themselves. (p. 485)

punishment An attempt to discourage a target behavior by the application of negative consequences whenever it does occur. (p. 435)

quality Value (linking different grades of a product and price), conformance to established specifications or standards, excellence (providing the best), or meeting and/or exceeding customers' expectations. (p. 185)

quality circle A group of employees from the same work area, or who perform similar tasks, who voluntarily meet regularly to identify, analyze, and propose solutions to problems in the workplace. (p. 523)

quality improvement team Personnel from interrelated functions who meet regularly to improve continuously the product or process for which they are responsible. (p. 524)

quality viewpoint One of the five principal viewpoints of management; emphasizes customer satisfaction through the provision of high-quality goods and services. (p. 60)

quota A restriction on the quantity of a country's imports (or sometimes on its exports). (p. 122)

ranking method A type of performance appraisal that compares employees doing the same or similar work. (p. 391)

ratio analysis Selecting two significant figures, expressing their relationship as a proportion or fraction, and comparing its value for two periods of time or with the same ratio for similar organizations. (p. 599)

rational model A series of steps that individuals or teams should follow to increase the likelihood that their decisions will be logical and well founded. (p. 252)

readiness A subordinate's ability to set high but attainable goals and a willingness to accept responsibility for reaching them. (p. 459)

realistic job preview A screening technique that clearly shows candidates a job's tasks or requirements. (p. 379)

receiver The person who receives and decodes (or interprets) the sender's message. (p. 484)

reciprocal interdependence The type of technological interdependence in which all individuals and departments are encouraged to work together and to share information and resources in order to complete a task. (p. 343)

recruitment The process of searching, both inside and outside the organization, for people to fill vacant positions. (p. 375)

reengineering Changing the way work is carried out. (p. 695)

referent power Influence based on followers' personal identification with the leader. (p. 448)

reinforcement model A process approach to motivation that suggests that behavior is a function of its consequences (rewards or punishments). (p. 431)

related-businesses firm An organization that provides a variety of similar products. (p. 146)

relatedness needs The desires to establish and maintain interpersonal relationships with other people (the second level in Alderfer's hierarchy). (p. 416)

relationship-oriented leader A person who recognizes the importance of developing strong and positive emotional ties with followers. (p. 457)

relevant labor market The geographic and skill areas in which an employer usually recruits to fill its positions. (p. 376)

reliability A measure of the degree to which a test provides consistent scores. (p. 380)

replacement chart A diagram showing each position in the organization, along with the name of the person occupying the position and the names of candidates eligible to replace that person. (p. 374)

representation Membership in an outside organization for the purpose of furthering the interests of the member's organization. (p. 99)

resource allocation The earmarking of money, through budgets, for various uses. (p. 144)

resource allocator role The decisional role managers play when they choose among competing demands for money, equipment, personnel, and the like. (p. 13)

responsibility An employee's obligation to perform assigned tasks. (p. 317)

restructuring Reconfiguring—changing levels of authority, responsibility, and control—the organization. (p. 694)

reward power Influence stemming from a leader's ability to reward followers. (p. 448)

rewards Job outcomes that an employee desires. (p. 428)

risk The condition under which individuals can define a problem, specify the probability of certain events, identify alternative solutions, and state the probability of each solution leading to the desired results. (p. 241)

rite and ceremony Elaborate and formal activities designed to generate strong sentiments and carried out as a special event. (p. 537)

robots Reprogrammable, multifunctional machines. (p. 652)

role An organized set of behaviors, which for managers may be grouped into three categories: interpersonal, informational, and decisional. (p. 11) A set of related tasks and behaviors that an individual is expected to carry out. (p. 554)

role ambiguity Job-related experiences involving (1) inadequate information about the person's expected performance goals, (2) unclear or confusing information about expected on-the-job behaviors, and/or (3) uncertainty about the consequences of certain on-the-job behaviors. (p. 554)

role conflict Experiencing strong and inconsistent pressures or expectations. (p. 554)

role episode Attempts by one or more role senders to influence the behavior of a focal person and the responses of the focal person, which in turn, influence the role sender's future expectations of the focal person. (p. 555)

role expectations The views held by others about what an individual should or should not do. (p. 555)

role perceptions An employee's belief that certain tasks should be performed (i.e., certain roles should be played) in order to do a job successfully. (p. 427)

role pressure The result of role senders exerting demands on a focal person to meet their expectations. (p. 555)

role set The collection of roles that are directly related to the individual. (p. 554)

routine decisions Standardized choice made in response to relatively well-defined and well-known problems and alternative solutions. (p. 245)

routine service technologies Methods used by organizations operating in relatively stable environments and serving customers who are relatively sure of their needs. (p. 344)

rule Specification of a course of action that must be followed in dealing with a particular problem. (p. 269)

rule utilitarianism Primary reliance on following predefined rules or standards in order to obtain the greatest good for the greatest number. (p. 219)

satisfaction An attitude determined by the difference between the rewards that employees receive and those that they believe they should have received; the smaller the difference, the greater is the satisfaction. (p. 428)

satisfaction-progression hypothesis The idea that a lower level need must be reasonably satisfied before the next higher level need emerges as a motivator of behavior. (p. 416)

satisficing The practice of selecting an acceptable goal or alternative solution. (p. 255)

scalar principle The precept that states that a clear and unbroken chain of command should link every person in the organization with someone at a level higher, all the way to the top of the organization chart. (p. 315)

scapegoating The process of casting blame for problems or shortcomings on an innocent or only partially responsible individual, team, or department. (p. 258)

scenario A written description of a possible future. (p. 172)

scientific management A traditional management system that focuses on individual worker–machine relationships in manufacturing plants. (p. 45)

second-order outcome The result, good or bad, brought about by a first-order outcome, or behavior. (p. 425)

security needs The desires for safety, stability, and absence of pain, threat, and illness (the second level of Maslow's hierarchy). (p. 413)

selective perception The process of screening out information that a person wants or needs to avoid. (p. 493)

selective perception bias What people expect to see often is what they do see. (p. 257)

self-actualization needs Desires for personal growth, self-fulfillment, and the realization of the individual's full potential (the highest level of Maslow's hierarchy). (p. 414)

self-managed work teams Groups formed from workers and first-line managers who must work together daily to produce a product (or major component) and who perform various managerial tasks regarding their own operations. Their goal is to improve the way their jobs are done. (pp. 22, 419)

self-managing team Five to fifteen employees who work together daily to produce an entire good (or major identifiable component) or service. (p. 525)

self-understanding The ability to recognize a person's own strengths and weaknesses. (p. 447)

selling style Building confidence and motivation through supportive behavior. (p. 460)

semantics The study of the way words are used and the meanings they convey. (p. 500)

sender The source of information and initiator of the communication process. (p. 483)

sequential interdependence The type of technological interdependence in which the flow of information and resources between individuals and departments is serialized. (p. 343)

similarity error A bias in favor of candidates that look or act like the interviewer. (p. 379)

simulation A representation of a real system. (p. 174)

single-business firm An organization that provides a limited number of products to one segment of a particular market. (p. 146)

skill-based pay Compensation that is linked to people's skills and knowledge. (p. 383)

skills Abilities related to performance that are not necessarily inborn and that for managers may be grouped as technical, interpersonal, conceptual, and communication. (p. 25)

skills inventory A detailed file maintained for each employee that lists his or her level of education, training, experience, length of service, current job title and salary, and performance history. (p. 374)

skunkworks Islands of intrapreneurial activity within an organization. (p. 725)

slack resources Extra resources—materials, funds, and time—that an organization stockpiles in order to be prepared to respond to environmental changes. (p. 353)

smoothing style Minimizing or suppressing real or perceived differences while focusing on the other's views of the situation. (p. 559)

social audit An attempt to identify, measure, evaluate, report on, and monitor the effects the organization is having on its stakeholders and society. (p. 230)

social responsibility The degree to which a company recognizes what being a good community and global citizen means and acts accordingly. (p. 17)

socialization The process by which people learn the values held by an organization or the broader society. (p. 100)

sociotechnical systems Consideration of the needs of both employee and organization in devising ways to satisfy customer demand. (p. 692)

span of control principle The precept that states that the number of people reporting directly to any one manager must be limited. (p. 315)

specialization The process of identifying particular tasks and assigning them to individuals or teams who have been trained to do them. (p. 302)

spokesperson role The informational role managers play when they provide others, especially those outside the organization, with information that is the official position of the organization. (p. 12)

stable environment A setting characterized by few changes in products, technology, competitive forces, markets, and political forces. (p. 333)

staff authority The right to direct and control subordinates who support line activities through advice, recommendations, research, technical expertise. (p. 323)

staffing The process by which organizations meet their human resources needs, including forecasting future needs, recruiting and selecting candidates, and orienting new employees. (p. 373)

stakeholder control Pressures from outside sources on organizations to change their behaviors. (p. 586)

stakeholder social responsibility The belief that managers and other employees have obligations to identifiable groups that are affected by or can affect the achievement of an organization's goals. (p. 227)

stakeholders Groups having potential or real power to influence the organization's decisions and actions. (p. 227)

standard operating procedure A series of rules that employees must follow in a particular sequence when dealing with a certain type of problem. (p. 269)

standardization The uniform and consistent procedures that employees are to follow in performing their jobs. (p. 302)

standards Criteria against which qualitative and quantitative characteristics are evaluated. (p. 593)

statistical process control The use of statistical methods and procedures to determine whether production operations are being done correctly, to detect any deviations, and to find and eliminate their causes. (p. 661)

status A person's social rank in a group. (p. 499)

stereotyping Making assumptions about individuals solely on the basis of their belonging to a particular gender, race, age, or other group. (p. 493)

stock options The right given to an employee to buy the company's stock at a specified price. (p. 385)

strategic business unit (SBU) A division or subsidiary of a firm that provides a distinct product and often has its own mission and goals. (p. 149)

strategic planning The process of developing and analyzing the organization's mission and vision, overall goals, and general strategies and allocating resources. (p. 141)

strategies The major courses of action that an organization takes to achieve its goals. (p. 143)

stress The individual's responses—emotional, physical, and cognitive—to any situation that places excessive demands on that person. (p. 566)

stressor Any situation that places special demands on the individual. (p. 567)

subjective probability The likelihood that a specific outcome will occur, based on personal judgment and beliefs. (p. 241)

subsidy A direct or indirect payment by a government to its country's firms to make selling or investing abroad cheaper for them—and thus more profitable. (p. 122)

substitute goods or services Goods or services that can easily replace others. (p. 92)

subsystem One or more interrelated parts comprising a component of a system. (p. 56)

supportive behavior Reliance on two-way communication, listening, encouraging, and involving followers in decision making. (p. 459)

supportive leadership Being friendly and approachable and showing concern for followers' psychological well-being. (p. 463)

survey feedback An OD method that allows managers and employees to provide feedback about the organization and receive feedback about their own behaviors. (p. 699)

symbol Anything visible that can be used to represent an abstract shared value or special meaning. (p. 536)

system An association of interrelated and interdependent parts. (p. 55)

systems viewpoint One of the five principal viewpoints of management; solving problems by diagnosing them within a framework of inputs, transformation processes, outputs, and feedback. (p. 55)

T

tactical planning The process of making detailed decisions about what to do, who will do it, and how to do it with a normal time horizon of one year or less. (p. 144)

tariff A government tax on goods or services entering the country. (p. 122)

task environment External forces (e.g., customers or labor unions), that directly affect an organization's growth, success, and survival. (p. 86)

task structure The degree to which a job is routine. (p. 457)

task-oriented leader A person who structures the job for employees and closely watches their behavior. (p. 457)

team A small number of employees who are organizationally empowered to establish some or all of its own goals, to make decisions about how to achieve those goals, to undertake the tasks required to meet them, and to be individually and mutually accountable for their results. (p. 521)

team building An OD method that helps teams operate more effectively by testing and improving their structure, processes, and member satisfaction. (p. 700)

team-based management by goals A philosophy of and an approach to management that helps integrate strategic and tactical planning. (p. 181)

technical skills The ability to apply specific methods, procedures, and techniques in a specialized field. (p. 26)

technological interdependence The degree of coordination required between individuals and departments to transform information and raw materials into finished products. (p. 343)

technology The method used to transform organizational inputs into outputs. The knowledge, tools, techniques, and actions used to transform materials, information, and other inputs into finished goods and services. (pp. 60, 95)

telling style Providing clear instructions and specific directions to others. (p. 460)

theory X A leadership style whereby leaders tell subordinates what's expected of them, instruct them in how to perform their jobs, insist that they meet certain standards, and make sure that everyone knows who's boss. (p. 452)

theory Y A leadership style whereby leaders consult with their subordinates, seek their opinions, and encourage them to take part in planning and decision making. (p. 452)

time-and-motion study Identifying and measuring a worker's physical movements, analyzing the results, and eliminating movements that slow production. (p. 45)

top managers Managers who are responsible for the overall direction and operations of an organization. (p. 7)

total quality management Emphasis on the reduction of defects in processes and products and on consumer needs. (p. 23) An organizational philosophy and strategy that make quality a responsibility of all employees. (p. 657)

total-factor productivity The ratio of total outputs to total inputs. (p. 644)

traditional quality control Product inspection during or at the end of the transformation process. (p. 657)

traditional social responsibility The belief that organizations should serve the interests of shareholders. (p. 227)

traditional viewpoint The oldest of the five principal viewpoints of management; stresses the manager's role in a strict hierarchy and focuses on efficient and consistent job performance. (p. 40)

training Improving an employee's skills to the point where he or she can do the current job. (p. 394)

traits Individual personality characteristics that can affect a person's job performance. (p. 427)

traits models Leadership models based on the assumption that contain physical, social and personal characteristics are inherent in leaders. (p. 450)

transformation process The technology used to convert inputs into outputs. (p. 55)

transformational leadership Leading by motivating. (p. 470)

turbulent environment An external environment that is complex, constantly changing, and both ambiguous and unpredictable. (p. 88)

turnkey operation A business or outlet (such as a franchise) that is ready to open when purchased or leased. (p. 718)

two-factor model Herzberg's content approach to motivation, which states that distinct kinds of experiences produce job satisfaction (motivator factors) and job dissatisfaction (hygiene factors). (p. 419)

Type A behavior pattern A person who is aggressively involved in a chronic, incessant struggle to achieve more and more in less time, and if required to do so, against the opposing efforts of other things or other persons. (p. 570)

Type B behavior pattern A person who is often contemplative, nonaggressive, realistic in goals pursued, and not hypercritical of self or others. (p. 570)

U

uncertainty The condition under which an individual does not have the necessary information to assign probabilities to the outcome of alternative solutions. (p. 242)

uncertainty avoidance Hofstede's value dimension that measures the degree to which individuals or societies attempt to avoid the ambiguity, riskiness, and the indefiniteness of the future. (p. 85)

union shop An organization whose agreement with a union stipulates that, as a condition of continued employment, all employees covered by the contract must already be or must become union members within a specified period of time. (p. 376)

unity of command principle The precept that states that an employee should have only one boss. (p. 314)

unrelated-businesses firm An organization that provides diverse products to many different markets. (p. 147)

upward channel A channel by which subordinates send information to superiors. (p. 490)

utilitarian model Judging the effect of decisions and behavior on others, with the primary goal of providing the greatest good for the greatest number of people. (p. 218)

V

valence The value or weight that an individual attaches to a first- or second-order outcome, which can motivate behavior and influence decisions. (p. 425)

validity A measure of the degree to which a test measures what it's supposed to measure. (p. 380)

value The relationship between quality and price. (p. 654)

value congruence The ability to understand the organization's guiding principles and employees' values and reconcile the two. (p. 447)

value of reward The importance that a person places on benefits to be obtained from a job. (p. 427)

value system Multiple beliefs (values) that are compatible and supportive of one another. (p. 83)

variable interval punishment schedule Providing punishment at irregular time intervals. (p. 436)

variable interval reinforcement schedule Providing reinforcement at irregular intervals of time. (p. 436)

variable ratio punishment schedule Providing punishment after a varying number of target behaviors have occurred. (p. 436)

variable ratio reinforcement schedule Providing reinforcement after a varying number of target behaviors have occurred. (p. 436)

vertical information system An information processing strategy that managers can use to send information efficiently up the organization. (p. 348)

vesting The employee's right to receive specified benefits from the company's retirement plan. (p. 371)

virtual reality A surrogate environment created by communications and computer systems. (p. 176)

vision An organization's fundamental aspirations and values, usually appealing to its members' hearts and minds. (p. 142) The ability to imagine different and better conditions and ways to achieve them. (p. 447)

voice recognition systems Methods of analyzing and classifying speech or vocal tract patterns and converting them into digital codes for entry in a computer system. (p. 651)

W

wellness programs Promotion of employees' physical and psychological health. (p. 571)

whistleblowers Employees who report unethical or illegal actions of their employers to external stakeholders. (p. 222)

work-force diversity The racial, gender, age, and ethnic mix of the work force. (p. 19)

Z

zone of indifference The decisions or orders that a subordinate will accept without question. (p. 317)

Organization Index

Name Index

Subject Index

Note: Only the first page number is presented for each time the subject appears. Many entries span more than one page.

Photo Credits

CHAPTER 1: p. 4, © Nikolai Ignatiev/Matrix; **p. 24,** © Barbara Laing/Black Star; **CHAPTER 2: p. 46,** Culver Pictures; **p. 51,** Culver Pictures; **CHAPTER 3: p. 81,** Courtesy of GM Hughes Electronics; **p. 99,** © Robert Wallis/SABA. Courtesy of Baxter International Inc.; **CHAPTER 4: p. 116,** © Jeffrey Aaronson/Network Aspen; **p. 127,** Michael St. Maul Sheil/Black Star; **CHAPTER 5: p. 143,** © Ian Berry/Magnum; **P. 150,** Courtesy of FlightSafety International; **CHAPTER 6: p. 173,** © Louis Psihoyos/MATRIX; **p. 176,** © 1994 Bob Sacha; **p. 184,** © Jose Azel/Aurora; **CHAPTER 7: p. 210,** © Ann States/SABA; **p. 229,** © Christopher Pillitz/Matrix; **CHAPTER 8: p. 242,** © Louis Psihoyos/MATRIX; **p. 248,** © Phil Huber/Black Star; **CHAPTER 9: p. 279,** © 1994 Cary S. Wolinsky/Stock, Boston; **p. 281,** © 1989 Robert Holmgren; **CHAPTER 10: p. 305,** © Ann States/SABA; **p. 316,** Courtesy of Fluor Daniel; **CHAPTER 11: p. 336,** © Tom Tracy; **p. 354,** David Fields/ONYX; **CHAPTER 12: p. 371,** © Chris Corsmeier; **p. 387,** © 1993 Kevin Monko/Kelsh Wilson Design; **CHAPTER 13: p. 414,** © Nina Berman/SIPA-PRESS; **p. 433,** © Larry Hamill 1993; **CHAPTER 14: p. 448,** McDonnell Douglas Corporation; **p. 455,** © 1993 Don B. Stevenson; **CHAPTER 15: p. 496,** © 1995 Gary Spector; **p. 499,** © Jay Dickman; **CHAPTER 16: p. 524,** © George Simian; **p. 535,** Kenneth Jarecke/Contact; **CHAPTER 17: p. 569,** Duane Burleson/Sygma; **p. 571,** © Max Aguilera-Hellweg; **CHAPTER 18: p. 597,** © 1994 Ted Rice; **p. 598,** © Sandy May Photography; **CHAPTER 19: p. 616,** © Rocky Kneten; **p. 619,** Courtesy of Hams Corporation; **CHAPTER 20: p. 661,** © 1994 Jose Azel/AURORA; **p. 663,** © Will Panich/Courtesy of Baxter International, Inc.; **CHAPTER 21: p. 682,** © Will Crockett; **p. 697,** David R. Frazier Photolibrary; **CHAPTER 22: p. 709,** © David A. Zickl; **p. 724,** © John Madere 1994.